T0144208

SMART COMPUTING

PROCEEDINGS OF THE INTERNATIONAL CONFERENCE ON SMART MACHINE INTELLIGENCE AND REAL-TIME COMPUTING (SMART COM 2020), PAURI, GARHWAL, UTTARAKHAND 246194, INDIA 26–27 JUNE 2020

Smart Computing

Editors

Mohammad Ayoub Khan
University of Bisha, Bisha, Saudi Arabia

Sanjay Gairola, Bhola Jha & Pushkar Praveen
Govind Ballabh Pant Institute of Engineering & Technology, Ghurdauri, Pauri, Garhwal, Uttarakhand, India

CRC Press
Taylor & Francis Group
Boca Raton London New York Leiden

CRC Press is an imprint of the
Taylor & Francis Group, an **informa** business

A BALKEMA BOOK

CRC Press/Balkema is an imprint of the Taylor & Francis Group, an informa business

© 2021 Taylor & Francis Group, London, UK

Typeset by MPS Limited, Chennai, India

Library of Congress Cataloging-in-Publication Data
Applied for

Published by: CRC Press/Balkema
Schipholweg 107C, 2316 XC Leiden, The Netherlands
e-mail: enquiries@taylorandfrancis.com
www.routledge.com – www.taylorandfrancis.com

ISBN: 978-0-367-76552-1 (Hbk)
ISBN: 978-0-367-76557-6 (Pbk)
ISBN: 978-1-003-16748-8 (eBook)
DOI: 10.1201/9781003167488

Smart Computing – Khan et al (Eds)
© 2021 Taylor & Francis Group, London, ISBN 978-0-367-76552-1

Table of contents

Track 2: Machine intelligence and data science

Track 3: Real-time and VLSI system

Smart Computing – Khan et al (Eds)
© 2021 Taylor & Francis Group, London, ISBN 978-0-367-76552-1

Preface

It's a pleasure and privilege to present the proceedings of the two-day International conference, SMART COM 2020, held at G.B. Pant Institute of Engineering & Technology (GBPIET), Pauri, Uttarakhand, India on 26th and 27th June, 2020. This international conference was held online and was the first of its kind, that discussed the burning topics from the fields of computer science, robotics, embedded systems, VLSI, Communications and renewable energy. All the participants joined online from across the world and it is a matter of pride for all to be a part of this wonderful event. The objectives set for the conference were:

– To bring together academics, researchers & professionals.
– To create opportunities to gain insight into advancement in the field.
– To promote the discipline of contemporary computing & applications.
– To participate in technical sessions, panel discussions and knowledge sharing Forums.

The objectives are going to be completely fulfilled by this proceeding where the presented papers by keynote speakers and researchers are available in the form of one book in one place. The proceeding consists of 113 research papers covering the theme and the reader will definitely benefit from this sea of knowledge. The theme was initially categorised into the following tracks:

Track 1: Smart System and Future Internet
Track 2: Machine Intelligence and Data Science
Track 3: Real-Time and VLSI Systems
Track 4: Communication and Automation Systems

The interest in the topic led to six more special tracks by the leading researchers in the field. These tracks are as follows:

Special Track 1: Blockchain for Internet of Things
Special Track 2: Soft Computing Techniques, Wavelets, Machine Learning, Hybrid Models for the accurate forecasting in all area of research
Special Track 3: Artificial Intelligence and Nature Inspired Algorithms
Special Track 4: Mathematical Modelling for Signal and Image Processing
Special Track 5: Recent Trends on VLSI Design and Embedded Systems
Special Track 6: Circuit, System Design and Optimization Technologies

These special sessions have been a huge attraction for researchers and readers shall definitely benefit from the papers associated with these tracks.
I once again welcome you to relive the experience, shared in the conference.

-S Gairola
Conference Chair

Smart Computing – Khan et al (Eds)
© 2021 Taylor & Francis Group, London, ISBN 978-0-367-76552-1

Distinguished Speakers

Dr. Vinod Kumar
Vice Chancellor
JUIT

Dr. S. N. Singh
Vice Chancellor
MMMUT Gorakhpur

Dr. Bhim Singh Professor
IIT Delhi

Dr. A. K. Ray
Professor
IIT Roorkee

Dr. Aparajita Ojha
Professor, IIITDM
Jabalpur

Dr. Rajkumar Buyya
Professor, University of
Melbourne

Dr. M. Ayoub Khan
Associate Professor
University of Bisha,
Saudi Arabia

Dr. Nguyen T. Khang
Associate Professor
Ton Duc Thang
University

Dr. Pragati Kumar
Professor, Delhi
Technical University

Dr. Raj Senani
Professor
NSUIT

Dr. A. K. Gautam
Professor
G.B.P.I.E.T.

Smart Computing – Khan et al (Eds)
© 2021 Taylor & Francis Group, London, ISBN 978-0-367-76552-1

Committee and messages

Preface
**TEQIP-3 Sponsored International Conference on Smart Machine Intelligence
and Real-Time Computing**

(SMART COM 2020)

TEQIP-3 Sponsored International Conference on Smart Machine Intelligence and Real-Time Computing (SMART COM 2020) is a premier conference, organized by the department of Electronics, Computer Science & Electrical Engineering during June 26-27, 2020 at Govind Ballabh Pant Institute of Engineering & Technology, Pauri Garhwal, Uttarakhand. The aim of the International Conference on "Smart Machine Intelligence and Real-Time Computing" is to bring together the researchers, scientists, engineers and research students in areas of Engineering and Technology, and it provides them a national forum for the dissemination of original research, new ideas and practical development experiences.

The conference has the focus on the frontier topics in the field of smart machine intelligence, real-time computing and related fields. SMART COM 2020 is organized with a vision to address the various issues to promote the creation of intelligent solutions in future. It is expected that researchers will bring new prospect for collaboration across disciplines and gain ideas facilitating novel concepts. The theme of this conference will motivate the researchers to adopt the outcome for implementation.

The conference will provide an exceptional platform to the researchers to discuss the practical solutions, scientific results and methods in solving intriguing problems with people who are actively involved in emerging research fields.

We would like to express our sincere thanks to all speakers, authors, member of the advisory committee and members of the organizing committee that have made this conference a success.

उत्तराखण्ड राज्य

CM Message

It gives me pleasure to know that the G. B. Pant Institute of Engineering and Technology, Ghurdauri, Pauri-Garhwal, Uttarakhand is organizing International Conference on Smart Machine Intelligence & Real Time Computing (SMARTCOM 2020) on June 26-27, 2020 and this souvenir is being brought to commemorate this occasion. In recent times, the role of Technical Education to carry out proactive research and development activities for the interest of all stakeholders has become more challenging and demanding. I am glad to note that the institute has been striving to explore the quality of teaching-learning and research for enhancing the quality of professional services.

(Trivendra Singh Rawat)

Chief Minister of Uttarakhand
Chairman, Board of Governors
GBPIET Society

Chief Patron Message

I am pleased to know that Department of Electronics, Computer Science and Electrical Engineering, Govind Ballabh Pant Institute of Engineering and Technology Pauri, Garhwal is organizing International Conference on "Smart, Machine Intelligence and Real-Time computing" (SMARTCOM-2020) during 26th and 27th June 2020.

This conference will provide excellent platform to technical experts, academia, and researchers to share their knowledge and expertise in the field and to get acquainted with recent research trends in technology development. I am sure, the students, engineers and researchers from various places will get benefit from this conference deliberation. I appreciate the effort taken by organizers, in organizing such a conference on this topic. As computing has become part of our daily life and the conference is devoted to advancement in contemporary Computing and Application, it is going to benefit society at large and would be very fruitful to the nation.

With this belief, I wish the organizers a successful event and I expect it will be a grand success.

Prof. S. N. Singh
Vice Chancellor
Madan Mohan Malaviya University of Technology
Gorakhpur India

Director Message

I am pleased to learn that the Institute is organizing International Conference on Smart Machine Intelligence & Real Time Computing (SMARTCOM 2020) on June 26-27, 2020.

The events in the conference are targeted towards researchers, practitioners, professionals, educators and students to share their experience, innovative ideas, issues, recent trends and future directions in field of Engineering and Science and Technology. It includes keynote addresses from Academicians and paper presentations by research scholars. It is a matter of joy for us to welcome all the dignitaries and participants to this conference.

The institute campus is studded with wealth of knowledge, innovation and technology. GBPIET in itself is a niche of opportunities to all aspiring engineers and researchers.

In a nutshell, the conference promises to transcend to a new and unprecedented level of excellence. It is thus the zenith where technology and skill meet opportunities and guidance. It is a milestone that one would not dare to miss. I wish SMARTCOM 2020 a grand success. I whole-heartedly congratulate all members of the organizing team.

Dr. M. P. S Chauhan
Director, G. B. Pant Institute of Engineering & Technology
Ghurdauri, Pauri-Garhwal, Uttarakhand

جامعة بيشة
UNIVERSITY of BISHA

General Chair Message

It is a pleasure to welcome you to SMART COM 2020, the 1st International Conference on Smart, Machine Intelligence and Real-Time Computing which is being held at GBPIET, Pauri, Uttarakhand, INDIA. Despite of the tough time of pandemic, the organizing committee was highly encouraged to organize the conference.

In this conference we bring together researchers and practitioners from academia, industry, and government to exchange their research ideas and results and to discuss the state of the art in the areas of smart technologies, machine intelligence, VLSI, Embedded system, and Real-Time System. We are overwhelmed with the response we received from the authors. We received around 300 papers from across the globe. To publish the proceedings and special issues, we collaborated with world leading scientific publishing partners CRC Press/Balkema, Taylor & Francis Group, Inderscience, European Alliance for Innovation (EAI) and Bentham Science.

I am highly thankful to Dr. Mahipal Singh Chauhan, GBIET, Director and conference organizing committee to give this opportunity to as a General Chair. I also would like to thank program committee members, reviewer board, web committee, publication committee and volunteers for the dedication, time, and strong support. I wish you a very pleasant and fruitful experience at SMART 2020.

Dr. Mohammad Ayoub Khan
General Chair, SMART COM 2020
Associate Professor, University of Bisha, Saudi Arabia

Conference Chair Message

I am glad to note that the institute is organizing the International Conference SMARTCOM on June 26–27, 2020. Anticipating that the outcome of this technological conference will certainly give us the solution of local/regional problems.

I am indeed happy to share that the institute provides quality education to thousands of students. It is a matter of great satisfaction that the engineers turned out by the institution are providing valuable service to people not only in this state but also in other parts of India and even outside.

I congratulate one and all on this joyous occasion and convey my best wishes to the conference.

Dr. Y. Singh
Prof. & Head
Department of Electronics & Communication Engineering

Conference Chair Message

On behalf of Department of Computer Science and Engineering, I feel a proud privilege to welcome the delegates and the participants to the International Conference on Smart Machine Intelligence and Real-Time Computing (SMART-COM 2020).

Through Technology, people have created a much better world and still there is tremendous research going on for further innovating technology to create value for mankind. SMART COM 2020 offers a global platform to explore the role of innovative technologies and gives an opportunity to researchers, educators and students, to enrich and learn about the latest developments and thrust areas of Engineering and Technology. I hope that this conference will provide many opportunities to participants to share practical innovative ideas and research for the betterment of our society.

I appreciate the efforts of the entire team to give this international conference its much needed color and dynamism. I wish them great success for the successful conduct of the entire event and hope that this mission will be carried out with even more dynamism in the years ahead.

Dr. H. S. BHADAURIA
Prof. & Head
Computer Sc. & Engineering

adhiṣhṭhānaṁtathākartākaraṇaṁ cha pṛithag-vidham
vividhāś cha pṛithakcheṣhṭādaivaṁchaivātrapañchamam

**"The body, the doer, the various senses, the many kinds of efforts, and Divine
Providence—these are the five factors of action."** – Bhagwat Gita Verse 14, Chapter 18.

Conference Chair Message

SMART COM 2020 is a platform for discussing smart technologies in the field of Computer
Science, Electrical and Electronics Engineering. I am sure that it will prove to be a milestone in
the history of GBPIET, Pauri and act as a catalyst for many more technical and society developmental activities in future. The efforts of GBPIET people along with members from collaborating
organisation have made this Conference possible, of course with blessings from divine providence.

The COVID-19 scare has changed the status of conference to a Virtual one, simultaneously
opening avenues of new learning. I must congratulate all my Colleagues, organising committee
members and participating candidates for shifting to virtual mode and taking on the challenge of
handling this voluminous task online. I believe that the two days of conference, June 26-27, 2020,
shall be full of wonderful technical learning.

Kudos to all.

Prof. S. Gairola
HOD (EED), GBPIET PAURI
and Conference Chair SMART COM 2020

Technical Conference Chair Message

On behalf of the Technical Program Committee, it is my pleasure to welcome you to an exciting technical program offered by the international conference on "Smart, Machine Intelligence and real time (SMART) Computing-2020. The technical program of SMART-2020 consists of online technical paper presentations and keynote speeches addressing emerging technologies and latest research and development in all areas of smart systems and future internets, machine intelligence and Data Science, Real-time and VLSI systems, communication and automation systems.

SMART-2020's technical program starts on Friday, 26 June 2020, with four parallel technical Tracks including 12 keynote speeches. Throughout the two days of the conference, a total of 20 technical sessions covering the key areas of smart systems and future internets, machine intelligence and Data Science, Real-time and VLSI systems, communication and automation systems will be presented. This conference will provide an excellent online platform for presenting research work and to get acquainted with recent research trends in technology development. Researchers from all over the country and abroad will gather on virtual platform (through online) to discuss their views and expertise on the recent advances in the field during this international conference.

We received over 250 submissions from different countries. Over 350 technical experts from all over the world participated in the peer review process. Based on the review results, the technical program committee accepted 150 general conference papers for presentation and publication. Since the whole world is suffering from a pandemic COVID-19 disease due to corona virus, we have dropped workshop papers, and demonstrations. The conference proceedings will be published by CRC Press/ Balkema, Taylor & Francis group and will be submitted to Clarivate Analysis (formerly known as Thomson Reuters/ISI), Web of Knowledge, SciVerse, SCOPUS, EI Compendex, Google scholar, etc for evaluation for indexing. The extended version of selected papers will be recommended for publication in reputed journals as well.

We would like to extend our deepest appreciation to the keynote speakers, sessions organizers, and the entire technical program committee, organizing committee and steering committee teams. The success of the technical program would not have been possible without their tremendous volunteer effort. We are most grateful to the reviewers who have so diligently supported the peer review process. The Best Paper Award and Best Student Paper Award may also be awarded during conference.

Finally, we would like to express our sincere thanks to state and centre government to provide the funding to the conference through TEQIP Phase-III project. We thank Director, Registrar and their supporting staff of the institute for their support in organizing this mega event "SMART-2020". Last but not least, we would like to extend our sincere thanks to over 1000 authors all around the world for their quality contributions, which resulted in an outstanding technical program. We look forward to welcoming you to GBPIET, Pauri Garhwal and offering you a rewarding and exciting experience.

Sincerely
Prof. A. K. Gautam
Technical Program Chair, SMART 2020

Registrar Message

It gives me immense pleasure that our institute is organizing Virtual Conference on Smart Machine Intelligence and Real Time Computing (SMARTCOM 2020) on June 26–27, 2020. This conference provides an opportunity for meeting of International Researchers, Engineers, Scientists and specialists in the various research and development fields of Engineering and Technology. The conference offers a premise for global experts to gather and interact intensively on the topics of Electrical and Electronics, Electronics and Communication, Computer Science and Information Technology. I hope eminent speakers will cover the theme virtual reality from different perspectives. I am privileged to say that this conference will definitely offer suitable solutions to global issues. The success of this Conference is solely due to the dedication and efforts of innumerable people who started working on the preparations for almost a half year in many ways to make this Conference become a reality. Eventually I express my special thanks and appreciation to all. I wish SMARTCOM 2020 all the best for its success.

Mr. Sandeep Kumar
Registrar
G. B. Pant Institute of Engineering and Technology
Ghurdauri, Pauri-Garhwal, Uttarakhand

TEQIP Co-ordinator Message

It gives me immense pleasure to be a part of hosting and sponsoring the International Conference on Smart Machine Intelligence and Real Time Computing" (SMARTCOM 2020) on June 26-27, 2020. This conference is fully sponsored by Technical Education Quality Improvement Program (TEQIP)-III which is a World Bank project being executed by MHRD, Govt. of India. TEQIP will always be at the forefront for sponsoring such activities meeting the objectives of improving Quality and Equity of Engineering Institutions.

On behalf of TEQIP-III Coordinator, I take this opportunity to welcome all the delegates of the conference and anticipate that the conference serves as a locus for interdisciplinarity, a space for discourse and collaboration in terms of technologies for achieving smart solutions through innovations.

I would like to express my appreciation to one and all for their dedicated involvement and efforts to materialize the conference. I wish SMARTCOM 2020 a grand success.

Dr. Bhola Jha
(TEQIP-III Coordinator)
Associate Professor
Electrical Engineering
G. B. Pant Institute of Engineering and Technology

INDIAN INSTITUTE OF TECHNOLOGY, DELHI
DEPARTMENT OF ELECTRICAL ENGINEERING
HAUZ KHAS, NEW DELHI-11016, INDIA

Dr. BHIM SINGH
CEA Chair Professor
B.E.(Electrical), M. Tech. Ph. D.
FIEEE, FIET, FNA, FNAE, FANc, FNASc,
FIE(I),FIETE, FTWASc
LMISTE, LMNIQR, C. ENGR, JC Bose Fellow

Message

I am aware that the International Conference SMART COM 2020 is being organised by G. B. Pant Institute of Engineering and Technology (GBPIET), Pauri, Uttarakhand with a great theme based on SMART technologies. So many researchers investigated the topics involved and this conference, are the need of the hour. The deliberations during the conference on Internet of Things, Soft Computing Techniques, Machine Learning, forecasting, Artificial Intelligence, Nature Inspired Algorithms, Signal and Image Processing, VLSI Design, Embedded Systems, Optimization Technologies, Smart Systems, Future Internet, Machine Intelligence, Data Science, Communications, Automation Systems and Renewable Energy are to definitely invoke new ideas. The participation is expected definitely to lead to further innovations and technological changes.

   I congratulate the Organising Committee of GBPIET, Pauri for providing this platform to the research community. My best wishes to all of you.

Dr. Bhim Singh
CEA Chair Professor

Message

It is my immense pleasure that Govind Ballabh Pant Institute of Engineering & Technology is organizing an international conference on "Smart Machine Intelligence & Real-Time Computing (SMARTCOM-2020) on 26–27th June, 2020 in the difficult time the world is facing today, i.e. Pandemic COVID-19.

The scientific community is well aware that in the recent past there have been many breath-taking developments in these two most important areas of computer science.

The theme of the conference generally includes artificial intelligence, smart machine, machine learning, pattern recognition, Automation, Communication, IOT, Reactive computing, Scheduling real time tasks, Modeling timing constraints, Real time operation etc., the uses of which are very relevant today. Similarly, in the area of Automation hundreds of ever-increasing algorithms have been developed and are being developed based on both non-nature and nature inspired processes, primarily for optimization and control of services, plant or systems. I do hope, some of these will be discussed in this conference.

It is heartening to see a large number of leading experts, senior professionals and engineers will participate and address their erudite views on these important topics.

I am very delighted to perceive that it gives a tough challenge to unfold the complexities of this highly technology-oriented topics which might help in many ways to eradicate the present crisis.

I congratulate the organizers for choosing these two topics befitting the current scenario & trend in research in electronics, & Computer Science and would be found most apt in the given circumstances.

The delegates will have ample opportunity to listen to the various speakers covering a large spectrum of the current and future issues and to decide one's own goal/actions that need to be taken to meet the challenges years ahead.

I am also sure this conference will provide a valuable "input" and "take away" for the participants to overcome the unsolved problems of uncertainty currently faced by the scientific community on use of artificial intelligence & real-time computing.

This will motivate, inspire the scientific community, create some thought-provoking ideas which will propel the research in these areas to a new orbit of growth and take our country forward.

The papers to be presented in the various sessions will definitely help in information dissemination, creating awareness and provide impetus for further Research & Development in technological exploration in computer science for the benefit of mankind.

I extend my warm welcome to all the Delegates, Authors, Co-authors and Scientific fraternity & good wishes to all for happy and fruitful exchange of knowledge.

I sincerely convey my greetings to the organizers, wish for a grand success of the conference & eagerly look forward to the feedback of the active participants.

Prof. (Dr.) A.K. Ray
Retired Professor and Emeritus Fellow

Message

Truong Khang NGUYEN was born in Ho Chi Minh City, Vietnam, in 1983. He received his B.S. degree in Computational Physics from the University of Science, Vietnam National University, Ho Chi Minh City in 2006, and his M.S. and Ph.D. degrees in Electrical and Computer Engineering from Ajou University in Suwon, Korea in 2013. From Oct. 2013 to Dec. 2014, he worked at Division of Energy Systems Research, Ajou University, Korea as a postdoctoral fellow. He has been appointed Research Associate Professor of Ton Duc Thang University in 2019. He is currently Assistant Director and also Head of Division of Computational Physics at Institute for Computational Science, Ton Duc Thang University in Ho Chi Minh City, Vietnam. He has authored and co-authored almost 100 peer-reviewed ISI journal articles and 40 conference papers. He has written one book chapter in the area of terahertz antenna and filed one patent on terahertz stripline antenna. He received the award by Central Committee of the Vietnamese Student Association in 2012 and by Vietnamese Embassy in Korea in 2013 for Vietnamese Student in Korea with excellent research achievements. His current research interests include Microwave Antenna for Wireless Communication; Terahertz Antenna for Compact and Efficient Source; Nano Structures and Nano Antenna for Optical Applications; and Computational Micro/Nano Fluidics.

Truong Khang NGUYEN

Conference Chair Message

It is a matter of pleasure to note that G.B. Pant Institute of Engg And Technology, Pauri Garhwal U.K. is organizing an international conference on Smart Machine Intelligence and Real Time Computing (SMARTCOM 2020). Machine Intelligence and Computing have witnessed new dimensions in recent years, due to explosive growth in hardware technologies, data, and artificial intelligence. I am hopeful that young researchers and participants will be greatly benefited by keynote lectures. Organizers have done a commendable job by keeping the schedule in spite of the current pandemic scenario. I wish a grand success to the conference.

Aparajita Ojha
Professor, Computer Science and Engineering &
Chief Investigator, Electronics and ICT Academy
PDPM Indian Institute of Information Technology,
Design and Manufacturing, Jabalpur (India)

Message

It gives me immense pleasure to note that the Gobind Ballabh Pant Institute of Engineering & Technology (GBPIET), Pauri, is organizing an international conference on smart machine intelligence and real-time computing, "SMART COM 2020" in association with Andhra University College of Engineering, Visakhapatnam. I am happy to observe the strident progress made by GBPIET since its inception in 1989. I congratulate the institute for taking the lead in organising this conference on a theme which has assumed great significance with increased used of digital technologies in our lives. I am also pleased to note that the institute is an active participant in the prestigious World Bank sponsored project-TEQIP. As informed by the organisers, a very good number of research papers are being presented in this conference even when this conference is being organised in virtual mode. I wish a very good luck to the institute for undertaking this endeavour which will go a long way in adding to the body of knowledge in the emerging area of Machine-Learning and allied Digital Technologies.

Prof. Pragati Kumar
Professor
Department of Electrical Engineering,
Delhi Technological University
New Delhi

Message from Co-Editor-in-Chief of the EAI Endorsed Transactions on Cloud Systems

As Co-Editor-in-Chief of the EAI Endorsed Transactions in Cloud Systems, I am delighted that the Journal is associated with SMART COM 2020. The focus areas of SMART COM 2020 are highly relevant to the Journal. From hosting the applications running across smart cities, to facilitating the analytics of collected data, the cloud is ubiquitous throughout our day-to-day lives. Indeed, our lives would have become even more difficult throughout our current Covid-19 experience without this infrastructure. Specific to SMART COM 2020, real-time computing has become even more important in our highly dynamic world, monitoring cases of the Covid-19 virus and tracking its movement worldwide. Extracting intelligence reliably and quickly from collected data has similarly become a priority in attempts to protect society from Covid-19's worst impacts.

In line with this, I am excited to invite extended SMART COM 2020 papers to be submitted to the Cloud Systems Journal, and look forward to becoming exposed to the most recent advances in the field. I thank Dr. Khan for his invitation to associate the Cloud Systems Journal with SMART COM 2020, and I sincerely wish everyone involved good luck for the conference.

Dr Cathryn Peoples
Co-Editor-in-Chief of EAI Endorsed Transactions on Cloud Systems
The Open University & Ulster University, United Kingdom

Chief Patron
Dr. S.N Singh, Vice-Chancellor, MMMUT Gorakhpur, India

Patron
Dr. Mahipal Singh Chauhan, Director, GBPIET Pauri Garhwal, India

General Chair
Dr. Mohammad Ayoub Khan, Senior Member IEEE, University of Bisha, Saudi Arabia

Conference Chair(s)
Dr. Yashvir Singh, Professor, GBPIET Pauri Garhwal, India
Dr. Harvendra Singh Bhadauria, Professor, GBPIET Pauri Garhwal, India
Dr. Sanjay Gairola, Professor, GBPIET Pauri Garhwal, India

Technical Program Chair
Dr. A.K. Gautam, Senior Member IEEE, Professor, GBPIET Pauri Garhwal, India
Dr. Manoj Kumar Panda, Professor, GBPIET Pauri Garhwal, India
Dr. Annapurna Singh, Associate Professor, GBPIET Pauri Garhwal, India
Dr. Mamta Baunthiyal, Associate Professor, GBPIET Pauri Garhwal, India
Dr. S K Verma, Assistant Professor, GBPIET Pauri Garhwal, India

Organizing Secretaries
Mr. Sandeep Kumar, Registrar, GBPIET Pauri Garhwal, India
Dr. Rajesh Kumar, Professor, GBPIET Pauri Garhwal, India
Dr. Bhola Jha, Associate Professor, GBPIET Pauri Garhwal, India
Dr. K.S Bhatia, Associate Professor, GBPIET Pauri Garhwal, India
Dr. A.R. Verma, Assistant Professor, GBPIET Pauri Garhwal, India
Mr. Pushkar Praveen, Assistant Professor, GBPIET Pauri Garhwal, India
Mr. Manoj Kumar, Assistant Professor, GBPIET Pauri Garhwal, India
Mr. Surjeet Singh Patel, Assistant Professor, GBPIET Pauri Garhwal, India
Dr. Bhumika Gupta, Associate Professor, GBPIET Pauri Garhwal, India
Mr. Papendra Kumar, Assistant Professor, GBPIET Pauri Garhwal, India
Dr. S.R. Verma, Assistant Professor, GKV, Haridwar, India

Track Chair
Dr. Yatindra Kumar, Associate Professor, GBPIET Pauri Garhwal, India
Dr. Fahad Algarni, Assistant Professor, University of Bisha, Saudi Arabia
Dr. Mohammad Tabrez Quasim, Assistant Professor, University of Bisha, Saudi Arabia
Mrs. Manisha Bhatt, Assistant Professor, GBPIET Pauri Garhwal, India
Mr. Jitendra Singh Rauthan, Assistant Professor, GBPIET Pauri Garhwal, India
Mr. Sandeep Kumar, Assistant Professor, GBPIET Pauri Garhwal, India
Mr. Abhishek Gupta, Assistant Professor, GBPIET Pauri Garhwal, India

Publication Chair
Dr. Balraj Singh, Assistant Professor, GBPIET Pauri Garhwal, India
Dr. Gaurav Varshney, Assistant Professor, NIT, Patna
Mr. Ajay Kumar, Assistant Professor, GBPIET Pauri Garhwal, India
Mr. Abhilekh Barthwal, Assistant Professor, GBPIET Pauri Garhwal, India
Dr. M. Sangeetha, Associate Professor, Coimbatore Institute of Technology, Coimbatore
Mr. Kamal Kumar Gola, Assistant Professor, Teerthanker Mahaveer University, Moradabad
Mrs. Sikha Arya, Assistant Professor, SRMS College of Engineering, Technology & Research, Bareilly

Advisory Committee
Dr. Rajkumar Buyya, Professor, University of Melbourne, Australia
Dr. Kiyoharu Aizawa, Professor, University of Tokyo, Japan

Smart Computing – Khan et al (Eds)
© 2021 Taylor & Francis Group, London, ISBN 978-0-367-76552-1

Conference venue

Govind Ballabh Pant Institute of Engineering & Technology, Pauri Garhwal, India

Govind Ballabh Pant Institute of Engineering & Technology, Pauri is an Institute with total commitment to quality and excellence in academic pursuits. The College was established in 1989, as an autonomous body, with a view to fulfill the ever-growing demand for well-trained professionals. It is one of the few premier colleges imparting technical education in the state of Uttarakhand.

The Institute started its first academic session from 1991-92 with a limited intake. The Institute was then affiliated to the Hemwati Nandan Bahuguna Garhwal University, Srinagar (Garhwal). From the academic year 2006-2007, the college got affiliated to the Uttarakhand Technical University, Dehradun year by year and getting disaffiliated from the H.N.B. Garhwal University. Since the academic year 2012-2013, the college got fully autonomous.

Department of Electronics & Communication Engineering

The Department of Electronics and Communication Engineering is proud to be the first department of the college established in the year 1991 to offer Bachelor's degree. Presently the department has a sanctioned intake of 60 students per year at the B.Tech level. The Department started its Master's Degree program in Digital Signal Processing in 2005 with intake of 10 students. Department has a rich tradition in research and training programs leading to Ph.D. degree in emerging areas of Electronics and Communication Engineering. In addition to well-equipped curriculum related laboratories, the department has many state of the art facilities for assisting research and development in solid state devices, VLSI, digital signal processing, microstrip antenna and wireless technology.

Department of Computer Science Engineering

The department of Computer Science and Engineering was established in the year 1992, has come out a long way on the frontier lines of software research and development. The department keeps in pace with the IT changes and regularly updates its laboratories with the latest computing facilities, licensed software and IT infrastructures to give exposure to the students to the state of the art technologies. Presently, Department offers Bachelor's degree in Computer Science & Engineering with an intake of 60 students. The Department has also started Master's degree program in Computer Science & Engineering in 2010 with intake of 18 students. The PhD program has been offered since 2013 and there are in all 14 PhD scholars registered currently in the various research areas such as mobile computing, digital image processing, ad-hoc networks, etc.

Department of Electrical Engineering

The Department started B.E. program in Electrical Engineering in 1997. It is envisaged to prepare Electrical Engineering graduates with adequate information on large-scale systems simulation and analysis tools, design capabilities and conceptual background for handling industrial process, embedded instrumentation and control strategies. The Department has also started PG course in Power Electronics & Drives. The department is offering doctoral courses under the guidance of highly qualified, experienced and dedicated faculty to provide both classroom teaching and practical instructions. The Department has qualified and experienced faculty in all the related fields of Electrical Engineering viz. Electrical Power System, Electrical Machines, Control, Instrumentation, Microprocessors, Power Electronics and Digital Signal Processing.

Acknowledgement

We would like to express our cordial thanks to all who helped make this conference a success. We sincerely thank our honorable Chief Patron Dr. S.N Singh, Vice-Chancellor, MMMUT Gorakhpur and Patron, Dr. Mahipal Singh Chauhan, Director, GBPIET Pauri Garhwal for their whole-hearted support for this conference.

The talk by Dr Mohammad Ayoub Khan, General Chair, the Keynotes by professors from Taiwan, Australia, Saudi Arabia, various IITs, IIITs DTU, etc. were key features of this conference.

We thank our director, Dr. Mahipal Singh Chauhan from the deepest corner of our heart. We would also thank Mr. Sandeep Kumar, Registrar, Director, GBPIET for his support to make the conference successful. We thank the advisory and technical committee for their significant contribution to this conference. We also thank all of our sponsors for sponsoring this event and making it a great succes.

This conference would not have been successful without the support of Management of GBPIET Pauri Garhwal. Our sincere thanks go to entire family of GBPIET Pauri Garhwal including faculty, staff and students for their assistance and hard work in organizing the conference.

And last but not least, we express our deep sense of gratitude to all the invited speakers, presenters, authors and the members of organizing committee without whose support this conference could not have been successful. We are deeply indebted to all contributors to this conference and all the reviewers for their patience and cogent views of papers, who have helped us with their expertise and thoughtful advice to shape this event effectively.

Our very special thanks go to all programme and organising committee members who have gone out of their way to help in shaping the event.

Finally, we offer our sincere thanks to Dr. Sanjay Gairola, Professor GBPIET for her continuous effort in the preparation, organisation and handling of the conference administration.

Track 1: Smart system and future internet

Smart Computing – Khan et al (Eds)
© 2021 Taylor & Francis Group, London, ISBN 978-0-367-76552-1

Toward semantic representation of middleware services

Alaa Abd Elhamid Radwan & Mohammad Tabrez Quasim
College of Computing and Information Technology, University of Bisha, Bisha, Saudi Arabia

ABSTRACT: Middleware is a middle-tier software that supports communication between two or more different applications and shared services. Managing the complexity and heterogeneity of distributed infrastructures is an important aspect of middleware. Middleware can provide a simple programing environment for the developer of a distributed application to support communication, information exchange, object management, and message sending, in addition to providing many functions for building distributed systems. Many classifications and definitions have been provided for middleware that emphasize giving middleware and its factors global appeal. In this paper, an ontology for middleware services is proposed to provide a global appeal for middleware, and to enrich the description of middleware services. Using this ontology, we can discover and classify incoming services into their appropriate forms according to the specifications and characteristics. The proposed ontology is helpful for users to find suitable services according to their own preferences.

Keywords: Middleware, OOM, RPC, MOM, DBM, TPM, ABM, WBM, ontology

1 INTRODUCTION

Middleware is a very vague term and there are many definitions which describe the basic concept. Middleware can be precisely defined as follows: A software layer that lies between the operating system and applications on each side of a distributed computing system in a network (Sacha, 2019). Transparency in location is also a very vital feature provided by middleware, which simply means that the components can travel between computers without making any changes to other components (Jean, 2005; Ajay, 2008). A proposed classification of middleware can appear as depicted in Figure 1. These categories are not always clearly isolated from one another as many types of middleware overlap in some of the provided services. The great benefit of middleware is to provide API services (through many distributed software) that work between the application and the operating system and network to enable the application to achieve the goals listed below (Amo, 2006; Max, 2006).

There is an urgent need to shed light on middleware services and their factors. Some classifications of middleware include (Chris, 2004; Cambel, 1999; Myerson, 2002):

- Object-oriented middleware (distributed object middleware);
- Remote procedure call;
- Message-oriented middleware;
- Database middleware;
- Transaction middleware;
- Agent-based Middleware; and
- Web-based Middleware.

However, this is not the complete list as we also can find some other software included in the category. Now, we will begin to briefly discuss each type of previous middleware service.

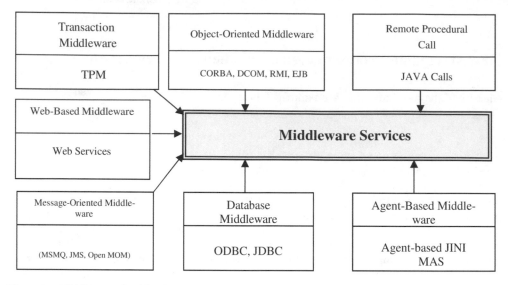

Figure 1.   Middleware classification and services.

Table 1.   OOM characteristics.

Property	Value
Request Reference	Distributed Object
Connection Point	Client/Server Stubs
Connection Mode	Synchronous (mainly)
	Asynchronous (limited)
Scalability	Limited
Message/Transaction	Supported
Heterogeneity	Language Independent

The remainder of this article is organized as follows. Section 2 presents a detailed discussion on the framework on middleware services. Section 3 presents the proposed ontology. Finally, a conclusion is presented in Section 4.

2   MIDDLEWARE MODELING

2.1   *Object-oriented middleware (OOM)*

Object-oriented middleware (OOM) is based on the simple concept of invoking an operation in an object that is available in another system, but unlike that of the client and server concept, in this concept there is a client and an object (Quasim, 2013a, 2013b). The characteristics of OOM are shown in Table 1. OOM provides a mechanism to allow methods to be invoked on remote objects and provides services to support the naming and location of objects in a system-wide manner (usually called Object Directory, Yellow Pages, etc.) in addition to object references, inheritance, and exceptions. Some of the examples of middleware systems in this category includes the OMG's CORBA, Microsoft COM, Java RMI, and Enterprise Java Beans (EJB) (ERL, 2003; OMG, 1995; Siegel, 2001)

Table 2.   Procedural middleware characteristics.

Property	Value
Request Reference	Remote Procedure
Connection Point	Client/Server Stubs
Connection Mode	Synchronous
Scalability	Limited
Client state	Blocked (Mainly)
Heterogeneity	Language independent

Table 3.   MOM characteristics.

Property	Value
Network communication	Messages
Connection Point	Client/Server
Connection Mode	Synchronous/Asynchronus
Scalability	Limited
Heterogeneity	Limited

2.2   *Remote Procedural Middleware (RPC)*

Sun Microsystems developed Remote Procedure Calls (RPCs) in the early 1980s, and RPCs now are integrated into different operating systems such as Unix and Mircrosoft Windows. The characteristics of the procedural middleware is show in Table 2.

2.3   *Message-oriented middleware (MOM)*

Message-oriented middleware (MOM) is another important middleware that establishes communication between applications through messages. MOM allows both synchronous and asynchronous communication models which lead to two different types of MOM: message queuing and message passing. A third model also exists which is known as the "publish and subscribe" model. The characteristics of MOM are shown in Table 3.

2.4   *Transaction Middleware (TM)*

In order to support the concept of distributed transaction across different hosts, the transactional middleware (TM) or transaction processing monitors (TPMs) were designed. The characteristics of TPM are shown in Table 4. Although it is compulsory for a transaction to enable ACID (Atomic, Consistent, Isolated, and Durable) properties, it usually supports the two-phase commit (2PC) protocol to implement these types of transactions and properties (Speer, 1994; Ozen, 1991).

2.5   *Database Middleware (DBM)*

Database middleware (DBM) is responsible for establishing communication among different applications and a local/remote database. However, the DBM cannot allow two-way communication as well as transfer calls/objects between client and server (Linthicum, 2019). It is often chosen to complement other middleware types of DBM that may be varying according to data source (e.g., flat file, relational DB, object database) or connection type such as native middleware, call-level interfaces (CLIs), and database gateways. CLIs provide a single interface to several databases. CLIs, such as OLE DB, ODBC, and JDBC, provide a single interface to several databases. They are capable of translating the common interface call into a number of database dialects, and also

5

Table 4. TPM characteristics.

Property	Value
Request Reference	Distributed transactions
Connection Point	Client/Server Component
Connection Mode	Synchronous/Asynchronous
Scalability	High
Client state	Blocked (Mainly)
Heterogeneity	Medium

Table 5. Agent-based middleware characteristics.

Property	Value
Request Reference	Messages
Connection Point	Client/Server
Connection Mode	Negotiation/Synchronous
Scalability	High
Client state	Unblocked
Heterogeneity	High

translating the response back in an understandable form to the requesting application (Microsoft Corporation, 1992). Database gateways are capable of integrating different databases for access from a single-application interface.

2.6 *Agent-based Middleware (ABM)*

Agent-based middleware (ABM) is suggested as a solution for solving problems and challenges that arise when creating applications that operate in dynamic, heterogeneous environments to manage the resources of distributed systems due to the increased flexibility in adapting to the dynamically changing requirements of such systems (Watson, 1996). The agent environment provides a set of services shielding agent developers from the low-level details of the underlying platform, as depicted in Figure 2. The characteristics of ABM is shown as follows in Table 5.

Advantages of ABM:

1. Modularity—different modules made up by groups of agents may be changed easily
2. Autonomy and pro-activity properties of agents are well suited for reasoning
3. Scalability and adaptability
4. MAS allows for the interconnection and interoperation of multiple existing legacy systems (Lin, 2004; Fabio, 2007)

2.7 *Web-based Middleware (WBM)*

Web-based middleware (WBM) is a new approach to system architecture service-oriented architecture (SOA) that was introduced by web services. The SOA can be defined as a software architecture that defines all functions as independent services with well-defined executable interfaces, which can be called in defined sequences to form business processes (Barry, 2007).

Existing CORBA and DCOM solutions may conform to the above definition, but this is web services technology that can really allow for wide application integration (Microsoft Press, 2003). Web services have a collection of underlying technologies, as depicted in Figure 3.

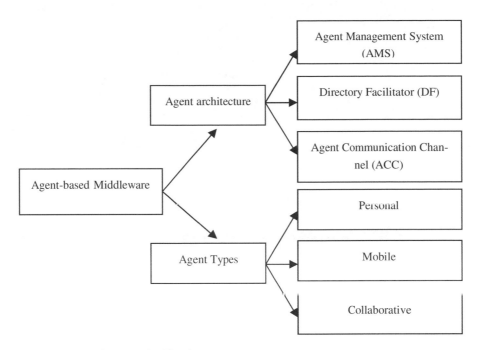

Figure 2.   Agent-based system classification.

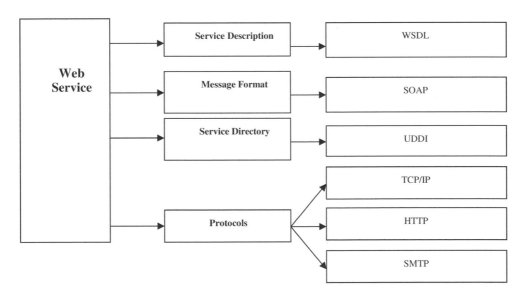

Figure 3.   Web services stack.

3   BUILDING MIDDLEWARE ONTOLOGY

In recent years' ontologies have become a topic of interest in computer science. Ontology gathers information about certain fields of interest, and describes the concepts in the domain as well as the relationships that hold between those concepts. In the following section we will present a

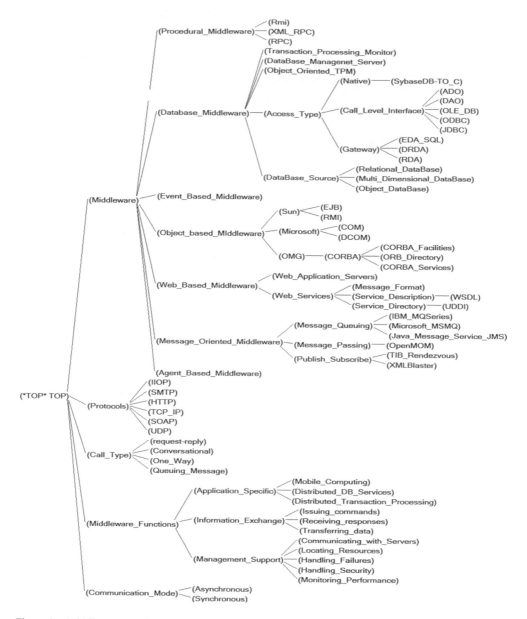

Figure 4.   Middleware ontology graph.

middleware ontology structure that can be used for many purposes, including enterprise integration, database design, information retrieval, and information interchanges.

3.1   Components of Middleware OWL Ontologies

Ontology provides a generic way of representing domain knowledge for a specific application. This can also be understood as a shared conceptualization formal and explicit description. Ontologies enable the creation of a common vocabulary of a domain, its context, and its relationships. Classes in ontology can be related to the class concept as in object-oriented programming. Real-world objects are grouped and compose collections of elements with similar features.

An ontology file consists of Individuals, Properties, and Classes (W3C Recommendation, 2019; Matthew, 2004; Allemang, 2011). Classes are interpreted as sets that contain individuals. Classes may be organized into a super-class-subclass hierarchy, which is also known as taxonomy. Subclasses specialize ("are subsumed by") their super-classes. For example, consider that the classes Middleware and MOM–MOM might be a subclass of middleware (so middleware is the super-class of MOM). Our proposed middleware ontology structure is depicted in Figure 4.

4 CONCLUSION

In this paper we have presented a survey about middleware services and its characteristics as a first step toward building an ontology to list classes and properties of middleware. Some of the classes in our ontology are not actually a tangible unit that can be parsed as a standalone service; instead, they are middleware functions that we could include in our program to provide a service such as database middleware services and agent middleware.

REFERENCES

Abuhasel, K.A., Khan, M.A. (2020). A secure Industrial Internet of Things (IIoT) framework for resource management in smart manufacturing. *IEEE Access*, 8: 117354–117364. DOI: 10.1109/ACCESS.2020.3004711.

Ajay, D., Mukesh, S. (2008). *Distributed Computing: Principles, Algorithms, and Systems*. Cambridge University Press.

Allemang, D., Hendler, J. (2011). *Semantic Web for the Working Ontologist*. 2nd ed. Elsevier Science.

Arno, P., Kay, R., Frank, P. (2006). *Distributed Systems Architecture: A Middleware Approach*. Morgan Kaufmann.

Barry, D.K. (2007). *Web Services and Service-Oriented Architecture*. Morgan Publishers, 2003.

Campbell, A.T., Coulson, G., Kounavis, M. (1999). Managing complexity: middleware explained. *IT Professional*, IEEE Computer Society.

Chris, B., Peter, B. (2004). *IT Architectures and Middleware: Strategies for Building Large, Integrated Systems*. 2nd ed. Addison-Wesley.

Erl, T. (2003). *Service-Oriented Architecture: Concepts, Technology, and Design*. Morgan Publishers.

Fabio, B., Giovanni, C., Dominic, G. (2007). *Developing Multi-Agent Systems with JADE*. John Wiley and Sons Press.

Horridge, M., Knublauch, H., Rector, A., Stevens, R.D., Wroe, C. (2004), *A Practical Guide to Building OWL Ontologies Using the Protégé-OWL Plugin and CO-ODE Tools*. The University of Manchester. August 27.

Jean, D., Tim, K., George C. (2005). *Distributed Systems: Concepts and Design*. 4th ed. Addison-Wesley.

Khan, M.A. (2020). An IoT framework for heart disease prediction based on MDCNN classifier. *IEEE Access*, 8: 34717–34727. DOI: 10.1109/ACCESS.2020.2974687

Khan, M.A. et al. (2020). *Decentralised IoT, Decenetralised IoT: A Blockchain Perspective*. Springer, Studies in Big Data. DOI: https://doi.org/10.1007/978-3-030-38677-1

Khan, M.A., Abuhasel, K.A. (2020). Advanced metameric dimension framework for heterogeneous industrial Internet of Things. *Computational Intelligence*, 1– 21. https://doi.org/10.1111/coin.12378

Khan, M.A., Algarni, F. (2020). A healthcare monitoring system for the diagnosis of heart disease in the IoMT cloud environment using MSSO-ANFIS. *IEEE Access*, 8: 122259–122269. DOI: 10.1109/ ACCESS.2020.3006424.

Khan, M.A., Quasim, M.T., et.al. (2020). A secure framework for authentication and encryption using improved ECC for IoT-based medical sensor data. *IEEE Access*, 8: 52018–52027. DOI: 10.1109/ACCESS.2020.2980739

Krakowiak, S. (2019). What is middleware. ObjectWeb.org. https://web.archive.org/web/20050507151935/ http://middleware.objectweb.org/. Accessed 2019.

Lin, P., Michael, W. (2004). *Developing Intelligent Agent Systems: A Practical Guide*. John Wiley and Sons Press.

Linthicum, D. (1999). Database-oriented middleware. *DM Review Magazine*, November.

Max, H. (2006). Operating Systems and Middleware: Supporting Controlled Interaction. Course Technology (2006).

http://www.dmreview.com/toc.cfm?issueid=1255. Accessed 2019.

Microsoft Corporation. (1992) *Object Linking and Embedding Programmers Reference*. version 1. Microsoft Press.

Microsoft Press (2003). Developing XML Web Services and Server Components with Microsoft Visual Basic. NET and Microsoft Visual C#. NET.

Myerson, J.M. (2002). *The Complete Book of Middleware*. Auerbach Publications.

OMG. (1995). *The Common Object Request Broker- Architecture and Specification*. OMG.

Ozsu, M., Valduriez, P. (1991). *Principle of Distributed Database Systems*. Prentice Hall inc, 1991.

Quasim, M.T. (2013). An efficient approach for concurrency control in distributed database system. *Indian Streams Research Journal* [Online], 3(9). DOI:10.9780/22307850.

Quasim, M.T. (2013). Security issues in distributed database system model. *International Journal of Advanced Computer Technology*, 2(xii): 396–400.

Siegel, J. (2001). *CORBA 3 Fundamentals & Programming*. John Wiley & Sons.

Speer, T., Storm, M. (1994). Digital's transaction processing monitors. *Digital Technical Journal*, 3(1): 18–32.

W3C Recommendation. (2019). OWL WEB ONTOLOGY LANGUAGE. http://www.w3.org/TR/2004/REC-owl-guide-20040210. Accessed 2019.

Watson, M. (1996). *Programming Intelligent Agents for the Internet*. McGraw-Hill.

Smart Computing – Khan et al (Eds)
© 2021 Taylor & Francis Group, London, ISBN 978-0-367-76552-1

A survey on energy-efficient networking and its improved security features

Usha Chauhan, Divya Sharma, Shriyash Mohril & Gaurav Pratap Singh
School of Electrical, Electronics and Communication Engineering, Galgotias University, Greater Noida, India

ABSTRACT: In today's fast-moving world, information sent from one end of the globe is received at the other end in a blink of an eye. Behind this phenomenon is a large backbone network in which various worldwide servers are interrelated in order to share information between them. The networking devices (routers, switches, etc.) are the most crucial part of a network as they are used as a medium to propagate information from source to destination. In recent years, various advancements have been made to improve the efficiency, security, and energy consumption of networks using various methodologies and reference models.

Keywords: Router, switch, network, methodology

1 INTRODUCTION

At its core, network security refers to information security on the network, which requires that the flow of network systems and secured data is not subjected to fortuitous or malicious damage, disclosure, or modification. Therefore, processed data is exposed to attack. Data safety measures should be taken on all data communication networks, including the lawfulness of the data confirmed and the lawfulness of the communication data guaranteed. A network handling a huge amount of data and information shall be kept in the external storage (Bakre & Badrinath 1995). With the development of computer networks and Internet technology, the problem of security in the data network and the Internet has become a crucial issue. Unauthorized users such as hackers are manipulating users' precious data in order to gain access to information (Lebeck et al. 2000). Therefore, the question arises: what is the need of network security?

Network security is defined as the practice by which we can protect the vital information present over the network(Alrajeh et al. 2013). The key goals of network security are as follows.

A. *Avoidance of information disclosure.* The protection of vital information is a major task in order to furnish confidentiality and privacy. Some methods by which confidentiality can be maintained are passwords, biometric verifications, data encryption, user IDs, etc.

B. *Sustaining veracity.* It should not only guarantee information secrecy but also ensure the accuracy and consistency over its entire life. Some measures to ensure truthfulness include controlling the physical environment of network terminals and servers and maintaining difficult authentication practices. Shielding the data is a major challenge that can be rectified by using a cryptography technique in order to promote data integrity.

C. *Ensuring accessibility.* Only sanctioned persons should have the right to access data at the right time. Accessibility can be ensured by preparing hardware repairs as soon as possible and by maintaining a correctly functioning operating system. Redundancy methods should be deployed for the regular backup of information services that are highly critical (Pathan et al. 2006).

Along with security, the efficiency of a networking device is also important. An efficient network improves the speed of networking devices. So in order to establish an ideal network both efficiency

DOI 10.1201/9781003167488-2

and network security should be taken into consideration. This paper presents various threats to the network and various processes to rectify them. Here, we will also use the Cisco Packet Tracer Simulator to apply security features to the networking device. An efficiency parameter is also discussed as well as a brief description about several approaches to improve the efficiency of the network (Schurgers & Srivastava 2001).

2 EFFICIENCY OF NETWORK

It has been observed that there is a noteworthy environmental and economic problem caused by the high-energy intake of Information and Communication Technology (ICT) equipment. Nowadays, network organizations are becoming a large portion of the energy impression in ICT. With recent developments, the concept of green networking or energy efficiency has come into the picture. The main concern in the path of network industry is to minimize the energy intake of network infrastructure due to the budding economic profits, environmental impact, and ethical responsibility (Karlof & Wagner 2003). This paper suggests that reducing the energy consumption of LAN switches and routers, as well as connected hosts, is of interest for environmental, economic, and operational reasons (Ogheneovo & Ibiba 2014). It is forecasted that in this decade the energy consumption of computing equipment will grow significantly unless energy efficiency mechanisms are implemented in computing systems. This problem disturbs mutually highperformance computing services such as end-user equipment and data centers. Energy consumption should be made more proportional to the system load so that the energy efficiency of computing and networking systems can be ominously improved to avoid poor energy efficiency (Kaur 2014).

According to the life-cycle assessment, the highest amount of energy is consumed during the usage phase of network devices. The major input constraints affecting the energy efficiency are link load bandwidth and traffic matrices during the usage phase (Singh 2016). The waste caused by network idle energy is very large. With constant improvement of performance in router, scale, and hardware integration, the power consumption of the router presents exponential growth; even in the idle state, network equipment takes a huge amount of energy. The problem of Internet energy saving has progressively become a new research direction of the future network. When the device's idle time exceeds a certain threshold, the device will enter standby or hibernation, and when the device's sleeping time reaches a certain threshold, the equipment is awakened. Due to sleeping time being limited, energy saving condition is poor and the data packet will be discarded during inactivity. The wake-on-arrival (WoA) strategy is an improved, timer-driven strategy and puts specific interface equipment into working condition. When the interface detects a packet arriving, it will awaken the device. However, the varieties of equipment that can support WoA are few. In addition to energy saving on its own, some studies focus on the link between energy-saving equipment. Data shows that when the Ethernet link rate increases from 100 Mbps to 1 Gbps, power intake has increased by 2–4 watt, and when the Ethernet link rate increases to 10 Gbps, power consumption has increased by 10–20 w. Nonetheless, the current Ethernet in power consumption in idle and non-idle conditions is almost the same, and measured data indicates that the link utilization of the Ethernet is mainly between 1 and 5%. So when the link is in the low consumption rate, reducing the link rate can effectively reduce the energy consumption within the limited performance impact. Through automatically adjusting the full-duplex transmission of Ethernet link exchange rate, adaptive link technology adapts to different link utilization and makes the link transmission rate and the link load proportional (Habibullah et al. 2017)

3 MAJOR FACTORS AFFECTING EFFICIENCY OF NETWORK DEVICES

A. Hardware. Hardware alignment plays an important role in determining the efficiency of the networking device. If the hardware is not scalable according to the need of the network, it reduces the efficiency of the device.

B. Bandwidth. It is one of the most valuable resources which affects the efficiency of a networking device A limited amount of bandwidth is provided to different devices on which they operate so proper utilization of provided bandwidth can upgrade the efficiency of the device.

C. Network load. Each networking device is designed with a limited number of ports as well as with limited load handling capacity. Sometimes with an increase in load, the efficiency of the device is reduced and hence its performance is degraded.

4 TECHNIQUES TO IMPROVE EFFICIENCY

A. Pause power cycle (PPC) for reducing LAN switch energy use. Ethernet links are very lightly utilized—in general, traffic is busty with infrequent high-rate peaks. The proposed Pause Power Cycle (PPC) exploits this property to reduce energy use (Christensen 2008). The basic idea of PPC is to use existing Ethernet PAUSE flow control frames sent from a first-level LAN switch to connected hosts (and other network equipment) to stop traffic flow on links incoming to the switch. During a coordinated link-off time, switch components such as the switch core and/or line cards can be powered down. Obviously, a major concern with PPC is what effects it may have on higher layer protocols and application performance. PAUSE frames sent to hosts may cause presentations to block (but, there will be no packet loss). PAUSE frames sent to other network equipment may cause packet loss due to a buffer overflow. These effects will only occur if a link off period coincides with a traffic burst. If packet loss occurs, TCP (as used by most network applications) will likely recover the lost packets, possibly even invisibly to a user (Christensen 2008).

B. Clustering approach Clustering means grouping of nodes using some approach to forward data efficiently. In this approach, a cluster head is elected for each cluster. This approach is used to avoid flooding and overloading the network, and also improves the performance of system by reducing battery power consumption. In order to minimize overloading, intra-group communication must be maximum and inter-group communication must be minimum. The clustering method has been widely pursued by the research community to achieve this scalable objective. Various clustering algorithms are used to reduce isolate groups for hibernating and switched off part of the network (Alrajeh et al. 2013).

5 NETWORK SECURITY

The major challenge in the field of networking is the security of the network from intruders. In order to safeguard precious data of various organizations, network administrations, and companies' effective safety measures are needed to incorporate. The Internet is connected to us without any boundaries. In this scenario, network security is essential because any organizational network is accessible from any computer all around the globe. Network security can be defined as shielding various websites from different forms of attack. Security means seeing attacks, threats, weaknesses, countermeasures, and acceptable risks in the network. Networking devices such as routers and peripheral devices security must be implemented as these devices buffer data. Therefore, routers are required to be secured enough as data cannot be easily stolen by means of malware like a "Trojan Horse" (Reviriego et al. 2012).

6 CLASSIFICATIONS OF NETWORK SECURITY

A. Network access control. User access must be selective in nature so that a limited user should have access to the network. Each user and each device should be recognized to avoid probable attackers. Various security policies can be implemented to the network by giving limited access to the disobedient devices. This process is said to be network access control (NAC).

B. Antimalicious software. Spyware, viruses, ransomware, and Trojan worms fall under the category of malicious software. Generally, it has been observed that malware can infect a network by lying latent for days or even weeks. To fix damage, remove the malware and anomalies; the best antimalware programs are required to implement over the network which can scan and stop the virus upon entry level.

C. Application security. Any software and applications that are used in both onbe's personal and professional life need to be protected because applications may contain loopholes, or vulnerabilities, that attackers can use to penetrate through the network. Application security comprises of both hardware and software in order to close these loopholes.

D. Behavioral analytics. In this, normal behavior is compared with the abnormal network behavior by using various behavioral analytics tools. By using this tool, we can check to see if activities have deviated from the norm.

E. Data loss prevention. This is a technique used by various organizations that can stop people from uploading, forwarding, or even printing critical information in an unsafe manner so that data breaching can be reduced.

F. Email security. Email gateways are the major source of security breaches in an organization. Hackers employ social engineering tactics and personal data to disclose the confidentiality of the organization. In order to prevent the loss of sensitive data, an email security application is required to block incoming attacks and control outbound messages.

G. Firewalls. Firewalls are the hardware or software entities that create obstacles between a trusted internal network and untrusted outside networks, such as the Internet. Firewalls deploy various sets of rules to block unwanted traffic.

H. Mobile device security. Cybercriminals can easily target mobile devices and apps so several parameters can be used to protect mobile devices from intruders. With the advancement of internet banking (BHIM, UPIs) attackers can easily target these banking portals.

I. Security information and event management. Security management and event management (SIEM) products pull together the information that your security staff needs to identify and react to threats. These products come in different forms, including virtual and physical appliances and server software (see Figure 1; Ramanathan & Rosales-Hain 2000).

L. Web security. Web security is a process by which web-based threats from malicious websites are thwarted. It will protect your web network on site or in the cloud.

M. VPN. VPN stands for virtual private network. It is a service that creates a private, secure network over a public one. If a user is connected through a VPN, all traffic becomes encrypted and the IP address gets replaced with the address of a VPN server (Sun 2015).

Figure 1. Security management and event management (SIEM).

7 DISSCUSSION

In this paper, we described the efficiency and network security in order to illustrate the security features of networking devices (Yuan & Yang 2015). We are using Cisco stimulation software (Cisco Packet Tracer). In Figure 1, we demonstrate a network containing routers, switches, and PCs, which are in turn connected with straight-through and crossover wires, respectively. In Figure 2, we show security password command is being applied on the IOS command line interface of a router. In Figure 3, we demonstrate how an applied password is encrypted as "1mERr$N3N8TZcJuMRiso.b3tRIVO" from an applied password "Indian army". Even in

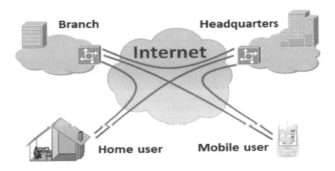

Figure 2.   Virtual private network (VPN).

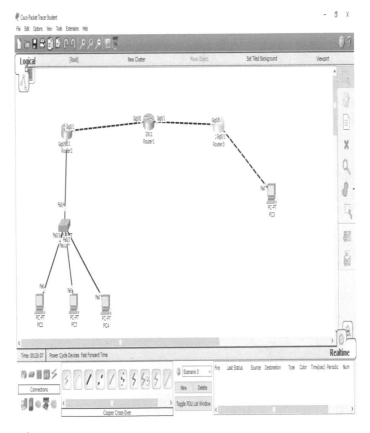

Figure 3.   Network.

large-scale industries and at home, we can secure our networking devices to protect our useful data (routers, switches, hubs) from hackers' attacks. The command line interface of the router is shown in Figure 4, while the output produced from password encryption is shown in Figure 5.

Figure 4. Command line interface.

Figure 5. Password encryption.

8 CONCLUSION

This survey paper explains how router-level security can be enhanced. To elaborate the process, methodologies of the networking have been used. That includes the router-level security password encryption. To make this possible, the Cisco network stimulation software (packet tracer) has been used for structural analysis and observation. This software involves the programming in basic C language. This project demonstrates the two levels of securities in which one has to first log in at the console port and then verify user access. For the first level, the login password is "singhmohril", and at the second level the password "Indian army" is used. Also, the password has been encrypted as "1mERr$N3N8TZcJuMRiso.b3tRIVO". So, if one wants to enter into the console port to compromise the router this level of security will discourage such a possibility. Hence, such measures are done to maintain the high network information security by reducing the probability of attack.

REFERENCES

Alrajeh, N.A., Khan, S., and Shames, B., 2013. IDS in Wireless detector networks: A Review. *International Journal of Distributed Detector Network*, 1, 7.

Bakre, A. and Badrinath, B.R., 1995. I-TCP: indirect TCP for mobile hosts. *In: Proceedings – International Conference on Distributed Computing Systems*. IEEE, 136–146.

Christensen, K., 2008. *Green Networking: Reducing the Energy Use of LAN Switches and Connected Hosts*.

Habibullah, K.M., Rondeau, E., and Georges, J.P., 2017. Reducing energy consumption of network infrastructure using spectral approach. *In: Technology for Smart Futures*. Springer International Publishing, 235–250.

Karlof, C. and Wagner, D., 2003. Secure routing in wireless sensor networks: Attacks and countermeasures. *In: Ad Hoc Networks*. Elsevier, 293–315.

Kaur, G., 2014. Reliability of wireless sensor networks. *International Journal of Advanced Research in Computer Engineering & Technology (IJARCET)*, 3, 1926–1928.

Lebeck, A.R., Fan, X., Zeng, H., and Ellis, C., 2000. Power aware page allocation. *In: International Conference on Architectural Support for Programming Languages and Operating Systems – ASPLOS*. 105–116.

Ogheneovo, E.E. and Ibiba, S.K., 2014. Modeling Network Router, Switches and Security Using Cisco and OPNET Simulation Software. *IOSR Journal of Engineering (IOSRJEN) ISSN (e)*, 2250–3021.

Pathan, A.S.K., Lee, H.W., and Hong, C.S., 2006. Security in Wireless Sensor Networks: Issues and challenges. *In: 8th International Conference Advanced Communication Technology, ICACT 2006 – Proceedings*. IEEE Computer Society, 1043–1048.

Ramanathan, R. and Rosales-Hain, R., 2000. Topology control of multihop wireless networks using transmit power adjustment. *In: Proceedings – IEEE INFOCOM*. IEEE, 404–413.

Reviriego, P., Sivaraman, V., Zhao, Z., Maestro, J.A., Vishwanath, A., Sanchez-Macian, A., and Russell, C., 2012. An energy consumption model for energy efficient ethernet switches. *In: Proceedings of the 2012 International Conference on High Performance Computing and Simulation, HPCS 2012*. 98–104.

Schurgers, C. and Srivastava, M.B., 2001. Energy efficient routing in wireless sensor networks. *In: Proceedings – IEEE Military Communications Conference MILCOM*. 357–361.

Singh, H., 2016. Network Security, A Challenge. *International Journal of Advanced Research in Computer and Communication Engineering*, 5 (3).

Sun, Y., 2015. Research on Security Issues and Protection Strategy of Computer Network. *The Open Automation and Control Systems Journal*, 7 (1), 2097–2101.

Yuan, L. and Yang, J., 2015. Design of an Energy-Efficient Wireless Router Switch. Atlantis Press, 449–452.

Smart Computing – Khan et al (Eds)
© *2021 Taylor & Francis Group, London, ISBN 978-0-367-76552-1*

The efficiency of a virtual lab in studying a digital logic design course using Logisim

Abdelrazig Suliman & Mohammad Tabrez Quasim
College of Computing & Information Technology, University of Bisha, Saudi Arabia

ABSTRACT: Analyzing students' attitudes and preferences in selecting teaching methods is one of the most important factors for measuring learning outcomes. The evaluation process is constantly evolving and requires the use of the best methods with flexibility, simplicity and low cost. This study aimed to design and understand the effectiveness of using virtual machines in the development of skills to use the design tools of the digital logic laboratory at the Faculty of Computing at the University of Bisha, Saudi Arabia. The purpose of the proposed platform is to reduce the cost of the system and the loss and damage elements of logic circuits while using the digital laboratory. The open-source Logisim software has been used for an easy-to-use graphical environment, enabling students to design and simulate digital circuits. In order to measure the effectiveness of this virtual software a questionnaire was given to the students. The application of statistical methods, where the study reached several results, included finding positive trends for students toward the use of virtual machines in teaching.

Keywords: Virtual lab, logic simulation, combinational circuits, the gates, the arithmetic, plexers, sequential circuits, Logisim Software

1 INTRODUCTION

A Digital Logic Design course was developed at the University of Bisha to introduce students to the fundamental theory and basic design blocks of digital circuits. Students of theoretical fundamentals delve into Boolean algebra and logic gates. The fundamental gates are AND, OR, NOT, XOR, and NOR. These gates constitute the basic units for all digital logic design, and combinational logic including: design of half-adder and full-adder–half-sub; full substructure; design of encoder & decoder; and synchronous sequential logic which includes sequential logic circuit (flip flop-shift registers-counters) (Akintomiwa 2014; Harris & Harris 2012).

To complement both the theoretical background and the design of digital circuits, the course includes experiments that progress at an equivalent pace with the course lectures (AbdElrazig 2015).

The educational software tool Logisim has been used by the faculty of computer and information technology at the University of Bisha in two introductory undergraduate engineering courses related to digital circuit design and an introduction to computer architecture. Logisim is an open source for designing and simulating digital logic circuits It is simple enough to facilitate learning the most basic concepts related to logic circuits (Logisim 2019a, 2019b). The first objective of this paper is to describe the modality of using the Logisim educational software tool in learning digital circuits design, applied within the course. The second objective of the paper is to review the student evaluation survey results on the use of the Logisim educational software tool within the course.

DOI 10.1201/9781003167488-3

2 RELATED WORK

Several virtual laboratories have been developed in logic design (Ichsan 2017; Schuurman 2013; Kurniawan 2017). In Abuzalata (2010), 13 different functions (VIs) were designed, including a complete set of programmable logic controller (PLC) functions in order to realize a programmable PC-based virtual PLC. In Borodzhieva (2018), a synthesizing process of decoder and its optimization was designed using Logisim. Team members exchange information and help each other in the course unit's tasks. Moreover, its objective is to motivate learners to perform the tasks where the success of the whole team depends on each student's work.

In our study, a Logisim software was used to simulate all digital circuit course labs. Student surveys for course topic tasks were investigated and analyzed which show their opinion and paradigm to reflect the factor scopes in their usage. Finally, the concluded result was discussed.

3 MATERIALS AND METHODS

In this paper, we describe how we designed and implemented a virtual lab at the University of Bisha Faculty of Computer and Information Technology. Logisim software has been used to build a digital logic circuit course.

The experiments are implemented and published at the lab of the University of Bisha using Logisim. These experiments include the following.

i. The gates includes NOT Gate, Buffer, AND/OR/NAND/NOR Gate, XOR/XNOR/Odd Parity/Even Parity Gate, and Controlled Buffer/Inverter.

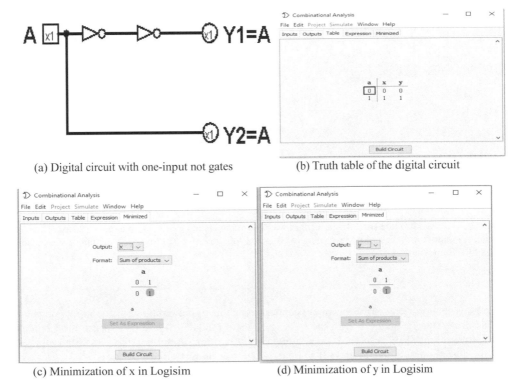

(a) Digital circuit with one-input not gates (b) Truth table of the digital circuit

(c) Minimization of x in Logisim (d) Minimization of y in Logisim

Figure 1. The NOT gate, buffer circuit. (a) Digital circuit with one-input not gates. (b) Truth table of the digital circuit. (c) Minimization of x in Logisim. (d) Minimization of y in Logisim.

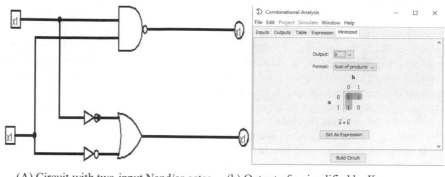

(A) Circuit with two-input Nand/or gates   (b) Output of x simplified by K-map

(c) Output of y simplified by K-map   (d) Boolean function of x

(e) Boolean function of y   (f) Truth table of the digital circuit

Figure 2.   The and/or/nand/nor gate. (a) Circuit with two-input Nand/or gates (b). Output of x simplified by K-map. (c) Output of y simplified by K-map (d) Boolean function of x. (e) Boolean function of y. (f) Truth table of the digital circuit.

In this section we describe the process of designing the digital circuit with one-input not gates, as illustrated in Figure 1 with the basic gate logic modules. We will also use the Logisim software tool in order to find: (a) a digital circuit with one-input not gates; (b) truth table of the digital circuit; and (c) and (d). Output of x, y was simplified by K-map.

- In Figure 2 is a basic gate or/Nand Gate. We will also use the Logisim software in order to find (a) or/nand circuit with two-input Nand, Or gates; (b) and (c) Output of y and x, in (d) and (f) find Boolean function of x, y. In Figure 2, (f) finds the Truth table of the digital circuit.

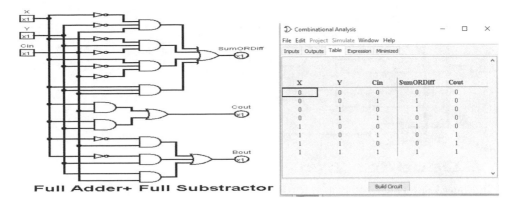

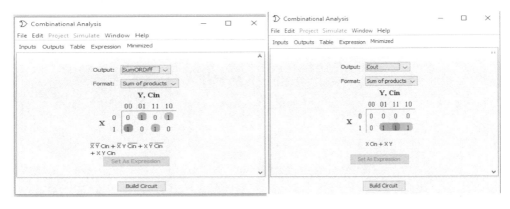

(a) Digital circuit with 4-bit adder subtractor circuit   (b) Truth table of the digital circuit

(c) Output of Y, Cin simplified by K-map   (d) Output of Cout

Figure 3.   The full adder and full substractor. (a) Digital circuit with 4-bit adder subtractor circuit. (b) Truth table of the digital circuit. (c) Output of Y, Cin simplified by K-map (d) Output of Cout.

ii. The arithmetic includes combinational components that perform arithmetic values on unsigned and two complement values. Includes adder, subtractor, multiplier, and divider.
The full adder and full substractor has three inputs, the same three singlebit binary inputs x, y and Cin, and four outputs–Sum, Diff, Cout and Bout. The corresponding digital circuit, truth table, Output of 7, Cin, Cout, and Bout simplified by K-map Boolean function (results a, b, and d) are shown in Figure 3.

iii. Plexers include control components, all of which are combinational, but their purpose is generally for routing values like multiplexer, de-multiplexer, and decoder.
The corresponding decoder circuit, truth table, and Output of D0, D1, D2, and D3 simplified by K-map (results a, b, d, c, d, and f) are shown in Figure 4.

iv Sequential circuit output depends not only on the current values of the inputs, but also on their past values. These hold the secret of how to memorize information, like flip-flop, register and counter.

The corresponding R-S flip-flop circuit, truth table, and Output of x, y simplified by K-map (results a, b, c, and d) are shown in Figure 5.

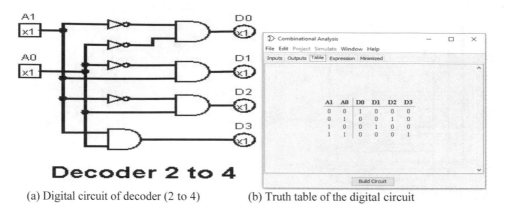

(a) Digital circuit of decoder (2 to 4) (b) Truth table of the digital circuit

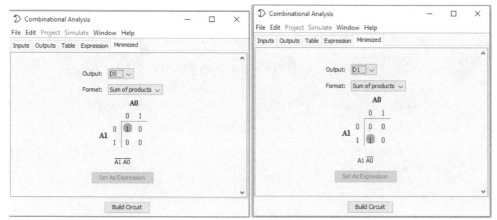

(c) Output of D0 simplified by K-map (d) Output of D1 simplified by K-map

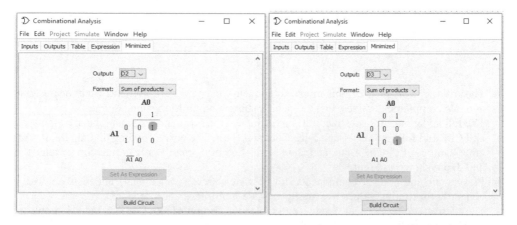

(e) Output of D2 simplified by K-map (f) Output of D3 simplified by K-map

Figure 4. The decoder. (a) Digital circuit of decoder (2 to 4). (b) Truth table of the digital circuit. (c) Output of D0 simplified by K-map. (d) Output of D1 simplified by K-map. (e) Output of D2 simplified by K-map. (f) Output of D3 simplified by K-map.

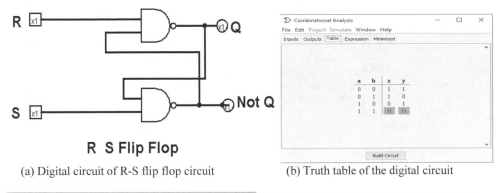

(a) Digital circuit of R-S flip flop circuit   (b) Truth table of the digital circuit

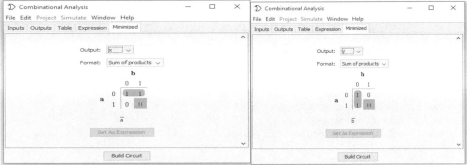

(c) Output of x simplified by K-map   (d) Output of y simplified by K-map

Figure 5.   The R-S flip-flop. (a) Digital circuit of R-S flip flop circuit. (b) Truth table of the digital circuit. (c) Output of x simplified by K-map. (d) Output of y simplified by K-map.

4   STUDENT EVALUATION OF USING A LOGISIM EDUCATIONAL SOFTWARE TOOL IN LEARNING DIGITAL CIRCUIT DESIGN

Various examples of design of a digital logic design course using the Logisim software tool were given to fouryear undergraduate students. Some of the tasks that were assigned to them for realization are described below

- Combinational logic circuit
  - The Gates include Constant, NOT Gate, Buffer, AND/OR/NAND/NOR Gate, OR/XNOR/Even Parity Gate, Controlled Buffer/Inverter.
  - The arithmetic includes adder, subtractor, multiplier, and divider.
  - Plexers includes multiplexer, de-multiplexer, decoder.
- sequential logic circuit
  - Like Flip-flop, register and counter.

The efficiency of the Logisim software tool in achieving its educational goal of helping students in a digital logic design course was assessed through an anonymous student survey in the form of a questionnaire. The survey consisted of 24 students who successfully realized the given task, and the questionnaire consisted of 23 questions. On the questionnaire, Likert-type questions (5=completely agree, 4=mostly agree, 3=partly agree, 2=mostly disagree, 1=completely disagree) were related to the evaluation of the Logisim educational software tool and its usage in teaching the course.

Results of the study question "What are the students' attitudes toward using the program Logisim in teaching" are provided in Table 1.

Table 1. Illustrates students' attitudes toward using the default program Logisim for a digital logic design course.

#	Question	Average	S.D.	Attitude Type
1	Using the tool of the virtual program helped me achieve the course learning objectives.	4.05	0.74	Positive
2	Using the virtual program helped me achieve the course learning outcomes.	3.95	0.8	Positive
3	The practicable note of using the virtual program is clearly understood and interesting.	3.81	0.93	Positive
4	The interface of the virtual program is easy to understand and use.	4	0.82	Positive
5	By using the tool of the virtual program, I managed to create logical circles quickly and precisely.	3.86	0.69	Positive
6	The tool of the virtual program is capable of training to detect and correct errors in logic circuit design.	4.14	0.69	Positive
7	The tools of the virtual program can be used to conceptualize logic circuit design concepts in ways that are more concrete.	4.29	0.49	Positive
8	Learning using the virtual program does not provide suitable opportunities for learning, but it is used for fun and entertainment only.	2.29	0.49	Negative
9	I find it difficult to deal with the virtual program in education.	2.14	1.07	Negative
10	Learning using the virtual program has more benefits than harms.	2.43	0.79	Positive
11	I greatly benefited from building logical circuits by using the virtual program tool.	4	0	Positive
12	Learning using the virtual program requires more effort than I can	2.14	0.38	Negative
13	Learning using the virtual program makes the lecture interesting.	2.29	0.76	Positive
14	Learning using the virtual program reduces the chances of learning a weak student.	4	0.58	Negative
15	Learning using the virtual program is a waste of time.	3.57	0.53	Positive
16	Learning using the virtual program makes the lesson fun.	3.71	0.76	Positive
17	Learning using the virtual program increases the activity of students to understand the course.	4	0.58	Positive
18	Learning using the virtual program accustoms the student to structured thinking.	4	0.58	Positive
19	Learning using the application of virtual program consolidates information in the student's mind.	3.86	0.69	Positive
20	By using the tool of the virtual program, I was able to build basic and non-basic logic circuits.	3.86	0.69	Positive
21	By using the tool of the virtual program, I was able to build associative logical circuits such as addition, subtraction, and others.	3.86	0.38	Positive
22	Using the tool of the virtual program, I was able to build logical sequences such as circuits, recorders, etc.	3.86	0.38	Positive
23	Learning to design digital logic course through the virtual programs makes me like it.	4.14	0.69	Positive
	Total	3.58	0.63	

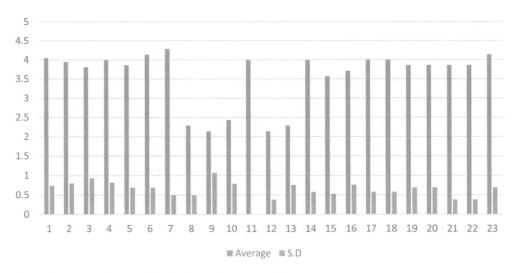

■ Average ■ S.D

Figure 6.   Mean and standard deviation of the questionnaire.

Table 1 indicates that the study has mostly positive attitudes because their arithmetic mean is larger and the approval rate is higher than the rate of disapproval. It was found that statement (7) (the tools of the virtual program can be used to visualize the concepts of logic circuit design of the course in more tangible ways) is the most appropriate statement in the arithmetic mean, followed by statement (23) (learning to design digital logic course through the virtual programs makes me like it), with an arithmetic mean of 4.29. Hence, the researchers believe in the necessity of employing the program in teaching.

As shown in Table 1, there are negative attitudes of students toward negative statements in the questionnaire, which are represented in the statements (8), (9), (12), and (14), which means that their attitudes are positive toward positive statements and negative (reject) toward negative statements. In general, there is complete satisfaction with the virtual programs, when the total arithmetic mean is 3.57 and the standard deviation is 0.63.

The following figure indicates the mean and standard deviation of the attitude questionnaire items for the use of the virtual Logisim program for the digital logic design course.

Figure 6 illustrates the mean and standard deviation of the items of the questionnaire trend towards the use of the program Logisim default for the design of digital logic decision. The results in Table 1 show that students have high attitudes toward using the Logisim default program for the course of digital logic designing.

5   DISCUSSION OF THE RESULT

The superiority of the Logisim program can be attributed to a number of reasons including the following.

  i. The interaction of the student with the program is an experiment conducted in a safe environment away from the risks that one may face in the case of using the real laboratory, and this is evidenced by their positive logical attitudes toward the use of the program, as shown in Table 1.
 ii. Student can repeat the experiment more than once so that they can focus on the experience.
iii. Students are able to conduct the experiment clearly, wherever the free program is available.

6 CONCLUSIONS

This paper discussed the use of the Logisim software tool for teaching students the design and analysis of a digital logic circuits course. The use of the tool was evaluated through a survey-based methodology, which was carried out with the students who used Logisim for the implementation of specific digital design and analysis tasks. The analysis of the survey results confirmed that students are interested in using this software because of its simplicity of use, effectiveness, free availability, system independency, and verifiability. On the other hand, some student answers lead to the conclusion that it is necessary to provide more pre-solved tasks of designing digital circuits in Logisim, in order for the educational objectives to be achieved. The research presented in this paper will help teachers to improve their teaching topics with various Logisim examples, so that the learning objectives and outcomes are better achieved for the next generations of students. Also, the introduction of remote experiments built on field-programmable gate arrays into teaching digital circuits design should be explored from the aspect of better achievements of the learning objectives and outcomes.

REFERENCES

AbdElrazig S, 2015 "Interactive Design Modules for Logic Design Course". Baharin (econf2015).
Abuzalata M.K., M.A.K. Alia. 2010. Design of a Virtual PLC Using Lab View. Maxwell Scientific Organization
Akintomiwa, A., 2014 "Using Logisim as the basis for teaching digital logic and computer architecture," European University Cyprus, 2014.
Borodzhieva, Plamen Manoilov. 2018. Decoder Synthesis in Teamwork Using Logisim. Bulgaria (ET2018).
David Harris; Sarah Harris. 2012. Digital Design and Computer Architecture, 2nd Edition. Morgan Kaufmann
Harris David; Sarah Harris. 2012. Digital Design and Computer Architecture, 2nd Edition. Morgan Kaufmann
Ichsan M., W. Kurniawan, 2017 Design and Implementation 8 bit CPU Architecture on Logisim For Undergraduate Learning Support. 2017. (SIET).
Khan, M.A. and V. K. Antiwal (2009), "Location Estimation Technique using Extended 3-D LANDMARC Algorithm for Passive RFID Tag," 2009 IEEE International Advance Computing Conference, Patiala, 2009, pp. 249–253, doi: 10.1109/IADCC.2009.4809016.
Khan, M. Ayoub and A. Q. Ansari (2011), "Quadrant-based XYZ dimension order routing algorithm for 3-D Asymmetric Torus Routing Chip (ATRC)," 2011 International Conference on Emerging Trends in Networks and Computer Communications (ETNCC), Udaipur, 2011, pp. 121–124, doi: 10.1109/ETNCC.2011.5958499
Khan, M.A., Sharma, M. and Prabhu, B.R. (2009). A survey of RFID tags. International Journal of Recent Trends in Engineering, 1(4), p.68. Academy publisher, Finland
Khan M.A. Sharma M, R. B. Prabhu, "FSM based FM0 and Miller encoder for UHF RFID Tag Emulator," 2009 IEEE International Advance Computing Conference, Patiala, 2009, pp. 1317-1322, doi: 10.1109/IADCC.2009.4809207.
Kurniawan W., M. Hannats Hanafi Ichsan, 2017 , "Teaching and Learning Support For Computer Architecture and Organization Courses Design on Computer Engineering and Computer Science for Undergraduate: A Review (EECSI 2017), Yogyakarta, Indonesia, 2017.
Logisim, 2019a URL: http://www.cburch.com/logisim/, Accessed 6 November 2019.
Logisim, 2019b source, URL https://sourceforge.net/projects/circuit/, Accessed 2 Oct 2019.
S. Tyagi, A. Q. Ansari and M. A. Khan (2010), "Dynamic threshold based sliding-window filtering technique for RFID data," 2010 IEEE 2nd International Advance Computing Conference (IACC), Patiala, 2010, pp. 115–120, doi: 10.1109/IADCC.2010.5423025.
Tyagi S., Ansari A.Q., Khan M.A. (2011) Extending Temporal and Event Based Data Modeling for RFID Databases. In: Nagamalai D., Renault E., Dhanuskodi M. (eds) Advances in Parallel Distributed Computing. PDCTA 2011. Communications in Computer and Information Science, vol 203. Springer, Berlin, Heidelberg, https://doi.org/10.1007/978-3-642-24037-9_43
Tyagi, S., M. Ayoub Khan, and A. Q. Ansari (2010), "RFID Data Management," in Radio Frequency Identification Fundamentals and Applications Bringing Research to Practice, Cristina Trucu, Ed. InTech, February 2010, DOI:10.5772/8001.

Smart wheelchair with fall detection provision: A telemedicine application

Richa Rai, Shubham Pratap Singh & B. Mohapatra
Galgotias University, Greater Noida, Uttar Pradesh, India

ABSTRACT: This work aims to propose a cost-effective healthcare management system with a wheelchair that provides fall detection mechanism. The system works with the help of the Internet of Things which informs the doctors to supervise the patient in terms of medical aspects, irrespective of the place, whether the patient is in hospital or at their home. In this project, various sensors or smart devices are used and the parameters like human body temperature, pulse rate, etc. are recorded in the cloud. Furthermore, the data is uploaded to a website, and a database will be stored for future reference. The real time is presented in graphical form and may be monitored across the globe. The developed system may be integrated with telemedicine applications.

1 INTRODUCTION

In this era, there has been tremendous growth in the development of medical devices that provide better healthcare services. These devices are very useful for medical professionals to provide a state-of-the-art medical service to patients at distant locations. In fact, the ever-increasing Internet of Things (IoT) enables medical equipment to provide better healthcare service to those living in rural areas [1, 2, 3].

An attempt has been made to develop an innovative system that puts forward a smart wheelchair to detect when an individual falls, and to provide information about the medical condition of the patient. The equipment comprises sensors to track the health parameters of the patient. Sensors are used to detect collision and wheelchair fall, and with the help of internet technology the equipment alerts the doctors or loved ones about the medical condition so that they can help in case of emergency [4].

Wheelchair fall detection provision is a technology that will enable a system to monitor an elderly or paralyzed perso's condition in an emergency at the time of collision (or a sudden impact of the wheelchair) and check on the patient's health apart from the conventional methods(e.g. in the home or in a clinic). This not only provides better healthcare services to the patient but is also done so at a reduced cost and from a distant location. With the help of this equipment, quality of treatment increases, difficulty in traveling is reduced, and the cost of treatment also reduces. This considerably improves people's quality of life as it allows a patient to be more independent, restricts their difficulties, and minimizes overall financial costs [5]. This equipment provides the above goals by delivering healthcare right at their door step. In addition, the patient and the people associated with the patient's family feel comfortable with knowing that the patient is being monitored properly around the clock and will be supported if any problem arises

1.1 *Enhancement using IOT*

The IoT is basically the junction of a device, application, sensor, or network connection that improves this property of gathering and exchanging of the data. The objective of IoT in this work is the regular management of a patient's health for checking those elementary measurements and derives a better output, against the available history in the database. There might be some cases where the medical instructor could not be informed in time about some incidence of an emergency, even if 24 × 7 monitoring is there. Moreover, this may lead to some difficulty in transmitting and receiving the information data with the medical instructor as well as with the family members and friends. The technology which improves the details has been presented previously but there is a lack in security, feasibility (economically lesser) rate, and most of the common people in developing countries such as in India could afford such expensive equipment. Therefore, it is imperative to develop a system which will be simple to use.

This paper introduces a smart wheelchair with fall detection, and patient's health care system controlled by Arduino. In this project, a system is developed to continuously monitor a patient's current state and medical parameters, such as pulse-rate and body temperature. The data is then published on a web server and the data could be fetched and thrown back onto a website in a graphical form or on a datasheet, by an authorized ID and password only. And whenever a person sitting on a wheelchair falls for some reason or has a sudden collision with some obstacle, an alarm will ring and the people nearby can be informed about such an incident. If a person is all good despite such an accident then he can just switch the alarm off. This work or the idea behind this might not be very new, but here the difference is we are going to publish an acute system and within a feasible rate also using an Arduino–UNO board [6]. The primary aim of the project is to continuously monitor a patient's state of rest and continuously send a body's parameter on the website and the people related to the patient can fetch the data accurately. The project or the work presented here has more opportunities in the further development as it works in the absence of caretakers. This work can also be modified by adding more medical parameters that can help if a patient is suffering from a particular disease or disorder.

1.2 *Objective*

To develop a system that is capable of providing real-time medical information about a patient anytime, anywhere. To interpret and predict any disease or disorder in its preliminary stage using the data mining techniques, which will be easy for decision making. To detect whether an elderly or paralyzed person has fallen from a wheelchair, and if so then an alarm will be ring out. To build a system so as to monitor a patient's medical condition anywhere in the world and his physical state whether he is comfortably seated on a wheelchair or not, without being physically present with them.

2 PROBLEM DESCRIPTION

To develop a healthcare system with provisions for detecting patient falls that will also be useful for telemedicine applications. Over the course of the last few decades, India has seen a significant growth in the quality of its healthcare services. However, the situation still is not that much better, and according to WHO, Indians are lagging behind some of their neighboring countries.

Many neighboring countries, such as Bangladesh, Bhutan, and Sri Lanka, have a better healthcare ranking than India. When we come to South Asia, Bangladesh has made the most improvement when compared to other countries outlined in Table 1. It has an improvement of almost 30 points, amending or enhancing it from 1990–2016. Contrasted to this, the rankings of Afghanistan and Pakistan are the worse during this period. India's rank is also at its worse than that of many other countries that are much poorer than India such as Botswana (122), Equatorial Guinea (129), Sudan (136), and Namibia (137). Even Yemen (140) performed better than India. The major obstacle of India's growth in the healthcare system is the negligence of mostly rural areas. It is not like rural areas are not being serviced, but the thing is that the advanced services are not provided in such places as they are mostly provided in uban hospitals. According to a health organization approximately 32% of hospitals and 15% of hospital beds are situated in rural areas, where most

Table 1. Health assistance questionnaire ranking in South Asia [11].

Country	HAQ index Score, 2016	HAQ index Rank, 2016	Improvement in Score, 1990–2016
India	41.2	145	16.5
Pakistan	37.6	154	10.8
Bangladesh	47.6	132	29.8
Afghanistan	25.9	191	10.1
Sri Lanka	70.6	71	23.2
Nepal	40	149	19.1
Bhutan	47.3	134	27.2

(3/4th) of the population of India resides [12]. Also, most doctors are not willing to be a part of rural areas whether it be due to salary issues or societal pressures.

In India, the lack of of medical professionals such as doctors, nurses, or anyone related to this profession is the basic and the major problem in the healthcare field. In 1999–2000, in India there were only 6 doctors per 10,000 people in India, and when we talk about different countries, that doctor/patient ratio is 25:10,000 in the United States and 20:10,000 in China. And here, there is only one allopathic government doctor for every 10,926 people in India which contradicts the WHO that recommend a doctor/population ratio of 1:1000 [12]. In India, of all the healthcare services such as homeopathic, Ayurvedic, Unani, and allopathic, allopathic is somewhat expensive therefore it is not easy to afford for common people. The price of important medicines has also increased.

2.1 System Architecture

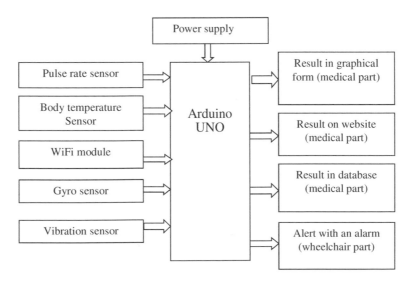

Figure 1. System model.

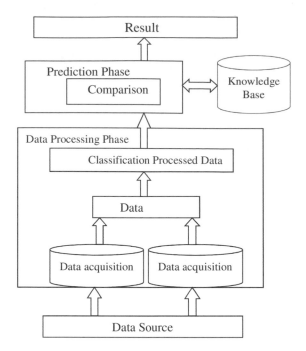

Figure 2. Basic data flow.

3 WORKING PRINCIPLES

In our project, we are working on two aspects which will be combined on a single automated system for monitoring medical parameters such as body temperature and pulse rate, and along with this we have implemented a smart wheelchair fall detection. Here *smart* stands for the capability of doing multiple tasks, and furthermore we are going to expand or elaborate our as mentioned system.

First, we are going to explain our smart healthcare part, wherein there are two parameters which will be acquired by two different sensors: bodytemperature sensor and pulse-rate sensor. Now, with the help of the 8266 WiFi module, we are uploading both the parameters acquired by the two sensors to a website in the form of graphical representation, and the same will be stored in a database by which we can make a track record of a patient's health. We have used here a baud rate of 115200, which will help with the communication between the WiFi module and Arduino board.

In addition, we explain a second part of this project i.e., smart wheelchair fall detection, wherein we are use a gyro sensor and a vibration sensor so as to keep in contact with the person sitting in the wheelchair. In the event of an elderly or paralyzed person's falling from the wheelchair, the gyro sensor makes an alarm so as to inform a loved one that the wheelchair has fallen and in the case when a collision has occurred and the wheelchair has not been tilted or fallen but the person sitting on it has fallen down, than again the vibration sensor comes into play and makes an alarm to inform someone nearby so as to help that needy person as soon as possible, and if everything is alright then the person may switch off the alarm [7, 8, 9].

Figure 2 shows the flow of information and how our project or system is working and producing a meaningful output. Starting from the data source and flowing through the data processing phase and coming up with an output. This project will further expand on how some of the symptoms are pointing to a chronic disease or another abnormality. Now, in the first level, unprocessed raw data from different sensors would be obtained, and then compared with some aspects and then at last stored on the web server.

Table 2. Real-time experimental value of human body temperature and pulse rate

Created at	Entry ID	Field1 (Body Temperature)	Field2 (Pulse Rate)
2020-02-02 13:41:18 UTC	1	34	72
2020-02-02 13:45:16 UTC	2	34	74
2020-02-02 13:48:35 UTC	3	34	74
2020-02-02 13:49:00 UTC	4	37	75
2020-02-02 13:51:16 UTC	5	35	74
2020-02-02 13:51:32 UTC	6	34	76
2020-02-02 13:51:47 UTC	7	35	78
2020-02-02 13:53:41 UTC	8	35	78
2020-02-02 13:53:57 UTC	9	34	79
2020-02-02 13:54:13 UTC	10	34	80
2020-02-03 04:27:25 UTC	11	36	85
2020-02-03 04:27:42 UTC	12	35	84
2020-02-03 04:27:58 UTC	13	34	84
2020-02-03 04:28:16 UTC	14	35	84
2020-02-03 04:40:00 UTC	15	35	82
2020-02-03 04:40:38 UTC	16	35	82
2020-02-03 04:40:54 UTC	17	34	82
2020-02-03 04:41:13 UTC	18	36	83
2020-02-03 04:41:30 UTC	19	37	83
2020-02-03 04:41:46 UTC	20	37	81

The data acquired by these sensors are patient's realtime data. The information provided by them would be used as a supplement in further levels for exploring if the patient is going through any kind of disease or disorder. This would help in making the system smarter and more efficient. Therefore, it will categorize the condition or the symptoms with the help of the stored database that the results are normal or not, if not which type of disease it could be.

3.1 *Methodology*

In the first level, unprocessed raw data from different sources such as IoT modules would be collected and preserved in the server. This module includes different sensors such as temperature and pulse sensor. In the second level, the consistent information and data collected are stored in the database. Then the system processes the data that was stored by classifying, filtering and dividing in different categories. This real-time patient health information is processed further by the healthcare professional or the associated members based on the symptoms that the patient has.

The information would be used as supplementary in the next level for predicting in case the patient is suffering from any kind of disease or disorder. This would help in making the system more robust and efficient. The third level is the analysis or predication phase. Here we may use the data mining techniques in predicting the types in a smarter way. Hence, the disease or disorder may be realized by using the existing database and categorizing the result in different categories such as normal, ideal symptoms etc.

4 RESULTS AND DISCUSSIONS

As we had discussed earlier, due to the insufficient number of healthcare professionals in India, this system was developed so that a single doctor can monitor multiple patients at a time without travel. Furthermore, there will be fewer requirements off hospitals and hospital beds, and through this we would also promote telemedicine The result of all of this will consist of output information

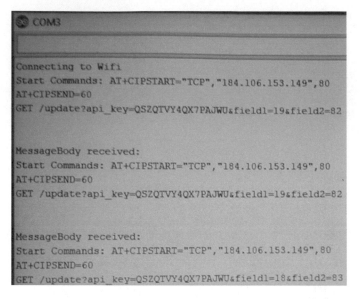

Figure 3.   Result observed in the monitor where Field1 denotes body temperature and Field2 denotes body pulse rate.

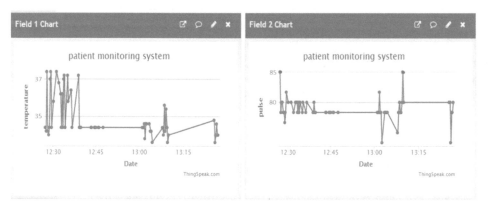

Figure 4.   Graphical results observed on the website: Field1 is body temperature and Field2 body pulse rate.

from our serial monitor, uploaded to our website, that detects things such as temperature and pulse rate [10, 11].

Now, in the case of smart wheelchair fall detection, an alarm will blow upon wheelchair collision and at the time when the wheelchair has been tilted with an angular velocity of plus (+) 5°/sec and minus (−) 5°/sec, it will blow the same alarm to indicate that something wrong has occurred.

4.1 *Discussion*

The system is easy to make but it needs a lot of study so that one can effectively make a system that can produce an appropriate output or a result and still be cost effective. The major issue with this system is internet connectivity because there are some areas where there could be some issues in internet being readily available. The baud rate should be precisely selected so that our WiFi module could connect effectively with the Arduino UNO. Here, in this system we have used an analog vibration sensor and by coding it to a digital form we can use it in this project or in this system.

5 CONCLUSIONS

This project was concerned with a smart wheelchair with fall detection, and a patient's health care system controlled by Arduino UNO. The main aim of our project was to continuously monitor a patient's current state and medical parameters such as pulse rate and body temperature and also check on whether or not the patient's wheelchair is in the correct condition. The data is then published on a web server and could be fetched and thrown back onto a website in a graphical form and on a datasheet, by an authorized ID-password only, which will be accessible only to the person who has this ID and password.

If a patient sitting in a wheelchair falls for some reason or has a sudden collision with some obstacle, an alarm will start to blow and the nearby people can be informed about the incident, and if the person is all good despite the collision then he or she can just switch the alarm off. Although this work is not very new, here the difference is that we are going to publish an acute system and it will be in a feasible rate also, using an Arduino-UNO board. The basic feature of the project is to continuously monitor a patient's wheelchair condition and continuously send their body's parameters to the website so that the people related to the patient can access the data accurately. The project or the work presented will have more opportunities for usage in the future because realistically no one can be present with a patient physically at all times. The informative data arranged by this system has so much value, and this work also can be modified by adding more medical parameters such as EEG, ECG, etc. These things would be implemented with the help of IoT and will enable medical professionals to monitor their patients, regardless of location.

REFERENCES

[1] Jung, S.J., & Chung, W.Y. (2011). Flexible and scalable patient's smart wheelchair with fall detection in 6LoWPAN. *Sensor Lett.* 9, 778–785.
[2] Chung, W.Y et al. (2007). A cell phone based smart wheelchair with fall detection with self-analysis processor using wireless sensor network technology. *In Proc. 29th Annu. Int. Conf. Eng. Med. Biol. Soc., Lyon, France.*
[3] Lawton G.(2004) . Machine-to-machine technology gears up for growth. *Computer, 37* 12–15.
[4] Kim, C et al. (2011). Global wireless machine -to- machine standardization. *IEEE Internet Compute, 15,* 64–69.
[5] Khan, M. A., Quasim, M. T, et.al, (2020), A Secure Framework for Authentication and Encryption Using Improved ECC for IoT-Based Medical Sensor Data, in IEEE Access, vol. 8, pp. 52018-52027, 2020. DOI: 10.1109/ACCESS.2020.2980739
[6] Abdullah, Amna et al. (2015). Real time wireless health monitoring application using mobile devices. *International Journal of Computer Networks & Communications (IJCNC), 7.*
[7] B.K, Bhoomika & Muralidhara, K.N. (2015) Secured Smart Healthcare Monitoring System Based on IOT. *International Journal on Recent and Innovation Trends in Computing and Communication, 3.*
[8] Motika, Goutam & Prusty, Abinash (2011). Wireless Fetal Heartbeat Monitoring System Using ZigBee& IEEE 802.15.4 Standard. *Second International Conference on Emerging Applications of Information Technology, 978-0-7695-4329-1/11, 2011 IEEE DOI 10.1109/EAIT.2011.89.*
[9] Mahalle, S.M & Ingole, P.V. (2013). Design and Implementation of Wireless Body Area Sensor Network Based Health monitoring system. *International Journal of Engineering Research & Technology, 2, 105– 113.*
[10] Prakash, M. et al (2016). A Smart Device Integrated with an Android for Alerting a Person's Health Condition: Internet of Things. *Indian Journal of Science and Technology, 9 (6).* DOI: https://doi.org/10.17485/ijst/2016/v9i6/69545
[11] Mahesh Kumar, D. (2012). Healthcare Monitoring System Using Wireless Sensor Network. *641 014.Volume 04, Issue 01 Pages: 1497-1500 (2012), ISSN: 0975-0290.*
[12] Https://www.firstpost.com/india/world-health-day-2019-access-quality-of-care-ranks-india-among-lowest-globally-4480939.html

Smart Computing – Khan et al (Eds)
© 2021 Taylor & Francis Group, London, ISBN 978-0-367-76552-1

AlphaZero: The new boss

Gulista Khan & Akshat Kumar Jain
Faculty of Engineering, Teerthanker Mahaveer University, Moradabad, UP, India

Gaurav Bathla
Chandigarh University, Chandigarh, Punjab, India

ABSTRACT: A core novelty of Alpha Zero (Google Deepmind project) is the mix of tree search and deep learning, which has proven very efficient in board games like Chess, Shogi, and Go. These games have a discrete action space, however many reinforcement learning domains have an impact in the real world, for example in robotic control, navigation, and self-driving cars. This paper presents the effectiveness of such concepts through extensions of Alpha Zero. The paper shows the theoretical comparison of two search tree algorithms (Monto Carlo and Alpha Beta search tree) using two different engines of Chess (Stockfish and AlphaZero), thereby providing the first step toward unsupervised learning.

1 INTRODUCTION

Over the last few decades, research has taken place on ways to surpass the human brain with computational power. Many scientists have worked for this, such as Charles Babbage with the mechanical Turk and Alan Turing, Claude E. Shannon, and John von Neumann designing algorithms for the same challenge. When designing the model for Chess, different scientists give different approaches. For example, John von Neumann who proposed two different algorithms, the first one based on the brute force search and the second one that works on the concept of an intelligence strategy that can simulate human intelligence (i.e., think like a human).

There are some highly specified systems that have been successful in Chess and also have had an impact on real-world domains such as robotics, industrial control, or intelligent assistants. Primarily, these systems use model-based reinforcement learning (RL) that first learn the model of the environment's dynamics, and then plan with respect to the learning model. Or, we have model-free RL, i.e., when they took the rules from the optimal policies/value functions and start from scratch.

1.1 *IBM's Deep Blue*

The IBM Deep Blue supercomputer that defeated the world Chess champion, Garry Kasparov, in 1997 employed 480 custom Chess chips. This technique describes the design philosophy, general architecture, and performance of the Chess chips, which provided most of the deep blue computational power. The article was given by IBM in 1999 given an engine for this technique that was under the IEEE micro.

1.2 *Stockfish*

Stockfish is an open-source Chess engine developed by Tord Romstud, Marco Costalba, and Joona Kiiski. This project started in November 2008, and since then it has only evolved. Stockfish can

DOI 10.1201/9781003167488-5

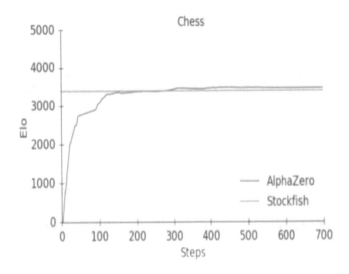

Figure 1.   Elo rating of Stockfish vs. AlphaZero.

Table 1.   Summary of AlphaZero results.

ReR	Win	Draw	Loss
Chess vs. 2016 TCEC world champion Stockfish	28	72	0

compare 70,000,000 moves per second as a player, and has been evaluated by human grandmasters since 2008. Also, its search extensions are highly optimized using a game-specific heuristic.

1.3   *AlphaZero*

AlphaZero, the latest technology, uses two main methodologies. The first one is deep neural networks and the second one is a general RL algorithm, as explained by Julian et al. (2020). It starts learning the game from scratch (like babies learn games from scratch) but obviously with more computational power.

In the next part of this paper, the authors explain the differences of Alpha Zero vs. Stockfish—AlphaZero learned Chess by self-play and Stockfish has had a data set training for the past 10 years as an open-source Chess engine.

2   LITERATURE REVIEW

On December 4, 2017, Google's AlphaZero took on Chess in Google headquarters in London. In just 4 hours, AlphaZero had surpassed Stockfish 8.

In Figure 1, the x-axis represents the measure of time which is concluded as training steps in the thousands and the y-axis represents the Elo rating in the game of Chess. The figure clearly shows that after just nearly 300 steps AlphaZero surpassed Stockfish.

As shown in Table 1, none of the matches are lost by AlphaZero, i.e., either AlphaZero draws or wins the match only.

The condition for this game is that both engines will be allowed to have 1 min per move. Stockfish is the strongest skill using 64 threads and the same algorithm setting and architecture (except input/output planes) for all games.

2.1 Anatomy of a World Champion Chess Engine: Stockfish

In Figure 2, it is clearly visible how many technologies Stockfish uses in its range.

Anatomy of a World Champion Chess Engine

Domain knowledge, extensions, heuristics in 2016 TCEC world champion *Stockfish*:

Board Representation: Bitboards with Little-Endian Rank-File Mapping (LERF), Magic Bitboards, BMI2 - PEXT Bitboards, Piece-Lists, **Search**: Iterative Deepening, Aspiration Windows, Parallel Search using Threads, YBWC, Lazy SMP, Principal Variation Search. **Transposition Table**: Shared Hash Table, Depth-preferred Replacement Strategy, No PV-Node probing, Prefetch **Move Ordering**: Countermove Heuristic, Counter Moves History, History Heuristic, Internal Iterative Deepening, Killer Heuristic, MVV/LVA, SEE, **Selectivity**: Check Extensions if SEE >= 0, Restricted Singular Extensions, Futility Pruning, Move Count Based Pruning, Null Move Pruning, Dynamic Depth Reduction based on depth and value, Static Null Move Pruning, Verification search at high depths, ProbCut, SEE Pruning, Late Move Reductions, Razoring, Quiescence Search, **Evaluation**: Tapered Eval, Score Grain, Point Values

Figure 2.   Depicting the anatomy of a world champion Chess engine.

2.2 Anatomy of AlphaZero

Giambattista et al. (2020) explained self-play reinforcement learning with Monte Carlo Tree Search, as shown in Figure 3.

Anatomy of AlphaZero

Self-play reinforcement learning + self-play Monte-Carlo search

~~**Board Representation**: Bitboards with Little-Endian Rank-File Mapping (LERF), Magic Bitboards, BMI2 - PEXT Bitboards, Piece-Lists, **Search**: Iterative Deepening, Aspiration Windows, Parallel Search using Threads, YBWC, Lazy SMP, Principal Variation Search. **Transposition Table**: Shared Hash Table, Depth-preferred Replacement Strategy, No PV-Node probing, Prefetch **Move Ordering**: Countermove Heuristic, Counter Moves History, History Heuristic, Internal Iterative Deepening, Killer Heuristic, MVV/LVA, SEE, **Selectivity**: Check Extensions if SEE >= 0, Restricted Singular Extensions, Futility Pruning, Move Count Based Pruning, Null Move Pruning, Dynamic Depth Reduction based on depth and value, Static Null Move Pruning, Verification search at high depths, ProbCut, SEE Pruning, Late Move Reductions, Razoring, Quiescence Search, **Evaluation**: Tapered Eval, Score Grain, Point Values Midgame: 198, 817, 836, 1270, 2521, Endgame: 258, 846, 857, 1278, 2558, Bishop Pair, Imbalance Tables, Material Hash Table, Piece-Square Tables, Trapped Pieces, Rooks on (Semi) Open Files, Outposts, Pawn Hash Table, Backward Pawn, Doubled Pawn, Isolated Pawn, Phalanx, Passed Pawn,~~

Figure 3.   Depicting the anatomy of AlphaZero.

Table 2. Moves per second by Stockfish and AlphaZero.

Positions/Second	Stockfish	AlphaZero
Chess	70,000,000	80,000

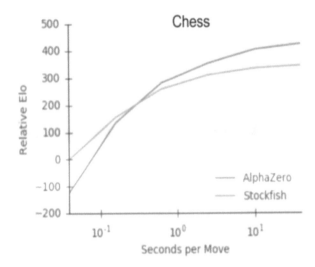

Figure 4. Moves per second by Stockfish and AlphaZero.

3 ANATOMY OF ALGORITHMS

Now, we see how AlphaZero dominated Stockfish 8 in the 100-game match and did not lose a single match against it. This is especially impressive when we consider that Stockfish was already 10 years old when the match happened between these two engines, so it had had much more experience. Furthermore, when we dig deeper, we see that even though Stockfish 8 checks 70,000,000 moves per second and AlphaZero checks around only 80,000, the matches still went in favor of AlphaZero.

David et al. (2016, 2018) explained that the Monte Carlo Tree Search (MCTS) could be used in AlphaZero instead of the Alpha-Beta Tree Search which had been previously used in earlier systems.

3.1 *Scalability with Search Time*

As was explained in previous research (Thomas et al. 2017; Donald et al. 2001; M. Campbell et al. 2002; Coulom 2008; David et al. 2016; Hoki et al. 2014; Hsu 2002; Jouppi et al. 2017; Tomoyu et al. 2011; Maddison et al. 2014; Ramanujan et al. 2012; Romstad et al. 2017; Veness et al. 2009), the Alpha-Beta search has dominated these domains for the past 50 years and there have been many studies that suggested MCTS, or any other algorithm, could not be competitive. However, here the authors concluded that MCTS not only outperforms the other programs, but actually scaled up more efficiently than the Alpha-Beta search (Thomas et al. 2017). Furthermore, Figure 4 and Table 2 depict moves per second by Stockfish and AlphaZero.

3.2 *AlphaZero Self Play*

Figure 5 shows some of the best matches that AlphaZero played against itself during the self-play training through RL. This set clearly demonstrates some of the key concepts and the brilliancy of RL.

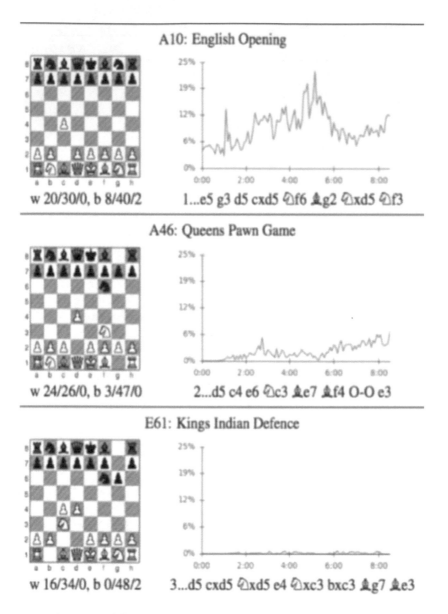

A10: English Opening

w 20/30/0, b 8/40/2   1...e5 g3 d5 cxd5 ♘f6 ♗g2 ♘xd5 ♘f3

A46: Queens Pawn Game

w 24/26/0, b 3/47/0   2...d5 c4 e6 ♘c3 ♗e7 ♗f4 O-O e3

E61: Kings Indian Defence

w 16/34/0, b 0/48/2   3...d5 cxd5 ♘xd5 e4 ♘xc3 bxc3 ♗g7 ♗e3

Figure 5a.   Opening moves AlphaZero self-play.

Figure 5(a) depicts AlphaZero trained for 9 hours by playing 44 million games against itself. AlphaZero's openings are amazing. AlphaZero plays in a universal and balanced way, having both, the best of humans and best of computers. AlphaZero's tactical strength is overwhelming, but it comes together with a deep strategic knowledge, only seen until now exclusively with humans, as you can see in the game using the Berliner Defence, which wins in 87 movements. AlphaZero plays very well in blocked positions, as shown during the two games played with the French Defence too.

Figure 5(b) shows the opening moves of AlphaZero. AlphaZero's openings are amazing: it has discovered and even overcomes five centuries of human effort in hardly 2 hours of training. When AlphaZero plays with black pieces, it shows a very solid position and rapidly occupies the center in a symmetrical way, similar to Karpov's style. When playing with white pieces, AlphaZero likes

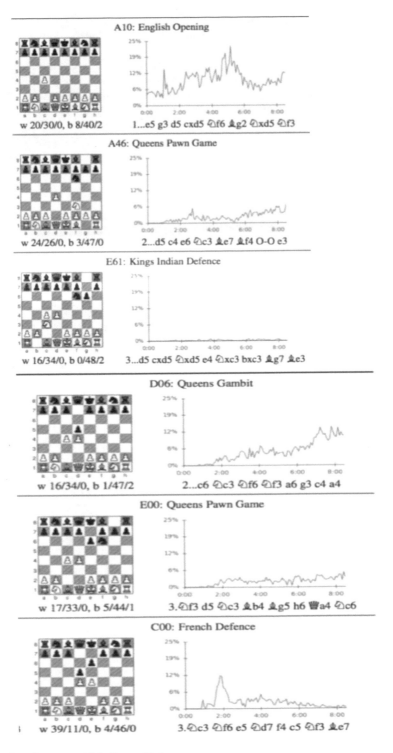

Figure 5b. Opening moves AlphaZero self-play.

39

to start with the Queen, but in an aggressive way, similar to Kasparov's style. AlphaZero loves to give away pieces in the long term, with tactical sacrifices such as Tal's and other positional ones who could be signed by Petrosian. The way AlphaZero plays against the Queens Indian Defence is sublime, from another galaxy, with outstanding ideas such as the sacrifice of the pawn in c4 during the match that ends in only 68 movements. What is also impressive is AlphaZero's relentless execution of its positional advantage in some of the matches where AZ plays inferiorly, as it is its faultless technique in the final positions. We could easily say, without risk of making a mistake, that, from the analysis of the 10 games, AlphaZero plays close to perfection (Tomoyu et al. 2011; Maddison et al. 2014; Raghuram et al. 2010; Romstad et al. 2017; Silver et al. 2017; Veness et al. 2009).

Figure 6 depicts the games play by Stockfish and AlphaZero.

THE 10 GAMES OF THE ALPHAZERO-STOCKFISH MATCH (Grouped by openings)

Berlin Defence (ST vs AZ)

1.e4 e5 2.♘f3 ♘c6 3.♗b5 ♘f6 4.d3 ♗c5 5.♗xc6 dxc6 6.0–0 Elite players are holding up castling with 6.♘bd2!? Too subtle for a SF without a book of Openings.

6...♘d7! To take the pawn to f6 according to the structure of pawns (white bishop, black pawns) and recycling the knight: a very human concept.

7.c3?! 7.♘bd2 0–0 8.♕e1?! (8.♘c4=) 8...f6 9.♘c4 ♖f7 10.a4 ♗f8 11.♔h1 ♗c5 12.a5 ♘e5 13.♘cxe5 fxe5 14.♘xe5 ♖f6 15.♘g4 ♖f7 16.♘e5 ♖e7 17.a6 c5 18.f4 ♕e8 19.axb7 ♗xb7 20.♕a5 ♘d4 21.♕c3 ♖e6 22.♗e3 ♖b6 23.♘c4 ♖b4 24.b3 a5 25.♖xa5 ♖xa5 26.♘xa5 ♗a6 27.♗xd4 ♖xd4 28.♘c4 ♖d8 29.g3 h6 30.♕a5 ♗c8 31.♕xc7 ♗h3 32.♖f2 ♖d7 33.♕e5 ♕xe5 34.♘xe5 ♖a7‡ 35.♘c4 g5 36.♖c1 ♗g7 37.♘e5 ♖a8 38.♘f3 ♗b2 39.♖b1 ♗c3 40.♘g1 ♗d7 41.♘e2 ♗d2 42.♖d1 ♗e3 43.♔g2 ♗g4 44.♖e1 ♗d2 45.♖f1 ♖a2–+ (0–1 in 67 moves).

7...0–0 8.d4 ♗d6 9.♗g5 ♕e8 10.♖e1 f6 11.♗h4 ♕f7 12.♘bd2 a5 13.♗g3 ♖e8 14.♕c2 ♘f8 15.c4 c5 16.d5 b6 17.♘h4 g6 18.♘hf3 ♗d7 19.♖ad1 ♖e7 20.h3 ♕g7 21.♕c3 ♖ae8 22.a3 h6 23.♗h4 ♖f7 24.♗g3 ♖fe7 25.♗h4 ♖f7 26.♗g3 a4 27.♔h1 ♖fe7 28.♗h4 ♖f7 29.♗g3

♖fe7 30.♗h4 g5 31.♗g3 ♗g6 32.♘f1 ♖f7 33.♘e3 ♘e7 34.♕d3 h5 35.h4 ♘c8 36.♖e2 g4 37.♘d2 ♕h7 38.♔g1 ♗f8 39.♘b1 ♗d6 40.♘c3 ♗h6‡

41.♖f1 ♖a8 42.♔h2 ♗f8 43.♔g1 ♕g6 44.f4 gxf3 45.♖xf3 ♗xe3+ 46.♖fxe3 ♔e7 47.♗e1 ♕h7 48.♖g3 ♗g7 49.♖xg7+ ♕xg7 50.♖e3 ♖g8 51.♖g3 ♕h8 52.♘b1 ♖xg3 53.♗xg3 ♕h6 54.♘d2 ♗g4 55.♔h2 ♔d7 56.b3 axb3 57.♘xb3 ♕g6 58.♘d2 ♗d1 59.♘f3 ♗a4 60.♘d2 ♗e7 61.♗f2 ♕g4 62.♕f3 ♗d1 63.♕xg4 ♗xg4 64.a4 ♗b7 65.♘b1 ♘a5 66.♗e3 ♘xc4–+ (0–1 in 87 moves)

French Defence (AZ vs ST)

1.d4 d5 2.♘c3 ♘f6 3.e4 d5 4.e5 ♘fd7 5.f4 c5 6.♘f3

6...cxd4?! It seems too early to take. 6...♘c6 7.♗e3 ♗e7 8.♕d2 a6 9.♗d3 c4?! SF does not know how to play this without a book. (Best considered move is 9...b5) 10.♗e2 b5 11.a3 ♖b8 12.0–0 0–0 13.f5! a5

14.fxe6 fxe6 15.♗d1! b4 16.axb4 axb4 17.♘e2 c3 18.bxc3 ♘b6 19.♕e1 ♘c4 20.♘c1 bxc3 21.♕xc3± (1–0 in 95 moves).

7.♘b5!? An idea relatively new and very promising. 7...♗b4+ 8.♗d2 ♗c5 9.b4 ♗e7 10.♘bxd4 ♘c6 11.c3 a5 12.b5 ♘xd4 13.cxd4± ♘b6 14.a4 ♘c4 15.♗d3 ♘xd2 16.♔xd2 ♗d7 17.♔e3 b6 18.g4 h5 19.♕g1 hxg4 20.♕xg4 ♗f8 21.h4 ♕e7 22.♖hc1 g6 23.♔e2 ♔d8 24.♖ac1 ♕e8 25.♖c7 ♗b4 26.♖xc8+ ♗xc8 27.♖c6 ♗b7 28.♖c2 ♔d7 29.♘g5 ♗e7 30.♗xg6!

30...♗xg5 31.♕xg5 fxg6 32.f5! ♖g8 33.♕h6 ♕f7 34.f6 ♔d8 35.♕d2 ♗d7 36.♖c1 ♔d8 37.♕e3 ♕f8 38.♕c3 ♕b4 39.♕xb4 axb4 40.♖g1 b3 41.♔e3 ♗c8 42.♔b3 ♗d7 43.♔b4 ♗e8 44.♖a1 ♔c7 45.a5 ♗d7 46.axb6+ ♔c6 47.♖a6+ ♔b7 48.♔c5 ♖d8 49.♖a2 ♖c8+ 50.♔d6 ♗e8 51.♔e7 g5 52.hxg5 1–0

Figure 6. Games play by Stockfish and AlphaZero.

40

4 CONCLUSION

Deep learning (DL) and RL have attracted massive attention for over a decade. Unlike traditional artificial algorithms such as fuzzy logic and neural networks which are more academically driven, DL and RL are more application-oriented, something that can bring unimaginable changes in our society. The paper shows the effectiveness of RL and DL over other approaches by direct match using Chess as a medium. Clearly, RL has an advantage over other approaches. From a technological point of view, they can be applied in prediction, anomaly detection, decision-making support for control, etc. For business, they can be used in robotic control, navigation, self-driving cars, and other great applications.

REFERENCES

Campbell, M. Hoane, A.J., & Hsu. F. 2002, DeepBlue. In ArtificialIntelligence,134:57–83, 2002.

R. Coulom. 2008. Whole-history rating: A Bayesian rating system for players of time-varying strength. In International Conference on Computers and Games, Vol. 5131:113–124.

David, Omid E, Netanyahu, Nathan S & Wolf, Lior. 2016. Deepchess: End-to-end deep neural network for automatic learning in chess. In International Conference on Artificial Neural Networks, pp 88–96.

Donald, F, Martin, B, C. Smith. 2001, Temporal difference learning applied to game playing and the results of application to shogi. In Theoretical Computer Science, Vol. 252(1–2):105–119.

Giambattista Parascandolo, et al. 2020. Divide-and-Conquer Monte Carlo Tree Search For Goal-Directed Planning. In ArXiv: 2004.11410v1.

Hoki, Kunihito & Kaneko, Tomoyuki. 2014. Large-scale optimization for evaluation functions with minimax search. In Journal of Artificial Intelligence Research(JAIR),Vol 49:527–568.

Hsu, Feng-hsiung 2002. Behind Deep Blue:Building the Computer that Defeated the World Chess Champion. In Princeton University Press. Technology and Culture Vol 44(3):634–635.

P. Jouppi, Norman, Young, Cliff, Patil, Nishant et al. 2017, In-datacenter performance analysis of a tensor processing unit. In Proceedings of the 44th Annual International Symposium on Computer Architecture, ISCA '17, pages 1–12. ACM, 2017.

Julian, Schrittwieser et al. 2020. Mastering Atari, Go, Chess and Shogi by Planning with a Learned Model. Vol 2, NIPS'15, Pp 2944–2952. In ArXiv:1911.08265v2.

Maddison, Chris J. et al. 2014. Move evaluation in Go using deep convolutional neural networks. In International Conference on Learning Representations,ArXiv:1412.6564, 2014.

Ramanujan, R., Sabharwal, A. & Selman, B. 2012, Understanding sampling style adversarial search methods. arXiv preprint:1203.4011.

Romstad, T., Costalba, M., Kiiski, J. 2017, Stockfish: A strong open source chess engine, Open Source available at https://stockfishchess.org/. Retrieved November 29th, 2017.

Silver, David & Hubert Thomas et al. 2018, A general reinforcement learning algorithm that masters chess, shogi, and Go through self-play. In AAAS Science Journal. Vol 362(6419): 1140–44.

Silver D. et al. 2016. Mastering the game of Go with deep neural networks and tree search. Nature, Vol 529(7587):484–489, January.

Silver D. et al. 2017, Mastering the game of go without human knowledge. In Nature, Vol 550:354–359, 2017.

Anthony Thomas, Tian Zheng & Barber, David. 2017, Thinking fast and slow with deep learning and tree search. In Advances in Neural Information Processing Systems 30: Annual Conference on Neural Information Processing Systems 2017, 4–9 December 2017, Long Beach, CA, USA, pp 5366–5376.

Tomoyu et.al. 2011. Analysis of evaluation-functional learning by comparison of sibling nodes. In Advances in Computer Games - 13th International Conference, ACG 2011, Tilburg, The Netherlands, November 20–22, 2011, Revised Selected Papers, pp 158–169.

Veness, J., Silver, D., Blair, A. & Uther, W. 2009. Bootstrapping from game tree search. In Advances in Neural Information Processing Systems, pages 1937–1945.

Smart Computing – Khan et al (Eds)
© 2021 Taylor & Francis Group, London, ISBN 978-0-367-76552-1

Machine learning techniques for the prediction of music

Ashish Sharma & Akanksha Bansal
Department of Computer Engineering & Applications, GLA University, Mathura (UP), India

ABSTRACT: Data mining refers to collecting useful information from a mass of data or data repository. Here the mining used based on music is called multimedia mining. There are so many representations of music which we refer to as multilayer representation. The primary aim of this kind of data mining is to recognize the similarities and differences between different pieces of music, as well as discover spectral patterns within them. The data generated to be encoded is done so by musical instruments, sensors, actuators, etc. The present article depends on the forecast of music as one of the subjects which concerns advanced music handling. In this examination, music acoustic highlights were removed utilizing computerized signal picture handling strategies. Afterward the grouping of music classifications and music proposals were made using artificial intelligence techniques.

1   INTRODUCTION

Music is a very important and interesting field of research. Basically, music plays an entertaining role which is necessary for our life so as to provide freshness to the mind, turning a boring time into an extra-curricular activity. This idea was discovered after reading a paper related to this subject, so the main purpose of this paper is to discover the difference between all the techniques regarding the spectral patterns of music. In the interim, music is a method of connection that reflects and establishes social relations (regardless of whether they are subcultures, associations, gatherings, or countries) and epitomizes social presumptions about these relationships. This implies that the feeling of socio-culture is significant for understanding what music can do and permit. For instance, if similar music is situated in these unique circumstances, it can work significantly to be crafted by country. This presentation is the method of physical articulation of music that can occur at any point when a tune is sung, a piano is played, a drum is beat, etc. In any case, an understanding of a melody or piece can change and develop as it is performed. In old-style music, a melodic work is initiated and written in music documentation by a writer and concludes when the arranger is satisfied with its structure and instrumentation. In traditional music, instrumental entertainers, vocalists, or conductors may continuously change the expression or rhythm of a piece. Entertainers have substantially more adaptability in present-day and conventional music to make changes to the state of a melody or piece. In that capacity, regardless of whether a band plays a melody in the well-known method or customary music style, they may make changes to it, e.g., presenting a guitar solo or consolidating a presentation.

The remainder of the paper is organized as follows. Section 2 provides a literature review, Section 3 presents a technical discussion of the machine learning model, Section 4 considers the comparison model, Section 5 provides experimental result, and finally Section 6 presents a conclusion and future work.

2   LITERATURE REVIEW

We all are humans, and we all are live in the beautiful nature by some creative thing that is called music. Without music, human interpretation cannot be done successively. Music is one of the

DOI 10.1201/9781003167488-6

beautiful creatures that surrounds our life and it is very important to human life. Music provides a freshness to our minds so that our mind reflects on the positive and we feel happy all the time (Thiruvengatanadhan 2019). Here, we find some musical songs by which we can make a spectral pattern (Brotzer et al. 2019).

Music plays a significant part in humanity's growth and has inspired many people to do great things (Taniguchi et al. 2008). Music is a complex structure of musical ingredients with diverse genres and dimensions. We have so many different kinds of music such as Bhangra, Pop, and Jazz, as well as remix songs, etc. The music data is in the form of sound. The common elements are are pitch, dynamics, and rhythm where pitch refers to the sound of noise, dynamics refers to the movement, and rhythm refers to the repeating patterns of music like tap, clap, etc. Timbre is a term used to classify all music and it defines the tone and color quality of the music. The word "beat" refers to the regularly occurring pattern of rhythmic stresses in music. The word "tempo" is the speed of the beat expressed in the terms of beat per minute (BPM). It is very hard to do work on a large dataset and it is a very hazardous problem found in nature. Basically, it finds the structure of the musical patterns that occurs in musical forms. By taking the common melody patterns we extract the BPM and spectrogram (Bagul et al 2014). The multilayer-like star model, graph model, stratified model, etc. represent the formats of music representation. Music summarization refers to the indexing of the music and classification based on machine learning algorithm (Avanzini et al. 2019) It represents the similarities and differences of the multilayer song (Baratè et al. 2019).

The classification of music is divided into pure and vocal, and based on that it differentiates the characterization of the musical performance very well using algorithms (Xu et al. 2005). It is totally based on some instruments that the separation of the data is generated. Smart musical instruments are digital instruments that were used to communicate with musical Internet of Things(IoT), and they also specify the design formats by collecting the required information about it (Panchwagh et al. 2016). The data is all about images, audio, video, text, etc. The work is to classify the data mining on classifiers and pre-processing methods. Using these two methods, we can easily classify the terms, and also split the data into two separate forms. Data extraction and classification are processed in a music genre classification (Thiruvengatanadhan 2019). Classification of music is a crucial step toward rapid growth and is useful in indexing music.

Some days, scanning and arranging are the main features of the music classification system. This paper describes a technique that uses support vector machines (SVMs) to classify songs using spectral features. It deals with how can we treat the subsystem of the signals that are transmitted in the real word (Thiruvengatanadhan 2019). The speech and music recognition tells us the task of an augmented work reality. The work rate is increased due to the improvement of the internet and network bandwidth frequency. As we know, speech and music both are the synonyms of the sound or noise that is produced. The work is divided into two areas: the classification and the clustering method process. The spectral analysis is analyzed to the input audio signal to select a spectral pattern by it. Moreover, it gives the specific pattern of it. Finally, we give a sinusoidal wave of voice and music. The music has been categorized into audio categories such as musical instrument, voice chanting, speech, and mixed categories such as instruments and singing.

An important goal of extracting the characteristics is to compact the music signal to a vector thatis indicative of the meaningful information it seeks to describe. Acoustic characteristics called spectral features are extracted in these works. Music has also been divided into genres and sub-genres not only on the basis on music but also on the lyrics as well. Various gigabyte scale music information datasets are available along with metadata and online music streaming services. Based on the enormity of these datasets, scalable machine learning models are required that can categorize music information according to different criteria such as artist, genre, and music similarity (Chen et al. 2019). Some methods of classification are done by the neural network where artificial intelligence (AI) also works efficiently and effectively.

The dataset of music consists of 1000 classes into 2 different data such as the separation of music into the various forms like rock, classical, jazz, country, blues, disco, hip-hop, metal, pop, and reggae.

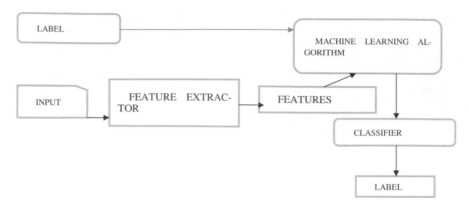

Figure 1. The machine learning model.

Table 1. Features extraction.

Group	Features
Spectral features	Zcr, spectral centroid, spectral roll-off, mfcc, chroma, spectral flux, pitch
Temporal features	Energy, entropy, rms

3 THE MACHINE LEARNING MODEL

The proposed model consists of the input phase where the music files are loaded from the data set, then the pre-processing is done on the files as shown in Figure 1. The main module is a feature extractor module which finds the user-specified features. After extracting the features, specific algorithms such as SVM (Support Vector Machine), NB (Naïve Bayes), RF (Random Forest), DT (Decision Tree), and Multi-class SVM are applied, and as a result it classifies the music. The main goal of this model is that as we collect the data of the music, then the pre-processing is done to get the valuable terms which are necessary for the training. Extract the music and after that one can extract the data. Divided, the data into the clusters are known as clustering. In the end, we generate a summary that provides knowledge of the music. This process is known as full summarization of the music. The result is evaluated based on classification. There are main classifications of music genres such as blues, classical, country, electronic, folk, jazz, new age, and reggae. All these are classifications based on the music that played in our musical life and these all are very humorous in nature to be listening to.

Feature Extraction Process: This is used to extract some features behind it using software before using the classification process to be done. The noisy data removed or extracted by using the pre-processing method and then it runs through the machine learning algorithm. The proposed features are derived as zero-crossing rate, periodicity, and second-order statistics of each Spectral Peak Sequence (SPS). The speech–music classification is performed by training classifiers on these features.

4 MUSIC SPECTRAL PATTERN TECHNIQUES

4.1 Support Vector Machine (SVM)

There is a hyperplane that divides the two different separation areas in the N-dimensional space of the given data points. The respective data points show that the closest hyperplane as well as its respective position and its orientation based on decision boundary.

Table 2. Dataset table.

Dataset name	Number of columns	Classification
Data	1000	On the basis of label belongs to genre.
Data_2genre	200	On the basis of label belongs to number.

4.2 *Naïve Bayes*

A collection of classification algorithms that is based on Bayes' Theorem. It is the part of one algorithm that belongs to the family algorithm where we shared all the features that classified to one another.

4.3 *Random Forest*

A Random Forest is a strategy that is equipped for performing both relapse and order process errands with the utilization of numerous choice trees and this procedure called a Bootstrap Aggregation, or stowing. There is one explicit approach to bunching all the individual choice trees and consolidating them to all settlements on the various choice trees that give the last yield with respect to it.

4.4 *Decision Tree*

A choice tree is a flowchart-type structure path by which each inward hub speaks to a test on a property. Each branch speaks to the result of the test, and each leaf hub speaks to a class mark (choice taken in the wake of processing all traits).

4.5 *Multi-class SVM*

Regarding multi-class problems, there is a simplest way to extend SVMs by using the so-called one-vs.-rest method. K-linear SVMs will be trained separately for K-class problems where the respective data from the other classes form the negative classes (Sharma et al. 2019).

5 RESULT

The popular finding of all the songs that have peak duration, that is, there is a cap in all of the filter spectra (Bagul et al 2014). Better audio produced by using the respective instruments give the sufficient output of it (Turchet et al. 2019).

Dataset: The dataset consists of a huge amount of a data in a prescribed format. A ataset containing the related information regarding the theory also gives valuable information about it or is the used information about it. Dataset results in the form of classes are similar or dissimilar. The similar or dissimilar data comes out in the Yes/No format. The dataset used https://www.kaggle.com/insiyeah/musicfeatures.

Table 3 provides information which consists of the 11 attributes that are important for any music.

Experimental Result-Classification based on the predicted result: Finally, the multi-class SVM provides much better results as compared to other machine learning algorithms.

6 CONCLUSION

The study of the pleasant sequences tells us that replication of the similarities in the song will lead to increased popularity. And, it generalized the musical spectral patterns of music by the software

Table 3. The most common attributes in the dataset.

Attributes	Description
Filename	The file name is given in a dataset.
Tempo	The speed at which a passage of music is played.
Beats	Rhythmic unit in the music.
Chroma stft	Short time Fourier Transform (stft).
Rmse	Root mean square error (rmse).
Spectral centroid	Indicates where the center of mass of the spectrum is located.
Spectral bandwidth	The wavelength that is given to the interval by which the spectral quantity of the radiated must be less than its corresponding value.
Roll-off	Roll-off is the step of a transmission function with respected frequency.
Zero-crossing rate	The rate at which the signal changes from its positive side to its negative side or back.
Mfcc	Mel-frequency cepstral coefficients (mfcc) are the coefficients that collectively make up the mfcc environment.
Label	It contains a string to depicting the genre.

Table 4. Experimental based table.

Algorithm	Accuracy (Data Set)	
	Data	Data_2genere
Support Vector Machine	61%	62%
Naïve Bayes	55%	56%
Random Forest	58%	62%
Decision Tree	46%	51%
Multi-class SVM	61%	64%

that is given by the goldware software. There is a need for an efficient and accurate technique for analyzing and synchronizing the representation of the layer. It analyzes the multi-representation and it organizes the layered work representation that is needed of it. The characterization, classification, and summarization of pure and vocal music is done and also the image compressed to be done.

Finally, the audio content takes the respective spectral patterns by using the multi-class SVM algorithm and then the classification processes are done so that the data is classified. We create a model in a very efficient way, and also provide a sufficient result of it on the basis of the rating that is produced. This reveals the efficient salient repetition structures and also improves the performance of the layered structure that is exploited. It enhances the complexity and interactivity and shows the structure very well. The classification is done in a very efficient and simple way. The representation of sinusoidal tracking waves formed, and the peak value was found when the graph is represented.

There is a scope of the work that the analysis of their work be extended within the combination of these two representations on behalf of its order to maintain and obtain the better understanding of the respective genre divisions through the clustering process. Moreover, the second or other way of representing the use of distinct distances classify the newly generated melodies to divide the existing songs into the respective clusters. The music generated, i.e., tempo, rhythm generation, and the use of its valuable harmonic information generates the melodies that also are studied in the future. There is an amazing system to achieve a great thing we have, that is we easily find a basic spectral pattern regarding these music songs and have eventual results about it. Also, this work is so enlarged in the world and the research never ends.

REFERENCES

Avanzini, Federico, and Luca A. Ludovico. 2019, Multilayer Music Representation and Processing: Key Advances and Emerging Trends. *International Workshop on Multilayer Music Representation and Processing (MMRP). IEEE, 2019.*

Bagul, Mitali, Divya Soni, and K. Saravanakumar. 2014, Recognition of similar patterns in popular Hindi Jazz songs by music data mining. *International Conference on Contemporary Computing and Informatics (IC3I). IEEE, 2014.*

Bahuleyan, Hareesh. 2018, Music genre classification using machine learning techniques. *arXiv preprint arXiv:1804.01149 (2018).*

Baratè, Adriano, Goffredo Haus, and Luca A. Ludovico. 2019, State of the art and perspectives in multi-layer formats for music representation. *International Workshop on Multilayer Music Representation and Processing (MMRP). IEEE, 2019.*

Bhattacharjee, Mrinmoy, S. R. M. Prasanna, and Prithwijit Guha. 2018, Time-frequency audio features for speech-music classification. *arXiv preprint arXiv:1811.01222 (2018).*

Brotzer, J. M., E. R. Mosqueda, and K. Gorro. 2019, Predicting emotion in music through audio pattern analysis. *MS&E 482.1 (2019): 012021*

Chen, Ke, et al. 2019, The effect of explicit structure encoding of deep neural networks for symbolic music generation. *International Workshop on Multilayer Music Representation and Processing (MMRP). IEEE, 2019.*

Giraldo, Sergio, et al. 2018, Automatic assessment of violin performance using dynamic time warping classification. *26th Signal Processing and Communications Applications Conference (SIU). IEEE, 2018.*

Li, T. L., Antoni B. Chan, and Andy HW Chun. 2010, Automatic musical pattern feature extraction using convolutional neural network. *Genre 10 (2010): 1x1.*

Panchwagh, Mangesh M., and Vijay D. Katkar. 2016, Music genre classification using data mining algorithm. *Conference on Advances in Signal Processing (CASP). IEEE, 2016.*

Sharma, Ashish, Anant Ram, and Archit Bansal. 2019, Feature Extraction Mining for Student Performance Analysis. *Proceedings of ICETIT 2019. Springer, Cham, 2020. 785–797.*

Tang, Yichuan. 2013, Deep learning using linear support vector machines. *arXiv preprint arXiv:1306.0239 (2013).*

Taniguchi, Toru, Mikio Tohyama, and Katsuhiko Shirai. 2008, Detection of speech and music based on spectral tracking. *Speech Communication 50.7 (2008): 547–563.*

Thiruvengatanadhan, R. 2019, Music Classification using Spectral Features and SVM. (2019).

Turchet, Luca, and Panos Kudumakis. 2019, Requirements for a file format for smart musical instruments. *International Workshop on Multilayer Music Representation and Processing (MMRP). IEEE, 2019.*

Xu, Changsheng, Namunu Chinthaka Maddage, and Xi Shao. 2005, Automatic music classification and summarization. *IEEE transactions on speech and audio processing 13.3 (2005): 441–450.*

Yadav, D. P., et al. 2019, Feature extraction based machine learning for human burn diagnosis from burn images. *IEEE Journal of Translational Engineering in Health and Medicine 7 (2019): 1–7.*

Smart Computing – Khan et al (Eds)
© *2021 Taylor & Francis Group, London, ISBN 978-0-367-76552-1*

An election system using blockchain

V. Dhiman, U. Kumar, A. Narla, A. Kumar, V. Sharma & N.P. Singh
National Institute of Technology Hamirpur, Hamirpur, Himachal Pradesh, India

ABSTRACT: Blockchain is a relatively new technology. Although it is not entirely new, people are not very aware of it because it has not been put into use in most parts of the world. But those who have studied blockchain know about its merits and how it can help replace some old techniques and produce better results. Using blockchain for this purpose leads to several benefits, and helps in conducting elections that are fair, transparent and independently verifiable. In this paper, we present a new method of conducting elections that use the features of blockchain to achieve the desired properties of transparency, privacy and decentralization. We show how our method can be used to implement elections at the national level, especially in countries like India where a huge amount of money is spent on conducting elections.

1 INTRODUCTION

In democratic nations, elections have become an important source for determining in whose hands the power to rule the nation lies. Holding elections on a small scale such as in a class or university is feasible and economically feasible, but it becomes tedious for a city or a nation. Generally, elections determining ruling leaders are held once every five years in democratic nations. India is the largest democracy in the world, and in order to carry out the election process smoothly and securely, a large amount of money is spent on the equipment used during the process, and for the security forces.

Recently, allegations have been made that the Electronic Voting Machines, popularly known as EVMs, which have been used during the election process in India, have been tampered with. There is no sure way to confirm or deny these allegations, because the data regarding votes is kept highly confidential.

In order to tackle this problem, we can use a decentralized technique to store the details of the votes, which can be verified later if the need arises. One such technique is "blockchain." Blockchain technology consists of a distributed network that consists of a large number of interconnected nodes (Quasim 2020). Each node has its own copy of the distributed ledger, which contains the complete history of all transactions processed by the network. There is no single source of authority that controls the network. Instead, if a majority of the nodes agree, they accept a transaction. In this network, the users remain anonymous. The blockchain application can also be developed for many applications based on Internet of Things (IoT) such as healthcare, industrial IoT, and security (Abuhasel 2020; Khan 2020a, Khan 2020e; Quasim 2019).

These features of blockchain suggest that it can be used to achieve the basic requirements of elections—privacy, immutability and verification. Apart from these, security is achieved due to the decentralization feature of blockchain. Hence, this blockchain method can prove to be better than the existing methods of voting and can greatly reduce the cost of holding elections in a nation.

 DOI 10.1201/9781003167488-7

2 RELATED WORKS

The idea of blockchain evolved after analyzing "Bitcoin," which is a peer-to-peer electronic cash system (Nakamoto 2008). After that, several researchers have tried to use the features of blockchain for different purposes. One such purpose is voting in elections. An electronic voting system highlighting features like anonymity, transparency, and robustness was proposed in 2016 (Lee et al. 2016). This was followed by several other attempts to use blockchain for the purpose of electronic voting.

The features of authentication, anonymity, accuracy, and verifiability were added to the e-voting system model. Such a system was reliable, secure, and anonymous (Ayed 2017). An analysis was done on how the adoption of blockchain into a kind of digital repertoire would solve common issues involved in voting systems. This then led to transparency in elections, enhancement of voter confidence, and increased auditability (Moura & Gomes 2017).

Later, an e-voting method based on blockchain that allowed re-voting was proposed and implemented (Kubjas 2017). A voting protocol based on blockchain that satisfied the properties of fairness, eligibility, privacy, verifiability, and coercion-resistance was proposed soon after. It also allowed the change or cancellation of a vote (Hardwick et al. 2017). An e-voting system in which the underlying technology used was a payment scheme that offered anonymity of the transactions was implemented later (Tarasov & Tewari 2017).

Soon after, an EVS that is based on the Bitcoin protocol and blind signatures was developed. This was quite different from the other e-voting systems used until then. Using the protocols like bitcoin protocol, blind signature protocol, and digital signature protocol, the proposed EVS had the properties of anonymity, fairness, robustness, and verifiability (Cruz & Kaji 2017). An e-voting application without a trusted third party was also proposed, which involved the use of a combination of blockchain technology with a secret-sharing scheme as well as homomorphic encryption (Hsiao et al. 2017).

After that, an effort was made to leverage the benefits of blockchain, such as cryptographic foundations and transparency, for achieving an effective scheme for e-voting, which was implemented using a multichain platform (Khan et al. 2018). An EVS using blockchain which preserves a participant's anonymity while being open to public inspection was developed later (Patil et al. 2018).

An EVS known as crypto-voting was proposed later, and it consisted of three phases: preparatory activities and formation of electoral lists; management of voting; and count of votes. It also covered aspects like safe timing for voting abroad and automatic management of electoral lists (Fusco et al. 2018).

A new protocol using blockDAG that is a directed acyclic graph of blocks was introduced, which explained how vote rigging, hacking of EVMs, and election manipulation are the major issues in the current voting systems. This led to the creation of a novel voting model which used a blockchain-based protocol, PHANTOM (Srivastava et al. 2018). After that, a novel EVS that combines the features of blockchain, ring signature, and fingerprint authentication for additional security was proposed. This method of using fingerprints for voter verification made the system highly secure and eliminated duplicate votes (Suralkar et al. 2019).

3 PROPOSED METHODOLOGY

Considering the developments made until now as listed above, we can describe the requirements for our model, as well as its structure.

3.1 *System requirements*

3.1.1 *Eligibility*
We need to ensure that only people who are at least 18 years old and who possess a valid Aadhar number are allowed to vote.

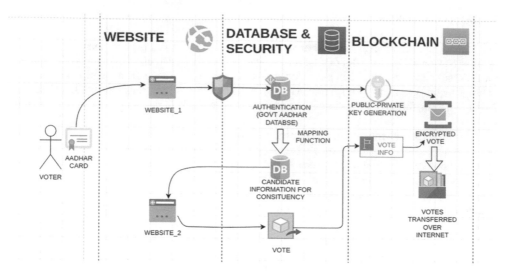

Figure 1. Structure of the proposed model.

3.1.2 *Privacy*
We need to ensure that the details of the voters, candidates, votes and counts are kept private and are not accessible to anyone.

3.1.3 *Transparency*
At any point of time after casting the vote, the voter should be able to verify the details of the his/her vote easily. This is useful to disprove the allegations of the tampering of votes.

3.1.4 *Concurrency*
Since millions of voters may vote at the same point of time, there will be as many new blocks to be added. Proper care should be taken to ensure that the server does not crash, and that all the new blocks are added to the correct chains.

3.1.5 *Decentralization*
The main problem with centralization is that it may be hacked or modified by an attacker. To avoid this, a method using decentralization must be used.

3.1.6 *Immutability*
Once a vote is cast, it should not be possible for anyone to modify it. This helps in ensuring that the tampering of votes does not take place.

3.2 *Proposed model*

Figure 1 shows the three important phases of the election system: the website, the database and the blockchain. In order to ensure that the above requirements are met by our model, we plan the model as follows

3.2.1 *Website*
The website that can be used as the voting tool by voters consists of a homepage that provides a few functions such as casting a vote, verifying one's vote etc. When a new person enters the webpage in order to vote, he/she clicks on the required option and is diverted to a new webpage that verifies his/her credentials. If the details are found to be correct, the voter's details are verified from the

database. If he/she is eligible to vote and his/her vote has not been cast yet, then he/she is diverted to the next webpage.

In the new webpage, the voter must enter his/her email-id. Once it is entered, a private key is generated and sent to that email-id. The voter must copy this key and paste it in the provided box. If entered correctly, he/she is redirected to the next page.

On this new webpage, the details of the available candidates in the constituency of the voter are displayed in tabular format. In each row of the table, the first column contains the serial number. The second one contains the name of the candidate. The third row contains the name of the political party to which the candidate is affiliated to. The fourth column consists of the official symbol of the corresponding political party. Additionally, a row for "None of the Above" or "NOTA" may be placed, if required.

After the voter selects the candidate of his choice, he is asked to confirm the selection, and after confirmation is received, the voting process is completed. The voter can verify his vote by going to the homepage and choosing the link to verify a vote. This process is simpler, and just needs the voter to enter the public key that he received in his e-mail after voting.

3.2.2 *Database*
A Database Management System (DBMS) is needed to efficiently, securely, and quickly store and retrieve data related to the voting process. There are multiple tables used in the database (Quasim 2013a). One table stores the details of all Aadhar card holders, another stores the details of the contesting candidates, another stores the details of the various political parties contesting in the elections, and yet another consists of the voters who have voted. Since millions of voters may log in at the same time, the database needs to store and retrieve data very quickly and accurately. Consistency should be maintained, and failed transactions should be taken care of properly (Quasim 2013b).

3.2.3 *Blockchain*
Blockchain, as the name suggests, is a "chain" of blocks. A block is an aggregated set of data. The collected data is processed to fit in a block through a process called mining. Mining refers to finding a cryptographic hash for the set of data contained in a block. Each block could be identified using this cryptographic hash (also known as a digital fingerprint). Every time a block is mined it can be added to the existing chain of blocks.

In this way, all the data could be connected via a linked list structure. The transactions that are included in a block depend on the miner. In our case, the transactions will be included on the basis of their timestamps. Each transaction to be included is verified using digital signatures (public key cryptography).

The blockchain is the main feature of this method that is embedded with cryptography techniques like a public–private system. The hashing functions used here provide the features of encryption, identification, confidentiality, integrity and distributed elections.

People present at a location different from their constituency can cast their votes from any location through this model, by the use of a mapping function which maps them to their respective constituency.

4 IMPLEMENTATION

Figure 2 shows how the blockchain is implemented for our purpose. Each vote by a citizen is converted into the encrypted format and transferred to the mining sites in the network which is the first phase of the blockchain. The block being mined is sent to other nodes in the network, so as to update their own copy of the distributed ledger maintaining consistency and integrity. When the voting process ends, the next stage involves the counting of votes. The ledger is made available for distribution to the public for the verification process. The implementation is described in detail in the following sections.

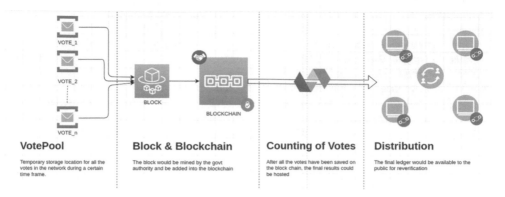

VotePool	**Block & Blockchain**	**Counting of Votes**	**Distribution**
Temporary storage location for all the votes in the network during a certain time frame.	The block would be mined by the govt authority and be added into the blockchain	After all the votes have been saved on the block chain, the final results could be hosted	The final ledger would be available to the public for reverification

Figure 2.   Blockchain implementation.

4.1   *Mapping of constituency*

This provides for mapping of the vote to a constituency by applying a suitable mapping function which will be directly linked to the database. In the election models used currently, the physical presence of voters is required in their respective constituency, and they can't cast their vote if they are residing at a different location during the time of elections. But with the help of blockchain in elections and mapping of people to their constituencies with the use of address they have provided during their registration of Aadhar card, the voter has the ability of casting his vote from any location.

4.2   *Generation of vote*

The voter will be authenticated using his Aadhar number. Using the Aadhar number, the voter will be shown the list of the contesting political parties and their respective candidates in his constituency. A public–private pair will be generated for the voter.

4.3   *Casting of vote*

The input to each blocking transaction is the single vote which is provided to the voter over the voter's public key. The voter can then select one of the candidates by transferring the vote (token) to a political party by using the public key of the political party.

4.4   *Block structure*

The public key voter as well as the public key of the political party of the receiver act as the input and output to a type of pseudo transaction happening between the voter and the political party. Moreover, the timestamp and the mapped constituency is added into the block. Finally, the block generated above is encrypted using the private key of the sender which creates a digital signature and can thus be later verified.

We can generate the signature by using the message and private key of the voter as input parameters. We can also verify a vote by using the message, signature and public key of the voter as input parameters. The output of the verification function is either true or false. Upon successful verification of the vote, true is returned.

4.5   *Mining of block*

The voting transaction created in the above steps is transferred from the local machine to the mining sites located at the desired locations preferably at the district level.

4.6 *Proof-of-work*

The computation performed by the mining nodes acts as the proof-of-work for mining the block. Moreover no reward is provided to the miner. Proof-of-work acts as the piece of data used for the purpose of the verification which is otherwise tough to produce.

4.7 *Proof-of-stake*

The Proof-of-stake concept refers to the extent to which a node can be mined based upon the mining rights provided by the programmer.

4.8 *Ledger updating and termination*

The mined block is then broadcast over the network and the other nodes would then update their own blockchain by adding the new block. Finally the voting process is terminated at a specific time and all the votes cast after that time will be simply discarded.

4.9 *Counting*

The votes cast to a respective candidate/political party are calculated by first mapping the vote to the correct constituency and then calculating vote share in the constituency by using the public key of the party stored in the blocks.

4.10 *Public disclosure*

The results as well as the blockchain are disclosed to the public.

5 LIMITATIONS

Although the proposed model does not have any defects in implementation, there may be some external problems for the proper functioning for the model. Some of them are as follows.

5.1 *Limited internet connectivity*

In a developing country like India, internet services are not available in all parts of the country. So, our model cannot be used to collect votes from rural parts of the country. A large percent of the Indian population is in rural areas, and this is one limitation for the successful implementation of our proposed model.

5.2 *Inability to change a vote*

In case a voter chooses a wrong candidate while voting, he can't change it later. He can vote only once. So, proper care should be taken by the voter before casting the vote.

5.3 *No control over voters*

Although this method of voting allows a voter to vote from any location, we can't ensure that a person's vote is not influenced by others by pressuring or bribing him. This is out of the scope of programming and can only be put in check by the society itself.

These limitations can be overcome by educating people and providing internet connection to all the regions in the country.

6 DISCUSSION

Through this research paper, we can see how the blockchain technology can be used to revolutionize the process of conducting elections in a fair and secure way. Although this paper uses the example of national elections, this model works well for small-scale elections at the classroom level, university level and municipal level. The implementation is also simple, thus making it easy to organize the whole election process. Despite the simple structure, this method of elections is much more secure than the existing ones.

The characteristics of blockchain like transparency, immutability and decentralization have been used here. One additional feature of this method is the ability to vote from any location. Generally, people move to far-off places for several reasons like education, employment, vacation etc. This makes them ineligible to vote in their constituency during the elections if they can't be present physically at the place. But in our method, we use the mapping function to overcome this problem. This makes it possible for millions of people who are away from their constituency to cast their vote from their current location. This increases the voter turnout and can lead to healthy elections.

7 CONCLUSION

In this paper, we have proposed a new method of conducting elections by using blockchain technology. The entire system is decentralized and secure. The voting process is very simple and hassle-free. This method has several advantages over the existing methods. If implemented, this method of conducting elections can lead to fair and cost-effective elections, for small-scale as well as large-scale ones. As more people begin to understand the power of blockchain, they'll support its applications such as this one, and make complex things simpler and safer. This method can be used by the bodies conducting elections at the municipal and national level to conduct fair and transparent elections at a low cost. The voter turnout can improve greatly too, which greatly affects the election results.

AUTHORS' CONTRIBUTIONS

V.D. and U.K. conceived of the presented idea. U.K. and V.S. analyzed the existing voting methods. A.N. and A.K. worked on the implementation of the website, while V.S. worked on the implementation of blockchain along with V.D. and U.K. All the authors discussed the obtained results. A.N. and V.D. wrote the final manuscript after taking input from all the other authors. N.P.S supervised the project.

REFERENCES

Abuhasel K. A. and M. A. Khan, (2020), "A Secure Industrial Internet of Things (IIoT) Framework for Resource Management in Smart Manufacturing," in IEEE Access, vol. 8, pp. 117354–117364, 2020, doi: 10.1109/ACCESS.2020.3004711.

Ayed, A.B. 2017. A conceptual secure blockchain-based electronic voting system. *International Journal of Network Security & Its Applications, Vol 9(3): 1–9.*

Cruz, J.P. & Kaji, Y. 2016. E-voting System Based on the Bitcoin Protocol and Blind Signatures. *IPSJ Transactions on Mathematical Modeling and Its Applications, Vol 10(1): 14–22.*

Fusco, F., Lunesu, M.I., Pani, F.E. & Pinna, A. 2018. Crypto-voting, a blockchain based e-Voting System. *10th International Conference on Knowledge Management and Information Sharing: 223–227.*

Hardwick, F.S., Gioulis, A., Akram, R.N. & Markantonakis, K. 2018. E-voting with blockchain: an e-voting protocol with decentralisation and voter privacy. *2018 IEEE International Conference on Internet of Things (iThings) and IEEE Green Computing and Communications (GreenCom) and IEEE Cyber, Physical and Social Computing (CPSCom) and IEEE Smart Data (SmartData): 1561–1567.*

Hsiao, J.H., Tso, R., Chen, C.M. & Wu, M.E. 2017. Decentralized E-Voting Systems Based on the Blockchain Technology. *Advances in Computer Science and Ubiquitous Computing Lecture Notes in Electrical Engineering: 305–309.*

Khan M. A. (2020), An IoT Framework for Heart Disease Prediction Based on MDCNN Classifier, in IEEE Access, vol. 8, pp. 34717–34727, 2020. DOI: 10.1109/ACCESS.2020.2974687

Khan, MA, Abuhasel, KA. (2020).Advanced metameric dimension framework for heterogeneous industrial Internet of things. Computational Intelligence. 2020; 1–21. https://doi.org/10.1111/coin.12378

Khan, K.M., Arshad, J. & Khan, M.M. 2018. Secure Digital Voting System based on Blockchain Technology. *International Journal of Electronic Government Research (IJEGR), Vol 14(1): 53–62.*

Khan M.A. et al, (2020), Decentralised IoT, Decenetralised IoT: A Blockchain perspective, Springer, Studies in BigData, 2020, DOI: https://doi.org/10.1007/978-3-030-38677-1

Khan, M. A., Quasim, M. T, et.al, (2020), A Secure Framework for Authentication and Encryption Using Improved ECC for IoT-Based Medical Sensor Data, in IEEE Access, vol. 8, pp. 52018-52027, 2020. DOI: 10.1109/ACCESS.2020.2980739

Khan, M.A. and Algarni F., (2020) "A Healthcare Monitoring System for the Diagnosis of Heart Disease in the IoMT Cloud Environment Using MSSO-ANFIS," in IEEE Access, vol. 8, pp. 122259–122269, 2020, doi: 10.1109/ACCESS.2020.3006424.

Kubjas, I. 2017. Using blockchain for enabling internet voting.

Lee, K., James, J.I., Ejeta, T.G. & Kim, H.J. 2016. Electronic Voting Service Using Block-chain. *Journal of Digital Forensics, Security and Law, Vol 11(2): 123–136.*

Moura, T. & Gomes, A. 2017. Blockchain Voting and its effects on Election Transparency and Voter Confidence. *Proceedings of the 18th Annual International Conference on Digital Government Research: 574–575.*

Nakamoto, S. 2008. Bitcoin: A Peer-to-Peer Electronic Cash System.

Patil, H.V., Rathi, K.G. & Tribhuwan, M.V. 2018. A study on decentralized e-voting system using blockchain technology. *International Research Journal of Engineering and Technology, Vol 5(11): 48–53.*

Quasim, M.T. (2013). Security Issues in Distributed Database System Model , COMPUSOFT, An international journal of advanced computer technology, 2 (12), December-2013 (Volume-II, Issue-XII) Quasim, M.T. (2013), An Efficient approach for concurrency control in distributed database system, Indian Streams Research Journal, 2013(Volume-3, Issue-9).

Quasim, M.T., Khan M.A, Algarni F., Alharthy A., Alshmrani G.M.M, (2020), Blockchain Frameworks. In: Khan M., Quasim M., Algarni F., Alharthi A. (eds) Decentralised Internet of Things. Studies in Big Data, vol 71. Springer, DOI: https://doi.org/10.1007/978-3-030-38677-1

Quasim, M. T., Khan M. A, et.al, (2019), Internet of Things for Smart Healthcare: A Hardware Perspective, 2019 First International Conference of Intelligent Computing and Engineering (ICOICE), Hadhramout, Yemen, 2019, pp. 1–5. DOI: 10.1109/ICOICE48418.2019.9035175

Srivastava, G., Dwivedi, A.D. & Singh, R. 2018. Crypto-democracy: A Decentralized Voting Scheme using Blockchain Technology. *International Conference on Security and Cryptography, Vol 2: 508–513.*

Suralkar, S., Udasi, S., Gagnani, S., Tekwani, M. & Bhatia, M. 2019. E-Voting Using Blockchain With Biometric Authentication. *International Journal of Research and Analytical Reviews (IJRAR), Vol 6(1): 77–81.*

Tarasov, P. & Tewari, H. 2017. The Future of E-Voting. *IADIS International Journal on Computer Science and Information Systems, Vol 12(2): 148–165.*

Smart Computing – Khan et al (Eds)
© *2021 Taylor & Francis Group, London, ISBN 978-0-367-76552-1*

Detection and prediction of infectious diseases using IoT sensors: A review

Mohammad Meraj & Surendra Pal Singh
CS & IT Department, NIMS University, Jaipur, Rajasthan, India

Prashant Johri
School of Computer Sciences & Engineering, Galgotia University, Greater Noida, India

Mohammad Tabrez Quasim
College of Computer & IT, University of Bisha, Saudi Arabia

ABSTRACT: Infectious diseases affect a large number of human beings. A lot of investigation is being conducted throughout the world on infections diseases. There are many interactive hardware platform packages in the healthcare market such as the Internet of Things (IoT), including smart tracking, smart sensors, and clinical device integration. Emerging technologies like IoT have a notable ability to keep patients secure and healthy and also enhance how physicians supply care. Healthcare IoT also can bolster an affected person's pride by permitting patients to spend more time interacting with their medical doctors. The most considerable advantage to IoT in healthcare is that it supports doctors in undertaking significant clinical work in a profession that is already experiencing a worldwide professional work shortage. This paper investigates the basis exploration of the applicability of IoT in the healthcare system.

Keywords: IoT, healthcare, infectious disease, prompt detection

1 INTRODUCTION

1.1 *IoT impact on healthcare*

Interactive hardware platform packages like the Internet of Things (IoT) include customized sensors that are designed to sense and respond to typical behaviors or situations, offering high performance (Khan 2020a; Quasim 2019). As in healthcare, a deep investigation has been performed on various infectious diseases. The complex data gathering with the secure connection has enabled the use of blood glucose meters, fertility sensors, and flu monitors, either by individual consumers or at medical institutions; ice sensors ensure that temperatures are insufficient to protect notify technicians when vaccines and injections are available; and remote monitoring equipment enables patients to recover at home, while still benefiting from healthcare professionals who monitor the situation (Jaafar et al. 2020). In terms of infection prevention and control, the power of IoT can be categorized into three different zones:

- testing parameters
- performance behaviors
- interaction with data

1.2 *Analysis of human behaviors*

The spread of diseases in healthcare is a research zone for researchers. Unfortunately, there has been a lack of evidence-based methods (Figure 1).

DOI 10.1201/9781003167488-8

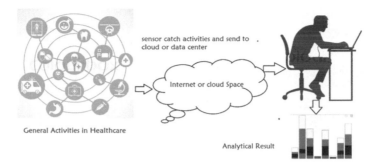

Figure 1.   Smart disease surveillance based on IoT.

Analysis of human behavior is very essential for the right kind of investigation through sensors and the data gathered from the sensors.

1.3 *Collaboration with IoT*

The opportunity to get involved and collaborate locally and globally through targeted, context-relevant stages and groups is exciting and intriguing. A systemic investigation-infection control technique was introduced in "Surveillance Syndrome" (Furness 2016), which includes organized gathering and analysis based on the status of symptoms seen in hospitals and other medical centers. Signal recruitment is a faster way to detect a public health outbreak or infection in a specific institution than current methods pending lab results on the shelf. Internet-based reporting tools, easy to use in emergency rooms, nurse's centers, and doctors' offices, will allow the rapid collection of relevant information. Information and analysis will be more accessible, opened up the interplay between machines and humans, and reduced response times and intervention strategies.

1.4 *IoT monitoring and disease*

The IoT (Khan 2020b) is changing lives in Johns Hopkins University's Global Clinical Health Education Center, which uses a network to react to patient participation and helps doctors and nurses share real-time health information in the care setting. Johns Hopkins University used this model in the investigation of tuberculosis on pregnant women. With increasing skepticism of this outbreak, healthcare devices could be the IoT device network to obtain highly sensitive data to identify the source of this devastating disease. If an outbreak is confirmed, the same network can be used or developed to provide the required medication, medical equipment, and other diagnostic tools.

1.5 *Real-time application of IoT*

IoT has various applications in real time like smart homes, industrial monitoring, non-civilian purposed monitoring, remote location monitoring, E-healthcare, etc. (Sivaram et al. 2020). The use of IoT devices also has very cost-effective and reliable use in engineering applications. The device could support the existing operating system and can handle it through a monitor or any suitable display (Figure 2).

With the rapid population growth of the elderly worldwide, the healthcare system is under tremendous pressure. Care for patients requires a variety of things such as hospitals, doctors, as well as more important checkup devices. This requires an explanation that reduces the problem on the healthcare system while continuing to provide patient healthcare (McCue 2015). With the arrival of smart devices and its adoption of jobs, it is extensively investigated as a possible explanation to

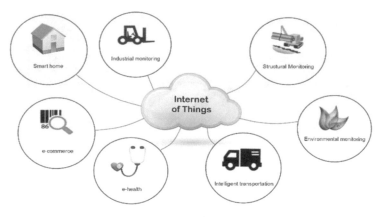

Figure 2. Application of IoT and surroundings.

shrink the burden on types of healthcare. The aiding rehabilitation through continuous observations of progress and emergency healthcare can save life of many people (Furness 2016).

2 RESEARCH BACKGROUND

Focusing on the general collection, analysis, and interpretation of local disease pattern data helps to identify outbreaks of major health-related symptoms (Mathew et al. 2015). In developing countries like India, the performance of single surveillance systems is often hampered by data quality and availability. The IoT concept enables access to information about tagged objects or people by browsing the Internet address or data entry associated with a specific functional RFID with a visual function. In a "Smart recruitment" based on the IoT, the smart device will process and send the required information to the spine network, which is located on a large server that keeps records of the patients in each hospital. This spinal network will process and provide information to the Department of Health for faster, smarter, and easier to understand trends. As all information is provided through smart devices, this will help government agencies take the necessary steps without causing excessive delays.

Demonstrate the theoretical framework of a mobile medical system that produces user diagnostic results (UDR) based on the life-balance results delivered by medical agents and other sensors (Verma & Sood 2018). In addition, the formal model includes keywords, concepts, disease diagnostic methods, and generation awareness strategies. The main motivation for generating results with various diagnostic applications is to use different IoT measurement sets to analyze life better over a given period of time. In addition, the proposed SQL Server Integration Services (SSIS) is a patient method that can extract results from the data gathered by sensors for further health, observing and delivering the specific task.

Parthasarathy & Vivekanandan (2018) proposed a universal design created on the concept of IoT to process sensory evidence and is separated from the most important clinical limitations for joint pain. The most notable scientific parameter that confirms bone formation is related to ROC research assistance. Experimental results show that in the symptoms of arthritis and certain cardiovascular diseases, the levels of uric acid and C-reactive protein in the blood are averaged 8.50 and 3.50 mg/L, respectively. Human vehicle validation is used to isolate the onset of osteoporosis.

In this article, they propose a systematic way of defining smart gadgets for the E-smart healthcare system (Laplante et al. 2017). They demonstrate and present a related quality of work from the E-smart healthcare system especially the essential to regard care as a necessity. In this article, they present a formal framework for defining and later providing assistance in defining, developing, and using IoT in healthcare. This approach involves defining a common category of program types, classifying healthcare settings, and using a systematic way to describe the components of a particular use case. Using this approach to describe (e.g., explain) healthcare, IoT can lead to stand-outs, reuse, collaboration, best practices, and more.

Rapid discovery is an area of intense research that has attracted the efforts and interest of many fields and companies (Lopez-Barbosa et al. 2016). However, the public interest in such devices has also grown, leading to major changes in the design and ideas of these methods of development and data generation. Therefore, future clinical trials should include communication with pre-existing technologies such as smartphones and networks, using automation of manufacturing. On the basis of this project, three key models have been analyzed based on various sensing technologies to highlight the development methods and tools for developing future clinical diagnostic equipment and data capture and application.

Sattar et al. (2019) presented a paper for wound monitoring through IoT-based system. They proposed a system develop IoT-based intelligent wound assessment for wound status. They used the ID3 algorithm as a decision tree for categorizing the attributes through MATLAB. This proposed system based on entropy and information gain for the splitting the tree and feature reduction.

This article introduces the origins and concepts on the impacts of smart devices and applications (Liu & Wang 2017). This article outlines important issues related to IoT technology and service development. The most appropriate parameters for the application are suggested. Although they present the best applications for the IoT, this article may not cover the challenges IoT may face in future practical applications, and future research may begin in this regard.

The proposed work plays an important role in a person's well-being (Muthukumar et al. 2019). Our work considered the beneficial effects of moisture storage and developed an IoT sensor-based module that monitors room temperature and updates the condition to room occupants. The system also regulates air-conditioners and air-conditioning in the living room to maintain optimal humidity levels between 45% and 55%. An upgraded module is an effective and very effective solution for hospitals because in such cases where the risk of an outbreak is high.

In this article, they propose a human-based conceptual framework for healthcare for the elderly and disabled (Husain et al. 2015). The platform is designed to monitor the health of the elderly and disabled and give them an emergency response when their health is unfamiliar. They focus on three aspects:

(a) content fraud (per person) from mobile devices;
(b) instant response;
(c) contextual mobile services to remote users.

Zhu et al. (2020) illustrated how the infectious disease spread and turned up as a pandemic. They demonstrate that the IoT system becomes an important tool for healthcare centers to handle in a pandemic scenario. They found the IoT system is fast, user-friendly, and affordable to control the infectious disease.

Ravi et al. (2019) explored the infectious disease like malaria among humans. This is a quite long and difficult task for detection. As this problem is not very life-threatening, it may be converted in the serious problem. As the author found that few parameters like blood sugar, body temperature, and heartbeat have significantly correlated with malaria. They proposed a model based on logistic regression to achieve maximum accuracy and speed in detection of the process.

3 IMPLEMENTING EFFECTIVE INFECTION PREVENTION MECHANISMS

Based on this analysis, they can recommend the use of data from the IoT network to take preventive measures, or even decide whether the proposed control measures are being used effectively. For example, with the outbreak of influenza in the United States, IoT-enabled devices can track handwashing and virus usage and collected data that can be used to track its impact on influenza transmission in real time. However, getting the job done right needs appropriate preparation and vigilant use of the right knowledge stages and implements. With IoT technology, it has become more realistic to actively identify and prevent the blowout of transferable infections.

4 EXPLORATION OF OUTCOME

In an assessment of this incipient technology is adding value to the sanitation systems of medical institutions, companies are advised to provide unlimited evidence of the effectiveness of their products. Merely discussing facts and statistics of healthcare-related illnesses (HAIs) or the ability of a product of smart devices that kill viruses is not enough. Prior databases (Quasim 2013a, 2013b) provide the right kind of help in the establishment of gadgets through IoT. Unless companies can provide evidence that their products have reduced overall HAIs over a period of time and space, cash-strapped health plans to slow down the use of IoT-based smart application and devices. Technology can coordinate efforts to prevent infection by many hospitals through the spread of disease, including cleaning and disinfecting (people and machines) and hygiene practices by medical to their own treatments and help to reduce disease spreading and provides important messages to healthcare patients with a better decision-making tool.

5 CONCLUSION

The IoT devices are very capable to handle various things. The work with accuracy provides the IoT has a very power full device of present era. The multipurpose use of the device uplifts the various existing gadgets much capable to handle the complex task also. This paper is the exploration of various filed where the IoTs are working. This investigation is deeply focused on the use of IoT with the disease, especially in infections. This research found that the spreading of this disease may turn up as the epidemic. So the control of the infectious disease is waiting this kind of research investigation.

REFERENCES

Furness, Colin, 2016, Syndromic Surveillance for Healthcare-Associated Infections.InfectionPrevention.tips, accessed February 22, 2016: http://infectioncontrol.tips/2016/02/15/syndromic-surveillance-for-healthcare-associated-infections/

Hussain, A., Wenbi, R., da Silva, A. L., Nadher, M., &Mudhish, M. 2015.Health and emergency-care platform for the elderly and disabled people in the Smart City. Journal of Systems and Software, 110, 253–263.

Jaafar Alghazo, Geetanjali Rathee, Sharmidev Gupta, Mohammad Tabrez Quasim, Sivaram Murugan, Ghazanfar Latif, and VigneswaranDhasarathan 2020. A Secure Multimedia Processing through Blockchain in Smart Healthcare Systems.ACM Trans. Multimedia Comput.Commun. Appl. 0, ja. DOI: https://doi.org/10.1145/3396852

Khan, Mohammad Ayoub, et al, 2020a, DecentralisedIoT, Decenetralised IoT: A Blockchain perspective, Springer, Studies in BigData, 2020, DOI: https://doi.org/10.1007/978-3-030-38677-1

Khan, M.A., M. T. Quasim, N. S. Alghamdi and M. Y. Khan, 2020b "A Secure Framework for Authentication and Encryption Using Improved ECC for IoT-Based Medical Sensor Data," in IEEE Access, vol. 8, pp. 52018–52027, 2020. DOI: 10.1109/ACCESS.2020.2980739

Laplante, P. A., Kassab, M.,Laplante, N. L., &Voas, J. M. 2017.Building caring healthcare systems in the Internet of Things. IEEE systems journal, 12(3), 3030–3037.

Liu, R., & Wang, J. (2017). Internet of Things: Application and prospect. In MATEC Web of Conferences (Vol. 100, p. 02034).EDP Sciences.

Lopez-Barbosa, N., Gamarra, J. D., &Osma, J. F. 2016.The future point-of-care detection of disease and its data capture and handling. Analytical and bioanalytical chemistry, 408(11), 2827–2837.

Mathew, A., SA, F. A., Pooja, H. R., & Verma, A. 2015. Smart disease surveillance based on Internet of Things (IoT). International Journal of Advanced Research in Computer and Communication Engineering, 4(5), 180–183.

McCue, TJ 2015. $117 Billion Market for Internet of Things in Healthcare by 2020. Forbes.com, accessed February 22, 2016:http://www.forbes.com/sites/tjmccue/2015/04/22/117-billion-market-for-internet-of-things-in-healthcare-by-2020/#4f6f7f924711

Muthukumar, S., Mary, W. S., Rajkumar, R., Dhina, R., Gayathri, J., & Mathivadhani, A. 2019. Smart Humidity Monitoring System for Infectious Disease Control. In 2019 International Conference on Computer Communication and Informatics (ICCCI) (pp. 1–3).IEEE.

Parthasarathy, P., &Vivekanandan, S. 2018. A typical IoT architecture-based regular monitoring of arthritis disease using time wrapping algorithm. International Journal of Computers and Applications, 1–11.

Quasim, M.T. (2013a). Security Issues in Distributed Database System Model, COMPUSOFT, An international journal of advanced computer technology, 2 (12), December-2013 (Volume-II, Issue-XII).

Quasim, M.T. (2013b), An Efficient approach for concurrency control in distributed database system, Indian Streams Research Journal, 2013(Volume-3, Issue-9)

Quasim, M. T., M. A. Khan, M. Abdullah, M. Meraj, S. P. Singh and P. Johri, 2019 "Internet of Things for Smart Healthcare: A Hardware Perspective," 2019 First International Conference of Intelligent Computing and Engineering (ICOICE), Hadhramout, Yemen, 2019, pp. 1–5. DOI: 10.1109/ICOICE48418.2019.9035175

Ravi, A., Gopal, V., Roselyn, J. P., Devaraj, D., Chandran, P., &Madhura, R. S. (2019). Detection of Infectious Disease using Non-Invasive Logistic Regression Technique.In 2019 IEEE International Conference on Intelligent Techniques in Control, Optimization and Signal Processing (INCOS) (pp. 1–5).IEEE.

Sattar, H., Bajwa, I. S., Amin, R. U., Sarwar, N., Jamil, N., Malik, M. A., &Shafi, U. (2019).An IoT-based intelligent wound monitoring system. IEEE Access, 7, 144500–144515

Sivaram, M., Rathee, G., Rastogi, R. et al, 2020. A resilient and secure two-stage ITA and blockchain mechanism in mobile crowd sourcing. J Ambient Intell Human Comput (2020). https://doi.org/10.1007/s12652-020-01800-x

Verma, P., & Sood, S. K. 2018. Cloud-centric IoT based disease diagnosis healthcare framework. Journal of Parallel and Distributed Computing, 116, 27–38.

Zhu, H., Podesva, P., Liu, X., Zhang, H., Teply, T., Xu, Y …& Li, Y. (2020). IoT PCR for pandemic disease detection and its spread monitoring. Sensors and Actuators B: Chemical, 303, 127098.

Smart Computing – Khan et al (Eds)
© 2021 Taylor & Francis Group, London, ISBN 978-0-367-76552-1

A comparative analysis on allocation of resources in the cloud computing environment

Ambika Gupta
Computer Engineering and Applications, GLA University, Mathura, India

ABSTRACT: In the real-time scenario the most popular, emerging technology named cloud computing becomes an individual's demand. The demands for the resources increase day by day, hour by hour, and minute by minute. For getting the availability of the sufficient number of resources there must be an optimal allocation for these resources so that it is easy to access the resources. The dynamic allocation of task management or resource management is not an easy procedure; there are a number of challenges such as provisioning of data centers across virtual machines, sharing virtual memory, etc. For improving resource utilization at a maximum level there is a comparative study analysis on the basis of various procedures available for resource allocation among virtual machine processing nodes. This survey identifies a conclusion for achieving the appropriate task management as well as optimal resource allocation in the cloud computing environment. Further future work can be extended toward the implementation of the derived approach.

1 INTRODUCTION

There are various deployment models and service models in the cloud computing environment in which it is necessary to allocate the resources optimally across multiple data processing nodes in geographical regions. Multiple numbers of procedures are available to allocate the resources but there are many challenges such as utilized cost, bandwidth consumption, and data security (Abuhasel & Khan 2020). The resource allocation methodology also ensures about quality of service parameters while providing the service to the users online via the Internet.

This requires allocating the resources from the collection of resources that are remotely available to a particular task. For doing the same, a proper framework is there in which four important modules need to be followed. First, on the basis of user requirements every task is needed to be grouped in the form of a complete batch. In the second step of the framework the number of the required resources must be recognized for allocation. In the next step, the allocation of required resources has been done as per the requirement. Finally, the resource scheduling has to be done for making the cloud environment optimal or appropriate just to provide Quality of Service for ensuring the service-level agreement from cloud providers to consumers. The complete framework (Parikh et al. 2017) for task scheduling is shown in Figure 1. The activity of allocating a number of resources definitely improves the overall system performance. As the system is already lacking in a sufficient number of resources, to improve the efficiency in less cost and in less time consumption it is required to better organize the limited resources (Devarasetty & Reddy 2019).

There are various resources elements which are given as follows (Frederic Nzanywayingoma & Yang 2018):

1.1 *Resource monitoring*

The monitoring of resources for client and cloud subscribers can be done.

DOI 10.1201/9781003167488-9

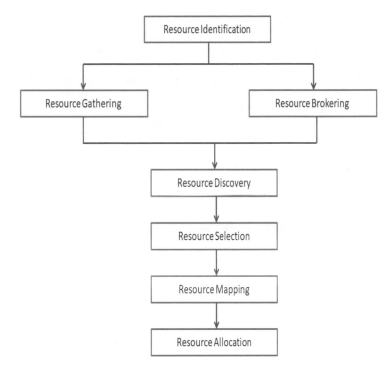

Figure 1.   A framework for resource allocation (Parikh et al. 2017).

1.2   *Resource allocation*

It defines the allocation of resources across various node servers.

1.3   *Resource discovery*

It defines discovery and resource provisioning.

First, in this paper we see the perspective of various possible methodologies for resource allocation on data centers so that the user finds better response time and performance. This paper outlines the comparative analysis among many algorithms for attaining the quality of service as well as a service-level agreement for customer relationship management in terms of appropriate resource allocation. The remaining part of the paper is classified as follows. Section 2 deliberates about related work available on task management and resource allocation. Section 3 deals with the detailed comparative analysis among various available algorithms. Section 4 introduced the problem statement as well as architecture. Section 5 concludes the research work and provides future enhancements.

2   LITERATURE REVIEW

There are various algorithms discussed on resource management system as follows. There is no visibility of any service to the clients among all these services such as infrastructure as a service (IaaS), platform as a service (PaaS), and software as a service (SaaS). Only they can have utilized the same and it is almost comparable to the black-box testing phenomenon where simply an on-demand network access or utility computing kind of model is fully utilized but again the resources allocation is the necessary condition for the same. Therefore, many algorithms available have been discussed below.

Liu et al. (2010) give an algorithm known as the compromised-time-cost (CTC) scheduling algorithm. In the first step of the algorithm, there is a description of minimizing the cost for execution. After that, the various scheduling algorithm applied just to reduce the overall time and cost consumed. Finally, in the last step there is an identification of heavily loaded servers and less loaded server nodes to optimize the resources evenly.

Singh et al. (2015) discussed various functions of resource organization in cloud computing such as provisioning of resources, task scheduling, maintaining a track of resources, etc. The provisioning of resources is to identify the requirement on a particular node server then appropriate allotment of resources for the same to ensure the Quality of service (QoS) parameters in a cloud-computing environment.

Jennings & Stadler (2015) categorize the resources into two main categories: one that is for infrastructure management must be manageable by cloud providers and another one is to execute the workload that is for clients or cloud consumers. Within the margins of service-level promises to provide the appropriate QoS the allocation of resources has been done as per the storage and network parameters.

Manvi & Shyam (2013) discussed the various components of resource management such as resources allocation, assignment, adjustment of resources, and corresponding mapping. Gonzalez et al. (2017) discussed every aspect of optimization for time and execution for the entire migration system. Some of these aspects are cost optimization, dynamic provisioning, energy efficiency, etc. Parikh et al. (2017) describe the better management of resources in cloud computing for user's utilization of cloud resources in terms of energy reduction and cost reduction.

3 WORKLOAD MANAGEMENT

Singh & Chana (2015) proposed a framework for cloud workload in which there are multiple steps given as follows. On the basis of requirements, the analysis of the workload was done in the first step. From a set of resources, find out the appropriate resource that has been done in the second step. After that, the scheduling has been done in the final step, as shown in Figure 2.

For evaluating the performance there are two aspects: one is real and the one is by using simulation (Batista et al. 2015). After that, a detailed analysis is required for better resource provisioning. For experimental setup a simulation tool is required that is CloudSim used to perform the implementation for a large-scale cloud-computing environment. To save the energy and effectively use all the resources, it is required to perform the better provisioning (Qu et al. 2020).

There are certain steps to be followed in the given sequence diagram, as shown in Figures 3 and 4.

Step 1. For maintaining QoS, client and provider must sign a service level agreement.
Step 2. Client will send the request to admission control.
Step 3. There must be a request queue in this state of the procedure.
Step 4. After that virtual resource provisioning must be set.
Step 5. Identify the resource availability.
Step 6. Request information will be sent to the appropriate node.
Step 7. Allocation of the resources must be done.
Step 8. Collection of execution information will be done.
Step 9. Send information to the resource management module.
Step 10. Meanwhile, aservice level agreement must be maintained in the entire procedure.

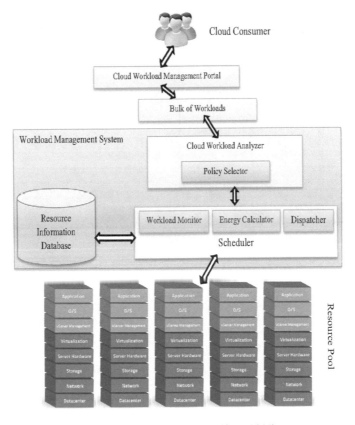

Figure 2.   Cloud workload management framework (Singh & Chana 2015).

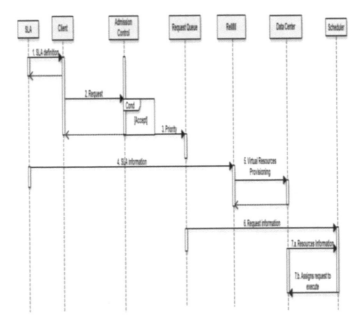

Figure 3.   Diagram for processing a client request.

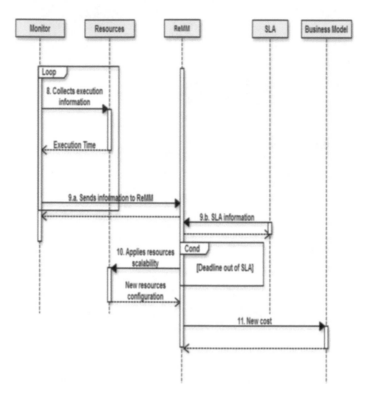

Figure 4.   Sequence diagram for maintaining a service-level agreement.

4   CONCLUSION

This research work deliberated on some key factors for resource management in the cloud computing environment. Various dissimilar aspects of better resource utilization in terms of lower cost and bandwidth optimization, etc. along with the QoS parameters have been surveyed. This paper gives an idea to develop an effective approach for dynamic framework in the context of better performance. And the work gives the real-time benefit of maximum resource utilization in cloud computing environment.

REFERENCES

Abuhasel K. A. and M. A. Khan, (2020), "A Secure Industrial Internet of Things (IIoT) Framework for Resource Management in Smart Manufacturing," in IEEE Access, vol. 8, pp. 117354–117364, 2020, doi: 10.1109/ACCESS.2020.3004711.

Batista BG, Estrella JC, Ferreira CHG, Filho DML, Nakamura LHV, Reiff-Marganiec S, et al. (2015) Performance Evaluation of Resource Management in Cloud Computing Environments. PLoS ONE 10(11): e0141914. doi: 10.1371/journal. pone. 0141914.

Jennings B, Stadler R. 2015. "Resource management in clouds: Survey and research challenges". J Netw Syst Manag 2015, 23(3):567–619.

Manvi SS, Krishna Shyam G. 2013. Resource management for Infrastructure as a Service (IaaS) in cloud computing: A survey", Journal of Network and Computer Applications, http://dx.doi.org/10.1016/j.jnca. 2013.10.004i.

Nelson Mimura Gonzalez, Tereza Cristina Melo de Brito Carvalho, Charles Christian Miers. 2017. Cloud resource management: towards efficient execution of large-scale scientific applications and workflows on complex infrastructures, Journal of Cloud Computing: Advances, Systems and Applications, 6:13, DOI 10.1186/s13677-017-0081-4.

Frederic Nzanywayingoma & Yang Yang (2018): Efficient resource management techniques in cloud computing environment: a review and discussion, International Journal of Computers and Applications, DOI: 10.1080/1206212X.2017.1416558.

Prasad Devarasetty, Ch. Satyananda Reddy. 2019. Research of Task Management and Resource Allocation in Cloud Computing", International Journal of Innovative Technology and Exploring Engineering (IJITEE) ISSN: 2278-3075, Volume-8, Issue- 6S4.

Zhiguo Qu, Yilin Wang, Le Sun, Dandan Peng and Zheng Li. 2020. Study QoS Optimization and Energy Saving Techniques in Cloud, Fog, Edge, and IoT", Hindawi Complexity, Volume 2020, Article ID 8964165, 16 pages, https://doi.org/10.1155/2020/8964165.

Singh S, Chana I, "Cloud resource provisioning: survey, status and future research directions" Knowledge Information System 2015, 49(3):1005–69. https://link.springer.com/article/10.1007/s10115-016-0922-3.

Sukhpal Singh, Inderveer Chana, QRSF: QoS-aware resource scheduling framework in cloud computing, J Supercomput (2015) 71:241–292, DOI 10.1007/s11227-014-1295-6, Published online: 16 September 2014.

Swapnil M Parikh, Narendra M Patel, Harshadkumar B Prajapati 2017. Resource Management in Cloud Computing: Classification and Taxonomy, arXiv: 1703.00374v1 [cs.DC].

Smart Computing – Khan et al (Eds)
© *2021 Taylor & Francis Group, London, ISBN 978-0-367-76552-1*

A pragmatic approach to IoT and distributed system framework era

Ujjwal Kumar & N. Suresh Kumar
School of Computing Science and Engineering, Galgotias University, Greater Noida, India

ABSTRACT: The idea of the Internet of Things (IoT) is a large number of distinct things or physical items interconnected via the Internet. The term Internet of Things was coined by Kevin Aston. Two things that helped IoT to flourish in its early stage was the use of less power devouring small-sized portable chipsets with enabled wireless communication techniques and formulating and using IPV6 protocol which enhanced the range of a number of the connected devices and also provided them with unique identifiers. The most basic approach for IoT is a centralized approach which mainly includes a client–server system with a centralized node/processor which governs nodes below it. They are also subject to security attacks as they are a transparent system with visible central node and cloud architecture. Now to counter these limitations we use a distributed approach. This uncommon issue intends to be an abridgment of the most recent advancement on IoT identified with new reflection or multi-agent ways to deal with circulating assignments among edges and the Cloud—new methods and correspondence principles for sharing data to build range productivity while keeping information consistent and accessible, and new meta-information, strategies, and equipment/programming capacities to help haze organization in conveyed databases. Simultaneously, a completely conveyed model will likewise fall flat, as the expense and specialized requirements that the sensors have will not permit overwhelming registering and capacity assets to be coordinated into the sensors.

1 INTRODUCTION

To understand how IoT works we have to dive deep into the architecture of IoT. The first level is made up of small devices like sensors and actuators. A sensor senses the data, and actuators are used to provide mechanical response according to the processed data. The second level is a gateway along with data acquisition in this sensor that generally collects the data and then sends it to the next level with the help of networks. The next level is pre-processing data into a mannered way such that it is easier to store and access. The fourth and final level is cloud storage. It simply analyzes the data with real-time technologies and other methods and keeps it in storage. The basic structure of a distributed computing system consists of tons of physical computers distributed over a long area and every individual system has its own memory for their respective processors. Although the computing done in this system is parallelly done they are far more different than any parallel computing device. The reason is that they are loosely coupled, meaning that fault at one unit won't affect the other nearby unit. For IoT we will use a similar famous distributed approach called "Edge Computing". With the help of edge computing the data is processed at the local unit itself rather than taking it to a centralized processor. It consists of mainly two components: cloud and gateway. The gateway consists of local IoT devices and networking. The Cloud section contains all the apps, analytics tools, and data storage facilities. With the help of edge computing, IoT achieves low latency rates, less load on the network, efficient and fast computing, low cost, and high security. In any case, much the same as the case with various new advances, handling one issue can make others. From a security position, data at the edge can be annoying, particularly when it's being dealt

DOI 10.1201/9781003167488-10

with by various gadgets that probably won't be as secure as a unified or cloud-based framework. As the quantity of IoT gadgets develops, it's basic that IT comprehends the potential security issues around these gadgets, and to ensure those frameworks can be made sure about. This incorporates ensuring that information is encoded and that the right access control techniques and even VPN burrowing is used. Continuously, in any case, the best bit of leeway of edge figuring is the ability to process and store data speedier, enabling for progressively profitable consistent applications that are essential to associations. Before edge figuring, a remote filtering of an individual's face for facial confirmation would need to run the facial certification check through a cloud-based help, which would set aside a great deal of effort to process. With an edge enrolling model, the figuring could run locally on an edge server or entry, or even on the mobile phone itself, given the extending power of PDAs. Information is handled nearer to the source, not in an outer server farm or cloud, which diminishes slack time. Enterprises spend less on information the board answers for nearby gadgets than for cloud and server farm networks. With an expanding number of IoT gadgets, the information age keeps on increasing at record rates. Accordingly, organize transmission capacity turns out to be progressively constrained, overpowering the cloud and prompting a more prominent bottleneck of data. With lower idleness levels, applications can work all the more effectively and at quicker speeds. Edge application organizations diminish the volumes of data that must be moved, the subsequent traffic, and the detachment that data must travel. That gives lower latency and diminishes transmission costs. Estimation offloading for nonstop applications, for instance, facial affirmation counts, showed broad improvements in like manner times, as displayed in early research. Further research exhibited that using resource-rich machines called cloudlets close to versatile clients, which offer administrations ordinarily found in the cloud, gave upgrades in execution time when a portion of the assignments are offloaded to the edge hub.

2 LITERATURE SURVEY

The first-ever distributed system was implemented in ARPANET in 1966 when 3 ARPA researchers Larry Roberts and Bob Taylor [6] discovered an efficient way to establish a communication link between far located army posts. During 1980 "Usenet" was discovered to work on the concept of UUCP (Unix to Unix copy). [6] Symposium on Principles of Distributed Computing (PODC) was the first major conference held in 1982 for discussing enhancement in the distributed computing area [7]. The first fully functional consumer-focused distributed system was content delivery network (CDN), launched by Akamai [16] in 1997. It introduced the concept of the use of cache memory. As soon as in 2006, Amazon introduced its first cloud-based elastic compute cloud, the door for edge computing was open [14]. In 2012, the concept of IoT achieved a high ground when fog computing was introduced by CISCO. This provided the required scalability and high speed to enable the IoT enterprise we are witnessing today. Murkiness enlisting was begun by Cisco in 2012. It is a structure-level plan prepared for scattering handling, accumulating, and control functionalities wherever between a united cloud and a device on the edge of the framework. Fog enrolling supports a standardized framework prepared for dealing with the data raised necessities of sweeping IoT applications. As a scattered resource, fog enlisting gives accommodating gadgets to watching, directing, and ensuring about resources across frameworks and between devices. Not in the slightest degree like various models discussed underneath, in any case, fog preparing works with the cloud to improve the value and decreasing lethargy by using neighborhood ISP servers as an arbiter [8]. One of the most important current technologies using distributed computing is Mobile Edge Computing (MEC). Versatile Edge Computing is a key structure thought in edge figuring and is viewed as an essential part of the enablement of IoT helpfulness for what's to come. By definition, MEC outfits an IT organization condition with circulated figuring limits at the edge of an adaptable framework. Specifically, this building incorporates MEC applications that run as Virtual Machines on a virtualized establishment. These applications can help out the compact edge stage such that

Table 1. Representation of breakthrough in the field of edge computing.

Year	Technologies
1966	ARPANET
1980	Usenet
1984	Fido Net
1997	CDN (akamai)
2006	Amazon Cloud
2012	Fog Computing

supports frameworks and life-cycle components of the application. In short, MEC courses of action develop a RAN in closeness to adaptable endorsers. This plan offers lower idleness, better region, higher transmission limit, and improved responsiveness while similarly engaging incalculable new sorts of employments. MEC advancements are starting at now feasible and significant; proof of concept (POC) structures are fit for arranging and progressing multi-shipper adventures, and use cases continue shaping into a varying and helpful edge enlisting condition. Fused data the officials anticipate that start should complete responsiveness. Mobile phones must send data to the related cloud, which plays out the appropriate examination and either sends it back to a comparable contraption or on to the accompanying zone on the framework. Adaptability overhauled little extension cloud data center or cloudlets may facilitate a segment of the solicitations this technique puts on the framework by setting up a PC or gathering of PCs that is enough dependable, resource-rich, and all-around related with ensuring high framework functionality. Cloudlets [8] fill in as middle people in the related edge enrolling design they have, as they give really proximate specialists of the concentrated cloud anyway with improved quality and openness. Tests have shown that cloudlets are fit for lessening framework response time fundamentally and decline essentialness usage by another two-fifths. These investigations have confirmed that cloudlets and virtual machine frameworks that assist them with offering a promising response for inaction challenges made by dynamically scattered enlisting over the IoT. A historical development of ARPANET to fog computing is shown in Table 1.

3 PROPOSED SYSTEM

We propose a simple medi-fog system in which we use an IoT-based implantable cardioverter-defibrillator (ICD) [2] to monitor and assist cardiac arrest prone patients. This framework proposed can be utilized to recognize and foresee any uncommon circumstance of a patient, for example, heart failure or over-the-top ascent and fall of blood pressure. This information will be caught by a sensor and will be sent to the mist servers. The clinics will have the entrance of the patient's information and can promptly make a move. The patient who has enlisted to a specific emergency clinic, just their information can be seen by that specific hospital. This information will be private and should be made sure about, with the goal that nobody else splits in. The patients don't have to share the information truly with the emergency clinics, unblemished the medical clinics can get to the fundamental information required at whatever point the patient needs test. The sensors connected to the patient will collect data and send it to local fog nodes which are eventually connected to the server. After the data is processed in the Cloud and analyze it will instruct local ICD [2] node to perform the required action with the help of provided actuators. The proposed model is shown in Figure 1.

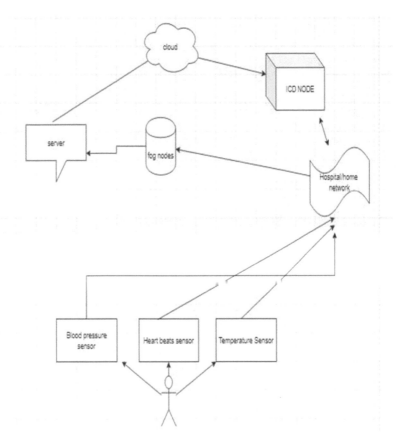

Figure 1. The architecture of the proposed model.

4 CONCLUSION

This paper discusses the idea of the IoT, the distributed computing paradigm. We discussed the four architectural blocks of IoT and their importance in the IoT ecosystem, the importance of distributed computing in IoT and how the concept of edge computing and fog computing is changing the future of IoT. Then we proposed our model of fog computing-based healthcare system and IoT-enabled ICD equipment. Furthermore, as an advancement to this project we will focus on building an effective IoT-based system to detect any type of virus outbreak and predict its severity. At present, IoT is currently used to manage certain pieces of the COVID-19. IoT can be used to follow the start of an outbreak, overlaying geographic information structure [15] on IoT flexible data from spoiled patients can finish two things. Upstream, it can help illness transmission experts as they kept searching for open-minded zero; downstream, it can help recognize all the individuals who have come into contact with the spoiled patients and may, thusly, also be tainted. General prosperity work power can screen which patients remain secluded, and which patients have infiltrated the confine. The IoT data will, in a like manner, help them with discovering who else may be introduced given the break. The structure will have the choice to build up its establishment quickly to interface the pieces of data grouping, taking care of, and limit, with the objective, that the system can scale and stretch out for disease following, preventive seclude, and the industrious thought of the spoiled.

REFERENCES

[1] Wiley STM/Editor Buyya, Srirama: Fog and Edge Computing: Principles and Paradigms, Chapter 1/Internet of Things (IoT) and New Computing Paradigms.

[2] Implantable cardioverter defibrillator [online] https://en.wikipedia.org/wiki/Implantable_cardioverter-defibrillator

[3] Yerra, Lakshminarayan, MD. Reddy, Pratap C., MD., "Effects of Electromagnetic Interference on Implanted Cardiac Devices and Their Management" Cardiology in Review 2007; 15: 304–309. Lippincott Williams & Wilkins, 2007.

[4] F. Xia, L. T. Yang, L. Wang, A. Vinel, "Internet of things," International Journal of Communications Systems, vol.25, no. 9, September 2012, pp. 1101–1102.

[5] Joshua R. Stachel, Ervin Sejdić, Ajay Ogirala, Marlin H. Mickle, The Impact of the Internet of Things on Implanted Medical Devices including Pacemaker

[6] Edge-Computing[online] https://en.wikipedia.org/wiki/ Edge-computing

[7] Scott Fulton III, Understanding Edge Computing, August 9, 2019.

[8] Samantha Joule Fow, IoT on the Edge, Opportunities and Challenges in Distributed Computing, January 24, 2020.

[9] A. Greenberg, J. Hamilton, D. A. Maltz and P. Patel, "The Cost of a Cloud: Research Problems in Data Center Networks," SIGCOMM Computer Communication Review, vol. 39, no. 1, pp. 68–73, Dec. 2008.

[10] M. Sun, M. Zheng, J. C. S. Lui, and X. Jiang, "Design and implementation of an android host- based intrusion prevention system," in Proceedings of the Annual Computer Security Applications Conference, 2014, pp. 226–235.

[11] A. Shabtai, U. Kanonov, Y. Elovici, C. Glezer, and Y. Weiss, "An-dromaly: A Behavioral Malware Detection Framework for AndroidDevices," Journal of Intelligent Information Systems, vol. 38, no. 1Feb. 2012.

[12] G. Dini, F. Martinelli, A. Saracino, and D. Sgandurra, "MADAM: AMulti-level Anomaly Detector for Android Malware", Modelsand Architectures for Computer Network Security: Computer NetworkSecurity, 2012.

[13] P. Hari, K. Ko, E. Koukoumidis, U. Kremer, M. Martonosi, D. Ottoni, S. Peh, and P. Zhang, "SARANA: Language, Compiler and Run-time System Support for Spatially Aware and Resource-aware Mobile-Computing," Philosophical Transactions of the Royal Society of LondonA: Mathematical, Physical and Engineering Sciences, vol. 366, 2008.

[14] M. Satyanarayanan, P. Simoens, Y. Xiao, P. Pillai, Z. Chen, K. Ha, W. Hu, and B. Amos, "Edge Analytics in the Internet of Things," IEEE Pervasive Computing, vol. 14, no. 2, pp. 24–31, Apr 2015.

[15] Sylvia He PhD, Using the Internet of Things to Fight Virus Outbreaks, Mar 12, 2020.

[16] Ismet Aktas, Cloud and edge computing for IoT: a short history

[17] Varghese, N. Wang, S. Bharbhuiya, P. Kilpatrick, and D. S. Nikolopoulos, "Challenges and Opportunities in Edge Computing," Proceedings of the IEEE International Conference on Smart Cloud, 2016, pp. 20–2.

[18] Abuhasel K. A. and M. A. Khan, (2020), "A Secure Industrial Internet of Things (IIoT) Framework for Resource Management in Smart Manufacturing," in IEEE Access, vol. 8, pp. 117354-117364, 2020, doi: 10.1109/ACCESS.2020.3004711.

[19] Khan, MA, Abuhasel, KA. (2020).Advanced metameric dimension framework for heterogeneous industrial Internet of things. Computational Intelligence. 2020; 1–21. https://doi.org/10.1111/coin.12378

Smart Computing – Khan et al (Eds)
© *2021 Taylor & Francis Group, London, ISBN 978-0-367-76552-1*

Smart farming using IoT

K. Revanth, S.M. Arshad & C.P. Prathibhamol
Department of Computer Science and Engineering, Amrita Vishwa Vidyapeetham, Amritapuri, India

ABSTRACT: In early days, farmers farmed in a very mundane way by figuring the ripeness of the soil as well as considering the area type. They didn't ponder regarding the water level, climatic conditions, or humidity. Agriculture has always played a vital role in our country, India. Issues concerning agriculture have become a matter of prime importance. Over the last ten years, there has been huge progress in science and technology-related domains. This technology can benefit the agricultural field in many ways such as predicting the suitable crop based on Nitrogen, Phosphorus, and Potassium content in the soil, water conservation, increase in yield production, increase in quality and quantity of the yield, remote monitoring, etc. The Internet of things (IoT) has provided us with better ways of farming by installing various sensors and motors. In this paper, an IoT-based smart farming model is used. Machine learning-related algorithm is used to predict the yield of the crop as per the sources. This is equipped with so many sensors for measuring and calculating environmental conditions required for farming. It consists of NodeMCU and so many sensors for calculating and analyzing the entire process. It helps the farmers to collect accurate data about the weather and soil conditions so that they can make accurate decisions about farming. This constructive model will help farmers by executing tasks like soil moisture sensing, humidity sensing, water level detection, temperature measurement, detection of animal intrusion along with the total gain of the crop is predicted in the farm automatically. Based on the conditions switching on/off the motors is very helpful for them, when they are in the field as they need not bother about the dryness or excess moisture in the fields. Therefore, this model of IoT synced with machine learning algorithm is very helpful in farming.

1 INTRODUCTION

In many countries, agriculture has played an important role in economic development. In developed countries, there are abundant techniques for farming but in some developing countries like India, the farmers are still using ancient techniques to cultivate crops. These techniques are useful when the climatic conditions are suitable for farming. Taking over the ancient methods farmers cannot increase quantity and quality of the yield. Even though when they are using spiritual techniques in agriculture that will effect more in case of expenses but gives less productivity. The farmers cannot predict temperature change, humidity conditions, climatic scenarios, etc. But day-by-day technology is growing abundantly in the agriculture sector as well. As the Internet of Things (IoT) is one of the most populated recent technology which helps to the development of agriculture field. It can make things simple and easier from the viewpoint of a farmer. He/she can also be getting as desired output, a better yield of the crop as to what is grown in the fields.

Merging of IoT with machine learning concepts can be used to calculate the humidity, temperature, soil moisture, possible to predict the weather conditions, and predict the next suitable crop in a particular season. It would be cheaper so that all the farmers can use these techniques for farming where the conventional systems can be very costly such that not all farmers may have a chance to afford it. The main aim of this research work is to produce a cost-effective system where all farmers could benefit to the maximum.

DOI 10.1201/9781003167488-11

2 LITERATURE SURVEY

Nowadays, based on the shortage crisis of farm production, all the departments are trying their best to support the farmers as best as they can. Scientists in all the areas are working on the development of the production and supporting the farmers on a direct or indirect basis. In [1], the authors had proposed an IoT-based solutions to help farmers to yield better results. This is to increase the harvest by using modern methods like using sensors in the field. The authors have researched and discovered measures related to finding the humidity, temperature, soil moisture, and so many other factors that affect the result of the harvest. The researchers in [2] have developed a model based on the real-time monitoring system for agriculture using IoT. The model works with the help of Wireless Sensor Networks. Due to the uneven distribution of rainfall, it is very difficult for a farmer to monitor and control the equal distribution of water to all crops in the whole farm. By real-time monitoring system, one can easily prevent this kind of problem.

In [3], the authors have implemented an IoT-based system with the help of the ESPN8266 device. This was the first step in building an IoT device. It consists of a user interface, hardware devices like sensors, processors, and actuators. This MCU is used for collecting data from firmware by using sensors. NodeMCU is an open-source and LUA programming language-based firmware developed for ESP8266 Wi-Fi chip. The authors in [4] described the various applications for agriculture using IoT. IoT helps us monitor climate conditions, soil moisture, temperature, humidity, greenhouse automation, crop management, and many more. The work in [5] is regarding the IoT to bring it to reality. This term represents a general concept for the ability of network devices to sense and collect data from all around the world and share it on the internet so that each and every one can make use of it. The paper [6] deals with crop prediction. It is the art of predicting crop yields before the harvest takes place. The task is to predict the suitable crop for the farmer on which soil they have. Based on the temperature and moisture humidity crisis in that particular term of the crop, the prediction of the yield can be done, which helps the farmers to know how much yield they will get after the ripening of the crop. The concept of embedded systems was brought in the framework by the researchers in [7].

Temperature and humidity play a vital role in farming. IoT comes into the picture here by significantly enhancing the efficiency of the mechanism and systematically decreasing human involvement, and thereby overall improving the efficiency of the crop. In order to reduce the load on the farmer, the authors in [8] and [9] have used a soil moisture sensor for smart farming. This sensor can be placed in the middle of the farm to get accurate results. No need to check the water content manually. Water supply is the most important thing in farming, with the help of soil moisture sensors, if the water content is less, then the motor will automatically pump water into the field. It will greatly decrease human effort and saves a lot of time for farmers. The paper [8] deals with the wireless sensor network, whereas paper [9] deals with Aurdino hardware. The researchers in paper [10] have implemented smart farming by using machine learning algorithms to predict the crop and intercrop cultivation based upon the soil type.

3 PROPOSED SYSTEM

This system is designed to collect the values of temperature, soil moisture, humidity, and analyze human detection from the fields which helps the motors to turn on and off which maintains the water level of the crop based on the requirement. Also, an algorithm is employed to predict a suitable crop and yield according to the situation. The task is to provide suitable fertilizers to the crop which is highly essential in optimum yield.

The communication between the IoT system and the algorithm is achieved by using serial communication which automatically sends the values as input to the algorithm for testing, where the algorithm is already trained with the dataset. Then the system predicts the suitable crop for the soil and also the fertilizers required for the optimum yield. Bio-fertilizers which are suitable for the

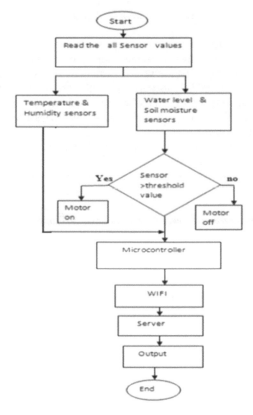

Figure 1. Hardware processing.

soil to boost the immunity system of the plant can also be predicted with the help of N, P, and K contents of the soil.

The number of seeds or stems needed to be purchased by the farmer will be suggested by the system. The process of the plantation of the crop will be shown and the material to be purchased to maintain the crop will also be suggested in advance. In some crops, intercrops can also be cultivated. The suitable crop for the intercrop cultivation is also suggested. The irrigation process is a must for the cultivation of a crop. So the process of irrigation for a particular crop is also recommended. A proper amount of fertilizer should be provided for the crop. Different crops have different quantity of fertilization and the amount of fertilizer to be used will also be suggested (Figure 1).

4 METHODOLOGY AND DATASET

In this architecture used, there are three sensors in total, namely temperature, soil moisture, and humidity sensor. These sensors need to be placed in different areas in the field. The soil moisture sensor is placed in the soil to read the water content present in the soil. Temperature and humidity sensors are placed in the middle of the field to get accurate readings. These sensors take inputs and send outputs to the NodeMCU to which all the three sensors are connected. These sensors will collect data from the field and send it to NodeMCU.

All the sensors will have a specific threshold value and that value is predefined in the NodeMCU. When a sensor reaches its threshold, a response will be sent to its node and it will be triggered according to the input sent by the sensors. A motor is attached to the node, which is used to pump water into the field.

The micro-controller is connected to the Internet, which is assigned to the MCU. Whenever a particular internet network is available, it connects to it. When the node gets connected to the internet, it will start transmitting data to a website designed for collecting data from the sensors. The data will be transmitting frequently through MCU provided by the sensors. This data will be updated every few seconds so that there won't be any mistakes, even when they are minor ones. All the data will be recorded for further calculations. For this process, we are using Thing speak or Blynk as an interface to get data.

For predicting the data there are two different types of methods, one is manual testing in which all the values required for the testing are given manually and then it is predicted. And another is an automatic way of testing where the values are automatically taken from the sensors and the algorithm starts the testing and shows the prediction and the data. The training algorithm uses the dataset for the training purpose and the values from the sensors and manual inputs for testing. The system is set to function with the k-nearest neighbor (k-NN) algorithm which is a classification algorithm. It considers the "k" nearest neighbors as a reference and predicts the class in most of the "k" neighbors are classified. In our situation, we are using the neighbor's value "k" as 3. The algorithm predicts the class belongs to the input soil values. Based upon the predicted class, the crop, fertilizers, bio-fertilizers, and required material are suggested.

The dataset is in the excel format which consists of classification data depending upon the N, P, and K values. The fertilizers that are to be suggested are also in the dataset according to different classes.

5 HARDWARES REQUIRED

5.1 *Soil moisture sensor*

The soil moisture sensor is used to sense the moisture content in the soil. The sensor consists of two probes which are used to calculate the resistance; the electricity passes in between the probes from the soil. In wet soil the conductivity is high and resistance power will be low. In the dry soil, the conductivity will be low and the resistance will be high.

This sensor can be used in both analog and the digital way, by connecting to any interface like ardino. The sensor is connected to the comparator which consists of a LED to show the connectivity. This sensor gives the values from 0–1023, the moisture is measured in the percentage so we can map these values from 0–100. When we set the threshold in the digital interface the comparator compares the values given by the sensor and the threshold given by the interface and turns on the led to green which is initially red (Figure 2).

Figure 2.   Soil moisture sensor.

5.2 DHT sensor

A DHT sensor is a combination of a capacitive humidity sensor and the temperature sensor (thermistor). It is very low in cost. The thermistor senses the temperature from 0–50° with an accuracy of 2% and measures the humidity up to 20–80% with an accuracy of 5%. For measuring the temperature, sensor uses a negative temperature coefficient thermistor, which makes a difference in resistance when the change in temperature. This sensor is made up of semiconductor ceramic. The humidity sensor consists of electrodes that make a difference in capacitance when the change in the humidity. The integrated circuit (IC)measures the capacitance and resistance and converts the values into digital form (Figure 3).

Figure 3.   DHT sensor.

5.3 5V DC pump

The pump used in the hardware is a normal 5V DC submersible motor that pumps the water when it is turned on by the relay (Figure 4).

Figure 4.   5V DC pump.

5.4 5V relay

The relay is commonly used in the electronics segment to turn on and off the appliances, we used the relay to turn on and off the motor. The relay consists of two segments Normal open and Normal close, which is On and Off. The relay is simply a circuit. The relay has a signal port which is connected to a signal port of the NodeMCU. When the signal from the MCU is high the circuit in the relay is connected and stays Normally open then the motor will turn on. When the signal is low then the circuit is open then it will be Normally closed which turn's the motor off (Figure 5).

Figure 5.   5V relay.

5.5   *NodeMCU ESP8266*

NodeMCU ESP8266 is a WiFi-enabled microcontroller which is developed with TCP/IP Protocol. To connect the electrical equipment to the internet this is used. It is a system-integrated chip that integrates all the components of a computer or other electronic systems. This is the micro-controller in which all the sensors are connected and the micro-controller is connected to the user interface. From the MCU we are collecting all the values from the sensors and sending the values to the system. For that, we can use think speak or Blync as API. It has powerful on-board processing capabilities and sufficient storage that allow it to be integrated with minimal development up-front and minimal loading during runtime through its General Purpose Input/output (GPIOs) (Figure 6).

Figure 6.   ESP8266.

6   RESULT AND ANALYSIS

The hardware needs to be placed in the field. The sensors must be placed carefully at particular locations like soil moisture sensors in the soil and DHT sensor in the middle of the field. The relay for the motors should be connected as per the power supply needed to the motor.

Whenever the sensor values reach the threshold, like soil moisture level is up to a threshold that means humidity is high, the micro-controller turns the motor on. Later, when a sufficient amount of water is present in the field, the sensor transmits the data to the micro-controller and it turns the motor off. Likewise, the required amount of water level is maintained in the field. After inputs are given to the algorithm, the testing will be done and the result will be shown on the designed web page. The suitable fertilizers, cultivation process, irrigation process, and compatible intercrops are shown on the web page (Figures 7–11).

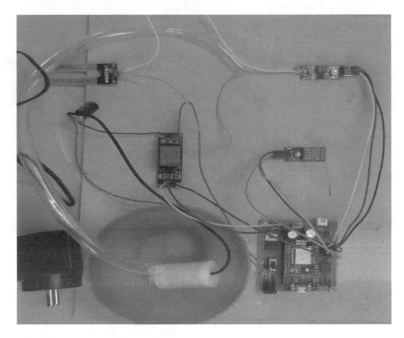

Figure 7.   The way of connecting hardware devices.

Temperature Requirement

Sr. No.	Stages	Temperature (ºC)		
		Minimum	Suitable	Maximum
1.	Seed germination	11	16-29	34
2.	Seedling growth	18	21-24	32
3.	Fruit set (day) (night)	10	15-17	30
		18	20-24	30
4.	Red colour development	10	20-24	30

Figure 8.   Temperature requirement.

Fertilizers

As the fruit production and quality depends upon nutrient availability and fertilizer application so balance fertilizer are applied as per requirement. The nitrogen in adequate quantity increases fruit quality, fruit size, color and taste. It also helps in increasing desirable acidic flavor. Adequate amount of potassium is also required for growth, yield and quality. Mono Ammonium Phosphate (MAP) may be used as a starter fertilizer to supply adequate phosphorus during germination and seedling stages. Calcium availability is also very important to control soil pH and nutrient availability. Sandy soils will require a higher rate of fertilizer, and more frequent applications of these fertilizers due to increased leaching of essential nutrients. The seedlings are sprayed with starter solution of micronutrient. Before planting farm yard manure @ 50 ton per hectares should be incorporated. Normally tomato crop requires 120kg Nitrogen (N), 50kg Phosphorus (P_2O_5), and 50kg Potash (K_2O). Nitrogen should be given in split doses. Half nitrogen and full P_2O_5 is given at the time of transplanting and remaining nitrogen is given after 30 days and 60 days of transplanting.

Soil and tissue analyses should be taken throughout the growing and production season to insure essential nutrients are in their proper amounts and ratios. Tissue analysis of a nutritionally sufficient plant will show the following nutrient status:

	Nitrogen	Phosphorus	Potassium	Calcium	Magnesium	Sulphur
%	4.0-5.6	0.30-0.60	3.0-4.5	1.25-3.2	0.4-0.65	0.65-1.4
	ppm	Manganese	Iron	Boron	Copper	Zinc
		30-400	30-300	20-60	5-15	30-90

In the present situation it has been realized that the use of inorganic fertilizers should be integrated with renewable and environmental friendly organic fertilizers, crop residues and green manures.

Figure 9.   Prediction of suitable fertilizers.

Tomato Cultivation Guide   Revenue/Hectare: Rs426000

Climatic Requirements

Figure 10.   Prediction of suitable crop.

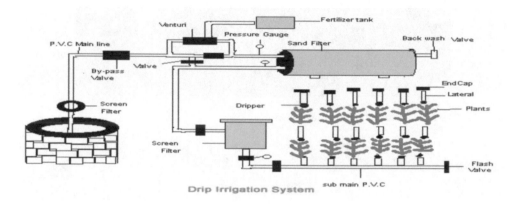

Figure 11.   Suitable irrigation system.

7 CONCLUSION

Agriculture is an essential sector throughout the world. Farmers are using ancient techniques of farming which are not reliable in the future as the new generation of farmers are not getting habituated to the mundane methods. If the farmers can do farming in a modern way with sophisticated techniques, then it will increase the yield of crops. Thereby our economy also will be improving to a larger extend. To make farming easy and more profitable, IoT will be very helpful in collecting the data from the fields and machine learning will play a keen role in the prediction of crops and fertilizers suitable for the soil. The system can be improved by adding more sensors like detecting the diseases and bug detection of the crops to alert the farmer in advance to take the necessary precautions. Designing a platform that connects the farmers and dealers in that area could make it easy for the farmers to sell their products at the best prices.

REFERENCES

[1] Gayatri, M.K. Jayasakthi, J. & Anandhamala, G.S. 2015. Giving Smart Agriculture Solutions to Farmers for Better Yielding Using IoT. In *IEEE International Conference on Technological Innovations in ICT for Agriculture and Rural*.

[2] Nalajala, P. Kumar, D.H. Ramesh, P. & Godavarthi, B. 2017. Design and implementation of modern automated real time monitoring system for agriculture using internet of things (IoT). *J. Eng. Appl. Sci*, 12.

[3] Wan, Z. Song, Y. & Cao, Z. 2019. Environment dynamic monitoring and remote control of greenhouse with ESP8266 NodeMCU. In *2019 IEEE 3rd Information Technology, Networking, Electronic and Automation Control Conference (ITNEC)* (pp. 377–382). IEEE.

[4] Zhang, L. Dabipi, I.K. & Brown Jr, W.L. 2018. Internet of Things applications for agriculture. *Internet of Things A to Z: Technologies and Applications*, pp. 507–528.

[5] Karimi, K. & Atkinson, G. 2013. What the Internet of Things (IoT) needs to become a reality. *White Paper, FreeScale and ARM*, pp. 1–16.

[6] Mucherino, A. Papajorgji, P. & Pardalos, P.M. 2009. *Data mining in agriculture* (Vol. 34). Springer Science & Business Media.

[7] Chavan, C.H. & Karande, P.V. 2014. Wireless monitoring of soil moisture, temperature & humidity using zigbee in agriculture. *International Journal of Engineering Trends and Technology (IJETT)*, 11(10), pp. 493–497.

[8] Kestikar, C.A. & Bhavsar, R.M. 2012. Automated Wireless Watering System (AWWS). *Int. J. Appl. Inf. Syst.(IJAIS)*, 2(3), pp. 40–46.

[9] Kumar, M.S. Chandra, T.R. Kumar, D.P. & Manikandan, M.S. 2016. Monitoring moisture of soil using low cost homemade Soil moisture sensor and Arduino UNO. In *2016 3rd international conference on advanced computing and communication systems (ICACCS)* (Vol. 1, pp. 1–4). IEEE.

[10] Khan M.A. et. al, (2020), Decentralised IoT, Decenetralised IoT: A Blockchain perspective, Springer, Studies in BigData, 2020, DOI: https://doi.org/10.1007/978-3-030-38677-1

[11] Khan ,M. A., Quasim, M. T, et.al, (2020), A Secure Framework for Authentication and Encryption Using Improved ECC for IoT Based Medical Sensor Data, in IEEE Access, vol. 8, pp. 52018–52027, 2020. DOI: 10.1109/ACCESS.2020.2980739

[12] Khan M. A.,(2020), An IoT Framework for Heart Disease Prediction Based on MDCNN Classifier, in IEEE Access, vol. 8, pp. 34717–34727, 2020. DOI: 10.1109/ACCESS.2020.2974687

[13] Khan M.A, and Algarni F., (2020) "A Healthcare Monitoring System for the Diagnosis of Heart Disease in the IoMT Cloud Environment Using MSSO-ANFIS," in IEEE Access, vol. 8, pp. 122259–122269, 2020, doi: 10.1109/ACCESS.2020.3006424.

[14] Lottes, P. Khanna, R. Pfeifer, J. Siegwart, R. & Stachniss, C. 2017. UAV-based crop and weed classification for smart farming. In *2017 IEEE International Conference on Robotics and Automation (ICRA)* (pp. 3024–3031). IEEE.

Smart Computing – Khan et al (Eds)
© *2021 Taylor & Francis Group, London, ISBN 978-0-367-76552-1*

ECG signal compression using dual-tree sparse decomposition of DWT filters and HRV analysis

Ranjeet Kumar
Madanapalle Institute of Technology & Science, Madanapalle, India
School of Electronics Engineering, VIT University, Chennai Campus, Chennai, India

Agya Ram Verma, Manoj Kumar Panda & Papendra Kumar
G. B. Pant Institute of Engineering & Technology, Pauri, India

ABSTRACT: A dual-tree sparse decomposition of discrete wavelet transforms technique is presented for the electrocardiogram (ECG) signals using a variable-length Huffman coding technique. In this method, a one-dimensional ECG signal is decomposed with as symmetry tree structure at each level using discrete wavelet transforms which outcomes from a larger quantity of insignificant coefficients. They are measured as zero amplitude value and represented as sparse datasets that improve the compression rate and Huffman coding helps to represent the signal with low bit rate data. These results compressed data codes of large ECG time-series datasets of the signal. Here, different wavelet filters evaluated for compression based on sparse data from wavelet decomposition. The performance of an algorithm in the term of compression 43.52% with a 99.9% correlation between original and recovered signals from compressed ECG data. Further, heart rate variability (HRV) analysis with correlation of R-R intervals in between the original and reconstructed ECG signal; it validates the reconstruction as well as sensitivity of compression technique towards data accuracy.

1   INTRODUCTION

A sparse decomposition based on discrete wavelet transform (DWT) technique proposed for data compression and evaluated for electrocardiogram (ECG) signals. An ECG signals are sensed and recorded using electrodes from patients' body for monitoring and cardiac functionality analysis. During the recording of the ECG signal, a huge volume of quantitative data is produced due to several reasons like time, high sampling rates, the number of channels, etc. Data compression techniques or tools also useful for ECG record management, transmission, and real-time ECG processing as well as telemedicine-based healthcare (Fong & Fong 2011).

In the last two decades, several techniques were presented for compression of an ECG signal as well as its analysis (Jalaleddine et al. 1990). These techniues are categorized in the literature as direct, parameter extraction, and transform and coding-based compression (Cox et al. 1968; Mueller 1978; Ruttimann 1979; Abenstein 1982; Nave 1993; Wang et al. 1994; Cardenas-Barrera 1999; Kumar et al. 2016a). Among these techniques, transform-based techniques attract more attention of researchers in the last few years due to its promised compressed efficiency with sustainable reconstruction ability and implemented in many healthcare systems.

A comprehensive review of these techniques is presented in the literature (Jalaleddine et al. 1990; Cardenas-Barrera 1999; Fong & Fong 2011; Kumar et al. 2016a) and the references therein. With regard to transform-based techniques, several data compression methods for ECG, speech and images are developed and standardized by technical communities (Kumar et al. 2013, 2016a; Patbhaje et al. 2017). Here, DWTs are very popular form compression of signals and images due to its robustness toward efficient compression and recoverability of signals and images from compressed data. In the particular case of an ECG signal, wavelet or transform technique further

DOI 10.1201/9781003167488-12

classified as one-dimensional (1D) and two-dimensional (2D) compression method. An ECG signal is the quasiperiodic nature of signal; therefore, 2D data processing is possible and compression achieved using inter-beat and intra-beat correlation (Chen 1998; Miaou & Yen 2002; Bilgin & Marcellin 2003; Chen 2008; Chen et al. 2008; Kumar et al. 2016a). In the last few years, different 2D compression techniques have come into the picture with higher compression with reconstruction quality. Although these techniques are offline techniques they are time-consuming methods due to their computation steps. as discussed in the literature (Lee & Buckley 1999; Ahmad 2001; Tai et al. 2005; Alexandre & Pena 2006; Sahraeian 2007; Lukin et al. 2008; Wang & Meng 2008; Wang 2008; Huang et al. 2009; Zhang et al. 2013; Kumar et al. 2013, 2015, 2016a, 2016b, 2017; Kumar & Kumar 2015b; Wang et al. 2016). In this paper, the principle of symmetric tree structure of signal decomposition is explored for 1D time-series data of an ECG signal. The details of the proposed method described in followed sections, a dual-tree DWT-based ECG signal compression using the Huffman Coding technique are evaluated, where the dual-tree DWT sparse decomposition structure is employed on the $1 \times M$ size or M sample length of an ECG signal record. The proposed method examined in terms of different fidelity parameters such as compression ratio (CR), percentage root-mean square difference (PRD), and correlation (Ranjeet et al. 2013; Kumar & Kumar 2015b, 2015a).

2 SPARSE DECOMPOSITION AND COMPRESSION

Sparse decomposition of a signal is representative of the signal with zero value coefficients. In the original form, stationary or non-stationary signals are having most of the non-zero value coefficients. Thus, using linear transformation and suitable signal processing technique, the signal can be represented as a sparse data set. In signal decomposition, a signal vector $x \in \mathbb{R}^n$ is decomposed as a linear combination of n numbers. Let x be the real-valued n-dimensional ECG signal which is decomposed with orthonormal wavelet transform basis $\psi = [\psi_1|\psi_2|\psi_3|\ldots|\psi_n]$ as $x = \psi c$, where c denotes the n-dimensional coefficient vector that contains the highly sparse nature data value of x in the wavelet domain. The coefficient vector c having most of the zero amplitude or near-zero amplitude value coefficients, does not have an effect on the signal quality or significant information. Therefore, to achieve the desired CR, the threshold value is initialized to make sparse data sets.

2.1 *Sparse decomposition of an ECG signal*

An electrocardiogram (ECG) signal with an original 1D signal or $1 \times M$ size of time-data series is considered in discrete form. It contains low- and high-frequency components that are analyzed by the signal decomposition using DWT, as shown in Figure 1. Basically, DWT analysis of signal deals with multiresolution analysis (MRA) that represents different sub-bands of frequency. Therefore, analysis of these bands indicates the significant and insignificant coefficients in terms of some features or characteristics like the energy of sub-bands (Mallat 1987; Kumar et al. 2013, 2016a).

In the DWT analysis, a set of low- and high-pass wavelet filter is exploited with decimation factor 2 using multi-rate signal processing; it raises the wavelet decomposition as illustrated in Figure 1. The wavelet filter iterates up to finite times that results multiresolution data of signal or time-series or spatial data decomposed, and process tending toward multiresolution analysis that consist of low- and high-frequency coefficients or approximation and detailed coefficients. At each iteration, DWT filter response or solutions represented as translation equation $\psi(n)$ and dilation equation $\phi(n)$ (Kumar et al. 2016a, 2016b) defined as:

$$\psi(n) = 2 \sum_k h_0[k]\phi(2n - k) \tag{1}$$

$$\phi(n) = 2 \sum_k g_0[k]\phi(2n - k) \tag{2}$$

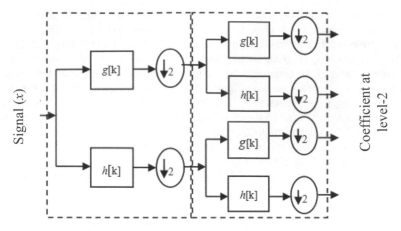

Figure 1. Wavelet filter decomposition of a signal (x): symmetric structure at level 2.

Here, $h_0[k]$ and $g_0[k]$ represent the high-pass and low-pass filters, respectively, in Figure 1 and Eqs. (1) and (2). Therefore, DWT decomposition structure for signal or array, wherein each level of coefficients decomposed as a parent note of the tree. Therefore, each level sub-bands contain the maximum energy of signal/data is concentered in an approximation coefficient and least energy in detailed band [3].

2.2 *Compression of ECG signal*

In the ECG signal, compression is important in terms of handling of large datasets in health record repository. Here, dual-tree or symmetric DWT decomposition structure, as illustrated in Figure 1, exploited for the decomposition time-series data or 1-D ECG signal. Let an ECG signal contain M length of data or coefficients, decomposed using the dual-tree-DWT analysis and signal assumed as a single-row image or data of **1 × M** size. The wavelet filters' decomposition on ECG signal computes the four sub-band data of a signal as compared to traditional DWT analysis and these results come as more sparse data; therefore, compression is attained based on thresholding, quantization, and suitable coding techniques.

This is illustrated in Figure 2 and discussed in the following several steps.

A. **2D DWT Decomposition.** In the first iteration, signal decomposed into two sub-bands and followed by the next iteration, each band decomposed into two more sub-bands, as shown in Figure. 1.

$$\text{i.e.,} \quad C(i) = DWT[x(k)]$$

$$= x^L(k) + x^H(k)$$

$$= [x^{LL}(k) + x^{LH}(k)] + [x^{HL}(k) + x^{HH}(k)]$$

where DWT coefficient $(0 \dots C(i)_{max})$ contains all the frequency components with maximum coefficient value $C(i)_{max}$.

B. **Thresholding**. Next to decomposition of the ECG signal, the thresholding process is initiated to remove the insignificant values based on the global threshold process, as illustrated in Equation (3), i.e.,

$$\bar{C}(i) = \begin{cases} 0 & if \, |C(i)| \leq Thr \\ C(i) & otherwise \end{cases} \tag{3}$$

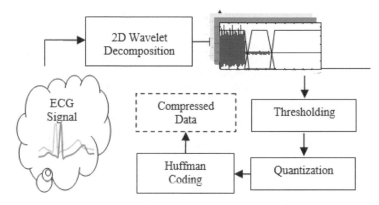

Figure 2.   2D DWT and Huffman coding based on ECG compression.

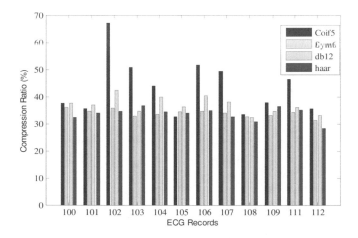

Figure 3.   Performance comparison in terms of CR of different wavelet filters with 11 different ECG records.

where $\bar{C}(i)$ represent the truncated wavelet coefficients by thresholding process.

C. **Quantization.** The wavelet coefficients are further computed using quantization process. The uniform quantization method exploited with step-size $\Delta = (C_{max} - C_{min})/L$, where L is the quantization level. In this process, a huge number of tiny-amplitude coefficients of high frequency bands is truncated as zero amplitude that help to achieve compressed data.

D. **Huffman Coding.** During thresholding and quantization process a consecutive zero amplitude coefficients are generated with significant coefficients data array that improve the sparsity of transformed data as shown in Figure 2. These data further compressed and coded by the Huffman coding technique that produces the compress data stream (Kumar et al. 2013).

At the end of compression process, the compressed data stream is obtained to store or transmit over the channel. The signal was recovered from the inversion process whenever it was needed for further review of clinical features as shown in Figure 3.

3   RESULTS AND DISCUSSION

In this paper, the compression technique for an ECG signal is presented based on the dual-tree DWT sparse decomposition. The statistical analysis that the compresses system produces more compact sparse data set by utilizing coding-based compression. Here, 11 different ECG records are carried from the MIT-BIH Arrhythmia Database (MIT-BIH, March 22, 2020). The proposed technique is exploited and examined with four different wavelets transform filters, namely Coif5 (coiflet), Sym6 (symlet), db12 (Debauches), and Haar, and these wavelet filters decompose the ECG signals for generating the sparse data in the compression process. Here, the proposed method evaluated using discussed fidelity parameters such as CR, PRD, and correlation which describe the compression amount, reconstruction difference, and similarity between the original and reconstructed signal, respectively. A brief analysis of performance of the proposed method are as follows.

Compression Ratio Algorithm is examined with different wavelet filters such as coiflet, Symlet, debouches, and Haar. These filters perform different to each. Figure 3 shows that compression scores of these filters are on 11 different ECG records. The average compression is 43.52%, 33.88%, 36.86%, and 33.72%, respectively, for coiflet, Symlet, debouches, and Haar as shown in Figure 4. In Table 1, the proposed techniques are compared with 2D DWT-based compression techniques. It also represents the performance of the algorithm that is better than the earlier referred techniques.

Fidelity Assessments. Signal reconstruction quality measure is also very important task that ensure the compression efficiency with low loss of data. The fidelity parameters to evaluate the signal reconstruction quality. In this paper, average PRD is 4.49%, 4.44%, 4.42%, and 10.85% for Coiflet, Symlet, debouches, and Haar, respectively, as illustrated in Figure 4 for 11 different ECG

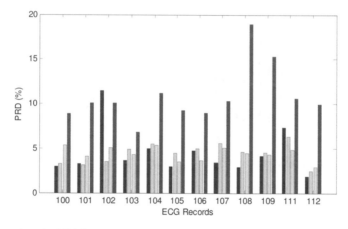

Figure 4.   Proposed method fidelity assessment (PRD) for 11 different ECG records using different wavelet filters.

Table 1.   Proposed technique performance comparison of with other techniques.

Method	Records	CR	PRD
Proposed	100	37.55	3.01
	107	49.36	3.42
	112	35.55	1.89
Wang & Meng (2016)	100	12	1.0
	107	12	2.1
	117	12	0.6
Wang & Chen (2008)		40	12.5
(Abo-Zahhad & Ahmed 2012)	117	13.00	1.14
	119	22	4.80
	205	32.2	0.66

records. Here, PRD shows the distortion in normal condition of reconstruction on the other hand PRD1 shows the distortion amount when mean value of signal is separated.

The algorithm is also evaluated through measure correlation between the original signal and reconstructed signal, as illustrated in Figure 5 for 11 different ECG records. The average correlation of signal is 0.999, 0.997, 0.998, and 0.978 for Coiflet, Symlet, debouches, and Haar, respectively. These results describe the efficiency of algorithm in terms of quality control and preservation of information.

HRV Analysis/Assessments. Heart rate variability (HRV) can measure in terms of variation of R-R intervals; it can be interpreted by doctors during the diagnosis as normal or abnormal health condition. Therefore, HRV analysis exploited for the assessment of reconstructed signal quality. In Figure 6, a comparison illustrated as comparison of R-R intervals in original and reconstructed signals Rec. 105 and 107. The R-R intervals in reconstructed signal are matched with the original signal value. Therefore, the proposed compression technique can be applicable for the ECG signal compression at minimum fidelity losses as discussed.

In this analysis, comparison of different wavelet filters illustrates the efficiency of the Coiflet filter is higher with comparison of other filters and comparable in term of other fidelity parameters.

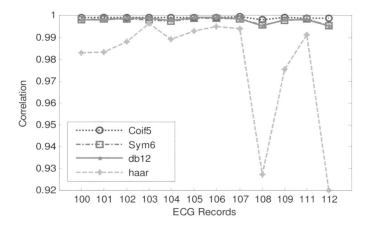

Figure 5. Correlation between original and reconstructed signals using four wavelet filters.

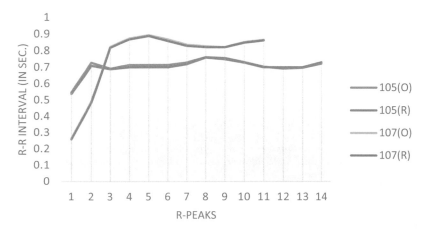

Figure 6. HRV analysis comparison in original and reconstructed signals Rec. 105 and 107 in terms of R-R intervals.

Another comparison listed in Table 1 with other methods represent the proposed method is efficient in compression as compare to others under the quality measures.

4 CONCLUSION

A method is proposed based on the dual-tree wavelet sparse decomposition applied on ECG signal for data compression. The results show the efficiency of generating larger sparse data as compares to other methods in terms of a good amount of compression. In the literature, several transform-based compression methods are listed based on the on multi-dimensional signal decomposition. In this work, symmetric signal decomposition property is utilized on a 1-D ECG signal instead of traditional wavelet decomposition. As per the results and analysis, the method has worked well in compression performance and is also good in comparison with existing techniques. Therefore, the proposed technique is suitable as well as applicable for ECG data compression in real time as well as offline processing. It is also applicable for other biomedical or real-time signals in continuing to monitor datasets.

ACKNOWLEDGMENT

This work is supported by the research grant for the project titled "Estimation of Heart rate Variability (HRV) Feature index and its classification: under Competitive Research of Technical Education Quality Improvement Programme (TEQIP-III) of Uttarakhand Technical University, Dehradun.

REFERENCES

J.P. Abenstein, W. J. T. (1982) 'New data-reduction algorithm for real-time ECG analysis', *IEEE Trans. on Biomed. Engineering*, 29(1):43–48.

M. Abo-Zahhad, S.M. Ahmed, A. Z. (2012) 'An Efficient Technique for Compressing ECG Signals Using QRS Detection, Estimation, and 2D DWT Coefficients Thresholding', *Modelling and Simulation in Engineering*. doi: 10.1155/2012/742786.

R.A.M. Ahmad, N. K. (2001) 'A two dimensional wavelet packet approach for ECG compression', in *Int. Symposium on Signal Processing and its Applications*, pp. 226–229.

E. Alexandre, A. Pena, M. S. (2006) 'On the use of 2-D coding techniques for ECG Signals', *IEEE Trans. on Info. Tech. in biomedicine*, 10(4):809–811.

A. Bilgin, M. W. Marcellin, M. I. A. (2003) 'Compression of Electrocardiogram signlas using JPEG2000', *IEEE Trans. on Consumer Electronics*, 49(4):833–840.

J.L. Cardenas-Barrera, J, V. L.-G. (1999) 'Mean-Shape Vector Quantizer for ECG signal compression', *IEEE Trans. on Biomed. Engineering*, 46(1):62–70.

D. H. Chen, S. Y. (2008) 'Compression of ECG signal using video coded technology-like scheme', *J. Biomedical Science and Engg.*, 1:22–26.

J. Chen, F.Wang, Y. Zhang, X. S. (2008) 'ECG compression using uniform scalar dead-zone quantization and conditional entropy codin', *Medical Engineering and Physics*, 30:523–530.

J.R. Cox, F.M. Nolle, H.A.Fozzard, G. C. O. (1968) 'AZTEC a preprocessing program for real-time ECG rhythm analysis', *IEEE Trans. on Biomed. Engineering*, 15(4):128–129.

B. Fong, A.C.M. Fong, and C. K. L. (2011) *Telemedicine Technologies: Information technologies in medicine and telehealth*. John Wilet & Sons.

Boqiang Huang, Yuanyuan Wang and Jianhua Chen (2009) '2-D Compression of ECG Signals Using ROI Mask and Conditional Entropy Coding', *IEEE Transactions on Biomedical Engineering*, 56(4):1261–1263

Jalaleddine, S. M. S. *et al.* (1990) 'ECG data compression techniques-a unified approach', *IEEE Transactions on Biomedical Engineering*, 37(4):329–343.

Kumar, A. *et al.* (2013) 'The optimized wavelet filters for speech compression', *International Journal of Speech Technology*, 16(2): 171–179.

Kumar, R. and Kumar, A. (2015a) 'Dual tree DWT analysis based electrocardiogram signal compression using zero coding technique', in *2nd International Conference on Electronics and Communication Systems, ICECS 2015*. doi: 10.1109/ECS.2015.7124983.

Kumar, R. and Kumar, A. (2015b) 'ECG signal compression algorithm based on joint-multiresolution analysis (J-MRA)', in *2nd International Conference on Electronics and Communication Systems, ICECS 2015*. doi: 10.1109/ECS.2015.7124982.

Kumar, R. *et al.* (2017) 'Efficient compression technique based on temporal modelling of ECG signal using principle component analysis', *IET Science, Measurement and Technology*, 11(3):346–353.

Kumar, R., Kumar, A. and Pandey, R. K. (2013) 'Beta wavelet based ECG signal compression using lossless encoding with modified thresholding', *Computers & Electrical Engineering*, 39(1):130–140.

Kumar, R., Kumar, A. and Singh, G. K. (2015) 'Electrocardiogram signal compression based on singular value decomposition (SVD) and adaptive scanning wavelet difference reduction (ASWDR) technique', *AEU – International Journal of Electronics and Communications*, 69(12):1810–1822.

Kumar, Ranjeet, Kumar, A. and Singh, G. K. (2016a) 'Electrocardiogram Signal Compression Based on 2D-Transforms: A Research Overview', *Journal of Medical Imaging and Health Informatics*, 6(2):285–296.

Kumar, R., Kumar, A. and Singh, G. K. (2016b) 'Electrocardiogram signal compression using singular coefficient truncation and wavelet coefficient coding', *IET Science, Measurement and Technology*, 10(4):266–274.

Kumar, Ranjeet, Kumar, A. and Singh, G. K. (2016b) 'Hybrid method based on singular value decomposition and embedded zero tree wavelet technique for ECG signal compression', *Computer Methods and Programs in Biomedicine*, 129:135–148.

Hanwoo Lee and Buckley, K. M. (1999) 'ECG data compression using cut and align beats approach and 2-D transforms', *IEEE Transactions on Biomedical Engineering*, 46(5):556–564.

V. Lukin, M. Zriakhov, A.A. Zelenskt, K. Egiazarian, A. V. (2008) 'Lossy compression of Multichannel ECG based on 2-D DCT and preprocessing', in *TCSET 2008*, 159–162.

Mallat, S. (1987) 'A compact Multiresolution Representation: The Wavelet Model', in *Proc. IEEE Computer society workshop on computer vision*, 2–7.

S. Miaou, H. Yen, C. L. (2002) 'Wavelet-based ECG compression using dynamic vector quantization with tree code vectors in single codebook', *IEEE Transactions on Biomed. Engineering*, 49:671–680.

MIT-BIH (March 22nd, 2020) 'Database, MIT-BIH Arrhythmia'. Available at: www.physionet.org/physiobank/database/mitdb.

W.C. Mueller (1978) 'Arrhythmia detection program for an ambulatory ECG monitor', *Biomed. Sci. Instrument.*, 41:81–85.

G. Nave, A. C. (1993) 'ECG Compression using long-term prediction', *IEEE Trans. on Biomed. Engineering*, 40(9):877–885.

Patbhaje, U. *et al.* (2017) 'Compression of medical image using wavelet based sparsification and coding', in *2017 4th International Conference on Signal Processing and Integrated Networks, SPIN 2017*. 394–398.

Ranjeet, K., Kumar, A. and Pandey, R. K. (2013) 'An efficient compression system for ECG signal using QRS periods and CAB technique based on 2D DWT and Huffman coding', in *2013 International Conference on Control, Automation, Robotics and Embedded Systems (CARE)*. IEEE, 1–6.

U.E. Ruttimann, H. V. P. (1979) 'Compression of the ECG by prediction or interpolation and entropy encoding', *IEEE Trans. on Biomedical Engineering*, 26(11):613–623.

S.M.E. Sahraeian, E. F. (2007) 'Wavelet-Based 2-D ECG data compression method using SPIHT and VQ coding', in *EUROCON 2007*, 133–137.

Wang, X. *et al.* (2016) 'ECG compression based on combining of EMD and wavelet transform', *Electronics Letters*, 52(19):1588–1590.

Wang, X. and Meng, J. (2008) 'A 2-D ECG compression algorithm based on wavelet transform and vector quantization', *Digital Signal Processing*, 18(2):179–188.

L. Wang, J. Belina, A.Vasinonta,M. Berner, S. R. (1994) 'Compression of ECG using a Code Excited Linear Prediction (CELP)', in *IEEE Proc. Advances: New Opportunities for Biomedical Engineers*, 1264–1265.

Zh. Wang, Y. C. (2008) 'A 2-D ECG compression algorithm based on modified SPIHT', in *Int. W. on wearable and implantable body sensor networks*, 305–309.

Zhang, Z. *et al.* (2013) 'Compressed sensing for energy-efficient wireless telemonitoring of noninvasive fetal ECG via block sparse bayesian learning', *IEEE Transactions on Biomedical Engineering*, 60(2): 300–309.

Smart Computing – Khan et al (Eds)
© 2021 Taylor & Francis Group, London, ISBN 978-0-367-76552-1

Cloud-based fully automated domestic wastewater disposal system in flood-affected urban cities

H.R. Goyal, K.K. Ghanshala & S. Sharma
Graphic Era Deemed to be University, Dehradun, India

ABSTRACT: In recent years, both administratively and ethically, the human-based disaster management program has been a concern. It can be more negative than healthy at times. There emerged a new Internet of Things (IoT) organization that was advanced enough to build a network that automatically connected people and forecasted every function and attribute of the flood to be considered using lesser interaction between human beings and all such innovations. In this study, a wastewater disposal system is developed and implemented to overcome the losses caused by urban inundations in urban regions. The platform consists of cloud-based IoT control on a real-time basis for the criticality of the wastewater disposal network. We have developed this architecture, technology, mathematical model, and application to satisfy the need to incorporate wastewater drainage systems in any urban area to prevent floods. The case study of floods in Mumbai 2005 illustrates this built framework. If we adopt this system, it will save more than 40% of damages and lives.

1 INTRODUCTION

Unpredictably, accidents happen all over the world where floods are the worst. Not only are the wildlife affected by floods but also buildings, body, vegetations, etc. In the case of the mountain of a cyclone or a low-pressure differential causing flooding of lakes and rivers, the floods usually occur because of heavy rains. The obstruction of the waste-line, or domestic wastewater pipes, is another big explanation for urban floods. The main examples of urban flooding are in Mumbai, where the flood causes more damage in this city each year during the rainy season (Zelenkauskaite et al. 2012). In the last three decades, urbanization in the developed world and industrialized nations has also taken place. Urbanization is more in terms of Asian content, particularly in India, and the municipal administration has created many challenges in city management. The greater the need for infrastructure, services, and so on for the migration of people from villages to urban areas, and particularly the less familiarity they have with the waste disposal (Bande & Shete 2017). Figure 1 shows the population migrating in the years 1960–2017 from the rural to the urban (Lirathni et al. 2018). From this statistic, we find that in 1960 the total population growth was approximately 21% in the year 1960, with the continuous rise of approximately 50% for 2017.

Also, they lead to the blockage of rivers and irrigation. Increased flooding occurs in urban areas due to the unplanned infrastructure during monsoon, cyclone, and low-pressure variations. It damages many lives, infrastructure, and so on. The earlier warning system needs to be established to prevent losses. In all areas of growth, India is moving forward. A clever urban development is needed so that we can use an intelligent wastewater disposal system.

The recent years have made things easier in the areas of smart, cloud and storage, artificial intelligence, and machine learning. Internet access in most villages and cities is currently open. To avoid flooding in urban areas, the sensors, motors, or other devices have been connected via the Internet (Goyal et al. 2020). The collection of Internet-linked tools for the mission in question is known as the Internet of Things (IoT). This work focuses on the development and growth of an IoT cloud-based wastewater network management and control.

DOI 10.1201/9781003167488-13

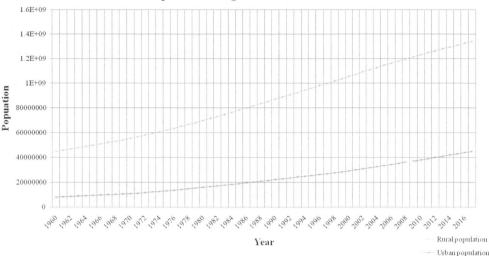

Figure 1.   Indian population year-wise vs. population migrated from rural to urban.

The rest of the paper is organized as follows. Section 2 explains the working of cloud-based IoT for flood management. Section 3 illustrates the traditional domestic wastewater disposal system in urban cities and how it is different from the modern wastewater disposal system. Section 4 explains the proposed methodology along with the algorithm. Section 5 titled implementation and result analysis we explained the implementation part along with the mathematical model and the conclusion and future work are explained in Section 6.

2   CLOUD-BASED IOT

Every year, floods are a natural phenomenon and a devastating cause of the destruction of life, agriculture, and infrastructure. The floods are affected by many factors of hydrological and meteorological characteristics which are peculiar to its existence. Several research studies are performed on flood management and the prevision system, which can support individual stack holders and the flood-prone mass (Suciu et al. 2017). The surveillance prediction paradigm is moving significantly from individual prevision systems to the smart flood prediction system (Goyal et al. 2020).

All this is made possible by the embedded communication system with the support of recent technological developments. However, the IoT was a mixture of an embedded architectural network without a hierarchy but an equal network of knowledge flows, which created a very human-like atmosphere thus negating the reality of losses of life, workers, and other underdeveloped crises (Abuhasel 2020, Khan 2020a–2020e; Quasim 2019a, 2020). Work is being carried out, the perceptible factors and qualities of the water, the temperature of its surroundings, and the linearity of nature, are all to be used as a learning record for creating a system (Gubbi et al. 2013). The system's calculations had to be based on mathematical models or hydrological models, basing it on certain algorithmic approach. Flood data has to be stored in a dynamic location with the nonlinear nature of access. Multifarious of the techniques used in these predictions include ingrained network systems working on specific algorithms (Babu et al. 2015). IoT -based Flood Monitoring system puts forth the basic design of Artificial Neural Network (ANN) for flood prediction has inescapable features included in its design enhancing its scalability and reliability for its utilization. Several of the researchers depict the use of Wireless Sensory Network (WSN) utilized with linear regression of multiple variables for real time for accurate flood prediction. Disparate communication technologies work on the same demographic of connectivity and interaction. Distinct of these researches are done on several other networks regarding even Arduino: Uno, being connected by an array of sensors, in turn, to respond to variations. All of these based on networks; our next focus would be very predictive like its communication in nodes. The Zigbee Technology works between the nodes and its connectivity utilizing CC2650 MCU as a paramount curator (Tai et al. 2015).

The next connective system has been proposed to be Nonlinear Auto Regressive with Exogenous Input or (NARX) model to abort the complications related to Nonlinear Flood Prediction Systems. These predict the occurrence of floods in certain areas of the world, some even to the lead time of 10 hr.

As of previously discussed, the elements are all separable components working as a part of or independent from a whole system network. For a shrewd understanding of the fellow systems that are to be discussed, we need to understand the network first (Xu et al. 2015).

A nexus creating interconnectivity between keys is simply what a fellow network is. In a developed system, the elements of conduct cancel out any human presence that was to be needed altogether, encapsulating the prediction team, the disaster management team, the reclusive team, and the information-sharing team. All of this that is to be managed are completed with least of human interaction to bothered about.

Several of the full blazing systems that are used here are system design, basing on a single board computer known as Raspberry Pi 3, and used in IoT application. Applications also work as a base for Wi-Fi protocols and communications.

It has efficient enough energy to operate to its lower input/output voltage of level 3.3V. The language-based is usually on is Python. This Raspberry Pi System utilizes itself as a single node being connected to a large WLAN network, working on a basic Wi-Fi hotspot for the elementary factor of Internet access (Biswas & Giaffreda 2014).

Another of these networks being used as a system is ANN analysis. From its basic definition, it's the mirroring of mammalian brain structure conducting certainly developed learning algorithms. It has a specifically interesting field of study regarding the observance of modification. Completing with system-based management, the more accurate representation of real-time data transfer is to be tested via specific disasters like flash flooding. A cloud-based management system works best for its instant reaction to modification (Quasim 2017, 2019b)). Certain of these systems have obtained recognizable developments, which includes Bluemix (IBM), working on basic mobile application and being supported by various programming languages has a huge array of access to the basic user (Souza et al. 2017). Figure 2 shows a typical cloud-based IoT system.

Cloud-based system management, MQ Telemetry Transport (MQTT), i.e., is based on Novel Messaging Transportation Protocol, aiming to publish "subscribe mode" to provide for a home control system for smart cities and billing systems. It is based on Minimized Network Bandwidth and Device Resource Requirement.

A further topic of discussion is Gateway Architecture, which has a previously discussed central element, i.e., the Raspberry Pi. If the temperature system, water-level, and speed sensor get inputted in Libelium Controller, that is sequentially connected with a battery supplied only to produce XBEE transmitter or alarm based on the specific circumstances (Marcian et al. 2018).

The advent of IoT has become a tangible phenomenon for many years in modern history, i.e., a patterned algorithm that generates different interactions. Any of these experiences varied from the existing understanding of internet-based interaction. From the originality of the past, the egress of the particular framework, which calls for further development, has gone to a further level. The program has built an all-pervading network for man to "keys" (day-to-day subjects of human use) and key-to-key interactions, based before on human-to-human interactions. Both these articulations provide a step for the expressiveness of scholarship. As for each key identified as a specific individual, the further interaction through the system was once accredited to those identifiers: first

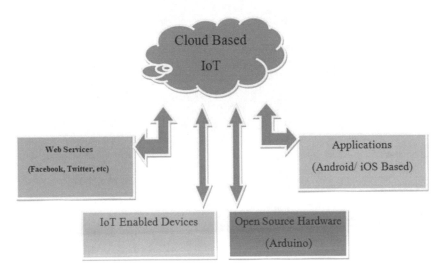

Figure 2. Cloud-based IoT system.

to be managed and subsequently to handle themselves and others (Jegadeesan et al. 2018). The outcome is not only a new creation but contact within itself.

The innovation, which integrates and cooperates between existing bodies, is an early concept and represents a breakthrough for a developing world filled with auto-sensory networks with less required but lived human interaction (Xu et al. 2018).

Self-maneuvering action as we speak of it would be a present one will live with, revolutionizing the way we concern the needs of quality human life. As much as IoT can be defined as the "World Wide Network of an interconnected object/devices, uniquely addressable based on communication protocols." By considering IoT as an ideal and not a defined architecture of hierarchy, one is embracing the model of complexity, based on the multi-dimensional system of the interlinked object. The new approach of the social network enables us to analyze and evaluate similar systems on multiple levels (Kamruzzaman et al. 2017).

Several existing quandaries can be solved with ease of access. Disaster management being, one of them, has IoT as a noticeable advantage to come forth with specifics of the advancement of interlinked connectivity come into play, evaluating up to obtainable measures. Hence, we come forth with the discussion of the cloud-based system using IoT for deluge facilitation, i.e., urban flood management (Ray et al. 2017).

3 TRADITIONAL DOMESTIC WASTEWATER DISPOSAL SYSTEM IN URBAN CITIES

Household or industrial wastewater, or some other wastewater, is disposed of (Datta & Sharma 2017). The wastewater disposal in any town/city is among the most important problems as it contains toxic gasses and is also hazardous to life. Every day thousands of liters of water, including households, factories, agriculture, and so on, are used by India in various applications. Each city municipal corporation is challenged by the fact that thousands of liters of wastewater are produced and properly disposed of. The traditional wastewater disposal system consists of the simple drainage/sewage pipeline connected to the places where human habitation is not present or we can say outside the urban area. Another way is just allowing the wastewater in the pass in rivers or lakes.

Figure 3 shows the typical traditional wastewater disposal system. This system is not suitable as far as the health and environment is concerned.

Household waste water (toilets, sink, etc.)   Commercial and industrial waste water

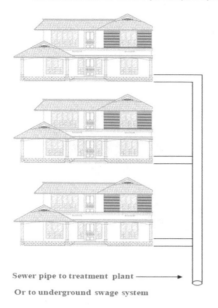 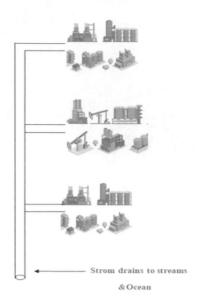

Sewer pipe to treatment plant ——→   ←—— Strom drains to streams

Or to underground swage system   & Ocean

Figure 3.   The traditional wastewater disposal system.

4   PROPOSED METHODOLOGY

In urban areas, the wastewater or wastewater treatment system is very critical. In India, as well as in many Asican countries, urbanization is spreading across the world very quickly. The local government has been unable to control the floods so that an automated disposal and monitoring system is required. Figure 4 shows the proposed methodology framework. The proposed method consists of different systems and subsystems and all perform different roles in the disposal of wastewater from time to time and during floods. The water flow sensor is installed in different locations of the wastewater disposal system. This sensor is connected to different subparts/systems such as controller, Wi-Fi module, GPS module, and motor/pump to discharge the water when the water level reaches the critical level.

All the sensors and control units are connected to the Cloud through ThingSpeak. The devices are monitored in real time. If the water level is normal then the application developed will show a green light, the yellow shows it in nearer to critical, but the red light indicates the danger or flood alert the stakeholders are informed based on the GPS location where the water level reaches the critical level.

In this module, we can locate if any blockage in the water disposal system based on the flow rate of the water. All these data are reviewed and stored on a real time-basis.

4.1   *System model*

Assumptions:

Let K be the number of locations.

Let the number of sensors each location is 2, i.e.,

- S1: Water Level Sensor (S11, S12.........S1K)
- S2: Water Flow Rate Sensor (S21, S22.........S2K)
- T1i and T2i are the threshold for sensor S1 and S2 respectively at the ith location.

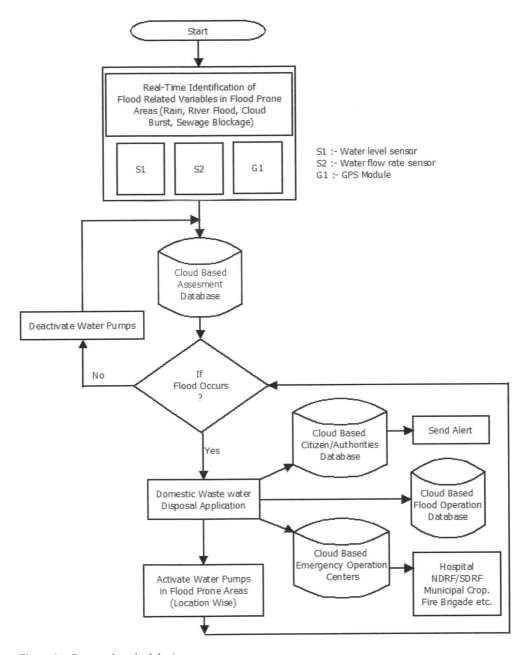

Figure 4. Proposed methodologies.

- Message_FO: Flood Occurred
- Message_FE: Flood Expected

Algorithm
    Step 1. Begin.
    Step 2. Read data from S11- - - -k and S21- - - -k.
    Step 3. Send data to a cloud-based database for the assessment.

Step 4. For i=0 to k.

Step 5. IF(S1i > T1i and S2i> T2i).

Step 6. Activate DWWD app.

Step 7. Switch ON water pump (with the help of actuator).

Step 8. Send message Message_FO through a cloud-based citizen/Authorities database.

Step 9. Update data to the Cloud regarding the operations for further analysis.

Step 10. Send information to various agencies.

Step 11. Else IF(S1i == T1iamd S2i == T2i)

Step 12. Send message Message_FE through a cloud-based citizen/Authorities database.

Step 13. Deactivate the water pump and go to Step 3.

Step 14. End.

5   IMPLEMENTATION AND RESULT ANALYSIS

The implementation consists of developing a hardware system that is capable of providing and controlling the wastewater disposal system along with the development of an application to monitor/control the system. This application is managed by the stakeholders. After implementation, the results obtained are analyzed.

5.1   *Assembled components of proposed model*

The components used in this study are assembled and are shown in Figure 5. The major components of this proposed modal are Arduino Uno, Wi-Fi module, GPS module, water flow rate sensor, ultrasonic sensor, and 5 V DC motor. These components are explained under the following heads.

5.1.1   *Arduino Uno*

Arduino Uno is a microcontroller used to control different sensors, motors, and so on. These controllers are widely used because of the low coast and good performance as compared to any other type of microcontroller. Figure 5 shows the Arduino Uno controller used in this study and

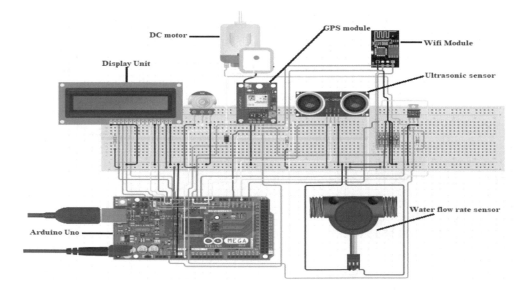

Figure 5.   Assembled components of proposed modal.

it is based on ATmega328. The programming of this controller is simpler and only required a computer with the Arduino computer program to make this controller work as we required. The power consumption is also too less.

5.1.2 *Water flow rate sensor*

A water flow tare sensor is commonly used where the flow rate of fluids is required to measure especially water. This device consists of a Hall Effect sensor which senses the flow rate based on the mechanism provided in the device.

Based on the water pressure or force, it converts that signal or sense and sends it back to the microcontroller. Figure 5 shows the water flow rate sensor.

5.1.3 *Ultrasonic sensor*

Ultrasonic sensor uses sonar to determine the distance of any object, obstacle detecting in robots, and so on. The range of detection varies from 1 in. to 13 ft. The device consists of a transmitter and a receiver end. Figure 5 shows the ultrasonic sensor. In our study, we use this sensor to find out the wastewater level to find out whether the water level is normal or critical for further.

5.1.4 *Wi-Fi module*

Figure 5 shows the Wi-Fi module which is used to control the wastewater disposal system on a real-time basis. This synchronized system that helps data collection from stations (station for all devices/sensors and so on). The data flow is from the Cloud to the stakeholders. This is integrated with a microcontroller.

5.1.5 *GPS module*

The GPS module is shown in Figure 5 and is used along with all the devices to send the location where the wastewater level reaches the critical level in the water disposal system. The stakeholder will access the data and location send by the device for further processing of the data to avoid the flood or any damage.

5.1.6 *DC motor*

DC motors are widely used in many applications. These applications vary from robot chaises motor to any industrial applications. In our study, we are using a 5V DC motor to the opening of valves for the wastewater disposal system when the water level reaches a critical level. Figure 5 shows the 5V DC motor.

5.2 *Mathematical model*

According to the proposed model, consider the rate of change in water flow S2 with time should be less than Threshold T2, Similarly, change in the amount of water level S1 with respect to time should be less than Threshold T1

Hence, differential equations governed as

$$\frac{dS_1}{dt} < T_1 \tag{1}$$

$$\frac{dS_2}{dt} < T_2 \tag{2}$$

For simplification, introduce arbitrary constants K_1 and K_2, Equations (1) and (2) becomes

$$\frac{dS_2}{dt} + K_2 = T_2 \tag{3}$$

The solution of these equations we obtain

$$S_1 = (T_1 - K_1)t + c_1 \tag{4}$$

$$S_2 = (T_2 - K_2)t + c_2 \tag{5}$$

Now, we know that amount of water level S_1 directly influenced the change in water flow S_2. So, we get

$$S_1 \, \alpha \, S_2 \Rightarrow S_1 = K_3 \, S_2 \tag{6}$$

where K_3 is arbitrary constant
where
S_1: Level of water
S_2: Change of water flow
T_1: Threshold limit of water level
T_2: Threshold limit of rate of water flow
t: Time

5.3 *Application development for a wastewater disposal system*

An android application domestic wastewater disposal system (DWWD) is developed to control the wastewater disposal system on real-time bases. Figure 9 shows the screenshots of the application.

This application consists of two types of users. The first user is the administrator and the other user is the stakeholders. The administrator will be able to view the data obtained from all the stations where the wastewater disposal systems control the pumps, and so on. The stakeholders can see the criticality of the water level in a given particular area/place. Figure 9 shows the interface of the two cities in Mumbai and they are integrated with the sensor system and so on to check the level of water and also it has the prevision controlling the pump remotely, the basic settings of the application, the data collected by the app, and the data is analyzed using plots generated in the application.

5.4 *Case Study on Mumbai 2005 floods*

The Mumbai flood in 2005 was the most destructive. There were many factors—some were natural and some were manmade. One of the natural reasons for this flood was 944 mm rainfall in 24 hr. It was the eight heaviest spots of rain recorded worldwide, but this factor can't be controlled. Despite that, there were so many manmade factors due to which this flood becomes a disaster. Some of the factors are the uncontrolled and unplanned development, destroyed mangrove ecosystem, and the main reason was the domestic wastewater disposal system which was not as per the current requirement. Many outfalls of disposal system were not equipped with flood gates; approximately 102 open pipes went directly into the sea, and only three outfalls were having flood gates. The disposal system is choked in many places; this is due to many people throwing plastics and other solid waste also in it. The waterways in the domestic wastewater disposal system that allowed the rainwater to drain out have been reduced drastically. Due to this destructive flood, many losses occurred. Around 582 people died due to landslide, tsunami rumors, vehicle suffocation, electrocution, wall collapse, etc., as shown in Figure 6.

More than 100,000 of the building were damaged either partially or fully, as shown in Figure. 7. Thousands of pubic vehicles were damaged as shown in Figure. 8.

If the proposed model is adopted in cities like Mumbai, then the proposed model works as shown in Figure 9. The different locations that control the unit along with the sensors is installed in the water disposal pipes and the data is collected and stored using the ThingsSpeak cloud platform and the mobile application is developed to control it. With this arrangement, we could have saved about 40% of losses in floods like Mumbai 2005.

Casualties

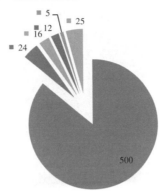

■ Landslide ■ Tsunami Rumor ■ Vehicle suffocation ■ Electrocution ■ Wall colapse ■ Water borne diseases

Figure 6.   Casualties during the Mumbai flood of 2005.

Building Damaged

■ Partly Damaged Residential Building   ■ Fully Damaged Residential Building

■ Commercial Establishments   ■ Classrooms

■ School Building

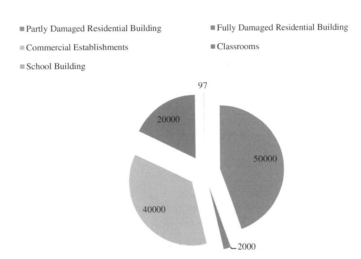

Figure 7.   Building damage during the Mumbai Flood of 2005.

5.5   *Result and discussion*

The results are divided into two subcategories: the first is the data collection and the data analysis, and the second is response time.

5.5.1   *Data collection and data analysis*

The device we developed for the wastewater disposal system consumes less power and we can operate this device with less power. The data is acquired through the ThingSpeak cloud platform which is more reliable in storing the data. This is the closed-loop system where we minimized human error to have a good system in place in times of floods or unforeseen situations.

The data collected for every second to days are automatically the graphs are plotted to see the flow rate in every area of the particular urban areas where this system is installed. Figure 9 gives a mobile application for easy control and understanding of the situation in every area. Such that the

Vehicles Damaged

■ Local Trains   ■ Taxis   ■ BEST buses

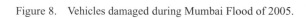

Figure 8.   Vehicles damaged during Mumbai Flood of 2005.

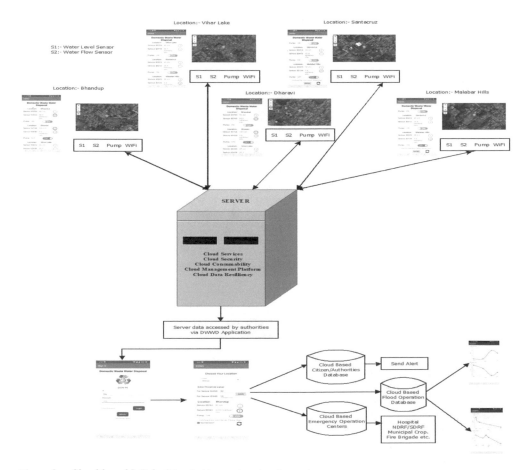

Figure 9.   Cloud-based IoT for Mumbai in wastewater disposal.

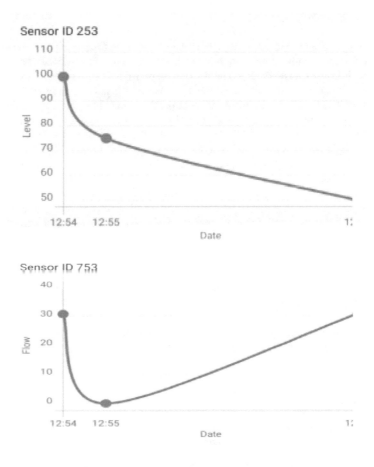

Figure 10. The data analysis of the data obtained from the sensors.

effective development of a system is carried out is more effective and efficient in avoiding more losses during urban floods.

The data is automatically collected from the sensors and the control system is transferred through ThingSpeak and the stored data in the cloud are used for the analysis in the future. Control and manage wastewater disposal system. Figure 9 shows the data automatically analyzed based on the flow rate and water level vs. date. With this, we can analyze the obstacle in the water flow and we can avoid the floods.

5.5.2 *Response time*

The proposed device is programmed and designed in such a way that we can overcome the drawbacks of this kind of devices developed by the researchers. The difference is that the response time is better than any other device in comparison to the available literature.

It is one of the best real-time based flow/flood monitoring systems for the urban wastewater disposal system is because of the response time.

6 CONCLUSIONS AND FUTURE WORK

The proposed model used to reduce losses from urban flooding is functional and real-time monitoring is more important. Another important thing is that we store the data and use them to understand the regular rate of flow of wastewater to enable us to prepare a redesign of the system for disposing of wastewater. It has three user interfaces: the administrator, disaster management, and the user. This design is easy to use. The administrator monitors the water flow rate for the disposal system and studies the flow response. If the flow rate reaches the critical level stated, then the emergency management team is well aware of further measures and the notifications are transmitted simultaneously to the people living in this area. With the case study, the Mumbai 2005 floods we explored what were the effects of urban flooding and compared the adoption of this modal to save more than 40% of losses.

The future work of this research may include the Raspberry Pi as a guide to making the proposed and built device more accurate and more sensitive. Second, after collecting and evaluating over several years, we should use artificial intelligence in designing the autonomous wastewater disposal system so that we can create a more robust system to save lives and the infrastructure, etc. from damage.

ACKNOWLEDGMENT

The authors are thankful to Mr. Nithin Kumar K C, Assistant Professor, MED, Graphic Era Deemed to be University, Dehradun for his guidance during this work.

REFERENCES

Abuhasel K. A. and M. A. Khan, (2020),"A Secure Industrial Internet of Things (IIoT) Framework for Resource Management in Smart Manufacturing," in IEEE Access, vol. 8, pp. 117354–117364, 2020, doi: 10.1109/ACCESS.2020.3004711.

Babu, S.M., Lakshmi, A.J. & Rao, B.T. 2015. A study on cloud-based Internet of Things: CloudIoT. *Global conference on communication technologies (GCCT), IEEE* : 60–65.

Bande, S. & Shete, V.V. 2017. Smart flood disaster prediction system using IoT & neural networks. *International Conference On Smart Technologies For Smart Nation (SmartTechCon)* : 189–194.

Biswas, A.R., & Giaffreda, R. 2014. IoT and cloud convergence: Opportunities and challenges. *IEEE World Forum on the Internet of Things (WF-IoT)* : 375–376.

Datta, P., & Sharma, B. 2017. A survey on IoT architectures, protocols, security, and smart city-based applications. *8th International Conference on Computing, Communication, and Networking Technologies (ICCCNT)* : 1–5.

Goyal, H.R., Ghanshala, K.K. & Sharma, S. 2020. Role of IoT devices in flood management system using social networking sites. *International Journal of Innovative Technology and Exploring Engineering*, Volume 9, Issue 4: 1986–1994. DOI: 10.35940/ijitee.D1620.029420

Gubbi, J., Buyya, R., Marusic, S., & Palaniswami, M. 2013. Internet of Things (IoT): A vision, architectural elements, and future directions. *Future generation computer systems*, 29(7): 1645–1660.

Jegadeesan, S., Dhamodaran, M., & Sri Shanmugapriya, S. 2018. Wireless Sensor Network based Flood and Water Quality Monitoring System using IoT. *Taga journal of graphic technology, Online ISSN*, (1748–0345).

Kamruzzaman, M.D., Sarkar, N.I., Gutierrez, J., & Ray, S.K. 2017. A study of IoT-based post-disaster management. *International Conference on Information Networking (ICOIN)*: 406–410.

Khan M. A., (2020), An IoT Framework for Heart Disease Prediction Based on MDCNN Classifier, in IEEE Access, vol. 8, pp. 34717–34727, 2020. DOI: 10.1109/ACCESS.2020.2974687

Khan, MA, Abuhasel, KA. (2020).Advanced metameric dimension framework for heterogeneous industrial Internet of things. Computational Intelligence. 2020; 1–21. https://doi.org/10.1111/coin.12378

Khan M.A, and Algarni F., (2020) "A Healthcare Monitoring System for the Diagnosis of Heart Disease in the IoMT Cloud Environment Using MSSO-ANFIS," in IEEE Access, vol. 8, pp. 122259–122269, 2020, doi: 10.1109/ACCESS.2020.3006424.

Khan, M. A., Quasim, M. T, et al., (2020), A Secure Framework for Authentication and Encryption Using Improved ECC for IoT-Based Medical Sensor Data, in IEEE Access, vol. 8, pp. 52018–52027, 2020. DOI: 10.1109/ACCESS.2020.2980739

Khan M.A. et al., (2020), Decentralised IoT, Decenetralised IoT: A Blockchain perspective, Springer, Studies in BigData, 2020, DOI: https://doi.org/10.1007/978-3-030-38677-1

Lirathni, H., Zrelli, A., Jridi, M.H., & Ezzedine, T. 2018. A Real-Time Flash-Floods Alerting System Based on WSN and IBM Bluemix Cloud Platform. *International conference on the Sciences of Electronics, Technologies of Information and Telecommunications*: 390–399.

Marcian, M.J., Sabarishwaran, S., Sudhagaran, D. & Sathiyapriya. S. 2018. Smart Drainage Monitoring and Clog Removal Using IoT, *International Journal of Scientific Research in Science, Engineering and Technology*, Volume 4, Issue 4:178–182.

Quasim, M.T., Khan M.A, Algarni F., Alharthy A., Alshmrani G.M.M, (2020), Blockchain Frameworks. In: Khan M., Quasim M., Algarni F., Alharthi A. (eds) Decentralised Internet of Things. Studies in Big Data, vol 71. Springer, DOI: https://doi.org/10.1007/978-3-030-38677-1

Quasim, M. T., Khan M. A, et al. (2019), Internet of Things for Smart Healthcare: A Hardware Perspective, 2019 First International Conference of Intelligent Computing and Engineering (ICOICE), Hadhramout, Yemen, 2019, pp. 1–5, DOI: 10.1109/ICOICE48418.2019.9035176

Quasim, M.T., and Mohammad Meraj, (2017), Big Data Security and Privacy: A Short Review, International Journal of Mechanical Engineering and Technology, 8(4), 2017, pp. 408–412. http://www.iaeme.com/IJMET/issues.asp?JType=IJMET&VType=8&IType=4

Quasim, Mohammad Tabrez, et al. (2019), 5 V'S OF BIG DATA VIA CLOUD COMPUTING: USES AND IMPORTANCE, Sci. Int (Lahore),vol.31(3),PP.367–371,2019

Ray, P.P., Mukherjee, M., & Shu, L. 2017. Internet of things for disaster management: State-of-the-art and prospects. *IEEE Access*, 5: 18818–18835.

Souza, A.S., de Lima Curvello, A.M., de Souza, F.L.D.S. & da Silva, H.J. 2017. A flood warning system to a critical region. *Procedia Computer Science*, 109:1104–1109.

Suciu, G., Scheianu, A., & Vochin, M., 2017, June. Disaster early warning using time-critical IoT on elastic cloud workbench. *IEEE International Black Sea Conference on Communications and Networking (BlackSeaCom)*: 1–5).

Tai, H., Celesti, A., Fazio, M., Villari, M., & Puliafito, A. 2015. An integrated system for advanced water risk management based on cloud computing and IoT. *2nd World Symposium on Web Applications and Networking (WSWAN)*: 1–7.

Xu, G., Huang, G.Q. & Fang, J. 2015. Cloud asset for urban flood control. *Advanced Engineering Informatics*, 29(3): 355–365.

Xu, X., Zhang, L., Sotiriadis, S., Asimakopoulou, E., Li, M., & Bessis, N. 2018. CLOTHO: A large-scale Internet of Things-based crowd evacuation planning system for disaster management. *IEEE Internet of Things Journal*, 5(4): 3559–3568.

Zelenkauskaite, A., Bessis, N., Sotiriadis, S., & Asimakopoulou, E. 2012. The interconnectedness of complex systems of the internet of things through social network analysis for disaster management. *Fourth International Conference on Intelligent Networking and Collaborative Systems*: 503–508.

Smart Computing – Khan et al (Eds)

Blockchain for secure IoT and edge computing: A survey

Shivani Wadhwa
Chitkara University Institute of Engineering & Technology, Chitkara University, Punjab, India

Gagandeep
Department of Computer Science, Punjabi University, Patiala, India

ABSTRACT: Blockchain is a buzzword that is enhancing the applicability of various technologies by providing them with security features. Blockchain supports Internet of Things (IoT) based devices by providing integrity and privacy to the data being produced. A massive number of such devices exist, which are generally low powered. To provide a computing environment for these devices, edge computing plays a very major role. Blockchain also consumes a lot of computation resources for mining a block. The edge computing supports blockchain and mobile devices by providing features such as low latency, local proximity, mobility support to the latency-sensitive, and compute-intensive applications. In this paper, the integration of these technologies is discussed, proliferating in various areas. Study area, techniques/algorithms used, problems, and solutions on the collaboration of these technologies are investigated. This paper explores the integration of IoT, mobile-edge-computing, blockchain, and it is evident that various technologies will be benefited.

1   INTRODUCTION

Nowadays, a growing number of smart devices are employing sensors which generate a huge amount of data by sensing the environment. Most of these smart devices are connected with mobile devices. Data generated by smart devices cannot be alone handled by these mobile devices as they are resource hungry and consume huge amounts of energy. So, there arises a need to merge computation-intensive data generated by smart devices to be linked with the resources that the network in close proximity can offer.

Data can be transferred to the Cloud, but because of delay and jitter in computations, Quality of Service (QoS) requirements of real-time devices are affected. Offloading computations to the Cloud induces communication and computation stress on the network.

The edge computing model brings resources of the network very close to the devices, i.e., at the edge of the current network. Integrating mobile devices with the edge nodes solves the issue of managing data or resource demand of mobile devices. Mobile Edge Computing (MEC) offers an IT operation system inside the radio access network which is in close proximity to the users of mobile devices (Hu et al. 2015). Mao et al. (2017) stated that the main function of MEC is to move computations of mobile devices, control of the network, and storage to the edges of the network.

Blockchain is a series of distributed ledgers that can be configured to record and monitor the value of anything. Whenever an entity of the distributed system receives new data in a blockchain, it shapes the data into the block. Miners help in generating blocks by solving complex puzzle, i.e., Proof of Work (PoW). This mining task consumes a lot of resources. Blockchain's Gartner projections will produce $3.1 trillion in new business value by 2030, but for its acceptance by 2023, companies should start exploring the technology. Gartner also predicted that by 2020, various new business models will turn up with smart contracts and other blockchain concepts.

Data generated by mobile devices should maintain integrity of the data and should be secured as well. Mining a block from the data it contains is a very computation-intensive task. MEC is an

DOI 10.1201/9781003167488-14

ideal platform for such types of computations. Edge nodes are deployed within the wireless access network from where computation resources can be accessed without any Internet delay. Tasks that can be offloaded to edge nodes are mining of blocks, consensus process, and computation-intensive applications.

2 APPLICATIONS OF BLOCKCHAIN

Blockchain has applications in various fields integrating it with different technologies. Blockchain is explored in a vast number of areas for security purposes. Figure 1 classifies the integration of various technologies, which provides the recent trends of research and guarantees that the combination of these technologies will bring successful results. Following are the applications that describe the use of blockchain.

Healthcare. Worldwide, many cities have started using blockchain technology to protect the private information created by smart healthcare devices being used for patients. Medical records of patients are increasing with time. Blockchain technology provides privacy and security to the patient's record by storing and maintaining electronic health record in an efficient way (Vora et al. 2018).

Supply Chain With the growing size of the businesses, the diversification of product portfolios, and a vast number of geographical areas need to be served and at the same time the supply chains are becoming too complicated to be handled. Blockchain manages the transactions of the supply chain and makes it more reliable. Tasks like tracking, sharing, and recording becomes very fast and scalable. Blockchain provides real-time distributed ledger of all transactions and movements among the stakeholders (Kamble et al. 2019).

Governmental Processes. Blockchain technology has brought a lot of innovation in governmental processes (Ølnes et al. 2017). The smart contract will automate some of the notary's intermediary roles in the purchase and sale of real estate. It has brought a transformation in land title projects, the involvement of multiple parties in transactions, information exchange, etc.

Digital Economy. Blockchain technology can also be used for shared economy applications like Airbnb, Uber, etc. It mainly helps in laying down platform for P2P automatic payment mechanism, cultural heritage, management of digital rights, foreign exchanges, etc. (Huckle et al. 2016). Such types of distributed applications are created by using Internet of Things (IoT) and Blockchain.

Energy Sector. Blockchain technology is emerging with the P2P energy transformation scenarios, managing energy in electric vehicles and smart grid, etc. (Casino et al. 2019). It is also responsible for de-carbonization in the energy sector by transforming into de-centralized energy sectors.

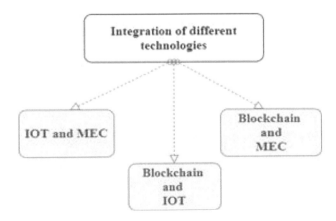

Figure 1.   Classification of integration of different technologies.

Education. Blockchain also supports ubiquitous learning environment and provides maintenance to educational records (Bdiwi et al. 2017). Teachers can information about the learning achievements of all students in the form of blocks in the blockchain. Based on blockchain, there exist school hubs that can support decision making.

Event Tickets. Event tickets are managed by blockchain on the basis of bar codes printed on the ticket. Blockchain provides security to the system by preventing sale of invalid tickets or sale of multiple copies of a ticket (Tackmann 2017).

3 INTEGRATION OF IOT AND MEC

Nowadays, huge numbers of computing applications like augmented reality, mobile gaming, smart environments, etc. are emerging. Earlier these applications were supported by Mobile Cloud Computing (MCC), but now current applications are very delayed sensitive and may need many resources for computations. For solving issues like high delay, computation-intensive tasks, resource-intensive tasks, there emerges a new paradigm called MEC. There are various opportunities that MEC can provide like compute and connectivity convergence, flexibility for application developers, streams of profits for service providers, and network equipment vendors (Ahmed & Rehmani 2017). Combining IoT with MEC brings a lot of advancement like IoT traffic is well-managed, improvement in the quality of service makes the system energy efficient, and many more. Table 1 states some of the work done on the area related to MEC and IoT.

Table 1. Analysis of the integration of IoT and MEC.

Ref.	Area	Algorithm	Problem	Solution
Li et al. 2019	MEC and IoT	No non-orthogonal multiple access technique	Latency constraints in wireless powered MEC. Time allocated for transferring energy and transmitting data is too long	Online energy consumption minimization algorithm is proposed Lyapunov optimization framework, iterative algorithm helps in optimal results
Mao et al. 2017	MEC and smart mobile devices	Gauss seidel method, Lyapunov optimization	Relation between weighted sum power consumption and execution delay	For multi-user MEC, online joint radio and computational resource management algorithm is developed
Xu et al. 2017	MEC and IoT	Markov decision process	Incorporating renewable energy into MEC for energy harvesting	Online post-decision state- (PDS) reinforcement learning optimizes the offloading and auto-scaling policy
Hu et al. 2015	Virtualized multi-access edge computing (vMEC), IoT,5G, Software Defined Networking (SDN) and Network Function Virtualization (NFV)	–	Management of IoT traffic	Container-based Virtualization Technology (CVT) improves the quality of service
			Scaling of devices due to high latency and low bandwidth	Combination of Virtual Network Functions (VNFs) and vMEC

(Continued)

Table 1. Analysis of the integration of IoT and MEC (Continued).

Ref.	Area	Algorithm	Problem	Solution
Bi & Zhang 2018	Wireless powered MEC and IoT	Binary computation offloading policy	Difficulty in selecting combinatorial computing modes	Coordinate descent (CD) method and alternating direction method of multipliers (ADMM) method are proposed to optimize computation rate

Table 2. Analysis of the integration of blockchain and IoT.

Ref.	Area of study	Algorithm or Technique	Problem	Solution
Casado-Vara et al. 2019	IoT and blockchain	Proposed adaptive control algorithm	Achieving optimal block number	Adaptive controller works by using queuing theory which improves the mining efficiency
			Searching of data takes too much of time	Hash map search is done
Hammi et al. 2018	IoT and blockchain	Elliptic Curve Digital Signature algorithm,l Smart contract	Security issues and fear of attack	Bubbles of trust, i.e., virtual zones are created on the basis of Ethereum
Kumar & Mallick 2018	IoT and blockchain	–	False authentication, data tampering, device spoofing of data generated by IoT devices	Distributed ledger based blockchain provides secu rity and integrity features to the data
Minoli & Occhiogrosso 2018	IoT and blockchain	–	Confidentiality and availability	Discussed inlayer IoT security using gateway-level blockchain
Huh et al. 2017	IoT and blockchain	RSA public key crypto systems, Smart contract	Managing thousands of connected IoT devices	Deployed smart contracts on Ethereum platform of blockchain
Reyna et al. 2018	IoT and blockchain	–	–	Discussed about the integration of IoT and block-chain and challenges related to the integration, IoT devices which can become blockchain components, IoT-blockchain-applications

4 INTEGRATION OF BLOCKCHAIN AND IOT

Nowadays, several smart devices are growing at a very fast pace with the inclusion of high-speed networks, and IoT is gaining world-wide acceptance. The information is shared among the devices with the standard protocols required for communication. Blockchain technology plays a vital role in managing the privacy and security of IoT devices. Problems that can be addressed by blockchain are identity and access management, data authentication and integrity, authentication, authorization and privacy of users, secure communication, etc. (Khan et al. 2020). When blockchain is integrated with IoT devices, blockchain can solve many security problems of IoT. The features of blockchain like auditability, immutability, security, and reliability are favorable for IoT technology and also bring autonomy in IoT but their combination increases the involvement of bandwidth as well as huge data. Table 2 illustrates the work done on the area related to blockchain and IoT.

5 INTEGRATION OF BLOCKCHAIN AND EDGE COMPUTING/MEC

Blockchain is providing support to other technologies but there is a large amount of computations for mining a block. To ensure a security mechanism for data released by smart devices, blockchain does a lot of computations. Generally, computations of blockchain are offloaded to edge nodes. The advantages of integrating blockchain with edge computing are that the computation required for mining of the blocks can be done on the edge devices which makes the system efficient and also reduces the time of generation of the block. Integration of MEC and blockchain is very much beneficial for mobile users as their devices are low powered and also provides security mechanisms to mobile devices. Table 3 highlights the work done on the area related to blockchain and edge computing/MEC.

Table 3. Analysis of integration of blockchain and edge-computing/MEC.

Ref.	Area of study	Algorithm/Technique	Problem	Solution
Guo et al. 2019	Improve authentication efficiency of edge nodes using blockchain	Asymmetric cryptography is designed	Attack on edge nodes and terminals	Assymetriccryptography which provides confidentiality and communication security
			Hit ratio and reduces delay	Caching strategy which implements BP (Belief Propagation) algorithm
Casado-Vara et al. 2018	Blockchain introduces edge layer in IoT architecture	Cooperative algorithm based on game theory which is distributed and self-organized	Data collected by IoT devices is not much secure	Algorithm improves quality of data as well as identifies false data detection
Xiong et al. 2018	Maximizesprofit of edge computing service provider	Stackelberg game model	Maximizes profit of edge computing service provider (ESP)	Attains optimal resource management by using uniform and variable pricing schemes for ESP
Seng et al. 2019	Offloading the computation among mobile user equipment and edge servers in MEC	Modified GS-based user matching algorithm	Searching edge servers/UEs conducting offloaded computations	Blockchain platform is developed that helps in coordinating computation offloading
			Checking analogous for offloading the computation tasks	GS-based user matching algorithm
Liu et al. 2018	Blockchain framework enabled by mobile edge computing (MEC)	Stochastic geometry methods, ADMM based algorithm	Huge computation demand by PoW during mining	Offloading decision and caching strategy is used for optimization, Distributed ADMM based algorithm is used to solve the scenario in an efficient manner
Zhang et al. 2019	Blockchain-empowered MEC	Non-cooperative Game	Joint computing offloading	Distributed algorithm is designed to achieve the Nash Equilibrium point
			Coin-loaning problem	Two smart contracts on Ethereum are designed

(Continued)

108

Table 3. Analysis of integration of blockchain and edge-computing/MEC (Continued).

Ref.	Area of study	Algorithm/Technique	Problem	Solution
Xu et al. 2019	Offloading computations of smart devices in edge by using blockchain	NSGA-III, SAW, MCDM	Inappropriate resource allocation schemes	NSGA-III is developed for computation off loading
			Un-optimized schemes for offloading	SAW and MCDM techniques confirms optimization
Jiao et al., 2018	Edge computing enables blockchain mining	Auction-based market model	Mining process consumes lot of energy and computational resources	Social welfare maximization auction for allocating resources from edge
Altman et al., 2019	Mining competition at the edge network	Nash equilibrium, association game	Budget of mining computation	Non-cooperative congestion game competition among Edge Service Providers
Pan et al., 2018	IoT accesses edge resources through blockchain	Edge chaiframework	Accessing resources of edge by IoT devices	Credit-based resource management
			Regulating behavior of IoT devices	Smart contracts

6 CONCLUSION

There are numerous applications of blockchain, like health care, supply chain, governmental processes, etc. which are bringing advancement in their processing. Integration of IoT and MEC provides the benefit of scalability and management of network traffic, gaining access to resources in their close proximity. The integration of blockchain and IoT ensures security, privacy, confidentiality, and integrity to the data being generated by smart devices. Integration of edge computing and blockchain provides a platform for offloading the data to the edge nodes for computation in a very efficient manner. Collaboration of these technologies will provide lot of enhancement in security features and improves the quality of service as there are various areas of their confederation which are not yet explored. This extensive literature survey throws light on the integration of IoT, blockchain, and edge computing, thus providing a base for future research.

REFERENCES

Ahmed, E. and Rehmani, M.H. 2017. Mobile edge computing: opportunities, solutions, and challenges. 2017: 59–63.
Altman, E., Reiffers, A., Menasche, D.S., Datar, M., Dhamal, S. and Touati, C. 2019. Mining competition in a multi-cryptocurrency ecosystem at the network edge: a congestion game approach, *ACM SIGMETRICS Performance Evaluation Review*, vol. 46: 114–117
Bdiwi, R., De Runz, C., Faiz, S. and Cherif, A.A. 2017. Towards a new ubiquitous learning environment based on Blockchain technology. *In IEEE 17th International Conference on Advanced Learning Technologies (ICALT)*: 101–102. IEEE.

Bi, S. and Zhang, Y.J. 2018. Computation rate maximization for wireless powered mobile-edge computing with binary computation offloading. In *IEEE Transactions on Wireless Communications*, vol. 17: 4177–4190.

Casado-Vara, R., Chamoso, P., De la Prieta, F., Prieto, J. and Corchado, J.M. 2019. Non-linear adaptive closed-loop control system for improved efficiency in IoT-blockchain management. In *Information Fusion*, vol. 49: 227–239.

Casado-Vara, R., de la Prieta, F., Prieto, J. and Corchado, J.M. 2018. Blockchain framework for IoT data quality via edge computing. In *Proceedings of the 1st Workshop on Blockchain-enabled Networked Sensor Systems*, 19–24.

Casino, F., Dasaklis T.K. and Patsakis C. 2019. A systematic literature review of blockchain-based applications: current status, classification and open issues. In *Telematics and Informatics*, vol. 36: 55–81.

Guo, S., Hu, X., Guo, S., Qiu, X. and Qi, F. 2019. Blockchain meets edge computing: A distributed and trusted authentication system. In *IEEE Transactions on Industrial Informatics*.

Hammi, M.T., Hammi, B., Bellot, P. and Serhrouchni, A. 2018. Bubbles of Trust: A decentralized blockchain-based authentication system for IoT. In *Computers & Security*, vol. 78: 126–142.

Hu, Y.C., Patel, M., Sabella, D., Sprecher, N. and Young, V. 2015. Mobile edge computing—A key technology towards 5G. In *ETSI white paper*, vol. 11: 1–6.

Huckle, S., Bhattacharya, R., White, M. and Beloff, N. 2016. Internet of things, blockchain and shared economy applications. In *Procedia computer science*, vol. 98:461–466.

Huh, S., Cho, S. and Kim, S. 2017. Managing IoT devices using blockchain platform. In *2017 19th international conference on advanced communication technology (ICACT)*: 464–467. IEEE.

Jiao, Y., Wang, P., Niyato, D. and Xiong, Z. 2018. Social welfare maximization auction in edge computing resource allocation for mobile blockchain," In *2018 IEEE international conference on communications (ICC)*: 1–6 IEEE.

Kamble, S., Gunasekaran, A. and Arha, H. 2019. Understanding the Blockchain technology adoption in supply chains-Indian context. In *International Journal of Production Research*, vol. 57: 2009–2033.

Khan M.A. et al. (2020), Decentralised IoT, Decenetralised IoT: A Blockchain perspective, Springer, Studies in BigData, 2020, DOI: https://doi.org/10.1007/978-3-030-38677-1

Kumar, N.M. and Mallick, P.K. 2018. Blockchain technology for security issues and challenges in IoT. In *Procedia Computer Science*, vol. 132: 1815–1823.

Li, C., Tang, J., Zhang, Y., Yan, X. and Luo, Y. 2019. Energy efficient computation offloading for nonorthogonal multiple access assisted mobile edge computing with energy harvesting devices, *Computer Networks*, vol. 164: 106890.

Liu, M., Yu, F.R., Teng, Y., Leung, V.C. and Song, M. 2018. Computation offloading and content caching in wireless blockchain networks with mobile edge computing. In *IEEE Transactions on Vehicular Technology*, vol. 67: 11008–1102.

Mao, Y., You, C., Zhang, J., Huang, K. and Letaief, K.B. 2017. A survey on mobile edge computing: The communication perspective. In *IEEE Communications Surveys & Tutorials*, vol. 19: 2322–2358.

Mao, Y., Zhang, J., Song, V. and Letaief, K.B. 2017. Stochastic joint radio and computational resource management for multi-user mobile-edge computing systems. In *IEEE Transactions on Wireless Communications*, vol. 16: 5994–6009.

Minoli, D. and Occhiogrosso, B. 2018. Blockchain mechanisms for IoT security. In *Internet of Things*, vol. 1: pp. 1–3.

Ølnes, S., Ubacht, J. and Janssen, M. 2017. Blockchain in government: Benefits and implications of distributed ledger technology for information sharing. In *Government Information Quarterly: 355–364*.

Pan, J., Wang, J., Hester, A., AlQerm, I., Liu, Y. and Zhao, Y. 2018. EdgeChain: An edge-IoT framework and prototype based on blockchain and smart contracts. In *IEEE Internet of Things Journal*, vol. 6: 4719–4732.

Reyna, A., Martín, C., Chen, J., Soler E. and Díaz, M. 2018. On blockchain and its integration with IoT. Challenges and opportunities. In *Future generation computer systems*, vol. 88: 173–190,

Seng, S., Li, X., Luo, C., Ji, H. and Zhang, H. 2019. A D2D-Assisted MEC Computation Offloading in the Blockchain-Based Framework for UDNs. In *ICC 2019-2019 IEEE International Conference on Communications (ICC): 1–6*.

Tackmann, B. 2017. Secure event tickets on a blockchain. In *Data privacy management, Cryptocurrencies and Blockchain technology*: 437–444. Springer, Cham.

Vora, J., Nayyar, A., Tanwar, S., Tyagi, S., Kumar, N., Obaidat, M.S. and Rodrigues, J.J., 2018, December. BHEEM: A blockchain-based framework for securing electronic health records. In *2018 IEEE Globecom Workshops (GC Wkshps): 1–6.IEEE*.

110

Xiong, Z., Feng, S., Niyato,D., Wang P. and Han, Z. 2018. Optimal pricing- based edge computing resource management in mobile blockchain. In *2018 IEEE International Conference on Communications (ICC): 1–6. IEEE.*

Xu, J., Chen, L. and Ren, S. 2017. Online learning for offloading and auto scaling in energy harvesting mobile edge computing, In *IEEE Transactions on Cognitive Communications and Networking*, vol. 3: 361–373.

Xu, X., Zhang, X., Gao, H., Xue, Y., Qi, L. and Dou, W. 2019. BeCome: Blockchain-enabled computation offloading for IoT in mobile edge computing. In *IEEE Transactions on Industrial Informatics.*

Zhang, Z., Hong, Z., Chen, W., Zheng, Z. and Chen, X. 2019. Joint Computation Offloading and Coin Loaning for Blockchain- Empowered Mobile-Edge Computing. In *IEEE Internet of Things Journal*, vol. 6(6): 9934–9950.

Smart Computing – Khan et al (Eds)
© *2021 Taylor & Francis Group, London, ISBN 978-0-367-76552-1*

E-waste management and energy conservation in industries

Shreyas M.S., K. Rakshak, A. Singh, A.M. Bhat & Anitha H.M.
Department of Information Science & Engineering, BMS College of Engineering, Bangalore, India

ABSTRACT: Green computing and innovation allude to the environmentally friendly use of PCs and certain other devices. Green computing requires the use of sustainable practices of devices such as CPUs, peripherals, and servers. Green innovation also plans to reduce resource consumption and enhance the disposal of electronic waste (e-waste). A two-phase model is proposed that deals with the e-waste effectively. The end goal is to use technology on both the hardware and software side to minimize pollution, increase energy efficiency, and also encourage material recycling. The usage and benefits of Eco-ATMs are explored in this paper. With regards to green computing, implementing it is getting simpler to a great extent because of the software and hardware solutions that permit one to adopt green standards. They likewise apply to all classes of systems. These green practices could revolutionize the industrial processes and operations which could be achieved efficiently by the following practices. First, by utilizing the energy resources that are in use to the maximum extent. Second, by disposing of the e-waste that is generated from the industrial processes and operations. This paper explores finding efficient practices in the management of energy resources and e-waste. The proposed approach efficiently manages energy resources and e-waste in industries by employing green computing approaches.

Keywords: Green Computing, E-Waste Management, Energy Conservation, Green Computing Revolution, Environmental Pollution

1   INTRODUCTION

Green computing is the process of making effective use of computational resources. Modern IT systems rely on a complex mix of people, networks, and frameworks as such a green computing strategy must be systemic in nature and should address more nuanced issues. Green computing is the utmost necessity in today's highly competitive world for protecting the environment and saving electricity along with operating expenses. Research on what kind of energy gains and operational gains can be achieved is important. It is therefore needed to examine the difference between what is seen today and what has to be done in order to obtain the advantages of Green computing. Each big change, too, begins with little initiatives. For example, some of the easy but successful interventions are setting the power options for switching to sleep mode when the computer or phones are not working. If the user is more than a few minutes away from the device, setting it to standby mode and switching off the monitor would save a massive amount of electricity. Interestingly, companies in every industry, from pseudo-profits to consumer goods, pay much more attention to their energy bills, as the amount spent on data center power has almost doubled in six years. The great news is that computer companies are thinking about sustainability and heading toward green programs. The rest of the paper is organized as follows. Section 2 presents the previous work, Section 3 gives e-waste management including its situation in India, Section 4 discusses the proposed approach, Section 5 explores the e-waste management case study and analysis, Sections 6 and 7 explain inferences and summary, and Section 8 concludes the paper.

DOI 10.1201/9781003167488-15

Grant et al. (2013) collated information from multiple datasets to examine the different components in electronic equipment, the source of exposure and its route of contamination by processing them in unhealthy ways. They have also analyzed the different categories of the population exposed to respective primary contaminants and their health effects by studying various other case studies by Ju et al. (2008), Yuan et al. (2008), Zhang et al. (2010), Wu et al. (2012), and Xu et al. (2012).

Robinson (2009) estimated the global e-waste production and predicted the future trends of e-waste production in the world. The authors have also mentioned the potential environmental contaminants contained in e-waste and its harmful consequences to e-waste workers, majorly of poor countries, through contact by skin and inhalation when the e-waste is burned off or undergoes dissolution by acid, also leading to contamination in the water and food chains in the local area.

Wath et al. (2011) discussed the composition of e-waste and the way they are categorized. The authors examined the e-waste management system in India where they mention the improper recycling methods used by the laborers and workers, causing serious environmental issues in India by contaminating the air, water, and land ecosystems. The e-waste management scenarios in countries like the U.S., UK and China, which includes the schemes implemented and the policies enforced by the respective governments, have been discussed. They have also presented with the treatment and processing options for e-waste to minimize the contamination in the environment.

Anam & Syed (2013) concentrated on applying green computing techniques by recycling to e-waste management. They planned to address the green policies in the computer industry and the concerns that had been posted about the initiatives and presented a report on the process of green computing and e-waste recycling. The authors concluded that the overall results of green computing are all positive, with its advantages, practicality, and uses. The impacts of green computing were wonderful not only for the user but for the whole globe as well.

Dominguez-Garcia & Hadjicostis (2010) speak about the use and application of distributed sources of energy. Many ancillary services are provided by the distribution side of the smart grid. The individual capacity of these resources to provide grid assistance may be quite limited, and their presence in significant numbers in many distribution channels means that they can collaboratively become an advantage for the provision of support services under adequate supervision. The photo-voltaic array mounts on a residential roof in a power electronics interface could provide a range of ancillary services. The author develops and analyzes distributed control strategies to allow certain distributed tools used for grid support services.

Ghamkhari and Mohsenian-Rad (2012) claim that they will have a significant approach to tackling the challenges of leveraging renewable sources of energy due to the flexibility of workloads in the Internet and cloud computing data centers. The data centers could be run with on-site renewable generators which would greatly reduce not only the energy consumption of data centers but also their carbon footprint. To achieve these goals, the authors suggest that the workload be optimally distributed among geographically scattered data centers according to the different types of available renewable energy resources in that geographic area. Many simulations were run, and Quality of Service (QoS) was ensured by tracking the queue lengths in real-time and effectively stabilizing the short queue lengths at each data center.

Roldan-Blay et al. (2017) suggested a new algorithm (DEROP - Distributed Energy Resources Optimization) for efficient control of the distributed energy resources in distributed generation facilities. DEROP's goal was to reduce energy supply costs in power hubs. Different types of energy storage systems and energy charges are built such as energy hubs. Their proposed algorithm iteratively manages each resource's energy flow optimally to achieve a cost-effective availability for data centers and data storage units to supply and demand. Eight different energy hub scenarios were simulated to demonstrate the algorithm's operation. Results show a strong degree of energy resource optimization by the efficient use of renewable energy sources and effective management of energy storage systems. It is concluded that the application of DEROP will achieve substantial cost savings (over 50%).

Bezakova (2013) commented on the need for sustainable computing and different approaches to implementing it. They noticed that one of the key factors of green computing was the consumer and had driven the businesses to look at the markets and consumers as the main drivers of their industry in the field of sustainable computing and concentrate on customer requirements. The authors' contribution also included the findings of research into the Slovak companies' approach to sustainable computing in the business climate in Slovakia. The authors concluded that sustainable IT services are important to business success.

3 E-WASTE MANAGEMENT

E-waste is a global concern that must be dealt with appropriate care. Some authors (Jadhav 2013) have researched the composition of e-waste, scenarios for e-waste globally and in India, and the diverse hazardous materials contained in the e-waste. The best practices are described to identify the hazardous materials, instructions for the manufacturer, and public knowledge about the proper disposal of e-waste. Proper e-waste management will assist in inefficient procurement and recycling right up to material production and disposal, ensuring that this massive piling up of e-waste creates profitable goods and business opportunities.

The impacts can be mitigated by innovative improvements to product design under Extended Producer Responsibility (EPR) and the use of environmentally friendly alternatives for hazardous substances (Uddin 2012). The study included the main e-waste sources, e-waste materials, and e-waste composition. It also included the analysis of the health effects of some rising e-waste constituents. Some of the environmentally sound e-waste treatment technologies are determined and classified them as different levels of treatment.

Informal e-waste recycling not only is linked to significant health and environmental implications, but also to the dearth of supply of formal recyclers and the safety issues of renovated electronic goods. Incomplete combustion of e-waste in the open environment and the processing of raw materials are the main sources of different toxic chemicals. For instance, the concentration of the sum of 22 PBDE (poly-brominated di-phenyl ethers) congeners contained in PM2.5 (16.8 ng m3) of air samples at Guiyu was 100 times higher than published data when recorded on a monthly basis. Experience has always shown that simply prohibiting or competing with informal collectors and informal recyclers is not a viable measure. New formal e-waste recycling systems should be part of the mix of existing informal sectors and more policies need to be put in attempts to encourage recycling rates, work conditions, and the efficiency of the informal role players (Chi et al. 2011; Wong et al. 2007).

3.1 *E-waste management in India*

The practical overview of India's conventional (Bansal & Agrawal 2017) and sustainable power source situation is explained with sources. Traditional energy sources, coal- and mineral oil-based force plants, which intensively contribute to the emanation of ozone-damaging substances are responsible for the greater part of the force age in India. The wise use of copious renewable power source assets such as biomass electricity, sunlight-based energy, wind energy, geothermal energy, and ocean energy is necessary to cope with the energy emergency. India has also gained the use of an array of advances in renewable energy sources for use in different fields. New energy solutions are also being implemented right now to tackle challenges and implement sustainability for what is to come. An ever-expanding population (Shahzad 2012) means an ever-developing energy need. Carbon sources can be assigned as inexhaustible and non-renewable. A few applications of renewable sources and the ultimate energy fate are discussed. The importance of renewable energy well-springs inferable from the setting of petroleum product problems. Deciding to use a sustainable source of energy would not only turn over the long haul into expense reserve assets but will also help ensure the situation from the dangers of outflows of non-renewable energy sources. Crusades of energy conservation education need to be launched at the administration level to make individuals aware of the importance of energy rationing. Web-based social networking will play a key role for individuals right now as regards energy sources and their use. It is emphasized diminishing the energy and carbon footprint of computers (Sen & Chowdhury 2016) and its related resources like monitors and printers using green computing. The issues related to green computing, dynamics of green computing standards, and analytical views of green computing in Indian IT companies must be incorporated. The power consumption of computer monitors and printers are taken into consideration. People should use energy star certified products, avoid the use of CRTs (Cathode Ray Tube), and use LCDs (Liquid Crystal Display) or LEDs (Light Emitting Diodes). Power plans for desktops and laptops should be brought in to use and avoid the informal disposing of computers.

4 PROPOSED APPROACHES

4.1 *E-waste management*

As technology is continually becoming close to being regarded as one of the staples of mankind, the increase in the production, usage, and disposal of electronic goods containing hazardous elements is paving the way to be the cause of pollution in a direct manner. Nowadays, electronic goods are being specifically designed to have shorter life spans, enabling people to dispose of their older devices only to be replaced by new ones. E-waste collection is done in a formal and informal manner, the former being a rather expensive one and hence making the latter an easier method of handling it by exporting to developing countries where recycling is cheap. Incineration of electronic goods produces toxic fumes, affecting the health of the workers, in ways like premature births, reduced birth weights, malformations, etc., who are not availed with protective gear. While some ideas of overcoming the E-waste problem are still under research, there are a few ideas which are in practice around the world.

- Designing safer products, with lesser toxic materials, is one way to reduce e-waste. Chemical engineers from Stanford University are developing a biodegradable circuit to replace the existing semiconductor-based circuits. Other scientists are looking into ways of pulverizing the e-waste into nano-dust, cooling it, and grinding it into homogeneous materials for reuse.
- It is also important to keep in mind that the electronic device can be repaired than having the thought of disposing of it in the first place.
- Producers should be made responsible for the electronic products they produce and the proper handling or disposal of e-waste the products generate.
- Installation of Eco ATMs will encourage people to dispose of their electronic possessions to certified recycling companies.

Figure 1 represents the proposed methodology to handle e-waste. This methodology includes two phases of e-waste handling as described below.

1. *Initial Phase*
   The biodegradable raw material can be used to produce electronic circuits for electronic goods. These raw materials undergo the production process to produce components for electronic goods. The finished product can be used until a certain period until its working exhausts. Here, there are two options that the user can opt for:
   - Deposit the electronic good as an e-waste in Eco-ATMs (e-cycling phase)
   - Replace outdated/non-working parts with new ones and reuse the same product.
2. *E-Cycling Phase*
   - Deposit the electronic good as an e-waste in Eco-ATMs (e-cycling phase). Post this:
     1. The e-waste is collected from the Eco-ATMs.
     2. The e-waste is then sorted.
     3. Those materials and components that can be upgraded and refurbished go through the up-gradation process and are packaged.

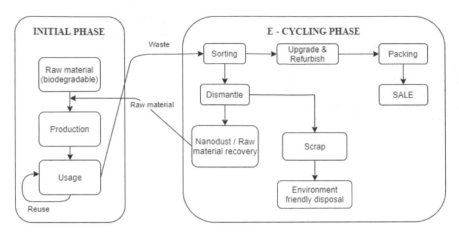

Figure 1. Method to handle e-waste.

4. The packed material can be then put up for sale.
5. For the components which cannot be upgraded, the materials can be dismantled which in most cases will lead to raw material recovery. This raw material may not be in a suitable form or shape so it is pulverized to nano-dust and this nano-dust can be used in the production process as a suitable raw material.
6. In cases where dismantled components are not useful, it can be categorized as scrap and can be disposed of in an environmentally friendly way.

• Considering the second option, the users can minimize the waste generated from their part by replacing outdated components with new ones while the skeleton of the electronic goods remain the same.

The e-waste statistics (Global E-waste Statistics Partnership 2019) of India, Italy, France, and U.S. are given below

Table 1. E-waste statistics—A comparison.

Metrics	India	Italy	France	U.S.
E-waste generated (in metric tonnes)	1.975	1.156	1.373	6.295
E-waste put on market (in metric tonnes)	3.276	1.137	1.567	8.109
E-waste generated (kg per capita)	1.5	18.9	21.3	19.4

where the metrics derived from (Eurostat 2018; Forti et al. 2018) can be formulated as:

$$Ewaste_{generated} = W_{formal} + W_{bin} + W_{others} \tag{1}$$

$$EEE_{Put\ On\ Market} = W_{domestic} + W_{import} - W_{export} \tag{2}$$

$$Ewaste_{PerCapita} = Ewaste_{generated}/population \tag{3}$$

where EEE = Electronic and Electrical Equipment; $Ewaste_{generated}$ = the size of the national e-waste market; $EEE_{Put\ On\ Market}$ = the size of the national e-goods market; $Ewaste_{PerCapita}$ = the amount of e-waste generated by a person in the country; W_{formal} = weight of e-waste collected formally; W_{bin} = weight of e-waste found in waste bins; W_{others} = weight of e-waste from other recycling streams; $W_{domestic}$ = weight of electronic electrical goods produced in a nation; W_{import} = weight of electronic and electrical goods coming from other countries; and W_{import} = weight of electronic and electrical goods distributed to other countries.

The numbers in Table 1 indicate that the U.S. has been producing large amounts of electronic and electrical equipment and so it is implied that the amount of e-waste produced is a huge number. The major contributor to such huge numbers, across all countries, is the IT industry which uses large number of huge servers, laptops, monitors, and other computer equipment. In most organizations, this equipment is discarded after 3–4 years.

Application of the proposed methodology with reuse of those equipment until they last or donating them to schools and colleges, is bound to reduce the amount of equipment given out to the recycling industry. In case, the equipment is not fit for use again, the recycling phase will ensure that only components of the equipment are sorted which can be refurbished or can be used as a raw material in the production of these equipment.

4.2 *Approaches to energy conservation and e-waste minimization*

Several efficient practices of utilizing green energy resources and e-waste minimization are:

- A green computer's features will include performance, fabrication, and materials, recyclables, service model, self-powering.
- Just about 15% of the money is expended on computing out of $250 billion annually expended on running computers worldwide. The rest is unnecessary idling, something that can be stopped.
- Reversible computing which also includes quantum computing promises a factor of several thousand to reduce power consumption.
- Replacing plastic filled with petroleum with bioplastics which are polymers based on plants. They need less oil and resources than traditional plastics to manufacture.
- It is necessary to optimize computers that can be operated with reduced power from environmentally friendly energy sources such as solar energy, pedaling a bike, turning a hand crank, etc.
- Energetically effective display choices include:
    - Avoiding the use of video card.
    - Use of a shared terminal, shared thin client, or desktop sharing software if required.
    - Using video output on motherboard normally lowers 3D performance and power consumption.
- Instead of having one device for each service or collection of services, one should then integrate each server into a larger virtualized network that makes full use of its resources and has a much smaller footprint on electricity.
- According to a case study done on virtualization of data centers at Schneider Electric (Electric 2012), before virtualization,
    - The total IT load (75% loaded) was 90 kW
    - The total server load (66% loaded) was 59 kW
    - PUE = 2

where

$$PUE = TotalFacilityEnergy/TotalITEnergy \qquad (4)$$

After the virtualization of the data centers,

- The total IT load (42% loaded) was 52 kW
- The total server load 22 kW
- 75% of the servers were virtualized
- Server consolidation ratio - 20:1
- PUE = 2.5

Furthermore, the electric bill $193,213 to $140,305. This shows the drastic effect virtualization can have on savings.

5 E-WASTE MANAGEMENT: CASE STUDY AND ANALYSIS

Recent trends (Saha 2018) in green computing and sustainable strategies are more generally defined as methods and processes for designing and producing eco-sustainable use of computing resources while preserving overall computing efficiency and finally disposing of them in an order to reduce the environmental impact. The efforts are taken in several multinational entities to take steps to reduce the negative environmental effects of their operations. It is seen that the work will be more inclined to automate data centers and cloud computing services in the coming years. The importance of the green computing approach (Jain 2011) on the earth for the people and benefit to the so-called triple bottom line and introduce the principle of green chemistry. Power supply and power control could be better controlled and modulated to allow better use of electricity. Berkeley University has introduced an initiative that uses Auto Shutdown Manager and wireless power meters to track energy usage and real-time reductions. They highlight that a fast CPU could be the biggest user of power on a computer whose load could be minimized by making use of state-of-the-art GPUs with higher computing capacity. In conclusion, adopting green computing activities such as software, equipment, power storage, recycling materials, and the government will help to minimize global warming.

5.1 *Analysis of e-waste sources in India*

According to the joint ASSOCHAM-NEC study (Manju 2018), only 20%, i.e., 8.9 Metric tonnes of the total e-waste produced in 2016, is documented to be collected properly and recycled, while the remaining e-waste is not recorded.

The study also shows the numbers on which the electronic item contributes more to the e-waste. Computer equipment accounted for almost 70% of waste material, telecommunications equipment for 12%, electrical equipment for 8%, medical equipment for 7%, and other equipment for the remaining 3%, as shown in Figure 2.

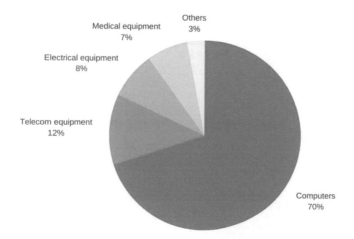

Figure 2.   Various e-waste sources in India.

6 INFERENCES

In 2019, the Indian government had proposed a resource efficiency policy. The requirement for such a policy is critical, as India's fast-paced economy consumes unsustainable resources, and the policy states that India has expanded its consumption of resources by six times, from 1.18 billion tons in 1970 to 7 billion tons in 2015. The recycling rates of India are much lower at 20–25% as compared to the European nations. With an annual growth of 30% of e-waste generated in the country, this methodology will enable a greener approach to e-waste management and increase the percentage of the materials recycled over time. Furthermore, the application of the methodology at an organizational level will also save them a huge amount of money by the utilization of recovered materials in e-waste that is fit to use as raw materials again during the production.

7 SUMMARY

Many IT industries, as well as academic institutions, should implement this green computing approach. There is debate about the implementation of this approach whether it is cost-effective or not. But many clients are very particular about the IT firms to follow green initiatives such as e-waste management. There are many issues associated with the implementation of this approach. The paper started with a discussion of e-waste, e-waste management situation in India, and presents an analysis of the green computing approach in India. Especially the developing country like India should incorporate the e-waste management so that the government will gain benefits with recycling and refurbishing. There are problems as well as solutions with this approach. It can be seen as the socio-economic gain. In order to achieve this proper planning and guidelines should be issued by the government. Environmental sustainability is achieved with green initiatives being followed by the IT sectors.

8 CONCLUSION

Green computing is not only beneficial from an economic point of view, but it is also important from an environmental point of view. They can help to mitigate global warming by adopting green computing practices such as software, hardware, power management, and material recycling. The approaches explored in this paper like the implementation and usage of Eco-ATMs will certainly impact the disposal and reuse of e-waste. Governments and telecommunications organizations are actively introducing new methodologies to reduce e-waste and allow more effective use of electricity. Authorities are now promoting electronic recycling to reduce e-waste. Energy utilization in industries could be optimized and will reduce the carbon footprint generated by the industries. Green computing definitely has come a long way, but with so many new technologies coming in with respect to protecting the environment, it is fair to assume that green computing is a fantastic step for a sustainable future.

REFERENCES

Anam, A. and A. Syed 2013, Green computing: E-waste management through recycling. *International Journal of Scientific & Engineering Research 4(5): 1103–1106.*
Bansal, S. and B. N. Agrawal 2017, Conventional and renewable energy scenario of India: present and future. *Invertis Journal of Renewable Energy 7(1): 29–34.*
Bezakova, Z. 2013, Green computing practices as a part of the way to the sustainable development. *IFIP Advances in Information and Communication Technology, 413: 579–587.*
Chi, X., M. Streicher-Porte, M. Y. Wang, and M. A. Reuter (2011). Informal electronic waste recycling: a sector review with special focus on china. *Waste Management 31(4): 731–742.*

Dominguez-Garcia, A. D. and C. N. Hadjicostis 2010, Coordination and control of distributed energy resources for provision of ancillary services. In *2010 First IEEE International Conference on Smart Grid Communications, pp. 537–542*. IEEE.

Electric, S. 2012, Energy efficiency data center overview.

Eurostat, E. 2018, Waste statistics-electrical and electronic equipment. November 2017.

Forti, V., K. Balde, and R. Kuehr 2018, E-waste statistics: Guidelines on classifications, reporting and indicators.

Ghamkhari, M. and H. Mohsenian-Rad 2012, Optimal integration of renewable energy resources in data centers with behind-the-meter renewable generator. In *2012 IEEE International Conference on Communications (ICC), pp. 3340–3344*. IEEE.

Grant, K., F. C. Goldizen, P. D. Sly, M.-N. Brune, M. Neira, M. van den Berg, and R. E. Norman 2013, Health consequences of exposure to e-waste: a systematic review. *The lancet global health 1(6), 350– 361.*

Jadhav, S. 2013, Electronic waste: A growing concern in today's environment sustainability. *International Journal of Social Science & Interdisciplinary Research 2(2): 139–147.*

Jain, N. 2011, Green computing practices: A solution to save environment. *International Journal of Advanced Research in Computer Science 2(3): 273–276.*

Ju, Y., G. Xu, L. Chen, and J. Shi 2008, Effects of the electronic waste pollution on the levels of thyroid hormone and its receptor expression in the parturient woman and the newborn. *Wei sheng yan jiu= Journal of hygiene research 37(5): 536–539.*

Manju Negi, A. S. 2018, India among the top five countries in e-waste generation: Assocham-nec study.

Robinson, B. H. 2009, E-waste: an assessment of global production and environmental impacts. *Science of the total environment 408(2), 183–191.*

Roldan-Blay, C., G. Escriva-Escriva, C. Roldan-Porta, and C. Alvarez-Bel 2017, An optimisation algorithm for distributed energy resources management in micro-scale energy hubs. Energy *132, 126–135.*

Saha, B. 2018, Green computing: Current research trends. *International Journal of Computer Sciences and Engineering 6(3): 467–469.*

Sen, D. and D. R. Chowdhury 2016, Green computing: Efficient practices and applications. *International Journal of Computer Sciences and Engineering, 4(1): 38–47.*

Shahzad, U. 2012, The need for renewable energy sources. *energy 2, 16–18.*

Uddin, M. J. 2012, Journal and confrence paper on (enviornment) e–waste management. *Journal of Mechanical and Civil Engineering 2(1): 25–45.*

Global E-waste Statistics Partnership, T. G. E. E-waste statistics, 2019.

Wath, S. B., P. Dutt, and T. Chakrabarti 2011, E-waste scenario in India, its management and implications. *Environmental monitoring and assessment 172(1-4): 249–262.*

Wong, M. H., S. Wu, W. J. Deng, X. Yu, Q. Luo, A. Leung, C. Wong, W. Luksemburg, and A. Wong 2007, Export of toxic chemicals–a review of the case of uncontrolled electronic-waste recycling. *Environmental Pollution 149(2): 131–140.*

Wu, K., X. Xu, L. Peng, J. Liu, Y. Guo, and X. Huo 2012, Association between maternal exposure to perfluorooctanoic acid (pfoa) from electronic waste recycling and neonatal health outcomes. *Environment international 48: 1–8.*

Xu, X., H. Yang, A. Chen, Y. Zhou, K. Wu, J. Liu, Y. Zhang, and X. Huo 2012, Birth outcomes related to informal e-waste recycling in Guiyu, China. *Reproductive Toxicology 33(1): 94–98.*

Yuan, J., L. Chen, D. Chen, H. Guo, X. Bi, Y. Ju, P. Jiang, J. Shi, Z. Yu, J. Yang, et al. 2008, Elevated serum polybrominated diphenyl ethers and thyroid-stimulating hormone associated with lymphocytic micronuclei in chinese workers from an e-waste dismantling site. *Environmental science & technology 42(6): 2195–2200.*

Zhang, J., Y. Jiang, J. Zhou, B. Wu, Y. Liang, Z. Peng, D. Fang, B. Liu, H. Huang, C. He, et al. 2010, Elevated body burdens of pbdes, dioxins, and pcbs on thyroid hormone homeostasis at an electronic waste recycling site in china. *Environmental science & technology 44(10): 3956–3962.*

Smart Computing – Khan et al (Eds)
© *2021 Taylor & Francis Group, London, ISBN 978-0-367-76552-1*

IoT-based skin disease: Monitoring a wearable application system

S. Juyal, S. Sharma, C. Kulshrestha, P. Juyal & A.S. Shukla
Graphic Era Deemed to be University, Dehradun, Uttarakhand, India

ABSTRACT: The paper proposes a wearable application system for Internet of Things- (IoT) based skin disease monitoring promoting two levels of classification, first to assist a physician in the diagnosis process and second to accurately track the pattern of recovery by monitoring. This device helps remote patients to attach at a remote location to a skin doctor. A novel approach for monitoring a patient's rehabilitation pattern is the proposed monitoring of the wearable application of IoT-based skin diseases. With machine learning, the program can identify and avoid skin disease to help doctors diagnose it. This also provides recovery charts based on severity levels in each follow-up plan for each condition. As part of a skin treatment and monitoring program, the suggested method of application can be implemented and referred to a doctor to diagnose and assess the patient more quickly. The device is being developed to collect patient data through image sensors (mobile-based). Automation based on machine learning is applied for skin disease detection and control.

1 INTRODUCTION

In recent years, with the emergence of the Internet of Things (IoT) and cloud technology, the healthcare industry has been dramatically changed. IoT-based health monitoring allows remote control, assistance for living, and other health services on request. In the field of healthcare, several researchers have suggested simple solutions for efficient health services by using various approaches. Skin surveillance is one of the evolving areas of healthcare that needs much attention, and which therefore focuses on the work suggested. This paper proposes an IoT-based system for monitoring wearable skin diseases, which allows a physician to track skincare patients remotely, including quicker diagnoses and daily monitoring. The program is built for people with skin conditions with or without skincare facilities at their location. The patient can photograph his ill skin; he can submit it on the diagnosis and reference website. The disease is identified automatically utilizing an algorithm of machine learning, and skin doctors access the information. Besides, the diseases are classified into various levels of severity and an index rating is assigned (rating 0–3) following a valid diagnosis of disease using classification data and physician experience. At each monitoring interval, the patient will upload the skin image, classify the level of severity of the application, and assign a seriousness index. These index values help to generate the patient recovery chart for recovery analysis during the surveillance phase. For a real-time skin monitoring system, the proposed system is applicable in a diagnostic device. Automation in the skin monitoring process of the proposed system will result in less diagnostic time. Automation reduces manual labor and is less vulnerable to human errors. A clear method for predicting success in recovery is proposed via the system. If the patient varies or if an adverse drug reaction is present, it is not so easily possible to remedy the condition in the manual system. Via easy use applications, the proposed work may play a key role in making skin monitoring far more available and affordable. Taking account of the capabilities of IoT technology, physically disabled patients will routinely visit a doctor to solve difficulties. The rest of the paper is organized as follows. Section 2 discusses work done in the field of skin monitoring using IoT. Section 3 discusses the methodology used for the

DOI 10.1201/9781003167488-16

proposed application system. Section 4 gives the result analysis of the proposed application system methodology followed by the conclusion in Section 5.

2   LITERATURE SURVEY

In the current section, we briefly describe research literature of skincare domain as much work has been done in the field of skin disease detection. This section discusses about the work done in the area so far. Deep convolutional neural networks, image classification algorithms, and data augmentation for detection and analysis of dermoscopic patterns and skin lesion are used by (Demyanov et al., 2016). Bhadula et al. (2019) discuss the classification of skin diseases using various machine learning methods and their comparative analysis. Wighton et al. (2011) proposed a supervised learning and MAP estimation-based model. It enables automated skin lesion diagnosis. Emre-Celebi et al. (2013) uses ensembles of thresholding methods to provide lesion borders detection in dermoscopy images. An IoT-based skin monitoring system that facilitates remote skin surveillance and helps patients in remote areas to access skincare services is proposed by Bhadula and Sharma (2020). An inventive method using support vector machine (SVM) and k-nearest neighbor algorithm was proposed by Ra et al. (2015). It performs auto segmentation and classification of skin lesions. Niu et al. (2006) experiments by applying the hue, saturation, value (HSV) color space and fuzzy C-means clustering algorithm on the color image of skin erythema. The result shows that dimensionality reduction can improve the time and precision of resulting segmentation. Ganeshkumar and Vasanthi (2017) detected the melanoma disease by applying preprocessing with edge detection technique to improve skin detection based on skin pixels, using different color models. Kotian and Deepa (2017) perform a study on auto-diagnosis skin disease system. Matlab software is used as a platform to implement image border identification and feature data mining. Kolkur et al. (2017) present a novel skin detection algorithm. Kumar and Singh (2016) relate skin cancer images through diverse types of neural networks and perform classification into different categories of skin cancer using Matlab. Esteva et al. (2017) used deep convolutional network to classify skin lesions. Their model was trained from images, using only pixels and disease labels on the input. Codella et al. (2017) proposed a technique for melanoma skin cancer detection. A combination of deep learning and proposed skin lesion ensemble method is used to propose a system. Schwarz et al. (2017) used ultra-imaging to present optoacoustic dermoscopy model. Skin analysis is proposed using the function of excitation energy and penetration depth measures. They presented the way to analyze absorption spectra at multiple wavelengths for visualization of morphological and functional skin features. A deep learning-based method for skin lesion and melanoma detection was proposed by Li and Shen (2018). The authors have discussed segmentation and feature extraction in relation with the center of melanoma by Lesions Indexing Network. Fully Convolutional Residual Network is used for detection. A review on skin disease diagnosis and detection using different machine learning algorithms is given by Pathan et al. (2018). Chao et al. (2017) present a comparative analysis of mobile apps for skin monitoring and melanoma detection. A comparison of different apps based on their potential in efficient image processing is given. The author also presented legal aspects of ethical, quality, and transparent development of apps for medical use. Lots of researchers have proposed there work so far in the area of skincare and IoT. This paper proposed a new approach that facilitates not only classification, but remote monitoring of patients by visualization of recovery patterns.

3   PROPOSED APPLICATION SYSTEM METHODOLOGY

This section describes the proposed application system methodology of the IoT-based skin monitoring system. The system is primarily designed to provide skin care for people living in remote areas with or without skin care facilities. The system also provides doctors in the diagnosis and monitoring process with the regular use of classification algorithms to predict the disease and its severity.

Before receiving care, patients and physicians must participate in the application through registration. Specific skin disorders are kept in a database and each disease is classified according to the guidance of the doctor in various rates of severity. Two phases of the scenario are explained. The first phase consists of a diagnostic aid and the second phase is a graphical and extreme control. The proposed scenario is illustrated in Figure 1.

Phase 1. Diagnosis Assistance phase mainly focuses on the classification of skin disease among several existing skin diseases available in the database. The patient uploads the skin picture after the application has been successfully registered. The picture is stored in the cloud from the computer and is graded using the algorithm. The classification algorithm forecasts the disease and produces the findings for the physicians. A registered doctor can access the picture at a remote location, predicted classification results, and the patient's basic information. The doctor diagnoses skin disease with his data and experience. In this way, this proposed application system can assist a doctor in making a fast diagnoses.

Phase 2. Severity check and graph generation phase starts after the correct diagnosis of the disease. In this phase, another classification algorithm runs to predict the severity of the disease. This is the second level of classification, performed to track the recovery of a patient. For the purpose of our work, each disease is sub-classified into four different levels according to their severity. Table 1 shows the different severity levels with the index number associated.

The image submitted by the patient is listed in four different grades (classes) and is identified with that picture by an index number corresponding to that grade. This index number generates a recovery graph that lets the doctor access the recovery history of the patient more easily, which

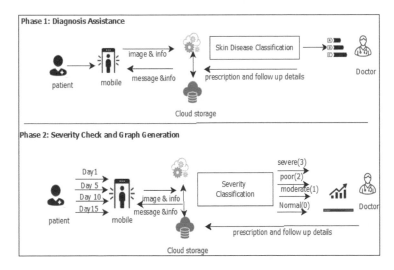

Figure 1. A scenario of IoT-based skin monitoring system.

Table 1. Different levels of severity.

S.No	Severity	Level index
1	Severe	3
2	Poor	2
3	Moderate	1
4	Normal	0

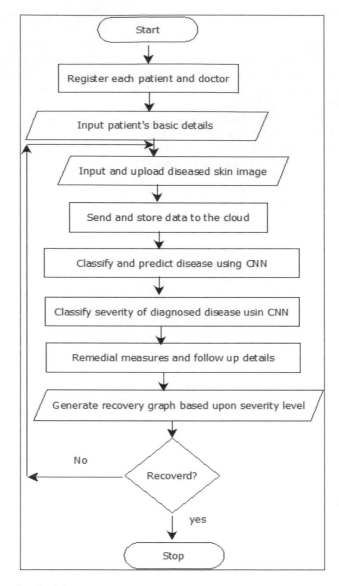

Figure 2. Proposed methodology.

follows additional medications. The following steps are defined for the proposed methodology used in remote skin monitoring and are also depicted in Figure 2.

Methodology Used:

1. Upload patient image.
2. Classify image and predict disease.
3. Classify the severity of the disease.
4. Allocate index according to severity.
5. Generate Recovery Graph.
6. Doctor's prescription and follow-up details.

4 RESULT ANALYSIS OF PROPOSED APPLICATION SYSTEM

In this article, three types of acne-type skin conditions could be described through the use of CNN, namely acne, Lupus Erythematosus, and SJS Ten; see Figure 3. Nearly 3000 skin samples for the creation and testing of the system have been collected. The pictures are taken at www.dermnetz.org. The dataset is separated into two sets, one for training (80%) and the other for testing (20%). The research data is qualified according to the disease in three different groups. The state of the skin is then graded and forecast with CNN.

Every disease's data set is further subcategorized into four classes according to its gravity: severe, poor, moderate, and normal (based on skin doctor's instructions). The patient is first authenticated and licensed.

The patient's skin picture will then be uploaded and stored in the cloud until registered. An algorithm for classification runs and predicts disease out of the available disease class database. The doctor will diagnose the illness and refresh the database for further evaluation in the absence of any of the diseases. The severity index is correlated with the disease after it is expected. The prescription and follow-up details are based on the severity. The patient uploads the image at each follow-up date and classifies the image as one of the four severity rates of the predicted disease. Increasing upload is associated with a severity index number that helps track the pattern of recovery.

A common angular front frame is used to build the Web application. MySQL database is used for data storage. Images are stored in the Cloud. PHP script files are used in the background to store and to access cloud data. The classification algorithm for producing PHP-acceding result is executed by a python script. The registration forms and simple forms that require a patient to register and log in using a mail id are shown in Figures 4 and 5. The figures indicates an application-classified disease based on the patient's image. During the monitoring intervals, Figure 7 shows the severity associated information. Figure 8 includes a detailed version of the graph, displaying the patient's recovery graph. Let X is a patient with a skin disorder. First, he sign in and enters his basic information and any previous medical records in the document. Patient X uploads the affected skin image which is processed in the cloud following positive registration. This picture is subsequently classified as acne by different groups of diseases. For diagnostic aid, a licensed doctor can access the report and the patient data and photos. If the condition has been confirmed, the patient will be provided with treatment and follow-up information. Patient X will upload his picture for monitoring again on the next monitoring day. At the beginning of the first follow-up, the acne condition for the patient was severe. Similarly, the photos are uploaded during each follow-up; the severity and index are established. In this way, the recovery pattern can be generated for each patient. At any point in time, patients and doctors can check recovery status. For patient X, recovery status is depicted through the graph given in Figure 8 as in order 3(severe), 3(severe), 2(poor), 2(poor), 0(normal), and 1(moderate) in different follow-up intervals. This graph is a novel idea to assist a doctor to monitor the recovery of the patient and also patient

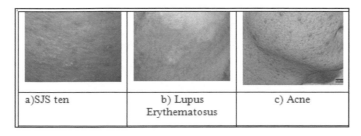

Figure 3.   Different categories of diseases.

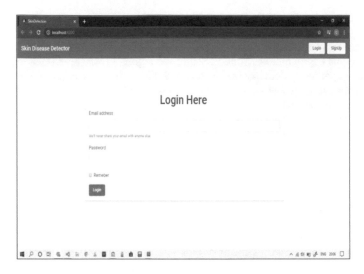

Figure 4. Login page for patients.

Figure 5. Detail entry form for patients.

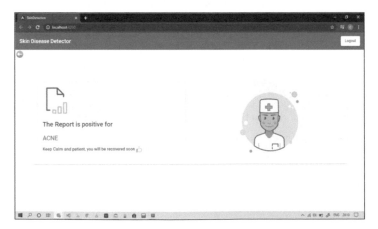

Figure 6. Report after diagnosis of disease.

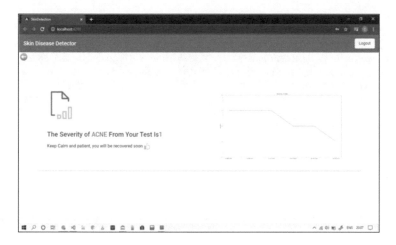

Figure 7. Severity level details of a patient after follow up.

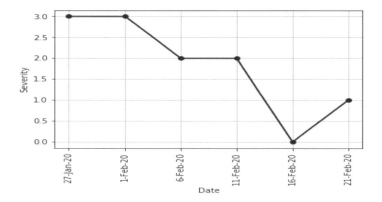

Figure 8. Recovery graph.

can track his recovery. Based on the recovery pattern prescription and follow up details can be updated.

5 CONCLUSION

The detection of skin disease is still in its infancy among the different areas of healthcare. Machine learning algorithms may be used to improve the process of skin-related identification and monitoring. Here we suggest a new application framework that can be part of the skin diagnostic system for the remote diagnosis and monitoring of skin disease. This proposed method of application will help skin doctors identify and track patients crossing their physical frontiers with their skin problems. We used the affected skin image (image sensor) as the main parameter for diagnosing and monitoring the patient in this proposed application. For research and implementation, minimal medical data are available. We will be able to incorporate temperature, moisture, tewl, and other skin sensors in the future to make the diagnosis and monitoring more effective and better. When properly applied, technology offers ample resources and a cohesive approach to the prevention of skin problems. This allows patients and doctors to treat skin diseases promptly.

REFERENCES

Bhadula, S. & Sharma, S. 2020. IoT-Based Skin Monitoring System. *International Journal of Recent Technology and Engineering (IJRTE). ISSN: 2277–3878, Volume-8 Issue-5, January 2020.*

Bhadula, S., Sharma,S., Juyal, P. & Kulshrestha, C. 2019. Machine Learning Algorithms based Skin Disease Detection. *International Journal of Innovative Technology and Exploring Engineering (IJITEE) ISSN: 2278–3075, Volume-9 Issue-2, December 2019.*

Chao, E., Meenan, C.K. & Ferris, L.K. 2017. Smartphone-based applications for skin monitoring and melanoma detection. *Dermatologic clinics, 35(4), pp.551–557.*

Codella, N.C., Nguyen, Q.B., Pankanti, S., Gutman, D.A., Helba, B., Halpern, A.C. & Smith, J.R. 2017. Deep learning ensembles for melanoma recognition in dermoscopy images. *IBM Journal of Research and Development, 61(4/5), pp.5–1.*

Demyanov, S., Chakravorty, R., Abedini, M., Halpern, A. & Garnavi, R. 2016. Classification of dermoscopy patterns using deep convolutional neural networks. *In 2016 IEEE 13th International Symposium on Biomedical Imaging (ISBI) (pp. 364–368). IEEE.*

Emre Celebi, M., Wen, Q., Hwang, S., Iyatomi, H. & Schaefer, G. 2013. Lesion border detection in dermoscopy images using ensembles of thresholding methods. *Skin Research and Technology, 19(1), pp.e252–e258*

Esteva, A., Kuprel, B., Novoa, R.A., Ko, J., Swetter, S.M., Blau, H.M. & Thrun, S. 2017. Dermatologist-level classification of skin cancer with deep neural networks. *Nature, 542(7639), pp.115–118.*

Ganeshkumar, M. & Vasanthi, J.J.B. 2017. Skin disease identification using image segmentation. *International Journal of Innovative Research in Computer and Communication Engineering, 5(1), pp.154–160.*

Khan, M. A. (2020), An IoT Framework for Heart Disease Prediction Based on MDCNN Classifier, *in IEEE Access*, vol. 8, pp. 34717–34727, 2020. DOI: 10.1109/ACCESS.2020.2974687

Khan M.A, and Algarni F., (2020) "A Healthcare Monitoring System for the Diagnosis of Heart Disease in the IoMT Cloud Environment Using MSSO-ANFIS," *in IEEE Access*, vol. 8, pp. 122259–122269, 2020, doi: 10.1109/ACCESS.2020.3006424.

Khan, M. A., Quasim, M. T, et al., (2020), A Secure Framework for Authentication and Encryption Using Improved ECC for IoT-Based Medical Sensor Data, *in IEEE Access*, vol. 8, pp. 52018–52027, 2020. DOI: 10.1109/ACCESS.2020.2980739

Kolkur, S., Kalbande, D., Shimpi, P., Bapat, C. & Jatakia, J. 2017. Human skin detection using RGB, HSV and YCbCr color models. *arXiv preprint arXiv:1708.02694.*

Kotian, A.L. & Deepa, K. 2017. Detection and classification of skin diseases by image analysis using MATLAB. *International Journal of Emerging Research in Management and Technology, 6(5), pp.779–784.*

Kumar, S. & Singh, A. 2016. Image processing for recognition of skin diseases. *International Journal of Computer Applications, 149(3), pp.37–40.*

Li, Y. & Shen, L. 2018. Skin lesion analysis towards melanoma detection using deep learning network. *Sensors, 18(2), p.556.*

Niu, H.J., Shang, K.K. & Liu, Y. 2006. Study of segmenting skin erythema images by reducing dimensions of color space. *Computer Engineering and Applications, 13(3), pp.219–221.*

Pathan, S., Prabhu, K.G. & Siddalingaswamy, P.C. 2018. Techniques and algorithms for computer aided diagnosis of pigmented skin lesions-A review. *Biomedical Signal Processing and Control, 39, pp.237–262.*

Ra, S., Suhilb, M. & Guruc, D.S. 2015. Segmentation and classification of skin lesions for disease diagnosis. *Procedia Computer Science, 45, pp.76–85.*

Schwarz, M., Soliman, D., Omar, M., Buehler, A., Ovsepian, S.V., Aguirre, J. & Ntziachristos, V. 2017. Optoacoustic Dermoscopy of the Human Skin: Tuning Excitation Energy for Optimal Detection Bandwidth With Fast and Deep Imagingin vivo. *IEEE transactions on medical imaging, 36(6), pp.1287–1296.*

Wighton, P., Lee, T.K., Lui, H., McLean, D.I. & Atkins, M.S. 2011. Generalizing common tasks in automated skin lesion diagnosis. *IEEE Transactions on Information Technology in Biomedicine, 15(4), pp.622–629.*

Smart Computing – Khan et al (Eds)
© *2021 Taylor & Francis Group, London, ISBN 978-0-367-76552-1*

IoT-based health monitoring system for infants

U. Chauhan, C. Tripathi & R. Yadav
SEECE, Galgotias University

ABSTRACT: This study defines an infant health monitoring system for working parents so that the parents can always have an eye on their loved ones. This system uses wireless sensor networks and the Internet of Things (IoT) to provide many lifesaving health parameters as well as video and audio of the infant. Arduino Uno microcontroller is the central processing unit of the system and it is used to control all the sensors. The system uses different sensors to provide many real-time health parameters, on the mobile phones of the parents. It also provides wakeup and crying alert messages to the parents. All the sensed data received from the sensors will be sent to the Cloud. The Cloud will then manipulate the data according to the parents' needs. The system can be deployed anywhere in any possible way as per the user.

Keywords: wireless sensor networks, IoT, Arduino Uno, cloud.

1 INTRODUCTION

It is really hard to take care of a little one especially when parents are working. While taking care of infants there are several things which usually parents forget and all they need is a message/alert on time, to do those small but important tasks for an infant. The proposed system acts like a warning system which will detect baby's health parameters and warn the parents about their child's health. This system can also send the collected or sensed data of infants to the concerned authority using the internet or even the radio signals, if required. Since the beginning of time, people have always had intentions to protect their newly born infants from different diseases. However, the way of caring is changed with the changing technology (Cao et al. 2007; Chowdary & Aruna 2011). Now babies are being cared for using different technologies and engineering inventions. In the 21st century, 95% of humans are busy in their own life. A health monitoring system for infants can be a quick fix for caring for infants accurately rather than keeping them in a childcare center or appointing a human for the infants. Always having an eye on a newborn baby is a tough job, and it is near to impossible for the parents to take their kids out with them especially when they are out for work. Hiring a nanny for newborns is an option. These approaches may not satisfy the parents and may not be able to fulfill their needs. In both methods, parents cannot fully trust the humans appointed for the caring of their baby (Aktas et al. 2017). For this angle, a monitoring system for newborn babies could be one of the most preferred solutions which will decrease parents' stress and concern.

2 LITERATURE REVIEW

An advanced system of automatic checking systems for infant care was explained in another paper and this paper explains a microcontroller-based system. In this study, the authors built an inexpensive system which can detect the noise when the baby starts to cry, and this noise detection system is connected to a system which swings the cradle of the baby. Once the system detects the noise, the swing system swings the cradle. The system will not stop swinging the cradle until the baby stops crying. A camera is also used in this system to provide live videos of the baby and baby's surroundings.

Another baby care system has been proposed by Savita P. Patil and Manisha R. Mhetre (2014). This system uses a global system for mobile communications (GSM) module. This infant monitoring system can sense body temperature, moisture, pulse rate, and movement of the baby and send these data using a GSM module. The central controlling unit in this system is a microcontroller.

Kranti Dive & Gitanjali Kulkarni (2013) proposed an infant monitoring system using a microcontroller. The system proposed in this paper has a door sensor, LDR sensor, and a sound sensor for monitoring babies. LED is used to display the sensed data and a buzzer is also connected which notify the parents in case of an anomaly.

3 SYSTEM ARCHITECTURE

Block diagram in Figure 1 describes the layout of the proposed system. The Arduino microcontroller is a central controlling unit and used for controlling all the sensor units and to send data to the Cloud.

When the baby cries, the sound sensor will detect it and send signals about it to the microcontroller. The PIR motion sensor will detect the baby's movement and inform the Arduino if something unusual happens. A camera will also be there in this system to get the live video of the baby and its surrounding. A Wi-Fi module is attached to the Arduino to connect our system to the internet wirelessly. A moisture sensor will be placed underneath the baby's sleeping mattress to detect whether it is dry or wet. This moisture sensor will be sending real time data to the Arduino and when the mattress becomes wet, Arduino Uno will send an alert to the parents (Cao et al. 2007; Simon et al. 2017). Temperature sensor will measure the body temperature of the baby after a fixed interval of time or whenever required and send this data to the microcontroller. Arduino is then sending this data to the cloud. Similarly, the heartbeat sensor will be measuring the heartbeat and will be sending data to the Cloud. Arduino microcontroller will be sending the data to the cloud where the data will be stored and manipulated as per the need of the user. For example, if parents want data in a mobile application the Cloud will be sending data to that application or if in case parents want a straight text message, the Cloud will be sending alert messages to them.

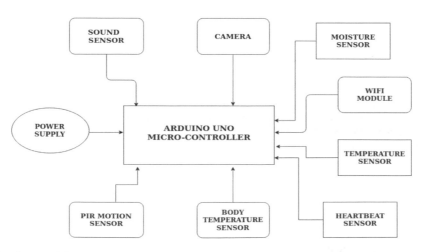

Figure 1.   Layout of the system.

3.1 *Components of the system*

- Arduino Uno
- Temperature sensor
- Moisture sensor
- Body temperature sensor
- Wi-Fi module
- Heartbeat sensor
- PIR motion sensor
- Sound sensor
- Camera module

- Arduino Uno

  The Arduino Uno is an open-source microcontroller which is based on the ATmega328P micro-controller. Arduino Uno is the central processing unit where all the sensed data gathers and is manipulated as per the code in the microcontroller. The Arduino Uno has 14 analog and digital input/output pins. These pins are used to interface Arduino Uno to different sensors and to different input/output devices. Arduino IDE is used to program Arduino Uno, via a type B USB cable (Palaskar et al. 2015; Smon et al. 2017).

- Temperature sensor - DHT11

  The DHT11 provides temperature and humidity of the surroundings. The DHT11 is connected to the Arduino using the digital input/output pins of the Arduino. This sensor provides temperature and humidity of the baby's room. It provides minimum 0°C and maximum 50°C temperature and minimum 20% and maximum 90% humidity with an accuracy of $\pm 1°C$ and $\pm 1\%$ which can be reduced by making some changes in the code.

- Moisture sensor

  Moisture sensor is an analog sensor which will detect the bed wetting by the baby. The moment water enters the mattress or nappy, the sensor output will be reduced, and vice versa will increase. By placing this sensor underneath the baby's mattress, the system can easily judge when the mattress should be changed hence making the baby more comfortable.

- Body temperature sensor - DS18B20

  In order to monitor the body temperature of the baby DS18B20 sensor module is used. The system uses a waterproof DS18B20 sensor module. Analog body temperature is taken from the sensor and changed to the actual temperature data using the microcontroller. The system can send real-time body temperature of the babies and can also generate an alert message, in case of an anomaly.

- Wi-Fi module - ESP8266

  The ESP8266 is a very inexpensive Wi-Fi module, with a full TCP/IP stack and can be easily connected to a microcontroller. Because of ESP8266 Arduino Uno is able to make simple TCP/IP connections by connecting to a Wi-Fi network. It supports serial communication hence compatible with Arduino Uno. ESP8266 is easily programmable with Arduino IDE.

- Heartbeat module - KY-039

  Heartbeat module counts the number of heartbeats in a minute. KY-039 uses IR LED and an optical transistor to detect pulsation in fingers. The sensor has two main components: the first one is an infrared phototransistor (sensor) and the second one is an infrared LED (IR LED). The amount of light passing through the finger which is in between the two components, i.e., IR LED and photoresistor. The heartbeat is sensed upon putting a finger on the sensor.

- PIR motion sensor

  Passive Infrared Motion Sensor is used to sense the motion of the baby. The PIR motion sensor has a range of up to 7 m which is adjustable. The system can be used with multiple motion sensors to increase the range. By using the PIR motion sensor the system can easily alert parents for any unusual moment of the baby.

- Sound sensor

  The sound sensor has a very sensitive capacitance mic for detecting different sounds. This module provides the noises around the baby. The sensitivity of the sound sensor is adjusted via the potentiometer on the sensor. The analog output voltage depends on the intensity of the sound received by the mic, so the threshold can be adjusted by the Arduino IDE code.
- OV7670 Camera module

  The camera module is used to provide real-time visuals of the baby. The Arduino IDE code can control image quality which includes hue, sharpness (edge enhancement), anti-blooming, color saturation, and color saturation. The OV7670 camera module can reduce noise, increase defect correction, and also support scaling and thus working properly even in harsh situations.

4   DESIGN AND IMPLEMENTATION

The hardware design of the system is presented by using mentioned peripherals and the cloud-based application. Data is taken from different experimental studies on infant health and infant caring and the data is used in this study.

4.1   *Hardware design*

As presented in Figure 2, the sensors used are finger heartbeat sensor, temperature sensor, body temperature sensor, camera module, moisture sensor, and sound sensor and are connected to the microcontroller Arduino Uno board via input ports on the board. The body temperature sensor should be touched either to the underarms or to the finger of the baby to get the precise results. The temperature sensor provides temperature as well as the perspiration around in the room of the baby. The moisture sensor should be placed in the baby's nappy or in the mattress for bedwetting detection. To collect the heartbeat data the finger of the infant should be touched to the sensor. Sound detection sensor detects different noises around the baby. It also detects the crying of the baby. The sound sensor is placed at a distance from the baby [1]. Camera module provides live videos when requested by the users. The ESP8266 connects the system to the internet.

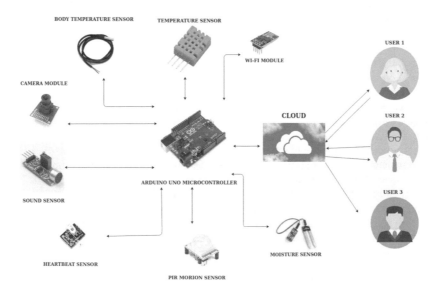

Figure 2.   Hardware connection diagram.

132

Table 1. Alarm codes and alarm conditions.

	ALARM CODE	ALARM CAUSES	ALARM CONDITION
1	A	High heartbeat	>135bpm
2	B	Low heartbeat	< 80bpm
3	C	High body temperature	>38 degree C
4	D	Low body temperature	<34 degree C
5	E	Bedwetting or perspiration	Wetness
6	F	Baby crying	Threshold value exceeded 15 times
7	G	Room temperature	According to the parents or weather

In the Arduino Uno microcontroller, first the data sensed from the different sensors are changed to digital data using the in-built analog-digital converter (ADC) module. After the modification of the analog data to the digital data, the digital data is used to determine the alarm circumstances. A set of alarms has been defined and each alarm has its own character. Alarm circumstances can be changed as per the user. The sensed data is compared with the predefined threshold values, these threshold values are taken from different experimental studies on infant health. A character code assigned to each alarm case (Cao et al. 2007). Character code or alarm code, different alarm cases and conditions related to these alarms are given in Table 1.

As presented in Table 1, an alarm is set up if the infant's body temperature goes above 38°C, character code C is assigned to this alarm condition. When the body temperature of the infant goes below 34°C an alarm would be generated with the character code D. An alarm is assigned to the high heartbeat condition with the character code A and for the low heartbeat condition character code B is assigned. Heartbeat conditions change with the age of infants. For example, 100–160 bpm (bit per minutes) are the heartbeat conditions for the 0–5 month-old baby whereas 80–140 bpm is for a 6–12 month-old baby.

In this study, the threshold values are taken from 80–135 bpm which is for 1–3 years. Character code E is assigned to the bedwetting and precipitation. For detection of baby crying, a sound level threshold is set. If this sound level reaches that threshold continuously or goes beyond threshold for a period of time, an alarm would be generated and character code F is assigned to it. For example, if the predefined value reaches the threshold value many times in a given period of time, let's say 10 sec, then an alarm will be created and parents will be notified. After an anomaly is detected by the microcontroller, it will send an alert to the cloud after which the parents will be notified. Alarms can be turned off the parents by a specific key on their mobile phones or on the website.

4.2 Cloud-based implementation

Microcontroller will send all the sense data to the cloud. As depicted in Figure 3, parents can opt for an Android-based application in which all the data and alert messages are sent to them by using an Android application or parents can use an SMS message notification in which the data and alert messages are sent to them by multiple SMS. Parents can also check the data on a website.

All the sensed data will be sent to the Amazon Web Services (AWS) cloud using MQTT protocol provides different cloud-computing platforms which will be used to manipulate the data and store the data. Once the data is stored it can be sent to the parents by using different AWS services. The system will use different AWS services.

a. AWS IoT Core
b. Amazon S3
c. AWS IoT Events
d. Amazon SNS
e. AWS Mobile Services

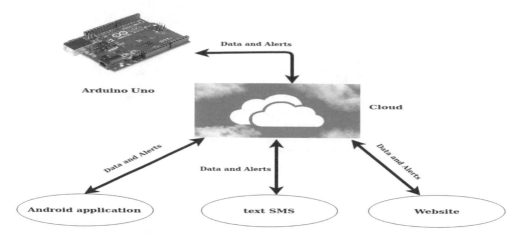

Figure 3.   Cloud-based application.

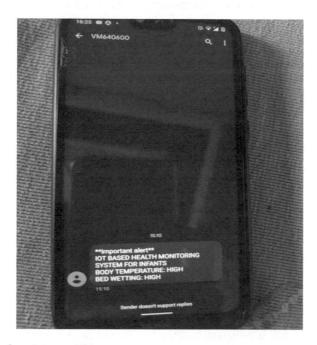

Figure 4.   Message from Amazon SNS.

- AWS IoT Core

    The microcontroller of the system is connected to AWS IoT Core. AWS IoT Core is a cloud service that lets different IoT devices securely and reliably connect to AWS. It also helps the system to use different AWS services easily. AWS IoT Core will be receiving messages from the Arduino. Once the messages are received it will be stored on AWS S3. AWS IoT Core can easily send the data to the HTTPS endpoint (website) by adding the required action. "Send a message to a downstream HTTPS endpoint" is the action required to send the data from the AWS IoT core to a specific website.

- AWS IoT Events

  AWS IoT Events is used to detect any anomaly and respond to that. AWS IoT Events will check for any anomaly/event in the data coming from the sensors and in case of an event it will take a predefined action. AWS IoT Events can be easily integrated with other services, which makes it more reliable for detecting an event and triggering action.

- Amazon Simple Storage Service (Amazon S3)

  Amazon S3 is an object storage service which will be used to store and protect the data coming from the microcontroller. Data stored in Amazon S3 will be sent to parents and could be used for future reference as well.

- Amazon Simple Notification Service (SNS)

  Amazon SNS will be used to provide notification to the parents. SNS is also a service provided by AWS. SNS will send the alert messages to the parents in case of an anomaly. Once the anomaly is detected by the AWS IoT Events it will take the action and command SNS to send the notification. SNS can send notifications to mobile users in more than 200 countries, hence SNS will also increase the range of the system.

- AWS Mobile Services

  All the data sensed from the sensors are displayed on an android application and AWS Mobile Services will be used to build and deploy the android application. This service will be integrated with other services like IoT Core, S3, and IoT Events to present the data to the parents.

5   CONCLUSION AND FUTURE SCOPE

This paper presents a real-time infant monitoring system for busy and working parents. The proposed system consists of sensors like finger heartbeat, body temperature, humidity and sound detection, a Arduino Uno microcontroller and AWS cloud-based application of the data collected from these sensors. In particular, the proposed system monitors the data and generates an alert for parents in case of an anomaly (Agios 2016).

The future scope of this system is that it can be developed using the more advanced microcontrollers. It can be implemented in a cradle or in the baby's room so that parents can know every bit of their baby in real time. The proposed system can be implemented with wireless sensors and with an Artificial Intelligence (AI) which will respond to the anomaly automatically and therefore parents will not be disturbed for every small things like when the baby starts crying the AI will detect and play a lullaby which will send the baby to sleep.

REFERENCES

Agezo, S. Zhang, Y., Ye, Z. Chopra, S. Vora, S. & Kurzweg, T. 2016. Battery-Free RFID Heart Rate Monitoring System, *IEEE Wireless Health (WH), Bethesda, MD,2016, pp. 136–142.*

Aktaş Faruk, Kavus, Emre, Kavus, Yunus. 2017. A Real-Time Infant Health Monitoring System for Hard of Hearing Parents by using Android-based Mobile Devices. *Journal of Electrical and Electronics Engineering,IU-JEEE Vol. 17(1), (2017), 3107–3112.*

Cao, H., Hsu, L-C, Ativanichayaphong, T, Sin, J. & Chiao, J-C. 2007.A non-invasive and remote infant monitoring system using CO2 sensors. *IEEE Sensors 2007 Conference, Atlanta, USA, 2007, pp. 989–992.*

Chowdary, P.S. & Aruna, S. 2011. Infant Monitoring System, *International Journal of Computer Science and Communication, vol. 2, no. 2, pp. 501–503, July-December, 2011.*

Deng, H. & Chen, S. Design and implementation of Android-based health and healthcare system.2016. *International Wireless Communications and Mobile Computing Conference (IWCMC), Paphos, CYPRUS,2016, pp. 164–169.*

Dive, P. & Kulkarni, P. 2013.Design of Embedded Device for Incubator for the Monitoring of Infants, *International Journal of Advanced Research in Computer Science and Software Engineering, vol. 3, no. 11, pp. 541–546, 2013.*

Khan M. A., (2020), An IoT Framework for Heart Disease Prediction Based on MDCNN Classifier, *in IEEE Access,* vol. 8, pp. 34717–34727, 2020. DOI: 10.1109/ACCESS.2020.2974687

Khan M.A, and Algarni F., (2020) "A Healthcare Monitoring System for the Diagnosis of Heart Disease in the IoMT Cloud Environment Using MSSO-ANFIS," *in IEEE Access*, vol. 8, pp. 122259–122269, 2020, doi: 10.1109/ACCESS.2020.3006424.

Khan, M.A., Quasim, M.T, et.al, (2020), A Secure Framework for Authentication and Encryption Using Improved ECC for IoT-Based Medical Sensor Data, *in IEEE Access*, vol. 8, pp. 52018–52027, 2020. DOI: 10.1109/ACCESS.2020.2980739

Palaskar, S. Pandey, A. Telang, A. Wagh and R. Kagalkar,R.2015. An Automatic Monitoring and Swing the Baby Cradle for Infant Care. *International Journal of Advanced Research in Computer and Communication Engineering, vol. 4, no. 12, pp. 187–189, 2015.*

Patil, S. & Mhetre, M. 2014. Intelligent Baby Monitoring System, *ITSI Transactions on Electrical and Electronics Engineering, vol. 2, no. 1, pp. 11–16, 2014.*

Rashid, Humayun, Ahmed, Iftekhar Uddin, Das, Remon, Reza, S.M. Taslim. 2017. Emergency Wireless Health Monitoring System using Wearable Technology for Refugee Camp and Disaster Affected People, *International Conference on Computer, Communication, Chemical, Materials and Electronic Engineering IC4ME2-2017, 26–27 January, 2017, pp. 144–147, 2017.*

Symon, Aslam Forhad, Hassan, Nazia, Rashid, Humayun, Ahmed, Iftekhar Uddin, Reza S.M. Taslim. 2017. Design and Development of a Smart Baby Monitoring System based on Raspberry Pi and Pi Camera. *4th International Conference on Advances in Electrical Engineering, Dhaka, 10.1109/ICAEE.2017.8255338.*

Smart Computing – Khan et al (Eds)
© 2021 Taylor & Francis Group, London, ISBN 978-0-367-76552-1

Smart irrigation system using IoT

P. Kumari
Department of Computer Science & Engineering, GBPIET, Pauri Garhwal, India

S.K. Singh
Department of Electronics & Communication Engineering, ABESEC, India

ABSTRACT: Nowadays, the whole world is using smart and automation-based systems through which one can benefit in terms of time and profit margin. These days technology affects all the fields such as automobile, irrigation system, etc., where manual systems are replaced. Now keeping this view in mind, this project is based on a smart irrigation system implemented using the Arduino-Uno microcontroller. The smart irrigation system consists of an Arduino-Uno, temperature sensor, humidity sensor, and control mechanism for water flow. The information getting from humidity sensor and temperature sensor will forward to data monitoring system by Arduino-Uno. At the monitoring place, the temperature and humidity levels are monitored and decided that which type of crops are presently in the field and how much moisture they need and then any decrease in wetness level below a limit will show the need for water and signal is given to the water pump for the water flow. As soon as the humidity sensor reading reaches a specific value the water pump will automatically turned off.

Keywords: Moisture sensors, Temperature sensor, Arduino-Uno, Microcontroller, IoT

1 INTRODUCTION

Around 70% of the Indian population directly or indirectly depends upon agriculture which is one of the major portions of India's GDP with a 17–18% share as per KPMG report and plays a major role in the Indian economy. Therefore, for economic growth of the country the development in the agricultural sector is necessary. Unfortunately, in India most of the farmers still use traditional irrigation methods which are manually operated. These irrigation systems become outdated and must be replaced with the latest smart systems.

Here, this project focuses mainly on minimizing the wastage of water and reduces the manual man power for irrigation (Gupta et al. 2016). The advancement in soil water monitoring with the smart devices make the commercial application of that system becomes useful for agriculture. The system is programmed in such a way that it can irrigate the field at regular time interval for predefined.

Due to the vastly distinct weather and soil conditions a variety of crops are cultivated in India. We know that water is one of the major parts that are required for the growth of the crop and the irrigation cost is also an important factor for the crop production cost. Table 1 shows few crops that are farmed in different seasons which are mainly based on the temperature and moisture available in the land. Using the availability of such a type of data, one can use a smart irrigation system for watering the land as per the requirement of the crop at that time or season, which will minimize the wastage of water as well as reducing the crop production cost.

DOI 10.1201/9781003167488-18

Table 1. Crops with temperature and humidity.

Crops	Temperature	Humidity
Rice	25–35°C	80%
Wheat	10–25°C	50–60%
Barley	16°C	40%
Maize	21–27°C	60%
Cotton	21–30°C	20%
Jute	25–30°C	70%

2 SYSTEM ARCHITECTURE

This block diagram shows that all components such as relay driver and temperature sensor are connected with the Arduino-Uno microcontroller and fixed on the printing circuit board and connected.

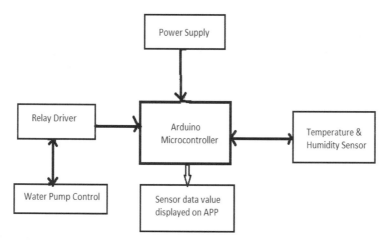

Figure 1. Block diagram of proposed system.

The main components that have used in this project are as follows

2.1 Arduino-Uno microcontroller

The Arduino-Uno iisi a imicrocontroller that is based ion itheiATmega328. It is ian i8-bit microcontroller iwith i32 KB iof iflash imemory iand i2KB iof iRAM (Gupta et al. 2016). iIt ihas i14 idigital input/output pins (6 ican ibe iused ias iPWM ioutputs, 6 ianalog iinputs),ia 16-MHz icrystal ioscillator, aiUSB connection, ia ipower ijack, ian iICSP iheader, iand ia ireset ibutton. It contains everything that needs to assist the microcontroller; simply connect it to a computer with a USB cable or power it with a AC-to-DC adapter or banery to turn into the start phase (Badamasi 2014).

a. *Temperature and Humidity Sensor*

SHT10 is a fully calibrated humidity and temperature sensor. It integrates sensor elements for humidity and temperature along with signal processing circuitry in a tiny package. It uses a capacitive sensor element for measuring relative humidity. For measuring temperature, it uses a band-gap sensor.

Figure 2.   Arduino-Uno board.

Pin	Name	Comment
1	GND	Ground
2	DATA	Serial Data, bidirectional
3	SCK	Serial Clock, input only
4	VDD	Source Voltage
NC	NC	Must be left unconnected

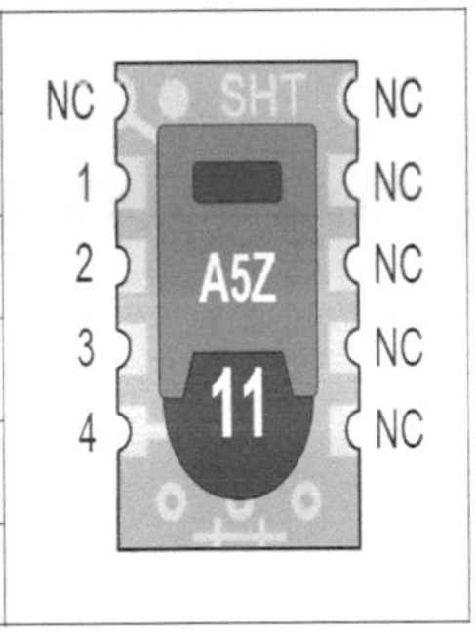

Figure 3.   Block diagram of SHT10.

b. *Relay Driver*

The one of the advantages using Arduino is that it can control higher voltage (120–240 V) devices such as fan, motors, lights, and other domestic appliances. The Arduino directly cannot control these devices because of its low operating voltage (5V). But using a 5 V relay it can switch the 120–240 V current and control the devices (Kansara et al.).

5V Relay Terminals and Pins

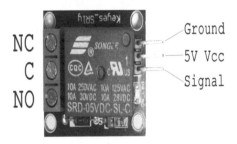

Figure 4.   Relay driver.

3   IMPLEMENTATION

This project is intended to design a smart irrigation system which switches the water pump on/off through sensing the humidity available in soil. In the field the use of proper irrigation is vital. But

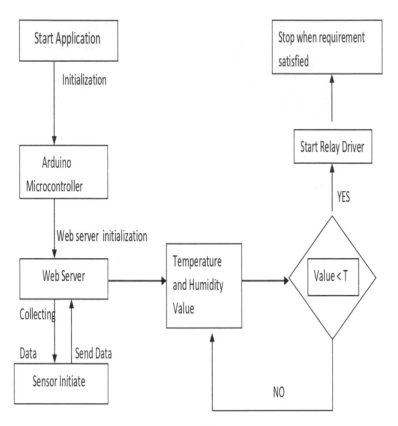

Figure 5.   Flow chart of proposed system.

using this type of advanced technology the irrigation will be better and reduces the wastage of water. In sensor-based Automated Irrigation System with IOT during which the irrigation will occur whenever there's a change in temperature and humidity of the environment. The flow of water is managed by a pump control mechanism. The flow of water is completed when a proof is sent through the microcontroller. The water to the basis of plant is completed and when the moisture level again become normal then sensor senses it and send a proof to microcontroller and also the flow mechanism stops working. When the soil moisture becomes a low-moisture sensor SHT10 senses and send a signal to microcontroller, then the microcontroller gives the signal to mobile and it activate the buzzer. This buzzer indicates that pump control mechanism has to be opened by pressing the button within the called function signals are sent back to the microcontroller. The microcontroller can increase system life and lower the facility consumption. There are two basic types of control for smart irrigation systems, weather-based and soil-based, each varying in its technical method of sensing and supplying information. The soil-based irrigation system is used here.

The device has three major parts: temperature and humidity sensing part, control section, and also the output section. SHT10 soil sensor (a resistance-type sensor) is used to detect the soil humidity and the ATMega328 microcontroller supported Arduino platform is used to control the device.

The designed irrigation system which is controlled by the control unit by switching it on and off counting on the soil moisture contents. Two stages of design were undertaken: hardware and software.

4 CONCLUSION

The designed irrigation system is cost effective and optimizes the wastage of water for agriculture production. The proposed system is simpler in use and turn-on/turn-off the water sprinkler depending upon the soil moisture levels. Therefore, through this device it can be concluded that there can considerable development in irrigation system with automation. Thus, this proposed system can be a solution for the problem faced by farmers in the traditional irrigation process.

REFERENCES

Abuhasel K. A. and M. A. Khan, (2020),"A Secure Industrial Internet of Things (IIoT) Framework for Resource Management in Smart Manufacturing," in IEEE Access, vol. 8, pp. 117354-117364, 2020, doi: 10.1109/ACCESS.2020.3004711.

Badamasi, Y.A. 2014. The working principle of an Arduino. *Electronics, Computer and Computation (ICECCO), 11th International IEEE Conference,* 2014.

Gluhak, A., Krco, S., Nati, M., Pfisterer, D., Mitton N., Razafindralambo, T. 2011. A survey on facilities for experimental Internet of Things research, *IEEE Communications Magazine 49,2011:58–67.*

Guru, S.G, Manoj, Naveen, P. , Raja, R.Vinodh, Nachiyar, V.Srirenga. 2017. SMART IRRIGATION SYSTEM USING ARDUINO SSRG *International Journal of Electronics and Communication Engineering – (ICRTECITA-2017) – Special Issue – March 2017.*

Kansara, Karan, Zaveri, Vishal, Shah, Shreyans, Delwadkar, Sandip , Jani, Kaushal Sensor based Automated Irrigation System with IOT. A Technical Review Karan Kansara et al.*(IJCSIT) International Journal of Computer Science and Information Technologies.*

Khan M. A., (2020), An IoT Framework for Heart Disease Prediction Based on MDCNN Classifier, in IEEE Access, vol. 8, pp. 34717–34727, 2020. DOI: 10.1109/ACCESS.2020.2974687

Khan, MA, Abuhasel, KA. (2020). Advanced metameric dimension framework for heterogeneous industrial Internet of things. Computational Intelligence. 2020; 1–21. https://doi.org/10.1111/coin.12378

Middleton, Peter, Kjeldsen, Peter & Tully, Jim.2013.Forecast: The internet of things, worldwide. 2013.

Khan M.A, and Algarni F., (2020) "A Healthcare Monitoring System for the Diagnosis of Heart Disease in the IoMT Cloud Environment Using MSSO-ANFIS," in IEEE Access, vol. 8, pp. 122259–122269, 2020, doi: 10.1109/ACCESS.2020.3006424.

Khan, M. A., Quasim, M. T, et al., (2020), A Secure Framework for Authentication and Encryption Using Improved ECC for IoT-Based Medical Sensor Data, in IEEE Access, vol. 8, pp. 52018–52027, 2020. DOI: 10.1109/ACCESS.2020.2980739

Khan M.A. et al., (2020), Decentralised IoT, Decenetralised IoT: A Blockchain perspective, Springer, Studies in BigData, 2020, DOI: https://doi.org/10.1007/978-3-030-38677-1

Sukriti, Gupta, Sanyam & Indumathy, K.2016. IoT based Smart Irrigation and Tank Monitoring System. *International Journal of Innovative Research in Computer and Communication Engineering (An ISO 3297: 2007 Certified Organization) Vol. 4, Issue 9, September 2016.*

Smart Computing – Khan et al (Eds)
© 2021 Taylor & Francis Group, London, ISBN 978-0-367-76552-1

Accident prevention using an auto braking system and accident detection using internet of things

Gitanjali Mehta, Yogesh Mishra, Uzair Ashraf, Shubham Dubey & Manoj Singh
Galgotias University, Greater Noida, India

Ruqaiya Khanam
Sharda University, Greater Noida, India

ABSTRACT: The frequency of accidents has increased in recent times due to an increase in the number of vehicles on the road and the carelessness of drivers. In addition, speeding is the primary reason for these accidents. This paper presents an auto-braking system that can be installed in any vehicle to prevent or mitigate an accident or collision if the driver loses control. However, if somehow the accident takes place on account of another vehicle that does not have this system installed, collision detection and communication system, also installed with the auto-braking system, will be utilized and the accident will be detected and communicated to the nearby hospital and registered authorities for providing necessary support to the victims because most of the casualties occur because of not getting help or an ambulance in time. Hence, the work is divided in two parts: (1) design of sensing and braking system; and (2) design of collision detection and communication system.

1 INTRODUCTION

The population explosion in India has made a direct impact in the market of automobiles. Everyone's need of vehicles for transportation has resulted in an increased number of road accidents. These accidents are mainly due to the poor quality of roads and carelessness of drivers which includes speeding. Unavailability of new technologies in vehicles is also a major cause of accidents. Transportation is a basic need for daily life, but an increased numbers of vehicles on the road causes traffic accidents. To reduce the severity of accidental impact, the technology used in the vehicles should be updated. The lack of appropriate traffic laws also lead to an increase in the number of road accidents. People are facing various problems because of lacking availability of secure traveling resources (Tian et al. 2019; Celesti et al. 2018; Chang et al. 2019; Coelingh et al. 2010; Pagadala et al. 2018).

The Indian government is not taking the required steps for implementation of stringent traffic laws so that the common man get the provision of secure travel. We use transportation to do many of our daily life works but it can create worst scenarios and even kill people through accidents. Transportation may have been developed for the ease of lifestyle, but it is also a reason for more than 1,000 road crashes and the age group which is most involved in these injuries is 15–29. India ranks first in fatal injuries caused by road accidents as per a report of the WHO (Celesti et al. 2018). In the absence of required actions, by 2020 a total number of 1.9 million deaths will occur annually as a result of road accidents due to unavailability of timely medical intervention(Celesti et al. 2018). So, for the betterment of the society the authors have come up with the idea of auto-braking system for the vehicles which will be helpful in prevention of collision or in reducing the impact of collision. Further, the authors have developed collision detection and communication system, a technology which will inform the concerned authorities as soon as possible to get the required medication and save lives in case an accident occurs.

DOI 10.1201/9781003167488-19

2 METHODOLOGY

The current system which is exists in this technology is useful for head-on collisions, whereas it is not as useful for backend or side-on collisions. We have tried to implement this system to be useful for both side and back collisions, also reducing the complexity of the system. Piezoelectric sensor

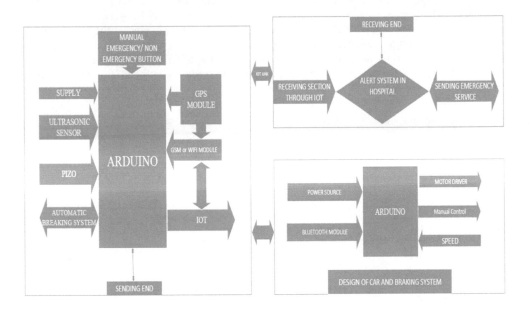

Figure 1.   Block diagram of the system

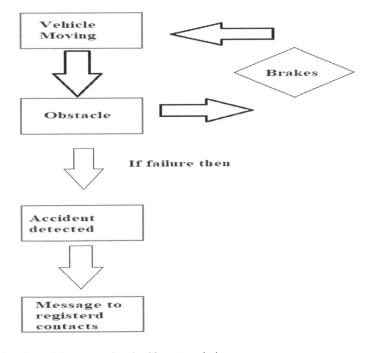

Figure 2.   Flowchart of the process involved in system design.

143

plates have been used to detect the collision from either side of the vehicle. Aurdino gets a signal when any vehicle is approaching very close to our vehicle. Certain distance is set as a preset value for head-on collision. And for side-on collision, this preset value is different and somewhat less than that of front or back collisions.

Figure 1 shows the block diagram of the proposed system. The Arduino-Uno is a microcontroller board based on the Microchip ATmega328P microcontroller. Arduino has made a huge impact in electrical and electronics world. In this work, it is used to detect the input from piezoelectric sensor and send the signal through GPS. A separate 9V portable power supply powers the Arduino board or we can use the supply of vehicle (Mahamud et al. 2017). GPS (global positioning system) is used to detect the location of anything on the earth. It uses longitude and latitudinal coordinates to find the position of the device. There is a transmitter and receiver in the GPS module in which

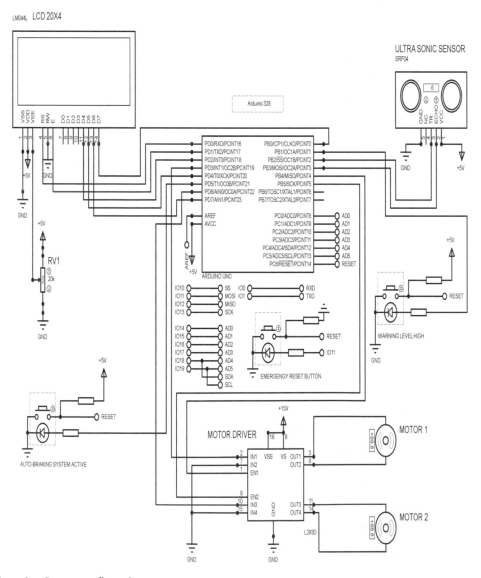

Figure 3.　System configuration.

transmitters transmit the signal to satellite and receivers receive the coordinates. In this project, GPS is used to communicate with nearby hospitals.

Piezoelectric sensors can detect the impact from any direction. A piezoelectric sensor is a type of transducer which takes pressure as input and converts it into an electrical signal. In this system when there is a collision between two vehicles a piezoelectric sensor is used in the front part which detects the collision and sends a signal to Arduino. In present time, every device can be connected with each other with the help of the Internet of Things (IoT), data is stored in the Cloud so that our time can be saved. IoT is used almost everywhere in today's world and after Industry 4.0 even large machines can be controlled from anywhere around the world (Verma et al. 2018; Mehta et al. 2018). Figure 2 shows the flowchart of the process involved in the designed system.

3 DESIGN PROCESS

While driving, the sensors monitor the distance between the vehicles. Working of a braking system can be divided into four parts: (1) When the distance between vehicles is more than 30 m system is not activated or it is disabled. (2) When distance is less than 30 m braking process will start. Motor starts decelerating or a little brake is applied by the system, and warning is given to the driver. (3) When distance is less than 10 m further deceleration of the motor takes place and an extra warning is given by system to driver. (4) When the distance is less than 4 m the whole system is fully automatic and there is no control of drivers in vehicles. An emergency brake is applied by the system. This will reduce the damage caused by the collision of two vehicles.

Figure 3 shows the System Configuration. Figure 4 show the Proteus simulation circuit. When the distance between the obstacles is less than 4 m the Auto Braking System will be activated and automatic brakes will be applied. When the distance between the obstacles is between greater than 4 m and less than 10 m, the Auto Braking System will generate a signal to the driver to limit the speed to desired value and alert the driver of the car. When the distance between the obstacles is between greater than 10 m and less than 30 m, the Auto Braking System will generate a signal to the driver to limit the speed to a desired rate. When the distance between the obstacles is greater than 30 m, the Auto Braking System will be active but will not generate any signal to motor driver. Figure 5 shows the hardware implementation of the proposed work.

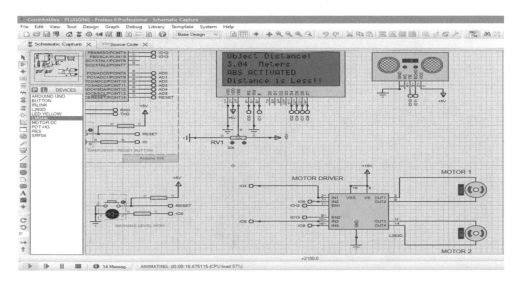

Figure 4. Simulation result when obstacle is less than 4 m and automatic brakes are applied.

Figure 5. Hardware implementation of the proposed work.

4 CONCLUSION

The objective of the proposed work is to prevent or reduce the severity of a collision. This safety feature will reduce those accidents which can be fatal or at least the impact can be reduced up to maximum extent. The speed of the vehicle is automatically reduced so as to reduce the impact of the collision. Even after an automatic emergency brake if there is a collision, then the sensing and communication part takes place. Piezoelectric sensor senses the impact and arduino detects the collision and send the signal to a nearby hospital through GPS. The advantages offered by the proposed system are that it is fully automatic, has simple electronic control unit, the components used are cost effective, automatic brakes are applied to prevent collision, and the system is helpful for front, as well as back, collisions.

REFERENCES

Celesti A., Galletta A., Carnevale L., Fazio M., Lay-Ekuakille A., Villari M., 2018, " An IoT Cloud System for Traffic Monitoring and Vehicular Accidents Prevention Based on Mobile Sensor Data Processing," IEEE Sensors Journal, 18. (12): 4795–4802.

Chang W., Chen L., Su K., 2019, "DeepCrash: A Deep Learning-Based Internet of Vehicles Sys-tem for Head-On and Single-Vehicle Accident Detection With Emergency Notification," IEEE Access, 7: 148163–148175.

Coelingh E., Eidehall A., Bengtsson M., 2010, "Collision Warning with Full Auto Brake and Pe-destrian Detection - a practical example of Automatic Emergency Braking," 13th International IEEE Conference on Intelligent Transportation Systems: 155–160.

Mahamud M.S., Monsur M., Zishan M.S.R., 2017, "An arduino based accident prevention and identification system for vehicles, IEEE Region 10 Humanitarian Technology Conference: 555–559.

Mehta G., Mittra G., Yadav V.K., 2018, "Application of IoT to optimize Data Center operations, International Conference on Computing, Power And Communication Technologies: 738–742.

Pagadala V., Rani S., Priya B.K., 2018, "Design and Implementation of the Prevention and Analysis of the Accident for Automobiles, International Conference on Advances in Computing, Communications and Informatics: 2283–2289.

Tian D., Zhang C., Duan X., Wang X., 2019, "An Automatic Car Accident Detection Method Based on Cooperative Vehicle Infrastructure Systems," IEEE Access, 7: 127453–127463.

Verma M.K., Mukherjee V., Yadav V.K., Mehta G., 2018, "Planning and optimizing the cost of DGs for Stability of Green Field Distribution Network, International Conference On Internet of Things: Smart Innovation and Usages, Birla Institute of Applied Sciences: 1–6.

Track 2: Machine intelligence and data science

Smart Computing – Khan et al (Eds)
© 2021 Taylor & Francis Group, London, ISBN 978-0-367-76552-1

Reservoir and irrigation management system using machine learning

M. Sangeetha, S.V. Ganka Manalan, P.V. Akshay Balaji, R.S. Harishkumar & K.R. Harish
Coimbatore Institute of Technology, Coimbatore, Tamilnadu, India

ABSTRACT: Dams act as a good source of water for irrigation, industrial requirements, generating hydroelectricity, and daily needs. They act as a natural habitat for various aquatic species. The water available in these resources are a source for various fundamental activities. Presently, there is a need to preserve the water and ensure proper and well-administrated water management. The smart reservoir management system makes use of the Internet of Things. In the event of a natural calamity such as a flood, due to a rise in the level of water in dam the smart system generates an alert automatically, thereby ensuring that the natural calamity does not affect the lives of people. This paper presents the design of an alert system that can predict rainfall in a particular zone as well as suggests crops that can be cultivated in that area.

1 INTRODUCTION

Dams act as one of the major resource suppliers for a city, as well as playing an important role in controlling floods and assisting in river navigation. Most dams are built for various purposes and their benefits are many. Water being one of the most precious natural resources, it needs to be preserved and utilized with the utmost care. During both the extreme conditions of water scarcity and excess water, and even with normal monitoring of the dam, safety parameters and water management are very necessary. In the modern age, dam safety needs to be based on weather parameters and physical parameters to be supported technically.

The Internet of Things (IoT) plays a vital role in gathering the data from sensor networks and other industrial devices to make the system smarter (Abuhasel 2020; Khan & Abuhasel 2020). The IoT is not only limited to the irrigation but it also has many applications such as healthcare, industrial security, etc. (Khan et al. 2020, Khan & Algarni 2020; Khan et al. 2020, Khan, Quasim et al. 2020). Generally, the dams and their ability to manage water are monitored through traditional surveillance techniques, except for the water level in some of the dams which is atomized. This data can be used to predict floods and alerts can be given so as to prevent damage. Water from the dams can also be managed smartly to help with irrigation. The collective water requirement for an area's nearby dam can be determined to manage open and close operations on the dam effectively.

The system detailed in "An IoT Based Dam Water Management System for Agriculture" (Chellaswamy et al. 2018) presents an IoT-based dam water management system (IoT-DWM) for reducing the wastage of water. The real data can be observed through different sensors placed in the agriculture area and updated in the cloud. The dam controller receives the real data of the particular area and estimates the water requirement. It is capable of sensing different parameters such as temperature and humidity. The drawback of the system is that there is no manual control and no disaster management modules, and it lacks any machine intelligence for calculating the water requirement. The system also does not provide any measure for the others to get information on the parameters.

In "IoT based Disaster Monitoring and Management System for Dams (IDMMSD)", Varghese et al. (2019) present a novel disaster monitoring and management system for dams that continuously monitor the water level of the dam, and also estimate the water inflow rate to the dam (considering various sensor measurements). It controls the movement of gates using IoT on a real-time basis. The project also includes an SMS warning system for farmers and common people and special SOS signals are sent to local fire stations, disaster management teams, police teams, and emergency response teams as the water level increases due to continuing rainfall. The shortcomings of the paper are that only the decision-making algorithm is simple and does not consider complex parameters such as rainfall.

In "Design of Flooding Detection System Based on Velocity and Water Level DAM with ESP8266", Yuliandoko et al. (2017) proposed a system for flood detection in dams based on the water level and the water flow rate/velocity. The system categorizes the status of the water as either secure, standby, alert, or danger based on the level and flow parameters. The system also provides emergency call facilities to take remedial actions. The drawback of the paper is that the detection system is based on only the level and flow of water. Other complex parameters such as rainfall, humidity, etc. also may be considered.

The rest of the paper is organized as follows. Section 2 presents system and architecture design. The method used is presented in Section 3. Implementation details are provided in Section 4. Finally, a conclusion is presented in Section 5.

2 SYSTEM DESIGN

The existing dam management is done manually with human interaction. It takes a lot of time between the farmers requesting the release of dam water for irrigation and the actual releasing of water. This delay in the releasing of water for irrigation can directly affect the quality of the crops. Flood prediction and smart alerts also are not available in the existing system. Lack of alerts during an emergency opening of dams also can result in the deaths of individuals.

The proposed system uses an ultrasonic sensor-based hardware module which is placed in the vicinity of the dam. This ultrasonic sensor in the module will determine the level of water in the dam, based on the reflected ultrasonic sound waves. When the level of water rises beyond safe levels, an alarm is sounded by the module. This alerts the authorities to release water. The water release process can be done manually as well as being automated. Before the water is released the authorities at the dam have to manually trigger the module which sends information about water release to a central database. The central database also transmits this information to the base stations near the river bank, such that any person who gets into the coverage area of the network receives messages about the release of water. The system also predicts the rainfall in a particular zone along with the crops that can be cultivated in that zone by using machine learning algorithms. This gives an added advantage to the user on how to maximize the crop yield. Figure 1 shows the architectural design of the system.

3 METHODOLOGIES USED

3.1 *Regression*

The regression analysis consists of a set of machine learning algorithms that allow us to predict a continuous outcome variable y based on the number of one or more statistical variables x.

In short, the purpose of the regression model is to create a mathematical equation that describes y as a function of x variables. Next, this statistic can be used to predict the result y on the basis of the new value of the forecast factor x.

Linear regression is the simplest and most popular way to predict continuous variables. It assumes a linear relationship between the outcome and the predictor variable. The linear regression equation can be written as

$$y = \beta_0 + \beta * x + e \tag{1}$$

where β_0 is the intercept, β is the regression weight or coefficient associated with the predictor variable x, and e is the residual error.

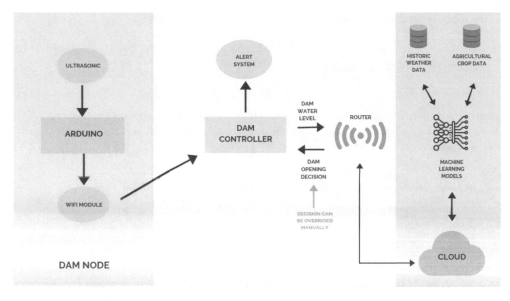

Figure 1. Architectural design.

3.2 *Neural networks*

Neural networks are set by algorithms that are very similar to the human brain and are designed to recognize patterns. They translate sensory information using machine understanding, labeling, or combining raw input. They can recognize the patterns of numbers, contained in pages, where all real-world information (pictures, sounds, text, or time series) should be interpreted. The resulting neural networks are made up of a large number of highly interconnected networks (neurons) that work together to solve a problem.

An artificial neural network (ANN) usually includes a large number of processors that work in parallel and are programmed on the target. The first tier receives raw input information, analogous to optic nerves in human visual processing. Each successive tier receives output from the preceding tier, rather than from the raw input—in the same way neurons proceed from the optic nerves receive signals from those close to them. The final tier releases the program result.

3.3 *Recurrent neural networks*

A recurrent neural network (RNN) is the latest neural network is an integrator of a neural feed network with internal memory. An RNN always appears in the environment as it performs the same function in all data entries while the current input result depends on one previous compiler. After the output is copied, it is copied and sent back to the recursive network. For decision making, it looks at the current input and output of the previous input.

Unlike feeder neural networks, RNNs can use their internal state (memory) to process input sequences. This enables them to use tasks such as non-recognition, handwriting recognition, or speech recognition. In some neural networks, all input is independent. But for RNN, all input is relative.

First, it takes the X_0 from the sequence of input and then it outputs h_0 which together with X_1 is the input for the next step. So, the h_0 and X_1 is the input for the next step. Similarly, h_1 from the next step is the input with X_2 for the following step, and so on. This way, it keeps remembering the context while training.

The formula for the current state is:

$$h_t = f(h_{t-1}, x_t) \tag{2}$$

Applying the Activation Function:

$$h_t = tanh(W_{hh}h_{t-1} + W_{xh}x_t) \tag{3}$$

where W is weight, h is the single hidden vector, W_{hh} is the weight at previous hidden state, W_{hx} is the weight at current input state, and tanh is the Activation function, that implements a nonlinearity that squashes the activations to the range [-1. . . 1].

3.4 *Random forest*

Random forest is a supervised learning algorithm that uses a classification method. A random forest is a way of betting and not a lifting process. Random forest trees are run in parallel. There is no interaction between these trees during the construction of the trees. It works by constructing a large number of decision trees during training and class extraction which is a class method (classification) or prediction (re-positioning) of individual trees. A random forest is a meta-model (i.e., includes a multiple prediction result) that includes multiple decision trees. Attribute selection is made using one of the following methods:

- Information Gain
- Gini Index
- Chi-Square

The information gain of a split can be calculated by using the following formula:
Information Gain (T, X) = Entropy (T) − Entropy (T, X)
The entropy is given by:

$$E(s) = \sum_{(i=1)}^{c} e_i \ln p_i \tag{4}$$

The Gini Index can be calculated as:

$$Gini = 1 - \sum_{(i=1)}^{c} (p_i)^2 \tag{5}$$

4 IMPLEMENTATION

Pseudo code:
Figure 2 shows the flowchart for the pseudo code provided in Algorithm 1.

Algorithm 1: Flow of Program

Input: Location
Output: Suggested crop, Dam opening decision
Collect the place of agriculture from the user
Forecast the weather condition for that place
if *Likely to rain during the season* **then**
    Based on the forecast, calculate the amount of rainfall and suggest the crop accordingly
    if *Water requirement is high for an area* **then**
        if *Water Available in nearby reservoir* **then**
            Place request to the reservoir authorities for opening
---

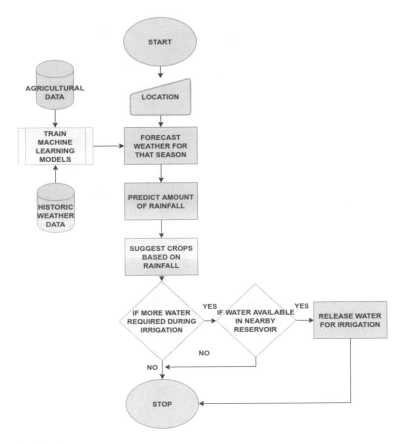

Figure 2. Flowchart for program.

Table 1. Sample data.

Time	Temperature Celsius	Pressure hPa	Humidity %	Wind Speed m/s	Condition
1-1-79 00:00	21.2	1014	98	1.34	Clouds
1-1-79 01:00	21.3	1014	98	1.16	Clouds
. . .	. . .	. . .	. . .	. . .	. . .
14-1-86 03:00	23.3	1013	90	1.66	Rain

4.1 *Dataset preparation*

Hourly weather data from Karur, India during the years 1979–2019 is used in the training of the models. The missing values in the dataset are filled with mean values and the data is normalized before feeding it to the machine learning models. The dataset consists of more than 3 Lakh rows of data. Table 1 shows a sample from the used dataset.

4.2 *Weather forecasting*

This module is used to forecast the weather parameters such as temperature, humidity, and pressure for the complete agricultural season. This forecast can then be used to predict if rainfall is likely to

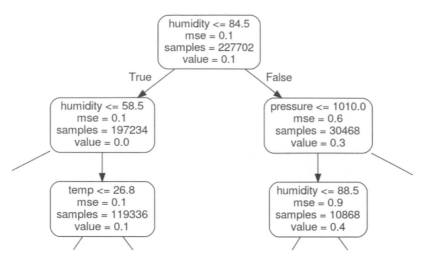

Figure 3.   A section from a single decision tree from the random forest.

occur or not. This module makes use of neural networks, especially Long Short-Term Memory type (LSTM) of neural network for predicting the time series data. LSTM is a type of RNN. The outputs from the previous states are also used as inputs to the current node for calculating the output. Thus, it is much suitable for time series analysis and forecasting. Weather parameters of the previous 30 days are given as input to the model to predict the weather parameter for the next day. Using this model, the weather for the entire month is forecasted.

4.3   Rainfall prediction

The forecast from the forecast module is fed into this module. This module will predict if rainfall will occur based on the forecasted parameters. A random forest is used for the classification of the weather condition. It takes the forecasted weather parameters and will find the weather condition for each day of the season. If the condition is rain, then a random forest regressor model is used to find the amount of rainfall. This amount of rainfall is calculated for all the rainy days and the total amount of water obtained from rain for that season is calculated. This data is used for the suggestion of which crop to irrigate so as to make optimal use of water resources and to increase the yield.

4.4   Crop suggestion

Based on the estimated rainfall, location, and soil moisture level, this module will suggest the optimum crop to cultivate to get the highest yield. Various crops are analyzed and based on the water quantity available; a suitable crop then is suggested to the user. The user is also presented with an option to select an alternative crop. The system is flexible so it can be adjusted to work on different varieties of crops.

4.5   Flood prediction

The water quantity in the dam is continuously monitored and the speed of the rise of water in case of rainfall is also monitored to detect if a flood will occur. In case of flood, suitable alert messages are passed to the authorities and the dam is opened automatically so as to prevent flood and maintain the water level in the dam.

5 PERFORMANCE ANALYSIS

The Crop Recommendation module has accuracy as high as 92%. The rainfall value prediction module has an accuracy of 86% and the predicted values are nearly as accurate as the actual value. The random forest classifier produces results with high accuracy of up to approximately 85% and performs better than the other classification models such as K-Means and support vector machine (SVM). The LSTM networks performed better than other methods such as ARIMA and SARIMA for weather forecasting. As seen in Figure 4, the training and validation loss reduces drastically. Figure 5 shows that the predicted weather parameters are the same or closer to the actual weather parameters.

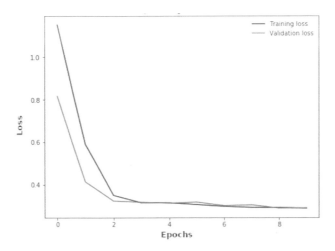

Figure 4. Multi-step training vs. validation loss.

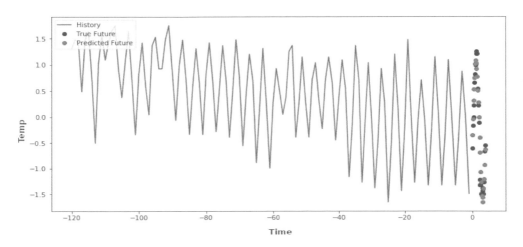

Figure 5. Forecast of weather parameters.

157

6   CONCLUSION AND FUTURE WORK

The Smart Reservoir System is implemented and tested. The weather parameters for a period of 30 days are provided by the system with relatively good accuracy. These parameters are then used by the application to provide reliable information regarding rainfall in the particular zone. This is further improvised by predicting the crop that can be cultivated in that area by using the rainfall parameters. The flood alert system has been designed to alarm the area in the event of a flood. By using an ultrasonic sensor, the level of water is measured and thresholds have been calculated according to the reservoir parameters. Google map overlay is also designed to give live updates on Google maps in the event of a flood. Figure 5 shows the forecasted temperature against the actual temperature. The application can be further enhanced by using additional parameters for rainfall prediction to provide more accuracy on the weather statistics of an area. The prediction on the crop that can be cultivated can also be improvised by using additional factors that can influence the yield and outcome of the irrigation. The alert system can be enhanced by using a flood flow-based overlay system rather than a simple overlay system to provide a more accurate alert on the areas that are likely to be flooded.

REFERENCES

Abuhasel K. A. and M. A. Khan (2020).A Secure Industrial Internet of Things (IIoT) Framework for Resource Management in Smart Manufacturing," in IEEE Access, vol. 8, pp. 117354–117364, 2020, doi: 10.1109/ACCESS.2020.3004711.

Chellaswamy C, Nisha J, Sivakumar K & Kaviya R, *An IoT Based Dam Water Management System for Agriculture*, IEEE COnference, International Conference on Recent Trends in Electrical, Control and Communication (RTECC), 2018.

Nikhil M. Dhandre, P. D. Kamalasekaran & Pooja Pandey, *Dam Parameters Monitoring System*, 7th India International Conference on Power Electronics (IICPE), IEEE 2016.

M. Julia Flores, Arm E. Nicholson & Rosa F. Ropero, *Dynamic OOBNs Applied to Water Management in Dams* IEEE International Conference on Knowledge Engineering and Applications (ICKEA), 2016.

Khan M. A (2020), An IoT Framework for Heart Disease Prediction Based on MDCNN Classifier, in IEEE Access, vol. 8, pp. 34717–34727, 2020. DOI: 10.1109/ACCESS.2020.2974687

Khan, MA, Abuhasel, KA (2020). Advanced metameric dimension framework for heterogeneous industrial Internet of things. Computational Intelligence. 2020; 1–21. https://doi.org/10.1111/coin.12378 DOI: 10.1109/ACCESS.2020.2980739

Khan M.A, and Algarni F(2020), "A Healthcare Monitoring System for the Diagnosis of Heart Disease in the IoMT Cloud Environment Using MSSO-ANFIS," in IEEE Access, vol. 8, pp. 122259–122269, 2020, doi: 10.1109/ACCESS.2020.3006424.

Khan, M. A., Quasim, M. T, et al. (2020), A Secure Framework for Authentication and Encryption Using Improved ECC for IoT-Based Medical Sensor Data, in IEEE Access, vol. 8, pp. 52018–52027, 2020.

Khan M.A. et al (2020), Decentralised IoT, Decenetralised IoT: A Blockchain perspective, Springer, Studies in BigData, 2020, DOI: https://doi.org/10.1007/978-3-030-38677-1

Kosandal, R. (2019). *Weather forecasting with Recurrent Neural Networks.* [online] Medium. Available at: https://medium.com/analytics-vidhya/weather-forecasting-with-recurrent-neural-networks-1eaa057d70c3 [Accessed 16 Feb. 2020].

Quasim, M. T., Khan M. A, et al., 2019, Internet of Things for Smart Healthcare: A Hardware Perspective, 2019 First International Conference of Intelligent Computing and Engineering (ICOICE), Hadhramout, Yemen, 2019, pp. 1–5. DOI: 10.1109/ICOICE48418.2019.9035175

Quasim, M.T., Khan M.A, Algarni F., Alharthy A., Alshmrani G.M.M, (2020), Blockchain Frameworks. In: Khan M., Quasim M., Algarni F., Alharthi A. (eds) Decentralised Internet of Things. Studies in Big Data, vol 71. Springer, DOI: https://doi.org/10.1007/978-3-030-38677-1

Sai Sreekar Siddula, Phaneendra Babu & P.C. Jain, *Water Level Monitoring and Management of Dams using IoT*, 3rd International Conference On Internet of Things: Smart Innovation and Usages (IoT-SIU), IEEE, 2018a.

Sai Sreekar Siddula, P.C. Jain & Madhur Deo Upadhayay, *Real Time Monitoring and Controlling of Water Level in Dams using IoT*, IEEE Conference, 8th International Advance Computing Conference (IACC), 2018b.

Albert Joshy Varghese, Abin Thomas Jolly, Astile Peter & Bhavana P Rajeev, *based Disaster Monitor- ing and Management System for Dams (IDMMSD)* IEEE Conference, 1st International Conference on Innovations in Information and Communication Technology (ICIICT), 2019.

Herman Yuliandoko, Subono, Vivien Arief Wardhany, Sholeh Hadi Pramono & Ponco Siwindarto, *Design of flooding detection system based on velocity and water level DAM with ESP8266*, 2nd International conferences on Information Technology, Information Systems and Electrical Engineering (ICITISEE), IEEE, 2017.

Smart Computing – Khan et al (Eds)
© 2021 Taylor & Francis Group, London, ISBN 978-0-367-76552-1

Crop disease identification using state-of-the-art deep convolutional neural networks

P.S. Thakur, T. Sheorey & Aparajita Ojha
PDPM IIITDM, Jabalpur, Madhya Pradesh, India

ABSTRACT: Deep Convolutional Neural Network (CNN) based prediction models have shown their capabilities in various problems of classification and regression on image datasets. Deep CNNs have also been used by researchers for plant disease identification. In this work, we evaluate the performance of some well-known CNN architectures VGG16, ResNet50, DenseNet121, NASNet, and MobileNet V2 for plant disease identification. Although VGG16 outperforms all the other models with an accuracy of 99.61% on PlantVillage dataset, MobileNet v2 shows a comparable performance with only 2.3 million trainable parameters as against VGG16 having 33.7 million parameters.

1 INTRODUCTION

Deep learning is an emerging AI technology inspired by human brain's neural system. It has led to remarkable improvement in a variety of complex tasks in different fields such as computer vision, speech recognition, machine translation. For classification problems involving image data, CNNs are especially designed to extract patterns and to handle high dimensional data. Several Deep CN models have been proposed over the years for different types of problems. AlexNet, VGG, ResNet, Inception, DenseNet, NASNet, MobileNet are some of the state-of-the art CNN architectures used in classification and regression tasks.

Crop monitoring and pest control is a significant issue worldwide. Early-stage crop disease identification can help overcome the problem of crop damage and related revenue loss. In the developing world, crop monitoring and disease identification is primarily dome by field experts or farmers. These processes are time consuming and often lead to delay in decision for pest control and medicinal treatment. To tackle the problem, technology-enabled solutions have been proposed by several research groups (Pantazi et al. 2019; Singh et al. 2016; Singh & Misra 2015; Dandawate 2015) and have also been successfully implemented. For plant disease identification, several machine learning approaches have been introduced over the years (Mwebaze & Owomugisha 2016; Al-Hiary et al. 2011; Rumpf et al. 2010). These include logistic regression, random forest and SVM. More recent methods apply deep CNN frameworks. One of the major challenges when applying deep learning methods is the lack of problem-specific data availability. CNN's architecture needs a large amount of data for training. Hughes & Salathe (2015), have been working on development of plant diseases data repository. More than 50,000 images have been shared by them on PlantVillage platform (Mohanty et al. 2016).

Due to large number of parameters in CNNs, training deep learning models from the scratch is a time-consuming task. To develop accurate models with less computational cost fine-tuning (Pan & Yang 2010) is a good idea where knowledge gained from one domain can be transferred to other applications. However, selecting a suitable CNN model is always a challenge, some CNN models outperform other models in accuracy, but the number of trainable parameters is large, leading to large memory and computational needs. On the other hand, CNN models with a smaller number

DOI 10.1201/9781003167488-21

of layers do not provide expected level of accuracy. Mohanty et al. (2016) have used a CNN model with 5 layers for plant disease identification and have reported the model accuracy of 85.53%. In another research work, Ferentinos (2018) have used AlexNet, GoogleNet, Overfeat, and VGG16 models and have reported that VGG16 performs best with 99.53% accuracy.

The concept of CNN and deep learning can also be applied to many other real-time applications to make the system smarter (Abuhasel 2020; Khan 2020a, 2020e; Quasim 2020a, 2020b). As a part of a project on real time crop monitoring and prevention from spread of disease in farms, we evaluate the performance of three well known CNN models namely, VGG16, ResNet50, DenseNet121, and two more recently introduced models NASNet, and MobileNetV2 on PlantVillage dataset. Each model has its own advantage, but selection of a model to build an end-to-end solution itself is a challenge, due to various constraints such as memory requirement, processing time and other relevant issues. The present study helps in selecting a right CNN model for online deployment of a solution on crop monitoring and prevention from spread of disease.

Rest of the paper is organized as follows: Section II contains a review of related works in the area of plant disease identification, Section III describes different model architectures used in the present study and Section IV presents comparative analysis of performance of these models, and Section V contains conclusion and future scope of work.

2 RELATED WORK

A CNN based architecture was proposed by Kawasaki et al. (2015) for automatic disease diagnosis in plants. They used 800 images of cucumber leaves. Due to small dataset size, they trained the model with 4-fold cross-validation. The model consists of three stacks of CONV-POOL-NORM layers and a fully connected layer. The reported accuracy is 94.9% as a binary classifier.

Fujita et al. (2016) proposed a disease diagnosis system on 7,520 cucumber leaves images with 4-fold cross-validation. In preprocessing step, they performed the cropping of the center image, rotation, trimming, resizing and mirroring as data augmentation. In the model, four stacks of CONV layers are present for classification which gives 82.3% accuracy.

Brahimi et al. (2017) worked on detection of diseases in tomato leaves in PlantVillage dataset of 14,828 images with nine categories. They compared the performance of AlexNet and GoogleNet models on this dataset and achieved 99.18% accuracy on GoogleNet.

Wang et al. (2017), started with apple black rot disease manual annotation over PlantVillage dataset, and trained a predefined model from the scratch as well as with fine-tuning. As per their results, VGG16 model with transfer learning performs best with test accuracy of 90.4%. Experts divided the crop into maturity stages. As per the study, disease increases as the stage of plant matures.

Ferentinos (2018) worked on CNN based architecture for plant disease detection with the dataset of 58 classes containing 87,848 images of 25 different plant species. The reported the best accuracy of 99.53% with VGG16 architecture when compared with AlexNet, GoogleNet, and Overfeat architectures.

Brahimi et al. (2019) proposed the CNNs based plant disease detection approach with a concept of binary classifiers: tutor and student; inspired from auto-encoder architecture so that training can be more transparent and interpretable. VGG16 architecture with skip-connections and deconvolution blocks was used with PlantVillage dataset with data split in the ratio of 6:4 into training and validation datasets.

Focus of recent research on crop disease identification is to apply cross-domain knowledge and speed up the training process by way of transfer learning or fine tuning pretrained models (Coulibaly et al. 2019; KC 2019; Shijie et al. 2017). Mohanty et al. (2016) have applied AlexNet and GoogleNet models for disease identification. Multiple train-test splits are done, and both the methods of parameter learning, i.e., random weight initialization and transfer learning are applied to obtain the best performing CNN model. They have reported that the split of 80-20 provided the best performance with an accuracy of 99.35% on GoogleNet architecture.

Too et al. (2018) performed a comparative plant disease classification of PlantVillage dataset on VGG with 16 layers, ResNet with 50, 101, 152 layers; Inception V4 and DenseNet with 121 layers. As per the study, they achieved the best accuracy of 99.75% using DenseNets 121 layers model after 30 iterations with high computation time.

3 ARCHITECTURE AND APPROACH

To perform the present evaluation study, we have used some of the top ILSVRC (Olga et al. 2015) CNN models and some more recent models as detailed below.

3.1 *VGG16*

Simonyan & Zisserman (2014) contributed to the progress of convolutional networks with 3x3 convolution filters at a depth of 16 layers. In ILSVRC 2014 they secured the second rank in object detection and localization task. They used a stack of sixteen convolution layers; five of these CNN layers were followed by max-pooling layers. At the end of the architecture, two fully connected layers were used, each of them with 4096 neurons.

In the present work, the same model is used, except that the top softmax layer is replaced by a 38 units softmax layer for classification task on PlantVillage Dataset.

3.2 *ResNet*

It is well known that the depth of neural networks severely affects performance of a deep learning model due to vanishing gradient problems. To overcome this, residual networks were introduced by He et al. (2016). They use shortcut/ skip connections for identity mapping, where the input of one layer was skipped for one or more layers and was added with a later layer output. ResNet provided two main advantages, training cost was significantly reduced and deeper networks could be used (like 152 layers) without the problem of vanishing gradients.

In the present work a ResNet model with 50 layers is used. We have truncated the topmost softmax layer, and added a new dense softmax layer with 38 units.

3.3 *DenseNet*

Huang et al. (2017) proposed a model based on densely connected architecture where every layer is connected to all other layers. In a deep learning model, when the input passes through multiple layers, information of the input vanishes when it reaches to the last layer. Training can be more efficient if connection between layers from input to output can be minimum. Therefore, each layer connected to all other layers. In the network, feature maps of the previous layers as input to next layers. This setting can reduce the number of parameters to learn with the reusability of feature-maps. It can also overcome the problem of vanishing gradient and overfitting.

In the present work, only the softmax layer is modified to the one having 38 units for classification.

3.4 *NasNet*

In Neural architecture search network (NASNet) (Zoph et al. 2018), the concept of knowledge transferability is deployed in a very innovative way. The authors in (Zoph et al. 2018) train a simple model on a small validation dataset to achieve some accuracy level and call this model as a "cell." Then they use the arrangement of multiple cells as a "search space" to train on a massive dataset.

They use normal cell and reduction cell for reducing feature map size to the half. The model provides simplicity to structure and can be applied with varying input sizes.

As mentioned for the previous models, only the softmax layer is modified in the present work to the one having 38 units for classification.

3.5 *MobileNet v2*

As the name suggests, the model is useful for mobile or low computation devices (Sandler et al. 2018). The model is based on skip-connections with the narrow bottleneck. Initially model expands the low-dimensional input, and at output the high-dimensional feature vector is degraded to a small size. For fine tuning we replace the topmost layer of MobileNet model with 38 units output layer.

4 RESULT AND ANALYSIS

4.1 *Dataset*

For classification, an openly available dataset of PlantVillage (Mohanty et al. 2016) covering 14 crops' images and 26 diseases is used. It contains 54,306 images including healthy plant leaves images in 38 classes.

Datatset is divided into 8:2 ratio for training and testing set, respectively (Kawasaki et al. 2015). Training set is again divided in the ratio of 8:2 training and validation set. After splitting, the training set, val-idation set and test set contain 34,727 images, 8702 images and 10,876 images respectively.

All the networks take input images of the size 224 × 224. Input samples are passed through the stack of convolutional and pooling layers, and then the fully connected layers after flattening the activation maps. ReLU activation function is used for non-linearity in all the convolution and fully connected layers. Finally output layer uses softmax function for classification. Figure 1 shows the block diagram of a generic CNN model for image classification task.

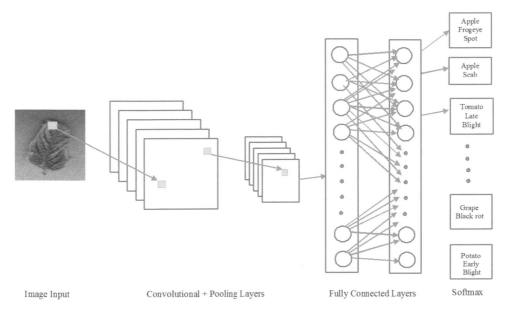

Figure 1. A generic convolution neural network for crop disease identification.

4.2 System configuration

For performance computation NVIDIA Quadro P5000 Graphics Processing Unit (GPU) with 16GB RAM, and Windows 10 operating system is used with Keras, Matplot library, and CuDNN python libraries.

4.3 Training

All the models were trained for 30 epochs with a batch size of 64 and Stochastic Gradient Descent (Ruder 2016) (SGD) was used as the optimizer. The learning rate was 0.001 with a weight decay 1e-6 and 0.9 Nesterov momentum. Performance of all the trained models was evaluated using accuracy metric and cross entropy loss.

4.4 Discussion

Transfer-learning approach is performed on VGG, ResNet, DenseNet, NASNet, and MobileNet. The results are compared based on number of parameters, testing accuracy, testing loss and computation time. As shown in Table 1, in terms of test loss DenseNet performs better; VGG 16 provides the best test accuracy. However, all other models also have test accuracy comparable to that of VGG16. MobileNetV2 requires less computational time and number of parameters are significantly low as compared to VGG16. The study shows that fine-tuning helps in reducing computation costs. Figures 2–11 show graphical representation of accuracy and loss during the training of various models.

Table 1. Performance measure of various models.

Model	No of parameters	Training		Validation		Testing		Time (secs)
		loss	accuracy	loss	accuracy	loss	accuracy	
VGG16	33.7 M	0.0000076	100	0.0221	99.55	0.0225	99.61	78.21
Resnet50	24.3 M	0.000238	99.99	0.0330	99.23	0.03123	99.36	65.76
DenseNet	7 M	0.00095	100	0.0226	99.41	0.0182	99.54	79.55
NasNet	4.3 M	0.0011	99.97	0.0011	99.47	0.0211	99.50	71.97
MobileNetV2	2.3 M	0.000938	99.99	0.0248	99.38	0.027	99.40	60.89

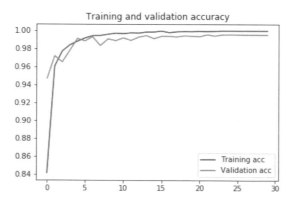

Figure 2. VGG 16 training and validation accuracy.

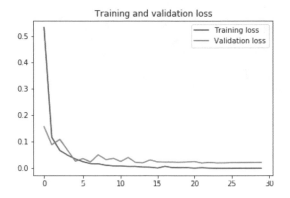

Figure 3. VGG16 training and validation loss.

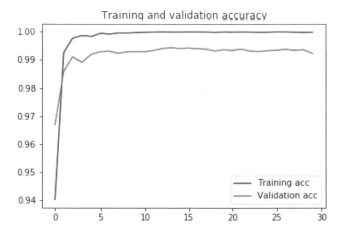

Figure 4. ResNet50 training and validation accuracy.

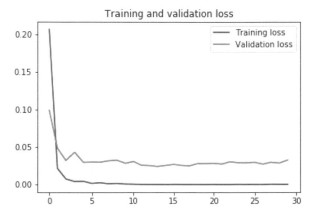

Figure 5. ResNet50 training and validation loss.

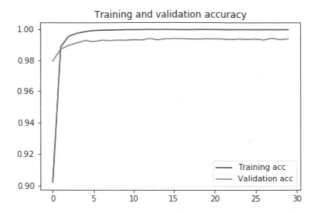

Figure 6.   DenseNet training and validation accuracy.

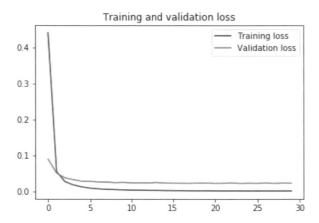

Figure 7.   DenseNet Training and validation loss.

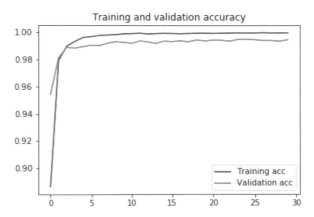

Figure 8.   NASNet training and validation accuracy.

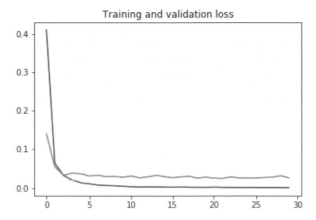

Figure 9.   NASNet training and validation loss.

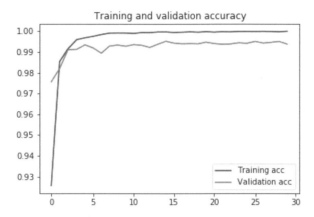

Figure 10.   MobileNetV2 training and validation accuracy.

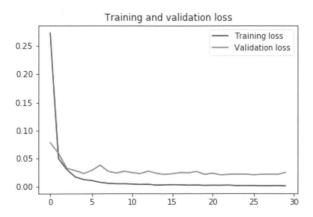

Figure 11.   MobileNetV2 training and validation loss.

167

5 CONCLUSION

Advancement in the computational power and availability of a large amount of data attracted most of the real-world applications to shift to deep learning approaches for data processing. In this work we conclude that all the state-of-the-art CNN models show comparable performance in plant disease identification problem on PlantVillage dataset. We conclude that MobileNetV2 can be used when speed and/or computation time are the priorities. VGG16 provides highest accuracy(99.6) but has around 33.7 million trainable parameters. Thus, it requires both higher computational resource as well as memory.

The work will be extended for real-time disease detection and localization on different types of crops.

REFERENCES

Abuhasel K. A. and M. A. Khan, "A Secure Industrial Internet of Things (IIoT) Framework for Resource Management in Smart Manufacturing," in IEEE Access, vol. 8, pp. 117354–117364, 2020, doi: 10.1109/ACCESS.2020.3004711.

Al-Hiary, H. & Bani-Ahmad, S. & Ryalat, M. H. & Braik, M. S. & Alrahamneh, Z. 2011. Fast and Accurate Detection and Classification of Plant Diseases. *International Journal of Computer Applications. 17. 10.5120/2183-2754.*

Brahimi, M. & Kamel, B. & Moussaoui, A. 2017. Deep Learning for Tomato Diseases: Classification and Symptoms Visualization. *Applied Artificial Intelligence. 1–17. 10.1080/08839514.2017.1315516.*

Brahimi, M. & Saïd, M. & Kamel, B. & Moussaoui, A. 2019. Deep interpretable architecture for plant diseases classification. *111–116. 10.23919/SPA.2019.8936759.*

Coulibaly, S. & Kamsu-Foguem, B. & Kamissoko, D. & Traore, D. 2019. Deep neural networks with transfer learning in millet crop images. *Computers in Industry. 108.10.1016/j.compind.2019.02.003.*

Dandawate, Y. 2015. An Automated Approach for Classification of Plant Diseases Towards Development of Futuristic Decision Support System in Indian Perspective. *10.1109/ICACCI.2015.7275707.*

Ferentinos, K. 2018. Deep learning models for plant disease detection and diagnosis. *Computers and Electronics in Agriculture. 145. 311–318. 10.1016/j.compag.2018.01.009.*

Fujita, E. & Kawasaki, Y. & Uga, H. & Kagiwada, S. & Iyatomi, H. 2016. Basic Investigation on a Robust and Practical Plant Diagnostic System. *989-992. 10.1109/ICMLA.2016.0178.*

He, K. & Zhang, X. & Ren, S. & Sun, J. 2016. Deep Residual Learning for Image Recognition. *770–778. 10.1109/CVPR.2016.90.*

Huang, G. & Liu, Z. & van der Maaten, L. & Weinberger, K. 2017. Densely Connected Convolutional Networks. *10.1109/CVPR.2017.243.*

Hughes, D. & Salathe, M. 2015. An open access repository of images on plant health to enable the development of mobile disease diagnostics through machine learning and crowdsourcing.

Kawasaki, Y. & Uga, H. & Kagiwada, S. & Iyatomi, H. 2015. Basic Study of Automated Diagnosis of Viral Plant Diseases Using Convolutional Neural Networks. *9475. 638–645. 10.1007/978-3-319-27863-6_59.*

KC, K. & Yin, Z. & Li, B. & Wu, M. 2019. Transfer Learning for Fine-Grained Crop Disease Classification Based on Leaf Images. 1–5. 10.1109/WHISPERS.2019.8921213.

Khan M. A., 2020, An IoT Framework for Heart Disease Prediction Based on MDCNN Classifier, in IEEE Access, vol. 8, pp. 34717-34727, 2020. DOI: 10.1109/ACCESS.2020.2974687

Khan, MA, Abuhasel, KA. Advanced metameric dimension framework for heterogeneous industrial Internet of things. Computational Intelligence. 2020; 1– 21. https://doi.org/10.1111/coin.12378

Khan M.A, and Algarni F., "A Healthcare Monitoring System for the Diagnosis of Heart Disease in the IoMT Cloud Environment Using MSSO-ANFIS," in IEEE Access, vol. 8, pp. 122259–122269, 2020, doi: 10.1109/ACCESS.2020.3006424.

Khan, M. A., Quasim, M. T, et al, 2020, A Secure Framework for Authentication and Encryption Using Improved ECC for IoT-Based Medical Sensor Data, in IEEE Access, vol. 8, pp. 52018–52027, 2020. DOI: 10.1109/ACCESS.2020.2980739

Khan M.A. et al., 2020, Decentralised IoT, Decenetralised IoT: A Blockchain perspective, Springer, Studies in BigData, 2020, DOI: https://doi.org/10.1007/978-3-030-38677-1

Mohanty, S. & Hughes, D. & Salathe, M. 2016. Using Deep Learning for Image-Based Plant Disease Detection. *Frontiers in Plant Science. 7. 10.3389/fpls.2016.01419.*

Mwebaze, E. & Owomugisha, G. 2016. Machine Learning for Plant Disease Incidence and Severity Measurements from Leaf Images. *158–163. 10.1109/ICMLA.2016.0034.*

Olga, R. & Jia, D. & Hao, S. & Jonathan, K. & Sanjeev, S. & Sean Ma, Z. H. & Andrej, K. & Khosla, A. & Michael, B. & Alexander, C. B. & Li F. F. ImageNet Large Scale Visual Recognition Challenge. *IJCV, 2015.*

Pan, S. & Yang, Q. 2010. A Survey on Transfer Learning. *Knowledge and Data Engineering, IEEE Transactions on. 22. 1345–1359. 10.1109/TKDE.2009.191.*

Pantazi, X.E. & Moshou, D. & Tamouridou, A. A. 2019. Automated leaf disease detection in different crop species through image features analysis and One Class Classifiers. *Computers and Electronics in Agriculture. 156. 96–104. 10.1016/j.compag.2018.11.005.*

Quasim, M. T., Khan M. A, et al, 2019, Internet of Things for Smart Healthcare: A Hardware Perspective, 2019 First International Conference of Intelligent Computing and Engineering (ICOICE), Hadhramout, Yemen, 2019, pp. 1–5. DOI: 10.1109/ICOICE48418.2019.9035175

Quasim, M.T., Khan M.A, Algarni F., Alharthy A., Alshmrani G.M.M, (2020), Blockchain Frameworks. In: Khan M., Quasim M., Algarni F., Alharthi A. (eds) Decentralised Internet of Things. Studies in Big Data, vol 71. Springer, DOI: https://doi.org/10.1007/978-3-030-38677-1

Ruder, S. 2016. An overview of gradient descent optimization algorithms.

Rumpf, T. & Mahlein, A.-K. & Steiner, U. & Oerke, E.-C. & Dehne, H.-W. & Plümer, L. 2010. Early detection and classification of plant diseases with Support Vector Machines based on hyperspectral reflectance. *Computers and Electronics in Agriculture. 74. 91-99. 10.1016/j.compag.2010.06.009.*

Sandler, M. & Howard, A. & Zhu, M. & Zhmoginov, A. & Chen, L. 2018. MobileNetV2: Inverted Residuals and Linear Bottlenecks. *4510–4520. 10.1109/CVPR.2018.00474.*

Shijie, J., Peiyi, J., Siping, H. & Haibo, S. 2017. Automatic detection of tomato diseases and pests based on leaf images. *2537–2510. 10.1109/CAC.2017.8243388.*

Simonyan, K. & Zisserman, A. 2014. Very Deep Convolutional Networks for Large-Scale Image Recognition. *arXiv 1409.1556.*

Singh, V. & Misra, A.K. 2016. Detection of Plant Leaf Diseases Using Image Segmentation and Soft Computing Techniques. *Information Processing in Agriculture. 4. 10.1016/j.inpa.2016.10.005.*

Singh, V. & Misra, A. 2015. Detection of unhealthy region of plant leaves using image processing and genetic algorithm. *1028–1032. 10.1109/ICACEA.2015.7164858.*

Too, E. & Yujian, L. & Njuki, S. & Yingchun, L. 2018. A comparative study of fine-tuning deep learning models for plant disease identification. *Computers and Electronics in Agriculture. 10.1016/j.compag.2018.03.032.*

Wang, G. & Sun, Y. & Wang, J. 2017. Automatic Image-Based Plant Disease Severity Estimation Using Deep Learning. Computational Intelligence and Neuroscience. *2017. 1–8. 10.1155/2017/2917536.*

Zoph, B., Vasudevan, V., Shlens, J. & Le, Q. 2018. Learning Transferable Architectures for Scalable Image Recognition. *8697–8710. 10.1109/CVPR.2018.00907.*

Smart Computing – Khan et al (Eds)
© 2021 Taylor & Francis Group, London, ISBN 978-0-367-76552-1

Analytical study on melanoma detection using clinical images

Mohd Firoz Warsi
Research Scholar, Department of ECE, Galgotia University, Greater Noida, India

Usha Chauhan
Department of ECE, Galgotia University, Greater Noida, India

Ruqaiya Khanam
Department of ECE, Sharda University, Greater Noida, India

ABSTRACT: Malignant melanoma is the deadliest form of skin cancer. Generally, there are two different kinds of skin cancer: benign and malignant. As benign and malignant melanoma have similarities at the early stages, it is not easy to distinguish between them. However, early detection of melanoma is key as it can lead to a highly successful treatment rate. Moreover, early detection of melanoma can be increased with the use of Computer-Aided Diagnosis. Melanoma is the 15th most commonly occurring cancer in the world. In 2020, there were 100,350 new cases of melanoma, and the rates of skin cancers have been steadily increasing, now doubling approximately every 15 years. This paper presents different methods for initial stage melanoma skin cancer recognition using medical images.

1 INTRODUCTION

Skin covers about a 20-square-foot area of the human body (Better information 2016). Our skin plays an important role in maintaining body temperature and defending our body from UV rays. It also permits the feelings of touch, heat, and cold. The human skin contains three layers: (1) epidermis; (2) dermis; and (3) hypodermis. The three layers can be seen in Figure 1.

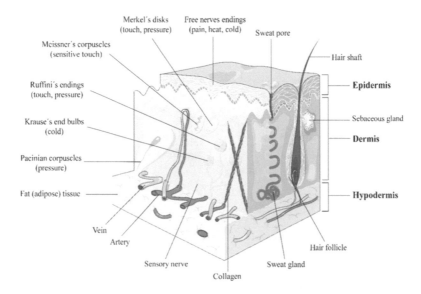

Figure 1. Structure of skin.

DOI 10.1201/9781003167488-22

Skin cancer is generally one of two types: benign and malignant. Benign consists of normal lesions but malignant is a dangerous form of skin cancer. It penetrates into the dermis layer and then, if not cured, can spread into the whole skin, as shown in Figure 2.

As per the records of the British Skin Foundation, melanoma cases are increasing very fast. Every year near about 100,000 fresh cases of skin cancer come into existence and approximately 2500 people die due to this deadly disease (The British Skin Foundation 2016). The Cancer Research UK tells us that the rates of melanoma cases will increase in the future, as shown in Figure 3. Melanoma is incurable in its last stage, but in its early stage it is curable. It is not easy to differentiate melanoma from other pigmented skin (Pariser & Pariser 1987). In the early-stage, melanoma can be detected by the "ABCDE" rule, Menzies method, or a 7-point checklist. Among the three methods, the ABCDE rule is the most frequently used. Here, "A" means "asymmetry", "B" means "border irregularity", "C" means "color variation", "D" means "diameter" (more than 6 mm), and "E" means "evolving over time".

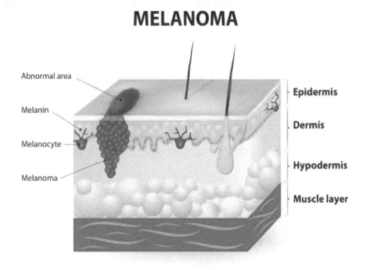

Figure 2. Melanoma spreading in skin.

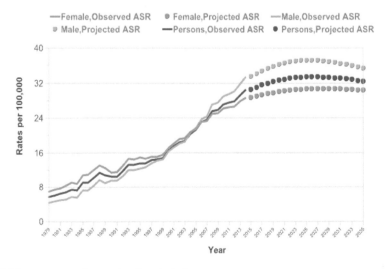

Figure 3. Melanoma cases observed and projected.

Figure 4.   Steps in skin cancer detection using CAD.

However, the most dangerous form of melanoma cannot be accurately detected by these methods. So, computer-aided diagnosis (CAD) is applied to detect the fatal form of melanoma with clinical images. This also supports the medical assessment of dermatologists.

Each CAD system for skin disease has the same steps with the same sequence as shown in Figure 4.

Pre-processing: The objective of the pre-processing is to do image enhancement, image sharpening, image restoration, and filtering and hair removal.

Segmentation: Image is divided into regions or categories, which are known as different objects or parts of objects.

Feature extraction: Here, visual content of images is captured for indexing and retrieval. Features like color, texture, and shape are extracted.

Classification: This refers to the labeling of images into one of a number of predefined categories.

2   LITERATURE SURVEY

An obscure skin lesion diagnosis is important to empower appropriate medications. If detected early, it essentially builds the survival rate. Here, we present a survey of the early examinations and framework for the detection of skin melanoma.

This study presents the CAD technique to classify hundreds of skin diseases according to disease taxonomy. Deep neural network is used for the classification ISIC and DermNet database. This method establishes accuracy of 80% and the area under curve (AUC) is 98% for 23 diseases on DermNet. Furthermore, it gives an accuracy of 93% and AUC of 99% on the ISIC database (Bajwa et al. 2020).

This research presents the automatic and early detection of melanoma with the CAD system. In this approach, Grey Level Co-occurrence Matrix (GLCM) is used for the feature extraction and the deep neural network (DNN) technique is used for the classification. The work has been done on the ISIC dataset. This method achieved accuracy of 81.75%, specificity of 88%, and sensitivity of 75.5% (Chandra et al. 2019).

A method to detect melanoma is introduced. In this method, the GrabCut algorithm is used for segmentation. Then features such as shape, color, and geometry are extracted.

The classification of extracted features is done with a support vector machine (SVM) with a Gaussian radial basis kernel (RBF). A database of 200 clinical images are used (100 benign and 100 melanoma) (Mustafa & Kimura 2018).

Two deep learning strategies, the Lesion Feature Network (LFN) and Lesion Indexing Network (LIN), are applied to tackle three primary undertakings, namely Lesion Segmentation, Lesion clinical Feature Extraction, and Lesion Classification for skin cancer detection. A convolutional neural network (CNN) technique is utilized on the ISIC 2017 dataset to assess the proposed deep learning system (Li & Shen 2018).

This work introduces a computer-based system which calculates the predictable deepness of lesions for analysis. A 3D image of a skin lesion is reconstructed using the predictable depth obtained from normal dermoscopic images. With the help of the 3D image reconstruction and depth, 3D and 2D shape, color, and texture features are extracted. Projected structure is planned to diagnose dermatofibroma, BCC, blue nevus, haemangioma, normal mole lesions, and seborrhoeic keratosis. Three types of dataset, ISIC (Melanoma Project), PH2, and ATLAS dermoscopy, are taken for experiments. Four feature sets are pooled and performance is calculated. Noteworthy performance enhancement is reported with the addition of expected depth and 3D features. The results obtained for classification are remarkable: sensitivity = 96%, specificity = 97% for PH2 dataset; and sensitivity = 98%, specificity = 99% for ATLAS dataset is achieved (Satheesha et al. 2017).

The extraction of texture feature and shape features is performed by the gray-level co-occurrence matrix (GLCM) and texture wavelet. These features are used to compare the work of different CAD classifiers. The projected method follows fixed wavelet grid network (FWGN). FWGN follows an algorithm named DOOMP. DOOMP stands for D-optimality orthogonal matching pursuit, used for image pre-processing, segmentation, and classification giving, specificity = 91.00, sensitivity = 92.61, and accuracy = 91.82 (Sadri et al. 2017)

The texture feature using GLCM and color features in hue, saturation, value (HSV) domain is extracted. These features are trained and tested with SVM classifier with the 3-fold cross validation technique. Results obtained using the above techniques are: specificity = 84%, sensitivity = 97%, and accuracy = 96% (Waheed et al. 2017).

The proposed system recognizes skin sores on pictures taken from a general camera. The pictures are separated by the ABCD rule and then a neural network classifier is used to enhance precision 76.9% on 463 images (Dubal et al. 2017).

The study suggests a system for melanoma detection. The ABCD rule was used to examine the data set of 201 images and the neural network system to get an accuracy of 97.5% far more than a specialist (75–85%) (Cueva et al. 2017).

In this paper, a skin cancer detection system with a pre-processing strategy for noise removal and image upgrade is introduced. GLCM is used for feature extraction. Then SVM is used to classify cancerous and non-cancerous images giving 95% of accuracy (Ansari & Sarode 2017).

In this work, an original melanoma recognition method is introduced that follows Mahalanobis distance learning (MDL) and constrained graph regularized non-negative matrix factorization (CGRNMF).

The projected method features dimensionality reduction with supervised machine learning. In this method both local manifold and global geometry are used to improve the discrimination power of the classification system. Edinburgh Dermofit Image Library and PH2 Dermoscopy Image Dataset are used for evaluations. This method gives the best performance with 94.43% sensitivity, 81.01% specificity, and 99.50% accuracy on PH2 dataset (Gu et al. 2017).This study introduced 19-layer CNNs for lesion classification. The authors utilized two databases which is ISBI 2016 and the PH2 database to assess the viability, productivity, and capacity of the proposed system. Investigations led by the author presumed that the proposed technique beat other best in-class calculations on these two databases (Gu et al. 2017)

Yu et al. (2017) proposed another technique for melanoma detection by utilized deep CNNs. He introduced that their framework, deeper networks, can procure more extravagant and discriminative highlights for more precise acknowledgment. To take a completely favorable point of view of deep networks, the author proposed an arrangement of plans to assure successful development and gain under controlled preparing information (Yu et al. 2017).

This work suggests a CAD system for the detection of malignant melanoma method by clinical images with joint reverse classification (JRC) and multi-scale lesion-biased representation (MLR). Training and testing of classifiers with the proposed method are done with PH2 database. The results show an accuracy of 92%, sensitivity 87.50%, and specificity 93.13% (Bi et al. 2016).

A robotized skin lesion investigation framework for early melanoma detection is used in this work. Hair finding and expulsion is done for successful order and extraction highlights of the skin lesion. The test results are checked on PH2 database (Joseph & Panicker 2016).

This paper reviewed the CAD system and inspected the latest methods used for these systems. Results and statistics by the recent methods are studied and reported. The author compared the performance of new work based on different parameters like computational time, color space accuracy, sensitivity, specificity, machine learning technique, etc. The result is put in table format to enhance the understanding of developing researchers in the emerging field of automatic skin cancer diagnosis systems. Automated skin cancer diagnosis systems research challenges in the different fields are also explained (Hameed et al. 2016).

This paper focuses on two renowned methods for texture feature extraction with Gabor filters and GLCM. SVM is used for classification of texture. In the first step, the techniques are applied in R, G, and B channels separately for the color image. The results show the enormous growth of accuracy in color texture extraction with GLCM. So, GLCM is adapted for evaluating probability matrices directly from the color image. Thirteen directions of a neighborhood system are proposed and 13 equations for probability matrices calculation are obtained. The projected method is known as color-level co-occurrence matrices (CLCMs) and results confirm it to be an influential method for texture and color classification simultaneously. Vistex and Outex databases are used for experimental evaluation with the help of the SVM-RBF classifier. The experimental results verify that the projected CLCM method got an F1 score around 40% superior to the fundamental GLCM method. This method proves over 90% achievement in texture color classification (Benco et al. 2014).

This study introduced two methods for recognition of melanoma and benign images applying on texture and color features. These proposed methods are global and local. Outstanding results were acquired by global methods. Lesion regions were separated in two sub-regions with specificity = 80% and sensitivity = 96% but the results of the local system were better: specificity = 75% and sensitivity = 100%. PH2 dataset of 200 dermoscopic images from Hospital Pedro Hispano is used for the training and testing of the suggested algorithm (Barata et al. 2013).

This is an original system to segment the images with CAD system. It uses color segmentation done by a customized K-means algorithm and texture segmentation by local binary pattern (LBP). Feature extraction is executed after segmentation process. The feature vectors are put in a neural network classifier having a number of layers for the classification of features.

The system achieved sensitivity >97% and specificity >93%. The proposed system is trained, tested, and verified with lesion images with free images on the Internet. It gives a simple use of an iPhone-based app to distinguish melanoma in an initial stage without biopsy (Cheerla & Frazier 2014).

A CAD system based on the ABCD rule is used to distinguish melanoma from non-melanoma lesions. First, morphological processing and fast marching schemes are used for a preprocessing task. Then, segmentation is done by an unsupervised approach for a lesion. Accuracy of this system is compared with GrowCut and mean shift Algorithms. The work also highlights the influence of results in feature extraction and classification. Features of the ABCD rule—(1) asymmetry; (2) border; (3) color; and (4) diameter—are computed. ANN is used to build a classification unit. A large dataset of 320 clinical images are used for evaluation. The results show that the proposed technique provides more exact segmented results than methods such as the mean shift approach and GrowCut algorithm (Messadi et al. 2014).

This research introduced a system where features like shape, color, and texture are calculated from the lesion part of the dermoscopic images. SMOTE, SVM, ensemble, and group of classifiers are proposed for classification. A 564 skin lesion image dataset is used for evaluation. The classification result in the proposed work is: specificity = 93.84%, sensitivity= 93.76%, and accuracy = 93.83% (Schaefer et al. 2013).

PH2 (a clinical image database) is presented which includes color images and the manual segmented images. This database has a set of 200 dermoscopic images, in which 80 images are

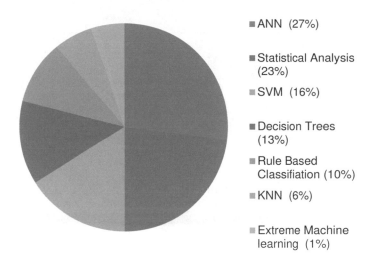

ANN (27%)

Statistical Analysis (23%)

SVM (16%)

Decision Trees (13%)

Rule Based Classifiation (10%)

KNN (6%)

Extreme Machine learning (1%)

Figure 5.   The usage percentage of machine learning methods in the literature.

non-melanoma, 80 images are benign, and 40 images are melanoma. Techniques like the ABCD rule, pattern analysis, the 7-point checklist, and the Menzies method are used to form this database. CAD has been projected to support the clinical estimation of clinical lesions. The PH2 database is based on manual segmentation of the skin lesion (Mendonça et al. 2013).

The proposed work gives an automatic system that detects malignant melanoma from clinical images. This system is defined by a set of following steps. First of all, a preprocessing technique is applied to modify the clinical image. After this, an attached component examination and a collection of directional filters are presented to identify the "lines" of the pigmentation. The second step involves feature extraction from the detected network. The third step includes an AdaBoost algorithm for the classification of every lesion of the pigment network. This algorithm was trained, tested, and verified on the PH2 dataset (200 medical images) from the database of Hospital Pedro Hispano (Matosinhos). Results show specificity $= 82.1\%$ and sensitivity $= 91.1\%$ (Barata et al. 2012).

Texture is a term known as the spatial difference of pixel intensities in an image. This definition is accepted and widely used in the skin cancer detection field. Texture analysis algorithms are used mainly for segmentation, classification, and synthesis. The aim of image segmentation is to create borders between dissimilar picture regions. Texture analysis methods determine the precise location where texture characteristic values vary significantly. Synthesizing image texture plays an important role in 3D graphics application to create extremely composite and practical-looking surfaces. Statistical texture analysis methods are continuously being developed by researchers and the variety of applications is rising. Fractal approaches present the ease of characterizing a textured section by a single evaluation. Statistical approaches are less application-specific than fractal approaches. Full 3D texture analysis approaches with algorithmic advances are tested to get great results. The numbers of publications in this area prove this as a challenging area of research (Nailon 2010).

Table 1 shows the summary of the reviewed papers which help are used fully in future research.

According to the survey, several machine learning and deep learning techniques have been used in the literature. As per the literature, the most widely used technique is ANN. Figure 5 shows a graph depicting the percentage of use of machine learning methods in the literature.

Numerous methods for feature extraction from dermoscopic images are also used in the literature. We demonstrate a summary of various feature extraction methods accepted in literature, as shown in Figure 6.

Table 1. Literature review.

Creator Name	Method Used	Results
Bajwa et al. (2020)	Deep learning with utilization of disease taxonomy	ISIC dataset – Accuracy = 93%, AUC = 99% DermNET Dataset-Accuracy = 80% AUC = 98%
Chandra et al. (2019)	GLCM for feature extraction and the DNN technique for classification	ISIC Dataset -880 melanoma and 773 non melanoma images. Accuracy = 81.75% Specificity = 88% Sensitivity = 75.5%
Mustafa & Kimura (2018)	GrabCut algorithm for segmentation. SVM·RBF for classification of melanoma images	Database of 200 clinical images. The result is significant. Images are classified as cancerous or non-cancerous.
Li & Shen (2018)	Two deep learning strategies: The Lesion Indexing Network (LIN) and the Lesion Feature Network (LFN) with CNN for segmentation, feature extraction, classification	Testing done on the ISIC 2017 database. Malignant and benign lesions are successfully differentiated.
Satheesha et al. (2017)	2D and 3D color and texture with shape features are extracted. SVM, AdaBoost, and bag-of features (BoF) classifiers are used.	Two datasets PH2 and ATLAS are used for testing. Sensitivity = 98%, Specificity = 99% (ATLAS dataset) Sensitivity = 96%, Specificity = 97% (PH2 dataset).
Sadri et al. (2017)	Texture features are extracted using GLCM. Segmentation and classification is done by FWGN.	Accuracy = 91.82%, Specificity = 91.00%, Sensitivity = 92.61%
Waheed et al. (2017)	Texture features and color features in HSV domain using GLCM are extracted. SVM with 3-fold cross folding are used for classification. Tested on PH2 database.	Accuracy = 96%, Sensitivity = 84% Specificity = 97% using MATLAB Accuracy = 95%, Sensitivity = 83% Specificity = 96% using Weka
Dubal et al. (2017)	ABCD rule for detection then neural network to enhance classification.	Database of 463 images and precision enhanced by 76.9%
Cueva et al. (2017)	ABCD rule for detection then neural network to enhance classification	Database of 261 images and accuracy enhanced by 97.5%
Ansari & Sarode (2017)	Texture features using GLCM are extracted.SVM for classification	Images are classified as cancerous or noncancerous. Accuracy = 95%
Gu et al. (2017)	Constrained graph regularized non-negative matrix factorization (CGRNMF) and Mahalanobis distance learning (MDL) methods are used for melanoma detection.	Sensitivity = 94.43%, Specificity = 81% using PH2 database Sensitivity = 99.50%, Specificity = 93.68% using Edinburgh Library
Yuan et al. (2017)	19-layer neural network used for image classification	Tested on the ISBI 2016 and the PH2 databases. The proposed technique beat other best-in-class calculations on these two databases.
Yu et al. (2016)	Deep CNNs are applied for classification between benign and malignant melanoma. FCRN for segmentation and classification are used on ISBI database.	Deeper networks can procure more discriminative highlights for more precise work than SVM and softmax classifier. Accuracy = 85.5%, Sensitivity = 54.7%

continued.

Table 1. Literature review (Continued).

Creator Name	Method Used	Results
Bi et al. (2016)	JRC and multi-scale lesion-biased representation (MLR) are used for melanoma detection	Testing and evaluation done on PH2 database. Accuracy = 92%, Sensitivity = 87.50%, Specificity= 93.13%
Joseph & Panicker (2016)	Robotized skin lesion investigation framework for melanoma detection.	Test results checked on PH2 database.
Hameed et al. (2016)	Survey paper on methods for melanoma diagnosis.	Performance of latest work with parameters like accuracy, sensitivity, and specificity, computational time, color space, and different machine learning techniques are compared and summarized.
Benco et al. (2014)	CLCM and GF technique is used for feature extraction. SVM is used as a classifier.	The projected CLCM method gets > 40% higher score than the basic GLCM method. It proves > 90% success in color texture classification.
Barata et al. (2013)	Two methods are used named—local and global—for detection of malignant melanoma using texture and color features.	Tested on 176 clinical images. Sensitivity = 100%, Specificity = 75% (local methods), Sensitivity = 96%, Specificity = 80% (global methods).
Cheerla & Frazier (2014)	Texture segmentation by LBP and color segmentation is performed by the K-means algorithm. A group of features are extracted from the segmented images. A multistage neural network is used as a classifier.	Sensitivity = 97%, Specificity = 93%
Messadi et al. (2014)	ABCD rule and ANN. Segmentation with unsupervised technique, GrowCut, and mean shift algorithm	Tested on 320 dermoscopy images. The proposed technique is capable of giving more precise results than methods like mean shift approach and GrowCut algorithm.
Schaefer et al. (2013)	Feature extraction (shape, color, and texture) is done from the lesion part of clinical images. Classification with SVM, SMOTE, ensemble, and their combination.	Training and testing are done on the dataset of 564 skin lesion images. Accuracy = 93.83%, Specificity = 93.84%, Sensitivity 93.76%.
Mendonca et al. (2013)	Dermoscopic image database called PH2 is presented.	In a total of 200 images, 80 images were non-melanoma, 80 atypical nevi, and 40 images are melanoma. The CAD system has been projected to help the clinical estimation of clinical images.
Barata et al. (2012)	Pigmented images detected using directional filter, feature extraction, and AdaBoost algorithm for classification.	Result tested on PH2 database. Sensitivity = 91.1%, Specificity = 82.1%.
Nailon (2010)	The texture extraction method with case studies is presented.	Full 3D texture analysis approaches with algorithmic advances are presented. There is zero loss of discriminatory power with 2D algorithms used in the coronal and sagittal planes.

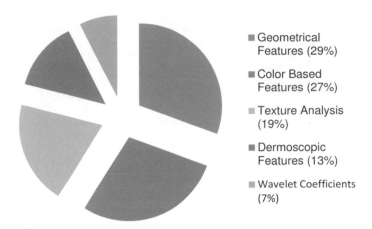

Figure 6.   The usage percentage of feature extraction methods in the literature.

3   CONCLUSION

Malignant melanoma cancer analysis system with CAD spot and differentiate skin cancer symptoms and detect melanoma in the initial stages. This paper gives a quick review that will assist future researchers to recognize and execute the techniques. In this paper, a survey of skin cancer with automatic detection methods is introduced. We have presented a summary of the 25 different research papers studied by us. This paper also highlights different techniques and methods used for skin cancer detection. During the survey it has been shown that by using different algorithms melanoma can be diagnosed, but with some disadvantages. To eliminate these disadvantages, the CAD system is introduced. ANNs have a great scope for melanoma detection using clinical images, and it is the most emerging technology in the field of skin cancer since it is more accurate than other classification methods. ANN is the most frequently used method (27%) in melanoma detection and provides the best result when used with color and texture feature extraction.

In this survey, different techniques are highlighted for melanoma detection so that, together, we can fight this lethal disease.

REFERENCES

Ansari, U.B. & Sarode, T. 2017. Skin Cancer Detection Using Image Processing. *International Research Journal of Engineering and Technology (IRJET)* 4.

Bajwa, M.N., Muta, K., Malik, M.I., Siddiqui, S.A., Braun, S.A., Homey, B., Dengel, A. & Ahmed, S. 2020. Computer-Aided Diagnosis of Skin Diseases using Deep Neural Networks. *Applied Sciences.*

Barata, C., Marques, J.S. & Rozeira, J. 2012. A system for the detection of pigment network in dermoscopy images using directional filters. *IEEE transactions on biomedical engineering* 59(10): 2744–2754.

Barata, C., Ruela, M., Francisco, M., Mendonça, T. & Marques, J.S. 2013. Two systems for the detection of melanomas in dermoscopy images using texture and color features. *IEEE Systems Journal* 8(3): 965–979.

Benco, M., Hudec, R., Kamencay, P., Zachariasova, M. & Matuska, S. 2014. An advanced approach to extraction of colour texture features based on GLCM. *International Journal of Advanced Robotic Systems* 11(7): 1–8.

Better information. better health. 2016. The skin (Human Anatomy), Available: http://www.webmd.com/skin-problems-and treatments/picture-of-the-skin.

Bi, L., Kim, J., Ahn, E., Feng, D. & Fulham, M. 2016. Automatic melanoma detection via multi-scale lesion-biased representation and joint reverse classification. *13th international symposium on biomedical imaging (ISBI), Czech Republic.*

The British Skin Foundation. 2016. Skin Cancer, Available: http://www.britishskinfoundation.org.uk/SkinInformation/SkinCancer.aspx.

Chandra, T.G., Nasution, A.T.M. & Setiadi, I.C. 2019. Melanoma and Nevus Classification Based on Asymmetry, Border, Color, and GLCM Texture Parameters Using Deep Learning Algorithm. *AIP Conference Proceedings 2193, Padang, Indonesia.*

Cheerla, N. & Frazier, D. 2014. Automatic Melanoma Detect ion Using Multi-Stage Neural Networks. *International Journal of Innovative Research in Science, Engineering and Technology.*

Cueva, W.F., Muñoz, F., Vásquez, G. & Delgado, G. 2017. Detection of skin cancer Melanoma through computer vision. In *2017 IEEE XXIV International Conference on Electronics, Electrical Engineering and Computing (INTERCON), Cuzco, Peru.*

Dubal, P., Bhatt, S., Joglekar, C. & Patil, S. 2017. Skin Cancer Detection and classification. *International Journal of Research and Analytical Reviews (IJRAR)* 7(1): 237–248.

Gu, Y., Zhou, J. & Qian, B. 2017. Melanoma detection based on mahalanobis distance learning and constrained graph regularized nonnegative matrix factorization. *IEEE Winter Conference on Applications of Computer Vision (WACV), CA, USA.*

Hameed, N., Ruskin, A., Hassan, K.A. & Hossain, M.A. 2016. A comprehensive survey on image-based computer aided diagnosis systems for skin cancer. *10th International Conference on Software, Knowledge, Information Management & Applications (SKIMA), Chengdu, China.*

Joseph, S. & Panicker, J.R. 2016. Skin lesion analysis system for melanoma detection with an effective hair segmentation method. *International Conference on Information Science (ICIS), Dublin, Ireland.*

Li, Y. & Shen, L. 2018. Skin Lesion Analysis towards Melanoma Detection Using Deep Learning Network. *Sensors*: 1–16.

Mendonça, T., Ferreira, P.M., Marques, J.S., Marcal, A.R. & Rozeira, J. 2013. PH 2-A dermoscopic image database for research and benchmarking. *35th annual international conference of the IEEE engineering in medicine and biology society (EMBC), Osaka, Japan.*

Messadi, M., Cherifi, H. & Bessaid, A., 2014. Segmentation and ABCD rule extraction for skin tumors classification. *Journal of Convergence Information Technology* 9(2): 21.

Mustafa, S. & Kimura, A. 2018. A SVM based diagnosis of melanoma using only useful image features. *International Workshop on Advanced Image Technology (IWAIT), Chiang Mai, Thailand.*

Nailon, W.H. 2010. Texture Analysis Methods for Medical Image Characterisation. *Biomed. Imaging.*

Pariser, R.J. & Pariser, D.M. 1987. Primary care physician's errors in handling cutaneous disorders. *Journal of the American Academy of Dermatology* 17: 239–245.

Sadri, A.R., Azarianpour, S., Zekri, M., Celebi, M.E. & Sadri, S., 2017. WN-based approach to melanoma diagnosis from dermoscopy images. *IET Image Processing* 11(7): 475–482.

Satheesha, T.Y., Satyanarayana, D., Prasad, M.N.G. & Dhruve, K.D. 2017. Melanoma Is Skin Deep: A 3D Reconstruction Technique for Computerized Dermoscopic Skin Lesion Classification. *IEEE Journal of Translational Engineering in Health and Medicine* 5: 1–17.

Schaefer, G., Krawczyk, B., Celebi, M.E. and Iyatomi, H., 2013. November. Melanoma classification using dermoscopy imaging and ensemble learning. *2nd IAPR Asian Conference on Pattern Recognition, Okinawa, Japan.*

Waheed, Z., Waheed, A., Zafar, M. & Riaz, F. 2017. An efficient machine learning approach for the detection of melanoma using dermoscopic images. *International Conference on Communication, Computing and Digital Systems (C-CODE), Islamabad, Pakistan.*

Yu, L., Chen, H., Dou, Q., Qin, J. & Heng, P.A. 2017. Automated Melanoma Recognition in Dermoscopy Images via Very Deep Residual Networks. *IEEE Transactions on Medical Imaging* 36(4): 994–1004.

Yuan, Y., Chao, M. & Lo, Y.C. 2017. Automatic skin lesion segmentation using deep fully convolutional networks with jaccard distance. *IEEE transactions on medical imaging* 36(9): 1876–1886.

Smart Computing – Khan et al (Eds)
© *2021 Taylor & Francis Group, London, ISBN 978-0-367-76552-1*

Automated brain hemorrhage segmentation using a deep neural network

V. Thapliyal, I. Kumar & P. Sharma
Graphic Era Hill University, Dehradun, Uttarakhand, India

H.S. Bhadauria & A. Singh
GB Pant Institute of Engineering & Technology, Pauri Garhwal, Uttarakhand, India

ABSTRACT: In this work, an automated brain hemorrhage segmentation using the deep neural network (DNN) has been proposed. A total of 157 patients, ages 23–69, are collected from different hospitals and laboratories, and the total number of 3038 images is collected. Initially, ground truth images are generated using preprocessing steps and validated through 3 experts having more than 20 years of experience. Data augmentation is performed to create a virtual image for training DNN models, and a convolutional neural network-based U-Net model is used. Extensive experimentations were performed using 6000, 8000, 10,000 samples with 20%, 30%, and 40% dropout, respectively. The same combination of experiments has been performed for *ReLU* and tanh activation function. After the investigations, it has been found that the maximum training accuracy of the proposed model is 98.8% using the ReLU activation function. Similarly, 93.3% of accuracy has been achieved by a tanh activation function.

Keywords: CT Imaging, brain hemorrhage, deep neural network, U-Net.

1 INTRODUCTION

According to the statistics reported in studies by Van et al. (2010), Qureshi et al. (2001), and Broderick et al. (2007), an average of 2.46 per 10,000 people each year are diagnosed with a brain hemorrhage. This report indicates the significance of detection or segmentation of hemorrhage as a primary task for the patients with neurological abnormalities or head injury. A hemorrhage is an unusual flow of blood in the body that can be external, i.e., visible outside the body, or internal, i.e., not visible outside the body. Hemorrhage can occur in any part of the body, but the most calamitous and typical of them is intracranial hemorrhage (ICH). In ICH, the blood flows inside the brain due to ruptured blood vessels, which causes swelling of clotted blood inside the brain within the tissues. This is known as a hematoma and it can cause life-threatening damage. It can occur in any age as observed in Van et al. (2010), Qureshi et al. (2001), and Broderick et al. (2007), Chilamkurthy et al. (2018), and Kuo et al. (2019, 2020). Depending upon the hemorrhage location, ICH is classified as follows.

 (i) *Epidural hematoma.* Bleeding occurs between the dura mater and the skull. This is fatal as the blood can cause high intracranial pressure.
 (ii) *Subdural hemorrhage.* A pool of blood occurs between the brain and its outermost covering.
(iii) *Subarachnoid hemorrhage.* Occurs in the area between arachnoid and pia mater known as the subarachnoid space.
(iv) *Cerebral hemorrhage:* This is bleeding inside the brain. This one is more dangerous than any other hemorrhage type and is harder to diagnose according to An (2017) and Caceres (2012).

DOI 10.1201/9781003167488-23

A computed tomgraphy (CT) scan or magnetic resonance imaging (MRI) can identify a brain hemorrhage (Bhadauria & Dewal 2014; Kumar et al. 2020) and can be used to highlight specific areas of that brain hemorrhage. A CT uses X-rays to produce a 2D image of structures inside the body, which are then converted to 3D structures using computers (Chang et al. 2018). It is a technique that is used worldwide to detect abnormalities in the body, such as tumors, abnormal blood vessels, bleeding inside the body, etc. It gives a clear picture of an area of your body or detects tumor location before radiotherapy.

In spite of technology, it is still a challenge even for experts to identify slight or faint abnormalities in the brain. Brain hemorrhage is a life-threatening situation that needs early and fast detection to be cured easily. Approximately 10,000 radiologists are practicing currently, with thousands CT scans done daily. However, radiologists are not always available every time, for example at night or in the case of some urgency. Therefore, research communities have to develop a computer-assisted system to perform a similar type of task in an efficient and optimized manner. The previously published work shows the developed system either based on the machine learning algorithm or without machine learning. Therefore, in this work, an automated brain hemorrhage segmentation using a Deep Neural Network (DNN) has been designed. The proposed work is validated as well as trained on real-time CT images, collected from different hospitals.

The rest of the paper is structured as follows. In Section 2, the current state of the art is described as well as the motivation behind the proposed work. Section 3, Materials and Methods, discusses dataset preparation and various methodologies. Section 4 discusses the obtained results and discussions are presented. Finally, Section 5 presents a conclusion.

2 RELATED STUDIES

Over the last few decades, so many semi-automated or fully automated computer-assisted frameworks have been proposed for the classification and segmentation of tiny artifacts, tumor cells, or brain hemorrhage detection with the help of CT images. It is worth mentioning that the semi-automated model required expert involvement so that such types of models take more time to make any decision regarding the problems. In the case of an automated model, machine learning (ML) techniques are widely applicable. It has also been observed that ML is not yielding efficient results for large datasets. Therefore, the present work is used to design a fully automated system for brain hemorrhage segmentation using a deep learning model.

The results of previous studies illustrate that the extensively used scheme for hemorrhage segmentation is strongly concerted around (a) thresholding (Weszka et al. 1974; Rawat et al. 2014); (b) fuzzy logics (Pham & Prince 1999); and (c) contour method (Caselles et al. 1993, 1995). Chan (2007) reports the hemorrhage segmentation using top-hat transform. The Otsu method (Otsu 1979) is also used for image segmentation as well as hemorrhage with fuzzy c-mean (Zaki et al. 2011) clustering algorithm. The variations of active contour (Caselles et al. 1995; Chan & Luminita 1999) are also used for medical image segmentation to with fuzzy set. In Bhadauria & Dewal (2014), fuzzy-based active contour is used to segment the hemorrhagic region using CT scan images.

Lee et al. (2019) focused on the classification of the hemorrhage based on their location. Its rating was based on data from previous CT scan images where the person suffered from a hemorrhage, and the stage to which the hemorrhage has reached was mentioned. Bhadauria & Dewal (2014) used spatial fuzzy c-mean and region-based active contour on brain CT imaging for brain hemorrhage detection.

From the previously published work, it has been found that the work based on hemorrhage classification is rigorously done in a semi-automated manner. Still, there haven't been many efforts to segment the hemorrhage region in a fully automated manner correctly. Classification of the hemorrhage is just a start; there are many more things that can be done using ML, especially neural networks. A segmentation model is proposed using a model that is inspired to some extent by the U-Net model. The proposed model is designed for the segmentation of hemorrhagic regions using brain CT images.

Table 1. Description of dataset.

Image Source	SGRMH	SMIH	JNMC	AMCC
Total Number of images	$35 \times 20 = 700$ {35 Patient and 20 images per patient)	$36 \times 20 = 720$ {36 Patient and 20 images per patient)	$35 \times 20=700$ {35 Patient and 20 images per patient)	$51 \times 18 = 918$ {51 Patient and 18 images per patient)
Scanner type	Philips Mx16	Philips Mx16	General Electric medical system	General Electric medical system
Image resolution	512×512 pixels	512×512 pixels	512×512 pixels	512×512 pixels
Thickness	2.5 mm.	2.5 mm.	3 mm	3 mm

2.1 Motivation

The motivation to propose this model came from facts that have been observed from past studies. After an extensive study of literature, it has been found that most of the work found is based on the semi-automated method that creates many errors and is more time-consuming. Such types of problems can be solved with the help of the development of an automated model. The development of an automated model is based on ML that is also an area of the author's interest. Therefore, a fully automated model has been proposed for correctly segmenting the hemorrhagic region using a CT image.

3 MATERIALS AND METHODS

3.1 *Dataset Preparation*

In this work, a dataset of 3038 brain CT images are used. All images are collected from four different sources, namely SGR Institute of Medical & Health Science (SGRMH), Dehradun, Shri Mahant Indresh Hospital (SMIH), Dehradun, Uttarakhand, Jawaharlal Nehru Medical College (JNMC), and Aligarh Muslim University, Aligarh and Amit MRI & CT Scan Center (AMCC), Moradabad, India from August 2017 to December 2019. The considered age group of patients lies between 23 and 69 years. The complete dataset is kept at an HP Z4 G4 workstation and Python environment is used for performing the experiments. The specification of the used workstation is mentioned as Intel Xeon W-2014 CPU @ 3.2 GHz, 64 GB RAM, 4GB NVIDIA Quadro P1000, 256 GB SSD, and 2TB SATA HDD. The brief description of dataset and scanner specification is given in Table 1.

3.2 *Proposed work*

The proposed workflow diagram of automated brain hemorrhage segmentation using DNN is shown in Figure 1. The designed method consists of three sections: a preprocessing section, model building section, and decision section. A brief description of each section is given here.

3.3 *Data Preprocessing*

There were a series of image preprocessing techniques used on the images such as the original images were first passed through cropping, thresholding, and masking which helped in removing the extra part of the image (Rawat et al. 2014) that was unnecessary such as the outer region of the head which in turn would have made the image unfit for training since it consisted of various regions which had a bit of a similar intensity as the hemorrhage region which might have caused trouble during the training process.

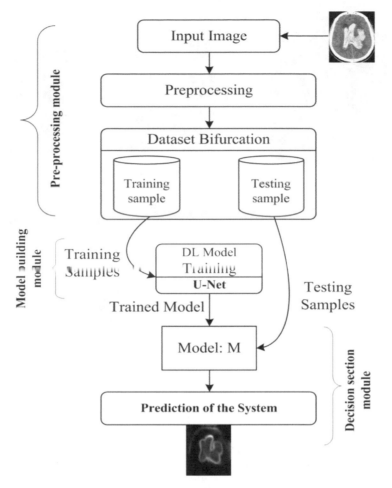

Figure 1. Proposed workflow diagram of automated brain hemorrhage segmentation using deep neural network.

Then by applying morphology, the mask (Rawat et al. 2014) of the images was created. Still, there was another trouble since the mask included the skull as it matched brightness intensity with the affected region, so the images were cropped based on the contour having a smaller area since the smaller area would be of the hemorrhage since it's inside the skull. Also in this phase, the authors created a bounding box around the ROI where the intensity was brighter inside the skull region.

Then by using thresholding followed by the convolution of the original and the masked image, we generate another image having only the affected region. The complete preprocessing steps and respective output of the sample input image is shown in Figure 2.

3.4 *Data Augmentation*

After thresholding, the images were augmented before sending them for the convolution stage. In order to train out the model during the process of the augmentation (Wang & Perez 2017; Lemley et al. 2017), a predefined probability was used in every operation. The probability of 0.3 indicates that 30 random images out of 100 images will be affected by the operation being performed for augmentation. The operations used were the rotation of maximum 50 degrees with the probability

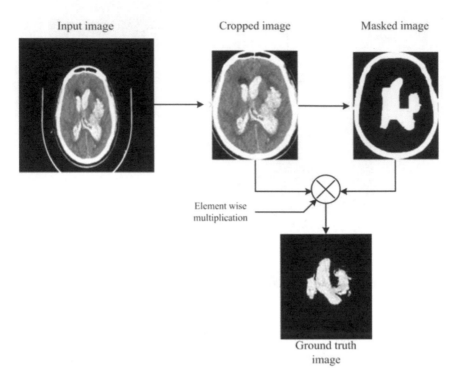

Figure 2.   Preprocessing step with output.

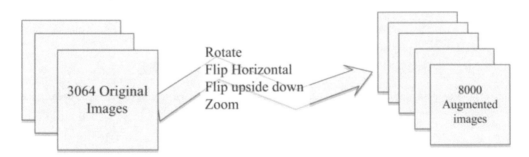

Figure 3.   Augmentation process flow.

of 0.8, image flipping left to right with a possibility of 0.5, zoom on random sections with a possibility of 0.5, and the zoom ratio between 0.1 and 0.8 flipping images upside down with a possibility of 0.5.

The final model used had 8000 images that were generated from the augmentation of 3064 original images and their ground truth (same operations as the original image were applied on the ground truth images during the development of augmentation). The description of data augmentation is shown in Figure 3.

3.5   Dataset bifurcation

The augmented dataset is further partitioned into training and testing samples. The used dataset for training was in Digital Imaging and Communication in Medicine (DICOM). All the patient's

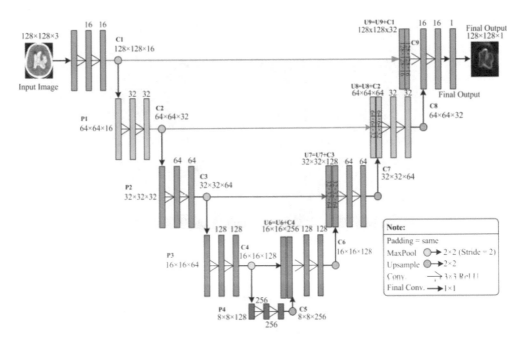

Figure 4.   Proposed U-Net architecture.

information was erased from the files before we received them. Therefore, processing these files, which initially was a challenge to process using python and openCV to read images, led to channel inversion since the typical image format is RGB. Still, openCV understands RGB, and even converting the image to RGB was not helpful. Still, then we found some libraries such as pydicom and some other libraries to read DICOM files and used them to load the images and used it to test the model and got around 97.0–98.0% accuracy.

3.6   U-Net Network Architecture

The used network architecture of U-Net (Ronneberger et al. 2015) is illustrated in Figure 4. It consists of a contracting or down-sampling part and an extracting or up-sampling part. The down-sampling part is on the left, and the up-sampling part is on the right. The down-sampling part follows a typical architecture of a convolutional network. It consists of repeated [3 × 3] convolutions (unpadded) and supported by the nonlinear activation function. Again, this is followed by a [2 × 2] max pooling with a stride of 2 during down-sampling, the number of feature channels was incremented in each next layer and during down-sampling, and during up-sampling (expansive path) each layer consists of a [2 × 2] (up-convolution) convolutional layer after up-sampling.

Since the down-sampling layer halves the number of feature channels we have to concatenate with the corresponding layer in the up-sampling phase. The cropping was necessary since we mainly required the area focused on the center generally and got a much better segmentation at the edges of the images.

The very end layer of the model has a sigmoid activation function, which helps to create the final output image. In total, the model consists of nine convolutional layers for the down-sampling and up-sampling procedures and then one for the output generation having a sigmoid activation function. The optimizer used was "Adam." The loss we monitored was the "binary cross-entropy" since we are dealing with binary images as segmentation training and output.

Cropped image	Ground Truth	Predicted Image

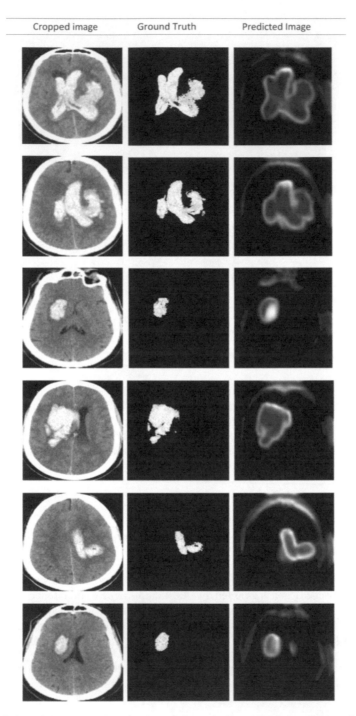

Figure 5. Prediction of the proposed work. *Note*: Column 1: Cropped Images; Column 2: Ground Truth Images; Column 3: Predicted Images.

Table 2. Obtained results using ReLU activation function.

Dropout	No. of images	Train 1 (accuracy) 50 epochs	Train 2 (accuracy) 50 epochs	Train 3 (accuracy) 50 epochs	Train 4 (accuracy) 50 epochs	Average accuracy
20%	6000	98.69	95.69	96.69	97.67	97.18
20%	8000	99.69	96.69	97.69	99.67	98.43
30%	8000	98.69	99.19	98.69	98.67	98.81
40%	8000	92.69	85.69	93.69	93.67	91.43
30%	10,000	98.69	94.69	97.69	98.67	97.43
40%	10,000	97.69	91.69	95.69	97.67	95.68

Table 3. Obtained results using ReLU activation function.

Dropout	No. of images	Train 1 (accuracy) 50 epochs	Train 2 (accuracy) 50 epochs	Train 3 (accuracy) 50 epochs	Train 4 (accuracy) 50 epochs	Average accuracy
20%	6000	94.69	92.69	91.69	93.67	93.18
20%	8000	93.69	92.69	91.69	89.67	91.93
30%	8000	91.69	93.19	94.69	93.67	93.31
30%	10,000	94.69	94.69	93.69	92.67	93.93
40%	10,000	96.69	92.69	87.69	93.67	92.68
40%	8000	94.69	93.69	92.69	91.67	91.18

3.7 Model-building Training

The model described is trained for 50 epochs in each test condition on the network and the average of the accuracy from the different tests has been taken as a measure to select which model to use to continue and refine the procedure and refine.

3.8 Testing

The model has been tested on a separate data which is in the form of DICOM images which was cleared of any information about the patient and then the pixel data was extracted which resulted in providing 200 images that were not used during the training of the model. They were also augmented to check the results under various conditions. The output of the designed model is shown in Figure 5.

4 EXPERIMENTS AND RESULTS

4.1 Description of experiments

Experiment 1: Automated Brain Hemorrhage Segmentation using Deep Neural Network with ReLU.

In this experiment, tedious work has been completed using dropout and different numbers of epoch using ReLU activation function. Initially, 6000 samples are used with 20% dropout and 4 different training methods were performed for 50 epochs. The obtained average training accuracy is 97.18% ((98.69 + 95.69 + 96.69 + 97.67)/4). Similarly, 8000 samples are used and achieved average accuracy is 98.43% with 20% dropout. The various combinations of dropout and the number of samples are tested, and the obtained training accuracy is reported in Table 2.

Experiment 2: Automated Brain Hemorrhage Segmentation using Deep Neural Network with tanh.

In this experiment, tedious work has been completed using dropout and different numbers of epoch using tanh activation function. Initially, 6000 samples are used with 20% dropout and 4 different training has been performed for 50 epochs. The obtained average training accuracy is 93.18% (94.69 + 92.69 + 91.69 + 93.67/4). Similarly, 10,000 samples are used and the achieved average accuracy is 93.93% with 30% dropout. The various combinations of dropout and the number of samples are tested, and the obtained training accuracy is reported in Table 3.

4.2 *Result Analysis*

From Table 2, it has been found that the highest training accuracy is 98.81% using ReLU activation function for 8000 samples and 30% dropout. Four different slots of training for 50 epochs is performed and the obtained accuracy is 98.69%, 99.19%, 98.69%, and 98.67%, respectively using ReLU activation function.

Table 3 shows the results of training accuracy using tanh activation function. It has been found that the 93.93% is the highest average accuracy for 10,000 samples with 30% dropout. Four different slots of training for 50 epochs are performed and the obtained accuracy is 94.69%, 94.69%, 93.69%, and 92.67%, respectively, using ReLU activation function.

5   CONCLUSIONS

According to the statistics reported in the literature, studies show that the death rate of people by brain hemorrhage is high. Therefore, detection or segmentation of the hemorrhagic region is an essential task. For this, various imaging modalities are used, but a CT scan is preferable due to its advantage and cost factor. In this work, a fully automated brain hemorrhage detection using DNNs is performed. For this brain, CT image samples are collected from four different hospitals and laboratories. Data augmentation is performed to create a virtual image for training DNN models, and CNN-based U-Net model is used. Extensive experimentations have been performed using 6000, 8000, 10,000 samples with 20%, 30%, and 40% dropout. The same combination of experiments has been performed for ReLU and tanh activation function. After the experiments, it has been found that the maximum training accuracy of the proposed model is 98.81% using the ReLU activation function. Similarly, 93.3% of accuracy has been achieved by tanh activation function. Thus, it has been noticed that ReLU activation function is more suitable for brain hemorrhage segmentation using a custom U-Net inspired CNN model.

REFERENCES

An, Sang Joon, Tae Jung Kim, & Byung-Woo Yoon. 2017. Epidemiology, risk factors, and clinical features of intracerebral hemorrhage: an update. *Journal of stroke*, *19*(1): 3–10.

Bhadauria, H. S., & Dewal, M. L. 2014. Intracranial hemorrhage detection using spatial fuzzy c-mean and region-based active contour on brain CT imaging. *Signal, Image and Video Processing*, *8*(2): 357–364.

Broderick, Joseph, et al. 2007. Guidelines for the Management of Spontaneous Intracerebral Hemorrhage in Adults: 2007 Update: A Guideline from the American Heart Association/American Stroke Association Stroke Council, High Blood Pressure Research Council, and the Quality of Care and Outcomes in Research Interdisciplinary Working Group: The American Academy of Neurology affirms the value of this guideline as an educational tool for neurologists. *Stroke* 38(6): 2001–2023.

Caceres, J. Alfredo, & Goldstein, Joshua N. 2012. Intracranial hemorrhage. *Emergency medicine clinics of North America*, *30*(3): 771–794.

Caselles, Vicent, Francine Catté, Tomeu Coll, & Françoise Dibos. 1993. A geometric model for active contours in image processing. *Numerische mathematik*, *66*(1), 1–31.

Caselles, Vicent, Ron Kimmel, & Guillermo Sapiro. 1995. Geodesic active contours. In *Proceedings of IEEE international conference on computer vision* (pp. 694–699).

Chan, Tao. (2007). Computer aided detection of small acute intracranial hemorrhage on computer tomography of brain. *Computerized Medical Imaging and Graphics*, *31*(4–5): 285–298.

Chan, Tony, & Vese Luminita. 1999. An active contour model without edges. In *International Conference on Scale-Space Theories in Computer Vision* (pp. 141-151). Springer, Berlin, Heidelberg.

Chang, Peter D., Edward Kuoy, Jack Grinband, Brent D. Weinberg, Matthew Thompson, Richelle Homo, Jefferson Chen et al. 2018. Hybrid 3D/2D convolutional neural network for hemorrhage evaluation on head CT. *American Journal of Neuroradiology*, *39*(9): 1609–1616.

Chilamkurthy, S., Ghosh, R., Tanamala, S., Biviji, M., Campeau, N. G., Venugopal, V. K., & Warier, P. 2018. Deep learning algorithms for detection of critical findings in head CT scans: a retrospective study. *The Lancet*, *392*(10162): 2388–2396.

Khan, Mohammad Ayoub. 2020. An IoT Framework for Heart Disease Prediction Based on MDCNN Classifier. *IEEE Access*, *8*: 34717–34727.

Kumar, Indrajeet, Chandradeep Bhatt, & Kamred Udham Singh. 2020. Entropy based automatic unsupervised brain intracranial hemorrhage segmentation using CT images. *Journal of King Saud University-Computer and Information Sciences*. 1–12.

Kuo, Weicheng, Christian Häne, Pratik Mukherjee, Jitendra Malik, & Esther L. Yuh. 2019. Expert-level detection of acute intracranial hemorrhage on head computed tomography using deep learning. *Proceedings of the National Academy of Sciences*, *116*(45): 22737–22745.

Lee, Hyunkwang, Sehyo Yune, Mohammad Mansouri, Myeongchan Kim, Shahein H. Tajmir, Claude E. Guerrier Sarah A. Ebert et al. 2019. An explainable deep-learning algorithm for the detection of acute intracranial haemorrhage from small datasets. *Nature Biomedical Engineering*, *3*(3): 173–182.

Lemley, Joseph, Shabab Bazrafkan, & Peter Corcoran. 2017. Smart augmentation learning an optimal data augmentation strategy. *Ieee Access*, *5*: 5858–5869.

Otsu, Nobuyuki. 1979. A threshold selection method from gray-level histograms. *IEEE transactions on systems, man, and cybernetics*, *9*(1): 62–66.

Pham, Dzung L., & Jerry L. Prince. 1999. An adaptive fuzzy segmentation algorithm for three-dimensional magnetic resonance images. In *Biennial International Conference on Information Processing in Medical Imaging* (pp. 140–153). Springer, Berlin, Heidelberg.

Qureshi, Adnan I., Stanley Tuhrim, Joseph P. Broderick, H. Hunt Batjer, Hideki Hondo, & Daniel F. Hanley. 2001. Spontaneous intracerebral hemorrhage. *New England Journal of Medicine*, *344*(19): 1450–1460.

Rawat, Jyoti, Singh, Annapurna, Bhadauria, H. S., & Kumar, Indrajeet. 2014. Comparative analysis of segmentation algorithms for leukocyte extraction in the acute Lymphoblastic Leukemia images. In *2014 International Conference on Parallel, Distributed and Grid Computing* (pp. 245-250). IEEE.

Ronneberger, Olaf, Philipp Fischer, & Thomas Brox. 2015. U-net: Convolutional networks for biomedical image segmentation. In *International Conference on Medical image computing and computer-assisted intervention* (pp. 234–241). Springer, Cham.

Van Asch, Charlotte JJ, Merel JA Luitse, Gabriël JE Rinkel, Ingeborg van der Tweel, Ale Algra, & Catharina JM Klijn. 2010. Incidence, case fatality, and functional outcome of intracerebral haemorrhage over time, according to age, sex, and ethnic origin: a systematic review and meta-analysis. *The Lancet Neurology*, *9*(2): 167–176.

Wang, Jason, & Luis Perez. 2017. The effectiveness of data augmentation in image classification using deep learning. *Convolutional Neural Networks Vis. Recognit*, *11*. 1–8.

Weszka, Joan S., Roger N. Nagel, & Azriel Rosenfeld. 1974. A threshold selection technique. *Ieee transactions on computers*, *100*(12): 1322–1326.

Zaki, W. Mimi Diyana W., M. Faizal A. Fauzi, Rosli Besar, & W. Siti Haimatul Munirah W. Ahmad. 2011. Abnormalities detection in serial computed tomography brain images using multi-level segmentation approach. *Multimedia Tools and Applications*, *54*(2): 321–340.

Smart Computing – Khan et al (Eds)
© 2021 Taylor & Francis Group, London, ISBN 978-0-367-76552-1

Digital image watermarking methods: A review

Satender Sharma & Usha Chauhan
SEECE, Galgotias University, Greater Noida, India

Ruqaiya Khanam
ECE Department, Sharda University, Greater Noida, India

ABSTRACT: Today private data content safety is an important point to consider. Watermarking, a data hiding technique, has been a popular research scope as of late. Watermarking is used for data safety and insurance, copyright administration, content verification and alter identification. This paper reviews the various methods of watermarking. Many of the advanced existing work is functionally described and compared based on robustness.

Keywords: Digital image processing, watermarking, discrete cosine transform, discrete wavelet transform, peak signal to noise ratio

1 INTRODUCTION

The digital image processing not only provides image security advancement but also provides a number of tools of security for image and video data. Practically, the incidents in digital fraud (Andalibi & Chandler 2015; Tirkel et al. 1993) have increased the requirement for advanced and updated methods of copyright safety to remove unauthorized copying and division. Largely due to its feasibility and perfection, watermarking has become a superiorly agreed-upon solution to this problem (Natarajan & Makhdumi 2009; Podilchuk & Delp 2001). Algorithms of digital watermarking insert the real media into specific recognizing information (the "digital watermark"; Andalibi & Chandler 2015), such as a seal, industry logo, biometric print, or serial numbers (Zhao & Ho 2010; Halder et al. 2010).

Watermarking is a technique for security, evidence of ownership, and right of possession protection on a large level; however, it is related to use in audio and video telecast controling, data honesty authentication, and photo marking and labeling (Nema & Mohan 2014). Watermarking is a growing field of research which has been explored for many decades. However, recent, laborious work has been done to get better a presentation, as the latest requirements and obligations posed by the newest applications inspiring the requirement of sustained study in this area.

The newest requirement is the capability of watermarking to stay alive in several repeated attacks. As of late, Multimedia Messaging Service (MMS) and online picture and video sharing of locales, e.g., Facebook, Twitter, Instagram, WhatsApp, and other public and customary news sources, have transformed into the most recent methods of scattering recordings and photographs. Generally, the raw images are a version of labor-intensive and/or machine processing (digitally processed) before being posted, chiefly when used on well-known social websites and software such as Instagram, Facebook, WhatsApp, etc. Furthermore, when a photo is transmitted through a noisy communication its size and clarity is also reduced. In last 10–15 years, it was too difficult to protect images from several attacks but now it is easy due to several watermarking methods.

A well-accepted bridge in digital image watermarking is logo watermarking; wherever an image is a watermark, generally a small user-specified image can be a watermark. Over the last 15 years, specified research has been done on logo watermarking

DOI 10.1201/9781003167488-24

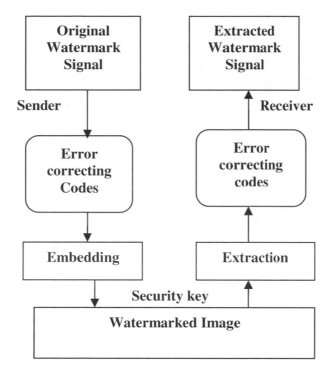

Figure 1. General watermarking technique

It is additionally required that there be an unseen logo watermark in a host image that is unnoticeable when positioned within the host image, and after extraction it must be visually identifiable. The prime profit of badge watermarking is the potential to pictorially evaluate the original logo with the extracted logo during validation (Braudaway 1997). It is very difficult to recognize the small changes in an image by the visual comparison method (Torralba & Freeman 2008). Thus, even an unskilled expert can easily identify if the original logo relates to the extracted logo. In recent applications, watermarking of an invisible logo is highly applicable, such as in audio and video watermarked quality monitoring (Brandao 2005; Wang et al. 2006; Baaziz et al. 2011) and codes in images or in medical images for hospital logo embedding (Vongpradhip & Rungraungsilp 2012; Bhalerao et al. 2012).

There is not any reference value or any appraisal algorithm to estimate quality measure without the use of original use and data, which is a most challenging area of research that has conventionally relied on the employment of geometric photo features (Andalibi & Chandler 2015; Chandler 2013). It has been seen that watermarking has an enormous outcome with respect to this activity, and more headway could be acknowledged through the utilization of logo (identification) watermarking.

Logo watermarking must overcome a number of challenging issues. First, the watermark that was extracted must be exact to the original. Thus, the watermark technique must be competent to make the image intact even after cyber-attacks so that the image does not downgrade.

Another issue faced by logo and other non-logo watermarking calculations, for example, duplicated monitor codes, originates from the detail that the checked logo is chosen by the client, not by the watermarking strategy. Hence, the technique maker cannot choose which information will be implanted. A successful logo calculation for watermarking must be able to hold a decent variety of logos that fundamentally limit the strategy from utilizing approaches which are adjusted to demanding information designs.

A basic watermarking method is explained in Figure 1 where the original image is embedded with the watermark at the sender's end and the watermark is extracted at receiver's end. Some error correction coding techniques are also used at the sending and receiving ends.

A. **Applications of digital image watermarking.** There are many applications of image watermarking which are given below (Podilchuk & Delp 2001).

- *Copyright Protection*. In the new look of host data copyright information is inserted in a host image, that helps to reduce the cases of copyright disputes.
- *Broadcast Monitoring*. To reduce unauthorized broadcasting, a watermark is inserted at the time of encryption which is used to authorize the broadcasting data at the time of visualizing. This verifies whether or not the content really is broadcasted.
- *Tamper Detection*. Tamper detection is done by fragile watermarks. When data is tampered or destroyed then it is seems that data is tampered.
- *Authentication and Integrity Verification*. In digital content, integrity authentication is done. This is done by a semi-fragile or fragile watermark that has poor robustness to alteration in an image.
- *Fingerprinting*. Unique authentication fingerprint insertion is an important application of watermarking.
  - *Content Description*. As a form of labeling and captioning the watermark can have some complete information of the host image. For this application watermark, the ability should be comparatively large and have no strict necessity of robustness.
- *Covert Communication*. Covert communication refers to the transmission of messages privately via embedded images. In this case, hidden data should not raise any doubt that a private message is being communicated.

B. **Attacks on Watermarked Image.** Several national and international attacks on watermarked images have distorted them. These attacks are judged by watermark methods and are classified as signal geometric attacks and processing attacks.

- *Signal Processing Attacks*. These are non-geometric and digital image processing attacks, e.g., Gaussian or salt and pepper noise, compression of image, sharpening, collusion, printing, scanning addition of noise such as gamma correction, filtering, brightness sharpening, averaging, etc.
- *Geometric Attacks*. Geometric changes in a photo are basic geometric attacks. These include row-column blanking, cropping, rotation, scaling, translation, warping etc. These attacks attempt to demolish the management of finding, thus making the discovery process hard or even impossible.

2 LITERATURE SURVEY

Imperceptible logo watermarking has previously been produced by utilizing binary logos (Andalibi & Chandler 2015).

G. Bhatnagar and Q. M. Jonathan Wu presented a watermarking algorithm in which the size of the host picture is smalletr than the watermark (Andalibi & Chandler 2015; Zeng & Lei 1999).

N. Saikrishna and M. Resmipriya use the Arnold ransform to scramble the watermark using a set of parameters that are classified by white and black textured regions (Andalibi & Chandler 2015; Voytais & Pitas 1998).

A. A. Abdulfetah, X. Sun, and H. Yang (Wu & Guan 2007) proposed a plan dependent on discrete wavelet transform (DWT) and the Human Visual System for video copyright security.

Two tumultuous guides are utilized in Wu & Guan (2007) to recognize the situation for installing the watermark in the host picture, and the pixel piece of the host picture for watermark inserting.

Two-fold logo watermarking additionally utilized discrete cosine transform (DCT) and DWT spaces. Abdulfetah et al. (2010) combined a noticeable decent variety of visual models with DWT and DCT to adaptively place the paired watermark in the host photograph.

In Ramanjaneyulu & Rajarajeswari (2011), a two-level DWT with specific, even sub-band (LH2), is applied to the host picture for creating a double watermark. For boundary investigation, a hereditary calculation is utilized to build the strength and subtlety of the information utilized.

Reddy & Varadarajan (2010) embed a pseudo-randomly shuffled version of the logo in either the LH, HL, or HH sub-band of the original image. Embedding is done by choosing a sub-band with maximum entropy.

In double logo watermarking, calculations for concealed logo watermarking have additionally been intended to work with dark scale logos, and significant steadfast exploration is done for the two classifications.

In Kundur & Hatzinakos (2010), a multi-goal combination-based watermarking procedure is anticipated for entering dim scale logos in the DWT space through a one-level DWT, and utilizing the four logo sub groups as a similar perspective on squares of the first picture.

Ganic & Eskicioglu (2004) merged DWT with singular value decomposition (SVD), where singular values of the host image are changed by the singular values of the watermark using special potency. Even though the same methods have also been used in many other methods including Bhatnagar et al. (2012) and Laiand Tsai (2010), these methods do not embed the watermark totally into the host image. For this reason, just the solitary worth framework is changed, and the two unitary lattices that are coming about totally vanish because of the singular worth disintegration. In the recovering stage, the un-assaulted unitary lattices work, in this way generally essential to evidently incredible heartiness measures.

Bhatnagar & Wu (2013) changed the components of the unique photograph utilizing the reversible expansion change, which is utilized by entering the dark scale logo in the middle solitary estimations of the changed picture. Next, to get a two-fold picture the toral automorphism followed via programmed thresholding is utilized by rearranging the watermarked picture, which is likewise installed in the first picture to improve the security and plausibility of logo recovery.

A few grayscale logo watermarking calculations have additionally been presented that rely upon the properties of the human visual framework (HVS), most amazingly, visual concealing. Reddy and Chatterji (2005) utilized a little logo in a unique picture in the DWT space utilizing a one-level SVD for the logo and a four-level spoiling for the first info picture. An uncommon method of visual veiling for recognizing watermarking loads for singular wavelet coefficients is utilized.

Hien et al. (2006) enter the logo in an easygoing commotion signal for security. At that point, the first info picture is decayed by excess DWT (RDWT), and the logo is inserted into the center recurrence RDWT sub-band. To display visual concealing for adaptively fluctuating the watermarking quality, a clamor versatility work is utilized.

By utilizing the DWT and visual veiling, logo watermarking is performed, as shown by Jin et al. (2006). To improve security, change is utilized for logo rearranging (Arnold and Avez 1968). At that point, this rearranged logo is gone into squares of the LL sub-band that has the largest sized coefficients. By weighted expansion the installing is done, where the loads are resolved that depend on models of luminance and commotion covering.

Foris and Levick (2007) used DCT and DWT with three HVS models for blending the watermarking. To choose "perceptually comparable" change coefficients three HVS models are utilized: (1) based on contrast affectability and luminance covering; (2) on territory of fixation and difference concealing; and (3) based on commotion veiling.

A complex watermarking calculation was presented by First and Qi (2007) in which a logo is installed in the DWT sub-groups of the first picture by adding substance-based inclusion through modulus. A PN code is haphazardly rearranged and scaled in record of the logo to install in the LL sub-band of photo by means of an expansion which is based on arithmetic modulus. The logo DCT is entered in the "perceptually same" squares of the HH, LH, and HL sub-groups through a weighted summation of coefficients, where decided loads depend on visual veiling.

A visual concealing and remarkable quality-based watermarking calculation is presented by Mohanty and Bhargava (2008). To start with, for watermark addition in a unique picture a district of intrigue is distinguished. At that point straightaway, by utilizing pictures, a blend logo is made;

hence, a watermark can be either (1) ready to be seen because of overestimates of concealing or (2) pointlessly far under the edge of terribleness because it belittles the covering. An increase in mixed-up appraisals of veiling can be possibly given by utilization of dynamic concealing measures.

Four examination measurements for obvious watermarking calculations are proposed by Navarro et al. (2018), in which the worldwide prominence, worldwide perceivability, and nearby prominence in the unique photograph has been considered. The quality of watermarked picture is assessed based on HVS and a pixel-based observable mutilation.

Later concealing typical pictures as veils demonstrated that remarkable covering impacts could be forced on ordinary pictures by veiling that could not be perceived by the existing calculative veiling models (Alam et al. 2013). The Logo fusion and a measurable picture that is incorporated in Yi et al. (2018) is assessed by twofold irregular stage encoding (DRPE) and DCT space watermarking plan. The DRPE is has been utilized for picture encryption Based on strength watermarking has been accomplished for various sizes of watermark pictures and host pictures. The computation is broken down and its PSNR value for various pictures are considered in watermarking(Voyatis and Pitas 1998)

3 COMPARATIVE STUDY OF WATERMARKING METHODS

Table 1 gives a comparative study of the literature provided in the above survey. The table compares various watermarking techniques done on the basis of robustness for different sized host images and watermark images. Each algorithm is analyzed and its PSNR values for different images are compared. In the above survey, the ALT mark algorithm has superior results than the others.

Table 1. Comparison of watermarking algorithms.

S. No	Method	Host Image Size	Watermark Size	PSNR										
				Barbara	Mandril	Cameraman	Peppers	Lenna	Parrot	Yacht	Eagle	Lady	Balloon	Montage
1	Size host image smaller than watermark (Zeng and Lei 1999)	128*128	512*512	34.89	32.35			31.1209	33.69					
2	An invisible logo watermarking using arnold transform (Voyatis and Pitas 1998)	512*512	64*64	48.92	48.89	48.9	48.89							
3	Robust adaptive video watermarking (Wu and Guan 2007)	177*144	20*36	39.98 to 41.0765										
4	Visual watermarks using DWT–SVD (Ganic and Eskicioglu 2005)	512*512	256*256					34.42						
5	Watermarking using fractional wavelet packet transform (Bhatnagar et al. 2012)	256*256	64*64					39.657		38.5669	41.972	38.9672	39.92	42.6181
6	Watermarking using DWT and SVD (Lai and Tsai 2010)	256*256	128*128 64*64	51.14										

(continued.)

Table 1. Continued

S. No	Method	Host Image Size	Watermark Size	PSNR										
				Barbara	Mandril	Cameraman	Peppers	Lenna	Parrot	Yacht	Eagle	Lady	Balloon	Montage
7	Watermarking based on redundant fractional wavelet transform (Bhatnagar and Wu 2013)	256*256	256*256	38.5681	40.7458			39.9853				39.7118		
8	Wavelet-based logo watermarking scheme (Reddy and Chatterji 2005)	512*512	64*64					44.7						
9	Watermarking-based HVS characteristic of wavelet transform (Jin et al. 2006)	256*256	16*16										39.11	
10	Implementations of HVS models in digital image watermarking (Foris and Levick 2007)	256*256	32*32					37.261						

4 CONCLUSION

To give security and copyright shield for authenticity identification, watermark entering and retrieving algorithms are required. This paper gives a detailed survey on several digital image watermarking schemes in different domains and their requirements. In this paper, on the basis of quality measure, the survey is undergone and classified in the manner of different schemes with their performance. It is concluded that techniques in frequency domain must be combined with other techniques to reduce distortions and to increase capacity that has strong robustness and high capacity against different types of attacks.

REFERENCES

Abdulfetah A. A., Sun X., Yang H., and Mohammad N., 2010 "Robust adaptive image watermarking using visual models in dwt and dct domain," Information tech. journal, vol. 9, no. 3, pp. 460–466.

Alam M. M., Vilankar K. P., and Chandler D. M., 2013 "A database of local masking thresholds in natural images," in SPIE, vol. 8651.

Andalibi M., and Chandler D. M., 2015 "Digital image watermarking via adaptive logo texturization". *IEEE TrTansactions on Image Processing 24*(12),pp.5060-5073.

Arnold V. I. and Avez A., 1968 "Ergodic Problems of Classical Mechanics. Benjamin, New York: Monograph Series.

Baaziz N., Zheng D., and Wang D., 2011 "Image quality assessment based on multiple watermarking approach," in IEEE 13th International Workshop on Multimedia Signal Processing (MMSP), pp. 1–5.

Bhalerao S., Mehta M., Dubey N., and Bhatele M., 2012 "Digital watermarking of medical images," in Proceedings of All India Seminar on Biomedical Engineering, pp. 111–116.

Bhatnagar G., Raman B., and Wu Q. M. J, 2012 "Robust watermarking using fractional wavelet packet transform," IET Image Process, vol. 6, no. 4, pp. 386–397.

Bhatnagar G. and Wu Q. M. J., 2013 "A new logo watermarking based on redundant fractional wavelet transform," Elsevier journal of Mathematical and Computer Modeling, vol. 58, pp. 204–218.

Brandao T., 2005 "Image communication quality assessment based on watermarking, an overview," Instituto de Telecomunications, Tech. Rep. vol.02.

Braudaway G., 1997 "Protecting publicly available images with an invisible image watermark," in Proc. Inter. Inter. Conf. Image Proc.

Chandler D. M., 2013 "Seven challenges in image quality assessment: Past, present, and future research," ISRN Signal Processing, vol. vol. 2013, no. Article ID 905685, p. 53 pages.

First E. and Qi X., 2007 "A composite approach for blind grayscale logo watermarking," in IEEE Int. Conf. Image Proc, Vol 3, pp. 265–268.

Foris P. and Levick D., 2007 "Implementations of hvs models in digital image watermarking," Radioengineering, vol. 16, no. 1.

Ganic E. and Eskicioglu A. M., 2005 "Robust embedding of visual watermarks using dwt-svd," J. Electronic Imaging, vol. 14, no. 4.

Halder R., Pal S., and Cortesi A., 2010 "Watermarking techniques for relational databases: survey, classification and comparison," Journal of universal computer science, vol. 16, no. 21.

Hien T. D., Nakao Z., and Chen Y. W., 2006 "Robust multi-logo watermarking by rdwt and ica," Elsevier journal of Signal Processing, vol. 86, pp. 2981–2993.

Jin C., Tao F., and Fu Y., 2006 "Image watermarking based hvs characteristic of wavelet transform," in International Conference on Intelligent Information Hiding and Multimedia Signal Processing.

KundurD. and Hatzinakos D., 2004 "Towards robust logo watermarking using multiresolution image fusion," IEEE Transaction on Multimedia, vol. 6, no. 1, pp. 185–197.

Lai C. C. and Tsai C. C., 2010 "Digital image watermarking using discrete wavelet transform and singular value decomposition," IEEE Transactions on instrumentation and measurement, vol. 59, no. 11.

Mohanty S. P. and Bhargava B. K., 2008 "Invisible watermarking based on creation and robust insertion-extraction of image adaptive watermarks," ACM Transactions on Multimedia Computing, Communications, and Applications, vol. 5, no. 2, pp. 1–24.

Natarajan M. and Makhdumi1 G., 2009 "Safeguarding the digital contents: Digital watermarking," DESIDOC Journal of Library and Information Technology, vol. 29, no. 2, pp. 29–35.

Navarro F., Hernández E. C., Miyatake M. N., Hernández M. C. A. and Meana H.M. P., 2018 "Visible Watermarking Assessment Metrics Based on Just Noticeable Distortion". *IEEE Access*, 6, pp.75767–75788.

Nema A. and Mohan R., 2014 "Digital image watermarking a review," Global Journal of Multidisciplinary Studies, vol. 3.

Podilchuk C. I. and Delp E. J., 2001 "Digital watermarking: algorithms and applications," IEEE Signal Proc Mag, vol. 18, no. 3, pp. 33–46.

Ramanjaneyulu K. and Rajarajeswari K., 2011 "Robust and oblivious image watermarking scheme in the dwt domain using genetic algorithm," Int. J. Advanced Eng. Technology, vol. 2, no. 3, pp. 85–92,.

Reddy A. A. and Chatterji B., 2005 "A new wavelet based logo-watermarking scheme," Pattern Recogn, vol. 26, pp. 1019–1027.

Reddy V. P. and Varadarajan D. S., 2010 "An effective wavelet-based watermarking scheme using human visual system for protecting copyrights of digital images," International Journal of Computer and Electrical Engineering, vol. 2, pp. 1793–8163.

Tirkel A.Z., Rankin G.A., Schyndel R.V., Ho W. J., Mee N., and Osborne C.F., 1993 "Electronic water mark," DICTA, pp. 666–673.

Torralba R.F.A. and Freeman W.T., 2008 "80 million tiny images: A large data set for nonparametric object and scene recognition," Trans. Pattern Anal. Machine Intell., vol. 30, no. 31, pp. 1958–1970.

Vongpradhip S. and Rungraungsilp S., 2012 "Qr code using invisible watermarking in frequency domain," in ICT and Knowledge Engineering, pp. 47–52.

Voyatis G. and Pitas I., 1998 "Digital image watermarking using mixing system," Computer Graphics, vol. 22, no. 4, pp. 405–416.

Wang Z., Wu G., Sheikh H., Simoncelli E., Yang E. H., and Bovik A., 2006 "Quality-aware images," IEEE Transactions on Image Processing, vol. 15, no. 6, pp. 1680–1689.

Wu X. and Guan Z. H., 2007 "A novel digital watermark algorithm based on chaotic maps," Elsevier journal of Physics Letters A, vol. 365, pp. 403–406.

Yi F., Kim Y., and Moon I, 2018 "Secure Image-Authentication Schemes With Hidden Double Random-Phase Encoding". *IEEE Access*, 6, pp.70113–7012.

Zeng B. L. W. and Lei S., 1999 "Extraction of multiresolution watermark images for resolving rightful ownership," Proc. SPIE, Security and watermarking of Multimedia Contents, vol. 3657, pp. 404–414.

Zhao X. and Ho A. T. S., 2010 "An introduction to robust transform based image watermarking techniques," Springer, Intelligent Multimedia Analysis for Security Applications, vol. 282, pp. 337–364.

Smart Computing – Khan et al (Eds)
© 2021 Taylor & Francis Group, London, ISBN 978-0-367-76552-1

Fake account detection using the machine learning technique

Rishabh Sharma & Ashish Sharma
Department of Computer Engineering & Applications, GLA University, NH#2, Delhi Mathura Highway, Post Ajhai, Mathura (UP) India

ABSTRACT: Online social media networks are becoming popular with great speed in this generation, and people's personal lives are becoming more closely linked to these sites. People use these networks to share videos, read news articles, advertise for products, etc. With the increasing growth of these networks, a huge quantity of a user's data can attract attackers and these attackers then can share false news and spread malicious lies. In addition, these social networking sites are now becoming a target medium for attackers to spread an enormous amount of false data. On account of this, researchers have begun to explore effective techniques for detecting these kinds of activities and fake accounts based on the classification methods. In this paper, different techniques of machine learning are explored to provide successful identification of a fake account. Various machine learning algorithms are used to solve such a problem with pre-processing techniques to identify fake accounts. Finally, the machine learning techniques are also compared, and the proposed approach provides better results than the previously used techniques to detect fake user accounts on these online social media networks

1 INTRODUCTION

An online social media network is an emerging platform that connects different people in one place. With the help of these networks, users can share photos, videos, etc. with their friends. These networks are also used by marketing sites such as Amazon, Myntra, Snapdeal, etc., to advertise their products. With the help of these online social networking sites, many famous personalities such as political leaders, superstars, sports persons, etc. are able to be present and share information with their followers. In short, it can be concluded that the online social media network is a platform in which all types of people—from film star to the common person—are connected in one place and able to share their information.

Currently, there are a lot of social media sites such as Twitter and Instagram that have advantages and disadvantages. The advantages of these online social media networking sites are that people can connected all in one place, as well as be introduced to many online sites advertising their products. The disadvantages, however, are that some users will create fake accounts in these sites in an effort to share false information such as fake news, racial discrimination, and much more. The main challenge here is to identify the fake accounts that are so frequently created every day on sites. Because many fraudulent accounts easily trap a user who does not have enough information regarding the information being presented, these days a great many researchers are attracted to the field of fake account detection.

In recent years, online social media networks like Twitter and Facebook have become increasingly popular. The open nature of online social media and the huge amount of subscriber information uploaded to these sites have made them more vulnerable to Sybil attacks (Douceur 2002). In 2012, an analysis of Facebook noticed abuse on their platform that included published hate speech, fake news, sensational and polarizing information, and many others. Researchers have become interested in analyzing this data, studying user behaviors, to detect abnormal activities (Kaur & Singh 2016).

DOI 10.1201/9781003167488-25

The increasing growth of social sites allows users to collect an abundance of user information. In today's time, Twitter is the platform of online social media networks on which people share their views, opinions, moods, and news. This openness can lead to arguments on many topics, such as current events, politics, etc. When a Twitter user tweets something then it goes to their followers, and the followers spread this information in a large network (Benevenuto et al. 2010). With the growth of these online social media networks, the work of researchers is to analyze the increase in user behavior.

One of the reports of Facebook said that 2.2 billion users were active on monthly basis and 1.4 billion users were active on daily basis. Facebook continues to grow with an annual increase of 11%, and it just announced that total revenue in the second quarter of 2018 was $13.2 billion with only $13.0 billion being from ads.

In their report on the first half of 2018 detailing the internal recommendation for upholding the people standard that covers activities in October 2017 to March 2018, Facebook outlined that inappropriate items can be removed from its network, including six categories of visual abuse, malware, fraudulent accounting, etc (Newcomb, Alyssa 2018). In addition, this Facebook report revealed that 88 million accounts on their network are fake.

Statistics on online social media accounts show that in the U.S 40% the parents and 18% of adolescents are very concerned about using fake accounts to sell or influence products (Erşahin, et al. 2017) Detecting these types of accounts in online social media networks has become a must for preventing malicious activities.

The rest of the paper is organized as follows. Section 2 provides a literature review. In Section 3, a technical discussion of different machine learning algorithms is presented. In Section 4, the comparison model is discussed. Finally, Section 5 presents the conclusion and future work.

2 LITERATURE REVIEW

Exploration of recent literature provides a list of methods used to detect spam. The classification system proposed is divided into the following stages: (1) false information, (2) detecting the malware based on the URL, (3) trend malware detection; and (4) false user detection (Masood et al. 2019). Gupta et al. (2013) conducted the exhaustive analysis of the elements influenced by the fast-growing illegal content. In this source, the researchers saw that users who had social media profiles were found to be circulating false information across an online social media network. To identify the fake accounts, researchers chose some accounts which are created after the Boston Marathon bombing in 2013 and after some time these accounts were removed from the social media network due to violations.

Detecting the malware based on the URL is identified by Chen et al. (2015), who conducted the evaluations of the different algorithms for the data mining for identification of the false information. The researchers used different features for detecting the efficiency of the identification of false information on social media. Such attributes are taken into account in the malware classification of the different algorithms for the identification of false information, and the attributes used by the researchers were also used in our experiment. Trend malware detection is explored by Gharge & Chavan (2017) who introduced a framework that is based on two concepts: (1) identification of false information lacking previous information of the people's account detail; and (2) identification of false information on the online social networking sites with the help of the topic which is trending at that time.

User detection is also a major aspect in this series, which is explored by Erşahin et al. (2017) who introduced the classification approach for the detection of the false user. In this paper, the authors used various features such as the number of followers. The authors created their dataset which consisted of 501 false accounts and 499 actual accounts. With the help of Twitter API, the author discovered the details of 16 features. The author then used two classification approaches for false user detection: (1) the Naïve Bayes algorithm before choice and (2) the Naïve Bayes algorithm after choice.

3   PROPOSED METHOD

The method that is discovered for predicting a fake account is presented in this section. The proposed methods are divided into two main parts—feature reduction and data classification—to develop the model that results in a small computation time with high classification accuracy.

3.1   *Preprocessing of data*

The feature of our dataset, i.e., the Microscopy Image Browser (MIB) dataset, represents the features in two different types such as categorical features such as tweets and numerical features such as follower count and default profile.

The proposed model is working as the process described by Khaled et al. (2018) first transformed the six categorical characteristics into numerical features to allow us to apply classification algorithms to them. To differentiate between fake and real accounts, a feature label has been added. The preprocessing phase resulted in 16 vectors of numerical features representing user activities on Twitter.

3.1.1   *Feature reduction*

There are many techniques for feature reduction, but four techniques are primarily applied in the feature reduction phase to determine the various patterns that were used in the process, i.e., Principal Component Analysis and Spearman Rank. In the present research solution, the Wrapper Feature Selection using a support vector machine (SVM) is used. The Wrapper Feature Selection is one of the best feature selection techniques used for the feature selection. In this method, various features were considered and test the various function. From all the features the best with the highest performance would be picked. All these are considered as a set that is extracted with the help of bit manipulation.

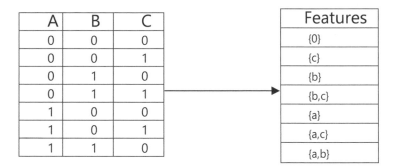

Figure 1.   Bit manipulation.

Using this technique, the feature set will perform best for a specific learning system, but this technique requires large computations for the large feature. In the MIB dataset, 16 feature vectors that represents 216-1 subset were obtianed. The data set was divided into 70% training data and 30% testing data. In next iteration, the data set also was divided into 80% training data and 20% testing data, and then further divided into 90% training data and 10% testing data. After this, all the features were trained and tested using an SVM. With the help of this model select the features that are up to 97%.

3.2   *Data classification*

In this section, the features which are obtained from the feature reduction will be processed on the models and the results will be compared. In this section, the features that will be obtained from the feature reduction will be divided into the training and testing parts using classification techniques like SVM using the 10 x 8-fold cross-validation to estimate the classifier's output.

3.2.1 *SVM-NN classification*

In the previous techniques, some researchers distinguish between real and fake accounts using different classification techniques such as SVM and neural network (NN). As a way to increase the accuracy of the model, Khaled et al. (2018) used a different algorithm which was called SVM–NN. Simply, the researchers used a hybrid model to improve the accuracy of the model, in which the model runs the NN classification on a value that is obtained from the SVM classifier. To get the best result, the NN feed-forward backpropagation algorithm is used. Although the model is good, they do not work on multi-class SVM. As in the case of face account detection, the user must be identifying the various parameters therefore multi-class SVM will support here to identify and validate the user in a very specific way so that the fake account which is a real fake account must be identified based on various parameters.

3.2.2 *Classification*

The model that is used was multi-class SVM. As the previous model was not able to work properly on the various parameters, there is need to design a model that can work on a multi-class problem. Therefore, in the proposed model, the multi-class SVM is applied with the NN technique.

3.2.3 *Multi-class SVM*

Regarding multi-class problems, the simplest way is to extend the SVMs with the help of the so-called one-vs.-rest method. K-linear SVMs will be trained separately for a K-class problem, where the data from the other classes form the negative cases (Tang 2013).

3.3 *Neural network*

Many algorithms were used to predict/calculate the accuracies of the model. There are many different techniques of the NN to train the model and give the results based on the previously trained data. But we used one of the algorithms to predict the accuracy of our model, i.e., the feed-forward backpropagation model.

3.3.1 *PNN*

It is a neural feed-forward that is used in the problem of classification and pattern recognition problem. It is faster and more accurate than multi-layer perceptron networks. It approaches Bayes' optimal classification and is relatively insensitive to outliers. The network contains four layers: an input layer, pattern layer, summation layer, and output layer. The probabilistic neural network (PNN) is slower than conventional neural network for classifying new cases. It requires more space to store the model. There are data patterns $y \in T\hat{}n$ which have predefined classes h=1...H, with the probability of y belonging to class h equals rg, the cost is y CG, and the probability density function is x1(y),x2(y),x3(y)....x g(y).

3.3.2 *MLP*

A multi-layer perceptron (MLP) is an NN connecting multiple levels in a directed graph which states a single path that will go only to one path. It is used in supervised learning and is a finite acyclic graph. It contains nodes which are neurons with logistic activation. With it we can calculate the complex functions by combing multiple neurons. It consists of three layers: the input layer, hidden layer, and the output layer.

3.4 *Logistic regression*

Logistic regression is a method for binary classification problems, and it uses a function which is called the logistic function to model the binary-dependent variable and it contains two values 0

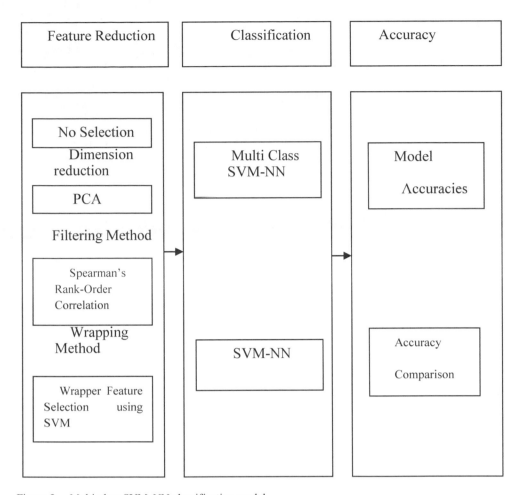

Figure 2.   Multi-class SVM–NN classification model.

or 1, true or false. It is used to predict the risk of developing the disease. In regression analysis, logistic regression is estimating the parameters of the logistic model (Sharma et al. 2020).

3.5 *Regression tree*

The regression tree is the iterative process that splits data into branches or partition. It has target values. Deciding on regression is much easier than another method. We can continue to split each branch into smaller groups.

3.6 *SVM*

SVM is the most popular supervised learning algorithm that is used for classification and regression. It constructs the hyperplane in high-dimensional space, and it separates the linear and nonlinear points. In this, the straight-line equation is being used (y=mx+c), and for mid-hyper-planes, mx+c will be equal to 0, when mx+c will be 1 then all positive values will be there, and when mx+c equals to -1 then negative values (Yadav et al. 2019).

201

3.7 Radial basis function

A radial basis function is a real-valued function which is defined as $\phi:[0,\infty) \to R$. It is a simple single-layer type of artificial NN. It gives the approximate value of the given functions.

4 PPERFORMANCE AND EVALUATION

The performance of the model /is performed and compared the newly built hybrid model, i.e., SVM–NN with the other classification model. In our paper, comparison of our model is done with the classification technique, i.e., SVM–NN.

4.1 MIB dataset

Use the MIB dataset (Cresci et al. 2015) to carry out the analysis which contains the dataset obtained from Twitter. The dataset was created after crawling nine million accounts and about three million tweets. The dataset contains both types of users, i.e., fake and real.

4.2 The fake project

The dataset of the Fake Project was initiated by a research project of the IIT–CNR in Italy. It created a Twitter account and monitored the users which followed that account after they started the verification program. They found that 469 out of the 574 accounts were correctly verified. So, it contains 469 volunteer accounts. The author referred to this dataset as "TFP" (Cresci et al. 2015).

Table 1. Accuracy of the feature vectors.

Feature Set	Multi Class SVM–NN			SVM–NN		
	Model accuracy	False-positive	False-Negative	Model accuracy	False-Positive	False-Negative
Wrapper–SVM (MIB Data Set)	0.971	0.019	0.002	0.965	0.027	0.007
The Fake Project Data Set	0.965	0.023	0.003	0.956	0.032	0.005

The result which is obtained from this model is useful to classify the accounts into two categories, i.e., real or fake account and to calculate the accuracy of our model we used the following formula:

$$\% \text{ Accuracy} = \frac{\text{All accuracy identify correctly}}{\text{Total no. of account}} \times 100$$

With the help of this formula, we can calculate the accuracy of the different models on the different subsets, as shown in Table 1. From the table, we see that the new approach called multi-class SVM–NN gives better accuracy with the previous algorithms, i.e., SVM and NN, with the highest accuracy of 0.971.

5 CONCLUSION

Today, in the information age, accurate and reliable information has become more valuable than ever. Social media has emerged as a source of fake accounts to share fake information. In the proposed study, new techniques were developed and tested on two data sets. Finally, the machine learning techniques were also compared and the proposed approach proves better results to the previously used techniques to detect fake user accounts on online social networking sites.

REFERENCES

Benevenuto, F., Magno, G., Rodrigues, T., & Almeida, V. (2010, July). Detecting spammers on twitter. In *Collaboration, electronic messaging, anti-abuse and spam conference (CEAS),* Vol. 6(2010): p. 12.

Chang, C. C., & Lin, C. J. (2011). LIBSVM: A library for support vector machines. *ACM transactions on intelligent systems and technology (TIST)*, Vol 2(3): 1–27.

Chen, C., Zhang, J., Xie, Y., Xiang, Y., Zhou, W., Hassan, M. M., …& Alrubaian, M. (2015). A performance evaluation of machine learning-based streaming spam tweets detection. *IEEE Transactions on Computational social systems*, Vol 2(3): 65–76.

Cresci, S., Di Pietro, R., Petrocchi, M., Spognardi, A., & Tesconi, M. (2015). Fame for sale: Efficient detection of fake Twitter followers. *Decision Support Systems*, Vol 80: 56–71.

Douceur, J. R. (2002, March). The sybil attack. In *International workshop on peer-to-peer systems*, Springer, Berlin, Heidelberg, pp. 251–260.

Erşahin, B., Aktaş, Ö., Kılınç, D., & Akyol, C. (2017, October). Twitter fake account detection. In *2017 International Conference on Computer Science and Engineering (UBMK),* pp. 388–392.

Gharge, S., & Chavan, M. (2017, March). An integrated approach for malicious tweets detection using NLP. In *2017 International Conference on Inventive Communication and Computational Technologies (ICICCT)*, pp. 435–438.

Gupta, A., Lamba, H., & Kumaraguru, P. (2013, September). $1.00 per rt# bostonmarathon# prayforboston: Analyzing fake content on twitter. In *2013 APWG eCrime researchers summit,* pp. 1–12.

Kaur, R., & Singh, S. (2016). A survey of data mining and social network analysis based anomaly detection techniques. *Egyptian informatics journal*, Vol 17(2): 199–216.

Khaled, S., El-Tazi, N., & Mokhtar, H. M. (2018, December). Detecting Fake Accounts on Social Media. In *2018 IEEE International Conference on Big Data (Big Data),* pp. 3672–3681.

Masood, F., Almogren, A., Abbas, A., Khattak, H. A., Din, I. U., Guizani, M., & Zuair, M. (2019). Spammer detection and fake user identification on social networks. *IEEE Access*, Vol 7: 68140—68152.

Newcomb, Alyssa. (2018) Online https://www.nbcnews.com/tech/social-media/facebook-reveals-how-much-abusive-content-it-removes-n874441

Sharma, A., Ram, A., & Bansal, A. (2020). Feature Extraction Mining for Student Performance Analysis. In *Proceedings of ICETIT 2019,* pp. 785–797.

Tang, Y. (2013). Deep learning using linear support vector machines. *arXiv preprint arXiv: pp.1306.0239.*

Yadav, D. P., Sharma, A., Singh, M., & Goyal, A. (2019). Feature extraction based machine learning for human burn diagnosis from burn images. *IEEE Journal of Translational Engineering in Health and Medicine*, Vol 7: 1–7.

Smart Computing – Khan et al (Eds)
© *2021 Taylor & Francis Group, London, ISBN 978-0-367-76552-1*

Improving visibility of hazy images using image enhancement-based approaches through the fusion of multiple exposure images

S.C. Agrawal

Department of Computer Engineering and Applications, GLA University, Mathura, UP, India

ABSTRACT: Haze is an atmospheric obscurity in which very small particles like dust, smoke, etc. are suspended in the air. These suspended particles reduce the visibility of image/video. This reduced visibility is the main cause of failure of various applications such as intelligent transportation, object recognition, target identification, underwater image enhancement, remote sensing, and so on. In this paper, we have proposed an image enhancement method to remove the effect of haze rather than a restoration-based method. The restoration-based methods first calculate the transmission based on some assumptions and are then followed by costly refinement process. The success of these methods depends on these assumptions. The proposed method utilizes three approaches, namely white balancing, multi-scale Retinex, and Gamma correction. The proposed method is validated through many experiments on hazy images. This analysis reveals that the proposed method performs well as compared to the existing methods in the field of dehazing.

1   INTRODUCTION AND RELATED WORK

The light scattered by the suspended particles in the air is mixed with the light received from the object by the camera. As a result, reflected light is attenuated. In addition, atmospheric light also entered the camera. These particles degrade the quality of the images in the form of visibility and contrast. The atmospheric model of haze is given by Singh & Kumar (2017):

$$H(x) = HF(x)t(x) + A(1 - t(x)) \tag{1}$$

$$t(x) = e^{-\beta d(x)} \tag{2}$$

where HF and H represent the haze-free image and the captured hazy image, respectively. A is the airlight or atmospheric light and t represents transmission medium. The attenuation of light reaching a camera is decided by the transmission function. The value of transmission lies in between 0 and 1. Furthermore, it depends on two factors: distance (d) and scattering coefficient β. It is a difficult problem because we have to estimate two unknowns A and t from hazy image H, in order to find hazy-free image HF. In the past, various types of image dehazing methods had been proposed. The first category of methods of image dehazing is image enhancement-based dehazing methods. These methods do not require any physical model of hazy image formation. They directly enhance the visual quality and contrast of the image. These methods mainly include spatial domain enhancement, e.g. histogram equalization, median filter, etc., gamma correction (Ju et al. 2018), Retinex method (Hu et al. 2014), morphological operations, and frequency domain enhancement.

The second category of image dehazing is image restoration-based methods. These methods need to compute the transmission map and used physical model. Tan (2008) proposed an effective method based on local contrast maximization. However "halo" effects are easily introduced in the dehazed image. Fattal (2008) proposed a modified image formation model with the assumption that transmission function and object surface shading function are not correlated. However, this

DOI 10.1201/9781003167488-26

method work is satisfactory only when a hazy image has a sufficient number of colors. Tarel & Hautiere (2009) proposed a fast and filtering-based approach for visibility restoration. He et al. (2011) proposed a dark channel prior to removing haze from a single input image. The dark channel states that in a patch of a haze-free image, minimum color channel has very low intensity. Zhu et al. (2015) proposed a machine learning-based method to estimate the depth of the hazy image. However, this method works fine in the presence of mild haze and leaves some portion of haze in the image. Berman & Avidan (2016) proposed a dehazing method based on non-local assumptions rather than local patches in the hazy image using clustering of RGB pixels.

The third category of image dehazing is fusion-based methods. Fusion-based methods generate the haze-free image by the progressive generation of multiple images. Ancuti & Ancuti (2013) proposed a method that utilized three weight maps: chromatic map, saliency map, and luminance on two derived images from a hazy image. Galdran (2018) also proposed a fusion-based method to remove the haze effects using Gamma correction and histogram equalization.

Another family of dehazing within image restoration methods is machine learning-based methods using convolutional neural networks such as fast all-in-one network (FAOD-Net) (Qian et al. 2020) and linear regression (Fan et al. 2017). Li et al. (2019) proposed a method based on polarization. Two sub-images are derived at orthogonal polarization states from the captured images, then a method called pseudo-polarimetric is used to remove the dense haze. Colores et al. (2019) proposed a method using morphological operations like opening, erosion, dilation etc.

The main contribution of the paper is to propose a single image dehazing method using image enhancement methodology. The proposed method uses the image enhancement approaches such as White Balancing (deals with color distortion), Multi-Scale Retinex (increases contrast and regulates dynamic range of pixels), and Gamma Correction (improves visibility). Finally, these enhanced images are fused in multi-scale fashion into a single haze-free image.

The rest of the paper is arranged as follows. Section 2 discusses the proposed methodology. Section 3 describes the experimental results on various challenging hazy images, and finally conclusions and future work are presented in Section 4.

2 PROPOSED METHODOLOGY

The framework of the proposed method is shown in Figure 1. In general, there is no any image enhancement algorithm which can entirely remove the effect of haze without color distortion and improved visibility. Thus, the proposed algorithm generates multiple images from the input hazy image. These images are fused to recover color, visibility, and contrast of the hazy images. The proposed method consists of two modules, namely progressive image generation and multi-scale Laplacian fusion. In the progressive image generation module, three images are generated using white balancing, multi-scale Retinex, and Gamma correction. Finally, the resulting images from these methods are fused in a single haze-free image in multi-scale fashion.

2.1 *Progressive image generation*

Progressive image generation step generates three different images from the captured hazy image using image enhancement-based operations as described in the next section.

2.1.1 *White balancing*

Chromatic casts are introduced in the captured image due to atmospheric light. Therefore, white balancing is used to generate first input image to eliminate the color casts. There exist many white balancing algorithms in the literature. We employed shades of gray color constancy algorithm (van de Weijer & Gevers 2005) in the proposed work due to its computationally efficient feature. The goal of white balancing algorithms is to estimate illuminant colors from the captured image.

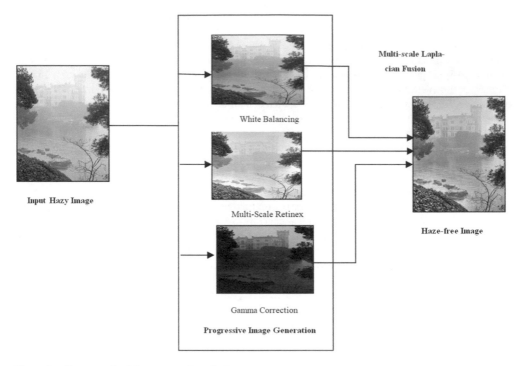

Figure 1.   Framework of the proposed method.

As seen in Figure 1, the Lambertian surface is dependent on many factors such as light source, surface reflectance, and camera sensitivity functions. The captured image can be modeled as follows:

$$f(x) = \int_w l(\lambda) \, r(\lambda, x) \, c(\lambda) d\lambda \qquad (3)$$

where $l(\lambda)$ is the light source, $r(\lambda, x)$ is the surface reflectance, and $c(\lambda)$ is the camera sensitive function, given by $c(\lambda) = \{R(\lambda), G(\lambda), B(\lambda)\}$. w and λ represent the visible spectrum and wavelength, respectively. The light source or its projection on the RGB channel is as follows:

$$l = \int_w l(\lambda) \, c(\lambda) d\lambda \qquad (4)$$

According to the gray world hypothesis (Buchsbaum 1980), scene reflectance is achromatic and given as follows:

$$\frac{\int r(\lambda, x)dx}{\int dx} = g(\lambda) = k \qquad (5)$$

The constant k lies between 0 and 1. The 0 value of k represents no reflectance and 1 total reflectance. Replacing r with f, the following expression can be obtained:

$$\frac{\int f(x)dx}{\int dx} = \frac{1}{\int dx} \int \int_w l(\lambda)r(\lambda, x)c(\lambda)d\lambda dx = \int_w l(\lambda)c(\lambda)d\lambda \int \frac{r(\lambda, x)dx}{\int dx}$$
$$= k \int_w l(\lambda)c(\lambda)d\lambda = kl \qquad (6)$$

A normalized light source is computed by:

$$l' = \frac{kl}{|kl|} \tag{7}$$

The image generated using white balancing is not able to remove the effect of haze but non-hazy regions are improved and it is also capable to remove color cast problem of hazy images, as shown in Figure 2(b).

2.1.2 *Multi-scale retinex*

Multi-Scale Retinex (MSR) theory was developed by Land and McCann (Cooper & Baqai 2004), which is based on the human visual system. MSR has numerous applications in the field of image enhancement. It can be used for contrast enhancement, color correction, shadowing removal, image dehazing, etc. Liu et al. (2019) also utilized the relationship between image dehazing and Retinex theory. They solved the image dehazing problem using minimization of a variational Retinex model. Total variational regularization is used to suppress halo artifacts. In Single Scale Retinex (SSR) algorithm, it is very difficult to determine a scale factor σ for the surround function which is used to balance between dynamic range compression and color rendition. This problem can be solved by considering different scales in MSR. The MSR output is defined as a weighted sum of several SSRs as follows:

$$MSR = \sum_{n=1}^{N} w_n R_{n_i} \tag{8}$$

$$= \sum_{n=1}^{N} w_n [\log I_i(x,y) - \log (S_n(x,y) * I_i(x,y))]$$

where N is the number of scales, Wn is the weight of each scale, I_i is the input image in i^{th} color channel, and R_{ni} is the Retinex output image at n^{th} scale and i^{th} color channel. S_n is the surround function at n^{th} scale, given by the following Gaussian function:

$$S_n(x,y) = C_n \, e^{-((x^2+y^2)/2\sigma^2)} \tag{9}$$

where σ is the filter standard deviation which controls the amount of contrast in an image whereas a normalized factor is represented by C. It is given as follows:

$$\int F_x(x,y)dxdy = 1 \tag{10}$$

Three scale factors are sufficient for most of the images and the weights can be identical. They are fixed as 5, 35, and 150. The image generated using MSR has good contrast and brightness and also a dynamic range of gray levels, as shown in Figure 2(c).

2.1.3 *Gamma correction*

Gamma correction given by $I_c = I^\gamma$ where I_c, I^γ, and γ are the gamma-corrected image, hazy image, and gamma correction factor, respectively. It has the ability (Ju 2018) to remove haze to some extents. A large value of γ is capable of removing haze in long-range regions but close regions gets oversaturated. On the other hand, the smaller value of γ is able to remove the problem of oversaturation in close range regions but is not able to remove haze in long-range regions. Therefore, we decide to take $\gamma = 5$ to get better details of long-range regions. Fusion procedure will take care of lost or oversaturated pixel's details of close regions from other two images generated in previous section. Resulting image is shown in Figure 2(d).

(a)	(b)	(c)	(d)

Figure 2. Resulting images of (a) progressive image generation, (b) hazy images, image generated using white balancing, (c) multi-scale Retinex, and (d) Gamma correction.

2.2 *Multi-exposure fusion*

The proposed method employs multi-scale Laplacian Pyramid decomposition (Mertens et al. 2007) to fuse multiple images generated by different methods. Let I be a haze-free image composed of $\{I_1, I_2, I_3\}$. I_1, I_2, and I_3 are the images generated after applying white balancing, multi-scale Retinex, and Gamma correction, respectively. The objective of multi-exposure fusion is to find optimal weights W_i. For each differently exposed image $I_i(x,y)$ as follows:

$$E = \sum_{i=1}^{n} W_i I_i(x, y) \tag{11}$$

where n is the numbers of multi-exposure images and E is a haze-free and correctly exposed image generated by the input images $I_i(x, y)$.

3 EXPERIMENT RESULTS AND DISCUSSION

We have used two datasets, Waterloo IVC dehazing dataset (Ma 2015) and a corpus of 500 foggy images dataset (Choi 2015), to test the capability of the proposed method. The performance of the proposed method is tested against recent and popular dehazing of state-of-the-art methods. We have used the following methods: Artificial Multi-exposure (AM) (Galdran 2018), Dark Channel (DC) (He et al. 2011), Color Attenuation prior (CP) (Zhu et al. 2015), and non-local dehazing (NL) (Berman & Avidan 2016). The proposed method is evaluated on the basis of subjective and quantitative parameters both. The visual analysis of each method is presented in Figure 3. We can notice the visibility and problem of over enhancement (i.e., color becomes darks) in the dehazed image of different methods.

3.1 *Subjective evaluation*

Figure 3 presents a comparative performance of the proposed method in the form of visual quality. The first image in Figure 3 is an example of the hazy image, in which haze is presented at the long-range regions. These types of images require dehazing in close range regions without color distortion, and improved visibility for the objects located at the far distance. Most of the methods produce an over-enhanced result with saturation of pixels around tress and leaves. The proposed method retains the color of the building and is free from over saturation. The second image depicts a road scene in which haze is present at the bottom of the image. In this case, all methods achieve good contrast enhancement and can remove haze except the NL method which leaves some portion of haze in the bottom part of the image. The difference in dehazing results for other images with the proposed method can be noticed in this figure.

Figure 3.   Dehazed results on hazy images using existing methods: (a) hazy image; (b) AM (Galdran 2018); (c) CP (Zhu et al. 2015); (d) NL (Berman & Avidan 2016); (e) DC (He et al. 2011); and (f) the proposed method.

3.2 Quantitative analysis

3.2.1 Visible edges-based method

Although the visual analysis plays a significant role in judging the performance of a dehazing method, we have also validated the proposed method through quantitative analysis using a visible edges-based method (Hautiere et al. 2008). This method uses three metrics to measure enhancement in contrast between a hazy and haze-free image: gradient ratio (r), rate of new visible edges ratio (e), and saturation of pixels ratio (σ). The comparative values of e, σ, and r for hazy images are shown in Figure 3, with other methods illustrated in Table 1.

Table 1. Comparison of value of e, σ, and r for the images, shown in Figure 3.

Image	AM (Galdren, 2018)			CP (Zhu, 2015)			NL (Berman, 2016)			DC (Hc, 2011)			The Proposed Method		
	e	σ	r	e	σ	r	e	σ	r	e	σ	r	e	σ	r
1	0.46	0.43	1.84	0.4	0.02	1.16	0.81	0.29	1.87	0.54	0.02	1.82	0.52	0	1.8
2	0.56	0	2.06	0.47	0.02	1.43	0.57	0.01	2.17	0.74	0	1.82	0.75	0.05	2.12
3	0.91	0	2.33	1.21	5.6	0.98	1.26	0.32	2.49	1.43	0.14	1.67	1.23	0.03	1.54
4	0.1	0.01	2.26	0.16	0	1.05	0.14	0	2.25	0.28	0	1.71	0.2	0.13	3.15
5	0.46	0.43	1.84	0.4	0.02	1.16	0.81	0.29	1.87	0.54	0.02	1.82	0.51	0.02	1.8
6	2.23	0	2.36	2.7	0.74	1.41	1.08	0.08	1.84	3.18	0.03	1.89	3.42	0.05	2.19
Average	0.79	0.15	2.12	0.89	1.07	1.20	0.78	0.17	2.08	1.12	0.04	1.79	1.11	0.05	2.10

In Table 1, it can be observed that most of the time DC and NL compete with the proposed method. However, some methods achieve the larger e value but of the cost of saturation. The proposed method overall produces good dehazing and performs better for all images and is comparable with the DC method. Values of these three indexes prove that the proposed method has better balance in terms of edges and texture details, does not suffer from over saturation, and visibility is also improved.

3.2.2 Fog aware density estimator

In addition, the fog aware density estimator (FADE) (Choi 2015) is also used to judge the performance of the proposed method. The FADE metric provides score to the haze-free image in terms of visibility based on features computed from haze-free image. The comparison of FADE score with existing method is illustrated in Table 2.

Table 2. FADE score on sample 500 foggy images.

Methods	DC (He et al. 2011)	NL (Berman & Avidan 2016)	AM (Galdran 2018)	CP (Zhu et al. 2015)	The Proposed Method
FADE score	0.39	0.31	0.56	1.04	0.38

The proposed method achieves the second ranking in FADE score and NL method achieves first ranking. The FADE metric segments the haze-free image into binary image. The value 0 in the segmented image denotes the haze is removed and while the value 1 indicates that the haze is not removed. The reason for highest FADE value for NL method is that this method suffers from the problem of over enhancement; therefore, gives higher weightage.

3.2.3 When ground truth image is available

The proposed method is tested on synthetic images from D-Hazy dataset (Ancuti et al. 2016) and two metrics PSNR and SSIM are used for evaluation. The performance comparison of the proposed method with other image dehazing techniques on some images is illustrated in Table 3 and qualitative evaluation is shown in Figure 4. We can see that the proposed method has the highest PSNR and second highest SSIM among all the methods in the comparison.

The visual analysis for sample hazy images is shown in Figure 4. It can be noticed that the proposed method has a better haze-free image in terms of better texture details, contrast, and visibility. The dehazed images of NL and DC suffer from over enhancement and over saturation as the colors of objects become darker than the grand truth images.

Table 3. Comparative analysis of PSNR and SSIM with existing methods for the images shown in Figure 4.

Image/ Method	AM (Galdren, 2018)		NL (Berman, 2016)		DC (He, 2011)		ML (Salazar, 2018)		The Proposed Method	
	PSNR	SSI:M	PSNR	SSIM	PSNR	SSI:M	PSNR	SSIM	PSNR	SSIM
Image 1	16.80	0.84	13.02	0.75	14.05	0.80	15.97	0.83	17.98	0.86
Image 2	19.67	0.86	13.76	0.74	12.65	0.70	20.34	0.89	18.31	0.87
Image 3	18.65	0.85	15.06	0.82	12.81	0.79	17.67	0.87	19.12	0.86
Image 4	20.69	0.82	18.35	0.85	16.27	0.85	17.81	0.89	19.79	0.78
Image 5	18.74	0.88	15.80	0.79	15.64	0.76	17.53	0.87	19.58	0.89
Average	**18.91**	**0.85**	**15.20**	**0.79**	**14.28**	**0.78**	**17.86**	**0.87**	**18.96**	**0.85**

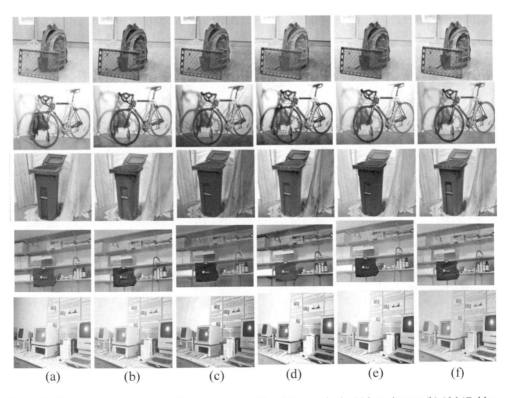

Figure 4. Dehazed results on synthetic hazy images with existing methods: (a) hazy image; (b) AM (Galdran 2018); (c) NL (Berman & Avidan 2016); (d) DC (He et al. 2011); (e) MLP (Salazar et al. 2018); (f) the proposed method.

4 CONCLUSIONS AND FUTURE WORK

In this paper, an image enhancement-based approach is used for single image dehazing. We generate three enhanced images using white balancing, gamma correction, and multi-scale Retinex. Finally, the resulting images are fused into a multi-scale fashion using pyramids of Laplacian and Gaussian decomposition. The proposed method is evaluated on various hazy images. The experimental analysis shows that the proposed method is able to enhance the visibility and contrast of the hazy image. The limitation of the proposed method is that it works well under only homogeneous haze. The future work investigates more enhancement-based approaches that can be utilized in the field of image dehazing that also will work on non-homogenous hazy images.

REFERENCES

Ancuti, C. O., & Ancuti, C. 2013. Single image dehazing by multi-scale fusion. IEEE Transaction on Image Processing 22(8): 3271–3282.

Ancuti, C., Ancuti, C. O., & Vleeschouwer, C. De. 2016. D-HAZY. A dataset to evaluate quantitatively dehazing algorithms. in Proc. IEEE Int. Conf. Image Process: 2226–2230.

Berman, D., & Avidan, S. 2016. Non-local image dehazing. In Proceedings of the IEEE Conference on Computer Vision and Pattern Recognition: 1674–1682.

Buchsbaum, G. 1980. A spatial processor model for object colour perception. J. Franklin Inst., 310(1):1–26.

Choi, L. K., You, J., & Bovik A. C. 2015. Referenceless Prediction of Perceptual Fog Density and Perceptual Image Defogging. IEEE Transactions on Image Processing 24(11): 3888–3901.

Cooper, T. J. & Baqai, F. A. 2004. Analysis and extensions of the Frankle-McCann retinex algorithm," J. Electron. Image 13(1): 85–92.

Fan, X., Wang, Y., Tang, X., Gao, R., & Luo, Z. 2017. Two-Layer Gaussian Process Regression With Example Selection for Image Dehazing. IEEE Transactions on Circuits and Systems for Video Technology 27(12).

Fattal R. 2008. Single image dehazing. ACM Transaction on Graphics 27(3).

Galdran, A. 2018. Artificial Multiple Exposure Image Dehazing. Signal Processing 149:135–147.

Hautiere, N., Tarel, J.P., Aubert, D., & Dumont, E. 2008 . Blind contrast enhancement assessment by gradient ratioing at visible edges. Image Anal. Stereol. J., 27(2): 87–95.

He, K., Sun, J., & Tang, X. 2011. Single image haze removal using dark channel prior. IEEE Transaction on Pattern Analysis Machine Intelligence 33(12): 2341–2353.

Hu, X. Y., Gao, X. H. & Wang, H. B. 2014. A novel retinex algorithm and its application to fog-degraded image enhancement. Sens. Transd. 175(7): 138–143.

Ju, M., Ding, C., Zhang D., & Guo, Y. J. 2018. Gamma-Correction-Based Visibility Restoration for Single Hazy Images. IEEE Signal Processing Letters 25(7): 1084–1088.

Ju, Mingye, Ding, Can, Zhang, Dengyin, & Guo, Y. Jay, 2018. Gamma-Correction-Based Visibility Restoration for Single Hazy Images. IEEE Signal Processing Letters 25(7).

Li, X. Hu, H., Zhao, L., Wang, H., Han, Q., Zhenzhou, C., H., & Liu, T.2019. Pseudo-polarimetric Method for Dense Haze Removal. IEEE Photonics Journal 11(1): 1–11.

Liu, Y., Shang, J., Pan, L., Wang, A., & Wang, M. 2019. A unified variational model for single image dehazing. IEEE Access 7: 15722–15736.

Ma, Kede, Liu,Wentao & Wang, Zhou. 2015. Perceptual evaluation of single image dehazing algorithms. IEEE International Conference on Image Processing.

Mertens, T., Kautz, J., & Reeth, F. V. 2007. Exposure Fusion. In 15th Pacific Conference on Computer Graphics and Applications 382–390. doi:10.1109/PG.2007.17.

Qian, W., Zhou, C., & Zhang, D. 2020. FAOD-Net: A Fast AOD-Net for Dehazing Single Image. Mathematical Problems in Engineering, Hindawi 2020(4945214).

Salazar-Colores S., Cruz-Aceves, I., Ramos-Arreguin J. 2018. Single image dehazing using a multilayer perceptron. J. of Electronic Imaging 27(4).

Salazar-Colores, S., Cabal-Yepez , Ramos-Arreguin E., Botella, J. M., G., Ledesma-Carrillo, L. M. & Ledesma S. 2019. A Fast Image Dehazing Algorithm Using Morphological Reconstruction. In IEEE Transactions on Image Processing. 28(5): 2357–2366.

Singh, D., & Kumar, V. 2017. Comprehensive survey on haze removal techniques. Multimedia Tools and Applications: 1–26.

Tan, R. 2008. Visibility in Bad Weather from a Single Image. In Proceedings of IEEE Conference on Computer Vision and Pattern Recognition. 1: 1–8.

Tarel, J.P., Hautiere, N. 2009. Fast visibility restoration from a single-color or gray-level image. In Proceedings of IEEE Conference on Computer Vision: 2201–2208.

Van de Weijer J. & Gevers, T. 2005. Color constancy based on the greyedge hypothesis. In Proc. IEEE Int. Conf. Image Process: 722–725.

Zhu, Q. S., Mai, J. M., & Shao, L. 2015. A fast single image haze removal algorithm using color attenuation prior (2015). IEEE Transactions on Image Processing 24(11): 3522–3533.

Smart Computing – Khan et al (Eds)
© *2021 Taylor & Francis Group, London, ISBN 978-0-367-76552-1*

Fuzzy logic-based performance analysis of cloud application system

Anupama Mishra & A.K. Daniel
Department of CSE, MMMUT Gorakhpur, India

ABSTRACT: Cloud computing offers applications, supporting technology, hardware, software, infrastructure, and integration for clients. Cloud computing has on-demand access to shared infrastructure. Cloud computing offers cloud application systems such as Email, gaming application, sound/video, and social media for clients. The user performance, throughput, and performance of cloud services are affected by delay, packet loss, and bandwidth parameters during the transmission between client and server. The proposed protocol determines the effects of delay, packet loss, and bandwidth parameters on the cloud application system using fuzzy logic decision-making techniques. The proposed fuzzy logic simulation shows the best user performance, throughput, and performance of cloud services by using delay, packet loss, and bandwidth parameters in cloud computing environments.

1 INTRODUCTION

Cloud computing infrastructure is implemented by the integration of NIST and IBM cloud computing reference architectures (Buzetti 2011). Cloud computing is distributed model which offers computing services and infrastructure to users in a demand-for-use payment model (Quasim 2019). The cloud computing environment is a demand-based allocation of resources, software, and hardware that are both virtualized and distributed from providers point to users. The system resources can be dynamically distributed based on the needs and user's expectations (Liu et al. 2011).

Cloud services can be classified into three different groups—Infrastructure as a Service (IaaS), Platform as a Service (PaaS), and Software as a Service (SaaS) (Ding et al. 2014; Buyya et al. 2013). IaaS requires ownership of the infrastructure used to manage activities, and provides resources such as hardware, virtual machines, virtual storage, and servers over the cloud. PaaS provides deployment tools and operating systems over the cloud without installation. SaaS is a software system implemented from cloud providers and used as a service to cloud users over the cloud. The cloud is categorized into three types as public cloud, private cloud, and hybrid cloud. Public cloud services such as application, storage, and infrastructure are accessible on pay-per-use to the public, e.g., Windows Azure services, Amazon Elastic Compute Cloud, and Google AppEngine. The private cloud services are accessible inside the corporate organization. The hybrid cloud is a collection of corporate organizations and the public cloud, e.g., EMC and IBM. The cloud computing can also be used in the Internet of Things (IoT) and blockchain to provide cloud infrastructure (Abuhasel 2020; Khan 2020a, 2020e; Quasim et al. 2019, 2020).

The cloud provider has responsibilities to offer quality of service (QoS) to different cloud users. QoS is the operational characteristics of a given service in terms of quantity/quality. The QoS covers both quantitative and qualitative services. Quantitative services are measured by values or numbers such as CPU utilization, accuracy, and data transfer rate, and cost can be measured quantitatively by using relevant software and hardware. Qualitative services accountability, agility, assurance, usability, security, and privacy is measured using an ordinal scale consisting of a set of predefined tags as good, bad, low, high, etc. (Yau & Yin 2011).

DOI 10.1201/9781003167488-27

The performance of the cloud application system is affected by the delay, bandwidth, jitter, packet loss, etc. The delay of the network involves propagation delay, processing delay, and congestion delay. The propagation delay refers to the ratio of time to travel data packets from the sender to the destination. The processing delay refers to the ratio of the time to process the data packets. When data packets do not reach its destination during transmission is known as packet loss. The maximum transmission power of the network is called bandwidth. The variation of delay between packets flow in the cloud application system is called jitter of the network. The cloud application system has a low delay and high bandwidth of the network to offer good quality video streams (Sonia & Singh 2012).

The paper proposes the performance analysis of cloud application system under delay, packet loss, and bandwidth using the fuzzy logic controller. The proposed protocol determines the effects of delay, packet loss, and bandwidth parameters on cloud application systems. The rest of the paper is structured as follows. Section 2 describes the related work. Section 3 discusses the proposed model. Section 4 provides validation and analysis, while Section 5 provides simulation and results. Finally, Section 6 concludes the paper.

2 RELATED WORK

The service mapper technique is used to map services between users and providers. This technique uses singular value decomposition for service ranking. The service mapper contains three layers. The first layer is called information gathering which is responsible for getting user expectations and determining services that can fulfill it. The second layer is to decompose the matrix into small dimension to enhance quality. The knowledge of the providers is placed at matrix rows and services are placed at matrix columns. The third layer receives singular and qualitative values of user expectations that are mapped on the selected service (Chan & Chieu 2010). This does not get the right response because a comparison of service is dependent on attributes that are restricted to large matrixes and are time-consuming.

In the service-level agreement, the matching method for the suitable cloud providers is selected by matching service level agreement parameters as per user expectations. This method has the following four steps. The first step considers the RDF models which contain cloud resources, properties, resource size, and so on. The second step converts the RDF models into a graph structure. The third step to construct a caused propagation graph using a pairwise connectivity graph. The fourth step obtains the original mapping using the RDF schema (Chauhan et al. 2011).

The Cloud Service Measurement Index has evaluated all the QoS attributes (functional and non-functional) from the cloud service measurement index consortium and ranking of services based on QoS attributes. The major problem of this approach is how to evaluate different attributes and how to rank the service provider attributes. The Service Measurement Index approach consists of three layers. The first layer is Cloud Broker. It gathers the user's expectations and meets their needs. The second layer is the monitoring of cloud services and their performance. The third layer is a service schedule to store the features that the cloud providers finalize (Limam & Boutaba 2010).

The Cloud Service Measurement Index is dependent on the analytical hierarchical process. The analytical hierarchical process technique performs weighted pairwise comparison of multiple parameters and finally selects the best cloud provider. Let n require metrics to compare and then make comparisons n (n-1)/2 for ranking the providers. The advantages of Service Measurement Index approach consider qualitative attribute standards across the procedure (Garg et al. 2013).

In the fuzzy logic model, the selection of cloud service is based on the specific quality of service (QoS) that is needed for the client. The appropriate service setup and run-time QoS data are obtained across trustworthy sources including monitoring systems, certified cloud providers' information, and customer feedback. The method of selecting the cloud service uses valid data input in the selection process. Established methods are focused on ambiguity data released by service providers, fuzzy view of consumer needs, and the inaccurate quality of service calculation provided by the history of real-time measurement and service usage (Masoumeh 2014).

In the Dynamic Cloud Service Trustworthiness model for trustworthiness in terms of various cloud services, the cloud service changes over time based on a variety of factors, such as the perception of the user, changes in technology, and addition of new needs for the end-user (Pandey & Daniel 2016).

The model changes the trustworthiness depending on the user's perception. The model estimates the trustworthiness of the entire cloud service by using a fuzzy-integrated estimation model (Pandey & Daniel 2017).

In the impact on cloud gaming, the application identified the differences in frame rate across different service situations like bandwidth, delay, and packet loss (Ryan 2013).

The cloud application services such as OnLive and Gaming applications play anywhere and anytime to users. We evaluate the effects of delay and packet loss on user experiences and performance of cloud application services (Claypool & Finkel 2014).

The study model also showed how delays appear at different geographical areas and how different browsers provide different delays. An experiment demonstrats the effect of bandwidth detected when trying to access Google cloud documents in cybercafé (Singh & Hemalatha 2012).

Cloud service providers with requirements such as usability, flexibility, finance, security, and network performance employ fuzzy logic to analyze the cloud service. The performance of another cloud service provider with regard to the other requirements for providing services as per the requirements for the user also as the QoS (Srivastava & Daniel 2019).

3 PROPOSED MODEL

Cloud application systems are usually placed in remote locations and managed by cloud infrastructure providers. The tasks of cloud application systems include cloud gaming, Email, file storage, file sharing, and social media. The cloud application systemw are based on client (desktop computer) and server systems. The client fetches user activity (request) and sends it to the cloud server. The server then processes the activity (request), encodes it, compresses the result (response), and then sends it back to the client (user). In the cloud, delays in sending, processing, and compressing of data packets occur every day. In this study, we examine the user performance, throughput, and performance of cloud services for a cloud application system during the transmission between client and server. The different network conditions such as delay, packet loss, and bandwidth affect the overall performance of the cloud application system. The proposed protocol determines the effects of delay, packet loss, and bandwidth parameters on the cloud application services system by using fuzzy control logic techniques. The proposed fuzzy logic model selects the best user performance, throughput, and performance of cloud services based on the delay, packet loss, and bandwidth parameter values. A Fuzzy Logic System (FLS) can be represented as a nonlinear graph of datasets (Mendel 1995). The fuzzy rule is based on systems of fuzzification and defuzzification components used for classification. The proposed model considered the concept of classification used in identification using machine learning (Mishra & Daniel 2020). The fuzzification unit has the ability to change crisp data into fuzzy sets and defuzzification transforms the fuzzy sets action into a crisp value to achieve real control action. The input variables, their fuzzy semantic quantities, and the terminology were summarized as follows: Delay (Lowest, Average, Highest), Packet Loss (Low, Medium, Heavy), and Bandwidth (Light, Sufficient, High). The result of the fuzzy semantic quantities and terminology are defined as the performance rating of cloud application system based on membership value of input variables. The performance analysis of the proposed protocol is based on network parameters such as delay, packet loss, and bandwidth.

3.1 *Delay*

The ratio of the time required for signals to move from the sender to the destination along with the connection length and the propagation speed over the particular medium can encounter delays. These delays are measured in milliseconds.

3.2 *Packet loss*

Packet loss occurs if data does not reach its destination during transmission. Packet loss occurs due to network errors or congestion. These errors result is packet loss during transmission and must be resent by the original sender. The packet loss is measured in percentage.

3.3 *Bandwidth*

The maximum transmission power of the network is called bandwidth. The maximum bandwidth connection provides better performance of cloud services. The traditional network is measured in bits per second and the modern network measured in megabits or gigabits per second.

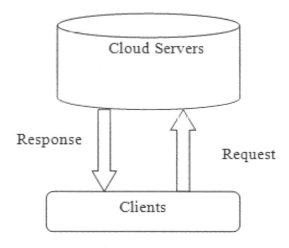

Figure 1.   Proposed model of cloud application system.

The proposed fuzzy-based decision-making protocol to determine the effects on cloud application system is analyzed. The input of fuzzy logic transforms into fuzzy sets. The fuzzy sets A, B, and C are defined as follows:

$$A = \{(\text{Del}, \mu_A\,(\text{Del}))\}, \text{Del} \in \text{delay}$$

$$B = \{(\text{PL}, \mu_B\,(\text{PL}))\}, \text{PL} \in \text{packet loss}$$

$$C = \{(\text{BW}, \mu_C\,(\text{BW}))\}, \text{BW} \in \text{bandwidth}$$

where Del, PL, and BW are particular components of delay, packet loss, and bandwidth in cloud computing. The membership functions μ_A, μ_B, and μ_C are used to determine the membership value in fuzzy sets. The delay, packet loss, and bandwidth membership functions are defined as follows:

$$\mu_A(\text{Del}) = \begin{cases} 0 & \text{if Del} \geq \text{TH}_2 \\ (\text{TH}_2 - \text{Del})/(\text{TH}_2 - \text{TH}_1) & \text{if TH}_1 > \text{Del} > \text{TH}_2 \\ 1 & \text{if Del} \leq \text{TH}_1 \end{cases}$$

$$\mu_B(\text{PL}) = \begin{cases} 0 & \text{if PL} \geq \text{TH}_2 \\ (\text{TH}_2 - \text{PL})/(\text{TH}_2 - \text{TH}_1) & \text{if TH}_1 > \text{PL} > \text{TH}_2 \\ 1 & \text{if PL} \leq \text{TH}_1 \end{cases}$$

$$\mu_C(\text{BW}) = \begin{cases} 0 & \text{if BW} \leq \text{TH}_1 \\ (\text{BW} - \text{TH}_1)/(\text{TH}_2 - \text{TH}_1) & \text{if TH}_1 < \text{BW} < \text{TH}_2 \\ 1 & \text{if BW} \geq \text{TH}_2 \end{cases}$$

where TH_1=Minimum threshold value and TH_2=Maximum threshold value.

Now apply the MIN–MAX rule on Del, PL, and BW fuzzy relationship:

$$\mu_A(\text{Del}) \wedge \mu_B(\text{PL}) \wedge \mu_C(\text{BW})$$

Let us consider the three-level membership values for input variables shown in Table 1.

Table 1.   Input values.

Input	Membership		
Delay	Lowest	Average	Highest
Packet Loss	Low	Medium	Heavy
Bandwidth	Light	Sufficient	High

The precedence order of output membership value are as follows:
P1>P2>P3>...........................>P25>P26>P27.

The relationships of fuzzy logic are described in Table 2.

Table 2.   Rule sets.

Delay	Packet Loss	Bandwidth	performance Rating
Lowest	Low	Light	P11
Lowest	Low	Sufficient	P3
Lowest	Low	High	P1
Lowest	Medium	Light	P15
Lowest	Medium	Sufficient	P6
Lowest	Medium	High	P5
Lowest	Heavy	Light	P19
Lowest	Heavy	Sufficient	P18
Lowest	Heavy	High	P12
Average	Low	Light	P13
Average	Low	Sufficient	P7
Average	Low	High	P2
Average	Medium	Light	P14
Average	Medium	Sufficient	P8
Average	Medium	High	P4
Average	Heavy	Light	P20
Average	Heavy	Sufficient	P17
Average	Heavy	High	P16
Highest	Low	Light	P23
Highest	Low	Sufficient	P10
Highest	Low	High	P9
Highest	Medium	Light	P24
Highest	Medium	Sufficient	P22
Highest	Medium	High	P21
Highest	Heavy	Light	P26
Highest	Heavy	Sufficient	P27
Highest	Heavy	High	P25

4   VALIDATION AND ANALYSIS

Let us consider five cloud application systems. Suppose a set of delay, packet loss, and bandwidth for cloud application services system are

delay={0.001, 0.002, 0.003, 0.004, 0.006},
packet loss={0.001, 0.0012, 0.0020, 0.0029, 0.0001}
bandwidth={2, 3.5, 10, 7, 8.5}

The membership function is according to the delay

$$\mu_{delay}\,(Del) = \begin{cases} 0 & \text{if } Del \geq 0.005(TH_2) \\ (0.005 - Del)/(0.003) & \text{if } 0.002 < Del < 0.005 \\ 1 & \text{if } Del \leq 0.002(TH_1) \end{cases}$$

The membership function is according to the packet loss

$$\mu_{packetloss}\,(PL) = \begin{cases} 0 & \text{if } PL \geq 0.003(TH_2) \\ (0.003 - PL)/(0.002) & \text{if } 0.001 < PL < 0.003 \\ 1 & \text{if } PL \leq 0.001(TH_1) \end{cases}$$

The membership function is according to the bandwidth

$$\mu_{bandwidth}\,(BW) = \begin{cases} 0 & \text{if } BW < 3Mbps(TH_1) \\ (BW - 3)/(5) & \text{if } 3 < BW < 8Mbps \\ 1 & \text{if } BW \geq 8Mbps(TH_2) \end{cases}$$

Now calculate the degree of membership of delay, packet loss, and bandwidth using the membership functions shown in Table 3.

Table 3. Degree of membership.

Delay	Membership	Packet Loss	Membership	Bandwidth	Membership
0.001	1	0.001	1	2	0
0.002	1	0.0012	0.9	3.5	0.1
0.003	0.66	0.0020	0 5	10	1
0.004	0.33	0.0029	0.05	7	0.8
0.006	0	0.0001	1	8.5	1

As per the fuzzy output, the above membership of delay are {0.001|lowest, 0.002|lowest, 0.003|average, 0.004|average, 0.006|highest}, packet loss are {0.001|low, 0.0012|medium, 0.0020|medium, 0.0029|medium, 0.0001|low}, and bandwidth are {2|light, 3.5|sufficient, 10|high, 7|sufficient, 8.5|high}

The fuzzy relationship of the membership value with delay and packet loss shown in Table 4.

Table 4. Fuzzy relationship.

Del/PL	0.001	0.002	0.003	0.004	0.006
0.001	1^1	1^1	1^0.66	1^0.33	1^0
0.0012	0.9^1	0.9^1	0.9^0.66	0.9^0.33	0.9^0
0.0020	0.5^1	0.5^1	0.5^0.66	0.5^0.33	0.5^0
0.0029	0.05^1	0.05^1	0.05^0.66	0.05^0.33	0.05^0
0.0001	1^1	1^1	1^0.66	1^0.33	1^0

The resultant value after the fuzzy operation with delay and packet loss is shown in Table 5.

Table 5. Result after fuzzy operation.

Del/PL	0.001	0.002	0.003	0.004	0.006
0.001	1	1	0.33	0.33	0
0.0012	0.9	0.9	0.66	0.33	0
0.0020	0.5	0.5	0.5	0.33	0
0.0029	0.05	0.05	0.05	0.05	0
0.0001	1	1	0.66	0.33	0

Let us consider the bandwidth from Table 3 and the resultant of delay and packet loss from Table 5. The result of the fuzzy relationship are shown in Table 6.

Table 6. Fuzzy relationship.

BW					
Del/PL	2	3.5	10	7	8.5
1	0	0.1	1	0.8	1
1	0	0.1	1	0.8	1
1	0	0.1	1	0.8	1
1	0	0.1	1	0.8	1

The possible delay, packet loss, and bandwidth, combined with the higher membership value from Table 5 and Table 6, are shown in Table 7.

Table 7. Output value.

BW		
Del/PL	10	8.5
0.001 | 0.001	1	1
0.001 | 0.0001	1	1
0.002 | 0.001	1	1
0.002 | 0.0001	1	1

The degree of membership of delay, packet loss, and bandwidth are shown in Table 8.

Table 8. Output of delay, packet loss, and bandwidth.

Delay	Degree	Packet Loss	Degree	Bandwidth	Degree
0.001	Lowest	0.001	Low	10	High
0.002	Lowest	0.0001	Low	8.5	High

Therefore, now all possible combinations of delay, packet loss, and bandwidth are available.

- Delay=0.001, Packet Loss=0.001 and bandwidth=10
- Delay=0.001, Packet Loss=0.001 and bandwidth=8.5

- **Delay=0.001, Packet Loss=0.0001 and bandwidth=10**
- Delay=0.001,Packet Loss=0.0001 and bandwidth=8.5
- Delay=0.002, Packet Loss=0.001 and bandwidth=10
- Delay=0.002, Packet Loss=0.001 and bandwidth=8.5
- Delay=0.002, Packet Loss=0.0001 and bandwidth=10
- Delay=0.002, Packet Loss=0.0001 and bandwidth=8.5

Any of the above combinations of delay, packet loss, and bandwidth can have the perfect performance of a cloud application system. But according to rule 3 from the rule sets, they have the best user performance, throughput, and performance of cloud service for cloud application system among all rule set combinations. When the delay is 0.001 ms, packet loss is 0.0001 (1 in 10,000 packets) and bandwidth is 10 Mbps (1 * 10^7 bits per second) for transmission of the data packets in the cloud. The output rating of the cloud application system for these values is "P1" as "delay is low, packet loss is less, and bandwidth is high." This will be the best among all for the transmission of data packets between client and cloud server. Thus, the protocol selects the best user performance, throughput, and performance of cloud services for cloud application systems with minimum delay, minimum packet loss, and maximum bandwidth parameters value in cloud environments

5   SIMULATION AND RESULTS

The proposed fuzzy logic techniques were simulated using a MATLAB fuzzy toolbox. Input variables are delay, packet loss, and bandwidth, as they are network parameters that affect the overall performance of the cloud application system during the transmission between client and server. In this study, we implement the membership value of input variables. The output variable of the fuzzy set considers the performance rating of the cloud application system based on the memberships of input variables. The fuzzy logic techniques have been proposed for the selection of the best cloud service based on the values of the user performance parameter .

Input variables have three membership functions, DELAY (Lowest, Average, Highest), PACKET LOSS (Low, Medium, Heavy), and BANDWITH (Light, Sufficient, High), as shown in Figures 2, 3, and 4. The range of input parameters is defined in Table 9.

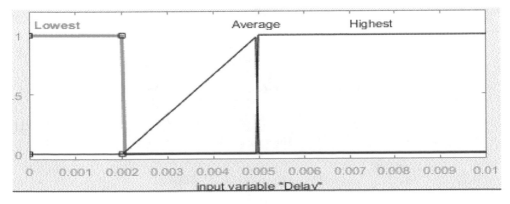

Figure 2.   Input membership value of delay with range "lowest", "average", and "highest".

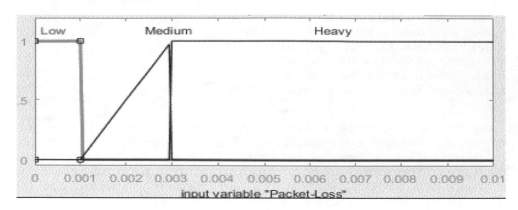

Figure 3. Input membership value of packet loss with range "low", "medium", and "heavy".

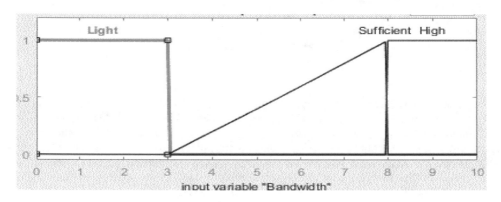

Figure 4. Input membership value of bandwidth with range "light", "sufficient", and "high".

Table 9. Range of parameters.

Parameters	Output membership	
	0 to 0.002 ms	Lowest
Delay	0.002 to 0.005 ms	Average
	0.005 and above	Highest
	0 to 0.001%	Low
Packet loss	0.01 to 0.003%	Medium
	0.003% and above	Heavy
	0 to 3 Mbps	Light
Bandwidth	3 to 8 Mbps	Sufficient
	8 Mbps and above	High

The output variable of performance rating has ranged from 0 to 100 and has 27 membership functions such as P1, P2, P3,............, P26, P27, as shown in Figure 5.

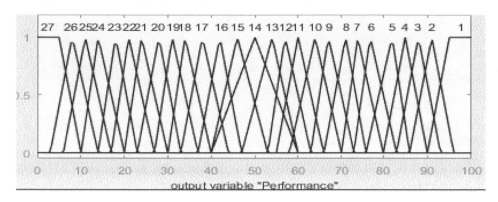

Figure 5.   Output of membership value.

The IF-THEN rule datasets are as follows:

Rule1:
IF (delay is lowest)^(packet loss is low)^ (bandwidth is light) THEN (Output is P11)

Rule 27:
IF (delay is highest)^(packet loss is heavy)^ (bandwidth is high)THEN (output is P25)

After defuzzification, the output is obtained from the fuzzy logic system shown in Figure 6.

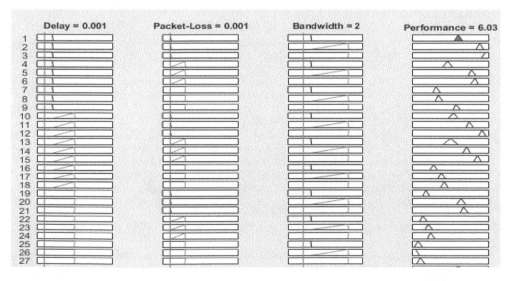

Figure 6.   Output of a cloud application system with respect to delay, packet loss, and bandwidth.

Table 10. Simulation result for selected inputs.

Delay	Packet Loss	Bandwidth	Performance rating
0.001	0.0001	10	96.4 (P1)
0.002	0.003	3	31.7 (P19)
0.005	0.0001	10	67.7 (P9)
0.0001	0.004	8.5	57.7 (P12)
0.002	0.005	7	34.7 (P18)

Using the above rule datasets and input variable membership functions, the following response is produced and shown in Table 10.

The above results show that as the delay increases the user performance decreases, as the packet loss increases the throughput decreases, and as the bandwidth decreases the performance of cloud services is decreased (the overall performance of cloud application system is decreased). But as the delay decreases the user performance is increased, as the packet loss decreases the throughput is increased, and as the bandwidth increases the performance of cloud services is increased (the overall performance of cloud application system is increased).

6 CONCLUSION

The proposed protocol determines the effects of delay, packet loss, and bandwidth parameters on a cloud application system. The proposed fuzzy logic protocol selects best user performance, throughput, and performance of cloud services by using delay, packet loss, and bandwidth parameter values in cloud computing. The simulation result shows that as the delay increases, the packet loss increases, and as the bandwidth decreases, the overall performance of cloud application system decreases. But as the delay decreases, the packet loss decreases, and as the bandwidth increases the overall performance of a cloud application system is increased.

REFERENCES

Abuhasel K. A. and M. A. Khan, (2020),"A Secure Industrial Internet of Things (IIoT) Framework for Resource Management in Smart Manufacturing," in IEEE Access, vol. 8, pp. 117354–117364, 2020, doi: 10.1109/ACCESS.2020.3004711.

Buyya R, Vecchiola C & Selvi S.T. 2013, Cloud Computing Architecture. *chapter 4*.

CCRA Team & Buzetti M. 2011, Cloud Computing Reference Architecture 2.0: Overview. *IBM Corporation.*

Chan H & Chieu T. 2010, Ranking and Mapping of Applications to Cloud Computing Services by SVD. *IEEE/IFIP Network Operations and Management Symposium Workshops.*

Chauhan Tejas, Chaudhary S, Kumar Vikas & Bhise M. 2011, Service Level Agreement Parameter Matching in Cloud Computing. *World Congress on Information and Communication Technologies (WICT),* 564–570.

Claypool Mark & Finkel David. 2014, The Effects of Latency on Player Performance in Cloud-based Games. *In Proceedings of the 13th ACM Network and System Support for Games (NetGames).*

Ding S, Yang S, Zhang Y, Liang C & Xia C. 2014, Combining QoS Prediction and Customer Satisfaction Estimation to Solve Cloud Service Trustworthiness Evaluation Problems. *Knowledge-Based Systems*, Vol 56: 216–225.

Garg S.K, Versteeg S & Buyya R. 2013, A Framework for Ranking of Cloud Computing Services. *Future Generation Computer Systems.*

Khan ,M. A., Quasim, M. T, et al., (2020), A Secure Framework for Authentication and Encryption Using Improved ECC for IoT-Based Medical Sensor Data, in IEEE Access, vol. 8, pp. 52018–52027, 2020. DOI: 10.1109/ACCESS.2020.2980739

Khan M. A., (2020), An IoT Framework for Heart Disease Prediction Based on MDCNN Classifier, in IEEE Access, vol. 8, pp. 34717–34727, 2020. DOI: 10.1109/ACCESS.2020.2974687

Khan, MA, Abuhasel, KA. (2020).Advanced metameric dimension framework for heterogeneous industrial Internet of things. Computational Intelligence. 2020; 1–21. https://doi.org/10.1111/coin.12378

Khan M.A, and Algarni F., (2020) "A Healthcare Monitoring System for the Diagnosis of Heart Disease in the IoMT Cloud Environment Using MSSO-ANFIS," in IEEE Access, vol. 8, pp. 122259–122269, 2020, doi: 10.1109/ACCESS.2020.3006424.

Khan M.A. et al., (2020), Decentralised IoT, Decenetralised IoT: A Blockchain perspective, Springer, Studies in BigData, 2020, DOI: https://doi.org/10.1007/978-3-030-38677-1

Limam Noura & Boutaba Raouf. 2010, Assessing Software Service Quality and Trustworthiness at selection time. *IEEE transactions on software engineering.*

Liu F, Hogan Michael, Sokol Annie & Tong Jin. 2011, NIST Cloud Computing Reference Architecture. *National Institute of Standards and Technology U.S Department of Commerce Special Publication 500–292.*

Masoumeh, Ranjan Rajiv, Joanna & Wang Lizhe. 2014, Fuzzy Cloud Service Selection Framework. *IEEE 3rd International Conference on Cloud Networking (CloudNet).*

Mendel J. 1995, Fuzzy logic systems for engineering: A tutorial. *Proceedings of the IEEE.*

Mishra Anupama & Daniel A.K. Feb 2020, Efficient protocol for Gender Identification using Machine Learning. *International Conference On Recent Trends in Artificial Intelligence, IoT, Smart Cities & Applications (ICAISC).*

Pandey Sarvesh & Daniel A.K. 2016, Fuzzy Logic Based Cloud Service Trustworthiness Model. *IEEE International Conference on Engineering and Technology (ICETECH).*

Pandey Sarvesh & Daniel A.K. 2017, QoCS and Cost Based Cloud Service Selection Framework. *International Journal of Engineering Trends and Technology (IJETT).*

Quasim, M. T.,Khan M. A, et al., (2019), Internet of Things for Smart Healthcare: A Hardware Perspective, 2019 First International Conference of Intelligent Computing and Engineering (ICOICE), Hadhramout, Yemen, 2019, pp. 1–5. DOI: 10.1109/ICOICE48418.2019.9035175

Quasim, M.T., Khan M.A, Algarni F., Alharthy A., Alshmrani G.M.M, (2020), Blockchain Frameworks. In: Khan M., Quasim M., Algarni F., Alharthi A. (eds) Decentralised Internet of Things. Studies in Big Data, vol 71. Springer, DOI: https://doi.org/10.1007/978-3-030-38677-1

Quasim, Mohammad Tabrez, et al. (2019), 5 V'S OF BIG DATA VIA CLOUD COMPUTING: USES AND IMPORTANCE, Sci.int(Lahore),vol.31(3), PP.367–371, 2019.

Ryan Shea, Liu Jiangchuan, Edith Ngai & Yong Cui. 2013, Cloud Gaming: Architecture and Performance. *IEEE Network.*

Singh Ajith & Hemalatha. 2012, Comparative analysis of Low latency on different bandwidth and geographical locations while using cloud-based applications. *Head department of Software systems. Kalpagam university Coimbatore:* IJAET ISSN: 2231–1963.

Sonia & Singh Satinder pal. 2012, Analysis of Energy Consumption in Different types of networks For Cloud Environment. *IJARCSSE.*

Srivastava Rashi & daniel A.K. 2019, Efficient Model of Cloud Trustworthiness for Selecting Services Using Fuzzy Logic. *Emerging Technologies in Data Mining and Information Security Advances in Intelligent Systems and Computing.*

Yau S & Yin Y. 2011, QoS-Based Service Ranking and Selection for Service-Based Systems. *IEEE International Conference on Services Computing.*

Smart Computing – Khan et al (Eds)
© 2021 Taylor & Francis Group, London, ISBN 978-0-367-76552-1

A graph clustering model to predict student retention using DAG

Anish Giri, Lakshmi Anand, Malavika P. Pillai, Sherin A. & Krishnaveni K.S.
Amrita School of Engineering, Amrita Vishwa Vidyapeetham, Amritapuri, India

ABSTRACT: Educational data mining is one of the prominent areas to explore information in the field of education. One of the major issues faced by universities nowadays is retention. Out of the many factors that influence this, curriculum structure has not received much attention. This paper models each student data as a Directed Acyclic Graph and applies the sub-graph mining method followed by the graph clustering method. The experimental results show that the proposed model gives an accurate and efficient way for predicting a student's chance of retention in a curriculum path.

1   INTRODUCTION

In recent times due to the vast availability of the educational data, Educational Data Mining (EDM) has helped the education sector to analyze, identify, rectify, and improve the process of education. This helps educators to improve the efficacy of teaching as well as identify and address the challenges of the students. It helps the students to enhance their performance and deliver better results. This field focuses on mining relevant patterns and relationships in order to extract useful information by applying different data mining, data analytical, and machine learning (ML) algorithms depending on the use case. Intelligent tutors that can be built to respond to and understand the students based on the data collected on their performance, etc. also make the learning experience more understandable and adaptable according to their abilities. It contributes to many other fields, including educational psychology and learning sciences, thereby enabling it to emerge as a prominent field of research.

Unlike the past, today the number of students that enroll for higher education has sharply increased. Along with the other contributing factors such as economy and the labor market, one of main reasons behind this trend is that young adults need to be capable enough to enter the job market with a qualification/degree. According to the National Center for Education Statistics (NCES), the overall college enrollment rate has increased since 2000. Even though the enrollment rates for the tertiary study levels are high, the numbers show that the challenge lies in the poor success rates and completion rates. Also, the youth unemployment rates are increasing despite the increasing number of graduates with professional degrees, indicating a decrease in the number of individuals entering the job market. There are a wide variety of factors that can contribute to this, including individual student factors, such as academic performance, physical and mental well-being of the individual, as well as family, economic issues, and external factors, such as national and local unemployment rates, climate changes, poor quality of teaching, lack of facilities, inexperienced staff, political environment, curriculum structure, etc.

When faced with such a situation, the students either discontinue their course study, i.e., dropout or take a break, complete the course over an extended period of time, or join another course. One of the most common scenarios is where the students take a long time to complete the degree as compared to the minimum required time as prescribed by the college. This is termed as student retention. Many ML methodologies have been applied on educational data to predict whether the student has a chance of retention or dropout. By applying certain analytical methods to educational data, universities can better understand the learning pattern of students and remodel the curriculum, in turn reducing dropout rates. It can also help the student to choose their curriculum path optimally.

DOI 10.1201/9781003167488-28

That is, if the curriculum path chosen is prone to retention then the students could reconsider the path taking their personal factors into account.

The proposed work mainly focuses on how to achieve reduced dropout rates by analyzing the role of the lesser-explored course curriculum structure in a student's reason for leaving school. This in turn would help universities to increase their retention rates, helping students to successfully graduate without any backlogs or without dropping out.

2 RELATED WORKS

Many works have focused on predicting student dropout and retention possibilities by taking different factors into account and using different algorithms. Many studies have been conducted to identify the contributing factors to student retention and finding ways to increase it.

2.1 Analytical algorithms

Statistical studies have been conducted on a large volume of data, plotting it against a variety of student factors to identify the reasons behind student dropout and retention rates. Moreover, learning analytics were applied in Taoyuan, a country with the second highest dropout rate.

2.2 Machine Learning (ML) algorithms

Some work has focused on predicting student performance which in turn is an indicator of possibility of dropout. On the other hand, some research is entirely dependent on finding the patterns in students' grade reports and others by analyzing students' personal factors. Many prediction models have used Bayesian classifications, classification models using Decision Trees and Apriori Concepts. Other approaches include assessment of student's enrollment details and student attendance. Also, other ML algorithms like Instance-Based Learning Algorithms, Logistic Regression, and Support Vector Machines have been applied.

2.3 Analyzing course structure

Following to the need of Fluminense Federal University, in a study, the curriculum structure was modeled into a Directed Acyclic Graph (DAG) and the methods' effectiveness was analyzed, finding retention patterns by checking its validity against actual statistical data obtained from another study conducted at the same university.

3 PROPOSED SYSTEM

The work so far in the given field includes analyzing the situation of the students in social and academic contexts. Instead of analyzing student behavioral patterns, the current proposed work aims at analyzing curriculum and identifying course patterns which may result in rentation or dropout.

If there is a problem with a course in a university which makes it likely to be dropped, then all that a student can do is to not opt for that course. In addition, the number of students who take that course unknowingly find it hard to complete and end up taking a longer time than required. This not only affects their timely graduation but also their mental health. This also prevents them from promptly joining the job market and starting to earn a living. This issue needs to be addressed by the universities to prevent this from increasing.

In order to find out the courses that cause dropout, we need to mine out the correlation between the number of retentions and the courses. For that we need to find out the patterns among courses where this retention has occurred. The best way to represent the course structure in a university is as a graph with nodes as the subjects and the edges representing the relationship between the subjects. As the course of study with a particular course as its pre-requisite cannot possibly be a pre-requisite of the latter, this relationship will always inherently be a DAG.

In order to analyze student course structure, the course path taken by the student as well as the ideal path of the curriculum, i.e., program flowchart offered by the university, needs to be modeled into a DAG. Here for the student's graphs, the edge weight corresponds to the number of times a course was repeated by the student. The edge weights for the program flowchart is taken as positive 1. The origin and end of the graphs are indicated by the nodes Admission and Conclusion. All the courses without any pre-requisites will be mapped to Admission and the courses that are not pre-requisites to any other course are mapped to Conclusion node.

Retention is said to happen when the student takes a next semesters to complete the course. Therefore, we need to discover the most expensive path taken by the student as it might contain the most repeated course taken by the student. Also, in order to check whether this path resulted in the retention we can check the most expensive path for that curriculum as it will indicate the maximum number of semesters that will be taken to finish that curriculum in an ideal case. In order to mine these, we must find out the longest paths in the DAGs. Being a DAG, the computationally expensive operation of finding frequent substructures is significantly reduced (linear) as cycles won't be present. So, representing graphs as DAG allows us to use efficient algorithms for mining out retention patterns with less effort.

With the above attained information, we can discover the patterns which can possibly lead to retention. In order to help the student from making the mistake of taking the wrong path and to equip him/her with information to make a well-informed decision regarding his/her course path, we expanded this to include a prediction model. This will also help us to verify how much of a contributing factor is this curriculum structure in the rising retention rates. Again, this might vary across universities.

In order to build a prediction model which will classify whether or not a student will face retention, we need a reference value relating to the students that has faced retention to compare the data points against. For that we took the longest paths of all the students that faced the retention. If the students' paths are similar to these then the student is more likely to face retention. So, we built one cluster each for seven curriculums by merging the longest path graphs and setting them as the cluster centroids. This is because now the cluster centroid will contain all the possible retention-causing paths as well as the paths that didn't contribute to retention. We then found out how much the retention-causing paths are similar to this centroid to find out the radius of the cluster. So, by doing this we can find out the reference required for classifying the students. The student graphs which falls within this radius is predicted as true as they are more similar to the retention causing paths and those which fall outside re predicted as false.

4 METHODOLOGY

The entire workflow has been divided into two phases. Phase 1 consists of pruning, pre-processing, and pattern generation steps and Phase 2 is concerned with sub-graph mining and the clustering model as shown in Figure 1.

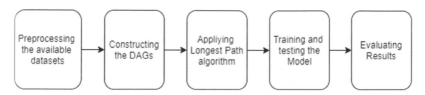

Figure 1. Overall system flow.

4.1 *Phase 1*

In Phase 1, we pre-processed the datasets and generated appropriate DAGs. Two types of DAGs were generated, namely student historical and program flowchart. The student historical is the graph

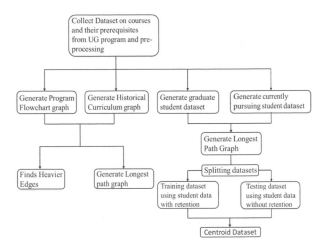

Figure 2. Stages for Phase 1.

generated from the grade reports which shows the curriculum path followed by the student including information on the time taken by the student to complete the course. The program flowchart is the graph representing the courses and its pre-requisites in a curriculum.

We split the entire dataset into training and testing. The splitting was done in a logical way rather than the traditional train/test split by partitioning the entire dataset. Instead, the training is done with the students who graduated and faced retention during that period and for testing, the data consists of those students who has not completed the undergraduate program. The students who faced retention make about 74.83% of the total number of students who graduated in that period. With respect to the data that we used for the ML model, 42.80% and 57.19% of it was taken for training and testing, respectively. We applied the SummB algorithm, which is a variation of the Bellman-Ford algorithm, on the graduated students' data to generate the longest path in the undergraduate program and the most expensive path in the student grade report. The longest path in the program flowchart graph indicates the maximum number of semesters a student takes to pass the undergraduate program if they are not faced with retention (that is the ideal path) and this is the principle that we use to validate the predictions. The expensive path indicates the maximum cost path which was taken by the student in order to pass the undergraduate program. That is, the path with a greater number of repetitions which likely caused retention for that student. The longest path in the undergraduate program and the most expensive paths in students grade report, helps to indicate the relation between minimum time conclusion of an undergraduate program and the time delay caused by retention in student's grade reports. Also, we find out the heaviest occurring edges to validate how accurate this approach can be.

4.2 *Phase 2*

In Phase 2, the longest paths obtained from the above phase for all the graduated students are merged together to form the cluster centroid. These include the longest paths pertaining to the graduated students in that period, including the ones who also had not faced retention. There are seven clusters, one for each curriculum. By using the training data, the similarity of the data point to the cluster centroids is discovered by using graph similarity measures. Here, datapoint is the student historical graph for students who faced retention. For aggregating the similarity scores, three measures of central tendencies are used, namely mean, median, and mode. The prediction is made by checking whether the testing datapoint falls within this similarity score. Testing and result analysis are also done in this phase. The graph similarity is measured using three formulae and the accuracy for each is found out.

Figure 3.   Stages in Phase 2.

5   RESOURCES USED

5.1   *Languages*

Python is the programming language used for writing the below-mentioned algorithms.

5.2   *Visualization tools*

Gephi is used for visualizing the graphs. The graphs to be represented are written as gexf file, which in turn can be viewed using the Gephi tool. *Graph viz* is also used for visualizing the graphs by creating a dot.gv file (Figure 5) Predefined packages like graphviz, network, etc. in Python are used.

5.3   *Datasets*

The real data from four program courses (two Computer Science and two Production Engineering programs) offered at Fluminense Federal University (UFF), a public federal university in Brazil, is used. The data includes ten years of student data from 2004–2014. Being a Brazilian university, the datasets are in Portuguese.

The datasets were obtained from from https://github.com/je?ersonjcosta/mgidu?/tree/master/english/web/examples/files. The following datasets are used to generate the required DAGs by the modules described in the subsequent sections.

5.3.1   *Prerequisites.csv*
This file contains the disciplines (subjects), their pre-requisites (subjects that needs to be completed before pursuing that course), the required time period of that course, and the period of its pre-requisite in a particular curriculum. Structure: idCurr, idDisc, periodDisc, cht, chp, idPreReq, periodPreReq.

5.3.2   *Accompainments.csv*
This file contains the curriculum taken by a student and the situation of that student in that curriculum, i.e., whether the student passed that course or not (e.g., Formado means Graduated). Structure: idStud, idStatus, Situation, yearSem, idCurr.

5.3.3   *Equivalences.csv*
This includes the equivalent disciplines, i.e., equivalent courses for a particular course in a particular curriculum. If a student didnot undertake a particular pre-requisite course as required, they can also take up an equivalent course as the pre-requisite. Structure: idCurr, idDisc, idEq.

5.3.4   *Historical.csv*
This contains the historical data of students that studied in the university in the given ten-year period. It contains the situation of the student in each discipline along with grade report and the number of times each discipline was taken by the student. The retention faced by the students can be observed using this data. Structure: idStud, yearSem, idDisc, grade, gradeSv, frequency, situation, discipline.

The code for the algorithms along with the datasets can be found at https://github.com/Malavika-P-Pillai/Prediciting-Possibility-of-Student-Drop-out. Intermediate datasets, i.e., DAGs, are generated by the code after pre-processing which is not included due to the huge size of the files. The DAGs are generated with the gSpan structure.

The GSpan algorithm is proposed to reduce duplicated graph generation without the need for searching frequent subgraphs that were previously discovered and do not extend any duplicate graph. The edges are sorted in lexicographic order.

```
g | graph id
v | id | code of discipline | period of discipline
e | id of the source vertex | code of source discipline (prerequisite) | id of the target vertex |
code      of source discipline | cost
```

The gSpan structure is as shown above. Here, the line that start with "g" indicates the graph id of the graph. In the program flowchart the graph ids are the curriculum ids and in historical graphs it is the student id along with the curriculum.

```
c|31.01.001|0-2-11-16-23-27-29-36-37-1
v|0|Admission
v|2|TCC04010
v|11|TCC04011
v|16|TCC04012
v|23|TCC04013
v|27|TCC04017
v|29|TCC04021
v|36|TCC04022
v|37|TCC04029
v|1|Conclusion
e|0|Admission|2|TCC04010|1
e|2|TCC04010|11|TCC04011|1
e|11|TCC04011|16|TCC04012|1
e|16|TCC04012|23|TCC04013|1
e|23|TCC04013|27|TCC04017|1
e|27|TCC04017|29|TCC04021|1
e|29|TCC04021|36|TCC04022|1
e|36|TCC04022|37|TCC04029|1
e|37|TCC04029|1|Conclusion|1
```

Figure 4.   The longest path file in gSpan structure.

For the longest path graph this becomes "c | graph id | longest path" (Figure 4). Line with "v" indicates the vertices/nodes. Nodes are the disciplines with their id which uniquely identify each course. The period of discipline is the minimum required number of semesters for the course. The line starting with "e" indicates the edges. That is the pre-requisite relationship between the disciplines. Cost refers to the edge weights.

For program flowchart the edge weights are 1 while for student graphs it is the number of times the subject was pursued by the student. The course code refers to the unique id assigned to that course in the vertices line.

This structure offers ease in the readability and in the application of different algorithms for forming cluster centroids by merging, verifying retention, etc. A sample of the longest path file generated for a curriculum in gSpan structure is shown Figure 4.

6.1 *Pre-processing*

6.1.1 *Create dataset program flowchart*
By using the prerequisites.csv file which contains the disciplines and its pre-requisites for each curriculum, all the possible course paths can be identified. There are 7 curriculums with course

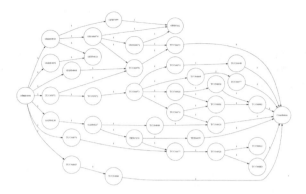

Figure 5. Program flowchart graph as visualized using GraphVizView.

id's 31.01.001, 31.02.001, 60.01.001, 42.01.001, 31.02.002, 31.01.002, and 63.01.001. In order to find the ideal path for a curriculum, the program flowchart for each of the seven curricula is generated. The output of the module is "datasetFlowchart.txt" that contains disciplines as nodes and the pre-requisite relationship as the edges. Here all the edge weights are 1.

6.1.2 Create historical

Like the previous module, this module also generates the DAGs with the gSpan structure for the student's data. This module generates the course structure for each graduated student, i.e., student historical graph. Same as before, the nodes are the subjects taken by the student in his most repeated curriculum. In order to generate this, all four dataset files are used. The most repeated curriculum by all the graduated students (that is, students with status as Formado) are taken from accompaniments.csv file. Moreover, for each subject in the curriculum if it is taken by the student, the edge is added by using pre-requisites file. The edge weight is added by taking the frequency by counting the number of times the student took the particular course using data from the historical file. Also, for some courses equivalent courses can be taken instead of another. In order to include those relations as well, equivalences.csv is used.

Figure 6. Student historical graph generated by GraphVizView.

6.1.3 Create testing historical

This module generates the data for testing the model. This is done by taking the students that are undergoing the course as per the available data, i.e., the students who have not graduated until 2014. The data is generated in the same manner as the above module except that the student's data with their status as not "Formado" is being taken.

6.2 Sub-pattern mining

6.2.1 Bellman–Ford

The generated graphs from the above pre-processing stages are fed to this module for finding the longest paths. Here, the Bellman–Ford Algorithm is used to find the longest paths. The DAG will contain the information on the number of times a student attended the course. This is used to find out the longest path of the given graph by multiplying the edge weights with negative one and finding different topological order from each node. Among these multiple topological orders, the path with the highest edge-weight sum is taken as the longest path. Here Bellman–Ford algorithm is used as it works fine on a graph with negative edge weights. Also, since the graphs won't have any cycles the complexity is reduced considerably. The longest path of curriculum denotes the maximum number of courses required to complete the particular curriculum if the student were to take it without any retentions, i.e., if each of the courses were taken only once what is the maximum number of semesters it will take in order to complete the particular course. The longest path in the student grade reports shows the time taken by the student to complete the particular curriculum. The longest path in the testing data shows the path that they took that is most likely to lead up to retention/drop-out. By checking this file for each of the seven curricula, we can find out the maximum required number of semesters to complete the course without any retention. This is used for validating the predictions and for finding the accuracy of our prediction model.

Figure 7.   Longest path in a program flowchart graph.

6.2.2 Split retention LP

This module splits the training data from the generated longest paths of students from the historical data. For training the model, only the historical graphs of students with the retention are taken. This is done by taking the sum of student's longest paths edge weights, which will give us the time taken by the student to complete the course. If the student has faced retention, then this value becomes higher than the number of nodes in the ideal path, i.e., the longest path in the program flowchart graph.

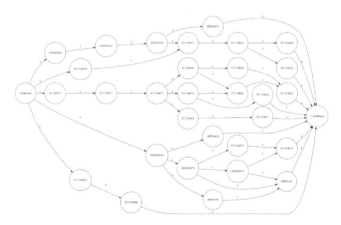

Figure 8.   Merged longest path of curriculum 42.01.001.

6.3 Training and prediction model

6.3.1 Merge longest path

In order to find the centroid for the graph clustering model, for each curriculum the longest paths of the students are taken and merged into a large single graph. Resulting in a graph containing, all

233

the paths that have led to the retention as well as the longest paths that did not lead to retention for the graduated students. This merged graph is used as a reference to compare the input student graphs for the prediction model as these graphs contains all the time-consuming paths that were encountered by the students during that 10-year period.

6.3.2 *Finding distance*

Finding distance finds similarity scores between the given graphs using the formulas shown below. Among the many graph inter-graph similarity scores these three are used. We chose these three for our model as some of the other distance measure formulas use the minimum common super graph which returns the testing data point path itself.

$$d_{MCS}(G1, G2) = 1 - \frac{|mcs(G1, G2)|}{\max(|G1|, |G2|)} \tag{1}$$

$$d_{WGU}(G1, G2) = 1 - \frac{|mcs(G1, G2)|}{|G1| + |G2| - |mcs(G1, G2)|} \tag{2}$$

$$d_{UGU}(G1, G2) = |G1| + |G2| - 2|mcs(G1, G2)| \tag{3}$$

Here, mcs is the maximum common subgraph, $|G_1|$ is the number of nodes in the graph, and $\max(G_1, G_2)$ returns the number of nodes in graph with maximum number of nodes.

First, our DAGs are modeled into networkx module's digraph model. Then to find out the maximum common subgraphs we iterate through each of the connected components sub-graphs in one of the graphs and checks whether that is present in the other. Among such connected components sub-graphs, the one with the maximum number of nodes is returned as the maximum common subgraph. Using this the similarity scores are computed as per the formula and returned.

6.3.3 *Finding threshold*

In order to train the model to correctly make the prediction, the longest paths of the students that faced retention are fed in and the similarity of those paths with the cluster centroid is found out by using the above-mentioned formulas. Then in order to aggregate the results, the mean median and mode for using formula is found out and appended to the merged longest path file for each curriculum as the thresholds. For making the prediction, the similarity scores are compared against this value.

6.3.4 *Model*

For the prediction model, we take the longest path of each student from the testing data as input. Then the similarity scores of these graphs with the centroid for the corresponding curriculum is discovered. If the similarity score is less than the threshold that means that the student graph is similar to the retention-causing paths. Therefore, there is a possibility of retention. So, the prediction is made as true for such cases.

In order to verify the correctness and find the accuracy of the model, the actual value is discovered by taking the sum of all the edge weights of the longest path and if it is less than the sum of edge weights of the longest path of the corresponding curriculum then we say the student has not faced retention. This is because the sum of edge weights in the longest path in the student graphs gives the time taken by the student to complete the course. If they have taken a greater number of semesters than expected by their curriculum then they have faced retention. The maximum number of semesters required to complete a curriculum is obtained from the sum of edges-weights of the corresponding program flowchart's longest path.

The accuracy measures used are precision and recall. Precision indicates how many were correctly classified as compared to the total predictions that were made as true. Recall is the number of true predictions made correctly as compared to the actual number of observations with true value.

Table 1. The confusion matrix for equation (1).

	Mean		Median		Mode	
	True	False	True	False	True	False
True	265	123	280	108	264	124
False	228	52	246	34	242	38

Table 2. The confusion matrix for equation (2).

	Mean		Median		Mode	
	True	False	True	False	True	False
True	265	123	279	109	263	125
False	228	52	229	51	225	55

6.3.5 *Heavier edges*

This module is used to validate the correctness of our approach. For a curriculum, using this module we can find out the number of students that took an edge by counting the number of times that edge has occurred in the datasetHistorical.txt file which contains the student grade report graphs. Also, by adding up all the edge weights for that edge in that file gives us the number of times the course was studied. This helps us slightly to see the retention patterns in an unbiased manner. By taking the ratio of the number of edges to sum of edges gives us how much fraction the structure of the course contributed to retention. That is, if out the total 500 times the course was taken there were 450 student retention cases that indicates an issue with the course structure.

6.4 *Visualization*

6.4.1 *CreateGraphVizView*

This module deals with generating the dot.gv file for visualising the graph using GraphVizView. Figure 6 is a student graph visualized by using the GraphVizView.

6.4.2 *CreateGexf*

This module deals with generating the gexf file for visualizing the graph using the Gephi tool. The above figure depicts the curriculum graph as visualized in the Gephi.

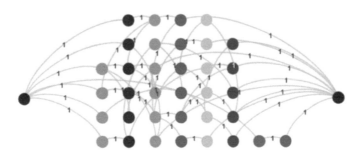

Figure 9. Example for a graph representing a program flowchart graph with all weights equal to 1.

7 TESTING AND RESULT ANLYSIS

As explained above, the testing was done by inputting the student's longest path graphs and finding the inter-graph similarity score between the input graph and the merged curriculum longest path graphs. It is compared with each of the measures of central tendency (mean, median, mode) of the threshold values. Validation is done by checking against the maximum number of semesters required and the maximum number of semesters taken by the student.

The last two equations rely on the union of the maximum common subgraph. Thus, explaining the similar accuracy measures for both. All the similarity scores except for the formula Equation (3) are normalized within the interval.

Table 3. The confusion matrix for equation (3).

	Mean		Median		Mode	
	True	False	True	False	True	False
True	265	123	279	109	263	125
False	228	52	229	51	225	55

Table 4. The accuracy measures for the three equations.

	Mean		Median		Mode	
	Precision	Recall	Precision	Recall	Precision	Recall
Equation 1	0.5375	0.6829	0.5323	0.7216	0.5217	0.6804
Equation 2	0.5375	0.6829	0.5492	0.7190	0.5389	0.6778
Equation 3	0.5375	0.6829	0.5492	0.7190	0.5389	0.6778

From the results the following observations can be made:

– The accuracy scores show that there is room for improvement for the model and that curriculum alone can't determine whether the student can/not face retention. This can be done by adding more factors such as student characteristics into it.
– The precision is almost the same across all three measures as well as formulas. So, the change in formulas has not much affected the number of students wrongly categorized.
– A variation was observed in the recall. The recall scores are higher when the median is used as a measure. High recall indicates that out of the total students who faced retention approximately 72% where correctly identified. This shows that a greater number of students followed a central behavior path as compared to the mean and most frequent paths.
– Also, for the second and third formula there is a slight positive variation for the precision for the median measure.
– From the confusion matrix, more and more students were classified as prone to retention vs. not. The number of false negatives is also high. So, this reinforces the statement that curriculum structure alone cannot be used as a feature for the retention pattern study.
– Although this cannot be used as a sole measure the accuracy shows that this is indeed one of the major contributing factors to retention rates. The influence of this factor will vary according to the university.
– Due to the similarity in mean behavior, the accuracy doesn't vary across different formulas
– However, by mining, the heavier patterns can give the university an idea about the paths that are more prone to retention (by using heavier edges).

8 CONCLUSION

As EDM has similarities to other fields like e-commerce, many of the popular data mining techniques can be applied in many scientific and commercial applications. This technique can be applied to fields where the relations can be modeled as a DAG. DAGs can be used to represent any set of elements with an order relation. By modeling a dataset as a DAG, efficient data mining algorithms can be applied with lesser time complexity (almost linear).

REFERENCES

Adam Schenker. 2003. *Graph-Theoretic Techniques for Web Content Mining Graph-Theoretic Techniques for Web Content Mining.*

Al-Radaideh,. A., Al-Shawakfa, E. M., Al-Najjar, M. I. 2006. *Mining student data using decision trees. In the Proceedings of the 2006 International Arab Conference on Information Technology (ACIT'2006).*

Amjad Abu Saa. 2016. *Educational Data Mining & Student's Performance Prediction.*

Bharadwaj B.K. and Pal S. 2012 *Mining Educational Data to Analyze Students Performance,* International Journal of Advance Computer Science and Applications (IJACSA), Vol. 2, No. 6, pp. 63–69.

Boris Perez, Camilo Castellanos, and Darıo Correal, Univ. Francisco de Paula Stder., Cucuta, Colombia, Universidad de los Andes, Bogota, Colombia. 2018. *Predicting Student Drop-Out Rates Using Data Mining Techniques: A Case Study.*

A Campello, LN Lins. 2019. *Methodology of analysis and treatment of dropout and retention in undergraduate courses at federal higher education institutions in Portuguese.*

CENSec@Amrita, Vazhayil, A., Harikrishnan, N.B., Vinayakumar, R., Soman, K.P, Amrita Vishwa Vidyapeetham. 2018. *PED-ML: Phishing email detection using classical machine learning techniques.*

D.J. Cook, L.B. Holder. 2006. *Mining Graph Data,* New Jersey: John Wiley and Sons.

Cristóbal Romero, Member, IEEE, Sebastián Ventura. 2010. *Educational Data Mining: A review of the state-of-the-art.*

Horacio Kuna, Ramon Garcia Martinez and Francisco R. Villatoro. 2010. *Pattern discovery in university student's desertion based on data mining.*

Jeffreson J Costa, Flavia Bernadani, Danilo Artigas, Jose Viterbo. 2019. *Mining Direct Acyclic Graphs to Find Frequent Substructures — An Experimental Analysis on Educational Data.*

Krishnaveni K.S, Rohith R Pai, Vignesh Iyer, Amrita Vishwa Vidyapeetham. 2017. *Faculty Rating System Based on Student Feedbacks Using Sentiment Analysis.*

Lakshmi Devi, K.,Subathra, P,Kumar, P.N, Amrita Vishwa Vidyapeetham. 2015. *Tweet sentiment classification using an ensemble of machine learning supervised classifiers employing statistical feature selection methods*

Madduri Venkata Sai Soma Manish, Rajesh Kannan Megalingam, Amrita Vishwa Vidyapeetham. 2019. *Applying and Evaluating Supervised Learning Classification Techniques to Detect Attacks on Web Applications.*

L.M.B Manhaes, S.M.S. Cruz, R.J. MCosta, J, Zavaletta, G. Zimbrao. 2019. *Prediction of students with risk of dropout using data mining techniques, in: XXII*

Saurabh Pal. 2013. *Analysis and Mining of Educational Data for Predicting the Performance of Students*

Shekhar Pandey, Supriya M, Abhilash Shrivastav, Amrita Vishwa Vidyapeetham. 2017. *Data Classification Using Machine Learning Approach.*

Shu-Fen TSENGad*, Chih-Yueh CHOUbd, Zhi-Hong CHENcd, Po-Yao CHAOcd. 2014. *Learning Analytics: An Enabler for Dropout Prediction.*

Senthil Kumar Thangavel, S.Rajendrakumar, T.V.Rajevan, Amrita Vishwa Vidyapeetham. 2019. *Deep Learning based Emotion Analysis Approach for Strengthening Teaching-Learning process in Schools of Tribal Regions.*

UFF. 2019. *Original research analyzes the causes of retention in students at UFF*

Xifeng Yan Jiawei Han Department of Computer Science University of Illinois at Urbana Champaign. 2002. *gSpan: Graph-Based Substructure Pattern Mining.*

C.H. Yu, S. Digangi, A. Jannasch-Pennell, C. Kaprolet. 2010. *A data mining approach for identifying predictors of student retention from sophomore to junior year.*

Y. Zhang, SOussena, T. Clark, K. Hyensook. 2019. *Using data mining to improve student retention in higher education: a case study.*

Smart Computing – Khan et al (Eds)
© *2021 Taylor & Francis Group, London, ISBN 978-0-367-76552-1*

Anomaly detection using machine learning algorithms

Y. Pant, A. Cheema & B. Negi
Computer Science and Engineering, Himalayan School of Science and Technology (SRHU), Dehradun, Uttarakhand, India

ABSTRACT: Anomaly detection techniques are a well-known area for solving a particular kind of problem when there is the presence of an anomaly. Anomaly is the deviation from standard or we can say normal (regular) pattern. Anomalies are the data points that do not match the expected pattern. Anomalies can occur in transactions like Credit Card Fraud, Campaign Response. It also can occur in Video Surveillance like in Traffic, and can also as Spam, Malware/Intrusion. As technology is evolving day by day, it gives us many profits but at the same time many losses are also incurred. Like with the evolution of the domain of e-commerce and online banking, there is a drastic increase in the usage of credit cards for payment. Mostly the shopping (online shopping) is done by making the use of credit cards and due to this big usage of the credit cards; we are also facing the problem of fraud and big damages. So, it is very important to detect fraud in transactions so that we do not have to face big financial losses. There are many Machine learning algorithms or techniques, both supervised and unsupervised are available for anomaly detection. Here we can classify the fraudulent transaction in credit card fraud as point anomaly, so for detecting it we can use supervised algorithms like SVM, KNN, Random forest algorithm, and unsupervised algorithms like Isolation Forest algorithm, LOF algorithm. In this paper, we are discussing our experiment on credit card fraud detection by using Unsupervised Anomaly Detection algorithm. Later, we will also compare the performance of all the algorithms that we are using (Isolation forest Algorithm and LOF Algorithm).

Keywords: Anomaly detection, Credit card fraud detection, Isolation forest algorithm, LOF algorithm, SVM, KNN

1 INTRODUCTION

Anomalies can be classified as point Anomaly, collective anomaly or contextual anomaly. Point anomaly is individual anomalous data instance with respect to the rest of the data e.g. sudden increase in the transaction value. Collective anomaly is, if the collection of related data instance is anomalous with respect to rest of the data. And last, Contextual Anomaly is the data instance that is anomalous in specific context, and not anomalous in other context .e.g. big drop in consumption at specific time like middle of month. Now a days, transactions are done offline and online both. In offline transactions we need a physical credit card and in online transaction we just need some information of card like pin no. and other user details. So, if fraudster wants to make fraudulent transaction then there is requirement of physical card in offline transaction and in online transaction fraudster needs to have some card's information and user's information. There are various types of frauds that can be made by fraudsters like bankruptcy fraud, Theft fraud/counterfeit fraud, application fraud, Behavioral fraud (Delamaire 2009). In bankruptcy fraud, users or we can say purchasers' purchases even after knowing that it is impossible for them to pay for their purchases. When bank sends them order to pay for their purchases then the purchasers recognize themselves that they are not able to recover their debts. At the end, all losses have to recover by bank itself. In the case of theft fraud, the fraudster steals the user's card and illegally uses it again and again

DOI 10.1201/9781003167488-29

until the card gets blocked. As soon as the original card user will report about the card theft, sooner will be the bank makes enquiry about it. In counterfeit fraud, the fraudster sees or copies your card no., code and more legal information of your card and uses it where no signature or credit card is required. Credit card fraud is very frequent in businesses or companies where they make use of internet for selling their services and items. So, the sellers that allow the clients to payment by credit card are very prone to risk, when fraudster uses stolen credit card's information to make payments then the businessperson or merchant can suffer from loss of money because of "charge back" policy (Delamaire 2009). Merchant have to charge for items or objects if the original card users make objections that they are not responsible for purchases. In the case of application fraud, fraudsters try to apply with wrong or false information that is different from information used before for a credit card. These types of fraud can be detected when the fraudster make application by the name of same individual with same information. And it can also be detected when identity fraudster comes into the game means application is made by the different name of individual but with same detail or information. In the case of behavioral fraud, fraudster theft the credit card's information illegally and fraudulently and by using that information then make transaction on the basis of regular or normal behavior of transaction made by the original or legitimate card holder. So, we have discussed above many kind of frauds that can be incurred in online transactions or offline transactions. As day by day new technology evolving, fraudsters take advantage of it and commit frauds in more intelligent manner by changing the behavior of fraud committed by them every time. Because of the fraud committed by fraudsters comes up with different behavior every time, so it is very difficult by the user to identify such no. of fraud every time and it is also difficult for authorities like bank authorities, credit bureau. So, many algorithms or models that we have discussed in abstract part of this paper are available to detect these frauds that may lead to loss of big amount of money and theft of confidential information of cardholder or original user. For finding the fraudulent transactions, in existing system Random forest algorithm, KNN (k–nearest neighbors) algorithm, Naïve Bayer's, Support Vector Machine methods are used. In this paper, we are discussing the use of isolation forest algorithm and local outlier factor algorithm for detecting the fraudulent transactions and how much these two methods are accurate in finding the fraudulent transactions. These both methods are unsupervised learning methods, so there is no need to have labeled data to form classifiers (Ounacer 2018) for normal and fraud cases but there is requirement of labeled data in the case of supervised methods like Random forest, KNN, clustering technique. Unsupervised methods work by recognizing that behavior of fraudulent activity is something different from normal one and that fraudulent activity acts as outlier and normal activity acts as inliers to the system. In real life scenario, obtaining labeled data is very difficult as in like anomaly detection where human makes labeling. So to deal with this problem we come up with unsupervised techniques or we can say anomaly detection techniques. In the case where we have large imbalance classification of data, it may be possible that supervised techniques are not efficiently works. So, in the case of imbalance data it is better to use unsupervised approach. Isolation forest algorithm is based on random forest algorithm, so if you know well about random forest technique then it is easy for us to implement the isolation forest algorithm which is used to reduce false positives and gives more correct predictions and also gives accuracy in detecting the frauds in normal transactions. We have many models and methods to detect frauds or outliers but different model works differently with different dataset or there may be a case that same model works differently with different dataset depending upon on which features we are focusing on to detect fraud cases in particular dataset. So, we have to experiment on a dataset by using different models to obtain the higher accuracy of detecting frauds. So by this, we can conclude that there is no fix one algorithm that we can apply on different dataset to detect fraud cases with same accuracy every time, a particular model or method can act differently with different dataset. As in transaction frauds become more frequent day by day, an estimation tells us that by 2020 frauds become more frequent (even at the rate of double digits) (Xuan 2018). There is another technique for fraud detection that is misuse method. For the determination of fraud among incoming transaction, this misuse method uses classification method. It learns the existing fraud pattern and prepare a model and based upon those existing patterns of fraud it classify whether the incoming transaction is fraudulent transaction or normal transaction. Anomaly detection learns about the pattern or behavior of normal transactions by observing the past or historic transactions made by the card holder and based upon it identifies whether the incoming transaction is fraud or not. It works in such a manner that if new incoming transaction have different pattern than the previously regularly observed pattern or we can say expected pattern, then this new incoming transaction will be considered as a fraudulent transaction. So, in anomaly detection method there is requirement of some samples of data to learn about the pattern and behavior of normal transaction so that later we can make predictions on new incoming transactions in terms of fraud or normal. In Random forest algorithm, there is an application of classification method where we classify the transactions as normal or fraud by getting the votes of all the base classifiers in random forest (Xuan 2018). In Random forest algorithm, there are two types of forest that we can use to train our model for classifying normal and fraud cases and those are CART-based (classification and regression trees) random forest and random tree-based random forest. In Random tree based random forest, base classifiers are simple decision trees. Here initially, we have standard training set, and by bootstrapping we make our own training set. Bootstrapping means we randomly select some samples of standard training set, and after this we make collection of these bootstrapped samples to make decision trees of random forest. In each decision tree, samples come from random selection. CART stands for classification and regression trees, here at initial stage bootstrapping of standard training set is done like in the case of random tree based random forest and here dataset at each node gets split by selection of attribute among set of attributes by using Gini impurity (Xuan 2018). Gini impurity is used to finding the dataset's uncertainty. Gini impurity describes that by what probability we classify the data point incorrectly. If the Gini impurity of left branch and right branch of current node which we have to split is zero, then we will get perfect split of current node (Xuan 2018). Fraud also can be detected by Clustering techniques. In 2002, there were two people who gave the two clustering techniques (Delamaire 2009) to detect the behavioral fraud that we have discussed above in this paper. One is peer group analysis and another one is break point analysis. In peer group analysis, several accounts are come into consideration. Here if two accounts behave or act differently at certain point or moment of time but they act similar previously, then those two accounts are taken into consideration. Now, fraud analyst has to deal with these types of accounts. But concept of break point analysis is slightly different from peer group analysis. In break point analysis, here the behavior of usage of card comes into consideration. We observe that how an individual uses his/her card on regular basis in terms of transactional amount, time slots or duration in which transaction is done by user and many other factors. Then at some point of time, if the behavior or pattern in which card is used by the cardholder changes, then that account is need to be reported. So, the key difference between peer group analysis and break point analysis is that, in peer group analysis two or more than two account or we can say group of accounts are required to identify the fraud but in break point analysis fraud is detected by seeing the activity of particular account means by observing its changed behavior in terms of card usage. There is another method that can be used for credit card fraud detection which is genetic programming and the concept of genetic programming is given by Bentley in 2000. For classification of credit card transactions into normal transactions or fraud transactions, genetic programming includes some logic rules for classification (Delamaire 2009). Bentley had 4000 transactions with about 62 features. So, each feature was tested with different logic rules every time and then finally the logic rule was came out best which predict more accurately means logic rule with higher prediction and true prediction. So, if we use this (genetic programming) method for credit card fraud detection then it can work efficiently. So, all these methods that we have discussed above in paper, make detection of frauds easier and accurate than if human predicts or analyzes by himself and also by Machine Learning algorithms we can continuously learn and improve our models so that they can give better or if possible best and accurate predictions. In Machine Learning, models or algorithms consume and update new data quickly. We can handle both unstructured and structured data by machine learning algorithms. Machine learning algorithms also give predictions about fraud even if we have imbalance data. Although we apply cleaning on our dataset at very initial stage and also try to balance our data by sampling (under sampling and oversampling) but if we play with imbalance data and directly apply machine learning algorithms or models on our dataset then there may be a case that it gives better result than when we are applying models on imbalance data (discussed on Kaggle website). Because during balancing and cleaning our dataset we have to take care of each and everything so that there is no loss of important features or data that must be taken into consideration when detecting frauds. So, many people try to apply model or algorithm on dataset after balancing it, if it is highly unbalanced like in the case of credit card frauds as in real scenario there are less no. of frauds than compared to legitimate transactions. But when people have compared their performance result of same model on same data (by balancing data first and by directly applying model on unbalanced data), then in some cases it is found that model gives better performance on unbalanced data than on balanced data. So, by this we can conclude that sometimes performance becomes worse when we apply model after balancing our data. So, in some cases there is no requirement of handling the unbalance data, it can be implicitly handled by our model whatever we are using like in our experiment that we will discuss later in this paper. As there are various methods are available for credit card fraud detection but along with this there are many challenges in credit card fraud detection like we have huge data, we can also have imbalance data to which we have to deal with because fraud cases are lesser in number than legitimate cases or normal transactions. There are many adaptive techniques to commit fraud that fraudsters have. As technology is evolving day by day, fraudsters are trying to commit frauds by using different patterns and techniques each and every time. And the big challenge in credit card fraud detection is availability of data to train and test our model because of confidentiality issues. So, some organizations, companies, banks provide data with virtual variables or features means after applying PCA (Principal Component Analysis) transformation that we will discuss later. When we have imbalance dataset or we can say class imbalance then AURC (Area Under Precision–Recall Curve) is used for measurement of accuracy of model in predicting the frauds instead of confusion matrix because it does not gives efficient and meaningful result in case of imbalance data. In AURC, performance measures are recall, precision, F–1 score, accuracy score, macro average, micro average, weighted average, support. From classification matrix we can know that how many false positives we predicted and how well our model is performing by checking the accuracy.

2 LITERATURE SURVEY

Shiyang Xuan, Guanjun Liu, Zhenchuan Li, Lutao Zheng, Shuo Wang, Changjun Jiang have used fraud detection technique that is Random Forest Algorithm to detect the Credit Card fraud. They have used two kind of Random Forest one is random tree based random forest and other is CART based random forest (Xuan 2018). Y. Kou, C. Lu, S. Sinvongwattana, Y. Huang have discussed various fraud detection system such as credit card fraud, telecommunication fraud, intrusion (Kou 2004). C. Aggarwal and P.S. Yu have used algorithm for outlier detection. These outliers presents with low density (Aggarwal 2001). V. Chandola, A. Banerjee, V. Kumar has discussed about outlier detection techniques, and also gave suspicious and normal pattern or behavior of each outlier detection technique (Chandola 2009). Ms. Amruta D. Pawar, Prof. Prakash N. Kalavandekar, Ms. Swapnali N. Tambe have given brief introduction of outliers, discussed about dataset that the attributes of data can be numerical and categorical. They have discussed about outlier detection classes such as supervised, semi-supervised, Unsupervised, Neural network based, rule based, Clustering based. They also have given detailed information about PCA (principal component analysis). They have discussed that PCA is used for dimensionality reduction. Correlated variables are transformed into uncorrelated variables by PCA. It is done due to confidentiality issue of data. They also discussed the steps involved in PCA and discussed that how PCA is used for Outlier detection (Pawar 2014). Hussein Abdou (UK), John Pointon (UK) and Linda Delamaire (UK) have discussed about various types of frauds such as bankruptcy fraud, theft fraud, behavioral fraud,

Application fraud. They also discussed about at which rate frauds were committed in European countries like Germany, Sweden, Ireland, United Kingdom and many others in 2003, 2004, 2005, 2006. They have also given detailed information about fraud detection techniques like Decision Trees, Genetic algorithms, Clustering Techniques, Neural Networks (Delamaire 2009). M. Suresh Kumar, V. Soundarya, S. Kavitha, E.S. Keerthika, E. Aswini have discussed about application of random forest algorithm for credit card fraud detection, In random forest algorithm decision trees are used for classification of data whether it is fraud or normal. When they applied this random forest algorithm on their dataset, they obtained accuracy of about 90% which is quite good performance of the algorithm. They have discussed each and every step involved in their experiment. Steps are data exploration, data cleaning, data preprocessing, partition of dataset into training and testing data, then performance measurement with the help of confusion matrix and lastly check the accuracy by which we can predict about algorithm and model that how well it makes true predictions about frauds. They also discussed about the software and hardware requirements, they mentioned that 4 GB RAM, window 10 and anaconda software is required for performing the experiment (Kumar 2019). Soumaya Ounacer, Hicham Ait El Bour, Younes Oubrahim, Mohamed Yassine Ghoumari and Mohamed Azzouazi have discussed various unsupervised techniques used for credit card fraud detection on their dataset and they have also made comparison to pick out best of them. They also have discussed about that why unsupervised techniques works efficiently in the case of anomaly detection and they came up with the fact that in unsupervised technique we do not need to have labeled data for classifiers. They have also mentioned the advantages and disadvantages of various anomaly detection techniques like LOF (local outlier factor), SVM (support vector machine), K–means method, Isolation forest Algorithm (Ounacer 2018). (Malini 2017) They have discussed about K–nearest neighbor technique for credit card fraud detection. It is supervised learning technique where nearest point comes into consideration for classification of transaction whether it is fraudulent or legitimate. If the point lies near to fraudulent transaction, when there is new transaction then that new transaction is considered to be the fraudulent transaction. But the major drawback of K–neighbor technique is that it cannot detect the anomalies in the real time transactions (means when transaction is taking place). In Existing system, researchers have discussed that Naïve Bayer's and cluster analysis requires normalization before their application to obtain the better result. M. Breunig, H-P Kriegel, R. T. Ng and J. Sander have discussed about method for Outlier detection that is LOF (Local Outlier Factor) which is density based. It assigns degree to the object of the system of being outlier. Degree defines that in what manner objects are isolated from their neighboring objects. There is one difference between all other outlier detection methods and this density based LOF (Local Outlier Factor method) is that this method assigns degree to the objects of being outliers and other methods describes the outlier as something different from normal (deviation from regular one) (Breunig 2000). Sahin and Duman have used SVM (Support Vector Machine) and decision tree for credit card fraud detection and also compared these two methods for checking which one is better in terms of detecting frauds and with best possible accuracy. They have created three partitions of available dataset with different proportion of normal transaction and fraudulent transaction. They have made various decision trees and SVM models and applied all those on every partition of dataset that they have made earlier and tested each model and finally predicted that which model performs best and with how much accuracy, then they finally came up with conclusion that decision tree model is better than SVM model (Sahin 2011).

3 OUR WORK

In our experiment and work we have used two unsupervised learning algorithms for credit card fraud detection. First is Isolation Forest algorithm and second one is LOF (LOCAL OUTLIER FACTOR) method. We have applied both of them on our dataset that we have collected from Kaggle and also made comparison between them in order to find that which one will give better result in terms of fraud detection. For measuring the performance of our two models on the dataset we have used many factors like precision, recall, F–1 score, support. We have used all these factors for performance measure because our dataset that we have collected from Kaggle is highly imbalance or we can say highly skewed, so accuracy is not the enough factors to determine the performance of algorithm or model on data. But here one point is to be noted that accuracy factor works well for performance measure if we have balanced data means we have same no. of suspicious data points and normal data points or we can say normal transactions. There are various steps that are involving in our work or experiments and those are mentioned below.

1. Collection of data
2. Data Exploration
3. Data Visualization in form of graphs and histograms.
4. Removal of null values (if any) from data and also deletion of rows or columns from available dataset if found not important for our experiment.
5. As data is very big, so some fraction of data is taken for the sake of computation and speed.
6. Determination of number of fraud and valid cases (transactions) in our available dataset.
7. Then define the classifiers that are named as Isolation Forest and Local Outlier Factor
8. Then apply those defined classifiers on our dataset.
9. And finally make predictions that which algorithm or model comes out with best result and those predictions are made by using various factors that are mentioned above in paper.

   Then after performing all these steps we have made some observations about algorithms or model that we have used. And all those are mentioned below.

   1. Errors:
      Isolation Forest = 71
      Local Outlier Factor = 97
   2. Accuracy:
      Isolation Forest = 99.75%
      Local Outlier Factor = 99.65%
   3. Precession and Recall:
      Isolation Forest = ~27%
      Local Outlier Factor = 2%

So, by all these observations we can conclude that Isolation Forest is performing well as compared to local Outlier factor with ~30% estimation of unsuspicious transactions or cases. One point is to be noted here that if we will take fraction of data more than that we have taken, and then result may be improve but it increases the computation. In our experiment, we have just taken 10% of available dataset.

3.1   *Isolation forest*

If you know well about random forest then implementation of isolation forest will be easy. Both are Ensemble methods and Isolation Forest Algorithm has basics derived from Random Forest Algorithm. Ensemble learning means that the learning agent learns and makes predictions by considering more than one case or scenario and not by depending on only one. We can understand it by an example that if a student wants to do engineering from reputed and result oriented college or university, then he/she should consult from more than one person and after analyzing all the points, he/she should make correct decision by taking admission in correct college or university. We mean by all this scenario is that, for better and accurate result the learner should trained by various datasets and should use various algorithms and consider various cases for correct prediction and not depending on by just one case. So, Random Forest works in similar way. It uses decision tree algorithm in randomized way. Here, we have input as a training data which we have to train. Initially we have original dataset with various numbers of attributes including target attribute that may have class like yes or no, and we make predictions according to target attribute (Table 1). Like in our experiment, we have target attribute as class defines normal and fraud cases. Now we have to generate bootstrap dataset means we have to do sampling of dataset, we have to pickup random samples of dataset and put them into bootstrap section and here duplication is also allowed (Table 2). Now using this Bootstrap dataset, we have to plot a decision tree (Figure 1) in randomized fashion means randomly select variables for root node assuming that the variable we are selecting for the root node is better for splitting samples. And then randomly select subset of variables at each step. Now, we come up with test tupple that is holding variables we used in decision trees and also holding test attribute. This test tupple asks that these variables that it holding holds some value and asks the value for task attribute, either it is yes or no (as in our experiment fraud or normal). So, apply this test tupple in each decision tree, means take the opinion of each decision tree whether it is yes or no. Now count voting of decisions. By this we can conclude that accuracy (for prediction) of more than one model is better than as compared to accuracy of only one model. This above process is shown in table below.

Table 1.   Original dataset.

	A	B	C	Target
1	-	-	-	Yes
2	-	-	-	No
3	-	-	-	Yes
4	-	-	-	Yes
5	-	-	-	No

Table 2.   Bootstrap dataset.

	A	B	C	Target
2	-	-	-	No
1	-	-	-	Yes
1	-	-	-	Yes
3	-	-	-	Yes
4	-	-	-	Yes

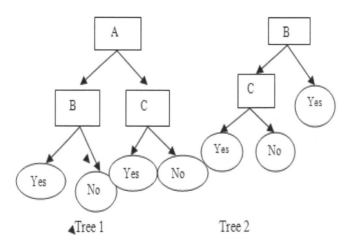

Figure 1.   Random forest = decision tree 1+decision tree2 + . . .

Here 1, 2, 3, 4, 5 are ensembles and A, B, C are different attributes. Target attribute has two classes yes/no.

As from Table 2, we can see that there duplication is allowed as we have ensemble 1 two times in this bootstrap section and here we do not follow any order for selection of samples of original dataset, we just select them randomly.

Always Remember, whenever you have an outlier in your dataset and you are going to use isolation forest algorithm to detect it, the initial and main thing is to understand how isolation forest works. Random Forest uses multiple decision trees and division will be going as shown in figure.1. On any number of decision trees Isolation Forest also works but for each and every split along with the leaf node, it provides some value. Like it just selects some value for the leaf node which will indicate that based on the number of depth "we go", this value will be increasing. Let just consider that value as a "score". Some score value will be there and as a splitting goes on along with the depth, so this score value will be increasing for the leaf node. But suppose if we have an outlier, remember outlier is a value which will not be actually nearer to the other value that we have in the leaf node, it will be completely separated. Suppose we have some dataset which is populated densely, and also have some data which is not dense means only some data points are there. Now if we are trying to distribute this less densely dataset then this will be split quickly and those data points will be assigned with lower value (lesser score). But those value of dense data (inliers) dividing more and more and we will get various different leaf node and the score value will be keep on increasing for those.

So Why Isolation Algorithm Works:

- When decision trees are created by Isolation algorithm, the outlier will be split initially at the initial depth itself, because outlier is a completely different value. So the root node should be selected in such a way so that the outlier will get split.
- Based on the particular score (low score), we can understand that it will be an outlier. Then it will be understood that how many outlier/errors are there.
- Isolation algorithm completely works on anomaly score.

In Figure.2, at node B we will get lower score value that shows that B will be an outlier and cannot be divided further. At node M we will get high score value (higher depth).

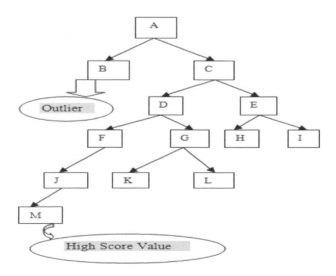

Figure 2.   Isolation tree.

245

Isolation of normal data points requires more time and computation as compared to isolation of fraud cases or data points. Because number of fraud cases are lesser than the number of normal cases as we can see in credit card transactions. So, Isolation algorithm works by isolating the fraud cases rather than the normal cases. It is different from other algorithms that detect the fraud cases by taking the density, separation distance under consideration. As in our experiment it is also giving better performance than Local Outlier factor (LOF) algorithm even with the availability of highly unbalanced dataset.

3.2 Local Outlier Factor (LOF)

- Outlier is something different in expected pattern.
- Outlier detection can be used in Credit Card Fraud, Cyber Security Attack etc.
- *Why Local Outlier?*
- Global outliers are far from the other data points itself but local outliers are only far from the nearby points.
- Similar points would be considered inliers and other points would be considered outliers.
- LOF (Local outlier Factor) considers the relative density of data point. If data point has less density than its neighboring points then it will be an outlier and if it has nearer density as neighboring data points has, then it will be normal or legitimate.
- Local outlier factor algorithm can detect outliers on skewed datasets (as used in our experiment).

Challenge of big data is to detect outliers; it takes much more time because data is big. So, solution is that we can distribute data such as Hadoop and Spark.

How to Identify Outlier:

There are two techniques to identify outliers that are discussed below.

1. Z–score (standard normal distribution)
2. IQR (Inter–Quartile Range)

Let suppose features that we are focusing on for our Final prediction as 1, 2, 3, 4, and 5.

Let data (features) = [1, 2, 3, 4, 5]

Let Mean $(\mu) = 3$

Let standard deviation $(\sigma) = 1$

Standard normal distribution is $\mu = 0$, $\sigma = 1$ and we can get it by $Z = (X - \mu)/\sigma$

Here Z defines that in which standard normal deviation i.e. *I*, *II* or *III* this dataset that we have taken above falls into. If our dataset not falls within the *III* standard normal deviation or away from *III* deviation then it will be an outlier. In IQR, you should need to know what is percentile e.g. 9, 4, 5, 6, 7, 1, 2, 10, 3, 8. Here, First of all sorting mechanism happens over here. After sorting, we will get a sequence as 1, 2, 3, 4, 5, 6, 7, 8, and 9. Now, 1 is representing as 0% means in a sequence there are 0 numbers that are less than 1 in a sequence. 2 is representing as 10% means 10% of total sequence are less than 2. In IQR, we focus on 25% and 75%. IQR = 75%-25%.

STEPS

1. Arrange the data in increasing order.
2. Calculate first $(q1)$ and third quartile $(q3)$.
3. Find inter quartile range.
4. Find Lower Bound $q1*$ 1.5.
5. Find upper Bound $q3*$ 1.5.
6. Any value below the lower bound or above the upper bound is an outlier.

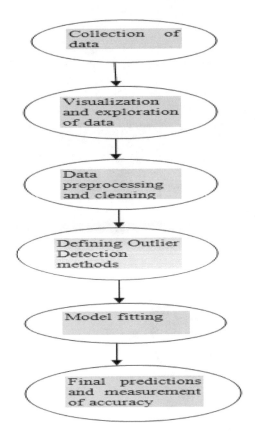

Figure 3.   Flow of process.

4   OUTPUT OF EXPERIMENT

4.1   *Data collection*

	A1		f_x	Time						
	A	B	C	D	E	F	G	H	I	J
Time	V1	V2	V3	V4	V5	V6	V7	V8	V9	
0	-1.35981	-0.07278	2.536347	1.378155	-0.33832	0.462388	0.239599	0.098698	0.363787	
0	1.191857	0.266151	0.16648	0.448154	0.060018	-0.08236	-0.0788	0.085102	-0.25543	
1	-1.35835	-1.34016	1.773209	0.37978	-0.5032	1.800499	0.791461	0.247676	-1.51465	
1	-0.96627	-0.18523	1.792993	-0.86329	-0.01031	1.247203	0.237609	0.377436	-1.38702	
2	-1.15823	0.877737	1.548718	0.403034	-0.40719	0.095921	0.592941	-0.27053	0.817739	
2	-0.42597	0.960523	1.141109	-0.16825	0.420987	-0.02973	0.476201	0.260314	-0.56867	
4	1.229658	0.141004	0.045371	1.202613	0.191881	0.272708	-0.00516	0.081213	0.46496	
7	-0.64427	1.417964	1.07438	-0.4922	0.948934	0.428118	1.120631	-3.80786	0.615375	
7	-0.89429	0.286157	-0.11319	-0.27153	2.669599	3.721818	0.370145	0.851084	-0.39205	
9	-0.33826	1.119593	1.044367	-0.22219	0.499361	-0.24676	0.651583	0.069539	-0.73673	
10	1.449044	-1.17634	0.91386	-1.37567	-1.97138	-0.62915	-1.42324	0.048456	-1.72041	
10	0.384978	0.616109	-0.8743	-0.09402	2.924584	3.317027	0.470455	0.538247	-0.55889	
10	1.249999	-1.22164	0.38393	-1.2349	-1.48542	-0.75323	-0.6894	-0.22749	-2.09401	
11	1.069374	0.287722	0.828613	2.71252	-0.1784	0.337544	-0.09672	0.115982	-0.22108	
12	-2.79185	-0.32777	1.64175	1.767473	-0.13659	0.807596	-0.42291	-1.90711	0.755713	

Figure 4.   Data collection.

4.2 Inspection of data

```
In [7]: #Load the dataset from the csv file using pandas
        data = pd.read_csv('creditcard.csv')
        data.head()
```

Out[7]:

	Time	V1	V2	V3	V4	V5	V6	V7	V8	V9	...	V21	V22	V23	V24	V2!
0	0.0	-1.359807	-0.072781	2.536347	1.378155	-0.338321	0.462388	0.239599	0.098698	0.363787	...	-0.018307	0.277838	-0.110474	0.066928	0.12853!
1	0.0	1.191857	0.266151	0.166480	0.448154	0.060018	-0.082361	-0.078803	0.085102	-0.255425	...	-0.225775	-0.638672	0.101288	-0.339846	0.16717!
2	1.0	-1.358354	-1.340163	1.773209	0.379780	-0.503198	1.800499	0.791461	0.247676	-1.514654	...	0.247998	0.771679	0.909412	-0.689281	-0.32764!
3	1.0	-0.966272	-0.185226	1.792993	-0.863291	-0.010309	1.247203	0.237609	0.377436	-1.387024	...	-0.108300	0.005274	-0.190321	-1.175575	0.64737!
4	2.0	-1.158233	0.877737	1.548718	0.403034	-0.407193	0.095921	0.592941	-0.270533	0.817739	...	-0.009431	0.798278	-0.137458	0.141267	-0.20601!

5 rows × 31 columns

Figure 5.   Inspection of data.

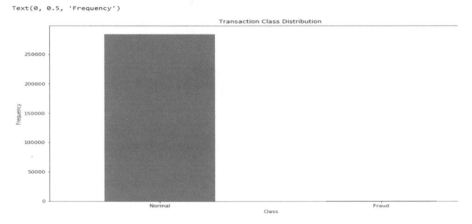

Figure 6.   Inspection of data.

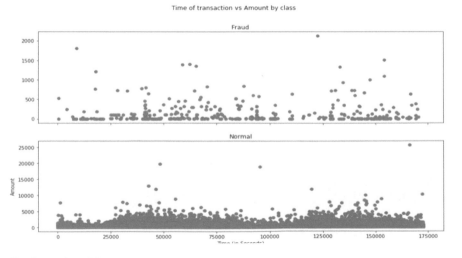

Figure 7.   Inspection of data.

4.3 Cleaning, preprocessing of data

```
In [28]:  # some sample of data
          data = data.sample(frac = 0.1,random_state = 1)
          print(data.shape)

          (28481, 31)

In [29]:  #Determine number of fraud cases and valid cases in dataset
          Fraud = data[data['Class'] == 1]
          Valid = data[data['Class'] == 0]
          outlier_fraction=len(Fraud) / float(len(Valid))
          print(outlier_fraction)
          print('Fraud Cases: {}'.format(len(Fraud)))
          print('Valid Cases: {}'.format(len(Valid)))

          0.0017234102419808666
          Fraud Cases: 49
          Valid Cases: 28432
```

Figure 8. Cleaning, preprocessing of data.

4.4 Defining methods and model fitting

```
#define a random state
state = 1

#define the outlier detection methods
classifiers = {
        "Isolation Forest":IsolationForest(n_estimators=100, max_samples=len(X),
                                        contamination = outlier_fraction,
                                        random_state = state),
        "Local Outlier Factor":LocalOutlierFactor(
        n_neighbors = 20, algorithm='auto',
        leaf_size=30, metric='minkowski',
        p=2, metric_params=None,
        contamination = outlier_fraction,
        novelty = False)
}
```

Figure 9. Defining methods and model fitting.

4.5 Final predictions and result

```
Isolation Forest: 71
Accuracy Score :
0.99750711000316
Classification Report :
                precision  recall  f1-score  support

            0      1.00     1.00      1.00     28432
            1      0.28     0.29      0.28        49

    accuracy                          1.00     28481
   macro avg       0.64     0.64      0.64     28481
weighted avg       1.00     1.00      1.00     28481


Local Outlier Factor: 97
Accuracy Score :
0.9965942207085425
Classification Report :
                precision  recall  f1-score  support

            0      1.00     1.00      1.00     28432
            1      0.02     0.02      0.02        49

    accuracy                          1.00     28481
   macro avg       0.51     0.51      0.51     28481
weighted avg       1.00     1.00      1.00     28481
```

Figure 10. Final predictions and result (a) isolation forest (b) local outlier factor.

249

5 CONCLUSIONS

Credit Card fraud is an unlawful act which should be detected and prevented timely otherwise it can cause big loss to someone's economy and also businesses that completely work by using E-commerce can also suffer from big harm and loss. So, the main focus of this paper is to exploring and implementing those anomaly detection techniques that can be used for credit card fraud detection. And we have used two unsupervised Anomaly detection techniques for detecting fraudulent transactions in the dataset that we have collected from Kaggle platform. Those two techniques that we have used are Isolation forest algorithm and Local Outlier detection (LOF) and we have also made comparison between them in order to check how well they are performing and which one is best. In our experimental process, first we explored the data, preprocessed the data, defined both the models and applied models on some fraction of data as data is big and needs much more computation and then came to final result and observed that Isolation Forest performing well .

REFERENCES

Aggarwal, CC. and Yu. P. S. 2001, Outlier Detection for High Dimensional Data. Proc. ACM SIGMOD International Conf. Management of Data.

Banerjee, R., Bourla, G., Chen, S., Purohit, S., Battipaglia, J. 2018, Comparative Analysis of MachineLearning Algorithms through Credit Card Fraud Detection: 1–10.

Breunig, M., Kreigel, H-P., Ng, R.T., Sander, J. 2000, LOF: Identifying Density Based Local Outliers. Proc. ACM SIGMOD Int'l Conf. Management of Data.

Chandola, V., Banerjee, A., Kumar, V. 2009, Anomaly detection: A Survey. *ACM Computing Surveys*, Vol. 41(3): 1–58.

Delamaire Linda, Abdou Hussein, Pointon John. 2009, Credit Card Fraud and Detection Techniques: A review. *Banks and Bank Systems*, Vol 4(2).

GithubRepository: https://github.com/krishnaik06/Credit.

Hyder, John, Naaz Sameena. April 2019, Credit Card Fraud Detection using Local Outlier Factor and Isolation Forest. *International Journal of Computer Sciences and Engineering IJCSE*, Vol. 7(4): 1060–1064.

Kou, Y., Lu, C., Sinvongwattana, S., Huang, Y. 2004, Survey of Fraud Detection Techniques. IEEE International Conference on Networking, sensing & Control, Vol 21–23(3).

Kumar, M. Suresh, Soundarya, V., Kavitha, S., Keerthika, E.S., Aswini, E. 2019, Credit Card Fraud Detection using Random Forest Algorithm. 3rd International Conference on Computing and Computing and Communication Technologies: 149–153.

Machine Learning Group, "Credit Card Fraud Detection", Kaggle, 23-Mar-2018.

Malini, N., Phil, M. 2017, Analysis on Credit Card Fraud Identification Techniques Based on KNN and Outlier Detection: 3–6.

Ounacer Soumaya, Bour Hicham Ait El, Oubrahim Younes, Ghoumari Mohamed Yassine, Azzouazi Mohamed. December 2018, Using Isolation Forest in Anomaly Detection: the case of Credit Card Transactions. *PEN*, Vol 6(2): 394–400.

Pawar Amruta D., Kalavadekar Prakash N., Tambe Swapnil N. Mar- Apr 2014, A Survey on Outlier Detection Techniques for Credit Card Fraud Detection. *IOSR Journal of Computer Engineering (IOSR-JCE)*, Vol 16(2): 44–48.

Sahin, Y., Duman, E. 2011, Detecting Credit Card Fraud by Decision Trees and Support Vector Machines. *Lecture Notes in Engineering and Computer Science*, 2188(1).

Thennakoon Anuruddha, Bhagyani Chee, Premadasa Sasitha, Mihiranga Salitha, Kuruwitaarachchi Nuwan. 2019, Real-Time Credit Card Fraud Detection using Machine Learning. 9th International Conference of Cloud Computing, Data Science and Engineering (Confluence), doi: 10.1109/CONFLUENCE.2019. 8776942: 488–493.

Xuan Siyang, Liu Guanjun, Li Zhenchuan, Zheng Lutao, Wang Shuo, Jiang Chanjun. 2018, Random Forest for Credit Card Fraud Detection. IEEE.

Smart Computing – Khan et al (Eds)
© *2021 Taylor & Francis Group, London, ISBN 978-0-367-76552-1*

Leaf descry with ayurveda facts using images

P. Singh & Y. Pant
Computer Science Department SRHU, Dehradun, Uttarakhand, India

ABSTRACT: Modern research continues to study the use of medicinal plants in healthcare and that is probably because the majority of people believe in the traditional way of treatment. So is the case in India, which had an ancient flow/heritage of traditional medicines used to heal and boost physical and mental well-being. However, the use of indigenous plants for medicinal applications is not well documented. Therefore, a database that contains the application of plants (their leaves) for various diseases (that can be treated at home) is an asset for people as well as for researchers. Therefore, we propose an efficient method for the identification of the plant and its medicinal values using the CNN model, just by clicking the picture of a leaf. Our database facilitates its access offline on any smartphone, thus providing its services in the low and/or no network zone as well (e.g., forest).

1 INTRODUCTION

Traditional plants are still widely used as an alternative to allopathic medicinal-based therapy (western-style medicine) for the treatment of various diseases and ailments (Singh 1986). The consumption of traditional/ayurvedic medicines for the treatment of diseases never went on the record. Moreover, the research associated with products derived from traditional plants (leaves) is progressing day by day. Specifically, developing countries continue to heavily rely upon plant-derived medicines for their primary healthcare, probably because of its inexpensive process economics (Pan et al. 2013). This usage came from ancient times, where medicinal plants were trusted as a therapeutic agent for treating diseases like cholera, typhoid, gonorrhea, etc. Medicinal plants were used not only as an ointment but also to maintain good health and mental condition. Recently, there has been increased global interest in traditional herbal medicine, becoming mainstream in many developed countries (Pandey et al. 2013). Approximately two-thirds of the world's population is now depending upon herbal medicine for primary healthcare because of better compatibility and adaptability with the human body in addition to the least side effects (Oladeji 2016).

Since drugs contain plant extracts (active ingredients obtained from plants) and plants (leaves) themselves can be used as home remedies, proper documentation of the various plants (leaves) is necessary. But, so far, all the plants are not well documented at one repository and thus the availability of information for public use is sparse. Therefore, people lack the knowledge of selecting the right plant (leaves) for the particular ailment that is possible to be treated at home. Practitioners of Ayurveda might be better aware of the differentiation of the plant leaves and, thus, the pros and cons of its respective applications, but, this is not an easy task for others. Hence, the consolidation of this information and its accessibility to the public solves the mentioned problem. Sometimes, in the process of selecting a herb, we may encounter the wrong plant that can cause itching, allergies, and may be fatal at times. This scenario is quite common in rural or suburban areas, where we may encounter many plants/trees unknown to us. There are around 1 million species of trees on Earth (25% of all plants) that still many remain undiscovered (Welzen 2005). This projects the complexity of the identification of various plants (trees, leaves) around.

This paper presents an easy application to identify any plant by just scanning the leaf using a smartphone camera. This application will provide facts in reference to Ayurveda, thus helping people use the right plant (leaves) for their home remedies.

DOI 10.1201/9781003167488-30

In implementation to make ease of the identification process: The color input was converted into a binary image for outline extraction, and then 2D characteristics were extracted from that outline. The grouping of the features is done by using Move Median Centers (MMC) classifier. By using the combination of the characteristics, it generated an accurate result with the recognition rate around 90%. However, it wasn't successful for the leaves of "Amla" and "Touch Me Not" that are very similar in shape. This indicates that the morphological identification of leaves isn't possible in cases like identical-looking leaves. Nam and Hwang moved a step ahead and tried to improve the accuracy by including the vein data into the outline data of plant leaves. A dataset of 1,032 plant leaf images was used. They tried to match the result in the database rather than plant identification (Friis & Balslev 2003). Jeon and Rhee created two models using GoogleNet by regulating the network depth. Their recognition rate was more than 94%, even after there is a 30% damaged leaf dataset (Jeon & Rhee 2017).

In this paper, we have worked on the training and recognition of leaves using a convolutional neural network (CNN) model. We have used the backpropagation algorithm to train the model. We have tried to achieve more accurate results for identifying even similar plants. We have discussed the transfer learning mechanism to bring the output to the mobile devices. We will also target the speed of recognizing the plants' real time even in the offline mode. The paper aims to overcome the mentioned drawbacks of presenting an Android application that offers the easiest plant identification platform. Nowadays, Android is one of the most popular operating systems used in every handhold device; that implementation makes it usable for every person. To implement and use the machine learning (ML) model into an Android we have used TensorFlow lite. Moreover, it eliminates the requirement of the active Internet connection for accessing the application. In this paper, we have discussed all the ML methods to fulfill the implementation requirements.

2 METHOD OF LEAF RECOGNITION

2.1 *Feature extraction*

Feature defines the behavior of an image; it plays a vital role in the field of image recognition. First, before extracting features, images are preprocessed. In the technique of preprocessing of image thresholding, normalization, etc., methods are being implemented. After preprocessing, the features extraction techniques are applied to extract the features that will be helpful in different applications like character recognition.

2.2 *Machine learning*

Machine learning is the field of study that provides computers with the potential to be held without being explicitly programmed. If there is an equation and input given, it is very easy to find the output using the given equation for any input but if there is only input and output given then it is pretty hard to detect the equation or the output of any random input. This defines the concept of predicting the outputs and figure out the algorithm using some given samples of inputs and outputs. In ML, input and output are simple predictors and what we want to predict, respectively.

2.3 *Datasets*

The dataset is the collection of different inputs and outputs based on different algorithms. In the dataset, some of the images are labeled and some are unlabeled. These labeled and unlabeled images are responsible for different algorithms used for the training machine. Those datasets in which images are labeled trained using techniques of supervised learning and for those having not proper labels we use unsupervised learning techniques. We have created our own dataset of around 100 plants. Around 50 images of each plant are there, which means the total dataset contains around 5000 plant images.

2.4 *Neural network structure*

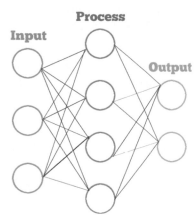

Figure 1.   Neural network structure.

- The red circle on the left represents the network's input layer where each circle represents an input neuron.
- The green circle on the right contains the output neurons and is the output layer of the network.
- The middle layer can be described as a hidden layer, which contains all the processing of the neural network as shown in Figure 1.
- Circles here represent neurons. Each neuron here is a function which takes the output neuron of the previous layer and provides a number between 0 and 1.

2.5 *Supervised learning*

We have trained the machine with well "labeled" data, which specifies that some of the data is already tagged with answers (correct). A supervised learning algorithm gets trained with the labeled training data and helps in predicting the outcomes for unseen data.

3   PLANT DETECTION AND MODEL TRAINING

3.1 *Edge detection*

Edge detection is a technique to process images and finding boundaries of the objects. It focuses on the detection of discontinuities in brightness.

3.1.1 *Canny edge detection*
In industry, the very standard edge detection technique is the Canny edge detection. It separates noise from the image before detecting the boundaries, and that makes Canny Edge Detection a very important method. Canny Edge Detection method is a better method to find the edges and the threshold value without even disturbing the edge features.

3.1.2 *Sobel edge detection*
This edge detection method uses Sobel approximation to find the edges of the derivative. This method is used for image segmentation. It led up to the edges to those points where it encounters the higher gradient. This technique performs a 2-D spatial gradient quantity on an image and thus the region of the high spatial frequency which corresponds to the edges gets highlighted.

3.2 *Image contrast stretching*

Contrast stretching (often known as normalization) is a simple image enhancement technique that provides an improvement in the image by stretching the range of its intensity values, e.g., the full range of pixel values that are allowed by the concerned image type.

3.3 *Corner detection*

In the field of computer vision systems, a corner detection is an approach used to extract certain kinds of features and deduce the contents of the image.

3.4 *Model compilation*

The compilation is a very important step. It is always required after the model definition. It includes both training from the scratch as well as loading a pre-trained file and increase weights to train again. The parameters required for the compilation process:

- **Regression:** Mean Squared Error.
- **Binary Classification (for two classes):** Cross Entropy or Binary Cross
- **Entropy:** Multiclass Classification (for more than two classes): Categorical Cross Entropy.

3.5 *Training model*

- **Convolutional neural network (CNN).** A network that has at least one convolutional layer. A typical CNN also includes other types of layers, such as pooling layers and dense layers.
- **Convolution.** The process of applying a kernel (filter) to an image.
- **Kernel/filter:** A matrix which is smaller than the input, used to transform the input into chunks.
- **Padding:** Adding pixels of some value, usually 0, around the input image
- **Pooling:** The process of reducing the size of an image through down sampling. There are several types of pooling layers. For example, average pooling converts many values into a single value by taking the average. However, maxpooling is the most common.
- **Maxpooling:** A pooling process in which many values are converted into a single value by taking the maximum value from among them.
- **Stride:** The number of pixels to slide the kernel (filter) across the image.
- **Down sampling:** The act of reducing the size of an image.

3.6 *Model fit*

Once the compilation is complete, the weights of the training dataset are adapted. The network training is performed using a backpropagation algorithm and is optimized using optimization function and loss functions were specified at the time of compilation. This backpropagation algorithm requires the network to be trained for particular epochs or rounds to the training dataset. Each epoch is grouped with input-output pattern pairs called batches. This defines the number of patterns that the network has to go through. It is important for memory optimization as well; we must have to ensure that too many input patterns should not be loaded into memory simultaneously.

3.7 *Network evaluation*

Now, when the model is trained and fit then it can be evaluated on the training dataset, but it will not reflect the useful predictions as all the data is known to the model. We can try evaluating the trained model on a different dataset which is unseen during testing. This can provide the overall performance of the network. The accuracy of the model can also be specified after applying the complied model on a different dataset.

3.8 *Transfer learning and tensor flow lite*

It allows the model to build in a time-saving way rather than starting from scratch. We will use our trained model to generate another model by re-training it to perform another task. Re-training needs fewer data to train a model instead of doing it from the beginning. We have our own trained and compiled model; we have to convert it into. tflite format.

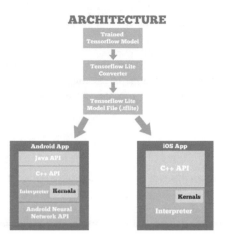

Figure 2. TensorFlow lite. architecture.

4 RESULT

This paper presented a survey of different methods for plant leaf detection using image processing techniques. There are many methods in automated or computer vision for detection and classification but there are still gray areas. Since all the plants cannot be identified using a single method, thus, this paper concludes the following:

- The k-nearest-neighbor method is perhaps the simplest of all algorithms for predicting the class of a test example.
- An obvious disadvantage of the k-NN method is the time complexity of making predictions.
- Additionally, neural networks are tolerant of noisy inputs.

Transfer learning allows to use a trained model and retrain it to enhance performance (additional dataset, shift to another platform, etc.). For example, an image classification model can be retrained

Figure 3. Live image detection of the plant part clicked by the mobile camera using the Leaf Descry program. The efficiency of the program is observed >97% accuracy.

to recognize a new category of images. It takes lesser time and consumes less amount of data than training from scratch.

We have trained 100 plant images with approx. >50 images (leaves, flowers) of each plant. Using Keras functions (conv2D, pooling, flatten, dense) we have compiled our model with more than 97% accuracy. Further applying the transfer learning algorithm provided by TensorFlow, the trained model is fitted for mobile devices. A retrained model and list of categories are rendered for later developing end-device applications.

5 CONCLUSIONS

We proposed a new technique to classify plants or leaves using a CNN model. We have created models using Keras which is an open-source neural network library. We evaluated the performance of our model using Relu and Softmax activation functions. We managed the loss using categorical cross-entropy during model compilation. The recognition rate was nearly 98% with a batch size of 64 and 10 epochs. After the model compilation, we applied the transfer learning to generate the mobile compatible model.

Finally, we have successfully brought the trained model to mobile devices and have eased the accessibility by offering the process offline.

6 FUTURE SCOPE

A country's economy is very much dependent on its agricultural productivity. Thus, the detection of diseases in plants hold importance for product quality and productivity. Sometimes, these diseases are hazardous, for example, little leaf disease in pine trees in the United States. Hence, automatic detection of plant diseases is required for early-stage detection as well as reducomgs manual monitoring work in big farms. The previous research on this filed has been limited as it involves human intervention.

ACKNOWLEDGMENTS

The authors appreciate the effort of Riya Yadav and Sandesh Singh of the Computer Sciences Department of SRHU, Dehradun for their contributions during the study. We would also like to show our gratitude to Mr. Bineet Kumar Joshi, assistant professor of the Computer Science Department, at SRHU for sharing his pearls of wisdom with us during this work.

REFERENCES

Friis and Balslev H. 2003, Plant diversity and complexity patterns: local, regional, and global dimensions. *Proceedings of an International Symposium*, Held at the Royal Danish Academy of Sciences and Letters, Copenhagen, Denmark: 25–28.

Jeon W. S. and Rhee S. Y. 2017, Plant leaf recognition using a convolution neural network. *Int. J. Fuzzy Log. Intell. Syst.*, Vol. 17(1):26–34.

Oladeji O. 2016, Natural Products: An Indian Journal The Characteristics and Roles of Medicinal Plants: Some Important Medicinal Plants in Nigeria. *Nat. Prod. An Indian J.*, Vol. 12(3): 1–8.

Pan S., Neeraj A., Srivastava K. S., Kishore P., Danquah M. K., and Sarethy I. P. 2013, A Proposal for a Quality System for Herbal Products. *J. Pharm. Sci.*, Vol. 102(12): 4230–4241.

Pandey M. M., Rastogi S., and Rawat A. K. S. 2013, Indian traditional ayurvedic system of medicine and nutritional supplementation. *Evidence-based Complement. Altern. Med.*, Vol. 2013.

Singh, Y. N. 1986, Traditional medicine in Fiji: Some herbal folk cures used by Fiji Indians. *J. Ethnophar macol.*, Vol 15(1): 57–88.

Welzen P. C. van, Slik F., and Alahuhta J. 2005, Plant Diversity and Complexity Patterns.

Smart Computing – Khan et al (Eds)
© 2021 Taylor & Francis Group, London, ISBN 978-0-367-76552-1

Sanjeevni—we care for life: Using big data-apache spark

Nipun Tyagi, Nikita Chauhan, Ayushi Singhal, Rijwan Khan,
Upendra Kumar Tiwari & Avinash Kumar Sharma
*Department of Computer Science and Engineering, ABES Institute of Technology, Ghaziabad,
Affiliated to AKTU Lucknow, India*

ABSTRACT: Roadways are one of the major types of transportation in India and with its highly significant impact on the Indian economy it cannot be avoided. With roadways there comes a concern of road safety and a high number of accidents. Many people lose their lives in road accidents for various reasons. The percentage of accidents is increasing to such a high level in India, causing loss of human life, because of a lack of proper real-time tracking of accident which could be passed to a nearby police station or hospital. This paper aims to provide a solution to this problem by providing information on the accident spot, which can be immediately be shared with a local police station or hospital with few necessary pieces of information such as photos, location, and video. The belief is that this increase in information will lead to the saving of human lives and a decrease in suffering. The idea behind the Sanjeevni mangemen system is that the device consists of hardware that detects whether or ot an accident took place and if it did would then send information such as location of the accident site via a fully automated system. Hence, this system has the ability to be a great contribution to society by saving lives with the help of Big Data technology like spark streaming, Hadoop, etc.

Keywords: Accident, Apache Hadoop, Apache Spark, Big Data, Hospital, Police Station, Transportation

1   INTRODUCTION

Unavoidable and unintentional accidents that result in multiple injuries or causalities occur in large numbers worldwide. Road accidents (Chong et al. 2005) are a result of many factors that can be broadly grouped as:

- human error
- road environment
- vehicular conditions.

In a country like India, there are many places which have poor road facilities which lead to many accidents and lead to a higher death rate due and an increase in property. Table 1 illustrates that in 2018 national highways in India contributed to only 1.94% of the total road network which accounted for 30.2% of total road accidents and represented 35.7% of the deaths . State highways accounted for 2.97% of the total road length which reported 25.2% of the accidents and 26.8% of the deaths. Other roads comprise of about 95.1% of the total roads which account for the remaining balance of 45% of the accidents and 38% of the deaths (Keerthi et al. 2013).

Table 2 shows the vehicle accident data (Deshpande 2014) which signifies that there is a need to reduce the number of accidents in order to save lives (Iyyappan & Nandagopal 2013).

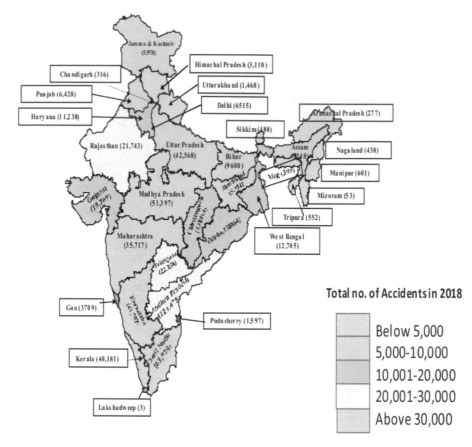

Total no. of Accidents in 2018

- Below 5,000
- 5,000-10,000
- 10,001-20,000
- 20,001-30,000
- Above 30,000

Figure 1. Statewise road accidents in 2018.

Table 1. Accidents, fatalities, and injuries in 2018.

Category of Roads	Length as on 31.3.17 Kms	% age Share in total	Accidents Number	% age Share in total	Persons Killed Number	% age Share in total	Persons injured Number	% age Share in total
National Highways	1,14,158	1.94	1,40,84	30.16	54,046	35.69	1,40,622	29.96
State Highways	1,75,036	2.97	1,17,50	25.17	40,580	26.80	1,21,579	25.90
Other Roads	56,08,477	95.10	2,08,631	44.67	56,791	37.51	2,07,217	44.17
Total	58,97,671	100	4,67,044	100	1,51,417	100	4,69,418	100

Table 2. Road accidents, fatalities, and injuries by types of collision in 2018.

Collision type	No of accidents	Persons killed	Person injured
Vehicle to vehicle	2,53,253 (54.32)	78,766 (52.02)	2,56,919 (54.73)
Vehicle to pedestrian	78,974 (16.91)	24,861 (14.96)	64,997 (13.85)
Vehicle to non-Motorized vehicle	22,248 (4.76)	8,753 (5.78)	20,035 (4.27)
Vehicle to Animal	5,902 (1.26)	2,267 (1.50)	4,917 (1.05)
Others	1,06,667 (22.84)	38,975 (25.74)	1,22,550 (26.11)
Total	4,67,044	1,51,417	4,69,418

1.1 *Accident challenges*

- **Lack of medical facilities.** If a person meets with an accident then that person wants immediate first aid to reduce the impact of the injury. However, due to a lack of nearby medical facilities the chance of death increases (Mitchison & Porter 1998).
- **Loss of life.** When an accident takes place there may be a chance that due to the high impact of the accident a fatality might occur.
- **Lack of ability to contact to family members.** Sometime the victim is not in a condition that he/she could contact their family member to inform them about the accident.

The Sanjeevni system makes sure that the accident information is given to the nearest police station and hospital. The system provides the current Global Positioning System (GPS) (Sonika et al. 2014) location, images, and video streaming of the accident spot which will help to make faster decisions. This system has an advantage from the earlier developed system, as it could provide information like image, location, and voice recording of the accident spot even if no network is available. If an injured victim does not receive any emergency medical care at that very moment or at the earliest time possible it can make a large difference in his/her chances of survival, as every single minute matters. The Sanjeevni system would contribute to the saving lives as well as provide the Government of India the ability to take preventive measures according to the data present in the database.

1.2 *Benefits of using Sanjeevni*

- Significant decrease in deaths caused by road accidents.
- To communicate or inform about the accident even if the network availability is not available.
- Fast alert notification by message to emergency care centers like a police station and hospital.
- To provide the utmost aid or support even in deserted or isolated areas.

2 PROBLEM STATEMENT

The transportation industry roughly contributed to 6.3% of India's GDP in the years 2017–18. The Indian Government plans to invest Rs 7 trillion (US$ 107.82 billion) over the next 5 years, for the construction of 200,000 km national highways, with the budgeted investment of US$82 billion by the year 2022 (Gholston & Anderson 2005; Panwhar et al. 2000). This proposed plan would result in better and more effective mobility across India, would take lesser travel time, and free up time for people. At the same time, many road accidents take place with no proper management system available to cater to such accidents which increases the chance of loss of life. At the spot of the incident, the sufferer does not need to receive immediate medical attention (first aid). As there is a lack of communication system established which would convey the incident occurred to the nearby/local hospitals or authorities who could take the necessary immediate actions. The Sanjeevni system will be there as the solution to such problems and will aim to save lives as every life matters.

3 COMPONETS UNSED IN EXPERIMENTAL SETUP

3.1 *Global Positioning System (GPS)*

GPS provides information about location and time that can be accessed from any place on earth. The location that GPS provides will be pictured (visualized) by using Google Earth and this will help in tracking the vehicle's movement and its location. GPS does not require any input; it takes location automatically (Sriram & Ramya 2013).

Figure 2.   GPS.

GPS consist of three components.

- **Satellite:** They send the signal to track the locations automatically.
- **Ground Station:** They consist of the radars which ensure us that the location provided is correct.
- **Receiver:** They are the signals received in the phone to track the person's location.

GPS module will require a 10 Hz update rate, with 14 channel trackers which provide exact location. Having two serial ports, UART (Universal Asynchronous Receiver Transmitter) which provides communication between microprocessor and GPS module and SPI (Serial Peripheral Interface) interfaces which is used to send data between a micro-controller and peripheral devices. It requires a 28-mA operating current and high sensitivity. GPS would track the car to get its correct location so that help can be provided immediately (Prabha et al. 2014; Kumar and Kim 2005).

3.2   *GY-521 accelerometer*

This device measures the acceleration by change in capacitance, which is the rate of change of the velocity of an object. The SI unit of acceleration is meter per second square (m/s^2). The GY-521 has an Invent Sense MPU6050 chip which contains a 3-axis accelerometer (range is ± 2, ± 4, ± 8, $\pm 1\,6$ g) and a 3-axis gyro meter (range is ± 250, ± 500, ± 1000, $\pm 2000°$/s).

GY-521 contains a total 8 pins:

- **VCC:** 3.3 V pins or 5 V.
- **GND:** Ground pin.

Figure 3.   GY-521 Accelerometer.

- **SCL (Serial clock Line) and SDA (Serial Data Line):** Responsible for primary I2C communication.
- **XCA (Auxiliary Clock Line) and XDL (Auxiliary Data Line):** Conducts auxiliary I2C communication.
- **ADO:** It is slave or master interface.
- **INT:** Interrupt pin.

3.3 *ESP8266 WiFi*

Wi-Fi is Wireless Fidelity, which is one of the most used wireless networks in the world. It uses 802.11 standards developed which is released by the Institute of Electrical and Electronic Engineers (IEEE) in 1997. It utilizes low-cost 2.4 GHz UHF and 5 GIIz SHF ISM radio groups and provides Internet connectivity. It will be used to transfer the data like location, images, and video to the database (Lv & Qiu 2017).

Figure 4.   Wi-Fi module.

Wi-Fi module will act as an access point (can create hotspot) and as a station (can connect to Wi-Fi). This eases in fetching the data and at the same time will upload it on the database; it will also fetch data like images, location, and videos from the database using Spark API.

3.4 *Arduino Uno microcontroller*

Arduino is an open-source computer hardware and software company. The Arduino community design utilizes a microcontroller-based development board known as Arduino Modules. Arduino Uno is a microcontroller board based on 8-bit ATmega328P microcontroller.

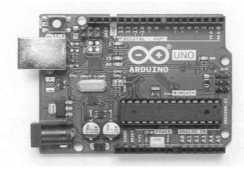

Figure 5.   Arduino Uno module.

Figure 6.   Ultrasonic sensor.

The ATmega328 has 32 KB memory (with 0.5 KB used for the boot loader) (Badamasi 2014). It also has 2 KB of SRAM and 1 KB of EEPROM (which can be read and written with the EEPROM library). In our system, Arduino Uno helps in communication between sensors on a single circuit board (platform).

3.5   *Ultrasonic sensor*

An ultrasonic sensor is used to measure the distance to an object using ultrasonic sound waves. An ultrasonic sensor uses a transducer to send and receive ultrasonic pulses that relay back information about an object's proximity (Carullo & and Parvis 2001). The ultrasonic meter performs the measurement of the height of a vehicle body from the ground. The ultrasonic pulse is generated using a piezoelectric transducer and the echo reflected by the ground is received by another piezoelectric transducer (Stiawan et al. 2017). The two transducers are mounted close to each other to make up the measuring head, i.e., the time between the transmission and the reflected signal. The distance is determined by the following formula:

$$\text{Distance} = 1/2 \, T \times C$$

where T = Time
C = Speed of sound

3.6   *ESP32-CAM*

The ESP32 is a low-cost system-on-chip (SoC) series created by Express if Systems. ESP32-CAM is a very small camera module with the ESP32-S chip, OV2640 camera, and several GPIOs to connect peripherals, it also has a micro SD card slot which is used to store images taken with the camera which can be used to store information. It has both Wi-Fi and Bluetooth capabilities, which make it an all-rounded chip for information transfer. ESP32-CAM has 160 MHz clock speed and built-in 520 KB SRAM, external 4MPSRAM, and requires external 5V power source for its proper functioning.

Figure 7.   ESP32 CAM.

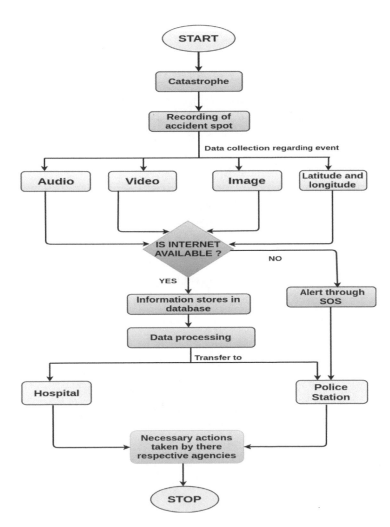

Figure 8.   Flow chart of proposed algorithm.

263

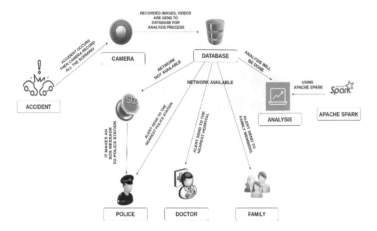

Figure 9.　Working flow diagram.

```
sketch_apr26a §
#include<Wire.h>
const int MPU=0x68;
int16_t AcX,AcY,AcZ,Tmp,GyX,GyY,GyZ;

void setup(){
  Wire.begin();
  Wire.beginTransmission(MPU);
  Wire.write(0x6B);
  Wire.write(0);
  Wire.endTransmission(true);
  Serial.begin(9600);
}
void loop(){
  Wire.beginTransmission(MPU);
  Wire.write(0x3B);
  Wire.endTransmission(false);
  Wire.requestFrom(MPU,12,true);
  AcX=Wire.read()<<8|Wire.read();
  AcY=Wire.read()<<8|Wire.read();
  AcZ=Wire.read()<<8|Wire.read();
  GyX=Wire.read()<<8|Wire.read();
  GyY=Wire.read()<<8|Wire.read();
  GyZ=Wire.read()<<8|Wire.read();   |

  Serial.print("Accelerometer: ");
  Serial.print("X = "); Serial.print(AcX);
  Serial.print(" | Y = "); Serial.print(AcY);
  Serial.print(" | Z = "); Serial.println(AcZ);

  Serial.print("Gyroscope: ");
  Serial.print("X = "); Serial.print(GyX);
  Serial.print(" | Y = "); Serial.print(GyY);
  Serial.print(" | Z = "); Serial.println(GyZ);
  Serial.println(" ");
  delay(333);
}
```

Figure 10.　Code for proposed system.

```
Accelerometer: X = -2548 | Y = -10164 | Z = 13216
Gyroscope: X = -1344 | Y = 8570 | Z = -17221

Accelerometer: X = 9376 | Y = -2088 | Z = 11720
Gyroscope: X = -1328 | Y = 6078 | Z = -7911

Accelerometer: X = 11172 | Y = 3568 | Z = 9476
Gyroscope: X = -1328 | Y = 1972 | Z = -545

Accelerometer: X = 9912 | Y = 3596 | Z = 10232
Gyroscope: X = -1328 | Y = -814 | Z = -1631

Accelerometer: X = 9416 | Y = 3696 | Z = 13872
Gyroscope: X = -1312 | Y = -4830 | Z = -3169

Accelerometer: X = 5176 | Y = 8624 | Z - 13636
Gyroscope: X = -1296 | Y = 2636 | Z = 2758

Accelerometer: X = 444 | Y = 6552 | Z = 12536
Gyroscope: X = -1328 | Y = -1342 | Z = 2037

Accelerometer: X = -2376 | Y = 5396 | Z = 14204
Gyroscope: X = -1360 | Y = -564 | Z = 7762

Accelerometer: X = -5528 | Y = 3144 | Z = 11552
Gyroscope: X = -1344 | Y = -2063 | Z = 2823

Accelerometer: X = -7704 | Y = 1752 | Z = 14556
Gyroscope: X = -1328 | Y = -1478 | Z = 1295

Accelerometer: X = -3308 | Y = -372 | Z = 17244
Gyroscope: X = -1312 | Y = -3916 | Z = -15910

Accelerometer: X = 3988 | Y = 80 | Z = 11500
Gyroscope: X = -1344 | Y = -2064 | Z = -3398

Accelerometer: X = 6348 | Y = -2528 | Z = 15384
Gyroscope: X = -1328 | Y = -4426 | Z = 4329

Accelerometer: X = -2708 | Y = -10300 | Z = 11756
Gyroscope: X = -1312 | Y = -12884 | Z = 2164

Accelerometer: X = -9316 | Y = -12248 | Z = 8976
Gyroscope: X = -1328 | Y = -3713 | Z = 1125

Accelerometer: X = -8268 | Y = -12544 | Z = 7832
Gyroscope: X = -1328 | Y = 1168 | Z = -3016

Accelerometer: X = -3248 | Y = -12672 | Z = 6268
Gyroscope: X = -1344 | Y = -15739 | Z = 2735
```

Figure 11. Output of accelerometer.

4 WORKING PROCEDURE

This Sanjeev system will provide real-time information about accident spots which would include its location using GPS, images, and videos of the accident spot.

The device is installed in the car, which would continuously record the videos and pictures of the road using ESP32-CAM, which would be sent to the cloud (database) using ESP8266 Wi-Fi. The accelerometer would provide information about the acceleration, 3-axis accelerometer (angle), and 3-axis gyro meter (angle), and the ultrasonic sensor provides information about the distance between the objects. The ultrasonic sensor and accelerometer would be used to detect whether the accident took place or not, i.e., if the acceleration of the vehicle is greater than 4 g ($>$4 g) and the presence of any object is detected then the alert would be sent that an accident had taken place.

```
Locat7.817710  Date/Time: 9/3/2013 04:52:51.00
Location: 30.240455,-97.817710  Date/Time: 9/3/2013 04:52:52.00

Done.

Location: 30.236640,-97.821456  Date/Time: 9/3/2013 04:51:03.00
Location: 30.236640,-97.821456  Date/Time: 9/3/2013 04:51:04.00
Location: 30.239700,-97.815856  Date/Time: 9/3/2013 04:52:00.00
Location: 30.239772,-97.815681  Date/Time: 9/3/2013 04:52:01.00
Location: 30.240457,-97.817710  Date/Time: 9/3/2013 04:52:51.00
Location: 30.240455,-97.817710  Date/Time: 9/3/2013 04:52:52.00

Done.
```

Figure 12.   Output of GPS.

Figure 13.   Analysis of data.

Figure 14.   Map shows highly accident-prone area, low accident-prone area, and no accident-prone area.

The pictures and videos of the accident spot will be shared with the nearby police station and the hospital and with their family members, informing them about the accident. If in case there is no Internet connectivity, then Save our Soul (SOS) will be sent to the police station so that they could take necessary action. In any of the situations, the notification about the accident would be sent to the police or/and hospitals near the accident spot.

5 CONCLUSION

In today's time, the number of the accidents are increasing day by day. In many cases, the victim does not get timely medical facilities due to no timely information about the accident on the road. This contributes to a high death rate (road accident) due to a lack of medical attention on time. This raised a need for a system that will provide on-time information regarding the accident spot, wherein the victim(s) will get medical attention and proper treatment on time. The proposed Sanjeevni system is an ideal solution to this life-or-death battle by notifying others about the accident. This system will significantly decrease the number of deaths by capturing the moment of an accident by using a camera and sharing the information about the accident to the nearest police station, hospital, and their dear ones. As the system provides real-time data that will be an upload to the database and the message is sent via Wi-Fi along with the location of the accident detected with the help of the GPS module. This will provide the medical facilities to the victim on time, hence reducing the chances of death. In case the network is not available, then an SOS alert will be sent to the nearest police station. This system is user friendly and will make the world a better place by making it safer to drive and helping to save lives.

6 FUTURE SCOPE

The information provided by the Sanjeevni system can be used to denote which area has the maximum probability of an accident. This would aler the driver about possible roadway danger and help the government to take necessary action according to the data available to reduce any future loss of life.

REFERENCES

Badamasi, Y.A., 2014, September. The working principle of an Arduino. In *2014 11th international conference on electronics, computer and computation (ICECCO)* (pp. 1–4). IEEE.

Carullo, A. and Parvis, M., 2001. An ultrasonic sensor for distance measurement in automotive applications. *IEEE Sensors journal*, *1*(2), p.143.

Chong, M., Abraham, A. and Paprzycki, M., 2005. Traffic accident analysis using machine learning paradigms. *Informatica*, *29*(1).

Deshpande, P., 2014. Road safety and accident prevention in India: a review. *Int J Adv Eng Tech*, *64*(2), p.68.

Gholston, S.E. and Anderson, M.D., 2005. A GIS accident system to accompany CARE (No. UTCA Report 03304). *University Transportation Center for Alabama*.

Iyyappan, M.S. and Nandagopal, M.V., 2013. Automatic accident detection and ambulance rescue with intelligent traffic light system. *International journal of advanced research in electrical, electronics and instrumentation engineering*, *2*(4), p.1319.

Keerthi, C.R., Shanmukh, G. and Sivaram, R., 2013. Various accident detection technologies and recovery systems with victim analysis. *International Journal of Advanced Trends in Computer Science and Engineering (IJATCSE)*, *2*(3), pp.07–12.

Kumar, M. and Kim, T., 2005, April. Dynamic speedometer: dashboard redesign to discourage drivers from speeding. In *CHI'05 extended abstracts on Human factors in computing systems* (pp. 1573–1576).

Lv, C. and Qiu, B., 2017, September. Design and research of WiFi intelligent car based on computer vision technology. In *2017 5th International Conference on Mechatronics, Materials, Chemistry and Computer Engineering (ICMMCCE 2017)*. Atlantis Press.

Mitchison, N. and Porter, S., 1998. Guidelines on a major accident prevention policy and safety management system, as required by Council Directive 96/82/EC (SEVESO II). *European Commission, Joint Research Centre, Institute for Systems Informatics and Safety, Report EUR, 18123*.

Panwhar, S.T., Pitt, R. and Anderson, M.D., 2000. Development of a GIS-based hazardous materials transportation management system. UTCA report, 99244.

Prabha, C., Sunitha, R. and Anitha, R., 2014. Automatic vehicle accident detection and messaging system using gsm and gps modem. *International Journal of Advanced Research in Electrical, Electronics and Instrumentation Engineering*, *3*(7), pp. 10723–10727.

Sonika, S., Sathiyasekar, K. and Jaishree, S., 2014. Intelligent accident identification system using GPS, GSM modem. *International Journal of advanced research in computer and communication engineering*, 3(2).

Sriram, A. and Ramya, P., 2013. Automatic Accident Notification System using GPS & GSM with 3G Technology for Video Monitoring. *International Journal of Emerging Trends in Electrical and Electronics (IJETEE)*, 1(2).

Stiawan, R., Kusumadjati, A., Aminah, N.S., Djamal, M. and Viridi, S., 2019, April. An Ultrasonic Sensor System for Vehicle Detection Application. In *Journal of Physics: Conference Series* (Vol. 1204, No. 1, p. 012017). IOP Publishing.

Smart Computing – Khan et al (Eds)
© *2021 Taylor & Francis Group, London, ISBN 978-0-367-76552-1*

A review paper on Machine Learning (ML)

Avinash Kumar Sharma & Neha Goel
Department of Computer Science, ABESIT, Ghaziabad, India

ABSTRACT: Machine Learning (ML) is one of the most enabling and consistent degrees of progress in Artificial Intelligence (AI). ML is a field of program building that interfaces with PCs to learn without being unequivocally balanced (Talwar 2013). One of the established goals of ML is to design a system to use the knowledge for default issues. In this article, we will concentrate on ML, AI assignments and issues, and different calculations. In this paper, a short audit and prospect of the enormous utilization of ML been made (Alpaydin 1999). It consists of various important algorithms of ML with their use cases which feature useful examples of where to use such types of algorithms.

Keywords: Machine learning, Supervised learning, Unsupervised learning

1 INTRODUCTION

Machine Learning (ML) is a piece of man-made thinking that licenses PC structures to pick up genuinely from models, data, and occurrence. By engaging a system to carry out express endeavors wisely, ML structures can do multiplex techniques by picking up from data, rather than sticking to a predefined theory (Makeig 2012). The essential great situation of using ML is that, when a figuring acknowledges how to oversee data, it can achieve its work. ML is the veritable assessment of checks and certified replicas that systems use to reasonably carry out a fixed aim. It is seen as a subset of man-made data. Machine understanding checks store up a keen model subject to test data, known as "orchestrating data", in order to pick figures or decisions without being unequivocally repaired to play out the task (Li et al. 2017). PC-based information figurines are used in a large approach of occupations, for instance, online correspondence restricting and system innovation, where it is absurd to develop an estimation of express rules for playing out the endeavor. Reproduced data is unflinchingly related to computational bits of data, which turns making checks using PCs. The evaluation of reasonable progress passes on strategy, theories, and application zones to the field of ML (Gregory 2009). Data mining is a field of study inside ML and spotlights on exploratory data assessment through execution learning. In its application across business issues, ML has, in a similar way, actuated sharp evaluation. As the sector expands, ML is building structures which may aid experts to offer an increasingly good or productive survey for unequivocal states (Shrivastava 2018). ML is assisting with comprehending the colossal volume of knowledge accessible to scientists, contributing new experiences into science and medication.

Here, we will try to cover up basic statistics as descriptive and inferential (Dey 2016). Then some concepts that will be used to describe a dataset. Next, we will be studying use cases of different ML algorithms, for example Linear Regression, Logistic regression, Decision trees, Random forest, support vector machine (SVM), Naive Bayes, K-means, and principal component analysis (PCA). These algorithms need to have a brief review. We will discuss it one by one. There are two types of learning—supervised and unsupervised. We will describe both of them.

2 DEVELOPING A LEARNING MACHINE

Numerous enormous information applications influence ML to work at the most elevated effectiveness. The sheer volume, decent variety, and speed of information stream have made it impracticable

DOI 10.1201/9781003167488-32

to abuse the characteristic capacity of people to examine information continuously. At the point when you have to anticipate or gauge an objective's worth, administered learning is the fitting decision. The subsequent stage is to choose, contingent upon the objective worth, between clustering (on account of discrete objective worth) and regression (on account of numerical objective worth) (Breiman 1984). The procedures of ML integrate models for enhancing the measurements. Since the measurements are fundamental to building up the answer for a given choice procedure, they should be chosen cautiously during the calculated stages (Bozzuto 2002). It is likewise critical to decide whether ML is a reasonable methodology for taking care of a given issue.

The activity of building ML algorithms can be defined as follows.

2.1 *Accumulate the information*

Choose the batch of every accessible fact that may be valuable in tackling the issue. Choosing each and every accessible information might be superfluous (Horvitz 2006). Contingent on the issue, information can either be recovered by an information stream application programming interface (API), or orchestrated through joining different information streams.

2.2 *Preprocess the facts*

Show the information in a way that is comprehended by the shopper of the information. Preprocessing incorporates accompanying three stages (Bozzuto 2002).

1. **Arrangement.** The information should be introduced in a usable organization, e.g., XML, HTML, and SOAP.
2. **Cleaning.** From time to time, the data should be normalized, discretized, found the center estimation of, smoothened, or isolated for compelling use.
3. **Sampling.** Information should be examined at standard or versatile intervals in a way to such an extent that repetition is limited without the loss of data for transmission by means of correspondence channels.

2.3 *Transform the data*

Change the data expressed to the computation and the data on the issue. Change can be as feature scaling, breaking down, or assortment.

2.4 *Teach the data*

Choose the readiness and testing datasets from the changed data. A figure is set up on the arrangement dataset and surveyed in opposition to the test set (Banaseka 2016). The changed getting ready dataset is dealt with to account for the withdrawal of facts.

2.5 *Test the facts*

Assess the calculation to test its adequacy and execution. A prepared model presented to a test dataset is estimated in opposition to forecasts built on that trial dataset which are demonstrative of the presentation of the model.

2.6 *Apply reinforcement learning*

Most control-theoretic approaches need a decent criticism system for steady tasks. By and large, the criticism information is scanty, postponed, or vague. In such cases, managed learning may not be pragmatic and might be subbed with reinforcement learning (RL). Rather than regulated learning, RL utilizes dynamic execution rebalancing to gain from the outcomes of associations with nature, without express preparing.

2.7 *Execute*

Apply the approved model to play out a genuine undertaking of expectation. The way toward preparing can exist together with the genuine undertaking of anticipating future conduct.

3 TYPES OF MACHINE LEARNING

ML errands are regularly characterized into three general classes, contingent upon the idea of the learning "signal" or "learning" accessible to a learning framework:

- Supervised learning
- Unsupervised learning
- Reinforcement learning

3.1 *Supervised learning*

A controlled learning estimation examines the organizing data and constructs an induced breaking point that can be employed for charting new models. It is the ML task of getting together a limit from a named organizing data. The status data contains an enormous measure of getting ready models.

Administered learning evaluation makes a numerical model of a colossal measure of data that holds both the fact sources and the perfect results (Hastie 2009). The data is known as organizing data and contains an abundance of getting ready models. Each status model has in any event one wellspring of data and a perfect yield, in any instance, called a supervisory sign. In the numerical model, each strategy model is tended to by an exhibitor vector and the masterminding data by a system. A perfect limit will allow the figuring to adequately pick the yield for inputs that were not a part of the strategy data. A count that upgrades the accuracy of its yields or checks after a while is said to have fathoms on how to carry out that task.

3.2 *Unsupervised learning*

It is the ML task of instigating an ability to delineate the secured structure from "unlabeled" data. Since the models set out to the understudy are unlabeled, there is no examination of the precision of the formation that is yielded by the pertinent estimation—which is one system for seeing execution getting from controlled learning and bolster learning (Mark 2012).

Free studying computation takes a lot of details that carry only wellsprings of information, and fine formation in the data, for instance, amassing or assembling server farms. The figuring, in that capacity, obtain from test data that has not been named, mentioned, or requested. Instead of reacting to examination, free learning computation sees shared traits in the data and reacts to the subject to the closeness or truancy of such split characteristics in each new bit of data (Gregory 2009). A concentrated use of solo learning is in the area of broadness approximation in bits of information; in any case, autonomous learning joins different zones including spreading out and illuminating information highlights.

3.3 *Reinforcement learning*

It is an area of ML that deals with taking the best suited action in any particular situation which may help in maximizing the reward (Kotsiantis 2007). It is used in many systems to deter-mine the best possible route or behavior which ensures the maximum possible reward in any specific situation. It is different from the supervised training as in that the system is trained using the correct answer but here the system has to find that itself means it learns from its own experiences.

4 SUPERVISED LEARNING ALGORITHMS

To put it simply, we train an algorithm and at the end pick the model that best predicts some well-defined output based on the input data. They are classified as regression and classification (Gregory 2009).

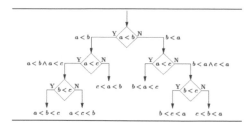

Figure 1.   Decision trees.

4.1   *Decision trees*

Decision trees are the base unit of yes/no deals that one needs to introduce to outline the likelihood of picking the right choice when in doubt (Kavukcuoglu 2009). As a strategy, it awards you to progress toward the issue in a separated serious and careful approach to manage appearing at the aftereffect of a veritable objective.

4.2   *Naïve Bayes classification*

Naïve Bayes classifier is a gathering of clear likelihood classifiers subject to put in Bayes' theorem with blameless self-rule suppositions in the middle of the characteristics (Kaelbing 1996). The featured picture is the condition—with P(A|B) being back probability, P(B|A) being the likelihood, P(A) is a class prior probability, and P(B) the marker prior probability.

Figure 2.   Naïve Bayes classifier.

A segment of this current reality models is:

- Decision Tree Naive Bayes classification
- Describe a report regarding advancement or administrative issues.
- Used for face affirmation programming

4.3   *Linear regression*

Linear regression is likely the most popular ML algorithm. Linear regression finds a line that best fits a scattered data point on a graph. A direct fall away from the certainty can be thought of as the assignment of fitting a linear line by an immense measure of center interests. There are particular potential techniques to perform or execute this, and "standard least squares" structure goes to these lines—draw a line, and sooner or later for the total of the server farms, calculate the upright segment in the middle of the point and the line, and union these up (Witten 2013).

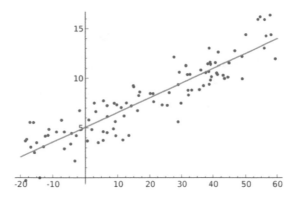

Figure 3.   Linear regression.

4.4   *Logistic regression*

Logistic regression is similar to linear regression, but it is suitable when the out-turn binary vital backslide is an unbelievable genuine strategy for showing a binomial outcome within any event one illustrative component. It measures the association between the all outward factor and in any event one self-governing variable by Ordinary Least Squares Regression assessing probabilities using a vital limit, which is the all-out determined course (Shih-wei 2009).

All around, backslides can be used in obvious applications, for instance:

– Credit scoring
– Evaluating the accomplishment paces of publicizing endeavors

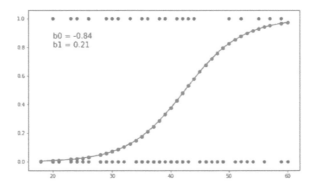

Figure 4.   Logistic regression.

4.5   *Support Vector Machines (SVMs)*

SVM is a supervised method used for classification problems (Breiman 1984). SVM tries to draw two lines between the data points with the largest margin between them. Given a great deal of motivation behind two sorts in N-dimensional spots, SVM makes a (N—1) dimensional hyperplane to detach those concentrations into two social occasions. The most concerning issues that are handled using SVMs (with sensibly changed executions) are demonstrated publicizing, individual join plot affirmation, picture-based sexual direction distinguishing proof, and immense degree picture request.

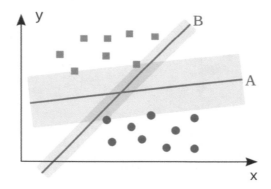

Figure 5. Support vector machines.

4.6 *Ensemble methods*

Random Forest is a very popular ensemble ML algorithm. The underlying idea for this algorithm is that the opinion of many is more accurate than the individual (Kavukcuoglu 2016).

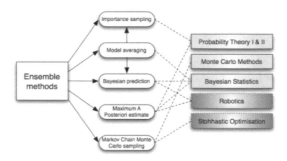

Figure 6. Ensemble methods.

In the Random Forest method, we use a group of decision trees. So how do achievement-gathering systems work and for what reason would they say they are superior to particular models?

– The typical out tendencies.
– They diminish the change.
– They are presumably not going to over-fit.

5 UNSUPERVISED LEARNING ALGORITHMS

Independent learning is useful in circumstances where the test is to discover certain associations in a given unlabeled dataset (things are not preassigned).

5.1 *Clustering algorithms*

It is the endeavor of gathering many articles with the ultimate objective that objects in a comparable social event (gathering) are more similar to one another than to those in various get-togethers (Pedregosa 2011). Clustering analysis can be done on the basis of features where we try to find subgroups of samples based on features or on the basis of samples where we try to find subgroups of features based on samples.

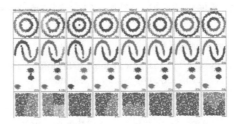

Figure 7.   Clustering analysis.

5.2 *Principal Component Analysis (PCA)*

PCA reduces the dimension of a dataset by squashing it onto a lower-dimensional line, or a hyper-plane/subspace. This retains as much of the original data's salient characteristics as possible. PCA is a true framework that uses a balanced change to change over a ton of view of conceivably associated factors into plenty of estimations of straightly uncorrelated components called head parts (Dietterich 1998).

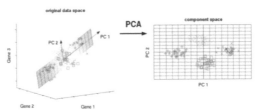

Figure 8.   Principal component analysis.

A portion of the utilization of PCA incorporates pressure, rearranging information for simpler learning, and representation. Notice that space information is significant while picking whether or not to go ahead with PCA.

5.3 *Singular Value Decomposition (SVD)*

In straight polynomial math, SVD is a separation of a certifiable compound cross section. For a provided m * n cross-section M, there is a decay with the ultimate objective that $M = U\Sigma V$, where U and V are entire lattices and Σ is a corner-to-corner structure.

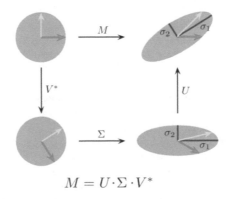

$$M = U \cdot \Sigma \cdot V^*$$

Figure 9.   Singular value decomposition.

In PC perception, the standard feature demand figurines utilized PCA and SVD so as to address features as a quick mix of "eigenfaces", and a brief timeframe later, encourage appearances to characters by methods for essential systems; yet, present-day methodologies are incredibly powerfully refined and diverse, paying little notice to everything relies upon in each functional sense hazy procedures (Hastie 2009).

5.4 Independent Component Analysis (ICA)

Independent Component Analysis (ICA) is a genuine methodology for uncovering secured components that underlie sets of self-emphatic components, estimations, or signs(Singh, S 2014). The ICA depicts a reproductive representation for the saw multicomponent data, which is normally depicted as an immense database of trials. In the model, the information elements are accepted to be a straight mix of some dull dormant components, and the mixing structure is in like way unclear. The inert elements are recognized as non-Gaussian and typically self-administering, and they are known as bits of the monitored data.

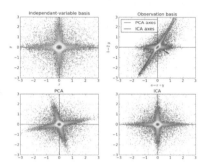

Figure 10.   Independent component analysis.

ICA is identified with PCA; however, it is a considerably more remarkable system that is fit for finding the basic components of sources when these great techniques bomb totally (Singh 2014). Its applications incorporate computerized pictures, record databases, monetary markers, and psychometric estimations. Presently, go forward and use your comprehension of calculations to make artificial intelligence applications that improve encounters for individuals all over the place.

6   CONCLUSIONS

Historically, machines have been employed to lessen the physical work needed to complete business, at any rate at present, with the nearness of ML people endeavor to create machines which are solid similarly as wise and subsequently ML has climbed to change into a locale of study that is ever in the blossom. This paper talks about the three classes of ML—controlled learning, autonomous learning, and fortification learning—and furthermore presents the various applications under them. The main clarification behind ML is to make checks that control the making of sharp machines along these lines decreasing the organization of the item as the machine learns at the chosen time of time to improve its presentation (Kotsiantis 2007). However, numerous degrees of advancements have been achieved in this field even then there exist apparent goals in the illuminating arrangement. It may be helped by incessantly being updated with the latest as learning is a solid procedure.

ML has demonstrated to be immeasurably helpful in a course of action in fields, for example, information mining, electronic reasoning, estimations, PC vision, sensible streamlining, and so on, and its centrality will, all things considered, stay always on the scale (Singh 2014). The businesses of ML are, moreover, ceaseless notwithstanding everything stays a working scope of investigation with tremendous improvement choices and an encouraging future. We conclude our paper by classifying various algorithms in their use case and will review every algorithm that is being surveyed where this paper focuses on the category and use case to which each algorithm belongs.

REFERENCES

Alpaydin, E. (1999). Combined 5x2cv F test for comparing supervised classification learning algorithms. Neural Computation, *11(8):1885–1892.*

Ayon Dey, 2016. *(IJCSIT) International Journal of Computer Science and Information Technologies, Vol. 7 (3), 1174–1179.*

Ball, Gregory R., and Sargur N. Srihari. 2009. Semi Supervised learning for handwriting recognition. Document Analysis and Recognition. *ICDAR'09. 10th International Conference on. IEEE.*

Ball, Gregory R., and Sargur N. Srihari. 2009. Semi Supervised learning for handwriting recognition. *ICDAR'09. 10th International Conference on. IEEE.*

Banaseka Kataka. 2016. A Review of Deep Machine Learning, *International Journal of Engineering Research in Africa.*

M. Bowles, "Machine Learning in Python: Essential Techniques for Predictive Analytics", *John Wiley & Sons Inc., ISBN: 978-1-118-96174-2.*

Chris Bozzuto. February 2002. Machine Learning: Genetic Programming.

Breiman, L., Friedman, J., Stone, C. J., and Olshen, R. A. (1984). Classification and regression trees.

Dietterich, T. G. (1998). Approximate statistical tests for comparing supervised classification learning algorithms. Neural computation, *10(7):1895–1923.*

Hastie, T., Tibshirani, R., and Friedman, J. H. (2009). In The Elements of Statistical Learning: Data Mining, Inference, and Prediction. *Springer, New York.*

Horvitz, Eric. 2006. Machine learning, reasoning, and intelligence in daily life: *Directions and challenges. Proceedings of. Vol. 360.*

James, G., Witten, D., Hastie, T., and Tibshirani, R. (2013). In An Introduction to Statistical Learning: With Applications in R. *Springer, New York.*

K. Kavukcuoglu, M. A. Ranzato, R. Fergus, and Y. Le-Cun, 2009. Learning invariant features through topographic filter maps, in Computer Vision and Pattern Recognition. *IEEE Conference on, 2009, pp. 1605–1612.*

L. P. Kaelbing, M. L. Littman, A. W. Moore, 1996 Reinforcement Learning: A Survey, *Journal of Artificial Intelligence Research, 4, Page 237–285.*

Khan M. A.,(2020), An IoT Framework for Heart Disease Prediction Based on MDCNN Classifier, in IEEE Access, vol. 8, pp. 34717–34727, 2020. DOI: 10.1109/ACCESS.2020.2974687

Khan M.A, and Algarni F., (2020) "A Healthcare Monitoring System for the Diagnosis of Heart Disease in the IoMT Cloud Environment Using MSSO-ANFIS," in IEEE Access, vol. 8, pp. 122259-122269, 2020, doi: 10.1109/ACCESS.2020.3006424.

S.B. Kotsiantis, 2007. Supervised Machine Learning: A Review of Classification Techniques, *Informatica 31, 249–268.*

Li, L. E., Chen, E., Hermann, J., Zhang, P., & Wang, L. (2017). Scaling Machine Learning as a Service. Proceedings of The *3rd International Conference on Predictive Applications and APIs. Proceedings of Machine Learning Research.*

Liao, Shih-wei, et al. 2009. Machine learning-based prefetch optimization for data center applications. *Conference on High Performance Computing Networking, Storage and Analysis. ACM.*

Makeig, S.; Kothe, C.; Mullen, T.; Shamlo, N. B.; Zhang, Z. & Kreutz-Delgado, K. (2012), 'Evolving Signal Processing for Brain-Computer Interfaces.', *IEEE 100 (Centennial-Issue) , 1567–1584.*

Mark J. Weal, Danius T. Michaelides, Kevin Page, David C. De Roure, Fellow, IEEE, Eloise Monger, and Mary Gobbi. April-June 2012., — *Semantic Annotation of Ubiquitous Learning?, Environments IEEE Transactions On Learning Technologies, Vol. 5, No. 2.*

Pedregosa, F., Varoquaux, G., Gramfort, A., Michel, V., Thirion, B., Grisel, O., Blondel, M., Prettenhofer, P., Weiss, R., Dubourg, V., et al. (2011). Scikit-learn: Machine learning in python. *Journal of Machine Learning Research, 12(Oct):2825–2830.*

W. Richert, L. P. Coelho, Building Machine Learning Systems with Python, *Packt Publishing Ltd., ISBN 978-1-78216-140-0.*

L. Rokach, O. Maimon, "Top – Down Induction of Decision Trees Classifiers – A Survey", *IEEE Transactions on Systems.*

Shrivastava, A. (2018). Usage of Machine Learning In Business Industries and Its Significant Impact. *International Journal of Scientific Research in Science and Technology, 4(8).*

Singh, S., Kumar, N. and Kaur, N., 2014. Design Anddevelopment Of Rfid Based Intelligent Security System. *International Journal of Advanced Research in Computer Engineering & Technology (IJARCET) Volume, 3.*

Stern, L. H., Erel, I., Tan, C., & Weisbach, M. S. (2017). Selecting Directors Using Machine Learning.

Talwar, A. and Kumar, Y., 2013. Machine Learning: An artificial intelligence methodology. *International Journal of Engineering and Computer Science, 2, pp. 3400–3404.*

Smart Computing – Khan et al (Eds)
© 2021 Taylor & Francis Group, London, ISBN 978-0-367-76552-1

Collision detection for USVs: An analysis on CV algorithms

Siddharth Kumar, Ram Manoj Potla, Gayathri Ravipati & G. Gopakumar
Amrita Vishwa Vidyapeetham, Amritapuri, Kerala, India

ABSTRACT: Floods are a lethal force of nature that not only cause heavy economical and infrastructural damage but most importantly take away invaluable lives. These floods can last days to weeks during which people in the affected regions get cut off from essential supplies. Rescue teams are deployed to save affected people, and in the process it is highly probable that the team members may lose their lives. We need to have a mode of transport for supplies to reach the flood victims that does not involve sending in human beings to the affected areas. Unmanned surface vehicles (USVs) are used in a wide range of areas where there is a risk to mankind. Since World War II, advancement has been seen in control systems and navigation for USVs, but we are still lacking in terms of the object detection prowess of these vehicles. A USV, armed with object detection capability interfaced with sensor data, has the potential to be the solution to the rescue ops problem. The challenge in this approach, however, would be to deploy computer vision algorithms on resource-constrained devices which would require a lot of optimization for accurate performance. Hence, we propose an analysis to identify the best algorithms for collision detection and design a cost-effective prototyping method for USVs.

1 INTRODUCTION

Floods are a fatal natural calamity that occur very frequently. It is estimated that floods cause more than $40 billion annually in damages (www.nationalgeographic.com). Moreover, floods result in huge human loss in countries like India as they take away hundreds of lives every year. The floods of Kerala in 2018 and 2019 alone took 584 lives. In the worldwide statistics, it was found that floods were responsible for the loss of 2.3 billion lives.

The reason behind such a high number of casualties is the fact that people are isolated from essential resources and as a result lose access to drinkable water, food, and other essentials. Flood-affected areas are contaminated with hazardous materials like sharp debris, untreated sewage, mud, etc., making the task of delivering supplies dangerous. Rescue operators use motor-powered boats, row boats, helicopters, etc. to transport and deliver supplies and even though they are effective, in most cases, harsh climatic conditions can limit their capability and also put the lives of the rescue operators at risk. After witnessing the struggles of people in Kerala in 208 and 2019, it is evident that there is a requirement for feasible and optimal technology-based solutions.

Unmanned Surface Vessels (USVs) are being used in the maritime industry as they serve the purpose and also have numerous advantages, e.g., they cut costs, increase efficiency, and enhance safety. In the future, we can expect the USVs to take charge of jobs that are dangerous to mankind, while humans remain in the operational loop for the majority of operations. There are two general classes of unmanned mobile vehicles: autonomous and teleoperated. The teleoperated class has USVs that can be remotely controlled by humans. An autonomous or unmanned surface vehicle is a boat that is operated without any crew on the surface of the water. Since USVs are generic platforms and are multi-purpose vehicles, they may be designed to be equipped with different types of sensors to suit different tasks. However, all of them follow the same architecture in terms of state transition as described in Figure 1.

DOI 10.1201/9781003167488-33

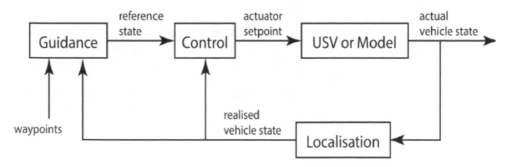

Figure 1.   Architecture of USV.

These USVs can truly navigate through unknown waters only when they are capable of having an accurate estimate of the obstacles that surround them and maybe approaching at various speeds. The need for these boats to have "vision: is paramount if they are to stand any chance at being able to perform rescue operations with utmost perfection without risking any human lives.

The current robust solutions for USVs are mostly used for oceanographic research and other marine operations. They make use of radar systems, infrared and other types of cameras and long-range communication., and tracking systems. Therefore, they are expensive and thus unaffordable to be deployed everywhere. This is the motivation behind the idea of designing a low-cost surface watercraft with collision detection capability, which can support flood relief operations. In order to integrate collision detection functionality, we will have to use cameras on-board in order to gain real-time footage of the movement of the boat. Coupled with data from peripheral sensors that are quite common in new age USVs it is possible for these boats to actively classify obstacles in its path. Once the classification is successful the resulting data can be used to reconfigure the course to destination in real-time avoiding any crashes in turbulent waters. In order to make this possible, we need to analyze various object detection models to understand which would be the best for the said use case.

The main challenge that arises is the fact that all of these object detection algorithms are resource-intensive. Our aim is to develop a cost-effective solution for prototyping the USVs. Therefore, we decided to optimize these algorithms to give peak performance even in resource-constrained devices. For this purpose, we have chosen a Raspberry-PI3 as the master device that will be used on the boat. We've chosen this device due to its low cost and 1 GHz processor that is powerful enough to process real-time data from a camera. However, it must be noted that an Internet of Things (IoT) system with autonomous navigation capability will have to rely on some kind of sensor for getting environmental awareness. If these sensors are faulty then the entire system will be in jeopardy.

In conclusion, with this project we aim to achieve the following goals. The primary goal is to analyze different object detection algorithms to identify the best classification functionality that can efficiently mark objects large enough to obstruct the path of the USV and so we will compare and contrast the performances of each of these algorithms and present it as a case study. The secondary goal is to design a proof of concept for an IoT system for a surface watercraft whose functionality is to assist during flood relief operations. We will identify the peripheral devices that will be required to take the prototype into production.

2   RELATED WORKS

A lot of research has been conducted on USVs for the needs of monitoring construction of marine structures, aiding global positioning systems (GPS) confusion, defense, and general robotics research. As per the stats over the last 27 years, it is found that there is an initiative for the development of USVs by both public and private sectors. MIT had created the very first USV named ARTEMIS back in 1993. ARTEMIS (Michael et al. 2013) was accustomed to collecting simple bathymetric data within the river in Boston. This was followed by a replacement USV for Autonomous Coastal Exploration developed during 1996 and 1997 to continue with the automated bathymetry experiments begun with ARTEMIS. By 2000, lots of modifications were made and after rigorous design iterations it had been renamed to AutoCat. These contributions have stimulated the researchers working for the same motive.

In the past decade, we have observed accelerated development during this field. The increase in popularity of machine learning and computer vision techniques has resulted in an exceeding pivot of sorts for USVs. A USV requires the flexibility to identify obstacles from in and around to far-sighted obstacles. Operation in shallow waters, as would be the case during floods, curbs the scale of USV and stops the utilization of auxiliary stabilizers. This puts additional limitations on the burden, energy utilization sensor types, and its positioning. The cost, weight, power efficiency, and wide field of view coverage of cameras are making it the go-to cost-effective sensor for USVs on a lower budget.

Unmanned ground vehicle (UGVs) have addressed the problem of obstacle detection previously. The UGV approach depends on ground plane estimation from range sensors. However, in recent years there has been some progress within the research of object detection in USVs. Rankin and Matthies (2010) propose a selected water body detector in wide-open areas from a UGV employing a monocular color camera. Their detector assumes that, in an undisturbed water surface, a change in saturation to brightness ratio across a water body from the resulting edge is uniform and distinct from other terrain types. They apply several ad-hoc processing steps to gradually grow the water regions for the initial candidates and apply a sequence of pre-set thresholds to get rid of spurious false detections of water pools. However, their method relies on the undistributed water surface assumptions, which is violated in coastal and open water applications.

Multiple unsupervised segmentation methodologies have been proposed in the literature. Recently, Alpert et al. (2012) proposed a way that begins from a pixel level and builds the visually homogeneous regions gradually making use of agglomerative clustering. They attained magnificent outcomes on a segmentation dataset containing objects that occupied a big portion of the picture. Since their algorithm incrementally merges regions, it's very slow for real-time applications even with lower resolution images, an alternative to start outing the segmentation from pixel level is to begin with an over segmented image following which these pixels can be grouped into superpixels (Ren and Malik 2003). Li et al. (2012) proposed a segmentation algorithm that uses multiple super-pixel over-segmentations and merges their result by a bipartite graph partitioning to attain state of the art results on a customary segmentation dataset. But there is no information related to segmentation on edge cases.

3 FRAMEWORK

As mentioned in the problem definition, our primary goal is to develop an autonomous surface vehicle that can act as a carrier of essentials in flooded regions while also being a reconnaissance tool. To achieve this goal, we have designed an Autonomous Navigation and Collision Detection System (ANCDS). This system allows the vehicle to detect objects in real time and mark the objects that could obstruct its path. The various features of this system are discussed in this chapter.

3.1 *Dataset*

Our dataset is a collection of videos of water bodies and obstacles in it. This data set is known as Marine Obstacle Dataset Detection (MODD). Our aim is to develop a USV that has a robust methodology for collision detection in flooded regions. This data set consists of all the scenarios that a USV could face in real-time environments. (Matej et al. 2015) has 12 videos in marine environments that are used as the training set. Videos are approximately 10 sec in length. To train our model, each video is split into 370 frames on average generating 4442 images. In the 12 videos,

Figure 2.   Sample images from the MODD dataset.

we have annotated all the videos in the training set following which we trained our model on this dataset. We also have four additional videos that were similarly split into frames and are used as test data. Figure 2 is a collection of some images of our dataset.

The frames of the videos in the dataset cover a wide range of angles a watercraft could encounter when en-route to a destination. In a flood scenario, the challenge would be to accurately identify the boundaries of the flooded region so as to have the ability to classify the obstacles in the right buckets. The MODD dataset shows it covers all possibilities of obstacle approach and shoreline proximity while also having frames of various obstacles ranging from boats to human beings in the water. Thus, our data set covers all the test scenarios that are required for a watercraft to navigate and allows us to test the algorithms with minimal bias.

3.2   *Proposed method*

After going through the related work that has been done on USVs in the past, we identified three common issues:

1. Lack of use of machine learning-based techniques in object detection,
2. The high cost of prototype development,
3. Lack of augmentation of sensor data with camera feed for object identification.

In order to overcome these challenges, we are interested in finding the ideal model that can be used for efficiently classifying objects in real time. To develop a cost-efficient model, we decided to build our architecture centered around a Raspberry PI-3 due to its exceptional processing power even though it is a constrained edge device. Since our solution is based on edge computing it brings forth a new challenge. Performing object classification on resource-constrained devices is a computationally expensive task considering the classification needs to occur in real time and a glitch during execution could be fatal in our use case. So, we are going to analyze the best object classification algorithms and, first, optimize them to efficiently run on a Raspberry-PI 3 following which we are going to rank based on four parameters:

1. Execution time
2. Precision of prediction
3. Model size
4. RAM usage

We will be analyzing the following models in the upcoming sections:

1. Semantic Segmentation
2. ImageAI
3. YOLO
4. EMI-RNN

As mentioned in Section 3.1, the MODD dataset will be used for the analysis and five cross-validation will be followed for testing to ensure the accuracy of the results. We have discussed in detail on design of our prototype in Section 4

3.2.1 Semantic segmentation

Semantic segmentation is used to locate multiple objects in the image and classify them by drawing bounding boxes around the objects found. Classification of the image is done into four major categories: sky, shore, sea, and any object in the sea. In semantic segmentation, each and every pixel of the image is assigned with a class index. So, the model can give the exact dimension of every object in the image, provided the segmentation is correct. There are different ways to perform it. U-net is a fully convolutional network that can be used in segmentation. This model uses convolutional, max-pooling, upsampling, and concatenate layers. In our case, initially, the input image runs through a few convolutional layers, the image gets convoluted with a kernel and after each convolution, max-pooling also takes place and reduces the image dimensions by half.

$$n_{out} = \left\lfloor \frac{n_{in} + 2p - k}{s} \right\rfloor + 1$$

n_{in}: number of input features
n_{out}: number of output features
k: convolution kernel size
p: convolution padding size
s: convolution stride size

Figure 3.   Equation for feature extraction.

After executing four convolutional layers. Most of the data related to the existence of objects in image is identified. But the spatial information, i.e., the object's location in the frame, is not calculated. Hence, the up-sampling along with merge is performed to retain the original image and get the complete information about it.

In the above model, altogether there are ten convolutional layers. The model is trained upon the MODD dataset instead of using the pre-trained models. Rectified linear activation function is implemented to extract various features from the given image. ReLu's definition is:

$$f(x) = alpha * x for x < 0, f(x) = x for x >= 0 \tag{1}$$

In our case, Unet model worked with efficiency because it is able to understand each pixel very well and classify it better when compared to other ones due to its U-shaped architecture (Olaf et al. 2015). Once the model is constructed, videos are divided into different frames, where the outcome is around 6000 images. Out of which, approximately 4000 are used for training, resulting in an accuracy of 82.12%. The semantic segmentation needs the dataset in such a way that each and every pixel needs to be annotated for the best results. As the annotations made in the dataset are approximated as boxes around objects, the accuracy is affected because of it. Implementing the same model, by converting images to grayscale format also didn't give better accuracy.

3.2.2 *Object detection with ImageAI*

Object detection with ImageAI helps to identify and track the objects that are present in the videos. ImageAI is the python library used to detect the objects. It provides simple and powerful approaches to training our own model using YOLO architecture on any set of images. This is done by using a pre-trained RetinaNet model, however this did not give promising results as the model is unable to detect the objects in images because we have pre-trained the model using the COCO dataset. The main aim of trying this out is to test if there are any models that could successfully detect the objects instead of training again on the dataset. The model is tested on the MODD dataset and accuracy is calculated.

3.2.3 *YOLO*

YOLO is an abbreviation for "You only look once." It is one of the best algorithms for image

Detection; it only looks through the entire image once and detects the image. Similar to ImageAI, YOLO is also on some predefined labels. YOLO first divides the entire image into segments and applies the algorithm on different segments to identify the objects.

Finally, it uses logistic regression to classify the objects. It uses a neural network for the detection of objects. YOLO is trained on the MODD dataset but it didn't give promising results when compared to ImageAI. Instead of running the model with predefined labels, we applied transfer learning with YOLO. As part of transfer learning, the model is trained on our dataset, which replaces all the last level nodes, i.e., instead of the predefined labels; we can specify our own classes as labels.

YOLO is used to identify small and large objects, so training is done with two classes. The results of the model are good comparatively and it could predict the objects in the image within a very less time. But the checkpoint size is big. For a model to work on edge devices the size is one of the main criteria. Even though YOLO could yield better results, it could not classify an object clearly. It is not able to differentiate the sea from the shore in certain instances. One of the most important things while building a USV is that there needs to be a distinction between the surroundings and sea so that the boat does not cross the sea boundary. All these failures don't make YOLO pertinent for our problem statement.

3.2.4 *EMI–RNN*

Don et al. (2018) proposed an exceptionally out-of-the-box mechanism for multiple instance learning problems to perform efficient classification in IoT devices that do not have high computing prowess. EMI–RNN is used to first identify boundaries between classes. The algorithms ability to identify class signatures early on, resulted in object identification in 15 ms. Window length is taken as 1/300 the size of the video and then divided the image into bags of overlapping n/300 windows (instances/frame) where n is the length of the frame. Following which, we isolated the instances based on identified signatures and relabeled the instances for training. The algorithm exploits the temporal structure of time series data and it removes common prefixes making early prediction effective.

> Algorithm:
> *1. Assign labels (Zi, yi), s. t. yi = yi, ∀τ*
> *2. Train classifier f on this mislabeled data.*   (2)
> *3. Score(si)=j=si f t (Z ij) and pick argmax si Score(si).*
> *4. Update labels. Repeat with new labels.*

We had picked EMI–RNN because of its exceptional results when used to classify numbers on the MNIST dataset. It outperformed all other algorithms with an execution time of 6.58 ms and an accuracy of 92.61%. However, we weren't able to test its performance on the MODD dataset due to technical difficulties interfacing the provided boundary box annotations to our model to give the desired results. Although in the time frame of the research we conducted there were some unknowns in the implementation methodology that we experimented with. Since then Microsoft research has open sourced new resources regarding the implementation of EMI–RNN which will be useful in our future works where we can qualitatively analyze EMI–RNN on the MODD dataset.

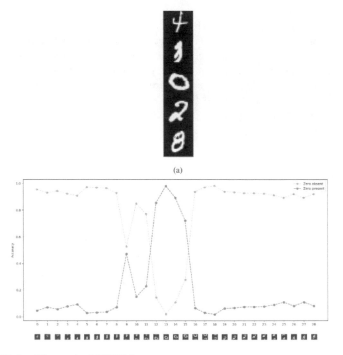

(a)

Figure 4. The "0" classifier on the MNIST dataset.

In theory, after observing the performance of the algorithm on the MNIST dataset we have reason to believe it has the potential to outperform other algorithms. So, it may be possible to observe higher precision based on testing methodology. We would like to explore this aspect in future works. Figure 4 illustrates EMI–RNN identifying if a "0" exists in a strip of numbers or not:

When the window containing pixels of zero is in the frame, we observe that the classification accuracy rises until all the pixels of class zero are in the frame. At this point, the confidence peaks, and the number is said to have been classified. Following this, the class signature moves out of the frame with each passing frame, and the accuracy slumps.

4 PROTOTYPE DESIGN

Considering all the specifications and the goals that we had envisioned, we have built innovative system designs for the watercraft. Figure 5 shows the block diagram. The main aspects of the system are discussed in this chapter. Our aim is to create a design of the prototype that can be used for testing purposes as a proof of concept. Following successful tests, the boat can be scaled up to real boats that can be augmented with sensors that are discussed in this section. This methodology proves to be an achievable and optimal one.

4.1 *Physical structural model*

A spherical design has been adapted for the watercraft. Two propellers are joined to the diagonally opposite sides of the sphere slightly above the equator. The watercraft can rotate in both clockwise and anticlockwise directions. It can move in all the six directions by varying the individual propeller's speed. The on-board electronics are positioned inside the hull and space is provided for the supplies. The ultrasonic sensors are placed outside the hull.

4.2 Hardware components

The cost and performance of the prototype depends on the components that are used in building it. Support for real-time computing in the hardware is essential due to the real-time constraints of all the subprocesses in our system. Due to this, costly high-performance hardware becomes a need. But the objective of the system is to benefit the masses and that will not be possible if the required components are expensive. So, a trade-off needs to be made between performance and cost. Additionally, an energy-efficient portable power source is required to get a long runtime for the system. Due to these constraints, we opted for the following components for the system.

1. **Microcontroller:** A Raspberry PI 3. It is based on a high-performance 4x ARM Cortex 1.2 GHz processor and 1 GB RAM. This makes it capable of executing processes with real-time constraints. The maximum current drawn is around 60 mA, making it suitable for low power applications. Our design uses two of them in a Master–Slave configuration, for implementing the various functionalities of the system.
2. **Wireless Transceiver:** Texas Instruments CC3100. It is a low-power WiFi module that can be easily integrated with the Raspberry-PI3 microcontroller.
3. **Propellers:** 5V Brushless Direct Current (BLDC) electric motor.
4. **Motor Driver:** L298 2A. It is a dual full-bridge driver and can supply a maximum output voltage of 46 V.
5. **Ultrasonic Sensor:** HC-SR04. It is a low-cost ultrasonic sensor. It has a range of about 4 m and an accuracy of 3 mm.
6. **GPS Module:** Ublox NEO – 6M. It is a low-power, high-performance GPS module.
7. **Magnetometer:** Honeywell HMC5883L. It is a low-cost magnetometer with an accuracy of $1-2°$.
8. **Camera:** Raspberry Pi camera model V2 is a high-quality 8-megapixel Sony IMX219 image sensor custom designed add-on board for Raspberry Pi, featuring a fixed focus lens. It's capable of 3280×2464 pixel static images, and also supports 1080p30, 720p60, and 640x480p60/90 video.

4.3 Hardware interfacing

All the hardware modules being assembled have different ways of interfacing with the microcontroller. So, we have documented each methodology for microcontroller interfacing between the required pairs as follows.

1. **Master–Slave microcontroller:** Out of the various methods used for interfacing two microcontrollers, we picked Synchronous Serial Interface (SSI) as it is better suited for a master–slave configuration. This interface provides a synchronized two-way communication between the connected devices. The clock signal generated by the master device is responsible for synchronization in the system which enables command and control over the communication channel.
2. **Wireless transceiver with master microcontroller:** Like the microcontroller, the wireless transceiver also supports both UART and SSI. For the reasons mentioned above, it is preferable to use the SSI.
3. **Propellers with motor driver:** There are two output ports in order to control the propellers. There is no need for any special interfacing techniques as the motors can be directly connected to the ports.
4. **Motor driver with master microcontroller:** Pulse width modulation (PWM) ports enable control over the propeller speed. So, the motor driver is interfaced with PWM ports of the master microcontroller.
5. **Ultrasonic sensor with slave microcontroller:** Every time the ultrasonic sensor senses a reflected sound wave it generates an output signal at its Echo pin. We connect this pin directly to

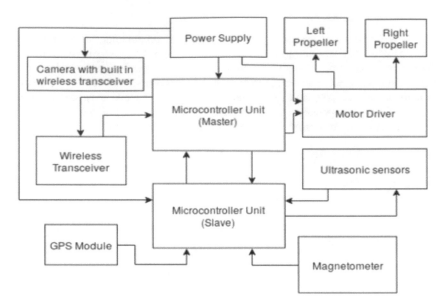

Figure 5. Prototype design.

an interruptible timer in order to reduce error in succeeding calculations. This helps in the estimation of time of each event accurately. The microcontroller has more than six General-Purpose Timers (GPTMs) with Input Edge-Time mode. In Input Edge-Time mode, the system can detect the time of rising edges with good precision.

6. **GPS sensor with slave microcontroller:** Unlike other sensors being used, the GPS sensor only supports the UART mode of communication.

7. **Magnetometer with slave microcontroller:** The magnetometer uses a synchronous serial-based communication protocol similar to the SSI. It is called the I-squared C (I2C) communication protocol. I2C is the only mode of communication offered by this module.

5 RESULTS AND DISCUSSION

5.1 *Qualitative analysis*

- In imageAI, a predefined retina-net model is used. It is pre-trained upon the COCO dataset. So, it cannot identify all the objects in the dataset. It can only identify a few ships. It cannot identify other small objects and any background. See Figure 6.
- In the case of YOLO, transfer learning has been done on the current dataset until 1,000 check-points. So, it could mostly identify large and small objects. But it cannot identify the reachable extent on the sea (i.e., it cannot segregate the sea with other backgrounds). There can be a situation where there are no objects in the sea but there is a large landmass on the way. So, the USV needs to know whether it could go in the current direction or the direction needs to be changed. See Figure 7.
- In the case of semantic segmentation, each pixel is assigned to a class. It could identify all the different objects in the frame. So, it could segregate the sea from the background and also be able to identify objects in the sea. Hence, it is better compared to other ones.
- The algorithms YOLO and ImageAI (with RetinaNet model) suffered to give higher precision and also took more time to execute on the Raspberry-PI3. The model size is also high in the case of these algorithms.

Figure 6.   Output of ImageAI.

Figure 7.   Output of YOLO.

5.2   *Quantitative analysis*

- To effectively analyze the performance of the above-mentioned algorithms we need to observe each algorithm's results in terms of the four set metrics. The aim is to produce an optimal performance on each metric. For optimal real-time performance, the algorithm will have to maximize accuracy and minimize the following three metrics. We will not be considering EMI–RNN in this evaluation since the data is from tests performed on the MNIST dataset. However, we have included its empirical data to point to its potential in our use case.
- Based on the observations from Table 1, we can conclude that semantic segmentation could yield a better result compared to the other ones.
- All of the above algorithms take less time, but out of all semantic segmentation 80 ms takes the least. Humans take around 390–600 ms to detect and react to an obstacle which implies the algorithm is much faster in comparison (news.mit.edu).

Figure 8.   Output of semantic segmentation.

Table 1.   Empirical data.

Algorithm	Accuracy	Execution time on Raspberry-PI 3	Model/ Checkpoint Size	RSS (Resident Set Size)
Semantic Segmentation	82.12%	80 ms	13 MB	55 MB
YOLO	50.23%	1.08s	180 MB	62 MB
ImageAI	40.65%	1.24 s	146 MB	127 MB
EMI-RNN (On MNIST)	92.61%	15 ms	23.4 KB	42 MB

- The models are stored in the form of.h5 files. The output model generated for semantic segmentation is around 13 MB which is very less compared to the other ones.
- Finally, coming to the RAM, we observe that the RAM usage is the least for semantic segmentation which proves that semantic segmentation is giving the most optimal solution based on the set metrics.

6   CONCLUSION

As rescue operations involve a lot of risks, technology should drive the humans in these scenarios. We have reached our goal by building an adaptive semantic segmentation model for the visual perception of the USV autonomous navigation. The semantic segmentation algorithm turns out to be the best algorithm for marine object detection based on our set metrics.

With this idea set as our goal, we proposed our system model to meet all our requirements. The cost of the proposed system model is under $500 which happens to be relatively cost-effective in comparison to the existing solutions. Like any other computer vision model, our model too gives sub-optimal performance because it has been trained on a small dataset. Better results can be achieved gradually over multiple rounds of self-training. Our experiments have shown that the proposed methodology enables our solution to be a multi-purpose tool because it has been trained on videos of mobile surface vehicles and covers various real-world scenarios.

However, one drawback could be that it has been trained on videos in daylight and may not perform as well in low light conditions. This is an aspect of the project we would like to work on in the future. Apart from these, we would also need to look at EMI–RNN with the knowledge that has recently come to light which might enable us to have a working model on the MODD dataset and if it can generate similar results as it did on MNIST it would be our go-to model for deployment. We have described a proof of concept of the IoT system. We aspire to develop a deployable version of the proposed prototype.

REFERENCES

A, Rankin. L, Matthies. 2010. "Daytime water detection based on color variation ". Int. Conf.Intell.Robots And Systems.

Benjamin, Drayer. Thomas, Brox. 2016. "Object Detection, Tracking, and Motion Segmentation for Object-level Video Segmentation". Arxiv.

Bharath, Hariharan. Pablo, Arbelaez. Ross, Girshick. Jitendra, Malik. 2014. "Simultaneous Detection and Segmentation". ECCV

Cihang, Xie. Jianyu, Wang. Zhishuai, Zhang. Yuyin, Zhou. Lingxi, Xie.Alan, Yuille. 2017. "Adversarial Examples for Semantic Segmentation and Object Detection". The IEEE International Conference on Computer Vision (ICCV).

CP, Prathibhamol. KV, Jyothy. B, Noora. 2016. "Multi label classification based on logistic regression (MLC-LR)". IEEE

Don, Kurian, Dennis. Chirag, Pabbaraju. Harsha, Vardhan, Simhadri. Prateek, Jain. 2018. "Multiple Instance Learning for Efficient Sequential Data Classification on Resource-constrained Devices.". NIPS

http://news.mit.edu/2019/how-fast-humans-react-car-hazards-0807

https://www.nationalgeographic.com/environment/natural-disasters/floods/

Jing, Tao. Hongbo, Wang. Xinyu, Zhang. Xiaoyu, Li. Huawei, Yang. 2018. "An object detection system based on YOLO in traffic scene". IEEE

M, Alpert. S, Galun. R, Basri. A, Brandt. 2012. "Image segmentation by probabilistic bottom-up aggregation and cue integration". CVPR.

Matej, Kristan. Vildana, Sulic. Stanislav, Kovacic. Janez, Pers. 2015. "Fast image-based obstacle detection from unmanned surface vehicles". IEEE

Michael, Blaich. Stefan, Wirtensohn. Markus, Oswald. Oliver, Hamburger. Johannes, Reuter. 2013. "Design of a Twin Hull Based USV with Enhanced Maneuverability". IFAC.

Mohammad, Javad, Shafiee. Brendan, Chywl. Francis, Li. Alexander, Wong. 2017. "Fast YOLO: A Fast You Only Look Once System for Real-time Embedded Object Detection in Video". Arxiv.

N, Deepika. VV, Sajith, Variyar. 2017. "Obstacle classification and detection for vision based navigation for autonomous driving". IEEE

Neena, Aloysius. M, Geetha. 2017. "A review on deep convolutional neural networks". IEEE

Olaf, Ronneberger. Philipp, Fischer. Thomas, Brox. 2015 "U-Net: Convolutional Networks for Biomedical Image Segmentation". Springer

Ross, Girshick. Jeff, Donahue. Trevor, Darrell. Jitendra, Malik. 2014. "Rich Feature Hierarchies for Accurate Object Detection and Semantic Segmentation". The IEEE Conference on Computer Vision and Pattern Recognition (CVPR).

Ross, Girshick. Jeff, Donahue. Trevor, Darrell. Jitendra, Malik. 2016 "Convolutional Networks for Accurate Object Detection and Segmentation". 'IEEE Transactions on Pattern Analysis and Machine Intelligence'.

X, Ren. J, Malik. 2003. "Learning a classification model for segmentation,". ICCV.

Xiang, Zhan. Wei, Yang. Xiaolin, Tang. Jie, Liu. 2018. "A Fast Learning Method for Accurate and Robust Lane Detection Using Two-Stage Feature Extraction with YOLO v3". MDPI

Z, Li. XM, Wu. SF, Chang. 2012."Segmentation using superpixels: A bipartite graph partitioning approach". CVPR.

Smart Computing – Khan et al (Eds)
© *2021 Taylor & Francis Group, London, ISBN 978-0-367-76552-1*

Brain tumor detection & segmented classification of CT-scan and MRI image

Sanjay Kumar, J.N. Singh & Naresh Kumar
School of Computer Science & Engineering, Galgotias University, Gr. Noida (U.P), India

ABSTRACT: Medical imaging is one field whose importance is growing as there is a rise in demand for automatic, quick, and effective diagnosis to provide imaging capabilities and quality higher compared to the human eyes. Brain tumors attributed as the second biggest cause of deaths due to cancer-related ailments in males aging between 20 and 39 and also the fifth large case in the case cancer caused deaths in women aged in the same range. Brain tumors induce a lot of pain resulting in numerous diseases unless cure properly. A part of the treatment of tumors is to diagnose it. Proper and timely identification of the tumors is in diagnosing benign and malignant type tumors. The main problem leading to an increase in cancer affected people around the globe is the ignorant behavior towards treating the rumor in its initial phases. Our paper discusses an algorithm that tells the patient details regarding the based on simple techniques of image processing. The involves noise removal, image sharpening along with some morphological functions, by dilution and erosion to get the background. The negative of the background-subtracted from various image sets resulting in an extracted image of the Brain tumor. The plot of contour versus c-label of growth and the border gives all the in order relating to the tumors further are useful to visualize and diagnose. The process identifies the shape, orientation, and dimensions of the brain tumor. Based on the doctors as well as the Patients can get an idea of how serious is the brain tumor is. They also get a color labeled having different levels of elevation show the seriousness of the brain tumor.

1 INTRODUCTION

Unusual growth of cells inside the spinal canal or the brain tumor is a brain tumor. Few tumors also turn out to be cancerous so that it is best to detect and cure the tumors before it is too late. The actual causes of a brain tumor cannot be unascertained is the symptoms are defined clearly those the patient might be suffering from brain tumors without even having any idea of the danger (Kumar 2019). The brain tumors do not necessarily always contain cancerous cells that may contain cancerous cells or not containing any cancerous cells.

The tumor appears like a solid mass on diagnosing it through medical imaging techniques. The brain tumors categorized into two types of name most important intellect growth and metastatic brain growth.

Most intelligence growth can identify as a condition in which a tumor develops inside the intelligence and tends to wait to present itself metastatic common sense tumors can be defined as the tumors developing in the body elsewhere and further spreading itself through the brain. The prevalent symptoms of brain tumors can range from suffering headaches to suffering from nausea and vomiting, also suffering from difficulty in walking or balancing. Brain tumor detection can be done with the help of a few diagnostic imaging modalities like CT scans and MRI scans (Kumar 2018). Both modalities are advantageous in detecting the tumors depending on the type of location and identifying the whole purpose of the required examination. In this paper, we have exerted on preferring CT images for use as they are easier to examine giving out precise calcification and also the accurate locations of the foreign mass. The CT images acquired from the CT tackle generate a two-dimensional cross-section of the brain. However acquire images of the brain could not extract

DOI 10.1201/9781003167488-34

the image of the tumor (Kumar 2018). Therefore, image processing techniques are required for determining the severity of the tumors depending on their sizes.

The reason for select CT imagery winning MRI images is as follow:

- CT is an earlier alternative as compared to MRI, thus making it more preferred choice in emergency situations such as trauma and neurological emergencies.
- CT is an economical and cheaper alternative compared to MRI.
- Unlike MRI, CT be fewer responsive if a enduring moves at the time of examination.
- The imaging process is very rapid, so CT is the easier to carry out on patients or serious weighted patient.
- CT poses no risks for patients having implanted medical devices like pacemakers or other vascular chips and simulators within them.

We focus on extraction of tumor from CT brain image and representing it in simpler forms which is understandable by everyone. Humans have a tendency to recognize and analyze colored images more effectively as compared to black and white images, thus here brain images are being represented by colored images by us to enable better understanding of the representation by the patient and medical personnel (Usman & Rajpoot 2017). The curve scheme and c-label plot of growth along with its border areas has been designed and programmed for giving a 3D visualization of the 2D image by representing in varying colors based on different intensity level

2 RELATED WORKS

In contrast to works in previous years, we have seen a major deviation of image representation globally, such as colored histograms, shape descriptors, and local features and descriptors like salient points, regional features, spatial feature models, and shape characterizations which are robust and local.

According to the authors Semantic Segmentation Using Deep Learning for Brain Tumor MRI via Fully Convolution Neural Networks. The benign growth consisting of cancerous cells can also grow abnormally. MRI is one tumor that keeps growing and rapidly and encroach the brain and also threatens life. It is commonly referred to as an intelligence tumor as the hateful consists of the cell is cancerous and capable of destroying nearby cells. Brain tumor image segmentation and identification of brain growth using FFT techniques of MRI images", published in "ACEEE International Journal on Communication, Vol. 02" conventionally, the wits tumor can be defined as a growth including neoplasm's which originate from the parenchyma of the brain also as of meanings and also the tumor in pituitary glands or from the structures indirectly affecting the tissues of the brain (Kumar 2020).

However, the majority of the techniques used are base on MRI modality rather than CT images due to the high-resolution image generated in MRI. Tumor image of the human body through CT helps doctors to detect illnesses such as brain tumors, colon cancer, etc… However, there are still some shortcomings as many times it is difficult to generate the key features of body parts in the images due to the limitations by image processing levels and the doctor's experience (Havaei et al. 2017).

3 OBJECTIVE PROBLEM DESCRIPTIONS

This paper aims to identify tumors in brain CT images. The key purpose of detecting brain tumors is providing help for clinical diagnosis. We aim to develop and impart an algorithm that detects and warrants the actual tumor presence. It is a foolproof method of detecting tumors developed by summating several techniques of CT brain images. The process utilizes various features such as filtering, adjusting contrast, image negation, subtracting image, dilation, erosion, and also creating an outline of the tumor (Shin et al. 2016). The project focuses on generating CT brain images in a simple and humanly understandable form. Humans tend to recognize and analyze colored images more effectively as compared to black and white brain images, thus here's brain images are being

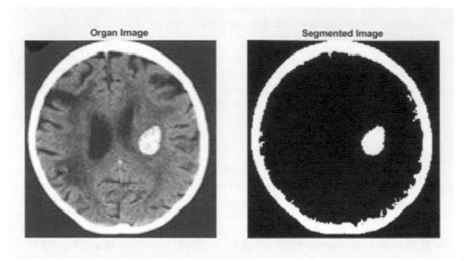

Figure 1. Organ image & segmented image.

represented by colored images by us to enable a better understanding of the representation by the patient and medical staff.

Our work aims to present necessary information in a simple form identifiable by the users, primarily the medical team performing the treatment of the patient (Long et al. 2015). With this paper, we aim to develop and impart an algorithm that results in extracting the cancer image from an MRI image. The resulting picture gives information like shape, orientation and dimensions of the tumor and plot of the contour versus c-label plot of a tumor and the boundary data give all the information relating to the tumors which further are useful to visualize and diagnose providing a base for the whole remedial process (Menze et al. 2014). Brain tumors along with its frontier provide information for the understanding of medical staff as humans recognize and analyze images effectively by different colors giving a 3D visualization of the 2D image by representing in different colors for different intensity levels.

4 PROPOSED METHOD

In this research paper we are collect brain tumor MRI and CT-scan Data sets and after that k-mean algorithm apply on the MRI & CT images for detection noise and tumor situation accurate situated.

4.1 *Noise removal*

Collared images of grayscale images might be the images that have inputted The first step, the image converted into a grayscale format image (Xiao et al. 2016). When it is the image converted to a grayscale image, the objective is filtering the image to make it sharp by eliminating any noise present. The algorithm applies to the unship filtering of the special filters sharpening by removing fewer intensity values.

4.2 *Erosion and dilation*

In this succession process of pre-processing, we have to predict the background. For doing so, some morphological operations are used, namely erosion and dilation. High erosions and lower dilation results in distorted skull bone images. This can be accomplished by keeping the structural radius of the eroding element greater than the dilating structural elements. The fundamental elements we utilize are a diamond.

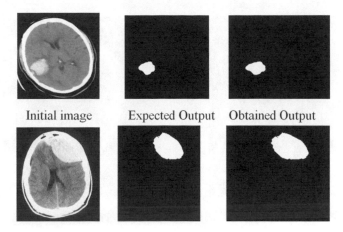

Initial image   Expected Output   Obtained Output

Figure 2.   Initial image & obtained output.

4,3   *Subtraction*

When we subtract the background and all negatives present in the background in the eroded image results into images having presence and also the absence of tumors (Xiao et al. 2016). The images consistboiundary of the skull and the region of tumors making them imperfect for further use.

4.4   *Threshold & test case*

The next task in the proposed algorithm is using Otsu's method for calculating image thresholds globally, which selects threshold to minimize intra group of students discrepancy between the white and also the black pixels giving us a clearer image of a region of cancer (Havaei et al., 2017).

4.5   *Curve and C-label*

Curvature over the entire purpose is steady is defined as the contour. The line of countries junction of equally elevated points above a certain level. The various levels are depicted using varying colored boundaries (Pereira et al. 2016). The contour-f function provides a better system view at each level by differing colors. C-label connections stature labels to 2Dimansion plot, thus giving an improved imminent into the picture (Long et al. 2015).

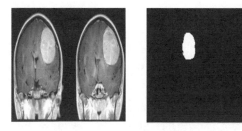

Figure 3.   Interface design & test case.

5   RESULTS

The focus of this paper is to detect and then create visuals of the tumor present within the brain through the CT images. Through imparting the model based on the architecture we have proposed,

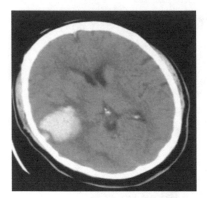
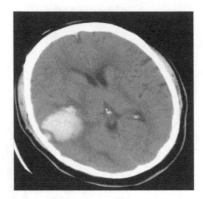

Figure 4.   Original image.

Figure 5.   Pre-processed image.

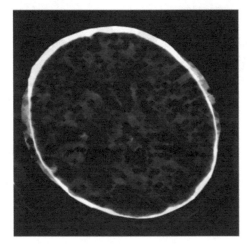

Figure 6.   Contrast adjustment.

the tumor is demarcated and obtained in the CT image. The received outputs are the showcased after every step in the algorithm by the following results:

• Transforming image to grayscale, as contour of final image has to be plotted which functions only on grayscale images.
• Low pass filter application, for eliminating any noised present in image

High pass filter applications, thus obtaining sharp images consisting of clearly defined and visible boundaries.

Morphological open should be preferred for use to get equal amounts of wearing absent and dilation level, to correctly estimate the image environment.

The shift of Figures 6 to Figure 5 and Figure 7 takes place by the below mentioned steps:

1. Background Negatio
2. Eroded image background Deletion
3. Background negative deletion of the images that are erod

Contrast identification of images subtracted:

After boundary detection in the MRI and CT image find the abnormal condition in the image showing through resultant image figure:

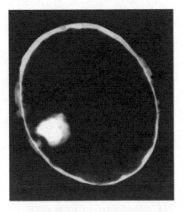

Figure 7.   Contrast adjustment.

Figure 8.   Boundary detection.

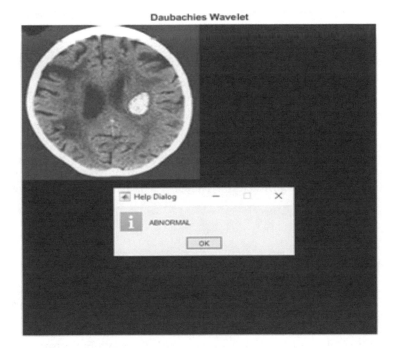

Figure 9.   Detected abnormal area.

This research paper according to the K-mean algorithm the abnormal tumor detection generates performance Graph in between error values and Iteration in Figure 10.

6   CONCLUSIONS

The enlargement inside the brain tumor brain process be careful an identify tumor reagen. In this paper main goal is to use Brain tumor MRI image find the region of the tumor contrast adjustment and subtraction of images to result in tumor region when background negative and the threshold image and boundary detection after boundary detection in the MRI and CT image find the abnormal condition in the image showing through resultant image. In this research paper

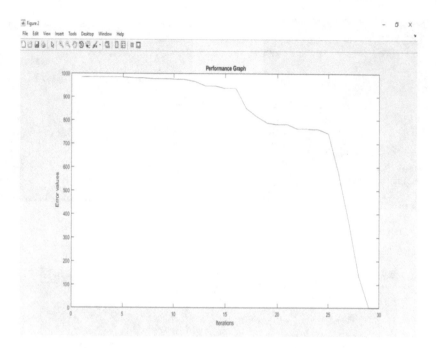

Figure 10.   Performance graph in error values & iteration.

according to the K-mean algorithm, the abnormal tumor detection generates performance Graph in between error values and Iteration. The process is the same from different parts of the body through MRI brain images be able to be alienated keen on four-part dispensation, just a picture and extract representation partition feature.

REFERENCES

Bauer, S., Nolte, L. P., & Reyes, M. (2011, September). Fully automatic segmentation of brain tumor images using support vector machine classification in combination with hierarchical conditional random field regularization. In International Conference on Medical Image Computing and Computer-Assisted Intervention (pp. 354–361). Springer, Berlin, Heidelberg.

Eason, G., Noble, B., & Sneddon, I. N. (1955). On certain integrals of Lipschitz-Hankel type involving products of Bessel functions. *Philosophical Transactions of the Royal Society of London. Series A, Mathematical and Physical Sciences, 247*(935), 529–551.

Havaei, M., Davy, A., Warde-Farley, D., Biard, A., Courville, A., Bengio, Y., … & Larochelle, H. (2017). Brain tumor segmentation with deep neural networks. *Medical image analysis, 35*, 18–31.

Khan M. A.,(2020), An IoT Framework for Heart Disease Prediction Based on MDCNN Classifier, in IEEE Access, vol. 8, pp. 34717–34727, 2020. DOI: 10.1109/ACCESS.2020.2974687

Khan M.A, and Algarni F., (2020) "A Healthcare Monitoring System for the Diagnosis of Heart Disease in the IoMT Cloud Environment Using MSSO-ANFIS," in IEEE Access, vol. 8, pp. 122259–122269, 2020, doi: 10.1109/ACCESS.2020.3006424.

Kumar, S., Negi, A., & Singh, J. N. (2019). Semantic segmentation using deep learning for brain tumor MRI via fully convolution neural networks. In *Information and Communication Technology for Intelligent Systems* (pp. 11–19). Springer, Singapore.

Kumar, S., Negi, A., Singh, J. N., & Gaurav, A. (2018a, October). Brain Tumor Segmentation and Classification Using MRI Images via Fully Convolution Neural Networks.In *International Conference on Advances in Computing, Communication Control and Networking (ICACCCN)* (pp. 1178–1181). IEEE.

Kumar, S., Negi, A., Singh, J. N., & Verma, H. (2018b, December). A deep learning for brain tumor mri images semantic segmentation using fcn. In *4th International Conference on Computing Communication and Automation (ICCCA)* (pp. 1–4). IEEE.

Kumar, S., Singh, J. N. and Kumar, N. (2020). An Amalgam Method efficient for Finding of Cancer Gene using CSC from Micro Array Data. International Journal on Emerging Technologies, 11(3): 207–211.

Long, J., Shelhamer, E., & Darrell, T. (2015). Fully convolutional networks for semantic segmentation. In *Proceedings of the IEEE conference on computer vision and pattern recognition* (pp. 3431–3440).

Maturana, D., & Scherer, S. (2015, May). 3d convolutional neural networks for landing zone detection from lidar. In 2015 IEEE international conference on robotics and automation (ICRA) (pp. 3471–3478). IEEE.

Menze, B. H., Jakab, A., Bauer, S., Kalpathy-Cramer, J., Farahani, K., Kirby, J., ... & Lanczi, L. (2014). The multimodal brain tumor image segmentation benchmark (BRATS). IEEE transactions on medical imaging, 34(10), 1993–2024.

Pereira, S., Pinto, A., Alves, V., & Silva, C. A. (2016). Brain tumor segmentation using convolutional neural networks in MRI images. IEEE transactions on medical imaging, 35(5), 1240–1251.

Ronneberger, O., Fischer, P., & Brox, T. (2015, October). U-net: Convolutional networks for biomedical image segmentation. In International Conference on Medical image computing and computer-assisted intervention (pp. 234–241). Springer, Cham.

Sharma, K., Kaur, A., & Gujral, S. (2014). Brain tumor detection based on machine learning algorithms. International Journal of Computer Applications, 103(1), 7–11.

Shin, H. C., Roth, H. R., Gao, M., Lu, L., Xu, Z., Nogues, I., ... & Summers, R. M. (2016). Deep convolutional neural networks for computer-aided detection: CNN architectures, dataset characteristics and transfer learning. *IEEE transactions on medical imaging, 35*(5), 1285–1298.

Usman, K., & Rajpoot, K. (2017). Brain tumor classification from multi-modality MRI using wavelets and machine learning. Pattern Analysis and Applications, 20(3), 871–881.

Usman, K., & Rajpoot, K. (2017). Brain tumor classification from multi-modality MRI using wavelets and machine learning. Pattern Analysis and Applications, 20(3), 871–881.

Xiao, Z., Huang, R., Ding, Y., Lan, T., Dong, R., Qin, Z., ... & Wang, W. (2016, October). A deep learning-based segmentation method for brain tumor in MR images. In *2016 IEEE 6th International Conference on Computational Advances in Bio and Medical Sciences (ICCABS)* (pp. 1–6). IEEE.

Xiao, Z., Huang, R., Ding, Y., Lan, T., Dong, R., Qin, Z., ... & Wang, W. (2016, October). A deep learning-based segmentation method for brain tumor in MR images. In 2016 IEEE 6th International Conference on Computational Advances in Bio and Medical Sciences (ICCABS) (pp. 1–6). IEEE.

Smart Computing – Khan et al (Eds)
© *2021 Taylor & Francis Group, London, ISBN 978-0-367-76552-1*

Automated short-answer scoring using latent semantic indexing

P. Anandakrishnan, Naveen Raj, Mahesh S. Nair, Akshay Sreekumar & Jayasree Narayanan
Department of Computer Science and Engineering, Amrita Vishwa Vidyapeetham, Amritapuri, India

ABSTRACT: Short answers are brief descriptions consisting of one to three sentences. They are evaluated by comparing the Student Answers with a Reference Answer. But scoring based on the term similarity alone can be inefficient given the fact that each student can answer in their own words. This approach doesn't take account of the contextual meaning of sentences. As a result, the performance of the system will be unsatisfactory. The proposed model focuses on the semantic relation between the student answer and reference answer by using Latent Semantic Indexing. Latent Semantic Indexing helps in representing the semantic similarity between documents in a reduced dimensional space using TF–IDF Document Matrix and Singular Value Decomposition (SVD). TF–IDF matrix reflects term importance instead of term frequency which is an improvement over previous research. The experimental result shows that both the Mean Squared Error and Mean Absolute Error have considerably decreased, compared to the term-based approach.

1 INTRODUCTION

In an education system, exams are a significant process. Exams should be conducted to evaluate the student's knowledge of the subject. This will give an overall idea of the extent of students' understanding of what had been taught. So, teachers can assess their students based on exam outcomes or scores. But the process becomes a difficulty if the tests were to be conducted to evaluate a bulk number of students (Pribadi et al. 2016; Mohler et al. 2011). Moreover, if there is a time constraint, the evaluation process becomes a burden. With the help of information technology, we can solve such difficulty in evaluating any number of student answers within a limited time.

There are generally two ways to evaluate a student's knowledge. They are Objective and Subjective testing (Pribadi et al. 2016). But the problem with Objective testing is that the students' level of absorbing information cannot be efficiently reflected by observing objective test scores (Feng 2008; Valenti et al. 2003). Instead, Subjective testing is much more appropriate when it comes to determining the student's level of knowledge. In Subjective testing, the students can answer in their sentences based on the level of understanding of the subject.

Two ways exist test a student's subjective knowledge. They are Automatic Essay Scoring (AES) and Automatic Short Answer Scoring (ASAS). In AES, the systems work by automatically evaluating long descriptive answers by the students. In ASAS, the system automatically scores student answers that are no more than three sentences. As the term short answer suggests, the answer is not too descriptive; instead, they are short explanations to subjective questions (Aziz et al. 2009). In this research paper, we are focusing on automatic short answer assessment using computational methods.

A short answer can be evaluated by comparing the similarity between the student answer and a given reference answer. A reference answer is nothing but the correct answer to every question which is being prepared by the teacher or human evaluator. So, an automated system must find an efficient way in computing similarity rate between student and reference answer.

Various research already suggests different methods to calculate the scores. One of them is the term "frequency method" or the term "overlapping method." This method proposes that a student tends to score more if more terms are in common with both student answer and reference answer.

DOI 10.1201/9781003167488-35

But this method becomes a disadvantage if the student is answering based on his knowledge in his sentences. Writing an answer in their sentences is not unacceptable (Feng 2008). This is actually what the teachers are evaluating for in their students. So, automatically evaluating student answers based on the overlapped words or common words could be a bad idea. The accuracy of such a developed system is less than 50% which is not at all desirable for efficient evaluation of students' knowledge.

This research states that a student can score more if his/her answers are more semantically similar to the reference answer. In a clear sense, if two sentences have similar meanings, they are similar semantically (Gomaa & Fahmy 2013). The semantic context is given more focus to efficiently handle various complexities contained in the student answer. Some previous research focuses on the semantic context of the answers. One of the references implemented an automatic grading system using semantic features, dependency graphs, and machine learning techniques (Krithika & Jayasree 2015). This system can predict whether an answer is correct or wrong given the correct answer. But, the process of grading an answer is much more difficult compared to predicting whether an answer is right or wrong.

In this research, Latent Semantic Indexing (LSI) is used to tackle the problem of identifying the semantic relationship between student and reference answers. LSI is an information retrieval technique widely used in topic modelling, document similarity, etc. (Islam & Hoque 2010; Kontostathis 2007). LSI works by reducing the original vector space to low-dimensional space. In doing so, the noise associated with the original vectors can be reduced. Moreover, the underlying aspects of finding similar documents are much more evident in the reduced dimension (Kontostathis 2007; Krithika & Jayasree 2015). So, this paper proposes an efficient method in computing student grades by drawing semantic relationships in Student answers with the help of LSI.

2 RELATED WORKS

There was an amount of research in the area of an automated grading system. From the previous researches, implementations can be categorized as corpus-based (Mohler & Mihalcea 2009; Gomaa & Fahmy 2012), string-based (Rodrigues & Araujo 2012; Omran & Aziz 2013), knowledge-based (Sankar 2015), and a combination of string-based, knowledge-based, and corpus-based (Siddiqi et al. 2010; Pribadi et al. 2016). Based on the approaches, Burrows (Gomaa & Fahmy 2012) categorized the system implementation as corpus-based (Rodrigues & Araujo 2012; Omran & Aziz 2013), concept mapping (Sukkarieh & Blackmore 2009), evaluation era (Eval), information extraction (Pulman & Sukkarieh 2005), and machine learning (Horbach et al. 2013). Some of those ASAS system implementations will be discussed here.

2.1 C-Rater

C-Rater was developed by the organization Educational Testing Service (ETS) (Pribadi et al. 2017; Sukkarieh & Blackmore 2009). This grading system uses rubrics to assess the student's answer. A rubric contains a set of rules or instructions in writing what is expected of the student. The score is computed by comparing the student answer and the subject concepts mentioned in the rubrics. The performance of the grader is highly accurate in assessing student answers. This is because the system uses a detailed analytical approach which resulted in an accuracy of about 85%.

2.2 IndusMarker

IndusMarker is another evaluation system that works by classifying right and wrong answers. The reference answers for the system are organized in an XML structure name QAML which stands for Question-Answer Markup Language (Pribadi et al. 2016, 2017; Siddiqi et al. 2010). The system works by making use of pattern matching between student and reference answers. This limits IndusMarker to handle only certain types of questions for its optimal evaluation. Also, care

Q.No	Question	Student Answer	Reference Answer
3.1	What does a function signature include?	It includes the name of the function and the types of its arguments.	The name of the function and the types of the parameters.
7.5	What is the difference between a circular linked list and a basic linked list?	A circular linked list has the last node point back to the head of the linked list.	The last element in a circular linked list points to the head of the list.
11.5	What is a recursive function?	A function that calls itself, in order to solve a problem.	A function that calls itself.
12.1	What is a pointer?	A variable that stores the address of a memory location	The address of a location in memory.

Figure 1.   Short answer dataset published by Mohler & Mihalcea (2009).

must be taken in organizing the keywords of reference answers in QAML as pattern matching is being used for student grading (Siddiqi et al. 2010; Pribadi et al. 2016). This could affect system performance and accuracy.

3   PROPOSED METHOD

This paper proposes a novel approach that focuses on text-to-text semantic similarity (Mohler & Mihalcea 2009). As an initial step, datasets are required. This system uses a dataset provided by Rada Mihalcea at umich.edu, which previous researchers used to work on (Mohler & Mihalcea 2009; Gomaa & Fahmy 2012; Sankar 2015). The dataset consists of a large collection of student answers and grades for a course in Computer Science consisting of 10 assignments having 7 questions each. For each question about 30 student answers were recorded along with the scores evaluated by the human evaluator. In this paper, not every question was used; instead, those questions of objective type were avoided. Figure 1 shows the visual representations of four sample questions, the corresponding student, and reference answers from the dataset.

3.1   *Text preprocessing*

As the term preprocessing suggests, some processing of the input data needs to be done before the development of the evaluation system (Yao et al. 2019). Student and Reference answers are the input data. General preprocessing methods are Substitution, Tokenization, and Normalization (Islam & Hoque 2010). Initially, tokenization is applied to segment the sentences into words so that it can be useful in the later developmental process. Thereafter, various substitution methods are applied. This includes case folding, removing punctuations, misspellings, HTML or XML scripts, and fixing contractions. Case folding is done to convert all texts to lowercase. Punctuation and special characters are removed so that the system can be more precise in predicting scores. Otherwise, unwanted characters can lead to the system working on interrupted data.

While dealing with stop words, both the cases with and without stop words were tested for performance analysis. Finally, normalization is applied so that words can be converted to their root words (Islam & Hoque 2010). General normalization processes are stemming and lemmatization. In this program, lemmatization alone is used. Lemmatization is resolving words to their canonical or dictionary form. Along with lemmatization, a Part of Speech (PoS) tagger is specified to convert the words into that particular part of speech. Here, which denotes verb is used as a PoS tag. This is done so that a word in any form can be reduced to their root form of the verb. For example, the

```
                    0           1        2        3
Ana        0.000000    0.000000    0.0    0.000000
a          0.005262    0.005894    0.0    0.003157
achieve    0.000000    0.000000    0.0    0.000000
again      0.000000    0.000000    0.0    0.000000
an         0.000000    0.079355    0.0    0.000000
...          ...         ...       ...      ...
usually    0.000000    0.000000    0.0    0.000000
which      0.024149    0.000000    0.0    0.000000
will       0.000000    0.000000    0.0    0.000000
```

Figure 2.   TF–IDF matrix constructed from student answer.

word simulates, simulating, and simulated gets converted to the root form-simulate. This helps the system in gathering information more systematically. Except for stop word removal, the rest of the preprocessing techniques are performed on the input data. Further processes are executed for both cases with and without stop word so that better results can be achieved by comparing both outputs. After preprocessing, term by document matrix needs to be built.

3.2   *TF–IDF Model*

Generally, in LSI a term by document matrix is built as an initial step. Here, by document, this implies both Student and Reference answers. A term by document matrix can be built as a Bag of Words Model or TF–IDF Model. In this system, a TF–IDF matrix of input document is constructed. Using TF–IDF can help in achieving better performance compared to the Bag of Words (BOW) Model. This is because in TF–IDF apart from computing term frequency, the weight of each term in the document is also calculated. The dimension of the constructed matrix is t × d, where t is the number of unique words in all of the documents, and d is the total numbers of documents. Given below are the steps in constructing a TF–IDF matrix:

- Calculate the frequency of every term for each document. Then divide it by the total no. of terms in each document. This gives the Term Frequency (TF) of each term in the corresponding document.
- That is, Term Frequency $= TF_{(t)} =$ (Number of times term t appears in a document)/(Total number of terms in the document).
- Compute the Inverse Document Frequency (IDF) of each term. This is the weight associated with each term which gives an idea about the importance of a term.
- Inverse Document Frequency $= IDF_{(t)} = \log_{10}$ (Total number of documents/Number of documents with term t in it).
- Finally, build a t × d matrix A with each row representing all unique terms or vocabulary created from the document and each column representing student answers along with the last column for reference answer. Each term's TF–IDF value can be computed by multiplying its TF value with its IDF value, i.e., $TF_{(t)} * IDF_{(t)}$ (Islam & Hoque 2010).

An example of the TF–IDF matrix constructed for Question 11.4 from the dataset is given in Figure 2. As mentioned earlier, the last column represents the reference answer in the TF-IDF matrix. To be concise, in the constructed t × d matrix, d, which is the number of columns is the sum of student answers and reference answer.

3.3   *SVD with Rank-K approximation*

After constructing term-document matrix A using TF–IDF, a mathematical function named Singular Value Decomposition (SVD) is applied to the d-1 columns of A. d-1 columns represent the

TF-IDF matrix of student answers. The last column representing the reference answer is taken as a one-dimensional array q.

- Performing SVD on the TF–IDF matrix A results in the decomposition of matrix into 3 different matrices (Islam & Hoque 2010; Furnas et al. 1988; Phadnis et al. 2014). That is, $A = U*\Sigma*V^T$.
- U is a t × d orthogonal matrix, S is a n × n diagonal matrix, and V is a d × n orthogonal matrix (Islam & Hoque 2010; Furnas et al. 1988).
- The diagonal elements of Sigma are called as Singular Values of A. The total rank of A is equal to the number of non-zero values of Sigma.
- Then comes the crucial part which affects the performance of the system. This is called k-rank approximation.
- The dimension of the obtained matrices U, Σ (Sigma), and V^T are reduced to k-dimensional space (Phadnis et al. 2014). In doing so, those columns which contribute noise to the model can be effectively reduced.
- A rank can be less than or equal to length of the document. In the constructed TF–IDF matrix, the number of student answers alone represents the length of the document.
- For the t x d matrix, A, d is equal to the number of student answers + 1. This is because 1, which represents the reference answer corresponds to the last column of the TF–IDF matrix. Therefore, a maximum rank approximation of d-1 is possible, that is, $k \leq d\text{-}1$.
- A rank-k approximation is implemented by keeping first k columns of U and V and the first k columns and rows of Σ.
- Using the k-dimensional U, V, and Σ matrices, coordinates, or vectors of student and reference answers are computed (Phadnis et al. 2014). The reduced dimension of U, V, and Σ are represented by Uk, Vk, and Σk, respectively, where k is the rank approximated for reduction.
- V_k which has a dimension of (d-1) × k holds the vector for student answers with each row representing vector for each student. So, each student answer is represented in a reduced k-dimension.
- New vector of the reference answer in k-dimensions can be computed using the Equation $q = q^T*U_k* S_k^{-1}$ (Islam & Hoque 2010; Furnas et al. 1988; Phadnis et al. 2014).

Now that the vectors for both student and reference answers are computed using LSI, their similarity can be calculated using appropriate distant metrics. Cosine distance is more often used to compute the similarity between two vectors. However, both Cosine and Euclidean distance have been used in this research for comparing the results (Phadnis et al. 2014). The distance calculated using these metrics is in the range of 0 to 1. So, two vectors are similar if their distance is closer to 0. And the corresponding similarity can be calculated by subtracting the distance from 1.

Likewise, after computing the distance between student and reference answer vectors, subtract it from 1 to get the similarity score. Finally, this score needs to be converted in the range of 0 to 5 by multiplying with 5. Thereafter, the system is evaluated for its accuracy.

3.4 *Model prediction and evaluation*

As mentioned before, the k-rank approximation is possible for the decomposed matrices (Kontostathis 2007; Kakkonen et al. 2008; Phadnis et al. 2014). So, the vectors of the student and reference answers can have k = 1 to d approximations. The scores calculated from all k-dimensional spaces can differ in value. Moreover, scores predicted using Cosine and Euclidean distance can also differ in value irrespective of the same rank used. All these factors need to be considered while choosing the optimal method.

The dataset contains the actual scores evaluated by the teacher or human evaluator. So, the predicted scores from all possible k-ranks are then compared with the actual scores to check for errors. There exist various metrics to estimate the error in predicting. Two common methods are Mean Absolute Error (MAE) and Mean Squared Error (MSE). The system checks for k = 1 to d ranks and shows the error associated with each rank. An optimal rank needs to be chosen which gives the least error (Kakkonen et al. 2008). A general trend follows that rank 1, 2, and 3 is giving

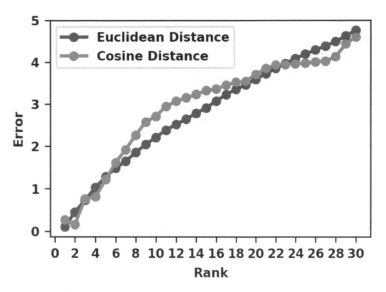

Figure 3. Dependency of absolute error with rank.

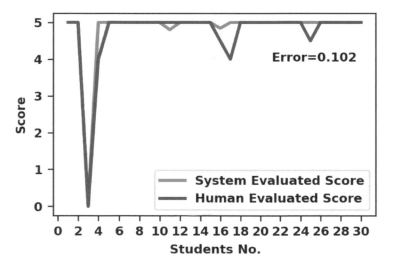

Figure 4. System evaluated score using Euclidean distance and rank-1 approximation.

the least absolute error of them all. It can also be observed that as the dimension-k increases, the error also increases (Kakkonen et al. 2008). This can be visualized from the graph given in Figure 3.

The next factor to be considered is the distance metrics used. Generally, Cosine distance is used in calculating similarity scores. In this system, both Cosine and Euclidean are used as mentioned before. The error associated with using each distant metric needs to be analyzed for its accuracy. From the experimental analysis, the absolute error observed for both Cosine and Euclidean computed score doesn't differ much. However, in particular cases, the Euclidean distance can perfectly fit into the original score much better than cosine distance with reduced error. This can be observed from the graph given in Figure 4.

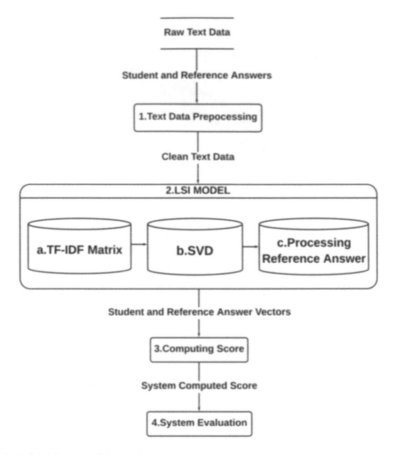

Figure 5.   Data flow diagram of the scoring system.

Table 1.   Comparison of different methods.

No.	Model Approach	Q.1 Absolute Error	Q.2 Absolute Error	Avg. Absolute Error
1	Jaccard Coefficient	3.43	2.96	3.195
2	Dice Coefficient	2.76	2.25	2.505
3	Cosine Coefficient	1.4	0.76	1.08
4	LSI Model	0.10	0.33	0.215

3.5   *Data flow diagram*

Figure 5 shows the data flow diagram for the developed system.

4   RESULT AND DISCUSSION

The accuracy of the proposed method is compared with the term-based method using common error metrics such as MAE and MSE. Table 1 analyzes different scoring methods by comparing their MEA for two different questions.

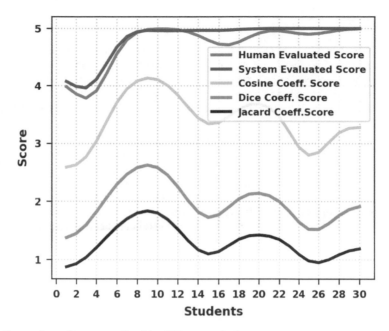

Figure 6.   Comparison of scores predicted by different methods.

From the table, it can be observed that the performance of the proposed method is considerably higher than the term-based approach. The table comprises of the MAE and its average measure associated with three common term-based methods and the proposed system for two selected questions.

The error observed for the Jaccard Coefficient is approximately 3 MEA and above. For the Dice Coefficient, it is 2.5 MEA. But, for the Cosine Coefficient, there were some serious decrements in error, which is an average of 1 MEA. Even though the Cosine Coefficient shows an improvement to the term-based method, the proposed system is still more accurate. That is, for LSI implementation, the error is less than 0.5 MEA, which means that there is an enormous decrease in the error compared to conventional methods.

The graph presented in Figure 6 compares the scores predicted by the proposed automatic scoring system, the conventional term-based system, and the human evaluated score for 30 students for a given question.

The significance of stop words, dimension reduction, and distance metrics used is that they all need to be analyzed to check how it affects accuracy. From the analysis, better performance was achieved when the stop words were not ignored. This is evident from comparing the experimental result observed from both the cases, with and without using stop words. However, the performance is more dependent on the dimensions and the type of distance metrics used. This is visualized in Figure 3, which shows that the least error is observed for rank 1 and 2, afterward the error increases.

As was discussed before, the semantic features need to be given priority over term commonness. A previous term-based approach like Jaccard, Dice, and Cosine Coefficient doesn't give importance to semantics at all. In spite of this, the paper followed a semantic approach arguing that giving priority to term frequency alone is not an efficient method in evaluating a student's answer. And when observing the results, it can be seen that what this paper stated proved to be correct. Thus, it can be finalized that the proposed system is more efficient and effective in evaluating student scores.

5 CONCLUSION

This paper proposed an advanced method for automatically computing a student score by considering semantic relationships. The LSI technique is used to draw latent semantic relation between terms and documents, which proved to be better than conventional term-based methods. This is done by LSI taking advantage of dimension reduction to map similar terms and documents (Kontostathis 2007). Using dimension reduction, noises in the original vector space are reduced which improves the system performance.

Even though the system performance is considerably high, better results can be achieved for certain dimensions or rank only. So, care must be taken while choosing the optimal dimension for capturing the semantic structure of the data. The current model approximates the rank to be 1 and 2 based on experimental analysis. In other words, the rank is drawn from a trial and error approach. To this day, no methods exist in finding optimal rank or dimensions. For further research based on the proposed system, one could try to find an advanced algorithm for finding an optimal k for dimension reduction. Moreover, one could try to draw the relation between rank and the size of the corpus (Islam & Hoque 2010). In this way, the score prediction could be made more precise.

REFERENCES

M. J. Ab Aziz, F. D. Ahmad, A. A. Abdul Ghani, and R. Mahmod, 2009, "Automated Marking System for Short Answer examination (AMSSAE)," 2009 IEEE Symp. Ind.Electron. Appl., no. Isiea: 47–51.

A. M. Ben Omran and M. J. Ab Aziz, 2013, "Automatic essay grading system for short answers in English language," J. Comput. Sci., Vol. 9: 1369–1382.

Z. Feng, 2008, "The algorithm analyses and design about the subjective test online basing on the DOM tree," Proc. – Int. Conf. Comput. Sci. Softw. Eng. CSSE 2008, Vol. 5: 577–581.

G. W. Furnas, S. Deerwester, S. T. Dumais, T. K. Landauer, R. A. Harshman, L. A. Streeter, K. E. Lochbaum, 1988, "Information retrieval using a singular value decomposition model of latent semantic structure", Proc. of 11th annual int'l ACM SIGIR conference on Research and development in information retrieval: 465-480.

W. Gomaa and A. Fahmy, 2012, "Short Answer Grading Using String Similarity and Corpus-Based Similarity," Int. J. Adv. Comput. Sci. Appl., vol. 3, no. 11: 115–121.

W. H. Gomaa and A. A. Fahmy, 2013, "A survey of text similarity approaches," Int. J. Comput. Appl., Vol. 68, no. 13: 13–18.

A. Horbach, A. Palmer, and M. Pinkal, 2013. "Using the text to evaluate short answers for reading comprehension exercises," Second Jt. Conf. Lex. Comput. Semant. (*SEM), Vol. 1 Proc. Main Conf. Shar. Task Semant. Textual Similarity, Vol. 1: 286–295.

T. Kakkonen, N. Myller, J. Timonen, E. Sutinen, 2008," Comparison of dimension reduction methods for automated essay grading", International Forum of Educational Technology & Society (IFETS): 275–288.

A. Kontostathis, 2007, "Essential Dimensions of Latent Semantic Indexing (LSI)," 2007, 40th Annual Hawaii International Conference on System Sciences (HICSS'07), Waikoloa, HI :73–73.

Krithika, R, Narayanan Jayasree, 2015, "Learning to Grade Short Answers using Machine Learning Techniques," in Proc.Third International Symposium on Women in Computing and Informatics: 262–271.

M. Mohler and R. Mihalcea, 2009, "Text-to-text Semantic Similarity for Automatic Short Answer Grading," Proc. 12th Conf. Eur. Chapter Assoc. Comput. Linguist. (EACL '09): 567–575.

Michael Mohler, Razvan Bunescu and Rada Mihalcea, 2011, "Learning to Grade Short Answer Questions using Semantic Similarity Measures and Dependency Graph Alignments, "Proceedings of the 49th Annual Meeting of the Association for Computational Linguistics, Portland, Oregon: 752–762.

M. Monjurul Islam and A. S. M. Latiful Hoque, 2010,"Automated essay scoring using Generalized Latent Semantic Analysis", 13th International Conference on Computer and Information Technology (ICCIT), Dhaka.

Phadnis, Neelam & Gadge, Jayant. 2014, Framework for Document Retrieval using Latent Semantic Indexing. International Journal of Computer Applications. 94. 10.5120/16414-6065: 37–41.

Feddy Setio Pribadi, Teguh Bharata Adji and Adhistya Erna Permanasari, 2016, "Automated Short Answer Scoring Using Weighted Cosine Coefficient", IEEE Conference on e-Learning, e-Management and e-Services.

Feddy Setio Pribadi, Teguh Bharata Adji, Adhistya Erna Permanasari, Anggraini Mulwinda, and Aryo Baskoro Utomo, 2017, "Automatic short answer scoring using words overlapping methods, "AIP Conference Proceedings.

S. G. Pulman and J. Z. Sukkarieh ,2005, "Automatic short answer marking," EdAppsNLP 05 Proc. Second Work. Build. Educ. Appl. Using NLP: 9–16.

F. Rodrigues and L. Araujo, 2012, "Automatic assessment of short free text answers," in CSEDU 2012 – Proceedings of the 4th International Conference on Computer Supported Education.

A. Sankar, 2015, "Towards an automated system for short-answer assessment using ontology mapping," Int.Arab J.e technology, vol. 4, no. Guha: 1989.

R. Siddiqi, C. J. Harrison, and R. Siddiqi, 2010, "Improving Teaching and Learning through Automated Short-Answer Marking," IEEE Trans. Learn. Technol., Vol. 3, no. 3: 237–249.

Srilekshmi M, Sindhumol. S, Chatterjee. S, Bijlani. K, 2017, "Learning Analytics to Identify Students At-risk in MOOCs," IEEE 8th International Conference on Technology for Education, T4E 2016 11 January, Article number 7814823: 194–199.

J. Sukkarieh and J. Blackmore, 2009, "C-rater: Automatic Content Scoring for Short Constructed Responses.," Proc. Twenty-Second Int. FLAIRS Conf. 290–295.

S. Valenti, F. Neri, and A. Cucchiarelli, 2003, "An Overview of Current Research on Automated Essay Grading," J. Inf. Technol. Educ., Vol. 2: 3–118.

L. Yao, Z. Pan and H. Ning, 2019," Unlabeled Short Text Similarity with LSTM Encoder," in IEEE Access, Vol. 7: 3430-3437.

Smart Computing – Khan et al (Eds)
© *2021 Taylor & Francis Group, London, ISBN 978-0-367-76552-1*

An Android-based travel safety app using machine learning

T.R. Krishnaprasad, Ravipati Jhansi & Sai Keerthana
Amrita School of Engineering, Amrita Vishwa Vidyapeetham, Department of CSE, Amritapuri, Kerala

ABSTRACT: Safety while traveling is increasingly gaining worldwide priority due to the increase in violent crimes. This paper proposes a machine learning model whose security rating results are sent to a mobile application based on the place to which the user is traveling so that the user can make an informed choice regarding the travel. This paper also provides real-time security at the place to which the user is traveling. The simulated results are evaluated and the results validating the efficiency of the model are presented.

1 INTRODUCTION

Everyone has a different perception of leisure and fun. For many, the idea of leisure and fun is associated with exploring new places; for others, it is moving along with like-minded peers to popular tourist places while many individuals prefer to travel alone. As per Ohlan (2017), tourism accounted for 9.8% of the GDP of the world in the year 2014. It can be easily inferred that, with such a surge in tourism, traveling constitutes a large part of the tourism industry on a worldwide scale. Violence anywhere in the world causes enormous pain and loss to the people. It has been observed that not only does the occurrence of crime in a place affect the decision of the person going to the place but also the perception about the place is also a deciding factor (George 2010). The Internet is one of the most widely used media for connectivity. Nowadays, mobile phones are not only used for talking but also for accessing the internet (Jisha et al. 2020). With the proliferation of a variety of sensor embedded mobile phones, data is no longer restricted to text alone, but also includes location, audio, and video to mention a few. According to Gartner, the worldwide sale of smartphones is expected to reach 1.57 billion by 2020 (Goasduff 2020). It is worth noting that among the mobiles, Android OS-based smartphones occupy about 84% of market shares (Nguyen-Vu et al. 2019). Also, there are many other applications of machine learning in the Internet of Things (IoT) in healthcare, personal security, and industrial IIoT (Abuhasel 2020; Khan, Quasim, et al. 2020; Khan 2020; Khan & Algarni 2020; Khan & Abuhasel 2020; Khan et al. 2020; Quasim et al. 2019).

Machine learning involves accumulating data in a specific domain and using different algorithms to evolve meaning out of the data collected (Nair and Mohan 2018; Anjali et al. 2019). The meaning thus extrapolated from this data gets more evolved from the additional data. This refinement of meaning is known as the "training" of data. This "trained" data can be used to predict or to classify unknown data that would be fed into the machine learning algorithm in the future. This paper utilizes certain machine learning principles from the data obtained from users for use in the prediction of a safety metric. The motivation of this paper is to provide a safety metric to travelers, particularly women, who traverse from a location A to another location named B so that the individual can have safer travel experience, irrespective of whether the place is a tourist destination or not. Due to the pervasiveness of Android phones, we have created an application on an Android which provides the user with a safety rating, using machine learning along with a real-time security scenario update concerning the destination to which the user is traveling. The rest of the paper is structured as follows. Section 2 covers related works, Section 3 provides the details of the proposed model, Section 4 mentions the experiments and results, while Section 5 provides future work.

DOI 10.1201/9781003167488-36

Table 1. Related work summary.

Name	Purpose	Method	Disadvantage
3-way women Safety device	Self-defense and alerting emergency numbers	Uses GPS via Android application, Raspberry Pi, and nerve stimulator	Does not inform of security risks
Travel decision modeling	To predict destination of users	Data from TripAdvisor is fed to a Gradient Boosting algorithm	Prevalent security scenario is not reflected
Travel planning and analyzing system	Travel recommendation to the first place, then second, and so on	Mesh spread, quarter-circle method	Safety is accounted for but only based on weather
Women safety system using IoT and ML	Alert emergency contact numbers	Sensing body temperature and pulse rate	Does not predict whether the place is relatively safe or not
Advanced women Safety system using IoT	Alert emergency contacts and send information to a nearby police station	Uses the KNN algorithm along with GPS	Does not inform the user about any disturbances

2 RELATED WORK

Sen et al. (2019) proposes an IoT-based women's safety device. The proposed device is a three-way safety module for it provides self-defense, evidence recording, and tracking information. The device is a combination of Android application, Raspberry Pi, and a nerve stimulator together with using GPS for the location of the individual. Keerthi and Lakshmi (2018) propose a machine learning model based on the Gradient Boosting algorithm to which data from the TripAdvisor is loaded to get the destination of the user. A method to recommend travel destinations based on weather patterns and via Google maps is proposed in Rathnayake (2018) using mesh- and quarter-circle based measuring techniques. In Muskan et al. (2018), the proposed method is for the automatic danger detection system. The device is customized to learn the individual pattern of temperature and heartbeat and if the situation is a danger then it finds out the threshold for generating an alarm and then automatically emergency alert messages and call is sent to emergency contacts along with the location of the individual. The danger condition is predicted using a machine learning algorithm called logistic regression. Varade et al. (2017) propose a model that along with sending messages to the emergency contacts also informs the individual about nearby police stations. The k-nearest neighbors (KNN) model is used along with GPS to inform the contacts of the individual. Thus, from the works mentioned earlier, we can understand that the works mentioned earlier do not reflect the degree of security risk, if any, at a given place to which the individual is traveling to.

3 PROPOSED MODEL

Our proposed model includes

- Data collection from users
- A client-based Android application
- A server-side data processing module
- A real-time client feedback module

3.1 *Data collection*

The application prompts the users to enter a safety metric on a scale of 1 to 10 (with 1 being less safe and as the value approaches 10, it stands for better safety). The users are provided with a user interface (UI) as shown in Figure 5 which provides them an option to select a place (both for entering the "from" and "to" places). The UI also has an option to enter the mode of traveling as

Table 2. Dataset sample.

The place from	Place to	Gender	Travel	Rating
Ernakulam	Chennai	Female	Train	8
Ernakulam	Chennai	Female	Train	7
Ernakulam	Chennai	Female	Train	9
Ernakulam	Chennai	Female	Bus	7
Ernakulam	Chennai	Female	Bus	9

Table 3. Curated dataset of Ernakulam to Chennai.

Gender	Travel	Rating
1	0	8
0	0	7
0	0	8
0	1	7
0	1	9

either via bus or via train along with asking for the gender of the user. The application asks the user to enter a rating based on their experience of traveling from a place say A to another place say B.

3.2 *The server-side data processing module*

This module is composed of the following components interacting with one another:

- Data receiving from the client
- Modeling the data via a Machine Learning algorithm
- Sending the result back to the client

3.2.1 *Data received from the client*

The data collected from the users has been tabulated into these five columns for efficient modeling: The Place From; Place To; Gender; Mode of Transport; and Rating. The mode of transport is restricted to either Train or Bus since they are the most preferred mode of travel. A snippet of the data set is given in Table 2. Based on the places of origin and destination, we curate the data set into numbers for efficient modeling. Thus, the data set for one pair of places will be different from a data set for another pair of places. The places from and to are not included in the data set so created, as the data is retrieved from the database and fed to the model. A snippet of curated data set is in Table 3.

As can be observed from Table 3, the data is converted into numbers where females and males are represented by the numbers 1 and 0, respectively. Likewise, Train and Bus are represented by 0 and 1 respectively.

The data so obtained is stored in the database for efficient data entry and retrieval

3.2.2 *Modeling the data via a machine learning algorithm*

To model the data and to derive an equation that would enable predicting the safety perception metric, the first step is to study the data. To study the data, we retrieve the data from the database, visualize a pair plot of the data set which is shown in Figure 2.

From Figure 2, we can understand that there is an almost linear correlation between the safety perception metrics of the female and male population. We can observe that the perception of safety amongst the females tends to go below 5 in several instances whereas for males it does not. From the pair plot, we can infer that the data set can be linearly separable. The data thus retrieved and

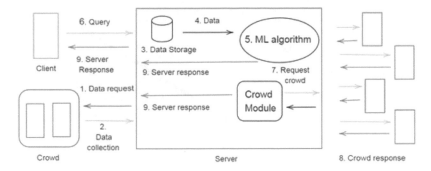

Figure 1.　Overview of the proposed model.

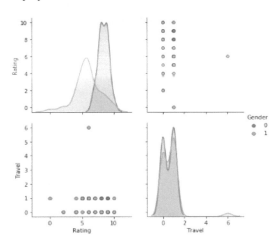

Figure 2.　Pair plot visualization.

studied is fed into a machine learning model (Step 4 of Figure 1). Hence, we modeled our data on Linear Regression Model and Support Vector Machine (SVM) model as the data can be linearly classifiable. We aim to run the data set on both the models and evaluate the efficiency of the result produced by both the models and based on the evaluation to finalize whether to opt for the Linear Regression model or the Support Vector Machine model (Step 5 of Figure 1). Regression Analysis is predicting the dependent variable value based on one or more independent variable(s). If there is only one independent variable that helps to predict the value of the dependent variable, that type of linear regression is known as simple linear regression. If there are multiple independent variables, then it is called a multivariable linear regression. For an intuitive understanding of linear regression, let us look at Figure 3 given below. As can be observed, the points which are colored red and those that are colored blue can be linearly separable. The data points are separated by a linear line having a slope, by following the equation

$$Y = m * X + c \tag{1}$$

where m is the slope of the line, X is the independent variable, and c is the y-intercept. For multiple linear regression, the equation will be

$$Y = m * X_1 + m * X_2 + c \tag{2}$$

where X_1 and X_2 are the independent variables and Y is the dependent variable and m is the slope. The idea is to come up with a line that delineates the red and blue data points and which is also the

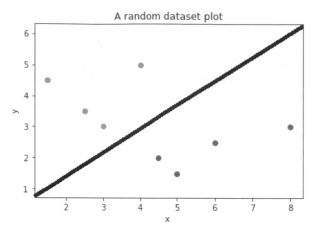

Figure 3.   A random data set scatter plot with linear regression.

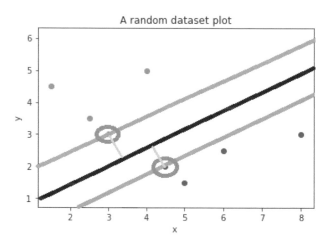

Figure 4.   A sample data set with SVM.

best fit in the scatter plot provided in Figure 3, such that it is possible to predict a value for any future independent variables.

SVM is another model of machine learning algorithm whereupon providing certain features of entities, the algorithm classifies the entity into specific categories.

SVM can also be used for regression analysis. Like linear regression, SVM also draws a line to delineate different classifications. There are different ways of drawing a line that separates two or more classes. However, one of the major differences between linear regression and SVM is that SVM incorporates margins and support vectors, as shown in Figure 4. The margin encompasses the area between the green lines. It denotes the separation of the classes. Thus, with a greater margin, more clearly are the data in the data set separated. The oval circles around the two data points, one in color red and another in color blue are known as the support vectors, as it is these two vectors that determine the area of margin. The support vectors are the data points that are the nearest to the line that separates either of the two sets of data points.

Figure 5. Registration, login, give rating, view rating pages.

4 SIMULATION AND RESULTS

The simulation of the proposed model consists of giving and viewing the security perception rating via the Android application (named A4Uy—Application for your safety) on the client-side, running the machine learning model on the server-side, and proving a real-time security update to the Android app user.

4.1 *Android application*

The Android application is developed using Android Studio. The user registers through the application into the service. At the time of registration, every user is asked the place of residence of the user. Let us say this user is called as User A. When User B needs to know about the real-time safety of that particular place, then the application issues a notification to User A. Thus, User B gets real-time information about the situation regarding the destination. The Registration page picture is given in Figure 5.

After registration, the user needs to login, through the Login page to each user must register with the application and Login, as shown in Figure 5. The machine learning algorithms are fed the input that is obtained by data sent by different users by clicking on the "Give Rating" link after logging into the application. Alternately, if the user is only interested in viewing the security rating of a particular place then the "View Rating" link has to be clicked. The application page of both the "Give Rating" and "View rating" is given in Figure 5.

4.2 *Server-side: machine learning models*

Data thus collected from the users via Android application is then stored in the server, retrieved, trained, and tested on the machine learning models. To train and test both the Linear Regression model and SVM model, sci-kit-learn (Pedregosa et al. 2011) library is used on the Anaconda python platform (Anaconda 2016). Matplotlib (Hunter 2007) library is used for visualization of the plots. The data set for training and testing both the models is divided into the ratio 80:20, respectively. The results after running the data on the Linear Regression model is given below in Figure 6.

The results after running the data on the SVM model is given in Figure 7. Once again, the measured value is given in the x-axis whereas the predicted value is given in the y-axis.

As we can observe by comparing Figures 6 and 7, the predicted values in the SVM model are much closer to the measured values in the Linear Regression model. A much more detailed analysis of the performance of both models is provided in Table 4. The MAE and the Root Mean Square

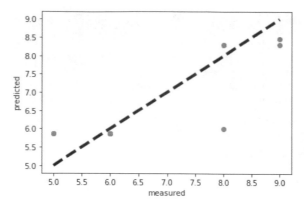

Figure 6.   The output of linear regression.

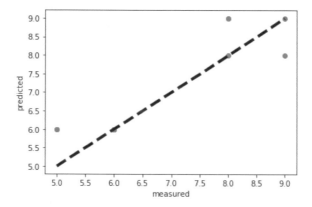

Figure 7.   Output of SVM.

Table 4.   Performance parameters.

Model	Mean Absolute Error	Root Mean Square Error	Input	Rating
Linear Regression	0.54	0.74	Female, Chennai, Train	5.8
Support Vector Machine	0.46	0.67	Female, Chennai, Train	6

Error (RMSE) are two performance metrics that can be used to evaluate the model's accuracy. MAE, as the name suggests, is the mean of absolute values of the predicted values subtracted from the actual values. RMSE goes further than MAE, in that it also calculates the square root of the MSE values. RMSE is also calculated as it provides weights to errors. The lesser the values of MAE and RMSE the better it is for the models. As we can observe from Table 4, MAE and RMSE values are lesser for SVM when compared to Linear Regression. Thus, for the proposed model, we chose the SVM model for predicting the safety perception rating.

4.3   Real-time security update of the destination

The simulation of our model also includes a real-time review of the prevailing security situation at the destination where a user is going. Figure 8 (review request) is the screen that gets displayed

Figure 8. Review request, review response.

when user M enters details given in Figure 5. A user of the place to which the user M is traveling to gets a notification asking him/her to give a real-time situation regarding the current safety scenario in the locality. The message entered by the native user is relayed to user M as given in Figure 8 review response page.

5 CONCLUSION AND FUTURE WORK

In times of increasing safety concerns, our mobile application provides users with both the safety perception metric of a place using prior data modeled on SVM with very little error margin. Our application also enables the user to make an informed decision about visiting the locality by having a real-time review of the place by the registered user(s) of the application who are native to the locality. As part of future work, we would like to add more parameters to the training data also to provide users with a GPS location of places within the locality which needs to be avoided.

REFERENCES

Anaconda. (2016). *vers. 2-2.4.0, Anaconda Software Distribution. Computer software.* Anaconda Software Distribution. Computer Software.

Anjali, B., Reshma, R., & Geetha Lekshmy, V. (2019). Detection of Counterfeit News Using Machine Learning. *2019 2nd International Conference on Intelligent Computing, Instrumentation and Control Technologies, ICICICT 2019*, 1382–1386. https://doi.org/10.1109/ICICICT46008.2019.8993330

Abuhasel K. A. and M. A. Khan, (2020), "A Secure Industrial Internet of Things (IIoT) Framework for Resource Management in Smart Manufacturing," in IEEE Access, vol. 8, pp. 117354–117364, 2020, doi: 10.1109/ACCESS.2020.3004711.

George, R. (2010). Visitor perceptions of crime-safety and attitudes towards risk: The case of Table Mountain National Park, Cape Town. *Tourism Management*, *31*(6), 806–815. https://doi.org/10.1016/j.tourman.2009.08.011

Goasduff, L. (2020). Gartner Says Worldwide Smartphone Sales Will Grow 3% in 2020. In *Gartner*. https://www.gartner.com/en/newsroom/press-releases/2020-01-28-gartner-says-worldwide-smartphone-sales-will-grow-3–

Hunter, J. D. (2007). Matplotlib: A 2D graphics environment. *Computing in Science and Engineering*. https://doi.org/10.1109/MCSE.2007.55

Jisha, R. C., Amrita, J. M., Vijay, A. R., & Indhu, G. S. (2020). Mobile App Recommendation System Using Machine learning Classification. *Proceedings of the 4th International Conference on Computing Methodologies and Communication, ICCMC 2020, Iccmc*, 940–943. https://doi.org/10.1109/ICCMC48092.2020.ICCMC-000174

Keerthi, R., & Lakshmi, P. (2018). Predictive analysis for modeling travel decision making. *Proceedings of the 2nd International Conference on Green Computing and Internet of Things, ICGCIoT 2018*, 44–49. https://doi.org/10.1109/ICGCIoT.2018.8753103

Khan, M. A., Quasim, M. T, et.al, (2020a), A Secure Framework for Authentication and Encryption Using Improved ECC for IoT-Based Medical Sensor Data, in IEEE Access, vol. 8, pp. 52018–52027, 2020. DOI: 10.1109/ACCESS.2020.2980739

Khan M. A. (2020), An IoT Framework for Heart Disease Prediction Based on MDCNN Classifier, in IEEE Access, vol. 8, pp. 34717–34727, 2020. DOI: 10.1109/ACCESS.2020.2974687

Khan M.A, and Algarni F., (2020) "A Healthcare Monitoring System for the Diagnosis of Heart Disease in the IoMT Cloud Environment Using MSSO-ANFIS," in IEEE Access, vol. 8, pp. 122259–122269, 2020, doi: 10.1109/ACCESS.2020.3006424.

Khan, MA, Abuhasel, KA. (2020).Advanced metameric dimension framework for heterogeneous industrial Internet of things. Computational Intelligence. 2020; 1–21. https://doi.org/10.1111/coin.12378

Khan M.A. et al, (2020), Decentralised IoT, Decenetralised IoT: A Blockchain perspective, Springer, Studies in BigData, 2020, DOI: https://doi.org/10.1007/978-3-030-38677-1

Muskan, Khandelwal, T., Khandelwal, M., & Pandey, P. S. (2018). Women safety device designed using IoT and machine learning. *Proceedings – 2018 IEEE SmartWorld, Ubiquitous Intelligence and Computing, Advanced and Trusted Computing, Scalable Computing and Communications, Cloud and Big Data Computing, Internet of People and Smart City Innovations, SmartWorld/UIC/ATC/ScalCom/CBDCom/IoP/SCI 2018*, 1204–1210. https://doi.org/10.1109/SmartWorld.2018.00210

Nair, J. J., & Mohan, N. (2018). Alzheimer's disease diagnosis in MR images using statistical methods. *Proceedings of the 2017 IEEE International Conference on Communication and Signal Processing, ICCSP 2017, 2018-January*, 1232–1235. https://doi.org/10.1109/ICCSP.2017.8286577

Nguyen-Vu, L., Ahn, J., & Jung, S. (2019). Android Fragmentation in Malware Detection. *Computers and Security, 87*, 101573. https://doi.org/10.1016/j.cose.2019.101573

Ohlan, R. (2017). The relationship between tourism, financial development, and economic growth in India. *Future Business Journal*. https://doi.org/10.1016/j.fbj.2017.01.003

Pedregosa, F; Varoquaux, G; Gramfort, A; Michel, V; Thirion, B; and Grisel, O. and Blondel, . and Prettenhofer, P., and Weiss, R. and Dubourg, V. and Vanderplas, J. and Passos, A. and, Cournapeau, D. and Brucher, M. and Perrot, M. and Duchesnay, E., Pedregosa, F., Varoquaux, G., Gramfort, A., Michel, V., Thirion, B., Grisel, O., Blondel, M., Prettenhofer, P., Weiss, R., Dubourg, V., Vanderplas, J., Passos, A., Cournapeau, D., Brucher, M., Perrot, M., & Duchesnay, É. (2011). Scikit-learn: Machine Learning in Python. *Journal of Machine Learning Research*. https://doi.org/10.1007/s13398-014-0173-7.2

Quasim, M. T., Khan M. A, et.al, (2019), Internet of Things for Smart Healthcare: A Hardware Perspective, 2019 First International Conference of Intelligent Computing and Engineering (ICOICE), Hadhramout, Yemen, 2019, pp. 1–5. DOI: 10.1109/ICOICE48418.2019.9035175

Quasim, M.T., Khan M.A, Algarni F., Alharthy A., Alshmrani G.M.M, (2020), Blockchain Frameworks. In: Khan M., Quasim M., Algarni F., Alharthi A. (eds) Decentralised Internet of Things. Studies in Big Data, vol 71. Springer, DOI: https://doi.org/10.1007/978-3-030-38677-1

Rathnayake, W. G. R. M. P. S. (2018). Google Maps Based Travel Planning Analyzing System (TPAS). *Proceedings of the 2018 International Conference on Current Trends towards Converging Technologies, ICCTCT 2018*, 1–5. https://doi.org/10.1109/ICCTCT.2018.8550996

Sen, T., Dutta, A., Singh, S., & Kumar, V. N. (2019). ProTecht – Implementation of an IoT based 3 -Way Women Safety Device. *Proceedings of the 3rd International Conference on Electronics and Communication and Aerospace Technology, ICECA 2019*, 1377–1384. https://doi.org/10.1109/ICECA.2019.8821913

Varade, M. S., Itnare, M. T., Parande, M. H., & Sonawane, M. P. (n.d.). *Advanced Women Security System Based on IoT*. 57–61.

316

Smart Computing – Khan et al (Eds)
© *2021 Taylor & Francis Group, London, ISBN 978-0-367-76552-1*

A novel approach for product cipher encryption algorithm using circular queues

B. Gupta
Department of Computer Science and Engineering, GB Pant Institute of Engineering & Technology, Pauri Garhwal, India

K.K. Gola
Department of Computer Science and Engineering, Faculty of Engineering, TMU, Moradabad, India

A. Bisht
Department of Computer Science and Engineering, GB Pant Institute of Engineering & Technology, Pauri Garhwal, India

S. Arya
Department of Computer Science and Engineering, SRMS College of Engineering Technology & Research, Bareilly, India

ABSTRACT: This paper aims to introduce a circular queue-based product cipher encryption algorithm in which the message or the plaintext is inserted into a series of circular queues where the letters in the circular queues are first replaced by some other letters including alphabets, numbers, or special characters and then the letters shift in a particular direction within the queue. Each circular queue may or may not have a distinct shifting offset and direction. In this way, the plaintext is altered into an unintelligent text. The concept of the shifting of letters in a circular queue is driven from the real-life safe lock systems where multiple rotator locks are rotated in such a way that only a particular position of every rotator lock unlocks the safe. As the size of plaintext increases, the number of queues and the size of queues will increase which will consequently increase the randomization of letters.

Keywords: Plaintext; Ciphertext; Encryption; Decryption; Product cipher.

1 INTRODUCTION

Information can be defined as the meaningful data that is derived from raw facts, however, for us, information is not merely a meaningful data but it's our personal data, official and private data, our bank account details, and much more. And with the modernization and computerization of physical information into digital data, everything in our computers, mobile phones, and tablets has become important and sensitive to us. While sending some message or information to someone, we can't afford to disclose or modify our sensitive data so it is imperative to secure the information in our systems and in the network as well from any kind of intrusion, forging, or modifications. So, to secure the information, there is a mechanism that can transform a readable message (plaintext) to an unreadable form of message (ciphertext) and that

DOI 10.1201/9781003167488-37

mechanism is called as "Encryption" (Van Camp 2014). The ciphertext can be transformed back into the plaintext simply by reversing the Encryption mechanism, which is known as "Decryption". The process of encryption of encryption and decryption is achieved by some sort of codes, (Mehdi et al. 2016) proposed a cyclic codes of length pn over Zp3 that can be used in encryption process.

With the evolution of computer systems, smartphones, and the Internet, a whole new virtual world has been created where everyone connected to internet can reach out to anyone located anywhere in the planet in fraction of seconds which consequently leads our information accessible to authorized as well as unauthorized users of internet. Various kinds of encryption algorithms are already developed but attackers, hackers, or cryptanalysts never stop trying to break the encryption. The term "security" is like a never-ending loop because no matter how strong the encryption is, hackers or cryptanalysts will eventually find a way to crack it one way or another and security experts will continue to develop even more secure encryption algorithms, and this process goes round and round, that's why the development of encryption techniques is inevitable (Tipton et al. 1997). Numerous attacks are out there that can disable our network and steal information. An improved cross-site scripting filter for input validation against attacks in web services was proposed by (Elangovan et al. 2014) to resist web attacks. Attacks via image and image infringement are also gaining some attention in field of cryptography. Digital watermarking scheme helps to eradicate these threats (Justin et al. 2015; Ambeth et al. 2015) proposed a discrete cosine transform–singularvvalue decompization- (DCT–SVD)-based digital watermarking scheme by human visual characteristics. Threats are pretty frequent in databases too nowadays that include information tampering. Waqas et al. (2016) introduced a prefix-oriented N4WA coding scheme for improved tampering detection in relational data. User authentication and authorization is a must in network or wireless communication. (Hu et al. 2014; Virender et al. 2016) proposed a scheme for the optimal node selection and improvement of user authentication protocol with anonymity for wireless communication. Biometric security measures are also used for authentication of users. One of the biometric authentications using adaptive decision boundaries was given by Fuad (2014). Identity theft and malwares lead to online fraudulent, so while making an online transaction one must check the quality of the online services and for that Zainab et al. (2015) published a paper on modeling and measuring the quality of online services. This paper aims to provide a circular queue-based product cipher encryption algorithm. Product cipher is a combination of two or more kinds of transformation and since the algorithm proposed in this paper uses two transformations, substitution and transposition, therefore it is termed as product cipher encryption algorithm (Henk et al. 2010). Generally, encryption algorithm uses either substitution or transposition transformation of the plaintext or the original message and in some cases a combination of both transformations can be used.

Substitution encryption algorithms are those in which a letter is replaced or substituted by another letter in order to hide the information in the message while transposition encryption algorithms simply changes the position of every letter within the message in order to randomize the letters to hide the information (Mazzeo 2006). In the proposed algorithm, the size of the plaintext to be encrypted is calculated first in order to determine the number of circular queues and the size of circular queues, and the size of every circular queue must be same. To encrypt a message into an unreadable form, every encryption algorithm uses a series of bits called a key. A key is an imperative factor to every encryption algorithm since it determines the particular transformation of plaintext into ciphertext and the size of the key establishes the difficulty in decrypting the ciphertext text (Goyal & Fernandez 1988).

In cryptography, keys are either symmetric or asymmetric and this circular queue-based product cipher encryption algorithm uses symmetric key or a single key to encrypt the message and decrypt it as well. In asymmetric key algorithms, there are two keys, one for encrypting the plaintext and other for decrypting the ciphertext (Hellman 2002). Few certificateless public key cryptography schemes are developed to solve the problem of key escrow (Huang and Tu 2015) proposed a method for secure certificateless one pass authenticated key agreement scheme. This algorithm uses a 512-bit key which is divided into 4 partitions where one part is used to determine the number of circular queues and the size of these queues, the second part is used for the substitution of letters, and the third and fourth parts are used for the transposition of the letters within the queues. When the size and number of circular queues are calculated, the letters of the plaintext are inserted into the circular queues and then substitution transformation is applied to the letters. After the substitution, transposition of letters within the queues is done for the randomization of letters in order to hide the information. When substitution and transposition are applied, the ciphertext is extracted from the circular queues and sent to the receiver over the network along with the key. Since key used in this algorithm is a symmetric key, therefore it must be transmitted over a secure channel. When a receiver receives the key and the ciphertext, the decryption process takes place and decryption of ciphertext is done by reversing the action of the encryption. By using the key, first the reverse transposition will be applied in order to bring the letters back to their original positions, after the transposition, reverse substitution will be applied to get the ciphertext back to the original plaintext. Hence, the message is successfully sent to the receiver without any alteration and disclosure while in transit.

2 A NOVEL APPROACH FOR PRODUCT CIPHER ENCRYPTION USING CIRCULAR QUEUES

The idea of using circular queues in the field of encryption is driven from the real-life combination locks as represented in Figure 1 which are pretty secure and easy to use in physical world. This paper focuses on the use of the concept of combination safe locks to map it to the virtual world or information security world to be specific. In combination safe locks there are several concentric circular locks with numbers printed on it and only the owner of the safe knows the exact pattern of every circular lock that will unlocks the safe. To lock the safe, the owner rotates the circular locks randomly and no one can open the safe without knowing the exact pattern of the lock. So, this concept of circular locks is used here to jumble and randomize the letters of the plaintext in order to hide the information within the message.

Figure 1. Real-life combination safe locks (http://www.gograph.com/clipart/rotary-combination-lock-safe-locking-mechanism-vintage-engraving-gg59235671.html).

2.1 *Flowcharts for the modules of algorithm*

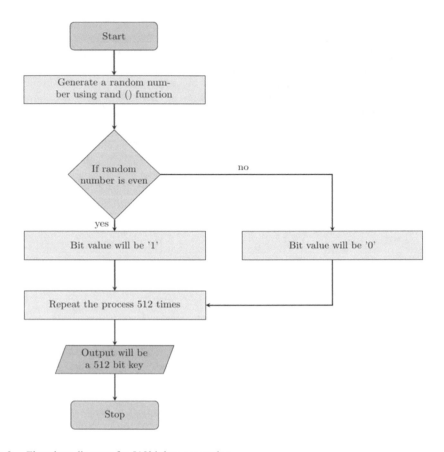

Figure 2.   Flowchart diagram for 512bit key generation

3   ALGORITHM

3.1 *Encryption*

3.1.1 *Key generation*
Step 1. Generate 512 random numbers using rand () function.
Step 2. If (random no. = even), then bit value = 1, else bit value = 0.
Step 3. A series of 512 bits is computed.
Step 4. Divide key into three parts: K1 with 256 bits, K2 with 128 bits, and K3 with 128 bits.

3.1.2 *Insertion of Plaintext in Circular Queues*
Step 5. Obtain the plaintext and count the number of letters (N) in it.
Step 6. If N is prime, check first bit of key K1.
Step 7. If Key_K1 [0] = 0, N = N + 1, else N = N + 2
Step 8. Factorize N and obtain the middle two factors F1 and F2.
Step 9. Number of circular queues = F1 and size of each circular queue = F2.
Step 10. Insert plaintext into the queues.

320

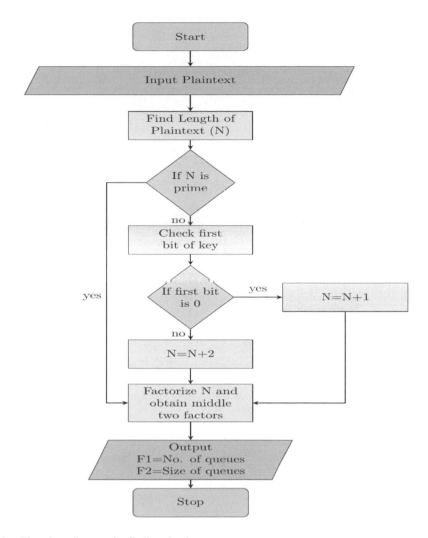

Figure 3. Flowchart diagram for finding circular queue parameters

3.1.3 *Substitution Encryption*

Step 11. Check bit values from key K1 to determine the direction to count the positions of letters in the circular queues.

Step 12. Obtain the ASCII value (AV) of the letters in the queues.

Step 13. For i = 0 to 255, if (key_K1 [i] ==1), then count the positions of a letter in clockwise direction within a queue (C),

else, count the positions in the counter-clockwise direction (C).

Step 14. Compute new ASCII value (NAV) = AV + C for every letter and substitute every letter with the letter obtained by the value NAV.

3.1.4 *Transposition Encryption*

Step 15. Check bit values from key K2 to determine the number of shifts for every queue.

Step 16. Check bit values from key K3 to determine the direction of shifts (clockwise/counter-clockwise),

For i = 0 to 127,

if (key_K3 [i]==0), then shift the letters in clockwise direction,

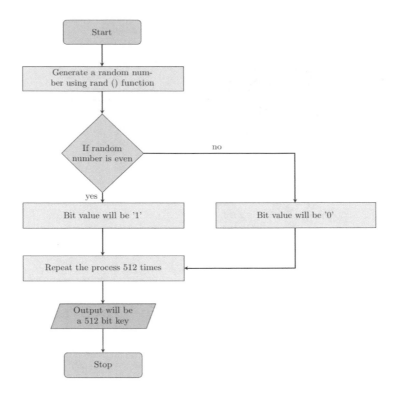

Figure 4.   Flowchart diagram for substitution encryption

else, shift the letters in the counter-clockwise direction

Step 17. Shifts the letters in each circular queues using the shift offset and shift direction obtained from Steps 14 and 15.

Step 18. Extract the ciphertext from the circular queues.

3.2   *Decryption*

3.2.1   *Transposition Decryption*

Step 19. Insert the ciphertext in the circular queues.

Step 20. Go to Step 15.

Step 21. Check bit values from key K3 to determine the direction of shifts (clockwise/counter-clockwise),

For $i = 0$ to 127,

if (key_K3 [i]==0), then shift the letters in counter-clockwise direction,

else, shift the letters in clockwise direction

Step 22. Shifts the letters in each circular queues using the shift offset and shift direction obtained from Steps 20 and 21.

3.2.2   *Substitution Decryption*

Step 23. Go to Steps 10, 11, and 12.

Step 24. Compute new ASCII value (NAV) = AV − C for every letter and substitute every letter with the letter obtained by the value NAV.

Step 25. Extract the plaintext from the circular queues.

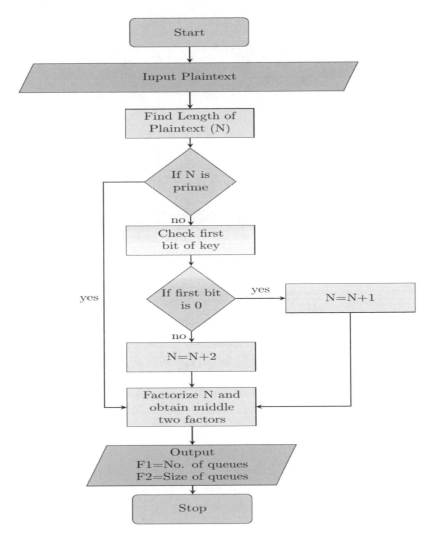

Figure 5.   Flowchart diagram for transposition encryption

4   IMPLEMENTATION OF THE PROPOSED ALGORITHM

4.1   *Encryption Example*

Consider the plaintext message CIRCULAR QUEUE BASED ENCRYPTION.

Step 1. The number of letters (N) including spaces is 31.

Step 2. A 512-bit random key (K) is generated which will be split into three parts.

Step 3. Since the size of plaintext is 31, which is a prime number and hence cannot be factorized, so we will check the first bit of K1, if it is 0, then add "1" to the size of plaintext and factorize it and if it is 1, then add "2" to it.

Step 4. Let the first bit be "1", then the size of plaintext will be 31+2=33, the factors of 33 are 33*1 and 11*3. We will take factor with minimum difference which is 11*3. Now the bigger integer will be used as the size of the circular queues and smaller integer will be used as the number of queues.

323

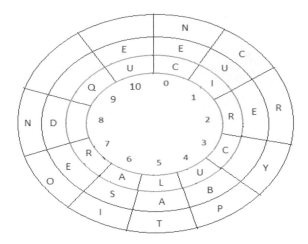

Figure 6. Letters in the circular queues before any transformation.

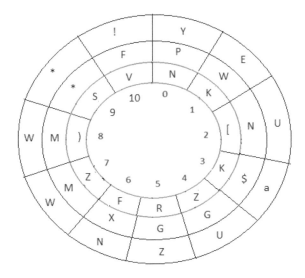

Figure 7. Letters in the circular queues after substitution.

Step 5. 1st Part (K1) with 256 bits will be used for substitution, 2nd Part (K2) with 128 bits will be used for transposition or shifting of letters within the queues and the 3rd Part (K3) with 128 bits will be used to determine the direction of the shifts in the circular queues.

Step 6. Now the letters in CIRCULAR QUEUE BASED ENCRYPTION are inserted in the circular queues as shown in Figure 6. The spaces will be inserted into the empty locations.

Step 7. Now we will use 256 bits from the key (K1) for the substitution. Foe r the first element of thfirst queue we will take the first bit of the key (K1). Let the first bit be "1", then we will count the elements of the circular queue in clockwise direction from C to U which is 11, then we will add 11 to the ASCII value of C which is 67, the new ASCII value obtained will be 78 which is the ASCII value of "N", so the letter "C" will be replaced by "N" and similarly all the letters will be replaced by some other letters using the key (K3). Refer to Table 1.

Step 8. After the substitution process, the letters in the circular queues will be changed, as shown in Figure 7.

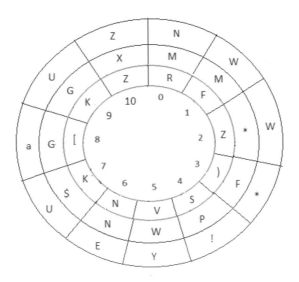

Figure 8. Letters in the circular queues after transposition.

Step 9. Now the 128 bits from the key (K2) will be used to determine the number of shifts in letters in each queue. We will split the 128 bits into fixed size blocks with the size same as the size of the circular queue in order to avoid the number of shifts from increasing more than the size of the queue, because if the number of shift is more than the size of the circular queue then it will not have any extra effect on the transposition.

Step 10. The size of circular queues is 11, so the 128 bits from key K2 will be divided into blocks of 11 bits, then we will count the number of 1's in every block and number of blocks of key bits will be equal to the number of circular queues, which in this case is 3. Now let the number of 1's (B1) in first block be "6". Similarly, let the number of 1's in second 11 bits block (B2) be "7" and in third block "B3" be "5".

Step 11. The binary values in the 128 bits from the 3rd part of the key (K3) will be used to determine the direction of the shift in every circular queue. For every "1" value, the shift will be in clockwise direction and for every "0", the shift will be in the counter-clockwise direction.

Step 12: Let the first bit be "1", then we will shift the letters in first circular queue to six positions in the clockwise direction and if second bit is "0", then the letters in second circular queue will be shifted to the seven positions in counter-clockwise direction. Similarly, if third bit is "1", then letters in third queue will be shifted to five positions in clockwise direction.

Step 13. Now, after the substitution and transposition, the letters in the circular queues will be as shown in Figure 8.

Step 14. We will extract the ciphertext from the circular queues by taking down the first letters in each queue, then the second letters in each queue and similarly for every element of the queues. We will get the ciphertext as follows:

RFZ)SVNK]KZMM ∗ FPWN$GGXNWW∗!YEUaUZ

Step 15. This algorithm uses a 512-bit symmetric key which means the same key will be used to encrypt the message and to decrypt it as well.

4.2 Decryption Example

Step 1. At the receiver's end, when the ciphertext and key is received, the key will hold the information necessary to decrypt the ciphertext back to its original form.

Table 1. Substitution encryption table.

Letter	ASCII Value	Bit value from K2	Counted number (C)	New ASCII value (OLD ASCII +C)	New Letter
C	67	1	11	78	N
I	73	0	2	75	K
R	82	1	9	91	[
C	67	1	8	75	K
U	85	0	5	90	Z
L	76	0	6	82	R
A	65	1	5	70	F
R	82	0	8	90	Z
Space	32	0	9	41	)
Q	81	1	2	83	S
U	85	1	1	86	V
E	69	1	11	80	P
U	85	0	2	87	W
E	69	1	9	78	N
Space	32	0	4	36	$
B	66	0	5	71	G
A	65	1	6	71	G
S	83	1	5	88	X
E	69	0	8	77	M
D	68	0	9	77	M
Space	32	0	10	42	*
E	69	1	1	70	F
N	78	1	11	89	Y
C	67	0	2	69	E
R	82	0	3	85	U
Y	89	1	8	97	a
P	80	0	5	85	U
T	84	1	6	90	Z
I	73	1	5	78	N
O	79	0	8	87	W
N	78	0	9	87	W
Space	32	0	10	42	*
Space	32	1	1	33	!

Table 2. Transposition encryption table

Circular Queue	Number of 1's in blocks from key K2	Bit value in K3	Shift
Q1	6	1	6 positions in counter-clockwise direction
Q2	7	0	7 positions in clockwise direction
Q3	5	1	5 positions in counter-clockwise direction

Step 2. By using the size of ciphertext, the number of circular queues and the size of the queues will be determined.

Step 3. Now the letters of the ciphertext will be inserted in the circular queues in the similar fashion as the insertion of the plaintext. After all the letters of the ciphertext are inserted into the circular queues, we will get letters in the queues just like as in Figure 5.

Step 4. The 128 bits from the second part (K2) and 128 bits from the third part (K3) will be used for the transposition of the letters back to their original positions. The size of circular queues is

Table 3.　Transposition decryption table

Circular Queue	blocks from key K2	Number of 1's in Bit value in K4	Shift
Q1	6	1	6 positions in clockwise direction
Q2	7	0	7 positions in counter-clockwise direction
Q3	5	1	5 positions in clockwise direction

Table 4.　Substitution decryption table

Letter	ASCII Value	Bit value from K2	Counted number (C)	New ASCII value (OLD ASCII +C)	New Letter
N	78	1	11	67	C
K	75	0	2	73	I
[	91	1	9	82	R
K	75	1	8	67	C
Z	90	0	5	85	U
R	82	0	6	76	L
F	70	1	5	65	A
Z	90	0	8	82	R
)	41	0	9	32	Space
S	83	1	2	81	Q
V	86	1	1	85	U
P	80	1	11	69	E
W	87	0	2	85	U
N	78	1	9	69	E
$	36	0	4	32	Space
G	71	0	5	66	B
G	71	1	6	65	A
X	88	1	5	83	S
M	77	0	8	69	E
M	77	0	9	68	D
*	42	0	10	32	Space
F	70	1	1	69	E
Y	89	1	11	78	N
E	69	0	2	67	C
U	85	0	3	82	R
A	97	1	8	89	Y
U	85	0	5	80	P
Z	90	1	6	84	T
N	78	1	5	73	I
W	87	0	8	79	O
W	87	0	9	78	N
*	42	0	10	32	Space
!	33	1	1	32	Space

11, so the 128 bits will be divided into blocks of 11 bits, then we will count the number of 1's in every block and the number of 1's in first 11 bits block (B1) will be "6", the number of 1's in second block (B2) will be "7" and "B3" is "5".

Step 5. Since the first bit in the K3 is "1", then we will shift the letters in first circular queue to six positions in counter-clockwise direction opposite to the direction as it was during encryption so as to reverse the process in order to retrieve the original message, the second bit is "0", then

327

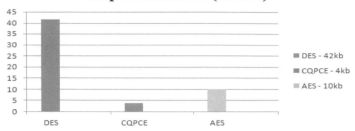

Figure 9.   Comparison on the basis of memory requirements of the algorithms.

the letters in second circular queue will be shifted to seven positions in a clockwise direction. Similarly, the third bit is "1" so the letters in the third queue will be shifted to five positions in the counter-clockwise direction; see Table 3.

Step 6. After the reverse transposition, we will reverse the substitution by using the 256-bit key and for the bit value "1", count the elements of the circular queue in the counter-clockwise direction and for every bit value "0", count the elements of the queue in the clockwise direction.

Step 7. Now, subtract the counted number (C) with the ASCII value of the letters and replace the letters with the letters obtained by the new ASCII value; see Table 4.

Step 8. In this way, we will get the original letters back in the circular queues and the original plaintext can be extracted from the queues by taking down the letters in a queue-wise manner.

Step 9. The plaintext obtained will be: CIRCULAR QUEUE BASED ENCRYPTION.

5   RESULTS AND COMPARISON

The implementation of the proposed algorithm shows that if we have a plaintext input as: CIRCU-LAR QUEUE BASED ENCRYPTION. Then, the substitution encryption applied on this plaintext will transform the plaintext to:

NK[KZRFZ)SVPWN$GGXMM*FYEUaUZNWW*! Which is obtained from the Table 1, then this encrypted text will further encrypted by the transposition transformation as shown in Table 2 which gives the following output:

$$RFZ)SVNK]KZMM * FPWN\$GGXNWW*!YEUaUZ$$

As shown in Table 1, the letters from the plaintext are substituted by other letters obtained by using their ASCII values and bit values from the key K1.

As shown in Table 2, the shifts of letters in each circular queue are determined by using the key bits from key K2 and key K3.

After extracting the ciphertext from the queues, we can transmit the message to the receiver and we also have to send the 512bit key through a secure channel to the receiver, since the proposed algorithm works on a symmetric key system, so the same key will be used to encrypt the message and decrypt it as well.

So, as shown in Table 3, we will decrypt the message by reversing the transposition or shifting of letters within the circular queues.

5.1   COMPARISON B/W DES, CQPCE, and AES

Using the data from the research paper by Akash et al. (2012), the comparison based on memory requirement, simulation speed and key size, between the three symmetric key encryption algorithms DES, CQPCE, and AES is given below in Figures 9, 10, and 11, respectfully.

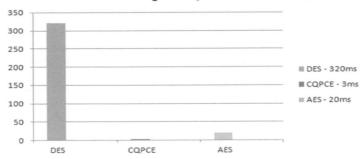

Figure 10. Comparison on the basis on simulation speed.

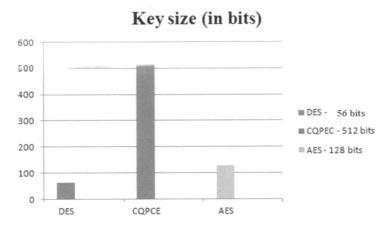

Figure 11. Comparison on the basis of key size of the algorithms.

Since, the DES and AES encryption uses too many computations to transform the plaintext to ciphertext, hence their code gets complex and contains too many operations which in turn increases their memory requirement. But in CQPCE, only operations are adding and subtracting the ASCII value and the shift operation, hence the memory requirement is comparatively low.

The DES and AES have too many rounds to complete the encryption and decryption process, so their simulation or execution time is much greater than CQPCE in which the process of encryption and decryption is pretty simple and fast.

DES uses 56-bit key size which is not considered as prone to brute force attack, AES uses 128 bits key size which is secure but not that extensive, CQPCE, on the other hand, uses the 512-bit key size which is the most secure among the three and most resilient to brute force attack.

6 CONCLUSION

The proposed circular queue-based product cipher encryption algorithm uses a symmetric key which is fast to transfer but requires a secure channel for transmission. Mathematical operations are very less in this algorithm which makes it faster to perform and despite so many algorithms for message encryption and decryption, no algorithm is safe enough to resist every attack and this circular queue based product cipher encryption algorithm is no exception. However, future work on this algorithm can make it more resilient to most of the attacks and proves to be a very efficient and simple form of encrypting and decrypting the message and achieve data security.

REFERENCES

Akash Kumar Mandal, Chandra Prakash & Archana Tiwari. 2012. Performance Evaluation of Cryptographic Algorithms: DES and AES, IEEE conference on Electrical, Electronics and computer science.

Ambeth Kumar Visam Devadoss, Ramakrishnan Malaishamy, Malathi Subramaniam & Ashok Kumar Visvam Devadoss. 2015. Performance improvement using an automation system for recognition of multiple parametric features based on human footprint, Kuwait Journal of Science, Kuwait University, pp 109–132.

A.Nadeem. 2006. A performance comparison of data encryption algorithms, IEEE information and communication technologies, pp.84–89.

Bin Hu, Qi Xie, Mengjie Bao & Na Dong. 2014. Improvement of user authentication protocol with anonymity for wireless communication, Kuwait Journal of Science, Kuwait University, pp 155–169.

Bloom, Jefrey A., Ingemar J. Cox, Ton Kalker, Jean-Paul M.G. Linnartz, Matthew L. Miller, C., & Brendan S. Traw. 1999. Copy protection for DVDvideo. Proceedings of the IEEE, IEEE Journals & Magazines.

Daemen, J., & Rijmen, V. Rijndael. 2001. The Advanced Encryption Standard." Dr. Dobb's Journal.

Diaa Salama Abd Elminaam, Hatem Mohamad Abdual Kader,Mohiy Mohamed Hadhoud. 2010. Evalution the Performance of Symmetric Encryption Algorithms, international journal of network security, pp,216–222.

Douglas Selent. 2010. Advanced Encryption Standard, Rivier Academic Journal.

Elangovan Uma & Arputharaj Kannan. 2014. Improved cross site scripting filter for input validation against attacks in web services, Kuwait Journal of Science, Kuwait University, pp 175–203.

Fuad M.Alkoot. 2014. Multimodal biometric authentication using adaptive decision boundaries, Kuwait Journal of Science, Kuwait University, pp 103–127.

Himani Agrawal and Monisha Sharma. 2010. Implementation and analysis of various symmetric cryptosystems "Indian Journal of Science and Technology, Vol. 3 No. 12.

Hellman. 2002. An overview of public key cryptography, M.E. Communications Magazine, IEEE Journals & Magazines.

Henk C. A. van Tilborg, Sushil Jajodia. 2010. Product Cipher, Superencryption, Encyclopedia of Cryptography and Security, Springer US.

Justin Varghese, Saudia Subash, Omer Bin Hussain, Mohammed Ramadan Saady, Bijoy Babu &Mohammed Riazuddin. 2015. Image adaptive DCT- SVD based digital watermarking scheme by human visual characteristics, Journal of Engineering research, Kuwait journals, pp 95–112.

Karthik.S1 & Muruganandam .A2. 2014. Data Encryption and Decryption by Using Triple DES and Performance Analysis of Crypto System, International Journal of Scientific Engineering and Research (IJSER).

Mazzeo. 2006. Special Issue on Cryptography and Security A. Proceedings of the IEEE, IEEE Journals & Magazines.

Mehdi Alaeiyan & Mohammad Hyrizadeh. 2016. Cyclic codes of length p^n over Z_p^3, Kuwait Journal of Science, Kuwait University, pp 15–24.

P. K. Goyal & E. B. Fernandez. 1988. Encryption using random keys-a scheme for secure communications, Aerospace Computer Security Applications Conference.

Prerna Mahajan, Abhishek sachdeva. 2013. A study of Encryption algorithms AES, DES and RSA for security, Global journal of computer science and technology network, web and security.

Tipton, Harold F. & Micki Krause, Editors. Information Security Management Handbook, 1996–97 Yearbook Edition, New York: Auerbach Publications.

Van Camp, Jeffrey. 2014. A study on cryptography attacks. Information Theory, IEEE Transactions, IEEE Journals & Magazines.

Virender Ranga1, Mayank Dave1 & Anil K. Verma. 2016. Optimal nodes selection in wireless sensor and actor networks based on prioritized mutual exclusion approach, Kuwait Journal of Science, Kuwait University. Pp. 150–173.

Waqas Haider, Muhammad Sharif, Hadia Bashir, Mudassar Raza & Mussarat Yasmin. 2016. Prefix oriented N4WA coding scheme for improved tampering detection in relational data, Kuwait Journal of Science, Kuwait University, pp 121–138.

William Stalling Cryptography and network security, Pearson education, 2nd Edition.

Zainab Mohammd Aljazzaf. 2015. Modelling and measuring the quality of online services, Kuwait Journal of Science, Kuwait University, pp 134–157.

Smart Computing – Khan et al (Eds)
© *2021 Taylor & Francis Group, London, ISBN 978-0-367-76552-1*

A systematic review on security metric in secure software development lifecycle

G.C. Sampada, T.I. Sake & Amrita
Sharda University, Greater Noida, Uttar Pradesh, India

ABSTRACT: A security metric evaluates the security performance, goals, and objectives of software and provides information that helps in the assessment of software security. With the advancement in technology, software is faced with lots of threats and risks to customers' data and privacy. Most of these threats are a result of security being considered as a feature of software and not taking it into account during the development of the software. Security metrics obtained during the development process go a long way to improve the core security properties of software, that is: confidentiality, integrity, and availability. Thus, it is of obvious importance to consider security across the software development lifecycle, hence, the use of software security metrics. This paper reviews the various security metrics that are meditated in the copious phases during the progression of the lifecycle with the aim of providing practitioners, managers, and researchers the substantial knowledge for further security assessment.

1 INTRODUCTION

The use of software has become a critical part of everyone's life. It is used to transfer sensitive and confidential information over networks. The development of software is an intensive process, which includes the gathering of the information, designing the software, implementing the design, testing the software for threats, risks, etc., and deploying the software. During these phases, software is vulnerable to threats, failure, and risks. These security threats can violate the integrity of the software by submerging vulnerabilities into the source code, software packages etc, or they can violate the confidentiality by disclosing details that permit attackers to procure and exploit the software and/or deny the access to the authorized users (Barbanov et al. 2018).

The vulnerability in software makes it more inclined to exploitation and attack and can also lead to the violation of the security policy of the software. Risks in software are the expectations that there will be certain loss and the software will incur certain damage (Kavita et al. 2014). By integrating the security policies in the development life cycle, software can be made more resistant and robust to vulnerabilities (Nazir & Nazir 2018).

Security in software ensures the secretiveness, uprightness, accessibility, liability, and non-repudiation of software. Software security embodies the internal weaknesses and the external attacks of the software (Wang et al. 2009). In order to minimize the incessant threats in software and ensure that it is reliable and secure, it is necessary to alert people Banerjee & Pandey (2010) presented a paper which features the utilization of security awareness techniques in order to build secure software. To resolve the problems encountered by software in the facet of security during development, a secure software development lifecycle (SDLC) was proposed (Duclervil & Liou 2019).

Figure 1 depicts the various stages of the evolution of secure software which comprises of five essential phases. The model was designed to improve security in the phases of software development. The accumulation, assaying, and officiating of the security requirements is a challenge to the organization (Souag et al. 2015). Scrutinizing and modeling the implicit threats that can affect the software is an important step during the designing of secure software (Desmet et al. 2005).

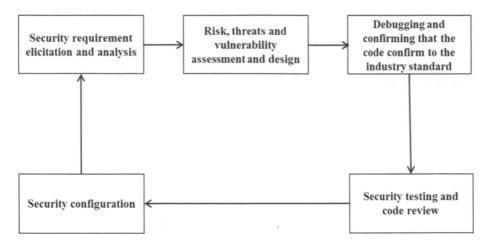

Figure 1.   Phases of development for secure software.

According to Hosseinzadeh et al. (2018), there are two significant security techniques that can be embedded in software: obscuring the code and providing the variation of software. The latter does not remove vulnerabilities from software but ensures that software is not exploited to some extent. In order to reduce the number of vulnerabilities and enhance the security in software, Banerjee & Pandey (2009) proposed 21 rules which when adopted by the developers, minimized the risk by up to 40.5%.

According to IEEE, "a metric is a degree of measurement to which a system can possess certain attributes." Security metrics are the indicators of the level of soundness property in software (Wang et al. 2009). According to Pendleton et al. (2016), there are four sub metrics that are based on the attackers' defense interaction characteristic. These are: metric of system vulnerability, metric of defense strength, metric of attack severity, and metric of situation understanding.

It is necessary to implement a security metric at the beginning of the development life cycle of software in order to minimize the vulnerabilities, introduce a mitigation process, characterize, evaluate, and enhance the soundness of the software. Similarly, the security metric can help in the quantification of the security of software. Khan & Zulkerine (2008) proposed a method to determine the vulnerability index during software development life cycle. This is to provide an insight on the vulnerabilities that exist along with the security index by utilizing the effect these vulnerabilities have during the development stage.

This paper presents a literature review of the security metrics that has been adopted in the various phases of the development life cycle of software published in the period of 15 years, from 2005–2020.

The main contribution of the paper is to provide an insight of the surveyed papers in relation to the metrics that have been proposed as well as techniques like vulnerability assessment and risk assessment that are adopted to guarantee the security of software.

This paper is organized as follows. Section 2 consists of a systematic literature review of related work. The security metrics for SDLC that have been proposed in various papers are introduced in Section 3. The findings are described in Section 4, whereas Section 5 concludes the paper.

2   SYSTEMATIC LITERATURE REVIEW OF RELATED WORK

With the amount of information being stored and disseminated using software intensive systems across the globe, there is an obvious need to seek to implement security metrics in the SDLC. Even though research in security metric is in its infancy, the related studies below outline established opinions in the said subject.

Metric that is based on the vulnerabilities present in software and the impact this vulnerability has on software are suggested in Wang et al. (2009). They have associated weaknesses and vulnerabilities of software with security metrics.

An algorithm to design a misuse case modeling tree in the security requirement gathering phase is presented in Poonia et al. (2020). The proposed algorithm provides the recognition and categorization of threat based on security requirement engineering and derives a security metric to fit into the SDLC. The algorithm is employed for retrieving, calculating, and filling the misuse case modelling worksheet. The output consists of copious strength of benchmarks and estimators in varied colors so that the quality assurance team can analyze and interpret the data. When the algorithm was used in an industry life project, it reduced the risk to 40.5%.

Security metrics to evaluate software vulnerability susceptibility from individual products was developed (Wright et al. 2013). These security metrics are Median Active Vulnerability and Vulnerability Free Days and are used to expedite the approximate liability of end-users to vulnerability in a product from software merchants. During the case study, it was found that it is unattainable for any browser to have even 50% vulnerability-free days in reality.

In Banerjee et al. (2018), the identification of vulnerability along with the classification of the misuse case is presented. This framework provides the development team with the obligatory inspection to plan and annihilate defects that may happen during the modelling of the misuse case and an alleviation strategy. The misuse case modeling aids in the definition of security metrics.

In Poonia et al. (2020), an extension of work done in Banerjee et al. (2018) was developed. It is also used to identify, define, interpret, and analyze the security metrics during the prerequisite gathering. This framework metric is based on the identification of the vulnerabilities using the common vulnerability scoring system, common vulnerability enumeration, etc., and then mapping these weaknesses with related misuse cases and provide a categorization of the vulnerabilities that has been identified by using the proposed framework metric that provide five criterion in order to determine the security level and also aiding the requirement engineers and the analyst to quantify software security based on those indicators and estimators.

The metric to ascertain the proportion of internal and external attack through the assay of abuse cases that was prevalent in the software or the system in use is developed in Banerjee et al. (2014). This model, however, did not provide the comprehension of the security dimension and the factors that influence the internal attack. Hence, an improvised model of the framework was provided in Banerjee et al. (2016), which minimizes the risk by 43.5%. Similarly, for the defensive perspective, the metric finds the ratio of flaw in the predicted misuse case model to the flaw in the observed misuse case model during the requirement engineering phase (Banerjee et al. 2014).

A metric based on Goal Question Metric (GQM) with the aim to assess the methods of software engineering to succor security quality requirement from the starting of the software development phase is proposed in Sultan et al. (2008). This technique aids the engineers to discover the security risk and intercept the risks by adopting metrics. The GQM proposed in Abdulrazeg et al. (2012) prioritizes on the development of the misuse case model. It aids in assisting it to detect and rehabilitate the vulnerabilities persistent in the software prior to advancing to other phases.

In object-oriented software security, GQM (Alam 2020) focuses on the observable security requirement to be acknowledged upon the baseline of the security and the metric derives the strategies for finding the security metric. To analyze the defect at source code level, code-level security metric is proposed in Chowdhury et al. (2008). The metric measures the source code quality properties that enhance program security as well as measure the soundness of software code security.

3 SECURITY METRICS FOR SDLC

According to Yadav et al. (2019), the metrics that are adopted during the development life cycle should be based on the relevance of metric in that phase, the experience based on the use of metric, the correctness of the metric, the necessity of the metric in the real world, and the feasibility of the metric. Below are outlines of the security metrics that need to be reviewed during the development process.

3.1 *Software metric based on vulnerabilities*

To ensure that a software runs smoothly without any error and security flaws, it is necessary to evaluate the vulnerability in the software. This describes the security metrics that are gotten from vulnerabilities within the software after development and before deployment. The knowledge of such metrics helps software vendors to make software failure predictions.

3.2 *Security metrics in the requirement gathering and analysis phase*

The annotation of requirements is the first stage of the development lifecycle. This phase set the foundation of all the proceeding phases. Thus, if the security metrics are adopted at this stage, then the cost of maintaining the software also reduces.

3.3 *Security metrics at the design phase*

Metrics in this phase helps software engineers evaluate security requirements and make design decisions with respect to critical classes. Any security error in this stage can have an adverse effect on the software.

3.4 *Security metrics in the implementation phase*

This phase turns the designs in the previous phase into reality. It involves metrics that are used to obtain the quality properties of the source with respect to the security of the system. Various steps should be undertaken to guarantee the security in this phase.

3.5 *Security metrics and their purposes in the testing phase*

Here, metrics are derived by assessing the test cases that are used to test security of the software to ensure the security as well as the quality of the software.

3.6 *Security metrics in the maintenance phase*

These metrics are obtained by considering the security changes made during the evolution of software. They are used to assess the recital of a system with respect to the security of the software.

4 FINDINGS

Security metrics are derived based on the software system under development since some projects are more complex than others. There are many metrics for the initial phase of the development lifecycle compared to the latter phases. This is a strict indication of how important it is to implement security at the very beginning of the SDLC.

The misuse case also plays an important part in identifying the security requirements in the system. Furthermore, the evaluation of vulnerability is significant for the security of the software as it offers essential understanding and software risk awareness together with an appropriate mitigation action. Apart from these, there are many exceptions affiliated with the enactment of the metrics.

The dynamic and the evolutionary property of software can cause hindrance during the prosecution of the metric as some of the metrics that were suitable for a particular version of the software may not be suitable for the other version.

5 CONCLUSION AND FUTURE SCOPE

In this paper, several security metrics have been reviewed considering the development phases in which they are implemented together with the purposes which they serve. These present the security metrics for which if followed can lead to the development of a threat-free software system. Care should be taken during the development lifecycle of any software, as new security metrics can be discovered, and also for the fact that security metrics differ from software to software.

The aim of this paper is to give insight to practitioners, managers and researchers the use of suitable security metrics in the software development lifecycle by categorizing security metrics that exist in the literature.

In the future, the outcome of this review paper can be realized to quantify the security during the development life cycle. Opposed to the manual calculation of the metrics, automated security metrics can be implemented to enhance the security of the software.

REFERENCES

Abdulrazeg, A. Ala. Norwawi, Md. Norita, & Basir, Nurlida. 2012, Security metrics to improve misuse case model. Proceedings Title: 2012 International Conference on Cyber Security, Cyber Warfare and Digital Forensic (CyberSec), Kuala Lumpur: pp. 94–99.

Alam, Mahtab. 2020, Object oriented software security: goal questions metrics approach. International journal of Information technology, vol. 12: pp. 175–179.

Banerjee, Arpita, Banerjee. C. Pandey, Samir Kumar, & Poonia S. Ajeet. 2016, Development of iMACOQR Metrics Framework for Quantification of Software Security. Pant M., Deep K., Bansal J., Nagar A., Das K. (eds) Proceedings of Fifth International Conference on Soft Computing for Problem Solving. Advances in Intelligent Systems and Computing, Springer, Singapore, vol. 437: pp. 711–719.

Banerjee, C. & Pandey, K Samir. 2009, Software Security Rules: SDLC Perspective. International Journal of Computer Science and Information Security. Volume 6. No. 1.

Banerjee, C. & Pandey, K Samir. 2010, Research on software security awareness: problems and prospects: ACM SIGSOFT Software Engineering Notes. October 2010. doi.org/101145/1838687.138701.

Banerjee, C. Banerjee, Arpita, & Muraka, P.D. 2014, Measuring Software Security using MACOQR (Misuse and Abuse Case Oriented Quality Requirement Metric: Attacker's Perspective. International Journal of Computer Application, vol. 93, no. 18: pp. 47–54.

Banerjee. C. Banerjee, Arpita. Poonia, S. Ajeet, & Sharma. S.K. 2018, Proposed Algorithm for Identification of Vulnerabilities and Associated Misuse Cases Using CVSS, CVE Standards During Security Requirements Elicitation Phase. Pant M., Ray K., Sharma T., Rawat S., Bandyopadhyay A. (eds) Soft Computing: Theories and Applications. Advances in Intelligent Systems and Computing, Springer, Singapore, vol. 584.

Barbanov, V. Alexander. Markov, S. Alexy. Grishin, I. Maksim & Tsirlov, L. Valentin. 2018, Current Taxonomy of Information Security Threats in Software Development Life Cycle. 12th International Conference on Application of Information and Communication Technologies (AICT), IEEE, Almaty, Kazakhstan: pp. 1–6.

Chowdhury, Istehad. Chan, Brian & Zulkerine, Mohammed. 2008, Security Metrics for source code structure. SESS'08: Proceedings of the fourth International Workshop on Software Engineering for secure system: pp. 57–64.

Desmet, Lieven. Jacobs, Bart. Piessens, Frank. & Joosen, Wouter. 2005, Threat Modelling for Web Services Based Web Applications. Chadwick D, Preneel B. (eds) Communications and Multimedia Security. IFIP – The International Federation for Information Processing, vol. 175. Springer, Boston, MA, 2005.

Hosseinzadeh, Shoreh. Rauti, Sampsa. Lauren, Samuel. Makela, Jari-Matti. Holvite, Johannes. Hyrnsalmi, Sami. & Lepponen, Ville. 2018, Diversification and obfuscation techniques for software security: A systematic literature review. Information and Software Technology, vol. 104: pp. 72–93.

Khan, A. Muhhamad Umair. Zulkerine, Mohammad. 2008, Quantifying Security in Secure Software Development Phase. 32nd Annual IEEE International Computer Software and Applications Conference, Turku, 2008: pp 955–960; doi 10.1109/COMPSAC.2008.173.

Nazir. Nosheen. Nazir, K. Muhammad. 2018, A review of security issues in SDLC. American Scientific Research Journal for engineering, technology and science, vol. 46, no. 1: pp. 247–259.

Pendleton, Marcus. Garcia-Lebron, Richard. Cho, Jin-Hee. & Xu, Shouhuai. 2016, A Survey on System Security Metrics. ACM Computing Surveys, vol. 49, no.4: 2016.

Poonia, S. Ajeet. Banerjee, C. Banerjee, Arpita, & Sharma, S.K. 2020a, Interpreting the Objective Outcome of the Proposed Misuse Case Oriented Quality Requirements (MCOQR) Framework Metrics for Security Quantification. Pant M., Sharma T., Basterrech S., Banerjee C. (eds) Performance Management of Integrated Systems and its Applications in Software Engineering, Asset Analytics (Performance and Safety Management), Springer, Singapore: pp. 101–106.

Poonia, S. Ajeet. Banerjee, C. Banerjee, Arpita, & S. K. Sharma. 2020b, Proposed Algorithm for Creation of Misuse Case Modeling Tree During Security Requirements Elicitation Phase to Quantify Security. Pant M., Sharma T., Basterrech S., Banerjee C. (eds) Performance Management of Integrated Systems and its Applications in Software Engineering, Asset Analytics (Performance and Safety Management). Springer, Singapore: pp. 21–28.

Sahu, Kavita. Rajshree, & Kumar, Rajeev. 2014, Risk management perspective in SDLC. International Journal of Advanced Research in Computer Science and Software Engineering, vol. 4, no.13: pp. 1247–1251.

Saniora, R. Duclervil & Liou, Jing-Chiou. 2019, The Study of the Effectiveness of the Secure Software Development Life-Cycle Models in IT Project Management. Latifi S. (eds) 16th International Conference on Information Technology-New Generations (ITNG 2019), Advances in Intelligent Systems and Computing, vol 800. Springer, Cham: pp. 91–96.

Souag, Amina. Salinesi, Camille. Mazo, Raul. & Comyn-Wattiau, Isabelle. 2015, A Security Ontology for Security Requirements Elicitation. Piessens F., Caballero J., Bielova N. (eds) Engineering Secure Software and Systems. ESSoS 2015. Lecture Notes in Computer Science, vol. 8978. Springer, Cham, 2015.

Sultan, Khalid. En-Nouaary, Abdelsam & Hamou-Lhadj, Abdelwahab. 2008, Catalog of Metrics for Assessing Security Risks of Software throughout the Software Development Life Cycle. International Conference on Information Security and Assurance (isa 2008), Busan: pp. 461–465.

Wang, Ju An. Wang, Hao. Guo, Minzhe. & Xia, Min. 2009, Security metrics for software systems. ACM-SE 47: Proceedings of the 47th annual southeast and regional conference.

Wright, Jason. McQueen, Miles. & Wellman, Lawerence. 2013, Analyses of two end-user software vulnerability exposure metrics (extended version). Information Security Technical Report. vol. 17, Issue 4.

Yadav, Neha. Yadav, Vibash. Mishra, & Prashant, Kumar. 2019, Software Matrices Selection for a SDLC Based Software Reliability Prediction Model. International Journal of Recent Technology and Engineering, vol. 8, Issue 2S6: pp. 959–963.

Smart Computing – Khan et al (Eds)
© *2021 Taylor & Francis Group, London, ISBN 978-0-367-76552-1*

Web development frameworks and its performance analysis—a review

S.P. Mishra & S.K. Srivastava
School of Computing Science & Engineering, Galgotias University, Gr. Noida, UP, India

ABSTRACT: Web application frameworks are quite popular in the multi-tier application domain. The framework fits the requirements of request-response object. Several different frameworks use a different kind of approach to solve a given task. If a wrong framework is chosen for the particular task then it can negatively impact the web application affecting its performance and scalability.

Our study highlights the best practices identified by the developers which can render better performance while analyzing the scalability issues when the load is increased. The study aims to benchmark ten frameworks and analyze their performances based on their responses from the server with some scalability factors.

This study can help developers to choose better application frameworks when data is sensitive and an application needs to fulfill requirements with better performance and scalability. We establish a link between client requests made per second and the response of the framework simultaneously.

Keywords: Web development practices, Scalability of web frameworks, web frame work performance.

1 INTRODUCTION

This era is greatly influenced by the internet and it has also penetrated the rural areas of the world serving a billion people. With great demand and user base, the quality of services provided has not been uniform and in this last decade, rapid development has been seen in mobile applications and web page (Pande et al. 2018). Thus, web technologies have been constantly improving, new technologies are emerging, and thus more people tend to use web services to improve their productivity while generating profits fulfilling customer needs and maximizing outcomes. In multitier applications, critical data travels across the Internet and requires additional security that impacts service costs. Developers and coders use various popular framework technologies to develop web applications to use such as Laravel, Symfony (Adam 2019), Struts, JSF, Spring, Angular, React, Flask, Ruby on Rails, Django, and many others.

Various web frameworks are used to make developers' jobs easier in providing these services with a well-built and structured design. Web frameworks have been an integral part of web application development which helps to construct the integral parts of the development without the need for re-inventing the sophisticated techniques. Software developers can easily implement solutions that make web applications dynamic, scalable, and strong while streamline and speed up the development process. A web framework or web application framework is a high-level solution framework that is designed for reuse of software pieces or code to act as a support system for the development of web applications, a step toward the library-based reuse that promotes a shared domain of functions and logic (Salas 2015).

Choosing an appropriate framework for web development that fits the developers' requirements is a typical task as a choice of an inappropriate framework leads to waste of time studying specifics of different languages, failure to meet the deadline and spending time in deciding proper actions to choose a different framework based on best practices. Basically, a best practice is a process, or a set of resources with a proven rate of success in achieving significant factors such as cost, quality,

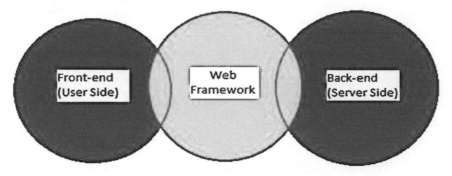

Figure 1. Web framework for application development.

scalability, performance, security, safety, environment, or other computable factors (Adam 2019; Salas 2015). In terms of framework scalability, it is important how a framework handles requests to and back the server.

This ensures a better quality of products including web services, web resources, and web APIs. A web framework work on the front-end or back-end part of any implemented application. It involves coding small to large modules of a web application thus automating the process. It is a tool that provides a hassle-free process of developing applications with abstraction and performance that complies with modern web standards.

There are various frameworks available to get a developer's work done. Node.js is a popular JavaScript platform that provides that is free of locks and is designed to advantage of the multi-core system (Link: nodejs.org/en/). React is also a JavaScript framework that has a virtual DOM architecture to deliver high performance. It is used in the Facebook technology stack (Kumar & Singh 2016). Java frameworks are also popular like JSF and Spring. Spring has asynchronous non-blocking architecture and is flexible, quicker, and safe with speed and simplicity. Its main advantage is that it contains a variety of modules to work with (https://spring.io/).

Therefore, frameworks provide gear to an application for handling requests, scaling up or scaling down, better response time, storing data to database, clean code, and so on. Framework performance and scalability have always been an important factor while considering the frameworks that provide easy integration and better communication as shown in Fig 1.

1.1 Framework Architecture

1.1.1 Model-View Controller (MVC)
This is an architectural pattern or design pattern which gives a reusable result to a common design pattern. Design patterns include solutions to availability, abstraction, performance, etc. The Model-View Controller (MVC) is used to separate the data according to the concerns and connect the space between user interface and code to fulfill the business requirements and thus perform a separate task for user interface and model design implementation. The Model part in MVC controls the data and business needs; View controls the visual or front-end part; and Controller provides interaction between the view and model layers (Kumar et al. 2017). Some examples of this architecture are Django, Ruby on Rails, Spring, and CodeIgniter.

1.1.2 Three-tier Architecture
This framework architecture has mainly three components: client, application, and database. The client usually runs the scripts on the server, the application contains the core business idea, and the database stores the related information such as Relational Database Management System (RDBMS).

This paper is organized as follows. Section 2 presents the comparative analysis of various frame-works that are based on the best practices. Section 3 details the data analysis of the frameworks

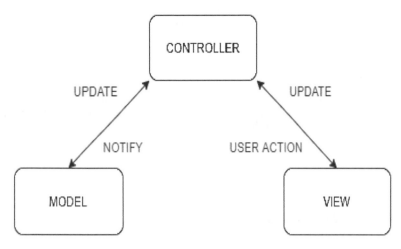

Figure 2. MVC architectural design.

based on the concurrency and response time of the users to evaluate the scalability factor, followed by a discussion of which development practice is comparatively performing better based on the above details. The final section includes a conclusion based on the best practices and web frameworks included and the future scope of this paper with concluding remarks.

2 COMPARATIVE ANALYSIS

A comparative analysis is the best way to find out the outcome and various best practices have evolved the web technological era leading to well-documented, widely used code that provides quality, security, flexibility, simple, and clean. Below is a comparison of various technologies (some are new and some have been around for some while) gathering most relevant practices by studies are mentioned in the Table 1.

2.1 *Cloud computing*

Cloud computing is widely used in many organizations and is still growing. It provides services such as software, platform, and infrastructure on the basics of pay-per-use and can be accessed from anywhere around the world. It provides various deployment strategies such that users can choose from a wide range of options (Adam 2019; flask.palletsprojects.com/en/1.1.x/deploying/#deployment; https://angular.io/guide/deployment; laravel.com/docs/5.0/filesystem; spring.io/projects/spring-cloud).

2.2 *HTML5*

The goal of developing a front-end framework is interactivity and responsiveness which include fluid animation, music, videos, and thus choose to integrate them into the website. HTML5 has made it possible to embed rich content into twebsites. It is primarily creating a declarative hypertext language to incorporate many application-like functions (Salas 2015; Benmoussa et al. 2019).

2.3 *Platform Support*

When developers write a particular application, they need to consider the hardware and OS demands also. It is worthless to input a lot of time and work into the development and then to find poor server performance because it is not suited for the platform (Salas 2015; Benmoussa et al. 2019; Maia 2015).

2.4 *Architectural Design*

The ease of development comes with a well-structured architecture such as MVC, MVVM (Model View-View Model), and MVT (Model View Template) which provide the abstraction of business logic and different modules of the application (Laaziri 2019; www.tutorialspoint.com/; Maia 2015).

2.5 *ORM*

Object Relational Mapping (ORM) is a way of sorting the data into the database from an architecture without involving the traditional approach which is much more typical. It reduces the complexities of code defines the mapping between the object model and database schema (Salas 2015; Benmoussa et al. 2019; Laaziri 2019).

2.6 *Documentation*

It is an important aspect of web development and maintenance. Documentation is essential in case any changes have to be made in the future but generally developers ignore it (symfony.com/doc/current/index.html#gsc.tab=0; compodoc.app/; docs.angularjs.org/guide; reactjs.org/docs/getting-started.html).

3 DISCUSSION ON FRAMEWORKS SCALABILITY ISSUES

The two important concerns for choosing a platform are performance and scalability. Analyzing web application performance means finding the performance of the request and response time of the web application. There are many ways to determine web application performance. Either you can build a physical system with benchmarking tools and establish simple scripts for complete research or purchase and study the analytical reports from an established organization like Gartner. TechEmpower is a website that started a project to compare the different web frameworks and platforms based on their performance and latencies under different environments and setups. It establishes benchmarking reports that if studied properly can help developers decide which platform to use. It's a colligative effort that is conducted in an open forum (Li & Jiang 2019).

The performance of a framework usually depends on factors according to the requirement according to the web application to be developed. Thus, the variety of tests performed to create a common basis for all the web frameworks are JSON serializations, database accesses, plaintext test, and server-side template composition.

TechEmpower provides data that can be used to determine scalability and performance results with the JSON test, single query test (framework's ORM), plaintext test (request-routing through HTTP pipeline), and fortune test (Database or ORM connectivity). Below are some graphs that were developed to show the detailed comparison of four majorly used framework platforms in modern web applications. These platform frameworks are compared with the total number of concurrencies at 16 to a concurrency at 128 of various platforms in a graphical manner. As shown in Table 1, the graphs depict the analysis of the performances of each of the platforms in terms of the responses per second. These tests are performed using Dell R440 Xeon Gold and 10 GbE of connectivity (https://www.techempower.com/benchmarks).

We will derive a relationship between the response time and the number of simultaneous users that can work on it. So first, we can need to find the response time (RP) required for a request and response action to be complete. In this decade, the performance of web applications has become the most important aspect for businesses as search engines like Google factor performance as

Table 1. Best web development practices comparison with Rails, JSF, Struts, Django, Angular, Laravel, Spring, React, Flask, and Symfony.

Best Practices	Web Frameworks									
	Ruby on Rails	JSF	Struts	Django	Angular	Laravel	Spring	React	Flask	Symfony
Cloud Computing	Yes (Amazon EC2, Rackspace, Heroku)	Yes (Oracle Public Cloud, Oracle WebLogic Server, Google App Engine)	Yes (Jelastic, Google App Engine)	Yes (dotCloud, Google App Engine, and Amazon EC2)	Yes (Firebase, Azure, Netlify, Amazon S3)	Yes (Amazon S3, Rackspace)	Yes (all major providers)	Yes	Yes (Heroku, App Engine, AWS, Azure)	Yes (all major providers)
HTML5 Support	No	Yes	No	Yes	Yes	No	No	No	Yes	No
Platform Support	Cross-platform	Cross-platform	Cross-platform	Cross-platform	Cross-platform	Cross-platform	Cross-platform	Cross-platform	Cross-platform	Cross-platform
Architectural Design	MVC	MVC	MVC2 (Pull MVC)	MVT	MVW	MVC	MVC	None, connected to flux	No defined model	MVC
ORM	Yes (Active Record)	Yes	Yes	Yes (Django ORM)	Yes (Angular Universal)	Yes (Eloquent ORM)	Yes (Hibernate, iBatis, JPA)	Yes	Yes (SQLAlchemy)	Yes (Doctrine ORM)
Documentation	Yes (RDoc)	Yes (JavaDoc)	Yes (JavaDoc)	Yes (Sphinx)	Yes (CompoDoc)	Yes (Apidoc)	Yes	Yes	Yes	Yes

Table 2. Data table of responses per second with best performance.

Web Frameworks	JSON Serialization	Plain-text	Single Query	Fortunes/ ORM
Rails	21818	20802	13057	8807
Django	63452	67880	19409	10304
Node.js	552075	9997327	143328	91086
Laravel	8681	7215	6023	5484
Spring	136364	70573	76780	30891
Flask	67749	90444	15526	10655
Symfony	22262	19741	740	1213

in their ranking which leads to performance equals better visibility and thus more users actively participating and which in turn increases revenue (Amza et al. 2002).

While the limit of pages a CPU can handle depends on the number of cores (nC), the maximum number of pages requested can be stated as $nC/Rp =$ maximum no of request (maxReq) it can handle. Thus, maxReq(mins) $*$ click frequency of users = maximum no of simultaneous result (maxUsers).

This analysis is based on the table of concurrency to platforms and frameworks that consider the best overall results with concurrencies varying from 16 to 256 to 16,384.

Summing up the results in the above architecture, we can safely say that Node.js infrastructure looks very efficient in overall results w.r.t the responses per second. Through this derivation, we can conclude that the Furthermore, scalability or handling users on a platform would be more difficult.

4 CONCLUSION

This paper provides a comparison of various web application development frameworks in terms of their best practices which included factors such as support for various functionalities and documentation. Therefore, the best practice helps in reducing the possible mistakes of choosing a particular framework and gives more insight into features to develop a web application. Also, the performance of frameworks has been deeply studied and the scalability factor has been evaluated. This helps us to understand the concurrency of users across various web systems and how can server handle the request and response at standard conditions.

5 FUTURE WORK

As for a future direction, it is suitable to study the performances and scalability factor of all the frameworks on the localized system proposed in the paper and also work on more future technologies. Although this paper has not considered cloud servers, it is left for future studies.

REFERENCES

Adam, Stenly, & Stevani. 2019. A New PHP Web Application Development Framework Based on MVC Architectural Pattern and Ajax Technology. *1st International Conference on Cybernetics and Intelligent System (ICORIS)*.

Amza, C., Cecchet, E., Chanda, A., Cox, A. L., Elnikety, S., Gil, R., ... & Zwaene-poel, W. 2002. Specification and implementation of dynamic web site benchmarks. In *5th Workshop on Workload Characterization* (No. CONF).

Architecture. *Tutorials Point India Limited*. www.tutorialspoint.com/

Benmoussa, K., Laaziri, M., Khoulji, S., Larbi, K. M., & El Yamami, A. 2019. A new model for the selection of web development frameworks: application to PHP frame-works. *International Journal of Electrical and Computer Engineering*, 9(1), 695.

Compodoc. *MIT*. compodoc.app/.

Deployment Options. Angular. 2020. *Google*. https://angular.io/guide/deployment.

Deployment Options. flask.palletsprojects.com/en/1.1.x/deploying/#deployment.

Developer Guide. *Google*. docs.angularjs.org/guide.

Facebook Inc., reactjs.org/docs/getting-started.html.

Filesystem. *Laravel LLC*. laravel.com/docs/5.0/filesystem.

Kumar, A., & Singh, R. K. 2016. Comparative Analysis of AngularJS and ReactJS. *Interna tional Journal of Latest Trends in Engineering and Technology*, 7(4), 225–227.

Kumar, V., Chopra, V., Makkar, R. S., & Panesar, J. S. 2017. DESIGN & IMPLEMEN-TATION OF JMETER FRAMEWORK FOR PERFORMANCE COMPARISON IN PHP & PYTHON WEB APPLICATIONS. *International Interdisciplinary Conference on Science Technology Engineering Management Pharmacy and Humanities.*

Laaziri, Majida, et al. "A Comparative Study of Laravel and Symfony PHP Frame-works." *International Journal of Electrical and Computer Engineering (IJECE)*, vol. 9, no. 1, Jan. 2019, p. 704., doi:10.11591/ijece.v9i1. pp704–712.

Li, Y., & Jiang, Z. M. J. 2019. Assessing and optimizing the performance impact of the just-in-time configuration parameters-a case study on PyPy. *Empirical Software Engineering*, 24(4), 2323–2363.

Maia, Italo. 2015. Building Web Applications with Flask Use Python and Flask to Build Amazing Web Applications, Just the Way You Want Them! *Packt Publishing.*

Node.js. *OpenJS Foundation*. nodejs.org/en/.

Pande, N., Somani, A., Samal, S. P., & Kakkirala, V. 2018. Enhanced web application and browsing perfor-mance through service-worker infusion framework. In 2018 *IEEE International Conference on Web Services (ICWS)* (pp. 195–202). IEEE.

Salas, María. 2015. Analyzing Best Practices on Web Development Frameworks: The Lift Approach. *Science of Computer Programming*, vol. 102.

Spring Cloud. *VMware Inc*. spring.io/projects/spring-cloud.

Spring Home. *VMware Inc*. https://spring.io/.

Symfony Documentation. Symfony SAS. sym-fony.com/doc/current/index.html#gsc.tab=0.

TechEmpower Web Framework Benchmarks, 2019 https://www.techempower.com/benchmarks.

Smart Computing – Khan et al (Eds)
© *2021 Taylor & Francis Group, London, ISBN 978-0-367-76552-1*

The impact of machine learning on processing big data in high-performance computing

Rohit
Department of Computer Science and Engineering, Uttarakhand Technical University, Dehradun, India

B. Gupta
Department of Computer Science and Engineering, GB Pant Institute of Engineering & Technology, Pauri Garhwal, India

K.K. Gola
Department of Computer Science and Engineering, Faculty of Engineering, TMU, Moradabad, India

ABSTRACT: In today's world, it is obvious that the use of digital data, i.e., big data, is rapidly expanding. Generation of useful information from proliferated data is an engrossing process that is referred to as "training of the data". Nowadays, trained data sets have a vital role in finding knowledge through machine learning (ML). This paper presents new ideas in ML or deep learning techniques for machines in the field of training data for high-performance computing. It represents the survey of various ML techniques or methods applied prior to training data sets for knowledge extraction in big data analytics to enhance high-performance computing like cloud computing or grid computing. This paper could be seen as the origin and basis of research and has a key value in the field of ML.

Keywords: Proliferated data, trained data sets, deep learning, machine learning, big data analytics, cloud computing, high-performance computing.

1   INTRODUCTION

Machine Learning (ML) has become an enhanced, forward-thinking, and advanced step in Artificial Intelligence (AI) in which given algorithms can be measured as pillars to make computers learn, acting as auxiliary intelligence by somehow generalizing the attractiveness in just storing, retrieving, and analyzing data items for high-performance computing such as cloud computing or grid computing. ML has taken an prominent position in a variety of fields, including computer science, statistics, forensic sciences, biology, medical practices, and psychology. The main impression of ML is about making a digital machine aware about past experiences. These types of job can be done by efficient classifier (Kotsiantis 2007).

ML, a phrase coined in 1959 by Arthur Samuel of IBM, is a branch of generalized AI in which a machine has been trained to automatically learn and improve based on past knowledge and experience without being clearly programmed to do so. ML has played a vital role in analyzing the observation of data generated from different areas to qualify the high-performance computing criterion. ML is the foundation for researchers in various fields (Shaikh & Ali 2017).

This rest of the paper is organized as follows. Section 2 delineates the ML algorithm and advances learning methods as background. Section 3 gives detailed reviews of different proposed and existing systems, models, frameworks, algorithms, methods/techniques. etc. as state-of-the-art. Section 4

DOI 10.1201/9781003167488-40

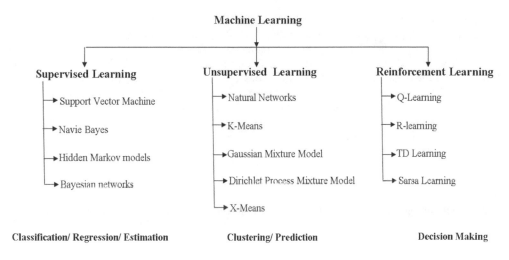

Figure 1. Classification of the machine learning approach.

presents a summary of the reviews taken from various researcher articles. Section 5 provides a conclusion as well as recommendations for future research.

2 BACKGROUND

In the field of high-performance computing ML, a vast collection of research exists that is properly bound for hypothesis, performance, properties, and synthesis of learning algorithms. It is a highly adjustable area that depends on rhythm in different types of fields like AI (Quasim 2015), optimality and optimization theory, statistical analysis, cognitive science, engineering, data science, and other sciences (Qiu 2016).

ML basically can be classified into three types of learning: supervised, unsupervised, and rein- forcement (Adam et al. 2008). Supervised learning requires training with labeled data which has inputs and desired outputs, but unsupervised learning does not require labeled training data and the system provides inputs without desired domain. Reinforcement learning enables learning from feedback received through connections with an exterior environment (Qiu 2016).

The supervised learning classification consists of two main steps: (1) the training step draws more scientific attention (Zheng et al. 2013) in which classification model is designed, fit on a small data set that does not represent facts for big data applications (Quasim 2019); and (2) the classification itself, where the trained model is applied to be assigned to unknown data to one out of a given set of class labels (Ayma et al. 2015). There are several algorithms described in Qiu (2016), Ghosh et al. (2009), Yue et al. (2015), Dong et al. (2010), Hajj et al. (2014), Bkassiny et al. (2013), Serrano & Giupponi(2010), Das et al. (1999), Sutton (1988), and Singh et al. (2000); see Figure 1.

3 REVIEWS

In 1950, the concept of "Turing Test" to find if a computer has real intelligence was first given by the scientist Alan Turing. After that, Arthur Samuel worked on a computer learning program to check the capability of learning in 1952. In 1967, the "nearest neighbor" algorithm was developed for basic pattern recognition. In 1952, Gerald Dejong was given the idea of explanation-based ML to analyze training data. After that, work was done on ML to convert the knowledge-driven approach to a data-driven approach in the 1990s. In 2006, Geoffrey Hinton introduced deep learning which explicated new algorithms for computers to predict the difference in objects and text in images or videos. After a huge discovery, Google invented ML methods in its X lab in 2012 that was able to browse YouTube in parallel to recognize the videos. Are closer to achieving artificial intelligence? Some researchers believe that this is actually the wrong question. They presume that a computer will never be able to imagine in the way a human brain does, and that comparing investigations which can be computed and algorithms for a computer to that of the human intellect is like comparing apples to oranges (Marr 2016). Hence, this section provides detailed reviews for the investigation of the most influential techniques.

Batista et al. (2004) examined the performance of different methods of learning from unfair data sets. Their result predicts the over-sampling technique, and the proposed model produces, very good results. In their work, over-sampling is thus commonly considered an encumbered method that predicts strong-willed results with more compounded methods. A large number of positive data set examples produced meaningful results by using the random over-sampling technique which is computationally cheaper than other techniques. Their work might be useful to understand the behavior of cleaning and balancing techniques.

Silla et al. (2008) presented a narrative approach to classify the music genre using ML techniques. They used different featured vectors and a pattern detection assembly method which reflects time and space decomposition schemes. They achieved the task using binary classifiers set, whose predictions are combined to create the final music genre label. They used the Latine Music Database of 3160 items distributed in 10 genres for experiments gives results that illustrate a projected ensemble approach which produced improved consequences over one extracted from global and individual classifier segments.

Bie et al. (2009) proposed taxonomy to classify approaches based on three fundamental characteristics: underlying framework, data representation, and algorithmic class. They had attempted to give an overview and propose taxonomy for some of the existing approaches to the Secure Sockets Layer (SSL).

Ince et al. (2010) worked on practicability of locating microcracks with using a multiple-sensor capacity of acoustic emissions which are produced through crack setting up and breeding. They used data from cracks in rock specimens which come through surface volatility test for experiment and these cracks simulate failure near a free facade like tunnel wall. They projected ML methods with support vector machine (SVM) and clustering analysis for finding the estimated clusters which successfully predict location where failures in the form of very disperse pattern are observed in surface volatility tests. Their method gives potential to be a component of a structural health monitoring system and also presents the competence of noisy signals filtrations and improves signal-to-noise ratio (SNR) to attain more consistent after effects (AE) cluster areas.

Training data enhances the performance of hybrid fuzzy algorithm. Its complexities were offered by Ishibuchi et al. (2011). They observed good effects for its execution with dissimilar sub-populations in parallel as well as non-parallel versions. They also obtained improved results training data subsets used for whole trained data in most of the cases.

Neethu (2013) proposed that intrusion detection involved an attribute selection technique to select relevant attributes applied on a classifier for classifying network data into two parts like normal classes and attack classes. The paper elaborated a framework of Network Intrusion Detection worked on Naïve Bayes and Principal Component Analysis algorithm make different network services patterns with labeled datasets by the services. The authors compare the method to the neural network and tree algorithm-oriented approach which gained less time consumption, higher detection rate, low cost, and provides about 94% accuracy using this approach which also generates some false positives.

Qu et al. (2013) explored the leeway of accessing big data generated by Discrete Fourier transform (DFT) techniques for the number of molecular structures, extracting pertinent molecular properties. The authors applied ML techniques to learn from the data. After training data, the ML model used structures to construct rapid predictions. Their approach was represented for hemolytic bond dissociation energy.

Smusz et al. (2013) tested ML techniques in two different modes: (i) immobile molecules generation by one test set and (ii) immobile molecules preparation in parallel by implementing test sets as for training. Their experiments give the result of five dissimilar protein targets, three samples for molecules illustration, and seven algorithms for classification with unstable parameters. They finally concluded that range of active molecules from databases with assorted structures and immobile compounds producing training set that should be envoy to the utmost possible amount for libraries suffered selection.

Kurczab et al. (2014) analyzed the number training sets which are in negative in nature, examples on the concert of performance of ML methods. They found an increment in the ratio of change in positive to negative training sets to really influence most of the inspected evaluating parameters of ML techniques in replicated virtual viewing experiments.

Emanet et al. (2014) developed predictive models by using a four-stage procedure of pulmonary sound signals analysis, feature extraction, decomposition of wavelets, and classification. In classification, they worked on classified respiratory of different sounds using Random Forest (RF) algorithm and AdaBoost with artificial neural networks. Their findings were Specificity with 95.0%, Sensitivity 90.0%, and Accuracy with 92.5%. Their outcomes reflect analysis of computerized lung sounds which relies on low-cost and non-invasive microphones, so that physicians can make faster and better diagnostic decisions by an embedded real-time microprocessor system even in the absence of X-ray and CT-scanners.

Raza et al. (2015) studied and worked for several ML methods for their accuracy in predicting the cancer class, i.e., tumor or normal. ML is efficiently fine when the number of attributes (genes) were larger than the number of samples which is seldom possible with gene facade data. They have relatively evaluated a variety of ML techniques for their correctness in class prediction of prostate cancer data set.

Ayma et al. (2015) presented data mining methods which are able to carry out classification on large data, expressing the benefits of working on clusters by using Hadoop framework. They concluded by experimental analysis that extraction performance of data is increases parallel with the amount of data being accessed. Also, the authors' outcomes presented that as increasing the number of nodes in cluster which does not essentially provide an equivalent decrement of execution times. Hence, the appropriate cluster designs pattern relies on the operations to be executed and on the size of input data.

Hasegawa et al.'s (2015) objective was to study to facilitate user operations by knowledge contexts pragmatic on a smartphone. They proposed a system for automatically adjustment of volume of the application to avoid interruptions in surrounding, and also reduce the user performance by estimating a suitable volume and by observing and learning on a usual basis. The system gives results on their experimental correctness of evaluation. They found the best accuracy with tree structure that is based on initial foreground application and sound volume in course of classifier.

Alistair et al. (2016) studied the issue of compartmentalization, corruption, and complexity concerned in the collection and preprocessing of critical care data in medicine. The authors worked on clinical data management systems (CDMS) which typically present caretaker teams with useful sequence, derived from huge, extremely heterogeneous, data sources that are frequently altering animatedly. They summarized the latest trend in ML in critical care and focused all components like acquirement of data, guarantee of quality, and final analysis. They worked for processing and validation of data acquired within the ICU. Many of these methods are required due to the fairly unique format of data collection.

Anna & Buczak (2016) focused on literature investigation of ML and data mining algorithms–data analytics of cyber analytics in support of intrusion detection. They used density-based methods which had been most resourceful, simple to employ, less constrained, or allocation-dependent and have elevated processing speeds. SVMs gained learning by extracting relationship rules or chronological patterns and much in anomaly detectors from the available usual traffic data. Efficiency of the techniques was not only one situation, but several criteria required to be taken into explanation, e.g., complexity, accuracy, time for classifying an unknown occurrence with a trained model of each data mining or ML.

Hordri et al.'s (2017) goal was to predict a systematic literature analysis on deep learning. They investigated and identified characteristics of deep learning, and influenced the efficiency of big data analytics. Their results exposed the five features of deep learning need to organize enhanced big data analysis. They concluded their idea was an active research area by which big data analytics became more efficient.

Alurkar et al. (2017) focused on categorizing email into two parts: spam and not spam. Their proposed system is a self-learning machine that is customizable to each user which is based on dataset will only give better accuracy when datasets rise in size which generates an optimal solution. Their proposed method trained the algorithm and classified previously classified datasets afterward the system enlarges the features to categorize received emails and exhibit them in an ordered manner. They find that the proposed system increases the productivity by reducing the distraction and also protect from malevolent attacks.

Sheshasaayee & Lakshm's (2017) proposed model gives training using optimized ML methods based on tree structure to forecast the temperature, using existing data-generated earlier. They replaced a map reduction framework by the Spark framework. They compared their findings on tree-structured ML techniques with respect to space and time utilization for minimization. Their model can be useful for many areas like fog, humidity, and pollution for uniformity to make out enhanced approximation future examination.

Sharma & Rani (2007) aimed to employ data mining and ML efficiency for illuminating the biological samples of pattern. They work for gene selection by their proposed technique for genomic profiles of cancerous. When sample size of the data is varied, their practice is oriented on the notion of using SVM and nearest-neighbor algorithms which gives a relative investigation of model concert. If the sample size amplifies, model production also increases; that gives the result of positive facet of robustness and adaptively of model.

Sukanya & Kuma (2017) analyzed the significance of big data and a range of steps involved in ML techniques in healthcare. They identified big data analytics which helped to comprehend target to success the goal of diagnosing, treating, healing, and helping all patients required for healthcare clinical system. They concluded that using new techniques of ML, it is easier to develop therapies and products.

Jaseena & Kovoor (2018) surveyed different deep learning methods for big data analytics in biometrics and discussed various issues and their solutions. Deep learning techniques may become ML that can be used to haul out the composite and nonlinear patterns observed in big data efficiently. The authors concluded in their paper after their comprehensive study that big data in biometrics can be handled easily.

4 REVIEWS AUTHOR'S TARGETS, SATISFIED FINDINGS, AND SHORT DESCRIPTION

In this section, we summarize the above-reviewed works in tabular format and present it in a more informative way. Table 1 describes in the short description of the researcher's/author's/reviewer's existing work, targets, and satisfied findings which make work more useful for forthcoming research in ML scope of research area. The table also shows that how ML is clutching the big data analytics day-by-day using earlier/previously defined tools, proposed approaches, algorithms, techniques, methods, or frameworks.

5 FINDINGS AND OUTCOMES

As per our survey, we discovered that if we applied many ML algorithms framework like supervised, unsupervised, reinforcement, and model-based learning with two presentations—vector and graph—then we can analyze the data in several approaches accordingly. These approaches may be

Table 1. Researcher/author's various targets with satisfying performance matrices and short description.

Authors	Technology/Framework/ Tools/Proposed Approach	Result/Short Description/Remark
(Batista et al. 2004)	Methods-Smote + Tomek and Smote + ENN proposed	Their work might be useful to understand the behavior of balancing and cleaning methods.
(Silla et al. 2008)	Pattern recognition assembly method	Method produced improved consequences obtained from global and individual classifiers.
(Bie et al. 2009)	Proposed taxonomy to classify approaches based on underlying framework, data representation, and algorithmic class	They give an overview and propose taxonomy for some of the existing approaches to SSL.
(Ince et al. 2010)	Projected ML methods with clustering analysis and SVM	Method gives structural health monitoring system component potential improved. Accordingly improves the SNR and also presents competence in noisy signals filtration.
(Ishibuchi et al. 2011)	Hybrid fuzzy GBML algorithm	Improved results of training data subsets used for entire training data mostly.
(Neethu 2013)	Framework-Network Intrusion Detection	Provides about 94% accuracy using this approach which also generates some false positives.
(Qu et al. 2013)	DFT methods	To achieve root mean of square deviation, proposed DFT model can be used to self-determining test sets.
(Smusz et al., 2013)	ML modes	They concluded that range of active range of molecules from databases sets with assorted formats and immobile compounds which create trained set that envoy to the utmost potential amount for libraries, suffered screening.
(Kurczab et al., 2014)	ML methods	Authors inspected evaluating parameters of ML approach in replicated virtual screening investigations.
(Emanet et al. 2014)	Four-stage procedure for analyzing pulmonary sound signals	Their findings were in three parameters: Specificity 95.0% Sensitivity 90.0% Accuracy 92.5%
(Raza et al. 2015)	Worked for several ML methods	They evaluated a variety of approaches of ML for correctness in prediction in variety of class of data sets of prostate cancer.
(Ayma et al. 2015)	Presented data mining package	Author's outcomes presented that as increasing the number of nodes in cluster which does not essentially provide an equivalent decrement of execution times
(Hasegawa et al. 2015)	Knowledge contexts pragmatic on a Smartphone	Authors found best accuracy with tree structure on initial foreground application and sound volume in course of classifier.
(Alistair et al. 2016)	Authors studied about the issue of compartmentalization, corruption, and complexity concerned in collection and preprocessing of critical care data in medical	They worked for processing and validation of data acquired within the ICU. Many of these methods are required due to the fairly unique format of data collection
(Anna & Buczak 2016)	Literature investigation of ML and DM method	SVMs gained learned by extracting relationship rules or chronological patterns as good and much in anomaly detectors data as accuracy, time, complexity for classifying with a trained.
(Hordri et al. 2017)	Prediction on systematic literature analysis on Deep Learning	They found that big data analytics became more efficient.
(Alurkar et al. 2017)	Proposed Self Learning system	Proposed system increases the productivity by reducing the distraction and also protect from malevolent attacks

(Continued)

Table 1.   Researcher/author's various targets with satisfying performance matrices and short description. (*Continued*)

Authors	Technology/Framework/ Tools/Proposed Approach	Result/Short Description/Remark
(Sheshasaayee & Lakshm 2017)	Proposed model optimizes ML methods based on tree.	Their model can be useful for different biological data for uniformity to make out improved judgment of future examination.
(Sharma & Rani 2017)	Proposed technique based on SVM and nearest-neighbor algorithm of ML.	Authors found aspect of robustness and adaptively of proposed model positively.
(Sukanya & Kuma 2017)	Analyze significance of big data and a range of steps involved in ML techniques	Authors are successful in goal of diagnosing, treating, healing, and helping all patients required for healthcare clinical system.
(Jaseena & Kovoor 2018)	Deep learning techniques	Deep learning techniques may become ML that can be used to haul out the composite and nonlinear patterns observed in big data efficiently.

Table 2.   Approach in percentage (%) can be applied for supervised framework according to the presentation of the 'd'.

Presentation	Heuristic	Exact (Expontial- Time)	Convex Relaxation	Exact (Polynomial- time)	Spectral relaxation	Convex/ spectral relaxation	Exact (spectral)
Vector	38	10	37	10	2	2	1
Graph	3	1	0	90	3	2	1

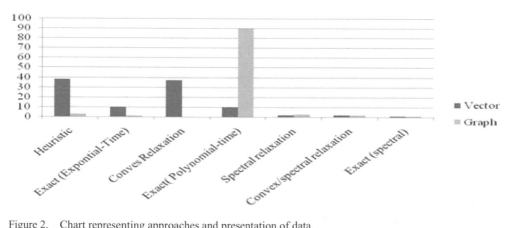

Figure 2.   Chart representing approaches and presentation of data.

on the basis of outcomes of the algorithms/methods/ framework. These approaches are exactness, exact (exponential-time), convex relaxation, heuristic, exact (polynomial-time), spectral relaxation, convex/spectral relaxation, etc., and we conclude the results of various frameworks and found the percentage of different approaches can be applied to various presentation in different framework, may or may not be applied on trained data.

Table 3. Approach in percentage (%) can be applied for unsupervised framework.

Presentation	Heuristic	Exact (Expontial-Time)	Convex Relaxation	Exact (Polynomial-time)	Spectral relaxation	Convex/ spectral relaxation	Exact (spectral)
Vector	90	2	0	2	2	1	1
Graph	2	1	5	5	80	2	5

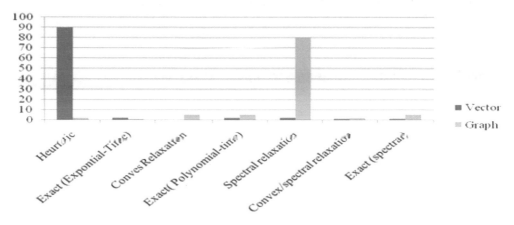

Figure 3. Chart representing approaches and presentation of data.

Table 4. Approach in percentage (%) can be applied to model-based framework according to the presentation of the data.

Presentation	Heuristic	Exact (Expontial-Time)	Convex Relaxation	Exact (Polynomial-time)	Spectral relaxation	Convex/ spectral relaxation	Exact (spectral)
Vector	90	2	0	2	2	1	1
Graph	2	1	5	5	80	2	5

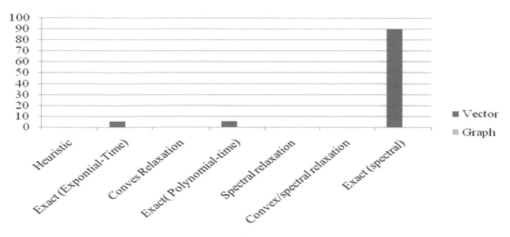

Figure 4. Chart representing approaches and presentation of data.

6 CONCLUSION AND FUTURE SCOPE

In this paper, we have studied and reviewed different paper articles written/presented by number of researchers given in different major fields in healthcare. We find and can focus on the view that ML techniques are becoming continuous increasingly popular in continuous manner. ML has been playing a vital role in big data analytics in various fields like clinical practice, biomedical research, network simulation/resources allocation, financial system, etc. Some researchers had given the idea how to train data set chosen from the big data used for learning. By comparing the effectiveness of different ML techniques/models used in various fields can assume that ML through algorithms using training datasets can be a better way to design the knowledge from the big data which improves big data analytics with effective performance.

In the future, this paper may be the base review paper for researchers/scholars in the field of ML and data training. As per the author reviews of different papers, as given in Tables 1–4 and Figures 2–4, we tried to showcase various reflected influenced idea of effective ML techniques in big data analytics to train the data for knowledge extraction. This survey will be an initial and effective approach in revolutionary trends in processing big data using ML.

REFERENCES

S. B. Kotsiantis. Supervised Machine Learning: A Review of Classification Techniques. *Informatica*, 31(3): 249–268, 2007.

T. A. Shaikh and R. Ali. Machine Learning: Messiah of 21st Century. *CSI Communications*, 08 (41), 2017.

Junfei Qiu, Qihui Wu, Guoru Ding, Yuhua Xu and Shuo Feng. A survey of machine learning for big data processing. *EURASIP Journal on Advances in Signal Processing*, 67, 2016.

B. Adam, I.F.C. Smith and F. V. Asce. Reinforcement learning for structural control. *Journal of Computing Civil Eng* 22(2), 13–139, 2008.

Q. Zheng, Z. Wu, X. Cheng, L. Jiang and J. Liu. Learning to crawl deep web. *Information Systems*, 38 (6), 801–819, 2013.

V. A. Ayma, R. S. Ferreira, P. Happ, D. Oliveira, R. Feitosa, G. Costa, A. Plaza, and Gamba. Classification algorithms for big data analysis, a map reduce approach. The International Archives of the Photogrammetry, *Remote Sensing and Spatial Information Sciences*, XL-3/W2, PIA15+HRIGI15 – Joint ISPRS conference, 2–27, 2015.

C. Ghosh, C. Cordeiro, D.P. Agrawal, M.B. Rao. Markov chain existence and hidden Markov models in spectrum sensing. In *Proceedings of the IEEE International Conference on Pervasive Computing & Communications* (pp. 1–6), 2009.

V. Yue, Q. Fang, X. WangLi and Weiy. A parallel and incremental approach for data-intensive learning of Bayesian networks. *IEEE Trans Cybern 99*, 1–15, 2015.

X. Dong., Y. Li, C. Wu and Y. Cai. A learner based on neural network for cognitive radio. In *Proceedings of the 12th IEEE International Conference on Communication Technology (ICCT)* (pp. 89–896). Nanjing, 2010.

A. E. Hajj, L. Safatly, M. Bkassiny and M. Husseini. Cognitive radio transceivers: RF, spectrum sensing, and learning algorithms review. *International Journal of Antenna Propagation*, 11(5), 479–482, 2014.

M. Bkassiny, S.K. Jayaweer, and Y. Li. Multidimensional dirichlet process-based non-parametric signal classification for autonomous self-learning cognitive radios. *IEEE Trans Wireless Communication*, 12(11), 541–5423, 2013.

A. G. Serrano and L. Giupponi. Distributed Q-learning for aggregated interference control in cognitive radio networks. *IEEE Transactions on Vehicular Technology*, 59(4), 182–1834, 2010.

T.K. Das, A. Gosavi, S. Mahadevan and N Marchalleck. Solving semi-markov decision problems using average reward reinforcement learning. *Management Science*, 45(4), 560–574, 1999.

R.S. Sutton. Learning to predict by the methods of temporal differences. *Mach Learn* 3(1), –44, 1988.

S. Singh, T. Jaakkola, V.L. Littman and C. Szepesvári. Convergence results for single-step on-policy reinforcement-learning algorithms. *Mach Learn*, 38, 28–308, 2000.

Marr, B. A Short History of Machine Learning – Every Manager Should Read, *Retrieved from http://.forbes.com /sites/bernardmarr/ 2016/02/19/a-short-history-of-machine-learning-every-manager-should-read/#3afc129615e7*, 2016.

Batista, Prati & Monard. A study of the behavior of several methods for balancing machine learning training data. *ACM SIGKDD Explorations Newsletter – Special Issue on Learning from Imbalanced Datasets*, (vol. 6, No.1, pp. 20), USA, 2004.

Carlos, N. Silla, J., Alessandro, L. Koerich, Celso, A. A. & Kaestner. (2008). A Machine Learning Approach to Automatic Music Genre Classification. *Journal of the Brazilian Computer Society*, 14(3), 7–18.

T.D. Bie, T.T. Maia, & Braga, A. P. (2009). Machine Learning with Labeled and Unlabeled Data. *European Symposium on Artificial Neural Networks – Advances in Computational Intelligence and Learning*, 22–24. Bruges, Belgium.

N. F. Ince, Chu-Shu Kao, M. Kaveh, A. Tewfik and J. F. Labuz. A Machine Learning Approach for Locating Acoustic Emission *EURASIP Journal on Advances in Signal Processing*, 895486, 2010.

H. Ishibuchi, S. Mihara and Nojima. Training Data Subdivision and Periodical Rotation in Hybrid Fuzzy Genetics-Based Machine Learning, In *Proceedings of the 10th International Conference on Machine Learning and Applications, IEEE*,1, 229–234, 2011.

B. Neethu. Adaptive Intrusion Detection Using Machine Learning. *International Journal of Computer Science and Network Security*,13 (3), 2013.

Xiaohui Qu, Diogo ARS Latino and Joao Aires-de-Sousa. A big data approach to the ultra-fast prediction of DFT-calculated bond energies *Journal of Cheminformatics*, 1 (1), 5–34, 2013.

S. Smusz,, Kurczab, and Bojarski,. The influence of the inactives subset generation on the performance of machine learning methods. *Journal of Cheminformatics*, 5–17, 2013.

Rafał Kurczab, Sabina Smusz and Andrzej J Bojarski. The influence of negative training set size on machine learning-based virtual screening, *Journal of Cheminformatics*, 6–32, 2014.

Nahit Emanet, Halil R oz, Nazan Bayram and Dursun Delen. A comparative analysis of machine learning methods for classification type decision problems in healthcare. *Decision Analytics*, 1–6, 2014.

K. Koshino and A. N. Hasan. A Comprehensive Evaluation of Machine Learning Techniques for Cancer Class Prediction Based on Microarray Data. *International Journal of Bioinformatics Research and Applications Archive*,11(5), 2015.

T. Hasegawa, H. Koshino, and H. Koshino. An experimental result of estimating an application volume by machine learning techniques. *Springer Plus*, 1–10, 2015.

E. Alistair, W. Johnson, M. Mohammad,, Ghassemi and S. Nemati. Machine Learning and Decision Support in Critical Care. *In Proceeding of the IEEE*, 104, (2), 2016.

E. Rezk, S. Babi, F. Islam and A. Jaoua. Uncertain training data set conceptual reduction: a machine learning perspective Fuzzy systems. *In Proceedings of IEEE International conference on Fuzzy Systems* (pp.1842–1849), 2016.

L. Anna, and Buczak. Machine Learning and Decision Support in Critical Care. *IEEE Communications Surveys & Tutorials*, 18 (2), 2016.

N. F. Hordri, A. Samar, S. S. Yuhaniz, S. M. Shamsuddin . A Systematic Literature Review on feature of deep learning in big data analytics. In *Proceeding of the International Journal of Advances in Soft Computing and its Applications*, (Vol. 9(1), pp. 32–49), 2017.

A. A. Alurkar, R.B. Ranade, S.V. Joshi, S. S. Ranade, P. A. Sonewar, P. N. Mahalle, & A. V Deshpande. A Proposed Data Science Approach for Email Spam Classification using Machine Learning Techniques *IEEE Xplore Digital Library*, 2017.

A. Sheshasaayee and J. V. N. Lakshmi. An insight into tree based machine learning techniques for big data Analytics using Apache Spark. In *proceeding of the International Conference on Intelligent Computing, Instrumentation and Control Technologies*, IEEE Xplore Digital Library, 2017.

Aman Sharma. & Rani, R. Classification of Cancerous Profiles using Machine Learning. In *proceedings of the International Conference on Machine learning and Data Science*, IEEE Xplore Digital Library, 31–36, 2007.

J. Sukanya and S. V. Kumar. Applications of Big Data Analytics and Machine Learning Techniques in Health Care Sectors. *International Journal of Engineering and Computer Science*, 6 (7), 21963–21967, 2017.

K.U. Jaseena and B. C Kovoor. A survey on deep learning techniques for big data in Biometrics. *International Journal of Advanced Research in Computer Science*, 9(1), 12–17, 2018.

Quasim, M.T., and Mohammad. Meraj, (2017), Big Data Security and Privacy: A Short Review, International Journal of Mechanical Engineering and Technology, 8(4), 2017, pp. 408–412. http://www.iaeme.com/IJMET/issues.asp?JType=IJMET&VType=8&IType=4

Quasim, Mohammad Tabrez, et.al. (2019), 5 V'S OF BIG DATA VIA CLOUD COMPUTING: USES AND IMPORTANCE, Sci.int(Lahore), vol.31(3), PP.367–371, 2019.

Quasim, M.T. (2015). Artificial Intelligence as a Business Forecasting and Error Handling Tool. COMPUSOFT, An international journal of advanced computer technology, 4 (2), February-2015 (Volume-IV, Issue-II).

Smart Computing – Khan et al (Eds)
© 2021 Taylor & Francis Group, London, ISBN 978-0-367-76552-1

Synchrophasor data management: A high-performance computing perspective

C.M. Thasnimol & R. Rajathy
Department of Electrical and Electronics Engineering (EEE), Pondicherry Engineering College, Puducherry, India

ABSTRACT: Wide Area Monitoring System (WAMS) consisting of Phasor Measurement Units (PMU) is an inevitable part of the modern power grid. PMU gives real-time measurements of power system state variables which could be employed for several time-critical applications such as fault detection, voltage control, islanding detection etc. Since the reporting rate of PMU is very high, advanced data processing and storage techniques are essential to dig useful information from PMU data. This paper presents an overview of utility big data issues related to PMU driven applications and their solutions through modern data storage and processing techniques.

1 INTRODUCTION

The traditional centralized power generation system is not capable of meeting the increased demand for electrical energy. Concerns about global warming and energy efficiency promote the transformation of power production from centralized to distributed. The large-scale penetration of distributed generation systems causes a two-way flow of energy and hence creates line overloading in both distribution and transmission systems. It may ultimately lead to blackouts. The analysis of previous interruptions all over the world shows the necessity of a proper information and communication system for the grid. Although Supervisory Control and Data Acquisition (SCADA) systems are efficient in giving a static view of the power system, it fails when it comes to dynamic event monitoring. The main reason is the low reporting rate of the SCADA system, which is only 2-3 samples per second.

The Wide Area Monitoring System (WAMS) gives a snapshot of the entire system. The Phasor Measurement Unit (PMU) provides synchronized measurements of voltage, current, frequency, and rate of change of frequency with the help of the Global Positioning System (GPS). PMU sends measurements to Phasor Data Concentrator (PDC). PDC receives measurements from multiple PMU, aggregate it, do time alignment and then send the compressed measurements to super PDC or the control centre.

The reporting rate of PMU is typically 30 measurements per second. The average size of a PMU data is 94 bytes, and the data generated from one PMU is about 80GB in one year. If there are 1000 PMUs installed the volume of data will come around 80TB in one year. At present, about 1500 PMUs are deployed throughout India, and around 3000 PMUs are about to install in the Indian power grid soon. Analysis of this massive volume of streaming PMU data is crucial for real-time monitoring and control purposes. Another equally important field is historical data analysis which has critical applications in post-event root cause analysis, feature comparison, and feature prediction.

The massive PMU data as such cannot provide any insight into the events occurring in the system. Processing this enormous volume of PMU data on time is necessary for applications like situational awareness, event detection, and anomaly detection. Conventional databases are inadequate for handling this massive data flow. Hence, modern databases and data analysis techniques

DOI 10.1201/9781003167488-41

are necessary to make the power system operators track valuable pieces of information from PMU data efficiently.

The data-driven power grid analysis is promising in terms of fast decision support but lagging behind the model-based applications in performance. It may be because of the lack of awareness about big data analysis platforms and techniques. This paper tries to fill this gap by discussing common big data issues related to PMU data handling for various power system applications and the multiple platforms and tools which will help to solve those issues. This article is organized as follows. The first section discusses the wide-area monitoring system and its big data characteristics in general. The applications of synchrophasor measurements are reviewed after that. The third section gives an overview of common issues in handling PMU data. The fourth section discusses the advanced data processing and storage platform for various PMU driven applications.

2 APPLICATION OF SYNCHROPHASOR DATA

The applications powered by synchrophasor data can be categorized into real-time and offline applications. Power grid applications that need to be completed within 2-3 minutes comes under the category of real-time applications. Examples are wide-area monitoring, voltage stability analysis, oscillation detection, islanding, mode meter, and state estimation. Due to its time criticality, all the real-time applications should be performed near to the data source itself. Usually, such applications are implemented by utilizing data stored in the data server's buffered memory. Offline data analytics are performed for applications that are not time-critical. Examples are historical data analysis, power plant model validation, frequency response analysis, post-event analysis, and baselining fault location. Data stored in the historian is used for offline analytics. After doing time alignment, bad data removal, and missing data filling, high-quality data is utilized for offline applications. Some critical applications powered by synchrophasor data are discussed in the following subsections.

2.1 *Voltage stability analysis*

Due to the increasing demand for electrical energy, the transmission and distribution lines are carrying power up to their capacity limits. Hence chances of occurring fault are higher than ever. Therefore, advanced fault prediction and detection techniques should be employed to enhance the reliability of the power system. Synchrophasor measurement-based voltage stability index is used (Li et al. 2016) to find out the lines which are operating under unsafe conditions, and an optimization method was developed to increase the voltage stability margin of those lines. Thevenin equivalent impedance, which is calculated from PMU measurement data, is employed (Lee & Han 2019) for predicting voltage instability. All these predictions may get adversely affected by the presence of gross errors in PMU data like synchronization errors, cyber-attacks etc. A robust recursive least square algorithm is proposed (Zhao et al. 2017) which employs robust estimator and projection statistics for predicting voltage instability. This method can mitigate the effects of gross errors on voltage instability prediction.

2.2 *Transient stability*

The increasing demand for electrical energy could be met adequately by the interconnection of several power networks. Any disturbance in any of the sections will affect the power transfer capability and hence will adversely affect the transient stability of the system (Wu et al. 2016). Traditionally, temporary stability monitoring is done by the tracking of power transfer limit on the interface. Instead of following this traditional practice, the best method is to monitor the generator phase angle difference which could be obtained from synchrophasor measurements. First, the critical generator buses are identified through transient stability simulations (Wu et al. 2016) and then the generator phase angle difference is calculated which will give an insight to the power transfer on the transfer interface and hence the transient stability of the system. A method to predict the impermanent stability margin is proposed (Wu et al. 2016), where the mode of disturbance technique together with transient energy function is employed to predict the transient instability. Mode of disturbance (MOD) is the group of generators that will go out of synchronism after a fault. An information directory is created which contains fault location, transient energy, and the MOD. Corresponding to the actual kinetic energy after the fault clearance, which is obtained from PMU data MOD are identified, and corrective actions are taken.

A sudden disturbance in a complex power network like heavily loaded transmission line outage will create rotor angle instability and will ultimately lead to transient instability of the system, if not resolved through emergency network reconfiguration. Finding out the appropriate control actions to correct the disturbance within less time is most important, but it is difficult in the case of a complex power system. A network restoration method is developed (Zweigle et al. 2016) to reduce the search space of control action. The network restoration algorithm will select that strategy which gives the lowest mean square system state error.

A transient stability assessment method based on synchrophasor data and Core Vector Machine (CVM) (Wang et al. 2016) is discussed, which consists of two phases offline and online. Feature selection, which represents the state of the system is the first step in the offline phase. Selected features from the synchrophasor data, generated by time-series simulation are used to train CVM. Later the real-time PMU data and the trained CVM are coordinated to find the transient stability of the system. The transient stability of the power system depends on the inertia of its components. With the high penetration of low inertia renewable energy sources, the total inertia of the power system became low, which causes oscillation of synchronous generator following a disturbance. Distributed storage devices can be employed for accelerating the stabilization of these oscillations by using real-time measurements from PMU (Ayar et al. 2017).

2.3 Out of step splitting protection

Out of step splitting protection can be implemented using only phase angle information without complex mathematical operations. There may be stable and unstable oscillations in a power system. Unstable oscillations (out of step oscillations) usually occurs following a fault in the system. The protective relays should not trip following stable oscillations but should respond immediately to an unstable oscillation. The rate of change of positive sequence impedance is used to differentiate between the short circuit, synchronous, and out of step oscillations. After detecting the presence of out of step oscillations the out of step centre is determined from PMU measurement (Zhang & Zhang 2017), and the entire power system is split into islanding sections to prevent blackouts.

2.4 Multiple event detection

Rafferty et al. (2016) proposed synchrophasor data-based multiple event detection. Frequency measurement is used to detect various events like loss of generation, loss of loads, and islanding detection. A considerable amount of data is generated from PMU every second. Hence, data analytics techniques are needed to extract useful information from this data. Principal Component Analysis (PCA) can be used to reduce the dimensionality of PMU data (Rafferty et al. 2016). To account for the time-varying nature of power system variables, moving window approach is also employed. Kernel Principal Component Analysis (KPCA) (Zhou et al. 2016b) is used to detect anomalies from the massive streaming micro-PMU data. To differentiate between various types of events, a novel discriminate method which necessitates only limited knowledge is employed. Hidden Structure Semi-Supervised Machine (HS3M) is applied (Zhou et al. 2017) for event detection, using unlabelled or labelled data.

2.5 State estimation

Power grid synchronization based on real-time state estimation is presented by Wang & Yaz (2016). The extended Kalman filter was employed to get an actual state of the system. Dynamic state estimation (DSE), otherwise known as forecast aided state estimation, uses historical data and real-time measurement data for estimating the system state. During sudden disturbances like line outage and generator outages etc. the system parameters will change, and the system state also will change. The use of historical data for state estimation will results in erroneous state estimation results under these circumferences. In order to handle inaccurate state estimation, Mixed-Integer linear programming based DSE is proposed by Aminifar et al. (2014). During sudden disturbance in the system, the forecasted values will be discarded from the estimation process to increase the quality of estimation. During normal conditions, the predictions will be included to improve the accuracy of the state estimation.

2.6 Fault detection

Rule-Based Data-Driven Analytics is employed for finding the location and type of fault from synchrophasor measurements (Liang et al. 2017). This method does not require any model or topology of the system. Pignati et al. (2017) proposed an algorithm for detecting the location type and the fault current using synchrophasor measurements. The fault detection algorithm relies on several parallel state estimator. Pignati et al. (2017) discussed a method to find out the location and type of fault using Time of Arrival (ToA) of the electromechanical wave. ToA can be computed from the phasor angle output of PMU using Artificial Neural Network (ANN). ANN will also give the type of fault. ToA and speed of electromechanical waves from fault point to PMU together with the topology of the network are employed to identify the faulty line. After identifying the faulty line by applying the binary search method, the exact location of the fault is determined.

2.7 Loss of Main (LOM) detection

If an embedded generator (generator at the distribution side) lost main supply it should be disconnected immediately from the utility; otherwise, restoration operations will cause severe hazards to safety personnel and out of synchronism re-closure will cause damage to the grid. Ding et al. (2016) proposed LOM detection using synchrophasor measurements. Peak ratio analysis of the rate of change of frequency is employed to find out the connectivity of the network. Laverty et al. (2015) developed a scheme to monitor the phase angle of the embedded generator continuously concerning a reference cite. The loss of synchronism of the integrated generator indicates the presence of LOM. Principal component analysis (PCA) was used by Guo et al. (2014) to detect islanding.

2.8 Topology update detection

The detection of topological changes is essential for state estimation and network monitoring. Undetected topological changes would stress the power system and ultimately will lead to blackouts. If a topology change occurs, there will be a unique variation in the voltage phasors that can be identified using sparsely located PMUs in that area. Ponce & Bindel (2017) discussed a fingerprint linear state estimator based topological detection method, which requires only a limited number of PMUs.

2.9 Oscillation Detection

Oscillations if not detected earlier, will cause the instability of the system and even leads to power outages. The oscillations can be of sustained or unsustained type. Sustained oscillations if not detected and solved earlier, will cause damage to equipment, power quality issues, and even blackouts. The peak of the coherence spectrum of synchrophasor measurement data is used to identify the oscillations. Zhou (2016) discussed a cross coherence method employing multiple channel PMU data. Multiple channel PMU data is used to avoid false alarming. This method is suitable for both low and high signal to noise ratio systems. The cause of each oscillation may be different and requires different countermeasures depending on the mechanism of oscillations.

A data-driven approach is proposed by Wang and Turitsyn (2016), to find out the source and mechanism of sustained oscillations from the synchrophasor data.

3 UTILITY BIG DATA ISSUES RELATED TO PMU DRIVEN APPLICATIONS

Proper management is required for the effective utilization of PMU data. Raw PMU data will not give much information about the power system events. Storage of this enormous volume of data itself a problem. We should employ proper data mining techniques for getting insights from the massive amount of data. Presentation of the data in a form readily understandable for the operator is another issue. Another most crucial problem is information security. Utilities are now concerned about all these problems and a lot of researches are going on in these. The following subsections discussed some of the significant issues related to power system big data.

3.1 *Heterogeneous measurement integration*

Conventionally, for storing the streaming data, WAMS and other power grid monitoring systems adopt the Relational DataBase Management System (RDBMS). RDBMS is not so useful in dealing with heterogeneous power system data. For handling this high-velocity massive PMU data high capacity server and hard disk are necessary, which will cost a lot. For integrating heterogeneous power grid measurement data, complex SQL languages and multi-table joint operations are needed, which will severely affect the read and write performance. Database scaling is the most crucial problem faced by traditional RDBMS when dealing with streaming data. PMU data types may differ depending upon the site of installation, which can only be understood from the configuration file. The two-dimensional table format of RDBMS is challenging to expand. Another option is to allocate fields for all types of data in the database, but it will increase redundancy. The authors Guerrero et al. (2017) proposed a different data source integration method called as metadata mining which is based on the meta-data in relational databases.

3.2 *Variety and inter-operability*

Although the concept of synchrophasors has emerged 30 years before, the PMU technology is still in its evolving phase. Most of the utilities are gradually moving from SCADA based monitoring system to PMU based system. The PMU available in utilities may be installed in different periods or manufactured by different vendors. Sometimes it may be a PMU enabled IED that can perform various functions in addition to generating synchrophasor data. PMU data types and structure may vary upon vendors. Utilities are forced to integrate communication modules, data concentrators, and visualization tools from different venders with PMU data processing. The integration and inter-operability of these heterogeneous data is the primary concern for the power utility. The term inter-operability signifies the ability of different utility applications and information technology systems to communicate, share data, and exploit most out of the utility data for the reliable operation of the grid (Moraes et al. 2012). Hardware independent inter-operability is the essential feature of any computing and data storage platforms when applied to the smart grid.

3.3 *Volume and velocity*

Synchrophasor data comes under the category of time series data. The storage and processing of time-series data is the primary concern of data scientists, especially when the volume of information is significant. Real-time data processing requirements also make the analysis complex. The conventional centralized control centre approach for storage and processing of massive streaming PMU data is not efficient as it involves significant latency issues, which are critical for time-critical smart grid applications. Also, high computing power and ultra-fast communication technologies are a must for a centralized approach. Another problem is the lack of a unified approach to store the time series data in a standard format that can be used by different applications. Systematic storage is the pre-conditioner for an efficient data analysis application.

3.4 Data quality and security

Cybersecurity is one of the main issues faced by the smart grid. Since most of the smart grid PMU applications have a high reliance on communication and sensing technologies, chances of getting vulnerable cyber-attacks are more. Cyber-attacks may trigger wrong decisions and may lead to the collapse of the entire power system. Paudel et al. (2016) discussed various types of cyber-attacks in terms of their attacking locations, their impacts and the existing strategies for alleviating their effects. A detailed survey of cybersecurity of PMU network is given by Beasley et al. (2014). Wang et al. (2019) developed a density-based spatial clustering method for cyber-attack detection and data recovery. An overview of cybersecurity concerning hybrid state estimation is provided by Basumallik et al. (2018). Mao et al. (2017) employed principal component analysis for the real-time detection of attacks and their locations. Paudel et al. (2018) demonstrate how the attackers are manipulating the PMU data with the knowledge of the state estimation process. They also show how the attackers are getting successful in bypassing the existing security measures adopted by the utility. Certificate-based authentication is proposed by Farooq et al. (2018), to secure the PMU communication network from man-in-the-middle attacks. It is implemented in real-time using python-based terminals.

3.5 Utilization and analytics

The raw PMU data will not give any information but will increase the burden of the data storage system. Measurement noises, outliers, & missing data pollutes PMU measurements, and this will affect the performance of PMU driven applications. PMU measurements taken at different events will differ in signal features. The signal features demanded by the steady-state applications are different from that of dynamic power system applications. The oscillatory signals in the PMU measurements originated under dynamic power system events will be treated as bad data for steady-state applications. Therefore, we have to do application-specific data analytics to dig the trends and patterns hidden in the PMU data.

Data mining is the interdisciplinary branch of computer science involving the extraction of useful information from an extensive database and processes it as an easily understandable form for further use. Today's grid will be smart only if we can extract valuable information from the massive data generated from all the intelligent meters and sensors and various types of forecasting data from weather, load and generation forecasts. A mathematical model will be created using this extracted information. Using real-time data and the mathematical model of the system, the current state of the system will be estimated, and this will help to determine the possible actions to be performed to solve potential problems. The time-critical power system applications like fault detection, service restoration, self-healing, and energy management need quick and efficient analysis of real-time and historical data. Various data mining techniques should be adopted to dig the customer load pattern, event detection, price forecasting, etc. from the raw data available from monitoring devices like AMI, SCADA, and PMU and various forecasting data. Table 1 lists different data mining techniques discussed in the literature.

3.6 Data visualization

Identification of weaknesses and prediction of potential problems are the main implications of Contingency Analysis (CA). As power system protection is very time-critical, CA results should be presented in an easily understandable way to assist the system operators in perceiving the security status of the system quickly and intuitively. Advanced visualization techniques are needed to efficiently present the overall security status and the level and location of contingencies. The critical challenge of visualization framework is to integrate information originated from different

Table 1. Data mining techniques.

Technique	Application
Normalized wavelet energy function (Kim et al. 2017).	Event detection.
Multivariate trend filtering scheme (Nadkarni & Soman 2018).	Estimation for microgrid
Fuzzy c-means (FCM) (Nadkarni and Soman 2018)	Locating the false data attacks.
Principal component analysis and second order difference method (Ge et al. 2015).	Real time event detection.
Low-rank matrix completion (Gao et al. 2016).	Missing PMU data recovery.
Moving Window principal component analysis (Rafferty et al. 2016).	Multiple event detection.
SVM (Nguyen et al. 2015).	Event detection.
Fourier based automatic ringdown analysis (Tashman et al. 2014).	Extracting dominant oscillatory modal content.
Dynamic programming based SDT (DPSDT) (Cui et al. 2018).	Event detection.
Random matrix theory (Pinheiro et al. 2017).	Anomaly detection and location
Euclidean distance-based anomaly detection schemes (Ahmed et al. 2018).	Covert cyber deception assault-detection.
Ensemble classifier bootstrap aggregation (Kaur & Hahn 2018).	Intrusion detection.
Data mining of code repositories (DAMICORE) (Gomes et al. 2018).	Islanding detection of synchronous distributed generators.
OPTICS (Wang et al. 2018).	To segment data and finds the outliers in the segmented data.
CNN (Zhu et al. 2018), RNN (Zhu et al. 2018)	Power system transient disturbance classification.
swinging door trending (Ma et al. 2018).	PMU data compression.
Principal component analysis (Gadde et al. 2016; Nadkarni & Soman 2018; Xie et al. 2014)	Dimensionality reduction of PMU data

Table 2. Visualization techniques.

Visualization technique	Description
GridCloud (Anderson et al. 2018).	Open source platform for real-time data acquisition sharing and monitoring.
FNET/GridEye (Liu et al. 2016).	Visualization of system stress.
Tableau (Munshi & Mohamed 2018), (Munshi & Yasser 2017).	SG data visualization.
Animation loops (Gegner et al. 2016).	Combine periodic snapshots of the grid into time-lapse videos defined across geographic areas.
Sparklines (Gegner et al. 2016).	Summarize trends in time-varying PMU data as word-sized line plots.
Google Earth (Gu 2018), (Gu et al. 2016).	SG data visualization.
GIS(Ashkezari et al. 2018).	To display real-time operational data.

data analytics tools and external sources and concisely present them in a single display. It is necessary for the operators and users for getting a quick insight into the current state of the power grid and for acting accordingly.

Stefan et al. (2017) presented an overview of visualization techniques for smart metering. A panoramic visualization scheme for SDN is presented by Du et al. (2018), which can visualize risk warning, fault self-healing, etc. FNET/GridEye is a low-cost GPS synchronized frequency measurement network. FNET/GridEye servers hosted at the University of Tennessee and Virginia Tech can visualize the system stress as animations of frequency and angle perturbations (Liu et al. 2016). Correlating PMU data with PMU location and system topology system stress is visualized as variations in frequency and phase angle (Liu et al. 2017) with the help of FNET/GridEye. Table 2 shows some of the visualization techniques discussed in the literature.

4 BIG DATA ANALYTICS PLATFORMS FOR PMU DATA PROCESSING

For getting intuitions about the real happenings in the power system from the signals originated from thousands of smart meters or PMU, we need a powerful computing platform. Several open-source projects are available to realize this high computing platform. One of such projects is Hadoop stalk which is a collection of open-source tools managed by Apache including Hadoop MapReduce, Hadoop Distributed File System, YARN, Cassandra, Storm, Spark and several other tools. Some of the tools within Hadoop stalk can handle only batch processing, and some others can handle both batch and stream processing. Batch processing is for processing static historical data, while stream processing is for streaming data like sensor data. MapReduce is basically for handling batch processing. Apache Storm and Spark are for streaming data processing,

4.1 *Hadoop*

Hadoop is an open-source platform developed by Apache Software Foundation. It has a Map-Reduce function and Hadoop Distributed File System (HDFS). Map Reduce consists of Map and Reduce operation. Map operation splits an extensive data set into many data sets of smaller size, and each one is assigned to a node or computer. At the Reduce stage, the results obtained from the cluster nodes are collected and aggregated into the final output. High scalability, fault tolerance, and computational parallelization are the most important features of Hadoop. Currently, the Hadoop framework is mostly employed for offline data analytics applications. The high computational time required by input and output files limits its use for online analytics. Hadoop MapReduce belongs to batch processing; hence, the system will wait until the batch reaches a predefined size. This will result in a high processing delay. Therefore, the Hadoop platform is not suitable for handling streaming PMU data. But it is most efficient for the batch processing of PMU data.

The oscillatory events in the power system and the presence of bad data may deteriorate the PMU measurement and will affect the satisfactory performance of PMU based steady-state applications. Therefore, PMU data should be appropriately filtered before giving to these applications. A MapReduce framework implemented with Hadoop is employed for a parallel detrended fluctuation analysis, utilizing a cluster of computer nodes (Khan et al. 2014). The large PMU data set is split into small sets, and each will be assigned to a mapping process. After doing fluctuation analysis on these small data sets by the mapping process, the results will be combined and compared with a threshold value during the reduce phase. This framework is employed for detecting transient events from the collected PMU data. The measurement data from the installed PMU was collected by OpenPDC software and were stored in a data historian who can store up to 100MB of data. All the real-time applications on the PMU data were performed in this phase. Once the data exceeds 100MB size, a data file will be created and will be stored in HDFS. The Hadoop framework will further fetch this data file for offline data mining applications. They have also proposed gene expression programming (Khan et al. 2017) for optimizing Hadoop performance by automatic tuning of Hadoop's configuration parameters.

A Hadoop based cloud computing platform is developed by Qu et al. (2013), to perform data mining and data processing of the massive WAMS data. Matthews and Leger (2017) proposed a MapReduce framework for real-time anomaly detection from the PMU data. In this work, the MapReduce algorithm was implemented in Phoenix++, which is an open-source multicore implementation of the MapReduce framework. The time-sliced PMU data in CSV file format is fed into the anomaly detection algorithm, which is implemented in Phoenix++. The system operators are intimated with an alarm if any anomaly is detected. Regardless of anomaly detection, the PMU data will be further stored in a database for offline processing.

On line monitoring of transmission line parameters is very important as it will help the system operators to take corrective actions before the malfunctioning of the grid. Hadoop based distributed transmission line parameter estimation from the massive PMU data is proposed by Sun et al. (2018)

Windowed sub-second event detection in the OpenPDC platform is employed by Trachian (2010) for real-time event detection from streaming PMU data. The instance-based learning approach is used to train Hadoop to detect the presence of a specific event.

4.2 *Apache spark*

Apache spark (2017) is a data processing engine with inbuilt modules for streaming, machine learning and batch processing. Resilient Distributed Data Sets (RDDS) is a list-like data structure, physically partitioned, with each partition resides in a different node. This way, Spark is achieving distributed and parallel processing capability. Compared to Hadoop, which relies on disk-based data processing, data computation speed is about 100 to 150 times higher. It can process both batch and streaming data efficiently. Spark is adaptable to a lot of programming languages like Python, Scala, SQL, and R. It can run over a variety of platforms like Hadoop and Mesos, or it can run stand-alone or in the cloud.

Aggregation and processing of enormous data for time-critical applications demand low latency and high-performance parallel processing. The power system data will be usually stored in low redundancy block distributed file systems such as HDFS, Apache Hive, etc., which are suffered from considerable latency due to high disk turnaround time. Latency requirements demanded direct streaming of data to real-time applications. The existing implementations of IEEE C37.118.2-2011 synchrophasor communication protocol like PyPMU, S3DK Synchrophasor Application Development Framework (SADF), Matlab library, etc. are not capable of streaming data directly to Hadoop, Spark, and other high-performance computing platforms. Menon et al. (2018) designed a streaming interface in Apache Spark. The interface was in scala language and is intended for receiving synchrophasor data directly to Spark applications for real-time processing and archiving. Zhou et al. (2016a) proposed a distributed data analytics platform for the FNET/GridEye synchrophasor measurement system. For real-time applications, PMU data is processed in the data centre's buffer memory itself. FNET/GridEye system and OpenPDC are acting as data servers. Near real-time applications utilize the data stored in data historian, which is realized through OpenHistorian2.0. Post-event and statistical analyses are performed in the analytics cluster, which is achieved through different data analytics platforms such as Apache Spark, R, and Pandas. The analysis algorithms are parallelized across multiple nodes for distributing the computational loads. An intrusion detection algorithm for synchrophasor data is designed by Vimalkumar & Radhika (2017), on the Apache Spark platform. A stream computing platform based on Infosphere has been developed by IBM (Hazra et al. 2011) for real-time voltage stability monitoring of the power system.

4.3 *HBase*

Apache HBase™(2017) is the Hadoop database. It is an open-source, distributed, scalable, and non-relational database that stores data as key-value pairs. The data is distributed horizontally between clusters of commodity hardware. It gives real-time read and writes functionality for a massive volume of data. A database management system based on Hbase is proposed by Wang et al. (2015), in which the data storage is organized according to the data access patterns of respective applications.

A cloud computing platform is proposed by Li et al. (2018), for a panoramic synchronous measurement system that integrates the measurement and fault recorders in high voltage side with the measurement system in the low voltage side. These heterogeneous measurement data is stored in non-relational database HBase. Hadoop architecture is utilized for heterogeneous processing of these massive data. After decoding the measurement data according to the corresponding configuration file, the information like analogue data, digital data and the status of switches, etc. are extracted and temporarily stored in memory. After standardization, the elimination of duplicate data and filling of missing data is done in HBase. Data pre-processing are done with MapReduce, together with various data analytics tools like Hive, Mahout, and Hadoop streaming.

4.4 *Storm*

Apache Storm is an open-source distributed computing platform for real-time processing of streaming data sets. It is scalable, fault-tolerant, and has multi-language support. Low latency and high encryption efficiency are advantages of Storm. Real-time encryption of the WAMS data is performed in the Storm platform. Zhang et al. (2015) proposed parallel data encryption and cloud storage platform for WAMS data. The encrypted information is stored in Hadoop's HDFS file system. HBase is employed for storing the index and keys of the WAMS data based on the source and the time of generation.

4.5 *Cloud-based platforms*

Zhang et al. (2018) presented a cloud-hosted Hadoop platform for analyzing massive historical PMU data. This platform consists of three layers, service layer, cluster layer, and application layer. Amazon EC2 and Amazon S3 constitute the first layer (service layer). Amazon EC2 is hosting the on-demand virtual servers demanded by Hadoop, and Amazon S3 provides scalable storage options and also host a static website for visualizing the data analysis results sent to S3. The cluster layer consists of Hadoop clusters running on virtual nodes hosted by Amazon EC2. The application layer hosts all the applications and analytics on PMU data. They have also presented a method for the detection of frequency excursion from the PMU data.

Mo et al. (2018) proposed a Saas platform for synchrophasor application. Through virtualization, the physical servers in the cloud are partitioned into virtual machines. Depends upon the processing requirement of the synchrophasor application, these virtual machines are allocated to the particular application. The end-user is not required to install the specific synchrophasor application on their local computers but can analyze by accessing the apps through a webserver. Pegoraro et al. (2017) proposed an adaptive state estimator for the distribution system. They have utilized a cloud-based IoT paradigm. The accuracy of the measurements is different under dynamic conditions than steady-state conditions. The weighting parameters of the state estimator algorithm are modified according to the detection of a dynamic state in the distribution system. The PMU data is transferred to virtual PMU (vPMU) at a high reporting rate. The cloud-hosted vPMU performs local processing and identifies the state of the distribution system, which is directly observed by that PMU. vPMU varies measurement reporting rate to state estimator applications according to different states of the system. The state estimator changes the weighting function of the WLS algorithm according to the reporting rate of vPMU.

The Linear State Estimator (LSE) utilizing only PMU measurements are subject to errors due to false data injection. This will degrade the reliability of the system, and hence False Data Detection (FDD) techniques should be incorporated in the LSE algorithm. This will increase the complexity of the state estimation process, and in turn, will increase its latency. A cloud-hosted parallelized LSE-FDD algorithm is proposed by Chakati et al. (2018). To fasten the state estimation with an increasing number of PMUs, the authors have used GPU (Graphical Processing Unit).

Shand et al. (2015) proposed a tool for power system model validation employing plug and play PMU. To identify the exact geographical and electrical positions of the PMU, the authors have used a GPS and cloud platform. This helps to detect the presence of bad data which arises due to an incorrect model of the system. Yang et al. (2018) proposed a PMU fog architecture for enhancing the QoS requirement of the WAMS communication system. By utilizing the computational capability of PMU devices, on-site pre-processing of data is carried out to detect and mark anomaly data. The market data is given higher priority for transmission to the control centre to mitigate the latency issues in the critical applications.

5 CONCLUSION

Now the trends are towards cross-disciplinary collaboration where advanced communication technologies, machine learning, artificial intelligence, signal processing, etc. should assist the smart grid monitoring system for realizing a cyber-physical intelligent grid system. It is critical to develop suitable data storage and computing platform and identify appropriate analysis techniques for various power system applications. Several advanced computing platforms for PMU driven applications are discussed in this paper.

REFERENCES

Ahmed, S., Lee, Y., Hyun, S.H., and Koo, I. 2018. Covert cyber assault detection in smart grid networks utilizing feature selection and euclidean distance-based machine learning. *Applied Sciences*, 8 (5): 772. doi: https://doi.org/10.3390/app8050772

Aminifar, F., Shahidehpour, M., Fotuhi-Firuzabad, M., and Kamalinia, S. 2014. Power system dynamic state estimation with synchronized phasor measurements. *IEEE Transactions on Instrumentation and Measurement*, 63 (2): 352–363. doi: 10.1109/TIM.2013.2278595

Anderson, D., Gkountouvas, T., Meng, M., Birman, K., Bose, A., Hauser, C., Litvinov, E., Luo, X., and Zhang, F. 2018. Gridcloud: Infrastructure for cloud-based wide area monitoring of bulk electric power grids. *IEEE Transactions on Smart Grid*, 10 (2): 2170–2179. doi: 10.1109/TSG.2018.2791021

Ashkezari, A. D., Hosseinzadeh, N., Chebli, A., and Albadi, M. 2018. Development of an enterprise geographic information system (gis) integrated with smart grid. *Sustainable Energy, Grids and Networks*, 14: 25–34. doi: https://doi.org/10.1016/j.segan.2018.02.001

Ayar, M., Obuz, S., Trevizan, R. D., Bretas, A. S., and Latchman, H. A. 2017. A distributed control approach for enhancing smart grid transient stability and resilience. *IEEE Transactions on Smart Grid*, 8 (6): 3035–3044. doi: 10.1109/TSG.2017.2714982

Basumallik, S., Eftekharnejad, S., Davis, N., Nuthalapati, N., and Johnson, B. K. 2018. Cybersecurity considerations on PMU-based state estimation. *In CyberSec 2018: Proceedings of the Fifth Cybersecurity Symposium in April 2018,* Article No.14: 1–4. doi: https://doi.org/10.1145/3212687.3212874

Beasley, C., Zhong, X., Deng, J., Brooks, R., and Venayagamoorthy, G. K. 2014. A survey of electric power synchrophasor network cybersecurity. *In IEEE PES Innovative Smart Grid Technologies, Europe, Istanbul, 2014*, 1–5. doi: 10.1109/ISGTEurope.2014.7028738

Chakati, V., Pore, M., Banerjee, A., Pal, A., and Gupta, S. K. 2018. Impact of false data detection on cloud hosted linear state estimator performance. *2018 IEEE Power & Energy Society General Meeting (PESGM)*, *Portland, OR* 1–5. doi: 10.1109/PESGM.2018.8586671

Cui, M., Wang, J., Tan, J., Florita, A., and Zhang, Y. 2018. *IEEE Transactions on Power Systems*, 34 (1): 454-466. doi: 10.1109/TPWRS.2018.2859323

Ding, F., Booth, C. D., and Roscoe, A. J. 2016. Peak-ratio analysis method for enhancement of LOM protection using m-class PMUS. *IEEE Transactions on Smart Grid*, 7 (1): 291–299. doi: 10.1109/TSG.2015.2439512

Du, J., Sheng, W., Lin, T., and Lv, G. 2018. Research on the framework and key technologies of panoramic visualization for smart distribution network. *Paper presented in 6th International Conference on Computer-Aided Design, Manufacturing, Modeling and Simulation AIP Conference Proceedings*, 20–24.

Farooq, S., Hussain, S., Kiran, S., and Ustun, T. 2018. Certificate based authentication mechanism for PMU communication networks based on IEC 61850-90-5. *Electronics*, 7(12): 370. doi: https://doi.org/10.3390/electronics7120370

Gadde, P. H., Biswal, M., Brahma, S., and Cao, H. 2016. Efficient compression of pmu data in wams. *IEEE Transactions on Smart Grid*, 7(5): 2406-2413. doi: 10.1109/TSG.2016.2536718

Gao, P., Wang, M., Ghiocel, S. G., Chow, J. H., Fardanesh, B., and Stefopoulos, G. 2016. Missing data recovery by exploiting low-dimensionality in power system synchrophasor measurements. *IEEE Transactions on Power Systems*, 31(2): 1006–1013. doi: 10.1109/TPWRS.2015.2413935

Ge, Y., Flueck, A. J., Kim, D.-K., Ahn, J.-B., Lee, J.-D., and Kwon, D.-Y. 2015. Power system real-time event detection and associated data archival reduction based on synchrophasors. *IEEE Transactions on Smart Grid*, 6(4): 2088–2097. doi: 10.1109/TSG.2014.2383693

Gegner, K. M., Overbye, T. J., Shetye, K. S., and Weber, J. D. 2016. Visualization of power system wide-area, time varying information. *EEE Power and Energy Conference at Illinois (PECI)*, Urbana, IL, 1-4. doi: 10.1109/PECI.2016.7459263

Gomes, E. A., Vieira, J. C., Coury, D. V., and Delbem, A. C. 2018. Islanding detection of synchronous distributed generators using data mining complex correlations. *IET Generation, Transmission & Distribution*, 12(17): 3935-3942. doi: 10.1049/iet-gtd.2017.1722

Gu, Y. 2018. Renewable energy integration in distribution system-synchrophasor sensor based big data analysis, visualization, and system operation. *preprint arXiv*. doi: arXiv:1803.06076v1

Gu, Y., Jiang, H., Zhang, Y., Zhang, J. J., Gao, T., and Muljadi, E. 2016. Knowledge discovery for smart grid operation, control, and situation awareness—a big data visualization platform. *North American Power Symposium* (NAPS), Denver, CO. 1–6. doi: 10.1109/NAPS.2016.7747892

Guerrero, J. I., Garc'ıa, A., Personal, E., Luque, J., and León, C. 2017. Heterogeneous data source integration for smart grid ecosystems based on metadata mining. *Expert Systems with Applications*, 79:254-268. doi: https://doi.org/10.1016/j.eswa.2017.03.007

Guo, Y., Li, K., and Laverty, D. 2014. Loss-of-main monitoring and detection for distributed generations using dynamic principal component analysis. *Journal of Power and Energy Engineering*, 2 (04): 423. doi: 10.4236/jpee.2014.24057

Hazra, J., Das, K., Seetharam, D. P., and Singhee, A. 2011. Stream computing based synchrophasor application for power grids. *In Proceedings of the first international workshop on High performance computing, networking and analytics for the power grid*, 43–50. doi: https://doi.org/10.1145/2096123.2096134

Kaur, K. J. and Hahn, A. 2018. Exploring ensemble classifiers for detecting attacks in the smart grids. *In Proceedings of the Fifth Cybersecurity Symposium*, 13: 1-4. doi: https://doi.org/10.1145/3212687.3212873

Khan, M., Huang, Z., Li, M., Taylor, G. A., Ashton, P. M., and Khan, M. 2017. Optimizing Hadoop performance for big data analytics in smart grid. *Mathematical Problems in Engineering*, 1–11. doi: https://doi.org/10.1155/2017/2198262

Khan, M., Li, M., Ashton, P., Taylor, G., and Liu, J. 2014. Big data analytics on PMU measurements. *11th International Conference on Fuzzy Systems and Knowledge Discovery (FSKD)*, Xiamen, 715–719. doi: 10.1109/FSKD.2014.6980923

Kim, D.-I., Chun, T. Y., Yoon, S.-H., Lee, G., and Shin, Y.-J. 2017. Wavelet-based event detection method using PMU data. *IEEE Transactions on Smart grid*, 8(3):1154–1162. doi: 10.1109/PESGM.2017.8274161

Laverty, D. M., Best, R. J., and Morrow, D. J. 2015. Loss-of-mains protection system by application of phasor measurement unit technology with experimentally assessed threshold settings. *IET Generation, Transmission & Distribution*, 9(2):146–153. doi: 10.1049/iet-gtd.2014.0106

Lee, Y. and Han, S. 2019. Real-time voltage stability assessment method for the Korean power system based on estimation of thévenin equivalent impedance. *Applied Sciences*, 9(8):1671. doi: https://doi.org/10.3390/app9081671

Li, H., Bose, A., and Venkatasubramanian, V. M. 2016. Wide-area voltage monitoring and optimization. *IEEE Transactions on Smart Grid*, 7(2):785–793. doi: 10.1109/TSG.2015.2467215

Li, Y., Shi, F., and Zhang, H. 2018. Panoramic synchronous measurement system for wide-area power system based on the cloud computing. In *13th IEEE Conference on Industrial Electronics and Applications (ICIEA)*, Wuhan, 764–768. doi: 10.1109/ICIEA.2018.8397816

Liang, X., Wallace, S. A., and Nguyen, D. 2017. Rule-based data-driven analytics for wide-area fault detection using synchrophasor data. *IEEE Transactions on Industry Applications*, 53(3):1789-1798. doi: 10.1109/TIA.2016.2644621

Liu, Y., Yao, W., Zhou, D., Wu, L., You, S., Liu, H., Zhan, L., Zhao, J., Lu, H., Gao, W., and Liu, Y. 2016. Recent developments of FNET/GridEye- a situational awareness tool for smart grid. *CSEE Journal of Power and Energy Systems*, 2:19–27. doi: 10.17775/CSEEJPES.2016.00031

Liu, Y., You, S., Yao, W., Cui, Y., Wu, L., Zhou, D., Zhao, J., Liu, H., and Liu, Y. 2017. A distribution level wide area monitoring system for the electric power Grid-FNET/GridEye. *IEEE Access*, 5:2329–2338.

Ma, Y., Fan, X., Tang, R., Duan, P., Sun, Y., Du, J., and Duan, Q. 2018. Phase identification of smart meters by spectral clustering. *In 2018 2nd IEEE Conference on Energy Internet and Energy System Integration*, 1–5. doi: 10.1109/EI2.2018.8582318.

Mao, Z., Xu, T., and Overbye, T. J. 2017. Real-time detection of malicious PMU data. *In 19th International Conference on Intelligent System Application to Power Systems (ISAP)*, 1–6. doi: 10.1109/ISAP.2017.8071368

Matthews, S. and Leger, A. S. 2017. Leveraging map-reduce and synchrophasors for real-time anomaly detection in the smart grid. *IEEE Transactions on Emerging Topics in Computing.* 7(3):392–403. doi: 10.1109/TETC.2017.2694804

Menon, V. K., Variyar, V. S., Soman, K., Gopalakrishnan, E., Kottayil, S. K., Almas, M. S., and Nordström, L. 2018. A spark™based client for synchrophasor data stream processing. *In International Conference and Utility Exhibition on Green Energy for Sustainable Development (ICUE)*, 1–9. doi: 10.23919/ICUE-GESD.2018.8635650

Mo, S., Chen, H., Kothapa, U., and Zhang, L. 2018. Synchrophasor applications as a service for power system operation. *In 2018 North American Power Symposium (NAPS)*, 1–5. doi: 10.1109/NAPS.2018.8600597

Moraes, R. M., Hu, Y., Stenbakken, G., Martin, K., Alves, J. E. R., Phadke, A. G., Volskis, H. A., and Centeno, V. 2012. PMU interoperability, steady-state and dynamic performance tests. *IEEE Transactions on Smart Grid*, 3(4):1660–1669. doi: 10.1109/TSG.2012.2208482

Munshi, A. A. and Mohamed, Y. A.-R. I. 2018. Data lake lambda architecture for smart grids big data analytics. *IEEE Access*, 6:40463-40471. doi: 10.1109/ACCESS.2018.2858256

Munshi, A. A. and Yasser, AR M. 2017. Big data framework for analytics in smart grids. *Electric Power Systems Research*, 151:369–380. doi: https://doi.org/10.1016/j.epsr.2017.06.006

Nadkarni, A. and Soman, S. 2018. Applications of trend-filtering to bulk pmu time-series data for wide-area operator awareness. *In Power Systems Computation Conference (PSCC), Dublin*, 1–7. doi: 10.23919/PSCC.2018.8443000

Nguyen, D., Barella, R., Wallace, S. A., Zhao, X., and Liang, X. 2015. Smart grid line event classification using supervised learning over PMU data streams. *Sixth International Green and Sustainable Computing Conference (IGSC)*, Las Vegas, NV, 1-8. doi: 10.1109/IGCC.2015.7393695

Paudel, S., Smith, P., and Zseby, T. 2016. Data integrity attacks in smart grid wide area monitoring. *In ICS-CSR '16: Proceedings of the 4th International Symposium for ICS & SCADA Cyber Security Research*, 1–10. doi: https://doi.org/10.14236/ewic/ICS2016.9

Paudel, S., Smith, P., and Zseby, T. 2018. Stealthy attacks on smart grid PMU state estimation. *In Proceedings of the 13th International Conference on Availability, Reliability and Security*, 1–10. doi: https://doi.org/10.1145/3230833.3230868

Pegoraro, P. A., Meloni, A., Atzori, L., Castello, P., and Sulis, S. 2017. PMU-based distribution system state estimation with adaptive accuracy exploiting local decision metrics and IoT paradigm. *IEEE Transactions on Instrumentation and Measurement*, 66(4):704–714. doi: 10.1109/TIM.2017.2657938

Pignati, M., Zanni, L., Romano, P., Cherkaoui, R., and Paolone, M. 2017. Fault detection and faulted line identification in active distribution networks using synchrophasors-based real-time state estimation. *IEEE Transactions on Power Delivery*, 32(1):381–392. doi: 10.1109/TPWRD.2016.2545923

Pinheiro, G., Vinagre, E., Praça, I., Vale, Z., and Ramos, C. 2017. Smart grids data management: a case for cassandra. *In International Symposium on Distributed Computing and Artificial Intelligence*, 87–95. Springer. doi: https://doi.org/10.1007/978-3-319-62410-5_11

Ponce, C. and Bindel, D. S. 2017. Flier: Practical topology update detection using sparse PMUS. *IEEE Transactions on Power Systems*, 32(6):4222–4232. doi: 10.1109/TPWRS.2017.2662002

Qu, Z., Zhu, L., and Zhang, S. 2013. Data processing of Hadoop-based wide area measurement system. *Automation of Electric Power Systems*, 37(4):92–97. doi: 10.7500/AEPS201111169

Rafferty, M., Liu, X., Laverty, D. M., and McLoone, S. 2016. Real-time multiple event detection and classification using moving window PCA. *IEEE Transactions on Smart Grid*, 7(5):2537-2548. doi: 10.1109/TSG.2016.2559444

Shand, C., McMorran, A., Stewart, E., and Taylor, G. 2015. Exploiting massive PMU data analysis for lv distribution network model validation. *50th International Universities Power Engineering Conference (UPEC)*, Stoke on Trent, 1–4. doi: 10.1109/UPEC.2015.7339798

Stefan, M., Lopez, J. G., Andreasen, M. H., and Olsen, R. L. 2017. Visualization techniques for electrical grid smart metering data: a survey. *IEEE Third International Conference on Big Data Computing Service and Applications (BigDataService)*, San Francisco, CA, 165–171. doi: 10.1109/BigDataService.2017.26

Sun, Y., Gao, Z., Hu, S., Sun, H., Su, A., Wang, S., Gao, K., and Ge, W. 2018. A method of estimating transmission line parameters using cloud computing based on distributed intelligence. *IEEE 17th International Conference on Cognitive Informatics & Cognitive Computing (ICCI∗CC)*, Berkeley, CA, 495–500. doi: 10.1109/ICCI-CC.2018.8482096

Tashman, Z., Khalilinia, H., and Venkatasubramanian, V. 2014. Multi-dimensional fourier ringdown analysis for power systems using synchrophasors. *IEEE Transactions on Power Systems*, 29(2):731–741. doi: 10.1109/TPWRS.2013.2285563

Trachian, P. 2010. Machine learning and windowed subsecond event detection on pmu data via Hadoop and the OPENPDC. *IEEE PES General Meeting*, Providence, RI, 1–5. doi:10.1109/PES.2010.5589479

Vimalkumar, K. and Radhika, N. 2017. A big data framework for intrusion detection in smart grids using apache spark. *International Conference on Advances in Computing, Communications and Informatics (ICACCI)*, Udupi, 198–204. doi: 10.1109/ICACCI.2017.8125840

Wang, B., Fang, B., Wang, Y., Liu, H., and Liu, Y. 2016. Power system transient stability assessment based on big data and the core vector machine. *IEEE Transactions on Smart Grid*, 7(5):2561–2570. doi: 10.1109/TSG.2016.2549063

Wang, X., McArthur, S. D., Strachan, S. M., Kirkwood, J. D., and Paisley, B. 2018. A data analytic approach to automatic fault diagnosis and prognosis for distribution automation. *IEEE Transactions on Smart Grid*, 9(6):6265–6273. doi:

Wang, X., Shi, D., Wang, J., Yu, Z., and Wang, Z. 2019. Online identification and data recovery for pmu data manipulation attack. *IEEE Transactions on Smart Grid*, 10(6): 5889-5898 doi: 10.1109/TSG.2019.2892423

Wang, X. and Turitsyn, K. 2016. Data-driven diagnostics of mechanism and source of sustained oscillations. *IEEE Transactions on Power Systems*, 31(5):4036-4046. doi: 10.1109/TPWRS.2015.2489656

Wang, X. and Yaz, E. E. 2016. Smart power grid synchronization with fault tolerant nonlinear estimation. *IEEE Transactions on Power Systems*, 31(6):4806–4816. doi: 10.1109/TPWRS.2016.2517634

Wang, Y., Yuan, J., Chen, X., and Bao, J. 2015. Smart grid time series big data processing system. *IEEE Advanced Information Technology, Electronic and Automation Control Conference (IAEAC)*, Chongqing, 393–400. doi: 10.1109/IAEAC.2015.7428582

Wu, Y., Musavi, M., and Lerley, P. 2016. Synchrophasor-based monitoring of critical generator buses for transient stability. *IEEE Transactions on Power Systems*, 31(1):287–295. doi: 10.1109/TPWRS.2015.2395955

Xie, L., Chen, Y., and Kumar, P. R. 2014. Dimensionality reduction of synchrophasor data for early event detection: Linearized analysis. *IEEE Transactions on Power Systems*, 29(6):2784–2794. doi: 10.1109/TPWRS.2014.2316476

Yang, Z., Chen, N., Chen, Y., and Zhou, N. 2018. A novel PMU fog based early anomaly detection for an efficient wide area PMU network. *IEEE 2nd International Conference on Fog and Edge Computing (ICFEC)*, Washington, DC, 1–10. doi: 10.1109/CFEC.2018.8358730

Zhang, S., Luo, X., Zhang, Q., Fang, X., and Litvinov, E. 2018. Big data analytics platform and its application to frequency excursion analysis. *IEEE Power & Energy Society General Meeting (PESGM)*, Portland, OR, 1–5. doi: 10.1109/PESGM.2018.8586512

Zhang, S., Sun, J., and Wang, B. 2015. A study of real-time data encryption in the smart grid wide area measurement system based on Storm. *In 3rd International Conference on Machinery, Materials and Information Technology Applications. Atlantis Press.*

Zhang, S. and Zhang, Y. 2017. A novel out-of-step splitting protection based on the wide area information. *IEEE Transactions on Smart Grid*, 8(1):41–51. doi: 10.1109/TSG.2016.2593908

Zhao, J., Wang, Z., Chen, C., and Zhang, G. 2017. Robust voltage instability predictor. *IEEE Transactions on Power Systems*, 32(2):1578–1579. doi: 10.1109/TPWRS.2016.2574701

Zhou, D., Guo, J., Zhang, Y., Chai, J., Liu, H., Liu, Y., Huang, C., Gui, X., and Liu, Y. 2016a. Distributed data analytics platform for wide-area synchrophasor measurement systems. *IEEE Transactions on Smart Grid*, 7(5):2397–2405. doi: 10.1109/TSG.2016.2528895

Zhou, N. 2016. A cross-coherence method for detecting oscillations. *IEEE Transactions on Power Systems*, 31(1):623-631. doi: 10.1109/TPWRS.2015.2404804

Zhou, Y., Arghandeh, R., Konstantakopoulos, I., Abdullah, S., von Meier, A., and Spanos, C. J. 2016b. Abnormal event detection with high resolution Micro-PMU data. *Power Systems Computation Conference (PSCC)*, Genoa, 1–7. doi: 10.1109/PSCC.2016.7540980

Zhou, Y., Arghandeh, R., and Spanos, C. J. 2017. Partial knowledge data-driven event detection for power distribution networks. *IEEE Transactions on Smart Grid*, 9(5):5152–5162. doi: 10.1109/TSG.2017.2681962

Zhu, Y., Liu, C., and Sun, K. (2018). Image embedding of PMU data for deep learning towards transient disturbance classification. *IEEE International Conference on Energy Internet (ICEI)*, Beijing, 169–174. doi: 10.1109/ICEI.2018.00038

Zweigle, G. C. et al. (2016). Transient instability mitigation for complex contingencies with computationally constrained cost-based control. *IEEE Transactions on Smart Grid*, 7(4):1961–1969. doi: 10.1109/TSG.2016.2536061

Smart Computing – Khan et al (Eds)
© *2021 Taylor & Francis Group, London, ISBN 978-0-367-76552-1*

A review of stock market analysis approaches and forecasting techniques

Chinthakunta Manjunath & M. Balamurugan
Computer Science and Engineering, School of Engineering and Technology, CHRIST (Deemed to be University), India

Bikramaditya Ghosh
MBA, Institute of Management, CHRIST (Deemed to be University), India

Addapalli V.N. Krishna
Computer Science and Engineering, School of Engineering and Technology, CHRIST (Deemed to be University), India

ABSTRACT: In the monetary market, the equity market plays a significant role and has always attracted the interest of many analysts and experts in the financial market. Stock market forecasting is an exigent problem due to the fact that it is immensely complex, chaotic, dynamic, and has a number of different variables that are involved. Many studies have emerged in the past several years exploring historical data of stock, sentimental, fundamental, and technical analysis using statistical, data mining, expert systems, and deep learning techniques for the better analysis or prediction of stock trading. However, there is a need for research that consolidates this available information pertaining to the different analysis used in statistical data mining, expert systems, and deep learning techniques. The key objective of this paper is to systematize and summarize extensive research that has contributed to the area of the financial market for analysis and forecasting of the stock market. This paper attempts to explore the existing literature on fundamental, technical, and sentimental analysis approaches used for stock market forecasting. This paper also deals with challenges and opportunities for research in this area.

1 INTRODUCTION

Stock market exchange is a forum to sell stocks and derivatives of a company at an agreed price. The stock market is driven by supply and demand for shares. One of the most investing places and new markets is in any country's stock market. Nowadays, many people relate to this sector indirectly or directly. Learning about stock market movements, therefore, becomes an important one. Recently, blended techniques of diverse predictive models have fascinated the interest of several researchers in numerous areas, particularly in financial time series analysis and forecasting. Therefore, with the stock market rising, humans are fascinated by the analysis of stock price and forecasting.

In the financial market, stock forecasting is usually considered one of the most interesting developments of our time, with significant and exigent issues with time series forecasting due to its nonlinear and unpredictable features and various input parameters (Abu-Mostafa & Atiya 1996). How to forecast a market price accurately remains an open problem about the economics of modern society. The volatility of the equity market is connected to various other factors such as political events, international influence, financial news, quarterly profit results, and contradictory trading behavior (Ticknor 2013). Many highly interrelated factors affect stock markets, including psychological, cultural, political, and company-specific variables. The financial data, such as

DOI 10.1201/9781003167488-42

bourse index values, stock prices, and the prices of the financial derivatives, are considered for forecasting (Zhong & Enke 2017).

There are various theories for forecasting equity market prices. There are two significant stock market forecasting theories. One is the Efficient Market Hypothesis (EMH) and the other is the theory of Random Walks (Falinouss 2007). EMH expresses that all accessible resource data are mirrored by the share prices. Therefore, the stock market cannot be over-performed. There are three types of EMH: (1) Soft EMH: only past data is used; (2) Semi-Strong EMH: All civic information is used; and (3) High EMH: public and private information is used. Random walk theory: Random walk theory assumes that stock prices cannot be calculated since stock prices are not based on the history of the stock. It also assumes that equity price has tremendous volatility and predicting future stock prices is infeasible (Attigeri et al. 2015).

Technical analysis and fundamental analysis are two traditional approaches to stock market prediction and these approaches are used in stock market forecasting (Rechenthin 2014). The research on the effectiveness of technical analysis is checked, and the empirical literature is divided into two categories: "early" studies (1960–1987) and "new" studies (1988–2004), based on test procedures (Park 2007). Technical and fundamental analyzes are the two primary methods of analyzing financial markets (Nguyen 2015). These two main approaches were used by investors to make decisions on financial markets in order to invest in equities and attain elevated returns at low risks (Arévalo et al. 2017).

Some new innovations and techniques have been implemented over the past few years to try to forecast stock values across several avenues (Chen 2016). Expert system models such as Support Vector Regression (SVR) and Artificial Neural Networks (ANNs) have been extensively used to predict stock financial time series data and give significant predictive accurateness (Selvamuthu et al. 2019). Trend reversal review of stock market movements for Indian benchmark indices using Naïve SVM-KNN-based machine learning models are used for stock market prediction (Kalyan et al. 2015).

The key studies of fundamental analysis, technical analysis, and sentimental analysis using statistics, data mining, expert systems, and deep learning techniques which have been published in recent years concentrate on the presentation of a documentary study. In this paper, the literature reviews the classification that was performed based on the OHLC (Open, High, Low, Close), technical analysis, fundamental analysis, and integrating fundamental analysis and technical analysis approaches. Various features used in the equity market forecasting are included in each grouping such as the nature of a dataset/features region, methodology, metrics, and performance. Bearing this in mind, we have the following.

- Summarize the research papers that describe mainly fundamental analysis, technical analysis, hybrid (combining fundamental analysis and technical analysis), and sentimental analysis of stock markets.
- Summarize modern approaches for stock analysis, prediction, and recent achievements.
- Finally, for the research review, we explore possible concerns and realistic future directions.

The rest of the paper is organized as follows. Section 2 describes the conceptual foundation of various approaches to stock market analysis. Section 3 gives a brief abstract of various stock market prediction techniques. Section 4 presents a literature review on OHLC, technical analysis, fundamental analysis, sentiment analysis, and the combination of fundamental and technical analysis techniques used for stock market forecasts. Section 5 describes the challenges and opportunities in the financial market for predicting the bourse. Finally, the paper concludes with Section 6, which describes the observations, conclusions, and recommendations for further study.

2 APPROACHES TO STOCK MARKET ANALYSIS

In the financial market, analysis and forecasting of stocks or stock market index can be done based on OHLC values, fundamental and technical indicators, and by doing sentiment analysis (this

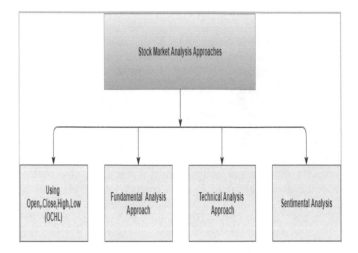

Figure 1.   Stock market analysis approaches.

involves taking financial data or stock data from social media) of stock or various indices of the stock market. Figure 1 shows a different approach to stock market analysis and these methods have gained interest and show potential results in the area of equity market analysis and forecasting.

2.1   OHLC

In this approach stock forecasting is done using Open, High, Low, and Close values of the stock. Sometimes along with theses values, the volume of the stock also considered for predicting the stock.

2.2   Fundamental analysis approach

Fundamental analysis in accounting and economics is a technique of finding the intrinsic value of security through the evaluation of the various microeconomic and macroeconomic variables. The ultimate aim of the fundamental analysis is to measure a security's intrinsic value. Therefore, its intrinsic value can be compared with its existing market price to help with investment decisions.
    Fundamental analysis consists of three principal components:

1. Analysis of Economics
2. Analysis of Industry
3. Analysis of Company

    Fundamental analysis is a very broad approach that involves a profound knowledge of economics, economy, and accounting. For example, fundamental analysis requires the capability to interpret statements of financial, understand macroeconomic trends, and the valuation techniques. To forecast the future growth of stock, it relies primarily on public data, such as an organization's historic earnings and a company's profit margins.

Top-down vs. bottom-up fundamental analysis
The basic investigation of the fundamental technique can either be top-down or bottom-up. A shareholder following the top-down method begins the study taking into account the health of the overall economy. A shareholder seeks to determine the overall monetary path by analyzing various macroeconomic variables, such as interest rates, inflation, and GDP levels, and to classify the industries and sectors of the economy that offer the best investment opportunities.

The shareholder then discusses detailed forecasts and future prospects within the listed industries and sectors. Ultimately, along with the most promising markets, stocks are evaluated and selected. Moreover, the solution is from the bottom-up. Instead of preliminary analysis on a superior scale, the bottom-up approach right away dives into the review of individual stocks. The underlying principle of investors using the bottom-up approach is that individual stocks are going to do a lot better than the entire economy. The bottom-up methodology focuses mainly on a mixture of microeconomic factors, such as a product's earnings and financial indicators. Using such a process, analysts create a comprehensive assessment of each company to achieve an improved understanding of its activities.

2.3 *Technical analysis approach*

Technical analysis is a method of forecasting the likely future value movement of a security like equity, commodity, currency etc based on market data and hypothesizing past value as an indicator of future performance. In the stock market technical analysts consider that present or past market price behavior is the most accurate sign of potential price action. Technical analysis is used not only by professional traders but also by fundamental analysts or traders to decide whether to buy in a market, the amount of goods, and lowrisk buy-in prices

2.4 *Text/news-based analysis*

Recent research has proven that a wide range of online facts in the community domain, such as a financial micro-blog, such as stocktwits, Google trends, data, and social media discussions, will have a noticeable effect on investors critiques on financial market (Loke 2017). The extractions of important financial news events are proposed to see a correlation exist between stock price and news (Zhang et al. 2018). The mining of subjective opinion expressed in the text with the help of sentimental analysis (Pang 2008).

3 STOCK MARKET PREDICTION TECHNIQUES

Many studies and work conducted on stock forecasting and its financial market analysis using traditional methods such as mathematical approaches to data mining. Recent advances in stock market research and forecasting include the use of pattern recognition, machine learning (ML), deep learning (DL), techniques for sentiment analysis, and hybrid approaches. Such methods use various stock markets strategies, such as OHLC, simple and technical data, social media news for analysis and stock price prediction, or various stock market indices. Recently the use of AI techniques such as machine learning and deep learning approaches has been gaining interest and showing promising results in equity analysis and bourse forecasting. Figure 2 demonstrates the taxonomy of various predictive techniques of common stocks.

3.1 *Statistical technique*

The use of statistical analysis has played a key role in helping to analyze and forecast the stock market. This section aims at various statistical methods to analyze the stock market and stock market forecasting are discussed.

The statistical ARIMA and machine learning models are combined to predict time series involving seasonality (Chen & Wang 2007). An analysis of equity market done using prophet variables and its performance measurements are evaluated in this work using statistical linear regression methods using R language with the S&P 500 Index (Seethalakshmi 2018). The use of statistical analysis dimensionality reduction technique such as Principle Component Analysis (PCA) improves the accuracy of the recurrent neural network model in financial time series forecasting (De-hua 2018).

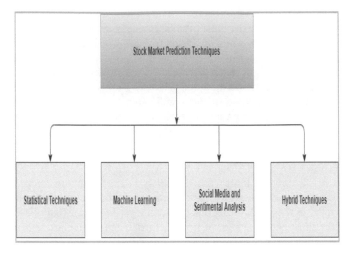

Figure 2.   Stock market prediction techniques.

3.2   *Machine learning*

Over the past decade, Artificial Intelligence (AI) has gained significant distinction, pushed by the use of a number of sophisticated applications such as smart robots, Autonomous Vehicles (AV), image, and automatic translations, medical and law usage, speech recognition, beating champions in games such as chess, poker, GO, and jeopardy (Makridakis 2017). The accomplishment of AIT is built on the use of algorithms able to learn through trial and error and improve their performance through the years, now not just via step-through-step coding instructions primarily based on logic, if-then regulations, and decision trees, that's the conventional programming sphere.

AI has well-known applications in the field of data processing, feature extraction, forecasting, and a considerable amount of research work has been carried out on how to use a specific class of it for time series forecasting, using Machine Learning (ML) Methods and Neural Networks (NNs). ANN is ideal for predicting operations in time series and different factors that may affect the efficiency of ANN (Zhang 1998). Predictions of the time series can be made for both discrete and intermediate multiple timescales. The analysis showed that ANN forecasts yield better results than the other approaches (Hamzaçebi et al. 2009). Numerous of papers applied different ML algorithms, indicating computational developments and progressed accuracy (Salaken et al., 2017). However, there is little analytical evidence regarding their relative success as a common forecasting tool and the ability for NNs to predict and forecast (Crone et al. 2011).

A PCA–LSTM-based machine learning algorithm hybrid Model for Stock Index Prediction is constructed and the multicollinearity of the stock price information data is processed using PCA and combined with the machine learning model LSTM network. The previous day's volume price information data as the input variable and the closing price of the next day stock price as the output variable is constructed and compared with the comparison model (De-hua & Jing-Jing 2018).

A stock selection and stock prediction model are developed to forecast stock prices using the support vector machine method and demonstrated that this approach has enhanced simplification compared to conventional methods (Lin et al. 2013). A machine learning model called a feed-forward multilayer perceptron with error backpropagation method a type of ANN is planned to forecast the stock prices. The conclusion shows that this model has given acceptable performance in forecasting the stock market (Wanjawa 2014). A two-stage fusion model consisting of various expert system techniques such as Artificial ANN, SVR, and RF are used for predicting bourse index and this fusion model tends to decrease predictive error overall (Jigar 2014).

372

A Trend Deterministic Data Preparation model is used for forecasting stock price, and bourse index movement via various machine learning techniques namely SVM, random forest, ANN, and Naive-Bayes. In this paper, stock price movement is used categorized as either "up" or "down" (Jigar 2015). The selection of stocks is performed based on fundamental and technical analysis data using expert system algorithms from ANN and SVM. Moreover, it was also experienced that the models constructed by using the SVM method in both types of analyses have shown more prominent results (Senol 2012). A diverse evolutionary machine learning methods are proposed such as DE, HMRPSO, PSO, and the outcome found that the recurrent FLANN model trained with the DE surpassed all supplementary FLANN models equally trained (Ajit 2017).

3.3 *Social media and sentimental analysis*

In this section, stock market analysis and stock market forecasting using social media and sentimental analysis techniques are discussed.

The correctness of the prediction model can be enhanced by means of the monetary ratio along with a model that can competently estimate sentiments. The influence of the price of the stock also including the other factors such as sentiments of the investor, news from various outlets, public opinion about the company, and actions that cause the complete stock market to swing (Loke 2017). The stock market can be accurately predicted by using data from technical indicators and by using additional methods, such as the use of a sentiment analyzer, to draw a meaningful correlation between investors' emotions and how investments in particular stocks affect them. The extraction of major financial news events to see a link between stock prices and news was another critical aspect of the prediction process (Zhang et al. 2018). In sentiment analysis the mining of subjective opinion articulated in the text, has been found to play a noteworthy role in numerous applications such as recommendation systems in product or movie, healthcare, politics, and in surveillance (Isah 2017).

3.4 *Hybrid techniques*

In this section, various hybrid techniques that combine more than one algorithm that is used in forecasting and analysis of the stock market are discussed.

A novel operator called Filling Operator is proposed to avoid early convergence problems and diminish the number of evaluations required. To improve the efficiency of a trading system that incorporates basic and technical indicators, an evolutionary methodology is used (Contreras et al. 2012). A convolutional neural network (CNN) and recurrent neural network (RNN) model combined to suggest a novel model for Stock Price Analysis. The outcome showed that the deep and wide area neural network (DWNN) model would reduce by 30% of the expected mean square error compared to the general RNN model (Ruixun et al. 2018). A generalized hybrid model is proposed, consisting of GARCH autoregressive model combined with the Long Short Term Model (LSTM) model to forecast stock price fluctuations (Ha 2018).

A stock selection approach is used to identify trends of stock using CNN model and then forecasted the equity prices using LSTM to maintain a hybrid neural network model for financial time series analysis to boost profit (Liu et al. 2017). An efficient stock trading decision made using an intelligent functional ANN that can provide investors with attractive benefits. The innovation of the method is the effectiveness of stock trading decision points by combining the CEFLANN neural network's learning ability with technical analysis (Dash & Dash 2016).

A smart and capable model for bourse price forecasting constructed usin Adaline Neural Network hybridization and customized Particle Swarm Optimization (PSO). The connoted Adaline and PSO model combination uses equity market fluctuations as a factor and uses PSO to refine and adjust Adaline representation weights to depict the Bombay stock exchange's open price (Das et al. 2019).

4 LITERATURE REVIEWS

Based on the stock market analysis approaches shown in Figure 1, this section covers a literature review work on, OHLC, fundamental and technical analysis approaches, sentiment analysis and combine fundamental and technical analysis techniques that have been useful for equity market forecasting.

4.1 *OHLC*

Several studies have done stock market forecasting using OHLC values of the stock or stock market index. Sometimes along with these values, the volume of the stock is also considered for predicting the stock.

An implementation of the RNN in tandem with LSTM methodology is proposed for bourse analysis and used for managing stock portfolio (Pawar et al. 2019). The next day pattern of a stock forecast made using the properties of network topology, SVM, and KNN algorithms. Integrating with complex network and expert system will give shareholder knowledge about strategies for profitability SVM learning theory is the methodology used in this research paper to predict stock trends. Here, the model is trained by the usage of actual historical data. This SVM learning theory gives us a one-step prediction (Hongduo 2019). AI approaches, unlike statistical techniques, can handle random, unpredictable, and nonlinear stock market data and have been commonly used to reliably forecast stock market indices (Chen & Hao 2017).

A novel neural model is proposed to boost efficiency of learning and prognostic ability by applying Back Propagation (HTBP) neural network model based on a fuzzy logic (Guan et al. 2018). A new model composed of an Adaline network designed by updated PSO to forecast open stock price (Das et al. 2019). Table 1 presents a summary of recent literature study applied to bourse forecasting based on OHLC.

4.2 *Fundamental analysis approach*

Fundamental analysis in accounting and finance is a method of determining the essential value of security through the evaluation of the various microeconomic and macroeconomic variables.

An amalgam machine learning algorithm is proposed using 60 financial and economic features to forecast each day return and the daily movement of the SPDR S&P 500 ETF stock market (Zhong & Enke 2017). The various financial ratio parameters for the selection of Portfolio in Indian Stock Market via Relative Performance Indicator Approach (RPIA) (Dhanya 2018). A hybrid LSTM model with numerous GARCH type models is proposed to forecast volatility of equity market with parameters of two or more GARCH-type models as inputs to the LSTM model. This model uses various fundamental data such as Gold price, Oil price, CB interest rate, and KTB interest rate as input to the model (Ha 2018). The institutional variables impact analyzed on the firm's stock market price performance on the NIFTY 50 Index. The study confirms that the performance of the fundamental ratios of the sector would be relevant and extremely helpful to investors and analysts in determining the better stocks belonging to different classes of industry (Nautiyal & Kavidayal 2018). Table 2 presents a summary of recent literature study applied to bourse forecasting based on fundamental indicators/fundamental analysis.

4.3 *Technical analysis approach*

Technical analysis is a method of forecasting the likely future value movement of a security like equity, commodity, currency etc based on market data and hypothesizing past value as an indicator of future performance.

Technical indicators are applied to eliminate chaotic from stock closing price information and the movement in stock prices are analyzed by using a robust kernel learning technique and Variational Mode Decomposition methods (Dash & Dash 2016). The calculation of various 50 technical

Table 1. Summary of literature applied to stock market forecasting based on OHLC (open, high, low, close).

Paper	Stock Exchange, Features and Country	Methodology	Prediction Type, Metrics and Results
Pawar et al. (2019)	AAPL (Apple Inc.), GOOG (Google), and TSLA (Tesla, Inc.) US	RNN LSTM	Next day's closing value MSE Loss :2.554e-04 Loss : 2.835e-04
Cao et al. (2019)	NASDAQ Composite Index (NASDAQ). Standard & Poor's 500 Index (S&P 500). Dow Jones Industrial Average (DJIA). US	KNN SVM KNN	Next-day volatility pattern. Prediction accuracy DJIA:74.83%S&P: 72.58% NASDAQ 72.45% SVM DJIA:74.97% S&P: 73.11% NASDAQ 74.57%
Guan et al. (2018)	Composite Index (SHSECI). fuzzified fluctuation dataset China	Fuzzy model. Back propagation Neural Network model.	Year Wise from 2007 to 2015. RMSE 2007 : 123.89 2008 : 57.44 .... 2015 : 59.69
Senapati et al. (2018)	Bombay stock exchange HDFC and JSPL 2012 to 2014. India	PSO ANN	Predicts next day open price of stoc Accuracy and MAPE HDFC 2012 ANN: 97.1 ANN-PSO: 99.1 MAPE (ANN-PSO):0.9 JSPL 2012 ANN: 97.7 ANN-PSO: 98.8 MAPE (ANN-PSO): 1.2

indicator values performed and added to the S&P500 open, high, low, close, and volume (OHLCV) data. To lessen the dimensionality of the technical indicators dataset ICA has been used and an optimal LSTM model is developed for the forecasting of stock prices (Sethia & Raut 2019). A new hybrid model incorporating technical and fractal analysis with ANN is introduced on the Warsaw Stock Exchange for the short-term forecasting of close values (Paluch 2018).

In the financial industry, the LSTM deep learning model results found better than traditional trading algorithms by performing technical analysis approach (Chenjie 2019). Neural networks and genetic algorithms are combined mutually in a stock trading decision system. The data characteristics provided as input to the neural network are the buy-sell trigger points for optimized technical analysis (Omer et al. 2017). Table 3 shows a summary of a recent literature study applied to stock market forecasting based on technical analysis/indicators.

Table 4 presents a summary of recent literature study applied to stock market forecasting based on integrating fundamental and technical analysis or indicators.

4.4 Social media data analysis

A stock prediction system is proposed incorporating both stock price data by means of technical analysis and news sentiments using the LSTM model and this model outperforms that only use either technical indicators or news sentiments, in both individual stock level and sector level (Savas 2019).

Table 2. Summary of literature applied to stock market forecasting based on fundamental indicators/fundamental analysis.

Paper	Stock Exchange Features and Country	Methodology	Prediction Type, Metrics and Results
Zhong & Enke (2017)	SPDR S&P 500 ETF 60 financial and economic features US	Deep Neural Network (DNN) Principal Component Analysis (PCA)	Daily. PCA-DNN PCs = 60 MSE: 0.3091. PCs = 31 MSE: 0.3095.
Jothimani & Shankar (2018)	Bombay stock exchange (BSE). National stock exchange (NSE) P/E ratio, Dividend yield, Beta, High index, P/B ratio, Close index. India	Automatic Linear Modelling ARIMA RBF Multi Layer Perceptron	index closing. Accuarcy. Results NSE dataset: Automatic linear modelling: 83.3% ARIMA R2 = 0.955 MLP SSE = 0.002 RBF SSE = 3.669
Kim & Won (2018)	KOSPI 200 index. Gold price Oil price CB interest rate KTB interest rate	LSTM. Multiple GARCH-type models	LSTM-based hybrid model with one GARCH-type W-LSTM MAE: 0.01322 MSE: 0.00279 G-LSTM MAE: 0.01271 MSE: 0.00252 E-LSTM MAE:0.01191 MSE:0.00216
Nautiyal & Kavidayal (2018)	NIFTY 50 Index EPS,DPS DIVP, EVA, Debt Equity Ratio.	FE and RE effects. FE 0.75 RE 0.61	Adjusted R2

Based on analysis of public opinion, a fresh stock assessment index was developed and the outcome shows that the fluctuation of equity prices is more sensitively to the intraday sentiment of individuals (Xiaodong 2020). A sentiment analysis is proposed on StockTwits a financial micro-blog using a variety of deep learning methods and compares the output of DL classifiers with conventional approaches to machine learning. (Dridi et al. 2019). A Sentiment Analysis for Effective Stock Market Prediction performed using Really Simple Syndication (RSS). This approach uses the amalgamation of both Sensex data and Really Simple Syndication (RSS) feeds data. The findings showed an analysis of perceptions of RSS news feeds has an effect on equity market price movement (Sv.Bharathi & Geetha 2017).

Table 5 presents a summary of a recent literature study applied to stock market forecasting based on social media data analysis.

5 CHALLENGES AND OPPORTUNITIES

In this section, challenges and opportunities in forecasting the stock market are discussed.

In the bourse forecasting, the future index, equity prices, and building buying and selling decisions are always exigent tasks. However, numerous stock analysts, shareholders, and venture capitalists are fascinated to participate in the analysis of the stock market and forecasting. Through

Table 3. Summary of literature applied to stock market forecasting based on technical analysis/ indicators.

Paper	Stock Exchange Features and Country	Methodology	Prediction Type, Metrics and Results
Bisoi et al. (2019)	Hang Seng Index (HSI), BSE S&P 500 Index (BSE), and Financial Times Stock Exchange 100 Index (FTSE). SMA25, %K, %D, MACD RSI, Wlr India China UK	Robust kernel extreme learning machine (RKELM). Variational Mode Decomposition (VMD).	Prediction of equity prices by the day ahead. Predicting daily trends Differential Evolution (DE).
Sethia & Raut (2019)	Standard and Poor's 500 Index data. MACD, Piviot point, MTM, ATR, SMA, EMA, Bollinger, Stochastic, fibonacci retracement, ROC US	ICA LSTM GRU SVM MLP	5th day Closing Price. Daily buying/selling strategy Model RMSE R^2 score LSTM 0.000428 0.948616 GRU 0.000511 0.938698 SVM 0.000543 0.934952 MLP 0.001052 0.874004.
Paluch & Jackowska-Strumillo (2018)	Technical Analysis SMA, EMA, RSI, ROC, Stochastic Oscillator, MACD, AD, BOS. Fractal Analysis RSI_FRAMA, MACD_FRAMA, BOS_FRAMA. Warsaw Stock Exchange (Poland)	ANN FA-ANN TA-ANN FA-TA-ANN	Day ahead of price closure. MSE ZYWIEC (Zywiec Brewery-company) FA–ANN : 0.00013 TA–ANN : 0.00077 FA–TA–ANN: 0.00041 ANN: 0.00206
Sang & Di Pierro (2019)	S&P 500 Index SMA, RSI, MACD US	LSTM AMZN stock	Yearly Annual cumulative Profit in dollars Using SMA, RSI, MACD are 332.11, 24.55.9.45. respectively.
Sezer et al. (2017)	Dow – 30 stocks. SMA, RSI, MACD, William % R. US	Genetic Algorithm (GA) Multilayer Perceptron (MLP)	Buy-sell-hold predictions. IBM stock Methodology & Return MLP+GA & 17.9% MLP & 8.19% BAH & 11.55%

the lofty return of the equity market and lofty risk, trading acts inspire capitalist to do their finest to make successful investment decisions. In the meantime, the rapid variation of monetary markets, exponential augmentation of financial data, growing intricacy of financial securities, and investment instruments in derivatives are added to research topics in the field of education and finance.

In today's world, a huge amount of stock information is generating every tick, we encounter several challenges in analyzing and dealing out this data to dig out useful patterns and analyze the impact on equity prices. These challenges consist of various issues like real-time deployment of stock market forecasting, algorithmic trading, short, medium, long-ter prediction of equity prices and stock index and impact of sentiment analysis in bourse.

The availability of large stock market time series data also provides various opportunities in this financial market domain such as market volatility or market hindrance prediction, analysis, and forecasting of the stock market by applying the latest machine algorithms and deep learning

Table 4. Summary of literature applied to stock market forecasting by integrating fundamental and technical analysis or indicators.

Paper	Stock Exchange Features and Country	Methodology	Prediction Type, Metrics and Results
Hoseinzade & Haratizadeh (2019)	S&P 500, DJI, NASDAQ, NYSE and RUSSELL. Close Price and Volume. Fundamental Data Treasury Bill, Oil Relative change of oil price(WTI), Relative change of oil price(Brent) Commodity, Relative change of silver spot U.S. dollar, Relative change of gas price, Relative change of gold spot U.S. dollar, Technical Data ROC – 5,10,15,20 EMA – 10,20,50,200	2D-CNN 3D-CNN	Next day's stock index value. Average F-Measure. 2D-CNNPred S&P 500: 0.4914 DJI : 0.4975 NASDAQ : 0.4944 NYSE: 0.4885 RUSSELL: 0.5002 3D-CNNpred S&P 500: 0.4837 DJI : 0.4979 NASDAQ : 0.4931 NYSE: 0.4751 RUSSELL: 0.4846
Bao et al. (2016)	CSI 300 index (China), Nifty50 index(India), Hang Seng index (Hong Kong), Nikkei 225 Index (Japan), S&P 500 index(US), DJIA index(US) Technical Indicators MA5,MA10, MTM6/MTM12, MACD,CCI, ATR,BOLL,EMA20, ROC,SMI,WVAD Macroeconomic Variable (Fundamental data) Exchange rate: US dollar Index Interest rate: Interbank Offered Rate	Wavelet transforms (WT). Stacked autoencoders (SAEs). Long-short term memory (LSTM)	Daily MAPE S&P 500 index WSAEs-LSTM : 0.011 WLSTM: 0.015 LSTM : 0.017 RNN: 0.018 Nifty 50 Index WSAEs-LSTM : 0.019 WLSTM: 0.029 LSTM : 0.034 RNN: 0.038
Contreras et al. (2012)	Technical Indicators MA,RSI, V(Volume), R(Resistance), Wight MA, Weight RSI, Weight V, Weight SR. Fundamental Indicators Price to Book Value(PBR), Return On Assets(ROA), Price to Earnings Ratio(PER), Sales Growth, Weight PER Weight PBV, Weight ROA, Weight SG Madrid Stock Exchange (Spain).	Simple Genetic Algorithm (sGA). GA – Filling Operator (GAwFO)	Daily Experimental Results for 100 companies. Buy and Hold Strategy: 180.62% accumulated return. TA and FA using the GAwFO Strategy: 830.09% accumulated return.

techniques. The stock price movements, market volatility, or market hindrance can be forecasted by performing novel data augmentation, extracting hidden information, identifying temporal dependencies on stock time series data, sentiment analysis on various stock social media data such as by extracting the financially sensitive information, political events, and global pandemics information.

Table 5. Summary of literature applied to stock market forecasting by using sentimental analysis.

Paper	Stock Exchange Features and Country	Methodology	Results
Yıldırım et al. (2019)	StockTwits, Dow Jones Industrial Average, US	Deep Learning (DL). Machine Learning (ML).	Success rate of both traditional and deep leaning classifiers analysis on for classifying bullish and bearish stocktwits data
Li et al. (2020)	Hong Kong Stock Exchange. Four different sentiment dictionaries. (LMFinance, SenticNet, SentiWordNet, Vader) Technical indicators.	LSTM model	LMFinance based models on test set – LSTM model Accuracy F1 0.376 0.270 0.554 0.513 0.550 0.518
Dridi et al. (2018)	Microblog messages News headlines message, US	Random Forest, Linear regression with SGD , Lasso with SGD , Ridge regression with SGD, Support vector regression	news headlines is 0.655 microblog messages it reaches 0.726
Sv.Bharathi & Geetha (2017)	RSS news feed data. Moving Average Indicates, ARBK from Amman Stock Exchange (ASE)	Dictionary based approach Sentence level sentiment score (SSS) algorith	Classification accuracy using the proposed method – ARBK Company Precision% 78.75%

6 CONCLUSION

In the financial world, the stock market is a lucrative investment in finance that can yield enormous wealth. The essence of the competitive environment of the stock world market is non-linear, unpredictable, and subject to pressures from so many outside factors. This paper offers a comprehensive literature review study of the stock market analysis methods, state-of-the-art algorithms and methodologies widely used in bourse forecasting, and addresses a few of the ongoing problems in this field that demand greater awareness and provide opportunities for potential growth and research. Based on literature review in this paper, the results show that SVM and deep learning methods good at extracting features from non-linear data and produced good acceptable results in time series data analysis of stock market forecasting. However, the use of advanced deep learning approaches and hybrid methods continues a number of research work to improve stock forecasting accuracy. By considering good external factors, technical indicators, sentiment analysis and combination of these indicators could provide a more accurate and precise prediction.

ACKNOWLEDGMENT

Many thanks to Dr. Balachandran K and Dr. Manohar M and the reviewers for their helpful comments and suggestions. I would also like to thank my institution CHRIST (deemed to be University), for providing all the resources.

REFERENCES

Abu Mostafa, Y.S, Atiya, A.F. 1996. Introduction to financial forecasting. Applied Intelligence, Vol 6: 205–213.

Ajit Kumar Rout, P.K. Dash, Rajashree Dash and Ranjeeta Bisoi. 2017. Forecasting financial time series using a low complexity recurrent neural network and evolutionary learning approach. Journal of King Saud University – Computer and Information Sciences, Vol 29(4): 536–552.

Arévalo, R, García, J, Guijarro, F, Peris Manguillot, A. 2017. A dynamic trading rule based on filtered flag pattern recognition for stock market price forecasting. Expert Systems with Applications, Vol 81:177–192

Attigeri, Girija V, Manohara Pai, M. M., Pai, R. M., and Nayak. 2015. Stock market prediction: A big data approach. TENCON 2015–2015 IEEE Region 10 Conference (2015): 1–5.

Bharathi.Sv, Geetha, and Angelina. 2017. Sentiment Analysis for Effective Stock Market Prediction. International Journal of Intelligent Engineering and Systems, Vol 10:146–154.

Chatfield C. 1993. Neural networks: Forecasting breakthrough or passing fad? International Journal of Forecasting, Vol 10: 43–46.

Y. Chen and Y. Hao, 2017. A feature weighted support vector machine and K-nearest neighbor algorithm for stock market indices prediction. Expert Systems with Applications, Vol. 80: 340–355.

Chen, K.Y. & C.H. Wang. 2007. A hybrid SARIMA and support vector machines in forecasting the production values of the machinery industry in Taiwan. Expert Systems with Applications, Vol 32: 254–64.

Chen, Tai-liang, and Feng-yu Chen. 2016. An intelligent pattern recognition model for supporting investment decisions in stock market. Information Sciences, Vol 346: 261–74.

Chenjie Sang & Massimo Di Pierro. 2019. Improving trading technical analysis with TensorFlow Long Short-Term Memory (LSTM) Neural Network. Journal of Finance and Data Science, Vol 5(1) : 1–11.

Contreras I., Hidalgo J.I., and Núñez-Letamendia L. 2012. A GA Combining Technical and Fundamental Analysis for Trading the Stock Market. In: Di Chio C. et al. (eds) Applications of Evolutionary Computation. EvoApplications. Lecture Notes in Computer Science, vol 7248.

Crone SF, Hibon M, and Nikolopoulos K. 2011. Advances in forecasting with neural networks?Empirical evidence from the NN3 competition on time series prediction. International Journal of Forecasting, Vol 27(3):635–660.

Dash R. & Dash PK. 2016. A hybrid stock trading framework integrating technical analysis with machine learning techniques. Journal of The Institution of Engineers (India): Series B, Vol 99: 555–563.

Das, Sumanjit & Mishra, Sarojananda & Senapati, Manas Ranjan.2019. Correction to: A Novel Model for Stock Price Prediction Using Hybrid Neural Network. Journal of The Institution of Engineers (India):Series B, Vol 100:387.

De-hua LIU & Jing-Jing WANG. 2018. A PCA-LSTM Model for Stock Index Prediction. DEStech Transactions on Engineering and Technology Research, Vol 10.

Dhanya Jothimani, Ravi Shankar, and Surendra S Yadav. 2018. Portfolio Selection in Indian Stock Market Using Relative Performance Indicator Approach. Flexibility in Resource Management, Vol 10:185–201.

Dridi, A., Atzeni, M, and Reforgiato Recupero, D. 2019. FineNews: fine-grained semantic sentiment analysis on financial microblogs and news. International Journal of Machine Learning and Cybernetics, Vol 10:2199–2207.

Falinouss, P. 2007. Stock trend prediction using news articles: A text mining approach. Master's Thesis, Lulea University of Technology, Sweden. diva2:1019373

Guan, Z. Dai, A. Zhao, and J. He. 2018. A novel stock forecasting model based on high-order-fuzzy-fluctuation trends and back propagation neural network. PLoS One, Vol 13(2): 1–15.

Hamzaçebi C, Akay D, and Kutay F. 2009. Comparison of direct and iterative artificial neural network forecast approaches in multi-periodic time series forecasting. Expert Systems with Applications, Vol 36(2): 3839–3844.

Hongduo Cao, Tiantian Lin, Ying Li and Zhang, Hanyu. 2019. Stock Price Pattern Prediction Based on Complex Network and Machine Learning. Complexity, Vol 2019: 1–12.

H. Isah. 2017. Social Data Mining for Crime Intelligence: Contributions to Social Data Quality Assessment and Prediction Methods. University of Bradford, 2017.

Ha Young Kim & Chang Hyun Won. 2018. Forecasting the volatility of stock price index: A hybrid model integrating LSTM with multiple GARCH-type models. Expert Systems with Applications, Vol 103: 25–37.

K. S. Loke. 2017. Impact of financial ratios and technical analysis on stock price prediction using random forests. International Conference on Computer and Drone Applications (IConDA), 38–42.

Pang, Bo & Lee, Lillian. 2008. Opinion Mining and Sentiment Analysis. Foundations and Trends in Information Retrieval, Vol 2: 1–135.

Jigar Patel, Sahil Shah, Priyank Thakkar, and K Kotecha. 2014. Predicting stock market index using fusion of machine learning techniques. Expert Systems with Applications, Vol 42(4): 2162–2172.

Jigar Patel, Sahil Shah, Priyank Thakkar, and K Kotecha. 2015. Predicting stock and stock price index movement using Trend Deterministic Data Preparation and machine learning techniques. Expert Systems with Applications, Vol 42(1):259–268.

Pawar K, Jalem RS, Tiwari V. 2019. Stock Market Price Prediction Using LSTM RNN. Proceedings of In Emerging Trends in expert applications and security.

Lin Y, Guo H, and Hu J. 2013. An SVM-based approach for stock market trend prediction. Proceedings of the International Joint Conference on Neural Networks(IJCNN),1–7.

Liu S, Zhang C, and Ma J. 2017. CNN-LSTM Neural Network Model for Quantitative Strategy Analysis in Stock Markets. International Conference on Neural Information Processing(ICONIP). Neural Information Processing, Vol 10635:198–206.

Makridakis, S. 2017. The forthcoming Artificial Intelligence (AI) revolution: Its impact on society and firms. Futures, Vol 90: 46–60.

Monica Adya & Fred Collopy. 1998. How effective are neural networks at forecasting and prediction?. A review and evaluation. Journal of Forecasting, Vol 17(56):481–495.

Nautiyal, N., & Kavidayal, P. C. 2018. Analysis of Institutional Factors Affecting Share Prices: The Case of National Stock Exchange. Global Business Review,Vol 19(3):707–721.

Nguyen, Thien Hai, Kiyoaki Shirai, and Julien Velcin. 2015. Sentiment Analysis on Social Media for Stock Movement Prediction. Expert Systems with Applications, Vol 42(24): 9603–9611.

Omer Berat Sezar, Murat Ozbayoglu, and Erdogan Dogdu.2017. A Deep Neural-Network Based Stock Trading System Based on Evolutionary Optimized Technical Analysis Parameters. Procedia Computer Science, Vol 114:473–480.

Paluch, Michal & Jackowska-Strumillo, Lidia. 2018. Hybrid Models Combining Technical and Fractal Analysis with ANN for Short-Term Prediction of Close Values on the Warsaw Stock Exchange. Applied Sciences, Vol 8(12): 2473.

Park, Cheol-Ho, and Scott H. Irwin. 2007. What do we know about the profitability of technical analysis?. Journal of Economic Surveys, Vol 21: 786–826.

Rechenthin, M.D., 2014. Machine-learning classification techniques for the analysis and prediction of high-frequency stock direction.

Robinson C, Dilkina B, Hubbs J, Zhang W, Guhathakurta S, and Brown MA. 2017. Machine learning approaches for estimating commercial building energy consumption. Applied Energy, Vol 208 : 889–904.

Rudra Kalyan, Nayak, Mishra, Debahuti, and Rath, Amiya. 2015. A Naïve SVM-KNN based stock market trend reversal analysis for Indian benchmark indices. Applied Soft Computing, Vol 35: 670-680.

Ruixun Zhang, Z. Yuan, and X. Shao. 2018. A New Combined CNN-RNN Model for Sector Stock Price Analysis. IEEE 42nd Annual Computer Software and Applications Conference (COMPSAC), Tokyo, pp. 546–551.

Salaken, Syed,Nguyen, Thanh and Nahavandi, Saeid. 2017. Extreme learning machine based transfer learning algorithms: A survey. Neurocomputing, Vol 267:516–524.

Savas Yıldırım, Dhanya Jothimani, Can Kavaklioglu and Aysc Basar. 2019. Deep Learning Approaches for Sentiment Analysis on Financial Microblog Dataset. IEEE International Conference on Big Data (Big Data), Los Angeles, CA, USA, 2019, pp. 5581–5584.

Sethia A. & Raut P. 2019. Application of LSTM, GRU and ICA for Stock Price Prediction. Information and Communication Technology for Intelligent Systems, Vol 107:479–487.

Seethalakshmi, & Ramaswamy. 2018. Analysis of stock market predictor variables using linear regression. International Journal of Pure and Applied Mathematics, Vol 119:369–377.

Senol Emir, Hasan Dincer, and Mehpare Timor. 2012. A Stock Selection Model Based on Fundamental and Technical Analysis Variables by Using Artificial Neural Networks and Support Vector Machines. Review of Economics & Finance, Vol 2:106–122.

Setty, D.V., T.M. Rangaswamy and K.N. Subramanya. 2010. A review on data mining applications to the performance of stock marketing. International Journal of Computer Applications, Vol 1: 33–43.

Selvamuthu, D., Kumar, V., and Mishra. 2019. A. Indian stock market prediction using artificial neural networks on tick data. Financial Innovation, Vol 5.

Sharda R. & Patil RB. 1992. Connectionist approach to time series prediction: An empirical test. Journal of Intelligent Manufacturing, Vol 3(1):317–323.

Soni & Sneha. 2005. Applications of ANNs in Stock Market Prediction: A Survey. International Journal of Computer Science & Engineering Technology, Vol 2: 71–83.

Ticknor, J. L.2013. A Bayesian regularized artificial neural network for stock market forecasting. Expert Systems with Applications, Vol 40: 5501–5506.

Wanjawa, Barack, and Muchemi, Lawrence. 2014. ANN Model to Predict Stock Prices at Stock Exchange Markets. ArXiv, abs/1502.06434.

Xi Zhang, Siyu. Qu, Jieun Huang, Binxing Fang and Philip Yu. 2018. Stock Market Prediction via Multi-Source Multiple Instance Learning. In IEEE Access, Vol 6 :50720–50728.

Xiaodong Li, Pangjing Wu and Wenpeng Wang. 2020. Incorporating stock prices and news sentiments for stock market prediction: A case of Hong Kong. Information Processing & Management, Vol 57(5):102212.

Zhong, Xiao, and Enke, David. 2017. Forecasting daily stock market return using dimensionality reduction. Expert Systems with Applications, Vol 67:126–139.

Zhang, Peter, and Patuwo, Eddy & Hu, Michael. 1998. Forecasting With Artificial Neural Networks: The State of the Art. International Journal of Forecasting, Vol 14(1):35–62.

Zhang, Le, and Suganthan, Ponnuthurai. 2016. A Survey of Randomized Algorithms for Training Neural Networks. Information Sciences, Vol 364.

https://corporatefinanceinstitute.com/resources/knowledge/trading-investing/fundamental-analysis/

Smart Computing – Khan et al (Eds)
© *2021 Taylor & Francis Group, London, ISBN 978-0-367-76552-1*

A nonlinear anisotropic diffusion model with forward-backward diffusivities for image denoising

Santosh Kumar, Khursheed Alam & Nitendra Kumar
Department of Mathematics, School of Basic Sciences and Research, Sharda University, Greater Noida, UP, India

ABSTRACT: In the present study, we give a very effective nonlinear anisotropic diffusion model to approximate the solution to minimizing the energy functional for additive noise removal. This model is obtained by multiplying the magnitude of the gradient in a nonlinear anisotropic diffusion model. To judge our models, we compared it with the existing model by numerical experiments using explicit numerical schemes with forward-backward diffusivity.

Keywords: Second-order PDEs, image denoising, nonlinear diffusion equation

1 INTRODUCTION

In the field of image processing, image restoration is a major problem. Given a noisy image $u_0 : \Omega \to R$,

$$u_0 = u + n, \tag{1}$$

where Ω is a bounded domain in R^2, u is the original real image, and r is an additive Gaussian white noise of standard deviation σ^2 with zero mean to add in the original images. We obtain the observed image u_0.

Rudin et al. (1992) introduced the first approach for image denoising by total variation norm and the solution of TV norm obtained by the gradient projection method. They proposed a constrained optimization-type numerical scheme for image denoising and edge detection. Rudin & Osher (1994) proposed another model for denoising and deblurring cases. The researchers looked toward the idea of total variation and have given improved and fast versions of the TV technique (Chan et al. 1999; Chang & I-Liang 2003; Marquina & Osher 2000; Rudin et al. 1992; Vogel & Oman 1996; Tripathi et al. 2021). Total variation denoising is a popular method and is considered as a bottom line for edge-preserving in image restoration. Marquina & Osher (2000) studied a time-dependent model using the multiply magnitude of the gradient of Rudin et al. (1992) model. The main analytic features of this model are (i) the image moves quickly to the steady solution with the help of level contours (ii) mean curvature for images through the gradient term.

Perona & Malik (1990) have given the first approach for removing noise by the nonlinear anisotropic diffusion equation. The rate of this equation is controlled by the edge-stopping function. In 1992, Catte et al. developed an approach and replaced the diffusivity $g(\nabla u)$ by $g(\nabla G_\sigma * u)$ in the Perona and Malik model. Many researchers have introduced different-different types of model for image restoration and edge detection via nonlinear diffusion, hyperbolic-parabolic, wavelet-based, complex diffusion, fourth-order equation, etc.; see Barbul & Moro (2019); Barbu et al. (2019); Chang & Hcrang (2004); Chen (2005); Ghanbari et al. (2014); Gilboa et al. (2004); Guo et al. (2012); Hajiaboli et al. (2012); Krissian et al. (2007); Kumar et al. (2016, 2018); Oiang et al. (2007); Rudin et al. (1992); Wang et al. (2018); Tripathi et al. (2021).

In 2005, Welk et al. proposed an additive noise removal-based anisotropic diffusion model. They have used forward-backward diffusivity in your experiments. We apply the technique of

Marquina & Osher (2000) in the Welk model, i.e., multiply the magnitude of the gradient in the anisotropic diffusion model, we get a new model for image denoising and we use forward-backward diffusivities in our experiments. The finite difference method to discretize old and new models with forward-backward diffusivities. The numerical results for an image denoising models are given in Tables 1 and 2 and Figures 2 and 3.

2 IMAGE DENOISING ALGORITHM

Welk et al. (2005) introduced a diffusion model for image restoration to use the non-convex regularization functional and given a minimizing the energy functional which as:

$$E(u) = \int_\Omega \phi(|\nabla u|^2 \ dx + \frac{\lambda}{2} \int_\Omega (u - u_0)^2) \ dx. \tag{2}$$

The Euler–Lagrange equation of the function E becomes:

$$0 = -\text{div}(\phi'(|\nabla u|^2)\nabla u) + \lambda(u - u_0), \quad x \in \Omega, \tag{3}$$

Using the method of gradient descent for $t \to \infty$ to a function of E is equivalent to:

$$u_t = \text{div}(h(\nabla u|^2)\nabla u) - \lambda(u - u_0),$$
$$u(x, 0) = u_0(x),$$
$$\frac{\partial u}{\partial \boldsymbol{n}} = 0, \quad x \in \partial\Omega. \tag{4}$$

Here, $\boldsymbol{n}$ represents the unit outer normal to $\partial\Omega$, $\partial\Omega$ is the boundary of Ω and homogeneous Neumann boundary conditions $\frac{\partial u}{\partial \boldsymbol{n}} = 0$, $x \in \partial\Omega$.

The diffusivity $h(s^2) = \phi'(s^2)$, is similar to the regularizer in E. Motivated by the Marquina and Osher (2000) model, we multiply Equation (4) by the magnitude of the gradient, we obtained a new model for image denoising:

$$u_t = |\nabla u| \ \text{div}(h(|\nabla u|^2)\nabla u) - |\nabla u|\lambda(u - u_0). \tag{5}$$

The original noisy image u_0 is taken as the initial guess and with the same conditions given in Equation (4). The diffusivity for both model (4) and (5), we have taken Charbonnier diffusivity $h(s^2) = \frac{1}{\sqrt{1 + \frac{|s^2|}{\gamma^2}}}$. The function h is related to the function $\phi(s^2) = \sqrt{\gamma^4 + \gamma^2 s^2} - \gamma^2$, where γ is a contrast parameter; see reference Charbonnier et al. (1994).

3 DISCRETE SCHEME

Let u_{ij}^n be the approximation of $u(x_i, y_j, t_n)$; we discretize

$$x_i = i\Delta x, \ y_i = j\Delta x, \ i, j = 1, 2 ...., N, \ t_n = n\Delta t, \ n \geq 1$$

where Δx represents the spatial step size and Δt represents the time step size.

The explicit scheme for nonlinear anisotropic diffusion model (4) as:

$$u_{ij}^t = \frac{1}{2\Delta x} \left((h_{i+1,j}^n + h_{i,j}^n)(u_{i+1,j}^n - u_{i,j}^n) - (h_{i,j}^n + h_{i-1,j}^n)(u_{i,j}^n - u_{i-1,j}^n) \right)$$

$$+ \frac{1}{2\Delta x} \left((h_{i,j+1}^n + h_{i,j}^n)(u_{i,j+1}^n - u_{i,j}^n) - (h_{i,j}^n + h_{i,j-1}^n)(u_{i,j}^n - u_{i,j-1}^n) \right) - \lambda(u_{i,j}^n + u_{i,j}^0)$$

The explicit scheme for nonlinear anisotropic diffusion model (5) as:

$$u_{ij}^t = q_{i,j}^n \frac{1}{2\Delta x} \left((h_{i+1,j}^n + h_{i,j}^n)(u_{i+1,j}^n - u_{i,j}^n) - (h_{i,j}^n + h_{i-1,j}^n)(u_{i,j}^n - u_{i-1,j}^n) \right)$$

$$+ \frac{1}{2\Delta x} \left((h_{i,j+1}^n + h_{i,j}^n)(u_{i,j+1}^n - u_{i,j}^n) - (h_{i,j}^n + h_{i,j-1}^n)(u_{i,j}^n - u_{i,j-1}^n) \right) - \lambda q_{i,j}^n(u_{i,j}^n + u_{i,j}^0)$$

where the diffusivity $h(|\nabla u|^2)$ is discretized by $h_{ij}^n = \phi'\left((\frac{u_{i+1,j}^n - u_{i+1,j}^n}{\Delta x})^2 + (\frac{u_{i,j+1}^n - u_{i,j-1}^n}{\Delta x})^2 \right)$ and $q_{i,j}^n = \sqrt{(u_{i,j}^x)^2 + (u_{i,j}^y)^2}$.

The explicit method for all models is stable and convergent for $\Delta t/\Delta x^2 = 0.5$ (Lapidus & Pinder 1983).

4 NUMERICAL EXPERIMENT

In this section, we have taken two grayscale images, Lena and Boat of (256×256) pixels and the pixel value lies between $[0,255]$. We begin our numerical experiment the intensities of the images lie between the range $[0, 1]$. We add Gaussian noise in the original images by the normal function in Matlab by the code imnoise (u, 'Gaussian', M, σ^2), for the mean M and variance σ^2, we get noisy images. We have used the value of Lagrange multiplier λ is 0.85 as given in the diffusivity parameter $\gamma = 5$ and $\Delta t/\Delta x^2 = 0.4$ as given in Chan et al. (1999), Chang & I-Liang (2003), Charbonnier et al. (1994) and Weickert (1998).

The peak signal to noise ratio (PSNR) as a metric to recover images as given below:

$$\text{PSNR} = 10 \, \log_{10} \left(\frac{k^2}{\frac{1}{mn} \Sigma_{i,j}^n [u_{ij} - x_{ij}]^2} \right) \text{dB}, \qquad (6)$$

where k is the maximum pixel value of original images, mn is the size of the images, u is the original image, and x the denoised image.

4.1 Tables

Table 1. Figure 2(a)–(b) corrupted images by Gaussian noise $\sigma^2 = 0.004, 0.006$, respectively. We applied the models (4) and (5) to noisy images we get denoised images.

Noisy images	PSNR for noisy images	Denoised images	PSNR for (Model-4)	Denoised images	PSNR for (Model-5)
Figure 2(a)	24.13	Figure 2(c)	26.83	Figure 2(e)	28.62
Figure 2(b)	22.39	Figure 2(d)	25.20	Figure 2(f)	27.16
		No. of iterations	400	No. of iterations	50

Table 2. Figure 3(a)–(b) corrupted images by Gaussian noise $\sigma^2 = 0.004$, 0.006, respectively. We applied the models (4) and (5) to noisy images we get denoised images.

Noisy images	PSNR for noisy images	Denoised images	PSNR for (Model-4)	Denoised images	PSNR for (Model-5)
Figure 3(a)	24.04	Figure 3(c)	27.34	Figure 3(e)	28.07
Figure 3(b)	22.32	Figure 3(d)	24.48	Figure 3(f)	27.70
		No. of iterations	400	No. of iterations	50

4.2 *Figures*

(a)   (b)

Figure 1.   (a–b) Original test Lena and boat images, respectively.

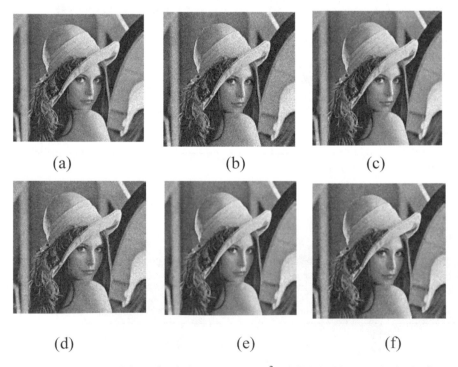

(a)   (b)   (c)

(d)   (e)   (f)

Figure 2.   (a–b) represents a different level of Gaussian noise $\sigma^2 = 0.004$, 0.006, respectively; (c–d) represent denoised images by model (4); (e–f) represent denoised images by our model (5), respectively.

Figure 3. (a–b) represents a different level of Gaussian noise $\sigma^2 = 0.004, 0.006$, respectively; (c–d) represent denoised images by model (4); (e–f) represent denoised images by our model (5).

5 CONCLUSIONS

In this study, a novel anisotropic model for image denoising was presented. The finite difference method is used to discretize our and existing models with forward-backward diffusivities. For the quality of the denoised image, we have used the PSNR value. The numerical experimental results confirm that our model (5) gives better-denoised images than the model (4). Model (5) has a smoother image and better PSNR value than the previous model at a small number of iterations. The model (5) converges very fast to obtain the smoothness images.

REFERENCES

Alvarez, L., Lions, P.L. & Morel, J.M. 1992, Image selective smoothing and edge detection by nonlinear diffusion II*. *SIAM Journal on Numerical Analysis*. 29(3): 845–866.
Barbu1, T. & Moro, C. 2019, Compound PDE-based additive denoising solution combining an improved anisotropic diffusion model to a 2D Gaussian filter kernel. *East Asian Journal on Applied Mathematics* 9(1): 1–12.
Barbu, T., Miranville, A. & Morosanu, C. 2019, A qualitative analysis and numerical simulations of a non-linear second-order anisotropic diffusion problem with non-homogeneous Cauchy Neumann boundary conditions. *Applied Mathematics and Computation* 350(1): 170–180.
Catte, F., Lions, P.L., Morel, J.M. & Coll T. 1992, Image selective smoothing and edge detection by nonlinear diffusion*. *SIAM Journal on Numerical Analysis*. 29: 182–193.

Chan, T.F., Golub, G.H. & Mulet, P. 1999, A nonlinear primal-dual method for total variation based image restoration. *SIAM Journal on Scientific Computing.* 20(6): 1964–1977.

Chang, Q. & I-Liang, C. 2003, Acceleration methods for total variation-based image denoising. SIAM *Journal on Scientific Computing* 25(3): 982–994.

Chang, Q. & Hcrang, Z. 2004, Efficient algebraic multigrid algorithms and their convergence. SIAM *Journal on Scientific Computing* 24: 597–618.

Charbonnier, P. & Blanc-Feraud, L., Aubert, G. & Barlaud, M. 1994, Two deterministic half-quadratic regularization algorithms for computed imaging. *In Proceedings of IEEE International Conference on Image Processing* 2: 168–172.

Chen, K. 2005, Adaptive smoothing via contextual and local discontinuities. *IEEE Transactions Pattern Analysis and Machine Intelligence* 27(10): 1552–67.

Ghanbari, B., Rada, L. & Chen, K. 2014, A restarted iterative homotropy analysis method for two nonlinear models from image processing, *International Journal of Computer Mathematics.* 91: 661–687.

Gilboa, G., Sochen, N. & Zeevi, Y.Y. 2004, Image enhancement and denoising by a complex diffusion process. *IEEE Transactions on Pattern Analysis Machine Intelligence.* 26(8): 1020–1036.

Guo, Z., Sun, J., Zhang, D. & Wu, B. 2012, Adaptive Perona-Malik model based on the variable exponent for image denoising. *IEEE Transactions on Image Processing*, 21(3): 958–67.

Hajiaboli, M., Ahmad, M. & Wang, C. 2012, An edge-adapting Laplacian kernel for nonlinear diffusion filters. *IEEE Transactions on Image Processing* 21(4): 1561–72.

Krissian, K., Westin, C.F., Kikinis, R. & Vosburgh, K. 2007, Oriented speckle reducing anisotropic diffusion. *IEEE Transactions on Image Processing* 16(5): 1412–24.

Kim, S. & Joo, K. 2006, Partial Differential Equation-based image restoration: a hybrid model and color image denoising. *IEEE Transactions on Image Processing* 15: 1163–1170.

Kumar, S., Sarfaraz, M. & Ahmad, M. K. 2018, Denoising method based on wavelet coefficients via diffusion equation. *Iranian Journal of Science and Technology, Transactions A: Science* 42: 721–726.

Kumar, S., Sarfaraz, M. & Ahmad, M.K. 2016, An efficient PDE-based nonlinear anisotropic diffusion model for image denoising. *Neural, Parallel and Scientific Computations* 24: 305–315.

Lapidus, L. & Pinder, G.F. 1983, Numerical solution of partial differential equations in science and engineering. *SIAM Rev.* 25(4): 581–582.

Marquina, A. & Osher, S. 2000, Explicit algorithms for a new time dependent model based on level set motion for nonlinear deblurring and noise removal. *SIAM Journal on Scientific Computing.* 22(2): 387–405.

Perona, P. & Malik, J. 1990, Scale space and edge detection using anisotropic diffusion. *IEEE Transactions on Pattern Analysis and Machine Intelligence* 12: 629–639.

Qiang, Q., Yao, Z.A. & Ke, Y.Y. 2007, Entropy solutions for a fourth-order nonlinear degenerate problem for noise removal. *Nonlinear Analysis.* 67: 1908–1918.

Rudin, L., Osher, S. & Fatemi, E. 1992, Nonlinear total variation based noise removal algorithm. *Physica D: Nonlinear Phenomena.* 60: 259–268.

Rudin, L. & Osher, S. 1994, Total variation based image restoration with free local constraints. *Proc. IEEE International Conference on Image Processing.* 60: 31–35.

Vogel, C.R. & Oman, M.E. 1996, Iterative methods for total variation denoising. *SIAM Journal on Scientific Computing.* 17: 227–238.

Wang, N., Shang, Y., Chen, Y., Yang, M. & Zhang, Q. 2018, A hybrid model for image denoising combining modified isotropic diffusion model and modified Perona-Malik model. *IEEE* 6: 33568–33581.

Weickert, J. 1998. Anisotropic Diffusion in Image Processing. Teubner Stuttgart.

Welk, M., Theis, D., Brox, T. & Weickert, J. 2005, PDE-based deconvolution with forward-backward diffusivities and diffusion tensors. *In scale space, LNCS, Springer Berlin*: 585–597.

Witkin, A.P. 1983, Scale-space filtering. *Proc. IJCAI Karlsruhe*: 1019–1021.

Tripathi P., Kumar N. and Siddiqi A. H., 2021, De-noising Raman spectra using total variation de-noising with iterative clipping algorithm. Computational Science and its Applications, Routledge & CRC Press Logo- Taylor & Francis Group. ISBN 9780367256234, 1st edition, Chapter 14. (In press).

Smart Computing – Khan et al (Eds)
© *2021 Taylor & Francis Group, London, ISBN 978-0-367-76552-1*

A survey and proposed methodology for the action recognition in sports

Seemanthini K., Amisha Kumari, Akanksha & M. Bhoomika
Department of ISE, DSATM, Bangalore, Karnataka, India

ABSTRACT: Several techniques have demonstrated the need to detect artifacts that are semantically relevant for identifying people in videos. There are no other techniques used to connect the project with the research to be translated in the direction of training for single deepening convolution neural network (CNN) by a broad text company. The proposed method discusses sports action recognition with a 3D convolutional network. Two different experiments are being performed. Two similar activities are distinguished: running and walking. The 3D convolution network has been shown to know space- and time-linked video sequence characteristics. The best thing was that the A1 architecture was at 85% We compared three different networks of this kind with the latter experiment on the UC F101 dataset.

Fifteen events have been picked. Architecture A1 has reached 80.7% precision. The results show that the 3D convolution architecture of the subtitle network can achieve relatively high precision. Computer vision and machine learning are among the most complex problems of automatic video analysis. An important part of this work concerns human activity identification because the majority of video semi-production occurs by humans and their behaviors. HAR is video based, but human activity recognition (HAR) is one of the most important and challenging applications in many fields. For hockey images, we introduce a multi-label deep HAR 3D CNN method; the recent performance of the CNNs for solving different challenges. Test method on two scenarios: a collection of k-binate interconnections vs. an individual k-output interconnection in a dataset that is accessible publicly.

Keywords: Convolution Neural Network, 3D Convolutional, Action recognition, Object recognition

1 INTRODUCTION

A substantial amount of research has centered on the identification of human activity in the computer vision environment. The objective of this study is to automatically identify and understand in a video what people do. Technically, we are trying to develop a profoundly concomitant neural network, a multi-purpose learning scheme, which simultaneously teaches activity recognition and objects recognition. Second, it enables us to use a large object identifying data set to increase the amount of training data available to us. Third, it helps us to integrate from a text that cannot be fully visible from the trained videos general knowledge about the target tasks, which increases the overall performance for action identification. An advantage of our approach is that we don't attempt to identify objects (Eum et al. 2019) in human activity scenes, but rather to derive the information of objects through the use of a specific network between the two activities, together with the major task (i.e., behavior identification). Networks of the neurons belong to our lives. Including industrial production to the pharmacy, they are used in many different sectors. They can be used to extract useful data information.

We chose to use 3D convergence networks to extract various activities from the video sequence. Videos can be easily understood by people. You can name the relations between video objects, detection, tracking, and saying. But the data is stored on computers. To be able to process computers, we need to find the appropriate explanation. Audio samples need to be evaluated accurately and useful data obtained from them. Over the past few years, the computer vision group has gone

DOI 10.1201/9781003167488-44

well. Continued work is being performed in many fields such as behavior prediction, incident detection, etc. Recognition of action (Brezovský 2018) in any particular sport is a major issue in computer vision to consider players ' activity. Human action recognition (HAR) has become the most interesting subject to be studied in recent years.

It is useful for a quick review to recapture some lengthy actual video. Such forms of video replay are mostly used to test the fault in any sport based on the action played by players on the field when playing either game. Here, we use convolutionary neural networks (CNNs) that fall under deep neural networks, most of which are used to explore symbolism. It is useful for a quick review to recapture some lengthy actual video. These types of recap of any video are mostly used to check out the fault in any sports based on an action that has been performed by players on the field while playing any sports. Here we use CNNs that are deep neural networks, most of which are used to analyze symbolism. The convolutional network in the design of correspondence between neurons was motivated by biological operations that resemble the organization of the visual cortex of the animal.

2 LITERATURE SURVEY

In the last few years, HAR has become a most agreeable topic to be researched. It has several types of applications, like intelligent video surveillance, intelligent human–machine interface, video storage, and retrieval and identity recognition. In this practice, we consider our first step with a large set of activities to define the shape and motion present in the videos.

In the field of computer vision, our main concerns here are human action and its classification into real-world recognition. Action recognition (Swears et al. 2014) is a basic activity that recognizes human action based on complete action in the picture.

On the contrary, action prediction is a before-the-fact video understanding task and is focusing on the future state. There is a huge difference between action recognition and action prediction lies in when to make a decision.

3 METHODOLOGY

3.1 *Using object recognition with action recognition*

To identify the objects in an image, specific events and behavior can be identified in the picture. To extract the object description using a similar method. Next, we choose to enhance the action recognition system by using the object recognition system to conduct the multi-task learning. We direct the program to perform the activity recognition function (Tejero-de-Pablos et al. 2016) with entirely different data sets.

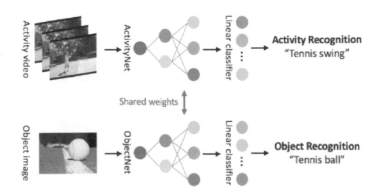

Figure 1. Action recognition in sports.

This increases the amount of training data for the entire system and also eliminates the need to detect objects from the videos selected manually.

We share weights in each layer of the process between the two tasks except the unique SoftMax classification task. In training the system, we push the parameter weights both for action recognition (Action Network and Object Recognition (Object Net) by refining the action recognition (Action Net) (Teng & Paramesran 2011) task from the network concern.

3.2 *3D convolutional network hockey plays hockey*

CNNs, with traditional convolution and pooling layers, are the methods used to significantly obtain the visages from the prerecorded data. We employ CNN generalizations to extract function not only from a single photographer but also from a frame segment 3D convolution and 3D grouping.

3.2.1 *Data pre-processing*

Resizing. Hardware limitations can require a large amount of processing memory even for a small batch of video data. All video frames have been dimensioned. Empirically, we find four-fold resizing optimal for our case.

Standardization of data. This is a required step in the neural system since the missing gradient is not standardized and can have an effect on the training process. We carry out standard normalization in this work.

Windowing. It means that the data is separated into fixed-size units/sequences, the instances, and their corresponding names. We use a window size of 15 overlapping window protocols and a five-frame overlap.

Labeling. All frame sequences obtained in the last step should be connected to an individual labeled vector. To obtain the final labeled vector, the majority rule applies to each part of the corresponding 15 vector marks (15 frames).

Training Dividing Test. We break the entire information into tippets after data pre-processing: training and testing. For modeling and hyperparameter selection, we divide trained data into trained and validated data sets, which in turn used finally to assess the models learned.

Unbalanced information management. We say addressing the issue of class inequality.

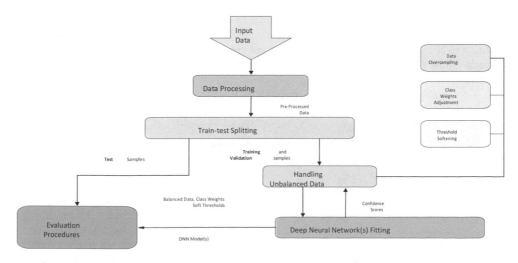

Figure 2.   Pictorial illustration of the research methodology.

3.2.2 *Training and network structure*

The inspiration of our network is classic CNN (Sozykin et al. 2018) architectures like ALEXNET and VGG, in general, a series of eminent nonlinear procedures, such as convolution, bundling, and the activation of single nonlinear units. Such techniques can be broadened to a 3D case to construct symbolic vectors in videos of local motions.

3.3 *Segmented video recognition approach*

Numerous aggregation techniques are available to detect segmented behavior. With segmented videos captured, the classification process is quietly accessible since each framework obtained from the video is the action. Our approach's basic component is a CNN that provides output by frame (or by segment). This is obtainable since customary two-stream CNNs with a recently developed deep CNN like I3D and InceptionV3. In v, the T-Shared represents a video where T is the video time and D is the dimensions of that function, the default grouping method is the significant mean grouping over time supplant by an associated video clip classification level.

One way to deal with this is the time hierarchy is shown in various lengths. Video input is divided into intervals of 1/2, 1/4, with 1/8, and maximum lengths per interval. We use these grouped functionalities to represent the K/D (K is the number of intervals in the time pyramid) and to classify the video clip using a fully connected layer. We also try to learn temporary filters, which can integrate a temporary local structure. Each container is fed with the width of the kernel $L \times 1$. This allows information from neighboring frames to be included in each time step representation. Then we use max-pooling over time and use a fully connected layer, as shown in Figure 5(c), to define the sequence. The intervals are preset and defined while the time-based grouping of pyramids allows some structure to remain unchanged. Previous research has shown that learning to pool the interval is useful when recognizing activity (Eum et al 2019). The intervals learned are regulated by three studied parameters, center 'g', 'δ' as width, and the other step is used to set 'N' as Gaussian parameters. Given 'T', the video length, we first calculate where the streaked Gaussians are located as:

$$gn = 0.5 \cdot T \cdot (gn + 1)\delta n = TN - 1\delta n \; \mu in = gn + (i - 0.5N + 0.5)\delta n \qquad (1)$$

The filters are then created as:

$$Fm[i, t] = 1Zm \exp(-(t - \mu i \, m) \, 2 \, 2\sigma 2 \, m) i \in \{0, 1 \ldots, N - 1\}, t \in \{0, 1, \ldots, T - 1\} \qquad (2)$$

where Zm is normalization constant.

We apply f to the matrix-multiplication video representation of $T \times D$, which results in a representation of $N \times D$ that is used as an input to completely linked layer for classification. Additional research used LSTMs for temporal structure video modeling. We also use the last hidden state as the input to a fully connected classification layer to compare a two-way LSTM with 512 hidden units. As a multi-label grouping, to minimize the cross-entropy, we formulate our tasks and train these models:

$$L(v) = czc \log(p(c) \log(1 - p(c))) \qquad (3)$$

where G(v) provides the time information (i.e., max pooling and LSTM, time convolution, etc.), and zc represents the basic realities label of class c.

3.4 *Uninterrupted video action recognition*

Uninterrupted detection of video activity is a difficult issue. Our goal here is to identify the activities taking place in every photo. Sequential events occur in several cases, often separated by no-activity frames, as opposed to segmented images. It allows the model to study to recognize the beginning and end of the actions. As an indication, we instruct as a per-frame classifier distinct fully connected layer. No temporal information in the features is used in this process. Through applying any approach to continuous videos on a temporary slider frame, the approaches given for the classification of segmented videos will be applied to continuous videos. Total pooling is used for each window (as in Figure 5(a)) and each pooled segment is defined.

We train the model to reduce the binary classification per frame:

$$L(v) = t, czt, c \log(p(c|H(vt))) + (1 - zt, c) \log(1 - p(c|H(vt))) \tag{4}$$

where vt is the per-frame or per-segment feature at time t, H(vt) means one of the practical methods of pooling, and zt, c is the soil truth class at t. Recent approaches have been proposed and proven efficient in continuous video detection in a study of the "super-events" (i.e., global video context). The method learns to model a series of N Cauchy distributions of time structure filters. The centers, xn, and widths of each distribution are μn.

Given T, filters are generated by the length of the video:

$$x\hat{}n = (T - 1) \cdot (\tanh(xn) + 1)2\gamma\hat{}n = \exp(1 - 2 \cdot |\tanh(\gamma n)|)F[t, n] = 1Zn\pi\gamma\hat{}n(t - x\hat{}n)\gamma\hat{}n2 \tag{5}$$

where Zn is a normalization constant, $t \in \{1, 2,...,T\}$ and $n \in \{1, 2,...,N\}$.

The filters are combined with learned soft weights per class, A, and the super event display is calculated as follows:

$$Sc = MmAc, m \cdot TtFm[t] \cdot vt \tag{6}$$

Where v is the T $\times$ D video representation.

4 CONCLUSION

The presented approach comes together with the survey on objects, humans, and scene features to recognize the actions in a better way. The available videos are marginally annotated to guide our approach. We do not know where, when, or what artifacts or scene features are used to define the action. An innovative way to build an integrated object and text-oriented CNN to handle the video recognition task for human activity, and we have trained the network with a shared network and a multiple-work training approach to identify the target activities and the set of objects.

REFERENCES

Brezovský, M., Sopiak, D., & Oravec, M. (2018, September). Action Recognition by 3D Convolutional Network. In 2018 International Symposium ELMAR (pp. 71–74). IEEE.

Eum, S., Reale, C., Kwon, H., Bonial, C., & Voss, C. (2019, May). Object and Text-guided Semantics for CNN-based Activity Recognition. In ICASSP 2019–2019 IEEE International Conference on Acoustics, Speech and Signal Processing (ICASSP) (pp. 1458–1462). IEEE.

Sozykin, K., Protasov, S., Khan, A., Hussain, R., & Lee, J. (2018, June). Multi-label class-imbalanced action recognition in hockey videos via 3d convolutional neural networks. In 2018 19th IEEE/ACIS International Conference on Software Engineering, Artificial Intelligence, Networking and Parallel/Distributed Computing (SNPD) (pp. 146151). IEEE.

Swears, E., Hoogs, A., Ji, Q., & Boyer, K. (2014). Complex activity recognition using granger constrained dbn (gcdbn) in sports and surveillance video.In Proceedings of the IEEE Conference on Computer Vision and Pattern Recognition (pp. 788795).

Tejero-de-Pablos, A., Nakashima, Y., Sato, T., & Yokoya, N. (2016, July). Human action recognition based video summarization for RGB-D personal sports video. In 2016 IEEE International Conference on Multimedia and Expo (ICME) (pp. 1–6). IEEE.

Teng, S. L., & Paramesran, R. (2011, November). Detection of service activity in a badminton game.In TENCON 2011-2011 IEEE Region 10 Conference (pp. 312–315). IEEE.

Smart Computing – Khan et al (Eds)
© 2021 Taylor & Francis Group, London, ISBN 978-0-367-76552-1

Intelligent system for question paper generation using Java

S. Kumar, U. Chauhan & A. Prakash
School of Electronics and Communication Engineering, Galgotias University, Greater Noida, India

ABSTRACT: With the world taking the step of automation in every desired field that can be touched, it's high time that it touches various aspects of the educational environment as well. The traditional question paper setting method to assessing the learning of a student needs to evolve. In this project, we present such a question bank management system which aims to fulfill all the desired criteria. It has controlled access to resources so that integrity and ethics of question paper setting is maintained. The randomization algorithm is used to address the issue of duplicates and same-meaning questions. Web applications today face a lot of threats from distributed denial-of-service (DDoS) attacks, authentication bypass and SQL injection. In this paper, we have tried to improve upon the security aspect of a question bank management system. By proper use of this question bank management system, question banking can continue to be used for a long time. All the required tools have been added and also any further development can be done with the help of plug-ins and traditional programming.

1 INTRODUCTION

Question bank management system is a management software in which we manage thousands of the questions in the database for academic purposes and assessment. In a traditional approach, faculty used to set question paper for the examination but after the exam there was no record of it. But in this system, the faculty can add the question in the database as per course outcome and as many as they want, unless and until there is a limit put by the software, and all the questions will be stored in the database. When the question setter needs to set paper for the examination they just click one button and using the shuffling algorithm the system generates a paper for the examination. The students can prepare for examination from the questions that are stored in the database which is read-only access for them. The faculty can also directly send the assignment and the quiz to students through this software, which will further increase interaction between the students and the faculty. This software is not limited only to colleges, but can also be used in various other academic institutions and for competitive examinations (Table 1).

Table 1. Comparison between manual and automated process of question paper generation.

Manual question paper generation	Automatic question paper generation
Human effort required	Automated software to do the job
Low security. High chance of paper leaks	High security. Last moment paper generation
Chances of repetition of questions	Totally random process
Less coverage and less variety	Wider coverage and wider variety
Slow process due to manual efforts	Fast process due to computer automation

DOI 10.1201/9781003167488-45

2 LITERATURE REVIEW

Learning is a lifelong process. We learn new things, lessons, and teachings, be it anything one can imagine every day. But sooner or later we forget it if there is nothing to keep track of it. We can't see where we are lacking, or what are the loopholes which need to be fixed. Thankfully, from ancient times there has been a system of regular assessments to address this issue. Every student was tested on various aspects of different skills that they had learned, by using the means present at that time to fulfill the purpose of learning.

Over time, things have evolved and the educational dimension is no exception. In the way of learning, the way of evaluation has changed over the time with the aim of fulfilling the same purpose. In modern times, evaluation through written examinations is a conventional procedure which has been followed in almost all educational institutions all over the world. Of course, there have been certain improvements in the mode of the examination which has gone from traditional methods of giving exams on OMR sheets, to modern-day online tests for various competitive examinations or institutional (academic organizations) examinations. However, we can observe that not much has changed in the aspects of setting a question paper. The traditional practice of manual question paper setting is still practiced in many of the schools or institutions. The process is very time taking and there is a high chance of manual mishaps here and there, which most of us would have witnessed during school and university examinations. The task becomes more challenging when the teacher has to cover a wider portion and wants to test his/her students on a diverse level of intellectuality, all in a single question paper. Meeting various course outcomes is an added challenge on top of it, while setting a question paper.

With time various advancements having been done regarding this issue, and also much of the research work is going on about which we will discuss in the following sections of the paper. Later, we will move our talk toward the question as to why there is a need to move to an automatic question bank management system.

Early works in this field go back to the year 2006 when Ittizar Aldabe focused his works on creating automatic questions. He called it Arikiturri. His work was based on Natural Language Processing (NLP) and Corpora methods. The system designed by him could sort out poorly developed questions.

E-learning was growing slowly and in the same year Li-Chun Sung brought forward his work for worldwide E-learning systems. The automatic quiz generator proposed by him made use of semantics network, WorldNet, and Google to develop questions for the quiz. The learners were evaluated based on their understanding of English text.

Moving forward, in the year 2010 Ming Liu brought forward his work on automatic question paper generator. This system used to take literature reviews as an input, and then questions were developed based on syntactic and semantic characteristics of words.

Recent works by various researchers make use of randomization algorithm and database management systems (DBMS).

2.1 *Traditional paper-based systems*

Traditional paper-based systems required human effort to set the question paper. There was a predefined syllabus and a predefined pattern for this which was designed by respective educational institutions. The question paper was then sent to higher officials in the hierarchy who had final say on this matter. After all this process only, a question paper was published for conducting the test.

2.2 *Limitations of paper-based dystem*

Covering everything in one sentence, I would like to say that even if almost all protocols are followed carefully; there is a high chance of manual mishaps here and there. There might be the issue of duplicacy due to lack of attention, or even questions with same meaning. Thus, it fails the purpose of randomization and various aspects of a good question paper. Time, availability of teachers, and other educational resources are also a major constraint. Also, there is a chance that a question paper leaks due to unethical practices, which we hear about in news from time to time.

Other limitations worth considering:

- Storage of question papers for a large-scale examination
- Last-minute modifications

Thus, there is enough reason to move on from traditional methods of question paper setting to more advanced methods.

3   CHALLENGES

3.1   *Course outcome mapping*

There are various course outcomes which are outlined by the course designing committee of the university at the start of the academic session. These outcomes state the skillset and knowledge which a student should be able to attain by the end of the course. Fair testing of skillsets to achieve the desired outcome is quite challenging. Setting a question paper for the same would be quite a demanding task.

3.2   *Duplicacy in meaning of questions*

Another challenge which is faced by question bank management software is the ability to differentiate between same meaning questions. These questions might not look to be duplicate but have same meaning.

For example, consider these two questions:

- What is Java?
- Define Java.

These questions might not be duplicates, but they convey same meaning. Thus, it becomes important to address such an issue.

3.3   *Module-wise allocation of questions*

A course consists of many well-prepared modules focusing on strengthening a particular area of skillsets. Providing equal weightage to all modules to keep satisfying course outcomes is a big challenge which needs to be addressed.

3.4   *Repetition of questions*

The same questions may appear many times during a question paper setting. One option to address this issue is to provide manual control to the person who is setting the question paper. But this may jeopardize the purpose of this software in some of the cases. So, it will be better to develop an algorithm which checks the questions at runtime.

3.5   *Template matching*

There is a well-defined template issued by the academic department of each educational institution. The challenge here is that question paper set by the software should match the prescribed template which is being followed.

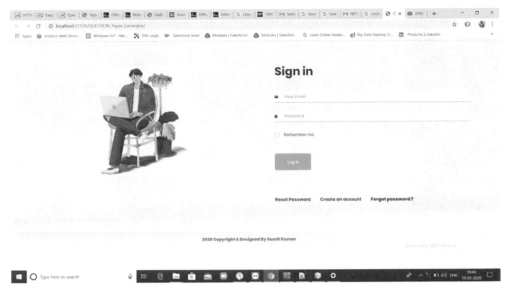

Figure 1. Login module.

4 IMPLEMENTATION

A software is combined working all different modules following a predefined framework. Implementation of question bank management software is done alongside the following modules.

4.1 Login module

This module is used to access to various users using question bank management system. Figure 1 presents the login module of the developed software

4.2 Administrator module

Administrator designs a blueprint which is to be followed by the teachers who are setting the question paper. In any scenario, the administrator has the final say regarding the question paper.

4.3 User module

This module provides access to the different contents of the question bank management software depending upon the role of the user. For example:

- A student can only have access to questions, he/she can't modify it.
- A teacher can set and modify the questions
- An administrator can modify the blueprint on which question paper is set (Figure 2).

4.4 Subject module

Question bank software is not limited to just one subject. This module provides the subject selection capability to the users (Figure 3).

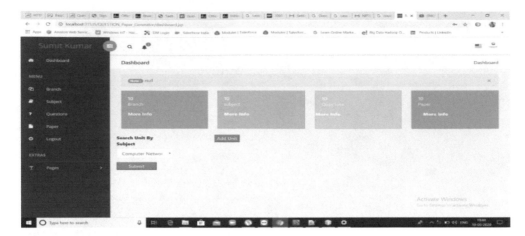

Figure 2.   User module.

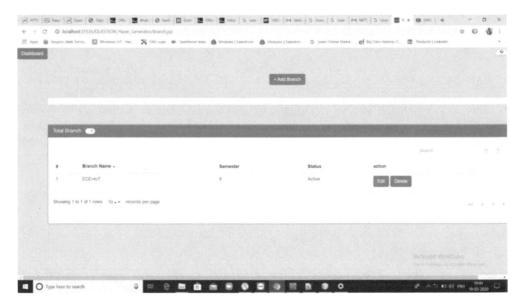

Figure 3.   Subject module.

4.5 *Exam-type selection module*

Various types of exams are conducted for the assessment of a student's learning. It can be a class test, quiz, assignment submission, mid-term examination, and end-term examination. All these assessments follow different blueprints and an exam-type selection module helps to a great extent with that (Figure 4).

4.6 *Paper pattern module*

As stated earlier, for various type of assessments, different blueprints for question paper setting need to be followed. Also, weightage assignment and course outcome differentiation is handled by this module (Figure 5).

398

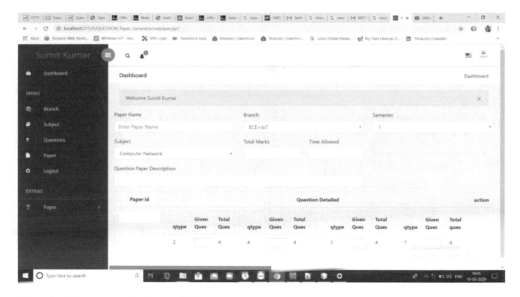

Figure 4.   Exam-type selection module.

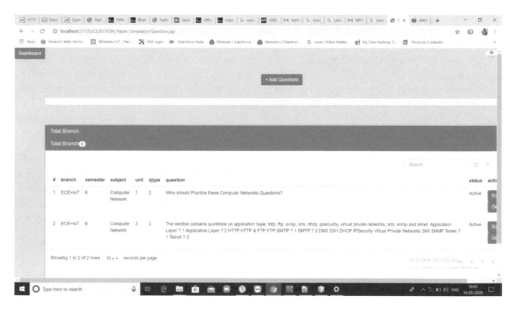

Figure 5.   Paper pattern module.

5   METHODOLOGY

5.1   *Instructor login*

Instructor will be provided with login ID and password after successful registration on the web application. After a successful login, he will have access to manually enter questions in the database which satisfy course outcome. The difficulty level of questions is set as easy, medium or hard. All the questions are stored as question bank in the database. While generating the question paper, the questions are sorted based on difficulty level and course outcome.

399

Flow Chart

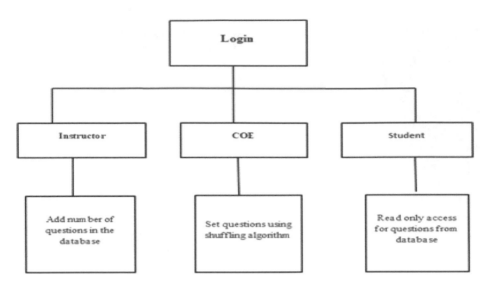

Figure 6. Flowchart depicting access method for different users of the designed software.

5.2 *Student login*

Student will be provided with login ID and password after successful registration on the web application. After a successful login, he will have access to the questions in the database. It will be read-only access and he can't modify it or tamper with it. Also, the web application can be used for online quizzes and submission of assignments online.

5.3 *COE login*

Controller of Examinations (COE) will be provided with login ID and password after successful registration on the web application. After a successful login, he can a generate question paper based on course outcomes and difficulty level with just a click of the button. With the help of randomization algorithm many sets of question papers can be generated; so that even in the case of a leak, various options will still be available till the last moment. All this will ultimately reduce the effects of malpractice in exams (Figure 6).

5.4 *Use of randomization algorithm*

This algorithm makes use of random numbers to decide next step in the sequential execution of the processes. For example, to choose the next pivot or randomly shuffling the array, the randomization quick sort method makes use of any random number.

5.4.1 *Steps Depicting Working of Randomization Algorithm*
Step 1. Generation of code by applying random function
Step 2. Generation of decimal digit in double format by random function
Step 3. Multiplication of random function by 10 to get single digit number
Step 4. Looping of numbers 1 to 6 to get a random 6 digit number into string format
Step 5. Conversion of string into integer
Step 6. The generated six-digit number used for identification of questions on the basis of bloom's taxonomy
Step 7. Numbers 0, 1, and 2 added at the end of six-digit number to show difficulty level

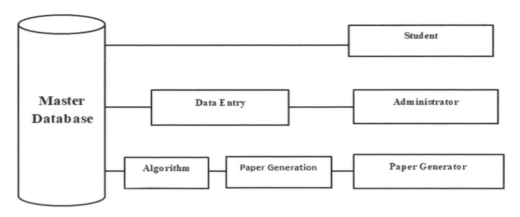

Figure 7.   Proposed model of the software.

6   PROPOSED MODEL

The proposed model for question bank management system is a revised work based on the work of earlier researchers. The algorithm used for sorting out the questions is randomization algorithm. The access to question bank management system is based on role-based hierarchy model, which means the action that a particular user can perform on this web application has already been defined by their roles. The central administrator will have complete control over the working of the software. For the generation of question paper: syllabus and course outcome mapping are considered for all questions, and also for generating multiple sets of question papers. Upon generation of the question paper, the paper is converted into an encrypted PDF and can be sent to the authenticated personnel on the click of a button.

Core functionalities of the application have been developed using Java, and the MySQL database has been used to store the questions. The interface has been made to look sleek and mobile compatible with the help of bootstrap framework. Security enhancements have been a major focus, which will be discussed in Section 7 (Figure 7).

7   WHAT'S NEW?

Crediting the work of previous researchers, we have tried to improve upon the security aspect of the software which couldn't be found in earlier works.

Any web-based application or software is vulnerable to following type of threats:

- DOS attacks
- Authentication bypass
- SQL Injection

7.1   *DOS attacks*

DOS attacks are intended external attacks which aim to prevent genuine usage of a service provided by an organization. In case of web-based apps, it can often lead to crashing.

Considering the usage of question bank management software on a large scale, it becomes important to address this security issue. An attacker with unfair intent may try to disrupt the working of the website and try to have unauthorized access to gain confidential information.

To address this issue, we have tried to embed black hole routing in our software which can work alongside sophisticated hardware.

7.2 *Authentication bypass*

To access a web-based service, valid session IDs are needed. Also, cookies are used to provide faster and customized service. Furthremore, execution of web-forms based authentication is done in client-side web browser scripts or through web browser.

So all in all, due to poor authentication mechanisms, the attacker can have access to everything just by manipulating some values in web forms or parameters. Thus, to address this issue we have enhanced our software with the following

7.2.1 *Session Handling*
- Session IDs don't get exposed
- Timing out of session IDs, so as to invalidate the ID after logout
- When a legitimate user logs in, the session IDs are recreated in the background

7.2.2 *Enhanced Authentication Mechanism*
- Improvement upon the password complexity making it a combination of alphanumeric and special characters
- Fool playing: Not providing the user with information that which part of data provided by him is incorrect, otherwise he/she may succeed with trial and errors method. Thus, it will always show "username or password incorrect", rather than showing "username incorrect" or "password incorrect".

7.3 *SQL injection*

In this method, the attacker tries to access the database contents by placing malicious contents in the SQL statements through inputs on the web page.

For a software like QBMS, which is a heavy web-input based software, not addressing this security aspect may cost a lot if exploited.

Thus, we have made following improvements to the software to make it less vulnerable to SQL injection:

- Use of parameterized queries: Parameterized queries help database to recognize the code and further differentiate it from the input data.
- Input validation: Defined format for each type of inputs, so that only valid inputs are accepted.

8 CONCLUSION

Constant assessment of developed skills goes a long way in keeping track of the progress of the students. A question bank management system moves away from traditional question paper setting method. It has proved to be beneficial and research and development is still in progress by many. The issue of duplicacy has been addressed by usage of enhanced artificial intelligence (AI). Question selection and course outcome mapping issues still need an optimization. Controlled access to resources or in another words role-based hierarchy goes a long way in maintaining the integrity of the system. A lot of security issues which web-based applications face regularly have been addressed. The software is completely usable and transition from old methods to new methods is rightly suggested while the remaining optimizations are worked upon.

9 FUTURE WORK

Even after improving upon security aspect, and carrying over the work of previous researchers, there are still a lot of areas which need improvement.

9.1 *Development with the help of machine learning*

With the help of machine learning, inputs fed by the teacher while setting the question paper can be checked at runtime and any mishaps can be notified instantly, thus avoiding any chance of future mishaps. There are various benefits of development of the software with machine learning, which have been left untapped and can be worked upon by future researchers

9.2 *Usage of a more efficient algorithm*

While randomization algorithm does the work of question selection for time being, a more efficient algorithm can be worked upon for future with the help of machine learning and artificial intelligence (AI).

REFERENCES

Fenil Kiran Gangar, Hital Gopal Gori & Ashwini Dalvi 2017. Automatic Question Paper Genertor system. *International Journal Of Computer Applications*(0975-8887) , Volume 166 – No. 10.

Itziar Aldabe, Maddalen Lopez de Lacalle, MontseMaritxalar, Edurne Martinez, & Larraitz Uria. 2006. ArikIturri: An Automatic Question Generator Based on Corpora and NLP Techniques. *ITS 2006, LNCS 4053*. pp. 584–594.

Li-Chun Sung, Yi-Chien Lin, Meng Chang Chen. 2006. The Design of Automatic Quiz Generation for Ubiquitous English ELearning System.

Ming Liu, Rafael A. Calvo & VasileRus. 2010. Automatic Question Generation for Literature Review Writing Support.

Surbhi Choudhary, Abdul Rais Abdul Waheed, Shrutika Gawandi & Kavita Joshi. 2015. Question Paper Generator System. *International Journal of Computer Science Trends and Technology*. Volume 3, issue 5.

Zalte S.V. , Jadhav C.C., Mangire A.A., Hole A.D. & Tulshi A.R. 2018. Automatic Question Paper Generator System. *International Journal Of Advanced Research In Computer And Communication Engineering*. Volume 7. Issue 3.

Smart Computing – Khan et al (Eds)
© *2021 Taylor & Francis Group, London, ISBN 978-0-367-76552-1*

Lower-limb muscle EMG analysis to predict ankle-foot activities for prosthesis control

Rohit Gupta & Ravinder Agarwal
EIED, Thapar Institute of Engineering and Technology, Patiala, Punjab, India

ABSTRACT: The human ankle-foot musculoskeletal structure is one of the complex structures of the human body. It has a large number of joints, ligaments, and muscles. The objective of this study is to analyze the muscular activity of the lower limb for different ankle-foot movements and to predict these movements for prosthesis control. The muscular activity of six lower-limb muscles has been recorded as an electromyography (EMG) signal. The experiment was conducted on the dataset of ten subjects, two non-weight bearings, and two weight-bearing ankle-foot movements. Analyzing EMG signal activity levels and reliability, a set of muscles have been proposed. Gastrocnemius and Tibialis Anterior muscles has been found as the most effective and reliable muscles to control ankle-foot movements. The average prediction accuracy has been found as $94.15 \pm 1.42\%$, $93.45 \pm 3.72\%$, and $93.27 \pm 3.34\%$ for LDA, SVM, and NN classifiers, respectively (ANOVA, p - value > 0.05).

1 INTRODUCTION

In the human body, the central pattern generator (CPG) generates the basic motor pattern to achieve any limb movement. The generated motor pattern transmitted to the muscles through a complex biological structure as an electromyogram (EMG) signal. Multiple muscles have been activated simultaneously to achieve any limb movement with particular force and torque (Gupta et al. 2018a). The human musculoskeletal structure is highly redundant in nature, i.e., the same limb movement can be controlled by the activation of a lesser number of muscles. It ultimately helps in establishing an efficient and practical man-machine interface for assistive and rehabilitative devices (Ivanenko et al. 2004).

The human lower body is consisting of a very diverse biomechanical structure. It works in a synergetic manner to achieve any limb movement. Particularly, the ankle-foot has 33 joints, 28 bones, and 112 ligaments. This compound structure is controlled by 20 intrinsic and 11 extrinsic muscles (Oatis 1988). The ankle-foot structure provides contact between the human body and the environment during various activities. The major movements of ankle-foot include dorsiflexion/plantarflexion and inversion/eversion of the foot. Both of these ankle-foot movements are controlled by six superficial muscles, namely: Gastrocnemius (Gast), Soleus (Sole), Tibialis Anterior (TiAn), Tibialis Posterior (TiPo), Peroneus Brevis (PeBr), and Peroneus Longus (PeLo), also known as prime muscle actuators (Riegger 1988). Each muscle has different characteristics; hence their contribution also differs in limb movement. The redundancy of the musculoskeletal model can be improved by selecting the optimal set of muscles, which provides sufficient information regarding ankle joint movements. This information is further transformed into a control signal to operate prosthesis.

The present work estimates the performance of the lower limb below knee muscles for various ankle movements using the EMG signal. Analyzing their fatigue level has assessed the performance of muscles and the consistency of their EMG signal over repeated limb movements, which includes ankle-foot movements during non-weight bearing and weight-bearing conditions. The outcome of the study provides a set of muscles, which will be able to provide reliable and consistent EMG

DOI 10.1201/9781003167488-46

signal to control ankle-foot movements. Further, the EMG signal of the selected set of muscles has been utilized for ankle-foot movement prediction.

2 MATERIAL AND METHODS

2.1 *Subjects and signal acquisition*

Total ten subjects have been recruited for the current study. All the subjects were volunteers and had no history of neural disorders. The signal recording protocol had been explained to all the subjects individually. Further, written consent had been signed by each subject before the experimenting. Also, they were permitted to withdraw at any time during the data collection. The method adopted for signal acquisition in the present research work is purely non-invasive. The experiment procedure adopted was as per the Helsinki declaration, 2013, and duly approved by the institutional research board.

EMG signal from six below-knee muscles (TiAn, Gast, Sole, TiPo, PeBr, and PeLo) has been recorded at a sampling frequency of 1000 Hz. EMG acquisition system has been developed around ADS 1298 and LabVIEW (Gupta et al. 2017). Ag–AgCl disposable electrodes have been used in a differential configuration, keeping the reference electrode on the knee. All the muscles and electrode placement positions have been identified by following SENIAM recommendations (SENIAM 2016).

The signal acquisition protocol had two phases; in the first phase, the EMG signal was recorded for non-weight-bearing ankle movements (DF/PF), whereas in the second phase, the signal was recorded for weight-bearing ankle movements (DFW/PFW). Figure 1 shows the ankle movements during the signal recording. The protocol followed for data recording was as follows.

Phase 1
- Subjects were instructed to sit straight on the table with hanging legs in a comfortable position. The subjects were free to take support from the back of his/her palm to keep himself/herself in a comfortable position
- The subject was trained for each ankle movement after explaining him all the ankle movements (DF/PF).
- After training appropriate resting time was provided.
- The sample recording for each movement was started when the ankle was in a neutral position and stopped after achieving the neutral position again while completing the complete RoM of a particular movement and holding the peak position for 3 sec.
- Twenty samples of each ankle movements were recorded one by one.
- If the subject demanded, appropriate resting time was provided in between sample recording.

Phase 2
- Subjects were asked to stand up straight on both legs comfortably.
- Subjects were trained for each ankle movement after explaining him/her the ankle movements, i.e., DF and PF, with bodyweight (DFW and PFW). DFW is standing on the heel while keeping the toes towards the tibia. PFW is standing on the toes while keeping the whole body straight.
- After training appropriate resting time was provided.
- The sample recording for each movement was started at a standing (neutral) position when heel and toe both were touching the ground.
- The subjects were asked to completing the ankle joint movement while holding the peak position for 3 sec.
- The sample recording was stopped when the subject ankle movement regain the neutral position.
- Twenty samples of each movement were recorded one after another.
- No resting time between the sample recordings was provided so that the acquired signal can be used for the muscle fatigue assessment.

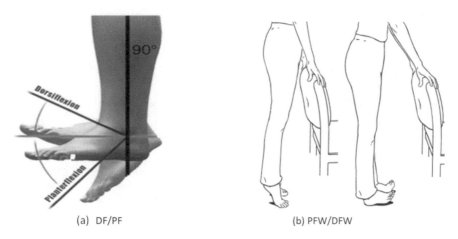

(a) DF/PF   (b) PFW/DFW

Figure 1.   Illustration of ankle movements used in presented study.

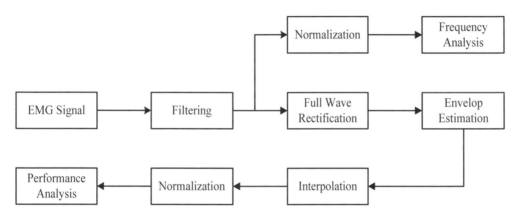

Figure 2.   Block diagram representation of signal processing for muscle selection.

2.2 *Signal processing*

Figure 2 shows the block diagram representation of steps followed for signal processing of the EMG signal. Each sample of EMG signal has been filtered through zero lag, 4th-order Butterworth band-pass filter with a frequency range of 10–450 Hz (Gupta et al. 2018b, 2019). Further, the filtered signal has been full wave rectified, and it envelopes has been estimated. For envelop detection, the rectified signal has been passed through a zero lag, 4th-order Butterworth low-pass filter having a cutoff frequency of 10 Hz (Dhindsa et al. 2016; Gupta et al 2020). The individual sample of EMG envelop has been interpolated over time base with 1000 points using cubic spline interpolation technique. Finally, the interpolated EMG envelop of each muscle has been normalized for individual activity using max normalization technique over all the subjects (Ivanenko et al. 2004; Hagio et al. 2015; Cappellini et al. 2006; Taborri et al. 2017).

2.3 *Data analysis*

The acquired EMG signal of both the phases of the experiment has been processed and analyzed separately for each subject. Dataset recorded during both the phases have been opted to access the consistency in the EMG signals for each activity and subject. Whereas for muscle fatigue analysis dataset of the only second phase of the experiment has been utilized. The activation duration and

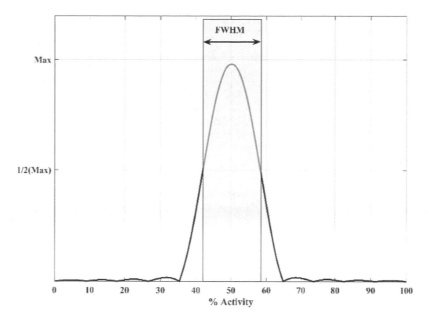

Figure 3.   FWHM illustration.

activation level of each muscle have been compared to access the performance of the muscle for individual activity and subject. The muscle activation duration has been quantified by the full width at half-maximum (FWHM) of the main peak of normalized EMG envelop (Cappellini et al. 2006). The activation level of muscle has been evaluated as the root mean square (RMS) of the normalized EMG envelop during FWHM.

Figure 3 shows the pictorial representation of FWHM. Both the parameters (FWHM and RMS) are directly proportional to the contribution made by the muscle during the activity (Mejia et al. 2018). Whereas, for each activity, the variation in these parameters, within the subject, signifies the reliability of the muscle. The fatigue has been quantified as median frequency (MF) in Hz. It is found to be a useful index for quantifying muscle fatigue during the dynamic condition. A degradation in MF signifies muscle fatigue, and the greater the reduction in MF higher muscle fatigue. The muscle having lower muscle fatigue has been preferred over the other muscles (Bonato et al. 2001).

2.4 Ankle-foot movements prediction

The EMG signal of the selected set of muscles has opted for ankle-foot activity prediction. Three are a total of four classes of activities, i.e., DF, PF, DFW, and PFW. For each activity, 20 samples of the EMG signal have been recorded and utilized for training and testing the activity prediction model. Each sample of EMG signal has been filtered through a zero lag, 4th-order Butterworth band-pass filter with a frequency range of 10–450 Hz followed by 50 Hz notch filter to remove powerline interference. After that, for each sample of filtered EMG signal Hudgin's time-domain (TD) feature set has been estimated. It is a set of four-time domain features, namely, means absolute value (MAV), window length (WL), zero crossings (ZC), and slope sign change (SSC) (Hudgins et al. 1993). Concatenating the TD feature set of all the selected muscles has constituted the feature vector for every sample of particular activity.

In the present research work, the performance of three different types of classifiers has been evaluated. The classiifers considered for present study are Support Vector Machine (SVM), Linear Discriminant Analysis (LDA), and Neural Network (NN) (Gupta et al. 2018). All the classifiers

Table 1. Average FWHM for all muscles and activities.

Ankle Movements	Muscles					
	TiAn	Gast	Sole	TiPo	PeBr	PeLo
PF	5.15 ± 2.50	47.45 ± 3.50	34.48 ± 4.45	15.15 ± 2.35	5.18 ± 1.45	8.48 ± 2.57
DF	57.24 ± 1.48	12.17 ± 2.48	17.24 ± 3.54	12.48 ± 1.45	7.41 ± 3.42	7.47 ± 2.35
PFW	34.48 ± 4.05	64.48 ± 1.45	52.47 ± 6.24	18.41 ± 2.47	14.37 ± 4.12	10.41 ± 3.48
DFW	78.75 ± 3.45	34.72 ± 4.58	34.65 ± 4.02	20.45 ± 3.04	15.89 ± 4.25	11.14 ± 4.05

were implemented using inbuilt functions available in MATLAB 2015a. 10-fold cross-validation was applied to validate the classifier performance. The performance of the prediction model has been quantified as % classification accuracy, as given by Equation (1) (Dhindsa et al. 2019):

$$\%Acc = \frac{correctly\ classified\ testing\ samples}{Total\ no.\ of\ applied\ testing\ sample} \times 100 \tag{1}$$

3 RESULTS AND DISCUSSION

Table 1 shows the average FWHM over all subjects for individual muscle and activities. It is presented as % of the activity duration, as illustrated in Figure 3. It signifies the duration for which the muscle has been activated during the activity. During PF activity, Gast and Sole muscles show significantly higher FWHM (47.45 ± 3.50% and 34.48 ± 4.45%, respectively) as compared to other muscles, whereas for PFW activity TiAn, Gast, and Sole muscles show higher activity duration (34.48 ± 4.05%, 64.48 ± 1.45%, and 52.47 ± 6.24%, respectively) as compared to other muscles. TiAn is an additional muscle that activated during PFW activity as compared to PF activity. It provides additional support during weight-bearing activity. It has been observed that the activation duration of Sole muscle for PF and PFW activity is inconsistent over the subjects as it carries the highest variation. In the case of DF and DFW activities, TiAn muscle shows significant activation duration (57.24 ± 1.48% and 78.75 ± 3.45%, respectively) as compared to other muscles. TiPo, PeBr, and PeLo muscles have shown insignificant participation in DF and DFW activities. However, their contribution has been found higher for weight-bearing activities (DFW and PFW) as compared to non-weight bearing activities (DF and PF). TiAn muscle has been found more reliable muscle for DF and DFW activities as it poses the lowest variation among all muscles. Similarly, for PF and PFW, Gast muscle has been found most reliable.

Table 2 shows the average RMS value during the FWHM for all muscles and activities. It signifies the activation level/contribution of the muscle during the activity. All muscles show higher activation level for weight-bearing activities (PFW and DFW) as compared to non-weight bearing activities (PF and DF). For PF activity, Gast and Sole muscles show the higher RMS value (0.60 ± 0.022 and 0.58 ± 0.031, respectively) as compares to other muscles while PF activity. Further, the Gast muscle has been found more reliable over Sole muscle as it shows lesser variation. Similar results have been found for PFW activates where Gast and Sole muscles outperformed over all other muscles with RMS value as 0.87 ± 0.044 and 0.75 ± 0.094, respectively. During DF and DFW activities, TiAn muscle contributed the most as compared to other muscles with an RMS value of 0.54 ± 0.02 and 0.84 ± 0.082, respectively. Also, its response has been found more reliable as compared to other muscles.

Figure 4 shows the average MF for each muscle. It has been estimated over the different number of activity repetitions to analyze the fatigue level of muscle. The reduction in MF over activity repetitions signifies the level of fatigue of the particular muscle. The results show a decline of 53%, 48%, and 33% in MF for TiPo, PeBr, and PeLo activities, respectively. TiAn and Gast

Table 2. Average RMS during the FWHM for all muscles and activities.

Ankle Movements	Muscles					
	TiAn	Gast	Sole	TiPo	PeBr	PeLo
PF	0.14 ± 0.019	0.60 ± 0.022	0.58 ± 0.031	0.24 ± 0.094	0.20 ± 0.047	0.31 ± 0.034
DF	0.54 ± 0.025	0.18 ± 0.035	0.12 ± 0.042	0.15 ± 0.042	0.14 ± 0.087	0.17 ± 0.054
PFW	0.25 ± 0.067	0.87 ± 0.044	0.75 ± 0.094	0.26 ± 0.052	0.52 ± 0.042	0.48 ± 0.068
DFW	0.84 ± 0.082	0.30 ± 0.048	0.35 ± 0.078	0.47 ± 0.087	0.27 ± 0.029	0.31 ± 0.078

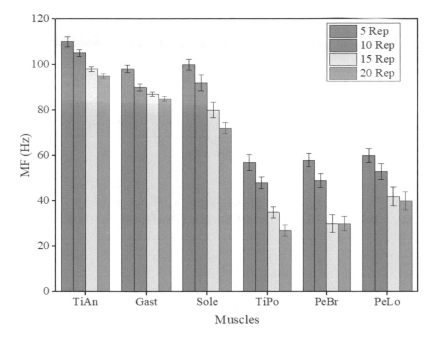

Figure 4. Average MF of each muscle for weight-bearing activities.

muscles show the least decrement in MF as 14% and 13%. TiAn and Gast muscles came out as least fatigued muscles for weight-bearing activities. The common muscles performing superior in all three compered parameters (activation level, activation duration, and muscle fatigue) are selected for further analysis. TiAn and Gast muscles have been found top-performing muscles over compared to parameters. Hence, TiAn and Gast muscles are selected for the prediction of ankle-foot movements.

Figure 5 shows the classification performance of all three classifiers for selected muscles (TiAn and Gast) and also for all six muscles. For each muscle, four TD features have been extracted. Hence, while opting only selected muscles, the feature vector has a total of 8 features, whereas while utilizing all 6 muscles, it has a total of 24 features. For selected muscle groups, the results show the best classification accuracy as 94.15 ± 1.42% for the LDA classifier. However, SVM and NN classifier also depicted satisfactory performance as 93.45 ± 3.72% and 93.27 ± 3.34%, respectively, without any statistically significant difference (ANOVA, p-value > 0.05). The performance of classifiers has been by utilizing all six lower limb muscles improved by 1.34%, 0.77%, and 0.61% for LDA, SVM, and NN classifiers, respectively (ANOVA, p-value > 0.05), whereas the number of features in the feature vector increased to 24 as compared to 8 features. The reduced set of features improves the computational performance and electronic circuitry burden of the system.

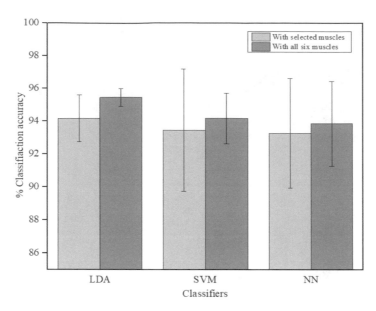

Figure 5. Average % classification accuracy of various classifies.

In terms of classifiers, all three classifiers possess comparatively the same performance. Hence, the LDA classifier is a suitable choice for real-time hardware implementation as it is a linear classifier, comparatively less complicated, and easily implementable at the embedded level.

4 CONCLUSION

A systematic analysis of the EMG signal of the lower limb below knee muscles for four different ankle-foot movements has been performed. It provides a methodology to select the most reliable and effective muscle over a group of muscles. A prediction model has been developed to predict the various ankle-foot movements utilizing selected group of muscles. The results have been validated for a group of ten subjects and six lower limb muscles. The results show that Gastrocnemius and Tibialis Anterior muscles are the best-suited muscles to predict ankle-foot weight-bearing and non-weight bearing activities. The best performance is depicted by the LDA classifier for a feature set of eight features. The proposed set of muscles and prediction model can be opted directly by the researchers to control ankle-foot prosthesis. In a future study, the experiment will be expended for dynamic ankle-foot movements during locomotion.

ACKNOWLEDGMENT

The authors would like to thank to the Ministry of Electronics and Information Technology (MeitY), Government of India for granting Visvesvaraya Fellowship. We would also thank Director, Thapar Institute of Engineering & Technology, Patiala for providing facilities for current research.

REFERENCES

Bonato, P., Roy, S. H., Knaflitz, M., & De Luca, C. J. 2001. Time-frequency parameters of the surface myoelectric signal for assessing muscle fatigue during cyclic dynamic contractions. IEEE Transactions on Biomedical Engineering, 48(7), 745–753.

Cappellini, G., Ivanenko, Y. P., Poppele, R. E., & Lacquaniti, F. 2006. Motor patterns in human walking and running. Journal of neurophysiology, 95(6), 3426–3437.

Dhindsa, I. S., Agarwal, R., & Ryait, H. S. 2017. Principal component analysis-based muscle identification for myoelectric-controlled exoskeleton knee. Journal of Applied Statistics, 44(10), 1707–1720.

Dhindsa, I. S., Agarwal, R., & Ryait, H. S. 2019. Performance evaluation of various classifiers for predicting knee angle from electromyography signals. Expert Systems, 36(3), e12381.

Gupta, R., & Agarwal, R. 2017. sEMG Interface Design for Locomotion Identification. vol, 11, 117–126.

Gupta, R., & Agarwal, R. 2018a. Continuous human locomotion identification for lower limb prosthesis control. CSI Transactions on ICT, 6(1), 17–31.

Gupta, R., & Agarwal, R. 2018b. Electromyographic signal-driven continuous locomotion mode identification module design for lower limb prosthesis control. Arabian Journal for Science and Engineering, 43(12), 7817–7835.

Gupta, R., & Agarwal, R. 2019. Single channel EMG-based continuous terrain identification with simple classifier for lower limb prosthesis. Biocybernetics and Biomedical Engineering, 39(3), 775–788.

Gupta, R., Dhindsa, I. S., & Agarwal, R. 2020. Continuous angular position estimation of human ankle during unconstrained locomotion. Biomedical Signal Processing and Control, 60, 101968.

Hagio, S., Fukuda, M., & Kouzaki, M. 2015. Identification of muscle synergies associated with gait transition in humans. Frontiers in human neuroscience, 9, 48.

Hudgins, B., Parker, P., & Scott, R. N. 1993. A new strategy for multifunction myoelectric control. IEEE Transactions on Biomedical Engineering, 40(1), 82–94.

Ivanenko, Y. P., Poppele, R. E., & Lacquaniti, F. 2004. Five basic muscle activation patterns account for muscle activity during human locomotion. The Journal of physiology, 556(1), 267–282.

Mejia Tobar, A., Hyoudou, R., Kita, K., Nakamura, T., Kambara, H., Ogata, Y., & Yoshimura, N. 2018. Decoding of ankle flexion and extension from cortical current sources estimated from non-invasive brain activity recording methods. Frontiers in neuroscience, 11, 733.

Oatis, C. A. 1988. Biomechanics of the foot and ankle under static conditions. Physical therapy, 68(12), 1815–1821.

Riegger, C. L. 1988. Anatomy of the ankle and foot. Physical therapy, 68(12), 1802–1814.

SENIAM, "Sensors location: Recommendations for sensor locations on individual muscles," 2016. Available: http://seniam.org/sensor_location.htm.

Taborri, J., Palermo, E., Masiello, D., & Rossi, S. 2017. Factorization of EMG via muscle synergies in walking task: Evaluation of intra-subject and inter-subject variability. IEEE International Instrumentation and Measurement Technology Conference (I2MTC) (pp. 1–6).

Smart Computing – Khan et al (Eds)
© 2021 Taylor & Francis Group, London, ISBN 978-0-367-76552-1

Metric dimension of join of a path with other families of graphs

B.S. Rawat
Department of Mathematics, Government Degree College, Pauri, India

P. Pradhan
Gurukula Kangri Vishwavidyalaya, Haridwar, India

ABSTRACT: In the present paper, we discuss the metric dimension of the joining of a path with a cycle. We generalized the results and developed a formula for metric dimension of joining a path and a star graph. Throughout the paper, finite and simple graphs have been considered.

Keywords: Resolving set, Basis, Metric Dimension

1   INTRODUCTION

The resolving set problem in graphs was studded from 1975 onward by Slater (1975) and Harary and Melter (1976). Consider,where w_i is the ith vertex of W, then $R_\theta(v/W) = \{d(v, w_1), ..., d(v, w_k)\}$, is metric representation of any vertex v of graph G. If $R_\theta(v/W) \neq R_\theta(u/W)$; $\forall u, v \in V(G)$ then W is called resolving set of G. Graph G can have more than one resolving set but the resolving set with the smallest number of elements is called the basis of graph G and the number of elements in basis is known as metric dimension β of graph G. Saenpholphat and Zhang (2003) observed that if W is a resolving set of a connected graph G and $W \subseteq W'$, then W' is also a resolving set of G. Khuller et al. (1996) used this idea robot navigation while Chartrand et al. (2000) found the relation among the order, diameter, and dimension of a graph G. Caceres et al. (2007) and Saputro et al. (2012) determined the metric dimension for Cartesian product and join of a star graph with K_1, respectively. Buczkowski et al. (2003) found $\beta(W_n)$ while Caceres et al. (2005) and Tomescu and Javaid (2007) obtained $\beta(f_n)$ and $\beta(J_{2n})$.

Motivated by Javaid (2007) and Saenpholphat (2003), we obtained some results related to metric dimension under the join operation of two graphs.

2   SOME EXAMPLES OF JOIN OF TWO GRAPHS

Table 1.   Some graphs which are obtained from join of two graphs.

G_1	G_2	$G_1 + G_2$
$\overline{K_m}$	$\overline{K_n}$	$K_{m,n}$
C_n	K_1	W_n
$\overline{K_n}$	K_1	$K_{1,n}$
$\overline{K_n}$	P_m	Fan Graph
$\overline{K_n}$	C_m	Cone Graph

DOI 10.1201/9781003167488-47

Khuller et al. (1996) derived the following results:

2.1 Path is only one graph whose metric dimension is 1.
2.2 Suppose $\{\alpha, \delta\} \subset V(G)$ is a basis for graph G, then
  (i) There is only one shortest path between α and δ.
  (ii) Degrees of vertices α and δ cannot have more than three.
  (iii) Other vertices lying on the shortest path between α and δ have degree at most five.

3 MAIN RESULT

Lemma 3.1. Let P_m be a path with $m \geq 9$ and G be any connected graph, then the basis of graph $P_m + G$ must contain $2r$ and $2r + 1$ vertices of P_m if $m = 5r - 1, 5r, 5r + 1$ and $5r + 2, 5r + 3$, respectively; $r = 2, 3, 4, \ldots$.

Proof: Let $u_i \in V(P_m)$, $v_j \in V(G)$ and $W = \{u_2, u_4, u_7, u_9, \ldots, u_{5r-3}, u_{5r-1}; v_1, v_2, v_3 \ldots v_k\}$; where $W = W_1 \cup W_2$ such that $|W_1| = 2r$, $|W_2| = k$. Since $d(u_i, v_j) = 1$; $\forall i, j$ therefore, first $2r$ coordinates of any v_j with respect to W are $(1, 1, 1, \ldots, 1)$ while first $2r$ co-ordinates of any u_i with respect to W will never be $(1, 1, 1, \ldots, 1)$. Therefore, $R_\theta(u_i/W) \neq R_\theta(v_j/W)$; $\forall i, j$. It implies that $R_\theta(u_i/W_1) \neq R_\theta(u_j/W_1) \Rightarrow R_\theta(u_i/W) \neq R_\theta(u_j/W)$; $\forall i, j$. Now the metric representations of $V(P_m) \backslash W_1$ with respect to W_1 in $P_m + G$ are as follows:

$$
\begin{aligned}
R_\theta(u_1/W_1) &= (1, 2, 2, .., 2) \\
R_\theta(u_3/W_1) &= (1, 1, 2, 2 \ldots, 2) \\
R_\theta(u_5/W_1) &= (2, 1, 2, \ldots, 2) \\
R_\theta(u_6/W_1) &= (2, 2, 1, 2 \ldots, 2) \\
R_\theta(u_8/W_1) &= (2, 2, 1, 1, 2 \ldots, 2)
\end{aligned}
$$

$$
R_\theta(u_{10}/W_1) = (2, 2, 2, 1, 2 \ldots, 2)
$$

.

.

$$
\begin{aligned}
R_\theta(u_{5r-2}/W_1) &= (2, 2, 2, \ldots, 2, 1, 1) \\
R_\theta(u_{5r}/W_1) &= (2, 2, 2, \ldots, 2, 2, 1) \\
R_\theta(u_{5r+1}/W_1) &= (2, 2, 2, \ldots, 2, 2, 2)
\end{aligned}
$$

Here, $R_\theta(u_i/W_1) \neq R_\theta(u_j/W_1)$; $\forall i, j$. Now, if possible, let $W' = W_1 - \{u_i\}$ be an ordered set which contains $2r - 1$ vertices of P_m. Then $\exists$ at least two vertices u_k and u_l in $V(P_m + G)$ such that $R_\theta(u_k/W') = (2, 2, 2, \ldots, 2) = R_\theta(u_l/W')$ or $R_\theta(u_k/W') = (1, 2, 2, \ldots, 2) = R_\theta(u_l/W')$. This implies that at least vertices of path are necessary for resolving all the vertices a path in $P_m + G$. Therefore, basis of graph $P_m + G$ must contain $2r$ vertices of P_m; if $m = 5r - 1$, $5r$, $5r + 1$, and $r = 2, 3, 4, \ldots$ Similarly using the same argument, we can show that basis of graph $P_m + G$ must contain $2r + 1$ vertices of P_m, if $m = 5r + 2$, $5r + 3$ and $r = 2, 3, 4, \ldots$

Lemma 3.2. Suppose $K_{1,n}$ be a star graph with $n \geq 2$ and G be any connected graph, then basis of graph $K_{1,n} + G$ must contain at least $n - 1$ vertices of $K_{1,n}$.

Proof: Suppose $\{v_1, v_2, v_3 \ldots, v_n, v_{n+1}\}$ be the set of vertices of $K_{1,n}$ and W be a basis for $K_{1,n} + G$. Suppose the basis of $K_{1,n} + G$ contains maximum $n - 2$ vertices of $K_{1,n}$; then $R_\theta(v_i/W) =$

$R_\theta(v_j/W)$; $\forall \ v_i, \ v_j \notin W$, which is a contradiction. So, any basis of $K_{1,n} + G$ must contain at least $n - 1$ vertices of $K_{1,n}$.

Lemma 3.3. Let P_m and $K_{1,n}$ be a path and a star graph, respectively, then $\beta(P_m + K_{1,n}) \geq 3$; for $m \geq 2, \ n \geq 1$

Proof: Let P_m and $K_{1,n}$ be a path and a star graph, respectively. Suppose W is a basis of $P_m + K_{1,n}$. Then, the following possible cases arise:

Case I: If $m = 2, \ n = 1$, then obviously $P_2 + K_{1,1} \cong K_4$ and therefore, $\beta(P_2 + K_{1,n}) = 3$.

Case II: $\beta(P_2 + K_{1,n}) \geq 2$ for $m = 2$ and $n \geq 2$. If suppose $\beta(P_2 + K_{1,n}) = 2$ then $W = \{u_i, v_j\}$; $u_i \in V(P_2)$ and $v_j \in V(K_{1,n})$ forms a basis of $P_2 + K_{1,n}$. Degree of each u_i in this case is at least four in $P_2 + K_{1,n}$, which is a contradiction as shown in result 2.2(ii). Therefore, W which contains only two vertices cannot be a basis for $P_2 + K_{1,n}$.

Case III: If $m > 2$ and $m > 2$, then similarly it is again a contradiction of result 2.2 (ii). Thus, we conclude that no two vertices of $P_m + K_{1,n}$ form a basis for $P_m + K_{1,n}$, i.e., $\beta(P_m + K_{1,n}) \geq 3$.

Lemma 3.4. Suppose P_m and C_n; $m \geq 2, \ n \geq 3$ be a path and a cycle, respectively, then $\beta(P_m + C_n) \geq 3$.

Proof: Let $V(P_m) = \{u_i | i = 1, \ 2, \ \ldots, \ m\}$ and $V(C_n) = \{v_j | j = 1, \ 2, \ldots, n\}$ be the sets of vertices of path and cycle, respectively. Suppose W is the basis of $P_m + C_n$, then clearly $|W| \geq 2$. Now, if we suppose $\beta(P_m + C_n) = 2$, then $W = \{u_i, v_j\}$ forms a basis of $P_m + C_n$ and degree of each u_i and v_j in this case is at least four in $P_m + C_n$, which is a contradiction as shown in result 2.2 (ii). Therefore, W containing only two vertices cannot be a basis for $P_m + C_n$, and hence $\beta(P_m + C_n) \geq 3$.

Theorem 3.5. Let P_m and $K_{1,n}$ be a path and a star graph, respectively, then

$$\beta(P_m + K_{1,n}) = \begin{cases} 2 \ ; & when \ m = 1, \ n = 1 \\ 3 \ ; & when \ m = 2, \ n = 1 \ or \ m = 3, 4, 5 \ and \ n = 1 \\ n + 1 \ ; & when \ m = 3, 4, 5 \ and \ n \geq 2 \\ n + 2 ; & when \ m = 6, 7, 8 \ and \ n \geq 2 \\ 2r + (n - 1) \ ; & when \ m = 5r - 1, \ 5r, \ 5r + 1 \ and \ r = 2, 3, 4, \ldots \\ 2r + n \ ; & when \ m = 5r + 2, \ 5r + 3 \ and \ r = 2, 3, 4, \ldots \end{cases}$$

Proof: Let $u_i \in V(P_m)$ and $v_j \in V(K_{1,n})$; such that degree of $v_j = 1$; $\forall \ 1 \leq j \leq n$ and degree of $v_{n+1} = n$. According to Lemma 3.2, the basis of $K_{1,n} + G$ must contain at least $n - 1$ vertices of $K_{1,n}$.

Case I: For $m = 1$ and $n = 1$, then $P_1 + K_{1,1} \cong K_3$ and therefore $\beta(P_m + K_{1,n}) = 2$.

Case II (a): For $m = 2$ and $n = 1$, then $P_2 + K_{1,1} \cong K_4$ and therefore $\beta(P_m + K_{1,n}) = 3$.

Case II (b): For $m = 3, 4, 5$ and $n = 1$, then $P_m + K_{1,1} \cong P_m + P_2$ and therefore $\beta(P_m + K_{1,n}) = 3$. Case III: For $m = 3, 4, 5$ and $n \geq 2$. Consider the set $W = \{v_1, v_2, v_3, \ldots, v_{n-1}, u_2, u_3\} \subset V(P_m + K_{1,n})$ with $|W| = n + 1$. Now the metric representations of $V(P_m + K_{1,n}) \backslash W$:

$$\begin{aligned} R_\theta(v_n/W) &= (2, 2, 2, \ldots, 1, 1) \\ R_\theta(v_{n+1}/W) &= (1, 1, 1, \ldots, 1, 1) \\ R_\theta(u_1/W) &= (1, 1, 1, .., 1, 2) \\ R_\theta(u_4/W) &= (1, 1, 1, \ldots, 2, 1) \\ R_\theta(u_5/W) &= (1, 1, 1, \ldots, 2, 2) \end{aligned}$$

Here, different vertices have different representations, therefore $\beta(P_m + K_{1,n}) \leq n + 1$. Now if possible, let $W_1 = \{v_1, v_2, v_3, \ldots v_{n-1}, u_i\}$; $|W_1| = n$, be a resolving set in this case, then $\exists$ a vertex $u_k \in V(P_m)$ different from $u_i \in W_1$ such that $R_\theta(v_{n+1}/W_1) = (1, 1, 1, \ldots, 1) = R_\theta(u_k/W_1)$, which is a contradiction that W_1 be a resolving set. So, any ordered set W_1 having cardinality less than $n+1$ cannot be a resolving set for $P_m + K_{1,n}$ in this case, i.e., $\beta(P_m + K_{1,n}) \geq n+1$. Therefore, $\beta(P_m + K_{1,n}) = n+1$.

Case IV: Consider the set $W = \{v_1, v_2, v_3, \ldots, v_{n-1}, u_2, u_4, u_6\} \subset V(P_m + K_{1,n})$ with $|W| = n+2$, for $m = 6, 7, 8$ and $n \geq 2$. Now the metric representations of $V(P_m + K_{1,n}) \backslash W$:

$$
\begin{aligned}
R_\theta(v_n/W) &= (2,2,2,\ldots,1,1,1) \\
R_\theta(v_{n+1}/W) &= (1,1,1,\ldots,1,1,1) \\
R_\theta(u_1/W) &= (1,1,1,..,1,2,2) \\
R_\theta(u_3/W) &= (1,1,1,\ldots,1,1,2) \\
R_\theta(u_5/W) &= (1,1,1,\ldots,2,1,1) \\
R_\theta(u_7/W) &= (1,1,1,\ldots,2,2,1) \\
R_\theta(u_8/W) &= (1,1,1,\ldots,2,2,2)
\end{aligned}
$$

We find that no two vertices have the same representations, therefore $\beta(P_m + K_{1,n}) \leq n+2$. Now we will show that $\beta(P_m + K_{1,n}) \geq n+2$. If possible, let $W' = \{v_1, v_2, v_3, \ldots v_{n-1}, u_i, u_j\}$; $|W'| - n+1$ be a resolving set in this case, then $\exists u_k$ and u_l in $V(P_m + K_{1,n})$ such that

$$
\begin{aligned}
R_\theta(u_k/W') &= (1,1,\ldots,1,2,2) = R_\theta(u_l/W') \\
&\text{or} \\
R_\theta(u_k/W') &= (1,1,\ldots,1,2,1) = R_\theta(u_l/W') \\
&\text{or} \\
R_\theta(u_k/W') &= (1,1,\ldots,1,2,2) = R_\theta(u_l/W') \\
&\text{or} \\
R_\theta(u_k/W') &= (1,1,\ldots,1,1,2) = R_\theta(u_l/W') \\
&\text{or} \\
R_\theta(u_k/W') &= (1,1,\ldots,1,1,) = R_\theta(v_{n+1}/W').
\end{aligned}
$$

These conditions are contradictions, so $\beta(P_m + K_{1,n}) \geq n+2$. Therefore, $\beta(P_m + K_{1,n}) = n+2$.

Case V: For $m = 5r-1$, $5r$, $5r+1$ and $r = 2, 3, 4, \ldots$; using Lemma 3.2, we construct an ordered set W which contains $n-1$ vertices of $K_{1,n}$ and $2r$ vertices of path P_m as given below: $W = \{u_2, u_4, u_7, u_9, \ldots, u_{5r-3}, u_{5r-1}; v_1, v_2, v_3, \ldots v_{n-1}\}$ such that $|W| = 2r + (n-1)$ Now the metric representations of $V(P_m + K_{1,n}) \backslash W$:

$$
\begin{aligned}
R_\theta(v_n/W) &= (1,1,1,\ldots,1;2,2,2,\ldots,2) \\
R_\theta(v_{n+1}/W) &= (1,1,1,\ldots,1;1,1,1,\ldots,1) \\
R_\theta(u_1/W) &= (1,2,2,..,2;1,1,1,\ldots,1) \\
R_\theta(u_3/W) &= (1,1,2,2\ldots,2;1,1,\ldots,1) \\
R_\theta(u_5/W) &= (2,1,2,\ldots,2;1,1,\ldots,1) \\
R_\theta(u_6/W) &= (2,2,1,2\ldots,2;1,1,\ldots,1) \\
R_\theta(u_8/W) &= (2,2,1,1,2\ldots,2;1,1,\ldots,1) \\
\\
R_\theta(u_{10}/W) &= (2,2,2,1,2\ldots,2;1,1,\ldots,1) \\
\cdot \\
\cdot \\
R_\theta(u_{5r-2}/W) &= (2,2,2,\ldots,2,1,1;1,1\ldots,1) \\
R_\theta(u_{5r}/W) &= (2,2,2,\ldots,2,2,1;1,1,\ldots,1) \\
R_\theta(u_{5r+1}/W) &= (2,2,2,\ldots,2,2,2;1,1,\ldots,1)
\end{aligned}
$$

415

Here, $R_\theta(u_i/W) \neq R_\theta(u_j/W)$. Therefore, $\beta(P_m + K_{1,n}) \leq 2r + (n-1)$. Now we will show that $\beta(P_m + K_{1,n}) \geq 2r + (n-1)$. Suppose $W_1 = W - \{u_i\}$ be an ordered set which contains $n-1$ vertices of $K_{1,n}$ and $2r-1$ vertices of P_m; where $|W_1| = 2r + (n-2)$ for the graph $P_m + K_{1,n}$; then $\exists u_k$ and u_l in $V(P_m + K_{1,n})$ such that:

$$R_\theta(u_k/W_1) = (1,1,\ldots,1,2,2) = R_\theta(u_l/W_1)$$
$$\text{or}$$
$$R_\theta(u_k/W_1) = (1,1,\ldots,1,2,1) = R_\theta(u_l/W_1)$$
$$\text{or}$$
$$R_\theta(u_k/W_1) = (1,1,\ldots,1,2,2) = R_\theta(u_l/W_1)$$
$$\text{or}$$
$$R_\theta(u_k/W_1) = (1,1,\ldots,1,1,2) = R_\theta(u_l/W_1)$$
$$\text{or}$$
$$R_\theta(u_k/W_1) = (1,1,\ldots,1,1,) = R_\theta(v_{n+1}/W_1).$$

These are contradictions. So, $\beta(P_m + K_{1,n}) \geq 2r + (n-1)$. Therefore, $\beta(P_m + K_{1,n}) = 2r + (n-1)$.

Case VI: Similarly, for $m = 5r + 2$, $5r + 3$ *and* $r = 2,3,4,\ldots$; we can show that out of $5r + 2$ or $5r + 3$ vertices of path P_m; $2r + 1$ vertices must be in any basis W for $P_m + K_{1,n}$ and by the result of Lemma 3.2; $n - 1$ vertices of $K_{1,n}$ must also be in W. Therefore, $\beta(P_m + K_{1,n}) = (2r + 1) + (n - 1)$ *i.e.* $2r + n$.

4 CONCLUSION

In this paper, we have discussed the graphs obtained from the joining of two graphs. Some fruitful results have been derived in the form of lemmas and on the basis of these results we obtained the metric dimension for $P_m + K_{1,n}$.

REFERENCES

Buczkowski, P.S., Chartrand, G. Poisson, C. & Zhang, P. 2003. K-dimensional graphs and their bases, *Periodica Math. Hung., 46(1) (2003), 9–15.*

Caceres, J., Hernando, C., Mora, M, Pelayo, I.M., Puertas, M.L., Seara, C. & Wood, D.R. 2005. On the metric dimension of some families of graphs, *Electronic Notes in Disc. Math., 22 (2005), 129–133.*

Caceres, J., Hernando, C. Mora, M. Pelayo, I.M., Puertas, M.L. Seara, C. & Wood, D.R. 2007.On the metric dimension of cartesian products of graphs, *Siam J. Discrete Math. , 21 (2007), 423–441.*

Chartrand,G.,Eroh,L.,Johnson,M.A.& O.R. Oellermann.2000. Resolvability in graphs and the metric dimension of a graph, *Discrete Applied Math.,105 (2000), 99–113.*

Harary,F., Melter,R.A.1976.On the metric dimension of a graph, *ArsCombinatoria, 2 (1976), 191–195.*

Imran,M.,Bokhary,S.A.H.,Ahmad,A.&Fenovcikova,A.S.2013.On class of regular graphs with constant metric, *ActaMathematicaScientia 2013,33B (1):187–206.*

Javaid, I, Rahim, M.T. & K. Ali.2008.Families of regular graphs with constant metric dimension.*Util. Math. 75 (2008) 21–33.*

Khuller, S. Raghavachari, B. &Rosenfeld, A.1996. Landmarks in graphs, *Discrete Applied Math., 70(3):217–229, 1996.*

Saenpholphat, V.& Zhang,P.2003.Connected rersolvability of graphs, *Czechoslovak Math. J. 53(128) (2003) 827–840.*

Saputro, S.W. Suprijanto, D., Baskoro,E.T. &Salman , A.N.M.2012.The Metric Dimension of a Graph Composition Products with Star, *J. Indones. Math. Soc. Vol. 18, No. 2 (2012), pp.85–92.*

Shahida, A.T & Sunitha, M.S.2014.On the Metric Dimension of Joins of Two Graphs, *International Journal of Scientific & Engineering Research, 5(9) September-2014, 33–38.*

Slater, P.J., 1975. Leaves of trees, *Proc. 6th southeastern conf. on combinatorics, Graph theory and computing, Congr. Number, 14 (1975), 549–559.*

Tomescu, I., Javaid, I. 2007.On the metric dimension of the Jahangir graph, *Bull. Math. Soc. Sci. Math. Roumanie, 50(98), 4(2007), 371-376.*

Smart Computing – Khan et al (Eds)
© 2021 Taylor & Francis Group, London, ISBN 978-0-367-76552-1

Metric dimension of the corona product of graphs

B.S. Rawat
Department of Mathematics, Government Degree College, Pauri, India

P. Pradhan
Gurukula Kangri Vishwavidyalaya, Haridwar, India

ABSTRACT: Operations on graphs are an important tool, not only for developing new graphs from original ones but also as a convenient way to consider a large graph as a combination of small ones and to derive its different properties, such as metric dimension, from those of smaller ones. This paper is focused on the metric dimensions of the corona product of a wheel and a cycle with a complete graph of one vertex.

Keywords: Corona Product of Graphs, Resolving set, Basis.

1 INTRODUCTION

The resolving set problem in graphs has been studied since 1975 (Slater 1975; Harary & Melter 1976). Consider $W = \{w_1, \ldots, w_k\} \subset V(G)$; where w_i is the ith vertex of W, then $R_\theta(v/W) = \{d(v, w_1), \ldots, d(v, w_k)\}$, is metric representation of any vertex v of graph G. If $R_\theta(v/W) \neq R_\theta(u/W); \forall u, v \in V(G)$ then W is called resolving set of G. Graph G can have more than one resolving set but the resolving set with the smallest number of elements is called the basis of graph G and the number of elements in the basis is known as metric dimension β of graph G. Saenphol-phat & Zhang (2002) observed that if W is a resolving set of a connected graph G and $W \subseteq W'$, then W' is also a resolving set of G. Khuller et al. (1996) used this idea for robot navigation while Chartrand et al. (2000) found the relation among the order, diameter, and dimension of a graph G. Caceres et al. (2007) and Saputro et al. (2012) determined the metric dimension for the Cartesian product and join of a star graph with K_1, respectively. Buczkowski et al. (2003) found $\beta(W_n)$ while Caceres et al. (2005) and Tomescu & Javaid (2007) obtained $\beta(f_n)$ and $\beta(J_{2n})$.

Motivated by Iswadi et al. (2008), Imran et al. (2013), and Shahida (2014), we obtained some results under the corona product of two graphs.

2 SOME USEFUL RESULTS

Khuller et al. (1996) derived the following results.

2.1 - Path is a graph whose metric dimension is one.
2.2 - Suppose $\{\alpha, \delta\} \subset V(G)$ is a basis for graph G, then
  (i) There is only shortest path between α and δ.
  (ii) Degrees of vertices α and δ can't have more than three.
  (iii) Other vertices lying on shortest path between α and δ have degree at most five.

DOI 10.1201/9781003167488-48

3 MAIN RESULT

Theorem 3.1. Suppose C_n be a cycle, then

$$\beta(C_n \odot K_1) = \begin{cases} 2; & \text{if } n \text{ is odd or } n = 4 \\ 3; & \text{if } n \text{ is even and } n \neq 4 \end{cases}$$

Proof: Suppose $V(C_n) = \{v_1, v_2, \ldots, v_n\}$ be the vertex set of cycle and u_i are pendant vertices corresponding to v_i; $1 \leq i \leq n$, then the following cases arise.

Case 1 (a): If n is odd. Consider the set $W = \{v_1, v_{\frac{n+1}{2}}\} \subset V(C_n \odot K_1)$; then the metric representations of $V(C_n \odot K_1) \backslash W$:

$$R_\theta (v_2/W) = \left(1, \tfrac{n-1}{2}\right); \qquad R_\theta (v_3/W) = \left(2, \tfrac{n-3}{2}\right);$$
$$R_\theta (v_4/W) = \left(3, \tfrac{n-5}{2}\right); \ldots R_\theta \left(v_{\frac{n-1}{2}}/W\right) = \left(\tfrac{n-1}{2}, 1\right);$$
$$R_\theta \left(v_{\frac{n+3}{2}}/W\right) = \left(\tfrac{n-3}{2}, 1\right); \ldots R_\theta (v_{n-2}/W) = \left(3, \tfrac{n-7}{2}\right);$$
$$R_\theta (v_{n-1}/W) = \left(2, \tfrac{n-5}{2}\right); \qquad R_\theta (v_n/W) = \left(1, \tfrac{n-3}{2}\right);$$
$$R_\theta (u_1/W) = \left(1, \tfrac{n+1}{2}\right); \qquad R_\theta (u_2/W) = \left(2, \tfrac{n+1}{2}\right);$$
$$R_\theta (u_3/W) = \left(3, \tfrac{n-1}{2}\right); \qquad R_\theta (u_4/W) = \left(4, \tfrac{n-3}{2}\right); \ldots$$

$$R_\theta \left(u_{\frac{n+1}{2}}/W\right) = \left(\tfrac{n+1}{2}, 2\right); \qquad R_\theta \left(u_{\frac{n+3}{2}}/W\right) = \left(\tfrac{n-1}{2}, 2\right); \ldots$$
$$R_\theta (u_{n-2}/W) = \left(4, \tfrac{n-5}{2}\right); \qquad R_\theta (u_{n-1}/W) = \left(3, \tfrac{n-3}{2}\right);$$
$$R_\theta (u_n/W) = \left(2, \tfrac{n-1}{2}\right);$$

Here, no two vertices have the same representations, therefore $\beta (C_n \odot K_1) \leq 2$. By using the result of Khuller et al. (1996), we obtain that $\beta (C_n \odot K_1) \neq 1$, that is $\beta (C_n \odot K_1) \geq 2$. Hence, $\beta (C_n \odot K_1) = 2$.

Case 1 (b): If $n = 4$. Consider the set $W = \{u_1, u_2\} \subset V(C_n \odot K_1)$; then the metric representations of $V(C_n \odot K_1) \backslash W$:

$$R_\theta (v_1/W) = (1, 2); \qquad R_\theta (v_2/W) = (2, 1);$$
$$R_\theta (v_3/W) = (3, 2); \qquad R_\theta (v_4/W) = (2, 3);$$
$$R_\theta (u_3/W) = (4, 3); \qquad R_\theta (u_4/W) = (3, 4)$$

Here, we find that different vertices have different metric representations, therefore $\beta (C_n \odot K_1) \leq 2$. Again by the same argument, $\beta (C_n \odot K_1) \geq 2$. Hence, $\beta (C_n \odot K_1) = 2$.

Case 2: If n is even and $n \neq 4$. Consider the set $W = \{v_1, u_{\frac{n}{2}}, v_{\frac{n}{2}+1}\} \subset V(C_n \odot K_1)$; then the metric representations of $V(C_n \odot K_1) \backslash W$:

$$R_\theta (v_2/W) = \left(1, \tfrac{n}{2} - 1, \tfrac{n}{2} - 1\right);$$
$$R_\theta (v_3/W) = \left(2, \tfrac{n}{2} - 2, \tfrac{n}{2} - 2\right);$$
$$R_\theta (v_4/W) = \left(3, \tfrac{n}{2} - 3, \tfrac{n}{2} - 3\right);$$
$$R_\theta \left(v_{\frac{n}{2}}/W\right) = \left(\tfrac{n}{2} - 1, 1, 1\right);$$
$$R_\theta \left(v_{\frac{n}{2}+2}/W\right) = \left(\tfrac{n}{2} - 1, 3, 1\right);$$
$$R_\theta \left(v_{\frac{n}{2}+3}/W\right) = \left(\tfrac{n}{2} - 2, 4, 2\right);$$
$$R_\theta (v_n/W) = \left(1, \tfrac{n}{2} + 1, \tfrac{n}{2} - 1\right);$$
$$R_\theta (u_1/W) = \left(1, \tfrac{n}{2} + 1, \tfrac{n}{2} + 1\right);$$
$$R_\theta (u_2/W) = \left(2, \tfrac{n}{2}, \tfrac{n}{2}\right);$$
$$R_\theta (u_3/W) = \left(3, \tfrac{n}{2} - 1, \tfrac{n}{2} - 1\right);$$
$$R_\theta \left(v_{\frac{n}{2}-1}/W\right) = \left(\tfrac{n}{2} - 1, 3, 3\right);$$
$$R_\theta \left(u_{\frac{n}{2}+1}/W\right) = \left(\tfrac{n}{2} + 1, 3, 1\right);$$

418

$$R_\theta\left(u_{\frac{n}{2}+2}/W\right) = \left(\tfrac{n}{2}, 4, 2\right);$$
$$R_\theta\left(u_{\frac{n}{2}+3}/W\right) = \left(\tfrac{n}{2} - 1, 5, 3\right);$$
$$R_\theta\left(u_n/W\right) = \left(2, \tfrac{n}{2} + 2, \tfrac{n}{2}\right);$$

Here, no two vertices have the same representation, therefore $\beta(C_n\Theta K_1) \leq 3$. Now we will show that $\beta(C_n\Theta K_1) \geq 3$ by using that $C_n\Theta K_1$ does not have resolving set with two elements. Suppose if possible W is a resolving set of $C_n\Theta K_1$ with two elements then, there are the following three possibilities.

(a) Both vertices belong to $\{u_i | 1 \leq i \leq n\}$; then, suppose one vertex is u_1 and other vertex is u_j; $2 \leq j \leq n$, i.e., $W = \{u_1, u_j\}$. Then we observe that $3 \leq d(u_1, u_j) \leq \tfrac{n}{2} + 2$. If $d(u_1, u_j) = 3$; then $\exists$ u_x and v_y of $C_n\Theta K_1$ such that $R_\theta(u_x/W) = (4, 3) = R_\theta(v_y/\tilde{W})$; a contradiction. If $d(u_1, u_j) = 4$; then $R_\theta(u_x/W) = (5, 3) = R_\theta(v_y/W)$ or $R_\theta(u_x/W) = (3, 3) = R_\theta(v_y/W)$; which are again contradictions. Similarly, other cases can be discussed and if $d(u_1, u_j) = \tfrac{n}{2} + 2$; then $R_\theta(v_{\frac{n}{2}}/W) = (\tfrac{n}{2}, 2) = R_\theta(v_{\frac{n}{2}+2}/W)$; a contradiction.
(b) Both vertices belong to $\{v_i | 1 \leq i \leq n\}$; then consider one vertex as v_1 and other vertex is v_j; $2 \leq j \leq n$ that is $W = \{v_1, v_j\}$. Then we observe that $1 \leq d(v_1, v_j) \leq \tfrac{n}{2}$. If $d(v_1, v_j) = 1$; then there exist two vertices u_x and v_y of $C_n\Theta K_1$ such that. $R_\theta(u_x/W) = (2, 1) = R_\theta(v_y/W)$; a contradiction. If $d(v_1, v_j) = 2$;
then $R_\theta(u_x/W) = (1, 3) = R_\theta(v_y/W)$; a contradiction. Similarly, other cases can be discussed and if $d(v_1, v_j) = \tfrac{n}{2}$; then $R_\theta(v_2/W) = (1, \tfrac{n}{2} - 1) = R_\theta(v_n/W)$; again a contradiction.
(c) One vertex of W belong to $\{u_i | 1 \leq i \leq n\}$ and other belong to $\{v_j | 1 \leq j \leq n\}$ that is $W = \{u_i, v_j\}$. Then we observe that $1 \leq d(u_i, v_j) \leq \tfrac{n}{2} + 1$. If $d(u_i, v_j) = 1$; then there exist two vertices v_x and v_y of $C_n\Theta K_1$ such that $R_\theta(v_x/W) = (2, 1) = R_\theta(v_y/W)$; a contradiction. If $d(u_i, v_j) = 2$; then $R_\theta(u_x/W) = (3, 1) = R_\theta(v_y/W)$; a contradiction. Similarly, other cases can be discussed and if $d(u_i, v_j) = \tfrac{n}{2} + 1$; then $R_\theta(v_2/W) = (2, \tfrac{n}{2} - 1) = R_\theta(v_n/W)$; a contradiction.

We obtain all the possibilities contradict, therefore $\beta(C_n\Theta K_1) \geq 3$. Hence, $\beta(C_n\Theta K_1) = 3$.

Theorem 3.2: Let W_n be a wheel; then

$$\beta\left(W_n\Theta K_1\right) = \begin{cases} 2; & n = 4, 5 \\ 3; & n = 3, 6 \\ \left\lceil \frac{n - f(n)}{2} \right\rceil; & n \geq 7 \end{cases};$$

$$\text{where } f(n) = \begin{cases} \left\lceil \frac{n-1}{4} \right\rceil; & n = 7, 8, 9, 10 \\ \left\lfloor \frac{n}{4} \right\rfloor; & n = 5k + 1 \\ \left\lceil \frac{n}{4} \right\rceil; & n = 5k + 2 \\ \left\lfloor \frac{n-1}{4} \right\rfloor; & n = 5k + 3 \\ \left\lfloor \frac{n-2}{4} \right\rfloor; & n = 5k + 4 \\ \left\lfloor \frac{n-3}{4} \right\rfloor; & n = 5k + 5 \end{cases}; \quad k = 2, 3, 4, \ldots$$

Proof: Suppose $V(W_n) = \{v, v_1, v_2, v_3, \ldots, v_n\}$ the set of vertices of wheel W_n and u, u_i are pendant vertices corresponding to vertices v and v_i; $1 \leq i \leq n$ respectively; then the following cases arise

Case 1: For $n = 4, 5$ Consider the set $W = \{u_1, u_2\} \subset V(W_n\Theta K_1)$; then the representations of $V(W_n\Theta K_1) \backslash W$:

$$R_\theta(v/W) = (2, 2); \qquad R_\theta(v_1/W) = (1, 2);$$
$$R_\theta(v_2/W) = (2, 1); \ldots; R_\theta(v_n/W) = (2, 3)$$
$$R_\theta(u/W) = (3, 3); \qquad R_\theta(u_3/W) = (4, 3); \ldots;$$
$$R_\theta(u_n/W) = (3, 3)$$

Here, $R_\theta(u_i/W) \neq R_\theta(u_j/W)$; $\forall i, j$; then $\beta(W_n\Theta K_1) \leq 2$. Since $\beta(W_n\Theta K_1) \geq 2$, therefore $\beta(W_n\Theta K_1) = 2$.

419

Case 2(i): For $n = 3$. Consider the set $W = \{v, v_1, v_2\} \subset V(W_n \Theta K_1)$; then the representations of $V(W_n \Theta K_1) \backslash W$:

$$R_\theta(v_3/W) = (1,1,1); \qquad R_\theta(u/W) = (1,2,2); \qquad R_\theta(u_1/W) = (2,1,2);$$
$$R_\theta(u_2/W) = (2,2,1); \qquad R_\theta(u_3/W) = (2,2,2)$$

Here, $R_\theta(u_i/W) \neq R_\theta(u_j/W); \forall i,j$. Hence, W is a resolving set with three elements. Now we show that $W_n \Theta K_1$ does not have resolving set with two elements. Suppose if possible W is a resolving set of $W_n \Theta K_1$ with two elements then, there are the following possibilities.

(a) One vertex of W is v and other vertex belong to $\{v_i | 1 \leq i \leq 3\}$, i.e., $W = \{v, v_i\}$; then $R_\theta(v_{(i+1) \bmod 3 + 1}/W) = (1,1) = R_\theta(v_{i(\bmod 3)+1}/W)$; a contradiction.
(b) One vertex of W is v and other vertex belong to $\{u_i | 1 \leq i \leq 3\}$, i.e., $W = \{v, u_i\}$; then $R_\theta(v_{(i+1) \bmod 3 + 1}/W) = (1,2) = R_\theta(v_{i(\bmod 3)+1}/W)$; a contradiction.
(c) Both vertices belong to $\{v_i | 1 \leq i \leq 3\}$, i.e., $W = \{v_i, v_j\}$; then $R_\theta(v_k/W) = (1,1) = R_\theta(v/W)$; a contradiction.
(d) Both vertices belong to $\{u_i | 1 \leq i \leq 3\}$, i.e., $W = \{u_i, u_j\}$; then $R_\theta(v_k/W) = (2,2) = R_\theta(v/W)$; a contradiction.
(e) One vertex of W belong to $\{v_i | 1 \leq i \leq 3\}$ and other vertex belong to $\{u_j | 1 \leq j \leq 3\}$, i.e., $W = \{v_i, u_j\}$; then $R_\theta(v_k/W) = (1,2) = R_\theta(v_l/W)$; a contradiction.
(f) One vertex of W is u and the other vertex belongs to $\{v_i | 1 \leq i \leq 3\}$, that is $W = \{u, v_i\}$; then $R_\theta(u_j/W) = (3,2) = R_\theta(u_k/W)$; a contradiction.
(g) One vertex of W is u and other vertex belong to $\{u_i | 1 \leq i \leq 3\}$ that is $W = \{u, u_i\}$; then $R_\theta(v_j/W) = (2,2) = R_\theta(v_k/W)$; a contradiction.
(h) One vertex of W is u and other vertex is v, i.e., $W = \{u, v\}$; then $R_\theta(v_j/W) = (2,1) = R_\theta(v_k/W)$, $\forall j \neq k$; a contradiction.

Case 2(ii): For $n = 6$. We consider the set $W = \{v_1, v_3, v_5\} \subset V(W_n \Theta K_1)$; then the metric representations of $V(W_n \Theta K_1) \backslash W$:

$$R_\theta(v_2/W) = (1,1,2); \quad R_\theta(v_4/W) = (2,1,1); \quad R_\theta(v_6/W) = (1,2,1); \quad R_\theta(v/W) = (1,1,1);$$
$$R_\theta(u/W) = (2,2,2); \quad R_\theta(u_1/W) = (1,3,3); \quad R_\theta(u_2/W) = (2,2,3); \quad R_\theta(u_3/W) = (3,1,3);$$
$$R_\theta(u_4/W) = (3,2,2); \quad R_\theta(u_5/W) = (3,3,1); \quad R_\theta(u_6/W) = (2,3,2)$$

Here all these representation are different. Therefore W is a resolving set with three elements. Now we show that $W_n \Theta K_1$ does not have resolving set with two elements. Suppose if possible W is a resolving set of $W_n \Theta K_1$ with two elements then, there are the following possibilities

(a) One vertex of W is v and the other vertex belongs to $\{v_i | 1 \leq i \leq 6\}$, i.e., $W = \{v, v_i\}$. If $2 \leq i \leq 5$, then $R_\theta(v_{i-1}/W) = (1,1) = R_\theta(v_{i+1}/W)$. If $i = 1, 6$ then $R_\theta(v_2/W) = (1,1) = R_\theta(v_6/W)$ and $R_\theta(v_1/W) = (1,1) = R_\theta(v_5/W)$, respectively, which are contradictions.
(b) One vertex of W is v and the other vertex belongs to $\{u_i | 1 \leq i \leq 6\}$, i.e., $W = \{v, u_i\}$. If $2 \leq i \leq 5$, then
$$R_\theta(u_{i-1}/W) = (2,3) = R_\theta(u_{i+1}/W).$$ If $i = 1, 6$ then $R_\theta(u_2/W) = (2,3) = R_\theta(u_6/W)$ and $R_\theta(u_1/W) = (2,3) = R_\theta(u_5/W)$, respectively, which are contradictions.
(c) Both vertices belong to $\{v_i | 1 \leq i \leq 6\}$; then suppose one vertex is v_1 and other vertex is v_j, i.e., $W = \{v_1, v_j\}$. If $j = 2, 6$; then $R_\theta(v_4/W) = (2,2) = R_\theta(u/W)$; a contradiction. If $j = 3$; then $R_\theta(v/W) = (1,1) = R_\theta(v_2/W)$; a contradiction. If $j = 4$; then $R_\theta(v_2/W) = (1,2) = R_\theta(v_6/W)$; a contradiction. . If $j = 5$; then $R_\theta(v/W) = (1,1) = R_\theta(v_6/W)$; a contradiction.
(d) Both vertices belong to $\{u_i | 1 \leq i \leq 6\}$; then suppose that one vertex is u_1 and other vertex is u_j, i.e., $W = \{u_1, u_j\}$. If $j = 2, 6$; then $R_\vartheta(v_4/W) = (3,3) = R_\theta(u/W)$; a contradiction. If $j = 3$; then $R_\theta(v/W) = (2,2) = R_\theta(v_2/W)$; a contradiction. If $j = 4$; then $R_\theta(v_2/W) = (2,3) = R_\theta(v_6/W)$; a contradiction. . If $j = 5$; then $R_\theta(v/W) = (2,2) = R_\theta(v_6/W)$; a contradiction.

(e) One vertex of W belongs to $\{v_i | 1 \leq i \leq 6\}$ and other vertex belong to $\{u_j | 1 \leq j \leq 6\}$, i.e., $W = \{v_i, u_j\}$. If $d(v_i, u_j) = 1$; then $R_\theta(v/W) = (1, 2) = R_\theta(v_k/W)$; where v_k is adjacent to v_i, a contradiction. If $d(v_i, u_j) = 2$; then there exist a vertex v_k such that $R_\theta(v_k/W) = (2, 3) = R_\theta(u/W)$; a contradiction. If $d(v_i, u_j) = 3$; then again there exist a vertex v_k such that $R_\theta(v_k/W) = (2, 3) = R_\theta(u/W)$; a contradiction.

(f) One vertex of W is u and other vertex is v, i.e., $W = \{u, v\}$; then $R_\theta(v_j/W) = (2, 1) = R_\theta(v_k/W), \forall j \neq k$; a contradiction.

(g) One vertex of W is u and other vertex belong to $\{v_i | 1 \leq i \leq 3\}$, i.e., $W = \{u, v_i\}$; then $R_\theta(v_j/W) = (2, 1) = R_\theta(v_k/W)$; where v_j and v_k are adjacent vertices of v_i, a contradiction.

(h) One vertex of W is u and other vertex belong to $\{u_i | 1 \leq i \leq 3\}$, i.e., $W = \{u, u_i\}$; then $R_\theta(v_j/W) = (2, 2) = R_\theta(v_k/W)$; where v_j and v_k are adjacent vertices of v_i, a contradiction.

Case 3: For $n \geq 7$. Let $\beta(W_n \Theta K_1)$ is odd; we consider $W = \{v_1, v_3, v_5\}$ for $n = 7, 8$; $W = \{v_1, v_3, v_6, v_8, \ldots, v_{n-6}, v_{n-4}, v_{n-2}\}$ for $n = 5k + 2$; $W = \{v_1, v_3, v_6, v_8, \ldots, v_{n-7}, v_{n-5}, v_{n-3}\}$ for $n = 5k + 3$; where $k = 2, 3, 4 \ldots$; then as similar as above we obtain that different vertices of $W_n \Theta K_1$ has different metric representation Therefore W is a resolving set with $|W| = \left\lceil \frac{n - f(n)}{2} \right\rceil$. Let $\beta(W_n \Theta K_1)$ is even; we consider $W = \{v_1, v_3, v_6, v_8, \ldots, v_{n-3}, v_{n-1}\}$ for $n = 9 \& n = 5k + 4$; $W = \{v_1, v_3, v_6, v_8, \ldots, v_{n-4}, v_{n-2}\}$ for $W = \{v_1, v_3, v_6, v_8, \ldots, v_{n-5}, v_{n-3}\}$ for $n = 5k + 1$; where $k = 2, 3, 4 \ldots$; then as similar as above we obtain that different vertices of $W_n \Theta K_1$ have different representation Therefore W is a resolving set with $|W| = \left\lceil \frac{n - f(n)}{2} \right\rceil$. Moreover, $\beta(W_n \Theta K_1) \leq \left\lceil \frac{n - f(n)}{2} \right\rceil$.

Now we will show that $\beta(W_n \Theta K_1) \geq \left\lceil \frac{n - f(n)}{2} \right\rceil$. Suppose that W is a resolving set of $W_n \Theta K_1$ with $|W| < \left\lceil \frac{n - f(n)}{2} \right\rceil$. If $W = \{u, v_1, v_2, v_3, \ldots, v_r\}; 1 \leq r \leq n$, then $\exists \alpha, \delta \in V(W_n \Theta K_1)$ such that $R_\theta(\alpha/W) = (1, 2, 2, \ldots, 2) = R_\theta(\delta/W)$. If $W = \{u, u_1, u_2, u_3, \ldots, u_r\}$; then $R_\theta(\alpha/W) = (1, 3, 3, \ldots, 3) = R_\theta(\delta/W)$. If $W = \{v_1, v_2, v_3, \ldots, v_r\}$; then $R_\theta(\alpha/W) = (2, 2, \ldots, 2) = R_\theta(\delta/W)$. If $W = \{u_1, u_2, u_3, \ldots, u_r\}$; then $R_\theta(\alpha/W) = (3, 3, 3, \ldots, 3) = R_\theta(\delta/W)$. If $W = \{v_1, v_2, \ldots, v_{r_1}, u_1, u_2, \ldots, u_{r_2}\}; 1 \leq r_1, r_2 \leq n$; then we obtain $R_\theta(\alpha/W) = (1, 2, 2, \ldots, 2, 3, 3, \ldots, 3) = R_\theta(\delta/W)$. We obtain that all the possibilities contradict, therefore $\beta(W_n \Theta K_1) \geq \left\lceil \frac{n - f(n)}{2} \right\rceil$. Hence, $\beta(W_n \Theta K_1) = \left\lceil \frac{n - f(n)}{2} \right\rceil$

4 CONCLUSION

In the present paper, metric dimension of a corona product of a cycle C_n and a wheel W_n with K_1 have been discussed. We have proved that $\beta(C_n \Theta K_1) = 2$; if n is odd number or $n = 4$ and $\beta(C_n \Theta K_1) = 3$; if n is even number other than 4. Thus, we conclude that metric dimension of a corona product of a cycle C_n with K_1 is constant for odd value of n.

REFERENCES

Buczkowski, P.S., Chartrand, G., Poisson, C., Zhang, P. 2003. k−dimensional graphs and their bases, *Periodica Math. Hung., 46(1) (2003), 9–15*.

Caceres, J., Hernando, C., Mora, M., Pelayo, I.M., Puertas, M.L., Seara, C. & Wood, D.R. 2007. On the metric dimension of cartesian products of graphs, *Siam J. Discrete Math. , 21 (2007), 423–441*.

Caceres, J., Hernando, C., Mora, M., Pelayo, I.M., Puertas, M.L., Seara, C.&D.R. Wood, 2005. On the metric dimension of some families of graphs, *Electronic Notes in Disc. Math., 22 (2005), 129–133*.

Chartrand, G. Eroh, L., Johnson, M.A.&Oellermann, O.R.2000. Resolvability in graphs and the metric dimension of a graph, *Discrete Applied Math., 105 (2000), 99–113*.

Chartrand, G. &Lesniak, L.2000. Graphs and Digraphs, *3rd ed., Chapman and Hall/CRC, 2000*.

Fehr, M., Gosselin, S. &O.R. Oellermann, 2006.The metric dimension of Cayley digraphs, *Discrete Math., 306 (2006), 31–41.*

Harary, F. & Melter, R.A.1975.On the metric dimension of a graph, *ArsCombinatoria, 2 (1976), 191–195.*

Imran, M., Bokhary, S.A.H., Ahmad, A., Fenovcikova, A.S.2013. On class of regular graphs with constant metric, *ActaMathematicaScientia 2013, 33B (1):187–206.*

Iswadi, H., Baskoro, E.T., Simanjuntak, R&Salman, A, N.M.The metric dimension of graph with pendant edges, *Journal of Combinatorial Mathematics and Combinatorial Computing, 65 (2008) 139–145.*

Khuller, S., Raghavachari, B. &Rosenfeld, A.1996. Landmarks in graphs, *Discrete Applied Math., 70(3):217–229, 1996.*

Saenpholphat, V. & Zhang, P.2002.Some results on connected resolvability in graphs, *Congr. Numer., 158 (2002), 5–19.*

Saputro, S.W., Suprijanto, D., Baskoro , E.T.& A.N.M.Salman.2012.The Metric Dimension of a Graph Composition Products with Star, J.*Indones. Math. Soc. Vol. 18, No. 2 (2012), pp.85–92.*

Shahida, A.T&M. S. Sunitha, On the Metric Dimension of Joins of Two Graphs, *International Journal of Scientific & Engineering Research, 5(9) September-2014, 33–38.*

Slater, P.J., leaves of trees, 1975.*Proc. 6th southeastern conf. on combinatorics, Graph theory and computing, Congr. Number, 14 (1975), 549–559.*

Tomescu, I., Javaid, I.2007.On the metric dimension of the Jahangir graph, *Bull. Math. Soc. Sci. Math. Roumanie, 50(98), 4(2007), 371–376.*

Smart Computing – Khan et al (Eds)
© *2021 Taylor & Francis Group, London, ISBN 978-0-367-76552-1*

Deep learning models for anomaly detection in wireless capsule endoscopy video frames: The transfer learning approach

S. Jain, A. Seal & A. Ojha
PDPM Indian Institute of Information Technology Design and Manufacturing, Jabalpur, India

ABSTRACT: Wireless Capsule Endoscopy (WCE) is a popular and widely accepted technique for the examination of gastro-intestinal (GI) tract and small bowel. A small capsule is swallowed by the patient equipped with a camera that records its journey in the form of a video. This video helps the doctor in visual examination of a patient's GI tract and intestine which further helps in the diagnosis of diseases. Several image processing and machine learning techniques have been proposed by the researchers for abnormal frame detection from WCE videos. Recent approaches have used deep learning frameworks for abnormality detection. In this study, transfer learning is employed using various available deep learning models for classification of normal images and images with abnormality. Three popular models—InceptionV3, Resnet50, and InceptionResnetV2—were trained and compared. It is found that the performance deep learning models is quiet better in comparison to traditional machine learning methods and InceptionV3 outperformed with 93% accuracy.

Keywords: Wireless capsule endoscopy, abnormal frame detection, deep CNN models, transfer learning.

1 INTRODUCTION

Wireless capsule endoscopy (WCE) is an effective technique for medical investigation of the gastro-intestinal tract. In contrast to traditional endoscopy (Kiesslich et al. 2011) which involves a long flexible tube pushed inside the patient's throat and rectum, capsule endoscopy is painless and easy going for patients (Iddan et al. 2000). A tiny camera is placed inside a small-size capsule which is swallowed by the patient. As the capsule moves through the digestive tract thousands of frames are captured by the camera in a complete video. These frames are continuously transmitted to a receiver unit tied around the waist of patient. WCE helps the doctors to examine small intestine even in the areas where traditional endoscopic procedures can't reach. WCE video is quiet lengthy which can extend from 8 and reach up to 10 hours with tens of thousands of frames. So, for a doctor to identify the anomalous frame, a great deal of attention and good amount of time needs to be invested. To make this examination simple and less time consuming, computer-aided automated diagnosis (CAD) systems are used, in which automatic detection of anomalous frames at initial level is done. Then the results are validated by medical experts.

Several approaches have been proposed for automatic detection of anomalous frames over the years. These include image processing-based techniques, machine learning-based methods and a combination of both types of methods (see, e.g., Liu & Yuan 2009; Li & Meng 2009; Iakovidis & Koulaouzidis 2014; Iakovidis et al. 2015). More recently, deep learning techniques have also been used to identify frames having different types of anomaly. While the Convolutional Neural Networks (CNNs) prove to be quite promising in many fields of applications, in medical image understanding they are still being explored as feature extractors, rather than providing complete solutions for the reason that datasets in medical domains are of relatively small size and are often highly imbalanced (Alom et al. 2018). Deep learning models require large datasets for learning the features and for providing accurate solutions. Transfer learning approaches have been introduced

DOI 10.1201/9781003167488-49

to overcome such problems of small datasets, and have been shown to be quite promising. In transfer learning, one uses a pretrained deep learning model from another domain and trains some layers of the CNN model on a given small dataset. In this paper, we investigate and compare three state-of-the-art deep CNN models for anomaly detection in WCE frames on a small WCE dataset.

The rest of the paper is organized as follows. Section 2 gives an overview of related state-of-the-art methods. In Section 3, deep learning models, WCE dataset, and metrics for evaluation of models are described. Section 4 shows a comparison of results obtained, and finally, our work is concluded in Section 5.

2 RELATED WORK

A variety of intestinal abnormalities have been found in patients, such as bleeding, ulcers, and polyps, and the available literature covers most of them. Methods of detecting anomalies can be categorized into three main groups according to the area inside frame used in the method. Many researchers have investigated the problem of bleeding detection or blood spot identification where color channels play an important role. Pixel-based methods for identification of anomaly were suggested by Liu & Yuan (2009) in which color histogram was computed based on pixel values of RGB color channels. Novozámský et al. (2016) proposed a new color model similar to CMYK color model which enhances the intensity of red color pixels in the image for bleeding frame detection. Ghosh et al. (2018) devised a block-based statistical color histogram technique for bleeding detection. There are techniques available in the literature where features are calculated by considering whole image at a time in contrast to pixel or block-based methods. Features from whole image can be extracted by using feature extractors such as speed up robust features (SURF) created by Bay et al. (2006), histogram of oriented gradients (HOG) proposed by Dalal & Triggs (2005), and scale-invariant feature transform (SIFT) given by Lindeberg (2012). It was found in the work presented by Iakovidis & Koulaouzidis (2014) and Iwahori et al. (2015) that they used SURF and HOG for extraction of textural information to detect lesion and polyps. Images in frequency domain like wavelet transformation in addition to spatial domain techniques can be used for feature extraction as suggested in the work by Barbosa et al. (2012). Local binary pattern was exploited by Li & Meng (2009) for textural feature extraction to detect ulcers in WCE frames.

Conventional machine learning techniques mentioned above require handcrafted features which are often over-specified, incomplete, and time-taking. Deep learning models, on the other hand, do not need handcrafted features. They automatically extract features to provide a solution. For image data, CNNs are employed as feature extractors, and have been established as effective tools. CNNs have also been used in anomalous frame identification in WCE (Jia & Meng 2016; Sekuboyina et al. 2017; Seguı et al. 2016; Iakovidis et al. 2018; Szegedy et al. 2017). Jia & Meng (2016) deployed CNN for bleeding detection in WCE frames. Sekuboyina et al. (2017) implemented CNN for abnormality detection in the WCE frames. Seguı et al. (2016) have also used CNN for computing generic features for motility characterization of small intestine. Iakovidis et al. (2018) employed CNN for detection of anomalous frames. Deep learning methods have proved their ability in the last decade for various challenging problems in artificial intelligence (AI). Deep learning methods due to inherent capability of generating feature maps has proven to be beneficial as given in the study by Iakovidis et al. (2018). Transfer learning, on the other hand, gives thrust in making use of existing deep learning models making use of pre-trained weights and training them again on the custom dataset. This motivated us to proceed with the study of WCE images for abnormality detection using deep CNN models. Therefore, existing pre-trained CNN models can be used for training WCE images. It will help in generalization of diseases to a single anomaly class by identification of patterns in deep layers. In this paper, we evaluate the performance of three state-of-the-art deep learning models, namely InceptionV3 by Szegedy et al. (2016), Resnet50 proposed by He et al. (2016), and InceptionResnetV2 made by Szegedy et al. (2017) for anomalous frame detection in WCE videos using the transfer learning approach.

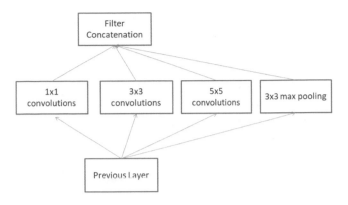

Figure 1. An overview of inception layer.

3 METHODS

A comparative analysis of deep learning models for classification of abnormal and normal WCE images is performed in this section. Advantages of transfer learning are exploited by retraining deep learning models initialized using imagenet pretrained weights. Since the dataset used for the study is very small, the concept of transfer learning proved to be quite beneficial for classification of WCE images. Three publicly available popular deep learning models, Inceptionv3 by Szegedy et al. (2016), Resnet50 by He et al. (2016), and InceptionResnetv2 by Szegedy et al. (2017) are used for the present study. The trained models are also compared with some recently introduced machine learning techniques. A brief description of WCE dataset, performance metrics, and training of these models is given in this section.

3.1 Models

3.1.1 Inception V3
This is the third version of an inception network proposed by Google known as GoogLeNet or Inception V3. GoogLeNet introduced the concept of inception layer which is a CNN layer with combination of layers (namely, 1×1 convolutional layer, 3×3 convolutional layer, 5×5 convolutional layer) with their output filter banks merged into a single output vector which act as input to the next stage, as shown in Figure 1. Along with the above-mentioned layers, there are two major additions in the naive inception layer in version 2. A 1×1 convolutional layer is added before applying another layer, which is mainly incorporated to reduce dimensions. A max-pooling layer also runs parallel, along with convolution layers. 5×5 filter is replaced by two 3×3 filter . So the convolutions are factorized to reduce the number of weights and parameters without pulling down the efficiency of the network, as shown in Figure 2. Moreover, they factorize convolutions of filter size nn to a combination of $1 \times n$ and $n \times 1$ convolutions. For example, a 3×3 convolution is replaced by first performing a 1×3 convolution, and then performing a 3×1 convolution on its output. It is found that this method to be 33% less expensive than a single 3×3 convolution. Three different types of inception modules were incorporated in Inception model version 3. InceptionV3 inherited all the upgrades of like factorization as well as also added new features like RMSProp optimizer, factorization of 7×7 convolutions and batch normalization. It is 48-layered CNN which can identify any image belonging to these thousand classes.

3.1.2 Resnet50
After the success of Krizhevsky et al. (2012) in LSVRC2012 (Russakovsky et al. 2015), researchers were attracted to use deep learning models which were deeper to learn more complex structures. But the problem of vanishing gradients turned to be a bottleneck for deeper networks. As the

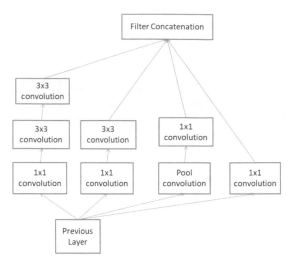

Figure 2. Factorizing convolution layers.

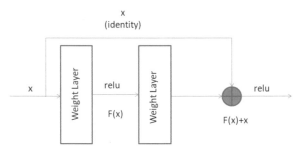

Figure 3. An overview of residual block.

model propagates back the error, the deep learning model eventually learns almost nothing, due to vanishing gradients. Resnet50 model proposed by He et al. (2016) has provided an efficient solution to this problem through skip connections which are shortcuts that jumps over certain layers. A skip connection gives outputs of an earlier layer to the forthcoming layers which can be considered as a residue of earlier layers and the network is known as deep residual network. An overview of a residual block is shown in Figure 3. Resnet50 is a 50-layered CNN model with residual blocks, trained on ImageNet dataset with a 1000 classes.

3.1.3 InceptionResnetV2

InceptionResnetV2 is the fourth version of inception network which takes the advantage of both inception layers and residual connections. This allowed Inception to gain all the benefits of the residual approach while retaining its computational efficiency as proposed in InceptionV3. It is a 164-layer deep network. In this network, Szegedy et al. (2017) optimized the residual block to lower the computational overload. Optimization is achieved by introducing 1×1 convolution without activation to increase the dimensionality of the filter bank before the addition to match the depth of the input shown in Figure 4. This is needed to compensate for the dimensionality reduction induced by the Inception block. Also, batch-normalization is applied on top of the traditional layers.

3.2 Dataset and Preprocessing

Video frames of capsule endoscopy were taken from the publicly available KID dataset Koulaouzidis et al. (2017) in our method. Both Dataset-1 and Dataset-2 are used in the present work. Images in

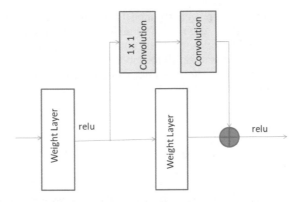

Figure 4. An overview of residual block in InceptionResnetV2.

Dataset-1 contain 77 images containing anomalies like angioectasias, apthae, chylous cysts, polypoid lesions, villous oedema, bleeding, lymphangiectasias, ulcers, and stenoses whereas Dataset-2 contains 593 images of abnormality classes like polypoid, vascular, and inflammatory lesions and it also contains 1778 normal images from the esophagus, stomach, small bowel, and colon. So, a total of 670 images with abnormalities and 1778 normal images were taken under experimentation. Since the images under abnormal category were approximately three times less than the normal category, data augmentation was applied using simple geometric transformations.

3.3 Performance Metrics

The performance of proposed work is measured on well known and widely accepted metrics (Sharma & Seal 2019) that are accuracy, precision, recall and f1-score metrics:

$$Accuracy = \frac{TP + TN}{TP + FP + TN + FN} \tag{1}$$

$$Precision = \frac{TP}{TP + FP} \tag{2}$$

$$Recall = \frac{TP}{TP + FN} \tag{3}$$

$$F1 - score = \frac{2 \times Precesion \times Recall}{Precision + Recall} \tag{4}$$

where TP, FP, TN, FN are true positive, false positive, true negative, and false negative results of frame identification.

3.4 Environmental Settings and Training

For experiments, dataset is divided into three subsets for training, validation, and testing keeping the ratio of 8:1:1. The training set contains 536 normal and 1422 abnormal images whereas validation and testing sets contain 67 normal and 178 abnormal images, respectively. Experiments are performed on a workstation with an Intel Xeon CPU 1660, 16 GB RAM, and an NVIDIA GeForce GTX 1080 GPU. CNN models are implemented in Python language. Models are initialized with the weights and bias parameters of pretrained models on ImageNet dataset (Deng et al. 2009) and transfer learning is applied by retraining them on KID dataset. All layers except the last four are frozen before training is performed. Frozen layers are not trainable whereas in all the other layers weights will get updated during training. Three dense layers are added at the end of the model. ReLu activation is added in the first two newly added dense layers and sigmoid activation at the last layer with two classes is applied. To prevent the model from overfitting, dropout regularization is incorporated. Batch normalization is also added to stabilize learning as an advantage of this small fluctuations in training and validation metrics were noted. A total of 100 epochs are executed and batch size of 32 is taken. It is observed that all the models perform well and results are very close but InceptionV3 shows better results among the three models. It can be concluded that any of these models can be employed for detection of anomalous frames in capsule endoscopy images.

4 RESULTS AND DISCUSSION

In this section, classification results of each model are analyzed and compared. Table 1 shows the performance comparison of all the three models using different metrics. It is seen that the highest accuracy is achieved using InceptionV3 model which is recorded as 93% percent whereas Resnet50 and InceptionResnetV2 are performing nearly the same with 90% accuracy. In terms of other parameters like precision, recall, and F1 score, InceptionV3 is performing consistently and leads in all the metrics. Analysis of these models is also done in terms of number of parameters learned. Table 2 shows the number of parameters computed in all three models. There exist two categories of parameters, one is trainable parameters that belong to the layers which are not frozen whereas non-trainable parameters are associated with frozen layers. Inception V3 has the least number of trainable parameters whereas ResNet50 has the highest number of trainable parameters but the performance was not as good as InceptionV3. Therefore, InceptionV3 can be considered as the best performing model with least computation of parameters.

To compare the deep learning models with some recently introduced machine learning techniques, we use InceptionV3, whose performance is the best among the three deep leaning models. For the purpose of comparison, two recent approaches introduced by Yuan et al. (2015) and Ghosh et al. (2018) are used. Table 3 shows comparison of these methods. Both of these methods by Yuan et al. (2015) and Ghosh et al. (2018) use handcrafted features. It can be seen that the deep learning model InceptionV3 outperforms the other two methods.

The problem of anomalous frame detection is quite challenging because of two possible reasons. First, the abnormalities are of different shape, size, and color. Second, the datasets are not publicly

Table 1. Performance evaluation of trained deep learning models.

Model	Accuracy	Precision	Recall	F1 score
InceptionResnetV2	0.90	0.87	0.81	0.83
Resnet50	0.90	0.92	0.82	0.85
InceptionV3	0.93	0.92	0.90	0.91

Table 2. Parameters learned in deep learning models considered in the study.

Model	Total Parameters	Trainable Parameters	Non-trainable Parameters
InceptionResnetV2	131, 410, 146	80, 269, 826	51, 140, 320
Resnet50	193, 460, 098	170, 927, 106	22, 532, 992
InceptionV3	24, 590, 242	2, 787, 458	21, 802, 784

Table 3. Performance comparison of anomaly detection methods.

Method	Accuracy	Precision	Recall	F1 score
Ghosh et al. (2018)	0.71	0.62	0.72	0.67
Yuan et al. (2015)	0.80	0.79	0.80	0.79
InceptionV3	0.93	0.92	0.90	0.91

available, and one is limited to only a small number of publicly available WCE with different sizes (Figure 5). As it can be seen in Figures 6 and 7, the frames were correctly classified. The reason behind this is probably due to visual characteristics of abnormality (angioectasia), that is, the bleeding region has different color characteristics and can be easily learned by a model, whereas in Figures 8 and 9 the abnormality (inflammatory, vascular) is very small in size and its texture and colors are close to normal region texture and color.

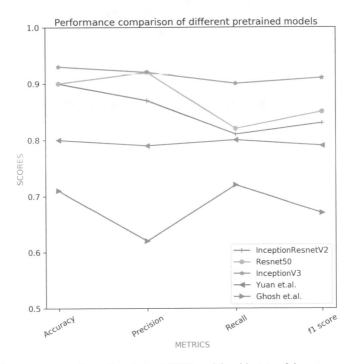

Figure 5.   Performance comparison of pre-trained CNN models with state-of-the-art conventional machine learning methods on different metrics.

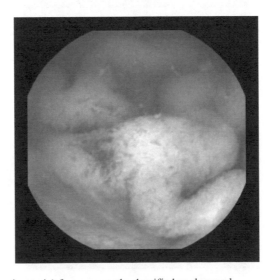

Figure 6.   Abnormal (angioectasia) frame correctly classified as abnormal.

429

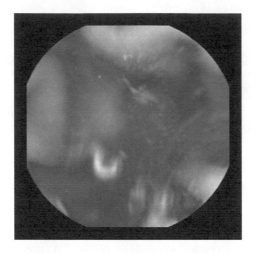

Figure 7. Normal frame correctly classified as normal.

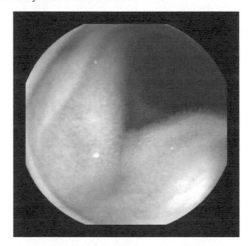

Figure 8. Abnormal (inflammatory) frame incorrectly classified as normal.

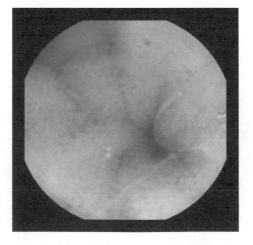

Figure 9. Abnormal (vascular) frame incorrectly classified as normal.

5 CONCLUSION

Deep learning techniques have played a significant role in computer vision. WCE is gaining popularity in endoscopic examination due to solutions provided by CAD systems using deep learning techniques are in the forefront of research and development in WCE domain. Due to limited number of publicly available datasets, which are smaller in size as well, deep learning approaches need to use transfer learning. In this work, we have investigated three most commonly used deep CNN models for anomaly detection in WCE video frames and have shown that they perform almost similarly on the KID dataset. To deal with the size of the dataset, augmentation helped us to some extent and good results were achieved. A comparison with two recently introduced machine learning techniques by Yuan et al. (2015) and Ghosh et al. (2018) shows that deep leaning models outperform existing machine learning methods using hand-crafted features. Localization of anomaly can be the future aspect of the current work.

ACKNOWLEDGMENTS

We are thankful to Prof. Dimitris K. Iakovidis and his colleagues, The Royal Infirmary of Edinburgh, Endoscopy Unit for providing us access to the KID dataset without which our aim of studying capsule endoscopy images and performing experiments could be quite difficult.

REFERENCES

Alom, M. Z., T. M. Taha, C. Yakopcic, S. Westberg, P. Sidike, M. S. Nasrin, B. C. Van Esesn, A. A. S. Awwal, and V. K. Asari (2018). The history began from alexnet: A comprehensive survey on deep learning approaches. *arXiv preprint arXiv:1803.01164*.

Barbosa, D. C., D. B. Roupar, J. C. Ramos, A. C. Tavares, and C. S. Lima (2012). Automatic small bowel tumor diagnosis by using multi-scale wavelet-based analysis in wireless capsule endoscopy images. *Biomedical engineering online 11*(1), 3.

Bay, H., T. Tuytelaars, and L. Van Gool (2006). Surf: Speeded up robust features. In *European conference on computer vision*, pp. 404–417. Springer.

Dalal, N. and B. Triggs (2005). Histograms of oriented gradients for human detection. In *2005 IEEE computer society conference on computer vision and pattern recognition (CVPR'05)*, Volume 1, pp. 886–893. IEEE.

Deng, J., W. Dong, R. Socher, L.-J. Li, K. Li, and L. Fei-Fei (2009). ImageNet: A Large-Scale Hierarchical Image Database. In *CVPR09*.

Ghosh, T., S. A. Fattah, and K. A. Wahid (2018). Chobs: color histogram of block statistics for automatic bleeding detection in wireless capsule endoscopy video. *IEEE journal of translational engineering in health and medicine 6*, 1–12.

He, K., X. Zhang, S. Ren, and J. Sun (2016). Deep residual learning for image recognition. In *Proceedings of the IEEE conference on computer vision and pattern recognition*, pp. 770–778. Iakovidis, D. K., D. Chatzis, P. Chrysanthopoulos, and A. Koulaouzidis (2015). Blood detection in wireless capsule endoscope images based on salient superpixels. In *2015 37th Annual International Conference of the IEEE Engineering in Medicine and Biology Society (EMBC)*, pp. 731–734. IEEE.

Iakovidis, D. K., S. V. Georgakopoulos, M. Vasilakakis, A. Koulaouzidis, and V. P. Plagianakos (2018). Detecting and locating gastrointestinal anomalies using deep learning and iterative cluster unification. *IEEE transactions on medical imaging 37*(10), 2196–2210.

Iakovidis, D. K. and A. Koulaouzidis (2014). Automatic lesion detection in capsule endoscopy based on color saliency: closer to an essential adjunct for reviewing software. *Gastrointestinal endoscopy 80*(5), 877–883.

Iddan, G., G. Meron, A. Glukhovsky, and P. Swain (2000). Wireless capsule endoscopy. *Nature 405*(6785), 417–417.

Iwahori, Y., A. Hattori, Y. Adachi, M. K. Bhuyan, R. J. Woodham, and K. Kasugai (2015). Automatic detection of polyp using hessian filter and hog features. *Procedia computer science 60*, 730–739.

Jia, X. and M. Q.-H. Meng (2016). A deep convolutional neural network for bleeding detection in wireless capsule endoscopy images. In *2016 38th Annual International Conference of the IEEE Engineering in Medicine and Biology Society (EMBC)*, pp. 639–642. IEEE.

Kiesslich, R., M. Goetz, A. Hoffman, and P. R. Galle (2011). New imaging techniques and opportunities in endoscopy. *Nature reviews Gastroenterology & hepatology 8*(10), 547.

Koulaouzidis, A., D. K. Iakovidis, D. E. Yung, E. Rondonotti, U. Kopylov, J. N. Plevris, E. Toth, A. Eliakim, G. Wurm Johansson, W. Marlicz, G. Mavrogenis, A. Nemeth, H. Thorlacius, and G. E. Tontini (2017, Jun). KID Project: an internet-based digital video atlas of capsule endoscopy for research purposes. *Endosc Int Open 5*(6), E477–E483.

Krizhevsky, A., I. Sutskever, and G. E. Hinton (2012). Imagenet classification with deep convolutional neural networks. In *Advances in neural information processing systems*, pp. 1097–1105.

Li, B. and M. Q.-H. Meng (2009). Texture analysis for ulcer detection in capsule endoscopy images. *Image and Vision computing 27*(9), 1336–1342.

Lindeberg, T. (2012). Scale invariant feature transform.

Liu, J. and X. Yuan (2009). Obscure bleeding detection in endoscopy images using support vector machines. *Optimization and engineering 10*(2), 289–299.

Novozámský, A., J. Flusser, I. Tacheci, L. Sulík, J. Bureš, and O. Krejcar (2016). Automatic blood detection in capsule endoscopy video. *Journal of biomedical optics 21*(12), 126007.

Russakovsky, O., J. Deng, H. Su, J. Krause, S. Satheesh, S. Ma, Z. Huang, A. Karpathy, A. Khosla, M. Bernstein, A. C. Berg, and L. Fei-Fei (2015). ImageNet Large Scale Visual Recognition Challenge. *International Journal of Computer Vision (IJCV) 115*(3), 211–252.

Seguı, S., M. Drozdzal, G. Pascual, P. Radeva, C. Malagelada, F. Azpiroz, and J. Vitria' (2016). Generic feature learning for wireless capsule endoscopy analysis. *Computers in biology and medicine 79*, 163–172.

Sekuboyina, A. K., S. T. Devarakonda, and C. S. Seelamantula (2017). A convolutional neural network approach for abnormality detection in wireless capsule endoscopy. In *2017 IEEE 14th International Symposium on Biomedical Imaging (ISBI 2017)*, pp. 1057–1060. IEEE.

Sharma, K. K. and A. Seal (2019). Modeling uncertain data using monte carlo integration method for clustering. *Expert Systems with Applications 137*, 100–116.

Szegedy, C., S. Ioffe, V. Vanhoucke, and A. A. Alemi (2017). Inception-v4, inception-resnet and the impact of residual connections on learning. In *Thirty-first AAAI conference on artificial intelligence*.

Szegedy, C., V. Vanhoucke, S. Ioffe, J. Shlens, and Z. Wojna (2016). Rethinking the inception architecture for computer vision. In *Proceedings of the IEEE conference on computer vision and pattern recognition*, pp. 2818–2826.

Yuan, Y., B. Li, and M. Q.-H. Meng (2015). Bleeding frame and region detection in the wireless capsule endoscopy video. *IEEE journal of biomedical and health informatics 20*(2), 624–630.

Smart Computing – Khan et al (Eds)
© 2021 Taylor & Francis Group, London, ISBN 978-0-367-76552-1

Analysis of conformable fractional SEIR model with treatment

Arti Malik, Nitendra Kumar & Khursheed Alam
Department of Mathematics, Sharda University, Greater Noida, Uttar Pradesh, India

ABSTRACT: This paper is based on a model of conformable fractional differential equation which explains the dynamics of certain epidemics. In this paper, we divide the population into susceptible, exposed, infectious, and recovered, and describe the treatment modalities. The analytical study of the present model shows two types equilibrium points (first is disease-free equilibrium and the second is endemic equilibrium). For both cases, local asymptotic stability has been proven. In the conclusion we present the numerical simulation.

1   GENERAL INSTRUCTIONS

First put forth is a brief introduction of fractional calculus [19]. Many mathematicians tried to define fractional derivative. Mostly an integral form for the fractional derivative is used. Two of the most frequently used are:

(i) Riemann–Liouville definition for $\propto \in [n-1, n]$, then $\propto$ derivative of f is

$$D_a^\propto f(t) = \frac{1}{\Gamma(n-\propto)} \frac{d^n}{dt^n} \int_0^t \frac{f(x)}{(t-x)^{\propto-n+1}} dx$$

(ii) Caputo definition for $\propto \in [n-1, n)$, the $\propto$ derivative of f is

$$D_a^\propto f(t) = \frac{1}{\Gamma(n-\propto)} \int_0^t \frac{f^n(x)}{(t-x)^{\propto-n+1}} dx$$

And all new definitions, which is simplest and most natural and sufficient definition of fractional derivative of order $\propto \in (0, 1]$

Definition. [19]-Conformable fractional derivative denoted by $T_\propto f(t)$, for $0 <\propto 1$ Of the function f:$[0,\infty[\to R[$ is defined as

$$T_\propto f(t) = \log_{\varepsilon \to 0} \frac{f(t + \varepsilon t^{1-\propto}) - f(t)}{\varepsilon}$$

For all > 0, $\propto \in (0, 1)$. If f is differentiable on $(0, a)$. Also $T_\propto f(0) = \log_{x \to 0^+} T_\propto f(t)$

Abdelhakim and Machado [20] observed that if f is $\propto$ differentiable in the conformable sense at $t > 0$, then it must be differentiable in the classical sense at t

$$T_\propto f(t) = t^{1-\propto} f'(t) \tag{1}$$

is satisfied.

Many analogous properties of classical derivative including mean value theorem and Roll's theorem hold true.

Fractional differential equations (FDE) is an extended form of ordinary differential equations (ODS), where fractional derivative is replaces the integral order derivative. Lately, there has been

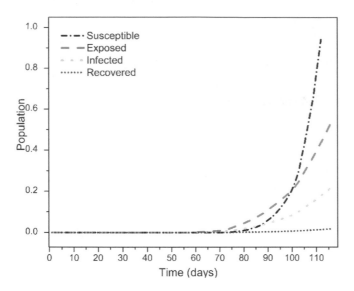

Figure 1. Dynamics of the system (2) without treatment.

many developments in fractional differential equations due to their applicability across various fields of engineering and technology

There is another derivative that is a natural extension of the usual derivative and known as conformable fractional derivative which helped us to understand different areas of engineering and science problems. This concept is used to study projectile motion Contreras.; problems of finance involve conformable fractional derivative, timeinverse parabolic problem, population growth, mixing problem, heat equation [23] and conformable fractional derivative that are also useful for explaining any infectious disease dynamics. There are many models, overly controlled by the system and different type of components. There are many examples of such types of models like SIR [2,3], SIS [7] SEIR-SEI [GAMS of dengue], and SEIR [12]. In the present paper we describe a SEIR model applying a treatment to reduce the number of infected persons as to control the disease.

The rest of this paper is organized as follows. The SEIR fractional model using conformable fractional derivative explained in Section 2. In the given model, we introduce the treatment as a control of those infected individuals by the disease. We analyze the diseasefree equilibrium point and the stability of these points. Section 3 is dedicated to cost optimization and reduction in cases of disease infection interested to minimize the cost of treatment and decreasing the individual infected by the disease. After this, we also study here the simulation of these models.

2 FORMULATION OF MODEL

Kermak and McKendrick present the SEIR epidemic model which is an additional form of the SIR model. In the SEIR model the total population segregated under four heads are determined by disease condition. The susceptible individuals S (those who are able to contract the disease), E indicates the exposed individuals (those persons who have been infected but are not yet infectious and are asymptomatic), the infectious individuals are I (those acting as carrier of disease), and R indicates the cured individuals (those who have been diagnosed and are now resistive to infection). In this study we introduce medical intervention as a way to reduce the number of patients. The model is shown in the following Figure 1.

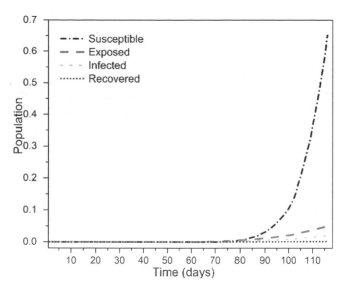

Figure 2. Dynamics of system (3) with treatment.

The SEIR model is governed by the following nonlinear deterministic system equation (2):

$$S'(t) = bN - \beta \frac{I(t)}{N} S(t) - bS(t)$$

$$E'(t) = \beta \frac{I(t)}{N} S(t) - (\sigma + b)E(t) \qquad (2)$$

$$I'(t) = \sigma E(t) - (\mu + q + b)I(t)$$

$$R'(t) = (\mu + q) I(t) - bR(t)$$

In the model, we assume that natural death, and birth rate b are equal, β is the transmission rate of the disease, μ the recovery rate without treatment, σ is the incubation rate and q is the treatment scale of the disease. N is the total size of population, thus

$$\dot{N} = \dot{S} + \dot{E} + \dot{I} + \dot{R}$$

So the population size is fixed w.r.t. time.

Another form of the model is fractional and the dependent variable of the total population under each of the four heads are represented as $= \frac{S}{N}$, $e = \frac{E}{N}$, $i = \frac{I}{N}$, $r = \frac{R}{N}$. Then the model (1) becomes

$$s'(t) = b - \beta i(t)s(t) - bs(t)$$

$$e'(t) = \beta i(t)s(t) - (\sigma + b)e(t)$$

$$i'(t) = \sigma e(t) - (\mu + q + b)i(t)$$

$$r'(t) = (\mu + q) i(t) - br(t)$$

In this paper, we replace the classical derivative and parameter $*$ by $*^{\alpha}$. Thus, dimension of both sides of the equation will be same. Therefore, our conformable fractional model is of the form

$$t^{(1-\alpha)}s'(t) = b^{\alpha} - \beta^{\alpha}i(t) s(t) + b^{\alpha}s(t)$$

$$t^{(1-\alpha)}e'(t) = \beta^{\alpha}i(t) s(t) - (\sigma^{\alpha} + b^{\alpha}) e(t)$$

$$t^{(1-\alpha)}i'(t) = \sigma^{\alpha}e(t) - (\mu^{\alpha} + q^{\alpha} + b^{\alpha})i(t) \qquad (3)$$

435

$$t^{(1-\alpha)}r'(t) = (\mu^\alpha + q^\alpha)i(t) + b^\alpha r(t)$$

with the initial conditions

$$s(0) = s_0, \quad e(0) = e_0, \quad i(0) = i_0, \quad r(0) = r_0, \quad s_0 e, \quad i_0, \quad r_0 \in R_0^+$$

Now we consider the functions s, e, i, r and their conformable fractional derivatives are continuous at $t > 0$ and the population size $t^{1-\alpha}N = 0$ is constant. Now analyze the uniqueness non-negativity and existence of the solution of the system (2).

Theorem 1. There is a non-negative and unique solution of the system of E quation (2).

Proof – We get the existence of the solution after using [11, theorem] and by [11, remark], we prove the uniqueness. At last we obtain a nonnegative solution. Observe first that

$$\dot{s}(t)\,|_{s=0} = b^\alpha t^{\alpha-1}, \quad \dot{e}(t)\,|_{e=0} = \beta^\alpha i(t)s(t)t^{\alpha-1},$$

$$\dot{i}(t)\,|_{i=0} = e^\alpha e(t)t^{\alpha-1}, \quad \dot{r}(t)\,|_{r=0} = (\mu^\alpha + q^\alpha)t^{\alpha-1},$$

after using some argumentation which used in the proof of [1, theorem 2] and using [1, lemma1]. Thus we come to the end that the feasible region of the system of equation (2) is given by

$$\Omega = \{(s, e, i, r) \in R^4 : s, e, i, r \geq 0 \text{ and } s + e + i + r = 1.\}$$

The solution of the system (2) is the equilibrium points.

$$\dot{s}(t)\,|_{s=0} = \dot{e}(t)\,|_{e=0} = \dot{i}(t)\,|_{i=0} = \dot{r}(t)\,|_{r=0} = 0.$$

S we come to the end instantaneously the following.

Theorem 2. At most two equilibrium points of the conformable fractional SEIR model (2):

1. a disease-free equilibrium $D_F = (1, 0, 0, 0)$
2. an endemic equilibrium point $D_E = (s^*, e^*, i^*, r^*)$, where

$$s^* = \frac{(\sigma^\alpha + b^\alpha)(\mu^\alpha + q^\alpha + b^\alpha)}{\beta^\alpha b^\alpha}, e^* = \frac{(\mu^\alpha + q^\alpha + b^\alpha)}{\sigma^\alpha}i^*, \quad i^* = \frac{b^\alpha(1-s^*)}{\beta^\alpha s^*}, \quad r^* = \frac{(\mu^\alpha + q^\alpha)}{b^\alpha}i^*,$$

if s^*, e^*, i^*, r^* are between 0 and 1.

The basic thought in epidemiology is the existence of threshold, a crucial value allowed to predict that the disease is epidemic or not depending certain parameters which are inherent in the disease. The value is $R_0 = \frac{\beta^\alpha b^\alpha}{(\sigma^\alpha + b^\alpha)(\mu^\alpha + q^\alpha + b^\alpha)}$ is called a basic reproduction number and defined the average number of the secondary infection that would appear in a entirely susceptive population. According to the interpretation of R_0 the endemic equilibrium points $D_E = (s^*, e^*, i^*, r^*)$ have the following relations:

$$W_E = \left(\frac{1}{R_0}, \frac{(\mu^\alpha + q^\alpha + b^\alpha)b^\alpha}{\sigma^\alpha \beta^\alpha}(R_0 - 1), \frac{b^\alpha}{\beta^\alpha}(R_0 - 1), \frac{(\mu^\alpha + q^\alpha)}{\beta^\alpha}(R_0 - 1)\right)$$ and exist only if $R_0 > 1$.

Now, we calculate the stability of the disease-free equilibrium point $W_F = (1, 0, 0, 0)$.

Now, we examine the Jacobian matrix of the system (3) which is given by

$$\begin{bmatrix} (-\beta^\alpha i - b^\alpha)t^{\alpha-1} & 0 & -\beta^\alpha s t^{\alpha-1} & 0 \\ \beta^\alpha i t^{\alpha-1} & (-\sigma^\alpha - b^\alpha)t^{\alpha-1} & \beta^\alpha s t^{\alpha-1} & 0 \\ 0 & \sigma^\alpha t^{\alpha-1} & (\mu^\alpha - q^\alpha - b^\alpha)t^{\alpha-1} & 0 \\ 0 & 0 & (\mu^\alpha + q^\alpha)t^{\alpha-1} & -b^\alpha t^{\alpha-1} \end{bmatrix}$$

Theorem 3. The disease-free equilibrium points W_F is locally asymptotically stable if $R_0 < 1$.

Proof.–The Jacobian matrix identify at W_F is as

$$\begin{bmatrix} -b^\alpha t^{\alpha-1} & 0 & -\beta^\alpha s t^{\alpha-1} & 0 \\ 0 & (-\sigma^\alpha - b^\alpha) t^{\alpha-1} & \beta^\alpha s t^{\alpha-1} & 0 \\ 0 & \sigma^\alpha t^{\alpha-1} & (-\mu^\alpha - q^\alpha - b^\alpha) t^{\alpha-1} & 0 \\ 0 & 0 & (\mu^\alpha + q^\alpha) t^{\alpha-1} & -b^\alpha t^{\alpha-1} \end{bmatrix}$$

The roots are real of characteristic equation and equal to

$$\lambda = -b^\alpha t^{\alpha-1} \vee \lambda = \frac{-(A+B) \pm \sqrt{(A-B)^2 + 4C}}{2}$$

where $A = (\sigma^\alpha + b^\alpha) t^{\alpha-1}$, $= (\mu^\alpha + q^\alpha + b^\alpha) t^{\alpha-1}$, and $C = \beta^\alpha \sigma^\alpha t^{\alpha-1}$. If $C/(AB) < 1$, the eigenvalues are negative and thus the disease-free equilibrium is locally asymptotically stable [22].

Theorem 4. If $R_0 > 1$, then endemic-free equilibrium point D_E is locally asymptotically stable.

Proof. The Jacobian matrix of W_E is calculated as
The eigenvalues are

$$\lambda = -b^\alpha t^{\alpha-1} \vee \lambda = \frac{-R_0(A + BR_0) \pm \sqrt{R_0(A-B)^2 + 4CR_0}}{2}$$

where $A = (\sigma^\alpha + b^\alpha) t^{\alpha-1}$, $= (\mu^\alpha + q^\alpha + b^\alpha) t^{\alpha-1}$, and $C = \beta^\alpha \sigma^\alpha t^{\alpha-1}$. Thus, eigenvalues are real and negative if $R_0 > 1$, proving the required result.

Theorem 5. If $R_0 > 1$, then endemic-free equilibrium point D_E is locally asymptotically stable.
Proof. The Jacobian matrix of W_E is calculated as

$$\begin{bmatrix} -b^\alpha R_0 t^{\alpha-1} & 0 & -\beta^\alpha t^{\alpha-1}/R_0 & 0 \\ b^\alpha (R_0 - 1) t^{\alpha-1} & (-\sigma^\alpha - b^\alpha) t^{\alpha-1} & \beta^\alpha t^{\alpha-1}/R_0 & 0 \\ 0 & \sigma^\alpha t^{\alpha-1} & (-\mu^\alpha - q^\alpha - b^\alpha) t^{\alpha-1} & 0 \\ 0 & 0 & (\mu^\alpha + q^\alpha) t^{\alpha-1} & -b^\alpha t^{\alpha-1} \end{bmatrix}$$

The eigenvalues are

$$\lambda = -b^\alpha t^{\alpha-1} \vee \lambda = \frac{-R_0(A + BR_0) \pm \sqrt{R_0(A-B)^2 + 4CR_0}}{2}$$

where $A = (\sigma^\alpha + b^\alpha) t^{\alpha-1}$, $B = (\mu^\alpha + q^\alpha + b^\alpha) t^{\alpha-1}$, and $C = \beta^\alpha \sigma^\alpha t^{\alpha-1}$
Thus, eigenvalues are real and negative if $R_0 > 1$, proving the required result.

3 OPTIMAL CONTROL PROBLEM OF THE DISEASE

One important concern is the therapeutics which are scant and correspond to financial cost; the issue at hand is to optimize the cost of treatment and to simultaneously contain the spread of disease. So the optimal control is illustrated by

$$Min\, J = \frac{1}{2}q^2 + \int_0^T i(t)dt$$

437

Subject to some initial conditions

$$s(0) = s_0, \quad e(0) = e_0, \quad i(0) = i_0, \quad r(0) = r_0,$$

and to the FDE (2). We use the Grünwald–Letnikov fractional derivative approximation formula to solve the problem numerically. Now fixed $T > 0$, and let $t_j = jT/N$, $J = 0, 1, \ldots \ldots N$, be a partition the total interval $[0, T]$. Then,

$$+O(h)$$

The above formula is the truncated Grünwald–Letnikov fractional derivative is a first-order approximation formula of conformable fractional derivative, where ω_k^α is a generalization of binomial coefficients to real numbers:

$$\omega_k^\alpha = (-1)^k \binom{\alpha}{k}$$

With help of the following optimization problem with equality constraints. We get

$$\min J = \frac{1}{2} q^2 + \sum_1^N i(t_k)$$

with the initial conditions

$$s(0) = s_0, \quad e(0) = e_0, \quad i(0) = i_0, \quad r(0) = r_0,$$

and the system

$$\frac{1}{h^\alpha} \sum_{k=0}^{j} \omega_k^\alpha x\left(t_{j-k}\right) - \frac{s(0)}{\Gamma(1-\alpha)}(t_j)^{-\alpha} = \left(b^\alpha - \beta^\alpha i\left(t_j\right) s\left(t_j\right) - b^\alpha s(t_j)\right) t^{\alpha-1}$$

$$\frac{1}{h^\alpha} \sum_{k=0}^{j} \omega_k^\alpha x\left(t_{j-k}\right) - \frac{e(0)}{\Gamma(1-\alpha)}(t_j)^{-\alpha} = \left(\beta^\alpha i\left(t_j\right) s\left(t_j\right) - (\sigma^\alpha + b'^\alpha)e(t_j)\right) t^{\alpha-1}$$

$$\frac{1}{h^\alpha} \sum_{k=0}^{j} \omega_k^\alpha x\left(t_{j-k}\right) - \frac{i(0)}{\Gamma(1-\alpha)}(t_j)^{-\alpha} = \left(\sigma^\alpha e\left(t_j\right) - (\mu^\alpha + q^\alpha + b^\alpha)\right) t^{\alpha-1}$$

$$\frac{1}{h^\alpha} \sum_{k=0}^{j} \omega_k^\alpha x\left(t_{j-k}\right) - \frac{r(0)}{\Gamma(1-\alpha)}(t_j)^{-\alpha} = \left(+q^\alpha - \beta^\alpha i\left(t_j\right) s\left(t_j\right) - b^\alpha s(t_j)\right) t^{\alpha-1}$$

take $j = 1, \ldots \ldots, N$. Take numerical simulation with reference to the values $b = 2 \times 10^{-4}$ and $\mu = \sigma = 1$. For different values of α and β, we take $s(0) = 0.8$, $e(0) = 0, i(0) = 0.2, r(0) = 0$ as initial condition. When take $\alpha = 0.5$ and $\beta = 10$, $q = 0.861469$ is the treatment rate.

4   CONCLUSION

The paper proposes a conformable fractional SEIR model along with treatment as a containment measure. The local stability and the equilibrium points were investigated. Following an optimal control method, we examine the benefits of this approach to eliminate the disease with tangible results. As expected the ratio of susceptible and exposed by the disease is lesser with medical intervention in the community.

REFERENCES

[1] I. Area, H. Batarfi, J. Losada, J. J. Nieto, W. Shammakh and A. Torres, On a fractional order Ebola epidemic model, Adv. Difference Equ., 2015 No 1 (2015), 278.
[2] C. Angstmann, B. Henry and A. McGann, A fractional order recovery SIR model from a stochastic process, Bull. Math. Biol., 78 (2016) 468–499.

[3] C. Angstmann, B. Henry and A. McGann, A Fractional-Order Infectivity and Recovery SIR Model, Fract, 1 No1 (2017), 11 pp.

[4] A. Atangana and A. T. Alqahtani, Modelling the spread of river blindness disease via the caputo fractional derivative and the beta-derivative, Entropy, 18 No 2 (2016) 40, 14pp.

[5] I. Area, H. Batarfi, J. Losada, J. J. Nieto, W. Shammakh and A. Torres, On a fractional order Ebola epidemic model, Adv. Difference Equ., 2015 No 1 (2015), 278.

[6] R. Casagrandi, L. Bolzoni, S.A. Levin and V. Andreasen, The SIRC model for influenza A, Math. BioSci, 200 (2006) 152–169.

[7] H. A. A. El-Saka, The fractional-order SIS epidemic model with variable population size, J. Egyptian Math. Soc, 22 No 1 (2014), 50–54.

[8] M. El–Shahed, F. A. El–Naby, Fractional calculus model for childhood diseases and vaccines, Appl. Math. Sci., 8 No 98 (2014), 4859–4866.

[9] R. Hilfer, Applications of Fractional Calculus in Physics, World Scientific, Singapore, 2000.

[10] W. O. Kermack and A. G. McKendrick, Contributions to the mathematical theory of epidemics, part 1, Proc. Roy. Soc. London Ser. A, 115 (1927), 700–721.

[11] W. Lin, Global existence theory and chaos control of fractional differential equations, J. Math. Anal. Appl., 332 No 1 (2007), 709–726.

[12] N. ¨ Ozalp and E. Demirÿrci, A fractional order SEIR model with vertical transmission, Math. Comput. Model., 54 No 1–2 (2011), 1–6.

[13] S. M. Salman and A. M. Yousef, On a fractional-order model for HBV infection with cure of infected cells, J. Egyptian Math. Soc, 25 No 4 (2017) 445–451.

[14] T. Sardar, S. Rana and J. Chattopadhyay, A mathematical model of dengue transmission with memory. Commun. Nonlinear Sci. Numer. Simul., 22 (2015) 511–525.

[15] D. Sierociuk, T. Skovranek, M. Macias, I.r Podlubny, I. Petras, A. Dzielinski and P. Ziubinski, Diffusion process modeling by using fractional-order models, Appl. Math. Comput., 257 (2015), 2–11.

[16] A. A. Stanislavsky, Fractional Oscillator, Phys. Rev. E, 70 (2004), 051103, 6pp.

[17] B. J. West, M. Turalska and P. Grigolini, Fractional calculus ties the microscopic and macroscopic scales of complex network dynamics, New J. Phys., 17 No 4 (2015), 045009.

[18] L. Zhang, G. Huang, A. Liu and R. Fan, Stability Analysis for a Fractional HIV Infection Model with Nonlinear Incidence, Discrete Dyn. Nat. Soc., 2015 (2015) 563127, 11 pp.

[19] Y. A. Khalil R, Horani MAI, S. M, Journal of Computational and Applied A new de nition of fractional derivative, Journal of Computational and Applied Mathematics 264 (2014) 65–70.

[20] T. Abdeljawad, On conformable fractional calculus, Journal of compu-tational and Applied Mathematics 279 (2015) 57–66.

[21] D. R. Anderson, D. J. Ulness, Properties of the Katugampola fractional derivative with potential application in quantum mechanics, Journal of Mathematical Physics 56 (2015).

[22] Almeida, Ricardo. "Analysis of a fractional SEIR model with treatment." *Applied Mathematics Letters* 84 (2018): 56–62.

[23] Siddiqi, A. H., Masood Alam, and Pragati Tripathi. "Inverse Problems in Conformable Fractional Differential Equation." *Indian Journal of Industrial and Applied Mathematics* 10, no. 1 (2019): 34–51.

Smart Computing – Khan et al (Eds)
© *2021 Taylor & Francis Group, London, ISBN 978-0-367-76552-1*

Analysis of conformable fractional derivative model of SEIR–SEI epidemic

Arti Malik, Khursheed Alam & Nitendra Kumar
Department of Mathematics, Sharda University, Greater Noida, Uttar Pradesh, India

ABSTRACT: The Zika virus is one of the flavivirus epidemics which strikes especially pregnant women and toddlers, through the Aedes mosquito. The aggregate-affected human population is divided into susceptible, exposed, infectious, and recovered (SEIR). Therefore, a mathematical model named SEIR–SEI has been proposed to predict the number of infected individuals. The subject work illustrates the 2016 eruption of the Zika virus in Brazil through the advancement of Conformable Fractional Epidemic model. This article proposes a fractional epidemic SEIR–SEI model and exhibits a comparative study of the number of susceptible individuals with the Conformable Fractional Epidemic model, through some graphs.

1 INTRODUCTION

The Zika virus infects humans to cause Zika fever. The symptoms seen in the patient includes sudden onset of fever muscle weakness, skin rash and arthritis (Brasil 2016; Organization 2016). Zika virus fever is transmitted by the mosquitoes Aedes (Fernandes 2016). Reports have shown that men who have recovered from Zika can still transmit the virus to their partner through semen for up to seven weeks after recovery from the illness. The first documented case of Zika virus dates back to 1947 in the Zkia forest of Uganda, hence the name Zika virus disease. About April 2015, the first Zika virus authochthonic case was reported in Brazil (Dick 1952; Moore 1975; Vigilancia 2016). Nearly 87 countries have reported mosquitoborne Zika transmission as of July 2016 (Faria 2016). Agencies investigating the Zika virus outbreak are finding an increased body of evidence about the link between Zika and microcephaly (Santos 2016). The national health authorities in Brazil have reported potential neurological and auto-immune complication of Zika virus disease. There is also the scientific consensus about the same in the World Health Organization (WHO 2017. To control the spread of disease requires an dependable mathematical model which can accurately forecast the spread of disease during the outbreak and which can be put to use practically along with all the modalities of disease control program (Naheed 2014; Huppert 2013; Ferguson 2016) of various agencies.

This remainder of this paper is organized into four sections. In Section 2, the mathematical model is described and in Section 3 the basics of fractional calculus have been introduced. Section 4 compares the graphs of the various frameworks and finally the last section is dedicated to the contribution of the present work and suggestions for the future work.

2 MODEL EQUATIONS

The following (nonlinear) autonomous system of ordinary differential equations defines the evolvement of infected individuals through the SEIR–SEI group:

$$\frac{dS_h}{dt} = -\beta_h S_h I_v$$

DOI 10.1201/9781003167488-51

Table 1. Table of values of the parameters.

	Values	References
$\propto_h$	1/5.9	[Ferguson,2016; Ioos 2014;Lessler 2016; Villela 2017]
$\propto_m$	1/9.1	[Wong 2013;Chouin − Camerio 2016; Ferguson2016]
γ	1/7.9	[Villela 2017;Ferguson 2016;21.Funk2016]
β_h	1/11.3	[Ferguson 2016]
β_v	1/8.6	[Ferguson 2016]
S_h	205,953,959	
E_h	8,201	
I_h	8,201	
I_m	2.2×10^{-4}	

$$\frac{dE_h}{dt} = \beta_h S_h I_v - \alpha_h E_h$$

$$\frac{dI_h}{dt} = \alpha_h E_h - \gamma I_h$$

$$\frac{dR_h}{dt} = \gamma I_h$$

$$\frac{dS_m}{dt} = \delta - \frac{\beta_m S_m I_h}{N} - \delta S_m$$

$$\frac{dE_m}{dt} = \frac{\beta_m S_m I_h}{N} - (\delta_m + \delta)E_m$$

$$\frac{I_m}{dt} = \alpha_m E_m - \delta I_m$$

$$\frac{dC}{dt} = \alpha_h E_h \tag{1}$$

While the total human population is depicted by N, $\frac{1}{\alpha}$ indicates the incubation period ("h" corresponds t humans and "m" for mosquitoes). $1/\delta$ indicates the life cycle of mosquito and $1/\Upsilon$ is the transmission rate, specifically when β_h is the mosquito to human rate, β_m is the human to mosquito rate.

On the right-hand side the first δ of $\frac{dS_m}{dt}$ indicates that there is no change to the total mosquito count during the entire calculation. The $\frac{dC}{dt}$ equation evaluates the total number $c(t)$ of the affected people until time t; that is the total number of individuals that has contracted the disease so far or has earlier infected or is in the infectious group at the given time. This is the Classical Integer model. The graph of susceptible human beings over the 50th week of outbreak using the parameters from Table 1 is given below as Figure 1

In Figure 1, X axis shows the time period in weeks and Y axis reflects the number of susceptible humans.

3 CAPUTO FRACTIONAL DERIVATIVE

Even though the Fractional Calculus is established mainly in the pure branch of Mathematics, since it can give a more realistic interpretation of the real problem, this has found application in engineering, biology, and the allied sciences in the recent era (Diethelm, 2002). The Fractional

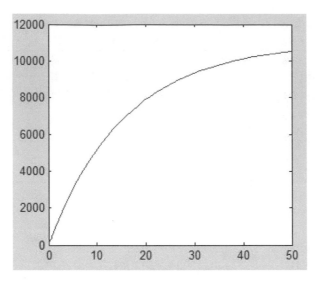

Figure 1.   Susceptible humans over 50th week as per integer order model.

Derivative may be defined as under:

$$
{}_a^c D_t^\alpha = {}_0 D_t^{-(n-\alpha)}
$$

$$
= \frac{1}{\Gamma(n-\alpha)} \int_0^t (t-\tau)^{n-\alpha-1} f^n(\tau) d\tau. \tag{2}
$$

Now we will consider the Caputo Derivative since it may be combined with the Classical Integer model:

$$
{}_a^c D_t^{\alpha_1} S_h = -\beta_h S_h I_v
$$

$$
{}_a^c D_t^{\alpha_2} E_h = \beta_h S_h I_v - \alpha_h E_h
$$

$$
{}_a^c D_t^{\alpha_3} I_h = \alpha_h E_h - \gamma I_h
$$

$$
{}_a^c D_t^{\alpha_4} R_h = \gamma I_h
$$

$$
{}_a^c D_t^{\alpha_5} S_m = \delta - \frac{\beta_m S_m I_h}{N} - \delta S_m
$$

$$
{}_a^c D_t^{\alpha_6} E_m = \frac{\beta_m S_m I_h}{N} - (\delta_m + \delta) E_m
$$

$$
{}_a^c D_t^{\alpha_7} I_m = \alpha_m E_m - \delta I_m
$$

$$
{}_a^c D_t^{\alpha_8} C = \alpha_h E_h \tag{3}
$$

From the above fractional order model, the graph of susceptible humans over the 50th week of outbreak using the same parameters as in Table 1 above can be drawn as under:

4   CONFORMABLE FRACTIONAL DERIVATIVE

The concept of Conformable Fractional Derivative has been studied by Khalil [2014].

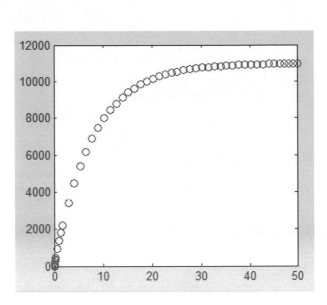

Figure 2. Susceptible humans over the 50th week as per the Caputo fractional order model.

Definition 1. The concept of Conformable Fractional Derivative [Khalil, 2014] is denoted by T_α of f for $0 < \alpha < 1$.

$$T_\alpha f(x) = \lim_{\varepsilon \to 0} \frac{f(x + \varepsilon x^{1-\alpha}) - f(x)}{\varepsilon}, \quad x > 0 \qquad (4)$$

provided the limit exists, in this case f is called α differentiable on $(0; \alpha)$ for the same, $\alpha > 0$ also

$$T_\alpha f(0) = lim_{x \to 0} T_\alpha f(x) \qquad (5)$$

It has been analyzed by Abdelhakin and Machado that if f is α differentiable in the conformable sense at $x > 0$, then it must be differentiable in the classical sense at x and

$$T_\alpha f(x) = x^{1-\alpha} f^i(x)$$

is satisfied.

Conformable Fractional Derivative also satisfies the properties provided by Katugampola as:

$$D^\alpha[p.f + q.g] = pD^\alpha[f] + qD^\alpha[g]$$

(Linear Property)

$$D^\alpha[fg] = f.D^\alpha[g] + g.D^\alpha[f]$$

(Product Rule)

$$D^\alpha[f(g)] = \frac{df}{dt} D^\alpha[g]$$

(Chain Rule)

The operator D^α satisfies

$$D^\alpha[y] = t^{1-\alpha} y \text{ or } D^\alpha = t^{1-\alpha} D.$$

For $1 < \alpha < 2$, $D^\alpha[y]$ that is anti derivative, I^α is as follows

$$(D^\alpha)^{-1} = (D)^{-\alpha} = I^\alpha = \int_\alpha^t \frac{1}{x^{1-\alpha}} dx$$

443

or

$$I^\alpha[D^\alpha[y]] = \int_a^t \frac{x^{1-\alpha}}{x^{1-\alpha}} y' dx = \int_\alpha^t y' dx = y$$

Definition 2. In Khalil [2014], let $\alpha \in (n, n+1)$ and f be an n-differentiable at t, where t > 0, then the conformable fraction derivative of order α is defined as

$$T_\alpha f'(t) = \lim_{\varepsilon > 0} \frac{f^{(|x|-1)} t + \varepsilon t^{(|x|-\alpha)} - f^{(|x|-1)} t}{\varepsilon}$$

where $[\alpha]$ is the smallest integer greater than equal to α.

Abdeljawad (2015) studied the Chain Rule, Gronwall Inequality and Integration of Parts formula and Laplace transform corresponding to the Conformable Fractional Derivative and Integral.

Various analogous properties of classical derivative including Roll's theorem, the Mean Value Theorem hold true. The concept of fractional derivative is defined in the following manner.

Definition 3. In Khalil (2014), Fractional Integral associated with the Conformable Fractional Derivative ($\propto$ derivative) is defined as:

$$I_\propto^a(f)(t) = I_t^a(t^{(\propto-1)}f) = \int_a^t \frac{f(x)}{x^{(\propto-1)}} dx \tag{6}$$

This definition has been given by Khalil et al (2014) that $T_\alpha I_\alpha^\alpha(f))(t) = f(t)$ are inverse of each other, namely $T_\alpha(I_\alpha^\alpha(f))(t) = f(t)$

For the t > a where f is continuous in the domain of T_α^a, it may be observed that $\alpha \in [0,1]$ and the integral is usual Riemann improper integral.

Definition 4. In Anderson (2015) Katugampola fractional derivative defined by $D^\alpha, 0 < \alpha < 1$ is defined as follows:

$$D^\alpha f(t) = \lim_{\epsilon \to 0} \frac{f^{(te^{\epsilon t})} - f(t)}{\epsilon} t > 0, \tag{7}$$
$$D^\alpha[f(0)] = \lim_{\epsilon \to 0} D^\alpha[f(t)].$$

Here, one interesting thing that arises is how conformable fractional derivative of a function f : $[0, \infty] \to R$ is related to minima and maxima of over $[0, \infty]$. The definition given by Kalugampala e-printarxiv:1410.6535, and studied in detail by Anderson (2015) is similar to conformable derivative based on the concept of limit rather than a fractional integral.

Here we consider the classical SEIR–SEI model in terms of Conformable Fractional Derivative:

$$t^{(1-\propto)} \frac{dS_h}{dt} = -\beta_h S_h I_v$$

$$t^{(1-\propto)} \frac{dE_h}{dt} = \beta_h S_h I_v - \alpha_h E_h$$

$$t^{(1-\propto)} \frac{dI_h}{dt} = \alpha_h E_h - \gamma I_h$$

$$t^{(1-\propto)} \frac{dR_h}{dt} = \gamma I_h$$

$$t^{(1-\propto)} \frac{dS_m}{dt} = \delta - \frac{\beta_m S_m I_h}{N} - \delta S_m$$

$$t^{(1-\propto)} \frac{dE_m}{dt} = \frac{\beta_m S_m I_h}{N} - (\sigma + \delta) E_m$$

$$t^{(1-\propto)} \frac{dI_m}{dt} = \alpha_m E_m - \delta I_m$$

$$t^{(1-\propto)} \frac{dC}{dt} = \alpha_h E_h \tag{8}$$

444

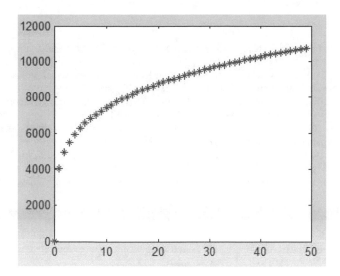

Figure 3.   Susceptible humans over the 50th week as per conformable fractional order model.

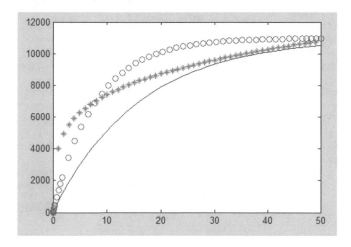

Figure 4.   Comparison of graphs: classical order model, Caputo model and conformable model.

From the above Fractional Order Model, the graph of susceptible humans over the 50th week of outbreak using same parameter from Table 1 reflects as under:

Below is the comparison of graphs of susceptible humans based on Integer Order Model, Caputo Fractional Order Model, and Conformable Fractional Order Model.

5   CONCLUSION

In the present paper we replaced Classical Derivative by Caputo Derivative and Conformable Derivative and studied the effects of this change which is visible in the graph. It is clear that in the time duration of 40–50 weeks, the numerical difference of susceptible persons as per the Conformable Model is almost equal to that of based on the Caputo and Classical Models.

REFERENCES

Abdeljawad, T. 2015. On conformable fractional calculus, Journal of computational and Applied Mathematics vol 279, 57–66.

Anderson, D. R. & D. J. Ulness, 2015. Properties of the Katugampola fractional derivative with potential application in quantum mechanics, Journal of Mathematical Physics vol 56,

Brasil, P. G. A. 2016. Zika Virus Outbreak in Rio de Janeiro, Brazil: Clinical Characterization, Epidemiological and Virological Aspects, PLOS Neglected Tropical Diseases vol 10, 1–13.

Chouin-Carneiro, 2016, T. A. Differential Susceptibilities of Aedes aegypti and Aedes albopictus from the Ameticas to Zika virus, PLOS Neglected Tropical Diseases: vol 10, 1–11.

Dick, G. S. Kitchen, 1952. A. Haddow, Zika virus isolations and serological specificity, Transactions of the Royal Society of Tropical Medicine and Hygiene vol 46, 509–520.

Diethelm, K. N. 2002. Analysis of Fractional Di erential Equations, Journal of Mathematical Analysis and Applications vol 265, 229–248.

Faria, R. R. d. 2016. Zika virus in the Americas: Early epidemiological and genetic ndings, Science vol 352, 345–349.

Ferguson, N. M. 2016. Countering the Zika epidemic in Latin America, vol. 353, (6297), 353–354.

Fernandes, R. S. 2016. Culex quinquefascia-tus from Rio de Janeiro Is Not Competent to Transmit the Local Zika Virus, PLOS Neglected Tropical Diseases vol 10, 1.13.

Funk, S. A. 2016. Comparative Analysis of Dengue and Zika Outbreaks Reveals Di erences by Setting and Virus, PLOS Neglected Tropical Diseases, vol 10(12):e0005173.

Huppert, A. G. 2013. Mathematical modeling and prediction in infectious disease epidemiology, Clinical Microbiology and Infection vol 19, 999–1005.

Ioos, S. 2014. Current Zika virus epidemiology and recent epidemics,vol 44(7):302–307.

Khalil, Y. A. & Horani, S. M. 2014, Journal of Computational and Applied A new de nition of fractional derivative, Journal of Computational and Applied Mathematics vol 264, 65–70.

Lessler, J. 2016. Times to key events in Zika virus infection and implications for blood donation: A systematic review, Bulletin of the World Health Organization vol 94, 841–849.

Lizarralde-Bejarano, D. P. S. 2017. Understanding epidemics from mathematical models: Details of the 2010 dengue epidemic in Bello (Antioquia, Colombia), Applied Mathematical Modelling vol 43, 566–578.

Moore, D. L. 1975. Arthropod-borne viral infections of man in Nigeria, 19641970, Annals of Tropical Medicine & Parasitology vol 69, 49–64.

Naheed A., M. Singh, D. Lucy, 2014, Numerical study of SARS epidemic model with the inclusion of diffusion in the system, Applied Mathematics and Computation vol 229 480–498.

Organization, W. H. 2016. Zika virus, https://www.who.int/news-room/ fact-sheets/detail/zika virus.

Organization, W. H. 2017. Zika virus, microcephaly and Guillain-Barr syn-drome situation report, Technical documents.

Santos, D. O. 2016. Zika Virus and the Guillain-Barre syndrome – Case series from seven countries. vol 375:1598–1601

Vigilancia, S. 2016. febre de chikungunya e febre pelo virus zika ate asemana spidemiologica, http// portalarquivos.saude.gov.br/images/pdf/2017/abril/06/2017-002-monitoramento-dos-casos-de-chikungu// nya-e-febre-pelo-v—rus-zika-ate-a-Semna-Epide,op;pgoca;-52//–.

Villela, D. A. 2017. Zika in Rio de Janeiro: Assessment of basic reproduction num-ber and comparison with dengue outbreaks., Epidemiology and infection, vol 145. 1649–1657.

Wong, P. S. 2013. Aedes (Stegomyia) albopictus (Skuse): A Potential Vector of Zika Virus in Singapore, PLoS Neglected Tropical Diseases vol 7(8): e2348.

Smart Computing – Khan et al (Eds)
© 2021 Taylor & Francis Group, London, ISBN 978-0-367-76552-1

Dark and low-contrast satellite image enhancement using DWT-SVD based on fuzzy logic technique

A.R. Verma & Pushkar Praveen
Department of ECED, G. B. Pant Institute of Engineering and Technology, Pauri, Uttarakhand, India

Bhumika Gupta
Department of CSE, G. B. Pant Institute of Engineering and Technology, Pauri, Uttarakhand, India

Surjeet Singh Patel
Department of EE, G. B. Pant Institute of Engineering and Technology, Pauri, Uttarakhand, India

ABSTRACT: This manuscript presents another way to deal with upgrading the dim and different satellite pictures utilizing Discrete Wavelet Transform–Singular Value Decomposition (DWT–SVD) dependent on Fuzzy rationale strategy. This procedure helps in wiping out high recurrence segments and clamor by deteriorating the picture into four repeat sub-bunches by using discrete wavelet change and registering the specific worth framework of LL sub-band. This particular worth lattice then goes through a Fuzzy Logic-based histogram adjustment (FHE). The covering limits of messiness, commotion, and target signals are isolated utilizing fluffy rationale. A fluffy induction motor is utilized to allot loads to various ghastly segments. Proposed conspire fundamentally functions admirably for upgrading dull and low difference satellite pictures. It recreates the upgraded picture by applying inverse wavelet Transform (IDWT). The test results show pervasiveness of the proposed methodology execution to the extent peak signal-to-noise ratio, mean square error, mean, and difference.

Keywords: DWT; SVD; Fuzzy Logic; IDWT.

1 INTRODUCTION

The satellite picture improvement is a significant advance for remotely detected cable and ethereal pictures as these are helpful in a few applications, for example, cosmology, land data, climatic data, climate, ranger service, fighting, fiasco monitory, geosciences concentrates, etc. [1,2]. When all is said and done, crude satellite picture have a moderately tight scope of brilliance esteem; hence, a complexity upgrade is much of the time used to improve the multiband cable pictures for better translation and representation [3,4]. One of the most significant superiority issues in satellite pictures originates from its complexity. Difference improvement is one of the most significant issues in picture preparing. Complexity is created by differentiation in concealing and splendor of the image. In case the separation of an image is especially centered around a particular range, the evidence may be misplaced in those domains which are extremely and reliably thought [1]. Essentially, the poor special visualizations emerge from the elements, for example, light, supplies, clamor, and so forth [2,3]. Commotion is the fundamental debasement factor for the satellite picture. Various kinds of clamor, for example, Gaussian commotion, multiplicative clamor, Poisson clamor, and so on exist in the environment which pollutes the nature of picture. We will probably improve the nature of picture by expelling clamor and high recurrence segments. There are a couple of plans, for instance, Generalized Histogram Equalization (GHE) [4–5], Singular Value Decomposition (SVD), gamma correction, Discrete cosine Transform (DCT), Discrete Wavelet Transform (DWT), and so forth. These strategies have been ad libbed later by joining at least two techniques together, for example, DCT–SVD [6], DWT–SVD, Fuzzy-rationale-based Histogram Equalization (FHE), and so forth. These techniques can be commonly ordered into two classifications: spatial area and recurrence space strategy. Spatial area techniques are utilized to work straightforwardly on pixels. The histogram balance strategies are one of the spatial area picture improvement procedures. Then again, recurrence area preparing procedures depend on adjusting the change space of a picture. The wavelet examination-based picture upgrade innovation is a recently evolved method [5]. The essential thought behind the utilization of change space is to upgrade picture by controlling the change coefficients. As of late, various upgrade calculations have been grown; nonetheless, every one of them can't be actualized in a versatile way. Accordingly, these procedures are a lot of comprehensive and experiential arrangements, just as not appropriate for all the pictures [5]. Be that as it may, to accomplish a strong strategy for dull satellite picture improvement with no loss of data is extremely troublesome in light of the fact that remote detecting picture displays progressively complex otherworldly character, for example, high-dimensional information investigation, choice of band, and a combination of acquired data. Thus, customary techniques to accomplish a vigorous upgrade for dim are not generally doable. As of late, heaps of strategies have been proposed utilizing wavelet change and different calculations, for example, nonlocal progressive word reference getting the hang of utilizing wavelets for picture de-noising, in which the multi-objectives construction and scarcity of wavelets are used by nonlocal word reference knowledge in each decay level of the wavelets [6–9].

This paper, as needs be, is an available improved philosophy for the overhaul of dull satellite pictures which relies upon versatile way utilizing DWT–SVD with fluffy rationale strategy. The wavelet investigation-based picture upgrade strategy is recently evolved procedure and being utilized as often as possible in many research regions. The crucial idea behind the wavelet speculation is to crumble the image in its four repeat sub-bands. These sub-bands are Low-Low (LL), Low-High (LH), High-Low (HL), and High-High (HH). The majority of the data exists in low recurrence band, so we preclude other high recurrence groups and apply the SVD in the LL band [10–17]. Since the LL sub-band has light data, SVD acted in LL sub-band for processing the versatile power change. At that point, IDWT is performed on this SVD picture alongside the other high recurrence parts (LH, HL, HH) so as to get the edge data of the picture. To identify the presentation of DWT–SVD with the fluffy rationale method, diverse amount parameters are utilized.

2 OVERVIEW OF DWT AND SVD

The discrete wavelet change is the on-going wavelet change utilized in picture preparing. Wavelet change is quicker, gives better pressure and is increasingly versatile. The principle preferred position of DWT is that it gives increasingly exact and proficient outcomes when contrasted with the fast Fourier transform (FFT) and DCT.

2.1 *Discrete Wavelet Transform (DWT)*

The DWT breaks down some random sign into a lot of essential capacities, which is known as wavelets. The wavelet change is the easiest method of performing Multi-Resolution Analysis (MRA). It is the procedure of putting away and handling the picture in different procedures. The DWT is an execution of the wavelet change using a discrete game plan of the wavelet scales and understandings agreeing to some described principles. By the day's end, this change separates the sign into regularly even course of action of wavelets. The fundamental idea of DWT is disintegrating the given data signal into four subparts using the property of conversion and augmentation, which is known as mother wavelet. The correct wavelet work is to be picked for wavelet crumbling of the image for getting wavelet constants. It is conceivable by utilizing a lot of limited motivation reaction channels, for example, low-pass and high-pass channels. A couple of channels are utilized to partition the recurrence into sub-bands. This procedure is rehashed recursively until the most minimal recurrence band of the given info picture is reached. The 2-D DWT decay of some random information picture can be acquired by utilizing 1-D wavelet change along the lines of the picture, first and afterward the resultants are deteriorated along the segments. This activity decay the given information picture into four subband pictures, which are known as LL, LH, HL, and HH recurrence groups [1,2]. This routine can be handled to acquire various "scale" wavelet disintegration. The DWT constants can be determined by taking the internal item between input sign and wavelet capacities. In this procedure, the DWT coefficients of one level can be determined from the DWT constants of the past level, which is spoken to as follows:

$$W_L(n,j) = \sum_m W_L(m, j-1)h(m-2n) \tag{1}$$

$$W_H(n,j) = \sum_m W_L(m, j-1)g(m-2n) \tag{2}$$

where WL (p, q) express the pth scaling constant at q^{th} level. WH(p, q) shows the pth wavelet constant at q^{th} level. Then again, h(n) and g(n) imply the widening constants comparing to scaling and wavelet works individually.

2.2 Overview of SVD

The Singular Value Decomposition (SVD), one of the most helpful apparatuses of direct polynomial math, is a factorization and deduction technique which successfully decreases any framework into a slighter invertible and square grid. One extraordinary element of SVD is that it tends to be done on any genuine m × n grid. The SVD method is spoken to by a rectangular network F, which can be disintegrated into the result of three frameworks. Each genuine lattice F can be separated into a result of three networks, calm as

$$F = USV^T \tag{3}$$

where U and V are known as symmetrical grids and S is recognized as particular estimations of network F, an inclining framework with nonnegative corner to corner sections in diminishing request. The askew passages of S are the confident square underlying foundations of the eigen approximations of AA^T and are known as the solitary approximations of A [22]. The decay F = USVT is known as a particular worth disintegration of an, and it tends to be composed as,

$$A = U_1 S_1 V_1^T + U_2 S_2 V_2^T + U_3 S_3 V_3^T + \ldots + U_n S_n V_n^T \tag{4}$$

Segments of U are recognized as left particular vectors of F, and sections of V are known as right solitary vectors of F [18]. Picture leveling utilizing SVD strategy relies on adjusting the solitary worth lattice acknowledged through SVD [22]. The total deterioration procedure is called as particular worth decay (SVD) of F which can likewise be composed as:

$$F = s_1 \begin{bmatrix} \cdot \\ u_1 \\ \cdot \end{bmatrix} [\cdot \quad v_1^T \quad \cdot] + \ldots + s_M \begin{bmatrix} \cdot \\ u_M \\ \cdot \end{bmatrix} [\cdot \quad v_M^T \quad \cdot] \tag{5}$$

where (for simplicity M N), $U = [u_1 \quad u_2 \quad \cdot \quad \cdot \quad u_M]$ and $V = [v_1 \quad v_2 \quad \cdot \quad \cdot \quad v_M]$ having sizes M × M and N × N are called unitary matrices and calculated as left FF^T and right F^TF eigen vectors correspondingly. Let $S = diag(s_1, s_2, \ldots s_M)$ with $s_1 \geq s_2 \geq \ldots \geq s_M \geq 0$, are singular values of F, then it can be written as:

$$F = \sum_{n=1}^{M} s_n u_n v_n^T = \sum_{n=1}^{M} F_n \tag{6}$$

where F_n are matrices of same sizes as F and are called modes of F [23].

The SVD speaks to the force data of picture, and any progressions on particular qualities change the power of the info picture. The principle favorable position of utilizing SVD for picture evening out is that S contains power data of the picture. Particular qualities give vitality data of the picture just as information on vitality dispersion.

449

3 FUZZY-SVD WITH IMAGE IMPROVEMENT

It is seen that the limits of messiness, clamor and object signals are not pointedly characterized [19]. That is the reason it is unimaginable to expect to separate solitary qualities precisely. At that point utilization of loads to hone the limits of messiness, commotion, and target signals is thought of. It is seen that when sn and Δ sn are high, at that point sn has a place with target and should be improved by applying substantial loads, in any case sn has a place with clamor and mess and should be smothered by doling out light loads [19]. Let w_n be the weight allocated to nth solitary worth; at that point the objective picture utilizing fluffy SVD is FFSVD:

$$F_{FSVD} = \sum_{n=2}^{M} F_n w_n \tag{7}$$

$$F_{FSVD} = \sum_{n=2}^{M} w_n s_2 u_2 v_2^T \tag{8}$$

The linear weight scheme is defined as follows:

$$W_n = \frac{\psi_1 s_n + \psi_1 \Delta s_n}{\psi_2} \tag{9}$$

where ψ_1 is constant used to regulator the effect of s_m and Δs_m and ψ_2 is regularizing constant.

3.1 Fuzzy logic-based Histogram Equalization (FHE)

In the ordinary histogram strategy, the remapping of histogram tops happens which prompts unwanted antiques and huge change in mean picture splendor. The proposed fluffy-based histogram adjustment jam splendor and furthermore improves the difference of the picture. It utilizes HSV shading space where just the V part is extended by safeguarding the chromatic data, for example, Hue (H) and Saturation (S). Extending the V part is performed under the upgrade parameters M and K [3]. This extending of V segment will give the changed adaptation of power esteem x_e [3].

The initial phase in the projected strategy is to change over the given RGB picture into HSV and afterward compute the histogram H(x) where x $\in$ V. There are two bounds, M and K, which control the degree at which the force esteem x must be escalated thus known as increase parameters. M is known as the normal power estimation of the picture is determined from the histogram as given in Equation (9). The parameter M isolates the histogram H(x) into two sections. The initial segment C1 contains pixels esteems in the range [0, M − 1] and the second part C2 in the range [M, 255]:

$$M = \frac{\sum_x XH(x)}{\sum_x H(x)} \tag{10}$$

The extending of V part depends on two fluffy enrollment esteems μD1 and μD2, firm for C1 and C2 class of pixels separately [3]. The other control parameter K is to process the upgraded power esteems xe. It chooses the extending point to which the power esteems x ought to be extended dependent on μD1 and μD2. From the test investigation, we for the most part allot K = 128 (the estimation of K depends upon the extent the stretching required), which gives improved results for the small contrast and dark-colored pictures. The fuzzy relationship value μ_{D1} for class C_1 is calculated from the fuzzy rule which is as follows.

3.2 The LARGER is the contrast among x and m, the SMALLER is the force of extending

The above standard shows that the pixels esteems nearer to M will be stretched advanced while values beyond from M will be lengthy lesser. Pixel esteems lying in the middle of will be expanded relatively. The above fluffy guideline can be scientifically spoken to as:

$$\mu_{D1}(x) = \frac{1 - (M - x)}{M} \tag{11}$$

where $x \in C_1$. After the relationship value for x is obtained, the increased value x_e for class C_1 can be calculated as follows:

$$x_e = x + \mu_{D1}(x)K \tag{12}$$

The fuzzy relationship value μ_{D2} for class C_2 is the fuzzy rule as follows.

3.3 *The LARGER is the contrast among x and e, the LARGER is the power of extending*

The above guideline shows that the pixels regard closer to E will be expanded lesser while values farther from E will be broadened higher. Pixel regards lying in will be long, respectively, [3]. To execute the above feathery standard the going with numerical depiction can be used:

$$\mu_{D2}(x) = \frac{E - x}{E - M} \tag{13}$$

where $x \in C_2$. After the participation esteem for x is acquired, the increased worth xe for class C2 can be gotten as follows:

$$x_e = (X\mu_{D2}(X)) + (E - \mu_{D2}(X)K) \tag{14}$$

The old x estimations of the V part are supplanted with the improved xe esteems that will make the V segment be extended bringing about difference and brilliance upgraded segment Ve. This better segment Ve can be joined with the Hue and Saturation segments in order to get upgraded picture HSVe which is at long last changed over to upgraded RGB picture [3].

4 PROPOSED METHODOLOGY

The proposed take a shot at improvement of satellite picture is done in two sections. The first is versatile force change strategy on prepared LL band the edges are moved in other sub-groups (i.e., LH, HL, and HH). In this way, isolating the high-recurrence sub-groups and applying brightening improvement utilizing fluffy rationale procedure in LL sub-band will shield the edge data from conceivable debasement. The subsequent one is SVD, which is a particular worth lattice as referenced in Section 2. The SVD contains the enlightenment data in the picture, with the goal that the alteration of solitary qualities will straightforwardly change the light of the picture, and other data existing in the picture will be as same as in the past and afterward resulting to recreating the last picture by utilizing IDWT. The last satellite picture won't just be upgraded concerning enlightenment, however, will likewise be more honed.

The following advances are to be embraced to perform primary computational procedure of the projected calculation.

(i) In the absolute initial step, a dull and low differentiation multispectral cable picture has been taken for the preparing. In the whole reproduction process, just dull pictures have been chosen to check the heartiness of the projected calculation. The mean estimations of info pictures are extremely low, which demonstrates dimmer power locales.

(ii) Adjust the satellite picture utilizing the general histogram evening out method to improve the power area for additional handling.

(iii) After the histogram adjustment, Figure 1-level DWT deterioration of the info picture for differentiates improvement of each band, for sample, NIR band, red band, and green band.

(iv) In the wake of getting DWT segments utilizing GHE and straight DWT segment, SVD is practical in a little recurrence segment LL for the figuring of S, V, and D.

(v) After SVD then apply fuzzy logic technique.

(vi) Compute new value F_{FSVD}.

(vii) After computing new F_{FSVD}, apply IDWT using F_{FSVD}, LH, HL, and HH.

451

(viii) At last, the improved upgraded multispectral cable picture is acquired deprived of obscuring and loss of data.

(ix) Ascertain the necessary execution parameters like peak signal-to-noise ratio (PSNR) and mean square error (MSE) to plaid in general superiority and quality of the improved picture.

5 RESULTS AND DISCUSSION

As a rule, crude satellite pictures have a generally restricted scope of brilliance esteems; thus, differentiate upgrade is every now and again used to improve the multiband cable pictures for improved translation and representation. There are a few techniques which have been utilized for cable picture improvement. In this paper, three procedures (DCT–SVD, DWT–SVD, and DWT–SVD utilizing fluffy rationale) are utilized for correlation reason. We have taken one diverse low differentiation satellite pictures. Figure 1 speaks to the info picture experiences the proposed calculation (DWT–SVD–FHE). Figure 1(a) shows low differentiation satellite picture. This picture at that point experiences the procedure of DWT appeared in Figure 1(b). DWT breaks down the pictures in four recurrence groups LL, LH, HL, HH. At that point, SVD is performed on pictures. Figure 1(c) shows the red SVD segment of the picture, 1(d) shows the green SVD part of picture, and 1(e) shows the blue SVD part of picture. Figure 1(f) shows consolidated SVD of the picture. Figure 1(g) shows the image in HSV colour space (fuzzified). Figure 1(h) shows fuzzified picture in

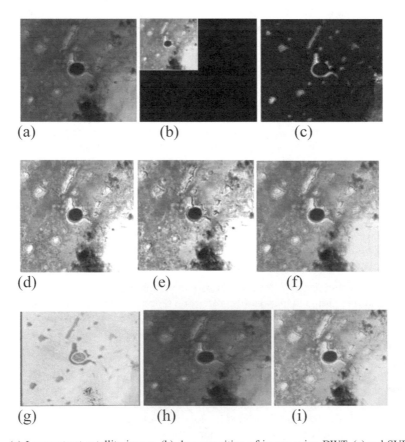

Figure 1. (a) Lowcontrast satellite image, (b) decomposition of image using DWT, (c) red SVD piece of image, (d) green SVD piece of image, (e) blue SVD piece of image, (f) combined SVD of image, (g) image in HSV color space (fuzzified), (h) shows fuzzified image in RGB color space and (i) finally enhanced image.

Table 1. Fedlity parameters.

input image		DCT–SVD		Output of DWT–SVD		DWT–SVD–FHE	
Mean (μ)	Variance (σ)	PSNR (α)	MSE (β)	PSNR (α)	MSE (β)	PSNR (α)	MSE (β)
0.2389	0.0422	$\alpha = 49.5644$	$\beta = 0.7188$	$\alpha = 49.5058$	$\beta = 0.7286$	$\alpha = 59.5538$	$\beta = 0.0726$

HSV shading space. Finally, HSV pictures is changed over back to RGB shading space. Figure 1(i) shows at last the improved picture. Quantitative execution measures arc significant in looking at changed picture upgrade calculations. In this segment execution of DCT–SVD, DWT–SVD, and the projected DWT–SVD utilizing FHE is assessed by thinking about constancy of the recreated picture to unique picture.

For this unkind, difference, PSNR and MSE constraints are thought of. Distinctive cable pictures are utilized to exhibit the aftereffect of this calculation. The following huge parameters are thought of:

$$\text{Mean}(\mu) = \frac{1}{RS} \sum_{x=1}^{P-1} \sum_{y=1}^{S-1} I(i,j) \tag{15}$$

$$\text{Variance }(\sigma) = \frac{1}{RS} \sum_{x=1}^{P-1} \sum_{y=1}^{S-1} (I(i,j) - \mu)^2 \tag{16}$$

Here, $I(i,j)$ is the power of the picture of size $R \times S$. Mean (μ) is the normal of all force esteems. It specifies standard magnificence of the image and change is the square of the deviation of the forces from the mean. PSNR processes top sign to clamor proportion in decibels between two pictures. It is quality estimation among unique and improved pictures. High PSNR implies better nature of the improved picture. MSE is another parameter to think about the upgraded and unique pictures. It gives the mistake framework between the two. Higher estimation of MSE implies the higher mistake and lower estimation of MSE speaks to bring down blunder. It is characterized as

$$\text{MSE}(\alpha) = \frac{\sum_{P,Q} [I_1(i,j) - I_2(i,j)]^2}{RS} \tag{17}$$

where I_1 is the original image and I_2 is the enhanced image of dimension $R \times S$. PSNR is calculated using the following equation:

$$\text{PSNR }(\beta) = 10 \log_{10} \frac{P^2}{MSE} \tag{18}$$

where P is the most extreme variance in input picture and PSNR is determined in dB. The proposed calculation is performed over a low-complexity satellite picture. Various parameters are determined and are summarized in Table 1.

6 CONCLUSION

This paper proposes a satellite picture differentiation and brilliance upgrade procedure dependent on DWT–SVD followed by Fuzzy rationale based FHE. The proposed method utilizes DWT to part a picture into lower and higher recurrence sub-groups. These sub-groups are LL, LH, HL, and HH. At that point SVD is performed over the low recurrence part of picture so as to improve enlightenment data. High recurrence parts are precluded from this procedure with the goal that limit data doesn't get contorted. After that acquired picture is gone through the FHE procedure. The picture is changed over into the HSV shading space. Histogram and other required escalation parameters are determined and gotten upgraded HSV picture is changed over back in RGB shading space. At that point backward DWT is performed over new LL, LH, HL and HH sub-groups. The projected method has been tried on different satellite pictures where mean difference, PSNR, MSE and graphic outcomes obviously display the predominance of projected procedure over traditional strategies.

REFERENCES

[1] Ashish, B.K., Kumar, A., & Padhy, P.K. 2011. "Satellite image processing using discrete cosine transform and singular value decomposion", Advances in Digital Image Processing and Information Technology, 205, 277–290.

[2] Aishwarya, K.M., Rachana, Ramesh., Sobarad, Preeti, M., "lossy image compression using SVD coding Algorithm".

[3] Bhandari, AK., Soni, V., Kumar, A., Singh, G.K., 2014, "Cuckoo search algorithm based satellite image contrast and brightness enhancement using DWT–SVD", ISA Transactions.

[4] Bhandari, A. K., Kumar, Anil., Siingh, G.K., Soni, Vivek. 2015. "Dark satellite image enhancement using knee transfer function and gamma correction based on DWT-SVD".

[5] Bhandari, AK., Soni,V., Kumar, A., Singh, GK. 2013 "Improved subband adaptive thresholding function for denoising of satellite image based on eolutionary algorithms", IET Signal Process, 7(8):720—30.

[6] Bhandari, AK., Kumar, A., Padhy, PK. 2012, "Improved normalized difference vegetation index method based on discrete cosine transform and singular value decomposition for satellite image processing", IET signal process, 6(7):617–25.

[7] Chitwong, S., Boonmee, T., Cheevasuvit,F. 2002, "Enhancement of color image obtained from the PCA-FCM technique using local area histogram equalization", Proc SPIE, 4787:98–106.

[8] Donoho, DL. 1995. "Denoising by soft thresholding", IEEE Trans Inf Theory, 41: 613–27.

[9] Donoho, DL., Jhonstone, IM. 1994. "Ideal spatial adaption by wavelet shrinkage", Biomertrika, 81(3):425–55.

[10] Gonzalez, RC. 2002. Woods, RE., "Digital Image Processing", 2nd edition. Singapore: Pearson Prentice-Hall.

[11] Gupta, V., Kumar, L., Kumari, U. 2011. "Color satellite image segmentationusing markov random field and, multiresolution wavelet trandsform", IJCAES.

[12] Iqbal MZ, Ghafoor A, Siddiqui AM. 2013. "Satellite image resolution enhancement using dual-tree complex wavelet transform and nonlocal means", IEEE Geosci remote sens let, 10(3):451–5.

[13] Kim TK, Paik JK, Kang BS. 1998. "Contrast enhancement system using spatially adaptive histogram equalization with temporal filtering", IEEE Trans Consum Electron, 44(1):82–7.

[14] Michailovich, OV., Tannenbum, A. 2006 ."Despeckling of ultrasoumd images", IEEE trans Ultrason, Ferroelectr Freq Control, 53(1):64–78.

[15] Magudeeswaran, V., Ravichandran,C.G., "Fuzzy logic-based Histogram Equlization for Image Contrast Enhancement", 891864.

[16] Rabbani, H. 2009. "Image denoising in steerable pyramid domain based on a local laplae prior", Elsevier J Pattern Recognit, 42(9): 2181–93.

[17] Riaz, M. M., Ghafoor, A. 2012. "Fuzzy logic and singular value decomposition based through wall image enhancement", June.

[18] Raju, G., Madhu,S. Nair, "A fast and efficient color image enhancement method based on fuzzy-logic and histogram".

[19] Zhang, B., Mukherjee, R., Abbas, A., Romagnoli, J. A. 2010, "Multi-resolution fuzzy clustering approach for image-based particle characterization".

Smart Computing – Khan et al (Eds)
© *2021 Taylor & Francis Group, London, ISBN 978-0-367-76552-1*

Vertical feature pyramid networks

Shivam Raj & Natasha Sebastian
Department of Electrical Engineering, Delhi Technological University, New Delhi, India

Anil Singh Parihar
Department of Computer Science Engineering, Delhi Technological University, New Delhi, India

ABSTRACT: In this paper, a new scalable configuration is introduced for arranging Feature Pyramid Networks (FPNs) known as Vertical FPNs or VFPNs. Our work is an alternative approach to the one commonly employed for computer vision tasks. The FPNs are parallelized for improved learning of complex features directly from backbone. Our hypothesis is validated by parallelizing EfficientDets FPNs. This method of scaling is an effective method to boost the performance and improve the mAP.

1   INTRODUCTION

Object detection is a computer vision task that is utilized to detect various objects in images. Due to the rapid growth of deep learning methods, the performance of object detectors has enhanced over the years.

One-stage object detectors like YOLO by Redmon et al. (2016) and SSD by Liu et al. (2016) surpass the previously existing two-stage detectors like Faster Region-Based Convolutional Neural Networks (RCNNs) by Ren et al. (2017) in terms of speed but lies behind in localization and object recognition accuracy.

There have been numerous changes over the recent years in the designing of object detectors to improve their efficiency. From anchor-based detectors such as YOLOv2 by Redmon and Farhadi (2017) and foreground-background class imbalance-based RetinaNet by Lin et al. (2017), to keypoint based detectors CornerNet by Law and Deng (2018), and CenterNet by Duan et al. (2019). On the other hand, EfficientDet by Tan et al. (2019) overcomes the task of representing and processing multi-scale features. This is done by using bi-directional feature pyramid networks (FPNs) for fusion of features and a compound scaling method.

For better accuracy in detecting an object in an image, it must extract more semantic features. Hence, the paper explores the techniques of feature fusion. FPNs play a crucial role in fusing of the features in this paper. Our work focuses on the previous bi-directional FPNs in EfficientDet. Parallel pathways have been used to merge the features and it has been comprehended how this increases the accuracy in comparison to the previous EfficientDet-D0 and EfficientDet-D1 architectures, achieving state-of-the-art performance.

2   RELATED WORK

2.1   *Feature fusion methods*

Feature pyramidal hierarchy in the works of Lin et al. (2017) is utilized to integrate the different scale feature maps. It comprises of a bottom-up and a top-down structure bridged together by lateral connections. This aids in capturing strong semantics at all levels with fine resolutions. PANet in

DOI 10.1201/9781003167488-53

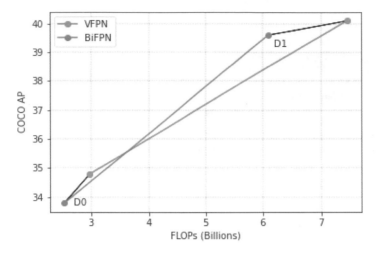

Figure 1. Performance enhancement with VFPN.

Liu et al. (2018) is another network that boosts information flow by adding a bottom-up path to the already existing FPNs and aggregates the features by adaptive feature pooling. Further, neural architecture search is used to discover new superior architectures like NAS-FPN by Ghiasi et al. (2019) for object detectors using FPNs.

2.2 *Bidirectional feature pyramid networks*

The BiFPN in EfficientDet follows the PANet architectural design. The nodes with one input edge are withdrawn, while extra edges are added where the original and output nodes are at the same level. The changes in the PANet structure are made taking into account the contribution of features and additional costs incurred.

When the features of various resolutions are fused via FPNs, they are simply resized and appended. Since the input features are at different resolutions they impart unbalanced features. Weighted feature fusion is used to tackle this matter. The weights help the nodes to learn the significance of each input feature, hence assist in the final fusion.

In this paper, the BiFPNs are arranged in parallel for better feature fusion. This technique diversifies the features and incorporates more features for better object recognition. The code is available at https://github.com/shivam-raj/automl/tree/master/efficientdet.

3 PROPOSED APPROACH

3.1 *Problem formulation*

FPN helps the network to learn from different parts of the backbone network (which is primarily responsible for feature extraction) and has been widely employed to solve a variety of computer vision tasks including Classification and Object Detection.

NAS–FPN introduced the concept of repeating FPNs, one after the other, for better performance. Tan et al. (2019) introduced BiFPN and achieved better performance by repeating BiFPN similar to NAS–FPN.

The limitation of stacking BiFPN in series is that you can only learn a fixed amount of features before the stacking of the FPNs make them saturated and henceforth, the following layers redundant. This is why one can't learn more complex features by adding more layers in series. Since one FPN only is learning from what the FPN layer behind them learns, this saturation occurs, increasing

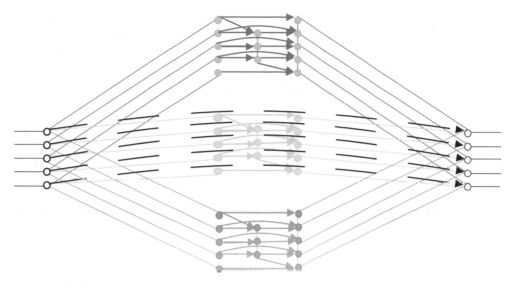

Figure 2.   Parallelized FPNs with three paths.

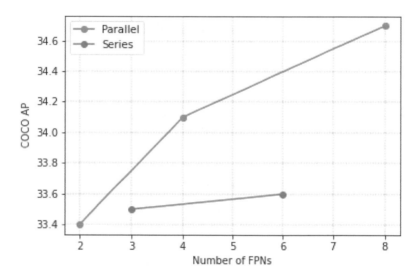

Figure 3.   Effect of stacking layers in different ways and their effect on COCO validation dataset.

the FPN depth after a certain depth stops having an effect on the network as a whole for better generalization.

Therefore, this saturation problem needs to be tackled by arranging the FPNs in a different configuration than the one introduced by PANet. Each of the FPNs need to learn different features from backbone, independent of each other so that the features learned by one FPN doesn't bottleneck the learning of other FPNs.

3.2   *Proposed solution*

Our approach revolves around stacking FPNs layers in parallel. Each FPN layer is allowed to learn from the backbone (in this case, EfficientNets in Tan et al. (2019) pre-trained on ImageNet database with auto augment). This way each FPN layer in parallel learns from the same backbone and are responsible for generalizing different features. Each of their contribution is being trained by fast attenuation method introduced by EfficientDet. Then every FPN layer in parallel is fed into a final FPN layer which accumulates the results of each FPN layer.

A weighted residual skip connection is introduced from the backbone to the final FPN layer which further feeds directly into the Class and Box Regressor. Since one FPN doesn't affect the learning of other FPNs in parallel (since their connections are independent of each other), the saturation of learning features is avoided this way. The contribution of each FPN is made to be learned on its own during the training process, though an ablation study may be conducted to remove the very weak learners and thus improve the efficiency of the network.

As is evident from Figure 3, one can see the evident effect of stacking layers in series and parallel. One can allow the network to learn more complex features which is helpful for the prediction task by stacking more FPNs in parallel.

The BiFPN configuration has already proven to work better for this network. As it is observed, there is no saturation of features occurring in the parallel configuration since random initialization of each of the FPN layers makes it possible for all of them to learn different features. Weighted connection assures the contribution of weak learners and strong learners.

4 EXPERIMENTAL SETUP

For the training and evaluation, the COCO dataset is used. The pre-trained EfficientNet B0 trained on ImageNet was used for feature extraction. The method of training is the same as EfficientDet. All models were trained on a TPUv3-8 device with 200 epochs with a batch size of 768. Focal Loss was used with $\alpha = 0.25$ and $\gamma = 1.5$ and aspect ratios $\{1/2,1,2\}$. The exponential moving average was used with a decay of 0.9998 and the activation function was Swish as in Ramachandran et al. (2017). The SDG optimizer is used with a weight decay of 4e-5 and a momentum of 0.9 was used. Learning rate increases from 0 to 0.16 for first epoch and then follows the cosine LR decay. For pre-processing, RetinaNet is used like in EfficientDet.

Table 1. Boost in performance with VFPN.

Model	AP	Params	FLOPs
EfficientNet-B0 + BiFPN	33.8	3.9M	2.54B
EfficientNet-B0 + VFPN	34.8	4.5M	2.98B
EfficientNet-B1 + BiFPN	39.6	6.6M	6.10B
EfficientNet-B1 + VFPN	40.1	7.8M	7.45B

5 RESULTS

Instead of increasing depth (in series), the paths can be scaled (in parallel) to get better accuracy. Although the cost of increasing paths is higher than increasing depth in terms of parameters, the accuracy achieved is higher than stacking multiple FPNs in series.

To prove the scalability of the network we train D1 model of EfficientDet replacing BiFPN in series with BiFPNs in parallel. An improvement of 0.5% mAP in D1 and 1.1% mAP in D0 on COCO test-dev dataset is observed. There is a FLOPS vs. accuracy trade off.

Better results can be achieved by increasing the paths, rather than increasing the depth of the network. This method of scaling the network works better than the one introduced by PANet.

Table 2. Performance on COCO test-dev dataset.

Model	AP_{test}	AP_{50}	AP_{75}	AP_S	AP_M	AP_L	AR_1	AR_{10}	AR_{100}	AR_S	AR_M	AR_L
VFPN-D1	40.1	59.4	43.0	18.8	44.7	56.6	32.8	51.4	54.4	29.0	61.1	74.1
EfficientDet-D1	39.6	58.6	42.3	17.9	44.3	56.0	–	–	–	–	–	–
VFPN-D0	34.8	53.3	36.9	12.9	39.4	52.6	29.5	45.5	48.1	19.3	55.7	70.2
EfficientDet-D0	33.8	52.2	35.8	12.0	38.3	51.2	–	–	–	–	–	–
DSSD513	33.2	53.3	35.2	13.0	35.4	51.1	–	–	–	–	–	–
YOLOv3	33.0	57.9	34.4	18.3	35.4	41.9	–	–	–	–	–	–
SSD513	31.2	50.4	33.3	10.2	34.5	49.8	–	–	–	–	–	–
GRP-DSOD320	30.0	47.9	31.8	10.9	33.6	46.3	28.0	42.1	44.5	18.8	49.1	65.0
R-FCN	29.9	51.9	–	10.8	32.8	45.0	–	–	–	–	–	–
YOLOv2	21.6	44.0	19.2	5.0	22.4	35.5	20.7	31.6	33.3	9.8	36.5	54.4

6 CONCLUSION

In this paper, a novel method of arranging FPNs is introduced which outperforms the current state of the art in terms of accuracy (in the low accuracy regime). This is scaled to the other backbone (namely EfficientNet B1) to showcase its scalability. A combination of increasing depth and paths may be used in search for better configuration in future works. We can also manually remove the weak learners which are contributing less to the final FPN layer to better the networks' efficiency.

REFERENCES

J. Dai, Y. Li, K. He, & J. Sun 2016. R-FCN: Object Detection via Region-Based Fully Convolutional Networks. In Proceedings of the 30th International Conference on Neural Information Processing Systems, 2016, pp. 379–387.

K. Duan, S. Bai, L. Xie, H. Qi, Q. Huang & Q. Tian 2019. CenterNet: Keypoint Triplets for Object Detection. 2019 IEEE/CVF International Conference on Computer Vision (ICCV), Seoul, Korea (South), 2019, pp. 6568-6577, doi: 10.1109/ICCV.2019.00667.

G. Ghiasi, T. Lin, & Q. v Le 2019. NAS-FPN: Learning Scalable Feature Pyramid Architecture for Object Detection. In 2019 IEEE/CVF Conference on Computer Vision and Pattern Recognition (CVPR), 2019, pp. 7029–7038, doi: 10.1109/CVPR.2019.00720.

H. Law & J. Deng 2018. CornerNet: Detecting Objects as Paired Keypoints. In European Conference on Computer Vision (ECCV), Sep. 2018.

T. Lin, P. Dollár, R. Girshick, K. He, B. Hariharan & S. Belongie 2017. Feature Pyramid Networks for Object Detection. 2017 IEEE Conference on Computer Vision and Pattern Recognition (CVPR), Honolulu, HI, 2017, pp. 936–944, doi: 10.1109/CVPR.2017.106.

T. Lin, P. Goyal, R. Girshick, K. He & P. Dollár 2017. Focal Loss for Dense Object Detection. 2017 IEEE International Conference on Computer Vision (ICCV), Venice, 2017, pp. 2999–3007, doi: 10.1109/ICCV.2017.324.

S. Liu, L. Qi, H. Qin, J. Shi & J. Jia 2018. Path Aggregation Network for Instance Segmentation. 2018 IEEE/CVF Conference on Computer Vision and Pattern Recognition, Salt Lake City, UT, 2018, pp. 8759–8768, doi: '10.1109/CVPR.2018.00913.

Liu W. et al. 2016. SSD: Single Shot MultiBox Detector. In Computer Vision – ECCV 2016, 2016, pp. 21–37.

Mingxing Tan & Quoc V. Le. 2019. Efficientnet: Rethinking model scaling for convolutional neural networks. ICML, 2019.

P. Ramachandran, B. Zoph, & Q. v Le 2017. Searching for Activation Functions. In arXiv e-prints, p. arXiv:1710.05941, Oct. 2017.

J. Redmon & A. Farhadi 2017. YOLO9000: Better, Faster, Stronger. 2017 IEEE Conference on Computer Vision and Pattern Recognition (CVPR), Honolulu, HI, 2017, pp. 6517–6525, doi: 10.1109/CVPR.2017.690.

J. Redmon, S. Divvala, R. Girshick & A. Farhadi, 2016. You Only Look Once: Unified, Real-Time Object Detection. 2016 IEEE Conference on Computer Vision and Pattern Recognition (CVPR), Las Vegas, NV, 2016, pp. 779–788, doi: 10.1109/CVPR.2016.91.

S. Ren, K. He, R. Girshick & J. Sun 2017. Faster R-CNN: Towards Real-Time Object Detection with Region Proposal Networks. In IEEE Transactions on Pattern Analysis and Machine Intelligence, vol. 39, no. 6, pp. 1137–1149, 1 June 2017, doi: 10.1109/TPAMI.2016.2577031.

Z. Shen et al. 2017. Improving Object Detection from Scratch via Gated Feature Reuse. In arXiv e-prints, p. arXiv:1712.00886, Dec. 2017.

M. Tan, R. Pang, & Q. v Le 2019. EfficientDet: Scalable and Efficient Object Detection. In arXiv e-prints, p. arXiv:1911.09070, Nov. 2019.

Smart Computing – Khan et al (Eds)
© 2021 Taylor & Francis Group, London, ISBN 978-0-367-76552-1

Modified Taylor wavelet Galerkin method for the numerical solution of one-dimensional partial differential equations

Ankit Kumar & Sag Ram Verma
Department of Mathematics and Statistics, Gurukula Kangri Vishwavidyalaya, Haidwar, India

ABSTRACT: In the present study, Modified Taylor wavelets Galerkin method-based approximation scheme is used to get out appropriate numerical solution of certain partial differential equations. The Modified Taylor wavelets are used with weight functions and these wavelets are supposed basis elements which permit the derivision of numerical solutions of partial differential equations. Some of the counter problems are given to show the numerical results extractive by proposed schemes which are compared with already established numerical methods, i.e., Coifman wavelet method, Finite Difference Method (FDM), Hermite Wavelet Galarkin Method (HWGM), and exact solution to set out the relevancy and efficiency of the introduced method.

Keywords: Wavelet, Modified Taylor Wavelet basis, Galerkin Method, Finite Difference Method, Numerical solution.

1   INTRODUCTION

For roughly 30 years, wavelets concept have been comparatively used in numerical techniques for solving complicated partial differential equations (PDEs) (Chui, 1992). In the subject of wavelet theory, contribution of fast wavelet transform introduced by Mallat and compact support orthogonal wavelets by Ingrid Daubechies (Daubechies 1988, Daubechies 1992) for PDEs received momentum in a pleasant way. Also, PDEs are used in the field of mechanical engineering such as elasticity, electrostatics (Farlow, 1993; Jost, 2002), etc. In recent years, many approximation schemes are applied to study the analytical solution of PDEs. Despite this we need wavelets Galarkin methods because it gives more accurate results. Wavelets Galarkin methods (Amaratunga and William, 1994; Mosevic 1977) has led tremendously vast usages in the area of mathematical science and in the field of engineering and it is becoming increasingly prominent in the advancement of numerical procedures for the study of PDEs over spectral procedures or finite difference method (FDM) (Chang et al. 2011). In this work, we use modified Taylor wavelet scheme which is to combine Galerkin method in solving PDES. This method depends on series approximation for the numerical solution by modified Taylor wavelets (MTWs) with unknown parameters. The rest of our paper is organized as follows. Section 2 deals with a basic definition of Modified Taylor wavelets and Section 3 consists of a procedure of the solution of the Modified Taylor Wavelet Galerkin Method. Numerical problems are demonstrated in Section 4. Finally, in Section 5 conclusions of the proposed work are discussed.

2   BASIC DEFINITION OF MODIFIED TAYLOR WAVELETS

A class of functions which is obtained by the translation and dilation of the single function ψ , called mother wavelet (or wavelet). The following wavelets are continuous if the dilation parameter

DOI 10.1201/9781003167488-54

ξ and translation parameter ζ vary continuously (Keshavarz and Ordokhani, 2019) such as

$$\psi_{\xi,\zeta}(z) = \frac{1}{\sqrt{|\xi|}}\psi\left(\frac{z-\zeta}{\xi}\right); \quad \xi, \zeta \in R; \ \xi \neq 0. \tag{1}$$

Here, translation ζ and dilation ξ are parameters in R. If we are setting parameters values, $\xi = \xi_0^{-k}$, $\zeta = n\zeta_0\xi_0^{-k}, \xi_0 > 1$, $\zeta_0 > 0$, where n, $k \in Z^+$ in Equation (1) then it is known as discrete wavelets. The discrete wavelets are written with the help of above equation such as

$$\psi_{k,n}(z) = |\xi_0|^{k/2}\psi\left(\xi_0^k z - n\zeta_0\right), \tag{2}$$

where $\psi_{k,n}(z)$ forms a wavelet basis for the square integrable functions space $L^2(R)$. Now, the Taylor wavelets $\psi_{n,m}(z) = \psi(k, \hat{n}, m, z)$ have four arguments: $\hat{n} = n - 1$, $n = 1, 2 \ldots 2^{k-1}$, here, order of Taylor polynomial is m and normalized time is z. They are defined on the interval $[0, 1]$ in (Keshavarz and Ordokhani, 2019),

Next, we define the following modified Taylor wavelets (MTWs) such as

$$\overline{\psi}_{n,m}(z) = \begin{cases} \sqrt{2}^{k-1} v_m\left(2^{k-1}z - n + 1\right), & if \ \frac{n-1}{2^{k-1}} \leq z < \frac{n}{2^{k-1}} \\ 0, & otherwise \end{cases} \tag{3}$$

where $v_m(z)$ are orthogonal Taylor polynomials which are obtained by applying well-known Gram-schmidt orthogonalization processes on normal Taylor Polynomials $\hat{T}_m(z)$; see Keshavarz and Ordokhani (2019), and m is the degree of the Taylor polynomial which is defined on the interval $[0, 1]$ and given by the aid of the following recursive formula:

$$v_m(z) = \sqrt{2m+1}\left(\frac{m!^2}{2m!}\right)L_m\left(2^k z - 2n + 1\right) \tag{4}$$

Here, $L_m(z)$ is usual Legendre polynomial (Razzaghi and Yousefi, 2001). For $k = 1$ in Equations (3) and (4), then some MTWs are given as

$$\overline{\psi}_{1,0}(z) = 1, \ \overline{\psi}_{1,1}(z) = \sqrt{3}\left(z - \frac{1}{2}\right), \ \overline{\psi}_{1,2}(z) = \sqrt{5}\left(z^2 - z + \frac{1}{6}\right).$$

2.1 Function approximation

A function $u(z) \in L^2(R)$ defined over $[0, 1]$ can be expressed as linear combination of modified Taylor wavelets series (MTWS) as

$$u(z) \cong \sum_{n=1}^{\infty}\sum_{m=0}^{\infty} \hbar_{n,m}\overline{\psi}_{n,m}(z), \tag{5}$$

where $\hbar_{n,m} = \langle u(z), \overline{\psi}_{n,m}(z)\rangle$ in which $\langle ., . \rangle$ denotes the inner product. If the given series (5) is truncated then, we have:

$$u(z) \cong \sum_{n=1}^{2^{k-1}}\sum_{m=0}^{M-1} \hbar_{n,m}\overline{\psi}_{n,m}(z) = H^T\psi(z), \tag{6}$$

where H and $\psi(z)$ are $2^{k-1}M \times 1$ matrices given by

$$H = [\hbar_{1,0}, \hbar_{1,1}, \hbar_{1,2,\ldots}, \hbar_{1,M-1}]^T; \quad \psi(z) = \left[\overline{\psi}_{1,0}(z), \overline{\psi}_{1,1}(z), \overline{\psi}_{1,2}(z)\ldots, \overline{\psi}_{1,M-1}(z)\right]^T.$$

3 PROCEDURE OF SOLUTION

Consider partial differential equation

$$\frac{\partial^2 u}{\partial z^2} + \chi \frac{\partial u}{\partial z} + \delta u = \bar{r}(z) \tag{7}$$

with the conditions

$$u(0) = a; \quad u(1) = b, \tag{8}$$

where χ, δ are may be constant or either a function of z or function of u and $\bar{r}(z)$ be a continuous function.

Now, we write Equation (7) as

$$\bar{R}(z) = \frac{\partial^2 u}{\partial z^2} + \chi \frac{\partial u}{\partial z} + \delta u - \bar{r}(z), \tag{9}$$

where $\bar{R}(z)$ is the residual for Equation (7), when $\bar{R}(z) = 0$ for the exact solution, $u(z)$ only which include the given conditions. Next, we consider a series solution of given differential Equation (7), $u(z)$ defined over $[0, 1)$ can be expressed in the terms of MTWs, satisfying the given conditions:

$$u(z) = \sum_{n=1}^{2^{k-1}} \sum_{m=0}^{M-1} \hbar_{n,m} \overline{\psi}_{n,m}(z), \tag{10}$$

where $\hbar_{n,m's}$ are unknown parameters to be determined, now differentiating Equation (10) two times with respect to z and putting the values of $\frac{\partial^2 u}{\partial z^2}, \frac{\partial u}{\partial z}, u$ in Equation (9). To find $\hbar_{n,m's}$ we chose weight function as supposed bases elements and integrating on boundary values together with the residual to zero (Cicelia, 2014), i.e.,

$$\int_0^1 \overline{\psi}_{1,m}(z) \bar{R}(z) dz = 0, m = 0, \ 1, \ 2, \dots .$$

Thus, we obtain system of linear equations with unknown parameters, on solving obtained system, we get unknowns. Then substitute these unknown parameters in test solution, approximate solution of Equation (7) is obtained.

4 NUMERICAL PROBLEMS

Problem 1: First consider the differential equation (Lofi and Mahdiani, 2007; Shiralashetti et al., 2019),

$$\frac{\partial^2 u}{\partial z^2} - \pi^2 u = -2\pi^2 \sin(\pi z), \ 0 \le z \le 1 \tag{11}$$

with the conditions

$$u(0) = 0; \quad u(1) = 0. \tag{12}$$

This problem has exact solution: $u(z) = \sin(\pi z)$.

The executions of Equation (11) as per the procedure of solution described in Section 3 are as follows. The residual of Equation (11) can be written as:

$$\bar{R}(z) = \frac{\partial^2 u}{\partial z^2} - \pi^2 u + 2\pi^2 \sin(\pi z). \tag{13}$$

463

Now selecting the weight function $\bar{w}(z) = z(1-z)$ for MTW bases to satisfying the given conditions (12), i.e.,

$$\Psi(z) = \bar{w}(z) \times \overline{\psi}(z)$$

$$\Psi_{1,0}(z) = \overline{\psi}_{1,0}(z) \times \bar{w}(z) = \left(-z^2 + z\right), \quad \Psi_{1,1}(z) = \overline{\psi}_{1,1}(z) \times \bar{w}(z) = \sqrt{3}\left(-z^3 + \frac{3}{2}z^2 - \frac{1}{2}z\right),$$

$$\Psi_{1,2}(z) = \overline{\psi}_{1,2}(z) \times \bar{w}(z) = \sqrt{5}\left(-z^4 + 2z^3 - \frac{7}{6}z^2 + \frac{1}{6}z\right).$$

Assuming the test solution of (11) for $k = 1$ and $m = 3$ is given by

$$u(z) = \hbar_{1,0}\Psi_{1,0}(z) + \hbar_{1,1}\Psi_{1,1}(z) + \hbar_{1,2}\Psi_{1,2}(z) \tag{14}$$

where $\bar{R}(z)$ is the residual of Equation (11). The "weight functions" are the same as the bases functions. Then by the weighted Galerkin method, we consider the following:

$$\int_0^1 \Psi_{1,m}(z)\bar{R}(z)dz = 0, m = 0, \ 1, \ 2 \tag{15}$$

For $m = 0, \ 1, \ 2$ in Equation (15), then we get a system of algebraic equation with unknown coefficients $\hbar_{1,0}, \hbar_{1,1}, \hbar_{1,2}$. After applying the method which is described in Section 3, we get these coefficients

$$\hbar_{1,0} = 3.70183, \hbar_{1,1} = 0.00, \hbar_{1,2} = -1.58128$$

On putting these values into Equation (14), we get the approximate solution. Obtained approximate solutions are compared with exact and other established method solutions. Table 1 shows that comparison between approximate solution and other method solution for given problem and Figure 1 shows that the proposed method has an appropriate convergence rate.

Table 1. Comparison between absolute errors in discussed problem 1.

z	Absolute error by FDM (Shiralashetti et al., 2019)	Absolute error by Coifman wavelet (Lotfi and Mahdiani, 2007)	Absolute error by HWGM (Shiralashetti et al., 2019)	Absolute error by proposed MTWGM
0.1	1.27E-03	1.51E-04	2.60E-04	2.48E-04
0.2	1.43E-03	1.25E-03	2.60E-04	2.50E-04
0.3	3.33E-03	2.80E-04	5.40E-04	5.45E-04
0.4	3.92E-03	1.97E-04	3.90E-04	3.85E-04
0.5	4.13E-03	4.00E-06	8.80E-04	8.78E-04
0.6	3.92E-03	2.95E-04	3.90E-04	3.85E-04
0.7	3.33E-03	6.55E-04	5.40E-04	5.45E-04
0.8	2.42E-03	1.03E-03	7.20E-04	7.37E-04
0.9	1.27E-03	1.36E-03	2.60E-04	2.38E-04

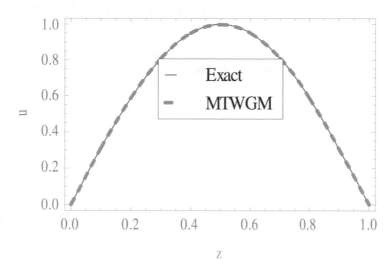

Figure 1. Comparison between exact and approximate solution for given problem.

5 CONCLUSIONS

In this paper, MTWs Galarkin method-based approximation scheme is used for solving PDEs. The efficiency of our method is observed through numerical problems, and figures and tables which shows that approximate solution obtained by the MTWGM gives comparable results with the exact solution and better than already established numerical methods. When the value of M increases, we get more accuracy in the approximate solution. Thus, the presented method is more effective for the solution of the above – introduced problem and other kind of differential equations.

REFERENCES

Amaratunga, K. & William, J. R. 1994. Wavelet-Galerkin solutions for One dimensional partial differential equations. *Inter. J. Num. Meth. Eng*, 37: 2703–2716.

Chang, J. Yang, Q. & Zhao, L. 2011. Comparison of B-spline method and finite difference method to Solve BVP of linear ODEs. *Journal of Computers*, 6(10): 2149–2155.

Chui, C.K. 1992. *An Introduction to Wavelets*. New York: Boston Academic Press

Cicelia, J.E. 2014. Solution of weighted residual problems by using Galerkin's method. *Indian Journal of Science and Technology*, 7(3): 52–54.

Daubechies, I. 1988. Orthonormal bases of compactly supported wavelets. *Communication on Pure and Applied Mathematics*, 41(7): 909–996.

Daubechies, I. 1992. *Ten Lectures on Wavelets*. USA: SIAM, Philadelphia, Pa.

Farlow, S.J. 1993. *Partial Differential Equations for Scientists and Engineers*. New York: Dover Publications.

Jost, J. 2002. *Partial Differential Equations*. New York: Springer Verlag.

Keshavarz, E. & Ordokhani, Y. 2019. A fast numerical algorithm based on the Taylor wavelets for solving the fractional integro-differential equations with weakly singular kernals. *Math meth Appl Sci*, 42: 4427–4443.

Lotfi, T. & Mahdiani, K. 2007. Numerical solution of boundary value problem by using Wavelet-Galerkin method. *Mathematical Sciences*, 1(3): 07–18.

Mosevic, J.W. 1977. Identifying differential equations by galerkin's method. *Mathematics of Computation*, 31: 139–147.

Razzaghi, M. & Yousefi, S. 2001. The Legendre wavelet operational matrix of integration. *International Journal of system science*, 32(4): 495–502.

Shiralashetti, S.C. Angadi, L.M. & Kumbinarasaiah, S. 2019. Wavelet based Galerkin method for the numerical solution of the one dimensional partial differential equations. *International Research Journal of Engineering and Technology*, 6(7): 2886–2096.

Smart Computing – Khan et al (Eds)
© 2021 Taylor & Francis Group, London, ISBN 978-0-367-76552-1

Fuzzy-based local fractional Fourier series using fuzzy numbers

S. Sokhal & S.R. Verma

Department of Mathematics and Statistics, Gurukula Kangri Vishwavidyalaya, Haridwar, Uttarakhand, India

ABSTRACT: In this article, the fuzzy local fractional Fourier series is introduced by using the triangular, trapezoidal fuzzy number within the interval $[-l, l]$ on the real axis $\Re$ and these fuzzy numbers are applied to examine the symmetry of the periodic local fractional Fourier series and satisfy the periodic function of fuzzy local fractional coefficients for real numbers.

Keywords: Local fractional fuzzy valued function, Triangular fuzzy number, Trapezoidal fuzzy number, Local fractional Fourier series.

1 INTRODUCTION

The first fuzzy set theory was presented by Zadeh (1965). Subsequently, Dubois & Prade (1978) presented the fuzzy number which play an important role in fuzzy applications. Fuzzy number (FN) is defined as a fuzzy set over the real line $\Re$ whose membership function is normal, continuous and fuzzy convex. The $L - R$ representation of a fuzzy number means dividing the membership function (MF) of a fuzzy number (FN) into two curves (Hanss 2004). There are many fuzzy numbers which are most common and used in various applications (Pathinathan & Ponnivalavan 2015). A fuzzy number is the generalization of a common, real number which refers to the possible value between 0 and 1 with its weight and this weight is called its membership function There are many cases in which it has been seen that the physical world looks more real than single-valued numbers by the use of fuzzy numbers. Statistics, computer programming, and engineering are the common fields in which fuzzy number has been used (Dubois & Prade 1980). The fuzzy number is the basic concept for fuzzy differential equations and fuzzy analysis, with this, it is also helpful for several applications. The Fourier series was introduced by J. B. Joseph Fourier (Tolstov 1976), but recently a new series has been developed by using the local fractional operator, known as the local fractional Fourier series (LFFS) (Baleanu & Xiao-Jun 2013), which works in a fractal space. Similarly, a new fuzzy local fractional Fourier series in this article is developed with fuzzy local Fourier coefficients using triangular, trapezoidal and pentagonal fuzzy numbers.

2 DEFINITIONS

2.1 *Fuzzy set*

If Y is the collection of things, then the fuzzy set (FS) D in Y be the ordered pair set, i.e.,

$$D = \{y, \mu_D(y) : y \in Y\},$$

with the membership function $\mu_D : Y \to [0, \ 1]$ in D

DOI 10.1201/9781003167488-55

2.2 Fuzzy number

If μ_D is the membership function (MF) of a fuzzy set D on real axis $\Re$ and satisfies some conditions, which are given as follows:

- $\mu_D(y) = 1$, $y \in \Re$ (i.e., fuzzy set is normal).
- $\mu_D[\lambda y_1 + (1 - \lambda)y_2] \geq \max[\mu_D(y_1), \mu_D(y_2)]$, for every $y_1, y_2 \in \Re$ and $\lambda \in [0, 1]$ (i.e. fuzzy set is convex).
- For every $\epsilon > 0$, $\exists \delta > 0$ s.t. $\mu_D(y_1) - \mu_D(y_2) < \epsilon$, whenever $|y - y_0| < \delta$, then fuzzy set D is said to be a fuzzy number (FN)

2.3 Triangular Fuzzy Number (TFN)

A TFN is a fuzzy number, which consists of three points namely say $D = \{d_1, d_2, d_3\}$ to form the triangular shape, whose membership function is given as follows:

$$\mu_D(y) = \begin{cases} 0, & y < d_1 \\ \frac{y - d_1}{d_2 - d_1}, & d_1 \leq y \leq d_2 \\ \frac{d_3 - y}{d_3 - d_2}, & d_2 \leq y \leq d_3 \\ 0, & y > d_4 \end{cases}, \tag{1}$$

and the λ-level set of TFN D is, $D_\lambda = [(1 - \lambda)d_1 + \lambda d_2, \ (1 - \lambda)d_3 + \lambda d_2]$.

2.4 Trapezoidal Fuzzy Numbers (TRFNs)

A trapezoidal fuzzy number (TRFN) consists of four points to make the trapezoidal shape, $D = \{d_1, d_2, d_3, d_4\}$, and its membership function (MF) $\mu_D(y)$ is defined as

$$\mu_D(y) = \begin{cases} 0, & y < d_1 \\ \frac{y - d_1}{d_2 - d_1}, & d_1 \leq y \leq d_2 \\ 1, & d_2 \leq y \leq d_3 \\ \frac{d_4 - y}{d_4 - d_3}, & d_3 \leq y \leq d_4 \\ 0, & y > d_4 \end{cases}, \tag{2}$$

with λ-level set, $D_\lambda = [(1 - \lambda)d_1 + \lambda d_2, \ (1 - \lambda)d_4 + \lambda d_3]$.

2.5 Local Fractional Integral (LFI)

For $G(y) \in C_\alpha(a, b)$, the local fractional integral (LFI) of function G within the interval $[\beta, \gamma]$ of order α is given as follows:

$$\Gamma(1 + \alpha)_\beta I_\gamma^\alpha G(y) = \int_\beta^\gamma G(s)(ds)^\alpha = \lim_{\Delta s \to 0} \sum_{j=0}^{N-1} G(s_j)(\Delta s_j)^\alpha, \tag{3}$$

where $\Delta s_j = s_{j+1} - s_j$, with $\Delta s = \max\{\Delta s_1, \Delta s_2, \Delta s_j, ...\}$, also $[s_j, s_{j+1}], j = 0, ..., N - 1$, and $s_0 = \beta$, $s_N = \gamma$, is the partition of the interval $[\beta, \gamma]$. Some basic LFIs of non-differentiable functions on fractal set are given in (Yang et al. 2015)

2.6 Local fractional Fourier series for a fuzzy valued function with period 2 l

Let the function $G^t \in C_\alpha(-\infty, \infty)$ and this function has period $2l$, then local fractional Fourier series of the function G^t is defined as:

$$G^t(y) = \frac{b_0}{2} \oplus \sum_{m=1}^{\infty} \left(b_m \cos_\alpha \left(\frac{\pi my}{l}\right)^\alpha \oplus c_m \sin_\alpha \left(\frac{\pi my}{l}\right)^\alpha \right), \quad m \in \mathbb{N}, \quad \alpha \in (0, 1) \qquad (4)$$

where b_0, b_m, and c_m are fuzzified local fractional Fourier coefficients, such as

$$b_m = \frac{1}{l^\alpha} \int_{-l}^{l} [G^t(y)]_\lambda \cos_\alpha \left(\frac{\pi my}{l}\right)^\alpha (dy)^\alpha; m \geq 0, \qquad (5)$$

$$c_m = \frac{1}{l^\alpha} \int_{-l}^{l} [G^t(y)]_\lambda \sin_\alpha \left(\frac{\pi my}{l}\right)^\alpha (dy)^\alpha; m \geq 1, \qquad (6)$$

which uniformly converges in $[0, 1] \forall m$ and the λ-level set of a local fractional fuzzy valued function G is

$$[G^t(y)]_\lambda = [G_\lambda^-(t), G_\lambda^+(t)], \quad for \ \lambda \in [0, 1] \qquad (7)$$

3 FUZZY LOCAL FRACTIONAL FOURIER SERIES USING TRIANGULAR FUZZY NUMBER

Let function G^t be the local fractional fuzzy valued function on a set D with period $2l$ on interval $[-l, l]$, whose membership function forms a triangular shape fuzzy number, Ewhich is given as

$$G^t_{\mu_D}(y) = \begin{cases} 0, & y < -l \\ \frac{y+l}{t^\alpha+l}, & -l \leq y \leq t^\alpha \\ \frac{l-y}{l-t^\alpha}, & t^\alpha \leq y \leq l \\ 0, & y > l \end{cases},$$

and is a fuzzy integral for the values of y, $t^\alpha \in [a, b]$, so from the definition of local fractional Fourier series for fuzzy valued function and using Equation (4), the λ-level set with the membership function (MF) of G^t is as

$$[G^t(y)]_\lambda = [G_\lambda^-(t), G_\lambda^+(t)] = [(\lambda - 1)l + \lambda t^\alpha, (1 - \lambda)l + \lambda t^\alpha]. \qquad (8)$$

So, the fuzzy local fractional Fourier coefficients b_0, b_m, and c_m for the TFN is given as,

$$b_0 = \frac{1}{l^\alpha} \int_{-l}^{l} [G^t(y)]_\lambda (dy)^\alpha = \frac{1}{l^\alpha} \int_{-l}^{l} [(\lambda - 1)l + \lambda t^\alpha, (1 - \lambda)l + t^\alpha \lambda] (dt)^\alpha$$

$$= \frac{\Gamma(1+\alpha)}{l^\alpha} [l(\lambda - 1), l(1 - \lambda)]_{-l}I_l^\alpha(1) = \frac{\Gamma(1+\alpha)}{l^\alpha} [l(\lambda - 1), l(1 - \lambda)] \frac{(2l)^\alpha}{\Gamma(1+\alpha)}$$

$$b_m = \frac{1}{l^\alpha} \int_{-l}^{l} [G^t(y)]_\lambda \cos_\alpha \left(\frac{\pi my}{l}\right)^\alpha (dy)^\alpha = \frac{\Gamma(1+\alpha)}{l^\alpha} [l(\lambda - 1), l(1 - \lambda)]_{-l}I_l^{(\alpha)} \cos_\alpha \left(\frac{\pi mt}{l}\right)^\alpha = 0$$

$$c_m = \frac{1}{l^\alpha} \int_{-l}^{l} [G^t(y)]_\lambda \sin_\alpha \left(\frac{\pi m y}{l}\right)^\alpha (dy)^\alpha = \frac{1}{l^\alpha} \int_{-l}^{l} [(\lambda - 1)l + \lambda t^\alpha, \ (1 - \lambda)l + \lambda t^\alpha]$$

$$\times \sin_\alpha \left(\frac{\pi m t}{l}\right)^\alpha (dt)^\alpha$$

$$= \frac{\Gamma(1 + \alpha)}{l^\alpha} \left[l(\lambda - 1)_{-l}I_l^{(\alpha)} \sin_\alpha \left(\frac{\pi m t}{l}\right)^\alpha + \lambda_{-l}I_l^{(\alpha)} t^\alpha \sin_\alpha \left(\frac{\pi m t}{l}\right)^\alpha, \right.$$

$$\left. l(1 - \lambda)_{-l}I_l^{(\alpha)} \sin_\alpha \left(\frac{\pi m t}{l}\right)^\alpha + \lambda_{-l}I_l^{(\alpha)} t^\alpha \sin_\alpha \left(\frac{\pi m t}{l}\right)^\alpha \right]$$

$$= \frac{\Gamma(1 + \alpha)}{l^\alpha} \left[\lambda_{-l}I_l^{(\alpha)} t^\alpha \sin_\alpha \left(\frac{\pi m t}{l}\right)^\alpha, \ \lambda_{-l}I_l^{(\alpha)} t^\alpha \sin_\alpha \left(\frac{\pi m t}{l}\right)^\alpha \right]$$

$$= \frac{2\Gamma(1 + \alpha)}{(m\pi)^\alpha} \left[\lambda(-1)^{m+1}, \ \lambda(-1)^{m+1} \right],$$

where $_{-l}I_l^{(\alpha)}g(y)$ is the local fractional integral in the interval $[-l, l]$. Now, putting the above coefficients in Equation (4), we get the required fuzzy local fractional Fourier series (FLFFS) as

$$G^t(y) = \frac{2^\alpha}{2}[l(\lambda - 1), \ l(1 - \lambda)] \oplus \sum_{m=1}^{\infty} [0, \ 0] \cos_\alpha \left(\frac{m\pi t}{l}\right)^\alpha \oplus \frac{2\Gamma(1 + \alpha)}{(m\pi)^\alpha}$$

$$\times [\lambda(-1)^{m+1}, \ \lambda(-1)^{m+1}] \sin_\alpha \left(\frac{m\pi t}{l}\right)^\alpha$$

$$\tag{9}$$

$$= \left\{ \frac{2^\alpha}{2} l(\lambda - 1) + \sum_{m=1}^{4} \frac{2\Gamma(1 + \alpha)}{(m\pi)^\alpha} \lambda(-1)^{m+1} \sin_\alpha \left(\frac{m\pi t}{l}\right)^\alpha, \ \frac{2^\alpha}{2} l(1 - \lambda) + \sum_{m=1}^{4} \frac{2\Gamma(1 + \alpha)}{(m\pi)^\alpha} \right.$$

$$\left. \times \lambda(-1)^{m+1} \sin_\alpha \left(\frac{m\pi t}{l}\right)^\alpha \right\}.$$

3.1 *Example*

Let us consider the membership value $\lambda = 0.6$, fractional order $\alpha = 1/2$, $t = 30°$ and the length $l = 1$ in Equation (9), then the Fourier fuzzy valued function (see Equation (8)) with the period $2l$ using local fractional Fourier series is $[G^{30}]_{0.6} = [-0.262352, \ 0.303333]$.

4 FUZZY LOCAL FRACTIONAL FOURIER SERIES USING TRAPEZOIDAL FUZZY NUMBER

Let G^t be the $2l$-periodic local fractional fuzzy valued function on a set D on $[-l, l]$, then the membership function of a TRFN (Pathinathan & Dolorosa 2018) is given below:

$$G^t_{\mu_D}(y) = \begin{cases} 0, & y < -l \\ \frac{y+l}{-t^\alpha + l}, & -l \le y \le t^\alpha \\ 1, & -t^\alpha \le y \le t^\alpha \\ \frac{l-y}{l-t^\alpha}, & t^\alpha \le y \le l \\ 0, & y > l \end{cases}$$

which is a fuzzy integral for every y, $t^\alpha \in [a, b]$, then from definition of subsection 2.6, the λ-level set of membership function of the function G^t is given as

$$[G^t(y)]_\lambda = [G_\lambda^-(t),\ G_\lambda^+(t)] = [(\lambda - 1)l - \lambda\, t^\alpha,\ (1-\lambda)l + \lambda\, t^\alpha].\tag{10}$$

The Fuzzy local fractional Fourier coefficients b_0, b_m, and c_m for the TRFN is

$$
\begin{aligned}
b_0 &= \frac{1}{l^\alpha}\int_{-l}^{l} [G^t(y)]_\lambda (dy)^\alpha = \frac{1}{l^\alpha}\int_{-l}^{l} [(\lambda - 1)l - \lambda\, t^\alpha,\ (1-\lambda)l + \lambda\, t^\alpha](dt)^\alpha\\
&= \frac{1}{l^\alpha}\Gamma(1+\alpha)\big[-l(1-\lambda)_{-l}I_l^\alpha(1), l(1-\lambda)_{-l}I_l^\alpha(1)\big] = \frac{\Gamma(1+\alpha)}{l^\alpha}\\
&\quad \times [-l(1-\lambda), l(1-\lambda)]\frac{(2l)^\alpha}{\Gamma(1+\alpha)},
\end{aligned}
$$

$$
\begin{aligned}
b_m &= \frac{1}{l^\alpha}\int_{-l}^{l}[G^t(y)]_\lambda \cos_\alpha\left(\frac{\pi m y}{l}\right)^\alpha (dy)^\alpha = \frac{1}{l^\alpha}\int_{-l}^{l}[(\lambda - 1)l + t^\alpha,\ (1-\lambda)l + t^\alpha]\\
&\quad \times \cos_\alpha\left(\frac{\pi m t}{l}\right)^\alpha (dt)^\alpha = 0,
\end{aligned}
$$

$$
\begin{aligned}
c_m &= \frac{1}{l^\alpha}\int_{-l}^{l}[G^t(y)]_\lambda \sin_\alpha\left(\frac{\pi m y}{l}\right)^\alpha (dy)^\alpha = \frac{1}{l^\alpha}\int_{-l}^{l}[(\lambda - 1)l - t^\alpha, (1-\lambda)l + t^\alpha]\sin_\alpha\left(\frac{\pi m t}{l}\right)^\alpha (dt)^\alpha\\
&= \frac{1}{l^\alpha}\Gamma(1+\alpha)\left[-\lambda_{-l}I_l^{(\alpha)}t^\alpha \sin_\alpha\left(\frac{\pi m t}{l}\right)^\alpha,\ \lambda_{-l}I_l^{(\alpha)}t^\alpha \sin_\alpha\left(\frac{\pi m t}{l}\right)^\alpha\right] = \frac{2\Gamma(1+\alpha)}{(m\pi)^\alpha}\\
&\quad \times \left[-\lambda(-1)^{m+1}, \lambda(-1)^{m+1}\right].
\end{aligned}
$$

We put the values of b_0, b_m, and c_m in Equation (4) to obtain the following Fuzzy local fractional Fourier series (FLFFS)

$$
\begin{aligned}
G^t(y) &= \frac{2^\alpha}{2}[-l(1-\lambda), l(1-\lambda)] \oplus \sum_{m=1}^{\infty}[0, 0]\cos_\alpha\left(\frac{m\pi t}{l}\right)^\alpha \oplus \frac{2\Gamma(1+\alpha)}{(m\pi)^\alpha}\\
&\quad \times [-\lambda(-1)^{m+1}\lambda(-1)^{m+1}]\sin_\alpha\left(\frac{m\pi t}{l}\right)^\alpha\\
&= \Bigg\{-\frac{2^\alpha}{2}l(1-\lambda) - \sum_{m=1}^{4}\frac{2\Gamma(1+\alpha)}{(m\pi)^\alpha}\lambda(-1)^{m+1}\sin_\alpha\left(\frac{m\pi t}{l}\right)^\alpha,\\
&\qquad \frac{2^\alpha}{2}l(1-\lambda) + \sum_{m=1}^{4}\frac{2\Gamma(1+\alpha)}{(m\pi)^\alpha}\lambda(-1)^{m+1}\sin_\alpha\left(\frac{m\pi t}{l}\right)^\alpha\Bigg\}
\end{aligned}\tag{11}
$$

4.0.1 Example

Let $t = 30°$, the membership value $\lambda = 0.6$ of the function G^t with fractional order $\alpha = 1/2$ and the length $l = 1$ in Equation (11), then from Equation (10) the obtained Fourier fuzzy valued function with period $2l$ using local fractional Fourier series is symmetric, i.e., $[G^{30}]_{0.6} = [-0.303333, 0.303333]$.

5 CONCLUSIONS

In the present article, the FLFFS is obtained by using fuzzy numbers and the obtained local fractional Fourier fuzzy valued function is periodic and symmetric for any membership value using TRFN but in case of TFN, the fuzzy valued function does not satisfy the symmetric condition. As the FLFFS is obtained using TFN and TRFN, in the same manner, using any other fuzzy number fuzzy local fractional Fourier series can also be obtained in the symmetric and non-symmetric form.

REFERENCES

Baleanu, D. and Xiao-Jun, Y. 2013. Local fractional Fourier series with applications to representations of fractal signals. *9th International Conference on Multibody Systems. Nonlinear Dynamics and Control.* 7B

Dubois, D. and Prade, H. 1978. Operations on Fuzzy numbers. *International Journal of Systems Science* 9(6): 613–626.

Dubois, D. and Prade, H. 1980. *Fuzzy set and system Theory and applications.* London (USA): Academic Press.

Hanss, M. 2005. *Applied Fuzzy Arithmetic: An Introduction with Engineering Applications.* Berlin, Heidelberg: Springer

Pathinathan, T. and Dolorosa, E. A. 2018. Fuzzy Fourier series using trapezoidal, reverse order trapezoidal and intuitionistic trapezoidal fuzzy number. *Journal of Computer and Mathematical Sciences* 9(12): 2004–2013.

Pathinathan, T. and Ponnivalavan, K. 2015. Reverse order Triangular, Trapezoidal and Pentagonal Fuzzy numbers. *Annals of Pure and Applied Mathematics* 9: 107–117.

Tolstov, G. P. 1976. *Fourier series.* New York: Dover publication.

Yang, X. J., Baleanu, D. and Srivastava, H. M. 2015. *Local fractional integral transform and their applications.* USA: Academic Press.

Zadeh, L. A. 1965. Information and Control Theory. *Fuzzy sets* 8: 338–353.

Smart Computing – Khan et al (Eds)
© 2021 Taylor & Francis Group, London, ISBN 978-0-367-76552-1

PDE-based time-dependent model for image restoration with forward-backward diffusivity

Santosh Kumar, Nitendra Kumar & Khursheed Alam

Department of Mathematics, School of Basic Sciences and Research, Sharda University, Greater Noida, UP, India

ABSTRACT: In the image processing community, image denoising and deblurring, data compression, edge detection, etc. are the most challenging and basic hurdles. We address a new nonlinear anisotropic diffusion model for image denoising and deblurring. To judge our model, we compared the existing model to obtain good results. To discretize for both nonlinear anisotropic diffusion models, we have used an explicit scheme and numerical experimental results are discussed.

1 INTRODUCTION

The Partial differential equations contain many applications in image restoration, edge detection, image denoising, etc. The original real image is corrupted by blur and noise and can be written as $u_0 : \Omega \to R$,

$$u_0 = r * u + n, \tag{1}$$

where u_0 is a blurry and noisy image and it is called an observed image, Ω is bounded in R^2, u is the original real image, r is the blurred kernel, and n is additive Gaussian white noise with zero mean and variance σ^2.

The total variation (TV) model has been proposed by many researchers but the first approach in this regard recalls the name (Rudin et al. 1992) for image denoising and edge detection. The solution to the imposed problem is obtained by the gradient projection method. Rudin & Osher (1994) proposed a multiplicative noise-based total variation model for image restoration. Kumar & Ahmad (2015) introduced a time-dependent model for removing additive noise. This model converges very fast for image denoising and edge detection. The first approach of the anisotropic diffusion model is given by (Perona & Malik 1990). The improved PM model, i.e., anisotropic diffusion model is given by Catte et al. (1992). The researchers looked toward the idea of anisotropic diffusion model and have given improved and fast versions of the anisotropic diffusion technique by various researchers such as Marquina & Osher (2000), Kumar et al. (2016, 2018), and Barbu et al. (2019). Total variation denoising is a popular method and is considered as a bottom line for edge-preserving in image restoration. A large statement is that this method can restore sharp edges but at the same time, might meet up with some stair casing (i.e., spurious edges) in-plane regions given by Vogel & Oman (1996). Chain et al. (1999) gave a value of Lagrange multiplier and introduced a new primal-dual implicit-quadratic methods for image denoising. De-convolution with total variation regularization by vibrational approaches is studied by many researchers (Chan & Wong 1998; Barbu et al. 2019; Barbu & Moro 2018), which deals with of the both classes of problems arising in non-blind and blind deconvolution. In 2005, Welk et al. proposed a de-convolution technique based nonlinear anisotropic diffusion model for image restoration. We have studied the Marquina & Osher (2000) model for image restoration and apply this technique in the anisotropic diffusion model given by Welk, i.e., multiply the magnitude of the gradient in the anisotropic diffusion model, we get a new model for additive blurred and noisy images.

DOI 10.1201/9781003167488-56

The rest article is organized as follows. Section 2 gives a technique to remove blurred and noise by an anisotropic diffusion model. In Section 3, we give an explicit scheme of models. The type of diffusivity is given in Section 4. The numerical experiment and conclusion are given in Section 5.

2 PDE-BASED IMAGE RESTORATION TECHNIQUE

Welk et al. (2005) introduced a de-convolution of a deblurring and denoising image of the minimizing energy functional can be written as:

$$E(u) = \int_\Omega \Psi(|\nabla u|^2 dx\, dy + \frac{\lambda}{2} \int_\Omega (r * u - u_0)^2 dx\, dy. \tag{2}$$

The first and second integrals are the smoothness term and the data term, respectively. The Euler–Lagrange equation of the functional E can be written as:

$$0 - -\text{div}(\Psi'\left(|\nabla u|^2\right)\nabla u) + \lambda r * (r * u - u_0), \quad x, y \in \Omega. \tag{3}$$

By the gradient descent method for $t \to \infty$ to a minimizer of E with homogeneous boundary conditions is equivalent to:

$$\frac{\partial u}{\partial t} = \text{div}(g\left(|\nabla u|^2\right)\nabla u) - \lambda\, r * (r * u - u_0),$$

$$\frac{\partial u}{\partial n} = 0, \quad x, y \in \partial\Omega. \tag{4}$$

Here, $\partial\Omega$ is the boundary of Ω and n is the outward normal to $\partial\Omega$. Motivated by the Marquina & Osher (2000) model, we multiply the magnitude of the gradient in (3) and it is equivalent to a new model for image restoration as:

$$\frac{\partial u}{\partial t} = |\nabla u|\text{div}(g\left(|\nabla u|^2\right)\nabla u) - |\nabla u|\lambda r * (r * u - u_0). \tag{5}$$

The diffusivity $g(s^2)$ is related to the energy functional $\Psi'(s^2)$.

3 DISCRETE SCHEME

The u_{ij}^n is the approximation of $u(x_i, y_j, t_n)$ and Δx and Δy are spatial and Δt is the time step size and we can define: $x_i = i\Delta x$, $y_i = j\Delta x$, $i, j = 1, 2, \ldots, N$, $t_n = n\Delta t$, $n \geq 1$.

We define the explicit scheme for nonlinear anisotropic diffusion model (4) as:

$$u_{ij}^t = \frac{1}{2\Delta x}(\left(g_{i+1,j}^n + g_{i,j}^n\right)\left(u_{i+1,j}^n - u_{i,j}^n\right) - (g_{i,j}^n + g_{i-1,j}^n)(u_{i,j}^n - u_{i-1,j}^n))$$

$$+ \frac{1}{2\Delta x}(\left(g_{i,j+1}^n + g_{i,j}^n\right)\left(u_{i,j+1}^n - u_{i,j}^n\right) - (g_{i,j}^n + g_{i,j-1}^n)(u_{i,j}^n - u_{i,j-1}^n))$$

$$- \lambda r * (r * u_{i,j}^n + u_{i,j}^0)$$

We define the explicit scheme for nonlinear anisotropic diffusion model (5) as:

$$
u_{ij}^t = \frac{1}{2\Delta x} s_{i,j}^n \big(\left(g_{i+1,j}^n + g_{i,j}^n \right) \left(u_{i+1,j}^n - u_{i,j}^n \right) - (g_{i,j}^n + g_{i-1,j}^n)(u_{i,j}^n - u_{i-1,j}^n) \big)
$$

$$
+ s_{i,j}^n \frac{1}{2\Delta x} \big(\left(g_{i,j+1}^n + g_{i,j}^n \right) \left(u_{i,j+1}^n - u_{i,j}^n \right) - (g_{i,j}^n + g_{i,j-1}^n)(u_{i,j}^n - u_{i,j-1}^n) \big)
$$

$$
- s_{i,j}^n \lambda r * (r * u_{i,j}^n + u_{i,j}^0),
$$

where the diffusivity $g\left(|\nabla u|^2\right)$ is discretized by

$$
g_{i,j}^n = \psi' \left(\left(\frac{u_{i+1,j}^n - u_{i-1,j}^n}{\Delta x} \right)^2 + \left(\frac{u_{i,j+1}^n - u_{i,j-1}^n}{\Delta x} \right)^2 \right) \text{ and } s_{i,j}^n = \sqrt{\left(u_{i,j}^x\right)^2 + \left(u_{i,j}^y\right)^2}.
$$

The explicit method for all models are stable and convergent for $\Delta t / \Delta x^2 = 0.5$ (Lapidus & Pinder 1983).

4 TYPES OF THE DIFFUSIVITY

In the de-convolution process, the diffusivity g and diffusivity parameters are very important. The total variation (TV) diffusivity $g(s^2) = \frac{1}{|s|}$ and regularized form $g(s^2) = \frac{1}{\sqrt{s^2 + \varepsilon^2}}$ is a popular choice (Rudin et al. 1992). The Parona–Malik (PM) diffusivity $g(s^2) = \left(1 + \frac{s^2}{\gamma^2}\right)^{-1}$ and the regularizer form $\psi(s^2) = \gamma^2 \log\left(1 + \frac{s^2}{\gamma^2}\right)$ given by (Chan & Wong 1998; Weickert 1998). Here, γ and ε are diffusivity parameters. Charbonnier diffusivity $g(s^2) = \frac{1}{\sqrt{1 + \frac{|s^2|}{\gamma^2}}}$ is associated by the regularizer $\Psi(s^2) = \sqrt{\gamma^4 + \gamma^2 s^2} - -\gamma^2$, where γ is a contrast parameter (Charbonnier et al. 1994; Weickert 1998). We have included Charbonnier diffusivity in our experiments.

5 NUMERICAL IMPLEMENTATION

The grayscale images, Lena and Boat of (256×256) pixels and pixel values, lie between [0,255]. In our experiment, we reduce the intensities of all real original images between [0, 1] in Matlab after that we add Gaussian white noise in original real images in Matlab by the function imnoise (I, "Gaussian", M, σ^2), M and σ^2 are mean and variance, respectively.

The Signal to Noise Ratio (SNR) of the level of noise can be defined as:

$$
\text{SNR} = \frac{||u - \bar{u}_0||_{L^2}}{\sigma} \text{ dB.}
$$

Here, u is the signal and u_0 is the mean of the signal, i.e., the ratio of the standard deviation of the signal over the standard deviation of the noise.

In the Blurred Signal to Noise Ratio (BSNR) we use the ratio of the level of the blurred kernel which is defined as:

$$
\text{BSNR} = 10 \log 10 \frac{blurred\,signal\,variance\,noise\,variance}{noise\,variance} \text{ dB,}
$$

The smoothness of the restored image, we use the metric Improvement Signal to Noise Ratio (ISNR) value as:

$$
\text{ISNR} = 10 \log_{10} \left(\frac{\sum_{i,j}^n \left[u_{ij} - (u_0)\,ij\right]^2}{\sum_{i,j}^n \left[u_{ij} - ((u_{new})\,ij\right]^2} \right) dB,
$$

Here, u_{new} is the restored image.

Using the Gaussian kernel it can be defined as:

$$r_\alpha(x, y) = \frac{1}{2\pi\alpha^2} \exp^{-\frac{(x^2-y^2)}{2\alpha^2}}.$$

Here, r_α is the blurring operator and the size of r_α is 5 with blurring parameter $\alpha = 2$ in the blurred kernel r_α. The Lagrange multiplier $\lambda = 0.85$, diffusivity parameter $\gamma = 5$ (Chan et al. 1999; Chang & I-Liang 2003), and $\frac{\Delta t}{\Delta x^2} = 0.4$ is used in our experiments.

5.1 Tables

Table 1. The results are given in terms of ISNR value.

Images in figures	ISNR for Model-4	Images in figures	ISNR for Model-5
2(c)	2.4620	2(e)	3.5833
2(d)	2.4686	2(f)	4.1082
No. of iterations	500	No. of iterations	50

Table 2. The results are given in terms of ISNR value.

Images in figures	ISNR for Model-4	Images in figures	ISNR for Model-5
3(c)	2.4120	3(e)	3.4858
3(d)	2.4231	3(f)	4.0192
No. of iterations	500	No. of iterations	50

5.2 Figures

Figure 2(a–b) and Figure 3(a–b) represent the blurred and noisy images of Lena and Boat, respectively, with the size of a Gaussian blurred kernel 5, the blurring parameter 2, and additive Gaussian white noise σ^2 =0.006, 0.008, respectively, wherein their SNR $\approx$ 4.97, 4.39 and BSNR $\approx$ 13.35, 12.18.

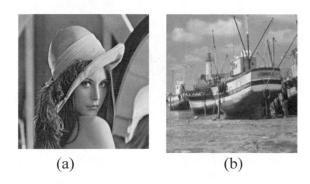

(a)   (b)

Figure 1. (a–b) Original Lena and Boat images, respectively.

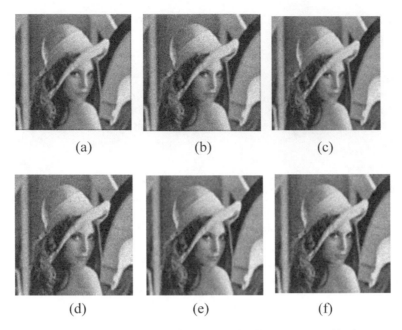

(a)   (b)   (c)

(d)   (e)   (f)

Figure 2.   (a)–(b) Noisy blur images with the size of Gaussian blur operator 5, blurring parameter 2, and Gaussian noise $\sigma^2 = 0.006$, 0.008, respectively; (c) and (d) restored image by model (4); (e) and (f) restored image by model (5).

(a)   (b)   (c)

(d)   (e)   (f)

Figure 3.   (a)–(b) Noisy blur noisy images with the size of Gaussian blur operator 5, blurring parameter 2, and Gaussian noise $\sigma^2 = 0.006$, 0.008, respectively; (c) and (d) restored image by model (4); (e) and (f) restored image by model (5).

6 CONCLUSION

In this paper, we proposed a nonlinear anisotropic diffusion model for removing additive blurred and noisy images. We have used the finite difference numerical explicit scheme to discretize our and existing models. Numerical results confirm that our model converges very fast to obtain smooth images. The results are given an ISNR metric. The ISNR value of our model is larger according to the existing model at a small number of iterations.

REFERENCES

Barbu, T., Miranville, A. & Morosanu, C. 2019. A qualitative analysis and numerical simulations of a non- linear second-order anisotropic diffusion problem with non-homogeneous CauchyNeumann boundary conditions. *Applied Mathematics and Computation* 350(1): 170–180.

Barbu, T. & Moro, C. 2018. Compound PDE-based additive denoising solution combining an improved anisotropic diffusion model to a 2D Gaussian filter kernel. *East Asian Journal on Applied Mathematics* 9(1): 1–12.

Catte, F., Lions, P. L., Morel, J. M. & Coll, T. 1992. Image selective smoothing and edge detection by nonlinear diffusion*. *SIAM Journal Numerical. Analysis.* 29: 182–193.

Chan, T. F., Golub, G. H. & Mulet, P. 1999. A nonlinear primal-dual method for total variation based image restoration. *SIAM Journal of Scientific Computing* 20(6): 1964–1977.

Chan, T. F. & Wong, C. K. 1998. Total variation blind deconvolution. *IEEE Transactions on Image Processing* 7: 370–375.

Chang, Q. & Chern I-Liang 2003. Acceleration methods for total variation-based image denoising. *SIAM Journal of Scientific Computing* 25(3): 982–994.

Charbonnier, P. & Blanc-Feraud, L., Aubert, G. & Barlaud, M. 1994. Two deterministic half-quadratic regularization algorithms for computed imaging. *In Proceedings of IEEE International Conference on Image Processing* 2: 168–172.

Kumar, S. & Ahmad, M.K. 2015. A time dependent model for image denoisng. *Journal of Signal and Information Processing,* 6: 28–38.

Kumar, S., Sarfaraz, M. & Ahmad, M.K. 2016. An efficient PDE-based nonlinear anisotropic diffusion model for image denoising. *Neural, Parallel and Scientific Computations* 24: 305–315.

Kumar, S., Sarfaraz, M. & Ahmad, M. K. 2018. Denoising method based on wavelet coefficients via diffusion equation. *Iranian Journal of Science and Technology, Transactions A: Science* 42: 721–726.

Lapidus, L., Pinder, G. F. 1983. Numerical solution of partial differential equations in science and engineering. *SIAM Review* 25(4): 581–582.

Marquina, A. & Osher, S. 2000. Explicit algorithms for a new time dependent model based on level set motion for nonlinear deblurring and noise removal. *SIAM Journal of Scientific Computing* 22(2): 387–405.

Perona, P. & Malik, J. 1990. Scale space and edge detection using anisotropic diffusion. *IEEE Transactions on Pattern Analysis and Machine Intelligence* 12: 629–639.

Rudin, L. & Osher, S. 1994. Total variation based image restoration with free local constraints. *Proc. IEEE International Conference in Image Processing* 31–35.

Rudin, L., Osher, S. & Fatemi, E. 1992. Nonlinear total variation based noise removal algorithm. *Physica D.* 60: 259–268.

Weickert, J. 1998. Anisotropic Diffusion in Image Processing. *Teubner Stuttgart.*

Welk, M., Theis, D., Brox, T. & Weickert, J. 2005. PDE-based deconvolution with forward-backward diffusivities and diffusion tensors. *In scale space, LNCS, Springer Berlin:* 585–597.

Vogel, C. R. & Oman, M. E. 1996. Iterative methods for total variation denoising. *SIAM Journal of Scientific Computing* 17: 227–238.

Smart Computing – Khan et al (Eds)
© 2021 Taylor & Francis Group, London, ISBN 978-0-367-76552-1

Bernstein polynomial multiwavelets direct method for certain physical variational problems

Sandeep Dixit
Department of Mathematics, University of Petroleum and Energy Studies, Dehradun, India

Shweta Pandey & Sag Ram Verma
Department of Mathematics and Statistics, Gurukula Kangri Vishwavidyalaya, Haridwar, India

ABSTRACT: In this article, variational problems are solved using a direct method derived from Bernstein polynomials multiwavelets (BPMWs). Based on the BPMWs, the operational matrix of integration is provided, which converts the variational problem into an algebraic equation system. Some numerical examples are given, and their findings are compared with the exact solution and some existing methods to demonstrate the efficiency and accuracy.

1 INTRODUCTION

Variational problems are an excellent instrument for the description of a variety of problems such as control theory (Weinstock 1974), image processing (Daubechies & Teschke 2004), and bone cell adhesion in orthopedic implants (Levy 2010). In general, form variational problems can be written as

$$J[\xi_0(x), \xi_1(x), \ldots, \xi_n(x)] = \int_{x_1}^{x_2} L[\xi_0(x), \xi_1(x), \ldots, \xi_n(x), \xi_0'(x), \xi_1'(x), \ldots, \xi_n'(x), x]dx, \quad (1)$$

Subject to the boundary condition for all functions

$$\xi_0(x_0) = a_0, \ \xi_1(x_0) = a_1, \ \cdots, \ \xi_n(x_0) = a_n; \ \xi_0(x_1) = b_0, \ \xi_1(x_1) = b_1, \ \cdots, \ \xi_n(x_1) = b_n. \quad (2)$$

Different numerical methods (Chen & Hsiao 1975; Horng & Chou 1985; Dixit et al. 2010) have been applied for the solution of variational problems. Different wavelet methods (Hsiao 2004; Razzaghi & Yousefi 2000; Glabisz 2004) were also used to solve of variational problems. In this article, orthonormal Bernstein polynomials multiwavelets (BPMWs) were used to develop a direct method to solve variational problems. First, representation of an unknown function is done by BPMWs with unknown coefficients; then the operational matrix of integration is utilized to get the coefficients using the necessary extremization conditions. The BPMWs becomes computationally attractive as the integral of product of two BPMWs function vectors gives an identity matrix. Comparison between the present method and Razzaghi & Yousefi (2000), Hsiao (2004), and Babolian et al. (2007) is made to show the superiority of the proposed method.

DOI 10.1201/9781003167488-57

2 BERNSTEIN POLYNOMIAL MULTIWAVELETS

The BPMWs $\psi_{i,j}(t) = \psi(d, i, j, t)$ are defined over the interval $[0, 1)$ as (Yousefi 2010)

$$\psi_{i,j}(t) = \begin{cases} 2^{d/2} b_j(2^d t - i), & \frac{i}{2^d} \leq t < \frac{i+1}{2^d}, \\ 0, & \text{otherwise}, \end{cases} \tag{3}$$

where d is dilation parameter ($d \in Z^+$), $j = 0, 1, 2 ..., N$ is the order of Bernstein polynomial, translation parameter $i = 0, 1, 2, ..., 2^d - 1$, and t is the normalized time. Here, $b_j(t)$ is orthonormalized Bernstein polynomials of order j.

3 FUNCTION APPROXIMATION AND THE OPERATION MATRIX OF INTEGRATION

We may expand $f(t) \in L^2[0, 1]$ as follows:

$$f(t) = \sum_{i=0}^{\infty} \sum_{j=0}^{\infty} e_{ij} \, \psi_{ij}(t), \tag{4}$$

where $e_{ij} = \langle f(t), \psi_{ij}(t) \rangle$ and $\langle ., . \rangle$ denotes the inner product on the Hilbert space $L^2(R)$. The infinite series (4) is truncated at levels $i = 2^d - 1$ and $j = N$, and the approximation of $f(t)$ is

$$f(t) \approx \sum_{i=0}^{2^d - 1} \sum_{j=0}^{N} e_{ij} \, \psi_{ij}(t) = E^T \, \Psi(t), \tag{5}$$

$$E = [e_{00}, \ldots, e_{0N}; e_{10}, \ldots, e_{1N}; \ldots; e_{(2^d - 1)0}, \ldots, e_{(2^d - 1)N}]^T, \tag{6}$$

$$\Psi(t) = [\psi_{00}(t), \ldots, \psi_{0N}(t); \psi_{10}(t), \ldots, \psi_{1N}(t); \ldots; \psi_{(2^d - 1)0}(t), \ldots, \psi_{(2^d - 1)N}(t)]^T. \tag{7}$$

where E and Ψ are matrices of order $2^d(N + 1) \times 1$.

Next, the BPMWs operational matrix of integration A ($2^d(N + 1)$-order) is given as

$$\int_0^x \Psi(t) \, dt = A_{2^d(N+1) \times 2^d(N+1)} \Psi(x), \tag{8}$$

As the integral of the product of two BPMWs function vectors is an identity matrix I

$$\int_0^1 \Psi(t) \, \Psi^T(t) \, dt = I, \tag{9}$$

Hence, I increases calculating speed and saves memory compared to Glabisz (2004) and Babolian et al. (2007).

4 THE BERNSTEIN POLYNOMIAL MULTIWAVELETS DIRECT METHOD

Consider the problem of evaluating the extremum of the functional

$$J(\xi) = \int_{x_1}^{x_2} L[x, \xi(x), \xi'(x)] \, dx, \tag{10}$$

Let the rate variable can be approximated as

$$\xi'(x) \cong \tilde{\xi}'(x) = \sum_{i=1}^{2^d-1} \sum_{j=0}^{N} e_{ij}\, \psi_{ij}(x) = E^T\, \Psi(x). \tag{11}$$

On integrating Equation (11) from 0 to x and using Equation (8), we express $\xi(x)$ as

$$\xi(x) = \int_0^x \tilde{\xi}'(x)dx + \xi(0) \approx E^T A_{2^d(N+1) \times 2^d(N+1)} \Psi(x) + \xi(0). \tag{12}$$

x can also be approximated in terms of $\Psi(x)$ as

$$x \cong B^T \Psi(x), \quad \text{where } B^T = [b_{00},\, b_{01},\, \ldots,\, b_{0N}] \tag{13}$$

All the other terms in functional given in Equation (10) are known functions of x, so can be expanded into BPMWs via Equation (13). On substituting Equations (11)–(13) in Equation (10), the functional $J(\xi)$ transforms into a function of e_{ij}

$$J = J\left(e_{00}, \ldots, e_{0N}; e_{10}, \ldots, e_{1N}; \ldots; e_{(2^d-1)0}, \ldots, e_{(2^d-1)N}\right). \tag{14}$$

To get the extremum of $J(x)$, we take partial derivatives of J w.r.t. e_{ij} and equate to zero

$$\frac{\partial J}{\partial e_{ij}} = 0, \quad i = 0, 1, \ldots, 2^d - 1, \quad j = 0, 1, \ldots, N. \tag{15}$$

On solving for e_{ij}, and substituting it in Equation (12), we get the solution.

5 NUMERICAL ILLUSTRATIONS

Absolute error functions associated with the subsequent examples are

$$E1(y) = |\xi(y) - \xi1(y)|, E2(y)\, |\xi(y) - \xi2(y)|. \tag{16}$$

where $\xi(y)$ is exact; $\xi1(y)$ and $\xi2(y)$ are approximated solutions for $d = 0$ and $d = 1$, respectively.

Example 1. Consider the following variational problem (Babolian et al. 2007):

$$J(\xi) = \int_0^1 [\xi'^2(x) + x\xi'(x)]\, dx \tag{17}$$

with boundary conditions

$$\xi(0) = 0, \xi(1) = unspecified, \tag{18}$$

An additional condition may be established from (Chen and Hsiao 1975)

$$F_{\xi'}|_{x=1} = 0, \ \xi'(1) = -\frac{1}{2} \tag{19}$$

The analytical solution via Euler's equation is

$$\xi(x) = \frac{-x^2}{4} \tag{20}$$

Suppose $\xi'(x)$ can be approximated as in Equation (11). We solve this example for $N = 3, d = 0$, and $N = 3, d = 1$. Now, substituting Equations (11)–(13) into Equation (17):

$$J \approx \int_0^1 [E^T \psi(x)\psi^T(x)E + E^T \psi(x)\psi^T(x)B]\,dx, \tag{21}$$

Now we are extremizing J subject to the condition (18), μ is the Lagrange multiplier; then we denote $\tilde{J}$ as

$$\tilde{J} \approx J + \mu \left(E^T \psi(1) + \frac{1}{2} \right). \tag{22}$$

Now, on taking $\partial \tilde{J}/\partial E^T = 0; \partial \tilde{J}/\partial \mu = 0$ we get

$$2E + B + \mu\psi(1) = 0 \quad E^T \psi(1) + \frac{1}{2} = 0. \tag{23}$$

On solving Equation (23), we get E^T and μ which gives the approximate solution $\xi(t) = E^T A \psi(t)$. Table 1 compares our results with exact and other numerical solutions. Figure 1 compares the exact and approximate solutions. Absolute error functions are shown in Figure 2.

Table 1. The approximated and exact solution, for Example 1.

t	Exact solutions	Approximated solutions by Haar method (Hsiao 2004)	Approximate solutions by Direct method method (Dixit et al. 2010)	Approximate solutions by TF Bernstein direct (Babolian et al. 2007)	Approximate solutions by proposed BPMWs direct method for $N = 6$	
					$d = 0$	$d = 1$
0.125	−0.003906	−0.0039	−0.003906	−0.003906	−0.00390625	−0.00390625
0.250	−0.015625	−0.0156	−0.015625	−0.015625	−0.015625	−0.015625
0.375	−0.035156	−0.0352	−0.035156	−0.035156	−0.0351563	−0.0351563
0.500	−0.062500	−0.0625	−0.062500	−0.062500	−0.062500	−0.062500
0.625	−0.0976563	−0.0977	−0.097656	−0.097656	−0.0976563	−0.0976562
0.750	−0.140625	−0.1406	0.140625	−0.140625	−0.140625	−0.140625
0.875	−0.191406	−0.1914	−0.191406	−0.191406	−0.191406	−0.191406
1	−0.250000	−0.2539	−0.250000	−0.250000	−0.250000	−0.250000

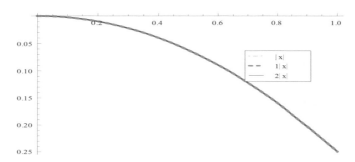

Figure 1. Comparison of the exact solution $\xi(x)$ with approximated solution $\xi 1(x)$ (for $d = 0$) and $\xi 2(x)$ (for $d = 1$).

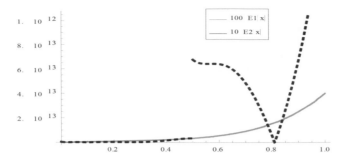

Figure 2. Comparison of absolute errors; $E1(x)$ and $E2(x)$.

Example 2. Take the following variational problem (Chang & Wang 1983)

$$J(\xi) = \int_0^1 [\dot{\xi}^2(x) + x\dot{\xi}(x) + \xi^2(x)]\, dx, \tag{24}$$

with boundary conditions

$$\xi(0) = 0, \xi(1) = \frac{1}{4}, \tag{25}$$

the analytical result using Euler's Lagrange equation is

$$\xi(x) = e^x \frac{2 - e}{4\left(e^2 - 1\right)} + e^{-x} \frac{e\left(1 - 2e\right)}{4\left(e^2 - 1\right)} + \frac{1}{2}. \tag{26}$$

The absolute errors for $N = 3$ and $N = 6$ are shown in Figures 3 and 4, respectively.

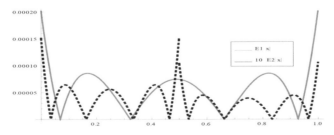

Figure 3. Comparison of absolute errors $E1(x)$ (for $d = 0$) and $E2(x)$ (for $d = 1$) for $N = 3$.

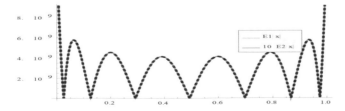

Figure 4. Comparison of absolute errors $E1(x)$ (for $d = 0$) and $E2(x)$(for $d = 1$) for $N = 6$.

482

6 CONCLUSION

The calculation procedures given in Chen & Hsiao (1975), Babolian et al. (2007), and Dixit et al. (2010) are usually too tedious, but the approximation property of orthonormal BPMWs, even with the small number of basis elements, gives satisfactory results and makes the computations very simple. The order of matrix in triangular orthogonal functions (Babolian et al. 2007) is of very large orders 32, 64, and 512, but we used BPMWs operational matrix of order 7 and 14 to achieve similar accuracy, which is shown clearly through figures and tables in the given examples.

REFERENCES

Babolian, E., Mokhtari, R. & Salmani, M. 2007. Using direct method for solving variational problems via triangular orthogonal functions. *Applied Mathematics and Computation* 191: 206–217.

Chang, R. Y. & Wang, M. L. 1983. Shifted Legendre direct method for variational problems. *Journal of Optimization Theory and Applications* 39(2): 299–307.

Chen, C. F. & Hsiao C. H. 1975. A Walsh series direct method for solving variational problems. *Journal of the Franklin Institute* 300(4): 265–280.

Daubechies, I. & Teschke, G. 2004. Wavelet-based image decomposition by variational functional. *Wavelet Applications in Industrial Processing.* 5266: 94–105.

Dixit, S., Singh, V. K., Singh, A. K. & Singh, O. P. 2010 Bernstein Direct Method for Solving. *In ternational Mathematical Forum* 5(48): 2351–2370.

Glabisz W. 2004. Direct Walsh-wavelet packet method for variational problems *Applied Mathematics and Computation* 159(3) 769–781.

Horng, I.R. & Chou, J.H. 1985. Shifted Chebyshev Series Direct Method for Solving Variational Prob lems . *Int. J. Sys. Sci.*16: 855–861.

Hsiao, C. H. 2004. Haar wavelet direct method for solving variational problems. *Mathematics and computers in simulation* 64(5): 569–585.

Levy, J. H. 2010. *Biomechanics Principles, Trends and Applications*. Nova: Nova Science Publisher.

Razzaghi, M. & Yousefi, S. 2000. Legendre wavelets direct method for variational problems. *Mathe matics and computers in simulation* 53(3): 185–192.

Weinstock, R. 1974. *Calculus of variations: with applications to physics and engineering*. Courier Cor poration.

Yousefi, S. A. 2010. B-polynomial multiwavelets approach for the solution of Abel's integral equation. *International Journal of Computer Mathematics* 87(2): 310–316.

Smart Computing – Khan et al (Eds)
© *2021 Taylor & Francis Group, London, ISBN 978-0-367-76552-1*

Traffic sign recognition using SVM and convolutional neural network

Renuka B. Ayyajjanavar & P. Jayarekha
BMS College of Engineering, Bangalore, Karnataka, India

ABSTRACT: Traffic Sign Recognition (TSR) is one of the most popular topics in image processing, which uses machine learning and deep learning techniques to identify the signs. TSR is an important feature of Advance Driver Assistant System (ADAS), which provides necessary information about the road. This helps to overcome road accidents and provides safety to drivers. This research gives implementation for TSR using Support Vector Machine (SVM) and Convolutional Neural Network (CNN) algorithm. Here, we are applying these two algorithms on German Traffic Sign Recognition Dataset (GTSRD) and computing the accuracy for both algorithms along with train time and prediction time. Then by analyzing the performance, we are suggesting the suitable algorithm for TSR.

Keywords: Traffic Sign Recognition, Advance Driver Assistant System, Support Vector Machine, Convolutional Neural Network, German Traffic Sign Recognition Dataset.

1 INTRODUCTION

According to recent survey from National Highway Traffic Safety Administration, 94% of accidents in the world are due to human errors. Sometimes the drivers cannot be able to identify objects from his position due to lack of attention while driving, reflection of lights during night time, fog, weather, etc. To overcome these problems, autonomous vehicles came into existence. Autonomous vehicles consist of Advance Driver Assistance System (ADAS). Among various ADAS functions, traffic sign detection is one of the precious tasks because ignorance of traffic signs causes accidents while driving. Traffic sign recognition (TSR) gives an alert to the driver to reduce the pressure while driving.

Developing automated traffic sign detection assist the driver while driving and guarantees the safety of the driver, other drivers, and also pedestrians. The main goal of traffic sign detection is to alert the driver while driving to prevent accidents. Sometimes it is difficult to detect the traffic sign by the system due to various environment conditions, for example: weather changes, light variations, complexity in identification of image, rain, and so on. The traffic sign in different light condition is shown in Figure 1.

Traffic sign (TS) is mainly categorized into three types based on its functions, which are as follows:

- Regulatory Signs: These signs are also called as control signs and gives information about traffic rules and regulations. These signs include stop sign, yield sign, etc.
- Warning Sign: Gives notice to driver about upcoming hazards or dangers like speed changes, lane merges, etc.
- Guide Sign: These signs give directional information to the drivers like routes and distance to the destination.

DOI 10.1201/9781003167488-58

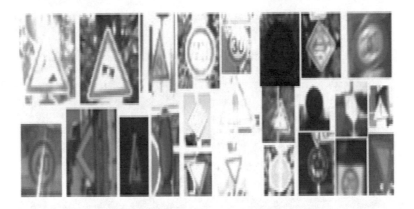

Figure 1.   Traffic sign in different light and weather conditions from GTSRB.

TS categories are again divided into subclasses based on their shape and information it gives to driver.

This paper gives two different approaches to recognize the traffic sign, i.e., Support Vector Machine (SVM) and Convolutional Neural Network (CNN) algorithm. We imported the SVM model from sklearn and applied it to the dataset. For CNN, different convolutional neural network layers are built to create model. After the creation of both the models, each model is applied to the German Traffic Sign Recognition Dataset (GTSRB) and finds accuracy and time taken by each model. At the end, it gives comparative analysis for SVM and CNN models.

2   RELATED WORK

2.1   *Traffic sign recognition*

Kaoutar et al. (2017) proposed work on traffic sign detection and recognition. Traffic sign recognition (TSR) plays vital role in ADAS and identification of these signs on the road while driving reduces the road accidents and saves the life of driver. Traffic sign recognition (TSR) is still an open challenge. For real time traffic sign detection author implemented color segmentation and CNN (C-CNN) algorithm.

Tarequl (2019) worked on the traffic sign detection and recognition, but here the author did not consider any specific place dataset. Instead, he collected set of common signs, then classified it based on shape and applied CNN for real-time identification of the signs.

Prashengit et al. (2017) proposed implementation of TSR using the Bangladeshi traffic signs dataset. After the collection of dataset the author first segmented the images using HSV (Hue, Saturation, Value) model and filtered it based on shape of sign. After the classification of image, author applied deep CNN to extract the features and observe the performance of network.

2.2   *SVM*

Yujun et al. (2015) gave a basic idea about how a SVM classifier will work. The author proposed a boundary detection technique using SVM and tried to improve the learning ability for the given dataset. This method reduces risk and increases confidence range for the identification of small images.

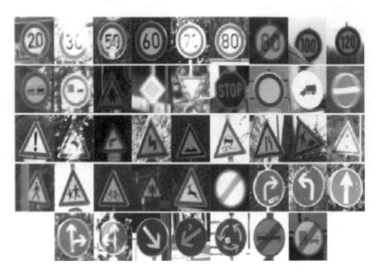

Figure 2.   Images of 43 traffic signs.

Wang (2008) created a survey on SVM algorithm techniques and divided it into three groups, i.e., variant-based, decomposition-based, and all other remaining algorithms in another group.

2.3   *CNN*

Rahul et al. (2018) proposed CNN for image detection and recognition. CNN mimics the function-alities of human brain. The author builds CNN which consists of multiple layers and applied it to MNIST, CIFAR-10 dataset, and then analyzed the performance of model on both the dataset.

Sun et al. (2019) proposed a CNN method to identify the TS. Here, the author first processed all images to highlight important features. Then applied the transformation method to detect signs on road. After successful detection of signs, deep CNN is created for recognition of only circular shaped images and achieved 98.2% of accuracy.

2.4   *Keras library*

Keras is open-source library which is written in python (Safat, 2019). This library is used for fast experimentation of deep neural network algorithms. Keras has the capability of running on top of the Tensor Flow library.

3   DATASET

GTSRB dataset is downloaded from the Kaggle website. It is an image classification dataset. This dataset has more than 50,000 images, which contains different photos of 43 traffic signs. This dataset contains 3 folders, i.e., Meta, Test, and Train folders. Meta folder contains all the 43 Train folders i.e., 0–42 folders, where each folder is considered as one class. Each class consists of images with different size and is used to train the model. Test folder contains all 43 traffic sign images with different sizes. This data is used to test the trained model.

All 43 sign images, which are present in the dataset is showed in Figure 2. These pictures gives information about speed limits, no entry symbol, directions like turn left or right, children crossing, etc.

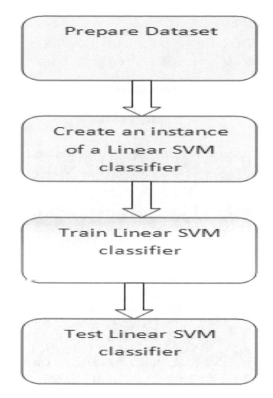

Figure 3.   Steps to build a linear SVM model.

4   IMPLEMENTATION OF SVM

SVM is machine learning supervised algorithm, which is used for classification and regression purpose (Yujun, 2015). Basic functionality of this algorithm is, it divides dataset into different classes based on their features and draws higher plane for proper classification.

To build the SVM model, matplotlib and sklearn modules are installed through pip command. Matplotlib is mainly used to plot graphs. SVM is imported from the sklearn module and also it is used to split the dataset into training and test dataset. Here we are using 80% of dataset to train the model and remaining 20% to test the model. Steps to build SVM model to train and test dataset is showed in Figure 3.

- Prepare Dataset: In this step the data will be split into train and test dataset.
- Create an instance of a linear SVM classifier: In this step we are creating instance of SVM classifier using scikit-learn module. Here we are explicitly mentioning kernel as linear to build linear SVM classifier.
- Train Linear SVM classifier: To train the model here we are using 31,367 images. The shapes of images are (30, 30, 3) i.e., height = 30, width = 30, and 3 indicates RGB value, means the images are colored images.
- Test Linear SVM model: After training model, we are testing the model for test dataset, which contains 7842 images.

After applying a linear SVM model to the GTSRB dataset, the total time taken to train the model is 68 min and time taken for prediction of 20% test dataset is 88 min. Accuracy for the prediction of test dataset using a linear SVM model is 94% is shown in Figure 4.

accuracy			0.94	7842
macro avg	0.93	0.94	0.94	7842
weighted avg	0.94	0.94	0.94	7842

Figure 4.   Accuracy for test dataset using the linear SVM model.

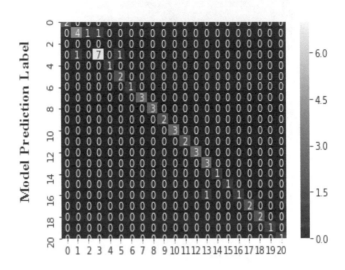

Figure 5.   Confusion matrix.

Confusion matrix for first 21 labels and for first 50 samples from test dataset is showed in Figure 5. Here, we can identify proper predictions and wrong predictions based on comparing the X and Y axis labels.

5   IMPLEMENTATION OF CNN

CNN is a deep learning algorithm (Rahul, 2018), which takess image as input and applies weights and biases to various objects present in the image and identifies all objects. To implement CNN on GTSRB dataset, the dataset is used similar to SVM model, i.e,, 80% of data to train model and 20% to test model. Steps involved in building CNN for dataset is shown in Figure 6.

- Explore dataset: Train folder contains 43 folders, each folder represents different classes. Here, we used OS module to iterate through all these classes and append all images and labels to data. To split the dataset sklearn module is used.
- Building CNN module: CNN consists of different layers like input layer, middle layer, and output layer. Figure 7 gives a brief idea about how to build different layers in CNN.
- Train the model with train dataset: After building the model, it will be fit with train dataset. Here we trained model with 64 batch size.
- Test model with test dataset: After training the model, Test folder dataset is tested to find the accuracy of the CNN model.

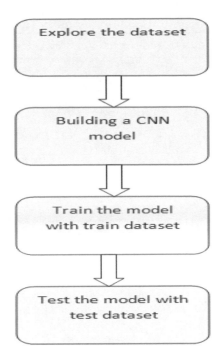

Figure 6.   Steps to build CNN for dataset.

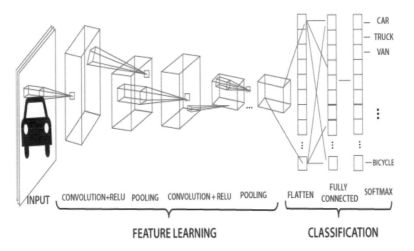

Figure 7.   Convolutional neural network.

After training the model on GTSRB dataset, accuracy and loss graph is plotted for 16 epochs, which is shown in Figure 8 and 9. For train dataset the accuracy is 98.46%. Time taken to train model is 36 min.

The time taken by CNN for the prediction of test data is just 14 sec and accuracy is 96%.

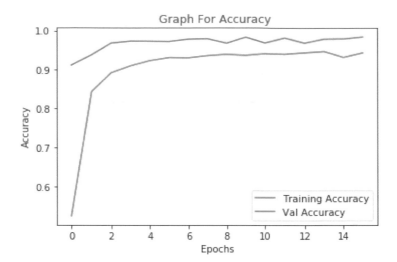

Figure 8.　Graph for accuracy.

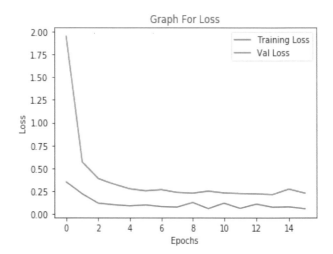

Figure 9.　Graph for loss.

6　COMPARISION OF ALGORITHMS

This section gives a clear idea about the performance of SVM and CNN algorithm on GTSRB dataset. Difference between the accuracy of both the algorithms is 2%, but training time and prediction time for both models has more of a difference, as shown in Figure 10.

The visualization of the accuracy and performance analysis of SVM and CNN is shown in Figures 11 and 12.

Based on analysis of accuracy and performance for both the algorithms on GTSRB dataset, we can conclude that a deep learning CNN works faster and gives more accuracy as compared to the machine learning SVM algorithm.

Algorithm Name	Time taken to train model	Prediction Time	Accuracy
SVM	68 min	88 min	94%
CNN	36 min	14 sec(0.23 min)	96%

Figure 10. Performance evaluation for SVM and CNN.

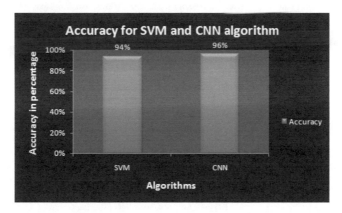

Figure 11. Accuracy for SVM and CNN.

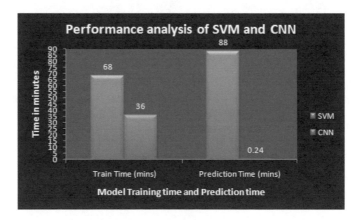

Figure 12. Performance analysis based on time.

7 CONCLUSION

Autonomous vehicles are driverless vehicles, which does not involve any human interactions. These vehicles works based on sensors collected information by perceiving surrounding environment, which involves static and dynamic objects, in that traffic sign identification also plays vital role. TSR is part of intelligent transport system in ADAS to build an autonomous vehicle. Identification of these signs while driving ensures the safety of customers. This paper gives basic idea about the working of SVM and CNN. Here we implemented these two algorithms on GTSRB dataset and analysis the result of both the algorithms and given clear visualization of algorithms result. From this analysis it is proved that CNN algorithm works better than the SVM.

In future work, we can identify traffic signs based on their shape, and also by applying different algorithms.

REFERENCES

Guosheng Wang. 2008, A Survey on Training Algorithms for Support Vector Machine Classifiers. International Conference on Networked Computing and Advanced Information Management.

Kaoutar Sefrioui Boujemaa, Afaf Bouhoute, Karim Boubouh, Ismail Berrada. 2017, Traffic sign recognition using convolutional neural networks. International Conference on Wireless Networks and Mobile Communications (WINCOM).

Prashengit Dhar, Zainal Abedin, Tonoy Biswas, Anish Datta. Dec 2017, Traffic Sign Detection- A New Approach and Recognition Using Convolution Neural Network. IEEE Region 10 Humanitarian Technology Conference (R10-HTC).

Rahul Chauhan, Kamal Kumar, Ghanshala Joshi. 2018, Convolutional Neural Network (CNN) for Image Detection and Recognition. International Conference on Secure Cyber Computing and Communication (ICSCCC).

Safat B. Wali, Majid Abdullah, Mahammad Hannan, Aini Hussain, Salina Samad, Pin Ker and Muhamad Bin Mansor. 2019, Vision-Based Traffic Sign Detection and Recognition Systems: Current Trends and Challenges. Sensors (Basel).

Tarequl Islam. 2019, Traffic sign detection and recognition based on convolutional neural networks. International Conference on Advances in Computing, Communication and Control (ICAC3).

Ying Sun, Pingshu Ge, Dequan Liu. 2019, Traffic Sign Detection and Recognition Based on Convolutional Neural Network. Chinese Automation Congress Conference.

Yujun Yang, Jianping Li, Yimei Yang. 2015, The Research Of The Fast Svm Classifier Method. 12th International Computer Conference on Wavelet Active Media Technology and Information Processing (ICCWAMTIP).

Track 3: Real-time and VLSI system

Smart Computing – Khan et al (Eds)
© 2021 Taylor & Francis Group, London, ISBN 978-0-367-76552-1

Smart glove for translating sign gestures to text

Tushar Verma, Suleman Khan, Vipul Kumar, Rijwan Khan & Pawan Kumar Sharma
Department of Computer Science and Engineering,
ABES Institute of Technology, Ghaziabad, Affiliated to AKTU Lucknow, India

ABSTRACT: Normally speech-disabled people use sign gestures to communicate with another person but for a normal person, it's very hard to understand sign language. So, our aim is to develop a device capable of translating sign language in order to make it easy for disabled people to communicate with the general public. For this, a smart hand gesture recognition system is proposed to reduce the communication gap between disabled and normal people (Hubbell 2014). The system is in the form of a glove, which consists of five flex sensors, one for each finger and a 3-axis accelerometer on the back of the palm, connected to an Arduino MEGA device. Flex sensors measure the bend of each finger and the accelerometer measures the slope of the palm. Data from these sensors is for each gesture collected to create a dataset (Deller et al. 2006). The system is based on American Sign Language. Machine Learning Algorithms train over these datasets to predict what gesture the user is making. The goal of this smart system is to minimize the communication gap and make day to day communication for disabled easy.

Keywords: smart glove, sensor, gesture, styling, insert

1 INTRODUCTION

According to the statistics of the World Federation of the Deaf and the World Health Organization, approximately 70 million people in the world are deaf-mute (Hubbell 2014). Sign language has an important role in the life of people with speech and hearing disorders for daily communication. Even then many people require a translator, which is expensive, or the other party is required to learn sign language. Both methods are not convenient and efficient in daily life. Each letter in the sign language has its own gesture. Many techniques are also used for Sign language translation like image processing, wearable sensors (Deller et al. 2006). Image processing requires high computational power and is quite complex. On the other hand, flex sensors are easy to use for users. In the era of emerging IoT, this method can be integrated with many applications such as smart healthcare, IIoT, smart bands, smart watches, bionic arms, etc. (Fels et al. 1994; Khan et al. 2020; Khan & Abuhasel 2020; Quasim et al. 2019; Quasim et al. 2020), (Abuhasel 2020)). This glove is developed using Random Forest Classifier for translation of sign language into text. The circuit of this glove is developed using flex sensors, 3- axis accelerometer and a gyroscope to collect data from the gestures and we are using machine learning for the classification of data.

In our country, there is no formal education for Indian Sign Language (ISL). So, we would be using American Sign Language for the development.

There are two main phases of operation for this project. The first phase is gathering data. This phase includes the recording and labeling of data.

After the completion of the first phase, the collected data is pre-processed. Which includes removing outliers and filling incomplete data.

In the second phase, the data is processed, and continuous predictions are made. For prediction, the machine learning algorithm is used. The model trains on the collected dataset and predictions are made.

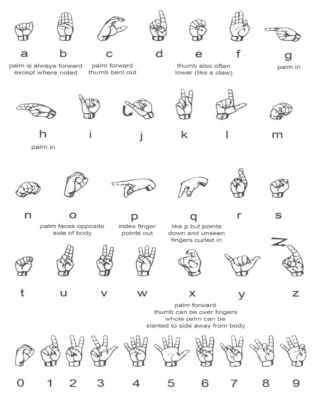

Figure 1. The ASL fingerspelling alphabet. https://www.nidcd.nih.gov/health/american-sign-language

2 LITERARY REVIEW

A summary of what we learned from the existing project in the same domain and understanding the behavior of individual systems. Priya Matnani (Matnani 2015) proposed the method in which hand, face and body gestures are used to communicate with the computer and other smart systems. It includes remote access of devices because of exposure to risks, controlling robotic arms and mechanical prosthetics. Real-time engagement in a simulation system. Laura Dipietro, Angelo M. Sabatini (Dipietro et al. 2008) discusses multiple glove-based systems. Like: a) Magnetic: Low cost, reasonable accuracy but susceptible to magnetic fields. b) Ultrasonic: The ultrasonic signal is used to determine the position. It can be easily obstructed, and transmission rate is slow. c) Optical: Through image processing. Computationally taxative and sensitive to lighting. d) Inertial: Measures the change in orientation of the hand. The paper also discusses the application of the smart glove in – interacting with/replacing hardware like mouse and keyboard, a communication system for deaf, analysis of hand or body movements for medical purposes. Solanki Krunal (Krunal 2013) introduces a glove-based system which uses flex sensors to determine hand gestures. Then the result is displayed on LCD along with speech. M. P. Paulraj, S. Yaacob, H. Desa, and W. Majid (Paulraj et al. 2009) uses a neural network for gesture recognition. Neural networks showed an accuracy of 98–99% as compared to other methods. This method, however, is only good for a system with high computational power. Kuo Chue Neo, Haidi Ibrahm and Wan Mohd Yusof Rahiman and Wan Abdul Aziz (Neo & Ibrahim 2011)– The system is based on image processing where the gestures are recognized using a camera. Abhishek Tandon, Amit Saxena Keshav Mehrotra, Khushboo Kashyap, Harmeet Kaur (Tandon et al. 2016). The system consists of flex sensors connected to a microcontroller. The inputs are in Indian sign language which is then converted into text and speech. The desired output is displayed on the phone screen through bluetooth. Tushar

Chouhan, Ankit Panse, Anvesh Kumar Voona and S. M. Sameer (Chouhan et al. 2014)– The smart glove is developed with the use of flex sensors, accelerometer and hall sensors and machine learning is then used to predict the hand gesture. Machine learning is based on MATLAB running on computer systems.

3 HARDWARE

3.1 *Arduino MEGA*

Arduino MEGA is a microcontroller board developed by Arduino.cc and based on Atmega 2560. Arduino provides all the necessary components for the working of the microcontroller along with an IDE (Integrated Development Environment). IDE can be used to write and upload code to Arduino and is compatible with Windows, MAC, and Linux. It can be connected to the computer using a simple USB cable. It supports both C and C++. It has 16 analog input pins, 54 I/O digital ports, voltage regulator and a crystal oscillator which acts as a clock (Kumar 2013).

3.2 *ADXL*

ADXL is a low power, 3-axis accelerometer. It supports both I2C and SPI interfaces. It can measure the tilt (static acceleration) and motion (dynamic acceleration). It provides a 13-bit resolution measurement at up to ±16 g. To power the module a 3.3V voltage is needed. Working ADXL345:

While the module faces up, Z_OUT is at the maximum which is +1 g; face down, Z_OUT is at the minimum. X_OUT increases along the Ax axis direction and Y_OUT along the Ay axis. See the picture below. Thus, when you rotate the module, you can see the changes in X_OUT, Y_OUT, and Z_OUT.

3.3 *Flex Sensor*

Flex sensor, a type of variable resistor. Its resistance is directly proportional to the angle of bent, higher the bend higher is the resistance. It usually comes in two sizes, 2.2 inches, and 4.5 inches. For our system, we have chosen 4.5 inches flex sensors.

For interfacing, one terminal of the flex sensor is connected to the A0 pin of the Arduino along with a 100k ohm resistor and the other terminal is connected to the ground pin.

Bend Resistance Range: 45K to 125K Ohms. Through this, the angle of the bent can be determined.

4 WORKING MODEL

Five flex sensors are attached on all the fingers (thumb, index, middle, ring, and pinky) and the accelerometer is placed on the back of the hand. Flex sensors the bent of the fingers (Sherrill et al. 2002) and accelerometer determine the tilt of the hand (Kabai 2008). All the sensors are connected to Arduino mega (Ghimire et al. 2018).

For a gesture, the sensor records the reading and the Arduino saves the data in a CSV file (Bishop 2006), (Dickson 2017). Once the dataset is prepared, the machine learning algorithm is used to train and develop a model.

After the data preparation and modeling, the model is then used to predict the meaning of the gesture performed by the user. The result is then displayed on the screen.

(a) Data Preparation– It is done in three steps.
(b) Dataset collection– The data at the serial port was collected and formatted into a structured csv (comma separated file) file.
(c) Data preprocessing – outliers, missing data, and then the collected data is randomized. After preprocessing, the dataset is then labeled for all five fingers and all 6 dimensions of MPU6050- 3 for accelerometer and 3 for the gyroscope.

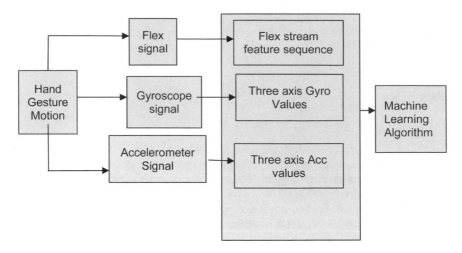

Figure 2. Working model.

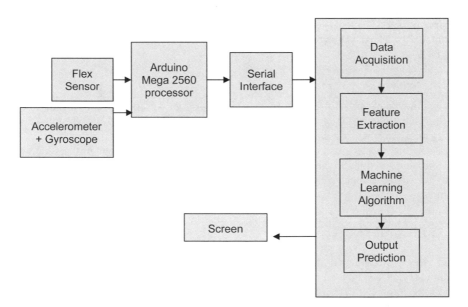

Figure 3. System block diagram.

4.1 *System block diagram:*

Once the dataset is prepared and preprocessed, the dataset is then trained with the machine learning algorithm – Random Forest Classifier (Ghimire et al. 2018). The trained model is then saved with the pickle library of python. Python then checks the data from the smart glove at the serial port through the serial interface. The inputted data is then processed through the saved model and the output is then displayed on the laptop screen.

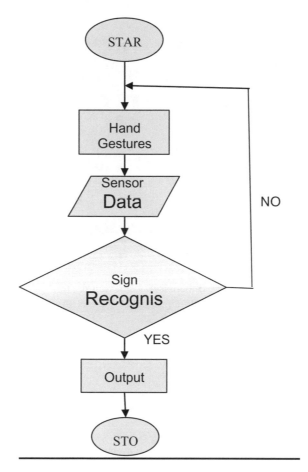

Figure 4. Flowchart.

5 FLOWCHART

6 PROPOSED ALGORITHM

Algorithm

A) Data Preparation at Arduino mega
    1. Start.
    2. Input – for a gesture.
    3. Read data from all six sensors.
    4. Write the sensor data into a CSV file.
    5. All the gesture inputted?
       A. If yes, goto B.
       B. Else, goto 2.
B) Dataset Preparation at Python end
    1. Start
    2. Read the dataset from the CSV file.
    3. Do preprocessing.
    4. Label the dataset.
    5. End
C) Prediction
    1. Start

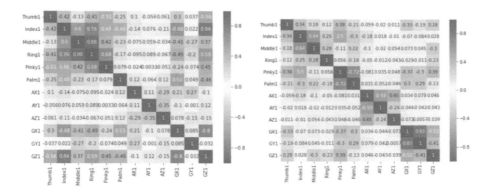

Figure 5.   Correlation plot for alphabet 'A' and 'B'.

2. Train the model using the dataset
3. Check the data at the serial port, if there is no data, wait for it.
4. After collecting data, predict the output through the trained model.
5. End.

7   RANDOM FOREST ALGORITHM

It is a supervised learning algorithm. It uses a tree-like graph to show the possible consequences. In the Random Forest algorithm, if there are enough trees in the forest, the classifier won't over fit the model (Ho 1995).

Pseudocode

1. Randomly select "n" features from total "m" features.
2. Calculate the node "d" using the best split point.
3. Split the node into daughter nodes.
4. Repeat a to c until a certain number of nodes is reached.
5. Repeat a to d to build the forest for "i" times.

8   CONCLUSIONS

This paper has presented the project of smart gloves for deaf and dumb communities. The primary objective of this project was to make a device that could read the sign language to help deaf and dumb people communicate more efficiently with the general population. Machine learning was used to train the datasets for the sign language. Speech disabled people can rely on sign language translators for communication, but this method is too expensive for common people (Ghimire et al. 2018).

A huge drawback of this model is the closeness of the dataset of the different alphabet and word with each other. Due to time limitations, we only were able to take 350 datasets for each alphabet and word.

Since the data showed a high correlation, the only way to increase accuracy is to increase the size of the dataset. Regardless of the issues mentioned, the designed glove could lower the communication gap between deaf dumb people and the general population to a certain level. The system is in prototype phase, future applications may include interacting with other smart systems, remote use of robots, writing an email.

REFERENCES

Abuhasel K. A. and M. A. Khan, 2020, "A Secure Industrial Internet of Things (IIoT) Framework for Resource Management in Smart Manufacturing," in IEEE Access, vol. 8, pp. 117354–117364, 2020, doi: 10.1109/ACCESS.2020.3004711.

Hubbell Daniel.2014, "Blogs: Microsoft".

Deller, M., Ebert, A., Bender, M. and Hagen, H., 2006, July. Flexible gesture recognition for immersive virtual environments. In *Tenth International Conference on Information Visualisation* (IV'06) (pp. 563–568). IEEE.

Fels, S. Sidney, and Geoffrey Hinton. Glove-Talk II: Mapping Hard Gestures to Speech Using Neural Networks: an Approach to Building Adaptive Interfaces. *University of Toronto, Department of Computer Science*, 1994.

Matnani, P., 2015. Glove based and accelerometer based gesture control. *International Journal of Technical Research and Applications*, 3(6), pp.216–221.

Paulraj, M.P., Yaacob, S., Desa, H. and Ab Majid, W.M.R.W., 2009, March. Gesture recognition system for Kod Tangan Bahasa Melayu (KTBM) using neural network. In 2009 *5th International Colloquium on Signal Processing & Its Applications* (pp. 19–22). IEEE.

Sherrill, D.M., Bonato, P. and De Luca, C.J., 2002, October. A neural network approach to monitor motor activities. *In Proceedings of the Second Joint 24th Annual Conference and the Annual Fall Meeting of the Biomedical Engineering Society] [Engineering in Medicine and Biology* (Vol. 1, pp. 52–53). IEEE.

Creative commons, "MegaQuickRef: *Arduino-info*," Wikispaces.

Solanki Krunal, M., 2013. Indian sign languages using flex sensor glove. *International Journal of Engineering Trends and Technology*, 4(6), pp.2478–2480.

Creative commons, "Product: SparkFun Electronics," SparkFun Electronics. "Electronic wings," *Electronic Wings*.

Kabai Sandor. 2008, "Gyroscope," *Wolfram Demonstrations Project*.

Khan M.A. et. al, 2020a, Decentralised IoT, Decenetralised IoT: A Blockchain perspective, Springer, Studies in BigData, 2020, DOI: https://doi.org/10.1007/978-3-030-38677-1

Khan, M. A., Quasim, M. T, et.al, 2020b, A Secure Framework for Authentication and Encryption Using Improved ECC for IoT-Based Medical Sensor Data, in IEEE Access, vol. 8, pp. 52018–52027, 2020. DOI: 10.1109/ACCESS.2020.2980739

Khan M. A., 2020c, An IoT Framework for Heart Disease Prediction Based on MDCNN Classifier, in IEEE Access, vol. 8, pp. 34717–34727, 2020. DOI: 10.1109/ACCESS.2020.2974687

Khan M.A, and Algarni F., 2020d "A Healthcare Monitoring System for the Diagnosis of Heart Disease in the IoMT Cloud Environment Using MSSO-ANFIS," in IEEE Access, vol. 8, pp. 122259–122269, 2020, doi: 10.1109/ACCESS.2020.3006424.

Khan, MA, Abuhasel, KA. 2020e. Advanced metameric dimension framework for heterogeneous industrial Internet of things. Computational Intelligence. 2020; 1– 21. https://doi.org/10.1111/coin.12378

Bishop, C.M., 2006. Pattern recognition and *machine learning. springer.*

Dickson, B., 2017. Exploiting machine learning in cybersecurity. *TechCrunch.*

Ho, T.K., Nokia of America Corp, 1999. *Classification technique using random decision forests. U.S. Patent* 5,930,392.

Dipietro, L., Sabatini, A.M. and Dario, P., 2008. A survey of glove-based systems and their applications. *IEEE transactions on systems, man, and cybernetics,* part c (applications and reviews), 38(4), pp.461–482.

Neo, K.C. and Ibrahim, H., 2011. Development of Sign Signal Translation System Based on Altera's FPGA DE2 Board. *International Journal of Human Computer Interaction (IJHCI),* 2(3), p.101.

Tandon, A., Mehrotra, A.S.K., Kashyap, K. and Kaur, H., A Review Paper on Smart Glove–Converts Indian Sign Language (ISL) into *Text and Speech. International Journal for Scientific Research & Development (IJSRD)* Vol, 4, pp.269–272.

Chouhan, T., Panse, A., Voona, A.K. and Sameer, S.M., 2014, September. Smart glove with gesture recognition ability for the hearing and speech impaired. In 2014 *IEEE Global Humanitarian Technology Conference-South Asia Satellite* (GHTC-SAS) (pp. 105–110). IEEE.

Ghimire, A., Kathmandu, N., Kadayat, B., Basnet, A. and Shrestha, A., *Smart Glove.* 2

Quasim, M. T., Khan M. A, et.al, 2019, Internet of Things for Smart Healthcare: A Hardware Perspective, 2019 First International Conference of Intelligent Computing and Engineering (ICOICE), Hadhramout, Yemen, 2019, pp. 1–5. DOI: 10.1109/ICOICE48418.2019.9035175

Quasim, M.T., Khan M.A, Algarni F., Alharthy A., Alshmrani G.M.M, (2020), Blockchain Frameworks. In: Khan M., Quasim M., Algarni F., Alharthi A. (eds) Decentralised Internet of Things. Studies in Big Data, vol 71. Springer, DOI: https://doi.org/10.1007/978-3-030-38677-1

Smart Computing – Khan et al (Eds)
© *2021 Taylor & Francis Group, London, ISBN 978-0-367-76552-1*

Krill Herd (KH) algorithm for text document clustering using TF–IDF features

Priyanka Shivaprasad More & Baljit Singh Saini
Computer Science Engineering, Lovely Professional University, Phagwara, India

Kamaljit Singh Bhatia
ECE, G.B. Pant Institute of Engineering and Technology, Pauri-Garhwal, India

ABSTRACT: The text document clustering is essential for providing navigation and searching methods by managing huge amounts of data into small and meaningful clusters. Due to a large number of text documents, document management tools are termed as a major topic for information retrieval. However, the conventional text clustering methods relate documents that utilize identical terminology and disregard conceptual similarity which may degrade the performance. This paper devises a KH algorithm for clustering a large number of documents. Here, the pre-processing is performed to eliminate noise and artifacts present in the data which is performed by stemming and stop word removal method. Moreover, term frequency–inverse document frequency (TF–IDF) is adapted for extracting the noteworthy features. The clustering of documents is carried out by acquiring features obtained from TF–IDF and applies the KH strategy to cluster text documents. The fitness function is newly devised considering mean square error and Jaccard similarity.

1 INTRODUCTION

The data is collected from various sources, which comprise a huge set of documents. Here, all documents consist of key-value pairs, and the attributes are assembled in subdocuments. The document assists litheness in developing model and facade ability to save structured data and assort them into the solitary set. Also, these datasets are acknowledged as schema-less and these schemas are adapted in handing data (Chevalier et al. 2015). The succession in technology and institution gathers large data, which masquerade different structure, velocity, and categories (Li et al. 2018). The amendment of the appropriate way might escort huge growth and facilitate associations to completely modify the information in the rising world which oblige sophisticated analysis of data and assist to facilitate pioneering models for handling large data and need of arrangement (Martinho & Santos 2016). The dataset provides a wrapper, which is used to retrieve the data based on the provided query. The documents which should be recovered are accessed to large datasets and queries (Karypis et al. 2000). In traditional datasets, the documents are managed in specific modes and the subject of a specific field is accessed based on queries. The queries are modeled, and these results are generated using indexing relations between different fields (Yarlagadda et al. 2019).

Text document clustering is an application of mining texts and a major issue of cluster analysis (Dörpinghaus et al. 2018). Recently, the count of published technical documents augmented exponentially. Thus, a proficient scientific document clustering model is of great interest among researchers for detecting research in-fronts in clustering. The citation networks (Zhang et al. 2019) are classified into three types, which involve co-citation, bibliographic coupling, and direct citation (Ailem et al. 2017; Yarlagadda et al. 2019). Several clustering strategies are employed for searching the documents or organizing the outcomes generated by search engines using specific

DOI 10.1201/9781003167488-60

queries. Here, agglomerative hierarchical clustering, K-means techniques, are frequently adapted for document clustering (Wan & Liu 2014; Srikanth & Sakthivel 2018). However, classical strategies are costly and require more endeavors for clustering document. Thus, incremental clustering strategies provide a trustworthy solution for minimizing the computation cost to deal with large datasets (Chevalier et al. 2015). The incremental clustering strategies are generally practiced in two phases. The initial phase is used for updating micro-clusters in real time whereas in other stages the clustering is performed with accumulated synopsis in which the request is given by the user (Martinho & Santos 2016). The incremental probabilistic latent semantic analysis technique is designed to compute the attributes which assist in revising the incremental hyperparameters (Chevalier et al. 2015; Yarlagadda et al. 2019).

This primary intention is to devise a KH algorithm to cluster a huge number of documents. Here, the pre-processing is performed to eliminate noise, artifacts contained in data, which is performed by stemming and the stop word removal method. Moreover, term frequency–inverse document frequency (TF–IDF) is utilized for extracting noteworthy features. The clustering of documents is carried out by acquiring features obtained from TF–IDF and applies the KH algorithm to cluster text documents. The fitness function is newly devised considering mean square error (MSE) and Jaccard similarity and is adapted for selecting the optimal centroids.

The main contribution of this paper: **Proposed TF-IDF-based KH strategy for clustering text document:** The proposed TF-IDF-based KH algorithm is employed for clustering documents. Here, the optimal solution is obtained for selecting the cluster centroid.

The remainder of the paper is structured as follows. Section 2 illustrates the introductory part of text document clustering. The survey of text document clustering techniques from four papers is elaborated in Section 3. Section 4 presents the challenges confronted by conventional text document clustering strategies. Section 5 demonstrates the KH algorithm for the clustering text document. The results of the methods and their performance are evaluated in Section 6. Lastly, Section 7 provides a conclusion.

2 MOTIVATION

Text document clustering is an emerging technique in browsing huge documents by categorizing the documents into a small number of controllable clusters. Numerous text document clustering algorithms are devised in the literary works for clustering the text data. However, the algorithm poses certain issues like synonymy and ambiguity which may produce erroneous grouping causing similarities among documents to be unnoticed. Moreover, the next section outlines four conventional strategies based on text document clustering whose limitations are considered for devising a novel model for a clustering text document.

3 LITERATURE REVIEW

The conventional strategies involved in text document clustering are illustrated along with their merits and demerits. Ailem et al. (2017) designed a generative mixture model, namely the Sparse Poisson Latent Block Model (SPLBM) to cluster huge data. This method was devised based on Poisson distribution, which utilizes contingency tables like a document-term matrix. The benefits of SPLBM can be modeled two-fold: (1) devise meticulous statistical models, which are cost-conscious (2) deal with data sparsity issues. The SPLBM algorithm was effective in handling complex and unbalanced datasets. However, the method failed to study the fuzzy norm based on the data log-likelihood for deriving the variational expectation–maximization (EM) algorithm. Sheri et al. (2019) designed an automated consensus-building measure based on text classifiers. The proposed method utilized the information of the cluster to constitute a dataset for training the classifier. This method was superior and produced effective results compared to other methods. However, it failed to test a combination of discriminative measures for improving performance.

Brockmeier et al.(2018) devised a strategy for clustering documents using the contents of the cluster by rapidly scanning the pertinent clusters. The selection of metaphors was based on the criteria of heuristic. Moreover, the descriptive clustering was adapted for predicting the subset of features. The document clustering was carried out using a multinomial regression model for cluster prediction. This method was useful in selecting the optimal feature for cluster prediction. Ahmadi et al. (2018) devised a document clustering strategy based on Cluster-based Sparse Topical Coding. Here, the modeling of the topic was performed for enhancing the clustering of the textual document by bag-of-words models and project them with topic spaces. The dormant descriptions of semantics were devised from the topic model, which were further used as features for initiating the clustering. The clustering of the document and topic modeling were combined in an amalgamated framework for attaining improved performance.

4 CHALLENGES

The challenges confronted by the conventional text document clustering strategies are as follows.

- The major drawback of the extended citation model is to envelop the documents using overviews, letters, editorials, and other document styles considering citation sentences and semantics (Zhang et al. 2019).
- The major drawbacks in clustering the document are based on bigotry information that occurs when the adequate training samples were not in the classifier. This issue generally occurs whereas the solutions of preliminary clustering did not pose any contracted documents. Moreover, consensus clustering is a complicated process on these datasets (Sheri et al. 2019).
- In Brockmeier et al. (2018), predictions of the cluster are done using logistic regression models, and prediction of the feature is based on logistic or multinomial regression models.

5 PROPOSED TF–IDF-BASED KH ALGORITHM

The clustering of text documents is considered an essential part of offering perceptive navigation and browsing strategies by arranging huge information into small clusters. Due to the profusion of text documents obtainable with communal document management models, high-quality partitioning of texts is focused on business intelligence. Here, the KH algorithm (Gandomi & Alavi 2012) is employed for clustering the text documents for enhancing the competence of clustering. Initially, keywords from the text are subjected to pre-processing for eliminating superfluous and redundant words from the document using stemming and stop word removal process. Once the document is pre-processed, the extraction of noteworthy features is performed using TF–IDF (Lee & Kim 2008) to determine keywords from the document. The extracted features are adapted for performing text document clustering to generate effective clusters. Figure 1 portrays a schematic illustration of the clustering text document using the KH algorithm.

Assume a document with different attributes, which is modeled as, B

$$B = \{B_{c,d}\}; (1 \leq c \leq e)(1 \leq d \leq f) \tag{1}$$

where $B_{c,d}$ represent document contained in a database B with d^{th} attribute in c^{th} data, f represent total attributes, and e specifies total data.

5.1 *Pre-processing of documents*

Pre-processing is performed for eliminating unnecessary words from the text database. The two major processes adopted in pre-processing the documents are the removal of stop words and stemming. The implication of pre-processing is to facilitate smoother processing of the input document. The text documents are usually large, which consist of redundant words and phrases that impact the

504

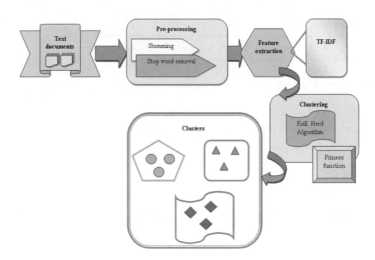

Figure 1. Proposed the TF–IDF-based KH algorithm for clustering text document.

text categorization. Thus, it is important to eliminate superfluous and incoherent words by adapting the pre-processing phase.

(i) *Stop word removal.* The words that are frequently utilized in the sentence involve preposition, articles, and pronouns. In computing, the stop words are removed before the processing of data. It is the process to eliminate stop words from large text documents. Here, the non-informative words are removed to minimize noise presented in the data. The elimination of stop words is utilized to prevent huge accumulation and facilitate faster processing for providing effectual results.

(ii) *Stemming.* This process is adapted for transforming the words into its stem. In huge data, different words are used which express a similar notion. The noteworthy method utilized for minimizing words to its root word is known as stemming. Several words are processed for minimizing the words to its basic form. For example, words like agree, disagree, and agreeing belong to the same word agree. The stemming is a simpler process, is comparatively precise, and does not need a suffix list.

5.2 *Extraction of features for text categorization using TF–IDF*

This section illustrates the noteworthy features mined from the text document and the implication of extracting features is to produce extremely pertinent features that facilitate improved text categorization using accessible documents. Besides, the intricacy of evaluating the document is expressed as the condensed features set. Furthermore, the extraction of features is adapted after pre-processing for extracting relevant features from the text document. Here, the extraction of features is performed after pre-processing wherein the extraction of keywords from documents is done with TF–IDF (Lee & Kim 2008). TF is adapted for computing the occurrence of each word in the document. IDF is employed for computing significant word which infrequently arises in the document. The TF–IDF is adapted for extracting the keywords to extract the noteworthy features. Moreover, the TF–IDF weighting model is utilized, which helps to state how significant a word is in the context of the document. The goal is to extract significant keywords for each text documents. Assume a document $B = \{B_1, B_2, B_3, \ldots, B_e\}$ represents aset of documents that belong to each domain. Let terms extracted from each document B be given as $K_c = \{k_{c1}, k_{c2}, k_{c3}, \ldots, k_{cm}\}$ are given wherein terms are extracted from the document c. For extracting important keywords from the document, the weights of each term must be computed. The formula for TF-IDF is expressed as:

$$TF - IDF_{xc} = TF_{xc} \times IDF_x \qquad (2)$$

Table 1. Solution encoding of KH algorithm.

1	2	3	4	5	6	7	8	9	10
3	3	1	1	3	2	3	1	2	3

where TF_{xc} indicates term frequency and DF_x represents the inverse document frequency. The term frequency is represented as

$$TF_{xc} = \frac{N_{xc}}{\sum_c N_{xc}} \tag{3}$$

where N_{xc} indicates the count of occurrence to be considered in B_c and $\sum_c B_c$ represents the count of occurrence of all term in B_c. The inverse document frequency is expressed as

$$IDF_x = \log \frac{|B|}{|\{B_c : k_m \in B_c\}|} \tag{4}$$

where $|B|$ indicates total document in the dataset, and $|\{B_c : k_m \in B_c\}|$ represents the count of documents when the term k_m appears. TF–IDF value consists of two components which involve TF and IDF. The base of the TF value is to evaluate frequent words in a document that are more significant. TF of a specific word from the given document is the number of occurrences from the document. This count is frequently normalized to avert bias to huge documents for computing the significance of the term k_m within the particular document B_c.

5.3 Clustering of a text document using KH algorithm

Here, the KH algorithm for text document clustering along with the newly devised fitness function is illustrated. The text document clustering facilitates the effective clustering of texts using TF–IDF features. The solution representation, fitness function, and KH algorithm are illustrated below.

5.3.1 Solution modeling

KH algorithm is utilized for the division of documents using a solution vector with length R wherein each decision variable fits into cluster centroid that belongs to z decision variable, which indicates the number of clusters Each solution poses a set of z centroids such that $c = \{c_1, c_2, \ldots, c_v, \ldots, c_z\}$ where c_v indicate v^{th} cluster centroid. For instance, consider ten documents that are modeled with three class labels z. For instance, class-1 consists of documents denoted by B_3, B_4, and B_8 which is represented in Table 1.

5.3.2 Evaluation of fitness function

Once the solution encoding is done, the fitness of each solution is evaluated for computing cluster centroids. The fitness is evaluated for determining the distance between centroid and data using MSE and the Jaccard coefficient. The fitness function is represented as

$$Fitness = X + (1 - Y) \tag{5}$$

where X represents the MSE and Y indicates the Jaccard coefficient. The best solution is obtained based on error, which is measured as a minimization function, and as a result, the solution with least MSE is chosen as the optimum solution. Here, the MSE is expressed as follows:

$$X = \frac{1}{R} \sum_{c=1}^{e} [N_v - N_v^*]^2 \tag{6}$$

where N_v is the expected output, N_v^* is the predicted output, and e indicates the number of documents, where $1 < c < e$. The Jaccard coefficient is adapted for computing the similarity between two documents which is expressed below. Assume E and D to be documents and thus the Jaccard similarity between the two documents is given as

$$Y = \frac{|E \cap D|}{|E| + |D| - |E \cap D|} \tag{7}$$

5.3.3 *Algorithmic steps of KH algorithm*

Here, the solution to the clustering problem is given by considering an optimization technique. The text document clustering has gained the interest of researchers to utilize it in several applications after maximizing the network information and dimension of the current appliance. Several applications use the text clustering method for easily dealing with huge information in information retrieval areas.

The KH (Gandomi & Alavi 2012) algorithm is a strategy that is utilized to solve global optimization issues based on simulation using the herding manners of krills. The position of krills is modernized based on three possessions of motions, namely movement produced by krill individuals, foraging activity, and random diffusion.

The fitness of the KH algorithm is a distance of sensing and is utilized for determining the adjoining optimal food. It is evaluated based on distance score using the uppermost density of krill individuals. The formulation of text documents using the KH algorithm is considered as an optimization issue for determining optimal clusters. The subsections illustrate KH operations based on clustering steps.

Step 1. Initialization. The foremost step is an initialization of solutions, whose positions are initialized in a random manner along with other algorithmic parameters as represented below:

$$A = \{A_1, A_2, \ldots, A_g, \ldots, A_h\}; 1 < g < h \tag{8}$$

where A_g indicates the gth solution and h represents the total number of solutions.

Step 2. Evaluation of fitness function. The best solution is determined based on the fitness function, which is termed as the minimization issue, and thus the solution generating less value of fitness is chosen as an optimal solution.

Step 3. Determination of update position. The KH algorithm (Gandomi & Alavi 2012) is employed for addressing the real-world issues, as they avoid local optima exploring the search space by exploring the global optimum. The KH algorithm is highly efficient and offers better performance while evaluating the solutions, and there is less parameter needed for fine-tuning and the KH algorithm is employed due to its simpler algorithmic structure. The briefer description of KH algorithm is stated below.

(i) *Lagrangian model of KH strategy.* KH algorithm adapts the Lagrangian model for making it apposite concerning the search space dimensionality. The space for a decision considering each krill is produced as

$$\frac{dA_g}{dp} = G_g + F_g + S_g \tag{9}$$

where F_g indicates motion influenced of gth krill, G_g indicates foraging motion of gth krill, and S_g denotes physical diffusion of gth krill.

The motion influenced by other krills

The inclination of the first group r_g is evaluated by objective effect, local effect, and head density. The motion of each position of krill individual is formulated as

$$F_g^{new} = F^{\max_{g} g^{tar}} \tag{10}$$

507

where $F^{\max}$ indicates maximum affected speed and r_g^{tar} indicates target effect. Thus, the first movement r_g is given as

$$r_g = r_g^{local} + r_g^{tar} \tag{11}$$

where r_g^{local} indicates local effect and r_g^{tar} indicates a coefficient value that generates global optimum. The effects of each neighbor concerning the movement of individuals' is evaluated as

$$r_g^{local} = \sum_{y=1}^{h} T'_{gy} * Z'_{gy} \tag{12}$$

$$Z'_{gy} = \frac{u_y - u_g}{\|u_y - u_g\| + \eta} \tag{13}$$

where u_y indicates the current position, u_g represents current neighbor, η specifies a positive number, and h indicates the count of krills.

$$T'_{gy} = \frac{\tau_g - \tau_y}{t^{wor} - t^{best}} \tag{14}$$

where t^{wor} and t^{best} indicate the best fit value. The best coefficient value of krill is expressed as

$$K^{best} = 2 \left(rand + \frac{p}{p_{\max}} O \right) \tag{15}$$

where p represents current iteration, $p_{\max}$ specifies max iteration, and $rand$ is the random number.

Foraging motion

Foraging motion contains two main elements that involve the location of food and the prior acquaintance regarding the location of food. The motion of gth individual is given as

$$G_g = W_n Q_g + \omega_n G_g^{old} \tag{16}$$

where W_n indicates foraging speed, G_g^{old} specifies last foraging speed, ω_n signifies inertia weight, and Q_g^{food} specifies food attractiveness and is formulated as

$$Q_g = Q_g^{food} + Q_g^{best} \tag{17}$$

where Q_g^{best} stands for best krill individual.

Physical diffusion

This procedure of KH algorithm is adapted as a random procedure for expressing maximum diffusion speed with directional vector and is given as

$$S_g = S^{\max \left(1 - \frac{p}{p_{\max}} O \right)} \tag{18}$$

where $S^{\max}$ indicates max diffusion speed and signifies a random number.

(ii) *Update position of KH algorithm.* The update is performed using the KH algorithm and is evaluated in such a way that the values corresponding to the minimum fitness are employed for selecting the best value for the fusion coefficient as per the equation. The krill herds are updated based on three motions. The update position of gth krill individual from the time p to $p + \Delta p$ is expressed as

$$A_g (p + \Delta p) = A_g (p) + \Delta p \frac{dA_g}{dp} \tag{19}$$

where $A_g(p + \Delta p)$ indicates the updated position of krill individual while moving in time p to $p + \Delta p$, $A_g(p)$ indicates the current position of krill individual, and Δp is constant.

508

Here, a genetic operator is utilized for enhancing the efficiency of krill herds, and the devised adaptive genetic utilizes mutation and crossover operators with a conventional differential evolution strategy. Crossover operator is a fundamental process devised based on evolution, and it deals with the swapping of a position to attain a globally optimal solution. This operator controls the probability of crossover value ranging in (0, 1). The mutation operator is termed as a significant process in optimization techniques; it helps to turn over the position of a solution to attain a globally optimal solution. The mutation operator is handled by mutation probability ranging in (0, 1).

Step 4. Evaluation of the optimal solution. The fitness of each solution is recomputed using Equation (5) along with the KH algorithm and is evaluated in such a way that the solution with less fitness is adapted for selecting optimal solution for clustering documents.

Step 5. Terminate. The stopping criterion is verified to mark the end of the optimization process. The stopping criterion is defined for better convergence of the algorithm, which comprises of maximal iterations, improvement percentage, and time-taken for execution.

6 RESULT AND DISCUSSION

The analysis of methods using the Jaccard coefficient, F-measure, and accuracy is illustrated with two datasets, namely Reuter's dataset and 20 Newsgroups data sets. The study is performed by varying cluster sizes.

6.1 *Experimental setup*

The testing of the methods is carried out in PC with 2 GB RAM, Intel i-3 core processor, andWindows 10 OS using PYTHON.

6.2 *Database description*

The dataset employed to perform the text document clustering includes the Reuter database and 20 Newsgroups database. The 20 Newsgroups data set (Newsgroup Database 2018) is donated by Ken Lang for the newsreader to refine the Netnews. The dataset is formed by accumulating 20,000 documents related to newsgroups, which is further partitioned evenly across 20 diverse newsgroups. This dataset is well known for experimentation of the text applications to deal with machine learning methods like text clustering and text classification. The dataset is arranged in 20 different newsgroups, each representing different topics. The Reuters-21578 Text Categorization Collection Data Set (Reuter Database 2018) is donated by David D. Lewis. The dataset comprises of documents that emerged on Reuters newswires in 1987. The documents are organized and indexed based on categories. The number of instances of the dataset is 21,578 with 5 attributes. The number of web hits achieved by the dataset is 163,417.

6.3 *Evaluation metrics*

The analysis of the methods is carried out based on three metrics, namely precision, recall, and accuracy.

6.4 *Competing methods*

The comparative methods include SPLBM (Ailem et al. 2017), hybrid fuzzy bounding degree + Rider Moth Flame optimization (RMFO) (Yarlagadda et al 2019), and proposed TF–IDF-based KH algorithm which are employed for the evaluation.

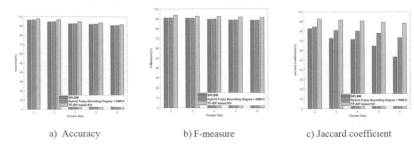

|a) Accuracy|b) F-measure|c) Jaccard coefficient|

Figure 2.   Analysis of methods with the Reuter database.

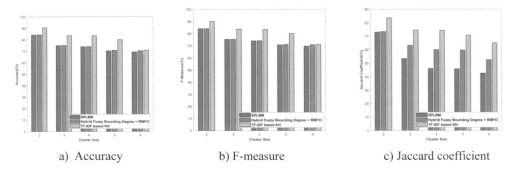

a) Accuracy   b) F-measure   c) Jaccard coefficient

Figure 3.   Analysis of methods using 20 Newsgroup databases.

6.5   *Comparative analysis*

The analysis of the proposed TF–IDF-based KH algorithm and classical methods is done with two databases, namely the Reuter database and 20 Newsgroups database.

6.5.1   *Comparative analysis using Reuter database*

Figure 2 elaborates the analysis of methods using the Reuter dataset considering accuracy, F-measure, and Jaccard coefficient metrics. The analysis of the method using the accuracy parameter is shown in Figure 2a. For cluster size $= 2$, the corresponding accuracy values computed by SPLBM, Hybrid fuzzy bounding degree + RMFO, and proposed TF–IDF-based KH are 96.218%, 96.416%, and 97.699%, respectively. Likewise, for cluster size $= 6$, the corresponding accuracy values computed by SPLBM, Hybrid fuzzy bounding degree + RMFO, and proposed TF–IDF-based KH are 90.506%, 90.694%, and 91.526%, respectively. The analysis of the method using the F-measure parameter is deliberated in Figure 2b. For cluster size $= 2$, the corresponding F-measure values computed by SPLBM, Hybrid fuzzy bounding degree + RMFO, and proposed TF–IDF-based KH are 90.839%, 90.933%, and 93.671%, respectively. Likewise, for cluster size $= 6$, the corresponding F-measure values computed by SPLBM, Hybrid fuzzy bounding degree + RMFO, and proposed TF–IDF-based KH are 88.370%, 88.461%, and 91.235%, respectively. The analysis of the method using the Jaccard coefficient parameter is deliberated in Figure 2c. For cluster size $= 2$, the corresponding Jaccard coefficient values evaluated by SPLBM, Hybrid fuzzy bounding degree + RMFO, and proposed TF–IDF-based KH are 82.586%, 84.611%, and 92.862%, respectively. Likewise, for cluster size $= 6$, the corresponding Jaccard coefficient values computed by SPLBM, Hybrid fuzzy bounding degree + RMFO, and proposed TF–IDF-based KH are 53.330%, 73.362%, and 88.295%, respectively.

6.5.2 *Comparative analysis using 20 Newsgroup database*

Figure 3 elaborates the analysis of methods using 20 Newsgroup databases considering accuracy, F-measure, and Jaccard coefficient metrics. The analysis of the method using the accuracy parameter is deliberated in Figure 3a. For cluster size = 2, the accuracy values computed by SPLBM, Hybrid fuzzy bounding degree + RMFO, and proposed TF-IDF-based KH are 84.292%, 84.467%, and 90.568%, respectively. Likewise, for cluster size = 6, the corresponding accuracy values computed by SPLBM, Hybrid fuzzy bounding degree + RMFO, and proposed TF-IDF-based KH are 69.451%, 70.564%, and 71.058%, respectively. The analysis of the method using the F-measure parameter is deliberated in Figure 3b. For cluster size = 2, the corresponding F-measure values computed by SPLBM, Hybrid fuzzy bounding degree + RMFO, and proposed TF–IDF-based KH are 84.120%, 84.208%, and 90.100%, respectively. Likewise, for cluster size=6, the corresponding F-measure values computed by SPLBM, Hybrid fuzzy bounding degree + RMFO, and proposed TF–IDF-based KH are 69.632%, 70.790%, and 71.048%, respectively. The analysis of the method using the Jaccard coefficient parameter is deliberated in Figure 3c. For cluster size = 2, the corresponding Jaccard coefficient values computed by SPLBM, Hybrid fuzzy bounding degree + RMFO, and proposed TF–IDF-based KH are 73.096%, 73.398%, and 83.644%, respectively. Likewise, for cluster size=6, the corresponding Jaccard coefficient values computed by SPLBM, Hybrid fuzzy bounding degree + RMFO, and proposed TF–IDF-based KH are 42.541%, 52.467%, and 61.932%, respectively.

7 CONCLUSION

This paper solves the issue of modifying the quality of text clustering based on the selection of apposite optimization techniques based on the KH algorithm. This algorithm is employed for clustering the text documents by determining the optimal centroids. Here, each document undergoes pre-processing for removing the noise and artifacts using stemming and stop word removal. The TF–IDF is adapted for extracting the significant features. The obtained TF–IDF features are adapted by the KH algorithm for grouping the text documents into suitable clusters. The fitness function is newly devised considering MSE and Jaccard similarity and is adapted for selecting the optimal centroids. The TF–IDF based KH algorithm outperformed other methods with maximal accuracy of 91.52%, F-measure of 91.23%, and maximal Jaccard similarity of 88.295%. In the future, the method will be expanded to initiate clustering on incremental data.

REFERENCES

Ahmadi, P., Gholampour, I. and Tabandeh, M., 2018. Cluster-based sparse topical coding for topic mining and document clustering. Advances in Data Analysis and Classification, 12(3), pp.537–558.

Ailem, M., Role, F. and Nadif, M., 2017. Sparse poisson latent block model for document clustering. IEEE Transactions on Knowledge and Data Engineering, 29(7), pp.1563–1576.

Brockmeier, A.J., Mu, T., Ananiadou, S. and Goulermas, J.Y., 2018. Self-tuned descriptive document clustering using a predictive network. IEEE Transactions on Knowledge and Data Engineering, 30(10), pp.1929–1942.

Chevalier, M., El Malki, M., Kopliku, A., Teste, O. and Tournier, R., 2015, September. Implementation of multidimensional databases with document-oriented NoSQL. In International Conference on Big Data Analytics and Knowledge Discovery (pp. 379–390). Springer, Cham.

Dörpinghaus, J., Schaaf, S. and Jacobs, M., 2018. Soft document clustering using a novel graph covering approach. BioData mining, 11(1), pp.1–20.

Gandomi, A.H. and Alavi, A.H., 2012. Krill herd: a new bio-inspired optimization algorithm. Communications in nonlinear science and numerical simulation, 17(12), pp.4831–4845.

Karypis, M.S.G., Kumar, V. and Steinbach, M., 2000, May. A comparison of document clustering techniques. In TextMining Workshop at KDD2000 (May 2000).

Lee, S. and Kim, H.J., 2008, September. News keyword extraction for topic tracking. In 2008 Fourth International Conference on Networked Computing and Advanced Information Management (Vol. 2, pp. 554–559). IEEE.

Li, N., Luo, W., Yang, K., Zhuang, F., He, Q. and Shi, Z., 2018. Self-organizing weighted incremental probabilistic latent semantic analysis. International Journal of Machine Learning and Cybernetics, 9(12), pp.1987–1998.

Martinho, B. and Santos, M.Y., 2016, December. An architecture for data warehousing in big data environments. In International conference on research and practical issues of enterprise information systems (pp. 237–250). Springer, Cham.

Newsgroup database, accessed on October 2018, <http://qwone.com/~jason/20Newsgroups/>

Reuter database, accessed on October 2018, <https://archive.ics.uci.edu/ml/machine-learningdatabases/reuters 21578-mld/>

Sheri, A.M., Rafique, M.A., Hassan, M.T., Junejo, K.N. and Jeon, M., 2019. Boosting discrimination information based document clustering using consensus and classification. IEEE Access, 7, pp.78954–78962.

Srikanth, D. and Sakthivel, S., 2018. Time and Space Efficient Web Document Clustering Using Rayleigh Distribution. Wireless Personal Communications, 102(4), pp.3255–3268.

Wan, X. and Liu, F., 2014. Are all literature citations equally important? Automatic citation strength estimation and its applications. Journal of the Association for Information Science and Technology, 65(9), pp.1929–1938.

Yarlagadda, M., Kancherla, G.R. and Atluri, S., 2019. Incremental document clustering using fuzzy-based optimization strategy. Evolutionary Intelligence, pp.1–14.

Zhang, S., Xu, Y. and Zhang, W., 2019. Clustering scientific document based on an extended citation model. IEEE Access, 7, pp. 57037–57046.

Smart Computing – Khan et al (Eds)
© 2021 Taylor & Francis Group, London, ISBN 978-0-367-76552-1

An efficient approach of image segmentation for noisy images

B. Gupta & A.R. Verma
GBPIET, Pauri, Garhwal, Uttrakhand, India

M. Joshi
TMU, Moradabad, U.P., India

R. Belwal
AITS, Haldwani, Uttrakhand, India

ABSTRACT: Segmenting an image is a vital concept in image processing where we sustain the subdivisions of an image in terms of its usability and significance in a multimedia application. Segmented images are essential for different image-processing procedures. The following paper represents a mechanism to acquire the segments of a noisy image. Initially, we input a noisy RGB image and perform RGB to gray conversion on it. We perform median filtering on it to remove salt and pepper noise. Then we processed it to find the edges so that image smoothing may be performed to reduce the number of connected components. As soon as we calculate the number of connected components, the task of segmenting and extracting an image's objects can be performed quite conveniently.

1 INTRODUCTION

We all are quite familiar with clustering in which we may form the group of data components in a sophisticated manner corresponding to which the data components in the same cluster hold the same set of features. We may assume an image as an altitudinal dataset consists of immense data which is essential to process in order to make it worthy and pertinent to an application (Sharma et al. 2015). The process of isolating an image into diverse non-overlying components in order to maintain the relevant texture and intensity is called an image segmentation. Segmenting an image is essential as we have to accomplish different tasks on image components to extract new features (Rao et al. 2009). Initially, we input a noisy RGB image and remove its noise using a median filtration technique so that it may be free from unwanted pixels. Median filters execute pixel by pixel and replace each noisy pixel with the median of its neighboring pixels (Ester et al. 1996). In a 2D-image, all the pixels within the radius are the participants to reduce the vulnerable pixels. Then we proceed to find the edges to obtain the connected components (Felzenszwalb & Huttenlocher 2004). These connected components may be a barrier in segmenting an image. Therefore, we have to find out the mechanism to reduce the number of connected components. For this we require the grouping information (Celebi et al. 2005). As an example, if the user does not acquire much knowledge about space, it will be very difficult for him to identify the database objects explicitly (Peng & Zhang 2012). Moreover, a spatial database may encompass an awful part of information in which, endeavoring to determine groups of information, may turn out to be dearer. Positions of groups may be furthermore self-motivated and multifaceted (Qixiang et al. 2003). Nearby, some renowned bunching calculations exist such as K-implies, K-medoid, Progressive Clustering, and Self-Organized Maps (James et al. 2008). By the by, none of these controls can deal with all these three referenced concerns completely (Pinaki et al. 2014).The number of connected components

DOI 10.1201/9781003167488-61

in an image are inversely proportional to the process of segmenting an image (Tuzel et al. 2009). Therefore, in this process we always intend to obtain all possible connected components and attempt to reduce its counting and diminish the latitude of connected components (Cheng 1995). An absurd portrayal signifying the distinction in the run-time for numerous pictures exploiting both the bunching calculations is introduced in Arbelaez et al. (2011). The current paper illustrates the procedural steps to obtain and extract the segments of an image.

2 PROPOSED APPROACH OF IMAGE SEGMENTATION

Segmenting an image is largely to segregate an image into numerous divisions (Chen et al. 2011). The objective of the division is to merely alter the depiction of an image rather than it is to further explore it. Segmenting an image is archetypally used to pinpoint items and borders in images (Yang et al. 2008), Further specifying, image segmentation is the procedure of conveying a marker to each pixel in an image so that pixels having the identical marker share firm features (Unnikrishnan et al. 2007). The following steps outline how to segment and extract image components:

2.1 *Feed the basic RGB image*

Initially, we feed a noisy RGB image. The image may be selected carefully as we have to deal with several complexity issues during segmentation. The selected image must be properly configured as per the requirement of segmentation and should contain some noisy pixels.

2.2 *RGB to grayscale transformation*

As soon as we input an image, our intention is to transform each R, G, B value component to its equivalent grayscale components as the task of edge detection can be tedious with RGB image components. The edges are not clearly identifiable with RGB image pixels. Grayscale simply reduces complexity from a 3-D pixel value (R, G, B) to a 1-D value. Many tasks do not respond better with RGB features.

2.3 *Apply median filtration to reduce salt and pepper noise*

Median filtration is the renowned percolation procedure which is cast off to eliminate noise from an image or signal. Such noise lessening is a distinctive preprocessing phase to mend the outcomes of earlier processing. Median filtering is precisely generally cast off to realm edges while eliminating noise. The central impression of the median filter is to execute over the signal item to item, substituting every item with the median of adjacent items. The median is intended by initially arranging entirely the pixel coefficients from the adjoining vicinity into arithmetic order and then substituting the pixel being measured with the central pixel coefficient. However, if the locality under deliberation holds an even amount of pixels, the mean of the two central pixel coefficients is cast off.

2.4 *Finding edges through edge detection*

Detecting an edge comprises an assortment of scientific procedures that object at detecting the fact in an image at which the image illumination deviates abruptly or further properly has cutoffs. The points at which image illumination variants abruptly are systematized into a collection of curled line fragments known as boundaries. Smearing an edge-finding procedure to a picture can expressively diminish the volume of facts to be handled and can so mesh out material that may be observed as rarer whereas conserving the vital operational characteristics of an image. If the image-finding task is fruitful, the succeeding undertaking of inferring the material in the real image could be markedly abridged.

2.5 *Smoothing image to reduce the number of connected components*

Image smoothing is performed to reduce the number of adjoining connected components in an image. It is achieved by convolving the image with a low-pass filter kernel. It is useful for removing noise. It actually removes high-frequency content from the image. Therefore, edges are blurred a little bit in this operation. It simply takes the average of all the pixels under the kernel area and replaces the central element. Flattening is also typically centered on a single value representing the image, such as the average value of the image or the middle value. It is essential for us to accomplish the smoothening of an image so that the associated components may be condensed. Smoothing provides a convenient environment to segmenting an image.

2.6 *Calculating connected components*

Now we tally the number of associated components to estimate the level of association in an image so that the image may be prepared for segmentation and extraction. Connected components may be labeled as 4-connected or 8-connected pixels. Here we are considering the 8-connected pixel interaction. It can be manipulated using the mathematical function bwlabel (arg1, arg2) which takes two arguments: arg1 is the 2-D nonsparse matrix which holds the image coefficients whereas arg2 is the level of connected pixel—it may be 4 or 8.

2.7 *Segmenting and extracting image components*

As soon as we have obtained the connected components in an image, our main task is to segment the image to extract its features by using the find function. In this way, we may locate indices of an image matrix with non-zero elements within the 0–255 range. Finally, after evaluating the dimensional size of the image matrix using size function, we can easily estimate the different segmenting components of an image.

To conclude, the outcome of segmenting an image could be acquired as a collection of delineations covering the whole image. Every single pixel in a section is identical with respect to certain features. The subsequent delineations can be supportive to contrivance 3-D remodeled images. We can summarize all these steps in a structural form using a flow chart which represents the flow of execution to evaluate the performance of the proposed approach of segmenting an image as shown in Figure 1.

3 IMPLEMENTATION

The proposed approach of segmenting an image is implemented using certain noisy RGB images to extract their sectional divisions and to detect their edges which resulted in the form of segmented image components. Results obtained on some image datasets can be represented in Figures 2 and 3.

4 RESULTS AND DISCUSSIONS

The obtained results signify the segmented components of an image in which we can easily detect the edges to discuss the behavior of a noisy image. These outcomes indicated the contrast between an original and segmented image. These segmented components again can be useful to reconstruct 3-D images.

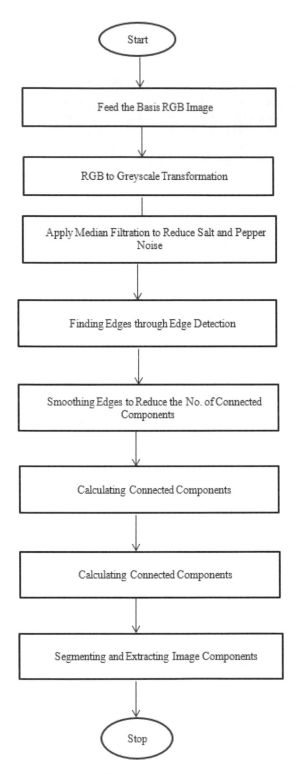

Figure 1.   Flowchart of the proposed algorithm.

Figure 2a.   Garden image.

Figure 2b.   Segmented portion of garden image.

Figure 3a.   Flower image.

Figure 3b.   Segmented portion of a rose.

5   CONCLUSION

This paper proposed an algorithmic approach in which we perform the divisional operation on noisy RGB images in which we may extract the segmented portions of an image. Initially, we converted them into greyscale to increase the edge visibility. Then we applied the median filter to remove the noise. After detecting the edges, we performed the smoothing operation to reduce the number of connected components. Then we proceeded to evaluate the number of connected components. These connected components must be at a minimum for the proper segmentation procedure. Finally, we extracted the segmented portions of an image to describe their features. Therefore, we have described the procedure to obtain the segments of an image which can be quite useful for noisy images.

REFERENCES

Arbelaez P., Maire M., Fowlkes, C.C. & Malik, J. Contour detection and hierarchical image segmentation. *IEEE Trans. Patt. Anal. Mach. Intell.*, vol. 33: 898–916, 2011.

Celebi, M.E., Aslandogan, Y.A. & Bergstresser, P.R.2005. Miningbiomedical images with density-based clustering. *Information Technology: Coding and Computing, 2005. ITCC 2005. International Conference on, Vol. 1, 4–6 April 2005: 163:168.*

Chen, X., Yang, X., Zhen, S., Lin, W., Zhang R. & Zhai G., "A new image quality assessment method using wavelet leader pyramids", *Opt. Eng.*, vol. 50, no. 6, 2011.

Cheng, Y.1995. Mean Shift, Mode Seeking, and Clustering. *IEEE Transactions on pattern analysis and machine intelligence, vol. 17, no. 8, August 1995.*

Ester, M., Kriegel, H.P., Sander, J. & Xu, X. 1996. A density-based algorithm for discovering clusters in large spatial databases with noise. *Proceedings of the 2nd International Conference on Knowledge Discovery and Data Mining (KDD'96), Portland: Oregon: 226–231.*

Felzenszwalb, P. & Huttenlocher, D.2004. Efficient graph based image segmentation. *Int. J. Comput. Vis., 2004, vol. 59: 167–181.*

James, C., Yixin, C. & Stephen R.2008. A Spatial Median Filter for Noise Removal in Digital Images *Computer Science and Information System, University of Mississippi, Southeastcon, 2008. IEEE, vol 1:618–623.*

Peng, B. & Zhang, L. 2012. Evaluation of image segmentation quality by adaptive ground truth composition. *Eur. Conf. Computer Vision, 2012*: 287–300.

Pinaki, P.A., Mukherjee, S. & Ghoshal D.2014. Digital Image Segmentation Using Median Filtering and Morphological Approach. *International Journal of Advanced Research in Computer Science and Software Engineering, Vol 4, Issue 1, January 2014.*

Qixiang, Y., Wen G. & Wei Z., Color image segmentation using density-based clustering *Multimedia and Expo, 2003. ICME'03. Proceedings. 2003 International Conference, vol.2: 401–404.*

Rao, S., Mobahi, H., Yang, A., Sastry, S. & Ma, Y.2009. Natural image segmentation with adaptive texture and boundary encoding. *Asian Conf. Computer Vision, 2009: 135–146.*

Shrama, A.D., Nath, D., Singh S. & Roy, B. 2015. Segmentation of images using density based algorithm. *International Journal of Advanced Research in Computer and Communication Engineering, Vol 4, Issue 5, May 2015: 273–27.*

Tuzel, O., Porikli F. & Meer P.2009. Kernel Methods for Weakly Supervised Mean Shift Clustering. *IEEE 12th International Conference on Computer Vision, 2009.*

Unnikrishnan, R., Pantofaru, C. &, Hebert M.2007.Toward objective evaluation of image segmentation algorithms. *IEEE Trans. Patt. Anal. Mach. Intell., 2007, vol. 29:929–944,.*

Yang, A., Wright, J., Ma, Y. & Sastry, S., "Unsupervised segmentation of natural images via lossy data compression", *Comput. Vis. Image Understand., vol. 11, no. 2, pp. 212–225, 2008.*

Smart Computing – Khan et al (Eds)
© 2021 Taylor & Francis Group, London, ISBN 978-0-367-76552-1

Résumé builder over rejuvenated AI features in website development

A. Malhotra, A. Sharma, D. Sharma & F. Ahmed
ABES Institute of Technology, Ghaziabad, Uttar Pradesh, India

ABSTRACT: This paper addresses valuable tips and methods and takes into consideration the building of and expert site along with analyzing issues in site advancement. Our project "CON-TRIRESUM" covers all enhanced features needed for anyone to develop their resume. These rejuvenated features will help the user to build a resume in less time with more modernized attributes, including a presentation video. An exceptional feature which makes the website unique among all is that it helps the user in transferring the resume to the respected companies of his own will. "CONTRIRESUM" will further examine how to make the procedure proficient and success-ful by refining the website at every single step of development. Once attending it, we will further experience issues often raised by the client along with how we can comprehend the specialized terms. This includes concerns such as code reusability, creation, organizational structure, necessity gathering, and much more. Our work relies on the usage of artificial intelligence in the selection of resumes and then automatically shares them to respective employers based on the skills of the candidates. Hence, classification algorithms play a major role here.

1 INTRODUCTION

Today, websites are the core of any business. A business' website should showcase its skill set and overall strengths. The project "CONTRIRESUM" showcases a business' reflection on their respective clients. To deliver the same, we started with the data collected from the market along with getting an in-depth understanding of the client's requirements. "CONTRIRESUM" meets every basic to enhanced requirement of a website's daily users by choosing the right model of development. After choosing the right model, it is re-evaluated by the client, thus cross-checking whether it will fulfill all the needs of the respective clients. Once completed, the next step is to examine a specific programming improvement architecture pattern based on the client's requirements. A programming language is the next step, making our project more secure and robust. While building our project we need knowledge about CSS, HTML, and Bootstrap with additional constraints of JavaScript. Along with that, we need certain attributes such as formatting of web pages, techniques for layout, knowledge about graphics, and multimedia aspects including images and various other functions of multi-page websites. By having such functionalities in our project, the next step goes on to the test server that is a local host that defines the layout of the web page. The reason behind doing this is for the development procedures by the respective developers so that the resume-building website does not have any disruptive functionalities (runtime errors, syntactical instances, and logical implications). All the developers, regardless of experience, need the right direction for developing their website in a tremendous way, so they need a preview of their code using an appropriate test server. The general test servers used in our project of building the website include XAMPP and WAMP for creating the PHP-based website.

2 RELATED WORK

A vast amount of work has been done in the field of website development classifications related to the software life cycle. The aim of this paper is to examine the new social technological era in various

DOI 10.1201/9781003167488-62

educational institutions which not only enhances a student's knowledge but also helps them in overall career opportunities. This paper examines the overall usage of social technologies in educational institutions. According to Taylor et al. (2002), website design depends on the requirement of the clients and what type of users will be interested in the website. Designing websites is done by using various techniques and these associated websites come under the user-centered design of the website. The interactive website and engagement with the Internet of Things (IoT) devices (Abuhasel 2020; Khan 2020a, 2020e; Quasim 2019, 2020) has an important role to play in AI enabled websites. JavaScript is used for creating dynamic web pages for client-side applications and is called a scripting language that runs on any supportive browser.

3 METHODOLOGY

The course of action involved in frontend and backend/website workflow is as follows.

- Anatomization
- Specification
- Design and Development
- Content Writing
- Coding
- Testing and Security
- Deploying the Website
- Maintenance and Update

3.1 *Anatomization*

For developing any website, one must know their audience for which they are developing the website which includes a better understanding of the website requirements such as how a website looks, the necessary content which is to be placed on which textual area, and the knowledge about the proper spatial organization so that your website doesn't look unmanaged and should have friendly customer engagement.

3.2 *Specification*

The acts of the specification include an enumeration of the analytical procedure that is grooming a Selective Service System to be developed including the sitemap and flow of various processes. It includes a set of potential use cases that describe user interactions that the software must provide to the user for perfect interlinkage.

3.3 *Design and development*

Development and invention for developing any website play a vital role in any project. It should have a properly layered structure and a decent design holding every specified trait requested by the client. In every designing process, requirement gathering is the primary key that holds the essential line-up. The requirements should be in such a way that it should cover every possible need enlisted by the client. The needs must be given to the specialized team of the development process. The main look of the website depends on the graphical interfaces and an impressive layout which holds the attention of every lead who is visiting the website for his needs. A blueprint of web pages and computer graphics includes navigation mock-up, template content, and placeholders. Once the blueprint is developed, it should be given to the respective client for the verification process so that if any changes are required, they could be done at that point in time. Doing this increases the involvement of the client and the developer should be aware if whether or not they are on the right track for building their project or website designing

3.4 Content writing

The content having the right keyword on the very first page of the website will make the customer believe the references he/she followed during the workflow. Writing the content for the web page includes the optimization techniques which should be well-defined and must not disguise the users visiting it. The right content is wholly responsible for attracting multiple genuine users reaching the website.

3.5 Implemented code for the website

Once the initial steps are followed then the crucial parts are taken into account. The coding schema is initiated with two subcategories that are Frontend and Backend. The languages used in Frontend are CSS, HTML, JavaScript, and jQuery, whereas Backend includes PHP with MySQL providing a stable database. The right code will make the website rank among various other competitors within the same domain. The right code also decreases the page loading time through having the correct meta titles with the right flowing mechanisms involved for the Backend process. The code should have accurate internal links and external links. The services, helper functions, and controllers for implementing the business logic prove to be the backbone of the entire web page. Services are more like an entity that is used multiple times within the segments of the code whereas the helper functions are used if the same code segment is required more than once. These functions are useful in the reusability of the code.

3.6 Testing and security

Testing is the chief step in website development not only because it's necessary but because it gives the right signal for the next procedure. Testing is done for the verification of the implemented code, i.e., whether the code results in the desired output. There must not be any broken links which in turn lead to spoiled issues. The in-all product should be handy and browser compatible. It is proven that every module should be tested accordingly in a website testing process which is termed as unit testing which decreases the amount of repeated work done by the tester. The testing process includes both the developer side testing (black box, white box, etc.) and client-side testing. Client-side testing ensures whether the website serves the purpose initially requested. One can keep an eye on the acceptance of the HTML code, the included CSS (inline or external), re-correction of used keywords, and built loops. If the website includes any payment procedures, mail services, or sign-up, a certain amount of meticulous testing is required. Security procedures ensure a review of the entire code as an integral part of the website. This prevents the software from malicious attacks and allows early perceptions of the flaws in the system. On the other hand, if we talk about the security check from the client-side perspective, all the data stored within the database must be kept private or encrypted. All these testing and security measures make the development process scalable and reliable.

3.7 Rolling out the website on web server

The selection of hosting services for any website development is a tough choice but ultimately it is the most essential task as well. If the website contains static content like CDN images or scripts, then we must choose a shared hosting service. Accordingly, if we create the website which will indulge high traffic and which will be used very frequently by the users, then you would be the one choosing VPS hosting. Using the VPS hosting service, it gives reliability and ensures the handling of high traffic on your website. A VPS host gives a boost to your website speed. Cloud hosting could be the best option if your website is a product-based website.

3.8 Maintenance of corresponding website

Once the website has rolled out on specific marketplaces, a major step that comes into play is the maintenance of the website. Monitoring the website from time to time must be done by matching each and every requirement of the client. The original clients as well as the newer ones that come up with modded requests. Maintenance work mainly deals with handing out customer's requests through a general follow-up. These requests revolve around the usage of the product and updates regarding it. Modernizing the website according to each and every user might help every team in increasing the engagement of the product which wasn't involved in the product or service list, resulting in increasing the organic traffic. No matter how focused or centralized the development team works, there is always room for new approval or updates which deal with bug fixes. Bug fixes should be maintained properly so that your website doesn't show any glitch for every different user.

4 IMPLEMENTATION

Website development is itself a vast platform that includes many software development steps. The thought process starts with the requirement gathering of the client. The client-side requirements are just the ideation on which developers must work. Developers who are associated with the website have their own approach to working, as the working approach can be different for different development teams. Website development initially requires a survey based on the data gathered. The gathered report once completed cannot be altered for every new analysis, as the need for different users keeps on changing on the basis of weeks or months. If we think about changing the website's necessary functionalities, we get restricted due to the associated web- servers because it requires huge cost investment and thus requires the storing space as well. After covering all the data mining phases, we move forward with the development of the PHP website through its frameworks and engines.

Objective:

- The objective is mainly to make the resume work of any new user efficient without dissipating much time to develop it as a whole.
- The other objective is to rejuvenate the AI features (Quasim 2015) into the resume-building website for automatically sharing the resume to the respective companies of the user domain.
- The goal is to understand all the programming concepts and to meet all the user requirements by improving the work efficiency. In other words, validating the resume for better outcomes.

Web projects require a PHP engine, a debugger, and a database server working on their distinct uses of the development. The details of the system environment for this research are:

- Web server: Apache web server, Lighttpd, IIS.
- Database: MySQL 5.1 or above, MariaDB 10.0 or above, Microsoft SQL Server 2005 or above.
- Operating System: Linux, Windows, etc.
- PHP Versions: For My SQL and MariaDB editions, PHP 5.4 or above with PHP XML extension. For SQL Server additions, PHP 5.4 or above with PHP XML extension with additional Microsoft SQL Server Driver for PHP.

For our project, we used the PHP framework CodeIgniter. CodeIgniter is open-source software that allows us to maintain modular grouping in the project. The framework is broadly based on the Model-View-Controller (MVC) approach. This approach is a software blueprint pattern that is used for creating and developing user interfaces (GUI) which splits the concerning programming logic into three related elements.

4.1 *Model*

A model is the dynamic data structure of the application and is independent of the user interface. The model is mainly responsible for stimulating the synchronous actions to develop an interactive approach and determine the state and behavior of the project. It holds the message protocol to add and remove dependence from the class collections. In addition to this, it sends update messages to the viewer. The model is built without any comprehension about view and controller. There is an

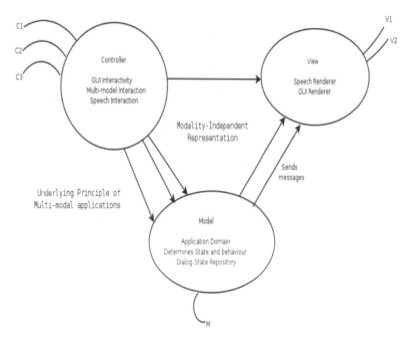

Figure 1.   MVC (model-view-controller).

implied alliance via a user-observer mechanism, where if the state of the model is changed specific introductions are introduced. Thus, the update messages are sent to the other two objects.

4.2   *View*

The view is responsible for the arrangement of the graphical and contentful output to the display screen connected. It isn't that the view contains only the elements needed for displaying but it also requests data from the model. They not only contain sub-views but also contain super views. The messages containing the graphical representations are passed from the standard system view of the application view through to the sub-views and super views. The ability to perform transformation and clipping between the levels is provided by a super view. In object-oriented terms, views consist of classes that give the functionality of a window onto a model. The examples are the Command Line Interface (CLI), Application Program Interface (API), and the Graphical User Interface (GUI).

4.3   *Controller*

A controller is responsible for bringing out the association between the interface and the other two objects. It also deals with interactions related to scheduling upon a timestamp and other view controller players that is the mouse button activity that correlates with input sensors. The controller can perceive events of the connected view and handles those events which are represented by the associated models. Briefly, the controller translates from GUI events to application-based logic.

To synchronize MVC four styles of communication are needed (in case of our dynamic project):

- The display has to authenticate itself as the viewer of the dashboard (View-Model).
- The dashboard must notify every time the user clicks the actionable button and thus attains the functionality (Model-View).
- If we as a user persist an icon or button the view must send proper events to the controller (View-Controller).

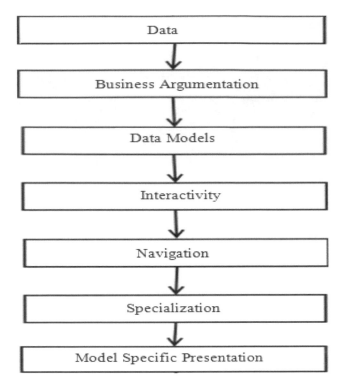

```
┌─────────────────────────────────────────┐
│                  Data                   │
└─────────────────────────────────────────┘
                   │
                   ▼
┌─────────────────────────────────────────┐
│          Business Argumentation         │
└─────────────────────────────────────────┘
                   │
                   ▼
┌─────────────────────────────────────────┐
│               Data Models               │
└─────────────────────────────────────────┘
                   │
                   ▼
┌─────────────────────────────────────────┐
│               Interactivity             │
└─────────────────────────────────────────┘
                   │
                   ▼
┌─────────────────────────────────────────┐
│                Navigation               │
└─────────────────────────────────────────┘
                   │
                   ▼
┌─────────────────────────────────────────┐
│              Specialization             │
└─────────────────────────────────────────┘
                   │
                   ▼
┌─────────────────────────────────────────┐
│        Model Specific Presentation      │
└─────────────────────────────────────────┘
```

Figure 2.   Complete controller translation.

- Events processed by the controller have domain controls which are assigned to the model (Control-Model).

  Why is MVC so effective when it comes to building up web-based projects?

- *Efficient Development Process*. MVC provides a modular approach, as in, if one is working on one part of the project, the other can modulate upon its sectional features as well. Thus, the general working of the overall project is not hindered.
- *Ability to provide numerous views.* The MVC pattern provides referential views and is necessary for a code reusable feature.
- *A dedicated support for JavaScript Query and jQuery Frameworks*. MVC integrates with language frameworks by which we are able to use AJAX and JS libraries easily. This phase tests the safety and effectiveness with a relatively larger group of 40–50 people with some specific medical conditions.

5   CONCLUSION AND FUTURE SCOPE

In this fast and developing world, everybody around us is busy on the Internet. From a young age to an older age, everybody is utlizing various websites for their basic needs. This is what gave us the idea of the development of a website. We tried to develop the website using various tools for the server. For the complete website development, we used languages such as PHP, HTML, CSS (Cascading Style Sheets) and JavaScript. Our website development process goes through the various software development processes by considering various architectural patterns that helped us in the overall development. In this, we have gone through various previous problems and tried to find the solutions. Including all the above factors we also used frameworks as these frameworks are useful in all aspects of website development. So, we are going to implement this scenario over an automated resume maker via this approach and this approach can be used to create any streamlined resume.

ACKNOWLEDGMENTS

The authors express their gratitude to Mr. Feroz Ahmed (Asst. Prof.) for his counsel, cooperation, and support in carrying out this research. We also thank Dr. K.K. Agrawal and Dr. Rizwan Khan for their continued motivation in developing the research work. The work itself is a true display of teamwork and patience. Our appreciation also goes to our colleagues in developing the project and people who have generously helped us out with their abilities.

REFERENCES

Abazi B. 2017. *PHP & MySQL with AJAX.*

Abuhasel K. A. and M. A. Khan, (2020), "A Secure Industrial Internet of Things (IIoT) Framework for Resource Management in Smart Manufacturing," in IEEE Access, vol. 8, pp. 117354-117364, 2020, doi: 10.1109/ACCESS.2020.3004711.

Gerner J, Naramore E, Owens M & Warden M. 2005 Professional LAMP: *Linux, Apache, MySQL and PHP5 Web Development.*

Kowtha N.R., Choon T.W.I. 2001. Determinants of website development: a study of electronic commerce in Singapore *in Information & Management, volume 39, Issue 3.*

Khan M.A. et. al, (2020), Decentralised IoT, Decenetralised IoT: A Blockchain perspective, Springer, Studies in BigData, 2020, DOI: https://doi.org/10.1007/978-3-030-38677-1

Khan, M. A., Quasim, M. T, et.al, (2020), A Secure Framework for Authentication and Encryption Using Improved ECC for IoT-Based Medical Sensor Data, in IEEE Access, vol. 8, pp. 52018–52027, 2020. DOI: 10.1109/ACCESS.2020.2980739

Khan M. A., (2020), An IoT Framework for Heart Disease Prediction Based on MDCNN Classifier, in IEEE Access, vol. 8, pp. 34717–34727, 2020. DOI: 10.1109/ACCESS.2020.2974687

Khan M.A, and Algarni F., (2020) "A Healthcare Monitoring System for the Diagnosis of Heart Disease in the IoMT Cloud Environment Using MSSO-ANFIS," in IEEE Access, vol. 8, pp. 122259–122269, 2020, doi: 10.1109/ACCESS.2020.3006424

Khan, MA, Abuhasel, KA. (2020). Advanced metameric dimension framework for heterogeneous industrial Internet of things. Computational Intelligence. 2020; 1–21. https://doi.org/10.1111/coin.12378

Leff, Avraham & Rayfield, James. 2001. *Web-application development using the Model/View/Controller design pattern.*

Nixon R. 2016. Learning PHP, MySQL, JavaScript, CSS & HTML5: *A Step-by-Step Guide to Creating Dynamic Websites.*

Pop, Paul D & AdamA, Adam. 2014. Designing an MVC Model: *Rapid Web Application Development.*

Taylor M.J., McWilliam J, Forsyth H & Wade S. 2002. Methodologies and website development: *A survey of practice in Information and Software Technology.*

Quasim, M. T., Khan M. A, et.al, (2019), Internet of Things for Smart Healthcare: A Hardware Perspective, 2019 First International Conference of Intelligent Computing and Engineering (ICOICE), Hadhramout, Yemen, 2019, pp. 1–5. DOI: 10.1109/ICOICE48418.2019.9035175

Quasim, M.T. (2015). Artificial Intelligence as a Business Forecasting and Error Handling Tool. COMPUSOFT, An international journal of advanced computer technology, 4 (2), February-2015 (Volume-IV, Issue-II).

Quasim, M.T., Khan M.A, Algarni F., Alharthy A., Alshmrani G.M.M, (2020), Blockchain Frameworks. In: Khan M., Quasim M., Algarni F., Alharthi A. (eds) Decentralised Internet of Things. Studies in Big Data, vol 71. Springer, DOI: https://doi.org/10.1007/978-3-030-38677-1

Smart Computing – Khan et al (Eds)
© *2021 Taylor & Francis Group, London, ISBN 978-0-367-76552-1*

SMART-driving license: An IoT-based system for a secure vehicle system

Nipun Jain, Nikita Bhadula & Mohd Daud
Student (CSE), ABES Institute of Technology, Affiliated to AKTU Lucknow, Ghaziabad, India

Ankita Dixit
Assistant Processor (CSE), ABES Institute of Technology, Affiliated to AKTU Lucknow, Ghaziabad, India

ABSTRACT: This paper represents the development of the idea of making the proposed mechanism for a SMART Driving License (DL) using the concept of the Internet of Things (IoT). The concept of SMART DL came into existence to provide a secure vehicle system by providing the prototype of an upgraded authorized version of a simple DL license by holding all the necessary information about the DL holder, car owner, and the vehicle with all their required documents into a single physical authorized device, using IoT (Eleonora 2016) so that the problems of fraud, theft, heavy challan, and terrorism could be stopped at a maximum extent. The system must contain a radio-frequency identification reader and a global positioning system for tracking purpose. The proposed mechanism for a SMART DL when inserted into the vehicle is that all the necessary information such as unique Identification (UID) number, vehicle number, location, etc., all go to the server (Cloud), and that information could be restored and viewed through a web- portal/application maintained, which could also be handled by the owner of vehicle as per his/her own requirement.

Keywords: IoT, Cloud-Computing, Arduino, RFID, SMART-DL, GSM module, GPS

1 INTRODUCTION

The SMART Driving License (DL) is an Internet of Things- (IoT) based project, which is basically a proposed mechanism for an upgraded version of a simple DL, but one that holds all the necessary information about a DL-holder vehicle owner and the vehicle, location, and all other required data in a single card (Singh 2017). The main objective of proposing this SMART-DL is to provide a secure vehicle system (Howard 1990).

The concept of proposing a SMART DL came into existence to enable the licensing authority and to ensure the secured storage of data, authentication of delinquent drivers, thefts, frauds, terrorism, etc., resulting in quite a secure vehicle system. Both the DL holder and vehicle owner benefit from using a SMART DL as the vehicle will not start until and unless the DL holder inserts his/her SMART DL, thereby eliminating someone forgetting their DL at home. In addition, information about the vehicle such as current location could be known.

The SMART DL is far more superior than a simple DL as it contains all the required information about a DL holder, vehicle owner, vehicle itself, and location. Moreover, it has a secured storage of data, which helps in authentication. Activities such as terrorism, fraud, theft, etc. could also be reduced to a great extent as all the information and tracking of a vehicle could be done when required. Another advantage of the SMART DL is that one no longer has to worry about forgetting DLs at home, tearing the DL, getting the DL wet, etc., thereby making it easy to install in a vehicle (Howard 1990) itself, hence heavy challans could get stopped.

DOI 10.1201/9781003167488-63

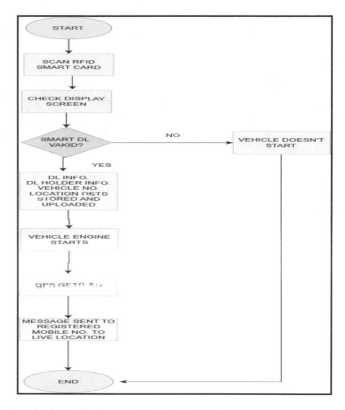

Figure 1. Flow chart for Smart DL designing and implementation.

2 PROJECT DESIGN AND IMPLEMENTATION

The proposed mechanism for the SMART DL system can be divided into hardware and software modules (Gupta et al. 2019). The methodology is discussed as follows.

2.1 *Hardware configuration of proposed system*

The system consists of a radio-frequency identification (RFID) reader which operates on radio waves for analyzing items people along with an ARDUINO, which is a processer to the system. The system also contains a Global Positioning System (GPS) for tracking purposes and Global System for Mobile Communication (GSM) for transmitting messages/signals. An Android application is also used for tracing and tracking the vehicle and the driver through their mobile phones from their respective places.

The system containing an RFID reader as a SMART DL, inserted into the holder of the vehicle, contains all the necessary information like Unique ID number (U.ID) (Nam-Yih 2000) vehicle number, location, and all get stored in the Cloud (acting as a server), and that information could be viewed/checked through the web portal/mobile application, which could be handled by the owner of the vehicle as per his/her need.

The point which needs attention is that designing the mechanism for SMART DL (Cummins 2003) is that the vehicle starts only when the SMART DL is inserted into the vehicle holder so that no one driving the vehicle could leave their respective DL at home. In addition, the vehicle and driver could be easily tracked therefore instances of heavy challan, fraud, theft, or terrorism could be tracked and retained, if need be.

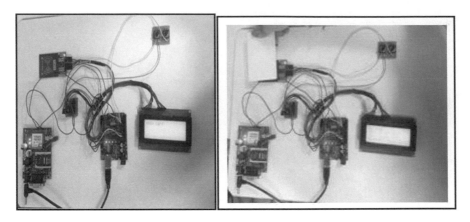

Figure 2.   Connections among hardware components of the proposed system (Kumar 2019).

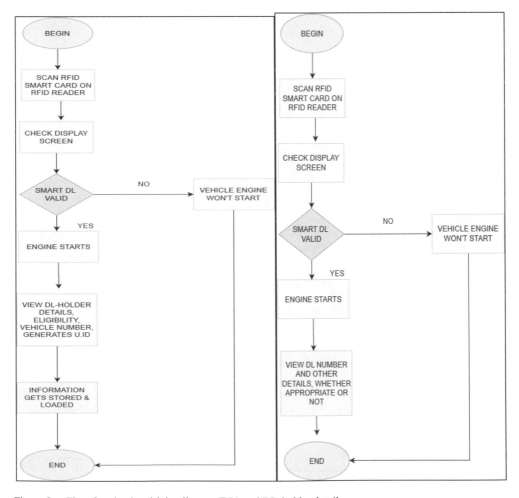

Figure 3.   Flow for viewing driving license (DL) and DL-holder details.

2.2 *Software configuration of the proposed system*

The SART DL system is an IoT-based system using it as a technology for its implementation (Tripathy 2019) and also using cloud computing as another necessary implementation technological model for the proposed mechanism of SMART DL.

In the proposed mechanism model for a SMART DL, an RFID reader is used to transmit information such as DL holder, vehicle, owner, and location to the processor (ARDUINO) and the Cloud (server). The Android application/web portal also contains data, linked to the server (Cloud), about the DL holder, vehicle, location, and owner. When the data stored in cloud matches to the information from the RFID reader, the engine of the vehicle starts; if it doesn't match, the vehicle does not start. For tracking and security purposes, a GPS sends the vehicle's live location.

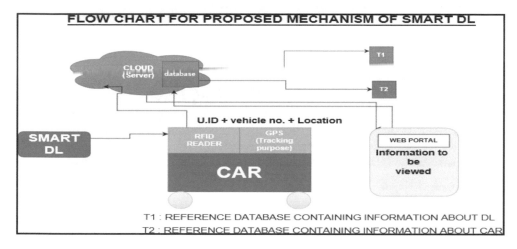

Figure 4.   Mechanism of SMART DL.

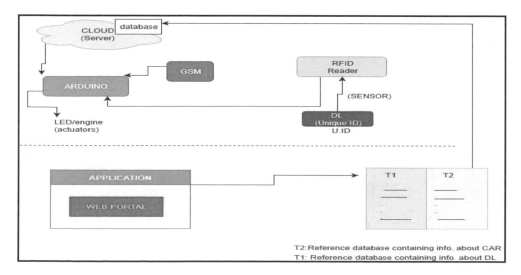

Figure 5.   Overview diagram of SMART DL.

3 TECHNOLOGY USED IN PAPER

The different technologies required while constructing the proposed mechanism of the SMART DL are as follows.

3.1 Internet of Things (IoT)

The IoT is an emerging and influencing paradigm that helps in enabling the communication between sensors and electronic devices through the Internet. From the air conditioners that one can control, with smartphones, smart cars provide the shortest route or smartwatch which tracks daily activities, IoT is a broad and expanded network with several connected devices. These devices receive and share data about how they are used and the environment in which they are being operated. It is progressively emerging as an innovation that puts an extensive variety of systems and frameworks together.

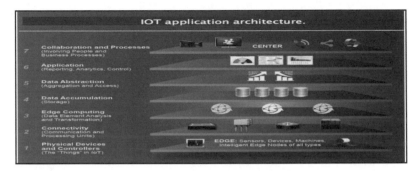

Figure 6.   Overview of IoT.

3.2 Cloud computing

Cloud computing is a completely new technology of IT infrastructure, with Internet resources and pay-as-you-go pricing. Instead of owning, buying, and maintaining physical data servers, you can access technology and its services, such as computing power, storage, and databases, on an as-needed basis from a cloud provider such as Amazon Web Services (AWS). Via cloud computing, one can access resources from the Cloud in real time. Cloud computing also makes it easy to expand to new regions and deploy globally in minutes. A real-time example of a cloud computing provider is Google's Gmail. Users can access files and applications from any device which has access to the Internet. We have two types of cloud: a public cloud and private cloud (Srivastava & Khan 2018). A public cloud consists of files, applications, storage, and services available to the public, an example of which is E-mail. A private cloud consists of cloud files, applications, storage, and services that are implemented and protected within a wall only specific users from a private organization can access.

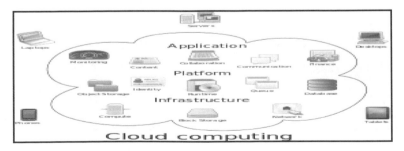

Figure 7.   Cloud computing.

3.3 Radio Frequency Identification (RFID)

RFID (Finkenzeller 2004) is a technology that works on the radio frequency of radio waves. Therefore, this particular technology is used to automatically identify and track the objects. The RFID tag possesses a tiny radio responder, radio transmitter, and receiver. In this technology, the RFID tag is used to get attached to the object which one wants to track. So, this RFID reader is continuously sending radio waves. Therefore, whenever the object is in the range of the reader then this RFID tag used to transmit its feedback signal to the reader, So, it is very similar to the technology which is used in a barcode. By using this technology, we can track even multiple objects at the same time, to a certain distance.

3.4 Global system for mobile communication module

GSM requires a SIM card just as mobile phones do, in order to activate communication with the networks and users. Also, it possesses an IMEI number which is used for identification purposes. GSM is basically a digital cellular technology which is used for transmitting signals, messages, data services and mobile voice. GSM digitizes and compresses data, then sends it down in their respective timeslots via a channel with two other streams of user data. GSM (Chao 2003) is designed to support image and data services with data rates up to 9.6 kbps and a globally accepted digital standard for cellular communications.

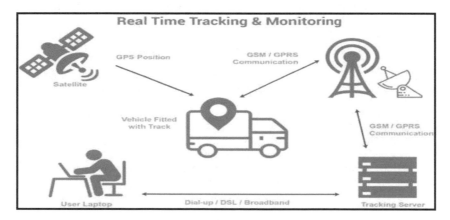

Figure 8. Overview of GSM module.

3.5 Global Positioning System (GPS)

GPS enables people to obtain position information anywhere in the world. A GPS receiver calculates distance between satellites and the receiver in order to generate position data. It is used for providing accurate location, time, and velocity information to many suitably equipped users. The main objective of GPS is to track (Philip 2004) vehicles for security purposes. It has many applications in several areas such as mapping, weather forecasts, vehicle location, equipment, military, and others.

4 CONCLUSIONS

This paper proposes the mechanism for a SMART DL for a secure vehicular system, intended to store all crucial information related to the vehicle and the DL holder. This RFID-based SMART

DL developed in this project will remove the need to carry other documents and provide security at a great extent by easily detecting fraud, delinquent drivers, duplication of DLs, theft, and heavy challans. The GPS will send the live location of the vehicle when needed and the GSM module for transmitting message signals to the vehicle's owner. This project is developed keeping in mind the security and safety of people, their vehicles, and the Indian government's smart and secure mission. Such a smart card will also promote the concept of smart living and security among the public.

REFERENCES

Automation (ICSIPCA), 2017.

Borgia Eleonora, 2016, Internet of Things: Research challenges and Solutions.

Ma Chao, "Design of SMS Interface Software and Hardware for Embedded GSM[J]", Microcontrollers & Embedded Systems, no. 8, pp. 15–17, 2003.

Cummins, P. (2003). A university wide smart card system. Retrieved from https://ro.ecu.edu.au/theses_hons/135.

K. Finkenzeller, RFID Handbook: Radio-Frequency Identi cation Fundamentals and Applications, Wiley, 2004.

Gupta Kunal, Kumar Dr. Sushil, Tripathy Dr. Malya Ranjan, 2019, Implementation of Smart Card for Vehicular Information, IJEAT, (Volume-8 Issue-5, June 2019).

J.A. Howard, 1990, Smart cards (for car security applications), IEE Colloquium on Vehicle Security. 25–25 Oct. 1990.

Khan, M.A. and V. K. Antiwal (2009), "Location Estimation Technique using Extended 3-D LANDMARC Algorithm for Passive RFID Tag," 2009 IEEE International Advance Computing Conference, Patiala, 2009, pp. 249–253, doi: 10.1109/IADCC.2009.4809016.

Khan, M.A and S. Ojha (2008), "Virtual Route Tracking in ZigBee (IEEE 802.15.4) enabled RFID interrogator mesh network," 2008 International Symposium on Information Technology, Kuala Lumpur, 2008, pp. 1–7, doi: 10.1109/ITSIM.2008.4631904.

Khan M.A. Sharma M, R. B. Prabhu, "FSM based FM0 and Miller encoder for UHF RFID Tag Emulator," 2009 IEEE International Advance Computing Conference, Patiala, 2009a, pp. 1317–1322, doi: 10.1109/IADCC.2009.4809207.

Khan, M.A., Sharma, M. and Prabhu, B.R. (2009b). A survey of RFID tags. International Journal of Recent Trends in Engineering, 1(4), p.68. Academy publisher, Finland

Lee Nam-Yih, 2000, Integrating access control with user authentication using smart cards IEEE Transactions on Consumer Electronics (Volume: 46, Issue: 4, Nov 2000).

Philip T. Blythe, 2004, Improving public transport ticketing through smart cards, Proceedings of the Institution of Civil Engineers Municipal Engineer 157, March 2004 Issue ME1 Pages 47–54.

Singh Abhishek, 2017, Designing and Implementation of Smart Card Technology for the Students of Higher Education, IJCSMC, (Vol. 6, Issue. 1, January 2017).

Srivastava, P. and Khan, R., 2018. A review paper on cloud computing. International Journals of Advanced Research in Computer Science and Software Engineering, 8(6), pp.17–20.

Stankovic John, 2014, Research Directions for the Internet of Things, IEEE Internet of Things Journal (Volume:1, Issue: 1, Feb. 2014).

S. Tyagi, A. Q. Ansari and M. A. Khan (2010a), "Dynamic threshold based sliding-window filtering technique for RFID data," 2010 IEEE 2nd International Advance Computing Conference (IACC), Patiala, 2010, pp. 115–120, doi: 10.1109/IADCC.2010.5423025.

Tyagi S., Ansari A.Q., Khan M.A. (2011) Extending Temporal and Event Based Data Modeling for RFID Databases. In: Nagamalai D., Renault E., Dhanuskodi M. (eds) Advances in Parallel Distributed Computing. PDCTA 2011. Communications in Computer and Information Science, vol 203. Springer, Berlin, Heidelberg, https://doi.org/10.1007/978-3-642-24037-9_43

Tyagi, S., M. Ayoub Khan, and A. Q. Ansari (2010b), "RFID Data Management," in Radio Frequency Identification Fundamentals and Applications Bringing Research to Practice, Cristina Trucu, Ed. InTech, February 2010, DOI:10.5772/8001.

Smart Computing – Khan et al (Eds)
© *2021 Taylor & Francis Group, London, ISBN 978-0-367-76552-1*

Parameter evaluation and performance analysis of a BIPVT system for the different climates of India: A comprehensive study

Amit Kumar Dash
Noida Institute of Engineering & Technology, Greater Noida, India

Sanjay Agrawal
School of Engineering and Technology, IGNOU, New Delhi, India

Sanjay Gairola
G.B. Pant Institute of Engineering and Technology, Pouri, Uttarakhand, India

Chetan Kumar Garg
Noida Institute of Engineering & Technology, Greater Noida, India

ABSTRACT: In this work overall exergy and efficiency of a building-integrated photovoltaic-thermal (BIPVT) system is analyzed based on which optimization with soft computing techniques are done. Algorithms such as the evolution algorithm is applied to complete the task. Second, on the basis of length, width of channel, and length of channel, optimization of the photovoltaic-thermal (PVT) module is designed. A comparison is made based on temperature variation as the weather conditions of India vary depending on the area. Dividing the whole year into four different weather conditions—sunny, cloudy, hazy, and mix of both—electrical efficiencies and exergy efficiency are calculated. Improvement is recorded in thermal gain, overall exergy, and overall efficiency for all weather conditions in four cities in India. Improvement recorded in exergy efficiency is 5.8–14.70% as compared to other systems discussed in literature

Keywords: Performance analysis; BIPVT module; Parameter evaluation; Genetic Algorithm

1 INTRODUCTION

Nowadays, due to the depletion in the production rate of conventional power plants, the whole world is searching for alternative methods of energy production. Fossil fuel can play a large role in this search. In addition, solar energy is a viable source of energy due to its abundance of availability. Most countries are trying to convert their energy production systems to more non-conventional plants.

Out of the total energy the earth receives, 80% of it is dissipated as loss and the remaining 20% is coverted to electrical energy. However, since the early 1980s one basic problem behind a photovoltaic (PV) cell is its efficiency which decreases w.r.t. temperature. Therefore, bringing the temperature within permissible limits of a cooling effect is a must.

Discussion has been made to compare the present system with previous ones. A literature review has been made on the periodic analysis of a PV system by applying the Fourier series (Tiwari & Hemsikha 2016) and results have been obtained by varying the input air (Debbarma & Baredar 2017). In addition to the review of building-integrated photovoltaic (BIPV) and building-integrated photovoltaic-thermal (BIPVT) systems this paper also describes application of the PV system. Agrawal & Tiwari (2011) gives an idea that the overall efficiency has been increased from 20% to 26% after changing the design parameters. Research has been made on amorphous silicon (Aggrawal & Tiwari 2010) and Sarkar & Kumar (2019) gives a brief idea about recent development related to the BIPV system and techniques related to generation of power.

DOI 10.1201/9781003167488-64

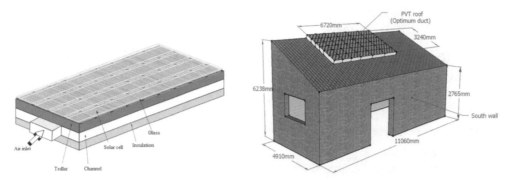

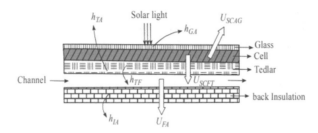

Figure 1.   PI controller response (simulation of model).

Figure 2.   Proposed BIPVT system.

Figure 3.   Side view of PVT module.

Many design parameters and performance evaluations have been made (Zondag & De 2002). Enviroeconomic analysis has been made for the calculation of carbon credits earned (Evola & Marletta 2014). Comparison has been made between a hybrid PIV system and normal solar system (Hunang et al 2001).

There is an overall increment of 1.1% of electrical efficiency from the previous 16% (Agrawal & Singh 2018). Solar isolation and radiation play an important role in deciding efficiency (Shukla & Sudhakar 2018). Air type and water collectors have been designed and performance analysis was described (Hee et al. 2014). Analysis has been made on the basis of thermal modeling developed for the system. Until now, it has been noticed that an average of 9% of electrical efficiency is generated in any BIPV system. Annual thermal and electrical output obtained for the best combination the ducts is 12.56 MWh and 4.22 MWh, respectively, for New Delhi (Omar & Sharaf 2019). Discussion has been made on thermal radiation in terms of exergy (Tripathy et al. 2015). An increment of 11.27% has been recorded in terms of the Genetic Algorithm (GA) application. Overall efficiency has been increased to 20.8% (Yang 2015).

2   PROPOSED MODEL

The proposed system that is going to be discussed is the BIPVT system where the whole system is integrated in a single roof. The design of a single module has been shown which is associated with the system. There are 48 panels which are connected in series and parallel. As we are going to calculate the exergy efficiency of different ares, here we have chosen Delhi, Bangalore, Jodhpur, and Srinagar for this.

The proposed system has been a system both in module form and side view, as detailed in Figures 1–3.

3 MATHEMATICAL/THERMAL MODELING

Modeling is designed by considering energy at each section of the whole system. To obtain it, energy balance formula is applied, i.e., how much energy is utilized and how much is lost. The following assumptions have been made:

- Perfect packing with no heat loss.
- Specific heat of air doesn't change with an increase of temperature.
- Change in system parameters is almost constant or varies slowly.
- Air flow throughout the duct is uniform.

There is a small incremental variation of bdx in Figure 1 of the PVT system.

$$T_{SC} = \frac{\alpha_{eff} I_{SL} + h_{SCA} T_A + h_{SCF} T_F}{h_{SCA} + h_{SCF}} \tag{1}$$

Efficiency and useful thermal energy may be calculated as

$$Q_{U,N} = n_R m_F C_{air} \left[\frac{h_F \alpha_{aff}}{U_L} I_{SL} + T_A - T_{F,i} \right] * \left[1 - \exp\left(\frac{-Nb U_L L}{m_F C_{air}} \right) \right] \tag{2}$$

$$\eta = \eta_{TC} \left[1 - \beta_0 \left\{ \frac{\alpha_{eff} I_{SL}}{U_{SCAG} + U_{SCFT}} - (T_{FO} - T_A) + \frac{U_{SCFT} h_F \alpha_{eff} I_{SL}}{U_L (U_{SCAG} + U_{SCFT})} \times \left\{ 1 - \frac{\exp\left(\frac{-Nb U_L L}{m_F C_{air}} \right)}{\left(\frac{Nb U_L L}{m_F C_{air}} \right)} \right\} \right. \right.$$

$$\left. \left. + \frac{U_{SCFT}}{U_{SCAG} + U_{SCFT}} \times \left\{ 1 - \exp\frac{\left(\frac{-Nb U_L L}{m_F C_{air}} \right)}{\left(\frac{Nb U_L L}{m_F C_{air}} \right)} \right\} (T_A - T_{FI}) \right\} \right] \tag{3}$$

The total thermal gain can be expressed from the law of thermodynamics:

$$\sum QUT = \sum QU,TH + \frac{QU,EL}{\eta C, power} \tag{4}$$

$$Q_{U,Th} = \frac{Q_{U,L} + Q_{U,U}}{1000} \tag{5}$$

Conversion efficiency of any system varies from 0.2–0.4 and the general equation of energy balance Equation (2) is given by

$$\sum ExOUT = \sum ExTH + \sum EXEL \tag{6}$$

where

$$\sum ExTH = Q_{U,N} \left[\frac{TA + 273}{TFO + 273} \right] \tag{7}$$

$$\sum ExEL = \left[\frac{\eta Am ISL}{1000} \right] \tag{8}$$

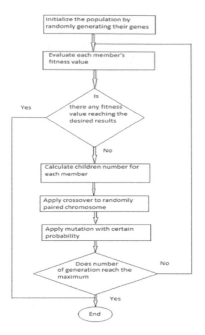

Figure 4. Flow chart of the genetic algorithm.

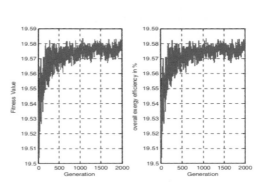

Figure 5. Performance of fitness function and exergy.

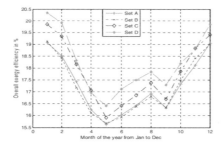

Figure 6. Performance of the exergy efficiency of Jodhpur.

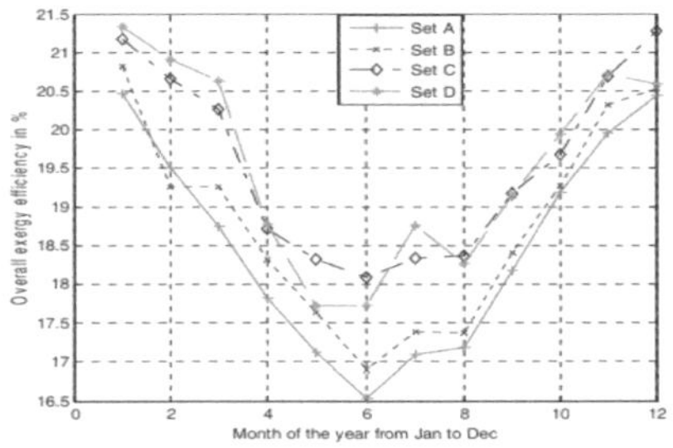

Figure 7. Performance of the exergy efficiency of Srinagar.

Input exergy can be expressed as

$$\sum \text{ExIN} = A_{Sc} N_C * I_{SL} \left[1 - \frac{4}{3}(\text{TA}/\text{TSUN}) + 1/3 \left(\frac{\text{TA}}{\text{TSUN}} \right)^4 \right] \tag{9}$$

Overall exergy can be expressed as

$$\eta_{EX} = \left(\frac{\text{ExOUT}}{\text{ExIN}} \right) \tag{10}$$

During the optimization process the input values are tested to maximize or minimize the function in a systematic way. In the GA it has to go through various processes such as reproduction, mutation, and selection. Within a given limit the input parameters to be applied are shown in Figure 3 (Figures 4–9).

Bangalore shows a change of 2% due to its weather conditions throughout the year in Figures 9 (Figures 10 and 11, Tables 1 and 2).

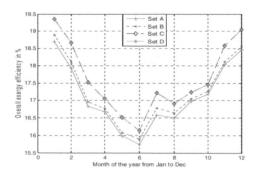

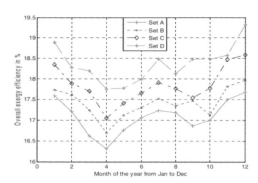

Figure 8. Performance of the exergy efficiency Delhi.

Figure 9. Performance of the exergy of New efficiency of Bangalore.

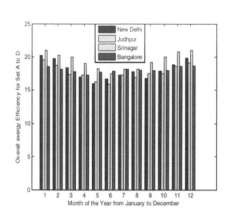

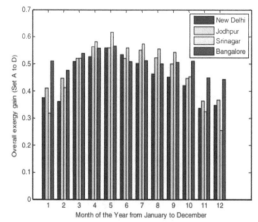

Figure 10. Variation of overall exergy efficiency.

Figure 11. Performance of overall exergy gain.

Table 1. Specification of the proposed system.

Parameter	Specification
V_{max}	425V
η_{ref}	16%
room specification	5580 mm × 4910 mm
wall height	2765 mm × 6238 mm
roof specification	11060 mm × 6144 mm
fitting of roof angle	35°

As from all the figures we can see that Set D gives better efficiency as compared to other weather conditions. Overall thermal gain can be observed from Figure 12. As compared to the earlier model, this system gives better results. As the experimental data has been taken for Srinagar, it is noticed that the thermal gain has improved a lot as compared to the proposed system of Agrawal and Tiwari (2011). Overall, monthly exergy gain can be calculated from the result which is given in Figure 11. As compared to the overall gain of Aggarwal and Tiwari of the previous design, this system generated better exergy gain (Figure 13).

The overall exergy efficiency of Srinagar recorded an efficiency of 20.8% which is much more than the previous system, and this happened in the month of December which can be seen from

Table 2.   Design parameters of the proposed system.

Design Specification	Related values
Length of Panel	1650 mm
Width of panel	800 mm
Output power	155 W
Depth of channel	255 mm
channel	Single input/output channel
C_{air} (J/kg K)	1005
C_r	0.38
A (ambient)	25°
h_0 (W/m^2)	$5.70 + 3.8 \times V_a$
h_i (W/m^2)	2.8
h_T (W/m^2)	$2.80 + 3 \times$ vair
K_c (W/m^2)	0.040
K_G (W/m^2)	0.80 (A: Clear days) (B: Hazy days)
K_i (W/m^2)	0.035 (C: Hazy and cloudy days)
K_T (W/m^2 K)	0.380 (D: Cloudy days)
L_c (mm)	0.3
L_G (mm)	34
L_i (mm)	11
L_T (mm)	3

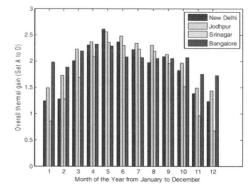 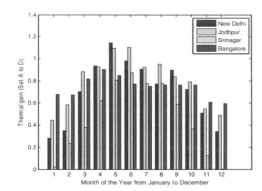

Figure 12.   Bar chart of overall thermal gain month wise. Figure 13.   Bar chart of thermal gain vs. cities.

Figure 10. As compared to the proposed system by Agrawal and Tiwari in 2011, the present system gives incremental exergy efficiency from 5.8 to 14.70 %.

4   RESULTS AND DISCUSSION

Various results have been discussed based on the result that was obtained on the basis of the optimization of different cities.

– In Figure 5, the similar value of exergy efficiency and fitness function shows that it is working properly. An observation can be done of constant increments of optimization, i.e., of the objective function.
– A detailed study was made for the month of January across the selected cities in India.
– Overall exergy efficiency was calculated for different cities in Figures 6–9.
– There is a steep change in efficiency for the whole year of about 4% in Delhi, Jodhpur, and Srinagar due to change in temperature.

5 CONCLUSION

For the four cities located in the different corners of India, exergy efficiency was calculated and then compared with the design of Agrawal and Tiwari (2011); there was a 2–5% increment in efficiency and exergy efficiencies.

- There is an observational increment of overall exergy efficiency over a year from 5.8–14.70%.
- Monthly overall exergy as well as thermal gain was improved as suggested by Agrawal and Tiwari (2011).

Appendix

$$\alpha_{eff} = \tau_g(\alpha_{sc} - \eta_{TC}) \quad m_F = \rho L d V_F$$

$$USCAG = \left(\frac{Lg}{Kg} + \frac{1}{hGa} \right)^{-1} \quad USCFT = \left(\frac{LT}{KT} + \frac{1}{hTF} \right)^{-1}$$

$$UFA = \left(\frac{Lin}{Kin} + \frac{1}{hIA} \right)^{-1} \quad hp = \left(\frac{USCFT}{USCAG + USCFT} \right)$$

$$Ufa = \left(\frac{1}{USCFT} + \frac{1}{USCAG} \right)^{-1}$$

$$U_L = UFA + Ufa$$

REFERENCES

Aggrawal, B. & Tiwari, G.N. 2010. Life cycle cost analysis of BIPVT system. Energy and Buildings 42: 1472–1481.

Agrawal, S. & Singh, S. 2018. Optimization and Performance Characteristics of Building Integrated Photovoltaic Thermal (BIPVT) System in Cold Climatic Conditions. Asian Journal of Water Environment and Pollution 15: 63–72.

Agrawal, S. & Tiwari A. 2011. A Survey on Development and Recent Trends of Renewable Energy Generation from BIPV Systems. Solar Energy 85: 3046–3056.

Debbarma, M. & Baredar, P. 2017. Comparision of BIPV and BIPVT: A review. Resource Efficient Technologies 3: 263–271.

Evola, G. & Marletta, L. 2014. Exergy and thermo economic optimization water cooled glazed hybrid PVT collector. Solar Energy 107: 12–25.

Hee, K., Kang, J. & Kim, J. 2014. Experimental performance of heating system in BIPVT system collectors. Energy conversion and management 48: 1374–1384.

Hunang, B.J., Lin, T.H. & Sun F.S. 2001. Performance evolution of solar Photovoltaic system. Solar Energy 70: 443–448.

Omar, Z. & Sharaf, M. 2019. Concentrated photovoltaic thermal solar collector systems, performance assessment. Energy conversion and management 121: 113–144.

Sarkar, D. & Kumar, A. 2019. Performance analysis of photovoltaic-thermal collector by explicit dynamic model. IETE Technical review, https://doi.org/10.1080/02564602.2019.1598294,

Shukla, A.K. & Sudhakar, K. 2018. BIPV based sustainable building in South Asian countries. Solar Energy 170: 1162–1170.

Tiwari, G.N. & Hemsikha, S. 2016. Periodic theory of building integrated photovoltaic thermal (BIPVT) system. Solar Energy 125: 373–380.

Tripathy, M. Sadhu, P.K. & Panda, S.K. 2015. A critical review on building integrated photovoltaic product and their applications. Renewable and sustainable energy reviews 61: 451–465.

Yang, T. & Andreas. 2015. Performance evaluation of air based BIPVT system with multiple inlets. In proc: Procedia Engineering 121: 2060–2067.

Zondag, H.A. & De, V.D.W. 2002. The thermal and electrical yield of a PV thermal collector. Solar Energy 72(2): 113–28.

Smart Computing – Khan et al (Eds)
© 2021 Taylor & Francis Group, London, ISBN 978-0-367-76552-1

An intelligent period monitor

Megh Singhal, Rashi Yadav & Himanshi Bhatnagar
ABES Institute of Technology, Affiliated to AKTU Lucknow, Ghaziabad, India

ABSTRACT: Periods—For most women this is a process that occurs every month accompanied with minor annoyances. But there are still a few women out there who face atrocities because they bleed every month. In rural India, menstruation circles around a culture of silence and shame. Keeping in mind the environment and mindset of the target lot that is living here, we are trying to come up with a solution to lessen the burden that they face in a major part of their lives. The purpose of this project is to make people aware of the fact that menstruation is a regular process that is healthy for a female body and not a disease to be afraid of. The vision of this work is to provide access to proper sanitation guidance related to menstruation, instill basic knowledge regarding the same, and break the stigmas associated with it.

Keywords: Menstruation, Rural areas, Female, Awareness, Sanitation

1 INTRODUCTION

The science behind menstruation says that it is the most fundamental part of the female reproduction process in which there is a periodic discharge of blood through the vagina—a result of the breaking down of the uterine walls, which marks the onset of puberty when it happens for the first time. Sadly, the knowledge gap between rural and urban women concerning this natural process in considerably broad.

Mensturation is a subject that is not freely talked about by the members of the community but somehow it is a conversation we all have. With television, the Internet, and more awareness and education, conversations around menstruation have become less inhibited (Willis 2017). In particular, the situation gets really bad when a person is from rural parts of the world where awareness is minimal as per required on a general note and is worse when the person is illiterate.

The reason behind choosing this specific topic is lack of awareness related to the personal health among women, especially the lack of knowledge about the menstrual cycle. Studies reported that many girls had lots of misconception about the physiological changes during their menstrual periods. Most of this information is acquired from their mothers, television, friends, and teachers. Taboos associated with menstruation affect women's emotional state, mentality, lifestyle, and health (Khanna et al. 2005).

Menstrual hygiene practices were found to be unsatisfactory among the rural women and various restrictions during menstruation were also in practice. Women need to be educated about the downside of using a cloth for the absorption of discharge and the use of sanitary pads for the same should be encouraged (Misra et al. 2013).

Given that menstruation is considered a women's private affair, young girls are taught from an early age that they have to manage it secretly without voicing the questions and concerns they have. From acting as an alarm to making sure the local dispensary keeps a check on the health issues the women face in the concerned region, the main aim of the project is to shed light on the importance of a healthy period and bring down the stigmas associated with it.

 DOI 10.1201/9781003167488-65

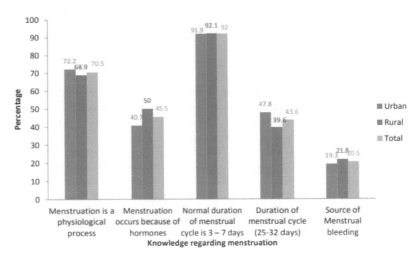

Figure 1. Depicts the percentage of women who have the appropriate knowledge about menstruation.

Keep in mind the fact that in certain areas of certain rural regions the male is the head of the family where his call holds the standing decision. Women belonging to this kind of society have no say in anything, not even issues related directly to them. To make sure this doesn't happen regarding menstruation and the concerns related to it, we'll educate the male counterparts about what it actually is and make sure there is open, yet private communication, between the two parties.

The stigma that comes along with periods won't end until people are educated the right way. Menstruation has always been a stressful topic to talk about. Addressing the period and expanding menstrual knowledge among the male fraternity is the clearest way to support girls/women when they need it the most. Women would benefit greatly by the knowledge given regarding the subject of concern which will help them understand the highs and lows of their menstrual cycles (Balamurugan et al. 2014). Figure 1. Shows the percentage of who have the appropriate knowledge about menstruation.

2 OBJECTIVE

Menstruation is a physiological process that is associated with the reproductive system but in most cases this phenomenon that is biologically healthy stamps the woman as unclean, if not entirely then at least during the days she is menstruating (Paria et al. 2014). Hygiene practices among the study population are found to be poor. The improving education level of the mothers can go a long way in improving menstrual hygiene practice along with educating young girls so that they impart the right hygiene practices among the future generations centering on menstruation (Sarkar et al. 2017). As for the matter of facts, this is a contribution toward the initiative under the Ministry of Health and Family Welfare to create awareness as well as encourage basic hygiene practices among the female community in rural areas of the nation.

This is a part of the National Health Mission. The main motive behind this idea is to increase awareness and access to the use of sanitary products and the disposal of it in ways that is not harmful to the environment. Women in the rural areas of many states/nations are not literate enough to understand the usage of apps whether or not the latter is developed for their own benefit.

There are a number of apps that can be seen which provide a medium to keep a track of everything related to one's health. There are a number of period trackers that keep us updated about everything concerning menstruation cycles. However, rural women hardly know how to use these apps.

The objective of this particular project here is the development of an app that provides all the facilities related to the periods/menstruation cycles but in the simplest way possible.

- Approximately 84% of the adolescent girls were taken by surprise when they got their first period.
- According to 2012 United Nations Population Fund study, around 60% of women diagnosed with common reproductive tract infections reported poor menstrual hygiene.
- A 2015 study on menstrual hygiene practices have shown that 15% of women use commercial sanitary protection, while 85% use homemade products.
- According to the National Family Health Survey, 2015–16 (NFHS-4) report, only 57.6% of women in India are using sanitary napkins—48.5% in rural areas and 77.5% in urban areas.
- In a 2015 study among 486 women in Odisha, urinary and vaginitis tract infections were twice as prevalent among women who used cloth during menstruation than those who used sanitary pads.
- A 2014 study found that a "huge information hole" is prevalent among the rural and urban adolescent girls about menstrual hygiene.

3 LITERATURE SURVEY

A number of surveys have been conducted centering around menstruation. All the surveys have shown and shed a light on the realities associated with menstruation and hygiene practices regarding the same. Of the 355 million menstruating girls' and women in India only 12% use a sanitary pad. 71% report to having no knowledge about the occurrence of it and 63 million live in homes without a toilet. The chances of developing reproductive and urinary tract infections go up as high as 70%.

India is ranked 125 out of 151 nations on the HDI Gender Inequality Index and menstruation is still cited as a barrier in achieving gender equality. Girl child education which plays an important role in the development of a nation faces a downfall as 20% of menstruating girls drop out of school upon reaching puberty. If this continues, an increase in the gender gap in terms of education and income seems like a plausible scenario.

In one survey of 995 women, 62% were unaware of the reason(s) of menstruation. Studies conducted with the target group have shown that 23% of girls drop out of school as soon as they start menstruating. 77% of them use an old cloth during periods that they then reuse (Garg 2017). Further, 88% use ashes, newspaper, or dried leaves to aid absorption of the discharge. All the conducted surveys and statistics clearly show how vulnerable girls and women are to stigmas associated with menstruation.

Through this project we will not only spread awareness about the topic of concern but also highlight the importance it holds in a woman's life. From providing easy access to the basic information to taking care of the health issues, it will do it all. All that the individual has to do is enter her name, the expected date, and the cycle break (Garg 2017).

4 EXISTING WORK and WHY DO WE NEED A NEW WORK ON?

There are many applications with the respective concern/objective such as Clue, Maya, etc. This proposal is different from the already existing applications in a number of ways. The main concern with the rural areas is the Internet connectivity. To overcome this barrier, we are focusing on providing offline data after one time connection. We tend to believe that awareness about menstruation does not only concern the female section but equally, the male section because it is seen that rural areas are generally male dominant.

This application is accessible to the dispensaries/clinics in the villages and small towns so that correct information is passed onto the next party. Things are being done for the betterment of the society in all aspects. "Charity begins at home" in this particular context is very much true when said "Healthiness begins at home!"

5 PROPOSED WORK

5.1 *Overview and expected outcome*

Considering the present-day scenario in rural areas here we are trying to come up with a solution to provide the required education related to the cause. In addition to the basic education to women of all age groups, we'll provide additional aid and assistance.

- We'll be specifically target females at an early age and also the ones who'll go through it at a certain point.
- Our project will also include health and hygiene measures to be taken during the postnatal phase.
- One of the major issues with people belonging to this area is little-to-no access to feminine hygiene products.
- To cover this concern, we'll try to build/establish a system where there is a reasonable and required supply at fairly affordable prices of feminine hygiene products.
- In the previously developed apps, a lot of information being asked for was not actually useful. This in-turn leads to the faults and failures in the accuracy of output. In our model, the information being asked for is minimal in order to accurately determine how and what the output should be delivered.
- The people of the rural areas don't have the in-depth knowledge of how a certain white substance which is ejected from time to time from the female body or how much white should it be labeled in order to be recorded, therefore these few things will be available as the content material of the application and not as the input required.
- Only a few steps lead to the better understanding of the scenario but not a thousand inputs leading to a confused output.
- Quality of output is more important than the quantity of it.
- Integration of sanitation projects, health education, and reproductive health programs is required, and the issue requires a more holistic approach (Garg & Anand 2015).
- Mass media may also be utilized to encourage menstrual hygiene among adolescents. These aspects should be kept in mind while planning any intervention, educational, or otherwise, regarding reproductive health of women (Singh et al. 2006).

5.2 *Use of artificial intelligence*

We plan on implementing artificial intelligence (AI) into this particular app. There are a number of ways through which it can be made faster and more convenient to use for both parties. One of those ways that we are considering to be the best and also the most useful in this case is to use AI to respond to the customers. What we mean by this is, as a business owner, there are probably hundreds of inquiries you need to respond to every day. Moreover, the majority are most likely from customers inquiring about everything from how cramps occur to what to do in case you miss a period. We can select one of the recommended answers or write one ourselves, save it, and then use it the next time someone has a similar inquiry. This will eventually improve our productivity.

6 CONCLUSION

This project not only has the potential to break the stigmas attached to menstruation but it will also let people know that menstruation is not dirty in any form. In fact, it's healthy and women and girls out there should not be ashamed of this. It should be, and can be, openly talked about. The female

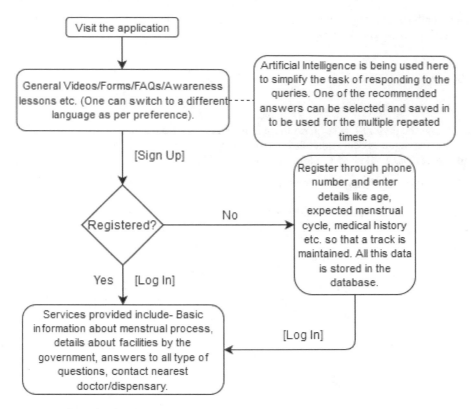

Figure 2.   Workflow of an intelligent period monitor.

community does not have to live under the cover of shame and hatred for something so natural. Awareness also needs to be created to abolish the unnecessary restrictions that are imposed on women to be followed during menstruation (Khanna et al. 2005). Not only is the strengthening of menstrual hygiene management (MHM) programs a must, but the disposal of MHM items needs to be addressed (van-Eijk et al. 2016). Thus, it is becoming clear that a multi-sector approach is needed.

7   FUTURE SCOPE

The future of this project mainly lies in the number of targeted people it is able to reach. Although there are a lot of similar applications out there, but applications are not indigenous nor they have been designed by keeping in mind the interest and need of people of rural areas.

Since the success of this project depends upon the audience it is catered to (the target audience is a major parameter), nothing is definite about its success. It isn't a commercial project. It's an awareness project where technology is used to simplify the cause it is working for.

REFERENCES

Angeline Grace G.*, Arunkumar M., Umadevi R, "Menstrual hygiene practices of women in a rural area of Kancheepuram district, India: a cross sectional study" 2019.
Baishakhi Paria, Agnihotri Bhattacharyya, and Sukes Das, "A Comparative Study on Menstrual Hygiene Among Urban and Rural Adolescent Girls of West Bengal" 2014.

Balamurugan SS, Shilpa SS, Shaji S., "A community based study on menstrual hygiene among reproductive age group women in a rural area", Tamil Nadu. J Basic Clin Reprod Sci. 2014(3):83–7.

Garg S, Anand T., "Menstruation related myths in India: strategies for combating it. J Fam Med Prim Care" 2015.

Garg, Anand. (Menstruation related myths in India: Strategies for combating it).

https://www.theweek.in/news/health/2019/09/26/creating-awareness-on-menstrual-hygiene-through-pictures. html

https://www.indiaspend.com/most-indian-girls-are-unprepared-for-menstruation-taboo-behind-unhygienic-practices/Ishita

Sarkar, Madhumita Dobe, Aparajita Dasgupta, Rivu Basu, and Bhaskar Shahbabu, "Determinants of menstrual hygiene among school going adolescent girls in a rural area of West Bengal" 2017.

Khanna A, Goyal RS, Bhaswar R., "Menstrual practices and reproductive problems: A study of adolescent girls in Rajasthan. J Health Manag" 2005;(7):91–107.

Misra P, Upadhyay RP, Sharma V, Anand K, Gupta V., "A community-based study of menstrual hygiene practices and willingness to pay for sanitary napkins among women of a rural community in northern India", Natl Med J India. 2013.

Singh A J., "Place of menstruation in the reproductive lives of women of rural North India. Indian J Community Med." 2006.

Shame, superstition and secrecy hurting menstrual hygiene, finds Tamil Nadu study [https://scroll.in/article/]

van-Eijk AM, Sivakami M, Thakkar M, Bauman A, Laserson KF, Coates S, et al., BMJ Open. 2016.

Willis. 2017. (Breaking the menstrual taboo: Why period stigma still holds women back) https://village volunteers.org/14825-2/Menstruation – A myth that needs to be broken[https://safecity.in/]

Smart Computing – Khan et al (Eds)
© *2021 Taylor & Francis Group, London, ISBN 978-0-367-76552-1*

Crop prediction

Megh Singhal, Akhilesh Singh, Aman Tiwari & Ankit Gupta
ABES Institute of Technology, Affiliated to AKTU Lucknow, Ghaziabad, India

ABSTRACT: India is an agricultural dependent country; its economy mostly depends on crop yield production and other agro-industry products. We are trying to bring an increment in the field of agriculture precision by getting better results in predicting crop production as compared to the research done in the field. With the use of machine learning (ML) techniques and efficient algorithms, a system can be built based on previous data of weather conditions and soil conditions that provide accurate and precise decision help. The proposed system will integrate and process the data obtained from stored repository, weather data, and by applying ML algorithm. This project helps in getting a solution for Smart Agriculture by monitoring the crop field which can assist the farmers in the process of increasing productivity to a great extent.

Keywords: Crop Prediction, Data Analytics, Machine Learning, Regression, Smart Agriculture

1   INTRODUCTION

In India, agriculture is one of the most practiced occupations and it is one of the most important sources of economy. Hence, we need to make the agriculture modern and head the farmers toward profit but there's always a risk to the farmers when it comes to deciding a particular crop in a specific season at a certain location as there are lot of certain factors affecting crop such as temperature, rainfall, humidity, etc. The crop may get destroyed if any of the above factors affect the crop. In order to save farmers from any such consequence, certain research has been done in the past and what we are trying is to perfect the prediction of the crop.

There are many ways available to improvise the production quantity and quality of the crop. In this project, we are using machine learning (ML) and data mining techniques [5][6]. Basically, data mining is used for analyzing the given data from various perspectives and summarizing it on the basis of given input conditions into some meaningful information [2][10]. This project also uses a prediction algorithm like regression and neighboring algorithms like k-nearest neighbor (KNN) algorithm to find out any pattern among the various data available. This as a result will predict the best crop available to grow in given weather and environmental conditions to maximize the profit as well as production then process it as per input conditions. As we are also taking the previous year's production into consideration, the prediction will be comparatively more accurate and productive. Still, this field requires a lot of research work and there is a lot of scope to pick various combinations of algorithms and strategies to increase precision of prediction algorithm [3][4].

2   RELATED WORK

Literature survey is one of the most important steps in any kind of research or project. Before developing we need to read various previous papers and researches of our domain. On the basis of this study we can discover drawbacks of the project and can start working with the reference of those previous researches and papers available.

DOI 10.1201/9781003167488-66

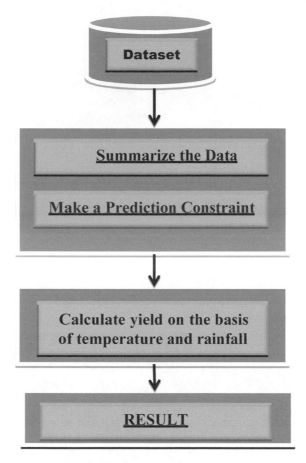

Figure 1.   Flowchart diagram.

Sadia Afrin, Mahrin Mahia, Rahbar Ahsan: To predict the crop yields with better quality and production. We need to analyze the soil properties and data related to climatic conditions to predict better crop yields and divide agricultural regions into different clusters, with various algorithms like K-means and linear regression.

Md. TahmidShakoor, Mr. KarishmaRahman, Mr. SumaiyaNasrinRayta, Mr. AmitabhaChakrabarty: Prediction of agriculture production with the help of using ML algorithms like Decision Tree, KNN, and regression algorithms.

Santosh K. Vishwakarma, Ashok Verma, Monali Paul: To predict better yielding, the crops are first analyzed and then on the basis of analysis these are categorized into similar categories and this categorization is done on the basis of data mining technique. This paper gives information about various classification rules like Naive Bayes and KNN.

3   ALGORITHMS AND TECHNOLOGIES

3.1   *Multi-linear regression*

Multiple regressions is basically an extended algorithm of linear regression. This algorithm plays an important role in this project as prediction is an important thing in this project. We use this algorithm to predict the value of a variable with the help of two or more inputs or variables available [1].

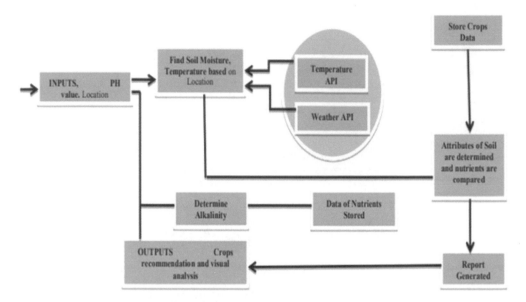

Figure 2.   Architecture of the system.

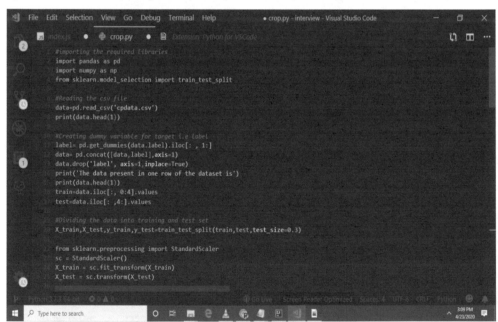

Figure 3.   Screenshot I of implementation on the visual studio platform.

Multiple regressions also allow us to calculate the overall fit or variance of the model and the relative contribution of each predictors to the total variance.

3.2   *K-nearest neighbor's algorithm*

To classify and apply regression in pattern matching and regression, we can also use the KNN algorithm in the nonparametric form of the algorithm. The main purpose of this algorithm is to

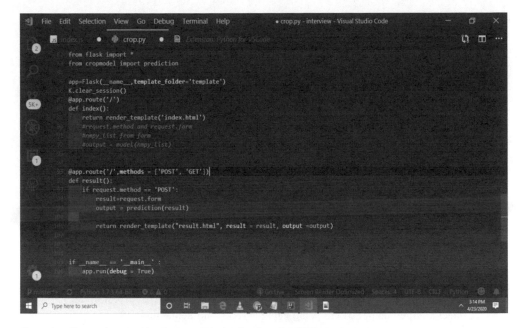

Figure 4.   Screenshot II of implementation on visual studio platform.

find patterns and then match them. Using this algorithm, we can get output for both classification and regression classification [8][9]. This algorithm categorizes objects into some classes. KNN categorizes the objects into classes. If found K = 1, then object is just simply assigned to the nearest neighbor class [7].

3.3   *Decision tree*

This algorithm uses the Greedy approach in choosing appropriate attribute. Hence, the attribute selected in the first step cannot be used anymore to get better classification. Also, it up to the training data which can provide poor results for the data which is not seen before [11] [12]. So, to overcome this drawback a different model is used. In this model results from various models are combined together. The result obtained from this model is generally better than any one of the individual models.

3.4   *RStudio*

RStudio is an important tool which was founded by J.J. Allaire. In the current scenario, R is the leading software for data analysis, statistics, analytics, and ML [13]. It is some more features than just a statistical package and as it is a programming language, so we can create our own objects, functions, and packages in a project.

4   PROPOSED SYSTEM

Our project aims to help farmers to grow crops with better chances of good quality and quantity production. To be accurate and precise in prediction of crops, the project analyses various inputs like temperature, humidity, rainfall data of the past, soil nutrients, and fertility of the soil. It reads data and summarizes it using various algorithms. It also takes input of some weather conditions which together helps in finding the best profitable crop available.

The dataset which we receive from various sources is then trained by some learning networks. This dataset is then processed using various algorithms and parameters are matched with the previous year data and a prediction constraint is made which is mainly responsible for prediction and with the help of which the system predicts most suitable crop to maximize the profit and quantity. It compares the accuracy of the prediction from various different network learning techniques and the most accurate result will be delivered to the end user. Also, with this prediction, the end user is given with proper recommendations about suitable fertilizers for every particular crop.

5 CONCLUSION

ML is a technique of artificial intelligence (AI) which helps the system to be able to learn itself without being programmed explicitly. The proposed project suggests the most suitable and profitable crop available on the basis of data received from various sources and on the basis of the previous year's data.

It takes data related to soil fertility, weather report, rainfall data, and also the previous year's data of production and prices into consideration as input and proposes the most profitable crops with good production available that can be cultivated in the current environmental conditions as output. In this project a large number of crops are being covered and hence under this project, a farmer may also get the information about the crops which can never be cultivated in that particular area.

6 FUTURE SCOPE

In the future, we can extend this project to find out the efficient algorithm on the basis of accuracy and efficiency metric to choose a more efficient and accurate algorithm for better crop prediction. We can also extend this project for better collection of valid details of soil fertility and location to accelerate the efficiency of the profit of farmer.

This system can also be extended to work as a mobile application to provide farmers easy access of the platform. We can also connect vehicles via the Internet of Things (IOT) so that easily real-time data can be passed to the servers and can also get the details of the suffering of the crop and also the quality and quantity of fertilizer to be used in the field. We can also implant sensors in the field to collect real-time data related to current situation of field.

REFERENCES

[1] Shastry, Aditya & Sanjayand H.A & Bhanushree E, 2017 "Prediction of crop yield using Regression Technique", International Journal of computing 12 (2) ISSN:1816-9503.

[2] Manjula E & Djodiltachoumy S, 2017 "A Model for Prediction of Crop Yield", International Journal of Computational Intelligence and Informatics, Vol. 6: No. 4.

[3] Choudhury Askar & James Jones, "CROP YIELD PREDICTION USING TIME SERIESMODELS".

[4] Sri Preethaa K. &, Nishanthini S. & Vani Shree K. 2016 "CropYieldPrediction",International Journal On Engineering Technology and Sciences – IJETS™ ISSN(P): 2349-3968, ISSN (O):2349–3976 Volume III, Issue III.

[5] Majumdar, Jharna & Naraseeyappa, Sneha & Shilpa, Ankalaki, 2017 "Analysis of agriculture data using datamining techniques: application of big data" Majumdar et al. J Big Data DOI 10.1186/s40537-017-0077-4.

[6] Ramesh, D &Vardhan, 2015 "Analysis of crop yield prediction using data mining techniques", International Journal of Research in Engineering and Technology, vol. 4, no. 1, pp. 47–473.

[7] Yethiraj N G 2012 "Applying data mining techniques in the field of Agriculture and allied sciences", Vol. 01, Issue 02.

[8] Thirumuruganathan, Saravanan 2016, A Detailed Introduction to K-Nearest Neighbor (KNN) Algorithm.

[9] Breiman, L., Friedman, J.H., Olshen, R.A., Stone, C.J., 1984. ClassificationAnd Regression Trees. Wadsworth.

[10] Vapnik, V & Chervonenkis, A 1974 Theory of Pattern Recognition, Nauka, *Moscow*.

[11] Haykin Simon Neural Networks A comprehensive foundation.

[12] Chen Jianhua Neural Network Applications In Agricultural Economics.

[13] Biom. J., R. C. JAIN & RANJANAAG UWALI.A.S.R.I. "Probability Model for Crop Yield Forecasting", *New Delhi*. 34 (1992) 4, 501–511. AkademieVerlag.

Smart Computing – Khan et al (Eds)
© 2021 Taylor & Francis Group, London, ISBN 978-0-367-76552-1

An efficient approach for a temperature monitoring system

Ambika Gupta, Sharad Gupta & Surbhi Sharma
Computer Engineering and Applications, GLA University, Mathura, India

ABSTRACT: There are temperature monitoring and predicting systems which will be designed by the combination of technologies such as Internet of Things and machine learning. This system will be able to monitor the temperature of the refrigerator and will send an alarming message via mail and SMS whenever the temperature of the system crosses the pre-defined threshold. This system will also be able to predict when in near future the temperature of the refrigerator will cross the threshold value with the help of analyzing the previous data generated by the LM35 sensor. It has been researched that the medicines which are kept under pre-defined temperature limits basically help better in the rehabilitation of the patient. The controller of the system will get a message when temperature is beyond the limits defined for a particular product. The temperature sensor will sense the temperature at each interval of 10 sec. This system can be used in pharmaceutical companies, cold storages where the quality of the product totally depends on the temperature they are kept on. Medicines are always kept under a prescribed temperature limit other than that they get rotten which will be a huge loss for the company as well as for the society. In this paper, a prototype was designed which is showing the functionalities those are stated above. An experimental approach to making a system like this able to run undeviatingly with accurate data collection and reliable control is introduced.

1 INTRODUCTION

Monitoring the temperature accurately is a tedious task. Humans monitor the temperature of the Earth to keep it habitable, server rooms to prevent servers from overheating, hospital rooms to make patients comfortable, and houses to provide a normal room temperature and predict the environmental climate. That is the reason why temperature monitoring systems are important. There are also various applications of temperature monitoring systems. For example, certain industrial equipment's and machinery need to be placed in a specified temperature limit. In order to monitor the temperature, data of temperature variations in real time is needed to be stored using some calibrated temperature sensor and further analyzed to predict the temperature variations if operating conditions changes due to any factor. There can be many other applications of temperature monitoring systems like human organ preservation, vegetable and fruit preservation, or in pharmaceutical companies. But designing an accurate temperature monitoring system can be expensive and challenging. The main challenge is how the system will communicate with the user if the temperature goes beyond the temperature limit defined by the user. The readings must be as accurate as the real environment temperature. Any activity in the surroundings can affect the value of temperature (https://www.boltiot.com/).

The main objective of this project is to build the circuit for temperature monitoring and Alert System in less cost using the Bolt IoT (Temperature-Sensor-Basics), LM35 sensor (lm35-temperature-sensor), and Python language for computer programming to get notified when an anomaly occurs or the temperature crosses the limit of required temperature, through any means like email, SMS, as well as a WhatsApp message. The LM35 sensor is inexpensive and weighs

DOI 10.1201/9781003167488-67

less. LM35 sensor has sensitivity of 10 mV/° C. When the temperature rises, the output voltage of the sensor also increases (LM35-temperature-sensor).

The proposed work eliminates the issue regarding the communication between system and user by using Bolt IoT. It is a system that is applied to detect temperature, display the value of temperature, and take action against the alarm when the temperature condition is exceeded from predefined temperature limits.

This paper has been organized as follows. Section 1 gives the introduction to the complete analysis and description of some of the related technologies. In Section 2 there are various related algorithms which have been proposed by various authors. In Section 3, there is a formulation of the Proposed Algorithm. After that, in Section 4 there is a complete experimental setup of the work. In Section 5, an analysis has been done. Finally, in Section 6, all the mentioned things have been concluded.

2   LITERATURE REVIEW

There are various algorithms discussed on temperature monitoring system as follows.

Sultana (2019) discussed preserving Propellant Actuating Devices (PADs) for storing of these PADs may increase its own lifetime and hence the benevolence of the aircraft. In this algorithm, a system is needed to kept in a storehouse which measures the temperature regularly and reflects the information to the end user, when the temperature is sensed by the sensors. At the end user site, the data is processed and stored in the database. The system analyzes the trend through some algorithm each time and reflects the information each time. When the temperature goes beyond the limit, it sends a message to the user or a buzzer gets turned "ON". In this way, the system can save the PDAs.

Besse et al. (2017) gave an algorithm which can produce energy in the form of heat. Thermal conduction and electrical conduction are the two mechanisms behind this. Nowadays, it is called Joule heating and is a result of the involvement of currents and atoms which are charged. The circuit uses charged particles which are expedited by an electric field but lose despair some of its kinetic energy every time they collide with an ion. Hence, measuring temperature through this mechanism was easy.

Mao et al. (2018) gave a methodology in which there are numerous patients that require treatment in comfortable zone in hospitals. Indoor temperature within hospitals plays an important role in patients' treatment and rehabilitation. Areas such as ICU, pharmacy, and operation rooms need several requirements of indoor air temperature. The storage of hospital drugs also puts forward strict requirements on the ambient temperature and humidity.

Thaker (2018) discussed different existing technologies whose aim of controlling and managing of various task also include dealing with temperature and addressing human needs. The efficient system needs to examine and monitor the conditions if it goes beyond the required values. It requires sensors to be placed on area of interest sites so that it can collect and predict the behavior. Through this paper, we are designing and executing an organized monitoring system by which the parameters are analyzed remotely and collected data is stored on cloud. Through this way we can generalize the trend.

Rao et al. (2018) discussed a methodology which is about knowing the symptoms of diseases is necessary otherwise the life of a person can be gone at any moment. IoT is such a technology which can measure a person's health, that is blood pressure level, temperature etc., remotely using some setups and can save the unanticipated death. The system consists of some equipment's that observes the patient health regularly and sends the data to the expertise doctor which responds it accordingly. In this way, the patient can be instructed regularly as well as remotely.

Waldman (2019) mentioned a technology in which there are millions of people in the United States who are diagnosed with diabetes. These diabetic people suffer from Diabetic Foot Ulcer (DFU). Decrement in DFU rates can be done by protecting patients by risk-based intercession. So, measuring skin heat can result out in protection of foot ulceration.

Evangeline (2017) discussed measuring temperature and humidity in the field is of prime importance. As ploughing of fields and making it right for the seed or crop to be grown demands a high amount of work, for proper growth of the crops, there is need for ambient temperature and humidity. The system regularly examines the environmental conditions of the field and produce the result accordingly. In this way the farmer can take the corrective measures so that one can get the valuable results.

3 PROBLEM FORMULATION

In pharmaceutical industries, the temperature of the capsules has to be maintained between -40 and $-30°$C. While the manufacturer is allowed to maintain the temperature of the tablets between -40 and $-30°$C, the temperature of the tablets must never remain between -33 and -30 stages for longer than 20 min at a time. Also, the manufacturer must preserve a log of when the cooling chamber for the production of the tablets is opened. Using this product, a method has proposed which can trigger an alert to the manufacturers when there is a possibility of the chamber being at unsuitable situation for extra than the predefined threshold.

Experimental Set-Up

The hardware set-up required is mentioned below and is shown in Figure 1.

1. **Bolt Hardware Module:** A Wi-Fi-enabled IoT module to act as an interface between sensors and cloud.
2. **Temperature Sensor (LM35):** LM35 is a sensor that measures the temperature by giving an analog output voltage which is proportional to the surrounding temperature. It can be used to measure the temperature between -55 and $150°$Celsius.
3. **Jumper Wires (Male to Female):** These are the wires that have pins for connection at both ends, which allows them to be used for joining two factors to every other besides soldering. They are generally used with breadboards and to make it easy to trade a circuit as per the requirement. The male end can plug into things, while the other end is used to plug matters into.
4. **Connecting Cable (Micro USB).** It is a shortened version of the Universal Serial Bus (USB) interface developed for the purpose of connecting cell devices such as mobile phones, MP3 players, GPS devices, picture printers, and digital cameras.

Some of the software technology required are discussed below.

1. **Bolt IoT cloud:** Bolt IoT cloud-based platform for managing and deploying IoT-based services.
2. **VMware workstation:** VMware Workstation is the widespread enterprise for strolling a couple of operating systems as virtual machines (VMs) on a single Linux or Windows PC.
3. **Bolt IoT mobile application:** A mobile app to connect Bolt IoT module to Bolt Cloud.
4. **Twilio API:** Used to send and receive messages
5. **Mailgun:** Used to send automated Emails.

4 PROPOSED ALGORITHM

Step 1. Hardware connections:
    1.1 Connect to Bolt Wi-Fi module to LM35 sensor using male to female jumper wires.
    1.2 Sensor's VCC pin is connecting to the 5V slot.
    1.3 Sensor's output pin is connected to A0 slot.
    1.4 Sensor's ground pin is connected to gnd slot.
Step 2. Set up Ubuntu Server using VMware in your desktop.
Step 3. Set up a twilio account and generate a twilio API key.

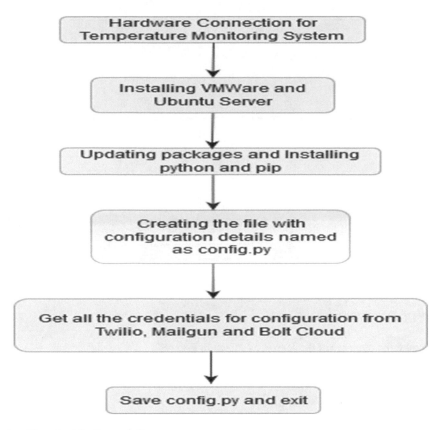

Figure 1. Flow chart for the work flow.

Step 4. Set up a Mailgun account and generate a Mailgun API key.
Step 5. Setup the Bolt python library in the Ubuntu Server:
    5.1 Update the packages on Ubuntu Server using the following command "sudo apt-get -y update".
    5.2 Install the python pip3 library.
    5.3 Install the Bolt IoT python library.
Step 6. Generate a Bolt API key.
Step 7. Make a Telegram Bot using Bot Father.
Step 8. Programming module:
    8.1 Create the configuration file containing the Bolt device SSID, Bolt API key, Mailgun API key, Twilio authentication token, sender and receiver mobile numbers, sender and receiver email id, telegram chat id and bot token, and sandbox URL from Mailgun.
    8.2 Now make a file for the anomaly detection code. The code can be illustrated in the following ways:
        8.2.1 Fetch the latest sensor value from a bolt device
        8.2.2 Store the values in a list that can be used later for computing Z-Score.
        8.2.3 Calculate Z-Score and threshold values
        8.2.4 Check whether sensor readings are in the specified range or not.
        8.2.5 If it is not, trigger the alert.
        8.2.6 Wait for 10 sec and then repeat from step 8.2.1
Step 9. End of the algorithm.

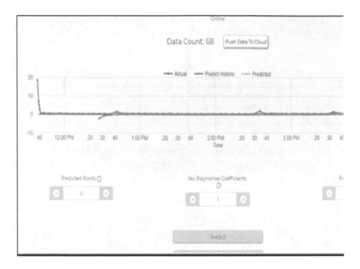

Figure 2.   The readings in a graph taken by sensor.

5   RESULT ANALYSIS

Here, we note the readings of the sensor, as shown in Figure 2.

6   CONCLUSION

There is a system which is able to monitor the temperature of refrigerators every 10-sec interval of time and on a regular basis analyze the collected temperature data, based on the analysis it predicts when the temperature of the refrigerator will cross the threshold. This system is also capable of detecting the anomalies. Anomalies in the case of temperature monitoring is whenever any person opens the refrigerator some of the cool air is lost and this loss of cool air reflects change in the current temperature pattern, so it should also be taken care while predicting the time when a refrigerator crosses the predefined threshold. The combination of IoT and machine learning (ML) give birth to inventions by these system predictions of temperature is done based on the data collected by sensors. This work successfully implements an IoT and ML-based temperature monitoring system. In the future, this temperature monitoring system can also be implemented in ICUs where the rehabilitation of the patients very much depends on the temperature the patients are kept.

REFERENCES

Abdullah U. A. Ali 2019 GSM based water level and temperature monitoring system, IJRDET- International Journal of Recent Development in Engineering and Technology, vol. 3, no 2, pp. 74 80.
Besse N. S. Rosset, J. J. Zarate, and H. Shea, "Flexible active skin: large reconfigurable arrays of individually addressed shape memory polymer actuators," Advanced Materials Technologies, Volume 2 no. 10, 2017.
Centers for Disease Control and Prevention. National Diabetes Statistics Report 2017: Estimates of Diabetes and Its Burden in the United States. Atlanta, GA: Centers for Disease Control and Prevention, US Department of Health and Human Services; 2017.
Mao M. Y. Jiang and Z. Chen 2018 "The design of household appliances controller in smart home" 3rd International Conference on Applied Mechanics and Mechanical Engineering, ICAMME (2018) November 14–15. Macau, China.
March2018 An Automated Thing Speak Weather Monitoring System using Raspberry PI'M. Ramesh, Dr. S. A.K. Jilani, Mr. S. Arun, MITS, Madanapalle, India.

Source URL: "https://www.boltiot.com/".

Source URL: "https://www.dnatechindia.com/LM35-Temperature-Sensor-Basics.html".

Source URL: "https:// www.electronicwings.com/components/lm35-temperature-sensor".

Stephanie B. Baker, Wei Xiang, and Ian Atkinson, "Internet of Things for Smart Healthcare: Technologies, Challenges, and Opportunities", Vol.5, 2019.

T. Thaker, "Esp8266 based implementation of wireless sensor network with linux based web-server," March 2018. International Journal of Engineering Trends and Technology (IJETT) – Volume 33.

Wang X Yun J Shi P Li Z Li P and Xing Y (2019), "Root Growth, Fruit Yield and Water Use Efficiency of Green House Grown Tomato under Different Irrigation Regimes and Nitrogen Levels", Journal of Plant Growth Regulation literature.

Smart Computing – Khan et al (Eds)
© 2021 Taylor & Francis Group, London, ISBN 978-0-367-76552-1

Battery health monitoring and controlling for HEV application

Kausik Bhaumik

Amity University, Uttar Pradesh, India

ABSTRACT: Hybrid Electric Vehicles (HEVs) with multiple energy sources can provide better and smoother vehicle performance, as well as contribute to fuel saving and emission reduction. With proper power control, HEVs can intelligently and adaptively provide better power conversion as well as save on fuel costs and improve battery health. Unlike many other control strategies, we focus on multiple conflicting challenges of minimizing the difference between power demand and supplied power as well as other challenges like minimizing fuel consumption while considering the health of the battery used in a hybrid vehicle. This paper uses a Genetic Algorithm (GA) in rule-based energy management whose important aspect of introduction is its ability to optimize multiple objectives. Here, we consider a battery-fuel cell hybrid vehicle. A given severity index is used to quantify the extent of the damage caused by various drive patterns on the battery. By prioritizing the battery life or battery fuel economy, is is not possible to model best the fuel consumption and vice versa. However, depending on the drive cycle there must be an intelligent optimization which considers low fuel consumption as well as better battery fuel economy while maintaining proper vehicle performance.

Keywords: HEVs, energy management, multi-objective genetic algorithm.

1 INTRODUCTION

Currently, we are very much concerned with the world's availability of fossil fuel and environmental needs, and electric vehicles (EVs) and hybrid electric vehicles (HEVs) are widely regarded as the most emerging needs in the automobile industry. There may be a history of developing EVs, however the improvements over the last decade are spectacular. In the last ten years, customers have also shown increased interest toward EVs, possibly due to concerns over saving fuel costs or environmental impact. The energy sources used in EVs (e.g., batteries) require particular care for the smooth and reliable operation of EVs. In [1], key technologies in the battery management system are suggested for EVs. On the other hand, [2] suggests the battery management system (BMS) monitor the system to work properly and perform the safety steps in case hazardous conditions arrive. To reduce fuel/energy consumption, greenhouse (GHG) emission, or to improve battery life, advanced power management strategies are required [3] [4]. Therefore, it is necessary to develop an intelligent control module that is suitable for monitoring and controlling the state of charge (SOC) and state of health (SOH) of a lithium-ion battery pack commonly used in HEVs. Shahverdi [5] suggested a bandwidth control strategy for a series of HEVs. On the other hand, Tani and Camara [6] suggested an energy management method of HEV based on the frequency approach. In [7], a systematic suggested approach to address the issue of choosing the proper model fidelity within model predictive control of HEV was introduced. In [8], the hybrid energy storage system composed of batteries and ultra-capacitors for an HEV was studied. Singh and Pratap [9] suggested a continuous slide mode controller design for HEVs. Most of these power management techniques are either not optimal or not occurring in real time. Very few of them considered multiple conflicting objectives. Degradation of components like batteries and fuel cells is inevitable. Considering EVs and HEVs, a faster degradation of the battery leads to a sooner End-of-Life (EoL) and therefore

DOI 10.1201/9781003167488-68

requires frequent replacement of a highly expensive battery. The main issue with batteries used in current EVs is their short life and health which is affected by the charge–discharge cycles and temperature. It is therefore important to model the cell-level dynamics associating cell degradation with severity associated with driving cycles. However, power management of HEVs and EVs often involve conflicting objectives, for example fuel consumption minimization of HEVs will be difficult to achieve without compromising on the battery life.

In this paper, using the concept of the severity map, the effective value of Ampere-hour (Ah) is computed. The optimal power split between the fuel cell and battery through the power management block is decided on two conflicting objectives, i.e., (1) minimization of fuel consumption and (2) minimization of Ah while maintaining the proper vehicle performance which means the difference between the power demand of the vehicle's motor and power supplied from the energy sources of the vehicle, i.e., battery and fuel cell. Vehicle performance should not be compromised. A 3D Pareto front is shown here as a convergence of multi-objective genetic algorithm (MOGA).

2   WEIGHTED AH MODELS AND SEVERITY FACTOR

The aging of the batteries degrades their state of health. According to [10], the parameters of the HEV/EV batteries defined correctly are rigid and calculations are relatively larger because of the complexity of the detailed aging process of lithium-ion batteries. Thus, these models being used in the BMS of a vehicle is usually impractical. The losses of the batteries degrade its state of health as per [11] and Equation (1):

$$Qloss = Ae^{\frac{-Ea}{RT}} . \quad (Ah)^z \tag{1}$$

where Ah represents Ampere-hour, "T" represents time in hour, "z" is exponent of time, "Ea" represents active energy, and "R" is gas constant.

In [12], a framework for predicting battery life was proposed which uses models that relate to parameters such as End-of-Life (EoL), such as Ah-throughput, number of cycles since production, or time since manufacturing. In this method, Onori [12] set a predetermined value of parameter and the battery is considered to have reached EoL when the battery exceeds that pre-determined value. In [13], battery health degradation is performed by accelerating aging for several months in the laboratory. Battery degradation and lifetime can be estimated as a function of certain parameters like voltage, current, temperature, SOC, and SOH. These parameters are estimated based on various modeling techniques. Out of these, weighted Ah-throughput models relate battery EoL to Ah-throughput as the actual amount of current being drawn/supplied to the battery. Based on the nominal/standard operating conditions (known C-rate, temperature, depth of discharge (DoD)), the actual operating conditions can be considered to be deviated from the standard by a severity factor σ as Equation (2):

$$\sigma \, (DoD, Tbatt) = \frac{Ah\_throughput_{nominal}}{Ah\_throughput_{actual}} \tag{2}$$

where the $Ah\_throughput_{actual}$ is given by Equation (3):

$$Ah\_throughput_{actual} = \int_{0}^{EoL} |I\,(t)|dt \tag{3}$$

with I(t) denoting the battery current.

The severity factor has been mapped as a function of DoD and temperature, as shown in Figure 2. It is used to calculate $Ah\_throughput_{effective}$ as Equation (4)

$$Ah\_throughput_{effective} = \sum WE.nE.AhE \tag{4}$$

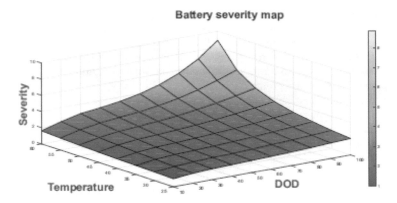

Figure 1. Severity factor map.

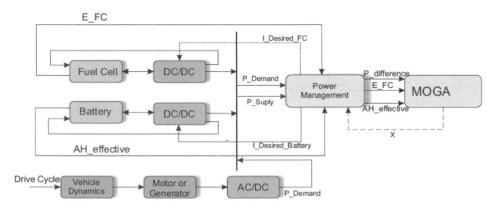

Figure 2. Block diagram.

where E denotes an event and W_E is the weight or severity associated with the event, n_E is the number of events, and AhE is the actual Ah-throughput associated with that event.

Here, we refer to severity factor as the weighting factors which is responsible for reduction of battery life. These severity factors are a highly nonlinear process as shown in Figure 1.

The damage variables of the batteries can be defined with age factor and factors. The severity factor function depends on how severely the the changes of cycles are occurring, i.e., temperature, SOC/DOD.

3 HEV MODEL

The hybrid vehicle powertrain considered in this paper is a battery-fuel cell hybrid in parallel topology. Both the sources are connected to individual bi-directional DC/DC converters. The demand side is backward modeled with vehicle dynamics, an AC motor, and AC/DC converter. The drive cycle is given as an input and the power demand at the bus is computed and compared with the power supplied by the battery-fuel cell combination. The task of the power management controller is to split the power between the battery and fuel cell in order to satisfy the power demand. Figure 2 shows the basic block diagram of the HEV model which has been modeled in MATLAB/SIMULINK. The whole model can be divided into three parts: (1) the power supplier part which consists of battery and fuel cell and their respective DC/DC converters; (2) the power management unit and the optimization algorithm used; and (3) the power demand part which

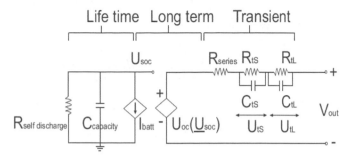

Figure 3.   Equivalent circuit model with respect to RC network.

consists of vehicle dynamics, motor or generator, and their corresponding AC/DC. All three parts are connected to a common power bus either for optimization or get the desired results.

3.1   *Battery model*

A comprehensive, accurate, and real run-time battery model is already proposed in [14]. Figure 3 describes this model.

Here,
Rts = Resistance in shorter time constant.
Cts = Capacitance in shorter time constant.
RtL = Resistance in longer time constant.
CtL = Capacitance in longer time constant.
Ibatt = Current source.
Vout = Output voltage.
Uoc = Open circuit voltage.
Capacity = Overall capacity of the battery.
Uts = Voltage across RC shorter time constant.
UtL = Voltage across longer time constant
If we denote capacitance in every RC network as parallel resistance R2. Here, C is denoted as R2. Resistance is denoted as R1.
Then from Figure 4, equivalent resistance of a RC network, Requivalent=R1||R2.

$$\Rightarrow \text{Requivalent} = \frac{R1\,(-R2)}{R1 + (-R2)} \tag{5}$$

If I is the current through RC parallel circuit, U is voltage across RC parallel circuit then,

$$\text{Voltage across RC parallel circuit } U = (\text{Requivalent}).I \tag{6}$$

$$\Rightarrow \text{Requivalent} = \frac{U}{I} \tag{7}$$

Again, for capacitor C,

$$U = \frac{1}{C}\int I \Rightarrow \dot{U} = \frac{I}{C} \tag{8}$$

Now, capacitive resistance

$$R2 = \frac{U}{I} = \frac{U}{\dot{U} * C} \tag{9}$$

561

Now from (5), Requivalent $= \frac{R1\left(-\frac{U}{U*C}\right)}{R1+\left(-\frac{U}{U*C}\right)}$

$$\Rightarrow \frac{U}{I} = -\left(\frac{(R1*U)}{(R1*\dot{U}*C)-U}\right)$$

By solving in terms of $\dot{U}$,

$$\dot{U} = -\left(\frac{I}{C}\right) - \left\{\frac{U}{(R1*C)}\right\} \tag{10}$$

Now, Voltage across series resistance, Us $= -(Rs*Ibatt)$

From Equation (10), voltage across RC short transient,

$$\dot{U}\text{ts} = -\left\{\frac{Uts}{(Rts*Cts)}\right\} - \left(\frac{Ibatt}{Cts}\right) \tag{11}$$

Similarly, voltage across RC long transient,

$$\dot{U}\text{tl} = -\left\{\frac{Utl}{(Rtl*Ctl)}\right\} - \left(\frac{Ibatt}{Ctl}\right) \tag{12}$$

Again, open circuit voltage, Uoc $= -\left(\frac{1}{Ccapacity}\int Ibatt\right)$

$$\Rightarrow \dot{U}\text{oc} = -\left(\frac{Ibatt}{Ccapacity}\right) \tag{13}$$

Usoc can also be express in terms of function of open circuit voltage such as (11):

$$\text{Usoc} = \text{f(Uoc)}$$

If we express Figure 4 in terms of equivalent ordinary differential equation (ODE), then from Equations (14), (15), and (16) will become

$$\dot{X} = \begin{bmatrix} 0 & 0 & 0 \\ 0 & -(Rts*Cts)^{-1} & 0 \\ 0 & 0 & -(Rtl*Ctl)^{-1} \end{bmatrix} X + \begin{bmatrix} -(Ccapacity)^{-1} \\ -(Cts)^{-1} \\ -(Ctl)^{-1} \end{bmatrix} Ibatt$$

Here, $X = \begin{bmatrix} Uoc \\ Uts \\ Utl \end{bmatrix}$

So, the output voltage is given in expression (14),

$$\text{Vout} = g(x1) + x2 + x3 + \text{RsIbatt} \tag{14}$$

3.2 Fuel cell model

According to Gou and Na [15], the equivalent circuit of proton-exchange membrane (PEM) fuel cell is shown in Figure 4, where C is the equivalent capacitor due to the double-layer charging effect.

The relation between the fuel cell stack voltage and current density is given in Equation (15):

$$\text{Vstack} = N\{E - A\ln\left(\frac{ifc+in}{io}\right) - (ifc+in)r - m\exp(nifc)\} \tag{15}$$

N denotes number of cells in stack others are given in [15].

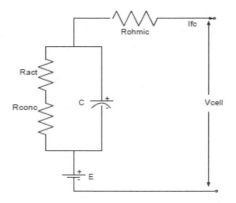

Figure 4. Equivalent circuit of PEM fuel cell.

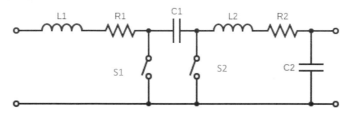

Figure 5. Cuk converter.

3.3 DC-DC converter model

Here, DC-DC converter is used to match the required power which has to supply. The converter consists of transistor switch, inductor, or capacitor as energy storage devices are normally used as linear voltage regulators. Here, we use a cuck converter which is explained in Figure 5.

This has two modes of operation: (1) where switch S1 is ON and switch S2 is OFF and (2) where switch S1 is OFF and switch S1 is ON.

In the model from Figure 5, when S1 ON and S2 OFF

$$V_{in} = (sL_1 + R_1) I_1 \tag{16}$$

Again,

$$0 = \left(\frac{1}{sC_1} + sL_2 + R_2 + \frac{1}{sC_2} \right) I_2 \tag{17}$$

Now,

$$V'_{C1} = \frac{I_1}{C_1} \tag{18}$$

and

$$V'_{C2} = \frac{I_2}{C_2} - \frac{I_{out}}{C_2} \tag{19}$$

$$I'_1 = \frac{V_{in}}{L_1} - \frac{R_1}{L_1} I_1 \tag{20}$$

$$I'_2 = -\left(\frac{V_{C1}}{L_2} + \frac{V_{C2}}{L_2} + \frac{R_2}{L_2} I_2 \right) \tag{21}$$

$$X' = \begin{bmatrix} (-R_1/L_1) & 0 & 0 & 0 \\ 0 & (-R_2/L_2) & (-1/L_2) & (-1/L_2) \\ 0 & (1/C_1) & 0 & 0 \\ 0 & (1/C_2) & 0 & 0 \end{bmatrix} X + \begin{bmatrix} 1/L_1 & 0 \\ 0 & 0 \\ 0 & 0 \\ 0 & -1/C_2 \end{bmatrix} U \qquad (22)$$

Or, the generalized expression can be written as

$$X' = A_1 X + BU$$

where $X = \begin{bmatrix} I_1 \\ I_2 \\ V_{C1} \\ V_{C2} \end{bmatrix}$ & $U = \begin{bmatrix} V_{in} \\ I_{out} \end{bmatrix}$

Similarly in mode 2, when S1 is OFF and S1 is ON

$$X' = \begin{bmatrix} (-R_1/L_1) & 0 & (-1/L_1) & 0 \\ 0 & (-R_2/L_2) & 0 & (-1/L_2) \\ (1/C_1) & 0 & 0 & 0 \\ 0 & (1/C_2) & 0 & 0 \end{bmatrix} X + \begin{bmatrix} 1/L_1 & 0 \\ 0 & 0 \\ 0 & 0 \\ 0 & -1/C_2 \end{bmatrix} U \qquad (23)$$

Or the generalized expression can be written as

$$X' = A_2 X + BU$$

where $X = \begin{bmatrix} I_1 \\ I_2 \\ V_{C1} \\ V_{C2} \end{bmatrix}$ & $U = \begin{bmatrix} V_{in} \\ I_{out} \end{bmatrix}$

4 POWER MANAGEMENT CONTROL

The role of power management controller is to provide the power from the power demand side to the power supply side through the corresponding DC-DC converters. In reality, the power management splits the demanded power between battery and fuel cell. As the optimal outcome is not based on the single objective, the power management needs to optimize the power between battery and fuel cell with some intelligent control which can deal with a multi-objective problem. There are many control strategies which were already discussed earlier, and most deal with a single-objective problem. The optimization is performed for minimization of power difference between power demand and power supplied from the source side and minimization of fuel consumption as well as maximization of battery fuel economy (i.e., minimization of battery health degradation). The logic of the rule-based power management block is shown in Figure 6.

The objective functions for optimizing using the MOGA are specified as Equation (24):

$$f(x) = \iiint_{t0}^{tend} \left(E_{FC} + a * AH_{effective} + b * P_{difference} \right) dt \to \min \qquad (24)$$

Which can be expressed as

$$f1(x) = \int_{t0}^{tend} E_{FC} dt \to \min \qquad (25)$$

$$f2(x) = \int_{t0}^{tend} AH_{effective} dt \to \min \qquad (26)$$

$$f3(x) = \int_{t0}^{tend} P_{difference} dt \to \min \qquad (27)$$

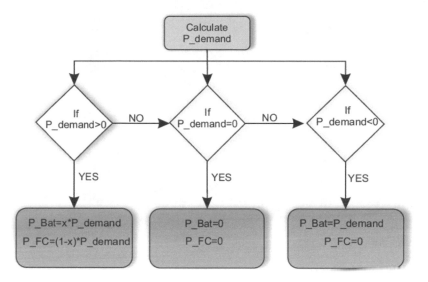

Figure 6. Rule-based power management block logic.

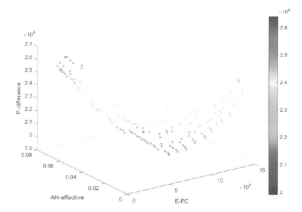

Figure 7. Three-dimensional pareto fronts of three objective functions.

So, Equation (24) can be written as

$$f(x) = f1(x) + a * f2(x) + b * f3(x) \qquad (28)$$

In Equations (24) and (28), "a" and "b" are the multiplying factor (a constant) which can be multiplied to any of the objective (here, we multiplied with AH_effective and P_difference) to take all the objective in a common frame.

A. Multi-objective Genetic Algorithm

The solution of three objective optimizations converged on a Pareto Frontier curve which is shown in Figure 7 which represents the trade of between fuel consumption (E_FC), battery health degradation (AH_effective), and power difference (P_difference).

Here, we use the MOGA to obtain the Pareto frontiers. The 3D Pareto curve is projected to 2D curves which is shown in Figures 8, 9, and 10. The color bar is according to the third objective, i.e., Power Difference (P_difference).

565

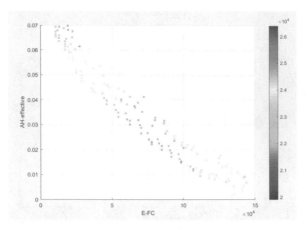

Figure 8.   AH_effective VS E_FC.

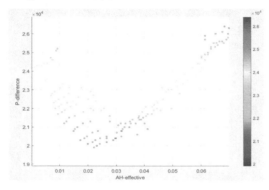

Figure 9.   P_difference VS AH_effective.

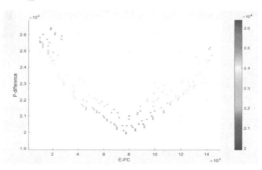

Figure 10.   P_difference VS E_FC.

From Figure 8, one can see battery health degrades (i.e., Ah_effective increases) when fuel consumption decreases and when AH_effective decreases fuel consumption increases. This is due to use of mass energy production from any one of those energy sources (fuel cell or battery) while very low production from other sources (battery or fuel cell).

5   RESULTS

The optimization plot is already shown in Figure 7. After optimization, the fuel consumption is shown in Figure 11.

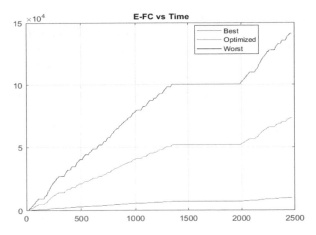

Figure 11. Fuel consumption.

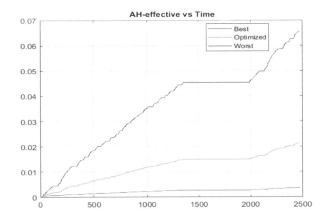

Figure 12. AH_effective of the battery used in HEV.

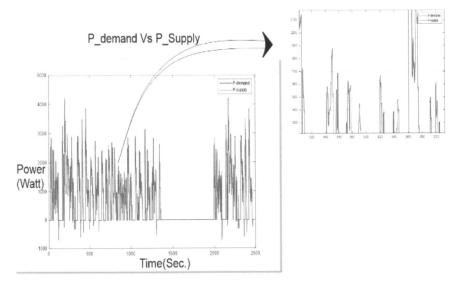

Figure 13. Power_demand vs. Power_supply.

If the optimization is done for only one objective (here fuel consumption) then the best, worst, and our optimized values are shown in Figure 11. Similarly, optimized AH_effective (battery fuel economy) along with their best and worst possible outcome is also shown in Figure 12.

Power demand of the vehicle and total power supplied by the battery and fuel cell are shown in Figure 13. The zoom portion describes how low the power differences is w.r.t. time.

So, we can conclude that without sacrificing battery fuel economy it's impossible to get the best fuel consumption for an HEV and vice versa.

REFERENCES

[1] Kailong LIU, Kang LI, Qiao PENG, Cheng ZHANG "A brief review on key technologies in the battery management system of electric vehicles" Frontiers of Mechanical Engineering, pages 47–64(2019).

[2] Conte F. V. "Battery and battery management for hybrid electric vehicles: a review" e & i Elektrotechnik und Informationstechnik, pages 424–431(2006).

[3] Shahverdi, M.; Mazzola, M.S.; Grice, Q.; Doude, M. "Pareto Front of Energy Storage Size and Series HEV Fuel Economy Using Bandwidth-Based Control Strategy". IEEE Trans. Transp. Electrification, pages 36–51, 2016.

[4] Shahverdi, M.; Mazzola, M.; Grice, Q.; Doude, M. "Bandwidth-Based Control Strategy for a Series HEV with Light Energy Storage System." IEEE Trans. Veh. Technol, pages 1040–1052, 2016.

[5] Shahverdi M., Mazzola, Q. Grice and M. Doude, "Bandwidth-Based Control Strategy for a Series HEV With Light Energy Storage System," in IEEE Transactions on Vehicular Technology, pages 1040–1052, Feb. 2017.

[6] Tani A., Camara M. B. and Dakyo B., "Energy Management Based on Frequency Approach for Hybrid Electric Vehicle Applications: Fuel-Cell/Lithium-Battery and Ultracapacitors," in IEEE Transactions on Vehicular Technology, pages 3375–3386, Oct. 2012.

[7] Sockeel N., Shi J., Shahverdi M. and Mazzola M., "Sensitivity analysis of the battery model for model predictive control implemented into a plug-in hybrid electric vehicle", IEEE Transportation Electrification Conference and Expo (ITEC), pages 493–500, 2017.

[8] Zhang L., Hu X., Wang Z., Sun F., Deng J. and Dorrell D. G., "Multiobjective Optimal Sizing of Hybrid Energy Storage System for Electric Vehicles," IEEE Transactions on Vehicular Technology, pages 1027–1035, Feb. 2018.

[9] Singh S. and Pratap B., "Continuous Sliding Mode Controller Design for Light Weighted Hybrid Electric Vehicle," IEEE 8th Power India International Conference (PIICON), Kurukshetra, India, pages 1–6, 2018.

[10] Safari M., Morcrette M., Teyssot A., Delacourt C., "Life prediction methods for lithium-ion batteries derived from a fatigue approach: Li. capacity-loss prediction of batteries subjected to complex current profiles", Journal of The Electrochemical Society, pages A892–A898, 2010.

[11] Wang J., Liu P., Hicks-Garner J., Sherman E., Soukiazian S., Verbrugge M., Tataria H., Musser J., Finamore P., "Cycle-life model for graphite-lifepo4 cells", J. Power Sources pages 3942–3948, 2011.

[12] Marano V., Onori S., Guezennec Y., Rizzoni G. and Madella N., "Lithium-ion batteries life estimation for plug-in hybrid electric vehicles," IEEE Vehicle Power and Propulsion Conference, Dearborn, pages 536–543, 2009.

[13] Stroe D., Swierczynski M., Kær S. K., Laserna E. M. and Zabala E. S., "Accelerated aging of Lithium-ion batteries based on electric vehicle mission profile," 2017 IEEE Energy Conversion Congress and Exposition (ECCE), pages 5631–5637, 2017.

[14] Chen M. and Rincon-Mora G. A., "Accurate electrical battery model capable of predicting runtime and I-V performance," IEEE Transactions on Energy Conversion, pages 504–511, June 2006.

[15] Gou B., Na W.K., and Diong B., "Fuel cells modelling, control, and applications", CRC Press, USA, Book 2010.

Smart Computing – Khan et al (Eds)
© *2021 Taylor & Francis Group, London, ISBN 978-0-367-76552-1*

Optimization of green signal using the firefly algorithm

S. Kar & U. Mittal
Lovely Professional University, Phagwara, Punjab, India

ABSTRACT: In the era of the 21st century, many developed and developing countries face the problem of traffic congestion. Few densely populated cities in India, like Bengaluru, Mumbai, and Pune Delhi, face such a problem even though India is so advanced in the field of science and technology. Many fields such as Advanced Transport Management System (ATMS) depend on the results for implementation of the traffic signal. To regulate the traffic demand, shorten the queue length and prioritize the emergency vehicle in intersections. Optimization of a traffic light signal includes many parameters such as vehicle density, flow rate, and delay to obtain efficient results. The author proposes swarm intelligence techniques to optimize the traffic light signal system. First, it detects the traffic density through sensors and, secondly, computed the results using swarm intelligence techniques. It works based on First Come First Serve (FCFS) in the intersection and road junctions.

Keywords: Traffic Congestion; ATMS; optimization; Swarm Intelligence; FCFS.

1 INTRODUCTION

India has one of the longest road networks in the world. There are many National Highway (N.H.), Express Highway (E.H.), and state roads spread all over the country. Among them, N.H. 44 is the longest and widest highway in India. Nowadays, most of the cities like Delhi have people who suffer from respiratory problems due to smog. The average waiting time of a vehicle in the intersection/road junction is responsible for smog. The green-phase traffic light is the way to move for the smooth movement of traffic. Many authors involve themselves in the field of optimization of traffic signals for many years. Some bold traffic signal management systems, such as TRANSYT (Transportation Research Center 1987), SCOOT (Hunt & Robertson 1982), and SCATS (Lowrie et al. 1982) are involved in the pre-calculated offline timing plan which is based on the current traffic scenario in the intersections and road junctions. Few authors placed stone for improving the traffic density of the intersection. Morgan and Little (1964) and Ma & Ruichun (2019) develop the maximum bandwidth traffic signal setting optimization program inspired from the maximum green-wave band-phase difference optimization. Little (1996) confirmed the Mixed Integer Linear Program Model (MILPM) with maximum green-wave bandwidth and the branch and bound method to conduct the optimal solution to the control model (Ma & Ruichun 2019). Messer et al. (1973) evolved the green-wave coordination control optimization timing software of progression analysis and signal system evaluation routine. Gartner et al. (1990, 1991) present a trunk-road two-way green-wave coordination control mode with variable bandwidth and used MINOS to act as the optimal solution to the mixed-integer linear program (Stamatiadis & Gartner 1996; Gartner & Stamatiadis 2002) for different traffic flow, conditions, and bandwidth demands in different intersections. As technological development increases with artificial intelligence (AI), some of the latest developments of the optimization of the green signal are artificial neural network (Chien & Ding 2002; Nubert et al. 2018), fuzzy expert system (Wei et al. 2001; Kaur et al. 2020), Petri nets (List 2004), Markov decision control (Yu & Stubberud 1997), swarm intelligence (Jovanovic et al. 2017; Siddavaatam & Sedaghat 2019; Rewadkar & Doye 2017), reinforcement learning (Yizhe 2018; Aslani 2018), and hybrid systems (Liang et al. 2019; Wei et al. 2019; Wang et al. 2018).

All the past developments inspire to propose an optimization strategy for "optimization of traffic light signal system with the involvement of artificial intelligence (AI) based on swarm intelligence (Ma & Ruichun 2019)." Swarm intelligence is derived from animal behavior while searching for food, detecting enemies, and survives in the tropical environment. Few animals depend on a special type of fragrance, a few depend on vision, a few depend on movement, and a few depend on light.

The Firefly Algorithm (FA) is a meta-heuristic approach for solving the computational optimization problem. The name is inspired by the behavior of a firefly which is found in the tropical region of America. The FA is a multi-agent system, in which a firefly recreates a look through lights, just like an artificial firefly. Fireflies have a unique flashing pattern and as the distance increases the flashing light becomes weaker and weaker due to absorption by air.

In this research, the selected path for the optimization, traffic density, flow rate, delay, and the presence of an emergency vehicle in the road, according to the parameters the firefly, changes its position and calculates the optimized time according to the parameter.

2 RELATED WORK

Ma & Ruichun (2019) proposes a green-wave traffic signal through the artificial fish swarm algorithm which is inspired from the movements of fish. It was proposed in the year 2002. The artificial fish swarm optimization algorithm works according to the visual scope of the water. When visual scope is crowded then a school of fish searches the empty visual scope. When visual scope is not crowded then a school of fish moves to the central or chase, moving toward the best point. This optimization strategy works accordingly to the optimization of a traffic light; traffic density is compared to the visual scope and searches for the best point of the road.

Renfrew (2009) proposed a green signal timing through artificial ant colony optimization (ACO) which is inspired from the movement of ants in search of food. The way ants choose the path forms the source and destination with the help of pheromones. The vehicle acts as a pheromone in the road. The time is predicted based on the presence of pheromones in the road.

Kareem (2018) implements PSO which compares the traffic density with the allotted green time. The study is based on the green time allocation and presence of traffic density on the road. The shortest green time is observed in the study. The study is on the different streets of the Iraq and found that the green time allocation is either shorter than the vehicle density or much longer than the vehicle density. Through PSO these times should be according to the vehicle density.

Singh (2019) proposed that VANET techniques use ant colony optimization. VANET searches for the base station through which each vehicle in the VANET architecture waits for the green signal, the ACO where ants can select the path from the source to destination using the presence of pheromones.

In Siddavaatam & Sedaghat (2019), the grey wolf was a swarm optimization technique which was used for the search space optimizing through wolf pack methodology. The wolf is divided into four categories: (i) Alpha Group, i.e., Leader group; (ii) Beta Group, i.e., Subordinate Wolves; (iii) Delta Group, i.e., scouts, sentinels, hunters, caretakers; and (iv) Omega Group, i.e., Lowest Ranking Wolves. Wolves are hunted like a following methodology in a certain space. These will be:

- Initialization
- Prey Encircling
- Hunting
- Attack
- Search Again

If we compare this with a search space of the road, the vehicle was encircled, and the optimization takes places in that road and the vehicle should go from that place. When it was optimized then it will search again for the optimization process on the other road.

Rewadkar & Doye (2017) implemented a network-modeled structure was the most vital and important elements for the vehicle to decrease the average waiting time of the vehicle. Everything relates to each other through a network. On the road, VANET was the most popular network model where each vehicle approaches the base station and each base station gives permission to the vehicle, but it was a static process. The dynamicity which is achieved through one of the swarm intelligence techniques, i.e., the Glow Worm Algorithm. The Glow Worm is a type of swarm intelligent technique. It was inspired from the insect glow worm. The algorithm wants a head station for the vehicle; the station gives permission to the vehicle dynamically like a VANET. It is efficient and less time consuming than VANET.

3 FIREFLY ALGORITHM

The principal study of swarm intelligence depends on the social behavior of the insects present in the tropical region. Swarm intelligence is the collective behavior of decentralized, self-organized which can be a natural and artificial system. The swarm intelligence system contains a population of agents which interact with the other mates and the environments for their survival. Each agent of the insect group only follows the rules and does not have a knowledge of the whole system. Some common examples of biological swarm intelligence optimization are: ant colony, artificial bee colony, firefly, grey wolf, etc.

The firefly algorithm proposed by Yang (2008) at Cambridge University is named after the flashing behavior of fireflies that are commonly found in the tropical forests of the United States. FA is a meta-heuristic approach for solving the mathematical optimization problem. Fireflies are unisex in nature, and produce cold light with the combination of oxygen. The flashing light can be yellow, green, or pale red light depending on the situation ahead of the firefly. Through these lights, fireflies behind them should know about the situation ahead be ready to retaliate according to the situation. As the distance, increases the lights become weaker and weaker with the absorption of air.

3.1 *Working methods of the firefly algorithm*

Step 1. Initialize the objective function: In this function, calculate the light intensity according to the distance. The light intensity varies from firefly to firefly. The mathematical formula is:

$$I(r) = \frac{I_s}{r^2}$$

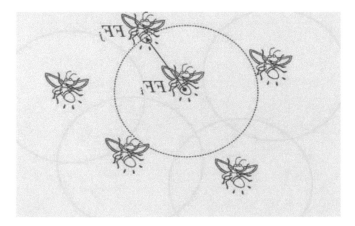

Figure 1. Firefly communication.

where I(r) is the light intensity and r^2 is the observer distance from the source.

Step 2. Generate the initial population of the firefly: Fireflies are unisex in nature. Firefly will increase the population by attracting the mating partner and through the randomization of the population. The formulation of generating the population of firefly is:

$$x_{t+1} = x_t + \beta_0 e^{-\gamma r^2} + \alpha \epsilon$$

Step 3. Determine the firefly's light intensity: Calculate the distance of every firefly in the population through their light intensity. A brighter light determines the nearest location. The formula for light intensity is:

$$I = I_0 e^{-\gamma r^2}$$

Step 4. Calculate the attractiveness of the firefly: Due to the bright light intensity of the firefly the mating partner will be attracted to the firefly. The formula is derived as:

$$\beta = \beta_0 e^{-\gamma r^2}$$

Step 5. Movement of a less bright firefly toward a brighter one: The movement of firefly to the brighter firefly:

$$x_i = x_i + \beta_0 e^{-\gamma r} i, j(x_i - x_j) + \alpha \epsilon$$

Step 6: Refurbish the light intensity, rank the firefly, and find the current best: In this stage, depending on the light intensity value, the fireflies are ranked according to the population and find the best optimized solution.

The firefly algorithm is used in many optimization problems such as the traveling salesman problem (TSP), digital image processing (DIP), feature selection, fault detection, etc.

3.2 *Flow chart of the optimization problem*

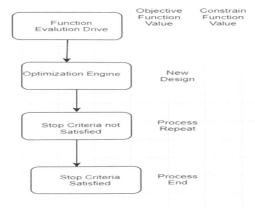

Figure 2. Flow chart of the optimization problem.

4   TRAFFIC SIGNAL OPTIMZATION USING THE FIREFLY ALGORITHM

The optimization problem consists of (ss, x, Ω), where "ss" is the search space, "x" is the objective function, and "Ω" is the set of constrains. Depending on the "Ω", f is minimized or maximized according to the search space.

The author's goal is to minimize the time of traffic signal control, whereas waiting time of the vehicle is minimized and time utilization in the intersection or road junction. In this research, the bright light which is illuminated from the fireflies is related with the performance of the machine. As we all know, the minimum and maximum green time of the traffic signal is bounded with some constrained value. The minimum time of the green signal is 0 sec and the maximum time of the green signal is 180 sec. The firefly algorithm defines the optimization of green signal time duration to minimize the average waiting time of the vehicle and the queue length of the vehicle is reduced.

The inputs for the optimization of green time duration of the traffic signal include the current traffic density (which is detected through the detection sensors), flow rate of the intersection/road (obtained by the number of vehicles passed during a point of time interval), delay (it is the reaction time of the driver and vehicle to ready to move from the queue), and emergency vehicle (presence of emergency vehicle) that lane will give a green signal on a priority basis.

The system will check for the emergency vehicle and calculate the traffic density; depending on the flow rate and delay, the predicted time of the traffics signal will be calculated.

This it is compared with the firefly algorithm; given priority to the emergency vehicle, calculate the traffic density detected by the sensors, calculate the flow rate of the road, calculate the delay time by the driver, and predict the time along with some additional time for the vehicles which are not detected by the sensors. Update the predicted time and calculated time for the other roads of the intersections.

5   CASE STUDY

This study addresses the optimization of the traffic light signal in the different parts of Jalandhar, such as Pap Chowk. The study will mainly be computed along the National Highway (N.H.) 44; the traffic density will increase in different times of the day and night. The different types of vehicles will run at different times of the day. The preferred time for a truck is during the late night and early morning. The captured video is used for training and testing of the system. 80% of the data is used for training purposes, and 20% of the data is used for testing purposes.

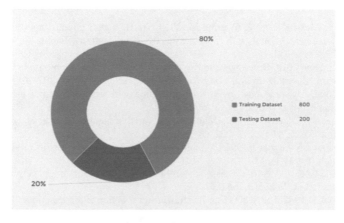

Figure 3.   Graphical representation of training and testing data.

6 STIMULATION AND RESULTS

The proposed algorithm is compared with the traditional traffic light signal system, the data available for the traffic signal time according to the traffic density, flow rate, delay, and emergency vehicle. The time prediction is on the FCFS basis in the intersection and the road junction. There is no specific cycle for the intersection.

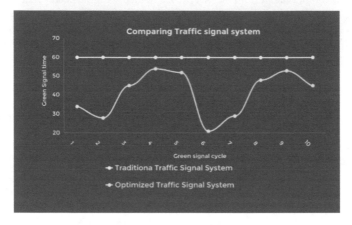

Figure 4.   Comparing traditional traffic signal with the computed (firefly algorithm) traffic signal.

7 CONCLUSION

Firefly algorithm is a new technique for optimization in swarm intelligence. In this paper, optimization of a traffic signal through the firefly algorithm was compared with the traditional traffic signal system on the described parameters. In the initial test, it proves that this system gives its best performance in every traffic situations. To enhance the performance of system, more training and testing of the system is required.

REFERENCES

Aslani, M, Seipel S, Mesgari M S, & Wiering M. 2018, Traffic signal optimization through discrete and continuous reinforcement learning with robustness analysis in downtown Tehran. Advanced Engineering Informatics, Vol:38: 639–655.

Ma Changxi, He Ruichun.2019, Green wave traffic control system optimization based on adaptive genetic-artificial fish swarm algorithm. *Neural Computing and Applications*, Vol: 31: 2073–2083.

Chien S, Ding Y.2002, Dynamic bus arrival time prediction with artificial neural networks. Journal of Transportation Engineering, Vol:128(5).

Gartner NH, Assmann SF, Lasaga F.1990, Multiband: a variable bandwidth arterial progression scheme. Transport Research, Vol:1287(1): 212–222.

Gartner NH, Assmann SF, Lasaga F.1991, A multi-band approach to arterial traffic signal optimization. Transport Research, Vol:25(1): 55–74.

Gartner NH, Stamatiadis C. 2002, Arterial-based control of traffic flow in urban grid networks. Mathematical and Computer Modelling, Vol:35(5): 657–671.

Hunt P, and Robertson D.1982, The SCOOT on-line traffic signal optimization technique. Traffic Engineering and Control, Vol:23(4).

List G, M. Cetin. 2004, Modeling traffic signal control using petri nets. IEEE Transaction on Intelligent Transportation Systems, Vol: 5(3).

Little John.1996, The synchronization of traffic signals by mixed-integer linear programming. Operations Research, Vol:14(4): 568–594.

Jovanovic, A, Nikolic, M, & Teodorovic, D. 2017, Area-wide urban traffic control: A Bee Colony Optimization Approach, Transportation Research Part C, Vol:77: 329-350.

Kaur G, Mittal U, & Kaur, K.2020, Fuzzy based traffic control system considering high priority vehicles. Smart Intelligent Computing and Applications, 397–403.

Kareem, Emad Issa Abdul. 2018, Traffic Light Controller Module Based on Particle Swarm Optimization (PSO). American Journal of Artificial Intelligence, Vol:2(1):12–21.

Liang X, Du X, Wang G, & Han, Z. 2019, Deep Reinforcement Learning for Traffic Light Control in Vehicular Networks. College of System Engineering, Vol:(21).

Lowrie P et al. 1982, The Sydney coordinated adaptive control systems – principles, methodology, algorithms. IEEE Conference Publication, Vol:207.

Messer CJ, Whitson RH, Dudek CL. 1973, A variable sequence multiphase progression optimization program. Transport Research, Vol: 445(1): 24–33.

Morgan John, Little John.1964, Synchronizing traffic signals for maximal bandwidth. Operations Research, Vol:12(6): 896–912.

Nubert J et.al. 2018, Traffic density estimation using a convolutional neural network. Machine Learning Project – National University of Singapore.

Renfrew, David, and Xiao-Hua Yu. 2009, Traffic Signal Control with Swarm Intelligence. Fifth International Conference on Natural Computation, 79 83.

Rewadkar D, & Doye D. 2017, FGWSO-TAR: Fractional glowworm swarm optimization for traffic aware routing in urban VANET. International Journal of Communication System.

Siddavaatam P, & Sedaghat R. 2019, Grey Wolf Optimizer Driven design space exploration: A novel framework for multi-objective trade-off in architectural synthesis. Swarm and Evolutionary Computation, Vol:49: 44–61.

Singh Gagan, Prateek Manish, Sastry Hanumat. 2019, Swarm Intelligence Based Efficient Routing Algorithm for Platooning in VANET through Ant Colony Optimization. International Journal of Innovative Technology and Exploring Engineering, Vol:8(9):1238–1244.

Stamatiadis C, Gartner NH.1996, Multiband: a program for variable bandwidth progression optimization of multi-arterial traffic networks. Transport Research, Vol:1554(1): 9–17.

Transportation Research Center.1987, Traffic network study tool: TRANSYT-7F software summary, University of Florida.

Wang Yizhe, Yang Xiaoguang, Liu Yang dong, Liang Hailun.2018, Evaluation and Application of Urban Traffic Signal Optimizing Control Strategy Based on Reinforcement Learning, Journal of Advanced Transportation, Vol:2018.

Wang S, Xie X, Huang K, Zeng J, & Cai Z. Deep Reinforcement Learning-Based Traffic Signal Control Using High-Resolution Event-Based Data. IEEE Transactions on Vehicular Technology.

Wei W et.al. 2001, Traffic signal control using fuzzy logic and MOGA, Proceedings of IEEE conference on systems, man, and cybernetics, Vol:2: 1335–1340.

Wei H, Chen C, Wu K, Zheng G, Yu Z, Gayah V, & Li Z. Deep Reinforcement Learning for Traffic Signal Control along Arterials. 2019.

X.-H Yu, & Stubberud A. 1997, Markovian decision control for traffic signal systems. Proceedings of the 36th IEEE conference on decision and control, 4782–4787.

Smart Computing – Khan et al (Eds)
© 2021 Taylor & Francis Group, London, ISBN 978-0-367-76552-1

Child tracking using IoT and GPS

Anjana Bhardwaj, Naman Garg, Dharya Khanna & Vivek Bhati
ECE Department, ABESEC Ghaziabad, India

ABSTRACT: This paper depends on Internet of Things (IoT). As we probably are aware in the present period everything depends on innovation. These days each individual is connected in many ways, where the most famous correspondence is the Web so it is the Web that accomplice individuals. This paper adduces an IoT based answer for help guardians to follow their kids in real time. Different devices are connected with a single device through channels of the web. The concerned gadget is connected with the server employing the Internet. The gadget can be used by guardians to follow their children progressively or for ladies' security. The contemplated arrangement takes the preferred area administrations given by the global system for mobile communication (GSM). It enables the guardians to get their kid's area on constant by Short Message Service (SMS). Here, a model (gadget) is made which is reenactment based. The work involves Atmega 328 as a microcontroller, alongside the global positioning system (GPS) and GSM module. Infused C center gather utilizing Keil and virtual recreation check utilizing Arduino is done. A server is made which will gather all the information created by our model framework and send the equivalent to the server utilizing general packet radio service (GPRS). A counterfeit server will be made. This gadget will likewise have the emergency help key (SOS), if anybody presses the key, an automatically generated call will be sent to the parents.

Keywords: Embedded System, Smart System, Internet

1 INTRODUCTION

The Internet of Things (IoT) implies the utilization of wisely connected gadgets and structures to use information assembled by installed sensors and actuators in machines and other physical items (Yang et al. 2011; Abuhasel 2020; Khan 2020a–2020e; Quasim 2019, 2020). IoT implies to the capacity of system gadgets to detect and gather information from our surroundings and after that shares the information over the Internet where it tends to be processed and used for a different reason.

The IoT is involved in acute machines collaborating and communicating with different machines, articles, conditions, and foundations. Pretty much every gadget today has an infused processor, commonly known as a microcontroller or MCU, alongside user interfaces (UIs); it can include programmability—regulations and control usefulness. The setback of the world and the inescapability of installed handling are the latchkeys to making objects—smart, your old toaster that precisely controlled the shading of your toast presently has an MCU in it, and the MCU controls the shade of your toast. The toaster completes its task even more dependably, moreover, trustworthily, and in light of the way that it is by-and-by an adroit toaster, it can talk with you electronically using its touchpad or switches. For example, in case I am running late for work, would I have the option to turn on my home lights for security reasons using my workstation or phone? Correspondence capacity and remote manual control lead to the resulting stage…how might I robotize things, subject to my settings having mobile cloud-based planning, to get things moving without my intervention? A conclusive goal of some IoT applications is to interface with the Internet to achieve the objective, for which they ought to at first advancement toward getting to be—smart MCU/embedded processor with a

DOI 10.1201/9781003167488-70

related novel ID by then associated and, finally, controlled. Those capacities would then have the option to engage another class of organizations that makes life less difficult for customers. The term Internet of Things was the first generated by Kevin Ashton in 1999 concerning creation arranges the board. Regardless, in the earlier decade, the definition has ended up being progressively far-reaching covering a wide extent of employments like human administrations, utilities, transport, etc.

Even though the meaning of "Things" has changed as innovation evolved, however, the primary objective of appearing well and good data without the guide of human mediation continues as before. The progression of the present Internet into a network of interconnected things does not simply accumulate information from the earth (sensing) and associates with the physical world (welcome/heading/control), yet furthermore uses existing Internet benchmarks to offer organizations to information trade, examination, applications, and correspondences. Controlled by the inescapability of contraptions enabled by open remote development, for instance RFID readers and tags (Khan 2008a, b, 2009a–c), Wi-Fi, and telephonic data benefits similarly as embedded sensor and actuator centers, IoT has wandered out of its beginning times and is practically changing the present static Internet into a joined Future Internet. The RFID and data management technologies plays an important role in the decision making (Tyagi 2010a, b, 2011).

The Internet uprising provoked the interconnection between people at an exceptional scale and pace. The accompanying rebellion will be the interconnection between things to make a sharp circumstance. Just in 2011 did the number of interconnected devices on the planet outperform the veritable number of people? At this moment, there are 9 billion interconnected devices, and it is predicted that number will rise to 24 billion by 2020. These days, over 80% of people, including adolescents around the age of seven or eight, have mobile cells. This is a direct result of various reasons. One of them is the earth-shattering features and limits that new mobile cells offer especially Android-based mobile cells. GPS offers surprising limits in finding the position and this can be used to make an astute application that helps in discovering a missing or lost child (Liu et al. 2019).

The essential idea of the IoT has been around for approximately two decades and has attracted various examiners and adventurers because of its fantastic surveyed influence in improving our stepbystep lives and society (Luo et al. 2019) The likelihood of IoT is especially significant for individuals with ineptitudes, as IoT advances can support human activities at a greater scale-like structure or society, as the contraptions can usually organize to go about as a full-scale system (Luo et al. 2019).

The invention of the Internet prompted an interconnection between individuals at an exceptional scale and pace. The following insurgency will be the interconnection between articles to make the acute domain (Zhang et al. 2012).

The wide variety of potential IoT applications needs an item progression condition that coordinates the applications, request, control, and guiding dealing with and the security of the center and system. While the centrality of programming in MCU courses of action has extended amid the past couple of years, for MCUs supporting the IoT, significantly more programming, instruments, and enablement will be required. A broad natural network with adequately open assistance is indispensable to engaging the headway of embedded planning centers and IoT applications (Wang et al. 2012).

These days, regardless, with advancement created at a snappy pace, a robotized vehiclefollowing structure is being used in a combination of ways to deal with track and show vehicle territories logically. In this endeavor, we are using the child instead of a vehicle. One contraption is associated with the server by methods for the Web. Using those contraptions, gatekeepers will pursue their adolescents continuously or women's prosperity. The mulledover plan abuses the zone organizations given by GSM since youngsters pass on that device. It allows the parent to get their child's location on a constant by Short Message Service (SMS).

2 LITERATURE REVIEW

Ten critical examples influencing IT for the accompanying five years were spread out by Gartner. The Internet is wandering into enormous business assets and client things, for instance, vehicles and TVs. The issue is that most endeavors and advancement venders are yet to research the potential results of an all-encompassing Internet and are not operationally or legitimately handled. Gartner perceives four major use models that are creating:

- Manage
- Monetize
- Operate
- Extend

These can be connected to individuals, things, data, and places, and in this manner, the supposed IoT will be prevailing by the Internet of Everything.

The IoT is positively not a singular development; it's a thought where most new things are associated The IoT convey various business openings and add to its multifaceted design. To oblige the conventional assortment of the IoT, there is a heterogeneous mix of correspondence developments, which ought to be balanced to address the necessities of IoT applications, for instance, imperativeness adequacy, security, and steadfastness. In this particular situation, the component of the arranged assortment may be scaled to different sensible system advancements that address the necessities of the IoT applications, grasped by the market.

Empowering advances for the IoT considered can be gathered into three classes:

a) Innovations that empower—things to gain relevant data,
b) Advancements that empower—thing to process logical data,
c) Advancements to improve security and protection.

The underlying two orders can be commonly grasped as helpful structure squares requiring consolidating—intelligence with things—which are without a doubt the features that differentiate the IoT from the standard Internet. The second rate class is not a valuable yet rather the acknowledged essential, without which the invasion of the IoT would be truly decreased. The IoT progression proposes that the earth, urban territories, structures, vehicles, dress, smaller contraptions, and various things have an ever-increasing number of attributes identified with them or possibly the ability to recognize, pass on the framework, and produce new information. Besides, the framework headways need to adjust to the new troubles, for instance, high data rates, thick swarms of customers, low inertia, low essentialness, insignificant exertion, and a massive number of contraptions The 5G circumstances that reflect future challenges and will fill in as executive for further work are a plot by the EC bolstered METIS adventure (Luo et al. 2019).

As the IoT winds up built up in keen processing plants, both the volume and the dimension of detail of the corporate information created will increase. Besides, plans of action will never again include just one organization, yet will rather include very unique systems of organizations and new esteem chains. Information will be produced and transmitted self-governing by keen machines and this information will have cross-organization limits. Various dangers are related to this new setting—for instance, information that was at first produced and traded to facilitate assembly and coordination exercises between various organizations could, whenever related to other information, all of a sudden give outsiders with exceedingly delicate data around one of the accomplice organizations that may, for instance, give them a piece of knowledge into its business procedures. New instruments will be required if organizations wish to seek the regular methodology of keeping such a learning mystery to secure their upper hand. New and managed plans of action will likewise be vital—the crude information that is produced may contain data that is important to outsiders and organizations may thus wish to make a charge for sharing them. Inventive plans of action like this will likewise require legitimate shields (prevalently in the state of agreements) in a request to guarantee that the esteem included is shared out reasonably, for example using dynamic evaluating models.

Various sorts of adroit contraptions are open on the planet. A couple of devices are for individual security and some are for vehicle following. This endeavor is proposed to be used by gatekeepers and expected to discover missing or lost children. It misuses how a significant number of adolescents have PDAs which is useful for this kind of condition. In this work, GPS is united with one of the basic organizations of a mobile cell phone which is GSM, even more unequivocally SMS, in one system.

An application at the parent's side will allow gatekeepers to send a region sale to the child side by then recuperating the region from the sales answer and showing it on the guide. Then again, the application at the adolescent's side amasses the essential information of the mobile cell phone that will be used to locate the intense phone. Information, for instance, GPS, encourages and time is collected and sent to the parentmobile cell phone that is pre-enlisted on the application. The correspondence between the parent and the adolescent applications is done using SMS. It will empower the system to work without the need of web affiliation in a like manner empowers the application to be completed on cuttingedge cell phones that make an effort not to help GPRS, 2G, or 3G web accessibility. The system sends the zone of the child's sharp device to a parent's mobile cell phone exactly when the parent wishes to watch out for the child (Liu et al. 2019).

Starting late, new contraption models have dropped to sizes wearable in a wristwatch limit. Some examination uses stay singular GPS chips near to a couple of other off-the-rack embedded improvement sections to make a GPS-based quantifiable wristwatch for sprinters. Some present things use accelerometers to aggregate data, for instance, speed. A GPS-based, watch-sized device could pass on logically dependable, higher exactness speed data similarly as region data. Sprinters could see this data to battle with themselves for their best time up. A couple of current courses of action exist for sprinters who need the helpfulness our thought about device offers. Mobile phones are frequently the most despicable aspect of particular gadgets, and applications exist which give GPS-based running information.

3 CONCLUSION

We have recently watched the usage of IoT increase. More articles are getting the chance to be embedded with sensors and grab the ability to convey.

This work demonstrates a model that relies upon the GPS tracker framework. Here, ARM-7 LPC2148 is to be used as a microcontroller, alongside the GSM and GPS modules. The composition PC programs are done using Keil and the generation check will be done by Proteus 8.1. A server will be made which will assemble all data created by the model framework. By the assistance of GPRS, the equivalent is sent to the server. The essential component of this application is to get the child's zone without its correspondence in the process with a direct and best technique, done by the use of GSM and SMS. The device will, in a like manner, have the emergency key (SOS). As an example of a crisis, on the offchance that anyone presses the key, a customized assistance message will be sent to any three enrolled adaptable numbers on the server, like any item thing or arrangement, however there is still room for improvement. Features can be added to improve the system. The pondered structure will be investigated, improved, and executed in later work.

ACKNOWLEDGMENT

The authors are extremely grateful to the editors for their recommendations and backing the development of this paper and to the Department of ECE, ABES Building College, for encouraging its improvement.

REFERENCES

Abuhasel K. A. and M. A. Khan, (2020), "A Secure Industrial Internet of Things (IIoT) Framework for Resource Management in Smart Manufacturing," in IEEE Access, vol. 8, pp. 117354–117364, 2020, doi: 10.1109/ACCESS.2020.3004711.

Feng Y.CH., Yuan Y., Lu X.Q., (2017), Learning deep event models for crowd anomaly detection, *Neuron computing*, vol. 219, pp. 548–556.

Khan M. A., (2020), An IoT Framework for Heart Disease Prediction Based on MDCNN Classifier, in IEEE Access, vol. 8, pp. 34717–34727, 2020. DOI: 10.1109/ACCESS.2020.2974687.

Khan, MA, Abuhasel, KA. (2020).Advanced metameric dimension framework for heterogeneous industrial Internet of things. Computational Intelligence. 2020; 1–21. https://doi.org/10.1111/coin.12378.

Khan M.A, and Algarni F., (2020) "A Healthcare Monitoring System for the Diagnosis of Heart Disease in the IoMT Cloud Environment Using MSSO-ANFIS," in IEEE Access, vol. 8, pp. 122259–122269, 2020, doi: 10.1109/ACCESS.2020.3006424.

Khan, M.A. and V. K. Antiwal, "Location Estimation Technique using Extended 3-D LANDMARC Algorithm for Passive RFID Tag," 2009 IEEE International Advance Computing Conference, Patiala, 2009, pp. 249–253, doi: 10.1109/IADCC.2009.4809016.

Khan, M.A and S. Ojha, "Virtual Route Tracking in ZigBee (IEEE 802.15.4) enabled RFID interrogator mesh network," 2008 International Symposium on Information Technology, Kuala Lumpur, 2008, pp. 1–7, doi: 10.1109/ITSIM.2008.4631904.

Khan, M. A., Quasim, M. T, et.al, (2020), A Secure Framework for Authentication and Encryption Using Improved ECC for IoT-Based Medical Sensor Data, in IEEE Access, vol. 8, pp. 52018-52027, 2020. DOI: 10.1109/ACCESS.2020.2980739.

Khan M.A. et. al, (2020), Decentralised IoT, Decenetralised IoT: A Blockchain perspective, Springer, Studies in BigData, 2020, DOI: https://doi.org/10.1007/978-3-030-38677-1.

Khan M.A., Sharma M., P. R. Brahmanandha, "FSM based Manchester encoder for UHF RFID tag emulator," 2008 International Conference on Computing, Communication and Networking, St. Thomas, VI, 2008, pp. 1–6, doi: 10.1109/ICCCNET.2008.4787699.

Khan M.A. Sharma M, R. B. Prabhu, "FSM based FM0 and Miller encoder for UHF RFID Tag Emulator," 2009 IEEE International Advance Computing Conference, Patiala, 2009, pp. 1317–1322, doi: 10.1109/IADCC.2009.4809207.

Khan, M.A., Sharma, M. and Prabhu, B.R., 2009. A survey of RFID tags. International Journal of Recent Trends in Engineering, 1(4), p.68. Academy publisher, Finland.

Kim J., Grauman K., (2009), Observe locally, infer globally: a space–time MRF for detecting abnormal activities with incremental updates, in CVPR, Miami, FL, pp. 2921–2928.

Lai Y.-C., Hsiao L.-Y., Chen H.-J., Lai C.-N., and Lin J.-W., (2013), A novel query tree protocol with bit tracking in RFID tag identification, IEEE Transactions on Mobile Computing, vol. 12, pp. 2063–2075.

Landaluce H., Perallos A., Onieva E., Arjona L., and Bengtsson L., (2016), An energy and identification time decreasing procedure for memoryless RFID tag anti-collision protocols, IEEE Transactions on Wireless Communications, vol. 15, pp. 4234–4247.

Liu Z. H., Wang J. J., Liu G., et al, (2019), "Discriminative low-rank preserving projection for dimensionality reduction," vol. 85, pp. 105768.

Luo F., Du B., Zhang L. and Tao D., (2019), Feature Learning Using Spatial-Spectral Hypergraph Discriminate Analysis for Hyperspectral Image, *IEEE Trans. Cyber.*, vol. 49, pp. 2406–2419.

Mohsenian-Rad A.-H., Shah-Mansouri V., Wong V. W., and Schober R., (2010), Distributed channel selection and randomized interrogation algorithms for large-scale and dense RFID systems, IEEE Transactions on Wireless Communications, vol. 9.

Quasim, M. T., Khan M. A, et.al, (2019), Internet of Things for Smart Healthcare: A Hardware Perspective, 2019 First International Conference of Intelligent Computing and Engineering (ICOICE), Hadhramout, Yemen, 2019, pp. 1–5. DOI: 10.1109/ICOICE48418.2019.9035175.

Quasim, M.T., Khan M.A, Algarni F., Alharthy A., Alshmrani G.M.M, (2020), Blockchain Frameworks. In: Khan M., Quasim M., Algarni F., Alharthi A. (eds) Decentralised Internet of Things. Studies in Big Data, vol 71. Springer, DOI: https://doi.org/10.1007/978-3-030-38677-1.

Soriano S. Lopez and Parron J., (2015), Wearable RFID tag antenna for healthcare applications, in IEEE-APS Topical Conference on. IEEE, pp. 287–290.

Tyagi S., Ansari A.Q., Khan M.A. (2011) Extending Temporal and Event Based Data Modeling for RFID Databases. In: Nagamalai D., Renault E., Dhanuskodi M. (eds) Advances in Parallel Distributed Computing. PDCTA 2011. Communications in Computer and Information Science, vol 203. Springer, Berlin, Heidelberg, https://doi.org/10.1007/978-3-642-24037-9_43.

Tyagi, S., A. Q. Ansari and M. A. Khan, "Dynamic threshold-based sliding-window filtering technique for RFID data," 2010 IEEE 2nd International Advance Computing Conference (IACC), Patiala, 2010a, pp. 115–120, doi: 10.1109/IADCC.2010.5423025.

Tyagi, S., M. Ayoub Khan, and A. Q. Ansari, "RFID Data Management," in Radio Frequency Identification Fundamentals and Applications Bringing Research to Practice, Cristina Trucu, Ed. InTech, February 2010b, DOI:10.5772/8001.

Vahedi E., Ward R. K., and Blake I. F., (2014), Performance analysis of RFID protocols: CDMA versus the standard EPC gen-2, IEEE Transactions on Automation Science and Engineering, vol. 11, pp. 1250–1261.

Wang J., Hassanieh H., Katabi D., and Indyk P., (2012), Efficient and reliable low-power backscatter networks, in Proceedings of the ACM SIGCOMM, pp. 61–72.

Yang L., Han J., Qi Y., Wang C., Gu T., and Liu Y., (2011), Season: Shelving interference and joint identification in large-scale RFID systems, in INFOCOM, Proceedings IEEE, pp. 3092–3100.

Zhang Z., Lu Z., Chen Q., and Yan X., (2012), Design and optimization of a CDMA-based multi-reader passive UHF RFID system for dense scenarios, IEICE transactions on communications, vol. 95, pp. 206–216.

Smart Computing – Khan et al (Eds)
© *2021 Taylor & Francis Group, London, ISBN 978-0-367-76552-1*

Richter's predictor: Modeling earthquake damage using random forest

Bharat Lal & S.P.S. Chauhan
SCSE Department, Galgotias University, Greater Noida, Gautam Buddha Nagar, India

Usha Chauhan
EEE Department, Galgotias University, Greater Noida, Gautam Buddha Nagar, India

ABSTRACT: This research work deals with Richter's Predictor, using the datasets which consider 39 features, available at a driven data platform, each row of dataset representing a unique result. By using approaches such as k-nearest neighbor (KNN), Decision Tree, artificial neural networks (ANNs), and Random Forest predict the damage caused by the earthquake in Nepal based upon their level of accuracy and performance of the training model. First, we applied Random Forests using some features. In this work, important features are selected with the help of the Random Forest approach. We obtained the highest accuracy when we selected an important feature by giving numeric values 0.02.

1   INTRODUCTION

The Nepal earthquake occurred on April 25, 2015 (local time 11:56 am) with a magnitude of 7.8. Its hypocenter was located in the Gorkha region which is why it's also known as the Gorkha earthquake. It was the highest damage-labeled earthquake in terms of buildings, roads, infrastructure, etc. Almost 10 billion U.S. dollars of Nepal's economy was lost due to that earthquake according to the Center for Disaster Management. It was the event that caused the most damage when compared to the 1934 Bihar–Nepal earthquake. According to disaster management reports, almost 8,510 deaths occurred and 199 went missing as a result. Moreover, after that disaster, several landslides and earthquakes occurred in the mountain areas. With the help of this paper, we can easily find earthquake damage in future earthquake events. The 2015 mainshock had a long-term impact on the nature, people, growth, infrastructure, etc. First, we analyzed this problem as a time-dependent problem. Later, this problem transforms into a classification problem because we can easily predict seismic damage grade based on features. The Random Forests classifier method is used to develop the best model which can be used to predict a seismic damage label by an earthquake. In this model, we consider 38 input features and 3 seismic damage grades of buildings as an output. During earthquake prediction, the Random Forests classifier gave the best results compared to other models.

2   RELATED WORK

2.1   *Random forest*

In this method, we used the ranger package for selection of important features based on a random permutation. Random Forest uses Decision Tree for the classification problems. A decision tree is like a flowchart where each branch denotes a test outcome, each internal node denotes a test on an attribute, and each external node denotes a class label. Decision trees provide classification of the instance based on instances sorting which classified by the tree from the root to leaf node.

DOI 10.1201/9781003167488-71

When new samples come, we thenpush into a decision tree and assign a label on that sample after predicting the result based on voting. It is the best method compared to a single decision tree.

The random forest approach is a supervised learning algorithm. In this paper, we applied a random forest approach because later we consider Nepal's earthquake problem as a classification problem for improving the accuracy of our models. It creates multiple decision trees on given data sets then predict the results from each decision tree. In this case, we can get the final result on the bases of voting and average the result. The random forest has certain desirable characteristics:

(i) It reduces the over-fitting of the model.
(ii) Its robustness to outliers and noise.
(iii) It's faster than a decision tree algorithm.

2.2 *KNN*

k-nearest neighbor (KNN) is a simplest and more-used method for a classification problem. It is also known as a lazy learning algorithm because it required a training step before classification. Therefore, KNN can only be used for small datasets which is considered only a limited feature.

2.3 *Libraries used*

NumPy, Matplotlib, Pandas, TensorFlow, Keras, Scikit-learn.

3 METHODOLOGY

3.1 *Data collection and pre-processing*

We downloaded data sets from a driven data portal. Datasets consider 260,602 samples with 3 damage building grades. Every row of the dataset denoted by a unique building ID that was hit by the 2015 Nepal earthquake. The available dataset considers the information on the building which was destroyed during the earthquake. We converted all the categorical column values into numeric values because categorical values do not help during the training of the model. Thus, all categorical values converted into numeric values. The building ID column is not useful for training the model. After dropped building ID columns we obtained a (260601, 38) matrix with 38 input features.

3.2 *Data partitioning and sampling*

We divided the dataset into one part for training and the remaining part for testing of the model. After that, we predicted building damage results from this training model. We randomly sampled 4/5 of it (208,480 data samples) to the training of the classifier and the remaining 1/5 of it (52,121 data samples) to the testing of the classifier. We divided the training part data into training input and output the same for testing phase data. We applied a different method for data analysis such as dimensionality reduction, clustering, ensemble method, etc. Table 1 shows damage grade of the building based on different age groups.

Table 1. Damage grades of buildings related to different age groups.

Age Groups	<5	<5–10	<10–25	<25–50	<50–100
Damage Grade (1)	12803	4360	5963	1565	244
Damage Grade (2)	31751	22370	53443	29736	9682
Damage Grade (3)	15184	12166	33152	19964	6094

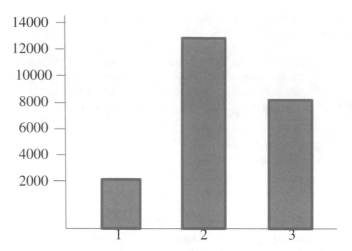

Figure 1. The show number of the building with each damage grade.

3.3 *Assessing classifier performance*

By using the test data, we evaluated the performance of trained models which is already available in given datasets. We are predicting the building level of damage from 1–3. The level of damage is an ordinal variable. During prediction, ordering is important for the level of damage variable.

We can also consider this problem as an *ordinal regression* problem. An ordinal regression problem is sometimes described as a classification and regression problem. We used the F1 score for measuring accuracy of the model. The F1 score of an algorithm balances on the basis of precision and recall. Recall denotes correctly the measure result by the model. For a better result, we need to balance precision and recall of the classifier. We have three types of damage labels of the building so we will use a micro-averaged F1 score:

$$F_{micro} = \frac{2.P_{micro}.R_{micro}}{P_{micro} + R_{micro}} \tag{1}$$

where

$$52P_{micro} = \frac{\sum_{k=1}^{3} TP_k}{\sum_{k=1}^{3}(TP_k + FP_k)} \tag{2}$$

$$R_{micro} = \frac{\sum_{k=1}^{3} TP_k}{\sum_{k=1}^{3}(TP_k + FN_k)} \tag{3}$$

In python language, we can easily calculate a micro-averaged F1 score using sklearn machine learning library. Here, k represents for class values 1, 2, 3 and FN is False Negative, TP is True Positive, and FP is False Positive.

3.4 *Model and hyperparameters*

We used different models for training and testing purposes but we get the highest accuracy when we applied a random forest classifier algorithm multiple times.

3.5 *Random forest*

The random forest method is used for a machine learning regression and classification problem. It used multiple decision trees instead of a single decision tree. In this algorithm, the final result

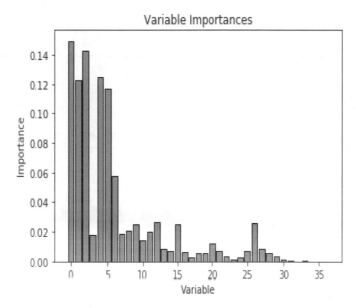

Figure 2.   Graph shows features' importance.

was evaluated on the bases of voting. Forests mean is a group of decision trees. Randomly sampled 4/5th of data (260,601, 38) is used for training of the model and 1/5th of the data is used for testing. We have set our number of estimators, i.e., some decision trees to 750 and 11 input features for ensemble decision tree on the dataset. We find 70% of a F1 score in this algorithm.

3.6   K-nearest neighbors

KNN is a simple and easy-to-use machine learning supervised algorithm. There are two types of learning: supervised and unsupervised. In supervised learning, we already have an input and output variable and we used you use a method to map input from the output. We can be used to solve both classification and regression problems:

$$Y = f(X) \tag{4}$$

Our goal is to map input from the output and trained model. With the help of a trained model, we predict an output for a new sample. When we are applying KNNs with 2000 neighbors then we get an F1 score of 63.95%. We face an over-fitting situation when we consider more neighbors. This is not a good model as it gives precision and recall for classes 1 and 3 equal to zero as they are minor classes. Therefore, this model cannot predict classes 1 and 3 accurately.

3.7   Decision tree classifier

Applying the decision tree classifier with auto hyperparameters similarly, it is observed that the score is 64.47%.

3.8   Artificial neural network

We used 5 hidden layers; 0.05 dropouts with tanh and ReLU activations functions for training the model.

Artificial neural networks (ANNs) consider one input layer, one output layer, and one or more than one hidden layer. We get precision and recall close to zero when we choose the different

Table 2. Classification report of the decision tree classifier.

	Precision	Recall	F1-score	Support
Damage Grade (1)	0.49	0.48	0.48	5138
Damage Grade (2)	0.69	0.70	0.70	29051
Damage Grade (3)	0.61	0.60	0.61	17932
Accuracy			0.6447	52121
Macro avg	0.60	0.59	0.60	52121
Weighted avg	0.64	0.64	0.64	52121

Table 3. Classification report of ANN.

	Precision	Recall	F1-score	Support
Damage Grade (1)	0.61	0.36	0.45	4985
Damage Grade (2)	0.66	0.87	0.75	29673
Damage Grade (3)	0.73	0.42	0.53	17463
Micro avg			0.67	52121
Macro avg	0.67	0.55	0.58	52121
Weighted avg	0.68	0.67	0.65	52121

Table 4. Comparison between various models.

Model	Micro-averaged F1 score
KNN	63.95
ANN	67
Decision Tree	64.47
Random Forest	70

hidden layers and hyper-parameters. This is because of the imbalanced dataset. In imbalanced datasets, the class distribution is not uniform among the classes. The uniform distribution is not possible in imbalanced datasets. It is treated as a special case for the classification problem. Also, data imbalance does not reflect an equal distribution of classes within a dataset. In our dataset, damage grade=2 is denoted as a major class and damage grade=1 and 3 denoted as a minor class. Therefore, it is difficult for the model to predict the accurate result for damage grade=3 class. When a datasets considers some class in major form and some class in minor form, then the bagging, boosting, and stacking method is best for solving this type of problem. Cross-validation doesn't work when a dataset considering one class is a major form and the other class is in minor form. We can overcome this issue using the boosting and bagging method.

4 EXPERIMENT RESULT

On applying different models like the decision tree classifier, KNN, neural network, and random forest, we get different accuracy scores. Table 4 shows the comparison between F1 scores of models.

We get the highest F1 score when applying the random forest classifier method compared to other methods.

5 CONCLUSION

In this study, we conducted research for earthquake prediction through computer science-based intelligent techniques and interaction of seismology-based earthquake precursors. A robust multilayer prediction model is generated using maximum seismic features. We consider 38 seismic features for this problem. We used important features for the training of an earthquake prediction model for better result. The prediction model consists of the Random forest Classifier (RFC) method. It's provides an initial estimation for prediction. Thus, the model is trained and tested successfully by using the RFC algorithm with the improved result by selecting important features and a training model.

REFERENCES

Ader, T., Avouac, J. P., Liu-Zeng, J., Lyon-Caen, H., Bollinger, L., Galetzka, J., et al. 2012. Convergence rate across the Nepal Himalaya and interseismic coupling on the Main Himalayan fault: implications for seismic hazard. *J. Geophys. Res.* 117, B04403.

Ambraseys, N. N., and Douglas, J. 2004. Magnitude calibration of north Indian earthquakes. *Geophys. J. Int.* 159, 165–206. doi:10.1111/j.1365-246X.2004.02323.x.

Avouac, J. P. 2003. Mountain building, erosion and the seismic cycle in the Nepal Himalaya. *Adv. Geophys.* 46, 1–80. doi:10.1016/S0065-2687(03)46001-9.

Bilham, R. 2004. Earthquakes in India and the Himalaya: tectonics, geodesy and history. *Ann. Geophys.* 47, 839–858. doi:10.4401/ag-3338.

Center for Disaster Management and Risk Reduction Technology (CEDIM). 2015. *Nepal Earthquakes – Report #3*. Available at: https://www.cedim.de/english/index.php United Nations Office for the Coordination of Humanitarian Affairs (UN-OCHA). 2015. Available at: http://www.unocha.org/nepal.

Chaulagain, H., Rodrigues, H., Spacone, E., and Varum, H. 2015. Seismic response of current RC buildings in Kathmandu Valley. *Struct. Eng. Mech.* 53, 791–818. doi:10.12989/sem.2015.53.4.791.

Goda, K., and Atkinson, G. M. 2014. Variation of source-to-site distance for megathrust subduction earthquakes: effects on ground motion prediction equations. *Earthquake Spectra* 30, 845–866. doi:10.1193/080512EQS254M.

Harbindu, A., Gupta, S., and Sharma, M. L. 2014. Earthquake ground motion predictive equations for Garhwal Himalaya, India. *Soil Dynam. Earthquake Eng.* 66, 135–148. doi:10.1016/j.soildyn.2014.06.018.

Morales-Esteban A, Martínez-A'lvarez F, Troncoso A, Justo J, Rubio-Escudero C. Pattern recognition to forecast seismic time series. Expert systems with applications. 2010; 37(12):8333–42.

United States Geological Survey (USGS). (2015). Available at: http://earthquake.usgs.gov/earthquakes/eventpage/us20002926#scientific_finitefault.

Smart Computing – Khan et al (Eds)
© 2021 Taylor & Francis Group, London, ISBN 978-0-367-76552-1

Smart shoes for the blind

Geetanjali Raj, Sumit Gupta, Mohit & Shubham Singh
ECE Department ABESEC Ghaziabad, India

ABSTRACT: A typical human being is bestowed with five sensory organs, from which the eye plays the most crucial role for them to interact with their environment. Visually challenged people in this world face more difficulties than those who have lost one of their other senses. The 21st century is an era of innovation. We have witnessed many breathtaking innovations in various disciplines, therefore we thought we should do something to make the lives of the visually impaired easier as they are entitled to equal rights and equal opportunities. Previously, many products have already been created in order achieve this goal but they were either inefficient or too expensive. Therefore, we decided to accept the challenge and make a low-cost product to help the visually impaired. Everyday challenges faced by a visually challenged person are not correctly understood, which is what we address in this project. There are approximately 286 million visually impaired people in the world and this paper presents an idea-turned-into-reality tool that would help them navigate the world freely. The goal is to prompt others also to develop more meaningful problem-solving products for the visually impaired.

1 INTRODUCTION

There are approximately 286 million people in the world with visual impairments, of which 39 million are 100% visually impaired and 246 million have less than 60% visual impairment. Moreover, about 90.3% of the visually challenged people worldwide belong to the low-income class, with 81.8% of people with blindness being senior citizens aged 55 and over. These are a serious number. Major eye problems worldwide are uncorrected refractive defects in the eye, but cataracts are still the major cause of visual impairment in middle and low-income segment countries (Shah et al. 2017). The number of visual impairments due to infectious diseases has decreased immensely in the last 20 years According to reports of global estimation for visual impairment, 75% of all visual impairments can be prevented or cured.

Years ago, people with visual impairments used to face many difficulties in moving around. They always needed assistance or support for moving around (Udgirkar et al. 2016). This has inspired a lot of inventors around the world to develop a permanent solution to these problems, so that they can move more freely and can feel more independent. One such innovation is the Go Robotic cane which suggests "Navigating indoors can be especially challenging for people with low vision or blindness. While existing GPS-based assistive devices can guide someone to a general location such as a building, GPS isn't much help in finding specific rooms.

The Smart Shoes we have developed are not only objects to guide someone over a path, but also will act as an SOS signaling tool for blind people so that they can reach people around in case of an emergency (Chew 2012). We can conclude that our project is a tool that can assist a visually impaired person in his daily life.

DOI 10.1201/9781003167488-72

We had gone through every other product on the market aimed to improve the movability of the blind. As there is always room for improvement on a product, we came up with a concept of developing a handfree small device such that they can walk freely without the use of their hands giving them liberty to move around without them asking for help from someone else. We know we are using various modules which will consume power for operations, for that we converted the energy consumption regime of the system to lowpower mode of operation, and joined some power-generating modules over the shoegenerating power such that the shoes become energy independent. Moreover we also concentrated to keep the device small in order to promote more maneuverability and keep it lightweight so that it will not feel bulky to the wearer when he or she wears the smart shoes. We believe that this device should be inexpensive so that anyone could afford it, and can be used by a large mass, connected with a mobile application making it more user accessible giving voice assistant to the user via a smartphone, in order to ease the user interface as a user won't hassle in controlling the product.

2   SMART SHOE PROJECT

Visually challenged people face various problems in navigating themselves while moving the open environment, as in a crowd or in a place with various obstacles. So, we decided to make a prototype of two concepts, bridging the two alreadyknown concepts: ranging path detection and SOS signaling. Hence the smart shoe project tells the user right path to move (using voice commands, making project more user friendly) as well as in the case of emergency will also send the SOS signals to people around in order for urgent medical assistance (Gangwar 2013). Initial experiments show that our device enables human users to navigate safely in indoor and outdoor environments. Blindness refers to a complete loss of functional vision. However, blindness has a very much broader meaning, such as the varying vision of a human being in varying circumstances such as weather, light, climate and environment. The science behind the vision of a human being is when light rays strikes at retina, a surface behind eye lenses, the nerve cells there generate electrical signals and nerves carries those electrical signals towards the brain (Farrajota et al. 2013). So blindness can occur in only two scenarios, if athe n inadequate amount of light is striking over the retina or there is a problem in transferring electrical signals to the brain; any or both of them can cause blindness in the person.

3   METHODOLOGY

The project illustrates a proof-of-concept (POC) and prototype model of a smart idea to provide a confident aid for walking to the blind person; it will also act as an SOS signal emitter for the blind person alerting his family members in case of an emergency. This system is intended to provide voice assistance to the user while walking on foot via using ultrasonic sensor which detects the surroundings and informs the person when an object approaches too close for the user. The system consists of microcontroller atmega328p, ultrasonic sensor, gyroscopic sensor, SIM900A module a smartphone, a vibratory circuit and a Bluetooth unit. When the object will be detected in front of the shoe and if any person coming in front of it will alert him with the use of our Android application and vibratory circuit, connected to the shoe via Bluetooth unit, it will guide them to turn in which direction giving sensation to the user using vibratory circuit too, making our project more user friendly. Now let assume a case where we have gyroscopic sensor which will track the movement of the user 500 times a second If a sudden fatal jerk is experienced or an accident is observed by the sensor, it will automatically send a distress signal or SOS of the GPS Location (acquired by GPS module) of the shoe, to the family members of the user, using SIM900A module sending them the location of the user and the local authorities a distress signal to rush toward the ward. To deal with the power budget of the system, we have used autocharging system for the shoe (piezoelectric sensor array with battery circuit in it, charging batteries while walking and

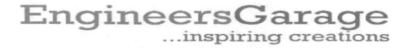

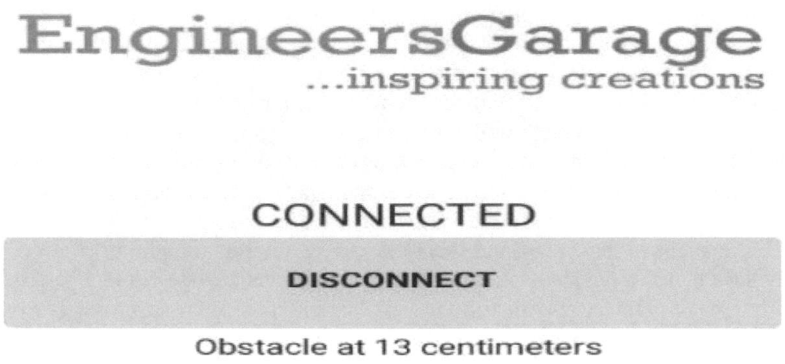

EngineersGarage
...inspiring creations
CONNECTED
DISCONNECT
Obstacle at 13 centimeters

Figure 1. Voice commands by the application.

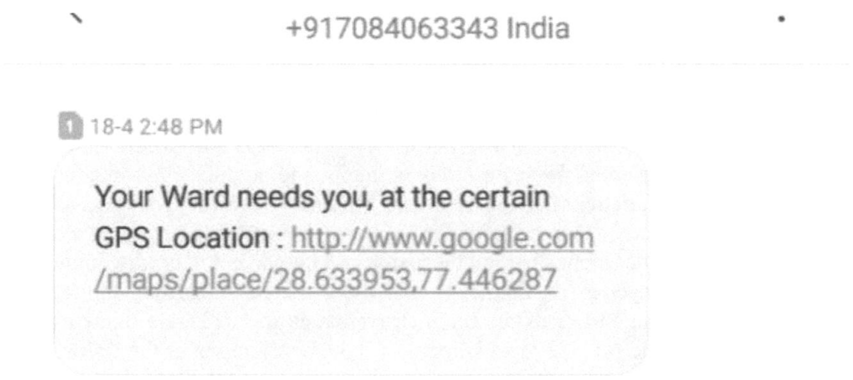
+917084063343 India
18-4 2:48 PM
Your Ward needs you, at the certain GPS Location : http://www.google.com/maps/place/28.633953,77.446287

Figure 2. The SOS SMS, with the location of the user in case of emergency.

powering the whole shoes) attached with the battery qualifying the power backup problem, making the working uninterrupted.

4 RESULTS

As we have already illustrated working on the whole module above, here are some pictures of: the Application for voice commands, the SOS signal in the form of SMS, and the location as we open the SMS on our smartphone (it will jump over Google maps, giving out the pinpoint location where the event have occurred).

In order to create a more user-friendly experience, we developed our own application which will provide the user voice access to the shoes, as voice is more logical in giving out instruction to the user than sensation or vibration.

It will automatically show the pinpoint location where the event has occurred or urgency is required.

Figure 3.   Pop-up tab when we open the SOS SMS, in any smartphone.

5   CONCLUSION

We conclude that the proposed system is quite successful and practical. The problem in existing system is the quality of hardware, poor reliability of ultrasonic sensors, low detection, and range of the GPS This problem should be eliminated with efficiency of object detection, giving out voiceassistant support to the user, and accident or havoc system so that in case of any emergency situation This project was focused on providing the user more comfort in movement as well as being able to act as a resource of communication for them, by which in case of emergency they can get the proper medical assistance they require. Hence, we conclude that this project provides independence for the visually challenged people, making them able to move around more freely in the outdoors.

6   FUTURE SCOPE

Future work will be a leap ahead, making the efficiency of system 10X better than it is now. We are planning to attach one highresolution camera and a thermal imaging camera into the system. Then the images acquired by the array of the cameras will be processed by AI and ML software, giving out more accurate information about the environment to a blind person in order to make him more informed and able to take this decision more precisely. It also would be able to detect the overall characteristics of the object coming ahead of the user. Matching percentages must always be more than 75%, and as in the case of a blind person, any flaw could be fatal to the wearer; hence we have to make the system a reliable one. We are focused on making the object more userfriendly and reliable, so that they can walk like a normal human being when wearing our designed smart shoes.

REFERENCES

Central Michigan University, January 2009, A Review on Obstacle Detection and Vision, International Journal of Engineering Sciences and Research Technology", Vol.4, (Issue No.1) pp. 1–11.

Chew S., April 2012, Electronic Path Guidance for Visually Impaired People, International Journal Of Engineering And Science (IJES), Vol.2, (Issue No.4), pp.9–12.

Gangwar S., June 2013, A Smart Infrared Microcontroller-Based Blind Guidance System, Hindawi Transactions on Active and Passive Electronic Components,Vol.3, (Issue No.2) Page No. 1–7.

Shah Hardik R, Uchil Dhiraj B., Rane Sanveg S., Prasanna Shete, April 2017, Smart Stick for Blind using Arduino, Ultrasonic Sensor and Android, International Journal of Engineering Science and Computing, Volume 7 (Issue No.4), Page No. 10929–10933.

Farrajota José, Miguel, Rodrigues Joao M.F., June 2013 A Smart Infrared Microcontroller Based Blind Guidance System, Hindawi Transactions on Active and Passive Electronic Components,Vol.3, (Issue No.2) pp.1–7.

Udgirkar Seema, Sarokar Shivaji, Gore Sujit, Kakuste Dinesh, Chaskar Suraj, September 2016, Object Detection System for Blind People, International Journal of Innovative Research in Computer and Communication Engineering, Vol. 4, (Issue 9).

S. L. Shimi and Dr. Chatterji S., November 2014, Design of microcontroller based Virtual Eye for the Blind, International Journal of Scientific Research Engineering & Technology (IJSRET), Vol.3, (Issue No.8), pp.1137–1142.

Wahab Mohd Helmyab, Talibetal Amirul A., January 2013, A Review on an Obstacle Detection in Navigation of Visually Impaired, International Organization of Scientific Research Journal of Engineering (IOSRJEN), Vol.3, (Issue No.1), pp. 01–06.

Smart Computing – Khan et al (Eds)
© 2021 Taylor & Francis Group, London, ISBN 978-0-367-76552-1

Autonomous car and driver drowsiness detection using a face and eye detection technique

Priyanka Singh Saini, Kirti Mandal, Sonia Sharma, Khushbu Bansal, Pallavie Tyagi & Sanjay Kumar Singh
ABES Engineering College, Ghaziabad, Uttar Pradesh, India

ABSTRACT: The motive of this paper is to build an obstacle-avoidance car that starts moving with the detection of the human eye (driver here) and immediately stops when the driver's eyes are closed for more than the normal human blinking time. This scenario is all about drowsiness and the drunken driver. It can reduce the number of accidents that occur due to the drowsiness of drivers. The system consists of a car with ultrasonic sensors, a microprocessor, and a microcontroller. Depending on the sensors, the microprocessor directs the controller to move the car in the desired direction. Face and eye detection are done on a separate system and are connected to the vehicle wirelessly. Generally, we have combined both the microprocessor and the microcontroller to ease the working of the microcontroller.

Keywords: Raspberry Pi 3, Arduino UNO, Face, and eye detection, obstacle-avoidance car, drowsiness detection.

1 INTRODUCTION

The number of deadly road accidents has increased over recent years. The main reasons for these accidents are driver drowsiness and alcohol consumption. According to a global report generated by the WHO (WHO 2009), there is a record of about 180 countries which reflect that the total number of road accident-based death cases are around 1.2 million per year, with India having a record of about .134 million in damages to personal health every year and a vast number of them being due to drunk driving cases.

A way to decrease these accidents is to use the advanced techniques for driver assistance. This project mainly focuses on the system that can control the car to start and stop with the eye detection technique. When this set-up identifies the face and eyes of the driver, the car starts and moves autonomously by avoiding the obstacles in its path; when the driver's eyes are closed, as in the state of drowsiness, the car stops moving.

1.1 *Face detection*

Face detection is a computer-oriented technology that is implemented in a variety of applications that recognize human faces in digital images. Face detection is one of the types of visual tasks that is easy for a human, but in computer vision this task is quite difficult. Below is the block diagram of the face detection technique. First, data is collected. Then, in image pre-processing, the data gets ready for the next module. Under the normalization of image and illumination, the adaptation processes are done. Feature extraction processes collect useful information which is used for facial recognition. Finally, classification is done to classify the face and non-face images that are based on the features that are extracted.

DOI 10.1201/9781003167488-73

Algorithms of face detection mainly focuses on the recognition of human faces. It is the same as an image detection technique in which the human image is matched bit-by-bit, and the images are stored in the database. First, the regions of eyes are detected by testing all regions in a grey-level image. Then the preferred algorithm is used to generate all face areas that are possible which includes the iris, eyebrows, and mouth corners (Rizv 2011).

1.2 *Methods of face detection*

Face detection is sectioned into these following steps.

1. **Pre-processing.** It reduces the variances of the faces, and before feeding it into the network the images are processed. All the positive features are obtained in this process by snipping the images with front faces to include the only front view. Then all the snipped images are corrected using standard algorithms.
2. **Classification.** In this process, a neural network is applied to classify the images as non-faces or faces by training on these positive image samples. Here, we use Haar Cascade Classifiers.
3. **Localization.** The prepared neural networks are then applied to search for the faces in an image and if the presence of a face is determined, then they place them in a bounding box.

   The Haar cascade classifier is a useful detection method for object detection or face detection which was brought forward by Paul Viola and Michael Jones in their published paper, "Rapid Object Detection using a Boosted Cascade of simple Featured" in 2001. It is a procedure of machine learning where the training of a cascade function from negative and positive images has been done (Carullo 2001).

Most importantly, an algorithm requires many positive samples of images which are kinds of faces and negative images that without faces train and prepare the classifier, and then features are taken from it.

1.3 *Haar cascade detection in openCV*

A Haar Cascade Classifier can be used to detect the object for which it has been trained from the source. It is trained by superimposing a positive image over a set of negative images. Better results are obtained either by using high-quality images or by live video-streaming and increasing the several stages for which the classifier is trained.

In figure 1, face and eyes are detected in the form of square boxes as shown.

The first step is to collect the Haar features from the live stream or image. The Haar features consider adjacent regions which are rectangular at a particular place in a detection window (Ghaleb 2018).

- A total sum of the weak classifier is the final classifier. Their final step has around 6500 features.
- Instead of applying 6500 features on a window, they are merged into phases of classifiers and then applied individually.
- In the first stage, if the window will fail then we can't move to the remaining features on it. However, if it passes, then the feature of the second stage is applied and the process is continued. Finally, the window which passes all the stages is a face.
- Many pre-trained classifiers already consist of openCV for eyes, face, smiles, etc. Those classifiers are in the form of files of XML that are stored in the same folder where openCV/data/haar cascades are present (Padilla 2012).

1.4 *Existing system*

In the simple robot, the algorithm is used where the person was controlling the car using the remote. Here, the algorithm works as an autonomous car where the sensor is present which can see the

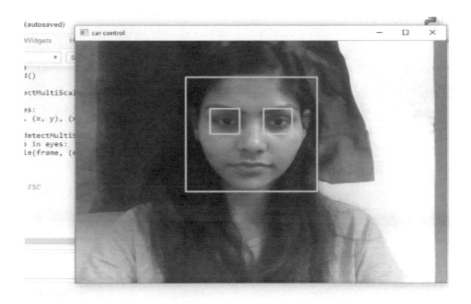

Figure 1.   The human face and eye detection.

obstacle and drive the car continuously under the surveillance of eye detection technology where when the person inside the car feels drowsy, then the car will stop moving forward.

The eye and face detection has been done separately and here they are combined with the obstacle the car avoided, so basically the car is started and stopped by the system that detects the face and eye of a person.

1.5   *Obstacle-avoidance car*

Various sensors are used to detect obstacles like Infrared Sensor (IR), cameras, and ultrasonic sensor. Here, three ultrasonic sensors are used in a car: the left one detects the obstacle in front of it similarly to the middle one and the right one. The car can move in forward and in the left-right direction according to the detection of an obstacle (Kumar 2018).

The ultrasonic sensor emits a high- and low-frequency signal. If they detect any obstacle or object, then they reflect an echo signal which is taken as input through the Echo pin in the sensor (Ebrahim 2016).

First, the trigger and Echo pin is initialized as low. When the object is detected, the echo pin will give a high input to the microprocessor. Then the function is called to calculate the distance between the robot and sensor. Every time, the function waits for a pin to go high and starts the timing, and then when the pin goes low, the timing is stopped. It returns pulse length in microseconds. The timing received implies the distance or length of the pulse. If the distance is less than the set distance then the robot moves right or left according to it (Louis 2016).

1.6   *Software components*

1. Windows: For face and eyes detection
2. Arduino IDE: For programming of an Arduino
3. Rasbian: For the Raspberry Pi 3 operating system
4. Python IDE: For python programming

Figure 2.   Obstacle-avoidance car.

HARDWARE COMPONENTS

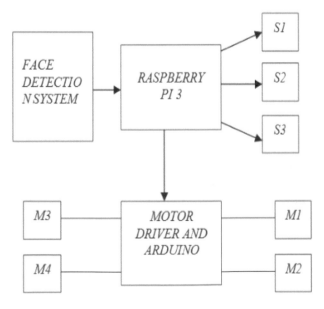

Figure 3.   Set-up module of hardware components.

FLOW OF PROPOSED SYSTEM

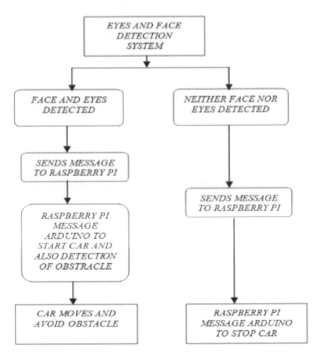

Figure 4.   Flowchart of proposed system.

1.7   *Hardware components*

1. **Raspberry Pi 3.** Raspberry Pi 3 is a microprocessor also known as a mini CPU that can be used in various applications. It is the upgraded version of Raspberry Pi computers, which comes in the credit-card-sized electronic board. As we know, it is effective with python so we used this model for face detection and understanding the programming. In project 3, ultrasonic sensors, namely S1, S2, and S3, are connected with rpi3 (Components 2017).
2. **Arduino UNO.** It is a microcontroller which is based on the ATmega328. There are 14 digital input/output pins in which 6 pins can be utilized as pulse width modulation (PWM) output, a ceramic resonator of 16 MHz, an ICSP header, 6 pins of analog inputs, a USB port, a reset button, and a power jack 7V to 12V. It is connected to four DC motors (Maksimović 2014).
3. **HC SR04.** It is a four-pin module for measuring distance and sense of the object. The module has two eyes like a structure in the front which forms the transmitter and receiver of an Ultrasonic Sensor. The sensor works with the simple formula:

$$\text{Distance} = \text{Speed} \times \text{Time}$$

In our project, we have used three HC SR04 sensors for the left, right, and front direction (Zhmud et al. 2018).
4. **Motor driver L293D.** It allows the DC motor to drive in either direction. By following incoming signals from the microcontroller, the motor driver determines the motion as well as the rest of the motor. Three sensors are used to sense the obstacle on the path for the left and right side and front. As soon as the obstacle is detected on the path, the IR sensor will detect it and react according to that (WHO 2009).

2 FUTURE SCOPE

- In the future, we can use the alcoholic sensor for a drunk driver.We can also execute a drowsiness detection system in aircraft to alert a pilot which can prevent him from drowsiness conditions.
- The device can be used for recognizing the face of a person (by name) under observation.

3 CONCLUSION

The idea of this project has driven by the fact that a drunk driver is unable to control his/her vehicle while unconscious. Moreover, by the time he/she realizes the accident this technology could have helped them. Due to this reason, many researchers try to make out a solution to resolve this issue. In this research, we will engender a model to prevent accidents to happen. The role purpose of working on this idea is to advance a system to detect fatigue symptoms in the driver and then control the speed of the vehicle. Under the monitoring case, the system can decide whether the eyes of the driver are opened or closed. If the eyes stay closed for more than 2 sec, a warning signal will be generated, and the vehicle stops moving. Our motive to building the system is that it can help the driver while driving even if the he feels drowsy.

REFERENCES

Alessio Carullo. 2001, An Ultrasonic sensor for distance measurement in an automotive application. *IEEE Sensors Journal*, VOL. 1, NO. 2: 5

Ebrahim Ayad Ahmed. *2016*, Ultrasonic sensor for distance measurement. *Process Tomography & Instrumentation System*, pp. 9–14.

Ghaleb Mugahed. 2018, Design of an Obstacle-avoiding Robot car Based on Arduino Microcontroller. 7–11

Kumar Ashu. 2018, Face Detection Techniques: A Review. *Artificial Intelligence Review*, DOI: 10.1007/s10462-018-9650-2: 3–19

Louis Leo. 2016, *International Journal of Control, Automation, Communication and Systems (IJCACS)*, Vol.1, No.2.

Maksimović Mirjana. 2014, Raspberry pi as the internet of things hardware: Performances and constraints. *Conference: IcETRAN 2014*, Serbia. 2–5.

Padilla.R. 2012, Evaluation of Haar Cascade Classifiers for Face Detection. *International Journal of Computer, Electrical, Automation, Control, and Information Engineering* Vol:6, No:4: 2–5.

Rizvi Qaim Mehdi. 2011, A Review on Face Detection Methods. 2–7.

World Health Organisation (WHO). 2009, Global Status Report on Road Safety.

Zhmud V A et al. 2018, Application of ultrasonic sensor for measuring distances in robotics. *Journal of Physics Conference Series* 1015(3):032189: 3–8.

Smart Computing – Khan et al (Eds)
© *2021 Taylor & Francis Group, London, ISBN 978-0-367-76552-1*

Design of 6T SRAM cell on different technology nodes

Sphurti Shukla, Surbhi Singh, Khushbu Bansal, Pallavie Tyagi & Sanjay Kumar Singh
ABES Engineering College, Ghaziabad, Uttar Pradesh, India

ABSTRACT: Over the last five decades, researchers have been downsizing complementary metal–oxide–semiconductor (CMOS) electronics to accomplish effective execution regarding speed, power blow-out, size, and unwavering quality. Our motive is to make the general electronics that use gadgets such as PCs progressively smaller size, better speed, and mini power utilization. The scaling of CMOS is done to accomplish pace and decrease memory size. Static Random Access Memory (SRAM) is used to store information in convenient gadgets. Presently, 6T (6 transistor) SRAM is more favored than 8T and 9T in light of the fact that 6T SRAM cell gives a very low delay when contrasted with 8T and 9T SRAM and, furthermore, the power dissipation is half of what is dissipated in 8T and 9T SRAM. This paper acquiesces the design and realization of 6T SRAM bit cell in 180 nm, 90 nm, and 45 nm CMOS technology on cadence virtuoso EDA tool. The performance characteristics of 6Transistor Static RAM has been evaluated with reference to power and delay.

Keywords: 6T SRAM, bit cell, power, delay

1   INTRODUCTION

Commonly, Static Random Access Memory (SRAM) is used as a static memory cell which is mostly promoted in different electronic ground work. It is very fast and dissipates less power when compared with other memory cells. It doesn't require refreshing sporadically. Because of this, SRAM is the pre-eminent memory cell used by very large-scale integration (VLSI) researchers and planners. Inevitably, persistent advancement is continuing for better the realization of SRAM cells. By virtue of this, various sorts of SRAM cells are accessible like 6-Transistor SRAM cell, 7-Transistor SRAM cell, 8-Transistor SRAM cell, 9-Transistor SRAM cell, and so on (Sharfkhani 2006). Most regular SRAM cells utilized in automated electronics good is the 6-Transistor SRAM cell. 6-Transistor SRAM can hold 1-bit of data information. The data-bit remains in the memory so far as power is given to cell. The two main design issues in SRAM read and write operation are the power dissipation and propagation delay (Saun 2019).

2   STATIC RANDOM ACCESS MEMORY (SRAM)

SRAM cells are divided into three groups depending on the load type used in the flip-flop inverter. They are classified as 4-Transistor cells, 6-Transistor cell, and Thin-Film Transistor (TFT) cell. Power is of two types—static and dynamic—when we performed the read and write operation. Some power is consumed and this power is known as dynamic power but when SRAM does nothing then the power consumed is known as static power (Saun 2019). Among those three forms is commonly used 6-Transistor SRAM. SRAM cells will hold the information data until the power supply is available to it and when the supply power is off, the information data is not available, i.e., it got lost. It does not require any repeated refreshment operation as in dynamic RAM; here the information data is held by SRAM flip-flop not by the capacitors. The SRAM bit cell is made of a latch circuit

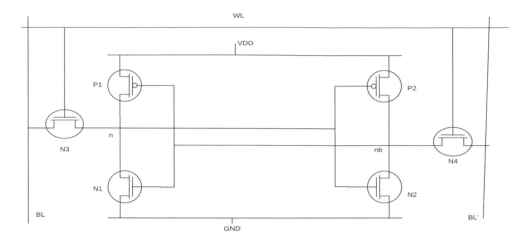

Figure 1.   6T SRAM bit cell.

which generally stores one bit of data. In the circuit, the word line is present to access the data that is done with the aide of bit line.

3   6-T CMOS SRAM CELL

Nowadays, the designing of SRAM-based memory 6T SRAM is very popular. It is designed by connecting two CMOS inverters in back-to-back fashion. The most significant benefit in the described topology is that it has low-static power dissipation which is restricted by little leakage current. This circuit has many dominances like high noise margin and capability to operate at low-power supply voltage (Panda 2017). Figure 1 demonstrates the delineative of six transistor SRAM memory cell. As in 6-T Generic SRAM, the word-line WL is loaded to the power supply. Because N-type metal-oxide-semiconductor (NMOS) is a far more potent driver unlike PMOS, no gap happens when writing a 0 into the cell. The disappearance of the Memory Node Q pull-down NMOS let's us write a 1 into the cell. Writing a 1 is obtained by compaction BL to VDD for bit rows. The bit-line BL is dismissed while writing 0 and then word-line WL is disposed (Majumdar 2011).

To decide W/L proportions of the transistors, various structure criteria must be examined. The two essential necessities which manage W/L proportions are that the stored data in the memory should not change during the read operation and data modification should be permitted during the write process. Therefore, the designing criteria of (W\L) proportions of the must satisfy the above two requirements. There is a swap-off that exists between speed and power. So, if we structure a SRAM cell to such an extent that it conveys minimum power with improvement in speed (Panda 2017). Then it will be very beneficial. The operation of SRAM memory is classified into three categories: standby mode, write mode, and read mode. The strength and speed of the SRAM cell can be expanded by expanding the supply voltage but an increment in supply voltage prompts increment in the power dispersal of circuit as power dissipation varies with square of supply voltage (Saun 2019).

Calculation of delay

SRAM delays are generally described as the time this requires for a SRAM cell to read or write an attributes. When a node routers, the time gap between 10% and 90% of the voltage swing is computed as delay (Maunder 2011).

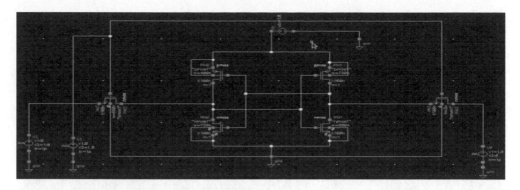

Figure 2.   6T SRAM schematic cell in 180 nm technology.

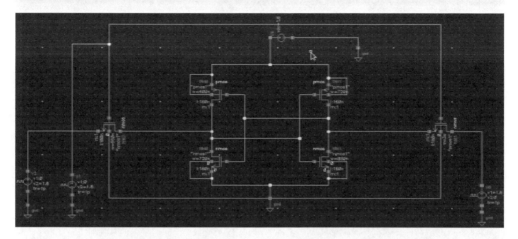

Figure 3.   6T SRAM schematic cell in 90 nm technology.

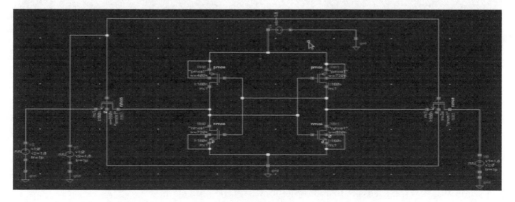

Figure 4.   6T SRAM schematic cell in 45 nm technology.

4   IMPLEMENTATION METHODOLOGY

6T SRAM bit cell is realized in a cadence virtuoso tool on 180 nm, 90 nm, and 45 nm technology
nodes as, shown in Figures 2, 3, and 4, respectively. The circuit is designed using 6 transistors

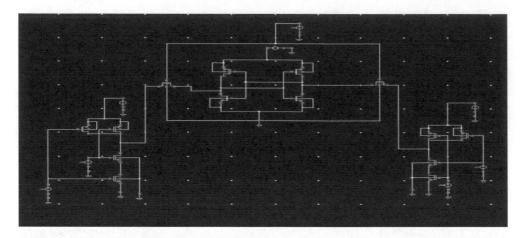

Figure 5. 6T SRAM schematic cell with write driver.

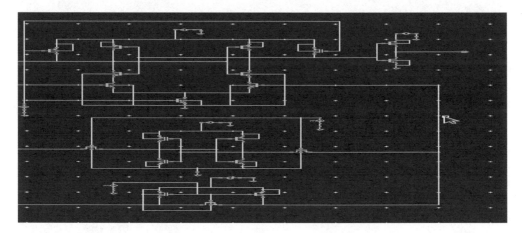

Figure 6. 6T SRAM schematic cell with read driver.

among which N3 and N4 are the access transistors which are used to access the bit line and bit line bar shortly known as BL and BL'. BL and BL' are employed to read the data stored in bit cell and to write the data into the bit cell. BL and BL' act as an input line when we have to write into the memory, and these will act as output line when we have to read from the memory.

In a schematic, WL depicts word line and it is used to ON the access transistors N3 and N4 for read and write operations (Sharfkhani 2006). When WL is 1 read and write operation is performed and when WL is 0 the access is lost and memory is in the hold state.

Generally, for write operation the dimensions of a pull-up transistor is not more than the access transistor because if we keep the size of a pull-up transistor greater than the access transistor then there is a possibility that the node will not completely discharge and it will be pulled up by the up-transistor. For the read operation to perform successfully the sizes of the pull-down transistor, access transistor, and pull-up transistor are in the ratio 3:2:1. Figure 5 shows the SRAM with write driver circuit. The driver circuit is very important as it helps in the smooth operation of SRAM. Figure 6 shows the SRAM with read driver circuit.

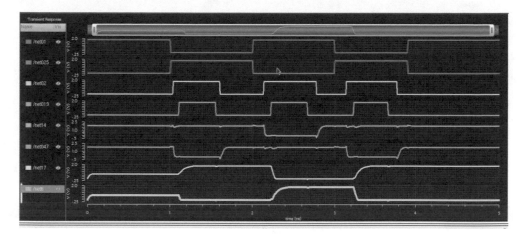

Figure 7.   Simulation cycle of the write operation.

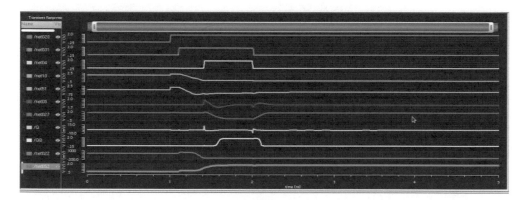

Figure 8.   Simulation cycle of read operation.

5   SIMULATION RESULT

After simulation on cadence virtuoso, with different technology nodes, i.e., 180 nm, 90 nm, and 45 nm write cycle and read cycle of SRAM is shown in Figures 7 and 8, respectively. Delay and power is calculated for both read and write operations.

6   RESULT ANALYSIS

In this paper, we calculated power and delay for SRAM read and write cycles on different technology nodes, i.e., 180 nm, 90 nm, and 45 nm on the cadence design suite. From the results we can say that when we move down in technology node both power and delay are shrinking voltage-critical and W/L of transistor are two important parameters on which delay depends, whereas power dissipation depends on the supply voltage (Sah 2015). Tables 1–4 display the power and delay reductions with the scaling of technology.

Table 1. Power analysis of write operation for 6T SRAM cell.

S.No	Technology	Power*
1.	180 nm	207.29
2.	90 nm	37.98
3.	45 nm	30.46

*Power in microwatts

Table 2. Power analysis of read operation for 6T SRAM cell.

S.No	Technology	Power*
1.	180 nm	197.4
2.	90 nm	62.5
3.	45 nm	42.8

*Power in microwatts

Table 3. Delay analysis of write operation for 6T SRAM cell.

S.No	Technology	Delay*
1.	180 nm	2.75
2.	90 nm	1.70
3.	45 nm	0.56

*Delay in nanoseconds

Table 4. Delay analysis of read operation for 6T SRAM cell.

S.No	Technology	Delay*
1.	180 nm	2.15
2.	90 nm	1.3
3.	45 nm	0.35

*Delay in nanoseconds

7   CONCLUSION

In this paper, simulation is over using a cadence virtuoso design suite on discrete technology nodes 180 nm, 90 nm, and 45 nm. The design depicts that with the shrinking of technology power dissipation drops down and delays also. In the future, we will work on some power gating techniques in SRAM cell read and write operations using the+ cadence virtuoso design suite on discrete technology node 180 nm, 90 nm, and 45 nm

ACKNOWLEDGMENT

We would like to thank ABES Engineering College for imparting the cadence virtuoso design suite to perform our work successfully

REFERENCES

Majumdar Budhaditya and Basu Sumana, 2011, Low Power Single Bitline 6T SRAM Cell with High read stability, international *conference on recent trends in information system.*

Randall Geiger, Philip E. Allen and Noel Strider, 2010, VLSI *Design Techniques for Analog and Digital Circuits,* McGraw-Hill.

Kathuria J., Khan M.A., Abraham A., Darwish A. (2014) Low Power Techniques for Embedded FPGA Processors. In: Khan M., Saeed S., Darwish A., Abraham A. (eds) *Embedded and Real Time System Development: A Software Engineering Perspective. Studies in Computational Intelligence*, vol 520. Springer, Berlin, Heidelberg. https://doi.org/10.1007/978-3-642-40888-5_11

Sharfkhani Mohammed, 2006, Design and Analysis of Low Power SRAM *thesis report, Waterloo University Canada.*

Neil H.E. Weste, David Money Haris, 2010, CMOS *VLSI Design* Pearson Education Jacob Baker R. 2019, *CMOS: Circuit Design, Layout and simulation*, Wiley-IEEE Press.

Allen Phillip E., Holberg Douglas R. 2007, CMOS Analog Circuit Design, Textbook, *Oxford University Press*, Second Edition.

Sah Kumar Rohit, Hussein Inamul, Kumar Manish, 2015, Performance Analysis of a 6T SRAM Cell in 180nm CMOS Technology, *IOSR Journal of VLSI and Signal Processing (IOSR-JVSP) Volume 5, Issue 2, Ver. I: 20–22.*

Saun Shikha and Kuma Hemant, 2019, Design and performance analysis of 6T SRAM cell on different CMOS technologies with stability characterization, *IOP Conference Series: Materials Science and Engineering,* doi:10.1088/1757-899X/561/1/012093.

G. Shivaprakash and D. S. Suresh,2016, Design of low Power 6T-SRAM Cell and Analysis for High Speed Application, *Indian Journal of Science and Technology,* vol 9(46).

Panda Kumar Siba, 2017, Analysis of 6T SRAM Cell in Different Technologies, *2nd National Conference on mechatronics Computing and signal Processing (MCSP-2017).*

Etienne Sicard and Sonia Delmas Bendhia, 2007, Advanced CMOS Cell Design, *INSA Electronic Engineering School of Toulouse, France* McGraw-Hill.

Smart Computing – Khan et al (Eds)
© *2021 Taylor & Francis Group, London, ISBN 978-0-367-76552-1*

Interactive pH measurement system

Himani, Navneet Sharma, Manidipa Roy & Sanjay Kumar Singh
Department of Electronics and Communication, ABES Engineering College, Ghaziabad, India

ABSTRACT: pH meters are essential lab and industry equipment that are extensively used for measurement of pH values of the unknown solutions. pH meters currently available use cumbersome diagnostic techniques that require lots of measurement precautions, calibrations and standardization. The novel interactive pH meter is developed to overcome the existing problem. Interactive pH meter provides the efficient way to measure the readings and the microcontroller ensures that the calculations are done on standard measurements, eliminating the use of temperature compensation. A touch-screen display has been used for providing an interactive graphical user interface (GUI) to the user. This paper provides designing of an interactive, portable, and cost-effective pH meter that is capable of measuring pH values without temperature compensation and storing pH values measured. The acquired pH values are then transferred to a computational system, connected to the network through internet gateway for Internet of Things (IoT).

1 INTRODUCTION

pH meter is invariably used to quantify a pH value (e.g., negative log of hydrogen ion concentration) of a test sample. The value ranges from approximately 0 for strong acids to 14 for strong bases. Pure water has a pH of about 7 (neutral). As shown in Figure 1, the determination of pH is of great importance and utilized on a routine basis in many industrial processes such as water treatment process, determination of concentration of an analyze (e.g., DNA, RNA, protein, toxin, metal, etc.), soil fertility measurement, quality of various water (e.g., municipal water, swimming pool, etc.), medical diagnosis (e.g., blood/urine chemistry), and many more. pH value depends on the temperature of the ambient environment and/or test sample. Hence, in the conventional pH measurements the pH meters also need a temperature compensation factor, which is directly proportional to the temperature. To provide the temperature compensation factor, a temperature sensor (e.g., thermometer) is also provided with the pH meter (Karastogianni et al. 2016). The temperature values of the thermometer are manually fed to the equipment to generate accurate readings. pH meter is an electronic device and comprises a special measuring probe (e.g., ion-selective field-effect transistor or a glass electrode) that is connected to an electronic meter which in-turn displays the pH readings in decimal. The pH meter must be calibrated before it is used against buffer solutions of known hydrogen ion activity. For the calibration of pH meters, the user manual is required to run a calibration protocol. This manual calibration results in the great cause of inconvenience to a user as a large number of instructions are required to effectively take on the measurements of unknown pH value. Most of the pH meters present today need user manuals to operate on them, this results in a gross ineffective way to work on, where a large number of instructions are required to effectively take on the measurements of unknown pH value (Rose et al. 2018).

This paper proposes an interactive pH meter which provides the efficient way to measure the readings and the microcontroller ensures that the calculations are done on standard measurements, so that temperature compensation is not required. The feature such as interactive touchscreen increases the ease of measurement. Also, the measured values if stored could produce graphical

DOI 10.1201/9781003167488-75

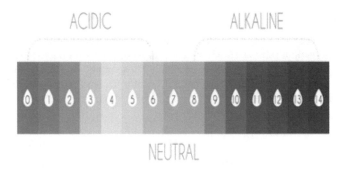

Figure 1. pH scale.

results for analysis and maintenance of record. Portability of the system has enhanced the usage of the equipment. The designed system is operated on mobile app using IoT, thereby increasing the reach out for the acquired data (Fatani et al. 2018; Kingsta et al. 2019). Since IoT devices are embedded with Internet connectivity, sensors, and other hardware, it allows the systems communication and control via the Web.

The objective is to create a prototype of interactive pH meter using IoT which interacts and guides the user to take readings effectively and distribute on the network and the computing device can be selected from a laptop computer, cellular telephone, home computer, smartphone, tablet, or a personal digital assistant (PDA). It does not require temperature compensation as the present standard pH values and corresponding voltages generate calculative multiplicand for the microcontroller to measure unknown pH. The equipment proposed and developed is cost effective and portable to enhance its capability of being installed in remote locations. The design uses Data Logger to store the measured data corresponding to date and time of measurement (Rehman & Halai 2011). The designed system is operated on a mobile app using IoT, thereby increasing the reach-out for the acquired data.

2 CONCEPTS AND THEORIES

Keeping in mind the novelty of this unmatched design, certain features of the new development are hereby discussed.

2.1 Internet of Things (IoT)

The Internet of Things (IoT) is often rendered as a connecting mechanism which uses devices such as smartphones, sensors, actuators, and Internet TVs to connect to the Web where these devices are smartly connected simultaneously. This will allow a new category of communication among devices, people, and between the devices itself to attach the Arduino to the Web, a Wi-Fi chip ESP8266 is employed. ESP8266 contain a TCP/IP stack and a Tensilica L106 (32-bit microcontroller) that features a 16-bit RSIC and extra-low power consumption. The clock speed of CPU is 80 MHz. The maximum speed that can be achieved is of 160 MHz (Fatani et al. 2018).

2.2 Human Machine Interface (HMI)

The system is operated by Nextion NX4024T032 3.2-Inch HMI Intelligent Smart USART UART Serial Touch TFT LCD Screen Module, Human Machine Interface (HMI) is an easy and effective method to operate the system without the use of any user guide and the results are displayed on the screen. The instructions are designed so as to instruct the user step-by-step for the operation of the system. The HMI is designed to automatically be interfaced with Aurdino Microcontroller.

2.3 Arduino Uno

Arduino Uno is a microcontroller, based on the ATmega328P microcontroller. It has 6 analog inputs, 14 digital input and output pins, a 16 MHz quartz crystal, a USB connector to communicate to computing device, power jack to provide power, an ICSP header, and a reset switch. The calculations regarding pH on the basis of incoming voltages from the pH sensor is executed in the Arduino microcontroller and the corresponding pH value is displayed on the HMI.

2.4 Data logger

A data logger also called a data recorder is an electronic device that records data over time. This data could be accessed through USB. Previous data can be stored along with date and time. The data could be retrieved by RJ 45 and graphical analysis of pH values w.r.t time can be done (Hammond et al. 2005).

2.5 Software design

For the development of the digital pH meter, the programming of the microcontroller is in C language with the use of g-μ Vision IDE-Kiel. The development software and hardware allows to easily program the chip. Programming module is needed for calculating the pH value in addition to having communication with HMI for interactive control of the device and display. The code has been written in Arduino programming language and transferred to the controller with the help of programmer.

3 WORKING PRINCIPLE

In the system proposed, the equipment will be interactive, thereby omitting the use of user manuals. An HMI resistive touchscreen is housed in the front panel which interactively instructs the user to work on the equipment. The equipment operates on very low power; therefore, using the system on battery is effectively possible. The advanced microcontroller allows the compensation of temperature, as the corresponding standard pH and voltage values are used to generate equation which is altered by the voltage/pH ratio (Yuan et al. 2017). The data is stored on the data logger with relation to the time. This data can be later extracted by RJ45 Jack provided and graphical output may be generated. The Microcontroller Arduino Uno is connected to pH sensor, as shown in Figure 2.

The pH sensor is a transducer, whose resistive value changes with the pH level, which in turn deviates the voltage provided by microcontroller. This deviation of voltage is measured by microcontroller. The greater the deviation, the greater is the pH value. The power supply of 12 V DC is provided to the microcontroller. An interactive HMI is connected to the microcontroller as an I/O device for functioning and the readings. The system is also connected to a Real-Time Clock (RTC). The RTC value is used for data logger and also the real time is displayed on the LCD screen of HMI (Figure 3). A buzzer is used for sound notification.

The USB output is connected to the device to carry data to a computational device, which in turn is connected to the IP gateway for the connectivity to the network, the data is been shared with any logged on an IoT device and can be fetched and used on any compatible device on the Internet (Abhyankar et al. 2019). The device is also equipped with a battery bank, so that it may be used as a portable unit.

An equation of straight line (1) is used for the formulation of exact pH value:

$$(y - y_1) = \frac{(y_2 - y_1)}{(x_2 - x_1)}(x - x_1) \tag{1}$$

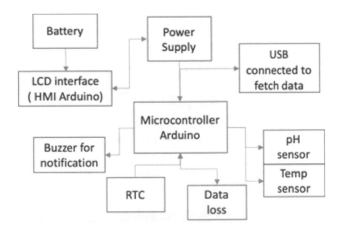

Figure 2.   Block diagram of the set-up.

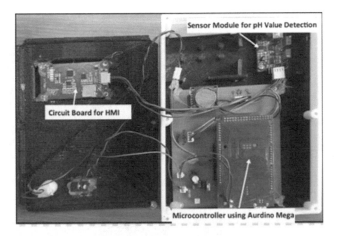

Figure 3.   Layout of components.

As the temperature changes the slope of the line, every time the temperature changes, the two calibration voltage changes which changes the slope of the line. Thus, giving exact reading for pH.

4   METHODOLOGY

As there is no calibration which is required on the basis of temperature, the pH is measured in seven simple steps.

Step 1. Unit is termed ON. The welcome screen shows the logo and prompts the user to GET STARTED (Figure 4).

Step 2. The system prompts the user to set the pH solution at 4 pH and records the corresponding voltage value (Figure 5).

Step 3. Rinse the measurement probe with distilled water.

Step 4. The system prompts the user to set the pH solution of 7 pH and records the corresponding voltage value (Figure 5).

Step 5. Rinse the measurement probe with distilled water. The system formulates the straight-line equation with the two voltage values acquired in Step 2 and Step 4.

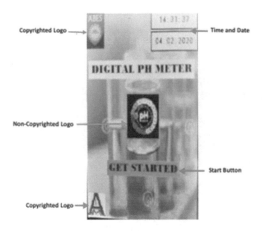

Figure 4.   Welcome screen.

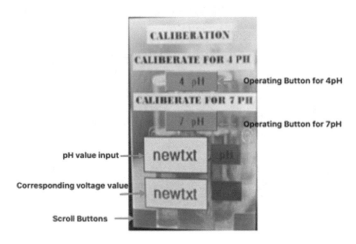

Figure 5.   System prompts for pH 4 and pH 7 solution.

Table 1.   Readings of pH.

S.No.	pH value to be measured	pH value measured	% error in pH value	Temperature °C mV	Voltage
1.	2	2.01	0.5	20	4
2.	12	12.02	0.16	20	1
3.	10	10.04	0.4	20	1.5

Step 6. Insert the probe in an unknown pH solution.

Step 7. pH value is formulated by the microcontroller on the basis of a straight line and is displayed on the screen (Figure 6).

Table 1 shows the readings in pH and mill volt of different solutions at 200°C temperature. The readings show that the percentage error is very small and the system is working properly.

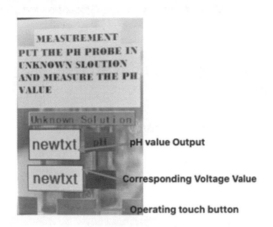

Figure 6. Formulated output of pH.

5 RESULTS AND CONCLUSION

The output of the novel temperature-compensated pH meter was tested using standard measurements of, e.g., citric acid/sodium hydroxide/hydrogen chloride solution having pH 4.00, boric acid/potassium chloride/sodium hydroxide solution of pH 9.00, citrate/hydrochloric acid solution having pH 2, phosphate/sodium hydroxide buffer solution of pH 12, ammonium chloride/ammonia solution of pH 10–11, etc. at different temperatures of 200°C, 400°C, and 600°C. The pH value has exactly matched the standard value, irrespective of the change in temperature.

REFERENCES

Abhyankar, V.V., Gavade, S. A., & Bhole, K. S., 2019, System Development for Simultaneous Measurement and Control of pH and Moisture of Soil, International Conference on Nascent Technologies in Engineering (ICNTE): 1–5.

Fatani, A., Kanawi, A., Alshami, H., Bensenouci, A., Brahimi, T., & Bensenouci, M., 2018, Dual pH level monitoring and control using IoT application, 15th Learning and Technology Conference (L&T):167–170.

Hammond, P.A., Ali, D., & Cumming, D. R. S., 2005, A system-on-chip digital pH meter for use in a wireless diagnostic capsule, IEEE Transactions on Biomedical Engineering, 52(4): 687–694.

Karastogianni, S., Girousi, S., Sotiropoulos, S., 2016, pH: Principles and Measurement, Encyclopedia of Food and Health:333–338.

Kathuria, J., Khan, M.A., Abraham, A., Darwish, A. (2014), Low Power Techniques for Embedded FPGA Processors. In: Khan M., Saeed S., Darwish A., Abraham A. (eds) Embedded and Real Time System Development: A Software Engineering Perspective. Studies in Computational Intelligence, vol 520. Springer, Berlin, Heidelberg. https://doi.org/10.1007/978-3-642-40888-5_11

Kingsta, R.M., Saumi, A. S. & Saranya, P., 2019, Design and Construction of Arduino Based pH Control System for Household Waste Water Reuse, 3rd International Conference on Trends in Electronics and Informatics (ICOEI):1037–1041.

Rehman, R., & Halai, M., 2011, Conceptual model of digital pH meter in telemedicine, IEEE 14th International Multitopic Conference: 87–89.

Rose, L., G. R. S. D, & Mary, X. A., 2018, TDS Measurement Using Machine Learning Algorithm, International Conference on Circuits and Systems in Digital Enterprise Technology (ICCSDET):1–4.

Yuan, S., Wang, H., & Islam, S. K., 2017, A monolithic low-power highly linear pH measurement circuit with wide input detection range and easy calibration, IEEE International Symposium on Medical Measurements and Applications (MeMeA):344–348.

Smart Computing – Khan et al (Eds)
© *2021 Taylor & Francis Group, London, ISBN 978-0-367-76552-1*

Differential amplifier analysis on different technology nodes using Cadence Virtuoso

Pallavie Tyagi, Khushbu Bansal & Sanjay Kumar Singh
ABES Engineering College, Ghaziabad, India

Pushkar Praveen
GBPIET, Pauri-Garhwal, India

ABSTRACT: This paper proposes the designing of a differential amplifier using two separate technology nodes. The differential amplifier is the fundamental building block in the designing of analog ICs and it controls many of the performance parameters of an IC such as Gain, the product of Gain and bandwidth, and Common Mode Rejection Ratio (CMRR). In this paper, high gain differential amplifiers have been designed on 180 nm and 90 nm. The simulated results are obtained by using the Cadence Virtuoso and based on these results comparison is made between the two differential amplifiers which are designed on different technology nodes.

Keywords: CMRR, Gain, Gain- Bandwidth product, Power dissipation, Differential amplifier

1   INTRODUCTION

The Electronics industry has undergone phenomenal improvements in the area of VLSI technology, during the past few decades and these big improvements in the industry came in as a consequence of the development of MOS transistors. The integration of either small scale, medium scale, large scale, ultra large scale, or Giga scale (GSI) technology has contributed to several benchmarks in the electronics industry.

Nowadays, low power has emerged as the key aspect in the field of electronics. Apart from area and speed, power dissipation has become a crucial performance consideration while designing the chip in the Nano regime. Due to enhanced sophistication below 100 nm, reducing power consumption is a very challenging task. Leakage current also plays a vital role in the low power VLSI design and it is also a significant part of integrated circuits overall power dissipation. Low power architecture is becoming more difficult as MOS scaling progresses. As we go down, new factors come into the picture and start playing crucial roles in this field, bringing this low power tale a new twist.

2   LITERATURE REVIEW

2.1   *Differential amplifier*

The initial differential amplifier was originally developed for use with vacuum tubes and subsequently introduced with discrete bipolar transistors. However, the emergence of integrated circuits has made the differential amplifier popular in both bipolar and MOS technologies. Differential amplifiers are widely used as an input stage in several forms of analog ICs, say operational

DOI 10.1201/9781003167488-76

amplifiers, voltage comparators, voltage regulators, video amplifiers, control amplifiers and balanced modulators/ demodulators (Rashid et al. 2009).

When two voltage signals are applied at the input stage of the differential amplifier, it senses them and gives their amplified difference at the output. It rejects the signals that are common to the two inputs. The gain of this amplifier is very high. A differential amplifier's performance is measured by the differential gain that occurs in response to a differential voltage between its two input terminals and a common mode gain that occurs in response to a voltage common to both input terminals (Sackinger & Guggenbuhl 2008 and Wang et al. 2012). These circuits provide higher immunity against environmental noise and also less susceptible to interference. It also has less harmonic distortion and a larger voltage swing. Differential circuits require simpler biasing techniques and provide higher linearity (Allen Phillip & Holberg Douglas 2007 and Razavi 2002). Differential amplifiers need large area as compared to their single-ended counterparts. Additionally, various benefits of the differential amplifiers greatly surpass the possible increase in the area (Grasso & Pennisi 2005 and Nakamura 1992).

The differential amplifier consists of two identical transistors and the output voltage of the differential amplifier can be measured in two ways:

1. Single-ended output or unbalanced output.
2. Balanced output or double ended output or differential output

A single-ended signal is calculated against a fixed potential, usually the ground. On the contrary, the differential signal is calculated between two nodes of equal and opposite signal excursions against a set potential. The differential amplifier has two types of input: (i) Dual input (ii) single input. The most widely used differential amplifier is dual input differential output mode, this is also known as Fully differential mode (Sedra Adel & Smith Kenneth 1998).

Using a direct connection between successive stages of differential amplifiers, a multistage amplifier with the desired gain can be produced. These amplifiers eliminate the need for coupling and bypass capacitors and therefore capable of amplifying dc as well as ac input signals (Bangadkar et al. 2015 and Hurst 2004). The differential amplifier has been the prevailing alternative in the current high-performance analog and mixed-signal circuits, providing many essential properties.

To enable high- performance analog signal processing in today's environment, several analog design techniques, and methodologies have been demonstrated.

3 CIRCUIT DIAGRAM

In this paper, we have designed a MOS differential pair amplifier with an active load (Current Mirror) as shown in Figure 1. The external biasing is removed in this circuit and a current mirror is used as an active load to design the differential amplifier. This arrangement's main objective is to convert a completely differential input into a single-ended output.

The transistors M3 and M4 are identical to each other. To boost the gain, the transistor M4 is used. If the gate to source voltage of transistor M1 is increased by a small amount, then-current Id1 is increased by ΔId1 and at the same time current through transistor M2 i.e. Id2 decreases by ΔId2. Current of transistor M3 and M4 also increases by ΔI. This is achieved because of the mitigated drain current of transistor M2 and increased drain current of transistor M3. M3 and M2 are selected in a way that M3 supports M2 in increasing the performance voltage.

4 RESULTS

Simulation results are obtained by using the Cadence Virtuoso tool. Here the differential amplifier circuit with the current mirror as an active load is simulated on 180 nm and 90 nm technology nodes as shown in Figure 2. A comprehensive analysis such as transient analysis, frequency analysis, and dc analysis is performed and a comparison is made on both the technology nodes in terms of gain,

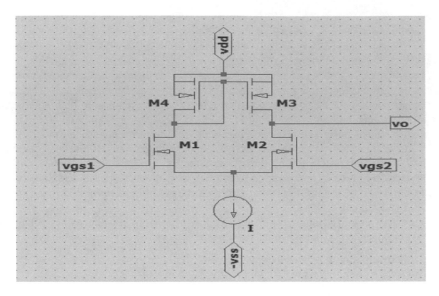

Figure 1. A differential amplifier with an active load.

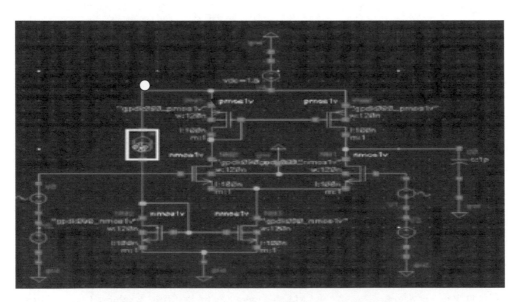

Figure 2. The differential amplifier with an active load (180 nm).

bandwidth, phase margin, and power dissipation. Magnitude and phase plots are shown in Figure 4 and Figure 6. Transient analysis for 180 nm/90 nm technology nodes is shown in Figure 3 and Figure 5. Through phase margin we can determine the closed-loop stability, and for no oscillation to occur phase margin must be greater than 0^0. In our work, on both technology nodes PM is sufficient.

Table 1 summarizes the results obtained from the simulation on both the technology nodes.

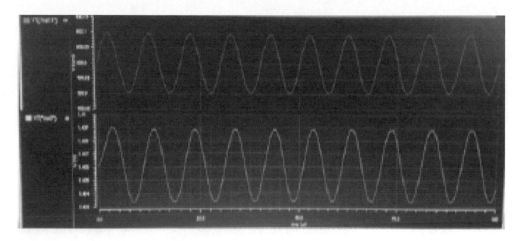

Figure 3.   Transient response (180 nm).

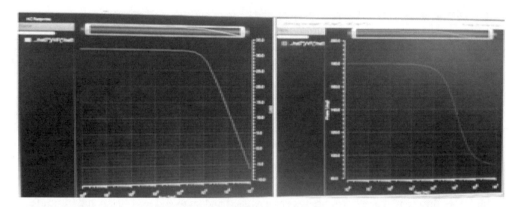

Figure 4.   Magnitude and phase response (180 nm).

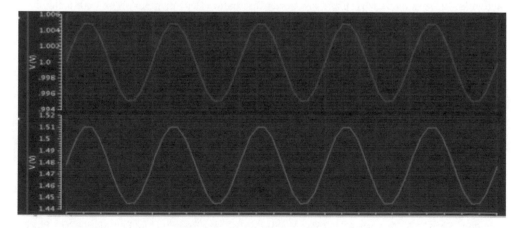

Figure 5.   Transient response (90 nm).

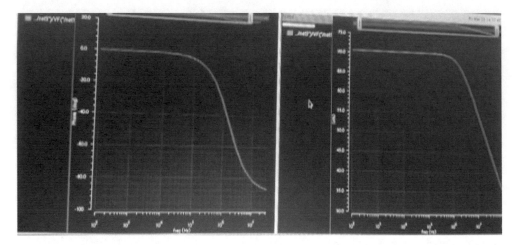

Figure 6. Magnitude and phase response(90 nm).

Table 1. Comparison between 180 nm/90 nm technology.

Sr. No.	Specifications	Expected Values	Obtained Results	Obtained Results
1	Technology Node	180 nm/90 nm	180 nm	90 nm
2	Gain	$\geq$30 dB	$\geq$31.37 dB	$\geq$71.36 dB
3	3-dB Bandwidth	$\geq$5 MHz	$\geq$5.67 MHz	$\geq$18.54 MHz
4	Phase Margin	$>45^0$	45.23^0	88.23^0
5	Power Dissipation	$\leq$3 mW	$\leq$0.188 mW	$\leq$0.245 mW

5 CONCLUSION AND FUTURE SCOPE

In this paper differential amplifier circuits are designed and analyzed on 180 nm and 90 nm technology nodes. Due to increased complexity as we move across the lower technology nodes, power dissipation is minimized but the reliability of the circuit degrades. So balancing power vs performance is a very challenging task. In this work, we obtain high gain (more than 30dB), good bandwidth (greater than 5MHz), and low power dissipation (less than 3mW) on both technology nodes. Although, there is more improvement is required in power dissipation i.e. $\leq$ 1 MW, by using some effective power reduction techniques. Some gain boosting techniques can also be employed in future work.

REFERENCES

Allen Phillip E., Holberg Douglas R. (2007), *CMOS Analog Circuit Design, Textbook*, Oxford University Press, Second Edition.

Bangadkar Bhushan, Lamba Amit, Bhure Vipin (2015), Study of Differential Amplifiers using CMOS, *IJERGS*. Volume 3(2), Part 2: 279–283.

Grasso A.D. and Pennisi S. (2005), High-Performance CMOS Pseudo-Differential Amplifier, *IEEE International Symposium on Circuits and Systems (ISCAS)*: 1569–1572.

Hurst Gray, Lewis & Meyer. (2004), *Analysis and Design of Analog Integrated Circuits*, John Wiley & Sons, Fourth Edition.

Kathuria J., Khan M.A., Abraham A., Darwish A. (2014) Low Power Techniques for Embedded FPGA Processors. In: Khan M., Saeed S., Darwish A., Abraham A. (eds) Embedded and Real Time System Development:

A Software Engineering Perspective. Studies in Computational Intelligence, vol 520. Springer, Berlin, Heidelberg. https://doi.org/10.1007/978-3-642-40888-5_11.

Nakamura Katsufumi and Richard Carley L. (1992), An Enhanced Fully Differential Folded-Cascode OP Amp, *IEEE Journals of Solid-State Circuits*, vol. 27(4):563–568.

Rashid S.M.S., Roy A., Ali S.N., Rashid A.B.M.H. (2009), Design of A 21 GHz UWB differential low noise amplifier using .13 μm CMOS process, *in ISIC*: 538–541.

Razavi Behzad. (2002), *Design of Analog CMOS Integrated Circuits*, Tata McGraw-Hill Edition.

Sackinger E. and Guggenbuhl W (2008), Design of Fully Differential CMOS Amplifier for Clipping Control Circuit, *World Applied Science Journal* 3(1): 110–113.

Sedra Adel S. and Smith Kenneth C. (1998), *Microelectronic Circuits*, 4th edition, Oxford University Press.

Wang L., Yin Y.S., Guan X.Z. (2012), *Design of a gain-boosted telescopic fully differential amplifier with CMFB circuit*, IEEE: 252–255.

Smart Computing – Khan et al (Eds)
© *2021 Taylor & Francis Group, London, ISBN 978-0-367-76552-1*

Social distance monitoring and alarm system

Shilpa Srivastava & Sanjay Kumar Singh
Department of ECE, ABES Engineering College, Ghaziabad, UP, India

Pushkar Praveen
GBPIET, Pauri Gharwal, Uttralkanad, India

Ashish Khare
Pyramid Consulting Pvt. Ltd., Noida, UP, India

ABSTRACT: In the present time of the Covid-19 crisis and in the future also, social distancing is the need of the hour. There are numerous problems regarding the maintaining of social distancing in places of public gathering. People management, tracking, and control by police and security in charges is a herculean task. During public gatherings the authorities find it a tedious task to manage, control, and guide the crowd. In order to avoid any mishappening, a real-time control system is the current need. Such a system is proposed and implemented in this paper. It uses a sensor used to monitor continuous high density of crowd thereby alerting the control station through the Global System for Mobile Communication (GSM). This system consists of two parts: overcrowding detection and an alarming unit. As soon as crowd density starts to increase the chances of maintaining social distance decreases so the sensor detects and alarms the authority via GSM.

1 INTRODUCTION

In the current scenario, crowd management and control systems using wireless communication and radio-frequency identification (RFID) have become the need of the hour. Security and alarm systems are needed which can limit the number of people without physical intervention of the authority. It becomes possible by using Wireless Sensor Networks or other communication protocols to track the movement of public [3]. In this paper, we have tried to present the idea of using GSM. Existing applications use only GSM which is primarily focused on the identification and listing the information. Faced by the real-time identification of medical emergencies, guidance of people and congestion management at checkpoints without any security physically being present on the checkpoint is of concern. Providing a real-time solution along with low cost requires robust tracking system is the most common problem so that the crowd so the authorities can be alarmed beforehand [1]. Many designs have been proposed and implemented in the past with limited success using RFID [2]. The major difficulty is that the crowd movement is at the same time and tracking/identifying the movement and general behavior of public goes hand in hand. The other approach is continuous tracking and monitoring of crowd in real time is the need of the hour. It is needed to setup a real-time system to manage the crowd, and monitoring a large gathering of people can be processed by the data collected by the sensors at specific checkpoints becomes of great signifance for the authorities simultaneously in a large group avoiding any flaunting of norms which can be sensed beforehand by using various sensors integrated together with Arduino and Global System for Mobile Communication (GSM) thereby alarming and avoiding any physical presence of the controlling and managing authority [4]. Due to the high population, crowd management and control is of great significance in India.

DOI 10.1201/9781003167488-77

2 RELATED WORK

The authorities face the problem of locating and guiding people and congestion management at different checkpoints [5]. Various technologies are used for tracking and monitoring the crowd. Some technologies consist of integration of different types of sensors connected via any wireless system. Graphic User Interfaces (GUIs) and Operating Systems (Oss) help detecting the presence of crowds in areas with the help of wireless technologies like Bluetooth, ZigBe,e and Wi-Fi. A significant limitation is in this architecture; this is due to the GUIs. The problem of interference lies within the RFID system such as stationary-to-stationary readers, in crowded places because the RFID system also uses the same frequency bands [6]. This results in a serious problem with regard to spectrum congestion and interference between various networks. Interference problems also lead to misdetection of important tags and reading the same tags multiple times.

3 PROPOSED METHODOLOGY

The proposed block diagram is shown in Figure 1. The proposed system consists of Arduino, GSM module, buzzer and LCD, display, IR sensor, and temperature sensor-integrated together. Figures 2–5 show the various components used. Lastly, it consists of PC server connected with a GSM module.

3.1 *Working*

Overcrowding detection tracking is implemented in the same controller. The infrared (IR) sensor receives the data and sends to the microcontroller. It uses Arduino ATmega 328 which is connected via a GSM to a PC server and then to an alarm system such as a buzzer. A simple diagram helps us to understand the connection of GSM and controlling via a PC.

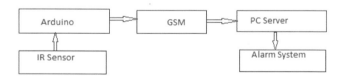

Figure 1. Block diagram of monitoring system.

3.2 *Crowd detection unit*

The proposed system comprises of SD card, loudspeaker, and liquid-crystal display (LCD). Monitoring of the load at regular intervals is done by the IR sensor for avoidance of overcrowd scenario. IR sensor will capture the real-time scenario of the area to be monitored. The overcrowding threshold is set to monitor which will be different for different stampede-like conditions depending upon a number of factors taken into account. The IR sensor will continuously analyze the real-time scenario for a stamped threshold [5]. If the population density in a particular area becomes greater than the threshold set then stampede warning is sent to microcontroller via IR Sensor and simultaneously announcements are done through buzzers from previously saved data. Crowd detection unit comprises of GSM module, IR sensors, and buzzers.

4 MONITORING SYSYTEM

In a monitoring system we will monitor with the help of IR sensor and LCD display. If the all sensors get ON then buzzer will sound and gate will be closed. A prototype of the above for a

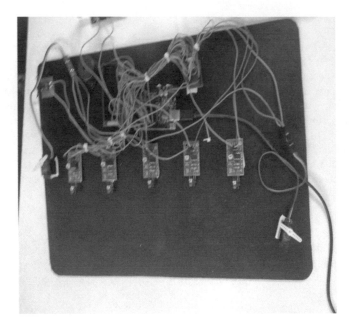

Figure 2.   Layout of project and connection of modules.

Table 1.   Status of monitoring system.

Level	LCD Display	No. of Persons	Alarm
1	Y1	1	No
2	Y2	2	No
3	Y3	3	No
4	Y4	4	No
5	Y5	5	Yes

crowd or gathering of five people at most is shown. For different values of load which corresponds to the number of people, Y1–Y5 are indicated by different levels are indicated by Levels 1–5. The IR sensor will turn ON when its corresponding load is present indicating the number of people entering. As the number of people entering is increases to five which is the maximum limit of persons entering, the buzzer will ring indicating that the maximum limit of persons entering has reached and further entry should be barred thereby closing the entry. This will eventually help in maintain the social distancing between the persons (Table 1, Figures 6–8).

5   CONCLUSION

The main goal of this project is to develop a real-time pre-alerting system to avoid overcrowding in public places where the large gathering of people takes place. The architecture proposed here uses the GSM modem which provide real-time tracking of a crowd via sensors connected with Arduino and in be detected beforehand to any alert for any mishappening and take immediate action in time in case if it arises. In addition to detecting overcrowding, the system is also capable of alarming the control room and closing any further entry of people without requiring their physical presence. This system is low cost and can be easily installed in malls, shopping plazas, stores, offices, banks, and other public places where the probability of public gathering is high. It can further be connected

Figure 3.   Layout of project and connection of module for Level 1.

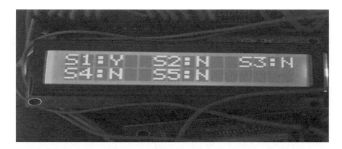

Figure 4.   Level 1, LCD indicating Y1 for Level 1.

Figure 5.   Layout of project and connection of module for Level 4.

to the entry gate which can be closed after the limit to which the number of people entered has crossed without any physical requirement of the security in charge. The load indicating the entry of the number of persons allowed to enter can be changed on requirement. This also will help in maintaining the social distance barrier and avoiding a fight with the security in charge. Future enhancement in the project can be to integrate it with a thermal sensor to detect people with higher

Figure 6.   Level 4, LCD indicating Y1, Y2, Y3, Y4 for Level 4.

Figure 7.   Level 5 LCD indicating Y1, Y2, Y3, Y4, Y5.

Figure 8.   Layout of project and connection of module for Level 5.

body temperature thereby thermal screening can also be implemented and restrict their entry thus avoiding any potential positive Covid-19 from entering.

REFERENCES

Barahim, M.Z.; Univ. of Mauritius Reduit, Reduit; Doomun, M.R.; Joomun, N. Low-Cost Bluetooth., *MobilePositioning for Location-based Application Internet*, 2007. ICI 2007. 3rd IEEE/IFIP International Conference in Central Asia, 2007.

Kathuria J., Khan M.A., Abraham A., Darwish A. (2014) Low Power Techniques for Embedded FPGA Processors. In: Khan M., Saeed S., Darwish A., Abraham A. (eds) *Embedded and Real Time System Development: A Software Engineering Perspective. Studies in Computational Intelligence,* vol 520. Springer, Berlin, Heidelberg. https://doi.org/10.1007/978-3-642-40888-5_11.

Khan, M.A and S. Ojha(2008), "Virtual Route Tracking in ZigBee (IEEE 802.15.4) enabled RFID interrogator mesh network," 2008 *International Symposium on Information Technology,* Kuala Lumpur, 2008, pp. 1–7, doi: 10.1109/ITSIM.2008.4631904.

Mantoro, T., *Hajj Locator: A Hajj pilgrimage tracking framework in crowded ubiquitous environment,* Multimedia Computing and Systems (ICMCS), 2011 International Conference, April 2011.

Mitchell, R.O., Dept. of Computer. Sci. & Eng., Univ. of Yanbu, Yanbu, Saudi Arabia, Rashid, H. Dawood, F.Al Khalidi, A., *Hajj crowd management and navigation system: People tracking and location based services via integrated mobile and RFID systems,* Computer Applications Technology (ICCAT), 2013 International Conference, 2013.

Mohamed Mohandas, Mohamed Haleem, Mohamed Deriche, and Kaviarasu Balakrishnan, *Wireless Sensor Networks for Pilgrims Tracking,* IEEE Embedded Systems Letters, Vol. 4, No. 4, December 2012.

Mohandas M, *Pilgrim tracking and identification using the mobile phone,* Consumer Electronics (ISCE), 2011 IEEE 15th International Symposium, 2011.

Xiaoli Wang; Wong, A.K.-S.; Yongpmg Kong, *Mobility tracking using GPS, Wi-Fi and Cell ID,* Information Networking (ICOIN), 2012.

Smart Computing – Khan et al (Eds)
© 2021 Taylor & Francis Group, London, ISBN 978-0-367-76552-1

Low-power VLSI design of arithmetic and logic circuits using the multiple-threshold CMOS technique

Prachi Kataria, Anuwarti Rai, Aanchal Singh, Ashwin Anand, Raman Kapoor &
Sanjay Kumar Singh
Department of ECE, ABES Engineering College, Ghaziabad, India

ABSTRACT: An exponential increase in the transistor density on a single substrate in an integrated circuit has paved the way for tremendous growth in the semiconductor industry. Very Large-Scale Integration (VLSI) of these transistors on a single substrate boosts performance, but also causes multiple issues related to delay and power consumption. It is important to boost performance but keep the trade-offs related to delay and power to a minimum. This has resulted in researchers moving towards low-power design techniques. Such techniques are different from conventional design techniques in such a way that power is consumed as and when needed. This helps in minimizing the total power consumed by any circuit. The aim of the work presented in this paper is to demonstrate the capability of the multiple-threshold complementary metal oxide semiconductor (MTCMOS) technique to achieve low power consumption with approximately same delay time in a single circuit. Standard arithmetic and logical circuits have been simulated at the 45 nm technology node and critical parameters, namely power and delay have been calculated using the MTCMOS technique and compared with conventional CMOS design. It is shown by studying some elementary yet frequently used circuits that by using transistors of different threshold levels (as in MTCMOS technique) power consumption is significantly reduced.

1 INTRODUCTION

The semiconductor industry has come a long way by following the trend of downscaling as guided by Moore's law. Devices with critical dimensions of the order of few microns faced issues that were primarily related to the area consumed, circuit performance, price, and reliable operation. With increased device density per chip due to aggressive downscaling, the leakage current multiplies which has resulted in significant attention being diverted toward the power consumption of an integrated circuit (Bohr & Young 2017; Subramaniam 2010; Zhao et al. 2010). Modern applications which include wireless and portable devices have severe power constraints because battery capacity inversely affects the size, weight, and compactness of the device. Since classical scaling has caused device dimensions to reach their physical limits, it is important to look for approaches which do not affect performance but also assist in controlling the power consumption levels (Rao et al. 2003; Hamzaoglu & Stan 2002; Ghani et al. 2000). Hence, a detailed comparison of a widely known complementary metal oxide semiconductor (CMOS) design technique with conventional CMOS designs is presented here. The comparison is extended to some of the most widely used circuits in Very Large-Scale Integration (VLSI) design.

In today's technology, low-power and high-speed systems are highly preferable. Circuit designers are constantly required to optimize the power consumed by any circuit (Benini et al. 2001; Hamada et al. 1998; Gupta & Padave 2016). The issue of power consumption gains further prominence in high-density circuits as the cumulative power dissipation rises significantly. Parasitic current components, especially the sub-threshold leakage reduces the value of useful current which is responsible for a circuit's desired performance (Kao et al. 2002). This ultimately reduces the

    DOI 10.1201/9781003167488-78

lifetime of the battery of any portable device. Hence, there is a need to employ different techniques that can reduce power consumption in digital VLSI circuits (Kaur & Noor 2011). The current which flows between the source and the drain when the magnitude of the voltage at the gate terminal is below its threshold voltage (V_{th}) is the undesired sub-threshold leakage current. Physical scaling down of device dimensions requires the reduction of V_{th} and supply voltage (V_{DD}) also. This can subsequently lead to an exponential increase in the power consumed when the device is electrically off, i.e., in the sub-threshold region (Bohr & Young 2017).

There are primarily three sources of power dissipation in a typical CMOS circuit. These are (1) dynamic, (2) static, and (3) short-circuit power dissipation. The dynamic and short circuit power dissipation usually occurs when the load supplied by a CMOS circuit switches its logical state or both the p-channel metal–oxide–semiconductor (PMOS) and n-type metal-oxide-semiconductor (NMOS) transistors are momentarily ON. In either case, at least one type of device is always ON. On the contrary, static power is the power consumed when one or more transistors are in OFF state or due to the defects in the gate dielectric or at its interface with the channel. Also, parasitic currents at the p-n junctions formed at the source and drain ends contribute to static power. It has been shown earlier that due to the scaling effects, dynamic power has shown a reduction with subsequent technology node. However, the static power especially due to leakage currents has risen significantly as we have progressed from one technology to another (LeelaRani & MadhaviLatha 2014). As we have advanced from the 180 nm feature size to 65 nm technology node, the leakage component of static power has risen almost three-fold.

Hence, optimization of power consumed in an integrated circuit is now one of the major concerns (Khursheed et al. 2018; Priyanka 2018; Zhao et al. 2010). Several techniques have been proposed to reduce leakage power. It is also worth noting that in comparison with bipolar technology, CMOS technology (which is the workhorse of the semiconductor industry) exhibit higher levels of static power. Much of this static power is due to the inherent defects in the bulk and at the interface at the gate terminal (Bohr & Young 2017). These undesirable issues associated with static power consumption can be resolved by utilizing multiple-threshold and asynchronous methodologies into the conventional CMOS technology.

1.1 The MTCMOS technique

Several approaches are possible for realizing low power circuits. The multiple-threshold complementary metal oxide semiconductor (MTCMOS) technique has emerged as a viable technique in reducing the power consumed during standby mode (Hemantha et al. 2008; Rao 2012). MTCMOS logic provides low power and high-speed designs with no area overhead. While low-power design strategies at various abstraction levels have been presented before (Priyanka 2018), it is also known that there exists a trade-off between savings, speed, and error as design hierarchy is changed (Gupta & Padave 2016). As described earlier, the reduction in V_{th} and V_{DD} following dimensional scaling can cause a significant rise in the current levels when the gate voltage is below V_{th}. The device-specific parameter, V_{th} is generally considered constant. However, for optimal operation of sub-micron devices, the effect of V_{th} on the device operation can be exploited to control leakage power (Thamarai et al. 2014). This is the basis of the MTMOS method of device design.

Multiple-threshold is a different kind of CMOS design technique that deviates from conventional device design. It is already known that metal oxide semiconductor field effect transistor (MOSFET) has a fourth terminal (the substrate or the body), which is normally not discussed and largely ignored. The substrate which is normally grounded can be used to tune the value of V_{th} for any given device. This is because a voltage applied to the substrate and hence the source will attract or repel majority charge carriers and hence require a lower or higher voltage at the gate to cause strong inversion. This is analogous to the tuning of the V_{th} of a metal oxide semiconductor field effect transistor (MOSFET). In addition to this body bias approach, modifications in the fabrication steps by incorporating separate doping stages for PMOS can also result in an MTCMOS circuit. On the level of circuit design and simulation, the MTCMOS technique can be implemented using a separate set of transistors commonly known as the sleep transistors. Conventionally, a CMOS logic gate

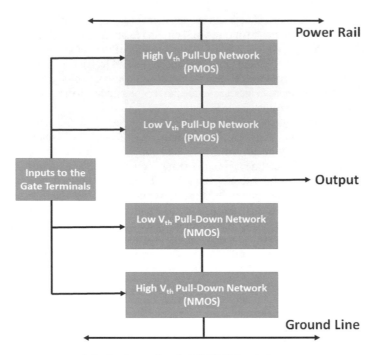

Figure 1. A common approach for implementing the MTCMOS technique.

has two segments: (1) a pull-up network consisting of PMOS transistors which pulls the output towards high logic; and (2) pull-down network consisting of NMOS transistors which pulls the output signal down towards the ground (or low) logic. The pull-up and pull-down network usually consists of transistors with low V_{th} to allow fast switching. A common approach of implementing MTCMOS logic involves sandwiching conventional CMOS logic (as described above) between a set of PMOS and NMOS transistors with relatively high levels of V_{th} (LeelaRani & MadhaviLatha 2014). These high V_{th} transistors are commonly known as sleep transistors and owing to their high levels of V_{th} greatly help in reducing the static power as it requires higher voltages to turn them ON. Figure 1 shows the arrangement described above.

With certain additional sequential circuitry, high-performance and low-power operation can be implemented. The sequential circuit will toggle between active and sleep transistors and have a memory element to retain the state during the standby stage. Hence, a circuit designed using the MTCMOS technique toggles between the active and sleep modes depending upon the transistors selected. This provides lower delays and higher speed (active mode) and lower power consumption and lower speed (sleep mode). In this paper, we explain the implementation of the NAND gate, full adder, and an ALU using MTCMOS technology. These circuits have been chosen as they are widely used in large numbers.

In this paper, we present the application of the MTCMOS technique of VLSI design to some frequently used logic and arithmetic circuits like NAND gate, full adder, and an arithmetic logic unit. The application of the MTCMOS technique is simple yet effectively explains the benefit of power consumption. Since almost every integrated circuit would use these circuits extensively it is worth knowing how much power can be saved by applying the proposed technique. Additionally, the impact of MTCMOS can be easily understood for the learning process as other parasitic parameters have the least impact on such basic components.

This paper has been organized as follows. Section 2 focuses on experimental details. Section 3 presents the schematics and discusses the results of power and delay estimation. Section 4 concludes the paper.

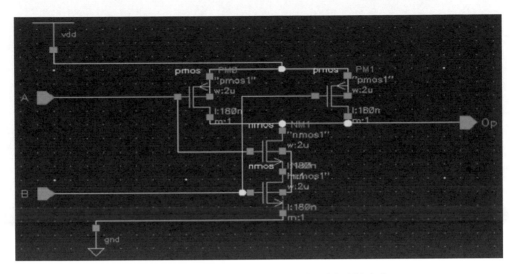

Figure 2. Two-input NAND gate implementation using conventional CMOS design.

2 EXPERIMENTAL

The Cadence Design Suite–Virtuoso has been extensively used to design schematics using conventional CMOS and MTCMOS technique in this work. The designs have been implemented on the 45 nm technology node which makes the results highly relevant in the current scenario. The circuit schematics have been drawn in the Virtuoso schematic editor L and the analog design environment feature has been used to estimate parameters like static power (using DC analysis) and delay (using transient analysis).

3 RESULTS AND DISCUSSION

3.1 *NAND gate design*

A conventional CMOS circuit consists of a pull-up network and a pull-down network. A network of p-channel transistors executes the pull-up operation while a set of n-channel transistors is employed to implement pull-down operation in any CMOS circuit. Here, all p-channel MOSFETs are to be driven by another p-channel device or from the external power source (VDD). Similarly, all n-channel MOSFETs should be driven by another n-channel device or from the ground. The pull-up circuitry consists of a parallel combination of PMOS transistors while the pull-down network has NMOS transistors in series. Consequently, the output is LOW only when the NMOS network provides passage to the ground which happens only when both the inputs exceed V_{th}. Figure 2 shows the schematic of a standard NAND gate obtained using the schematic editor in Cadence Virtuoso.

In the MTCMOS technique, p-channel MOSFETs (the sleep PMOS transistors) are connected in the middle of the power supply voltage (VDD) and the logic circuit. Similarly, n-channel MOSFETs (the sleep NMOS transistors) are inserted between the logic circuit and zero potential (i.e., the ground). These sleep transistors are designed to exhibit high values of V_{th}. Figure 3 shows the schematic of a two-input NAND gate using this technique. During the active mode of operation, MOSFETs with the high value of V_{th} (sleep transistors) are turned ON, while during sleep mode, these devices are turned OFF as they possess a high value of V_{th}. This ensures power reduction during both the operating modes.

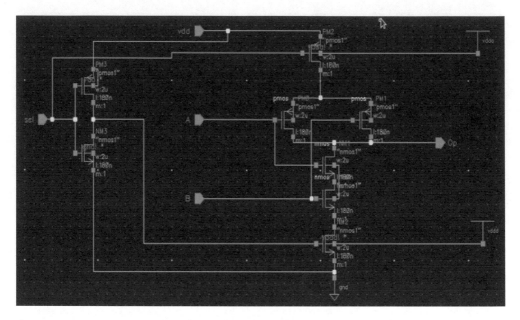

Figure 3.   Two-input NAND gate implementation using MTCMOS technique.

3.2   Full adder design

To implement a circuit that adds two numbers and generates the carry signal, a full adder digital logic circuit is required. Figure 4 shows the schematic of the conventional one-bit full adder circuit. It consists of three inputs and two outputs as highlighted. Adder logic performs addition during the active mode when sleep transistors are ON. During standby mode, the adder circuit is cut off from supply rails due to turn OFF provided by the high V_{th} sleep transistors [5]. If A and B are the signals to be added and C_{in} is the input carry to the full adder circuit, the two outputs SUM and CARRY are represented by the following Boolean function:

$$SUM(S) = (A\ XOR\ B)$$

$$Carry(C) = (A\ AND\ B)\ OR\ (A\ XOR\ (B\ AND\ C_{in}))$$

For implementing a full adder using the MTCMOS technique, an asleep transistor with high V_{th} is used either as a footer (NMOS) or a header (PMOS) to the conventional circuit. The schematic of the proposed MTCMOS full adder circuit with an N-Type sleep transistor connected as footer between ground rail and the logic circuit is shown in Figure 5. A virtual ground (with potential slightly higher than ground) is connected to the logic gate ground rails. The real and virtual grounds are linked to each other via the sleep transistor.

3.3   Design of a 4-bit ALU

Here, we present a 4-bit ALU that is capable of performing the typical arithmetic and logical operations. It consists of logical and arithmetic units like gates like AND, OR, ADDER, SUBTRACTOR, and MUX. The 4-bit ALU presented here can be used as a building block for large size ALUs. The ALU presented here consists of five multiplexers and the design is similar to the circuit of 74S181 by Texas Instruments. Due to its complexity and density, it can consume a large amount of power even in the OFF state. Figures 6 and 7 present the schematic of a 4-bit ALU using conventional and MTCMOS techniques, respectively.

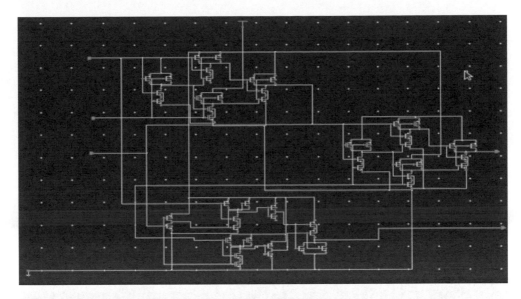

Figure 4.   A full adder implementation by conventional CMOS technique.

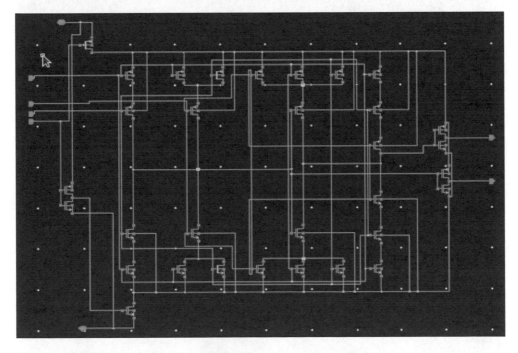

Figure 5.   MTCMOS implementation of a full adder.

The increased complexity and density of the design can be seen from the schematic which also highlights the need and capability of an automated system for electronic design.

Finally, DC and transient analysis were carried out on each of the design presented above. The values of static power and delay obtained for each design are presented below in Table 1. Overall, the general trend of using the MTCMOS technique is that static power reduces, however, due to the extra circuitry required for implementing the MTCMOS technique the propagation delay between

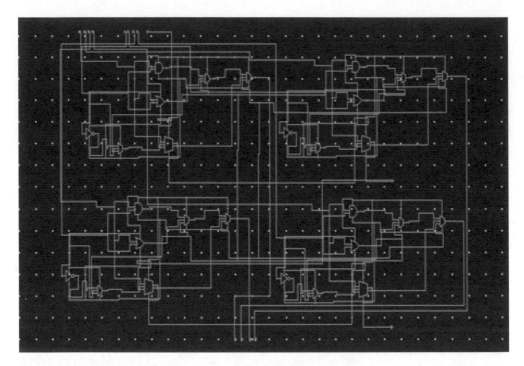

Figure 6. Four-bit ALU schematic obtained using conventional CMOS design.

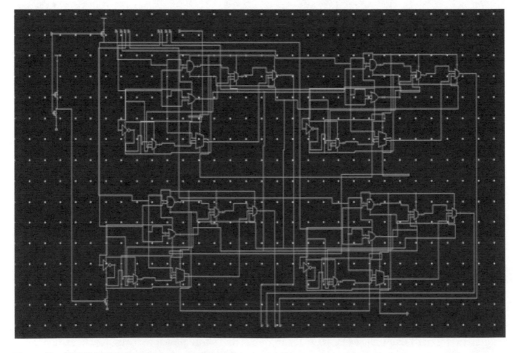

Figure 7. MTCMOS schematic of a 4-bit ALU.

Table 1. Comparison of static power and delay for conventional CMOS and MTCMOS.

Circuit	Technique	Static Power (W)	Delay (sec)
NAND Gate	CMOS	3.76×10^{-12}	2×10^{-10}
	MTCMOS	2.34×10^{-12}	3×10^{-10}
Full-Adder	CMOS	2.36×10^{-12}	2.3×10^{-11}
	MTCMOS	2.88×10^{-12}	3×10^{-11}
4-bit ALU (Addition)	CMOS	2.8×10^{-11}	3.8×10^{-11}
	MTCMOS	2.1×10^{-11}	4.3×10^{-11}
4-bit ALU (Subtraction)	CMOS	2.5×10^{-11}	2.3×10^{-11}
	MTCMOS	1.8×10^{-11}	2.5×10^{-11}
4-bit ALU (OR operation)	CMOS	2.6×10^{-11}	3.1×10^{-11}
	MTCMOS	1.6×10^{-11}	3.3×10^{-11}
4-bit ALU (AND operation)	CMOS	2.3×10^{-11}	3.5×10^{-11}
	MTCMOS	1.7×10^{-11}	4.1×10^{-11}

input and output increases. Hence, there is a trade-off needed between power and delay for the best optimization of circuit performance.

4 CONCLUSION

This paper presents a multi-threshold CMOS logic, an effective standby leakage control technique. MTCMOS technique can significantly reduce the static power consumed by digital by making use of low threshold and high threshold MOS transistors. From the simulation results, we can conclude that MTCMOS can achieve a reduction of static power which can prove beneficial in realizing portable devices that consume relatively low power while in OFF-state. On the contrary, there is an expected delay of signal propagation between input and output. The fact that the results have been presented for the 45 nm technology node enhances the viability of the method.

ACKNOWLEDGMENT

The support provided by the management of ABES Engineering College, Ghaziabad, and AICTE for setting up of Centre of Excellence in VLSI Design is duly acknowledged.

REFERENCES

Benini, L., Micheli, G. D. & Macii, E. (2001) Designing low-power circuits: practical recipes. *IEEE Circuits and Systems Magazine,* 1, 6–25.

Bohr, M. T. & Young, I. A. (2017) CMOS Scaling Trends and Beyond. *IEEE Micro,* 37, 20–29.

Ghani, T., Mistry, K., Packan, P., Thompson, S., Stettler, M., Tyagi, S. & Bohr, M. (2000) Scaling challenges and device design requirements for high performance sub-50 nm gate length planar CMOS transistors. *2000 Symposium on VLSI Technology. Digest of Technical Papers (Cat. No.00CH37104).*

Gupta, S. & Padave, S. (2016) Power Optimization for Low Power VLSI Circuits.

Hamada, M., Takahashi, M., Arakida, H., Chiba, A., Terazawa, T., Ishikawa, T., Kanazawa, M., Igarashi, M., Usami, K. & Kuroda, T. (1998) A top-down low power design technique using clustered voltage scaling with variable supply-voltage scheme. *Proceedings of the IEEE 1998 Custom Integrated Circuits Conference (Cat. No.98CH36143).*

Hamzaoglu, F. & Stan, M. (2002) *Circuit-level techniques to control gate leakage for sub-100 nm CMOS.*

Hemantha, S., Dhawan, A. & Kar, H. (2008) *Multi-threshold CMOS design for low power digital circuits.*

Kao, J., Narendra, S. & Chandrakasan, A. (2002) *Subthreshold leakage modeling and reduction techniques.*

Kaur, K. & Noor, A. (2011) Strategies & methodologies for low power vlsi designs: A review. *International Journal of Advances in Engineering & Technology ©IJAET ISSN,* 1, 2231–1963.

Khursheed, A., Khare, K. & Haque, F. (2018) Designing of ultra-low-power high-speed repeaters for performance optimization of VLSI interconnects at 32 nm. *International Journal of Numerical Modelling: Electronic Networks, Devices and Fields.*

Leelarani, V. & Madhavilatha, M. (2014) Design of MTCMOS Logic Circuits for Low Power Applications. *IJEST,* 6, 438–443.

Priyanka, A. D. A. Y. (2018) Analysis of Optimization Techniques for Low Power VLSI Design. *IJSRSET,* 4, 369–375.

Rao, M. P. K. A. N. S. (2012) A Low Power and High Speed Design for VLSI Logic Circuits Using Multi-Threshold Voltage CMOS Technology *International Journal of Computer Science and Information Technologies,* 3, 4131–33.

Rao, R., Burns, J. L. & Brown, R. B. (2003) *Circuit techniques for gate and sub-threshold leakage minimization in future CMOS technologies.*

Subramaniam, P. (2010) Power management for optimal power design. *Edn -Boston then Denver then Highlands Ranch Co-,* 55, 40–45.

Thamarai, P., Balaguru, K. & Kumaran, E. B. (2014) Optimizing 2:1 MUX for low power design using adiabatic logic. *Middle – East Journal of Scientific Research,* 20, 1322–1326.

Zhao, P., Wang, Z. & Hang, G. (2010) Power optimization for VLSI circuits and systems. *2010 10th IEEE International Conference on Solid-State and Integrated Circuit Technology.*

Smart Computing – Khan et al (Eds)
© *2021 Taylor & Francis Group, London, ISBN 978-0-367-76552-1*

IoT-based advanced weather monitoring system

Pranavi Yadav, Nimish Nigam, Ranjeeta Yadav & Sanjay Kumar Singh
ABES Engineering College, Ghaziabad, India

ABSTRACT: The proposed system is a progressive solution for weather monitoring at a particular place and make the data available over the Internet. The system makes use of the cutting-edge technology Internet of Things (IoT) which aids to connect the embedded system to a network and also to the devices for their operation. The designed system monitors the environmental parameters such as wind speed, temperature, and humidity followed by generating real-time data which can be processed and saved onto a cloud. This data can then be viewed in an application so that necessary and timely actions can be taken. The system makes use of sensors, motor, and other electronic components for the monitoring of weather parameters.

1   INTRODUCTION

Internet of Things (IoT) is one of the many contemporary technologies which has revolutionized the world and is continuing to do so. It has enabled us to monitor and control various electronic appliances remotely with the use of a sensor network having the ability to sense, process, and transmit the data to a cloud. The cloud is a service providing the capability of storage, complex computation, and produce the information in a more convenient form. From the Cloud this information can be made available through various user-friendly interfaces such as web or mobile applications, depending upon their appropriateness and requirements [1]. The Internet is the heart in this transformation playing a vital role in productive, reliable, and prompt communication of data from devices to the cloud and vice versa.

With the changing times and technology, human needs are also changing. This creates a need for developing smart systems which are able to sense the changes in the environment and thus control the connected devices. Sensor devices arc planted at different locations in order to gather the data and when it senses a change in the area of interest [2]. An environment is accoutered with a combination of sensor devices, microcontroller, and a software application capable of notifying and self-monitoring the environment then it is often referred to as a smart environment [3]. In such kinds of environments, the "things" have the ability of sensing changes in temperature, pressure, humidity, carbon levels, noise, etc. The aforesaid system is an example of embedded system which has a hardware part comprising of all the sensors and electronic components and a firmware written for it. This embedded system enables the user to remotely control its appliances through wireless communication [11]. Integration of such intelligent systems in human life has made its life a lot more effortless and interactive.

2   LITERATURE REVIEW

In today's world, many weather and health monitoring systems are designed by engineers making use of various technologies. Meteorological departments of various countries and states are still using age-old technology or does not have an accurate means to monitor weather parameters resulting in

DOI 10.1201/9781003167488-79

situations such as loss of life, crop failure, damage to property, and food shortages in the case of natural disasters. Some of them are mentioned below along with their references:

2.1 Manual weather monitoring system

Many weather stations still work using the age-old analog technology for weather forecasting and observations [3]. They deploy multiple instruments such as thermometers for temperature, barometers for atmospheric pressure, wind vanes, rain gauge for precipitation, etc. to observe changes in weather conditions [14]. The majority of these instruments are based on simple applications of analog technology. Their observations are later manually recorded and stored [12]. The acquired information is then sent to the news reporting stations, channels, and radio for reporting weather conditions.

Limitations:
1. Such weather-monitoring stations consist of obsolete technologies which are not in much use today. It also uses heavy machinery consisting of various moving parts that demand regular maintenance and need to be replaced frequently.
2. Power consumption is another issue that poses a limitation as the instruments are usually located far from main power supply, further adding to its cost.
3. Usage of thermometers for measuring temperature; however accurate is still infrequent and periodically requires manual checking of any change in temperature.
4. Manual transfer of data collected is required to a laptop or PC from the logger through a cable.
5. Use of enormous and heavy instruments demands for a huge space and poses difficulty of installation in far-away places.
6. Instruments which are incredibly expensive which further scales up the sky-high cost of maintenance and installation.
7. Warnings issued are often delayed due to slackened analog system leading to loss of lives and property.

2.2 Weather monitoring using master–slave communication

In the preceding research [1], a microcontroller-based single-master and multi-slave communication is developed. But the microcontroller still communicates through unicast communication, i.e., the master can give commands to only one slave at a time arranged in a star topology in a network. The slave with the corresponding address will respond and function according to the master's commands [11]. Along with the master-slave configuration, the Modbus Protocol is used for data communication between different devices.

Limitations:
1. In the above systems, communications are between a single master and a single slave in a single-master–multi-slave configuration.
2. Masters can give orders to only one slave at a time.
3. Slaves can communicate only with the master and not with other slaves in the network.

3 PROPOSED SYSTEM

The proposed system is a leading solution for weather monitoring that incorporates IoT, making the real-time data easily available on a user-friendly interface which the consumer can access through a thin client like a web browser or a mobile application. Thus, making it a convenient alternative for the user to directly check the figures and weather conditions of its area online beforehand without the need of a weather forecasting agency. The system also an attractive feature of push notifications on the client's mobile in case the weather conditions worsens, which can alert the consumer to take necessary preventive measures in time.

It has further advantages of:

- Inexpensive
- Installation is not so complex
- Requires less maintenance
- Energy efficient, can be operated on solar energy also.

System monitors change in weather conditions such as wind speed, temperature, and humidity, followed by provision of live reporting of the weather stats over a customized web page and/or through a mobile application.

The system deals with monitoring weather and climate changes like:

1. Temperature, humidity by using the DHT 22 sensor
2. Wind speed using a DC motor with a fan. Text and indenting

4   SYSTEM ARCHITECHTURE

The main processing unit in the implemented system consists of a microcontroller ATmega 328 which is basically a mini computer. All the sensors and the modules are to be connected to this microcontroller [5]. This minicomputer can then fetch the data from the sensors for further processing and analysis. The processed data is then updated on the local network via the Wi-Fi microchip ESP 8266 connected to it.

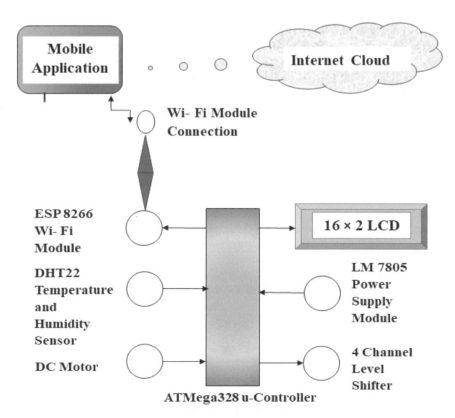

Figure 1.   Block diagram of the proposed system.

635

5 SOFTWARE IMPLEMENTATION

The code written for the hardware design plays a crucial role in its working. This code is referred to as a firmware once it is burnt in the microcontroller. There are two stages in the development of our software: initialization and simulation of hardware. Lastly, transmitting the data to a mobile application for user interface.

5.1 *Firmware of initialization and simulation of hardware*

Arduino IDE: It is an open-source integrated development environment to program the microcontroller. The IDE is platform independent, i.e., can be run on Windows, MAC OS, or Linux [6]. It can be used with any Arduino board. Once the code is written and tested it can be used to retrieve data from the sensors and transmission on to a cloud. The electronic components are integrated with the controller after their individual testing [12]. Now to make the Wi-Fi module work as a client it has to be initialized by sending AT commands in a defined pattern. Finally, DHT 22 a digital temperature and humidity sensor provides real-time readings for both the parameters simultaneously. We use MATLAB analytics service of ThingSpeak to visualize the live data stream on the mobile app, once the sensor data is fetched and processed by the microcontroller and uploaded onto the Cloud [15]. ThingSpeak provides quick visualization of the real-time data transmitted by our embedded system in a presentable form.

5.2 *Mobile application*

Blynk is the most popular application designed for IoT. It can store, visualize, and display sensor data. One can also control hardware devices from remote locations. It is a digital dashboard with easy to use widgets, pin manipulation without the need of writing a code, makes device to device communication possible, and send emails, tweets, and also push notification.

6 COMPARISON

IoT technology is brought into play in many different ways so no single network solution can be completely called wireless or wired. Everything depends on certain factors some of them being location, requirements, range, bandwidth, power consumption, connectivity, and security.

6.1 *Wired technology*

1. As compared to the wireless, wired connections are expensive owing to the cost of installation, labor involved, and cost of the wiring.
2. In order to connect them to the sensors, at times they need to be buried inside the floors, ceilings, and walls, hence their mobility is low.
3. It requires a lot of pre-planning to extend a wired system as it involves hardware that needs to be purchased and configured to make it fully operational and thus are less scalable.

6.2 *Wireless IoT implementation*

1. With advancement in technology and lower cost of manufacturing, implementation of wireless technology such IoT is cost effective.
2. Requires just the configuration and can be up for operation in a very short span of time. It also involves no hardware installation.
3. Unlike most wired networks, wireless IoT implementation are not bulky, inexpensive, and are the common solutions.

7 CONCLUSION

In the course, our objective is to come up with a highly accurate and an inexpensive automated weather monitoring system. The embedded system proposed would be capable of observing the changes in the environmental parameters and periodically update the consumer over an app thus making it smart and interactive. The smart system will also be able to generate short-term push notifications when the figures cross a warning limit. The sensors are to be deployed in the environment which needs to be monitored in order to collect the data for analysis. The information after processing of the collected data can be accessed by the consumer through Wi-Fi.

8 FUTURE POTENTIAL

- A few more sensors can be integrated and connect the system to the satellite making it a global feature.
- To implement the system for a town or a village, a WAN can be brought into use [7].
- There is a great potential of this real-time system in the navigation of aircrafts, military, and defense as well [9].
- To provide better precautionary measures and development of medication, it can be implemented in medical institutes for the research and study of the harmful effects of changing weather conditions on health [12].
- It can be deployed in farms to alert the farmers of high speeds, humidity, and temperature conditions to cover its harvested crops or regulate their irrigation patterns, respectively.

REFERENCES

[1] Amale, Patil. 2019. IOT Based Rainfall Monitoring System Using WSN Enabled Architecture. In IEEE, Conference Paper 2019.

[2] Halder, Sivakumar. 2017. Embedded based remote monitoring station for live streaming of temperature and humidity. In IEEE, Conference Paper, 2017.

[3] Kamelia, Nugraha, Effendi, Priatna. 2019. The IoT-Based Monitoring Systems for Humidity and Soil Acidity Using Wireless Communication. In IEEE 5th International Conference on Wireless and Telematics (ICWT), Yogyakarta, Indonesia, 2019: pp. 1–4.

[4] Kapoor, Barbhuiya. 2019. Cloud Based Weather Station using IoT Devices. In IEEE Region 10 Conference (TENCON), Kochi, India, 2019: pp. 2357–2362.

[5] Khotimah, Krisnandi, Sugiarto. 2011 Design and implementation of Remote Terminal Unit on Mini Monitoring Weather Station Based on Microcontroller. In 6th International Conference on Telecommunication Systems, Services, and Applications (TSSA), Bali, 2011: pp. 186–190.

[6] Kumar, Math, Nagaraj, Dharwadkar. 2018. IoT Based Low-cost Weather Station and Monitoring System for Precision Agriculture in India. In IEEE, Conference Paper, 2018.

[7] Khan M.A. et. al, (2020), Decentralised IoT, Decenetralised IoT: A Blockchain perspective, Springer, Studies in BigData, 2020, DOI: https://doi.org/10.1007/978-3-030-38677-1

[8] Khan, M. A., Quasim, M. T, et al., (2020), A Secure Framework for Authentication and Encryption Using Improved ECC for IoT-Based Medical Sensor Data, in IEEE Access, vol. 8, pp. 52018–52027, 2020. DOI: 10.1109/ACCESS.2020.2980739

[9] Khan M. A.,(2020), An IoT Framework for Heart Disease Prediction Based on MDCNN Classifier, in IEEE Access, vol. 8, pp. 34717–34727, 2020. DOI: 10.1109/ACCESS.2020.2974687

[10] Khan M.A, and Algarni F., (2020) "A Healthcare Monitoring System for the Diagnosis of Heart Disease in the IoMT Cloud Environment Using MSSO-ANFIS," in IEEE Access, vol. 8, pp. 122259–122269, 2020, doi: 10.1109/ACCESS.2020.3006424.

[11] Khan, MA, Abuhasel, KA. (2020).Advanced metameric dimension framework for heterogeneous industrial Internet of things. Computational Intelligence. 2020; 1–21. https://doi.org/10.1111/coin.12378

[12] Khan, M Ayoub, M. Sharma and R. B. Prabhu(2009), "FSM based FM0 and Miller encoder for UHF RFID Tag Emulator," 2009 IEEE International Advance Computing Conference, Patiala, pp. 1317–1322, doi: 10.1109/IADCC.2009.4809207.

[13] Khan, M.A and S. Ojha (2008), "Virtual Route Tracking in ZigBee (IEEE 802.15.4) enabled RFID interrogator mesh network," 2008 International Symposium on Information Technology, Kuala Lumpur, 2008, pp. 1–7, doi: 10.1109/ITSIM.2008.4631904.

[14] Khan, M.A. and V. K. Antiwal(2009), "Location Estimation Technique using Extended 3-D LANDMARC Algorithm for Passive RFID Tag," 2009 IEEE International Advance Computing Conference, Patiala, 2009, pp. 249–253, doi: 10.1109/IADCC.2009.4809016.

[15] Khan, M.A., Sharma, M. and Prabhu, B.R.(2009). A survey of RFID tags. International Journal of Recent Trends in Engineering, 1(4), p.68. Academy publisher, Finland.

[16] Khan M.A. Sharma M, R. B. Prabhu, "FSM based FM0 and Miller encoder for UHF RFID Tag Emulator," 2009 IEEE International Advance Computing Conference, Patiala, 2009, pp. 1317–1322, doi: 10.1109/IADCC.2009.4809207.

[17] Khan M.A., Sharma M.,P. R. Brahmanandha(2008), "FSM based Manchester encoder for UHF RFID tag emulator," 2008 International Conference on Computing, Communication and Networking, St. Thomas, VI, 2008, pp. 1–6, doi: 10.1109/ICCCNET.2008.4787699.

[18] Khan, M. Ayoub and A. Q. Ansari (2011), "Quadrant-based XYZ dimension order routing algorithm for 3-D Asymmetric Torus Routing Chip (ATRC)," 2011 International Conference on Emerging Trends in Networks and Computer Communications (ETNCC), Udaipur, 2011, pp. 121–124, doi: 10.1109/ETNCC.2011.5958499.

[19] Kathuria J., Khan M.A., Abraham A., Darwish A. (2014) Low Power Techniques for Embedded FPGA Processors. In: Khan M., Saeed S., Darwish A., Abraham A. (eds) Embedded and Real Time System Development: A Software Engineering Perspective. Studies in Computational Intelligence, vol 520. Springer, Berlin, Heidelberg. https://doi.org/10.1007/978-3-642-40888-5_11

[20] Lohchab, Kumar, Suryan, Gautam, Das. 2018. A Review of IoT based Smart Farm Monitoring. In Second International Conference on Inventive Communication and Computational Technologies (ICICCT), Coimbatore, 2018: pp. 1620–1625.

[21] Mittal, Mittal, Bhateja, Parmaar, Mittal. 2015. Correlation among environmental parameters using an online Smart Weather Station System. In IEEE, Conference Paper, 2015.

[22] Rahut, Afreen, Kamini. 2018. Smart weather monitoring and real time alert system using IoT. In IRJET, Vol 5, Issue:10, Oct 2018.

[23] Rao, Sridhar. 2018. IoT based smart crop-field monitoring and automation irrigation system. In IEEE, Conference Paper, 2018.

[24] R, Kavitha, Praveena, Parvathi. 201. Design and Implementation of Weather Monitoring System using Wireless Communication. In International Journal of Advanced Information in Engineering Technology (IJAIET) ISSN: 2454–6933 Vol.4, No.5. 2017.

[25] Sahitya, Balaji, Naidu, Abinaya 2017. Designing a Wireless Sensor Network for Precision Agriculture Using Zigbee. In IEEE 7th International Advance Computing Conference (IACC), Hyderabad, 2017: pp. 287–291.

[26] Singh, Jerath, Raja. 2020. Low Cost IoT Enabled Weather Station. In International Conference on Computation, Automation and Knowledge Management (ICCAKM), Dubai, United Arab Emirates, 2020: pp. 31–37.

[27] Suriyachai, Pansit. 2018. Effective Utilization of IoT for Low-cost Crop Monitoring and Automation. In IEEE, Conference Paper, 2018.

[28] S. Tyagi, A. Q. Ansari and M. A. Khan(2010), "Dynamic threshold based sliding-window filtering technique for RFID data," 2010 IEEE 2nd International Advance Computing Conference (IACC), Patiala, 2010, pp. 115–120, doi: 10.1109/IADCC.2010.5423025.

[29] Susmitha, Sowmyabala. 2015 Design and Implementation of Weather Monitoring and Controlling System. In International Journal of Computer Applications Volume 3, issue 2, March–April, 2015.

[30] Tyagi, S., M. Ayoub Khan, and A. Q. Ansari(2010), "RFID Data Management," in Radio Frequency Identification Fundamentals and Applications Bringing Research to Practice, Cristina Trucu, Ed. InTech, February 2010, DOI:10.5772/8001.

[31] Tyagi S., Ansari A.Q., Khan M.A. (2011) Extending Temporal and Event Based Data Modeling for RFID Databases. In: Nagamalai D., Renault E., Dhanuskodi M. (eds) Advances in Parallel Distributed Computing. PDCTA 2011. Communications in Computer and Information Science, vol 203. Springer, Berlin, Heidelberg, https://doi.org/10.1007/978-3-64224037-9_43

[32] Ucgun, Kaplan. 2017. Arduino based weather forecasting station. In IEEE, Conference Paper, 2017.

[33] Xiaojun, Xianpeng, Peng. 2015. IOT-based air pollution monitoring and forecasting system. In IEEE, Conference Paper, 2015.

[34] Zhou, Ling. 2010. HCI-based bluetooth master-slave monitoring system design. In International Conference on Computational Problem-Solving, Lijiang, 2010: pp. 406–409.

Smart Computing – Khan et al (Eds)
© 2021 Taylor & Francis Group, London, ISBN 978-0-367-76552-1

Survey on applications of AI in medical science

F. Ahmed & A. Tiwari
ABES Institute of Technology, Ghaziabad, Uttar Pradesh, India

ABSTRACT: Artificial Intelligence (AI), also called machine intelligence, is defined as the ability of machines to display human-like intelligence by learning, problem solving abilities, speech and language, adapting to the environment, etc. Continuous development is being made in this field to make machines capable enough of making the best decisions on their own while requiring minimal human intervention. With the rapid pace of expansion, AI is now also entering into the field of medicine at a very explosive rate. Its capability of utilizing datasets for exploratory analysis and then producing results based on patterns and analysis makes it popular enough for the diagnosing and detection of diseases and helps in their treatments. It involves a data-driven decision-making process with machine learning algorithms. But the two important factors, i.e., safety and effectiveness, have a key role to play in determining the role of AI in medical science. This paper explores the applications of AI in medical science along with the challenges and benefits in the future.

1 INTRODUCTION

In medical science there is a wide scale of applications for Artificial Intelligence (AI). The impact of AI can be seen in various fields of medical science in the form of technological improvements (Quasim 2015). The applicability of various machine learning algorithms is visible in the usage of health bands, fitness watches, etc. Currently, only very specific settings in clinical practice benefit from the application of AI, such as the detection of atrial fibrillation, epilepsy seizures, and hypoglycemia, or the diagnosis of disease based on histopathological examination or medical imaging (Briganti & Moine 2020). The introduction of AI in medical science has led to many revolutionary changes. AI has been used efficiently for disease diagnosis, radiology, and to study drug interactions. Patient data can be recorded easily and can be safely stored for long period of time. Machines are able to analyze the symptoms of various diseases and relate them with the age groups and regions of patients to draw a relation and predict solutions. We use smart watches to record our pulse, breathing rate, oxygen, etc. Smart applications are designed to predict the risk of various diseases and suggest preventive measures. Robots can be seen in assisting in major surgical and laser operations. The training of AI algorithms is taking place at a very profound level, and it can be understood from the fact that medical practitioners even train these machine learning algorithms from ample amounts of datasets to make those algorithms able to identify a new parasite or bacteria. AI simplifies the lives of patients, doctors, and hospital administrators by performing tasks that are typically done by humans, but in less time and at a fraction of the cost. Although the pace of AI in the detection of disease is faster than medical professionals as seen in an instance of detecting cancer (Davenport & Kalakota 2019); it's devastating affects cannot be ignored if compromised. One of the most powerful implementations of IBM is IBM Watson which can also be seen in assisting the oncology branch of medicine by accumulating medical records, journals, and reports of clinical trials. Comparatively, Google's Cloud Healthcare application programming interface (API) includes clinical diagnostics offerings and other AI solutions that help doctors make

DOI 10.1201/9781003167488-80

more informed clinical decisions regarding patients. AI used in Google Cloud takes data from users' electronic health records through machine learning—creating insights for healthcare providers to make better clinical decisions. Some of the large-scale implementations of AI in the medical field are as follows:

– Faster data collection and processing
– Growth of genome sequencing databases
– Understanding the pattern of spread of viruses
– Data logs in rare diseases
– Improved precision with less chances of human error
– Assistance to doctors in complicated surgeries

2 BACKGROUND

The British mathematician Alan Turing was one of the founders of modern computer science and AI. He defined intelligent behavior in a computer as the ability to achieve human-level performance in cognitive tasks; this later became popular as the "Turing test" (Ramesh 2004). John McCarthy of Stanford University, an American computer scientist, first devised the term AI in 1956 as the science and engineering of intelligent machines. The potential of AI in medical science has been expressed by several researchers. In 1998, Hoong (Klaus 2007) summarized the potential of AI techniques in medicine. Many intelligent systems have been developed for the purpose of enhancing healthcare and provide better healthcare facilities, reduce cost, etc. As expressed by many studies, intelligent systems were developed to assist users (particularly doctors and patients) and provide early diagnosis and prediction to prevent serious illness. Even though the system is equipped with "human" knowledge, the system will never replace human expertise as humans are required to frequently monitor and update the system's knowledge. Therefore, the role of a medical specialist and doctors (or medical practitioner) is important to ensure system validity (Hussain et al. 2008). From its advent in the early 20th century, AI has now made inroads in almost every field such as transportation, security, medical science, etc. One of the biggest AI breakthroughs in drug development came in 2007 when researchers tasked a robot named Adam with researching functions of yeast. Adam scoured billions of data points in public databases to hypothesize about the functions of 19 genes within yeast, predicting 9 new and accurate hypotheses. Adam's robot friend, Eve, discovered that triclosan, a common ingredient in toothpaste, can combat malaria-based parasites. With large-scale advances in machine learning, robotics, and computational power in the 21st century, AI has grown the most rapidly. The use of deep learning has given a definite boost to the applicability of AI in medicines. The work in Chen & Chen (2018) explains the usage of neural network-based multiscale Gaussian matching filter for diagnosing coronary angiogram X-ray images for improvement in classification of images. It describes support vector machine (SVM) to detect pneumothorax. It also describes the designing of decision support systems for predictions related to fractures in hip bones. Similarly, a work discusses an algorithm developed by Kim et al. for the prediction of prostate cancer. To carve out an accurate segmentation of tumors from three-dimensional images, the algorithm discussed in Chen & Chen (2018). The work in the present system is for healthcare and industrial IoT (Abuhasel 2020; Khan 2020a–2020e; Quasim 2019, 2020).

3 APPLICATIONS, ACCOUNTABILITY, AND EFFECTIVENESS

3.1 *Applications*

AI has various applications and usages in the present world.

3.1.1 *Maintaining medical records and other data*

There are several applications available to store the data of each patient as a separate record so that for any future reference, the full medical history of the patient can be examined. The information about various diseases has also been stored and can be shared with the whole world in the case of a global pandemic.

3.1.2 *Virtual nurses*

AI has now made several algorithms which allow applications to act as virtual nurses. These nurses have all the data feeds in their algorithms and can effectively handle minor problems of patients and provide better health tips.

3.1.3 *Doing repetitive jobs like X-ray, CT scan, etc.*

The repetitive tasks such as taking an X-ray of a patient or doing a CT scan are made much easier with the advancement in AI. Now the process is automated with little human intervention so it reduces time and removes chances of human error.

3.1.4 *Digital consultation*

Due to availability of various applications with AI features, people do not have to book an appointment with a doctor for every small problem. Now people can get consultation from trusted sources at their home with a few clicks.

3.1.5 *Health monitoring*

We see that many gadgets such as smart watches and bands offer the facility to monitor pulse, heartbeat, oxygen level, blood pressure, and many other things in a single go. These applications are easy to use and provide accurate health monitoring.

3.1.6 *Precision medicine*

With the help of AI algorithms, applications have been designed which can prescribe medicines to patients on the basis of the symptom which the patients have entered. Certain algorithms are also developed which can suggest medicines for new viruses and diseases by studying their genome.

AI has been widely used in performing image detection and analysis in almost every field of medical science such as radiology, pathology, dermatology, neurology, etc. The development and use of deep learning algorithms has further enhanced the capabilities of image processing by which we cannot only process the images but also analyze those images to detect severe health conditions such as tuberculosis on a chest X-ray, lung nodule on a chest CT, breast mass on a mammography, and much more. Considering the field of radiology alone, AI has a number of applications beyond image processing. These applications include patient scheduling, improving imaging appropriateness, scanner efficiency, patient safety, billing, content-based image retrieval work list optimization, follow-up care of patients, staffing optimization, work lists optimization, and many more. There are many significant advantages of AI in the field of medical imaging which is not only limited to image processing but also analyzing these images for health conditions of the patients and predicting their health condition accurately. The medical professionals need to make themselves used to the new technologies so that they can easily comply with these technological advancements and make effective use of these technologies for the welfare of mankind. Although many new algorithms have been introduced which have taken the use of AI in medical fields to a new height but there is still much room for more advancements as many fields are still unexplored and new opportunities are waiting to be explored and used for reducing the workload of medical professionals and reducing the chances of human errors by providing accurate results. The active use of AI in the medical field has led to the introduction and implementation of AI methods and algorithms in every aspect of medical science and the analysis and treatment of neurological diseases is also one of its major applications. Due to high risks associated with neurological diseases and its high mortality rate, the implementation of AI to study the patterns and changes in

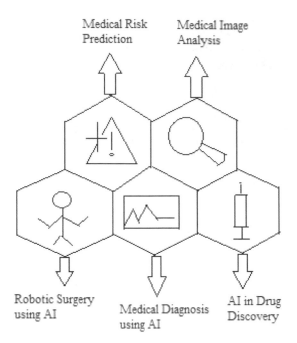

Figure 1.   Applications of AI.

the human brain and designing of algorithms for their better treatment is a better option rather than the conventional factors. The application of AI in neuro-imaging has been successful in handling a wide range of tasks involving stages from imaging study's acquisition through interpretation which includes study protocoling, shortening image acquisition time, MRI, etc. The quality of the labeled data and the inclusion of dataset from a wider range have led to a greater accuracy in results and have been successfully implemented for people all around the world. Some new technologies and devices have led to use of AI in various ways such as the preprocessing of brain images, protocoling, execution, image construction, segmentation of the images for better study and analysis, the labeling of tissue infected after a brain stroke, the classification of tumor, and the detection of various other diseases. The biggest advantage of using AI in the medical field is that it can exceed human capabilities and overcome human limitations by handling a very large amount of data and it is less prone to errors which can be caused by humans due to fatigue and workload. The use of AI has provided a boom to this field as things which seem to be impossible in the past have now become possible. We have never imagined that we will be able to obtain clear images of the vital organs and analyze and study them effectively to obtain accurate results. Since the introduction of AI in the medical field, it has now become one of the most important factors in the medical science with a huge potential and future scope. Chest pathology is one of the areas where AI has made big advancements. The use of a computer for chest pathology has been attempted for a long time but the recent developments in the field of AI have caused significant advantages in this area. The vital parts of chest pathology include detection and the monitoring of a number of health conditions related to the heart and lungs which includes pulmonary embolism, cancer detection, lung nodule detection, interstitial lung disease, parenchymal lung, airways diseases, etc. The use of the machine learning approach for lung nodule detection and lung cancer detection include treatment advice and outcome predictions have been much more accurate than ever and have raised great hopes for their future scope. The use of the machine learning approach and computer-assisted diagnosis and detection of the deadly diseases have shown accurate results. Lung texture analysis, pixel wise density analysis of lung CT images and their assessment using more automated techniques using advanced algorithms of data science and machine learning, is very promising. Various software tools have been designed and developed to help in classifying and quantifying parenchymal and airway diseases and more advanced versions of these tools are in the development phase. Although the introduction of AI in chest pathology is new and its role is limited, it has shown to have great potential and has given more accurate results so its role in the future is much more promising as a great deal of work is going on developing new algorithms and overcoming the present limitations and shortcomings. In this world of innovation, the AI and machine learning developers do not aim to limit the progress of AI in the medical field to image processing and classification only, rather they are developing intelligent systems with methods of operation which are comparable to or even more accurate and advanced then the human intelligence. The area of cardiovascular diseases is one of the major fields where we see large-scale application and implementation of AI in the medical world. The entire process focuses on patient scheduling, image acquisition, image reconstruction, image classification, and development of prognostic information with the help of machine learning and deep learning algorithms. The overall impact of AI on the whole process of cardiovascular diseases in the field of medical science are a decision support system to provide evidence-based care, image acquisition, processing, reconstruction, analysis, interpretation, diagnosis, and studying image with help of other data sets available for new findings. There are many practical uses of AI in this medical field which are very efficient and accurate. They include methods such as echocardiography, computer tomography to evaluate cardiac anatomy, magnetic resonance imaging, nuclear imaging, outcome prediction based on composite data, and development of algorithms for clinical practices. The application of AI in medical field in echocardiography, CT scan, and MRI have moved ahead of simply providing and analyzing images to transformation and depiction of living biological tools as a quantitative dataset. The predictions and results have been accurate and the chances of errors are significantly low so the dependency on the AI algorithms has greatly increased. The ability of algorithms to interpret the medical conditions and provide cure have been beneficial and has a greater scope in the near future. When we consider and analyze the health condition of patients and the impact of diseases on their body at various stages, what we observe is that that many deadly diseases which can be cured at an early stage without being fatal to the life of patient, rather they go undetected in their early stage due to hidden symptoms and no serious issues thus becoming fatal in their later stage. It is very unpredictable for a medical professional or a common person to predict the possibility of an underlying disease until its symptoms are shown. Here AI plays a major role in medical science by warning the patients and their health professionals at an early stage about an underlying disease which can be fatal in the near future. Breast cancer is one such case which is primarily responsible for the death of thousands of women per year in different parts of the world. Breast cancer is a very frequent cancer and is fatal at a later stage, hence early detection and cure of this disease is necessary to prevent the mortality rate. AI and machine learning developers have designed and developed many algorithms and tools which can be a part of our daily life and will continuously monitor our health condition. If any serious issue is detected, it will immediately inform the person and related doctor. There are two stages for early detection of cancer which are screening and early diagnosis. The use of AI in mammography has been more successful compared to computer-aided detection (CAD). The major goals of AI professionals in mammography in the field of medical science is to develop deep learning algorithms which are able to recall decision support and provide accurate results for lesion localization, density stratification, and risk prediction. This will help to ensure early screening of cancerous cells and will tend to decrease the mortality rate. Since the concept of AI for detection is new and has been recently introduced, hence it also has some goals to achieve and challenges to face. These are memory constraints, data issues, dataset bias, under fitting or over fitting curve, and certain uncertain results. Hence, the focus of AI developers is to design a general adversarial network with active learning and regulations. Tomosynthesis and genomic studies are the targets of near future but the advent of the AI and machine learning algorithms have positively impacted the field of medical science. The introduction of any method or technique in the treatment process in a medical field require excessive testing and successful trials to check any of the side effects and if they are suitable for use on humans. Same is the case with AI which tend to bring a revolution in the field of medical science by reducing costs, saving time, providing greater accuracy, promoting automation, and setting high standards in treating patients. First, we need to check whether the uses of new techniques of AI are safe for humans and are achieving proposed result or not. This can be ensured with the help of clinical trials. The clinical trial ensures that the images and technologies are standardized or not. We see that medical imaging is a key feature in diagnosis which helps to provide insights on several diseases which may remain undetected otherwise. A clinical trial is the experimental evaluation of a product, substance, medication, and diagnostic or therapeutic technique that, in its application to human beings, aims to assess its effectiveness and safety. Any new technology needs to pass the four phases of clinical tests before being accepted. These phases are listed below.

3.1.7 *Phases*
3.1.7.1 Phase 1
This phase includes study regarding any possible side effects. It is usually done with a small group of 10–15 people who have no alternate treatment option for their medical condition.

3.1.7.2 Phase 2
This phase tests the safety and effectiveness with a relatively larger group of 40–50 people with some specific medical conditions.

3.1.7.3 Phase 3
This is the last phase before the release of any new technology in the market so it is tested for both side effects and effectiveness on a relatively large number of people.

3.1.7.4 Phase 4
This is the phase after the new technologies have been approved by the experts. Now the technology is continuously tested on large masses for its effects on a variety of people and to increase the content of data input for the algorithms.

Some steps need to be followed before the start of clinical trials and during the clinical trials. These steps are image acquisition protocol design, site validation, and quality assurance. Various kinds of AI algorithms used are classification and segmentation algorithms.

3.2 *Accountability*

Accountability is one of the four components required in a governance model for AI in healthcare which also includes fairness, transparency, and trustworthiness. We know that from the stage of proposal to final deployment in the market, an AI model for healthcare has to go through software developers, government agencies, health services, medical professional bodies, patient interest groups, and others. Hence, we need accountability at each level to ensure the reliability and effectiveness of the model so that the security of patients can be ensured. Therefore, we see that accountability is the most important and most challenging factor. We need to set and assign the accountability at each stage so that we can monitor and evaluate the safety and accuracy of the devices and programs run by AI in the medical sector. The stages at which we can check the accountability are as follows.

3.2.1 *Approval*
This stage includes taking permissions from the authorities for the marketing and use of AI-based products in the healthcare system and government bodies. It becomes very necessary for the officials to check the product and algorithms on various parameters including safety. This means that when the AI software has a significant medication that affects the safety or effectiveness, the developer would have to revert back and maintain an approach toward ensuring the safety and quality of

AI-based product. It is the duty of the officials not to create unnecessary hurdles in the path of developers and not to allow any product with risks associated.

3.2.2 *Introduction*

Once the product is passed from the security concerns of the officials, it comes to the introductory stage where the healthcare professionals review the products based on their needs and requirements and the scale of use and growth of product in the available scenarios. The reviewing panel may consist of the available medical staff and trained professionals but they may not be fully aware about the scope and uses of the introduced technology and they need to be very careful while analyzing the product and they need to deeply understand even the smallest feature of the model so that they can identify even the minimum risks associated and could get the full information about the smallest benefits which the proposed model can give to the humanity and the medical system.

3.2.3 *Deployment stage*

This is the final stage while considering introducing a new software or product related to AI in the field of healthcare. Once the authorities have approved the product and the healthcare professionals are satisfied with the performance than the product is ready to be deployed in the market. It is a very crucial stage as a new technology has been introduced to the people who literally have no idea about its working principles and may also have trust issues.

Thus, a balanced and responsive approach has to be taken into consideration while deploying the product so that it may be in a user-friendly way to ensure the trust of the people. A committee also needs to be set up to be responsible for maintaining the product and preventing any security risks. Thus, after ensuring the above factors, an AI-based product is finally ready to be launched in the market to be introduced to the general public to provide maximum assistance to health professionals and maximum benefit to common people.

3.3 *Effectiveness*

The introduction of deep learning, machine learning, big data, and computing infrastructure revoked the interest in AI that has gone on since the late 1950s. Its implementation has many challenges such as protection of patients, privacy, and the general public in the use of AI in medical science. Overcoming their challenges focused on healthcare can be achieved on meeting the requirements of ethical challenges. It is these major challenges, in a way, that it comprises the people's privacy that need to be satisfyingly maintained in order to prevent psychological and reputational harm to the patients, that's why they need to provide the explicit data only. This can be maintained by the effective trust between the public and health professional systems. It is the duty of professionals or, we can say, an ethical duty. To maintain the patient's trust and promote the safeguard duty among them. Sometimes it may lead to the mistrust due to transparency of the AI and deep learning algorithms, it may lead to an opaque decision-making process, hidden even to the developers—this situation known as the black issue. Black box issues present many challenges in the output of the AI models guaranteeing safety in unusual input situations. Clinicians must have proper knowledge of AI models and their algorithms in order to understand and explain the on-going process and make an effective decision so that they will be able to satisfy a patient's vital trust. This knowledge is necessary for explaining the errors that may arise due to the use of the AI software in clinics.

ACKNOWLEDGMENT

We would like to express my gratitude to Dr. Rizwan Khan, Head of Department, ABES Institute of Technology, Ghaziabad, for promoting me and guide me along with his immense help which enables me to complete this work.

REFERENCES

Abuhasel K. A. and M. A. Khan, (2020), "A Secure Industrial Internet of Things (IIoT) Framework for Resource Management in Smart Manufacturing," in IEEE Access, vol. 8, pp. 117354–117364, 2020, doi: 10.1109/ACCESS.2020.3004711.

Briganti, G. & Moine, O.L. (2020). Artificial Intelligence in Medicine: Today and Tomorrow. *Frontiers in Medicine. vol.–7. pp. 27.*

Chen, Y.K. & Chen, Y.F. et. al. (2018). Artificial Intelligence in Medical Application. *Journal of Health Engineering. 2 pages*

Davenport, T. & Kalakota, R. (2019). The potential for artificial intelligence in healthcare. *Future Health Journal. Vol–6(2):94–98.*

Hussain, W., Ishak, W.H.W. & Siraj, F. (2008). Artificial intelligence in medical application: an exploration.

Kuhn, K.A., Warren J.R., & Leong T.Y. (2007). Studies in Health Technology and Informatics. *MEDINFO 2007. vol–129*

Khan M.A. et. al, (2020), Decentralised IoT, Decenetralised IoT: A Blockchain perspective, Springer, Studies in BigData, 2020, DOI: https://doi.org/10.1007/978-3-030-38677-1

Khan, M. A., Quasim, M. T, et.al, (2020), A Secure Framework for Authentication and Encryption Using Improved ECC for IoT-Based Medical Sensor Data, in IEEE Access, vol. 8, pp. 52018–52027, 2020. DOI: 10.1109/ACCESS.2020.2980739

Khan M. A., (2020), An IoT Framework for Heart Disease Prediction Based on MDCNN Classifier, in IEEE Access, vol. 8, pp. 34717–34727, 2020. DOI: 10.1109/ACCESS.2020.2974687

Khan M.A, and Algarni F., (2020) "A Healthcare Monitoring System for the Diagnosis of Heart Disease in the IoMT Cloud Environment Using MSSO-ANFIS," in IEEE Access, vol. 8, pp. 122259–122269, 2020, doi: 10.1109/ACCESS.2020.3006424.

Khan, MA, Abuhasel, KA. (2020). Advanced metameric dimension framework for heterogeneous industrial Internet of things. Computational Intelligence. 2020; 1– 21. https://doi.org/10.1111/coin.12378

Quasim, M.T. (2015). Artificial Intelligence as a Business Forecasting and Error Handling Tool. COMPUSOFT, An international journal of advanced computer technology, 4 (2), February-2015 (Volume-IV, Issue-II).

Quasim, M. T., Khan M. A, et.al, (2019), Internet of Things for Smart Healthcare: A Hardware Perspective, 2019 First International Conference of Intelligent Computing and Engineering (ICOICE), Hadhramout, Yemen, 2019, pp. 1–5. DOI: 10.1109/ICOICE48418.2019.9035175

Quasim, M.T., Khan M.A, Algarni F., Alharthy A., Alshmrani G.M.M, (2020), Blockchain Frameworks. In: Khan M., Quasim M., Algarni F., Alharthi A. (eds) Decentralised Internet of Things. Studies in Big Data, vol 71. Springer, DOI: https://doi.org/10.1007/978-3-030-38677-1

Ramesh, A. & Kambhampati, Chandra & Monson, John & Drew, Philip. (2004). Artificial intelligence in medicine. *Annals of the Royal College of Surgeons of England.*

Smart Computing – Khan et al (Eds)
© *2021 Taylor & Francis Group, London, ISBN 978-0-367-76552-1*

Microcontroller-based monitoring and alert system: A review

Deepti Rawat, Divya Mishra, Himanshu Chauhan, Tripti Mishra & Ranjeeta Yadav
Department of ECE, ABES Engineering College, Ghaziabad, Uttar Pradesh, India

ABSTRACT: The objective of this paper is to design and implement a microcontroller-based monitoring and alert system. It monitors the surrounding temperature and smoke level employing LM35 for monitoring the temperature, MQ2 as a smoke sensor, and the value of which are displayed the LCD screen. It focuses mainly on our homes. It also automatically controls the fan connected to the motor driver depending upon the temperature sensed by the microcontroller, thus also working as an automated control system. When the sensor value exceeds the threshold limit causing fire, the owner of the house will be alerted by SMS through SIM900 GSM module. Hence, it discusses about a low-cost microcontroller-based alert system.

1 INTRODUCTION

Home automation is building automation for the home called a smart home or smart house. It controls and monitors the heat, lighting, ventilation, security, etc. A programmable logic controller (PLC) is one of the major tools in automation, where it is used in industrial automation, not home automation. Also, nowadays many smart systems such as industrial automation, healthcare, and smart factories, are being developed using the Internet of Things (IoT) (Abuhasel 2020; Khan 2020a–2020e; Quasim 2020). Home or residential automation includes the interfacing of sensors and microcontrollers and programmed to perform a specific function. Home automation plays an important role to control the devices in our home through our mobile devices from anywhere around the world.

Fire accidents tend to happen frequently due to various causes and hence require advanced techniques to prevent such mishappenings. This technique is called home automation which is used to implement an alert system that monitors the temperature and smoke of our surroundings and more precisely our homes or where the device is installed. Fires usually occur suddenly and can cause a huge amount of destruction of property and life. Thus, it is very important to inform the fire department or fire brigade at the time of any such incident which is impossible if nobody is home. This project idea mainly aims at preventing such incidents when nobody is home.

Temperature, smoke, and humidity are parameters that should be continuously monitored at our homes. The rise in temperature in summers or the rise in moisture levels in winters both causes discomfort and can be a reason for health issues. Hence, both the temperature and smoke level should be monitored and maintained below their threshold values. This is done by LM35 and MQ2 temperature and smoke sensors, respectively. These sensors work when they are interfaced with the microcontroller. The electric fan minimizes the temperature by the airflow and is controlled by the variations in the temperature. In this paper, the idea describes how the temperature and humidity are monitored using respective sensors that are interfaced with the ATMEGA microcontroller. When the parameter value exceeds the threshold value the electric fan automatically starts to minimize the temperature and besides an alert SMS is sent to the owner of the house and the fire department using a GSM module to control the fire before everything is destroyed. The use of dehumidifiers to automatically control the humidity is also proposed in the paper.

DOI 10.1201/9781003167488-81

2 LITERATURE REVIEW

Nowadays, temperature and humidity systems are installed in temperature-controlled rooms (William 2012) that are used to store and preserve time and temperature-sensitive pharmaceutical products and food items. The temperature and humidity alert system should be linked with a monitoring system with high and low alarm setpoints. There should be visual or audible alarms together with an SMS text warning. Some of these are mentioned here for reference.

2.1 *Manual temperature monitoring system*

In many fields, people still work using the old methods of temperature and humidity measurement. They deploy multiple instruments such as thermometer for temperature, rain gauge for precipitation, etc. The majority of these instruments are based on analog technology and the records of these instruments are manually stored and analyzed for various applications. The main aim of this paper was to continuously monitor the environmental factors and broadcast them through various channels.

2.1.1 *Limitations*

- Such monitoring systems consist of obsolete technology which is not in use today. Also, the usage of heavy machinery consisting of various moving parts that demand regular maintenance and need to be replaced frequently.
- Power consumption is another issue that poses a limitation as an instrument is usually installed far from the main power supply, further adding to its cost.
- Usage of thermometer for temperature measurement, however, is inaccurate and not precise as per our requirement.
- There was no work in the dimension of warning and alert in the case of any threat, leading to loss of lives and property.

2.2 *Smart sensory system for environmental monitoring:*

The purpose of this paper was to develop a system (Goudal et al. 2014; Quasim 2019) that monitors environmental parameters like temperature, humidity, flammable gases, and smoke. This system uses open-source hardware and software at a low cost, and also helps us in applications such as creating smart buildings. SD cards store the data obtained from the sensors with an operating system that contains a web server and a database.

2.2.1 *Limitations*

- As the data are stored in SD cards, the possibility of data loss increases.
- There is no redundancy of data which results in a faulty system.
- As the sensor is exposed to gas once, it takes several minutes to take the next reading.

3 PROPOSED SYSTEM

In this project, we have implemented the low-cost digital meter using Peripheral Interface Controller (PIC) which acts as a monitoring and alert system to prevent fire accidents. We have used temperature sensor LM35 and humidity sensor DHT11 for monitoring temperature and humidity of the environment. Home security systems offer an early warning system, instead of smoke alarms in which many homeowners rely upon to warn them of fire outbreak. This warning is given through SMS using the Global System for Mobile Communications (GSM) module. The advantage of this system is as follows:

- Easy and affordable
- Low maintenance

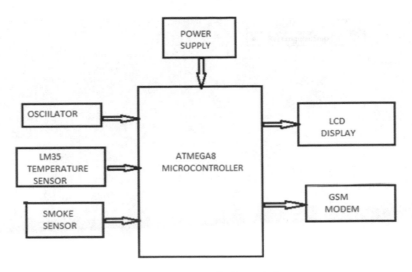

Figure 1. Block diagram of microcontroller-based monitoring and alert system.

- 24/7 monitoring
- Placement flexibility

4 SYSTEM ARCHITECTURE

The main processing unit in this system is ATMEGA Microcontroller. It is based on RISC architecture and is a low-power, high-performance 8-bit microchip. It operates on 1.8–5.5 volts. Temperature and humidity sensors (Hoque et al. 2013) are interfaced with the ATMEGA microcontroller. The LM35 temperature sensor is an integrated circuit whose output is proportional to Celsius temperature. DHT11 humidity sensor protects the infrastructure of the house from damage. When a certain parameter value exceeds the threshold value of the fan, an alert message is sent to the concerned person using GSM. And if there is an emergency, the fire department will receive an SMS alert containing the address of the specified location. LCD is also connected to the ports of the microcontroller which displays the measured values.

5 WORKING COMPONENTS

A. Temperature sensor

LM35 is a temperature sensor used to monitor the temperature. It is an integrated circuit whose output and Celsius temperature is directly proportional to. It is easy to connect to the readout circuitry due to its linear output and low output impedance characteristics. The operating range of LM35 is −55 to 150°C and has a scale factor of 0.01/°C. It has three pins +v, ground, and V_{out}.

B. MQ2 sensor

The (MQ2) module is useful for gas leakage detection in homes and industries. It helps detect CH4, H2, CO, LPG alcohol, and smoke. It is also possible to take measurements as soon as possible due to its high sensitivity and fast response time. Wide detecting scope, fast response, and high sensitivity make it useful for a wide range of applications.

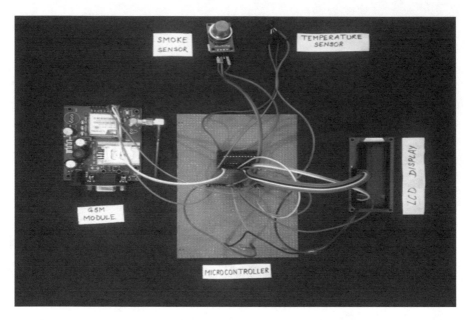

Figure 2. Working model of microcontroller-based monitoring and alert system.

C. ATMega microcontroller

It is a low-power, high-performance 8-bit microchip. It is based on RISC architecture. It has flash memory to read while writing capabilities. It operates on 1.8–5.5 volts. It has 1 KB EEPROM, 2 KB SRAM, 54/69 general-purpose I/O lines, 32 general purpose working registers. It has five software selectable power saving modes, an 8-channel 10-bit A/D converter, SPI serial port, and programmable watchdog timer with an internal oscillator.

D. GSM module

GSM stands for Global System for Mobile Communication. It is one of the most popular networks for mobile communication. GSM works with a wireless network. It enables users to communicate or connect with whomever they want. It is a hardware component with the capabilities of sending and receiving messages over a network. It uses an RS232 serial port for communication and SIM900A as a GSM module. Short Message Service (SMS) is a text messaging service component of telephone, World Wide Web, and mobile telephony systems.

E. LCD display

As one of the purposes is to display the measured values of temperature and humidity through a display device just like values appear on a digital meter. So, here we use an Liquid Crystal Display (LCD) screen and connected a 16X2 LCD module to the ports of the microcontroller which display the measured values.

F. Alert SMS

As here one of our main objectives is to use GSM to send an SMS to a particular mobile number or the concerned authority whenever the temperature or humidity exceeds above a certain limit. Also, the police or the fire department will get an SMS alert. GSM receives the mobile number either of a person or fire department via UART communication protocol which is given with the help of AT commands from the microcontroller.

6 FUTURE WORK

In this paper, the automated control of temperature is proposed which is extended to humidity control. Humidity is controlled by the implication of dehumidifiers, which reduces the humidity level by increasing the home temperature. To ensure the 220 V dehumidifier which is controlled by the microcontroller, the 5–220 V relay module is used and is connected between them. In place of a fan, an air conditioner can also be used.

7 CONCLUSION

It has been concluded that microcontroller-based monitoring and alert system using the GSM module works as a low-cost, easily usable system and within reach of every house or any workplace. There are various other advantages of using this low-cost digital microcontroller alert system as it is available in much-reduced size which can be placed anywhere without facing any difficulty. Also, it can be easily manufactured at a very reasonable cost and consumes less power.

The main objective of this research paper is to design and implement a low-cost system which is a simple, efficient, and wireless home automation system for fire detection and other disastrous threat by controlling excess temperature and humidity. The readings will continuously display on the LCD screen and when it exceeds the above comfort limit, the concerned authority will automatically receive an alert signal via GSM. GSM also allows us to communicate in any faraway isolated remote place and to access across all over the world. Therefore, the main idea behind this research is to ensure and overcome the efficient operation of controlling fire accidents so that we can protect many lives whether it is human or flora and fauna.

REFERENCES

Abuhasel K. A. and M. A. Khan, (2020), "A Secure Industrial Internet of Things (IIoT) Framework for Resource Management in Smart Manufacturing, " in IEEE Access, vol. 8, pp. 117354–117364, 2020, doi: 10.1109/ACCESS.2020.3004711.

Bakrania S.D., Wooldridge M.S. (2010), The effects of the location of Auadditives on combustion generated SnO2 nanopowders for CO gas-sensing, *Sensors*, Issue:10, pp.700–7017.

Goudal KC, Preetham V R and Shanmukha Swamy M N. (2014), Microcontroller based real-time weather Monitoring device with GSM. *International Journal of Science, Engineering and Tech-nology Research (IJSETR)*, Volume 3(7), July 2014.

Tomer Hemlata, Mangla Kapil, "Study and Development of Temperature & Humidity monitoring system through Wireless Sensor Network (WSN) using Zigbee module". *Hemlata Tome Tnt. Journal of Engineering Research and Application* ISSN: 2248–962

Hoque M.E, Rasid S.M, Roy Amit, Paul N, Alam Ferdous, Raseluzzaman Md. (2013), Development of an Automatic Humidity Control System. *International Conference on Mechanical, Ind-ustrial and Materials Engineering* 2013 (ICMIME20J3).

Khan M. A., (2020a), An IoT Framework for Heart Disease Prediction Based on MDCNN Classifier, in IEEE Access, vol. 8, pp. 34717–34727, 2020. DOI: 10.1109/ACCESS.2020.2974687

Khan, MA, Abuhasel, KA. (2020b).Advanced metameric dimension framework for heterogeneous industrial Internet of things. Computational Intelligence. 2020; 1– 21. https://doi.org/10.1111/coin.12378

Khan M.A, and Algarni F., (2020c) "A Healthcare Monitoring System for the Diagnosis of Heart Disease in the IoMT Cloud Environment Using MSSO-ANFIS," in IEEE Access, vol. 8, pp. 122259–122269, 2020, doi: 10.1109/ACCESS.2020.3006424.

Khan, M.A and S. Ojha (2008), "Virtual Route Tracking in ZigBee (IEEE 802.15.4) enabled RFID interrogator mesh network," 2008 International Symposium on Information Technology, Kuala Lumpur, 2008, pp. 1–7, doi: 10.1109/ITSIM.2008.4631904.

Khan M.A. et al., (2020d), Decentralised IoT, Decenetralised IoT: A Blockchain perspective, Springer, Studies in BigData, 2020, DOI: https://doi.org/10.1007/978-3-030-38677-1

Khan, M. A., Quasim, M. T, et al., (2020e), A Secure Framework for Authentication and Encryption Using Improved ECC for IoT-Based Medical Sensor Data, in IEEE Access, vol. 8, pp. 52018-52027, 2020. DOI: 10.1109/ACCESS.2020.2980739

Meghana. R. Kanitkar, Dr. J. S. Awati. "Design of Temperature and Humidity Monitoring Emb-edded System". International Conference on Computing, *Communication and Energy Systems (access-I6)*.

Quasim, M. T., Khan M. A, et al., (2019), Internet of Things for Smart Healthcare: A Hardware Perspective, 2019 First International Conference of Intelligent Computing and Engineering (ICOICE), Hadhramout, Yemen, 2019, pp. 1–5. DOI: 10.1109/ICOICE48418.2019.9035175

Quasim, M.T., Khan M.A, Algarni F., Alharthy A., Alshmrani G.M.M, (2020), Blockchain Frameworks. In: Khan M., Quasim M., Algarni F., Alharthi A. (eds) Decentralised Internet of Things. Studies in Big Data, vol 71. Springer, DOI: https://doi.org/10.1007/978-3-030-38677-1

William Theophilus, Setiawan Budi. (2012), A Microcontroller- based Room Temperature Monitoring System. *International Journal of Computer Applications* (0975–8887), Volume 53, September 2012.

Teich Tobias, Wolf Sebastian, Neumann Tim, Junghans Sebastian, Franke Susan. (2014), Concept for a Service-oriented Architecture in Building Automation Systems, *Procedia Engineering*, Volume 69: pp.597–602.

Smart Computing – Khan et al (Eds)
© 2021 Taylor & Francis Group, London, ISBN 978-0-367-76552-1

Multifunction filter using current conveyor

Rishabh Aggarwal, Preeti Anand, Shaurya Garg, Shailendra Bisariya & Sanjay Kumar Singh
ECE Department, ABES Engineering College, Ghaziabad, Uttar Pradesh, India

ABSTRACT: In this paper, we are using a current-controlled conveyor component with extra X terminal for implementing multifunction filer, this will ultimately decrease the complication of the circuits presently used. The proposed circuit has three input ports and only one output port to form a biquadratic filter consisting an only single functioning component called as current conveyor from second generation (CCII) along with two capacitors to obtain all standard filter transfer functions such as low pass, high pass, band-pass, and band-reject filter. Now in this a current conveyor is used instead of op-amp because of two reasons one is that it can work on high frequencies and another is that it gives bandwidth-gain better under small as well as large signal conditions. Also, we are working on 180 nm complementary metal–oxide–semiconductor (CMOS) technology parameter using CADENCE Virtuoso and the results are obtained using ORCAD PSPICE 17.2 simulation tool for precision.

1   INTRODUCTION

A Current Conveyor is an analog electronic device that shows the reflection between the three terminals. The circuit proposed here is an electronic amplifier which provides unity gain and works on current-controlled mode similar to the operational amplifier.

1.1   *Generations of current conveyor:*

- 1st generation (CCI)
- 2nd generation (CCII)
- 3rd generation (CCIII)

This work is based on the 2nd-generation Current Conveyor (CCII). Its other name is the current-controlled conveyor (CCCII). In 2nd-generation current conveyor (CCII), the current is zero in terminal Y. The voltage drop between gate to source or you can say base to emitter is zero, causing the source or emitter voltage at terminal X and terminal Y to be equal. The source or emitter has

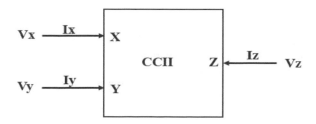

Figure 1.   Basic block diagram of CCII.

DOI 10.1201/9781003167488-82

almost zero input impedance at node X, whereas the input impedance at node Y is almost infinity at gate or base. Any current which flows at terminal X is reversed at terminal Z, but with infinite impedance. In other words, we can say that if the output current of terminal X is constant, the current flowing out of Z is going to have high-impedance and it will be CCII+. The inversion between terminal X and terminal Y current is represented as CCII−.

Now, simplicity of the building blocks of the current conveyor circuit gives us many advantages such as they make the circuit compact, effortlessly work on low voltages, the area is reduced, and energy usage is diminished to improvise at high-frequency functions. Current mode implementation of biquad filter was given by Minaei & Yuce (2007) while the current mode active-C filter was proposed by Senani (1996). Realization of biquad filters using current conveyor was presented by Altuntas & Toker (2002).

2 LITERATURE SURVEY

Senani (1996) shows multifunction biquadratic filters using DDCC. This circuit consists of 3DDCC, 2 capacitors, and 2 resistors grounded, respectively. The low voltage with low-power DDCC is used to obtain low-power consumption for the filters. By providing the appropriate connections at the input and output terminals, this circuit can act as LP, BP, HP, BS, and all pass current responses. This circuit provides benefits such as larger signal bandwidth, more noteworthy linearity, more extensive unique range, basic hardware, low-power consumption, and high input impedance. This filter performs LP, HP, BP, BS, and provides better output response. The power consumption of the circuit was 29.7 mW.

Gunes et al. (1999) shows the circuit implementation in a compact size, low-power dissipation, and low supply voltages which are important for circuit design. The main purpose of designing low voltage is to get similar performance with a low power supply, which reduces the total power consumption. Later, it will be evaluated that analog circuits will need supply voltage equal to or less than ±0.5 V. Thus, the low-power low-voltage design techniques are required for analog circuits. This MFCCCII was simulated by using SPICE 180 nm TSMC complementary metal–oxide–semiconductor (CMOS) technology and ±0.5 V is the supply voltage. This circuit gives better performance, low noise, and low power dissipation.

Ibrahim et al. (2005) shows a multifunction current-mode biquadratic filter performing LP, HP, BP, BR, and all-pass functions. The circuit rule depends on the 2nd-generation current controlled current conveyor (CCCII) one output terminal while having three input terminals. The circuit comprising of simply 2 CCCIIs and 2 grounded capacitors. The circuit is very comfortable to further develop into an integrated circuit architecture without any external resistor and using only grounded elements. The result shows that at ±1.5 V power supply voltages, the power consumption is approximately 1.87 mW. The circuit was operating with C1 = C2 = 1nF, IB1 = IB2 = 50 µA.

3 CIRCUIT DESCRIPTION

3.1 *Biquad filter design with Three-Input Single-Output (TISO)*

Figure 2 shows the schematic of the biquadratic filter circuit. It is obtained by using ORCAD PSPICE simulation tool in which we are working on CMOS.

Figure 3 shows CMOS implementation of Three-Input Single-Output (TISO), it consists of only one functioning component, i.e., Extra Current Controlled Conveyer (EXCCCII) with two capacitors for grounding purposes. The existing circuits consist of 2 CCCII (±), 2 capacitors, and they require 38 MOS transistors whereas our circuit needs only 31 MOS which is a benefit. Another advantage of the circuit is that by selecting the various value of input signal, the circuit can easily realize low-pass filter, band-pass filter, high-pass filter, and band-reject filter as shown in Table 1.

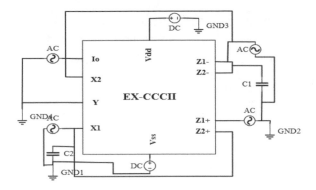

Figure 2. TISO schematic.

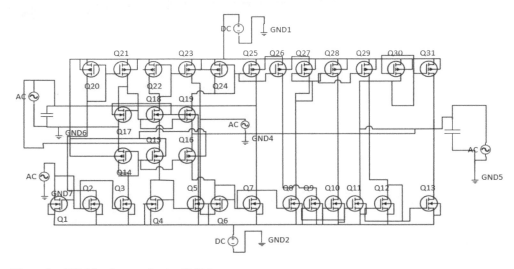

Figure 3. TISO implementation by CMOS.

Table 1. Realized filter functions.

Filters	I_1	I_2	I_3
LP	I_{in}	Zero	Zero
HP	I_{in}	I_{in}	I_{in}
BP	Zero	I_{in}	Zero
BR	Zero	I_{in}	I_{in}

4 SIMULATION RESULT

The width and length of CMOS transistors shown in the Figure 2 circuit are given in Table 2.

The circuit shown in Figure 2 has cut-off frequency (f_c) of 3.93 MHz and the value of capacitors (C_1 and C_2) is 50 Pico farad, the input current (I_{in}) is 100 mA, and the circuit operates at ± 1.25 V. Results obtained for the filter response are plotted and shown in Figure 4 for low-pass filter, Figure 5 for high-pass filter, Figure 6 for band-pass filter, and in Figure 7 for band-reject filter, respectively, by applying the selected input current to acquire the desired AC response.

Table 2. MOS dimensions.

Transistors	Width (mm)	Length (mm)
Q17, Q18, AND Q19	10	0.5
Q14, Q15, AND Q16	16	0.5
Rest all NMOS	6	0.5
Rest all PMOS	10	0.5

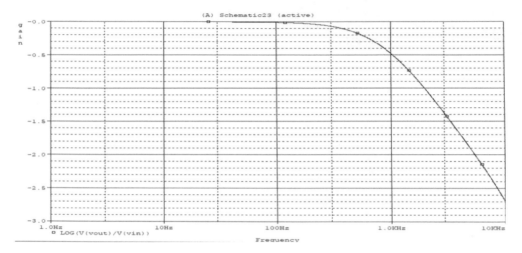

Figure 4. Response of LP filter.

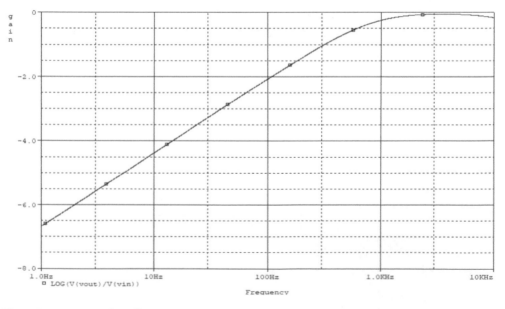

Figure 5. Response of HP filter.

4.1 *Low-pass filter response*

To obtain the filter response for low pass we take the value of I_1 as 100 mA, I_2 and I_3 as zero

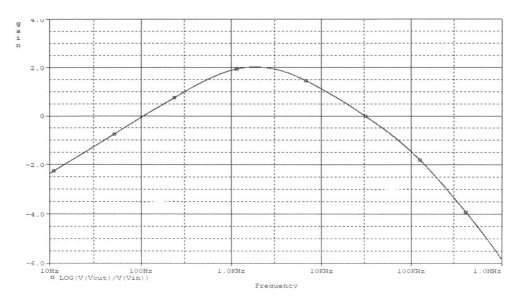

Figure 6.   Response of BP filter.

Table 3.   Comparative analysis of various research papers.

Research paper	Power consumption	Technology used	Frequency	Voltage	Type of current conveyor used
Senani (1996)	29.7 mW	CMOS 180 nm	1 khz	–	DDCC
Altuntas & Toker (2002)	4.8 mW	CMOS 180 nm	–	+.5 v and −.5 v	MFCCCII
Minaei & Yuce (2007)	1.87 mW	CMOS 180 nm	–	+1.5 v and −1.5 v	CCCII
Our proposed work	1.45 mW	CMOS 180 nm	–	+1.25 v and −1.25 v	EX-CCCII

4.2 High-pass filter response

To obtain the filter response for high pass we take the value of I_1, I_2, and I_3 as 100 mA.

4.3 Band-pass filter response

To obtain the filter response for band pass we take the value of I_2 as 100 mA, I_1 and I_3 as zero.

4.4 Band-reject filter response

To obtain the filter response for band reject we take the value of I_1 as zero, I_2 and I_3 as 100 mA

By comparing the different papers specifications with our paper specifications, it shows the better result in terms of power consumption, area, and complexity. In our proposed circuit, the number of transistors are less as compared to other circuits.

5 CONCLUSION

A biquad filter in current mode is introduced and realized by using a single extra X terminal current controllable current conveyor with two external capacitors which is sustainable for ICs fabrication. This multifunction biquad filter (Assaderaghi & Sinitsky 1997) with multiple inputs and a single

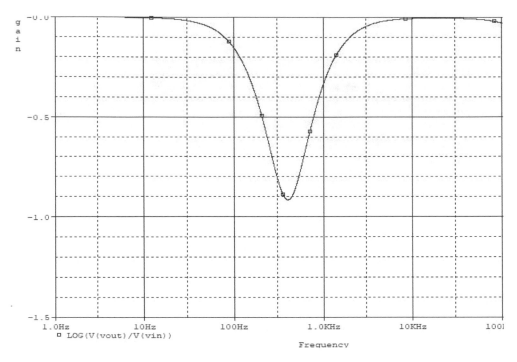

Figure 7.　Response of BR filter.

output provides similar performance as in the previous circuits along with key added advantages such as the total number of transistors is turned down. Hence, it consumes less area. Also, the total power consumption is minimized to a greater extent which is a boon in the low-power very large-scale integration (VLSI) application domain.

REFERENCES

Altuntas, E. and Toker, A. (2002). Realization of CM KHN biquads filter using CCCIIs. *AEU*, 56, pp. 45–49.

Assaderaghi, F. and Sinitsky, D. (1997). Dynamic Vth MOSFET for ultra LV VLSI. *IEEE Transactions on Electron Devices*, 44(3), pp. 414–422.

Gunes et al., (1999). Analyzing CM universal filter with minimum components by using DO-CCII. *Electron Lett*, 35, pp. 524–525.

Ibrahim et al., (2005). Analyzing a 22 MHz KHN biquad current mode filter by using DV-CCII and grounded passive elements. *IJEC*, 59, pp. 311–318.

Kathuria J., Khan M.A., Abraham A., Darwish A. (2014) Low Power Techniques for Embedded FPGA Processors. In: Khan M., Saeed S., Darwish A., Abraham A. (eds) *Embedded and Real Time System Development: A Software Engineering Perspective. Studies in Computational Intelligence,* vol 520. Springer, Berlin, Heidelberg. https://doi.org/10.1007/978-3-642-40888-5_11

Minaei, S. and Yuce, E. (2007). Current mode active C filter employing reduced number of CCCII. *Journal of Circuit Systems Comput*, 16, pp. 507–516.

Senani, R. 1996. A simple approach of deriving single input and multiple output CM biquad filters. *Frequenz*, pp 124–7.

Smart Computing – Khan et al (Eds)
© 2021 Taylor & Francis Group, London, ISBN 978-0-367-76552-1

Multiple object detection

Ankit Singh & Tushar Kumar
Galgotias University, Greater Noida, India

ABSTRACT: In the cutting-edge and swift world, finding a precise and proficient object recognition for headway in computer vision frameworks has been an integral part. With the emerge of faster (due to faster and better hardware too) and increasingly accurate deep learning techniques the prediction for finding a good and accurate model is of paramount importance. In this undertaking, we are aiming to incorporate the best possible technique to tackle object detection, with the goal of achieving higher accuracy in our Multiple Object Detection project. The major motivation in our task is to make colossal contribution to increasing the accuracy of object detection. In this venture, we resort to four models to tackle the problem, mainly Mask-RCNN (Mask Region Convolution Neural Network), Faster-RCNN (Faster Region Convolution Neural Network), SSD (Single Shot MultiBox Detection), and YOLO (You Look Only Once) trained on the most publicly and freely accessible dataset (MS-COCO).

Keywords: Faster-RCNN, Mask-RCNN, MS-COCO, NN, SSD, YOLO

1   INTRODUCTION

Our project was to find the best accuracy on MS-COCO (Microsoft Common Objects in Context) datasets of the Multiple Object Tracking (MOT) dataset. The MOT has been encouraging researchers to develop object tracking systems that can tackle more objects in a faster and accurate way. The common challenges were a large number of objects present in each data separated by very less distance, where the problem of plotting accurate bounding box comes into the picture. In small datasets, traditional methods could give us better results but in large datasets, they fail in detecting multiple objects. Background subtraction (or removal of unnecessary things) is the process of object detection to separate the background from the frame that we captured. The basic technique for the detection of a scene for moving subjects is to segregate pictures by outlines of the image or frame. During object detection process background can be treated either as dynamic or static. It is a tedious task to identify a class or object in a dynamic or changing background because of different elements like fluctuating in a light, unexpected change in a scene, impediment, shadow, and so forth both new and traditional-based methodologies are reviewed. In most of the situation, we saw that the traditional-based methodologies do not give a superior detection in moving or dynamic (changing background) conditions. In the MOT challenge, we used four alternate models starting with solid-state drive (SSD) with an inception network. The architecture of SSD utilizes a way to detect object by using a single-shot deep neural networks, using two networks that are regional proposals and feature extraction. A set of default boxes (like bounding boxes using ground truth) are mapped to the feature maps and then maps are computed bypassing the number of frames of images, we obtained from our video data. Second, we moved to YOLO (You Look Only Once) where the input frame images are divided into an SXS grid and come up with the bounding box (Huang et al. 2017). Hence, we finally tried faster-RCNN (Region Convolution Neural Network) which is based on RCNN which uses selective search to determine region proposals, pushed these through a classification network and bounding boxes then used a or SVM (Support Vector Machine) to classify the different regions. Instead of using default bounding boxes, faster-RCNN has a region proposed

DOI 10.1201/9781003167488-83

network (RPN) to generate a fixed set of regions. The RPN uses the convolutional features from the image classification network, enabling nearly cost-free region proposals. Finally, we tried Mask-RCNN architecture which is more suitable for pose estimation, but for segmentation and bounding box detection Mask-RCNN rise above all the other three models that we experimented. While for faster processing we can use YOLO, it's got better frames per second (FPS) than three of them but that also sacrifices some accuracy to get better results and we even try this with our webcam it performs well. We even tried on the local machine instead of Google Collab and it gives 20–25 FPS of speed on core i3 (running on CPU) 5th generation. We even tried it on graphics processing unit (GPU) on the local machine and on Collab. After that, we go for faster-RCNN but again it's resource-hungry but a better version than its previous generations such as RCNN and fast-RCNN, because it's made to perform like that. Faster-RCNN has two network regions and network-based proportion and its work with the concept of return on investment (ROI), where it predicts where an object can lie and then uses the next to output the image that's how it decreases its workload. Moreover, SSD uses a network called VGG, and the number is attached (like VGG16) to tell how deep the image layer is (like 16 layers deep). VGG is trained on the ImageNet database and you can load a pre-trained that is been trained on over one million images. In addition, Mask-RCNN is the masking of objects in a better and accurate way. It is aimed to solve the instance segmentation problem and it is also used to count no of objects. Mask-RCNN is an extended version of faster-RCNN and that's how it got speed as well as accuracy and it uses ResNet 101 to extract features from the image. In addition, it also uses the bounding boxes and ROI or RPN (Region Proposal Network) like the FRCNN (Ng 2018). Now when it comes to accuracy, we like to with Mask-RCNN which is also a superclass faster-RCNN and YOLO will be a great option for real-time video processing on Jetson you can get even 100+ FPS. Moreover, you can even try YOLO with the Drones that are not well equipped with the high-performance GPUs. Now when it comes to uses, we can use our model to check the current traffic and make a smart traffic system with that by checking how many cars on the road at which side and make our traffic system even more dynamic and also, we can control the pedestrian by checking them where the risk is more critical and object detection can be useful for the autonomous self-driving car. In autonomous car driving, we can check the pedestrian on the road and then can control the car (Dendorfer et al. 2019).

The most challenging scenario is the dim light condition to get the accurate results we get the video from the MOT site and with a good quality video of 1920*1080 and for that, we get ground truth and better hardware support.

2 RELATED WORK

In ongoing recent years, the community of computer vision has developed a sustained and unified benchmark for different types and numerous targets including object detection system, human or pedestrian detection, 3D remaking or reconstruction, "optical flow", single-object transient tracking, and including stereo estimation. Despite potential traps of such benchmarks, they have been proved and demonstrated to be the most helpful to propel the cutting edge in the respective area. For numerous objectives, we need an exact identification, and precise and accurate detection; in contrast, there has been very limited work on normalizing quantitative evaluation.

Some few exceptions are about notably PETS dataset and the famous MS-COCO dataset, aim mainly at surveillance applications. The 2009 version consisted of three subsets: S1 targeted at person count and density estimation (using bounding box); S2 targeted at people and object tracking; and S3 targeted at flow analysis and event recognition. The PETS team organizes a workshop approximately once a year to which researchers can present their outcomes and improve results than earlier years, and techniques are assessed under the same conditions. Recently, the KITTI benchmark was introduced for challenges in autonomous driving (technology where VEMO is introduced on), which included stereo/flow, odometry, road and lane estimation and distance between objects, object detection, and orientation estimation, as well as tracking. Some of the sequences and situations include crowded pedestrian crossings and crossroads, making the dataset very is a hard task, yet the camera position is consistently the equivalent for all circumstances (at a car's height). Soon, DETRAC (like KITTI), a new benchmark for vehicle tracking, is going to open a similar submission system to the one we proposed with MOD Challenge (Milan et al. 2016): "Another work that merits referencing is A. Alahi, V. Ramanathan, and L. Fei-Fei, in which the creators have collected a very huge amount of data with 42 million persons on foot trajectories." Since comment or annotation of such a huge collection of video data is infeasible, they use utilize a denser arrangement of cameras to create the "Ground Truth" trajectories. Despite the fact, we do not aim at collecting such an outsized measure of data or knowledge, the objective of our benchmark is some degree comparable: to push research in tracking forward by summing or generalizing the test data to a better and bigger set that is profoundly factor and hard to overfit. With the MOT16 release within the MOT challenge benchmark, they aim to increase the difficulty by including a variety of situations filmed from different angles, with different lighting conditions (mostly dark), and far more crowded scenarios when compared to MOT previous release.

3 METHODOLOGY

From the analysis of the different models and the study of different networks and architecture, we find out the models which will be best suited for our task, that is briefed below and they are very popular ones and maybe you already have heard of these techniques.

3.1 *SSD*

The SSD uses a VGG16 model, which is converted or changed over to a fully convolutional network. At that point, we connect some extra convolutional layers, that help to deal with no object and bigger size objects in a picture. We get the output of the VGG network, i.e., after done with Convolution Neural Network (CNN), is a 38x38 feature map. The additional layers produce 19×19, $10. \times 10$, 5×5, 3×3, 1×1 feature map maps. During training, SSD matches ground truth annotations (localization) with anchors or bounding box. Each element of the feature map has several anchors associated with it. The loss function used in SSD is the multi-box classification and regression loss to get accurate results. SSD objects have to parts first one to extract feature map from the image using VGG and second one to apply convolution filters to detect objects. It detects objects using the convolution Conv4_3 layer. SSD lower the image quality to get the speed and then it converts that image back to required quality like SSD300 (image size of $300 * 300$) and SSD512 (image size of $512 * 512$) (Girshick 2018). VGG also got a new model called VGG19 (19 deep layers) based on the same database ImageNet. Single Shot means that object detection and localization will happen in single-pass forward of the CNN and Multibox is a technique for bounding box regression while Detector means detection of object and classification at the same time. There is mainly two losses in SSD—the first one is location loss that works on testing purpose where we check that the how far bounding box from the ground truth annotation and the second one is about confidence loss where we find the how sure our network about any class or object and the main logic that SSD revolves around is priors that also we can say anchors in terms of faster-RCNN case and also it is precomputed and got a fixed size of the bounding box and that try to match closely to the ground truth. Another thing is intersection over union (IoU) ratio that tells the value between the ground truth and priors and it is always greater than 0.5; less than 0.5 will be a poor detection and approx. 0.9 will be in an excellent case. So, Multibox tries to fill the gap between ground truth and priors. So, the architecture of SSD contains the 11 priors that 8,6,4,3,3 and 1 (like $8 * 8$, $6 * 6$, and so on) feature map so we get a total of 1420 priors per image that enable our model to have robust behavior in all image scales and quality During training time, if the IoU is low or maybe even negative it may result from the negative example given to our model so it is advised that we should have negative to the positive ratio of 3:1 so that our network will get to know what constitutes an incorrect detection. To make our model more robust for various sizes of an object in input, we just resize images for additional example for our model used in training purpose based on IoU sizes so we can achieve this by flipping up the picture at a various angle to train our model better and there should be only one class per bounding box to remove inconsistency for model and the class with better confidence will get an in-place bounding box or for the object. The next we did just remove the no of bounding boxes present in the image what we do here is used a technique called Non-Maximum-Suppression (NMS) that will remove the bounding box having less than 0.45 of IoU value and threshold value to 0.1, this allows our model to show the most predicted class and noisie will be removed.

3.2 *YOLO*

Our framework separates the input picture into an SXS network (like 3×3). In the event, if the focal point an item falls into a framework's matrix or grid cell, that organized cell is liable for recognizing that article presents in the network or matrix. Every single-system/framework cell predicts B bouncing boxes and conviction (regard for prediction) scores for those boxes. The limitation of YOLO is that it forces solid spatial requirements on bouncing box expectations since each framework cell just predicts two boxes and can simply have one class (0 for no item). This spatial basic controls the amount of near to objects that our model can anticipate on the system network.

Each bouncing has five kinds of forecasts—x, y, w, h, and the last one is a certainty. So "x" and "y" are utilized to get the focus of the lattice cell and "w" and "h" is utilized for width and stature of the jumping box or object size on image and confidence is used to tell that how confidence the network about any class and then we want confidence in between the intersection over union or IoU and ground truth (Redmon 2018). Now that leads us to class-level confidence score or prediction value for each of the box and that encodes the probability for appearing an object or class inbounding for every image and how well the object fits for predictions. So, for training purposes, we need to use a better loss function for better accuracy, differential weights used for prediction(confidence) for the image that contains the boxes and objects.

Our model predicts the number (different) of bounding boxes every grid cell but at training time we mainly want only one predictor to get used for a single class in order to maintain the speed based on which predictor has better value in terms of IoU the same as ground truth. And every network gets better while it predicts the classes and bounding boxes for images and it improves its accuracy over time (Chablani 2017). As we have mentioned earlier, our model has some flaws and limitations like it struggles when it comes to smaller objects in a group of the same or other objects. It also struggles to generalize objects in different aspect ratios or configurations. This model utilizes harsh features for getting the bounding box because it lowers the quality of an image in multiple layers of the network, while the major source could be the incorrect localization of objects on the image. YOLO mainly predicts the grid boxes using a fully connected layer on the over convolutional network that leads to a network to learn better because the prediction of offset instead of coordinated but that also comes with a price because we remove fully convolutional network and used anchors instead that why we have less accuracy than faster-RCNN.

3.3 *Faster-RCNN*

Faster-RCNN has two sorts of systems: "Region proposal Network" (RPN) for creating ROI or region (utilizing BB) proposals and a system utilizing these propositions to perceive or detect objects.

RPN is utilized to pre-check which area contains objects. What's more, the corresponding BB will go to the detection process to recognize the item class and restoring the BB (utilizing class) of that object. As areas can be secured or covered with each other, NMS is used to diminish the number of recommendations (on different districts). The yield of an RPN (locale proposition organize) is a lot of boxes/recommendations (districts in bouncing boxes) that will be inspected by a classifier (model) and regressor to in the long run check the event of items. RPN predicts the chance of a grapple (utilizing bouncing boxes and ROI) being a foundation or closer view, and refine the stay. After RPN (pre-check), we get proposed areas with various sizes.

Network start computing task by taking an image as input and put into the backbone of CNN then it will resize the image not exceedingly more than 1000px. So, every pass of the network model should learn some that there is present any object at a particular location or not and also estimates the size of it. Our model does that by placing some set of anchors on the input image for each location. So, the anchors also indicate the size of objects in various locations (Ananth 2019). We also add some of the anchors' limitations to avoid confusion like whichever the anchor crosses the edge or boundary of the image it should be ignored as output feature map have like 40*60 locations and any anchor less than 0.3 confidence score will be labeled as negative. Moreover, for positive one two conditions should be satisfied: (1) the anchor with the highest IoU with bounding boxes and (2) IoU is greater than 0.7.

3.4 *MaskRCNN*

The Mask-RCNN is nothing but the network of faster-RCNN with an added fully convolutional layer performing instant segmentation for which instead of getting a bounding box around the object we are masking the shape of the object.

Like faster-RCNN there are two phases of Mask-RCNN and the two phases are associated with spine structure which is an FPN-type organize, a top-base pathway. Presently, from the start stage, there is a lightweight neural system RPN, which is liable to check all FPN and concentrates highlight maps and afterward, we use stays or bouncing boxes utilizing the ground truth to limit the items present in the picture and afterward it comes to the second stage in another neural system takes proposed districts from the first stage and afterward allocates them explicit zones of highlight map and creates object classes and do the concealing on article and boxing and it is fundamentally the same as the RPN (Girshick 2018). The contrast between faster-RCNN and cover is stage-two utilized a stunt called ROIAlign to find the important regions of a highlight map. Also, as we talked about IoU earlier, if the IoU value gets to 1 then we can say it's perfectly overlapped with ground truth notation and we already know the image is run through CNN and it does that using the nine anchors over any image and the uses NMS to reduce the number of anchors (Abdulla, Splash of Color: Instance Segmentation with Mask-RCNN and Tensor Flow 2018). Less than 0.5 of confidence will be removed using NMS as other models do the same kind of technique. (Abdulla, Mask R-CNN for object detection and instance segmentation on Keras and Tensor Flow 2018).

4 RESULT AND DISCUSSION

With the end goal of this task, we use pre-trained models tested and trained on MS-COCO dataset and YOLO pre-trained weights. COCO dataset consists of 330,000 images for free out of which 220,000 are known class or labeled, 1,500,000 object instances are available with 80 object categories type and 91 stuff categories. In our task, we have total of 14 videos, and also, we can get several other videos on the MOT challenge, out of that 7 are used for training and seven used for testing purposes. The total size of the dataset is about 5.5 GB with on average 800–900 frames for each video. For training videos, bounding box labels are provided. With the following format "bb" references bounding box.

<frame number> <frame_id> <bb_top_left_x> <bb_top_left_y> <bb_width> <bb_height> <x> <y> <bb_confidence> The annotated data provided by MOT challenge was present in XML format which was stored in a text file so that it could be implemented in our model and also the images were resized to the original video frame size so that bounding boxes could be plotted on the input videos from the ground truth XML file. In our dataset for faster-RCNN, we got an accuracy of about 95% for 50 epochs in all the objects but with more computation time than SSD. For, images of size 1920×1080 at FPS 30 we got an accuracy of around 55–70% in all our objects for SSD. In YOLO v2, we got an accuracy of about average 70–80% but it has faster computation

time when compared to SSD. The project is implemented and configured in Python3. Tensor Flow and pre-trained models were used for training the deep network and open CV was used for image preprocessing. Our project was trained on NVIDIA GPUs available in the cloud and also on our laptops for pre-trained models.

5 CONCLUSION

We can conclude from our project that the model of faster-RCNN was chosen for our project because it is fast and gives better accuracy concerning other models and we also can use Mask-RCNN due to its better accuracy but also sacrifices some speed and YOLO is better for low-end hardware configuration or when we need better FPS or real-time object detection. We also use the GPU present in our laptop by Nvidia which is mx150 using their cuda cores.

REFERENCES

Abdulla, W. 2018 Splas*h of Color: Instance Segmentation with Mask R-CNN And TensorFlow.*
Ananth, S. 2019. Faster R-Cnn For Object Detection.
Andrew N, Kian, K. Mourri, Y.B. 2018 *Convolutional neural networks.*
Chablani, M. 2017. Yolo you only look once real timeobject detection explained.
Dendorfer, P. Rezatofighi, H. Milan, A. Shi, J. Cremers, D. Reid, I. Roth, S. Schindler, K. Leal-Taixe, L. 2019. CPVR2019-Object Tracking and Detection Challenge – How crowded can it get?
Huang, J. Rathod, V. Sun, C. Zhu, M. Korattikara, A. Fathi, A. Fischer, I. Wojna, Z. Song, Y. Guadarrama, S. Murphy, K. CVPR 2017. Speed/accuracy trade-offs for modern convolutional object detectors.
Kaiming, H. Gkioxari, G. Dollar, P. Girshick, R. 2018 Mask R-CNN.
Khan, M.A and S. Ojha (2008), "Virtual Route Tracking in ZigBee (IEEE 802.15.4) enabled RFID interrogator mesh network," 2008 International Symposium on Information Technology, Kuala Lumpur, 2008, pp. 1–7, doi: 10.1109/ITSIM.2008.4631904
Milan, A. Leal-Taixe, L. Reid, I. Roth, S. Schindle, K. 2016. MOT16: A Benchmark for Multi-Object Trackin.
Redmon, Joseph, Farhadi, Ali. 2018. YOLOv3: An Incremental Improvement.
Waleed, A. 2017. Mask R-CNN for object detection and instance segmentation on Keras and TensorFlow.
Wei, L. Dragomir, A. Dumitru, E. Christian, S. Scott, R. Cheng-Yang, F Alexander C. Berg, 2016. SSD: Single Shot MultiBox Detector.

Smart Computing – Khan et al (Eds)
© 2021 Taylor & Francis Group, London, ISBN 978-0-367-76552-1

Design of current conveyor trans-conductance amplifier for low power applications: A review

Shailendra Bisariya, Raman Kapoor & Sanjay Kumar Singh
ECE Department, ABES EC, Ghaziabad, Uttar Pradesh, India

Pushkar Praveen
ECE Department, GBPIET, Pauri Garhwal, Uttarakhand, India

ABSTRACT: The Current Conveyor Trans-conductance Amplifier (CCTA) is a basic building block that can be utilized in linear as well as nonlinear applications of current-mode circuits. This paper provides a review of the CCTA implementations and its applications in analog signal processing. A number of parameters like power consumption, operating voltage, 3dB bandwidth, trans-conductance, number of transistors used for implementation, and technology used are taken into consideration keeping in mind the utility of CCTA in low-power very large-scale integration (VLSI) application areas. This review concluded with a remark on the best suitable CCTA structure for low-power applications and its future possibilities to use.

Keywords: Current Mode (CM), Low power, Analog signal processing, Current Conveyor Transconductance Amplifier (CCTA), Bulk-Driven (BD), Floating Gate (FG)

1 INTRODUCTION

The Current Conveyor Trans-conductance Amplifier (CCTA) was initially designed as an extension of the current feedback amplifier (Prokop & Musil 2005). Since then, this device is getting increasing attention and a number of functions have been implemented using the same. The simple implementation approach of the CCTA is by cascading the current conveyor with a dual output trans-conductance amplifier (Pandey et al. 2011). CCTA consumes less power and provides large bandwidth with a high slew rate. Due to these characteristics of this device, it seems to be a promising device for different analog signal-generating and processing applications.

Realization of CCTA has been shown by a number of researchers using either BJT, MOS, BICMOS, or bulk-driven technique (Kumar & Chaturvedi 2017; Khateb et al. 2015; Pandey et al. 2013; Raj et al. 2018; Chaturvedi & Kumar 2016; Pandey et al. 2011; Sotner et al. 2011; Jaikla et al. 2009; Siripruchyanun et al. 2009; Siripruchyanun 2008; Kumar & Pandey 2015; Jantakun 2015; Kumngern et al. 2012; Kumar & Pandey 2011; Prokop & Musil 2005; Tangsrirat 2014).

Use of CCTA has been found in a number of application areas. Researchers have proved its scope in filter designing whether low-pass, high-pass, biquad, or universal filter (Kumar & Chaturvedi 2017; Kumngern et al. 2018; Khateb et al. 2015; Pandey et al. 2013; Siripruchyanun et al. 2009; Siripruchyanun 2008; Kumar et al. 2019; Kumngern et al. 2017; Nonthaputha & Kumngern 2017; Budboonchu & Tangsrirat 2017; Agarwal et al. 2016; Kumar & Pandey 2015; Kumngern & Chanwutitum 2013; Verma & Gautam 2013; Maiti & Pal 2013; Kumngern et al. 2012; Thosdeekoraphat et al. 2012; Pandey & Paul 2011; Kumar & Pandey 2011; Herencsar et al. 2009; Mangkalakeeree et al. 2009; Prokop & Musil 2005). It has tremendous scope in implementing sinusoidal oscillator as shown by a number of researchers (Kumar & Chaturvedi 2017; Pandey et al. 2011; Sotner et al. 2011; Jaikla et al. 2009; Siripruchyanun et al. 2009; Sirpruchyanun 2008; Tangsrirat et al. 2015; Adirek & Worawat 2013; Thosdeekoraphat et al. 2013; Tanaphatsiri & Jaikla 2011; Kumngern 2010; Kumngem & Dejhan 2009; Lahiri 2009 and Tangsrirat 2014). A novel Schmitt trigger circuit in Current Mode is also prescribed (Siri-pruchyanun 2008). Multiplier and Divider were proposed by few researchers (Jaikla et al. 2009; Siripruchyanun 2008; Silapan et al. 2008). Its use as voltage and current amplifier and as a frequency modulator is also shown (Pandey et al. 2011; Sotner et al. 2011). Further PI, PD, and PID controllers were also implemented by using only one differential voltage block of CCTA (Shrivastava et al. 2019; Kumngern & Torteanchai 2016). Integrator circuit and an incremental decremental memristor emulator with high frequency was also designed by using CCTA (Linita et al. 2017; Ranjan et al. 2017).

It has been proved that CCTA can be utilized in implementing a number of linear as well as nonlinear application areas. Also, a survey on low-power circuit design techniques (Raj et al. 2015) shows the ways to design with low power dissipation. The major issue for designing with low power consumption is that area and delay should not increase.

This paper describes different structures of CCTA that have been realized to date whether it is BJT based structure, MOS based, or using bulk-driven technique. This paper also gives a comparative result to analyze different CCTA structures and also discuss the best suitable option for CCTA design which can be utilized in low-power application areas.

2 DESCRIPTION OF CCTA BLOCK

The symbolic representation of CCTA and model representing its behavior is shown in Figures 1 and 2. The CCTA has current conveyor CCIII at its input stage followed by the operational trans-conductance amplifier. The current output of this current conveyor enters into its intermediate Z terminal via a load connected from outside of the block. The voltage obtained at this Z terminal due to this conveyor current is converted into current Iout via a trans-conductance amplifier. At the two output terminals, this current I_{out} is received with opposite polarity.

The basic operation of CCTA can be explained as, if we apply a voltage V_y to the input "y" terminal then through a voltage buffer the same voltage V_x will be obtained on the second input terminal "x". Due to this voltage V_x, an input current I_x is obtained into "x" terminal which will provide a current I_y of equal amplitude but flowing in the opposite direction at terminal "y". Due to current follower action, I_y will then provide I_z of the same amount at the intermediate output terminal "z". The "z" terminal output impedance is comparatively high and follows the

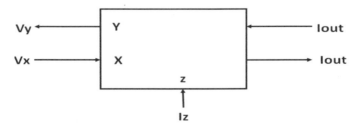

Figure 1.   Basic symbolic representation of CCTA.

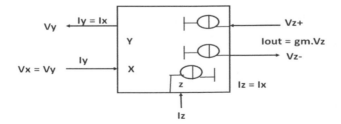

Figure 2.   Representation of behavioral model of CCTA.

characteristics of a current source that provides current I_z. This current then provides a voltage Vz at this intermediate terminal "z" which works as an input to the next stage of CCTA, i.e., trans-conductance amplifier. Now trans-conductance the amplifier converts this voltage into the output current and with dual-stage output current with dual polarity can be obtained as I_{out-} and I_{out+} in both inward and outward direction.

It can be easily observed that, the voltage obtained at "x" terminal is fixed by the voltage applied at "y" terminal, but the current produced at this "x" terminal is independent of the "y" terminal voltage. Further, the current obtained at node "y" is provided by terminal "x" and is not depending upon the voltage applied at "y" terminal. It can also be seen that CCTA in its ideal form have high impedance at the input terminal "y" due to the buffering action at the this node.

Mathematically, the characteristics of the CCTA can be written in matrix form as:

$$\begin{bmatrix} I_y \\ V_x \\ I_z \\ I_o \end{bmatrix} = \begin{bmatrix} 1 & 0 & 0 & 0 \\ 0 & 1 & 0 & 0 \\ 1 & 0 & 0 & 0 \\ 0 & 0 & +g_m & 0 \end{bmatrix} \begin{bmatrix} I_x \\ V_y \\ V_z \\ V_o \end{bmatrix}$$

where g_m is the trans-conductance of CCTA's trans-conductance amplifier stage and it depends on the value of input bias current.

3   IMPLEMENTATION OF CCTA

The concept of CCTA was first introduced with its implementation in CMOS technology (Prokop & Musil 2005). It was initially designed as an improvement over basic current feedback amplifier, which is basically originated from cascading of current conveyor with voltage buffer circuit. Initially, it was assumed to be used as a current mode device but later on it was found as a good choice for voltage-current hybrid circuits as well. The authors showed its utility in current sensing, inverting current amplifier as well as biquadratic active band-pass filter.

The current-controlled CCTA with its implementation using BJT was proposed, as shown in Figure 3 (Siripruchyanun & Jaikla 2008). A total of 17 transistors were used excluding 2 current

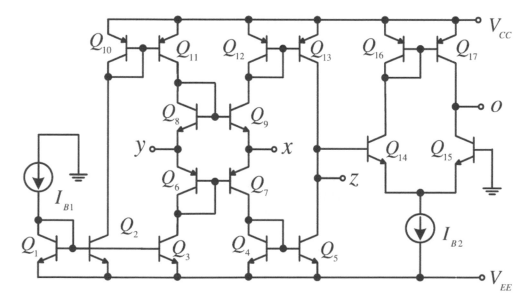

Figure 3.   BJT-based current-controlled CCTA (Siripruchyanun and Jaikla, 2008).

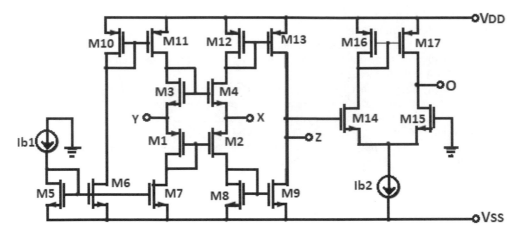

Figure 4. CMOS-based current-controlled CCTA (Siripruchyanun et al. 2009).

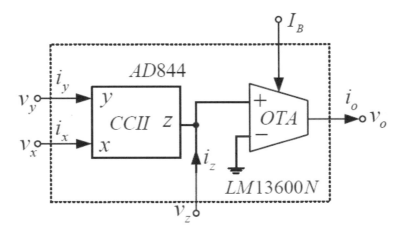

Figure 5. MOS-based differential difference CCTA (Pandey & Paul 2011).

sources. It was designed and simulated using PSPICE with parameters of BJT ALA400 array from AT&T. Using a supply voltage of ±1.5 V and a variation of base current from 0.1 μA to 3 mA result shows the trans-conductance value from 0.25–1 mS and a power consumption of 1.48 mW.

The current-controlled CCTA with its implementation using CMOS as shown in Figure 4 was also proposed (Siripruchyanun et al. 2009). This design was similar to the previous design (Siripruchyanun and Jaikla 2008) with only one change that BJT was replaced by MOS. A total of 17 transistors were used excluding 2 current sources. It was designed again using PSPICE and in this case of maximum bandwidth was 107.34 MHz and maximum power consumption was only 899 μW. The power consumption was much less in comparison to BJT counterpart which proves that MOS is a better choice in comparison to BJT as far as power consumption is concerned.

Implementation of a modified version of CCTA named differential difference CCTA is shown in Figure 5 (Pandey & Paul 2011). DDCCTA includes differential difference current conveyor block at input port, cascaded with a trans-conductance amplifier. Total number of transistors increased to 24 with a current source and hence the power consumption in this case is increased to 1.8 mW.

The advantage of using this topology was that it includes all the good properties of current-controlled CCTA as well as differential voltage trans-conductance amplifier. The filter circuits,

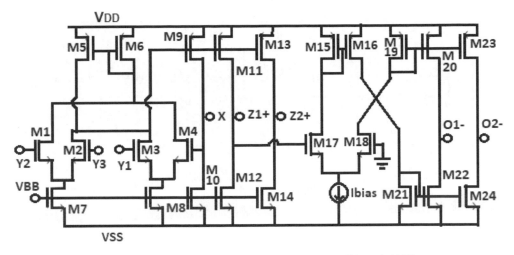

Figure 6.   Realization of CCTA based on commercially available ICs (Jaikla et al. 2009).

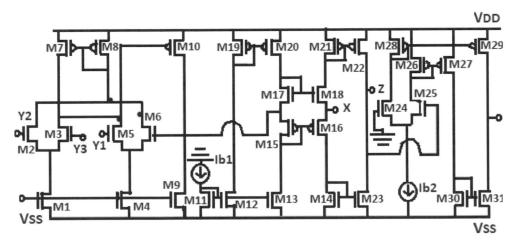

Figure 7.   CCDD-CCTA structure using MOS (Pandey et al. 2013).

oscillator, as well as voltage and current amplifiers were successfully implemented by using this CCTA element.

Implementation of CCTA using commercially available ICs was also being done (Jaikla et al. 2009) and the results were also verified using an experiment and PSPICE simulations. CCTA was implemented by cascading a second-generation current conveyor using ICAD844 to a trans-conductance amplifier using IC LM13600N, as shown in Figure 6.

Current gain-controlled CCTA was again designed by using commercially available ICs 2082 & 860 and two diamond transistors (Sotner et al. 2011). Electronic control was provided to transfer current from input to output port. The authors used this modified structure in designing an oscillator as well as frequency modulator circuit.

Further current-controlled with differential difference CCTA structure was proposed, as shown in Figure 7 (Pandey et al. 2013). The differential difference structure combined with current conveyor has the properties that differential and floating input circuits can be easily implemented. The implementation was done by using current-controlled differential difference CCII cascaded with OTA block.

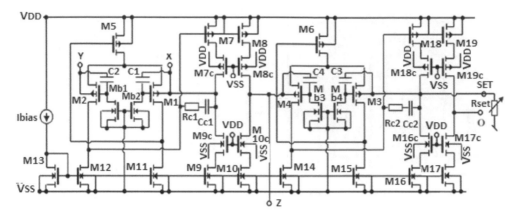

Figure 8. Bulk-driven quasi-floating gate CCTA implementation (Khateb et al. 2015).

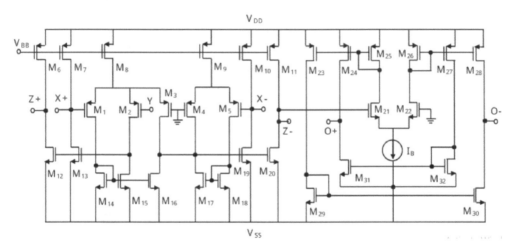

Figure 9. DXCCTA implementation (Chaturvedi & Kumar 2016).

The internal circuit consists of CMOS transistors, where M1–10 are used to produce differential difference voltage and M11–23 create a trans-linear loop and transistors M24–31 formed an OTA structure.

A design of CCTA extremely suitable for applications require low power consumption was proposed as shown in Figure 8 (Khateb et al. 2015). The technique of bulk-driven transistor with quasi-floating gate was used to operate comparatively at a much lower temperature around 0.3 V. Two OTAs were used to implement current conveyor and trans-conductor and unity gain feedback was provided in OTA to ensure proper functioning and linear operation. The power consumption in this case was much low approximately 34 uW only which proves its suitability for low power VLSI applications.

CMOS realization of CCTA with dual X terminal was presented, as shown in Figure 9 (Chaturvedi & Kumar 2016). DXCCII was used at the input stage followed by an OTA. Hence, this CCTA structure includes the properties of DXCCII like two terminals X+ and X- with low input impedance available at the input side with extra feature of inbuilt tuning. 0.18 um CMOS parameters were used for HSPICE simulation of the same with operating voltage of ±1.25 V. The maximum value of trans-conductance obtained was 1.74 mS with a power consumption of 1.43 mW.

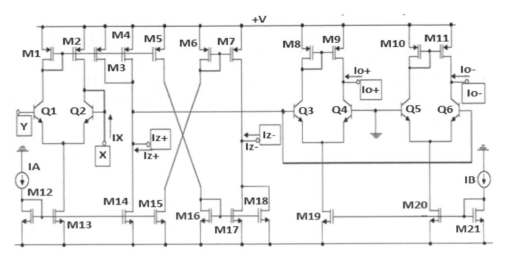

Figure 10.   BICMOS MOCC-CCTA structure (Raj et al. 2018).

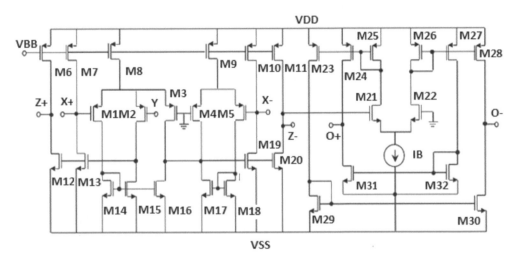

Figure 11.   Novel DXCCTA implementation (Kumar & Chaturvedi 2017).

A new concept for CCTA implementation was presented using BiCMOS technology with multiple-output and current-controlled method, as shown in Figure 10 (Raj et al. 2018). This block was designed as a modified version of CCCTA basic building block. This multiple-output CC-CCTA structure has two input, two output terminals and no current is allowed to pass through another terminal y since its impedance is high enough. There is small parasitic resistance appearing at the input terminal which varies according to the externally applied current. It utilizes the advantages of both bipolar and CMOS technology like higher trans-conductance due to BJTs, higher frequency but it has drawback that chip area will increase and also the power consumption. Using 0.35 μm process parameters for BiCMOS technology, PSPICE simulations were done and the obtained power dissipation was 0.9 mW.

A transconductance amplifier using CMOS technology with 0.18 μm n-well process parameters was also implemented (Kumngern et al. 2018) which again shows the usefulness of bulk driven techniques to implement CCTA structure in low power applications.

Analog building blocks using 0.5 V bulk-driven concept was also presented (Raikos et al. 2012). The importance of BD, FG, and also quasi-FG techniques and its usefulness in low power analog circuit applications, operating at low voltages were shown (Khateb 2014; Khateb et al. 2010).

A new design for CCTA implementation using CMOS logic was presented which used Dual-X terminals (Kumar and Chaturvedi 2017). This dual X terminal CCTA includes all the properties of DXCCII as well as OTA. The input terminals are having low impedance whereas other terminals are having high impedance including the intermediate terminal. Using this CCTA structure better dynamic range, bandwidth and low power consumption are obtained.

CMOS process parameters of 0.18 μm technology were taken for HSPICE simulation. Results obtained at 1.25 V supply voltage shows 3 dB bandwidth of 3.36 GHz, the maximum value of trans-conductance as 1.18 mS, and power consumption of 1.43 mW.

4 RESULTS AND COMPARISON

The result of different CCTA structures is compiled and shown in Table 1. The result includes different parameters of CCTA for comparing its structure and to find its utility for analog signal generating and processing circuits especially suited for low power applications.

Table 1. Result comparison of CCTA parameters.

Parameters Values	Kumar & Chaturvedi (2017)	Khateb et al. (2015)	Raj et al. (2018)	Chaturvedi & Kumar, (2016)	Pandey et al. (2011)	Siripruchyanun et al. (2009)	Siripruchyanun (2008)
			Reference paper				
Supply voltage (V)	±1.25	±0.3	±1	±1.25	±1.25	±1.5	±1.5
Power consumption (mW)	1.43	0.034	0.9	1.43	1.8	0.899	1.48
3dB Bandwidth (Iz/Ix) (MHz)	5000	40	47	5000	223	333.48	33.96
(Vx /Vy) (MHz)	3360	52		3360	236	4120	104.95
(Io/Ix) (MHz)				7500		107.34	29.24
(Io/Vy) (MHz)	1650		35	1650	201	115.22	29.17
Input current linear range (μA)	−100 to 100	−8.5 to 8.5		−60 to 60	−80 to 100	−700 to 700	−1000 to 1000
Rx range (kΩ)	0.14 to 0.29		18	0.14 to 0.29		0.491 to 15760	6.3 to 132
Bias current for controlling Rx range (μA)			50 to 150		0.01 to 450	0.01 to 95.29	0.1 to 7230
Transconductance maximum (mS)	1.18	0.04	2.88	1.74	1.6	1	1
Bias current for controlling transconductance range (μA)						1 to 180	0.1 to 7330
Ro (kΩ)	57.2			57.20	324	207.87	207.87
Rz (kΩ)	29.73			29.73	218	140.16	123.26
Ry (kΩ)	1831×10^9			1830×10^9		9320	7240
No. of transistors	32	31	27	32	24	17	17
Technology (μm)	0.18	0.18	0.35 BiCMOS	0.18	0.25	0.35	PR&NR200N
Simulation tool	HSPICE	PSPICE	PSPICE	HSPICE	PSPICE	PSPICE	PSPICE

This table clearly indicates that if the operating supply voltage is less than we can achieve minimum power dissipation 30 uW only, however trans-conductance also reduced accordingly to 40 uS (Khateb et al. 2015). Maximum bandwidth is obtained with the help of dual x CCTA up to 5 GHz (Kumar & Chaturvedi 2017; Raj et al. 2018) and maximum trans-conductance achieved is 2.88 mS using BiCMOS technology (Raj et al. 2018).

5 CONCLUSION

It is obvious that we can achieve the best trans-conductance by using BJT or BiCMOS instead of MOS transistors but if we want lesser area and less power dissipation the only the choice is MOS. Furthermore, DXCCTA gives maximum bandwidth so suitable for high-frequency applications but if we want less power consumption than either current-controlled CCTA (Siripruchyanun et al. 2009) or bulk-driven CCTA (Khateb et al. 2015) should be chosen.

The bulk-driven and floating gate concepts used to implement CCTA seems to provide a better option for implementing CCTA suitable for low-power application areas especially required for VLSI circuits in analog signal processing domain but their use is restricted to low voltage range only due to the drawback of bulk transistor operating reasons. So, wherever there is low operating voltage, in such applications like a pacemaker, etc., this bulk-driven CCTA design can be much useful.

ACKNOWLEDGMENT

The authors acknowledge the management, director, and dean of ABESEC Ghaziabad to provide wonderful facilities and a great environment to pursue this work.

REFERENCES

Adirek, J. and Worawat, S. N. 2013. Current-mode sinusoidal oscillator using CCCCTA. *Rev. Roum.Electrotech. Energ.,* 58(4): 415–423.

Agarwal R., Saxena N., and Bairathi R. 2016. Compact Design of Universal biquadratic filter using Basic CCTA. *8th International Conference on CICN*: 266–270.

Budboonchu, J. and Tangsrirat, W. 2017. Single input three output CM multifunction filter using single CCCTA. *14th International Conference on ECTI-CON,* 00(1): 242–245.

Chaturvedi B. and Kumar A. 2016. DXCCTA: A new active element. *1st IEEE International Conference on PIECES*: 1–6.

Herencsar, N., Koton, J. and Vrba, K. 2009. Single CCTA based universal biquadratic filters employ-ing minimum components', *IJCEE,* 1(3): 307–310.

Jaikla, W. et al. 2009. Practical implementation of CCTA based on commercially available CCII and OTA. *International symposium on ISPCS*: 1–4.

Jantakun A. 2015. CCCCTAs with Non-interactive CC for CO, FO and Amplitude. *Journal of Microelectronics, ECM,* 45(1): 47–56.

Kathuria J., Khan M.A., Abraham A., Darwish A. (2014) Low Power Techniques for Embedded FPGA Processors. In: Khan M., Saeed S., Darwish A., Abraham A. (eds) *Embedded and Real Time System Development: A Software Engineering Perspective. Studies in Computational Intelligence*, vol 520. Springer, Berlin, Heidelberg. https://doi.org/10.1007/978-3-642-40888-5_11

Khateb, F. 2014. BD FG and BD-QFG techniques for LVLP analog circuits design. *AEU – IJEC,* 68(1): 64–72.

Khateb, F. et al. 2010. Utilizing the BD technique in analog circuit design. *13th IEEE Symposium on DDECS*: 16–19.

Khateb, F. et al. 2015. Ultra LVLP CCTA. *IJPAP,* 53(7): 478–487.

Kumar P. and Pandey N. 2015. DVCCTA based wave active filter. *ICMSPTC:* 95–98.

Kumar, A. and Chaturvedi, B. 2017. Novel CMOS DXCCTA realization with CM multifunction filter and Quad oscillator. *CSSP. Springer US,* 37(6): 2250–2277.

Kumar, P. and Pandey, N. 2011. DV-CCTA based wave active filter. *ICMSPCT,* 20(4): 95–98.

Kumar, V. et al. 2019. New realization of multi-function filter using BD DD CCII. *ICCSP. IEEE:* 190–194.

Kumngern, M. 2010. Electronically tunable CM multiphase oscillator using CC- CCTAs, *IEEE Int. Conf. EDSSC.*

Kumngern, M. and Chanwutitum, J. 2013. An electronically tunable CM first-order APF using a CCCCTA. *International Conference on ATC*, (2): 733–736.

Kumngem, M. and Dejhan, K. 2009. OTA Based CM quadrature oscillator. *ISPACS:* 302–305.

Kumngern, M., Nonthaputha, T. and Klangthan, K. 2017. CMOS programmable universal filter using CCTAs. *2nd ICACOMIT:* 115–118.

Kumngern, M. and Torteanchai, U. 2016. CMOS programmable P, PI, PD and PID controller circuit us-ing CCTA. *ICEIC,* (1): 4–7.

Kumngern, M. et al. 2018. Sub-Volt BD trans-conductance amplifier and filter application. *IEEE APCCAS* (2): 1–4.

Kumngern, M., Torteanchai, U. and Sarsitthithum, K. 2012. Current tunable CM multifunction filter employing a modified CC-CCTA. *7th IEEE Conference on IEA*, 1: 1794–1797.

Lahiri, A. 2009. Explicit current output quadrature oscillator using 2nd generation CCTA. *Radioengi-neering,* 18(4): 522–526.

Linita, R., Reddy and Srinivasulu, A. 2017. An integrator circuit using DD-CCTA. *4th ICSCN:* 16–19.

Maiti, S. and Pal, R. R. 2013. Universal biquadratic filter employing single DCV-CCTA. *Lect. Notes Photonics Optoelectron.,* 1(2): 56–61.

Mangkalakeeree, S., Duangmalai, D. and Siripruchyanun, M. 2009. CM KHN Filter Using Single CC-CCTA: 306–309.

Nonthaputha, T. and Kumngern, M. 2017. Programmable universal filters using CCTA. *JCSC:* 26(7).

Pandey, N. and Paul, S. K. 2011. Analog filters based on CMOS DVCCTA. *IICPE:* 1–5.

Pandey, N., Kumar, P. and Choudhary, J. 2013. CCDD-CCTA and its application as wave active filter. *ISRN Electronics:* 1–11.

Pandey, Neeta and Paul, S. K. 2011. DDCCTA: A new analog building block for signal processing. *JECE:* 1–10.

Prokop R. and Musil V. 2005. New modern circuit block CCTA and some its applications. *14th ISASCE:* 93–98.

Raikos, G., Vlassis, S. and Psychalinos, C. 2012. 0.5V BD analog building blocks. *AEU – Int. J. Elec-tron. Commun,* 66(11): 920–927.

Raj N. et al. 2015. LP circuit design techniques: a survey. *IJCTE*, vol. 7(3): 172–176.

Raj, N. et al. 2018. MO-CC-CCTA using BiCMOS for analog signal processing. *Proceedings of the 4th International Conference on RAIT:* 1–5.

Ranjan, R. K. et al. 2017. Single CCTA based HF floating and grounded type of incremental/decremental memristor emulator and its application. *Microelectronics J. Elsevier*, 60: 119–128.

Shrivastava, P. et al. 2019. PI, PD and PID controllers using single DVCCTA. *IJSTTEE*, 43(3): 673–685.

Silapan, P., Tanaphatsiri, C. and Siripruchyanun, M. 2008. CC-CCTA Based novel grounded capacitance multiplier with temperature compensation. *IEEE Asia Pacific conference on Circuits and Systems:* 1490–1493.

Siripruchyanun, M. 2008. CC-CCTA based novel CM schmitt trigger and its application. *ISCIT,* (1): 416–421.

Siripruchyanun, M. 2008. CCCCTA: a building block for analog signal processing. *Electr. Eng.,* (1): 416–421.

Siripruchyanun, M., Silapan, P. and Jaikla, W. 2009. Realization of CMOS CC-CCTA and its applications. *JAPED,* 4(1–2): 35–53.

Sotner R. et al. 2011. Current gain CCCTA and its application in quadrature oscillator and direct frequency modulator. *Radioengineering,* 20(1): 317–326.

Tanaphatsiri, C. and Jaikla, W. 2011. Electronically tunable four phase quadrature oscillator employing CC-CCTA. *6th IEEE International Symposium on EDTA:* 89–92.

Tangsrirat W. 2014. Simple BiCMOS CCCTA design and resistorless analog function realization. *The Scientific World Journal,* Article ID 423979: 1–7.

Tangsrirat, W., Channumsin, O. and Pukkalanun, T. 2015. Single CC sinusoidal oscillator with current and voltage outputs using single CCCTA and grounded passive elements. *Rev. Roum. des Sci. Tech. Ser. Electrotech. Energ.,* 60(2): 175–184.

Thosdeekoraphat, T. et al. 2012. Resistorless CM universal biquad filter using CCTAs and grounded capacitors, 6(9): 499–503.

Thosdeekoraphat, T. et al. 2013. CCTAs based CM quadrature oscillator with high output impedances. *IJEE,* 1(1): 52–56.

Verma, K. and Gautam, S. 2013. Realization of voltage mode universal filter by using single DV-CCTA. 2: 93–96.

Smart Computing – Khan et al (Eds)
© *2021 Taylor & Francis Group, London, ISBN 978-0-367-76552-1*

Optimization of dynamic clock-based D flip-flop for low-power applications

Shruti Shrivastava, Usha Chauhan & Mohammad Rashid Ansari
Department of Electronics and Communication Engineering Galgotias University, Greater Noida, Uttar Pradesh, India

ABSTRACT: D flip-flops (DFFs) are of two basic types: static and dynamic. This paper focuses on dynamic DFF. The dynamic nature comes with clock and reset configuration in true single-phase clocked (TSPC). The clock and rest signal consumes a lot of power when it comes to its work and switching activity. This makes it an important research area where it is necessary to improve the power consumption of the TSPC-based DFF. Below 22 nm, due to effects like DIBL or GIBL, power consumption rises, which also needs to improve. In this paper, a new TSPC-based DFF is proposed for a low-power application with Multi-Threshold CMOS (MTCMOS) Logic sleep signal insertion to reduce the power consumption for low-power applications. This works uses low-power-based MOS like GNRFET to reduce the short channel effects in MOS. This focuses on low power by the use of GNRFETs in 22 nm technology.

Keywords: GNRFET, D Flip Flop, 22nm, MOSFET, VLSI

1 INTRODUCTION

D flip-flop (DFF) is basically considered to be the most fundamental memory cell in by far most digital circuits, which brings it a broad use, particularly under current conditions where high-density pipeline innovation is every now and again employed in digital-integrated circuits and gigantic flip-flop modules are indispensable segments (Jahangir et al. 2018). This paper focuses on TSPC-based DFF using GNRFET in 22 nm technology and proposal of new work related to it. The force productivity and decreasing the format region are two primary worries in the DFF structure (Arunlakshman 2014). Force utilization assumes a significant job in any coordinated circuit and is recorded as one of the three greatest difficulties in the International Innovation Guide for Semiconductors (Himanshu 2015). In any incorporated circuit, a clock conveyance system and flip-flop devour a huge measure of intensity as they make most extreme number of interior changes (Naresh 2012). Structuring low-force gadgets is currently a significant part of examination because of expanded interest for compact gadgets (Sanga 2016). Since metal-oxide (MOS) gadgets are across the board, there is an incredible requirement for less vitality devouring circuits, particularly for compact gadgets and workstations (El-hmaily et al. 2018). A memory component devours 70% of all out force in a coordinated circuit (Yoon 2008). As flip-flops are the primary territory of memory components utilized on any versatile gadget, the significant worry to lessen flip-flop vitality utilization will help decrease power utilization in an IC extensively (Mayank 2017). Flip-flops are major memory components and are utilized to store data (Maedeh 2014). They are utilized in development of RAMs, locks, move registers, counters, and other computerized circuits (Devendra & Choudhary 2015). This paper proposes new and simulated structures for DFF. The structures have power dispersal altogether not exactly the past flip-flop plans.

DOI 10.1201/9781003167488-85

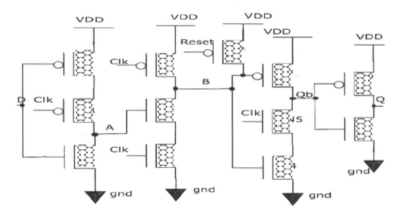

Figure 1.   TSPC-based D Flip-Flop GNRFET 22 nm.

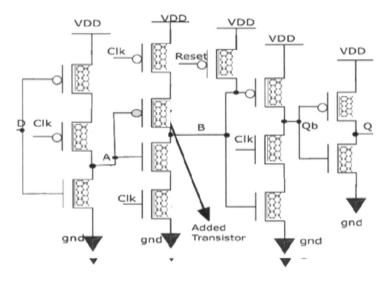

Figure 2.   Modified TSPC-based D Flip-Flop GNRFET 22 nm.

1.1 *Implementation*

Graphene Nano Ribbon Field Effect Transistor (GNRFET) has a nano ribbon structure on channel the area, as shown in Figure 1. It works similar to MOSFET and has similar characteristics and works with advantages of low power. True single-phase clocked (TSPC) technique which uses clock and reset signals for the working of DFF in TSPC mode. The circuits are shown in Figures 1, 2, and 3. For device-level simulation, the GNRFET spice model is taken from nanohub.org, the simulations are performed with the use of HSPICE software, and is tested for GNRFET sample file and also inverter circuit. The implementation is done on HSPICE software using the MOSFET and GNRFET spice model files. The waveform is generated on Avanwaves in Synopsys HSPICE Software.

In Figure 1, the TSPC-based DFF is implemented using GNRFET in HSPICE through node coding method. Similarly, Figures 2 and 3 are for GNRFET-modified and MTCMOS-proposed circuit, respectively.

In the above figure, on ground path an n-type GNRFET is added to prevent any leakage path which improves the power and delay in the circuit.

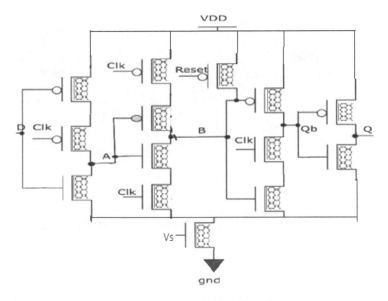

Figure 3.   Modified TSPC-based MTCMOS-based low-power proposed D Flip-Flop GNRFET 22 nm.

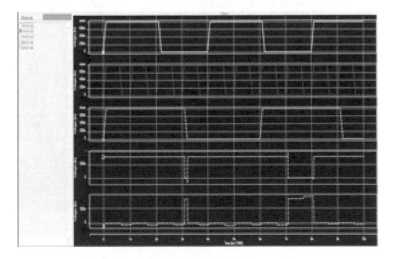

Figure 4.   Output and input waveforms for GNRFET-based TSPC circuit.

Waveform of TSPCD Flip-Flop after GNRFET implementation is shown in Figure 4.

Waveform for GNRFET-based 22 nm modified and proposed MTCMOS circuit are shown in Figures 4 and 5.

In Figure 6, according to sleep signal VS marked with number 14, gives sleep and active mode for MTCMOS. Also, the waveform output comes in accordance with the d input and sleep input, which is the main cause of power saving in proposed circuit.

2   RESULTS

In Figure 7, it is seen that the average power is lowest in case of TSPC DFF GNR based and highest in 22 nm MOS circuit constituting effects of a shorter channel.

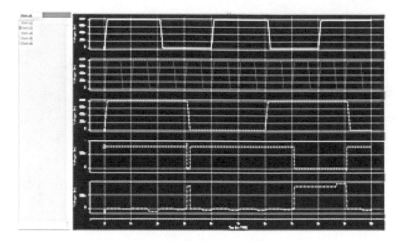

Figure 5.   Output and input waveforms for modified GNRFET-based TSPC circuit.

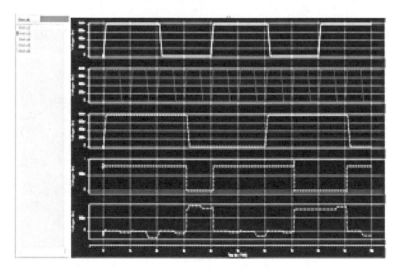

Figure 6.   Output and input waveforms for proposed modified GNRFET-based TSPC circuit with MTCMOS.

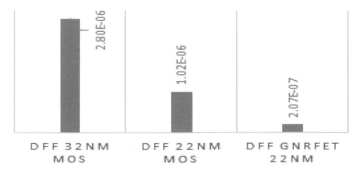

Figure 7.   Average power for 32 nm and 22 nm TSPC DFF MOS and GNR.

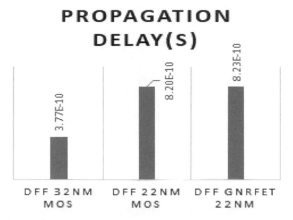

Figure 8. Delay for 32 nm and 22 nm TSPC DFF MOS and GNR.

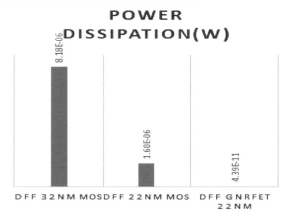

Figure 9. Power dissipation for 32 nm and 22 nm TSPC DFF MOS and GNR.

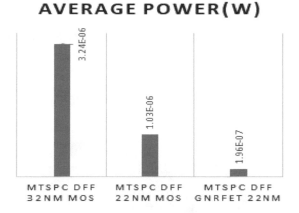

Figure 10. Average power for 32 nm and 22 nm modified TSPC DFF MOS and GNR.

In Figure 8, a similar case for a delay is seen as its lowest in GNRFET 22 nm-based circuit for a simple TSPC circuit.

In Figure 9, the power dissipation is lowest in GNRFET-based dynamic TSPC circuit.

Similarly, in Figures 10 and 11 the average power and delay are lowest in the case of modified TSPC DFF 22 nm configuration.

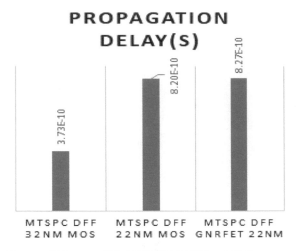

Figure 11.   Delay for 32 nm and 22 nm modified TSPC DFF MOS and GNR.

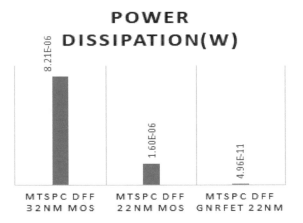

Figure 12.   Power dissipation for 32 nm and 22 nm modified TSPC DFF MOS and GNR.

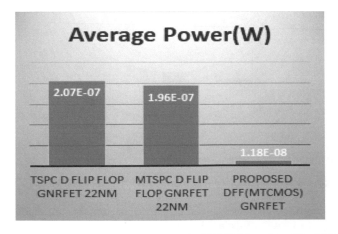

Figure 13.   Average power for 32 nm and 22 nm proposed MTCMOS-based modified TSPC DFF GNR.

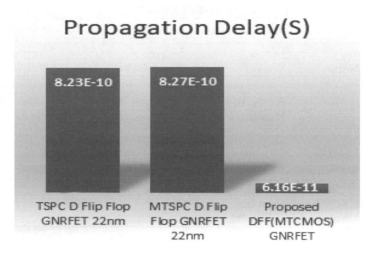

Figure 14.   Delay for 32 nm and 22 nm proposed MTCMOS-based modified TSPC DFF GNR.

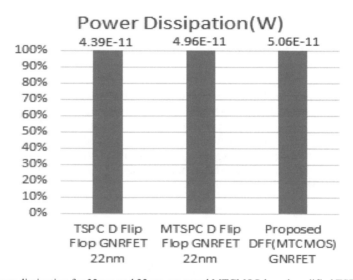

Figure 15.   Power dissipation for 32 nm and 22 nm proposed MTCMOS-based modified TSPC DFF GNR.

In Figure 12, the lowest power dissipation is considered in 22 nm modified TSPC DFF.

In the proposed MTCMOS-based modified TSPC DFF, in Figure 13 the average power is best, and the delay is best in Figure 14.

Delay is improved because the path of ground prevents extra leakage in the proposed circuit. For instance, if the output is 1, and the ground transistor is off, it balances it and reaches 1 value in shorter time. Similarly, if the output 0 needs to be achieved the ground path will give a faster flow due to the on transistor for MTCMOS. Hence, delay is improved.

As shown in Figure 15, the power dissipation for all GNRFET-based circuits are nearly the same, which does not give any negative impact on the proposed circuit. The results in tabular form are shown in Tables 1 and 2 below.

Table 1. Results in tabular form for MOS and GNRFET-based DFF.

	DFF 32 nm MOS	DFF 22 nm MOS	DFF GNRFET 22 nm
Average Power (W)	2.80E-06	1.02E-06	2.07E-07
Propagation Delay (S)	3.77E-10	8.20E-10	8.23E-10
Power Dissipation (W)	8.18E-06	1.60E-06	4.39E-11
	MTSPC DFF 32 nm MOS	**MTSPC DFF 22 nm MOS**	**MTSPC DFF GNRFET 22 nm**
Average Power (W)	3.24E-06	1.03E-06	1.96E-07
Propagation Delay (S)	3.73E-10	8.20E-10	8.27E-10
Power Dissipation (W)	8.21E-06	1.60E-06	4.96E-11

Table 2. Results in tabular form for GNRFET.

	TSPC D Flip Flop GNRFET 22 nm	MTSPC D Flip Flop GNRFET 22 nm	Proposed DFF (MTCMOS) GNRFET
Average Power (W)	2.07E-07	1.96E-07	1.18E-08
Propagation Delay (S)	8.23E-10	8.27E-10	6.16E-11
Power Dissipation (W)	4.39E-11	4.96E-11	5.06E-11

3 CONCLUSION

In this paper, the objectives are fulfilled by proposing a MTCMOS-based Dynamic DFF which has improved average power and delay. Also by the use of GNRFETs instead of MOS the power dissipation is improved. In 22 nm, the short channel effects are reduced by using MOS-like GNRFETs. GNRFET ribbon structures promises better low-power devices and hence a perfect substitute for the conventional MOS in lower technology length. The average power circuit is improved by 93.9%, propagation delay is improved by 92.5%, and power dissipation is nearly the same but improved by 99.9% when compared to its MOS counterparts.

REFERENCES

M. Arunlakshman, "Power and Delay Analysis of DoubleEdge Triggered D-Flip Flop based Shift Registers in 16nm MOSFET Technology", International Journal of Advanced Research in Electrical, Electronics and Instrumentation Engineering, Vol. 3, Issue 4, April 2014, pp. 4–9.

E. El-hmaily, Hader & Ezz-Eldin, Rabab & Galal, A.I.A. & Hamed, Hesham. (2018). High Performance GNR MTCMOS for Low-Voltage CMOS Circuits.

Maedeh Akbari Eshkalaka, N, Rahim Faezb, Saeed Haji-Nasiria "A novel graphene nano-ribbonfield effect transistor with two differentgate insulators" http://dx.doi.org/10.1016/j.physe.2014.10.0211386-9477/&2014 Elsevier.

Kathuria J., Khan M.A., Abraham A., Darwish A. (2014) Low Power Techniques for Embedded FPGA Processors. In: Khan M., Saeed S., Darwish A., Abraham A. (eds) Embedded and Real Time System Development: A Software Engineering Perspective. Studies in Computational Intelligence, vol 520. Springer, Berlin, Heidelberg. https://doi.org/10.1007/978-3-642-40888-5_11

Himanshu Kumar, Amresh Kumar, Aminul Islam "Comparative Analysis of D Flip-Flops in Terms of Delay and its Variability" IEEE, 2015, pp. 25–37.

Naresh Kumar, Umesh Dutta and DileepKumar, "Design of Low Voltage and Low Power D-Flip Flop". International Journal of Scientific Engineering and Technology, 2012, www.ijset.com, Volume No.1, Issue No.3, pp : 184–186.

Mayank Mishra, RonilStieven Singh, Ale Imran "Performance optimization of GNRFET Inverter at 32nm technology node", materials today proceeding, Volume 4, Issue 9, 2017, Pages 10607–10611.

Sanga, MohammadiBanadaki, Yaser& Srivastava, A &Sharifi, Safura. (2016). Graphene nano-ribbon field effect transistor for nanometer-size on-chip temperature sensor. 980203. 10.1117/12.2219346.

Jahangir Shaikh, HafizurRahaman, "High speed and low power preset-able modified TSPC D flip-flop design and performance comparison with TSPC D flip-flop", IEEE, 2018.

Devendra Upadhyay and Sudhanshu Choudhary "Understanding the impact of graphene sheet tailoring on theconductance of GNRFETs", Bull. Mater. Sci., Vol. 38, No. 7, December 2015, pp. 1705–1709.c©Indian Academy of Sciences.

Yoon, Youngki & Fiori, Gianluca& Hong, Seokmin&Iannaccone, Giuseppe & Guo, Jing. (2008). Performance Comparison of Graphene Nano-ribbon FETs With Schottky Contacts and Doped Reservoirs. IEEE Transactions on Electron Devices, 5 10.1109/TED.2008.928021.

Smart Computing – Khan et al (Eds)
© *2021 Taylor & Francis Group, London, ISBN 978-0-367-76552-1*

Design and simulation of CNTFET-based folded cascode Op-Amp for instrumentation amplifier

Priyanka Tyagi
Department of Electronic and Communication, Research scholar, AKTU, Lucknow, U. P, India

Sanjay Kumar Singh
Department of ECE, ABES Engineering College, Ghaziabad, U. P, India

Piyush Dua
Department of Engineering, College of Applied Sciences, Suhar, Sultanate of Oman

ABSTRACT: The carbon nanotube- (CNT) based folded cascode Op Amp has been designed for advanced applications. HSPICE tool has been used to discover the performance parameters. CNT-based folded cascode Op Amp showed better speed, low power, and small size. DC Gain in CNT-based folded cascode Op Amp is 67 dB as compared with complementary metal-oxide semi-conductor (CMOS) folded cascode Op Amp which has 33.52 dB, Output resistance is 173.4 ohms, as compared with CMOS-based, i. e., 233.39, average power is 2.8827 fW in comparison to 0.52 mW in CMOS-based folded cascade Op Amp. Furthermore, we have implemented both CMOS-folded cascode Op Amp and CNT-based folded cascode Op Amp for Instrumentation Amplifier. The simulation results show that CNT-based folded cascode Op Amp Instrumentation Amplifier has better DC Gain (152.27 dB) as compared with CMOS-based folded cascode Op Amp Instrumentation Amplifier (126.4 dB).

Keywords: CNTFET, folded cascode Op Amp, low power, DC gain, output resistance, frequency, Instrumentation Amplifier

1 INTRODUCTION

In the recent electronics world the supply voltage is the major parameter We can improve the power dissipation by reducing the supply voltage The size of the device was also reduced (Minh & Hong 2009; Sinha et al 2009) By scaling the voltage the performance of the circuit in terms of the band width and voltage also degraded which affected the performance of the circuit (Wong et al 1999; Wong 2002) To solve this problem in the metal-oxide–semiconductor field-effect transistor. (MOS-FET) the new technology is introduced that is carbon nanotube field-effect transistor (CNTFET) (Bachtold 2001) CNTFET device is same as the MOSFET expect it has carbon nanotube in place of the silicon channel (Philip Wong 2006) It provides the full voltage swing and reduces the size of the device (Zhang 2009) In the advance and ultra-fast application CNTFET was used as the basic element for designing (Appenzeller 2002) The lager channel Op Amp are going outdated in the future The performance evaluation of the traditional Op Amp design based on the large channel length is quite older technique (Skotnicki et al 2005) To balance the complexity of the design and enhance the efficiency of the system a new technique has to be adapted There are many complications when the complementary metal-oxide semiconductor (CMOS) technology scaled down

DOI 10.1201/9781003167488-86

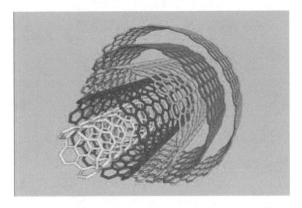

Figure 1. Carbon nanotubes (Avouris et al. 2003).

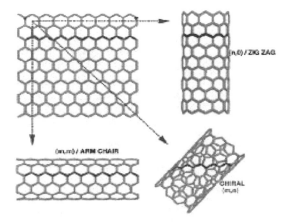

Figure 2. Different types of SWCNTs.

to the nano ranges The drawbacks of the scaling are the high shortchannel effect high dissipated power and increment in leakage current (Bate 1989) CNTFET has used to eliminate and reduce the drawbacks of the conventional CMOS technology (Agarwal et al. 2008).

2 CARBON NANOTUBES

In the field of nanotechnology, carbon nanotubes are the unique invention. The structure of CNT is the rolled graphene sheet having the sp^2 hybridization (Gordon et al. 1997). The properties of the carbon nanotubes such as lightweight, high aspect ratio, small size, good tensile strength was good enough to be used in the electronic devices (Saeed & Ibrahim 2013). These properties make the CNT most promising material in the field of electronics (Avouris et al. 2003; Avouris 2004). Figure 1 shows the structure of the nanotubes. There are two types of CNT 1: (1) single-wall carbon nanotubes (SWCNT); and (2) multi-wall carbon nanotubes (Chen 2006). Figure 2 shows the SWCNT structure.

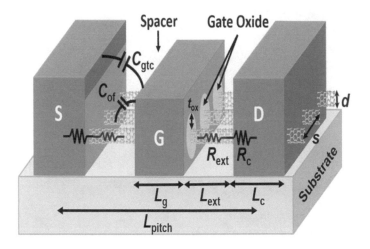

Figure 3.   Three-dimensional CNTFET structure.

CNTs have very good electronics properties We used the CNTFET in place of CMOS in the proposed circuit CNTs are good conductors and provide the full voltage swing and the better noise margin characteristics (Raychowdhury & Roy 2007) A basic 3D model of the CNTFET is shown in Figure 3 (Hashempour & Lombardi 2007).

3   PROPOSED FOLDED CASCODE OP AMP DESIGN

The schematic design of a folded cascode Op Amp based on the class AB output buffer has been shown in Figure 4. The maximum load applied to the Op Amp is 1 pF capacitor to analyze the frequency response. Folded cascode operational transconductance is planned for a range of carbon nanotubes (N). The CNTFET and MOSFET widths are chosen to be the same for a fair comparison. The widths of CNTFET and MOSFET are taken same for valid assessment of the results.

We study the simulated parameters such as the power dissipation and the delay. The parameters of the proposed design are compared with the traditional design of the op-amp. The CNTs have very wide applications in the electronics field. The very large-scale integration (VLSI) applications such as processor units, DSP systems and memory units can be designed using the CNTs (Lin et al. 2008). The Op Amp means the operational amplifier that can perform the many arithmetic operations. Thus, the proposed design can also be applicable for the summation unit, integration, subtraction, and differentiation. The various analog applications such as the rectifiers, comparators, peak detectors, clippers, and clampers. All these applications can be designed using the low-power CNTFET-based folded cascode operational amplifier (Op Amp) (Bendre et al. 2018).

4   PROPOSED INSTRUMENTATION AMPLIFIERS

There are basically two main parts in the instrumentation amplifiers (Baker 2000). The buffered amplifier XOP1, XOP2 and a basic differential amplifier XOP3 are the parts. For the measurements of the sensor we used the differential amplifier. Differential amplifiers were used when we must measure the signal produced by the sensor in the condition when neither terminal is connected to

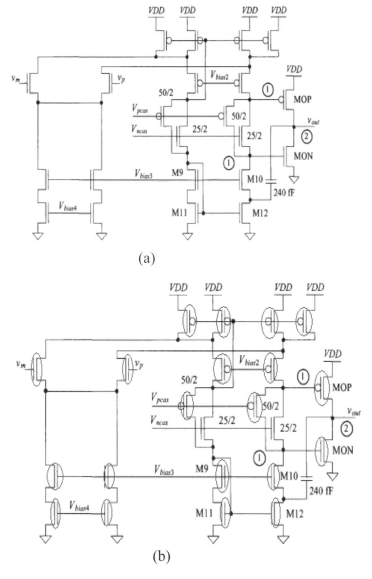

Figure 4.   (a) Conventional CMOS-based FC-OP-AMP and (b) proposed CNT-based FC-OP-AMP.

the ground. For high potential biased terminals, the differential amplifier directly measures the signal between the sensor terminals.

For achieving the gain in the Op Amp circuit, the buffered amplifier XOP1 and XOP2 is used. This amplifier also provides protection to the Op Amp from the sensor resistance and vice versa. Our proposed model of CNFET-based Cascode Op Amp the performance is better than CMOS-based Cascode Op Amp. Thus, the instrumentation amplifiers using CNFET is better than CMOS-based Instrumentation Amplifier. In Figure 5, the conventional and the proposed design of the Cascode-folded amplifier are shown.

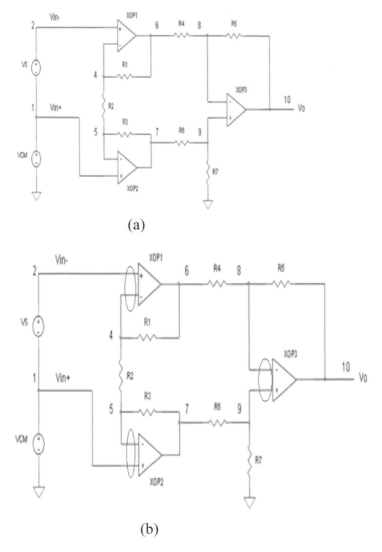

(a)

(b)

Figure 5.   (a) Conventional CMOS-based Instrumentation Amplifier using Folded Cascode Op-Amp and (b) proposed CNT-based Instrumentation Amplifier using cascode folded Op- Amp.

5   RESULTS

Now we will discuss the parameters of the proposed cascade folded OpAmp design Figure 6 shows the DC gain of the design with respect to the supply voltage The DC gain of the CNT is higher than the CMOS Op Amp Bandwidth of the conventional design and the proposed design are compared Figure 7 shows the representation of the response Figures 8 and 9 show the output resistance and the average power with respect to the supply voltages Then the main parameter comes that is the frequency response Figures 10 and 11 show the simulation results of the conventional CMOS op-amp and the CNT Op Amp at 45 nm node technology.

Figure 12 shows the average power simulation of the CMOS cascade Op Amp and Figure 13 shows the simulation of the CNT cascade Op Amp for average power for the 1 pf capacitive load

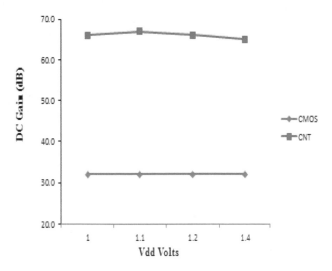

Figure 6.   Supply voltage vs. DC gain in CMOS–FCA and CNT-FCA.

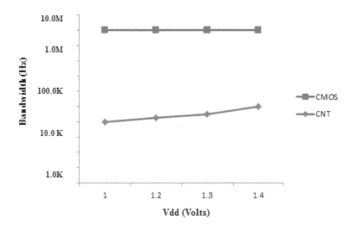

Figure 7.   Supply voltage vs. bandwidth in CMOS–FCA and CNT–FCA.

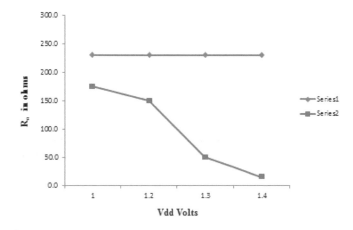

Figure 8.   Supply voltage vs. output resistance in CMOS–FCA and CNT–FCA.

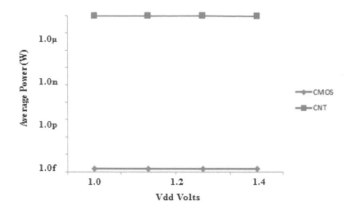

Figure 9.   Supply voltage vs. average power in CMOS–FCA and CNT–FCA.

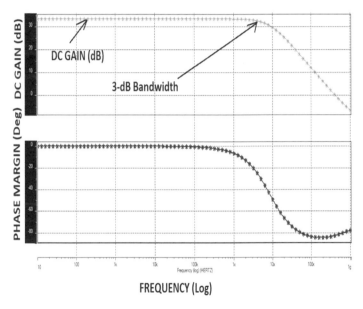

Figure 10.   CMOS–FC Op Amp design frequency response.

and the power supply at 0.9 V. Both figures show the comparision of the power dissipation for the folded cascode Op Amp. The average power dissipation of the CNT-based device is less and decreasing with the supply voltage. Tables 1 and 2 are shown below. The table will describe the comparitive analysis of the CMOS and CNTFET-based cascode-folded Op Amp.

6   CONCLUSIONS

We simulate the CNT-based folded cascode at 45 nm. We used the HSPICE tool to evaluate the mean power, DC voltage gain, bandwidth, and output resistance. In this paper, the Op Amp-folded

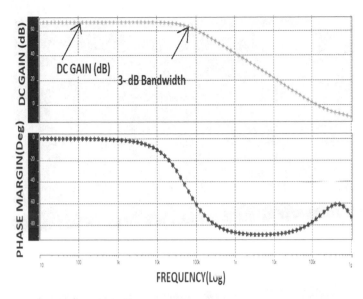

Figure 11.   CNFET–FC Op Amp design frequency response.

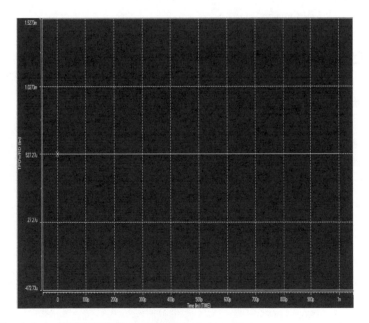

Figure 12.   Simulation of CMOS FC-Op Amp design power.

cascode simulation based on CNT was performed at 45 nm. The parameters such as DC voltage gain, mean power, bandwidth, and output resistance were evaluated using HSPICE Software. The CNTFET Op Amp-folded cascode is more efficient than the traditional design. The proposed CNFET-based cascode Op Amp is better than CMOS-based cascode Op Amp resulting in a more efficient Instrumentation amplifier. For the future scope we can modify the transconductance properties for the biomedical device's application.

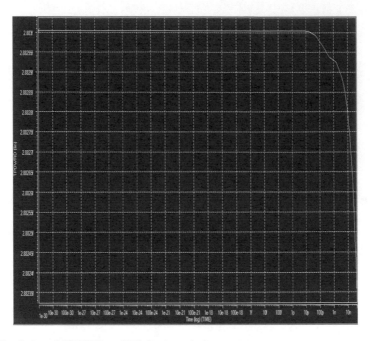

Figure 13.   Simulation of CNFET-based FC-Op Amp design power.

Table 1.   Comparison of folded cascodeOp Amp with $C_L = 1\,pf\,V_{DD} = 0.9\,V$ @ 45 nm.

S. No.	Parameter	CMOS-Folded Cascode Op Amp	CNT-Folded Cascode Op Amp
1	DC GAIN	33.52 dB	67 dB
2	3-dB Bandwidth	8.56 MHz	55.5 KHz
3	Output Resistance	233.39Ω	173.4Ω
4	Average Power	0.52 mW	2.8827 fW
5	Unity gain Freq.	423 MHz	139 MHz

Table 2.   Comparison of folded cascode-Op Amp-based instrumentation amplifier.

S. No.	Parameter	CMOS-Folded Cascode Op Amp	CNT-Folded Cascode Op Amp
1	DC GAIN	126.4 dB	152.27 dB
2	3-dB Bandwidth	39.376 MHz	14.96 KHz
3	Average Power	0.419 W	0.52 μW

REFERENCES

Agarwal T., Sawhney, A., Kureshi, A. K. &Hasan, M 2008. Performance comparison of CNFET andCMOS based full adders at the 32 nm technology node *Proc of VLSI Design and Test Symposium (VDAT), pp* 49–57 *Bangalore India*.
Appenzeller J. 2002 Carbon Nanotubes as potential building blocks for future nanoelectronics. *Elsevier, Microelectronics Engineering. vol* 64.

Avouris, P. 2004. Supertubes: The Unique Properties of Carbon Nanotubes May Make Them the NaturalSuccessor to Silicon Microelectronics. *IEEE Spectrum,* 41(8):40–45.

Avouris P., Appenzeller J., Martel R. & Wind S. J. 2003. Carbon nanotube electronics Proc *of IEEE 2003 pp* 1772–1784.

Bachtold A. 2001. Logic Circuits with Carbon Nanotube Transistor *Science Mag 294(11):2001.*

Baker R. J. 2000. CMOS Circuit Design Layout and Simulation *3rd Edition IEEE Series on Microelectronic Systems page 797.*

Bate R. T 1989. An overview of nanoelectronics *Texas Instruments Tech. J, July/Aug-1989:1.*

Bendre, V. S., Kureshi, A. K & Waykole, S. 2018. Design of Analog Signal Processing Applications Using Carbon Nanotube Field Effect Transistor-Based Low-Power Folded Cascode Operational Amplifier. *Journal of Nanotechnology*, 2018: 1–15.

Chen Z. 2006. An Integrated Logic Circuit Assembled on a Single Carbon Nanotube ScienceMag *BREVIA* 311(5768):1735–1735.

Gordon D. G., Montemerlo M. S., Love, J. C, Opiteck, G. J. &Ellenbogen, J. M. 1997. Overview of Nanoelectronics Devices *Proc. of IEEE* 85(4): *521–540.*

Hashempour H & Lombardi F. 2007. Circuit-level modeling and detection of metallic carbonnanotube defects in carbon nanotube FETs. *Proc of the conference on Design automation and test in Europe* April 2007: 841–846.

Lin, S., Kim Y. B. and Lombardi F. & Lee Y. J. 2008. A new SRAM cell design using CNTFETs. *IEEE ISOCC 24–25 Nov. 2008.*

Minh, P. and Hong Khoi, P. 2009. Carbon Nanotube: A novel material for applications. *APCTP-ASEAN Workshop on Advanced Materials & Nanotechnology Journal of Physics: Conf Series 187.*

Philip Wong H. S 2006. Carbon Nanotube Transistor Circuits-Models and Tools for Design and Performance Optimization. *ICCAD'06 Nov 5–9, 2006.*

Raychowdhury, A. &Roy, K. 2007. Carbon nanotube electronics: design of high- performance and low power digital circuits. *IEEE Transactions on Circuits and Systems-I: 54(11): 2391–2401.*

Saeed, K & Ibrahim. 2013. Carbon nanotubes–properties and applications: a review *Carbon Letters 14(3): 131–144.*

Sinha S., Balijepalli, A & Cao, Y. 2009. Compact Model of Carbon Nanotube Transistor and Interconnect *IEEE Trans on Electron Devices, 56(10):2232–2242.*

Skotnicki T., Hutchby, J. A., King, T. -J & Wong H. -S P & Breuf F 2005. The Road to the End of CMOS Scaling *IEEE Circuits Devices Magazine 21:16–26.*

Wong, H. S. P., Frank, D. J., Solomon, P., Wann, C. J & Welser, J. J. 1999. Nanoscale CMOS. *IEEE Proceedings 87(4):537–570.*

Wong H. S. P. 2002. Beyond the Conventional Transistor. *IBM Journal of Research & Development* 46(2): *133–168.*

Zhang, W 2009. Modeling of Carbon Nanotube Field – Effect Transistor with Nanowelding treatment *Elsevier Microelectronics Engineering* 40(12):1681–1685.

Smart Computing – Khan et al (Eds)
© *2021 Taylor & Francis Group, London, ISBN 978-0-367-76552-1*

Performance analysis of imputation methods on air quality dataset

A. Tyagi, A. Koul & M. Mahajan
Graphic Era Deemed to be University, Dehradun, Uttrakhand, India

ABSTRACT: A significant challenge that is confronting our modern and rapidly industrializing society is air pollution due to its detrimental consequences to the ecosystem, its species as well as personal health. Therefore, world governments and health organizations must take measures to reduce pollutants but, unfortunately, this requires effective data and its analysis. This poses an issue since most real-world data is unorganized and contains missing values. This paper addresses this issue and several imputation methods that can be used on an air quality dataset to fill these missing values so that the data does not suffer from the loss of valuable information. The imputation methods are compared using performance measures (discussed further in the paper) to observe which method is best suited for imputing air quality datasets.

1 INTRODUCTION

Air pollution is a pressing issue in today's industrial world, with repercussions (supported by the study conducted by Di et al. 2017) that are clear in the environment and personal welfare. According to The National Oceanic and Atmospheric Administration (NOAA), approximately 60,000 deaths in the United States each year are because of poor air quality. Costs of illness related to air pollution are estimated at $150 billion per year. To combat air pollution, effective decision making is required which can only be achieved through the analysis of informative data (Xu et al. 2016). Unfortunately, data in the real world is often disorderly and missing, which, if not handled with caution, can discredit the entire integrity of the data and any conclusions deduced from it. Missing data not only reduces the authenticity of the data, but it also decreases the efficiency of any decision-making process that relies on the data. In the case of the air quality dataset, it will limit the effectiveness of the countermeasures devised for overcoming the harmful effects of air pollution (Nugroho et al. 2019). A premature way of handling missing data would be by removing all columns and rows where any field is empty. Even though this provides a solution to the problem, it is the least effective solution since it results in the loss of relevant data (Rosenthal 2017). For example, if there is a row or column with various fields but only a select few are missing, the rest of the data present, which could contribute significant insight to the analysis, is also lost. It is for this reason that several imputation methods are utilized in data science to fill in the missing values from a dataset (each having its own merits and demerits), and the usage of one depends upon multiple factors such as the data type involved, the mechanism of missingness (see Literature Review section), and so forth. Each imputation method uses some basic characteristics of the underlying data and the inherent relationship and correlation between the various attributes to fill in the gaps with suitably predicted data, rendering the process more effective than just removing valuable data (Bertsimas et al. 2017). This paper will compare various imputation techniques to fill missing values in an air quality dataset and observe which has the best performance (Huque et al. 2018). The imputation methods discussed in this paper consist of k-Nearest Neighbor (kNN), Linear Interpolation (LI), Expectation-Maximization (EM), Multiple Imputation by Chained Equations (MICE), and Random

DOI 10.1201/9781003167488-87

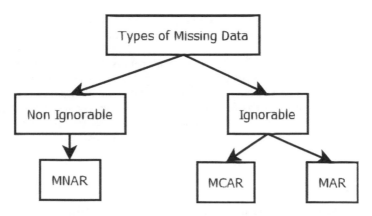

Figure 1.   Types of missing data.

Forest (Vitale et al. 2018). The performance of each method will be tested by calculating the root-mean-square error (RMSE) and the normalized root-mean-square error (NRMSE) to determine the efficacy of each method in imputing different missing values in an air quality dataset (Chai et al. 2014). The remaining sections of the paper are organized as follows: Section 2 discusses the related works and researches that have been carried out on similar domains or methods. Section 3 discusses the experimental results that were obtained, and the visualizations based on those results. Finally, Section 4 provides the conclusion of the research.

2   LITERATURE REVIEW

This section explores past research conducting in the field of data science that deals with the replacement of missing values in data. Graham (2009) mentions the 3 mechanisms of missingness in his paper: missing at random (MAR), missing completely at random (MCAR), and missing not at random (MNAR):

1. MCAR denotes that the property of missingness observed in the data is independent of the missing values and the observed values.
2. MAR denotes that the property of missingness observed in the data is independent of the missing values only.
3. MNAR denotes that the property of missingness observed in the data is dependent on the missing values.

Figure 1 depicts the three types of missingness of data based on whether they can be ignored:
The author explains the practical significance of each mechanism, such as mentioning MCAR is a special case of MAR where the cases for which the data are missing can be thought of as a random sample of all the cases. Pedersen et al. (2017) explore the different types of imputations such as single value imputation (where the missing data is replaced by a single value such as the mean) and multiple imputation where multiple copies of the dataset are created using multiple independent variables after which they are analysed and pooled into a single dataset using algorithms specific to that method. The author also mentions that multiple imputation is recognized as the standard method used in research for filling missing values and further elaborates on which method to use for each mechanism of missingness. Wulff et al. (2017) explain that Multiple Imputation by Chained Equations (MICE) is an iterative imputation process where, in the first iteration, the variable with the least missing values is approximated using only the data that is present. Next, the variable with the second least missing values is approximated using the present data as well as the imputed

values from the last process. This process continues until all variables have been imputed (which constitutes one iteration). According to the authors, typically 10 iterations are used while imputing data using MICE. Yuanyuan et al. (2019) use k- Nearest Neighbor (kNN) imputation to integrate forest attributes and sensing data since forest inventory data is limited to only sample plots and therefore lack complete spatial coverage. They state that kNN is a popular approach to predict forest attributes due to its ability to estimate multiple attributes simultaneously. Kokla et al. (2019) mention that LC-MS technology enables the measurement of abundant molecular features of a sample, but, because it generates vast arrays of data, it is also prone to losing data. In their study, they observed that random forest imputation was the best imputation method (among nine others) that gave the least Normalized Root Mean Squared Error (NRMSE) in the estimation of MCAR and MAR data. Mahmood et al. (2019) perform a comparative study between various imputation methods and Jadhav et al. (2019) test the performance of imputation methods using the mean NRMSE as a threshold. A lower value of the mean NRMSE indicates a better estimate for the missing values. Their study concluded that the kNN imputation method resulted in the lowest value of the error across all datasets used in their study. Nigam et al. (2015) discuss several methods used for assessing and calculating the air quality index (AQI) of a region based on the means and ratios of certain pollutants. In their study, they explore 5 different methods to calculate the AQI of a region. Overall, they suggest that the AQI (Chaudary et al. 2013) gives a meaningful evaluation of the air quality in a particular region (the higher the value of AQI, the more polluted and hazardous the air quality is).

3 EXPERIMENTAL RESULTS

The research is conducted using the standard air quality dataset provided by the Government of India. The dataset shows the major cause of air pollution in India is primarily because of four air pollutants:

1. Sulfur dioxide (SO2): The prime sources of sulfur dioxide in the air are industrial activities such as the combustion of fossil fuels and oil refineries. Other natural occurrences include decomposition of organic matter, sea spray, and volcanic eruptions.
2. Nitrogen dioxide (NO2): Its primary and secondary source is fossil fuel combustion, kerosene heaters, lightning, and biological processes in the soil.
3. Suspended Particulate Matter (SPM): SPM primarily consists of dust, mist, fumes, smoke, and aerosol (particulate matter is made up of solid particles and liquid droplets).
4. Respirable Suspended Particulate Matter (RSPM): Particulate matter that is smaller than 10 micrometers.

There are a varying number of missing values not only across the various pollutant attributes but also across the data for different states. The following 5 imputation methods were considered in this paper for comparative performance analysis:

1. k-Nearest Neighbor (kNN) (Song et al. 2017)
2. Linear Interpolation (LI)
3. Expectation-Maximization (EM)
4. Multiple Imputation by Chained Equations (MICE) (Zhang 2016)
5. Random Forest (RF) (Yadav & Ravi 2018)

The dataset used consists of data collected from many states and regions in India. As representative data, the paper shows the results obtained from three major polluted states: Delhi, Haryana, and West Bengal. The 5 chosen imputation methods mentioned above are applied on the datasets, creating a new dataset after each method is performed on the original dataset. After the missing values are filled in each imputation, the AQI is calculated in each dataset using the equation mentioned in Method V (Nigam et al. 2015). Parallelly, a new dataset is created with rows that contain no null or missing values from the original dataset. The process of this study is depicted in Figure 2:

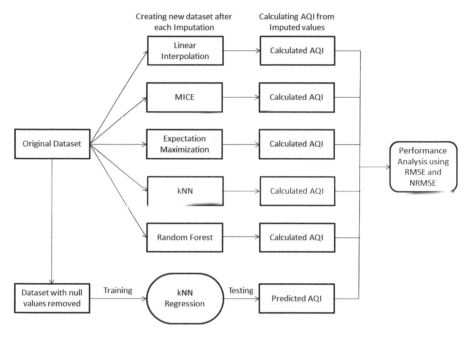

Figure 2.   Proposed procedure.

The Density plot of each pollutant in each of the datasets is depicted in Figures 3a–3g:

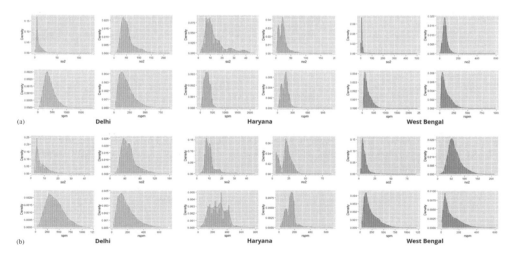

Figure 3.   (a) Original datasets. (b) Datasets with null (missing values) dropped.

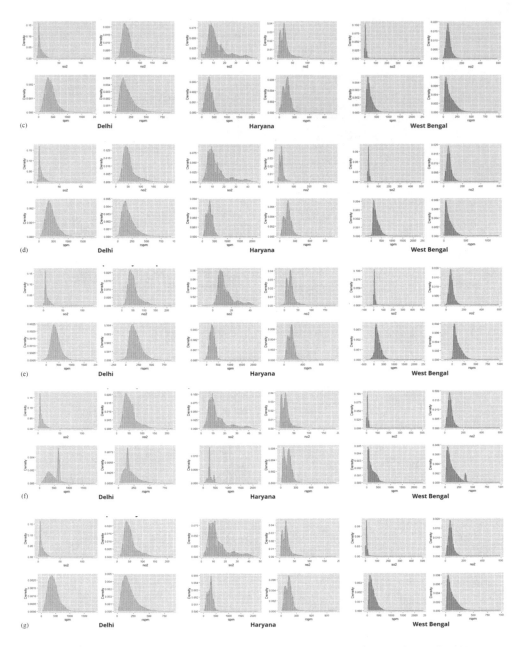

Figure 3.   (c) Datasets with k-nearest neighbor imputation. (d) Datasets with MICE imputation. (e) Datasets with expectation maimization imputation. (f) Datasets with linear interpolation imputation. (g) Datasets with random forest imputation.

Table 1. RMSE error.

State	kNN	MICE	EM	LI	RF
Delhi	15.8707	8.8681	36.8209	13.1456	**6.4314**
Haryana	16.8507	13.5221	23.5024	18.4498	**13.0861**
West Bengal	10.0542	13.0591	14.5717	12.0120	**8.6006**

Table 2. NRMSE error.

State	kNN	MICE	EM	LI	RF
Delhi	0.0222	0.0124	0.0516	0.0184	**0.0089**
Haryana	0.0265	0.0213	0.0371	0.0290	**0.0206**
West Bengal	0.01761	0.0228	0.0255	0.0210	**0.0151**

A kNN Regressor is trained using 70% of the non-null dataset to predict the AQI for each of the imputed datasets. Finally, RMSE and NRMSE (as shown in Eq. 1 and 2) errors are found using the predicted and calculated AQIs.

$$RMSE = \sqrt{\frac{1}{N}\sum_{i=0}^{N}(Predicted_i - Actual_i)^2} \qquad (1)$$

$$NRMSE = \frac{1}{Max - Min}RMSE \qquad (2)$$

Using the two errors mentioned above, the performance of each of the imputation methods is compared with the better performance being associated with a lower error. The following tables indicate the results obtained:

As the results show, random forest imputation was found to be the most effective imputation method among the 5 discussed in this paper for the air quality data set. This is depicted in Figures 4a and 4b.

4 CONCLUSION

This study analyzes the performance of various imputation methods on an air quality dataset and to determine which method is the most effective in filling missing data to take actions to address air pollution. Initially, five different types of imputation methods are performed on an air quality dataset, creating a separate dataset after each imputation. Then, using the imputed fields, the AQI is calculated for each of the imputed datasets. A new dataset is created by isolating the non-missing values in the original data set and 70% of it is used to train a kNN Regressor. Next, the regressor is used to predict the AQI for each of the imputed data, supplying the pollutants as the input. Finally, the performance of each imputation method is measured by calculating the RMSE and the NRMSE values through the predicted and calculated AQI values of each imputed dataset. The results indicate that random forest imputation is the best-suited method to impute missing values in this dataset. These results will aid in determining the best course of action to mitigate the risks of air pollution by enabling effective decision making against air pollution.

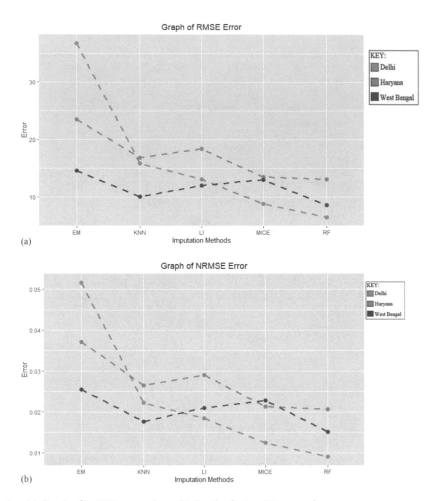

Figure 4.   (a) Graph of RMSE comparison. (b) Graph of NRMSE comparison.

REFERENCES

Ali, Wisam & Sabah, Mohammed & Khairi, Teaba. 2019, Choosing Appropriate Imputation Methods For Missing Data: A Decision Algorithm On Methods For Missing Data. *Journal of Al-Qadisiyah for computer science and mathematics,* Vol 11.

Bertsimas, Dimitris & Pawlowski, Colin & Zhuo, Y.D. 2017, From Predictive Methods to Missing Data Imputation: An Optimization Approach. *Journal of Machine Learning Research, Vol 18(196): 1–39.*

Chai, Tianfeng & Draxler, R.R. 2014, Root mean square error (RMSE) or mean absolute error (MAE)?. *Geoscientific Model Development Discussions (GMDD),* Vol 7: 1247–1250.

Chaudary, Priyanka & Singh, Dharmveer & Kumar, Jitendra & Singh, Sudhir. 2013, Assessment of ambient air quality in Northern India using Air Quality Index method. *Bulletin of Environmental and Scientific Research,* Vol 2(2–3): 12–17.

Di, Q. & Wang, Y. & Zanobetti, A & Wang, Y. & Koutrakis, P. & Choirat, C. & Dominici, F. & Schwartz, J. D. 2017, Air Pollution and Mortality in the Medicare Population. *The New England journal of medicine,* Vol 376(26): 2513–2522.

Graham J.W. 2009, Missing data analysis: making it work in the real world. *Annual review of psychology,* Vol 60: 549–576.

Huque, M.H. & Carlin, J.B. & Simpson, J.A. & Lee, K.J. 2018, A comparison of multiple imputation methods for missing data in longitudinal studies. *BMC Medical Research Methodology,* Vol 17(1):168–178.

Jadhav, Anil & Pramod, Dhanya & Ramanathan, Krishnan. 2019, Comparison of Performance of Data Imputation Methods for Numeric Dataset. *Applied Artificial Intelligence,* Vol 33(10): 913–933.

Kokla, M. & Virtanen, J.K. & Kolehmainen, M. & Paananen, J. & Hanhineva, K. 2019, Random forest-based imputation outperforms other methods for imputing LC-MS metabolomics data: a comparative study. *BMC Bioinformatics,* Vol 20(1): 492–502.

Nigam, Shivangi & Rao, B & Kumar, N & Mhaisalkar, V. 2015, Air Quality Index – A Comparative Study for Assessing the Status of Air Quality. *Research Journal of Engineering and Technology,* Vol 6(2): 267–274.

Nugroho, Heru & Surendro, Kridanto. 2019, Missing Data Problem in Predictive Analytics. *ICSCA '19: 2019 8th International Conference on Software and Computer Applications,* 95–100.

Pedersen, A. B. & Mikkelsen, E. M. & Cronin-Fenton, D. & Kristensen, N. R. & Pham, T. M. & Pedersen, L. & Petersen, I. 2017, Missing data and multiple imputation in clinical epidemiological research. *Clinical epidemiology,* Vol 9: 157–166.

Rosenthal, S. 2017, Data Imputation. *The International Encyclopedia of Communication,* 1–12.

Song, Y. & Liang, J. & Lu, J. & Zhao, X. 2017, An efficient instance selection algorithm for k nearest neighbor regression. *Neurocomputing,* Vol 251: 26–34.

Vitale, D. & Bilancia, M. & Papale, D. 2018, A Multiple Imputation Strategy for Eddy Covariance Data. *Journal of Environmental Informatics,* Vol 34(2): 68–87.

Wulff, Jesper & Ejlskov, Linda. 2017, Multiple Imputation by Chained Equations in Praxis: Guidelines and Review. *Electronic Journal of Business Research Methods,* 15(1): 2017–2058.

Xu, Bin & Luo, Liangqing & Lin, Boqiang. 2016, A dynamic analysis of air pollution emissions in China: Evidence from nonparametric additive regression models. *Ecological Indicators,* Vol 63: 346–358.

Yadav, M., & Ravi, V. 2018, Quantile Regression Random Forest Hybrids Based Data Imputation. *2018 IEEE 17th International Conference on Cognitive Informatics & Cognitive Computing (ICCI∗CC),* 195–201.

Yuanyuan, Fu & He, H.S. & Hawbaker, T.J. & Henne, P.D. & Zhu, Zhiliang & Larsen, David. 2019, Evaluating k-Nearest Neighbor (kNN) Imputation Models for Species-Level Aboveground Forest Biomass Mapping in Northeast China. *Remote Sensing.* Vol 11(17): 2005–2024.

Zhang, Zhongheng. 2016, Multiple imputation with multivariate imputation by chained equation (MICE) package. *Annals of translational medicine,* Vol 4(2): 30–34.

Smart Computing – Khan et al (Eds)
© *2021 Taylor & Francis Group, London, ISBN 978-0-367-76552-1*

Design and implementation of ALU-based FIR filter

Ruqaiya Khanam
Sharda University, Greater Noida, India

Gitanjali Mehta
Galgotias University, Greater Noida, India

Rani Astya
Sharda University, Greater Noida, India

ABSTRACT: In the field of technological advancement, researchers are continuously trying to improve the technology to make it better than before. In this proposed work, we use an algorithm to design an ALU-based FIR (Finite Impulse Response) filter. Basically, adder and multiplier are the main internal components of the ALU block in this 16- tap FIR filter. Multipliers and Adders (Floating Point) are used in the ALU (Arithmetic Logic Unit) block. These are the main parts of proposed architecture of FIR filter. This FIR filter architecture can be reduced its chip area and power consumption. Initially, the value of 16 input samples and 16 coefficients are obtained directly from a 16-tap filter using MATLAB software and then converted them into IEEE 754 standard forms. As a result, the proposed technique achieves 47 mW power and 16.4% reduction in area from conventional FIR filter design. Furthermore, HDL synthesis result shows power and area of the filter. The final simulation and the synthesis of proposed architecture is done by Xilinx ISE suite 14.7 software.

1 INTRODUCTION

Filters play an essential role in Digital Signal Processing (DSP). Filters are a system that passes certain frequency components and rejects other frequency components. Filters are designed for the specifications of the desired properties of the system. Field-programmable gate array (FPGA) is a prototype device which is used to implement a simpler algorithm. A filter helps in removing the unwanted signals along with the noise of the signal concerned. They are majorly classified into two types: finite impulse response (FIR) filters and infinite impulse response (IIR) filters. Both FIR and IIR filters have their own specific areas of working; this completely depends on its characteristics. In most cases, the FIR filters have been used on a larger scale due to its finite character of its inputs being monitored. An FIR filter (Figure 1) helps us to digitally realize practically any type of frequency. This is carried out with the help of multipliers, adders, and delays which can be used in series to get its output.

Linear-phase filters do not deform the phase but simply retard the input signal; therefore, simplifying its implementation. FIR filter can easily design for "linear phase". They perform by multi-rating applications, which is either increasing or decreasing the sample rate or even doing both sometimes. Increasing the sample rate is referred to as interpolation and decreasing the sample rate is called decimation. Some of the calculations are omitted by the FIR filter, thus its increased efficiency. Whereas in IIR filters the individual output has to be calculated even if it may be discarded later during the computation because the feedback must be included to the filter. Their numeric properties are desirable.

Practically, all DSP filters are realized by using finite-precision type of arithmetic, which uses a fixed number of bits. Depending on the nature of feedback being involved in the IIR filters,

DOI 10.1201/9781003167488-88

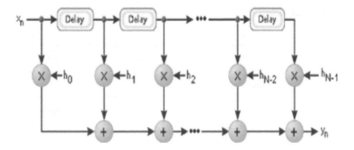

Figure 1.   Finite impulse response filter structure.

the numbers of bits used are more than that being used in an FIR filter. Thus, the designer has an advantage of solving fewer problems related to non-ideal type of arithmetic. They can be realized by the use of fractional arithmetic. During the use of Fixed-Point DSP, it is a very crucial consideration to be noted that FIR filters can be realized by the use of coefficients that has the magnitude of lesser value than 1.0 (if needed, the overall gain can be adjusted at the output of an FIR filter), thus simplifying the implementation or realization. An N-tap FIR filter which has a coefficient of h (k), whose output is described by:

$$y(n) = h(0). x(n) + h(1). x(n-1) + \ldots h(N-1). x(n-N-1) \qquad (1)$$

$$H(z) = \sum_{n=0}^{N-1} h(n).z^{-n} \qquad (2)$$

2   RELATED WORK

Das et al. (2018) proposed an area efficient architecture of FIR filter with distributed arithmetic (DA). Paliwal and Sharma (2018) designed an architecture of FIR filter with the help of Han–Carlson adder which is based on Vedic Multiplier for low power and delay. Some other researchers deal with the design of 32-bit type of Floating-point Processor containing MAC unit for its signal processing application. The convolutions (linear and circular) of signals are verified by Burud and Bhaskar (2018). Urdhva–Triyakbhyam sutra-based Vedic multiplier is used for designing both the filters (FIR and IIR) in the research work of Howel et al. Area, power, and delay are also optimized using various techniques of multiplication in Vedic multiplier which was done by Mittal, Nandi, and Yadav. This work presents all different designing techniques of FIR filter with different parameters by Chandra and Chtoupadhyay (2016). Liao et al. proposed a simple ALU-based universal FIR filter, which was designed with the help of certain components such as shift register and multiplexer. Here, additional RAM, ROM, and D Flip Flops were used which is for storage purposes. An online collection of electronic information shows different windowing methods for filter designing through labbookpages.co.uk site. Yamada and Nishihara presented fast and low-complexity FIR filter on FPGA board with wired-shifters, adders, and subtractor. FIR filter structure is modified in terms of length of critical path.

3   PROPOSED WORK

For designing the FIR filter, we need some basic elements such as adders, subtractor, multipliers, and accumulator. Floating point type of adder and multiplier are used in proposed design. In this paper, we use the concept of the ALU and break it down into a much simpler ALU-based FIR filter design by directly using only two types of components to perform multiple operations repeatedly for different operands.

Table 1.   Filter coefficients.

S.No.	Coefficient (h)	S.No.	Coefficient (h)
1	0.015547	9	0.492663
2	0.0046292	10.	−0.1126
3	−0.00447	11	−0.11894
4	−0.07023	12	0.021328
5	−0.02133	13	0.070228
6	0.118942	14	0.004473
7	0.112598	15	−0.04629
8	−0.49266	16	−0.01555

Table 2.   Filter inputs.

S.No.	Input (x)	S.No.	Input (x)
1	−1.22E-16	9	0.207912E-16
2	−0.40674E-16	10.	0.587785E-16
3	−0.74314E-16	11	0.866025E-16
4	−0.95106E-16	12	0.994522E-16
5	−0.99452E-16	13	0.951057E-16
6	−0.86603E-16	14	0.743145E-16
7	−0.58779E-16	15	0.406737E-16
8	−0.20791E-16	16	1.22079E-16

A much more efficient form of Adder, i.e., a floating-point-type adder and a floating-point type multiplier to form its ALU logic and then design the filter. Sixteen input samples and filter coefficients were taken using MATLAB software with an FDA tool. These values of input samples and coefficients were converted into their universally acceptable IEEE standard for representing floating-point numbers for the computing which is the IEEE 754 standard in Figure 2. 32-bit floating point representation is used in this approach for designing of the ALU-based filter. First, 16 tap filter generates its filter coefficients through MATLAB which is given below in Table 1.

The value of input is defined by "x". The coefficients will be defined by "h" as h (0), h (1), h (2), h (3), and so on. Input information of filter shows in Table 2. Values of filter input and coefficient are required to calculate output of a system. Put these values in Equations (1)–(2) to get its output. Figure 2 shows the simulation results of input and output sample.

Among all the approaches, the most difficult part was to choose the most suitable and simple yet effective type of multiplier and the adder used in the ALU, which took a bit of time to overcome. Finally, we used floating-point-type of adder and multiplier as well. Modeling of this proposed architecture is done by Verilog HDL and implementation design on FPGA board

4   RESULTS AND OUTCOMES

With proper clock input, we were able to get the output waveform, which could be finally seen in the output wave sample by further zooming the view of the image. The output values are in hexadecimal form. The values can be changed by changing the Radix. Hence, values are fixed depending on the 16 tap filter coefficients and input values, as they are also fixed. Our main focus is to try to decrease the filter area which has been done by using the same adder and multiplier again and again for a different number of times for each different operation. Hence, the chip area is decreased by such operation. Although due to the parallel nature of the operation, there is a little delay found. Input and output waveforms are shown in Figure 3 and zoomed output values are

```verilog
`define x0  32'b10100101000001101001100010011001 0
`define x1  32'b10111110110100000001111111001001
`define x2  32'b10111111100111110001111101011101
`define x3  32'b10111111011100110111100001110001
`define x4  32'b10111111011111101001100011111101
`define x5  32'b10111111010111011011001111010111
`define x6  32'b10111111000101100111100100011000
`define x7  32'b10111110010101100111001101100110
`define x8  32'b00111110010101001110011011001101
`define x9  32'b00111111000010110011110010001000 0
`define x10 32'b00111111010101101101101001111010111
`define x11 32'b00111111011111101001100011111101
`define x12 32'b00111111011100110111100001110001
`define x13 32'b00111111100111110001111101011101
`define x14 32'b00111110110100000001111111001001
`define x15 32'b00100101010000110100110001001100 10
```

Figure 2.   Simulation results of input and output sample.

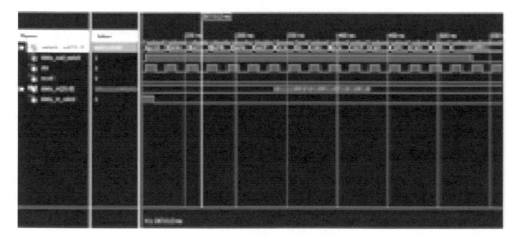

Figure 3.   Simulation results of input and output sample.

shown in Figure 4. In our design, the input size will be 32 bits in this design, i.e., single precision. As we know that the waveform will be in the form of an S-curve, half appearing in the x-axis and half appearing in the y-axis, and changing from a certain point to a negative value but the magnitude will always be the same.

There will be a formation of mirror image after the 8th sample, the 9th will be the same magnitude with the 8th, and so on, but the sign will be different. So, we can see that the result of the equation of the FIR filter will run until the 8th cycle in a normal way which is easy, but when it reaches the 9th cycle, the computation will change. The first memory location of the comparison memory in the VERILOG program of the filter will be re-used by overwriting the new values. The adders will keep adding the values and the multiplier will multiply the values for the next greater sample rate and this will continue until 16 total cycles as we have used only 16 tap filter. The basic structure of proposed FIR filter is shown in Figure 5.

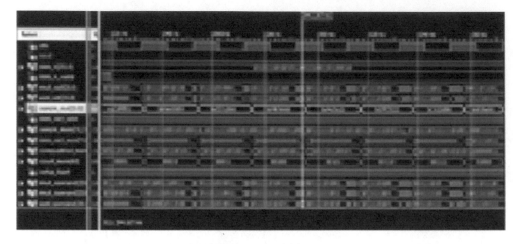

Figure 4.   Zoomed simulation view of the sample output values.

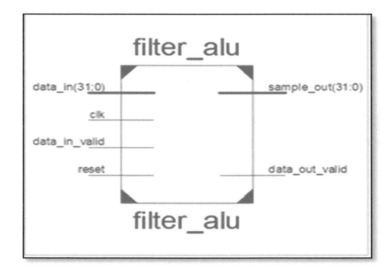

Figure 5.   RTL schematic view of ALU-based FIR filter.

Eventually, the chip area and power consumption are reduced in proposed work although power is combined with static and dynamic power. Therefore, the total used power of new filter is found 47 mW in this analysis. And another parameter is also achieved with approximately 16.4% reduced in terms of chip size with conventional filter. The power used by the FIR filter is shown in Figure 6.

5   CONCLUSION

In this paper, ALU-based FIR filter design has been implemented efficiently. It is found the use of floating type adder and multiplier in ALU block of FIR filter which results in effective area and power consumption. Low-power consumption is an important criterion for DSP and communication fields. However, in this design, we achieved less chip area to accommodate whole FIR filter design. Xilinx ISE suite is still very much effective and simple for working on filter designing, implementation, and synthesis. Hence, the implementation code is written in Verilog

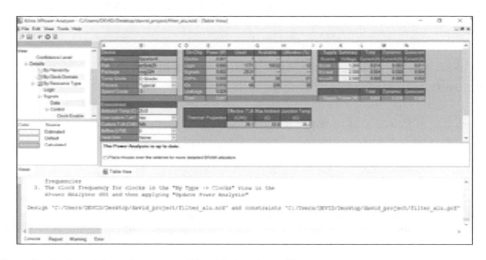

Figure 6.   Static and dynamic power used by ALU-based FIR filter.

HDL. Finally, filter realization and implementation results show that the proposed design decreases chip area nearly 16.4% as compared to the conventional method of designing besides that power consumption is also minimized to 47 mW. We can work on its speed also in the future and even try to work with 32 taps, 64 tap filters which will be much tunable in its parametric efficiency.

REFERENCES

Burud A., and Bhaskar P, 2018, "Design and Implementation of FPGA Based 32 Bit Floating Point Processor for DSP Application," International Conference on Computing Communication Control and Automation (ICCUBEA): 1–5.

Chandra A., and Chattopadhyay S., 2016 "Design of hardware efficient FIR filter: A review of the state-of-the-art approaches," International Journal Engineering Science and Technology, 19(1):212–226, Elsevier.

Das G., Maity K. and Sau S. 2018, "Hardware Implementation of Parallel FIR Filter Using Modified Distributed Arithmetic," IEEE International Conference on Data Science and Business Analytics (ICDSBA): 643–646.

Howal P.S, Upla K.P., Patel M.C, 2017 "HDL implementation of digital filters using floating point vedic multiplier," IEEE International Conference on Circuits and Systems (ICCS) :274–279.

http://www.labbookpages.co.uk, an online collection of electronic information.

Kathuria J., Khan M.A., Abraham A., Darwish A. (2014) Low Power Techniques for Embedded FPGA Processors. In: Khan M., Saeed S., Darwish A., Abraham A. (eds) Embedded and Real Time System Development: A Software Engineering Perspective. Studies in Computational Intelligence, vol 520. Springer, Berlin, Heidelberg. https://doi.org/10.1007/978-3-642-40888-5_11

Liao Y.B, Li P, Ruan A.W. and W.C. Li, 2010 "Design and Verification of an ALU-based universal FIR filter," COMPEL-The international journal for computation and Mathematics in Electrical and Electronic Engineering, 29(2):317–326.

Mittal A, Nandi A, Yadav D, 2017 "Comparative study of 16-order FIR filter design using different multiplication techniques," IET Circuits Devices Syst.,11(3):196–200.

Paliwal P, Sharma J.B 2018, "Efficient FPGA Implementation Architecture of Fast FIR Algorithm Using Han-Carlson Adder Based Vedic Multiplier," International Conference on Inventive Research in Computing Applications (ICIRCA) ISBN: 978-1-5386-2456-2.

Yamada, M. and Nishihara, A, 2001, "High-speed FIR digital filter with CSD coefficients implemented on FPGA", Conference on Asia South Pacific Design Automation: 7–8.

Smart Computing – Khan et al (Eds)
© 2021 Taylor & Francis Group, London, ISBN 978-0-367-76552-1

An assessment of SRAM using MOSFET and FinFET technology in VLSI

Rajesh Kumar Raushan, Mohammad Rashid Ansari & Usha Chauhan
Department of ECE, SEECE, Galgotias University, Greater Noida, UP, India

ABSTRACT: Static Random-Access Memory (SRAM) is the most important component circuit in the very large-scale integration (VLSI) microcontrollers, processors, and other memory devices. The purpose of this circuit is to store bits. The main basic component of this circuit is an SRAM cell. There are numerous works done in the field of designing an efficient SRAM cell. In this review paper, we study various existing SRAM and the techniques used to improve them under FinFET and MOSFET technology. Voltage scaling is a successful procedure for limiting the power consumption of SRAMs. Further, as SRAMs keep on involving a commanding segment of the absolute zone and power in present day ICs, the subsequent all-out power funds are huge. It is very important to design a noise efficient SRAM cell for better performance of the circuit.

1 INTRODUCTION

As the manufacturing process of integrated circuits (IC) goes into a nanometre regime, the density of transistors increased on chip, making it more susceptible to radiation-hardened errors in memory element mostly, Static Random-Access Memory (SRAM) (Chunyu et al. 2019). The power usage and dissipation also increased which requires protracted packaging and unflinching quality issues. Thus, the rule structure objective for very large-scale integration (VLSI) (huge scope coordination) fashioners is to meet execution essentials inside a force spending plan.

The memory is utilized to store the information and these are accessible according to our applications. The embedded memory, which is considered an unavoidable entity of microchip-controlled gadgets, connected to an enormous part of the System-on-chip (SoC). These versatile frameworks need ultra-low power consuming circuits to use a battery for a longer life span so as to increase the portability (Kim & Mazumder 2017). The standard activity in the sub-threshold region is very troublesome in conventional SRAMs, therefore the Dynamic Feedback Control-based SRAM cells are gaining most importance in current research trends due to its high stability.

As most of the circuits designed using SRAM are used in portable appliances that require very small power consumption, so that its battery life increases. This very low power consumption demand cannot be handled by conventional IC, therefore new innovative circuits need to be designed for it. Notwithstanding the way that voltage scaling has incited circuit activity in the sub-threshold region with least power usage, there is an exponential disadvantage of reducing in execution power (Amin & Gupta 2017).

The power utilization by bit lines during composing is relative to the bit line capacitance, square of the bit line voltage, and recurrence of composing. There is a powerful approach in which the vitality put away in the bit line capacitance that is regularly lost to the ground is gathered and siphoned once again into the source. This is known as vitality recuperation approach. Vitality put away in the bit lines is reused by the assistance of changes to neighboring piece lines so as to spare

DOI 10.1201/9781003167488-89

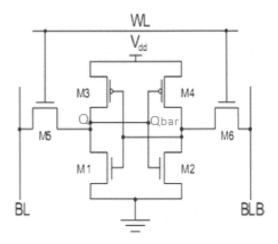

Figure 1.   Basic SRAM cell 6T structure.

vitality in bit line charge-reuse strategy. This technique diminishes the swing voltages to a low swing voltage. In light of whether vitality reusing is done distinctly during composing cycle or during both composition and understanding cycles, there are variations. The conventional structure of 6T cell of SRAM is shown in Figure 1. In this figure, it is seen there is one bit line and the other is bit line bar for inputs and a word line access is shown and the outputs are Q and Qbar. These cells have been modified into 8T, 9T, 10T, and so on designs for better power consumptions. Furthermore, a 14T is designed in a radiation-hardened environment for aerospace applications (Chunyu et al. 2019). Some of the cells are designed using FinFET technology for low power consumption.

The rest of the paper is organized as follows. In Section 2, a detailed review of previous papers is explained and discussed. Section 3 provides simulation results and discussion, and Section 4 concludes the paper.

2   LITERATURE REVIEW

In this section, a literature review of SRAM cells is discussed. Initially, a SRAM cell of 6T is designed, and further 8T and 9T configurations are made using stacking and power gating low-power techniques.

In Chunyu et al. (2019), a radiation-hardened technique is applied using MOSFET, which gives a 14T structure for SRAM under better performance and considerations. In Kim and Mazumder (2017), an ultra-low power 12T SRAM cell is designed with improved write margins using feedback elimination method. In Amin and Gupta (2017), low-power SRAM design in 45 nm is designed with the help of power gating techniques. Clock Gating Techniques review given in Kathuria et al (2011). In Ghasem & Fakhraie (2019), a high-speed SRAM design is proposed with 1K cells per one-bit line. The read and write operations are also enhanced. Apollos (2019) develops a new 9T design and compares with 6T design using CMOS logic and stacking methods. In Yu and Shiau (2016), a 5T SRAM cell is designed with single input and it has a reduced leakage current and power configuration. In Lim et al. (2014), 14-nm-based FinFET SRAM cell in 6T configuration is designed to improve the performance under power and delay. Similarly, in Jyoti et al. (2019), a 10T SRAM cell is defined with the use of FinFET technology and has very good performance optimization. In Lior et al. (2016), a 13T-based radiation hardened SRAM is designed with low voltage applications. In Kaushik and Noor (2013), the performance of SRAM is studied over the deep submicron region and effects of scaling is discussed. Techniques for network-on-chip used to increase processing speed was explained (Ansari et al. 2016) and performance comparison using

Table 1. Comparison of conventional SRAM cells.

	6T	8T	9T	10T	11T
Power	2.00E−06	2.12E−06	5.01E−01	1.03E−07	1.10E−05
Delay	1.08E+00	1.01E−08	1.16E−10	1.18E−11	1.18E−12
PDP	2.17E+00	2.20E+00	5.81E+01	2.32E+00	1.87E+00

various parameter is given in Ansari et al. (2015). In Tamil Selvan and Sundararajan (2019), 6T-based SRAM cell is designed using a carbon nano tubes field effect transistor. It has low power but due to carbon its stability is lower. In Biswarup and Chatterjee (2019), a 14T CMOS-based SRAM structure is defining by the author and is in 45 nm technology. In Lokesh et al. (2018), a special read and write operation control is defined for the CMOS-based 6T SRAM cell. Shirode and Gadhe (2013) is a reference paper using Schmitt trigger circuit to get better performance of the SRAM cell. In Khaleeq et al. (2019), an 8T SRAM cell with enhanced read noise is proposed.

In Munaf et al. (2017), the authors present a comparative study of SRAM conventional structures based on power dissipation. In Rukkumani and Devarajan (2015), a special logic known as charge recycling logic is used for 8T and 10T SRAM cell to improve the power and delay parameters. Performance of SRAM was improved by using MTCMOS techniques by authors in Sriwastava and Shubham (2017). In Chaitanya and Kannan (2019), a radiation-hardened 10T based memory structure is proposed that reduces leakage power and noise, and gives better performance. In Madhusudhan et al. (2018), leakage reduction techniques are applied to SRAM architecture.

In Tripathi et al. (2018), proposed fingering and multi-threshold techniques that results in 6T SRAM that in stand-by had very small leakage current and enhanced stability. Sriwastava et al. (2019) gave 14T SRAM based on MTMOS using transmission gate and voltage mode method, results in low-delay and low-power consumption design with 6T SRAM cell.

The predictive technology model was used to enhanced stability and lowering power consumption and dissipation in SRAM (Saun & Kumar 2019).

Ramin et al. (2015), proposed innovative RHD11 and RHD13, SRAM cells it that is more compact and had more stability toward single-event multiple effects.

Santosh et al. (2015) used two voltage sources for bit-lines, so as to reduce voltage swings because of transition from one state to other state. It showed less power dissipation compared to CMOS based traditional 6T SRAM cells, but has drawbacks as it has increased the number of transistors in cell, therefore there is an area overhead problem.

In data crypto-systems, non-invasive Side-Channel Attack (SCA) on memory devices based on SRAM and its security was given in Lerman et al. (2017). SCA resilient 10T SRAM of 7-nm was proposed in Chen and Oruklu (2019) that has coordinated leakage behavior avoiding against SCA. Low Power Techniques for Embedded Processors are given by Kathuria et al. (2014).

In Kato et al. (2020), the authors conducted experiments on 12-nm FinFET SRAM for angular sensitivity when attacked by radiation that makes single-event upsets. More parasitic bipolar effect was there when radiation is in parallel with world lines.

All of these resource sources review the many works that have been done in the field of SRAM using FinFET and MOSFET applications. The radiation hardened technology is gaining much importance and there is a need to improve the parameters using low power technology using FinFET and much work is required to be done in 22 nm technology and further below scaled down.

3 SIMULATION RESULTS AND DISCUSSION

In this work we simulated conventional SRAM using SPICE, following results have been analyzed, as given in Table 1.

In Figures 2, 3 and 4, the graphs and figures for power delay and PDP are shown.

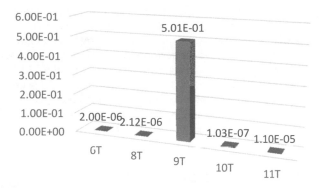

Figure 2.   Power comparison of warious SRAM.

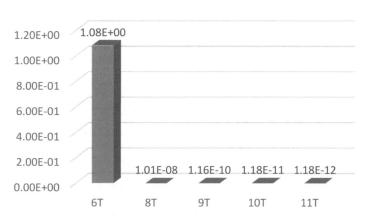

Figure 3.   Delay comparison of Various SRAM.

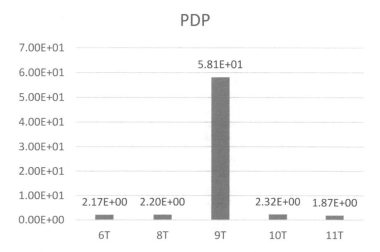

Figure 4.   PDP comparison of various SRAM.

4 CONCLUSION

Hence, in this paper, we have reviewed SRAM, and it is observed that power consumption is the major issue which needs to solved. Many cells namely, 8T, 9T, 10T, 11T are made under the consideration of power, speed and noise reduction. Many researchers have used FinFET and MOSFET in 32 nm technology to improve the performance of SRAM cell. The radiation-hardened effect is less severe in FinFET based SRAM compared with traditional SRAM.

The radiation hardened techniques are used to improve the SRAM which are basically built for 14T structure under aerospace application. The best configuration as per assessment is for 11T SRAM. The technology of this in future can be scaled down to lower nm technology and further aerospace application-based FinFET designing can also be implemented.

REFERENCES

Ansari A. Q. et al (2015), Performance evaluation of various parameters of network-on-chip (NoC) for different topologies, *proceedings of India Conference (INDICON), 2015 Annual IEEE*, 1–4.

Ansari A. Q. et al (2016) Modified quadrant-based routing algorithm for 3D Torus Network-on-Chip architecture, *Perspectives in Science, Vol.* 8, 718–721.

Ezeogu Chinonso Apollos (2019), Performance Analysis of 6T and 9T SRAM, *International Journal of Engineering Trends and Technology (IJETT) – Vol.* 67(4), 1–6.

Amin Asifa, Gupta Pallavi (2017), Low Power SRAM Designs, *International Journal of Engineering Sciences & Research Technology: Vol.* 6, 353–360.

Lior Atias et al. (2016), A Low-Voltage Radiation-Hardened 13T SRAM Bitcell for Ultralow Power Space Applications, *IEEE Transactions on Very Large Scale Integration (VLSI) Systems (Vol.* 24(8), 2622–2633.

M. Chaitanya, V. Kannan (2019), Design And Analysis Of RHBD Memory Cells And 4x4 RHBD 10T Memory Cell Architecture, *International Journal of Innovative Technology and Exploring Engineering (IJITEE) ISSN: 2278–3075, Vol.* 8(10).

K. Chen and E. Oruklu (2019), Side-Channel Attack Resilient Design of a 10T SRAM Cell in 7nm FinFET Technology, *2019 IEEE 62nd International Midwest Symposium on Circuits and Systems (MWSCAS), Dallas, TX, USA*, 860–863, doi: 10.1109/MWSCAS.2019.8884824.

Chien-Cheng Yu and Ming-Chuen Shiau (2016), Single-Port Five-Transistor SRAM Cell With Reduced Leakage Current In Standby, *International Journal of VLSI design & Communication Systems (VLSICS) Vol.* 7(4), 120–127.

Pasandi, Ghasem and Sied Mehdi Fakhraie (2019), A 256kb 9T Near-Threshold SRAM with 1k Cells per Bit-Line and Enhanced Write and Read Operations, *IEEE Transactions on Very Large Scale Integration (VLSI) Systems, Vol.* 23(11), 2438–2446.

Kim Jaeyoung, Mazumder Pinaki (2017), A robust 12T SRAM cell with improved write margin for ultra-low power applications in 40 nm CMOS, *INTEGRATION the VLSI journal* Vol. 57,1–10

Kathuria J. et al (2011), A review of Clock Gating Techniques, *MIT Int. J. Electron. and Commun. Engin., Vol.* 1(2), 106–114.

Kathuria J., Khan M.A., Abraham A., Darwish A. (2014) Low Power Techniques for Embedded FPGA Processors. In: Khan M., Saeed S., Darwish A., Abraham A. (eds) Embedded and Real-Time System Development: A Software Engineering Perspective. Studies in Computational Intelligence, vol 520. Springer, Berlin, Heidelberg.

T. Kato et al (2020), Angular Sensitivity of Neutron-Induced Single-Event Upsets in 12-nm FinFET SRAMs with Comparison to 20-nm Planar SRAMs, *IEEE Transactions on Nuclear Science, Vol.* 62(6), 2578–2584 doi: 10.1109/TNS.2020.2989446.

B.K. Kaushik, Arti Noor (2013), SRAM Cell Performance in Deep Submicron Technology", *International Journal of Computer Applications Vol.* 72(22), 0975–8887.

L. Lerman et al (2017), On the construction of side-channel attack resilient s-boxes, *International Workshop on Constructive Side-Channel Analysis and Secure Design. Springer,* 102–119.

Wei Lim et al (2014), Performance Evaluation of 14nm FinFET-Based 6T SRAM Cell Functionality for DC and Transient Circuit Analysis, *Journal of Nanomaterials, Hindawi Publishing Corporation, Vol.* 2014, 8–15.

S.B. Lokesh et al. (2018), Design of Read and Write Operations for 6t Sram Cell, *IOSR Journal of VLSI and Signal Processing (IOSR-JVSP) Vol.* 8(1), 43–46.

M. Madhusudhan Reddy et al.(2018), Low-Power Sram Cell for Efficient Leakage Energy Reduction in Deep Submicron using 0.022 μm CMOS Technology, *ARPN Journal of Engineering and Applied Sciences, Vol.* 13(4).

S. Munaf et al. (2017), Review on Power Dissipation Analysis of Conventional SRAM Cell Architecture, *International Journal of Advanced Research in Computer Engineering & Technology (IJARCET) Vol.* 6(11), 2278–1323.

M. Muzammil Khaleeq et al. (2019), Design of Low Power 8T SRAM Array With Enhanced RNM, *International Journal of Engineering and Advanced Technology (IJEAT) ISSN: 2249–8958, Vol.* 8(4), 1–6.

Biswarup Pal, Dr. Karunamoy Chatterjee (2019), Design of Low Power 14T SRAM using 45 nm CMOS Technology, *International Journal of Engineering Research & Technology(IJERT), Vol.* 8(07), 1–6.

Chunyu Peng, Jiati Huang, Changyong Liu, Qiang Zhao, Songsong Xiao, Xiulong W (2019), Radiation-Hardened 14T SRAM Bitcell With Speedand Power Optimized for Space Application, *IEEE Transactions on Very Large Scale Integration (VLSI) Systems, Vol.* 27(2), 407–415.

Ramin Rajaei et al (2015), Design of Robust SRAM Cells Against Single-Event Multiple Effects for Nanometer Technologies, *IEEE Transactions on Device and Materials Reliability, Vol.* 15(3).

Rukkumani V, Devarajan N (2015), Design and Analysis of 8T/10T SRAM cell using Charge Recycling Logic, *International Journal of Computer Science Engineering (IJCSE), Vol.* 4(04).

Santhosh B. G. (2015), Design And Implementation of 8T SRAM cell for Analysis of DC Noise Margin during Write Operation, *International Journal of Innovative Research in Electrical, Electronics, Instrumentation And Control Engineering, Vol.* 3(3).

S. Tamil Selvan, & M. Sundararajan (2019), Six Transistor Carbon Nanotube Field Effect Transistors Based RAM Design and Hardware Description Language Code Development, *International Journal of Recent Technology and Engineering (IJRTE), Vol.* 8(2S5), 124–131.

Jyoti Verma et al.(2019), Design 10-Transistor (10T) SRAM using FinFET Technology, *International Journal of Engineering and Advanced Technology (IJEAT), Vol.* 9(1), 24–30.

Shikha Saun and Hemant Kumar (2019), Design and performance analysis of 6T SRAM cell on different CMOS technologies with stability characterization, *IOP Conf. Series: Materials Science and Engineering, Vol.* 561.

Ujwal Shirode, Ajay Gadhe (2013), Read stability and read failure analysis of low voltage Schmitt- Trigger based SRAM bitcell, *International Journal of Engineering Research and Applications (IJERA), Vol.* 3(1), 876–879.

Subham Sriwastava, Kumar Shubham (2017), MTCMOS Based 14T SRAM Cell Optimized for High Performance Applications, *International Journal of Engineering Research & Technology (IJERT), http://www.ijert.org ISSN: 2278-0181, IJERTV6IS010040, Vol.* 6(01).

Tripti Tripathi et al (2018), A Novel Approach to Design SRAM Cells for Low Leakage and Improved Stability, *J. Low Power Electron. Appl. Vol.* 8(41). doi:10.3390/jlpea8040041

Track 4: Communication and automation systems

Smart Computing – Khan et al (Eds)
© 2021 Taylor & Francis Group, London, ISBN 978-0-367-76552-1

A comparative study of robust image watermarking using DCT transform with the windowing technique

Bhumika Gupta
Department of CSE, G. B. Pant Institute of Engineering and Technology, Pauri, Uttarakhand, India

A.R. Verma
Department of ECE, G. B. Pant Institute of Engineering and Technology, Pauri, Uttarakhand, India

Pushkar Praveen & Surjeet Singh Patel
Department of EE, G. B. Pant Institute of Engineering and Technology, Pauri, Uttarakhand, India

ABSTRACT: In this paper, a robust scheme which is efficient, yet much simpler in comparison to other watermarking authentication, has been proposed. This paper presents a watermarking technique in the Discrete Cosine Transform (DCT) domain, using the basic frequency domain property of images and window filters. In modern data communication networks, the images sent from the sender end may not be the same at the receiver end due to noisy channels, errors, and other factors. Noise can degrade the images at the time of capture or transmission. The proposed algorithm makes use of window filters to remove the noises which are usually encountered in image processing. The experimental result shows that the proposed technique is highly robust and simple enough for real-time implementation. With a little modification in the algorithm, further improvement in fidelity parameters such as mean squared error, peak signal-to-noise ratio, and correlation factor can be achieved for the extracted watermark.

Keywords: Image, DCT, watermarking, MSE, PSNR, NC.

1   INTRODUCTION

In the literature, several techniques have been developed for watermarking. Watermarking is divided into two categories according to the domain of operation: (1) spatial domain and (2) frequency domain. The first attempt to watermark digital data was in spatial domain. The main advantage of watermarking in the spatial domain, compared to algorithms in frequency domain, is the simplicity, which makes the hardware implementation much easier with lesser specification requirements and lesser execution time of the algorithm. Hence, real-time implementation of the algorithms is much easier. However, with the advancement of time, the drawback of this approach started to become evident. As spatial domain watermark was not able to withstand basic image operations like cropping, rotation, and others, the solution to this problem came with watermarking in the frequency domain. Other than spatial domain algorithms, several frequency domain techniques have been proposed to this day with much work ongoing [18–20]. In Bhargava et al. [1], a blind watermarking algorithm in the discrete cosine transform (DCT) domain was proposed using the correlation of DCT coefficients. However, although the logic was good, the algorithm complexity and implementation on hardware were not on par with the work invested. In Cox et al. [2], a simple DCT domain algorithm using block-dependent pseudo-random permutation was proposed but the algorithm is highly vulnerable to noise and basic image operations. In Das et al. [3], the algorithm makes use of the basic property of the DCT domain and embedded watermark in the

DOI 10.1201/9781003167488-90

low-frequency region but is vulnerable to lossy data compression. In Hsu and Wu [7], a spatial domain algorithm was proposed. Some other proposed algorithms are found in Hartung and Kutter [8], Shieh et al. [10], Mohanty et al. [14], and Mohammad et al. [16]. In Nikolaidis and Pitas [17], a wavelet domain algorithm is proposed with great potential although it still lacks the ease of implementation. The proposed algorithm provides an efficient, but much simpler, approach than other DCT domain approaches with results on par and with some modification even better than the others in DCT domain. Some of the proposed algorithms focus much on the steganography (hiding a secret message within an ordinary message), which is paid off with lesser robustness against noise attacks. If the modification made in DCT coefficients is significant there will be distortion in the reconstructed image. The proposed algorithm should be feasible for real-time hardware implementation with low execution time. Noise represents unwanted information which deteriorates the quality of the image. Noise is random variation which may arise due to the physical nature of the detection process and has various forms and causes. The acquisition process of an image includes converting the optical signal into electrical signals and then into digital signals [4]. Each process is a conversion process and if even a minute fluctuation is encountered in the process, a small random noise value is added at each step. Depending upon the type of disturbance, the noise can affect the image to a different extent. The proposed algorithm makes use of window filters to minimize the noise content to the level where it becomes insignificant. The algorithm is highly robust against noise attacks, has low execution time, is simple enough for real-time implementation, and has shown good results against basic image operations.

1.1   *Discrete cosine transform*

A DCT communicates a limited grouping of information focuses regarding a total of cosine capacities swaying at various frequencies. DCTs are significant for various applications in science and building, from lossy pressure of sound and pictures (where little high recurrence segments are disposed of) to numerical arrangements of incomplete differential condition. The DCT-based frequency domain watermarking approaches are quite popular nowadays, as with slight modification in the DCT coefficients these can be used to embed watermark bit 1 or 0. There are other frequency domain approaches which have proven to be much more efficient than DCT ones if properly used, such as discrete wavelet transforms (DWT), lifting wavelet transform (LWT), and discrete Hadamard transform (DHT). For the practical implementation of the watermarking algorithm, 8×8 block wise is the optimum choice as extensive research has been done in the development and implementation of 8×8 block-wise DCT. On further increasing the size of the block size to 16×16, the computation complexity increases with lesser increases in compaction efficiency in comparison to 8×8 block-wise DCT. If we decrease the size of block to 4×4, computation complexity is lesser than 8×8 block-wise DCT but the compaction efficiency is less than the 8×8 block DCT as shown in Figure 1. To achieve good imperceptibility, a watermark should be embedded in the low-frequency components whereas robustness occurs in high-frequency components [1, 5]. A typical example of hardware implementation of the DCT domain algorithm includes

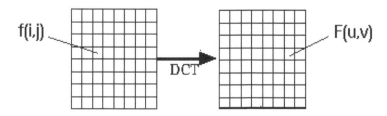

Figure 1.   Transformation from spatial to frequency domain.

watermarking algorithms used in JPEG-supported cameras and the optimum setting used is 8×8 block-wise DCT.

The general condition for a 1D (N information things) DCT is characterized by the accompanying condition:

$$F(u) = \left(\frac{2}{N}\right)^{\frac{1}{2}} \sum_{i=0}^{N-1} A(i) . \cos\left[\frac{\pi.u}{2.N}(2i+1)\right] f(i) \qquad (1)$$

The general condition for a 2D (N by M picture) DCT is characterized by the accompanying condition:

$$F(u,v) = \left(\frac{2}{M}\right)^{\frac{1}{2}} \sum_{i=0}^{N-1} \sum_{j=0}^{M-1} A(i) A(j). \cos\left[\frac{\pi.u}{2.N}(2i+1)\right].\cos\left[\frac{\pi.u}{2.N}(2j+1)\right] f(i,j) \qquad (2)$$

1.2 *Pseudo-random permutation*

So as to improve the perceptual imperceptibility, the qualities of the first picture ought to be remembered while planning the calculation model the alteration of high recurrence segment or high luminance district are less detectable. Such picture subordinate properties have been utilized in a few calculations to rearrange the pseudorandom permuted watermark to fit the affectability of natural eyes. As in Cox et al. [2], for each picture square of size 8×8, the differences (which is utilized as a proportion of intangibility under watermark inserting) are registered and arranged. For each sub examined watermark the measure of data is additionally arranged [5]. A run-of-the-mill and most normal method applied for pseudo-arbitrary changes of watermark squares incorporates a criss-cross requesting of DCT coefficients as appeared in Figure 2.

As a watermark is implanted into a specific area of each square, in this manner every watermark square might be scattered over its relating picture obstruct, rather than the whole spatial picture. A typical picture-editing activity can dispense with the watermark. To guarantee enduring the normal picture activity and as extra security, a quick pseudorandom number-crossing technique is utilized to permute the watermark to scatter its spatial relationship in connection with a key. In easier terms, it is a sort of unusual change (UP) whose qualities cannot be anticipated by a quick randomized calculation. These capricious stages might be utilized as building block for cryptographic frameworks with progressively complex properties. An enemy for an unusual stage is characterized to be a calculation that is offered access to a prophet for both forward and backward change activities. The enemy is given a test input W and is solicited to anticipate the incentive from

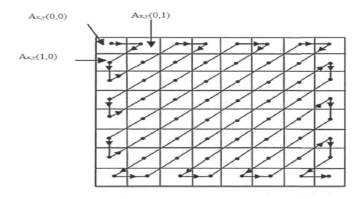

Figure 2. Zig-zag ordering of DCT coefficients.

work P. It is permitted to make a progression of questions to the prophet to assist it with making this forecast, however it is not permitted to inquire the estimation of W itself:

$$PP = PERMUTE(W, key) \tag{3}$$

2 PROPOSED WATERMARK ALGORITHM

In our methodology, a DCT-based calculation is created for watermarking the picture. Leave X alone, the first dark-level picture of size $M1 \times N1$, and the computerized watermark W of size $M2 \times N2$. It is normally favorable that the size of the watermarked picture is equivalent to that of bearer picture, yet a smaller watermark can likewise be chosen, as is done in the proposed calculation. For a $M1 \times N1$ picture, the all-out number of 8x8 squares will be $M1 \times N1/64$ (expecting M1 and N1 are products of 8). We mean a 8x8 DCT square of a picture by Ax, y ($1 \leq x \leq M1/8$ and $1 \leq y \leq N1/8$) where y is section record and x is the line list of the square. For pixel esteem in the scope of 0 to 255 (8 bits for every pixel), 128 is deducted from every pixel before taking DCT to bring pixel esteems to extend -128 to $+127$. The first coefficient in the top-left corner of the block is called the DC coefficient and the rest are AC coefficients. To achieve higher robustness, high-frequency DCT coefficients are modified and to achieve higher imperceptibility the low-frequency coefficients are modified. Extra columns and rows may be introduced during the algorithms to fill the gaps in the original image or in the watermark. Pseudo-random function shuffles the watermark bits in association with a key.

2.1 Embedding steps

1. The original carrier image is read and divided into several 8×8 blocks of the total size, and DCT is performed on each block.
2. The watermark image is read, and the above process is repeated.
3. Now a filtering operation is performed on the original image to clear the image of any noise traces which may interfere with the algorithm.
4. Now to add another level of encryption in our algorithm, permutation of the watermark bits is done in association with a key.
5. Now carefully choosing the region of embedding the watermark according to the requirement of our application—in the proposed algorithm robustness is highlighted.
6. Embedding the watermark bits: The watermark image bits are scanned and if the bit is 1 DCT, coefficients are modified by adding the special parameter value and if the bit is 0, DCT coefficients are modified by subtracting the value.
7. All the blocks are recollected to form the complete image and the inverse DCT operation is performed.
8. The final watermarked image is written into the file.

2.2 Extraction steps

1. The original watermarked image is read.
2. The filtering operation is performed to remove any noise that might have been introduced during the transmission.
3. The entire watermarked image is divided into the 8×8 blocks.
4. Watermark bit extraction. First, the DCT coefficient of the watermarked bit is taken as the reference and a check is performed to determine whether the difference in the coefficients is negative or positive. If the difference is negative, bit 1 is extracted; otherwise, bit 0 is extracted.
5. After all the watermark bits have been determined, the image is recollected to form the complete image and encryption is broken with the key and initial order of permutation.
6. The inverse DCT of the watermark image is performed.
7. The watermark extracted is saved into the file for further evaluations.

3 QUANTATIVE PARAMETERS

In this paper, we have utilized two constancy boundaries to show the quality of the proposed watermarking procedure. The first is top peak signal-to-noise ratio (PSNR), which is utilized to assess the nature of the picture delivered by proposed watermarking calculation, given as:

$$MSE = \sum_{i=0} \sum_{j=0} \frac{\{W(i,j) - \hat{w}|(i,j)\}^2}{M.N} \tag{4}$$

$$PSNR(dB) = 10 log 10 \left(\frac{255^2}{MSE} \right) \tag{5}$$

$$NC = \frac{\sum_i \sum_j w(i,j) \, \hat{w}(i,j)}{\sum_i \sum_j [w(i,j)]^2} \tag{6}$$

where w is the first picture and w is the watermarked picture. The subsequent boundary is standardized relationship coefficient (NCC) which is utilized to give data about the presence of the watermark and the comparability estimation between the reference (unique) watermark w and the extricated watermark w.

MSE and PSNR values obtained of the above images are as follows:

1. MSE = 2.3 and PSNR = 45
2. MSE = 10.02 and PSNR = 39
3. MSE = 17.2 and PSNR = 36

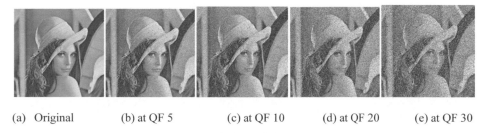

(a) Original   (b) at QF 5   (c) at QF 10   (d) at QF 20   (e) at QF 30

Figure 3. Lena image when subjected to Salt and Pepper noise at various QF and corresponding watermarked images.

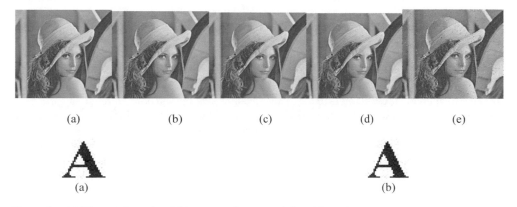

(a)   (b)   (c)   (d)   (e)

(a)   (b)

Figure 4. (a) Watermark used and (b) watermark extracted from Figure 3a.

Table 1. Fidelity parameter values for different techniques applied.

Technique used	MAE	MSE	PSNR	NC
Adaptive Filter	6.3206	4.3917	41.76	0.9981
Gaussian Filter	0.6429	4.9009	42.12	0.9991
Median Filter	0.6298	4.8127	41.43	0.9985

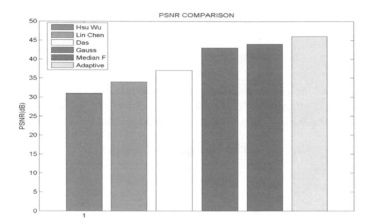

Figure 5. Performance comparison between various algorithms and the proposed one.

4. MSE = 30.39 and PSNR = 34
5. MSE = 43.70 and PSNR = 32

4 EXPERIMENTAL RESULTS AND DISCUSSIONS

To break down the exhibition of the proposed calculation in terms of subtlety, we have executed the proposed watermark inserting calculation on various pictures. If there should arise an occurrence of no assault, the first pictures taken are dark-scale pictures of size 512×512 and unique paired watermark of size 32×32 are contributions to our calculation. As seen in Figure 3(a), the first is a "Lena" picture and the related watermarked picture with no assault. After the execution of the calculation, the yield acquired regarding loyalty boundaries like PSNR is 45, MSE = 2.3, and NCC = 1. To test the power and dependability of the proposed calculation, distinctive fake clamors were created and added to the pictures like Gaussian, Salt and Pepper, Poisson, and Speckle. In the wake of applying these clamors to the distinctive info pictures and going through the proposed calculation, the outcomes regarding MSE, NCC, and PSNR are given in Table 1. By comparing the result of proposed algorithm with the algorithms proposed in Bhargava et al. [1], Cox et al. [2], and Das et al. [3], it can be clearly observed that the results are on par with the other proposed techniques. The performance of the algorithm, in terms of the extracted watermark, can be analyzed using the parameter NCC. As we know, the closer the value of NCC is to 1, the better the quality of the extracted watermark. If the value of NCC is 1, then the extracted watermark is exactly the same as the original one. The security requirement for the watermarking algorithm varies from application to application. Some watermarks are required to have the facility to detect, edit, or remove the watermark while the others are prohibited from doing so. If a higher level of security is required, then a 2-level encryption can be performed using 2 keys (key1 and key2). For a higher level of security, 3- or 4-level coding can be employed with some complicated loops.

5 CONCLUSION

In this paper, a simple yet efficient digital watermarking algorithm is proposed. Using the basic frequency domain property, an algorithm having high robustness is achieved, which is highly resistant to moderate noise attacks usually encountered in an image which may enter either during capturing, conversion, or transmission of data. Depending on the region of insertion of the watermark determines the imperceptibility and robustness of the watermark algorithm which vary depending on the application it is used for. The quality of the watermark extracted by the process is also good. The encryption algorithm used in this algorithm is a simple pseudo-random permutation and watermark bits. Depending on the application and importance of an image, this may be modified to achieve a higher degree of encryption. The results achieved are better than the previous proposed algorithms in the DCT domain, and with some modification the quality of the image can be achieved as high as 50dB PSNR.

REFERENCES

[1] Bhargava, Neeraj, Sharma, MM, Garhwal, Bhimanyu Singh, Mathuria, Manish.2012. Digital image authentication system based on digital watermarking, International Conference on Radar, Communication and Computing (ICRCC), Page 185–189, December.
[2] Cox, I.J, Kilian, J, Leighton, F.T, Shamoon.1997. Secure spread spectrum watermarking for multimedia, IEEE Transaction on Image Processing, Volume 6, Page 1673–1687.
[3] Das, Chinmayee, Panigrahi, Swetalina, Sharma, Vijay K, Mahapatra, K.K. 2014. A novel blind robust image watermarking in DCT domain using inter-block coefficient correlation, AEUE-International Journal of Electronics and Communications, Volume 68, Page 244–253.
[4] D. Lin, Shinfeng, Chen, Chin Feng.2000. A robust DCT based watermarking for copyright protection, IEEE Transactions on Consumer Electronics, Volume 46, Issue 3, August.
[5] Foo, Say wei, Dong, Qi.2011. A Normalization-based Robust Image Watermarking Scheme Using SVD and DCT, 18th IEEE International Conference on Image Processing (ICIP), Page 2757–2760.
[6] Furht, B, Kirovski, Darko.2006. Multimedia Watermarking Techniques and Applications, Taylor & Francis Group, New York: Auerbach Publications.
[7] Hsu, Chiou-Ting., Wu, Ja-Ling.1999. Hidden Digital Watermarks in Images, IEEE Transactions on Image Processing, Volume. 8, Number 1, January.
[8] Hartung F, M. Kutter. 1999. Multimedia watermarking techniques. Proceeding IEEE, Volume 87, Number 7, Page 1079–1107, July.
[9] Image Watermarking, Wikipedia available at: https://en.wikipedia.org/wiki/Digital_watermarking.
[10] JM, Shieh, DC, Lou, MC, Chang.2008.A semi-blind digital watermarking method based on singular value decomposition. Comp Stand Interfaces, Pages 428–440, January.
[11] Kaur, Sukhjinder.2015. Noise Types and Various Removal Techniques, International Journal of Advanced Research in Electronics and Communication Engineering (IJARECE), Volume 4, Issue 2, February.
[12] Kiran *et al.2015.* Digital Watermarking: Potential Challenges and Issues, International Journal of Computer Science Engineering and Technology (IJCSET), Volume 5, Issue 3, Page 48–50, March.
[13] Kalantari, NK, Ahadi, SM, Vafadust, M.2010. A robust image watermarking in the ridgelet domain using universally optimum decoder, IEEE Transactions on Circuits and Systems for Video Technology.
[14] Lu, Z.M, Zheng, H.Y, Huang, J.2007.A digital watermarking scheme based on DCT and SVD, Third International Conference on Intelligent Information Hiding and Multimedia Signal Processing, Volume 40, Page 3740–3752.
[15] Mohanty, Saraju P, Ranganathan, Nagarajan, Namballa, Ravi K. 2008. A VLSI Architecture for Visible Watermarking in a Secure Still Digital Camera (S2DC) Design, IEEE Transactions on Very Large Scale Integration (VLSI) Systems, Volume.13, Number.8, Page 1002–1012, August.
[16] Mohammad, Ahmad A., Alhaj, Ali, Shaltaf, Sameer. 2008. An improved SVD-based watermarking scheme for protecting rightful ownership, Volume 88, Issue 9, September.

[17] N. Nikolaidis, I. Pitas. 1998. Robust image watermarking in the spatial domain, Elsevier, Signal Processing, Volume 66, Issue 3, Pages 385–403, May.

[18] Nayak, Manas Ranjan, Bag, Joyashree, Sarkar, Souvik, Sarkar Subir, Kumar. 2017. Hardware implementation of a novel water marking algorithm based on phase congruency and singular value decomposition technique, International Journal of Electronics and Communications, Volume 71, Pages 1–8, January.

[19] Verma, Vivek Singh, Jha, Rajib Kumar.2015.Improved watermarking technique based on significant difference of lifting wavelet coefficients, Springer-Verlag London, Signal, Image and Video Processing, Volume 9, Issue 6, Page 1443–1450, September.

[20] Wallace, GK.1992. The JPEG still picture compression standard, IEEE Transaction on Consumer Electronics, Volume 38, Issue 1, February.

[21] Kathuria J, Khan M.A, Abraham A, Darwish A. (2014) Low Power Techniques for Embedded FPGA Processors. In: Khan M, Saeed S, Darwish A, Abraham A. (eds) Embedded and Real Time System Development: A Software Engineering Perspective. Studies in Computational Intelligence, vol 520. Springer, Berlin, Heidelberg. https://doi.org/10.1007/978-3-642-40888-5_11

Smart Computing – Khan et al (Eds)
© 2021 Taylor & Francis Group, London, ISBN 978-0-367-76552-1

Sensitivity analysis of stock consistency models for a paper machine headbox using Particle Swarm Optimization (PSO) based controllers

Parvesh Saini
Department of Electrical Engineering, Graphic Era Deemed to be University, Dehradun, India

Rajesh Kumar
Department of Electronics and Communication Engineering, G.B Pant Institute of Engineering and Technology, Ghurdauri, Pauri, India

Pradeep Kumar Juneja
Department of Electronics and Communication Engineering, Graphic Era Deemed to be University, Dehradun, India

ABSTRACT: This paper presents an analysis of the sensitivity function and complementary sensitivity function for stock consistency process models using Particle Swarm Optimization-(PSO) based conventional Proportional-Integral (PI) and Proportional-Integral-Derivative (PID) controllers. The analysis of these functions is required to test the effect of disturbances, noise, and variation in process dynamics on the process output, i.e., to check the robustness of the controllers. The PI controller has been designed using a fuzzy login-based PSO algorithm. The objective is to determine the optimal controller tuning parameters using a proposed algorithm such that the effect of process variations and disturbances is minimum on the process output. The peak values of sensitivity and complementary sensitivity functions have been obtained through MATLAB along with the closed-loop bandwidth of the proposed control system. Also, the time taken by proposed controllers to suppress the effect of disturbance and noise has also been evaluated. The comparison has been done between PSO–PI and PID controllers on the basis of the above-mentioned criterion. From the comparative analysis, it has been observed that the PSO–PI controller exhibits better robustness as compared to the PSO–PID controller.

1 INTRODUCTION

Most of the controller design are based on the mathematical modeling of the system. A mathematical model is the representation of the real-time system which is based on the knowledge available about the system. A mathematical model of any system helps in developing novel control techniques through proper investigation of the system's response to a wide variety of inputs deprived of compromising the actual plant. However, due to the absence of information about the various critical dynamics of a system (such as disturbances, noise, nonlinearities etc.), it is difficult to obtain a perfect mathematical model of the system. This is a serious concern in process industries when it comes to designing a control system for the given system. The mismatch of a mathematical model from its real-time representation leads to the deviation of the performance of the designed control system when implemented on a real-time system. Also, the controller designed may also not able to work on the unknown disturbances, uncertainties, or noises if it occurs in the system at any point of time. In other words, the controller may not be able to control the effect of disturbances, noises, or uncertainties on the behavior of the system. Such controllers do not possess robustness. A controller is said to be robust if it is capable of suppressing the effect of known and unknown disturbances, noises, and uncertainties on the system's response. Since robustness and performance are correlated, if a controller is not robust it cannot perform as desired on real-time systems.

DOI 10.1201/9781003167488-91

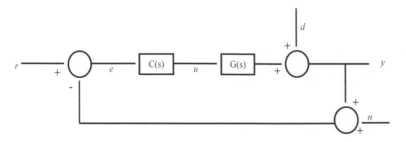

Figure 1. Block diagram of control system with disturbance.

There are various methods to assess the robustness of a control system. However, among all methods, sensitivity function and complementary sensitivity function are two such components which are generally used to test the effect of disturbances and noises on the system's response and hence robustness of a controller (Doyle and Stein 1981; Cruz et al. 1981). This paper deals with the robustness analysis of the PI controller designed using a Fuzzy-PSO (particle swarm optimization) algorithm for a paper machine headbox stock consistency. The robustness of the designed controller has been analyzed through assessment of sensitivity function and complementary sensitivity function. Consider a closed-loop control system, as shown in Figure 1.

In fact, supposing a preservative noise "n" appearing after the plant's output, the overall transfer function of the system (which is shown in Figure 1) is given by:

$$Y(s) = \frac{C(s)G(s)}{1 + C(s)G(s)} R(s) + \frac{1}{1 + C(s)G(s)} D(s) \tag{1}$$

Replacing "s" with "jω", Equation (1) is modified to

$$Y(j\omega) = \frac{C(j\omega)G(j\omega)}{1 + C(j\omega)G(j\omega)} R(j\omega) + \frac{1}{1 + C(j\omega)G(j\omega)} D(j\omega) \tag{2}$$

$$Y(j\omega) = T(j\omega)R(j\omega) + S(j\omega)D(j\omega) \tag{3}$$

where $G(j\omega)$ and $C(j\omega)$ are the transfer functions of the plant or process and controller, respectively.

The sensitivity function $|S(j\omega)|$ is the transfer function between the system's output and load disturbance (Zimenko et al. 2016). It describes the rejection of low frequency disturbances. It is mathematically expressed as:

$$S(j\omega) = \frac{1}{1 + G(j\omega)C(j\omega)} \tag{4}$$

and $T(j\omega)$ is known as the complementary sensitivity function and represents the closed-loop transfer function of the systems. This function describes the strength of the controller to suppress the effect of noise on the system and is expressed as:

$$T(j\omega) = \frac{C(j\omega)G(j\omega)}{1 + C(j\omega)G(j\omega)} \tag{5}$$

The sensitivity function of a control system is assessed by determining the value of peak value of the magnitude of S($j\omega$) for all frequencies. The peak value of $|S(j\omega)|$ is denoted by M_S and is expressed as:

$$M_S \overset{\Delta}{=} \max_{0<\omega<\infty} |S(j\omega)| \tag{6}$$

Similarly, the complementary sensitivity function is assessed by determining the peak value of the magnitude of $T(j\omega)$ and is known as resonant peak (M_T). It is expressed as:

$$M_T \overset{\Delta}{=} \max_{0<\omega<\infty} |T(j\omega)| \tag{7}$$

The sensitivity (S) and complementary sensitivity functions (T) can be derived from the assumptions of disturbances (which are low-frequency signals) and noise (which are high-frequency signals). Now, for a system to have robustness and better performance, the systems shall not be sensitive to these signals. This means that both S and T must be zero ideally. However, when the sum of S and T is analyzed we get the following equation:

$$S + T = \frac{1}{1 + GC} + \frac{GC}{1 + GC} = \frac{1 + GC}{1 + GC} = 1 \tag{8}$$

From Equation (8), it is observed that the sum of S and T is unity, which implies that both S and T cannot be zero simultaneously. Now, the consequence of this is that if S is zero then T is unity and if T is zero then S is unity, which further indicates the significant effect of noise or disturbances on the closed-loop response of the system. So, to have a control system with optimized robustness and performance, the peak value of magnitude of "S" (i.e., M_S) will exist between 1.2 and 2.0. Similarly, the peak value of magnitude of "T" (i.e., M_T) will exist between 1.0 and 1.5 (Zimenko et al. 2016; Astrom 2000; Yepes et al. 2011).

Apart from sensitivity and complementary sensitivity functions, another important parameter in a control system to assess the noise rejection capability and robustness is bandwidth of the control system. It is one of the inherent properties of the control system and indicates the system's response toward the changes in the input signal. It indicates the ability of the system to replicate the input signal. The closed-loop bandwidth of a control system is also one of the measures of a system's transient response characteristics. Large bandwidth points toward a fast transient response of a control system and low bandwidth indicates sluggish response. The cut-off rate is the slope of the closed-loop frequency response at high frequencies. The cut-off rate together with bandwidth indicates the noise-filtering characteristics and the robustness of the system. The difference between a useful signal and unwanted noise can be understood through the cut-off rate. If we want our system to follow the arbitrary input signal (which is changing with time) in an accurate manner, then the bandwidth of the system must be large. However, when we see it through the concept of noise, a larger bandwidth will give the opportunity for noise to enter into the system's response. Hence, it is again undesirable to have a large bandwidth. Hence, we need to maintain a trade-off in case of bandwidth. For a good design, a compromise on bandwidth is required. Also, a system with large bandwidth needs components which can exhibit high performance. Such components are costly and hence will add to the overall cost of the system. So, the large bandwidth not only lets the noise components in the system's response but also make the overall system costly (Doyle and Stein 1981).

2 PULP CONSISTENCY

Pulp or stock consistency is one such parameter related to a paper machine headbox which plays a vital role in the quality of the final product, i.e., paper. The knowledge of this particular parameter is very important because this knowledge leads to the optimization of the final product. There are three vital points where the pulp consistency is measured on a paper machine. The schematic representation of measurement of stock consistency is shown in Figure 2.

In this research, we have considered five different pulp consistency transfer function models (Nancy and Sell 1995; Tippett 2002). These are depicted in Table 1.

There are various control methodologies proposed for various stock consistency models. Ying et al. (1992) proposed a decoupling control scheme based on state feedback for a bilinear system. The proposed methodology has been implemented to control the stock consistency and stock level in a paper machine headbox. Similarly, Kokko et al. (2002) proposed an adaptive model predictive control (AMPC) technique to control stock consistency. The controller parameters are updated using the process model and the operating conditions. The performance of the proposed strategy for consistency control is assessed by comparing the simulation results with the results of the existing control approach. While Juneja et al. (2011) presented a paper that discusses the comparison of

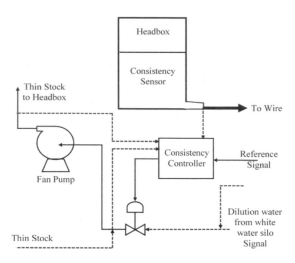

Figure 2.   Control methodology of stock consistency.

Table 1.   Transfer functions of consistency control process
in a paper mill (Nancy and Sell 1995; Tippett 2002).

Sl. No.	Transfer functions
Sys 1 (FOPDT)*	$G_1(s) = \frac{-2.035}{3.84s+1} e^{-6.84s}$
Sys 2 (FOPDT)*	$G_2(s) = \frac{0.03}{10s+1} e^{-5s}$
Sys 3 (FOPDT)*	$G_3(s) = \frac{-1.4}{3s+1} e^{-3s}$
Sys 4 (FOPDT)*	$G_4(s) = \frac{-2.08}{5s+1} e^{-5s}$
Sys 5 (FOPDT)#	$G_5(s) = \frac{-1.93}{3.51s+1} e^{-5.7s}$

different proportional-integral-derivative (PID) control techniques for stock consistency. The aim is to evaluate the performance of each control strategy to control stock consistency. Also, Juneja et al. (2011) proposed an advanced control technique that is based on a model predictive control (MPC). The proposed technique has been used to control stock consistency and stock level of a paper machine headbox. The process output is predicted by MPC in association with future time horizon. The aim is to optimize the performance index. Later, Juneja and Ray (2013) presents a comparative analysis of robustness of various controllers, for stock consistency, designed using different tuning techniques. Hamdy et al. (2014) proposed a controller which is non-fragile based on state feedback for bilinear multivariable system. The main aim is to address the inconsistency of the existing controllers to perform in presence of the variations in the controller tuning parameters, so that implantation problems could be resolved. The design methodology also make use of Linear Matrix Inequality (LMI). The proposed and designed methodology is implemented to control the stock consistency of a paper machine headbox.

3   CONTROLLER DESIGN

PSO was proposed by Kennedy and Eberhart (1995). It is one of the evolutionary algorithms. This algorithm makes use of artificial livings which are simulated to study their behavior, especially the swarm behavior of the elements such as fish, birds, bees etc. PSO is a technique which is used to optimize the response of a system through the population size of the elements. In this technique, the optimum point is obtained by initiating the set of solutions which are possible to find.

In this work, the proportional-integral (PI) and PID controllers have been designed using proposed Fuzzy–PSO algorithm. The objective function for PSO has been decided so as to optimize the performance and robustness of the control system. Fuzzy logic has been used to normalize the range of optimized parameters. The hybrid algorithm proposed is used to update the controller's parameters. The design of proposed Fuzzy-PSO algorithm is summarized below.

i. Define the upper and lower limits of variable using conventional technique.
ii. Generate or initialize the initial population.
iii. Check whether the generated/initialized population is within limits.
iv. If yes, then input the process model for each generated set of population.
v. If no, then update the values
vi. Determine the controller parameters (Kp, Ki, and Kd)
vii. Check the performance and robustness of the controller using controller parameters as obtained in step vi.
viii. If yes, stop.
ix. If no, then update the controller parameters until the optimized performance and robustness is achieved.

The optimal controller tuning parameters obtained from fuzzy-based PSO algorithms are depicted in Tables 2 and 3.

Table 2. PI controller parameters obtained through PSO.

Controller's Gain	Process Models				
	$G_1(s)$	$G_2(s)$	$G_3(s)$	$G_4(s)$	$G_5(s)$
K_p	−0.21	7.03	−0.43	−0.29	−0.24
K_i	−0.04	1.42	−0.12	−0.05	−0.05

Table 3. PID controller parameters obtained through PSO.

Controller's Gain	Process Models				
	$G_1(s)$	$G_2(s)$	$G_3(s)$	$G_4(s)$	$G_5(s)$
K_p	−0.34	7.48	−0.46	−0.51	−0.12
K_i	−0.05	1.02	−0.11	−0.05	−0.03
Kd	−0.37	1.39	−0.62	−0.53	−0.24

4 RESULT ANALYSIS

This section discusses the results obtained through proposed PI and PID controllers for all stock consistency models. Figure 3 depicts the peak values of magnitude plot of the respective sensitivity functions models. From Figure 3, it is observed that except for consistency model G1(s), the peak value obtained through the PID controller is lower as compared to the PI controller. This specifies that the PID controller is more effective in suppressing the effect of disturbances on the system's response.

However, when closely observed for high frequencies, the response through PID controller is oscillatory in nature except G2(S), while the response through PI controller damps out with higher frequencies. This phenomenon indicates that though a PID controller restrains the influence of disturbances on the response of the system. But for high-frequency noise signals, PI controller performs better in noise rejection. The respective maximum values of sensitivity function magnitude plots have been given in Table 4.

Similarly, the peak values (also known as resonant peak) of complementary sensitivity function have been depicted in Table 5. Generally, the value of resonant peak should exist between 1.0 and 1.5. Here, the peak values for both controllers on all consistency models is same (i.e., 1). For high frequencies, the value of resonant peak is zero for the PI controller. However, for the PID controller, the value of resonant peak is not zero for high frequencies except the model G2(s).

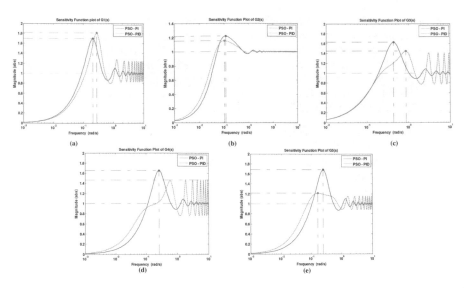

Figure 3. Sensitivity function plots of consistency models (a) $G_1(s)$, (b) $G_2(s)$, (c) $G_3(s)$, (d) $G_4(s)$, and (e) $G_5(s)$ (blue line – PI controller and red line – PID controller).

Table 4. Comparison of sensitivity function peak values.

| Consistency Model | Sensitivity Function (Peak Values) | |
	PSO – PI	PSO – PID
G1(s)	1.7013	1.8109
G2(s)	1.2200	1.1545
G3(s)	1.6293	1.4478
G4(s)	1.6547	1.4699
G5(s)	1.6860	1.2152

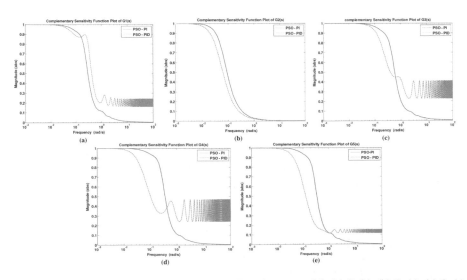

Figure 4. Complementary sensitivity function plots of consistency models (a) $G_1(s)$, (b) $G_2(s)$, (c) $G_3(s)$, (d) $G_4(s)$, and (e) $G_5(s)$ (blue line – PI controller and red line – PID controller).

Table 5. Comparison of complementary sensitivity function peak values.

Process Model	Complementary Sensitivity Function (Peak Values)	
	PSO – PI	PSO – PID
$G_1(s)$	1	1
$G_2(s)$	1	1
$G_3(s)$	1	1
$G_4(s)$	1	1
$G_5(s)$	1	1

Table 6. Comparison of load disturbance rejection time.

Consistency Model	Load Disturbance Settling Time (in seconds)	
	PSO – PI	PSO – PID
$G_1(s)$	20.3	35.8
$G_2(s)$	59.8	98.7
$G_3(s)$	10.5	17.7
$G_4(s)$	16.5	63.9
$G_5(s)$	17.5	48.9

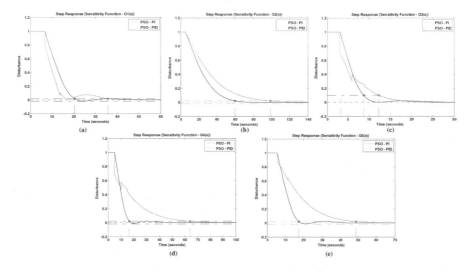

Figure 5. Sensitivity function step response of consistency models (a) $G_1(s)$, (b) $G_2(s)$, (c) $G_3(s)$, (d) $G_4(s)$, and (e) $G_5(s)$ (blue line – PI controller and red line – PID controller).

To check the compatibility of controllers in settling the effect of load disturbance on system's output, step response of sensitivity function of all consistency models (as depicted in Figure 5) have been evaluated. The respective settling time values have been given in Table 6. From the responses obtained, it is observed that the PI controller settles down the disturbance on output in less time as compared to the PID controller.

Table 7 depicts the comparison of bandwidth values of all models

Table 7. Comparison of closed-loop bandwidth.

Consistency Model	Bandwidth (rad/sec) (-3 dB drop)	
	PSO – PI	PSO – PID
$G_1(s)$	0.2280	0.2707
$G_2(s)$	0.0599	0.0391
$G_3(s)$	0.4304	0.2109
$G_4(s)$	0.2700	0.0601
$G_5(s)$	0.2643	0.0793

From Table 7, it is observed that except consistency model G1(s), in all other models, the closed-loop bandwidth of system with PI controller is large as compared to that of the PID controller.

5 CONCLUSIONS

This paper has presented a PSO-based technique to design conventional PI and PID controller for a paper machine headbox stock consistency model. The comparison of PI and PID controllers has been done on the basis of four components viz. sensitivity function, complementary sensitivity function, load disturbance settling time, and closed-loop bandwidth of the control system. On comparing the responses as obtained, it is observed that the PI controller produces enhanced performance in terms of the aforementioned components as compared to the PID controller.

REFERENCES

Cruz, J. B., et al. 1981. A relationship between sensitivity and stability of multivariable feedback systems. *IEEE Transactions on Automatic Control, Vol 26 (1): 66–74.*

Doyle, I. C., and Stein, G. 1981. Multivariable Feedback Design: Concepts for a Classical Vs Modern Synthesis. *IEEE Transactions on Automatic Control, Vol AC-26 (1): 4–16.*

Hamdy M., Hamdan I. & Ibrahim M. 2014. Non-fragile bilinear state feedback controller for a class of MIMO bilinear systems. 8th International Conference on Computer Engineering & Systems (ICCES), Cairo, 26–28 November 2013: 146–151.

Juneja Pradeep Kumar & Ray A. K. 2013. Robustness Analysis of Various Controllers Designed for Consistency of a Headbox. *Journal of Forest Products & Industries, Vol 2(6): 14–17.*

Juneja Pradeep Kumar, Ray A.K. & Mitra R. 2011. Model Predictive Control of Important Parameters in a Paper Machine Headbox. *Indian Chemical Engineer, Vol 53(3): 170–181.*

Juneja Pradeep Kumar, Ray A.K. & Mitra R. 2011. Various PID Controller Algorithms for Closed Loop Performance of Consistency Parameter of paper Machine Headbox in A Paper Mill. IPPTA: Quarterly *Journal of Indian Pulp and Paper Technical Association, Vol 23(2): 127–133.*

K.J. Astrom 2000. Model uncertainty and robust control. in Lecture Notes on Iterative Identification and Control Design. Lund, Sweden: Lund Institute of Technology, Jan. 2000: 63–100.

Karl Johan Åström & Richard M. Murray. 2008. Feedback systems: an introduction for scientists and engineers. Princeton University Press, Princeton, NJ.

Kathuria, J., Khan M.A., Abraham A., Darwish A. (2014) Low Power Techniques for Embedded FPGA Processors. In: Khan M., Saeed S., Darwish A., Abraham A. (eds) Embedded and Real Time System Development: A Software Engineering Perspective. Studies in Computational Intelligence, vol 520. Springer, Berlin, Heidelberg. https://doi.org/10.1007/978-3-642-40888-5_11

Kennedy, J., & Eberhart, R. C. 1995. Particle swarm optimization. In Proceedings of the 1995 IEEE International Conference on Neural Networks, 4: 1942–1948.

Kokko T., Lautala P. & Huhtelin T. 2002. Adaptive Model Predictive Control of Consistency. *IFAC Proceedings Volumes, Vol 35(1): 73–78.*

Nancy J. & Sell P.E. 1995. Process control fundamentals for the pulp and paper industry, TAPPI process control textbook, Tappi Press, Atlanta, GA.

Tippett J. 2002. Consistency control loop dynamic specification, *EnTech, Emerson process management.*

Ying Y., Rao M. & Shen S. X. 1992. Bilinear Decoupling Control and Its Industrial Application. American Control Conference, Chicago, IL, USA: 1163–1167.

Zimenko D et. al. 2016. Feedback sensitivity functions analysis of finite-time stabilizing control system. *International Journal of Robust and Nonlinear Control, Wiley, Vol 27(15): 2475–2491.*

A. G. Yepes, et al. 2011. Analysis and design of resonant current controllers for voltage-source converters by means of Nyquist diagrams and sensitivity function. *IEEE Trans. on Industrial Electronics, Vol 58(11): 5231–5250.*

Smart Computing – Khan et al (Eds)
© *2021 Taylor & Francis Group, London, ISBN 978-0-367-76552-1*

Artificial neural network modeling and control of paper machine headbox parameters

Rajesh Kumar
Department of Electronics & Communication Engineering
Govind Ballabh Pant Institute of Engineering & Technology, Ghurdauri, Pauri Garhwal, Uttarakhand, India

A.K. Ray
DPT, Indian institute of Technology, Roorkee, Uttarakhand, India

ABSTRACT: Artificial Neural Network (ANN) techniques have grown rapidly in recent years, due to high computational rate and a good ability to control nonlinear control. This paper presents classical and ANN controllers for headbox parameters. The ANN is simulated and analyzed using MATLAB Simulink. The neural network controller is used to determine real-time values for headbox parameters. A comparison is made between classical and ANN controllers.

1 INTRODUCTION

The paper machine is the last part of a long chain of processes for making paper. In fact, it is an important subsystem at the end of the entire paper-making system, consisting of the raw material preparation steps to the paper finishing stage. The stock is pumped from a primary fan pump to a series of centri-cleaners at a consistency of 0.6–1.0% consistency and then again to vacuum treatment and screening operation (Nissinen et al. 1997). Then comes the headbox that stores the stock for further processing. The headbox consists of a pond section, dispersing devices, and slice open equivalent to the width of a wet-end paper machine. In order to get a paper of desired quality various measurement and control systems have been attempted for sensing and controlling numerous parameters in the paper machine headbox.

2 MODELING OF PAPER MACHINE HEADBOX PARAMETERS

2.1 Modeling of stock flow

A simple flow diagram for a stock-flow control is shown in Figure 1. Flow can be measured with different types of flow meters, but an electromagnetic flow meter is widely used for corrosive acids, slurries, etc. especially for paper pulp. The measuring element, the magnetic flow meter (MFM), supplies the feedback signal for the flow controller, which in turn compares the measured flow with a set point and adjusts a flow control valve accordingly (Mirchandani 1989).

As far as a dynamic model of stock flow is concerned, the following linear stock flow model of the first order has been the representative one. As q is the volumetric flow rate and Q is the deviation from the steady-state value, one can write

$$\zeta \, dQ_0/dt + Q_0(t) = Q(t)$$

$$\zeta s Q_o(s) + Q_0(s) = Q(s)$$
$$Q_0(s)/Q(s) = [1/(1 + \zeta_p s)]$$

In reality, for flow control there are three elements joined in series: hydraulic flow in pipe, valve, and flow measuring devices. Nancy & Sell (1995) reported that the overall transfer function is

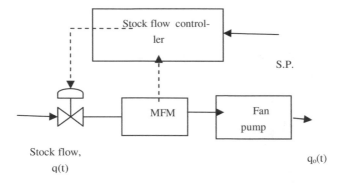

Figure 1. Flow control loop.

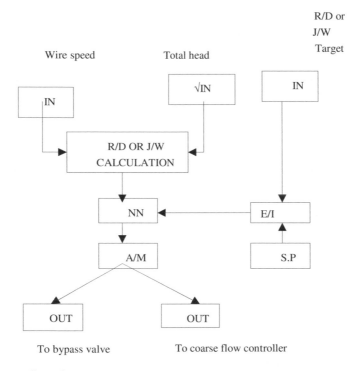

Figure 2. Loop configuration.

a third-order process with time constants of the order of 0.5 s, 0.8 s, and 2.0 s, respectively, and process gain of 1.5. This, when coupled with a PI controller and considering interactions with the other parameters of the system, the control problem becomes more complicated to analyze (Luyben 1990). To avoid this complexity, the majority of the Indian pulp and paper industry uses the coarse flow and fine flow control techniques for stock-flow to the headbox and its approach flow.

2.2 *Development of Artificial Neural Network (ANN) controller for the case of stock-flow control in an approach flow system*

Figures 1 and 2 show a simplified control-loop diagram for neural control of the head box system. Several important parameters must be properly determined in a neural network (NN) design such as the learning rate and the neuron numbers in each layer. The program runs n iterative training cycles

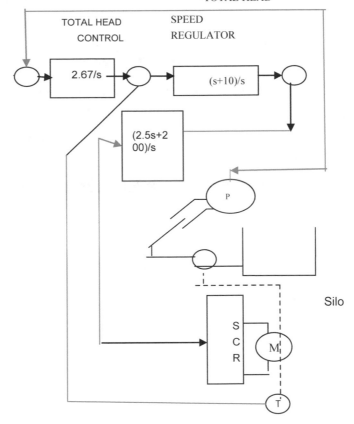

HEADBOX
TOTAL HEAD

Figure 3.   Paper machine headbox total head control.

for the NN with a fixed hidden neuron number. Relationships between wire speed and pressure or vacuum are applied to the headbox at various values of the coefficient of discharge, C_v, and coefficient of contraction, C_c, obtained from a theoretical model for industry as well as detailed models. Using the above artificial neural controller for stock-flow control has been designed and simulated. For the ANN controller, the back-propagation algorithm is used and trained using the MATLAB program.

2.3   Modeling of total head

Paper machine headbox total head control is one of the most important control applications on a paper machine. It achieves the transformation from stock to a sheet. It is also the fastest loop in the papermaking process (Edward & Murray 1999). The total head measurement on the side of the headbox and the proportional–integral (PI) controller, which adjusts the fan pump reference speed, is clearly a part of the conventional instrumentation. The paper machine headbox total head control scheme is shown in Figure 3 for the hydraulic headbox (Luyben 1990). The development of the overall transfer function and the analysis of the loops, including the cascade, are discussed. In this case, the dynamic of the current regulator and motor speed can be assumed approximated as first-order response with K_p of the order of 1.0 and reset time of the order of 0.6 s. The simulation result of the system is shown in Table 2.

Loop:1 Transfer function for armature regulator control loop, assuming transfer function of SCR controlled motor equal to 1.0

$$\text{Output/input} = [(2.5s + 200)/s]/1 + [(2.5s + 200)/$$
$$= (2.5s + 200)/(3.5s + 200) \tag{1}$$

Loop:2 Transfer function for speed regulator, current regulator, and motor loop

$$\text{output/input} = [(s + 10)/s][(2.5s + 200)/(3.5s + 200)][10/(0.2s + 1)]/$$
$$[1 + [(s + 10)/s][(2.5s + 200)/(3.5s + 200)][10/(0.2s + 1)]](1)$$
$$= [50(2.5s + 200)(s + 10)]/[s(3.5s + 200)(s + 5)]$$
$$= \frac{[50(2.5s + 200)(s + 10)]/[s(3.5s + 200)(s + 5)]}{1 + [50(2.5s + 200)(s + 10)]/[s(3.5s + 200)(s + 5)]}$$
$$[50(2.5s + 200)(s + 10)]/$$
$$[s(3.5s^2 + 200s)(s + 5) + 50(2.5s^2 + 225s + 2000)]] \tag{2}$$

Loop:3 Overall transfer function for total head control can be written as open-loop transfer function of total head control system can be written as under:

$[\text{Output/input}] =$

$[50 * 2.67 * 1.05(2.5s + 200)(s + 10)]/$

$[s(1 + 0.6s)\{(3.5s^2 + 200s)(s + 5) + 50(2.5s^2 + 225s + 2000)\}]$

$[140.175(2.5s^2 + 225s + 2000)]/$

$[(s + 0.6s^2)\{3.5s^3 + 217.5s^2 + 1000s + 125s^2 + 11250s + 100000\}]$

$[140.175(2.5s^2 + 225s + 2000)]/[(s + 0.6s^2)\{3.5s^3 + 342.5s^2 + 12250s + 100000\}]$

$[350.44s^2 + 31539.38s + 280350]/[2.15s^5 + 209s^4 + 7692.5s^3 + 72250s^2 + 100000s]$

Closed-loop transfer function

$$[\text{O/p/input}] = [350.44s^2 + 31539.38s + 280350]/$$
$$[2.15s^5 + 209s^4 + 7692.5s^3 + 72600.44s^2 + 131539.38s + 280350]$$
$$\text{Or } [70.09s^2 + 6307.87s + 56070]/$$
$$[0.43s^5 + 41.8s^4 + 1538.5s^3 + 14520.08s^2 + 26307.88s + 56070] \tag{3}$$

The stability test and tuning for the PI controllers are complete and the results of the simulation are shown for both analog and digital systems.

2.4 *Modeling for stock level*

The modeling of level control is well documented in all control literature, both for linear and nonlinear systems. Here we apply this model for the dynamics of stock level in the open headbox, or in closed air pressure headbox where interactions with other parameters are considered negligible. For the open headbox, the head due to stock level is the only driving force of the stock-flow as the external force implied on the stock is atmospheric pressure. For the closed headbox (air padded) the additional air pressure is added to the stock head and in hydraulic headbox the entire driving force is from the fan pump. As usual, it starts with the material balance across equipment at steady and unsteady state conditions as shown in the following paragraph. In this case, only the density of pulp suspension within the range of consistency 0.1–1.0% is included, resulting in slight variations of density from that of water. For practical calculation, however, the density can be assumed the density of water.

Nonlinear: $q_o = Ch^n$ where n may have values such as 0.5, 1.5, etc.

if $t = 0$, then $h = hs$, $q = q_s$, $q_0 = q_{0s}$

$$[Ad(h - hs)/dt + (h - hs/R)] = q - \mathbf{q}_s \tag{4}$$

or $AdH/dt + H/R = Q$

Taking Laplace transform for linear first-order system, one can get

$$AsH(s) + H(s)/R = Q(s)$$
$$RAsH(s) + H(s) = Q(s).R$$
$$\zeta sH(s) + H(s) = Q(s).R$$
$$\zeta sH(s) + H(s) = Q(s)R$$
$$H(s)[\zeta s + 1] = QsR$$
$$H(s)/Q(s) = [R/(1 + \zeta s)] \tag{5}$$

If R tends to infinite, Equation (5) reduces to $1/As$, the transfer function for a liquid level system with constant flow outlet, i.e., an integration.

Equation (4) is of first order

when, $H/R = q_0$ or $H = q_0 R$

$$q_0(t) - q(t) = A(q_0R)/dt = ARdq_0/dt$$
$$\zeta dQ_0/dt + Q_0(t) = Q(t)$$
$$\zeta sQ_o(s) + Q_0(s) = Q(s)$$
$$Q_0(s)/Q(s) = [1/(1 + \zeta s)] \tag{6}$$

Nonlinear system dynamics
If a valve is nonlinear,

$q(t) - q_0(t) = Adh/dt$

$q_0 = ch^{1/2}$

$q_0 = q_{0(s)} + q_0'(h_s) + qo''(h_s)(h - h_s)^2/2! + qo'''(h_s)(h - h_s)^3/3! + \text{----------}$

$q_0'(h_s) = 1/2ch_s^{-1/2} = (R_1)^{-1}$

$q_0 = q_{os} + 1/2ch_s^{-1/2}(h - h_s) = q_{os} + 1/R_1(h - h_s)$

if $q - q_0 = Adh/dt$, then

$q_{(s)} - [q_0(s) + 1/R_1(h - h_s)] = Adh/dt$

$(q_0 - q_{os}) - 1/R_1(h - h_s) = Ad(h - h_s)/dt$

$Q - (1/R_1H) = AdH\backslash dt$

$Q(s) - (1/R_1H(s)) = AsH(s)$

$H(s)/Q(s) = [R_1/(1 + \zeta s)]$

2.5 Modeling for stock temperature control

It is a well-known fact that a higher temperature of the stock will increase the drainage rate on the wire by reducing surface tension and viscosity of water. Stock temperature can be measured by different types of sensors–transmitters with reasonable dynamic characteristics. The sensors which provide measurement in terms of electrical signal such as thermocouples, resistance bulb thermometers, and thermistors are the most common types. The dynamic response of most sensors is usually much faster than the dynamics of the process itself. The time constants for various temperature-measuring devices vary widely depending upon the construction type. Luyben has reported for thermocouples of the order of 30 s with a heavy thermowell but Nancy reported this to be of the order of 2 s. The value of time constants of thermistors, semiconductors, and optical sensors (photoconductors and photovoltaic cell) is of the order of 0.3 s, 0.01 s, 10 ms, and 1–100 μs, respectively, whereas the same for resistance temperature detector (RTD), although possessing very fast dynamics, may have the values intermediate between thermocouples and thermistors (Hong Wang et al. 1997). For temperature control of the approach flow system, including the headbox, there are two kinds of dynamics available: one for the measurement system itself with an appropriate sensor and the other when the temperature of the stock is controlled in the system. However, the temperature control system can preferably be used before entering the headbox. In most cases, the temperature of stock in a headbox or silo with temperature as a feedback signal is controlled by modulating the amount of live steam as the manipulated variable entered into the silo or the flow of gas to a special gas-fired whitewater heater. The controller used is usually a conventional PI controller.

Dynamics of temperature measurement system (thermo well or thermocouple)
The energy balance equation on the thermowell can be expressed as

$$mC_P dT_m/dt = UA(T - T_m) \tag{7}$$

The above equation can be rearranged as

$$[(mC_P/UA)dT_m/dt] + T_m = T$$

Converting to deviation variables and taking the Laplace transform, one can write

$$(\zeta s + 1)T'_m(s) = T'(s) \text{ or } T'_m(s)/T'(s) = 1/(\zeta s + 1) \tag{8}$$

where m = mass, C_P = specific heat, T_m = measured temperature, T = surrounding temperature, U = heat transfer coefficient, and A = heat transfer area
    The dynamics of thermocouple–thermowell (Goel 2020) combined system when the resistance of thermowell is not neglected one can derive a second-order system with two first-order interacting system joined in series. In general, a temperature measurement system can be modeled as under:
    One capacity process

$$G(s) = T'(s)/T'_i(s) = K_P/(\zeta s + 1) \tag{9}$$

For two capacity processes

$$\zeta^2 d^2 T/dt^2 + 2\xi \quad \zeta dT/dt + T = T_i \tag{10}$$

$$G(s) = K_P/[\zeta^2 s^2 + 2\xi \quad \zeta rs + 1]$$

Two capacity processes joined in series (non-interacting type)

$$G_P(s) = K_P/(1 + \zeta_1 s)(1 + \zeta_2 s) \tag{11}$$

Dynamics of temperature control process:

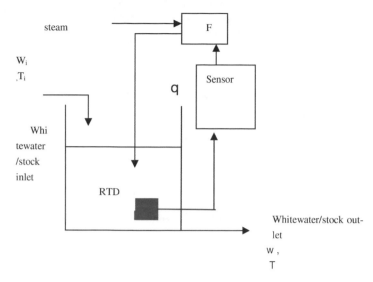

Figure 4.   Temperature control strategy.

Figure 4 is a typical temperature control system (shown as a purpose of model building) for heating a stock storage tank where steam is used as a manipulated variable. An unsteady state energy balance equation can be written as

$$\rho C_P V dT/dt = q + wC_P(T_i - T_o) - wC_P(T - T_o) \tag{12}$$

At steady state condition $dT/dt=0$, Equation (12) becomes

$$q_s + wC_P(T_{is} - T_o) - wC_P(T_s - T_o) = 0 \tag{13}$$

subtracting Equation [12] from Equation (13) one can write

$$q - q_s = wC_P[(T_i - T_{is}) - (T - T_s)] = \rho C_P V d(T - T_s)/dt \tag{14}$$

if deviation variables $Q = q - q_s$; $T_i' = T_i - T_{is}$; $T' = T - T_s$
    Equation (14) can be written as

$$Q = wC_P(T_i' - T') = \rho C_P V dT'/dt \tag{15}$$

Taking Laplace transform of Equation (15)

$$Q(s) = wC_P[T_i'(s) - T'(s)] = \rho C_P \, V \, sT'(s) \text{ or } T'(s)[(\rho C_P/w)s + 1] = Q(s)/wC_P + T_i'(s)$$

$$\text{or } T'(s) = [(1/wC_P)Q(s)]/(\zeta s + 1) + T_i'(s)/(\zeta s + 1)$$

If there is a change in $Q(t)$ only, then $T_i'(t) = 0$, the transfer function relating T' to Q

$$T'(s)/Q(s) = (1/wC_P)/(\zeta s + 1) \tag{16}$$

If there is a change in $T_i'(t)$ only, then $Q'(t) = 0$, the transfer function relating T' to T_i'

$$T'(s)/T_i'(s) = 1/(\zeta s + 1) \tag{17}$$

The equation is representing temperature control process as under

$$G_p(s) = [60/(0.2s + 1)]$$

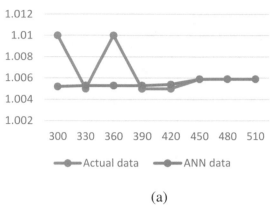

Comparison between actual and ANN data when
number of hidden neurons = 18, momentum = 0.8,
and learning rate = 0.9

(a)

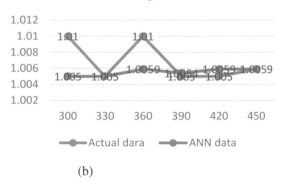

Comparison between actual and ANN data, when
number of neurons = 20, momentum = 0.8, and
learning rate = 0.9

(b)

Figure 5.   Comparison between actual and ANN data.

Table 1.   The range of ANN controller design parameters.

Number of hidden layers	Number of hidden neurons	Learning rate	Momentum
1.0	18–20	0.6	0.9

3   COMPARISON BETWEEN CONVENTIONAL AND ARTIFICIAL NEURAL NETWORK CONTROLLERs

3.1   *For stock flow control*

Figure 5a shows that the actual values of the J/W ratio are approximately equal to NN controller values when the speeds of the wire are changed with the variation of a number of neurons, momentum coefficient, and learning rate. Figure 5b shows that the number of hidden neurons in the hidden layer minimize the performance measure, when the speeds of the wire are 315.31, 375.375, 450.45, and 480.48 m/min. From the analysis of plots of ANN parameters as a function of error, it can be found that the NN parameters indicate satisfactory results of J/W values or total head at the values shown in Table 1.

J/W ratio profiles as a function of speed indicate that the ANN controller gives a better prediction than the same from the data obtained from industry. The plots also reveal that above the speed of 450 m/min the values obtained from an ANN simulated results and the data obtained from industry closely tally with each other. However, there are noticeable deviations in the range of values between 300.3 and 450 m/min.

3.2 *For total head*

The NN error goal 0.0001 is met at 100,200 epochs during training. The responses of the total head of headbox using PI and ANN controllers at a rated total head are shown in Figures 6 and 7. From the analysis of rise time, overshoot, and settling time of both controllers, it is revealed that the ANN controller provides better results. The performance indicators between the ANN and PI controller are more clearly shown in Table 2, which indicates that the ANN controller is more reliable than the conventional controller because the ANN controller reduces the delay time, and minimizes the overshoot.

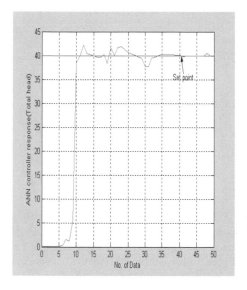

Figure 6.   ANN controller response.

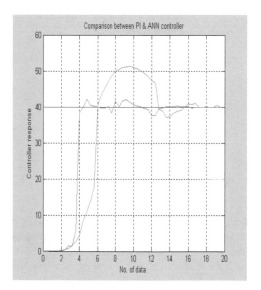

Figure 7.   PI and ANN controller response.

Table 2.   Comparison between ANN and PI controller for total head.

Performances criteria	ANN controller	PI controller
Minimum value	0.00003	0.00
Maximum value	42.25	51.25
Mean	32.24	31.88
Median	39.89	39.99
Standard deviation	15.88	19.14
Range	42.25	51.26
Maximum overshoot, %	≈5.6	≈28.1
Delay time, s	0.8	1.8

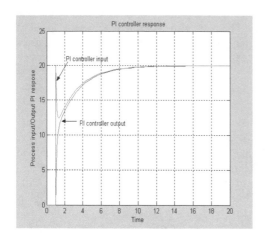
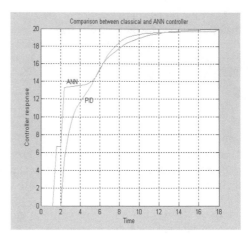

Figure 8. PI controller response (simulation of model). Figure 9. Temperature response.

Table 3. Comparison between PI and ANN controllers for stock level.

Performances criteria	PI data	ANN data
Delay time (s)	3.0	2.1
Settling time (s)	12.0	10.0
Mean value	14.91	15.8
Maximum value	19.93	19.93
Std.	6.79	5.91
Median	18.47	19.09
Range	19.93	19.93

3.3 *For stock level*

Stock-level response of headbox using a PI controller is shown in Figure 8. The performance of the PI and ANN are compared in Figure 9. The plot shows that the PI controller indicates the settling time of 12 s and delay time of 3 s whereas an ANN controller shows the same of the order of 10 s and 2.1 s, respectively. The performance of ANN and PI controller in terms of statistical data is also shown in Table 3. It concludes that the ANN controller is best suited for the stock-level control.

REFERENCES

Edward Peter J., Murray Alan F. 1999, "The application of neural networks to the papermaking in dustry", IEEE transactions on neural networks, vol 10, no.6, pp. 1456–1464.

Goel Rajiv. 2020, "Instrumentation and control for paper machines", IPPTA Journal, vol.14, no.4, pp. 61–65.

Hong Wang, Ai Ping Wang and Stephen R Duncan,1997: "Advanced process control in paper and board making", Pira international publishers, Surrey.

Luyben W.L, 1990: Process modeling simulation, and control for chemical engineers", McGraw-Hill Publishing company, IInd edition.

Mirchandani, G. and Cao W. 1989, "On hidden nodes for neural networks", IEEE Transactions on circuits and system, 36(5), pp. 661–664.

Nancy J. Sell P.E. 1995: "Process control fundamentals for the pulp and paper industry", TAPPI process control textbook, Tappi Press, Atlanta, pp. 428.

Nissinen A.I., Koivo H.N., and Huhtelin T.J. 1997, "Headbox control using a multivariable PI controller in a distributed automation system", Pulp & paper Canada, 98:5, pp. 38–41.

Smart Computing – Khan et al (Eds)
© *2021 Taylor & Francis Group, London, ISBN 978-0-367-76552-1*

Challenges of a wireless body area network: Architecture and applications

Indra Kumar Shah
Department of MME, IIT (ISM) Dhanbad, India
Department of EC, IPS Academy IES, Indore, India

Yogendra Singh Dohare
Department of EX, IPS Academy, IES Indore, India

Tanmoy Maity
Department of MME, IIT(ISM) Dhanbad, India

ABSTRACT: The addvancement of wireless networking technology made the life of people simpler and more comfortable. Some of the most relevant facilities are remotely monitoring, diagnosing, and treating patients without being present at health facility centers. Due to the advancement of Very Large-Scale Integration (VLSI) technology, sensor systems are flexible and small in size, therefore it is easy to place them on or off the body. Such sensor systems are also capable of transmitting physiological data over the wireless medium to remote location servers or health centers. This remote communication technology is known as Wireless Body Area Network (WBAN). This article presents a comprehensive survey on architecture, various communication technologies, applications, and challenges of WBAN. We also present a comparison between the Wireless Sensor Network (WSN) and WBAN.

1 INTRODUCTION

Our day-to-day life is impacted by information and wireless communication technologies in all aspects. Due to the ease of communication, our health sector also utilizes it most. By leveraging various telecommunication technologies, exercise monitoring (calorie analysis), electronic health tracking, online expert (physician) consultation, and diagnosis are possible (Gangwar 2013). In this era of advanced technology, wireless body area network (WBAN) is considered one of the leading candidates that are used in monitoring and consulting on human health. Due to the technological advancement in the health sector, these days patients are no longer forced to stay in health centers (hospital) for monitoring even in the treatment of chronic diseases, such as heart, kidney-related issues, etc. Electronic systems and connectivity now assist the healthcare system, offering greater physical autonomy and considerably reduced hospitalization (Patil et al. 2018; Abuhasel 2020; Khan 2020a–2020e, Quasim 2019).

The number of patients with chronic disease is steadily growing which needs significant medical facilities and treatment. To provide efficient treatment it is essential to improve the smart healthcare system. In this situation, the design of smart healthcare systems using WBAN is the main prerequisite. In the age of WBAN technology and mHealth, generally, sensors are mounted on the patient's body or implanted inside the body of the patient in some serious cases. Such sensors are interconnected wirelessly using various wireless technologies of short-range, such as Bluetooth, Wi-Fi etc. Communication devices such as mobile phones and personal digital assistants (PDAs) work as a gateway that forwards the sensed data to remote servers, for further analysis and medical assistanc, where doctors or medical software applications can provide the necessary assistance.

WBAN sensors are driven by small batteries, therefore long battery life is an important aspect In the case of wearable WBAN devices, the battery can be replaced easily, however the placement of the battery in the case of implanted sensors is not easy, and can even require surgery. It is therefore important that energy-efficient routing, clustering protocols, and architectures should be developed, which increases the life cycle of the used biosensor (Shah et al. 2020)

This paper highlights the architecture of WBAN along with its applications and challenges. The major contributions are as follows:

1. The constraints of the current WBAN architecture have been established.
2. Different medico and non-medico applications of WBAN are discussed.
3. Different implementation challenges are summarized.

2 RELATED WORK

Several research works were done to enhance the working of the WBAN Some of the papers on WBAN show communication architecture, technology, medical and non-medical applications, security, and propagation models (Ghamari et al. 2016; Hayajneh et al. 2014; Tob et al. 2013; Khan et al. 2012; Janabi et al. 2017; Alam & Hamida 2014; Cavallari et al. 2014; Ahmed et al. 2015). Details of the physical layer and MAC layer of the protocol stack are elaborated in Movassaghi et al. (2014) and Shah et al. (2020). This literature also discusses security issues. WBAN wearable devices for workers of oil industries and the use of GSM LTE are presented in Alam & Hamida (2014). Radio channel modeling of WBAN for energy consumption minimization is present in Jain et al. (2019). In Cavallari et al. (2014) analysis of different issues related to WBAN and interference mitigation are presented. Hayajneh et al. (2014) presents mathematical modeling of IEEE 802.15.6, IEEE 802.15.4, and simulation of lowpower Wi-Fi. The relation between cognitive radio and WBAN is demonstrated in Mainanwal et al. (2015). A survey on residential healthcare is demonstrated in Ghamari et al. (2016) in which smartphone-based architecture is also depicted. The latest energy-efficient routing protocol is presented by Khan et al. (2018)

3 WIRELESS BODY AREA NETWORK (WBAN) LAYOUT OF TEXT

3.1 *The architecture of WBAN*

WBAN is composed of small and versatile interconnected sensors, which are attached or implanted in the patient body to obtain various physical parameters such as blood sugar, body temperature, respiratory pressure, heartbeat, pulse rate, etc. Such devices are also used to track health complications such as the number of calories burned during exercise or after walking. A common architecture of the body area network is shown in Figure 1, consisting of three stages Level 1 is called Intra-BAN, which reflects wireless communication between variousbody sensors (Biosensors) and the master node. Level 2 denotes inter-BAN contact between the master node and gateways such as a cell phone and PDA. The links between the personal devices to the Internet are seen in Level 3 beyond BAN. The traffic generated by WBAN can be classifiedmainly into three categories

1. **Emergency traffic.** In the event of an emergency such as heart attack, if monitoring devices measure heartbeats below or above the threshold (set by doctors/physicians), monitoring systems produce an emergency warning for doctors to take the appropriate action. That kind of traffic is unforeseeable.
2. **Normal traffic.** Data generated by regular monitoring of patient condition creates normaltraffic, as in cancer diagnosis, recovery of disabilities, and the most severe heart disorders.
3. **On-demand traffic.** Due to data/information requested by doctors or healthcare workers for diagnostics

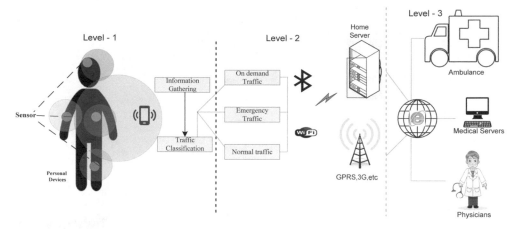

Figure 1. Architecture of WBAN.

Table 1. Comparison of different wireless technologies used in WBAN.

	MISC	WMTS	UWB	ZigBee	Bluetooth	WLANs
Range	Up to 10 m	>100 m	1.2 m	Up to 10 m	10–100 m	Up to 100 m
Date rate	19 or 76 Kbps	76 Kbps	850 Kpbs–20 Mbps	2.4 Ghz	721 Kbps	>11 Mbps
Bandwidth	3 Mhz	6 Mhz	>500 Mhz	5 Mhz	1 Mhz	20 Mhz
Frequency	402–405 Mhz	608–614, 1429–1431 Mhz	3–10 Ghz	2.4 Ghz	2.4 Ghz	2.4 Ghz
Multiple Access	CSMA/CA	Polling	Not definied	CSMA/CA	FHSS/GFSK	OFDMA
Transmission Power	−16 dbm	10 dbm	−41 dbm	0 dbm	4.20 dbm	24 dbm

3.2 *Technologies used in WBAN*

Lay specific wireless transmitting technologies, such as WMTS Medical Implant Communi-cation Services (MICS), IEEE802.15.6 (UWB), IEEE 802.15 (Bluetooth), IEEE 802.15.4 (Zig Bee), 802.11b/g (WLANs), etc., are used in WBAN. In Table 1, a comparison of these wireless technologies is shown (IEEE Standards)

Both WSN and WBAN consist of several sensors used for data sensing, but they are different in the implementation scenarios and use. Naturally, WSN does not use any specific challenge especially related to health monitoring, where the WBAN is used for specifically monitoring the health activities of the patients.

WSN is deployed in an area where human access is restricted (hazardous) or limited, where deployment of the WBAN node depends on different physiological parameters that have to be observed. In terms of protocol and transmission distance, WSN uses highpower radio for long-distance, wherein WBAN uses lowpower transmission because it is related to human health issues (IEEE Standards) WBAN provides a steady data rate when an incident happens and is used mainly periodically. In comparison, WSN is used for event-based tracking at an unpredictable interval In WBAN, strict protection and privacy are preserved and it could be relaxed for certain applications in terms of wireless sensors. Energy efficiency is another important issue in both WSN and WBAN. In some cases, WBAN devices need to implant in the patient body, where replacement of the battery is not easy; the battery is therefore expected to have a long service life (Gyselincks et al. 2007)

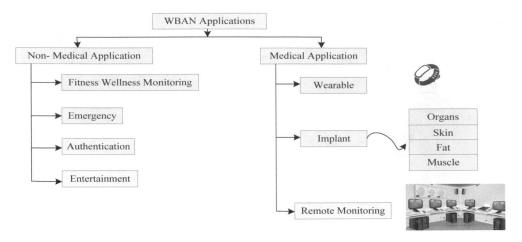

Figure 2. Applications of WBAN.

4 WBAN APPLICATIONS

WBAN applications can be generally divided into both medico and nonmedical systems. Further classification of WBAN is summarized in Figure 2.

4.1 *Medical applications*

WBAN can be further divided into wearable, implant, and remote monitoring categories depending on the medical perspective

1. **Wearable WBAN.** This type of WBAN device includes wearables such as fitness bands. Monitoring of allergic content in the air with location information that can provide physician feedback of asthmatic patients is an important application, and throughout this application the patient will avoid going to that vicinity. If a patient roams in that area an alarm will trigger to the patient and also to the physician so that they can make the necessary decisions (Quasim 2019)Wearable WBAN devices can be used to monitor battlefield conditions if WBAN devices are equipped with GPS and camera, then from the remote control room, necessary security and action decision can be made (Ullah et al. 2012) Physical parameters of an athlete can be monitored by wearable WBAN devices, and at the same time avoid injuries with real-time feedback.
2. **Implanted WBAN.** To monitor internal conditions of the patient's body, WBAN biosensors are implanted in the patient's body somewhere in the skin, muscle, and also sometimes in organs. To periodically monitor myocardial infraction, WBAN sensors are implanted and decrease the risk of cardiovascular diseases (Cavallari et al. 2014) Glueco cellphone technology is used to detect the condition of diabetes, WBAN sensors are implanted in blood vessels to monitor sugar levels and give an alarm when sugar level goes up or down at the threshold level. This can thus avoid various kinds of complications due to diabetes such as stroke, kidney failure, and lower limb amputation (Lewis 2008) A biopsy is a technique used to detect the status of cancer and is very costly. To monitor the cancerccell a WBAN sensor is implanted in the patient's body to continuously extract the cancer-related data (Teshome et al. 2019)
3. **Remote Monitoring.** WBAN sensors are capable of monitoring patient blood pressure, heartbeat, sugar level, and other physiological parameters on a continuous or periodic basis. Seamless connectivity of the Internet to the WBAN make it able to send the sensed data to remote physicians or medical healthcare applications. Patients are tracked remotely in WBAN telemedicine

using integrated health information systems and telecommunication technologies, which supports scientists, physicians, and other medical professionals around the world to serve more patients.

4.2 *Non-medico applications of WBANs*

WBAN technology is also used in non-medico applications other than medical applications, some of which are discussed below

1. **Health and Wellness Monitoring** WBAN biosensors can be used in offices to monitor the performance of the employees, by transmitting employee physiological data ambient temperature and lighting. By use of this information, the manager can improve the environmental conditions which lead to employee satisfaction and productivity.
2. **Emergency** For differently abled people such as those that are deaf, dumb, or elderly, it is sometimes impossible to sense ambient conditions such as fire. Deployment of WBAN sensor in such a situation makes their life safe and secure In the case of industry, where there may be a particular type of dangerous gas that is vulnerable to explosion, WBAN sensors (attached to the body) may play a major role in saving the workplace and even lives
3. **Authentication** Biometric parameters such as iris and face recognition, finger and palm scanning, retina and hand morphology, and body signals such as heart and brain waves provide special biometric signatures that are incredibly difficult to hack, clone, or counterfeit. Hence, WBAN can be used for secure authentication.

5 CHALLENGES OF WBAN

WBAN is an emerging technology and faces many challenges which include ethical, social, and technical challenges

1. **Energy efficiency** WBAN biosensors are generally powered by batteries, therefore energy efficiency is highly required because in implanted sensors battery replacement is not an easy task as can sometimes even require surgery (Tob et al. 2013)
2. **Data quality** Data collected by WBANs biosensors play a key role in the patient care process. Therefore, it is essential to maintain the quality of this gathered data so that correct decisions will possibly be based on sensed data.
3. **Heterogeneous devices and traffic** WBAN uses any kind of sensors and actuators. Therefore, the sensed measured data is also different. According to the application, data may be further classified as priority and non-priority. These data consist of biomedical, audio, and video sensor signals.
4. **Security, authentication, and privacy** Data generated by WBAN is essential, therefore it is essential to maintain security and data confidentiality, which means that only designated entities should have access to the transmitted information from WBAN.
5. **Environmental challenges.** Similar to WSN, WBAN signals also experience environmental challenges such as path loss, node mobility due to postural body movement of the patient, biological impediments, and body tissue absorption.
6. **Biocompatibility** Within the patient's body, WBAN biosensors are inserted, and tissues of the patient's body give symptoms of reactions. Because of this reaction, proteins of cells and other undesirable materials are deposited on the surface of the skin, known as bio-fouling; this creates degradation of sensor activity and leads to sensor failure (Hasan et al. 2019)
7. **Interference and coexistence** Interference occurs when the frequency band of WBAN biosensors and electronic devices presented around WBAN are the same, the proximity of the sensor node also creates interference (Chin et al. 2012)

8. **Hardware design** As WBAN sensors are mounted or implanted in the patient/human body, sensors must be constructed by material and technology which are as per the nature of the human body. Even size and antenna configuration are also important that are used in biosensors.

9. **Overheating** Due to continuous electrical and electromagnetic radiation, heating occurs in sensors which are attached directly with the patient's body, therefore overheating creates a serious problem. Therefore, it is essential to design temperatureaware protocols and hardware.

6 CONCLUSION

In the era of mHealth and telemedicine, WBAN is an important area of healthcare science. Recent literature on various research issues is presented in this survey article. This paper points out a few key differences between WSN and WBAN. Typical WBAN design and their weaknesses are also expanded. This survey also addresses numerous obstacles faced by WBAN. This paper also summarizes WBAN medico and the non-medico fields. By surveying different articles in this field, we also agree that the successful implementation of WBAN technology enhances the quality of human life whether medical or non-medical aspects are involved.

REFERENCES

Abuhasel K. A. and M. A. Khan, (2020), "A Secure Industrial Internet of Things (IIoT) Framework for Resource Management in Smart Manufacturing, " in IEEE Access, vol. 8, pp. 117354–117364, 2020, doi: 10.1109/ACCESS.2020.3004711.

Ahmed G., Jianhua Z., Fareed M. S.Fareed M. Z., 2015.Analyzing algorithms in Wireless Body Area Sensor Networks: A survey, 2015 *Fourth International Conference on Aerospace Science and Engineering (ICASE),* Islamabad, 2015, pp. 1–8.

Alam M.M., Hamida E.B., 2014.Surveying wearable human assistive technology for life and safety-critical applications: standards, challenges and opportunities, *Sensors*, vol. 14 (5), pp. 9153–9209, 2014.

Cavallari R., Martelli F., Rosini R., Buratti C. Verdone R., 2014.A Survey on Wireless Body Area Networks:Technologies and Design Challenges, *IEEE Communications Surveys Tutorials,* vol. 16, no. 3, pp. 1635–1657.

Chin C. A., Crosby G. V., Ghosh T., Murimi R., 2012. Advances and challenges of wireless body area net worksfor healthcare applications, 2012 International Conference on Computing, *Networking and Communications*(ICNC), Maui, HI, 2012, pp. 99–103.

Chu Hsueh-Ting, Chir-Chang Huang, Zhi-HuiLian, J. J. P. Tsai, 2006.A ubiquitous warning system for asthma-inducement, *IEEE International Conference on Sensor Networks, Ubiquitous, and Trustworthy Computing (SUTC'06),* Taichung, 2006, pp. 186–191.

Gangwar D.S., 2013. Biomedical sensor network for cardiovascular fitness and activity monitoring.*IEEE Point-of-Care Healthcare Technologies (PHT).* pp.279–282.

Ghamari M., Janko B., Sherratt R.S., Harwin W., Piechockic R., Soltanpur C., 2016.A Survey on Wireless Body Area Networks for eHealthcare, Systems in Residential Environments. *Sensors,* vol. 16, pp. 831, 2016

Gyselincks B., Borzi R., Mattelaer P., 2007. Human: emerging technology for body area networks, In: Wire lessTechnologies. CRC Press, pp. 227–246, 2007.

Hayajneh T., Almashaqbeh G., Ullah. S. Vasilakos, A.V., 2014.A survey of wireless technologies coexistence, *wban: analysis and open research issues, WirelessNetw.* Vol. 20 (8), pp. 2165–2199, 2014.

IEEE Draft Standard for Local and metropolitan area networksPart 15.4: Low-Rate Wireless Personal Area Networks (WPANs) Amendment 5: Physical Layer Specifications for Low Energy, Critical Infrastructure Monitoring Networks, *IEEE P802.15.4k/D4, February*, 2013, vol., no., pp. 1–154, 23 Aug. 2013.

IEEE Standards Coordinating Committee, 2006. IEEE Standard for Safety Levels with Respect to Human Exposure to Radio Frequency Electromagnetic Fields, 3khz to 300ghz, IEEE C95, pp. 1–1991.

Jain, NK, Yadav, DS, Verma, A.2019 A fuzzy decision scheme for relay selection in cooperative wireless sensor network. *Int J Commun Syst.* 32: e4121.https://doi.org/10.1002/dac.4121

Janabi Al, ShourbajiS. Al, ShojafaI. r, Shamshirband M., 2017. Survey of main challenges (security and privacy) *wireless body area networks for healthcare applications. Egypt.* Inf. J. 18 (2), 113–122.

Hasan Khalid, Biswas Kamanashis, Ahmed Khandakar, Nazmus S. Nafi, MdSaiful Islam.2019.A comprehensivereview of wireless body area network, *Journal of Network and Computer Applications*, 2019, pp. 178–198

Khan M. A., (2020), An IoT Framework for Heart Disease Prediction Based on MDCNN Classifier, in IEEE Access, vol. 8, pp. 34717-34727, 2020. DOI: 10.1109/ACCESS.2020.2974687

Khan, MA, Abuhasel, KA. (2020).Advanced metameric dimension framework for heterogeneous industrial Internet of things. Computational Intelligence. 2020; 1– 21. https://doi.org/10.1111/coin.12378

Khan M.A, and Algarni F., (2020) "A Healthcare Monitoring System for the Diagnosis of Heart Disease in the IoMT Cloud Environment Using MSSO-ANFIS," in IEEE Access, vol. 8, pp. 122259–122269, 2020, doi: 10.1109/ACCESS.2020.3006424.

Khan, M. A., Quasim, M. T, et.al, (2020), A Secure Framework for Authentication and Encryption Using Improved ECC for IoT-Based Medical Sensor Data, in IEEE Access, vol. 8, pp. 52018–52027, 2020. DOI: 10.1109/ACCESS.2020.2980739

Khan M.A. et. al, (2020), Decentralised IoT, Decenetralised IoT: A Blockchain perspective, Springer, Studies in BigData, 2020, DOI: https://doi.org/10.1007/978-3-030-38677-1

Khan R.A., Pathan A.S.K., 2018.The state-of-the-art wireless body area sensor networks: a survey, *Int. J. Distributed Sens. Netw.* Vol. 14 (4), pp. 1–23, 2018.

Khan S., Pathan A.S.K., Alrajeh N.A.2012, Wireless Sensor Networks: Current Status and Future Trends, CRCpress, Boca Ratun, FL.

Lewis D., "802.15. 6 Call for Applications in Body Area Networks Response Summary, " 1508040705-0006, 2008.

Mainanwal V., Gupta M., Upadhayay S. K., 2015.A survey on wireless body area network: Security technologyand its design methodology issue, *International Conference on Innovations in Information, Embedded and Communication Systems (ICIIECS),* Coimbatore, 2015, pp. 1–5.

Marinkovic S., Spagnol C., Popovici E.2009.Energy-Efficient TDMA-Based MAC Protocol for Wireless Body Area Networks, 2009*Third International Conference on Sensor Technologies and Applications, Athens,* Glyfada, 2009, pp. 604–609.

Movassaghi S, Abolhasan M., LipmanJ., Smith D., Jamalipour A., 2014.Wireless body area networks: a survey, *IEEECommun. Surv. Tutorials* vol. 16 (3), pp. 1658–1686, 2014.

Patil V., Thakur S. S., Kshirsagar V., 2018.Health Monitoring System Using Internet of Things, *Second International Conference on Intelligent Computing and Control Systems (ICICCS),* Madurai, India, 2018, pp. 1523–1525.

Quasim, M. T., Khan M. A, et.al, (2019), Internet of Things for Smart Healthcare: A Hardware Perspective, 2019 First International Conference of Intelligent Computing and Engineering (ICOICE), Hadhramout, Yemen, 2019, pp. 1–5. DOI: 10.1109/ICOICE48418.2019.9035175

Shah I.K., Maity T., Dohare Y.S 2020. Algorithm for energy consumption minimisation in wireless sensor network, *IET Communications,* vol. 14(8), pp. 1301–1310, doi: 10.1049/iet-com.2019.0465

Shah I. K., Maity T., Dohare Y. S., 2020. Weight Based Approach for Optimal Position of Base Station in Wireless Sensor Network, *International Conference on Inventive Computation Technologies(ICICT), Coimbatore, India,* pp. 734–738, doi: 10.1109/ICICT48043.2020.9112581.

Teshome A. K., KibretB., Lai D. T. H., 2019.A Review of Implant Communication Technology in WBAN: Progress and Challenges, *IEEE Reviews in Biomedical Engineering,* vol. 12, pp. 88–99, 2019.

Tob'on D.P., Falk T. H., M.Maier, 2013.Context awareness in WBANs: a survey on medical and non-medicalapplications, *IEEE Wireless Communications* vol. 20, no. 4, pp. 30–37, August 2013.

Ullah S, Higgins H., Braem B., Latre B., Blondia C., Moerman I., SaleemS., Rahman Z., Kwak K.S., 2012. *A comprehensive survey of wireless body area networksI.J. Med. Syst. Vol.* 36 (3), pp. 1065–1094.

Smart Computing – Khan et al (Eds)
© 2021 Taylor & Francis Group, London, ISBN 978-0-367-76552-1

Performance comparison of indirect vector-controlled induction motor drives using FLC, IMC, and PSO

Bhola Jha & Manoj Kumar Panda

G. B. Pant Institute of Engineering and Technology, Pauri, Uttarakhand, India

ABSTRACT: Induction motor has been the best choice for the indutries over many decades. Therefore many control schemes are evolved and practiced by the industrries. In the present decade the application of the soft computing approach, robust technique and optimizing methods in an asynchronous induction motor control is rising for the optimal performance of motor. In this paper, Fuzzy Logic Controller (FLC) as a soft computing technique, Internal Mode Control (IMC) as a robust technique and meta-heuristics approach as an optimization technique are tested for the optimal performance of vector control of asynchronous motor. The results are illustrated using MATLAB.

Keywords: Modeling, vector control, FLC, IMC, PSO

1 INTRODUCTION

Popular induction motors are also said to be like asynchronous motors which are robust in construction, have almost negligible maintenance, are low cost, and have high torque-to-weight ratio. Since the induction motor cost is low, industries have exploited that low-cost quality. The DC motor is very much popular for the variable speed that drives many applications because of independent working of armature and field. Therefore, the dynamic performance of a DC motor was found to be very good. However,, such independent or decoupling quality cannot be achieved in the case of an asynchronous motor. To make the stator and rotor of the induction motor to work independently, a method is developed which is known as vector control. Two approaches of vector control are direct control and indirect control. If the field angle is obtained through some sort of sensor, preferably a hall sensor, then that control is referred to as direct control and if it is obtained through rotor position then control is said to be as indirect control. This paper uses indirect method.

The principle of working vector control is the field orientation which makes the decouple control of real power and reactive power, i.e., torque and flux. A variety of research papers/literature and books are available for the vector control (see Bose 2002; Krishanan 2001; Novotney et al. 1986; Kraus et al. 2004; Slemon, et al. 1989; Bhimbra 2012; Menna et al. 2007a, Kar et al. 2011; Liying et al. 2007a; Zerikat et al. 2010a; Narayan et al. 2011a; Uddin et al, 2002a; Tripura 2011a; Subudhi et al. 2008a; Waheedabeevi, et al. 2012a). Other sources (Menna et al. 2007b; Kar et al. 2011; Liying et al. 2007b; Zerikat et al. 2010b; Narayan et al. 2011b; Uddin et al. 2002b; Tripura 2011b; Subudhi et al. 2008b; Waheedabeevi et al. 2012b) discuss the application of the extended Kalman filter, sliding mode control, and fuzzy to vector control of induction machine. Out of these techniques, the fuzzy introduced by Zadeh (1965) became more popular. Implementation of Internal Mode Control (IMC) robust controllers in an asynchronous motor control is a relatively new proposal. The IMC introduced by Garcia (1982) is explored in this paper. There are the other sources (Poitiers et al. 2001; Nagaria et al. 2009; Salman, and Badrzadeh 2015; Petersson et al. 2005) where IMC is employed.

At present, the trend of using heuristic or biological inspired optimization algorithm keeps on increasing. The constants of the PID controller can be obtained by this algorithm. Several search

 DOI 10.1201/9781003167488-94

optimization tools are available such as genetic algorithm (GA), particle swarm optimization (PSO), ant colony (AC), bee colony (BC), etc. Because of simplicity and accuracy, the PSO became much more popular. Kennedy and Eberhart developed this algorithm, and the basic concepts of this algorithm are available in Eberhart (2005), Hassan et al. (2005), and Debnath et al. 2013). This PSO is having wider applications almost in different aspects of technical concepts. There are several research papers (e.g., Uddin et al. 2008c; Allaoua et al. 2008; Das 2018; Raj et al. 2009a, 2009b; Bervani et al. 2012a, 2012b; Datta et al. 2011) published in the domain of electrical engineering.

The performance comparison of a decouple control of an induction motor is bestowed through fuzzy logic controller (FLC), IMC, and PSO in this article. The following are the main and novel contributions of this paper:

(1) Dynamic modeling and implementation of vector control.
(2) Implementation of FLC as a soft computing technique.
(3) Design and implementation of IMC as a robust technique (novel).
(4) On-line implementation of PSO algorithm as an optimization technique (novel).

Here, online means running of MATLAB-Simulink model using PSO code for tuning of PID controller.

This paper is arranged as follows. Section 2 explains the dynamic modeling and vector control, Section 3 briefs the fuzzy concepts, Section 4 presents the design of IMC, and Section 5 exhibits the PSO algorithm. Results are illustrated in Section 6 and Section 7 ends the paper with inferences and a conclusion.

2   MODELING AND CONTROL OF INDUCTION MOTOR

A very important step for the vector control implementation is the dynamic modeling of machine. The axis transformation from three phase to two phase and vice versa is needed for reducing the complexity, as shown in Figure 1.

The mathematical equations for the transformation of three-phase to two-phase and vice versa are given as Equation (A1) in the Appendix. The two-axis voltage in terms of d-q of stator and rotor in the field-oriented reference frame are demonstrated in Equation (A2) in the Appendix. In (A2), superscripts e denote this field-oriented reference frames.

Flux linkages of are related as

$$\left.\begin{array}{l} \lambda_{qs}^e = L_s i_{qs}^e + L_m i_{qr}^e \\ \lambda_{ds}^e = L_s i_{ds}^e + L_m i_{dr}^e \\ \lambda_{qr}^e = L_r i_{qr}^e + L_m i_{qs}^e \\ \lambda_{dr}^e = L_r i_{dr}^e + L_m i_{ds}^e \end{array}\right\} \quad (1)$$

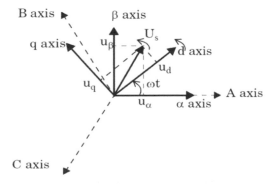

Figure 1.   Transformation of axes (from 3-phase to 2-phase).

$$\left.\begin{array}{l}\lambda_{qm}^e = L_m(i_{qs}^e + i_{qr}^e)\\ \lambda_{dm}^e = L_m(i_{ds}^e + i_{dr}^e)\end{array}\right\} \tag{2}$$

For a short-circuited squirrel cage rotor, rotor equations can be expressed by

$$\left.\begin{array}{l}R_r i_{dr}^e + p\lambda_{qr}^e + \omega_{sl}\lambda_{dr}^e = 0\\ R_r i_{qr}^e - \omega_{sl}\lambda_{qr}^e + p\lambda_{dr}^e = 0\\ where \qquad \omega_{sl} = \omega_s - \omega_r\end{array}\right\} \tag{3}$$

where

$$p = \frac{d}{dt} = timederivative$$

For reducing the number of variables, the rotor flux linkage λr can be considered to be on the d-axes. Hence, aligning d-axes.

$$\lambda_r = \lambda_{dr}^e \tag{4}$$

$$\lambda_{qr}^e = 0 \tag{5}$$

$$p\lambda_{qr}^e = 0 \tag{6}$$

The rotor equation now becomes

$$\left.\begin{array}{l}R_r i_{dr}^e + \omega_{sl}\lambda_r^e = 0\\ R_r i_{qr}^e + p\lambda_r^e = 0\end{array}\right\} \tag{7}$$

The currents of rotor and stator are related as

$$\left.\begin{array}{l}i_{qr}^e = -\frac{L}{L_r}i_{qs}^e\\ i_{dr}^e = -\frac{\lambda_r}{L_r} - \frac{L}{L_r}i_{ds}^e\end{array}\right\} \tag{8}$$

Now the current responsible for producing magnetic field and torque are as below:

$$\left.\begin{array}{l}i_f = i_{ds}^e = \frac{[1+T_r p]}{L_r}\lambda_r\\ i_T = i_{qs}^e = \frac{T_r \times \omega_s}{L_m}\lambda_r\end{array}\right\} \tag{9}$$

Rotor time constant:

$$T_r = \frac{L_r}{R_r} \tag{10}$$

The induction machine's torque is expressed as:

$$T_e = \frac{3}{2}\frac{P}{2}L_m(i_{qs}^e i_{dr}^e - i_{ds}^e i_{qr}^e) \tag{11}$$

Otherwise,

$$T_e = \frac{3}{2}\frac{P}{2}\frac{L_m}{L_r}(i_{qs}^e\lambda_{dr} - i_{ds}^e\lambda_{qr}) = K_{te}\lambda_{dr}i_{qs}^e = K_{te}\lambda_r i_T \tag{12}$$

Asynchronous motor's electromechanical equation can be given as

$$T_e - T_L = \frac{2}{P}J\frac{d\omega_r}{dt} \tag{13}$$

The working of AC drives is made equal to DC drives in this vector control for the decouple control of flux and torque. To achieve this decoupling, the vector of a stator current can be divided

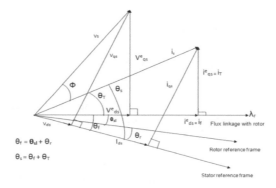

Figure 2.   Field-oriented phasor diagram of vector control.

into two parts: one component is in the same direction of the rotor flux linkages known as field producing current i_f and the other component is orthogonal to λ_r known as torque-producing current component i_T. The vector diagram is depicted in Figure 2.

The three-axis stator currents can be converted into two-axis components of currents in the field-oriented reference frames. From the stationary reference field, angle θ_f is measured:

$$
\begin{bmatrix} i^e_{qs} \\ i^e_{ds} \end{bmatrix} = \frac{2}{3} \begin{bmatrix} Cos\,\theta_f & Cos\,(\theta_f - 120°) & Cos\,(\theta_f + 120°) \\ Sin\,\theta_f & Sin(\theta_f - 120°) & Sin\,(\theta_f + 120°) \\ 0.5 & 0.5 & 0.5 \end{bmatrix} \begin{bmatrix} i_{as} \\ i_{bs} \\ i_{cs} \end{bmatrix} \tag{14}
$$

Stator current vector i_s can be calculated as

$$
i_s = \sqrt{\left(i^e_{qs}\right)^2 + \left(i^e_{ds}\right)^2} \tag{15}
$$

and angle of stator current vector is

$$
\theta_s = \tan^{-1}\left(i^e_{qs} \div i^e_{ds}\right) \tag{16}
$$

Rotor flux linkages and torque can be expressed as

$$
\lambda_r \; \alpha \; i_f
$$

$$
T_e \alpha \quad \lambda_r i_T \alpha i_f \; i_T
$$

It is now understood that the field current component of the current- and torque-producing component of the current appears to be direct current in steady state, due to zero relative speed with respect to the rotor field. Once it becomes DC then it is going to be very easy to control the motor.

The block diagram and flow chart diagram are shown in Figures 3 and 4, respectively, and are mentioned here along with step-wise mathematical terms:

$$
\theta_e = \int (\omega_r + \omega_{sl})dt = \int \omega_e dt \tag{17}
$$

$$
\omega_{sl} = \frac{L_m \times i_q}{T_r \times \lambda r} \tag{18}
$$

$$
\lambda r = \frac{L_m \times i_d}{(1 + T_r s)} \tag{19}
$$

$$i_d^* = \frac{\lambda^*r}{L_m} \tag{20}$$

$$i_q^* = \frac{2}{3} \times \frac{2}{P} \times \left(\frac{L_r \times T_e^*}{L_m \times \lambda_r} \right) \tag{21}$$

- The comparison between reference currents (i_d^* and i_q^*) and actual currents are done to generate the reference voltages V_d^* and V_q^*. This reference voltage V_{dq}^* is transformed to V_{abc}^* for the PWM inverter.
- PWM inverter voltage is applied to the stator after receiving the pulses from the above step to produce the commanded rotor flux linkages and torque. The magnitude of the current and its phase can be controlled by the inverter and thus machine's flux and torque can be decoupled by injecting the currents giving the flux-and torque.

The above Figure 3 (block diagram) and Figure 4 (computational steps) along with mathematical modeling all together creates a clear understanding of the vector control concept which is implemented using MATLAB. The machine parameters used in MATLAB is mentioned in Table 1.

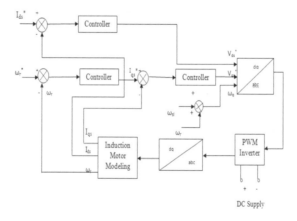

Figure 3. Vector control block diagram.

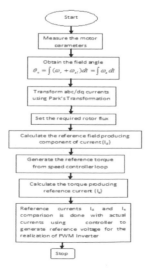

Figure 4. Computational flow diagram of vector control.

3   FUZZY LOGIC CONTROLLER

In the case of uncertainties and inaccuracies for complex problems, fuzzy logic is usually preferred for implementation. This fuzzy logic is introduced by Zadeh (1965b) and has the following advantages:

(1) mathematical model of a system is not required,
(2) nonlinearity and complexity can be handled easily,
(3) it increases the robustness,
(4) it does not require the system information,
(5) its principle of working is linguistic/human logic, i.e., IF/IF–THEN statement rules are their general instructions or structure. Apart from these advantages, the FLC has some disadvantages, i.e., high computational burden during hardware and software implementation.

There are three main components of a fuzzy system: fuzzification, fuzzy rule base inference engine, and defuzzification.

(A) **Fuzzification.** Error signals of crisp values are converted into fuzzy variables. The universe of discourse is established for all input and output variables. The suitable ranges are selected for bringing all the inputs–outputs to the universe of discourse. Three overlapping fuzzy sets are the division of each discourse. Each variable is a member of a subset with a degree of membership ranging from 0 to 1.
(B) **Fuzzy rule base inference system.** This system represents IF–THEN general instructions governing the input–output variables with membership functions. In this case, the variables are processed through inference engine executing the following rules which is shown in Table 2.

 (i) If the speed error (se)/current error (ce) is NE then the speed response (sr)/current response (cr) is NR.
(ii) If the speed error (se)/current error (ce) is ZE then the speed response (sr)/current response (cr) is ZR.

Table 1.   Machine parameters.

S. N	Parameters	Values
1	Stator resistance (Rs)	0.1830 Ω
2	Stator inductance (Ls)	0.0533 H
3	Rotor inductance (Lr)	0.0560 H
4	Rotor resistance (Rr)	0.277 Ω
5	Mutual inductance (Lm)	0.0533 H
6	Moment of inertia (J)	0.0165 Kg-m^2
7	No of pole pair (P)	2
8	Frequency (f)	50 Hz
9	DC Supply (Vd)	400 V
10	Viscous damping co-efficient (β)	1

Table 2.   Fuzzy rule base.

Fuzzy Rule Base Variables	se/ce (speed/current error)	sr/cr (speed/current response)
NE	NE	NR
ZE	ZE	ZR
PE	PE	PR

(iii) If the speed error (se)/current error (ce) is PE then the speed response (sr)/current response (cr) is PR.

Here, NE: Negative Error, ZE: Zero Error, PE: Positive Error, NR: Negative Response, ZR: Zero Response, PR: Positive Response. The snapshot of fuzzy rule viewer is shown in Figure 5.

From Figure 3 it is understood that there are two controllers, i.e., speed controller and current controller used in indirect vector control of asynchronous motor. Both controllers have the same Fuzzy Rule Base shown in Table 2.

In the speed controller loop, the input is speed error and the output is torque producing current component i^*_{qs}. The mathematical relationship is expressed as

$$i^*_{qs} = \int \Delta i_{qs} = f(\Delta e) \tag{22}$$

where Δe = speed error and f = nonlinear function.

Similarly, in current controller, current errors $\left(\Delta i_q = i^*_{qs} - i_{qs} \right)$ and $\left(\Delta i_d = i^*_{ds} - i_{ds} \right)$ are considered as input and reference voltages) $\left(v^*_{qs} \text{ and} v^*_{ds} \right)$ are considered as outputs to trigger the Voltage Source Converter (VSC) for obtaining the desired response. Here also, the inputs and outputs are related mathematically by a nonlinear function, as mentioned below:

$$v^*_{qs} or v^*_{ds} = \int \Delta i_q or \Delta i_d = f(\Delta e) \tag{23}$$

Here, $\left(\Delta i_q = \Delta e = i^*_{qs} - i_{qs} \right)$ & $\left(\Delta i_d = \Delta e = i^*_{ds} - i_{ds} \right)$.

Now it is required to select the membership function. In this paper, triangular membership is selected to reduce the computational burden. For the above-mentioned fuzzy rules, Mamdani-type fuzzy inference is applied. The snapshot of Mamdani-type FLC is depicted in Figure 6. The membership functions, fuzzy sets, and fuzzy rules, all are selected using hit and trial method to obtain optimum performance.

(C) **Defuzzification.** In this subsection, a centroid defuzzification method is applied to obtain a crisp value of output. In this method, the center of each membership function for each rule

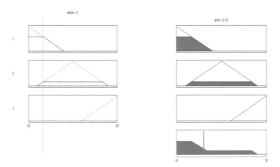

Figure 5.   Fuzzy rule viewer.

Figure 6.   FLC controller mapping input–output.

is evaluated first then final value of output is determined by taking the average of individual output, as expressed below:

$$i_{qs}^* = \frac{\sum_{k=1}^{n} i_{qs}^* \mu(i_{qs}^*)_k}{\sum_{k=1}^{n} \mu(i_{qs}^*)_k} \tag{24}$$

$$v_{qs}^* = \frac{\sum_{k=1}^{n} v_{qs}^* \mu(v_{qs}^*)_k}{\sum_{k=1}^{n} \mu(v_{qs}^*)_k} \tag{25}$$

$$v_{ds}^* = \frac{\sum_{k=1}^{n} v_{ds}^* \mu(v_{ds}^*)_k}{\sum_{k-1}^{n} \mu(v_{ds}^*)_k} \tag{26}$$

where N=total number of rules and μ =degree of membership grade with the kth rule.

4   INTERNAL MODE CONTROL AND ITS DESIGN

The Internal Model Control (IMC). The IMC control strategy is depicted in Figure 7. In fact, mismatch always occurs in the process-model. A resulting signal $\hat{d}(s)$ is derived through comparison of process and its model. Here, an unknown disturbance is $d(s)$ affecting the system.

The same input $U(s)$ is applied to process and its model. If $d(s)$ is zero then $\hat{d}(s)$ is a measure of the difference in behavior between the process and its model. If $G_p(s) = \widehat{G}_p(s)$, then $\hat{d}(s)$ is equal to an unknown disturbance. Thus, $\hat{d}(s)$ may be regarded as the information missing in the model $\hat{G}_p(s)$ and can therefore be used to improve the control. This could be done by subtracting $\hat{d}(s)$ from set point $R(s)$ which is very similar to affecting a set point trim.

The resultant equations are expressed below:

$$\hat{d}(s) = [G_p(s) - \widehat{G}_p(s) U(s) + d(s) \tag{27}$$

$$U(s) = \left[R(s) - \hat{d}(s)\right] G_c(s) \tag{28}$$

$$U(s) = \frac{[R(s) - d(s)] G_c(s)}{1 + [G_p(s) - \widehat{G}_p(s)] G_c(s)} \tag{29}$$

$$Y(s) = G_p(s) U(s) + d(s) \tag{30}$$

IMC transfer function is given below:

$$Y(s) = \frac{G_c(s) G_p(s) R(s) + \left[1 - G_c(s) \widehat{G}_p(s)\right] d(s)}{1 + [G_p(s) - \widehat{G}_p(s)] G_c(s)} \tag{31}$$

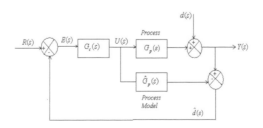

Figure 7.   IMC block diagram.

It is understood that if $G_c(s) = \frac{1}{\widehat{G_p}(s)}$ and $G_p(s) = \widehat{G_p}(s)$ then tracking and disturbance rejection both can be achieved. The accurate disturbance rejection can be realized if $G_c(s) = \frac{1}{\widehat{G_p}(s)}$ even if $G_p(s) \neq \widehat{G_p}(s)$.

The mismatch between process and its model should be minimum for improving the robustness. Since the frequency nature is usually high for this mismatch between the process and model behavior so, a low-pass filter $G_f(s)$ is usually placed to attenuate the effects of process-model mismatch. Therefore, the transfer function of internal model controller is given, i.e., $G_{IMC}(s) = G_c(s)G_f(s)$. To prevent differential control action, the proper value of $G_c(s)\,G_f(s)$ is selected. The resulting closed loop leads to

$$Y(s) = \frac{G_{IMC}(s)\,G_p(s)\,R(s) + \left[1 - G_{IMC}(s)\,\widehat{G_p}(s)\right]d(s)}{1 + [G_p(s) - \widehat{G_p}(s)]G_{IMC}(s)} \tag{32}$$

The Internal Model Principle expresses that the control can be obtained only if the control system expresses its essential features, either implicitly or explicitly. Model-based controller-designed IMC is presented by Garcia and Morari (1982b). The IMC is also helpful to tune the settings for conventional PI controllers. The IMC block diagram is now reduced to a conventional closed-loop structure, as shown in Figure 8.

$$G_{PI}(s) = \frac{G_{IMC}(s)}{1 - G_{IMC}(s)\widehat{G_p}(s)} \tag{33}$$

Below are the steps for designing IMC.

Step 1a. Transfer function of Induction Motor for the current control:

$$T.F = \frac{L_m V d}{(L_r L_s - L_m^2)s + L_s R_r} = \hat{G}_p(s) \tag{34}$$

Step 1b. The transfer function for IMC design of the speed controller of induction motor easily can be derived (mentioned in the Appendix) from electromechanical Equation (13) is:

$$T.F = \hat{G}_p(s) = \frac{k}{\tau s + 1} \tag{35}$$

Both transfer functions are of the first-order equation, where k = static gain of the system depending on the parameter numbers of poles P, L_m, R_r, λ_r, and τ = time constant, depending on moment of inertia.

The following steps of IMC design are same for current controller and speed controller.

Step 2. Set

$$G_{PI}(s) = \frac{G_{IMC}(s)}{1 - G_{IMC}(s)\hat{G}_p(s)} \tag{36}$$

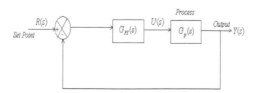

Figure 8.   Block diagram of IMC-based PI tuned controller.

Step 3. Put
$$G_{IMC}(s) = G_c(s)G_f(s) \tag{37}$$

Step 4. Set
$$G_f(s) = \frac{1}{(1 + \lambda_f s)^n} \tag{38}$$

Step 5. Set
$$G_c(s) = \frac{1}{\hat{G}_p(s)} \tag{39}$$

Here, λ_f is tuning parameter of the filter and n is the order of the filter, Here, $n = 1$ is taken as a model of first order.

Step 6. The filter tuning parameter λ_f can be selected in such a way to achieve proper tracking and disturbance rejection, both. There should be balance between the performance and robustness while selecting the value of λ_f. For smaller λ_f, the closed-loop system is fast and for larger λ_f, the closed-loop system is more robust, i.e., good disturbance rejection. In this case, λ_f is taken equal to 0.001 for both speed control as well current control.

5   PSO-BASED PID CONTROLLER

PSO is a search algorithm that works on the principle of flock of birds popularly known as a swarm. The swarm is able to search for food through a collaborative approach which works on the probability laws of finding the food or getting the best solution in a prescribed space. The following are merits of PSO:

- The accurate result is expected from PSO without involving many complex operations.
- This is flexible and robust because it works on the probability concept,
- The premature convergence may occur which enhances the search action capability.
- PSO optimization time taken is low.
- PSO can be applied in online mode.
- From any search point, this optimization can start, but there is good probability to get the optimal response.

Kennedy and Eberhart developed the PSO algorithm in 1990. As we know, the flock of birds/swarms are looking for food in a given prescribed space. That the availability of food is present somewhere is now obvious. However, the birds are not aware of their food. Yet, during each step of the journey on the food search they may know the distance of food. All the birds see are the closest birds to come near the location of food.

Here, a particle means bird and all the particles constitute a group or swarm. The position vector and velocity vector of each particle is represented as X (t) and V (t), respectively. The position of each particle is regarded as a solution of the problem. The particles must change their position and velocity to get the best or optimal solution considering their own floating experience, previous experience, and flock floating experiences. In this way, this collective technique helping to get the solution in an n-dimensional search space. The position and velocity of ith particle at time k or at K^{th} iteration number may be given as:

$$V_i(k) = [V_{i1}(k)V_{i2}(k)\ldots\ldots\ldots V_{in}(k)]^T \tag{40}$$

$$X_i(k) = [X_{i1}(k)X_{i2}(k)\ldots\ldots\ldots X_{in}(k)]^T \tag{41}$$

Particles must remember its best position and also storing all past values from the beginning. There are two best in PSO: one is local best and other is global best. Local best is also known as personal best. The local or personal best position of ith particle up to time k is given as:

$$P_{best}(k) = [P_{best,i1}(k), Pbest_{,i2}(k)\ldots\ldots P_{best,in}(k)] \tag{42}$$

759

The infusion of all particles is referred to as global best which can be given as follows:

$$G_{best}(k) = [G_{best,1}(k), Gbest_{,2}(k) \ldots \ldots G_{best,n}(k)] \tag{43}$$

Position and velocity of each particle at time $(k + 1)$ is obtained from the following equations:

$$V_{ij}(k + 1) = WV_{ij}(k) + C_1 Rand1_{ij}(P_{best,ij}(k) - X_{ij}(k)) + C_2 Rand2_{ij}(G_{best,j}(k) - X_{ij}(k)) \tag{44}$$

$$X_{ij}(k + 1) = X_{ij}(k) + V_{ij}(k + 1) \tag{45}$$

where V_{ij} and X_{ij} are the velocity vector V and position vector X of ith element for ith particle position.

$P_{best,ij} = j^{th}$ dimension of best position of ith particle at time k.

$G_{best,i} = j^{th}$ dimension of best global position.

W = inertia weight = 0.8

$Rand1_{ij}$ and $Rand2_{ij}$ = two random variables in the interval [0 1].

C_1 & C_2 = training factors or self-confidence (C_1) or swarm confidence (C_2) = 1 and 2.

k = time or iteration number = 10 = number of particles

Initializations of parameters are very crucial for the convergence. Here, the following procedure illustrated the PSO algorithm.

Step 1. Keep the values of parameters such as the number of particles, dimension, inertia weight, and training factors, Here, the number of particles = 10, dimension = 3, training factors = 1/2, and inertia weight = 0.8.

Step 2. Randomly initialize all the particles.

Step 3. Assigning of P_{best} vectors of all particles through random initial values generated in Step 2.

Step 4. Determine the local best position also known as fitness value for each particle.

Step 5. Calculate the global best position.

Step 6. Keeps on updating the particle velocity vectors and position vectors through the above equations.

Step 7. Update the P_{best} for each particle.

Step 8. Update G_{best}. If the outcome of G_{best} (k+1) is better than the outcome of G_{best} (k), then G_{best} (k) = G_{best} (k+1).

Step 9. If the solution converges then iteration will stop; otherwise return to step 6.

The objective of PSO is to get the optimum value of Kp, Ki and Kd of the PID controller for the speed controller/current controller loop. Here, the optimum means to minimize the objective function or fitness function. The objective/fitness function is selected as a speed error and current error. There are various performance indices to select the speed/current error such as integral of absolute error (IAE) $I_{AE} = \int |e(t)|dt$, integral square error (ISE) $I_{SE} = \int e^2(t)dt$, integral square of absolute error (ISAE) $= I_{SAE} = \int |e(t)|^2 dt$, and integral of time multiplied by absolute error (ITAE) $= I_{TAE} = \int t|e(t)|dt$. Here the error $e(t) = \omega_r^* - \omega_r or i_{qs}^* - i_{qs} or i_{ds}^* - i_{ds}$.

In this paper, integral square error (ISE) $I_{SE} = \int e^2(t)dt$ is selected as a one of the performance indices. In this way the particle moves in space with velocity vector V and position vector X for each iteration and checks for the optimization of objective function. The optimized value of each particle during the iteration is said to be local best denoted by P and optimum value of all the local best is known as global best denoted by G. Here the objective/fitness function is a performance index i.e. speed/current error integral square error (ISE) $I_{SE} = \int e^2(t)dt$.

The PSO algorithm flow chart is depicted in Figure 9 for ease of understanding.

This paper proposes an online technique to set the parameters of PID controller using the PSO algorithm to obtain the optimal performance of vector-controlled induction motor drives. The optimum values of the parameters of PID controller are Kp = 669.2552, Ki = 0.0159, and Kd = 0.4.

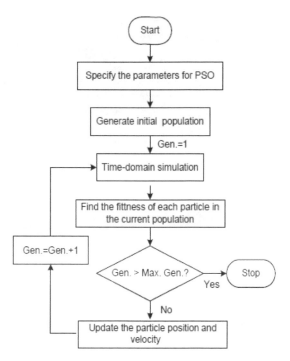

Figure 9.   Flow chart of PSO algorithm.

This nonlinear search technique has been applied to the linear system meeting the objective or fitness function which is nonlinear in nature.

6   RESULTS AND DISCUSSION

Figures 10(a), (b), and (c) compare the dynamic performances of torque using FLC, IMC, and PSO, respectively. This is obvious from the figures that a reference torque of 0 N-m initially and then 50 N-m from 1.2–1.5 sec, 30 Nm from 1.5–1.8 sec and again 50 Nm after 1.8 sec is tracked by actual torque in all the three cases.

This is now clear from the above figures that the torque performance using PSO is better than that of IMC and fuzzy. The magnitude of peaky transients appearing at the instants 0.8 sec in the torque waveform of Figure 10(b) using IMC is more comparatively, whereas it is much more at the instant 1.2 sec, 1.5 sec, and 1.8 sec using PSO which is shown in Figure 10(c). Under a steady-state case, the ripple contents in torque waveform is less using PSO followed by IMC and FLC.

Figures 11(a), (b) and (c) show the dynamic performance of speed using FLC, IMC, and PSO, respectively. At 0.8 sec, the reference speed is changed to 1400 rpm. It is clear that the actual speed tracks the reference values in all the cases. This is observed from Figure 11(a) and Figure 11(b) that there is a very little decrease in speed at 1.2 sec and little increase in speed at 1.5 sec and again decrease in speed at 1.8 sec and then continues with the same speed thereafter. This is only due to changes in torques at the respective times. The speed variation should not be much (usually below 5%) due to load torque variations. In Figure 11(c) of speed waveform, transient appears but no variation in the actual speed waveform is observed for the changes in load torque. The actual speed is above reference speed using FLC and IMC whereas it is below reference speed using PSO. The speed tracking and preserving the speed characteristics without ripple content is found better using IMC, but peaky transient at time 0.8 sec is little high as shown in Figure 11(c).

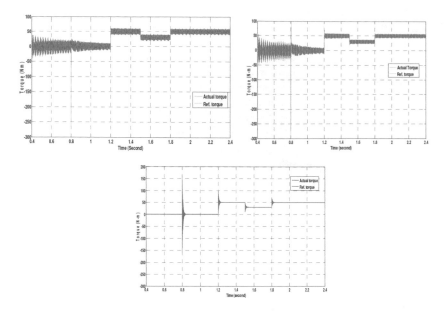

Figure 10. **(a)** Torque-time waveform using FLC. **(b)** Torque-time waveform using IMC. **(c)** Torque-time waveform using PSO.

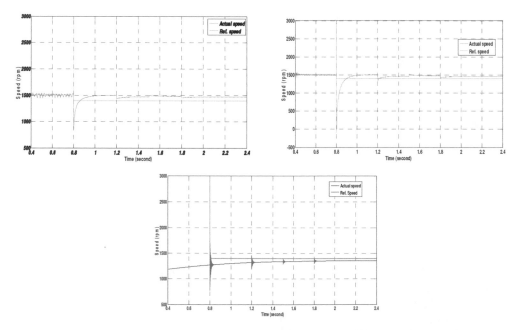

Figure 11. **(a)** Speed-time waveform using FLC. **(b)** Speed-time waveform using IMC. **(c)** Speed-time waveform using PSO.

Similarly, the current waveforms shown in Figures 12(a), (b), and (c) are shown using FLC, IMC, and PSO, respectively. The keen observation of current waveforms shown in Figure 12(a) and 12(b) indicating that there is a smaller decrease or increase in supply current in accordance with changes in load torque, but no such change is observed in Figure 12(c).

762

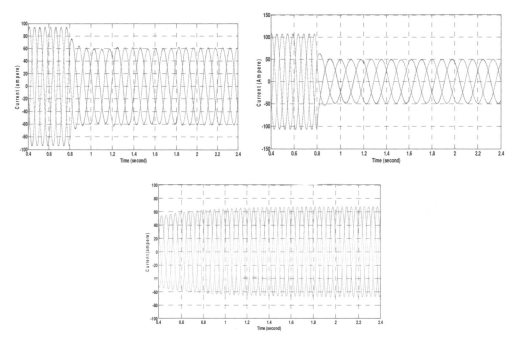

Figure 12. **(a)** Current-time waveform using FLC. **(b)** Current-time waveform using IMC. **(c)** Current-time waveform using PSO.

The adnd ded advantage of using IMC is that only one parameter, i.e., filter-tuning parameter λ_f, is required to select; but in FLC, membership function, fuzzy sets, and fuzzy rules all are required to select using hit and trial method. In PSO also, three parameters are required to get using PSO which takes a very long time for MATLAB code to terminate the optimum values.

7 CONCLUSION

Indirect method of vector control of an induction motor is presented using PSO, IMC, and FLC. The design of FLC, IMC, and PSO are presented. Under a steady-state condition, it is observed from performance comparison that the overall performance of IMC is comparatively good. This is found that the uncertainty is less in the case of IMC since only one parameter, i.e., filter tuning parameter λ_f, is required to select. For a very, very short period of time, the magnitude of peaky transient using IMC is more as compared to FLC and PSO, but the running performance of the motor using IMC is found to be reasonably good.

REFERENCES

Boumediene Allaoua et al. "The Efficiency of PSO Applied on Fuzzy Logic DC Motor Speed Control" Serbian Journal of Electrical Engg. Vol.5, No.2, 2008, pp. 247–262.
Sree Bash Chabdra Debnath, Pintu Chandra Shill, K. Murusae "PSO Based Adative Strategy for tuning of FLC" International Journal of Artificial Intelligence and Applications, Vol.4, No.1, jan.2013, pp. 37–50.
H. Bervani et al. "Intelligent Frequency Control in an AC Micro Grid: Online PSO-Based Fuzzy Tuning Approach" IEEE Transaction on Smart Grid Vol.3, No.4, Dec.2012, pp. 1935–1944.
Hassan Bervani et al. "Intelligent LFC Concerning High Penetration of Wind Power: Synthesis and Real Time Application" IEEE Transaction on Sustainable Energy, Vol.5, No.2, April 2013, pp. 655–662.

P. S. Bhimbra "Generalized Theory of Electrical Machinery" Khanna Publishers 2012.

Bimal K Bose "Modern Power Electronics and AC Drives" Prentice Hall 2002.

D. Das and A. Ghosh "Algorithm for PSO Tuned Fuzzy Controller of a DC Motor" International Journal of Computer Applications, Vol.77, No. 4, July 2013, pp. 37–41.

Manoj Datta et al. "A Frequency Control Approach by Photovoltaic Generator in a PV-Diesel Hybrid Power System" IEEE Transaction on Energy Conversion, Vol.26, No.2, June 2011, pp. 559–571.

R. C. Eberhart and Yuhui Shi "Comparision between Genetic Algorithm and PSO". Springer, Volume 1447 of the series Lecture notes in Computer Science, December 2005.

Garcia, C. E., and M. Morari. 1982. "Internal Model Control –1. A Unifying Review, *Ind. Eng. Chem. Process Des. Dev.*, **1982**, 21 (2), pp. 308–323.

M. Godoy Simoes and Fellix A. Ferret "Alternate Energy Systems: Design and Analysis with Induction Generator" 2nd edition, CRC Press-Taylor and Francis Group.

Rania Hassan, Babak Cohanim, Oliver de Weck "A Comparision of PSO and G.A" American Institute of Aeronautics and Astronautics, 46th AIAA/ASME/ASCE/AHS/ASC Structures, Structural Dynamics and Materials Conference, 18–21, April 2005, Autin Texas".

Kathuria J., Khan M.A., Abraham A., Darwish A. (2014) Low Power Techniques for Embedded FPGA Processors. In: Khan M., Saeed S., Darwish A., Abraham A. (eds) Embedded and Real Time System Development: A Software Engineering Perspective. Studies in Computational Intelligence, vol 520. Springer, Berlin, Heidelberg. https://doi.org/10.1007/978-3-642-40888-5_11.

B. N. Kar et al. "Indirect Vector Control of Induction Motor using sliding mode controller" IET International Conference on Sustainable Energy and Intelligent Systems, July 20–22, 2011, Chennai, 507–511.

P .C. Kraus, O. Wasynczuk, Scott. D. Sudhoff "Analysis of Electric Machinery", 2nd Edition, 2004, John Wilely and Sons.

R. Krishnan "Electric Motor Drives-Modeling, Analysis & Control" Prentice-Hall, 2001.

Liying Liu, Zhenlin Xu, Quieng Mei "Sensorless Vector Control Induction Motor Drive Based on ADRC and Flux Observer" IEEE Control and Decision Conference, June 17–19, 2009, 245–248, Guilin.

M. Menna et al. "Speed Sensorless Vector Control of an Induction Motor using spiral vector model ECKF and ANN controller" IEEE conference on Electric Machines and Drives EMDC, May3–5, 2007, Antalya, 1165–1167.

Deepak Nagaria, G. N. Pillai & H. O. Gupta "Modeling & Control of Wind Energy Conversion System Equipped with DFIG" International Conference on Energy & Environment, March 19–21, 2009, pp 902–908.

K.B. Narayan, K.B. Mohanty and M. Singh "Indirect Vector Control of Induction Motor using Fuzzy Logic Controller" IEEE, 10th International Conference on Environment and Electrical Engg.(EEEIC), 8–11, May, 2011.

D. W. Novotney, *et al.* "Introduction to Field Orientation and High Performance AC Drives," IEEE IAS Tutorial Course, 1986.

Andreas Petersson, Lennart Harnefors and Torbjorn Thiringer "Evaluation of Current Control Method for Wind Turbines Using Doubly-Fed Induction Machines" IEEE Transactions on Power Electronics, Vol. 20, No. 1, January 2005. pp 227–235.

F. Poitiers, M. Machmoum, R. Le Doeuff and M. E. Zaim "Control of Doubly-Fed Induction Generator for Wind Energy Conversion Systems" International Journal of Renewable Energy, Vol. 3, No. 3, December 2001, pp. 373–378.

S. K. Salman & Babak Badrzadeh "New Approach Modeling Doubly-Fed Induction Generator for Grid Connection Studies" www.2004ewec.info/files/23_1400_sksalman_01.pdf, 2015.

G. R. Slemon, "Modelling of Induction Machines for Electric Drives," IEEE Trans. on Industry Applications, Vol.25, No. 6, pp. 1126–1131, Nov. 1989.

B. Subudhi et al. "dSpace Implementation of Fuzzy Logic Based Vector Control of Induction Motor" IEEE Conference TENCON,2008, Nov.19–21, Hyderabad, 978-1-4244-2408-5.

C. Thanga Raj et al. "Particle Swarm and Fuzzy Logic Based Optimal Energy Control of Induction Motor for a Mine Hoist Load Diagram" IAENG International Journal of Computer Science,36:1, IJCS, 36_1_03, 2009a.

C. Thanga Raj et al. "Energy Efficient Control of Three-Phase Induction Motor-A Review" Internal Journal of Computer and Electrical Engg., Vol.1, No.1, April 2009b.

P. Tripura and Y. Srinivasa Babu "Fuzzy Logic Speed Control of Three Phase Induction Motor Drive" World Academy of Science, Engg. and Technology (WASET), International Journal of Electrical, Electronic, Computer, Energetic and Communication Engg. Vol. 5, No. 12, 2011, pp. 1769–1773.

M. N. Uddin, T. S. Radwan, M. A. Rahman "Performances of fuzzy-logic-based indirect vector control for induction motor drive" IEEE Transaction on Industry Applications, 2002, pp. 1219–1225.

M. Uddin. Sang Woo Nam "New Online Loss Minization-Based Controlled of Induction Motor Drives" IEEE Transactions on Power Electronics, Vol. 23, 2008, pp. 926–933.

Waheedabeevi, M. Suresh Kumar, A, Nair N. S "New Online Loss Minimization of Scalar and Vector Controlled Induction Motor Drives" IEEE International Conference PEDES2012a.

Zadeh "Fuzzy Sets" Inf. Control, Vol. 8, pp. 338–353,1965.

Zerikat M, Mechernene A, Chekroun S "High Performance Sensorless Vector Control of Induction Motor Drives using Artificial Intelligence Technique" IEEE International Conference on Automation and Robotics, Aug. 23–26, 2010, 67–75, Miedzyzdroje.

APPENDIX

$$\left.\begin{array}{l}\begin{bmatrix}V_{qs}^s\\V_{ds}^s\\V_{os}^s\end{bmatrix}=\tfrac{2}{3}\begin{bmatrix}Cos\,\theta & Cos\,(\theta-120°) & Cos\,(\theta+120°)\\Sin\,\theta & Sin\,(\theta+120°) & Sin\,(\theta+120°)\\0.5 & 0.5 & 0.5\end{bmatrix}\begin{bmatrix}V_{as}\\V_{bs}\\V_{cs}\end{bmatrix}\\[2em]\begin{bmatrix}V_{as}\\V_{bs}\\V_{cs}\end{bmatrix}=\begin{bmatrix}Cos\theta & Sin\theta & 1\\Cos(\theta-120°) & Sin(\theta-120°) & 1\\Cos(\theta+120°) & Sin(\theta+120°) & 1\end{bmatrix}\begin{bmatrix}V_{qs}^s\\V_{ds}^s\\V_{os}^s\end{bmatrix}\end{array}\right\}\quad\text{(A1)}$$

$$\left.\begin{array}{l}v_{qs}^e=(R_s+L_sp)\,i_{qs}^e+\omega_sL_si_{ds}^e+L_mpi_{qr}^e+\omega_sL_mi_{dr}^e\\v_{ds}^e=(R_s+L_sp)\,i_{ds}^e-\omega_sL_si_{qs}^e+L_mpi_{dr}^e-\omega_sL_mi_{qr}^e\\v_{qr}^e=(R_r+L_rp)\,i_{qr}^e+(\omega_s-\omega_r)L_mi_{ds}^e+L_mpi_{qs}^e+(\omega_s-\omega_r)L_ri_{dr}^e\\v_{dr}^e=(R_r+L_rp)\,i_{dr}^e-(\omega_s-\omega_r)L_mi_{qs}^e+L_mpi_{ds}^e-(\omega_s-\omega_r)L_ri_{qr}^e\end{array}\right\}\quad\text{(A2)}$$

Transfer function of the speed controller loop of induction motor for the IMC design

The IMC design of speed controller can be obtained from the electromechanical equation:

$$T_e-T_L=\frac{2}{P}J\frac{d\omega_r}{dt},\text{ where },T_e=\frac{3}{2}\frac{P}{2}\frac{L_m}{L_r}(i_{qs}^e\lambda_{dr}-i_{ds}^e\lambda_{qr})=K_{te}\lambda_{dr}i_{qs}^e=K_{te}\lambda_r i_T\quad\text{(A3)}$$

We have:

$$i_T=i_{qs}^e=\frac{T_r\times\omega_s}{L_m}\lambda_r=\frac{L_r\times\omega_s}{R_r\times L_m}\lambda_r\quad\text{(A4)}$$

Now Te and T_L can be expressed as below:

$$T_e=\frac{3P\lambda_r^2\omega_s}{4R_r}=k\omega_s\text{ where }k=\frac{3P\lambda_r^2}{4R_r}\quad\text{(A5)}$$

$T_L=\beta\omega_r$, where $\beta=$ viscous damping co-efficient.

From the electromechanical equation:

$$k\omega_s-\beta\omega_r==\text{J}^{'}\text{ Where J}^{'}=\frac{2}{P}J\quad\text{(A6)}$$

Now, the transfer function after taking Laplace transforms

$$\frac{\omega_r(s)}{\omega_s(s)}=\hat{G}_p(s)=\frac{k}{sJ^{'}+\beta}=\frac{k}{\tau s+1}\quad\text{(A7)}$$

where $\tau=\frac{J^{'}}{\beta}$ time constant of the system and $k=$ static gain of the system.

Smart Computing – Khan et al (Eds)
© *2021 Taylor & Francis Group, London, ISBN 978-0-367-76552-1*

Development of robust control algorithm for an inertially stabilized platform

Kumar Rajesh
*Department of Electronics and Communication, Govind Ballabh Pant Institute of Engineering and
Technology, Ghurdauri, Pauri Garhwal, India*

ABSTRACT: The aim of this paper is to design and analyze the line-of-sight stabilization of a two-axis gimbaled system with different disturbances. It also presents robust control algorithms for inertially stabilized platform. Linear Quadratic Gaussian with Loop Transfer Recovery robust controller has been designed and simulated for an inertially stabilized platform. The performance of the robust controller is also compared with a proportional-integral classical controller. The paper concludes that the Linear Quadratic Gaussian controller gives the better performance and stability objectives as compared to the Proportional Integral controller.

1 INTRODUCTION

Inertially stabilized platform (ISP) is widely used to stabilize the line of sight (LOS) of the gimbaled payload mounted on an Army tank to Navy systems, and used for airplanes, helicopters, and Unmanned Air Vehicles (UAVs). An ISP scheme can also be used for optical imaging systems. Control of LOS orientation is a prerequisite for a model-based control design, a dynamic model in which an electromechanical or optical sensor is used to sense the position of target or images. If a sensor is not placed properly on the gimbal, an ISP is essential. LOS stabilization system has the ability to control the position of an assembly or instrument when it is subjected to weather conditions, i.e., mass imbalance, cable restraint, viscous friction, air friction, etc. The several disturbances of torque are included in the two-axis gimbal model. The performance of the system is analyzed with two controllers, i.e., proportional–integral (PI) and linear quadratic regulator/loop transfer recovery (LQG/LTR). The PI controller is designed for the stabilization system. The LQG/LTR controller is also presented in the present investigation to improve robustness. If the control system is performing well in the presence of noise, the system is called robust.

2 SYSTEM DESCRIPTION

ISP usually consists of mechanical, electrical, and electronics devices called a mechanical assembly. It consists of a sensor or group of sensors, bearing, motor, and amplifier. The optical sensor or mechanical sensor is mounted on the gimbal, i.e., payload. Mirrors or other optical systems or mechanical devices are attached to the gimbal assembly. The electromechanical or optical sensor is connected to the land vehicle like an Army tank. Typically, the gimbal algorithm has been designed to track the position of the vehicle and stabilize about two axes, and, therefore, the latest systems require at least two gimbals for raw and pitch. The weight of two axes Gimbal may be a pound to several kilograms, while the weight of an ISP depends on controlling parameters mechanism, actuators, and sensors. But ISP weight and size may increase as number of axes and degree of freedom increased. Gimbal is rotated by direct drive motor installed on gimbal axes. This system has sensed the displacements and position of a gimbal, and LOS angular position describes the target angular position (or location). Gyro measures angular rate or angular rotation. A stabilization

DOI 10.1201/9781003167488-95

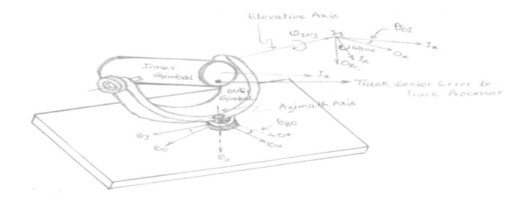

Figure 1.   Two-axis gibmal structure.

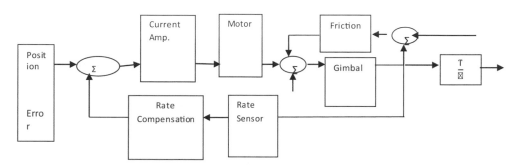

Figure 2.   Inner-stabilization control loop.

loop is a feedback control system (Hilkert). The purpose of the optimization is to reduce the mass and increase the values of the natural frequency for the first few modes of vibrations. Servo Robust PI Controller used for the control and stabilization of LOS of charge-coupled devices and a distance finder on a ground vehicle (Mokbel). To generate the controlling torque which is equal and opposite to disturbance torque by acting on the gimbaled payload in order to isolate the payload(Krishna Moorty). A feed-forward scheme is used for rejection of a disturbing torque for an inertially stabilized platform (Mortin). The system has a two degree-of-freedom gimbal which is connected to a land vehicle or Army tank. Due to dynamics errors, disturbances, moisture, wind, torque, and friction, the performance of the gimbal will be decreased. So, an advanced control technique is required.

In the proposed configuration the pointing system is directly mounted on an LOS axis. A two-axis gimbal is considered (elevation over azimuth). Two rate gyros are proposed for angular rate measurement. The different disturbances, i.e., mass imbalance torque, friction, and cable restraint torques affect the line of sight. The two-axis gimbal structure is shown in Figure 1 and an inner stabilization control loop is also shown in Figure 2.

3   DESIGN AND DEVELOPMENT OF ROBUST CONTROLLER FOR AN INERTIALLY STABILIZED PLATFORM

In this paper, a modern synthesis tools such as LQG/LTR control for optimization have been designed.

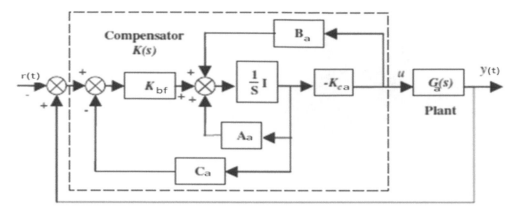

Figure 3. LQG/LTR control loop.

3.1 *Designing of linear quadratic Gaussian*

AN LQG controller is divided into two parts: LQR and Kalman filter. The LQR system is dealing with state regulation, output regulation. The quadratic performance index is calculated as, denoted by J:

$$J = \int_0^{\infty} (X^T a(t) \, Qc \, Xa(t) + U^T a(t) \, Rc \, Ua(t)) dt \tag{1}$$

Control law for LQR:

$$Kca = Rc^{-1} B_a^T Pc \tag{2}$$

The value of Pc is calculated by the Control Ricaati Equation (CRE), expressed as $A_a^T Pc + Pc\,A_a - Pc B_a R_c^{-1} B_a^T Pc + Qc = 0$; $Qc = q \, C_a^T Ca$, q > 0 and $Rc = \alpha I$, $\alpha > 0$
The scalar design parameters are q and α. The overall LQG modeling equation is

$$G_c = K_{ca}(A - k_{ca}c)x +_{Ba} u + k_{ca}y$$
$$G_p = \text{plant model, } \hat{x} = A\hat{x} + B_a u + k_{ca}(y - \hat{y}); \hat{y} = c\hat{x} \tag{3}$$

Putting the value of $\hat{y}$ in $\hat{x}$ model, the relation becomes

$$\hat{x} = A\hat{x} + B_a u + k_{ca}(y - c\hat{x}) \tag{4}$$

So, after determining the overall closed-loop system model, the closed-loop gain of the system, A_{CL} becomes

$$A_{CL} = \begin{bmatrix} A_a & -B_a K_{ca} \\ K_{bf} C_a \, A_a - B_a K_{ca} - K_{bf} C_a \end{bmatrix} \tag{5}$$

$$B_{CL} = \begin{bmatrix} 0 \\ -K_{bf} \end{bmatrix} \quad \text{and} \quad C_{CL} = [C_a \ 0] \tag{6}$$

The Kalman filter and LQR have designed and simulated on MATLAB platform to estimate the output, using the above equations. The Kalman function can be used to determine optimal state based on the noise or disturbance, shown in Figure 3.

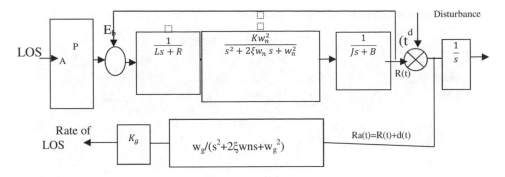

Figure 4. ISP control scheme.

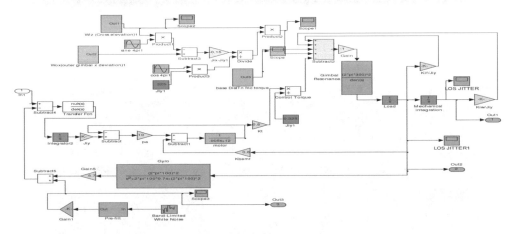

Figure 5. Simulink model of the plant with the LQG/LTR controller.

3.2 *ISP specifications (given by IRDE-DRDO, Dehradun, Govt. of India): Model should meet the following design specifications:*

Acceptable Residual Jitter	$\leq 80\ \mu$ radians
Closed loop (0 dB Crossover) bandwidth	≥ 30 Hz
Gain Margin	> 6 dB
Phase Margin	> 30 degrees
Damping Co-efficient ξ	0.3–0.7

Disturbances of the order of 10 Hz, and prominent disturbances is of the order of 3 Hz,

The inner stabilization robust controller has been modeled according to the given specifications, shown in Figure 4. Simulink models of the inner loop with the LQG/LTR controller have been developed on MATLAB Simulink tool platform, as shown in Figure 5.

LOS jitter and LOS rate responses with LQG/LTR controller are shown in Figures 6 and 7, respectively. The standard deviation of LOS jitter is of the order of 13 μrad in case of the LQG/LTR controller, while 22.15 μrad in the case of proportional controller, so LQG improves the performance of the inertially stabilized platform. Figure 7 reveals that open-loop magnitude response follows the target, and the gain margin of the order of 21.8 dB, the phase margin of the open-loop bode of the order of 58. The ISP with PI controller and LQG/LTR has been simulated with the provided specification to get the desired performance. Figures 8 and 9 reveal that the performance

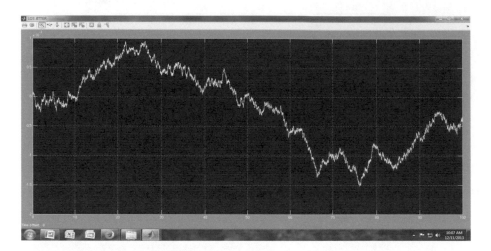

Figure 6. LOS jitter with LQG/LTR controller.

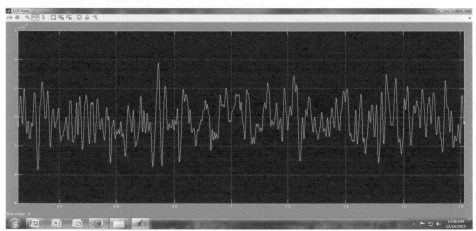

Figure 7. LOS rate.

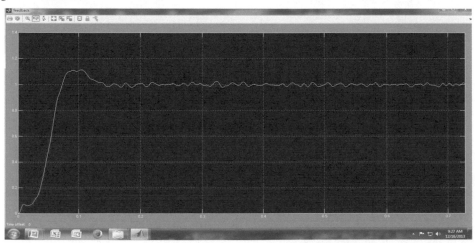

Figure 8. Closed-loop step response with PI controller, Peak overshoot = 11.5%.

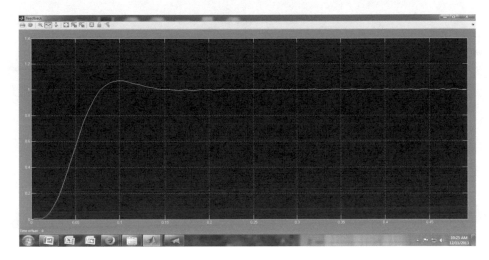

Figure 9.   Step response with the LQG/LTR controller.

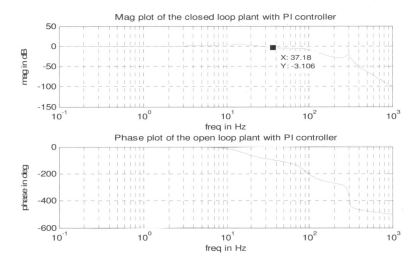

Figure 10.   Closed-loop bode response with PI controller.

parameters of PI and LQG controller such as overshoot, rise time, open, and closed-loop bode plots for PI and LQG controller are also shown in Figures 10, 11, 12, and 13, respectively. Figure 11 shows the stability factor with respect to body motion at 1 Hz. The gain at 1 Hz is 67.46 dB for LQG/LTR while 47.36 dB in the case of the PI controller.

4   RESULTS AND CONCLUSION

In the proposed work, one can design and develop robust models for a two-axis gimbal with PI controller and LQG/LTR controller for inert ally stabilized platform. The comparison has been

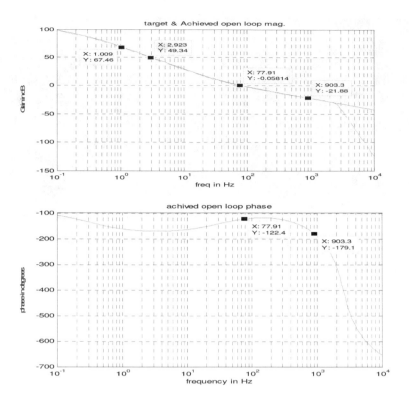

Figure 11. Open-loop bode response.

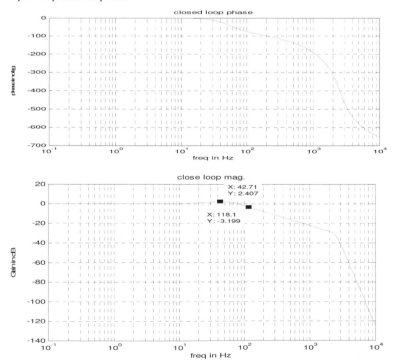

Figure 12. Closed-loop bode response.

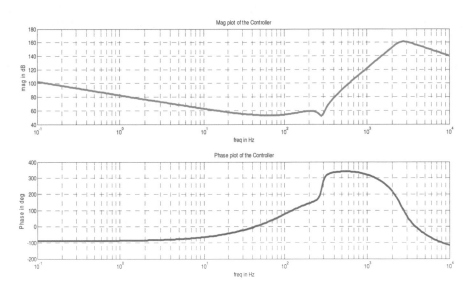

Figure 13. LQG/LTR controller bodeplot.

Table 1. Performance analysis.

Performance parameters	Proportional controller	LQG/LTR controller
GM (dB)	10.28	21.8
PM (deg)	46	58
Bandwidth	37	118.1
Los jitter (Std. Deviation)	22.15 μrad	13 μrad
Peak overshoot	11.5%	7%

made in terms of performance and stability objectives of the system. The comparative analysis (frequency and time response analysis) is shown in Table 1.

Table 1 concludes that the LQG/LTR controller gives the better performance and stability in comparison to the PI controller while system is affecting from weather and inherent conditions.

REFERENCES

Hilkert J. M. 2008. Inertially stabilized platform technology IEEE control system magazine, pp. 26–46.
Ho-Pyeong Lee and Inn-Eark Yoo, 2007. Robust Control Design for a Two-axis Gimbaled Stabilization System, IEEE AC paper # 1010, Version 3, Updated December 31.
Kathuria J., Khan M.A., Abraham A., Darwish A. (2014) Low Power Techniques for Embedded FPGA Processors. In: Khan M., Saeed S., Darwish A., Abraham A. (eds) Embedded and Real Time System Development: A Software Engineering Perspective. Studies in Computational Intelligence, vol 520. Springer, Berlin, Heidelberg. https://doi.org/10.1007/978-3-642-40888-5_11.
Krishna Moorty, J.A.R, Rajeev Marathe & V.R. Sule, 2002. H∞ control law for LOS stabilization for mobile land vehicles, Optical Engg., vol-41, no.11, Nov.2002, pp. 2935–44.
Martin Rezac and Zdenek Hurak. 2011. Vibration rejection for inertially stabilized double gimbal platform using acceleration feed forward, IEEE International conference on Control Applications (CCA), 978-1-4577-1063-6/11/$26.

Masten M.K. et al. 2008. Inertially stabilized platforms for optical imaging systems, IEEE control system magazine, pp. 47–64.

Mokbel et al. 2012. Design optimization of the inner gimbal for dual-axis inertially stabilized platform using finite element model analysis, International journal of modern Engg. Research, vol-2, issue-2, Mar-April 2012, pp. 239–44.

Prasatporn Wongkamchang and Viboon Sangveraphunsiri. 2008. Control of Inertial Stabilization Systems Using Robust Inverse Dynamics Control and Adaptive Control. Thammasat Int. J. Sc. Tech, vol-13, no-2.

Smart Computing – Khan et al (Eds)
© 2021 Taylor & Francis Group, London, ISBN 978-0-367-76552-1

An online-based approach for frequency control of a micro-grid using GWO

Bhola Jha & Manoj Kumar Panda
G. B. Pant Institute of Engineering and Technology, Pauri, Uttarakhand, India

ABSTRACT: This paper presents the Grey Wolf Optimization- (GWO) based frequency control of a micro-grid consisting of the Diesel Engine Generator (DEG), Fuel Cell (FC), Photo-Voltaic (PV) system, Flywheel Energy Storage System (FESS), Battery Energy Storage System (BESS), and Wind Energy Generator (WEG). The membership function of the Fuzzy Logic Controller (FLC) is tuned using a GWO technique. A comparative evaluation of frequency variation of a micro-grid using a conventional proportional–integral (PI) controller, PI plus FLC, and PI plus FLC plus GWO is investigated. It is found that the performance of three combined techniques, i.e., PI plus FLC plus GWO, is superior over the other two.

Keywords: Frequency, Micro-Grid, PI, FLC, GWO

1 INTRODUCTION

The depleting conventional energy resources may create a shortage of power for future generations. In such a situation, renewable resources such as solar, wind, fuel cell, etc., is an alternative option which can provide sustainable and pollution-free electricity (Freris 2008). Instability and uncertainty are the main problem in a renewable power system because of its dynamic behavior. There is deviation in load frequency because of the difference of total generation and demand. In a power system (Golpîra 2014; Ghafouri et al. 2015), load-frequency control (LFC) plays a vital role. Practicing engineers decide which type of controllers would be necessary for LFC issues (Panda et al. 2009; Yousef et al. 2014).

A wide range of literature review subjected to LFC issues has been found (Pandey et al. 2013; Parmar et al. 2012; Rahmani & Sadati 2013). Khuntia (2012) and Ansari & Velusami (201) have used artificial neural networks (ANNs) and Fuzzy Logic Controller (FLC) in an LFC problem. The time taken to train the neurons of an ANN is large which is one of the drawbacks of an ANN. Zadeh (1965) introduced the fuzzy set theory describing its difficulties, i.e., to determine exact membership function. Since the penetration of renewables keep on increasing the conventional controller capability is unable to limit the frequency variations within the required range. Therefore, several resources address the issues by implementing intelligent control or tuning the constants of proportional–integral (PI)/Fuzzy through optimization technique in either online/offline mode.

There are uncertainties in the membership function of Type 1 fuzzy which can be minimized by Interval Type-2 Fuzzy Logic systems (IT2FLS) (Liang & Mendel 2000). A Type-2 fuzzy system has a three-dimensional membership function which is an advantage of Type-2 fuzzy set over a two-dimensional membership function of Type-1 fuzzy set.

The extra third-dimensional membership function helps to regulate the uncertainty more efficiently. The applications IT2FLC in different areas of engineering was presented in (Castillo & Melin 2014). LFC of two-area generation rate constraint (GRC) nonlinearity power system using interval Type-2 fuzzy is described (Sudha & Santhi 2011). The IT2FLC-based feedback error learning (FEL) method is suggested for LFC (Sabahi et al. 2014). The literatures published are different in terms of their results and claim.

DOI 10.1201/9781003167488-96

In Saxena (2019), fractional order controller via internal mode control (IMC) for the LFC of a given power system is proposed. The IMC framework is made to act as a robust controller using the CRONE principle, model-order reduction, and FO filter which is applied to a single-area system and then extended to a two-area system. Xiong et al. (2018) address the time delay issues for the LFC of a three-area system. The delay causes a potential threat for the stability of a power system. To mitigate the threat, robust control with delay margin estimation using the linear matric inequality (LMI) method is introduced. The design of the Modified Active Disturbance Rejection Control (MADRC) scheme considering Extended State Observer (ESO) is proposed in Srikanth & Yagaiah (2018) to overcome the difficulties non-minimum phase dynamics. For this, constraint multi-objective functions are unified and a Teaching- Learning Based Optimization (TLBO) technique is applied. This MADRC is implemented to a given power system for load frequency. Aziz et al. (2018) addresses the frequency sensitivity of wind penetration into a grid and also the grid code compatibility. To support the frequency of a micro-grid, the vehicle-to-grid (V2G) concept is introduced in Khooban et al. (2017). This concept uses multi-objective fractional order fuzzy PID controller (MOFOFPID) whose parameters are tuned using modified black hole optimization algorithm (MBHOA). In Wang et al. (2016), a sliding mode pitch angle controller is designed for a Wind Energy Generator (WEG) to get proper output power. The sliding mode load frequency controller is designed as a secondary frequency regulation for a diesel power plant to bring back the system frequency in normal. For the improvement of dynamic performance, the sliding mode LFC is redesigned through the disturbance observer (DO). The frequency control approach for the PV generator in PV-diesel hybrid power system using fuzzy is proposed by Datta et al. (2011). Huge piercing of wind energy causing frequency deviation to the power system for which an experimental real-time implementation is demonstrated by Bervani et al. (2013).

Supplying electricity from a conventional big power plant to the rural/hilly areas of our country is one of the challenges due to huge transportation cost, operation, maintenance, transmission line erection, etc. Therefore, this paper addresses installing a micro-hybrid grid system which is feasible, reliable, and economically viable and at most meeting the demand of electricity locally. The durability of this grid system will be enhanced because the life span of individual energy resources is going to be increased. The grid should also ensure to give the quality of power at constant frequency which is usually typical because of presence of varying wind seed and solar irradiation of micro grid system. The proposed hybrid test system consisting wind energy, solar PV array, fuel cell, diesel engine generator, battery energy storage system, and flywheel energy storage system. The test system and its parameters are taken same as that of Bervani et al. (2012). Since proposed test system consisting of WTG and PV which are the major sources causing the frequency variations, so an intelligent optimized controller, i.e., GWO-based FLC and PI controller, is used for a diesel engine generator which is a conventional resource in which natural frequency change is not possible. This paper differs from that of Bervani et al. (2012) in terms of approach. In Bervani et al. (2012), FLC and PI are used and the parameters of PI, i.e., Kp and Ki, are tuned using particle swarm optimization (PSO) technique. In this paper, a novel approach, i.e., tuning the membership function of FLC using GWO, is proposed.

To demonstrate the capability of proposed method, the outcomes of the results are collated with respect to the fuzzy-PI controller and conventional PI controller.

This paper is arranged as follows. Section 2 narrates the test system and its modeling. Section 3 describes GWO and its implementation in the micro-grid system. Section 4 describes the outcome of results and their discussion. Inferences are mentioned in Section 5.

2 TEST SYSTEM DESCRIPTION

The dynamic nature of the power system is definitely affected by renewable energy sources. Nowadays, renewal integration to the grid keeps on increasing. Therefore, a standard test system proposed by Bevrani et al. (2012d) in *IEEE Transaction on Smart Grid* is taken for study where all the parameters are the same. A typical block-diagram of a test system is depicted in Figure 1.

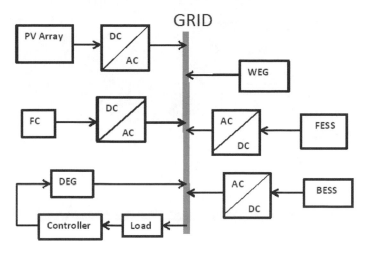

Figure 1. Proposed test system.

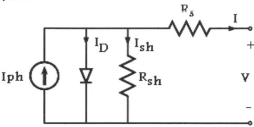

Figure 2. Solar PV circuit.

2.1 *Photovoltaic model*

The solar cell is nothing but a simple diode. The simple circuit representation of a solar cell is a diode with a parallel current source which is shown in Figure 2.

The photoelectric effect is the principle a working PV. As per this principle, light energy is transformed to electricity. For a photovoltaic module, the equation of an ideal solar cell in Onar et al. (2006) and (2012) is given by

$$I = I_L - I_R \left[\exp\left(\frac{V}{aV_t}\right) - 1 \right] \tag{1}$$

ahere I_L = photocurrent (A), I_0 = reverse saturation current (A), V = Diode voltage (V), V_t = thermal voltage, (V_t = 27.5 mV at 25°C), and a = ideality factor of diode. V-I characteristic of solar cell is rewritten:

$$I = I_L - I_R \left[\exp\left(\frac{V + IR_{Se}}{aV_i}\right) - 1 \right] - \frac{V + IR_{Se}}{R_{Sh}} \tag{2}$$

where R_{Se} is series resistance and R_{Sh} is shunt resistance in solar cell.

Since the low voltage (approximately 0.5V) is obtained from a PV cell so a number of series and parallel-connected PV cells are required for desired output power. V-I characteristic equation of a PV module is mentioned below, where N_s and N_p are series and parallel cells, respectively:

$$I^M = N_p I_L - N_p I_R \left[\exp\left(\frac{V^M/N_s + I^M/N_s}{AV_i}\right) \right] - \frac{(N_p/N_s)V^M + I^M R_{Se}}{R_{Sh}} \tag{3}$$

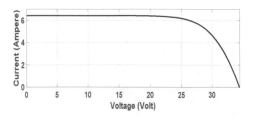

Figure 3. Solar I-V characteristics.

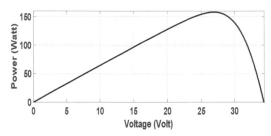

Figure 4. Solar P-V characteristics.

Solar I-V and P-V characteristics are obtained through simulation which are shown in Figures 3 and 4, respectively.

2.2 *Wind energy*

The basic equation concerning air or wind velocity as an input and the output power as a mechanical, generated by the rotor blades is mentioned by Simoes & Bevrani (2016)

$$P_{mech} = C_P(\omega, \sigma)\frac{1}{2}\tau a \upsilon_{wind}^3 \tag{4}$$

where P_{mech} = turbine output power (W), C_P = coefficient of performance of the turbine, ω = tip speed ratio, σ = blade pitch angle (°), τ = air density (kg (m^3)$^{-1}$), a = turbine swept area (m^2), and υ = wind speed (ms^{-1}).

Normalization and simplification can be done in Equation (5) for particular values of τ and a. Per Unit (p.u.) equation is as follows:

$$P_{mech-pu} = k_p C_{P-pu} \upsilon_{wind-pu}^3 \tag{5}$$

where $P_{mech-Pu}$ = p.u. power for given values of τ and a (p.u.), K_p = power gain for C_{P-pu} = 1 p.u., and $\upsilon_{wind-pu}$ = 1 p.u., C_{P-pu} = per unit (p.u.) performance coefficient, and $\upsilon_{wind-Pu}$ = per unit of base wind speed.

Speed-output power characteristics of turbine are shown in Figure 5 for various values of air or wind speed. Due to inertia of turbine, output power appears to be zero from 0–0.2 p.u. turbine speed.

2.3 *Diesel Engine Generator (DEG) model*

Transfer function of DEG model given as follows (Papathanassiou & Papadopoulos 2001):

$$P_d = -\left(\frac{1}{R} + \frac{K_I}{s}\right)\left(\frac{1}{T_{sg}s + 1}\right)\left(\frac{K_{\deg}}{T_{\deg}s + 1}\right)\Delta f_e \tag{6}$$

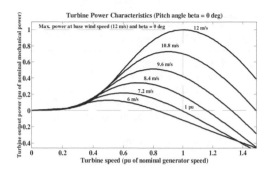

Figure 5.   Speed power characteristics of turbine.

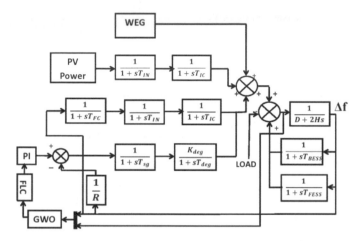

Figure 6.   Frequency response schematic diagram of MG.

where P_d = Power of Diesel Engine Generator, K_I = Constant of integral gain constant, R = Speed regulation, T_{sg} = Time constant of speed Governor, K_{deg} = Gain of DEG, T_{deg} = DEG time constant. In this paper, and $K_{deg} = 1$.

2.4   *Fuel cell, BESS, and FESS*

The fuel cell (FC) and battery energy storage system (BESS) convert chemical energy to electrical energy whereas the flywheel energy storage system (FESS) is popularly known as mechanical energy storage system. The details and description can be found in Wang et al. (2019), Mahmoud et al. (2019), Mousavi et al. (2017), and Hawke et al. (2011).

The transfer function of FC, BESS, and FESS are mentioned here:

$$\frac{1}{1 + sT_{FC}} \qquad \frac{1}{1 + sT_{BESS}} \qquad \frac{1}{1 + sT_{FESS}}$$

Here, T_{FC}, T_{BESS}, and T_{FESS} are the time constant of FC, BESS, and FESS, respectively. All are considered to be as a first-order system.

The detailed block diagram for the frequency response of a proposed micro-grid (MG) system is depicted in Figure 6.

Parameters and their values are mentioned in Table 1.

Table 1. Parameters values.

S.N	Name/Symbol of Parameter	Values
1	Damping coefficient, D (p.u./Hz)	0.015
2	Inertia Constant, H (p.u. s)	0.835
3	Fuel cell time constant, T_{FC}	0.26
4	Battery energy storage system time constant, T_{BESS}	0.1
5	Flywheel energy storage system time constant, T_{FESS}	0.1
6	Speed governor time constant, T_{sg}	0.08
7	Diesel engine time constant, T_{deg}	0.4
8	Inverter time constant, T_{IN}	0.04
9	Connector time constant, T_{IC}	0.004
10	Speed regulation, R (Hz/p.u.)	3
11	WEG rating (kW)	100
12	PV power rating (kW)	30
13	FC raing (kW)	70
14	DEG raing (kW)	160
15	FESS rating (kW)	45
16	BESS rating (kW)	45
17	Total load (kW)	410

Table 2. Fuzzy rule base.

$\Delta f \, \Delta P_L$	BN	MN	SN	SP	MP	BP
S	BN	MN	SN	SP	SP	MP
M	BN	BN	MN	SP	MP	MP
B	BN	BN	BN	MP	MP	MP

3 FUZZY LOGIC CONTROLLER

The fuzzy logic was developed by Zadeh (1965). This can be applied to the system where uncertainties and inaccuracies exist. The FLC has the following advantages:

(1) mathematical model of a system is not necessary,
(2) it can handle nonlinearity and complexity,
(3) it increases the robustness,
(4) it does not require the system information,
(5) principle of operation of FLC is linguistic rules, i.e., IF/IF–THEN general instructions or structure.

Apart from these advantages, the FLC has some disadvantages, i.e., high computational burden during hardware and software implementation.

A fuzzy system is made up of three components, i.e., fuzzification, fuzzy rule-based inference system, and defuzzification.

(A) **Fuzzification**. Error signals of crisp values are converted into fuzzy variables. The appropriate membership functions (triangular) for the input-output variables are selected. The universe of discourse is established for all inputs and outputs variables. The suitable ranges are selected for bringing all the inputs-outputs to the universe of discourse. Each discourse is split into three overlapping fuzzy sets. Each variable is a member of subset with a degree of membership ranging from 0 to 1.

(B) **Fuzzy rule-based inference system:** This system represents IF–THEN general instructions governing the input-output variables with membership functions. In this case, the variables are processed through inference engine executing the following rules which is shown in Table 2.

Here, BN: Big Negative, MN: Mean Negative, SN: Slight Negative, SP: Slight Positive, MP: Mean Positive, BP: Big Positive, S: Slight, M: Mean, and B: Big. In an FLC controller, the error comes out from GWO which meets the fitness/objective function dynamically considered as an input variable:

$$K = f(\Delta e) \tag{7}$$

where K = input of PI controller, Δe = errors (Δf), and f = nonlinear function.

Now it is required to select the membership function for the input and output variables. In this paper, triangular membership is selected to reduce the computational burden. For the above-mentioned fuzzy rules, Mamdani-type fuzzy inference is used. The membership functions, fuzzy sets, and fuzzy rules are all are selected using a hit-and-miss method to obtain optimum performance.

(C) **Defuzzification.** In this section a crisp value of output is obtained by using centroid defuzzi-fication approach in which the center of each membership function for each rule is evaluated first.

4 GREY WOLF OPTIMIZATION (GWO)

A GWO algorithm is a meta-heuristic search algorithm proposed by Mirjalili. It works on how the wolves are attacking the prey for their food. The GWO algorithm emulates the chain of command and trapping system of grey wolves in the environment. Four names of grey wolves are given: alpha (α), beta (β), delta (δ), and omega (ω) which are used to imitate or simulate the chain of command. While designing the mathematical model of GWO, α is considered as the best solution of the fittest function popularly known as a leader of wolves who is guiding others and asking them to participate in hunting. Accordingly, the second- and third-best results are beta (β) and delta (δ) commonly. The remaining individual outcomes are considered to be omega (ω).

The wolves undergoing through the various activities to get their food, i.e., searching, chasing, tracking, encircling, and then attacking the prey. This behavior can be mathematically modeled as

$$D = |\vec{C} . \overrightarrow{X_p(t)} - \overrightarrow{X_p(t)}|$$

$$\vec{X}(k+1) = \overrightarrow{X_p(t)} - \vec{A} . \vec{D}$$

Here, k denotes the number of iterations. D, A, and C indicate the coefficient vectors. X_p and X indicate the position vector of prey and grey wolf, respectively.

The vectors A and C can be determined as

$$\vec{A} = 2\vec{a} . \vec{p} - \vec{a}$$

$$\vec{C} = 2 . \vec{q}$$

where $\vec{a}$ vector linearly decreases from 2 to 0 during the iteration process, $\vec{p}$ & $\vec{q}$ are the random vectors in [0 1].

When the wolves stop moving, then it is understood that hunting is now over.

Out of many optimization algorithms, this GWO is implemented in this paper because of having the following features.

- Since this algorithm uses the concept of probability, it becomes flexible, robust, and easy convergence.
- It may lead to premature convergence which increases the search action capability.
- Less time of optimization.
- GWO can be implemented in online/offline mode. In this paper, a scaling factor of FLC is tuned in online mode.

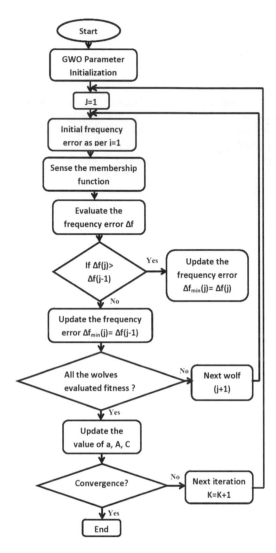

Figure 7.   GWO flow chart.

The objective of GWO is to obtain the optimum scaling factors of FLC. Here, the optimum means to minimize the objective function or fitness function. The objective/fitness function is frequency error $(\Delta f) = e$. There are various performance indices to select the error such as integral of absolute error (IAE) $I_{AE} = \int |e(t)dt|$, integral square error (ISE) $I_{SE} = \int |e^2(t)|dt$, integral square of absolute error (ISAE) $= I_{SAE} = \int |e(t)|^2 dt$, and integral of time multiplied by absolute error (ITAE) $= I_{TAE} = \int t|e(t)|dt$ In this paper, integral square error (ISE) $I_{SE} = \int e^2(t)dt$ is selected as a one of the performance index.

In this way the search agents (wolves) move and check for the optimization of the objective function for each iteration keeping the constraints of scaling factor to lie in between 0 and 1. Here the number of search agents are taken $= 10$ and number of iterations $= 5$.

The flow chart for implementing the GWO algorithm is depicted in Figure 7.

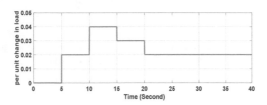

Figure 8.   Load profile on microgrid system.

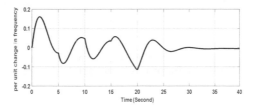

Figure 9.   Frequency change profile using PI controller alone.

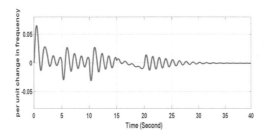

Figure 10.   Frequency change profile using PI and FLC controller.

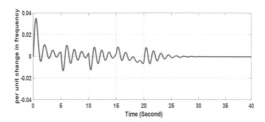

Figure 11.   Frequency change profile using PI, GWO, and FLC controller.

5   RESULTS ANALYSIS

The load change profile on a micro-grid is shown in Figure 8. There is an increase and decrease in load at 5 sec, 10 sec, 15 sec, etc.

The per unit change in frequencies by the PI, PI plus FLC, and PI plus GWO plus FL Controller are depicted in Figures 9, 10, and 11, respectively.

This is understood from the above figures that the per unit change in frequency decreases/increases in accordance with the per unit change in load by all controllers. The frequency variation is less by the proposed method, i.e., PI, GWO, and FLC.

6 CONCLUSION

A standard miro-grid model is selected for the study. Each component of micro-grid is simulated using MATLAB. The comparative evaluation of a frequency profile is validated.

REFERENCES

M. M. T Ansari., and Velusami S, (2010), Dual mode linguistic hedge fuzzy logic controller for an isolated wind diesel hybrid power system with superconducting magnetic energy storage unit, Energy Conversion and Management, 51(1):169–181. http://www.sciencedirect.com/science/article/pii/S0196890409003501.

Asma Aziz, Aman Than, Alex Stojcevski "Analysis of frequency sensitive wind plant penetration effect on load frequency control of hybrid power system" International Journal of Electrical Power and Energy Systems, 99 (2018), 603–617. https://doi.org/10.1016/j.ijepes.2018.01.045

Hassan Bervani et al., "Intelligent LFC Concerning High Penetration of Wind Power: Synthesis and Real Time Application" IEEE Transaction on Sustainable Energy, Vol.5, No.2, April 2013, pp655–662

H. Bervani et al., "Intelligent Frequency Control in an AC Micro Grid: Online PSO-Based Fuzzy Tuning Approach" IEEE Transaction on Smart Grid Vol.3, No.4, Dec.2012, pp.1935–1944.

H. Bevrani, and Hiyama T, (2016) Intelligent automatic generation control. CRC press.

O Castillo and Melin P, (2014). A review on interval type-2 fuzzy logic applications in intelligent control and information sciences 279:615–631. http://www.sciencedirect.com/science/article/pii/S0020025514004629

Manoj Datta et al., "A Frequency Control Approach by Photovoltaic Generator in a PV-Diesel Hybrid Power System" IEEE Transaction on Energy Conversion, Vol.26, No.2, June 2011, pp.559–571.

L Freris and Infield D (2008), Renewable energy in Power Systems, John Wiley & Sons, U.K., 2008.

A Ghafouri, Milimonfared J and Gharehpetian G B, (2015) Coordinated Control of Distributed Energy Resources and Conventional Power Plants for Frequency Control of Power Systems, in *IEEE Transactions on Smart Grid*,6(1):104–114.

M. Godoy Simoes and Fellix A. Ferret "Alternate Energy Systems: Design and Analysis with Induction Generator" 2nd edition, CRC Press-Taylor and Francis Group.

H Golpîra and H Bevrani (2014),A framework for economic load frequency control design using modified multi-objective genetic algorithm, Electric Power Components and Systems, 42(8):788–797. http://www.tandfonline.com/doi/abs/10.1080/15325008.2014.893545.

J. Hawke et al., A modular fuel cell with hybrid energy storage, IEEE energy conversion congress & exposition 2011.

Kathuria J., Khan M.A., Abraham A., Darwish A. (2014) Low Power Techniques for Embedded FPGA Processors. In: Khan M., Saeed S., Darwish A., Abraham A. (eds) Embedded and Real Time System Development: A Software Engineering Perspective. Studies in Computational Intelligence, vol 520. Springer, Berlin, Heidelberg. https://doi.org/10.1007/978-3-642-40888-5_11

Mohammad-Hassan Khooban et al., (2017) "Load Frequency Control in Microgrids Based on Stochastic Non-Integral Controller " IEEE Transaction on Sustainable Energy, DOI 10.1109/TSTE.2017.2763607.

S R Khuntia, and Panda S, (2012). Simulation study for automatic generation control of a multi-area power system by ANFIS approach, Appliedsoftcomputing,12(1):333–341. http://www.sciencedirect.com/science/article/pii/S156849461100322X

Q Liang, and Mendel J M, (2000). Interval type-2 fuzzy logic systems: theory and design, IEEE Transactions on Fuzzy systems, 8(5):535–550, http://www.sciencedirect.com/science/article/pii/S0142061515001520

Thair Shakir Mahmoud et al., The role of intelligent generation control algorithms in optimizing battery energy storage system size in microgrids: A case study from Western Australia energy Conversion and Management Volume 19615 September 2019, Pages 1335–1352.

S. M. Mousavi et al., A comprehensive review of flywheel energy storage system technology Renewable and Sustainable energy, Reviews Volume 67 January 2017, Pages 477–490.

Onar O C, Uzunoglu M, Alam M S, (2006). Dynamic Modeling, Design and Simulation of A Wind/Fuel Cell/Ultra-Capacitor-Based Hybrid Power Generation System. Journal of Power Sources 161(1):707–722. doi: 10.1016/j.jpowsour.2006.03.055.

G Panda, Panda S and Ardil C, (2009). Hybrid neuro fuzzy approach for automatic generation control of two–area interconnected power system. International journal of computational intelligence, 5(1):80–84. http://www.waset.org/publications/6556.

Papathanassiou S A and Papadopoulos M P, (2001), Dynamic characteristics of autonomous wind-diesel systems, Renewable Energy 23(2):293–311.

K S Parmar, Majhi S, and Kothari D P, D.P., (2012). Load frequency control of a realistic power system with multi source power generation. International Journal of Electrical Power & EnergySystems, 42(1):426–433, http://www.sciencedirect.com/science/article/pii/S0142061512001676.

S Pandey, Mohanty S R, and Kishor N,(2013). A literature survey on load–frequency control for conventional and distribution generation power systems. Renewable and Sustainable Energy Reviews, 25:318–334. http://www.sciencedirect.com/science/article/pii/S1364032113002815.

Qi C, and Ming C Z, (2012), Photovoltaic Module Simulink Model for a Stand-alone PV System. Science Direct International Conference on Applied Physics and Industrial Engineering, PhysicsProcedia, 24(A):94–100.

M Rahmani, and Sadati N, (2013). Two-level optimal load–frequency control for multi-area power systems. International Journal of Electrical Power & Energy Systems, 53:540–547. http://www.sciencedirect.com/science/article/pii/S0142061513002123

K Sabahi, Ghaemi S, and Pezeshki S, (2014). Application of type-2 fuzzy logic system for load frequency control using feedback error learning approaches. Applied Soft Computing, 21:1–11. http://www.sciencedirect.com/science/article/pii/S1568494614000921.

Sahaj Saxena "Load frequency control strategy via fractional- order controller and reduced- order modelling" International Journal of Electrical Power and Energy Systems, 104 (2019), 603–614. https://doi.org/10.1016/j.ijepes.2018.07.005

M. V. Srikanth, Narri Yagaiah "An AHP based optimized tuning of modified active disturbance rejection control: an application to power system load frequency control problems" ISA Transaction (2018), https://doi.org/10.1016/j.isatra.2018.07.001

K R Sudha and Santhi R V, (2011), Robust decentralized load frequency control of interconnected power system with generation rate constraint using type-2 fuzzy approach. International Journal of Electrical Power & Energy Systems, 33(3):699–707, http://www.sciencedirect.com/science/article/pii/S0142061511000135.

Chengshan Wang et al., (2016) "Frequency control of an isolated micro-grid using double sliding mode controllers and disturbance observer " IEEE Transaction on Smart Grid, DOI 10.1109/TSG.2016.2571439.

Yongqiang Wang, et al., Optimization of power plant component size on board a fuel cell /battery hybrid bus for fuel economy and system durability, International Journal of Hydrogen Energy Volume 44, Issue 335 July 2019 Pages 18283–18292

Linyum Xiong, Hao Li, Jie Wang "LMI based robust load frequency control for time delayed power system via delayed margin estimation" International Journal of Electrical Power and Energy Systems, 100 (2018), 91–103. https://doi.org/10.1016/j.ijepes.2018.02.027

H A Yousef, Khalfan A K, Albadi M H, and Hosseinzadeh N, (2014), Load frequency control of a multi-area power system: An adaptive fuzzy logic approach. IEEE Transactions on PowerSystems, 29(2):1822–1830.http://ieeexplore.ieee.org/document/6717058.

L A Zadeh, (1965), Fuzzy sets, Information and control, 8(3):338–353.

Smart Computing – Khan et al (Eds)
© *2021 Taylor & Francis Group, London, ISBN 978-0-367-76552-1*

Comparative study of wireless technologies used in home automation with AI

Lalan Kumar & Arushi Sharma
Department of Master of Computer Application, G. L. Bajaj Institute of Technology and Management, Greater Noida, Affiliated to AKTU Lucknow, India

ABSTRACT: This paper proposes the structure of the Internet of Things (IoT) in light of a home mechanization framework through a remote system. With the upgrade of robotization innovation life is getting more straightforward and simpler. The remote home robotization framework utilizing IoT is a framework that utilizes mobile gadgets to control the home apparatuses and their capacities via the web from anyplace. There are many well-known advances technologies for home automation such as ZigBee, Z-wave, Bluetooth, and so forth. With just a little tap we can enhance simple tasks of our daily routine, like operating the lighting for the whole house, gardening, giving access to the gate by maintaining security by ensuring wh's knocking at the door, maintaining the temperature level of the house, and many more things just to make life easier. The main source which is required to use these technologies is electricity and a smart way to merge these technologies must exist.

Keywords: HAS, IoT, Wi-F

1 INTRODUCTION

With a serious improvement of remote innovations, the home robotization framework is getting progressively advanced for controlling and monitoring (Ransing & Rajput 2015; Jamil & Ahmad 2015). Robotization assumes a significant role in our life. Home mechanization is whatever empowers us to utilize our home lighting, warming, security framework, and electronic machines all the more advantageously and proficiently. It gives us remote or programmed control of things around the home with the assistance of the Internet (Dickey et al. 2012; Folea et al. 2012). In this they have gadgets containing sensors. The sensors gather the information from the outside. These gadgets are constrained by remote control and cell phone applications too. These are connected through Wi-Fi or the Web. The exceptional development of remote advancements, for example, Bluetooth (Ullah & Celik 2016), GSM (Chinchansure & Kulkarni 2014), ZigBee (Han et al. 2014), and Wi-Fi (Courreges et al. 2016) sway us to utilize cell phones to do direction on home appliances (Vivek & Sunil 2015; Ahmim et al. 2016).

1.1 Different technologies

1.1.1 Bluetooth technology-based home automation
In home automation systems (HASs) using smartphones, Bluetooth and Arduino technology are cheap and secure. Piyare introduced HASs based on Bluetooth technology. This connection has been built between Arduino BT board and smartphone through wireless Bluetooth technology. Moreover, the device should have password protection for security purposes. Because of this, only authorized users can access the device. The drawback of this technology is that it can make a connection on limited Bluetooth range (Kumar & Lee 2014). The user cannot control appliances beyond the range.

DOI 10.1201/9781003167488-97

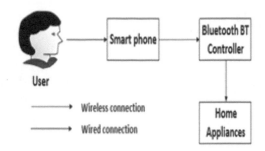

Figure 1.   Block diagram of a home automation system.

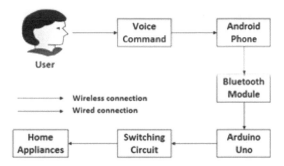

Figure 2.   Block diagram of voicecontrolled HAS.

1.1.2 *Home automation based on voice recognition system*

An HAS backed by a voice recognition system was introduced by Sen et al. (2015). A hardware architecture is developed to facilitate voice recognition based on home automation consisting of smartphone and Arduino UNO. The connection is established between these through Bluetooth technology. It built a voice recognition system through Android OS which is mainly used to develop a smartphone software and is able to command the home gadgets. This application converts a human voice into text then that text is sent to the Bluetooth module, which is directly linked to Arduino UNO. The Arduino UNO is connected to the home appliances.

1.1.3 *ZigBeebased home automation system*

Wireless home automation based on ZigBee has also been considered (Alshu'Eili et al. 2011). It comprises of three applications, and a wireless network is set up utilizing RF ZigBee. The fundamental modules are: handheld mouthpiece module, central commander module, and machine controller module. The small mouthpiece module utilizes the ZigBee convention, and the central controller module is dependent on the PC. In this framework, Microsoft discourse API is utilized as a voice acknowledgment module to fetch speech with fluently. The system records sound at an examining frequency of 8 kHz whereas human speech is most noteworthy recurrence at 20 kHz. A huge important portion of this system is the encoding of sound which may be done at a frequency in between 6 Hz to 3.5 kHz. These data bits are sent from a microcontroller to the RF ZigBee modular, its maximum transfer rate of 115,200 bits/s. The ZigBee communication protocol delivers the most extreme transfer rate of 250 Kbps, but 115.2 Kbps was being utilized by microcontrollers to send and receive data. This mechanization system was tried using voice commands of 35 male and female voices with distinctive English accents. Each person got his/her voice recorded up to 35 voice tests which added up to 1225 voice commands that were tested, and the framework accurately

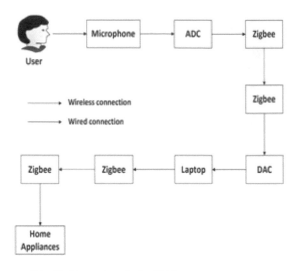

Figure 3. Block diagram of the ZigBee system in the HAS.

recognized 79.8% of people. The accuracy of this system is limited within a run of 40 m whereas the acknowledgment system is better, up to 80 m in clear line of transmission.

The other ZigBee-based home computerization framework examined and executed by analysts (Baviskar et al. 2015). This domestic automation can be operated in two ways: (1) estimation mode and (2) current sensor mode. The Java platform is utilized for tracking genuine-time control. Encourage the execution of the overall framework has been examined by utilizing different 978-1-5090-4059-9/16/$31.00 ©2016 IEEE 28 performance measurements including Circular Trip Delay time, the Idleness, or Gotten Flag Quality Pointer (RSSI).

1.2 GSM-based home automation system

A smart HAS is done by using Global System for Mobile (GSM). In this GSM technology the hardware included technology such as GSM modem, microcontroller, and smartphones. In GSM, the particular 2G SIM is inserted for making a connection with smartphones.

Because of this, a GSM modem controls the electric appliances through SMS requests. For making connections Arduino is also used. The Arduino has pins connected tovthe GSM modem through wiring and loads the particular program to Arduino. To communicate with the GSM modem, it uses an AT command or we can say an Attention command. With a GSM modem like SIM900A, we can change the status of the device or appliances with receiving commands through SMS. The reaction time of the GSM modem is very less; it is just 500 ms. Due to the broad zone of GSM network, the user can control appliances from anywhere in the world.

1.2.1 Home automation system based on EnOcean technology

Nowadays, various efforts are being put into the many technologies like home automation, IoT, etc. with the help of the EnOcean Technology (Sharma & Sharma 2014). A home automation business is also gaining a huge amount of profit with the help of EnOcean technology. The main reason behind it is its productivity putted along with the effectiveness which are also getting implemented in the different and unique electronic components. It is helpful in reducing the cost at a very good scale.

The networking technologies which are implemented very well in the terms of bandwidth is appreciable (Zakariyya et al. 2017). HASs need to be developed using various gadgets or physical

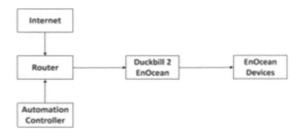

Figure 4. Block diagram of EnOceanbased automation system.

devices which could be implemented on the network which includes switches and various EnOcean devices.

2   COMPARATIVE ANALYSIS

This section consists of comparison of all the above-discussed HAS's system's advantages and disadvantages which are highlighted and also all of their common features. Different varieties of communications methods are used to send commands from the user interface to the main controller. Table 1 shows a comparison of cost, speed, and real-time application of different home automation systems.

HASs based on voice recognition play a vital role in the life of disabled people whowant to automate their home appliances by giving them voice commands. This module is also very secure because each and every individual has a different voice which is stored in the database of the system.

Bluetooth: Home automation based on a Bluetooth system gives complete control over the home appliances as long as the user is in the Bluetooth range. A PC or smartphone can be used as the receiver's device used for the Bluetooth system. Real-time systems have the real communication rate. It has the feature of great security and low cost. The Bluetooth network has a limited range of smartphones and gets out of range beyond 10 m. HASs will not be able to control it, as this is one of the major disadvantages of Bluetooth-based systems. The drawback of a Bluetooth HAS is that it is applicable within given range only (Khan & Amjad 2016). The Bluetooth technology used a PC or cell phone as a collector gadget. It has a high correspondence rate, extraordinary reliability, and minimum hard work, so it is very well actualized as an ongoing module.

ZigBee: ZigBee is based on IEEE802.15.4 network specification. The IEEE802.15.4 implies 16 bit and 64 bit addresses which theoretically can support more than 65,000 nodes on their network. It provides a range of 50 m and each node is dependent on other nodes. ZigBee requires very little power to operate, usually up to only 1 mW or less. But ZigBee still gives a range of 150 m which makes it an ideal choice for mobile devices. ZigBee provides a data transfer rate of 250 kbps. All these properties of ZigBee makes it an ideal choice for HASs.

GSM: The Global System for Mobile Communication was developed by implementing Time Division Multiple Access (TDMA). It is also called the 2G network. It utilizes 850 MHz, 900 MHz 1800 MHz and 1900 MHz frequency bands. The Subscriber Identity Module (SIM) is used to identify a user on the network. GSM has the theoretical ability to deliver data transfer rates of up to 384 lbps (Srivastava & Khan 2018). GSM technology can be accessed from anywhere independent of any other device or node wherever the 2G network is available.

EnOcean: The EnOcean is a very efficient technology. EnOcean's main focus is being energy efficient. It used very short messages for communication which greatly reduces network collisions which in turn require fewer replications, thus being energy efficient. It is not a feature-rich network but is very suitable for less complex networks. This property of EnOcean make is highly suitable for micro devices and can be very useful in implementing home automation.

Table 1. Comparison of different HASs.

System	Cost	Speed	Real-Time
Bluetooth	Cost is totally dependent on the requirement, usage and brand.	Depending on the range it is used with the speed up to 2 Mbps.	Yes
Voice Recognition	These are also less expensive as compared to the Bluetooth devices, for which different modules are available in the market.	It helps in enhancing the recognition authority by increasing the rate from 90–95%.	Yes
Zig-Bee	Just like the above two technologies ZigBee is also a less expensive module which is used when high speed and good communication systems are needed.	Using the ZigBee module we can get the speed of 100 Kbps to 1 Mbps.	Yes
GSM	This GSM module is expensive to use but mostly used by the users due to effective results in terms of speed, range, or both. Requires to use a GSM SIM to communicate by sending the messages.	As GSM module works on sending messages, hence speed is determined as per the messages that could be delivered per second/minute, e.g. 30 messages/min.	Yes
Internet, WiFi	It is costly in terms of electricity consumption as compared to the ZigBee, but also depends on the range in which it is required to use.	Although a smart home requires minimal speed of the Internet; on the other hand it varies on the number of gadgets being connected to it, e.g. basic speed requirement +5 mbps for the smart home (10 mbps for the video).	Yes
EnOcean	It is effective in terms of cost and time. It is battery less, wireless uses switches, radio technology, and sensors. It is long lasting too.	As this EnOcean technology uses the radio technology using sensors and buttons, works at a very good speed.	Yes

3 CONCLUSION

This paper consists of special home automation mechanization structures which are studied and also talks about their advantages and disadvantages. The Bluetooth remote system uses voice home automation which is suitable for old and disabled people. They can control the device only by voice. Another technology used the ZigBee module for the usage of remote systems. The user has full control over the home appliances. Another one is GSM technology. In this technology the client can control the home appliances by sending an SMS through the smartphone. Humans get a lot of benefits by the fast growth of IoT gadgets.

The next one is EnOcean technology, which we the find best among all the technologies. This is also used for wireless technology. It can be connected via a smartphone. It can be used to reduce energy consumption. Using radio technology, it includes the use of sensors and buttons which themselves increase its efficiency. Using this technology, we can save time, cost, and also develop any type of the structure for, e.g., flats, retrofits, newly constructed buildings, etc. EnOcean technology is also energy efficient because if we do wiring in the house it is very expensive and if use batteries, they require changing after a particular period of time, If we then throw out the batteries, that does damage to the earth. EnOcean technology also requires easy installation of some modules like sensors, buttons, and many more which are also flexible and adaptive to any change in the building structure as per the requirement or any natural disaster. It also requires less maintenance.

REFERENCES

Ahmim, A., Le, T., Ososanya, E. and Haghani, S., 2016, January. Design and implementation of a home automation system for smart grid applications. In *2016 IEEE International Conference on Consumer Electronics (ICCE)* (pp. 538–539). IEEE.

AlshüEili, H., Gupta, G.S. and Mukhopadhyay, S., 2011, May. Voice recognition based wireless home automation system. In *2011 4th international conference on mechatronics (ICOM)* (pp. 1–6). IEEE.

Baviskar, J., Mulla, A., Upadhye, M., Desai, J. and Bhovad, A., 2015, January. Performance analysis of ZigBee based real time Home Automation system. In *2015 International Conference on Communication, Information & Computing Technology (ICCICT)* (pp. 1–6). IEEE.

Chinchansure, P.S. and Kulkarni, C.V., 2014, January. Home automation system based on FPGA and GSM. In *2014 International Conference on Computer Communication and Informatics* (pp. 1–5). IEEE.

Courreges, S., Oudji, S., Meghdadi, V., Brauers, C. and Kays, R., 2016, January. Performance and interoperability evaluation of radiofrequency home automation protocols and Bluetooth Low Energy for smart grid and smart home applications. In *2016 IEEE International Conference on Consumer Electronics (ICCE)* (pp. 391–392). IEEE.

Dickey, N., Banks, D. and Sukittanon, S., 2012, March. Home automation using Cloud Network and mobile devices. In *2012 proceedings of IEEE Southeastcon* (pp. 1–4). IEEE.

Folea, S., Bordencea, D., Hotea, C. and Valean, H., 2012, May. Smart home automation system using Wi-Fi low power devices. In *Proceedings of 2012 IEEE International Conference on Automation, Quality and Testing, Robotics* (pp. 569–574). IEEE.

Han, J., Choi, C.S., Park, W.K., Lee, I. and Kim, S.H., 2014. Smart home energy management system including renewable energy based on ZigBee and PLC. *IEEE Transactions on Consumer Electronics 60*(2), pp. 198–202.

Jamil, M.M.A. and Ahmad, M.S., 2015, March. A pilot study: Development of home automation system via raspberry Pi. In *2015 2nd International Conference on Biomedical Engineering (ICoBE)* (pp. 1–4). IEEE.

Kathuria J., Khan M.A., Abraham A., Darwish A. (2014) Low Power Techniques for Embedded FPGA Processors. In: Khan M., Saeed S., Darwish A., Abraham A. (eds) Embedded and Real Time System Development: A Software Engineering Perspective. Studies in Computational Intelligence, vol 520. Springer, Berlin, Heidelberg. https://doi.org/10.1007/978-3-642-40888-5_11

Khan, R. and Amjad, M., 2016. Automatic generation of test cases for data flow test paths using K-means clustering and generic algorithm. *International Journal of Applied Engineering Research 11*(1), pp.473–478.

Kumar, S. and Lee, S.R., 2014, June. Android based smart home system with control via Bluetooth and internet connectivity. In *The 18th IEEE International Symposium on Consumer Electronics (ISCE 2014)* (pp. 1–2). IEEE.

Ransing, R.S. and Rajput, M., 2015, January. Smart home for elderly care, based on Wireless Sensor Network. In *2015 International Conference on Nascent Technologies in the Engineering Field (ICNTE)* (pp. 1–5). IEEE.

Sen, S., Chakrabarty, S., Toshniwal, R. and Bhaumik, A., 2015. Design of an intelligent voice controlled home automation system. *International Journal of Computer Applications 121*(15).

Sharma, H. and Sharma, S., 2014, March. A review of sensor networks: Technologies and applications. In *2014 Recent Advances in Engineering and Computational Sciences (RAECS)* (pp. 1–4). IEEE.

Srivastava, P. and Khan, R., 2018. A review paper on cloud computing. *International Journals of Advanced Research in Computer Science and Software Engineering 8*(6), pp.17–20.

Ullah, M.A. and Celik, A.R., 2016. An Effective Approach to Build Smart Building Based on Internet of Things (IoT). *Journal of Basic and Applied Scientific Research*, (6), pp. 56–62.

Vivek, G.V. and Sunil, M.P., 2015, November. Enabling IOT services using WIFI-ZigBee gateway for a home automation system. In *2015 IEEE International Conference on Research in Computational Intelligence and Communication Networks (ICRCICN)* (pp. 77–80). IEEE.

Zakariyya, S.O., Salami, A.F., Alabi, O.O. and Usman, A.M., 2017. Design of a Bimodal Home Automation System using ESP8266 and ATMEGA328 Microcontroller. *Computer Engineering and Applications Journal 6*(3), pp. 95–108.

Smart Computing – Khan et al (Eds)
© 2021 Taylor & Francis Group, London, ISBN 978-0-367-76552-1

Comparative analysis of various control schemes used in single-phase grid-connected photovoltaic systems

Pankaj Negi
Research Scholar, School of Renewable Energy and Efficiency, NIT, Kurukshetra (Hr), India

Yash Pal
Department of Electrical Engineering, NIT, Kurukushetra (Hr), India

Leena G.
Department of Electrical and Electronics Engineering, MRIIRS, Faridabad, India

ABSTRACT: This paper is about a comparison between proportional-integral controller (PI), Fuzzy PI controller, and model reference adaptive controllers (MRAC) which is used in a single-phase grid-connected photovoltaic (PV) system. A comparison has been made between the PI, Fuzzy-PI, and MRAC controller in the very-large circuit integration (VLSI) in terms of the response time and frequency response. The integrated system is modeled and simulated in MATLAB/SIMULINK and the simulation outcomes are compared.

Keywords: Proportional-Integral Controller, Fuzzy PI Controller, Photovoltaic System, MRAC controller, Simulation

1 INTRODUCTION

Nowadays, the pollution due to conventional energy resources are growing continuously which is a great concern for global warming. Renewable energy recourses are abundantly available in nature through various sources such as wind, solar, geothermal, gas micro-turbine, and fuel cell (Pal et al. 2018; Kumar et al. 2019) One of the biggest concerns in renewable energy field is that the generation of power depends on natural resources which are not in control of humans. There are various problems of voltage and power fluctuations, poor power quality, voltage and current harmonics, and low power factors.

A gridconnected photovoltaic (PV) system has become an important powergenerating system (Liu et al. 2018). The various current control schemes have been used in gridconnected PV system which effect on the quality of the current supplied to the grid by the PV inverter. Proportional-integral (PI) or proportional-integral-derivative (PID) controllers are the wellknown controllers in many processes. The mainly used tuning methods which are used industries are Cohen–Coon and Ziegler–Nichols (Rout 2016). In the PI controller, the control performance depends mainly on PI gains and also, the constant gain of PI controller cannot promise preferred rise time and overshoot for nonlinear loads. There are various unknown parameters in any process which reduces the preferred performances of control system in real time. Thus, during the transient practice in order to attain the improved performance it is essential to adjust the PI gain values. The fuzzy logic control (FLC) is one of the influential methods that can be useful for adjusting PI gains. FLCs, also known as intelligent controllers work on a basis of fuzzy logics algorithm used; the fuzzy logic algorithm determines the fuzzy controller output power and improve the system efficiency (Negi et al. 2018).

 DOI 10.1201/9781003167488-98

For the automatic adjustment of parameters an adaptive controller can be used in real time (Zhang et al. 2018). This adaptive controller can maintain a preferred level of control system performance output whenever there is a parametric variation or unknown parameters and for this model reference adaptive controllers are used. Every controller has its own advantages and drawbacks which have been analyzed in this paper.

The paper is organized as follows. In Section 2, the modeling of gridconnected PV system with PV system modeling and LCL filter modeling with its parameters is discussed in brief. The various controllers—PI, fuzzy PI and MRAC—are described in Section 3. Section 4 is integrated with outcome and conversation and in the last section, Section 5, is the conclusion

2 GRIDCONNECTED PV SYSTEM

Consider a singlephase gridconnected PV system which is basically made of PV array, Inverter circuits, filters circuits and a current controller [2] as shown in Figure 1. The inverter circuit is used to convert DC power which is coming from solar array into AC power. A filter circuits which is mainly LCL filters are used to remove the harmonics. Controllers are used for system stability. The basic model of the gridconnected PV system is briefly described in Negi et al. (2018).

2.1 PV system structure

The PV system formation is disclosed in the subsequent Equation (1):

$$i_{pv} = i_p - i_d - i_{sh\_r} \tag{1}$$

$$= i_p - i_o \left(\exp \left(\frac{q}{q_f KT \left(v_{pv} + i_{pv} r_s \right)} \right) - 1 \right) - \frac{v_{pv} + r_s i_{pv}}{r_{sh}} \tag{2}$$

Here, i_{pv} = PV cell output current
i_p = Photovoltaic current
i_d = diode reverse saturation current
i_{sh_r} = current via shunt resistance
i_o = reverse saturation current
v_{pv} = output terminal voltage of solar cell
r_s = series loss resistance
q_f = quality factor
r_{sh} = shunt resistance
K is Boltzmann constant and T is P-N junction temperature (^0K)
q = electron charge (1.6×10^{-19} C) and the PV current i_{pv} is given as

$$i_{pv} = \left(i_{pvg} + K_i \Delta T \right) \frac{G_{ir}}{G_n} \tag{3}$$

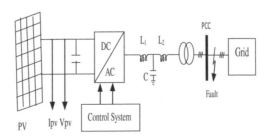

Figure 1.   Gridconnected photovoltaic (PV) system.

In Equation (3):
i_{pvg} = generated current at nominal conditions
K_i = the current temperature coefficients
G_{ir} = irradiance
G_n = irradiance at nominal conditions
ΔT = actual and the nominal temperatures difference (in ^0K)
   The PV system output power is written in Equation (4):

$$p_{pv} = v_{pv}i_{pv}\eta_{dc/dc} \tag{4}$$

where $\eta_{dc/dc}$ is represented as efficiency of DC/DC converter having ranges from 90–95%.

2.2   LCL filters

The LCL filters are mostly used in a gridconnected PV system and it mostly consists of $L_1 + R_1$, $L_2 + R_2$ and $C + R_c$ These filters are mostly used for harmonic reduction (Rout 2016). The pulse width modulation technique is used for the switching of semiconductors used in inverter circuits and also injects the harmonics. The mathematical model of LCL filter is given in Equation (5):

$$\begin{cases} L_1\dfrac{di_1}{dt} + R_1i_1 = v_i - v_c - R_ci_c \\[2mm] L_2\dfrac{di_g}{dt} + R_2i_g = v_c - v_g - R_ci_c \\[2mm] C\dfrac{dv_c}{dt} = i_c \\[2mm] i_1 = i_g + i_c \end{cases} \tag{5}$$

Figure 2 represents LCL filter per-phase model is defined where grid voltage is v_g and inverter output voltage is represent as v_i, the resistances are R_1 and R_2 inductors is represent as L_1 and L_2
   LCL filter is also represented in Figure 3 in the form of a block diagram. The resistance has been omitted for the circuit for the simplicity and Laplace TF of the LCL is specified in Equation (6):

$$G_{LCL\_f}(s) = \frac{1}{s^3L_1L_2C + s\,(L_1 + L_2)} \tag{6}$$

The resonant frequency of LCL filter is determined using Equation (7):

$$f_{res} = \frac{1}{2\pi}\sqrt{\frac{L_1 + L_2}{L_1L_2C}} \tag{7}$$

The other filters which are used for harmonic reduction are L and LC filters but LCL filters shows good performance compare to other filters [5]. A resonance peak is produced in LCL filter

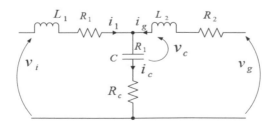

Figure 2.   Perphase model of LCL filter.

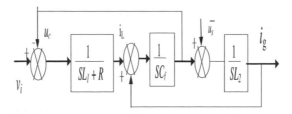

Figure 3.   LCL filter.

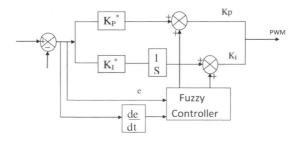

Figure 4.   Fuzzy PI controller.

at the resonant frequency hence at that point the system becomes highly unstable. To overcome this problem active damping is used for damping the filter resonance.

By relating the grid current and voltage the plant model transfer function can be represented in Equation (8):

$$H(s) = \frac{i_g}{v_i} = \frac{RCs + 1}{L_1 L_2 C s^3 + RC(L_1 + L_2)s^2 + (L_1 + L_2)s} \quad (8)$$

3   CONTROL SCHEMES

3.1   *PI controller*

The most frequently used controller is a PI controller because of its simplicity (Liu et al. 2018). The main problem with a PI controller is that the gain parameters which are a combination of proportional and integrator controller and the gain of the controller is not adaptive. This PI controller is not so much more efficient if there is alteration or variation in system parameters and in case of nonlinear system (Gao et al. 2018).

3.2   *Fuzzy PI controller*

Fuzzy logic control is based on fuzzy logics that examine analog input values in terms of logical variables and have a constant value between 0 and 1. The major components of FLC are fuzzy knowledge base, fuzzifier, fuzzy rule base, inference engine and defuzzifer. Fuzzy PI is a combination of FLC and PI controller and is considered in the current control loop of voltage source converter (VSC). The LCL filter block diagram revealed in Figure 4 is used as a plant system. The parameters of PI controller gain is synchronized by FLC as per the input signal i.e., error (*er*). There are if–then rules in the form of "If *er* and Δer then the value of K_p and K_i" which is used to decide control signals for K_p and K_i gains. Figure 5 shows the general structure of the FLC and Figure 6 shows the membership function which makes the control more robustness and sensitive (Negi et al. 2018).

The K_p and K_i gains parameters are adjusted using a fuzzy adjuster which is based on *er* and Δer as shown in Equation (9):

$$K_p = K_p^* + \Delta K_p$$
$$K_i = K_i^* + \Delta K_i \qquad (9)$$

Here K_p and K_i are desired gain of fuzzy-PI-based controllers. The values of K_p^* and K_i^* are considered offline based on the conventional method (Negi et al. 2018).

On the basis of knowledge working rules have been designed for adaptive values of K_i and K_p The number of rules can be designed as per the requirement in FLC. Some rules in the rule base can be uttered as

If (*er* is *NB*) and (change in error is *NB*) then (K_p is *PB*) and (K_i is *ZO*)
If (*er* is *NB*) and (change in error is *NM*) then (K_p is *PB*) and (K_i is *ZO*)
If (*er* is *NB*) and (change in error is *NS*) then (K_p is *NB*) and (K_i is *NB*)
If (*er* is *NB*) and (change in error is *ZO*) then (K_p is *PB*) and (K_i is *NM*)
If (*er* is *NB*) and (change in error is *PS*) then (K_p is *PS*) and (K_i is *NM*)
If (*er* is *NB*) and (change in error is *PM*) then (K_p is *PS*) and (K_i is *ZO*)
:
:
:

If (*er* is *PB*) and (change in error is *PB*) then (K_p is *NB*) and (K_i is *ZO*)

Similarly there are a total of 49 rules that have been designed to achieve the desired values of adaptive gain vales of K_i and K_p based on error and change in errors.

The inference method is used for the conversion of vague fuzzy control action to a precise control action. For defuzzify fuzzy variables into their physical domains as shown in Equation (10) there is a requirement of the center gravity method:

$$Kp = Kp * + \frac{\sum_{j=1}^{n} \mu.j(e, \Delta e)\Delta Kp.j}{\sum_{j=1}^{n} \mu.j(e, \Delta e)}$$

$$Ki = Ki * + \frac{\sum_{j=1}^{n} \mu.j(e, \Delta e)\Delta Ki.j}{\sum_{j=1}^{n} \mu.j(e, \Delta e)} \qquad (10)$$

$\mu = $ *membership function of fuzzy sets.*

3.3 MRAC technique

One of the most using adaptive controllers is the model reference adaptive controller (MRAC). In the MRAC technique the plant model is the following reference model. The error can be calculated by comparison of plant model and reference model. To make the system stable and with zero steady error the controller parameters can be adjusted based on the error that comes after comparison. The MIT rule or by the Lyapunov stability theory is mainly used in the MRAC controller (Zhang et al. 2019; Negi et al. 2020). Figure 7 shows the MRAC model as below.

The secondorder system of plant model is represented as $\frac{b}{S^2 + \alpha_1 S + \alpha_2}$ and the transfer function of closed loop is given in Equations (11) and (12).

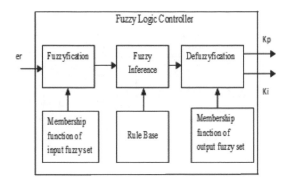

Figure 5.   General structure fuzzy logic control.

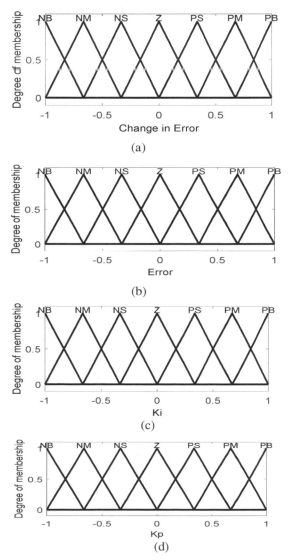

Figure 6.   Membership function of (a) error( ) (b) change in error (Δer) (c) output, and (d) output.

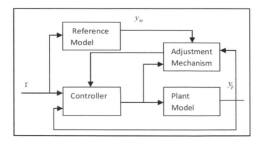

Figure 7.   Block diagram of a MRAC.

In (11), r(s) is the input and y_p (s) is the plant output:

$$\frac{y_p(s)}{r(s)} = \frac{b(k_p s + k_i)}{s(s^2 + \alpha_1 s + \alpha_2) + b(k_p s + k_i)} \tag{11}$$

$$\frac{y_p(s)}{r(s)} = \frac{b(k_p s + k_i)}{s^3 + \alpha_1 s^2 + (\alpha_2 + bk_p)s + bk_i} \tag{12}$$

The reference model is represented in Equation (13):

$$\frac{y_m(s)}{r_m(s)} = \frac{bm_2 s + bm_3}{s^3 + a_{m1}s^2 + a_{m2}s + a_{m3}} \tag{13}$$

where $\begin{array}{l} a_{m2} = \alpha_1, a_{m2} = \alpha_2 + bk_p, a_{m3} = bk_i, \\ b_{m1} = 0, b_{m2} = bk_p, b_{m3} = bk_i \end{array}$

The parameters of the PI controller values can find in

$$\frac{dk_p}{dt} = -\gamma_p \frac{\partial j}{\partial k_p} = -\gamma_p \left(\frac{\partial j}{\partial e}\right)\left(\frac{\partial e}{\partial y_p}\right)\left(\frac{\partial y_p}{\partial k_p}\right) \tag{14}$$

$$\frac{dk_i}{dt} = -\gamma_i \frac{\partial j}{\partial k_i} = -\gamma_i \left(\frac{\partial j}{\partial e}\right)\left(\frac{\partial e}{\partial y_p}\right)\left(\frac{\partial y_p}{\partial k_i}\right) \tag{15}$$

where

$$\frac{\partial j}{\partial e} = e, \ \frac{\partial e}{\partial y} = 1, D = \frac{d}{dt} \tag{16}$$

$$\frac{\partial y_p}{\partial k_p} = \frac{bD}{D^3 + \alpha_1 D^2 + (\alpha_2 + bk_p)D + bk_i}[r - y_p] \tag{17}$$

$$\frac{\partial y_p}{\partial k_i} = \frac{bD}{D^3 + \alpha_1 D^2 + (\alpha_2 + bk_p)D + bk_i}[r - y_p] \tag{18}$$

$\frac{dk_p}{dt}$ and $\frac{dk_i}{dt}$ can be derived by

$$\frac{dk_p}{dt} = -\gamma_p \frac{\partial j}{\partial k_p} =$$

$$-\gamma_p e \frac{bD}{D^3 + \alpha_1 D^2 + (\alpha_2 + bk_p)D + bk_i}[r - y_p] \tag{19}$$

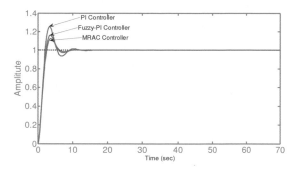

Figure 8.   MRAC Fuzzy PI and MRAC controller response.

$$\frac{dk_i}{dt} = -\gamma_i \frac{\partial j}{\partial k_i} =$$

$$-\gamma_i e \frac{b}{D^3 + \alpha_1 D^2 + (\alpha_2 + bk_p)D + bk_i}[r - y_p] \tag{20}$$

Here γ represents adaptation gain. The controller gain values Kp and Ki gain can be adjusted whenever there is a change in the output of the system.

4   SIMULATION RESULTS

To explore the current controller's performance it is simulated in Matlab/Simulink. Two cases have been considered to show the usefulness of the proposed controller and their comparison with other controllers. In Case 1 the time response of PI, Fuzzy PI and MRAC current controlled VSC has been analyzed which is plotted in Figure 8. In Case 2 a frequency analysis of the system using all three controllers has been analyzed, as shown in Figure 9.

Case 1 Time response analysis

In time response analysis the controllers are used for the system response and have been analyzed for unit step input. From analysis it has been analyzed that the MRAC is better than the Fuzzy PI and PI controller but it's so much more complex in designing.

From the time analysis graph the effect of various controllers on the gridconnected PV system performance has been analyzed. From Table 1 it has been analyzed that the MRAC is a better controller than the fuzzy PI and PI controller. Hence where a fast response and better settling time is required we can suggest using the MRAC controller.

4.1   Case 2 Frequency response analysis

In this case the frequency response analysis of the system stability has been analyzed with thehelp of the bode plot. The stability parameters like gain margin and phase margin is calculated for all current controllers. From the bode plot and frequency analysis it has been shown that all the controllers (PI, fuzzy PI and MRAC) make the system stable.

A PI controller is tuned with the help of Z–N method and in fuzzy controllers fuzzy rules has been implemented for PI controller gain calculations. A model reference adaptive controller is based on system feedback parameters and adjusts the gain of PI if there is change in system parameters. Figure 9 is the frequency analysis of gridconnected PV system using diverse controllers has been described.

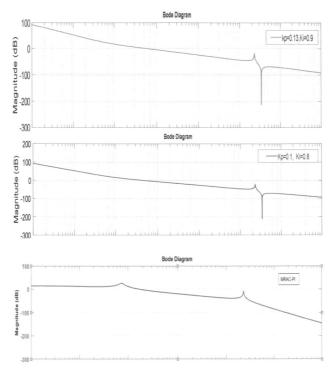

Figure 9. Bode plot grid-connected PV system using (a) PI controller (b) fuzzy PI controller, and (c) MRAC controller.

Table 1. Analysis of PI, Fuzzy PI and MRAC controller for step response.

System characteristics	PI	Fuzzy PI	MRAC
Rise Time	1.81	1.64	1.60
Settling Time	8.41	8.13	5.83
Overshoot	25.4	16.3	12.6
Peak	1.25	1.16	1.13
Peak Tine	3.44	3.60	3.85

Table 2. Frequency response of PI, fuzzy PI and MRAC controller.

Characteristics of system	PI Controller	Fuzzy PI	MRAC Controller
Gain Margin	2.3115	4.6961	7.6168
Phase Margin	0.3483	91.1334	86.178
Gain crossover frequency	2.2939e+04	2.2940e+04	2.2940e+04
Phase crossover frequency	87.1299	94.6633	69.2284

5 CONCLUSION

With the help of simulation, the effect of controller schemes on a gridconnected PV system is clearly visualized. Time response and frequency response has been analyzed for a gridconnected PV system for a variety of controllers. From Table 1 it can be analyzed that the MRAC is faster than the fuzzy PI and PI controllers and Table 2 is the frequency response of the system while using controllers and it shows that all the controllers make the system stable. The MRAC and fuzzy PI controller have comparable results and better than PI controllers.

Appendix

Table 3.   System parameters.

Name	Value
Fundamental frequency f1	50 Hz
Grid Phase voltage (RMS)	220 V
Switching Frequency fs	12 Khz
filter inductor L1 (Inverter side)	1.88 mh
filter inductor L2 (Grid side)	0.34 mh
Filter-capacitor C	6.6 μf

REFERENCES

Gao C, Chen Q, Zhang L, Quan S. 2018. Current multi-loop control strategy for grid-connected inverter with LCLfilter. *Youth academic annual conference of Chinese association of automation (YAC):* 712–716.
Kathuria J., Khan M.A., Abraham A., Darwish A. (2014) Low Power Techniques for Embedded FPGA Processors. In: Khan M., Saeed S., Darwish A., Abraham A. (eds) Embedded and Real Time System Development: A Software Engineering Perspective. Studies in Computational Intelligence, vol 520. Springer, Berlin, Heidelberg. https://doi.org/10.1007/978-3-642-40888-5_11
Kumar N, Singh B, Panigrahi B.K. 2019. LLMLF Based Control Approach and LPO MPPT Technique for Improving Performance of a Multifunctional Three-Phase Two-Stage Grid Integrated PV System. *IEEE transaction on sustainable Energy.*
Liu B, Wang L, Chen Z, Song S. 2018. Robust state feedback current controller with harmonics compensation for sinle stage grid connected PV inverter with LCL filter. *IEEE transaction on sustainable energy*: 1 12.
Negi P, Pal Y, Leena G. 2018.Stability Analysis of Grid-Connected PV System using PR Controller. *Journal of Advanced research in dynamic and control system, (JARDCS).* Vol.(10): 1191–1201.
Negi P, Pal Y, Leena G. 2018. Performance Analysis of Grid connected Photovoltaic system with Fuzzy logic control based VSC. *Journal of Advanced research in dynamic and control system, (JARDCS),* Vol (9):1439–1452.
Negi P, Pal Y, Leena G. 2020. Grid-Connected Photovoltaic System Stability Enhancement Using Ant Lion Optimized Model Reference Adaptive Control Strategy. *Differential Equations and Dynamical Systems.* Vol. 28(1).
Pal B, Sahu P.K, Mohapatra S. 2018. A review on feedback current control techniques of grid connected PV inverter system with LCL filter. *Technologies for smart city energy security and power (ICSESP):*1–6.
Rout P. 2016. PV Based autonomous HBCC microgrid performance analysis using adaptive PI and PI controller. *International Journal of Control Theory and Applications* Vol 9(33): 131–143.
Zhang Q., Zhou, L., Mao, M., Xie, B., Zheng, C. 2018. Power quality and stability analysis of large scale grid-connected photovoltaic system considering non-linear effects. *IET Trans. Power Electronics.* Vol (11): 1739–1747.

Smart Computing – Khan et al (Eds)
© 2021 Taylor & Francis Group, London, ISBN 978-0-367-76552-1

Energy-efficient and secured housing

Yogesh Pant & Atul Rawat
*Department of Computer and Information Sciences, Swami Rama Himalayan University,
Dehradun, India*

Abhishek Gupta & Ashwini Kumar Saini
CSED GBPIET, Pauri, Uttarakhand, India

ABSTRACT: In the fast-moving world of the 21st century, the gadgets which can save the time and money of a man can survive in the market for a prolonged period of time. So is the case with our home appliances and garden. Today, most of us are shifting toward automated gadgets which we can control easily by sitting in our own space. Such gadgets are available in the market at a relatively high price which is unaffordable for those in the Indian middle-class. Therefore, the purpose of this research was to find out the ways by which we can provide such features at a very negligible price and with much better connectivity and applications. Today, the basic ideas of automation are based on technologies like Wi-Fi, Bluetooth. or Internet, but they have their own limitations like range, data, speed, etc. So, the aim was to also find out a more reliable solution for such things. The other purpose was to provide basic security features like CCTV camera, fire alarm, etc., at a cost which is much lower than the current market price, making it affordable to almost everyone.

1   INTRODUCTION

The Energy-Efficient and Secured Housing model is a way which leads to a very smart and low-priced automation of home appliances without replacing the current gadgets being used at most of the houses and also providing some basic security features along with it. In most of the cases, technologies used in this field are Wi-Fi, Bluetooth, or infrared, but the problem is that for Internet-controlled gadgets there is a need for proper Internet speed which is still an issue here. With Bluetooth, Wi-Fi, and infrared, the problem is with a range which is less than 250 m in most of the cases (Zeinab & Elmustafa 2017). So, the aim was to find out a medium which is very reliable and has a very appreciable range. The result of this part of the work was the 2G network. Almost all parts of world today have 2G network connectivity and all we have to do in this system is to use this network as a medium for connectivity between us and our gadgets (Patel et al. 2018).

So now another question arises: How will we use that network for our purpose? The basic use of the 2G network was calling, SMS, and an Internet service for small purposes. We decided to use the SMS service and now the concept that used was the same as that of automatic response systems used in Customer Service Centers.

Internet of Things (IoT) is the current trending technology which is spreading its wings in every platform and controlling and managing physical objects and many more applications (Abuhasel 2020; Khan 2020a–2020e; Quasim et al. 2019). These objects could be any electronic appliances like light bulb, fan, motor for water pump, and many more which are used in our home day today. The main advantage of using these automation and remote-control system is that we can reduce the power consumption and waste of water which is an important asset. A home automation

                                                   DOI 10.1201/9781003167488-99

system could be implemented using a simple circuit using Raspberry Pi and other such systems are developed which is based on mobile networks like 3G and LTE.

For security purposes, we decided to design an Android application which can be used as a dedicated CCTV camera in old Android phones. The aim was to design an application which can receive and transmit video footage to another cellphone present at any part of the world even when the screen is turned off so that it can save the battery as well as being placed anywhere secretly, and also so that we can use the cellphone for a longer time. It was also ensured that if there is no cellphone present with the user or receiver then he can also watch the footage even on his desktop or laptop through a web browser. The other features used were like a fire alarm or motion detector which can be activated and deactivated easily by the user. The challenge was also to ensure that the whole automation system can be turned off easily by the user and appliances can continue to work in traditional way as earlier. The important thing was to keep this system very economical. So, with our best efforts and study, all these services can be provided at low cost on an Android phone which can be arranged very easily these days.

2 RELATED WORK

There are number of techniques for implementing a home automation system (HAS) based on wireless sensor technology and Wi-Fi but these systems which are based on Bluetooth technology are restricted with the range and other systems which are based on 3G and LTE networks are restricted with the quality of mobile network. As we are moving forward toward smart home and automation systems, the need of IoT technologies also increasing the communication of our home with the outer world. Another implementation of automation systems is based on different types of signals used for controlling and passing information; these systems include power circuits, dual-tone multiple-frequency (DTMF) identification circuits, and other warning tones circuits. DTMF generates a specific binary code for a particular dial tone key, and these signals receiving from the caller end are decoded by the controlling module and can perform any set of specific task, such as DTMF-based surveillance robot. The application of remotely controllable system is getting attention in recent years and also capable of highly flexible because of DTMF tones which can be generated by the system using a Global System for Mobile (GSM) network. A popular autonomous mobile robot "Tesco" is an example of its implementation. DTMF is also a good technique to give signals to the microcontroller and then automate the systems but the problem with the DTMF is that a limited number of keys present to generate the DTMF tones and no feedback to the user (Ghosh et al. 2015).

A GSM module is a particularly planned chip or circuit that is used to establish a connection between a gadget or an appliance operating on a GSM network and a system using the module. Modulator-demodulator is a significant part of the project. GSM or General Packet Radio Service (GPRS) module is powered by an electrical circuit and a connection circuit such as USB 2.0, RS-232. GSM modules with basic devices are able to provide all the basic services such as driving, SMS, and 2G Internet, and are able to communicate with the microcontroller using centralized communication. ATtention (AT) commands are the basis of the GSM module and there are many unique commands for performing certain tasks such as receiving a message, sending a message, receiving a call, dialing a number, etc. (Yuchen et al. 2011)

3 PROPOSED MODEL

The backbone of the project/research is the GSM technology. Global mobile communication system (GSM) is a portable communication system. The GSM concept was developed in Bell Laboratories in the 1970s. The GSM system was developed as a digital system using a time-varying time (TDMA) process. GSM is an open and digital mobile technology used to transmit cellular voice and data services running on 850 MHz, 900 MHz, 1800 MHz, and 1900 MHz frequency bands and has a

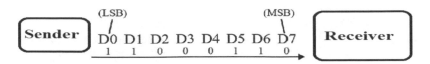

Figure 1. Serial communication.

capacity of 64 kbps to 120 Mbps data rates. It is widely used in cellular telecommunications in the world (Ur Rahman 2017).

3.1 *GSM architecture*

The GSM network has the following components.

Sub-Network. Sub-networks play an important role that provides basic network connection to cellular stations. The Home Location Register (HLR) and visitor location register (VLR) are the part of a Switching Center that provides access to diverse networks such as PSTN, ISDN, etc. It also contains a resource ownership register that keeps an account of all mobile devices where each cell is identified by its IMEI number. IMEI stands for International Mobile Equipment Identity.

Mobile Channel. A system with a processor, transceiver, and display that is controlled by a SIM card operating on the network is a mobile channel.

Base Station: A Base Station has a Base Transceiver Station contains radio transceivers and handles logistics communications. To provide connection between the mobile station and the mobile switch center it also has Base Station Controller (BSC). BSC manages the Base Transceiver station.

To make use of this GSM technology we used the GSM module as discussed earlier. The basic features provided by the GSM modules are:

- Short Message Service
- Improved signal efficiency
- SIM phonebook administration
- Compatibility with ISDN services
- The actual clock time for alarm management
- Better and high-quality speech
- Encryption makes calls more secure

GSM's standardized security features make it the most secure of the communication engineers. The confidentiality of the telephone and the GSM registrar is only guaranteed on the radio station (Ur Rahman 2017).

The GSM module connects with the microcontroller using serial communication with the help of RX and TX provided in both modules. The process of sending one-bit data at a time in telephone communication and data transfer is known as serial communication over a communication channel or computer bus. This is the opposite of parallel communication, where multiple data bits shred at a time in parallel order.

3.2 *Microcontroller module*

The IDE uses to code the microcontroller is the Arduino IDE and the used microcontroller is AtMega328p. The software-serial library is used for serial communication between the Microcontroller and the GSM module. The RX pin of the microcontroller is connected to the TX pin of the GSM module, and vice versa. The GSM module we used is the SIM 900A GSM module.

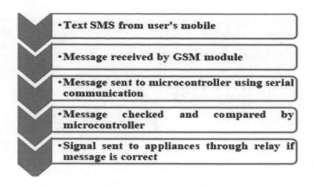

Figure 2. Basic working.

The sensors used in the prototype model include MQ-2 sensors for detecting methane, boo-lane, LPG and smoke, and PIR sensors (passive infrared sensors) for detecting any improper access inside the home. A steel exoskeleton beneath with the sensing element consists in a gas sensor module. This sensing element is currently subject to the connecting lead. This flow is called the heating flow; the sensing element absorbs and ionizes the gases closed to sensing element and then resistance of the sensing element will change, that leads to changes the current value of the outlet.

Passive Infrared Sensor (PIR) is an electronic sensor that deals infrared (IR) light radiation from objects in its view area. Different PIR sensors detect changes in the amount of infrared radiation applied to it, which varies depending on temperature and surface properties of objects in front of the sensor. When an object like a human pass through a wall-like background, the temperature of the sensor's space rises from room temperature to body temperature, and then returns. The change in infrared radiation changes the sensor output voltage and triggers detection. Objects of similar temperature but also different surface properties may have a different infrared emission pattern, so moving them relative to the background also sends a signal as a trigger for the detector (Khodzhaev 2016).

3.3 CCTV module

Platform as another service used for the purpose of CCTV application that provides the managed infrastructure, APIs, and tools needed to deliver Web real-time communication business capabilities.

Server SDKs. Software development kits (SDKs) integrate with the REST API and allow developers to create tokens and session IDs for their application. There are commercial and social supported libraries are available for Java, PHP and Python, Ruby on Rails, .NET, andNode.js, respectively.

Client Libraries. Client libraries enable video communication on a client's remote device. The commercial and social-supported libraries are available for Javascript, Android/iOS andPhoneGap, and Titanium, respectively.

4 MATERIALS AND METHODS

The equipment that are used in the prototype model are an ATMega 328p microcontroller, SIM900A GSM module, 5V 4 Channel Relay module, MQ-2 sensor, PIR sensor, any Android phone with android version above 5.0, piezo buzzer, and jumper wires. The GSM900 module is used as an interface between the microcontroller and the network. GSM module gets the message and forwards the message to the microcontroller along with the number it received the message from. Then program uploaded in the microcontroller compares the message with predefined set of strings

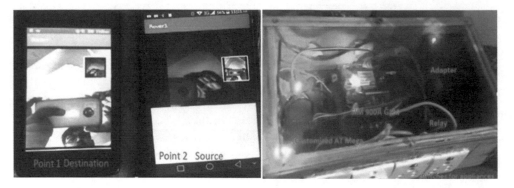

Figure 3.   CCTV application (left) and final module (right).

and also checks the number it received the message from to check the authenticity of the message. So, the algorithm of the program uploaded on the microcontroller.

In this way you can control as many appliances we want. Another aspect of this project was the use of the relay. As a microcontroller gives the output of only 5 Volts so we cannot directly control the AC appliances so a relay module is used. A relay is a switch which is operated electrically. Most of the relays work with the help of electromagnet to function a switch mechanically but there are many other mechanisms such as solid-state relays. They are used mainly when we need to control a powerful circuit by another less powered signal.

The sensors are also used with the appliances; MQ-2 sensor is used as analog sensor and PIR as digital sensor. Sensors were given the functionality as follows.

If (mq2_value>400) // 400 is the threshold value which can be increased or decreased
DIGITAL_PIN_BUZZER = 1 // Buzzer (Alert System) turned on
ElseDIGITAL_PIN_BUZZER = 0 // Buzzer (Alert System) turned off as soon as smoke is vanished
If (pin value == HIGH) // PIR sensor digital o/p is HIGH when motion is detected
DIGITAL_PIN_BUZZER = 1// Buzzer (Alert System) turned on
ElseDIGITAL_PIN_BUZZER = 0// Buzzer (Alert System) turned off as soon as motion is stopped
Alerts based on the sensors can also be sent to the user using the SMS.

On the CCTV camera, the Android system was created using Opentok Service. These objects require client and server-side objects.

5   RESULTS AND DISCUSSION

So, in this way GSM technology can be used for the purpose of long-distance control of the various devices and machines. Most mobiles have this technology and by using the right techniques, we can apply it in any field and use it for our benefits. But the limitation of the GSM is the availability of the GSM network. For sending or receiving calls and SMS it is mandatory to have a GSM or TDMA or code-division multiple access (CDMA) network in that area. However, the 2G/3G network is one of the most widespread networks these days and almost 75% of the Indian population has an access to the mobile phones. The OpenTok service can be used for the various purposes related to video streaming, archiving, etc. and implemented as a cheap wireless video surveillance system. Opentok services can use in any platform like Android, Windows, iOS, etc. The OpenTok platform helps in easily integrating the real-time, interactive video, messaging, screen sharing, and other audio video features in our application.

The overall cost of this whole setup is very low and can be used in various places like offices, schools, large buildings, etc. so that we can control a large number of appliances very easily by sitting in our place by using plug-and-play module (Figure 3a). Traditional CCTV setup requires a lot of hardware and wiring and is also very expensive but by using the OpenTok platform we can just use the old or cheap android mobiles available at a cost less than CCTV cameras and this method is more economical and we can also see the footages from anywhere. OpenTok platform also provides us with cloud storage of our recordings and we can download them in case we need them. Apart from OpenTok there are also various other platforms which work in the same way and we can use them as per our wish (Figure 3b).

6 FUTURE SCOPE

A NodeMCU can be used with this module which can send us the notifications or give the live updates continuously about any activity inside the house. Activities can be traced using the sensors. Various other sensors can be used for the purpose of detecting the water levels in the water tanks, measuring the intensity of the sun light, tracing the rain drops. etc. All these sensors can be used to make the owner of the house aware about any scenario. A Smart Face detection door lock or biometric or PIN-protected door lock can also be used for security purposes. All these measures can help in making the life easier and more comfortable.

REFERENCES

Abuhasel K. A. and M. A. Khan, (2020), "A Secure Industrial Internet of Things (IIoT) Framework for Resource Management in Smart Manufacturing," in IEEE Access, vol. 8, pp. 117354–117364, 2020, doi: 10.1109/ACCESS.2020.3004711.

Ghosh, S. & Konar, S. & Ghosh, S. & Ghosh, T. & Gope, S. 2015. Dual Tone Multiple Frequency Based Home Automation System. *International Journal of Engineering Research*, 4: 542–544.

Khan M. A., (2020a), An IoT Framework for Heart Disease Prediction Based on MDCNN Classifier, in IEEE Access, vol. 8, pp. 34717–34727, 2020. DOI: 10.1109/ACCESS.2020.2974687

Khan M.A. et al., (2020b), Decentralised IoT, Decenetralised IoT: A Blockchain perspective, Springer, Studies in BigData, 2020, DOI: https://doi.org/10.1007/978-3-030-38677-1

Khan, MA, Abuhasel, KA. (2020c).Advanced metameric dimension framework for heterogeneous industrial Internet of things. Computational Intelligence. 2020; 1–21. https://doi.org/10.1111/coin.12378

Khan M.A, and Algarni F., (2020d) "A Healthcare Monitoring System for the Diagnosis of Heart Disease in the IoMT Cloud Environment Using MSSO-ANFIS," in IEEE Access, vol. 8, pp. 122259–122269, 2020, doi: 10.1109/ACCESS.2020.3006424.

Khan, M. A., Quasim, M. T, et al., (2020e), A Secure Framework for Authentication and Encryption Using Improved ECC for IoT-Based Medical Sensor Data, in IEEE Access, vol. 8, pp. 52018–52027, 2020. DOI: 10.1109/ACCESS.2020.2980739

Khodzhaev, Z. 2016. Monitoring Different Sensors with ATmega328 Microprocessor. 10.13140/RG.2.2.27918. 25921/1.

Patel, S. & Shah, V. & Kansara, M. 2018. Comparative Study of 2G, 3G and 4G: 2–3.

Quasim, M.T., Khan M.A, Algarni F., Alharthy A., Alshmrani G.M.M, (2020), Blockchain Frameworks. In: Khan M., Quasim M., Algarni F., Alharthi A. (eds) Decentralised Internet of Things. Studies in Big Data, vol 71. Springer, DOI: https://doi.org/10.1007/978-3-030-38677-1

Quasim, M. T., Khan M. A, et al., (2019), Internet of Things for Smart Healthcare: A Hardware Perspective, 2019 First International Conference of Intelligent Computing and Engineering (ICOICE), Hadhramout, Yemen, 2019, pp. 1–5. DOI: 10.1109/ICOICE48418.2019.9035175

Ur Rahman, Z. 2017. GSM Technology: Architecture, Security and Future Challenges. *International Journal of Science Engineering and Advance Technology,* 5: 70–74.

Yuchun, M. & Yinghong, H. & Kun, Z. & Zhuang, L..2011. General Application Research on GSM Module: 525–528.

Zeinab, K. & Elmustafa, S.A.A. 2017. Internet of Things Applications, Challenges and Related Future Technologies: 2–5.

Smart Computing – Khan et al (Eds)
© 2021 Taylor & Francis Group, London, ISBN 978-0-367-76552-1

A review on massive Multiple-Input Multiple-Output (MIMO) system's combiners

Garima Kulshreshtha & Usha Chauhan
Galgotias University, Greater Noida, Gautam Buddh Nagar, India

ABSTRACT: Massive multiple-input multiple-output (MIMO) technology for wireless communication is considered a key technology for the future fifth-generation (5G) communication networks. To reduce the propagation loss of channel, MIMO systems with analog or digital hybrid precoders and combiners (HPC) architecture have been used. This review paper presents the various types of analog and digital HPC designs for the massive MIMO communication systems that were investigated within the last decade. The reviewed systems are useful for both single-user (SU) and multi-user MIMO (MU-MIMO) systems. The key parameter of the study was spectral efficiency (SE), signal-to-noise ratio (SNR), signal-to-interference pulse noise ratio (SINR), system sum-rate (SR) performance, computational complexity (CC), co-channel interference (CCI), inter-primary base station interference (IPBSI), multiuser interference (MUI), effective desired channel gain (EDCG), and minimum mean square error (MMSE).

1 INTRODUCTION

MIMO technology has become very popular nowadays in the modern wireless communication system. This technology provides optimal solutions for current challenges and increased demand for higher data rates (Pappa et al. 2018). In MIMO technology, the transmitter and receiver consist of multiple antennas up 100 or 1000 at the base station (BS). MIMO system is very useful in terms of reducing fading and interference in multipath in comparison with conventional antenna systems (Santumon & Sujatha 2012). A conventional antenna system uses a sequential manner to transmit the data symbols while MIMO system uses orthogonal frequency division multiplexing (OFDM) to send the data signal in parallel order, the benefit of sending data symbol in parallel order is that there is a less chance of missing the signal information because each data symbol is easily detectable (Larsson et al. 2014). Various channel estimation (CE) techniques/algorithms are being introduced to estimate the channel parameters like bit-error-rate (BER) and signal-to-noise ratio (SNR). Channel performance can be compared for various wireless channels using BER–SNR characteristics.

As the demand for wireless technology and Internet of Things (IoT) is increasing day-by-day in many applications such as healthcare, industrial IoT, and smart factories are being getting attention (Abuhasel 2020; Khan 2020a–2020e; Quasim 2019, 2020). The underlying infrastructure of these technologies is MIMO. Massive MIMO is a large-scale antenna system that is scalable to any degree depending on the requirement of desired antennas. The key feature of massive MIMO is spatial division multiplexing (SDM), in which data streams can propagate in many directions and paths; these streams can be additive or interfere destructively when unwanted by increasing the number of antennas beam can be more focused selectively in the desired direction to the specific user or mutli-users (MUs) (Marzetta 2015).

In Massive MIMO systems, channel capacity and spectrum utilization are major parameters to improve the performance of the MIMO system, apart from this various CE techniques and algorithms are proposed like Massive MIMO low-complexity channel algorithms like data-assisted

DOI 10.1201/9781003167488-100

CE, cooperative CE, blind CE, and many more estimation techniques (Khan & Singh 2018). To solve the design issues of multi-cell Massive MIMO uplink, a data-aided CE algorithm is used (Li 2014). If there are an infinite number of BSs, the data obtained by the decoder at the receiving end will be equal to the correlation between different users' data cross-contamination of pilot pollution and self-contamination created by CE errors. For appropriate solution a frequency selective CE algorithm has been proposed which implies the shared information between adjacent antennas to estimate the impulse response of individual channel at the receiving end, if compared with MMSE this algorithm has better performance (Masood et al. 2015).

The conventional singular value decomposition (SVD) and eigenvalue decomposition (EVD) CE are used in the high complexity for the actual defect calculation process, which follows fast-single compensation approximation power iteration (FSCAPI) subspace tracking algorithm. This algorithm is known for its minimum CC and better orthogonality (Xu et al. 2014). By the simulation results, it can be proved that FSCAPI semi-blind CE can find similar results to EVD–CE (Ngo & Larsson 2015). In the case of Massive MIMO, we use a large number of BS antennas thereby increasing the complexity of CE so for low CC. The analyzed massive MIMO system proposed low-complexity Bayesian CE and polynomial expansion CE (Shariati et al. 2013, 2014).

Signals produced by massive MIMO travels from multipath, therefore, it suffers from multiple access interference and free space path loss and these interferences add up with the signals so to combat these things "Precoders and Combiners" can be used separately or jointly (Gao et al. 2016).

Traditional precoder and combiner are used with the large number of radio frequency chains and energy-intensive analog-to-digital converters (ADCs) so it is impractical to use these systems in mm-wave communication due to higher carrier frequency and wide bandwidth (Wang et al. 2017). To deal with this problem an energy-efficient analog/digital hybrid precoders and combiner (HPC) is implemented which uses a large number of phase shifters (Ayach et al. 2014). For enhancing the effective channel gain a joint combiner and precoding design has been proposed in which each user selects a code word from the predefined codebook and a user selection algorithm is provided to select the users when the number of user increases than the number of transmission antennas (Li et al. 2011a,b).

2 MASSIVE MIMO SYSTEM MODEL

The massive MIMO systems (Moon et al. 2010; Yokota & Ochi 2015; Maza et al. 2020) have the N_{tr} number of transmitting antennas and the N_{re} number of receiving antennas shown in (Figure 1). The traditional Massive MIMO receiver system is based on the linear transformation (LT) technique to generate the output signal y^o. Here, input signal is assumed as a complex form because it is in the form of a QAM signal. The system presents the output signal vector (Hassan et al. 2015) in the complex form as per the given relation in Equation (1):

$$y^o = H^c s^t + n^c \tag{1}$$

where s^t is a complex input signal vector with dimension $N_{tr} \times 1$, H^c is a massive MIMO channel matrix with dimension $N_{re} \times N_{tr}$, n^c is additive white Gaussian noise (AWGN) vector of MIMO channel with dimension $N_{re} \times 1$, and y^o is output signal vector with dimension $N_{re} \times 1$.

The signals s^t, n^c, H^c, and y^o are shown in Equations (2), (4), (5), and (6), respectively.

$$s^t = \begin{bmatrix} s_1^t & s_2^t & s_3^t & \cdots & s_m^t & \cdots & s_{N_{tr}}^t \end{bmatrix}^T \tag{2}$$

where S_m^t is m^{th} transmitted signal or symbol and $1 \leq m \leq N_{tr}$. The mth transmitted symbol is also divided into its real and imaginary parts, as shown in Equation (3). Also, $(\cdot)^T$ denotes the transpose of the given vector

$$s_m^t = s_{m,R}^t + j s_{m,I}^t \tag{3}$$

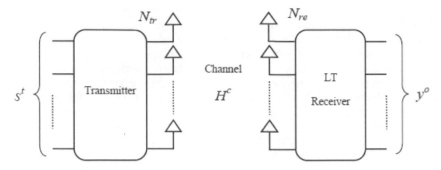

Figure 1. Block diagram of massive MIMO communication system.

where the mth transmitted signal or symbol s_m^t $s_{m,R}^t$ has and $s_{m,I}^t$ as the real and imaginary parts, respectively.

$$n^c = \begin{bmatrix} n_1^c & n_2^c & n_3^c & \ldots & n_n^c & \ldots & n_{N_{re}}^c \end{bmatrix}^T \qquad (4)$$

where n_n^c is the received channel noise signal component at the nth receiving antenna and $1 \le n \le N_{re}$.

$$H^c = \begin{bmatrix} H_{1,1}^c & H_{1,2}^c & H_{1,3}^c & \ldots & H_{1,m}^c & \ldots & H_{1,N_{tr}}^c \\ H_{2,1}^c & H_{2,2}^c & H_{2,3}^c & \ldots & H_{2,m}^c & \ldots & H_{2,N_{tr}}^c \\ H_{3,1}^c & H_{3,2}^c & H_{3,3}^c & \ldots & H_{3,m}^c & \ldots & H_{3,N_{tr}}^c \\ \ldots & \ldots & \ldots & \ldots & \ldots & \ldots & \ldots \\ H_{n,1}^c & H_{n,2}^c & H_{n,3}^c & \ldots & H_{n,m}^c & \ldots & H_{n,N_{tr}}^c \\ \ldots & \ldots & \ldots & \ldots & \ldots & \ldots & \ldots \\ H_{N_{re},1}^c & H_{N_{re},2}^c & H_{N_{re},3}^c & \ldots & H_{N_{re},m}^c & \ldots & H_{N_{re},N_{tr}}^c \end{bmatrix} \qquad (5)$$

where $H_{n,m}^c$ is a channel matrix coefficient between the nth receiving antenna and m^{th} transmitting antenna for $1 \le m \le N_{tr} \le 1 \le n \le N_{re}$ and

$$y^o = \begin{bmatrix} y_1^o & y_2^o & y_3^o & \ldots & y_n^o & \ldots & y_{N_{re}}^o \end{bmatrix} \qquad (6)$$

where y_n^o is n^{th} output signal and $1 \le n \le N_{re}$.

The AWGN must have zero mean value and covariance value $\sigma_{n^c}^2$. The input signal symbol also has a covariance value $\sigma_{s^t}^2$. The channel matrix coefficients are independent and identically distributed complex Gaussian distribution function (Ayach et al. 2014; Ni et al. 2017).

3 COMPARATIVE STUDY OF COMBINERS FOR MASSIVE MIMO SYSTEMS

The combiner of massive MIMO systems combines the received signals at the receiver end from the receiving antennas using different techniques or algorithms. These techniques or algorithms are investigated and updated day-by-day by the researchers. The techniques or algorithms combines the multiple signals receives at the multiple antennas and provide higher SNR as well as improve other performance parameters. The receive combiner bank (RCB) of the given traditional massive MIMO system is shown in (Figure 2). RCB is a combination of combiners. The output vector α of the RCB is given in Equation (7):

$$\alpha = C^T y^o = C^T H^c s^t + C^T n^c \qquad (7)$$

where C is the receive combining matrix (RCM) with dimension $N_{re} \times N_{tr}$. The RCM is described in Equation (8):

$$C = \begin{bmatrix} C_1 & C_2 & C_3 & \ldots & C_d & \ldots & C_D \end{bmatrix} \qquad (8)$$

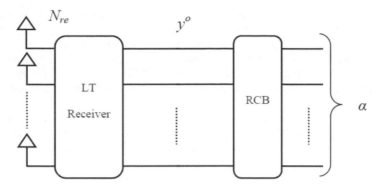

Figure 2. Block diagram of the massive MIMO receiver system.

The dimension of the C_d, d^{th} vector component of RCM is $N_{re} \times J$. The dimension of the channel matrix H^c is also $N_{re} \times N_{tr}$ but the complete matrix divided into D matrix sub-components. Dimensions of each component are $N_{re} \times J$, where $J \cdot D = N_{tr}$ and $J \ll N_{tr}$. The channel matrix H^c is described in Equation (9):

$$H = [H_1 \quad H_2 \quad H_3 \quad \ldots \quad H_d \quad \ldots \quad H_D] \tag{9}$$

The dth vector component of the output of RCB (Moon et al. 2010) for the massive MIMO system is described in Equation (10):

$$\alpha_d = C_d^T H_d s_d + C_d^T \sum_{u=1, u \neq d}^{D} H_u S_u + C_d^T n^c \tag{10}$$

The SINR of dth vector component ($SINR_d$) of the output of RCB in the traditional massive MIMO receiver system is also described in Equation (11):

$$SINR_d = \frac{E\left[\left\| C_d^T H_d s_d \right\|^2\right]}{E\left[\left\| C_d^T \sum_{u=1, u \neq d}^{D} H_u S_u \right\|^2\right] + E\left[\left\| C_d^T n^c \right\|\right]} \tag{11}$$

where $E[\,\cdot\,]$ is the expectation or mean value of the given signal.

The massive MIMO systems are useful for the detection of multiuser systems, reduces CC, improves diversity, and reduces symbol interference. The output signal is shown in Equation (1) when this signal passes to the RCB it separates the transmitted symbol as shown in Figure 2. RCB collects inputs with channel noise and generates output as per the traditional algorithm of the RCB. The $SINR_d$ has a channel noise vector n^c; this noise parameter decreases SINR of the traditional massive MIMO receiver system.

This section presents the comparative study of different types of combiners presented by the researchers from 2010–2019 for MIMO and massive MIMO systems. The references for this research belongs to the years 1962–2019.

A new group-wise receive combiner design (RCD) presented by Moon et al. (2010) for MIMO–SDM systems. The proposed linear combiner is based on the corresponding group-wise selection (GD) method. It is suggested for MU detection using code division multiple access for the MIMO systems. The main advantage of the proposed design is to reduce the complexity of the maximum likelihood detection. The traditional GD and the proposed GD have only 10% and 25% multipliers concerning conventional detection. Therefore, it has low complexity and fewer power consumption circuits. The conventional and some other detection are taken as reference from the period of research 1982–2009.

Li et al. (2011a,b) considered practical MU–MIMO systems where each user has multiple receive antennas and a limited feedback channel is available at the BS. An HPC scheme also proposed. This proposed system eliminates the co-channel interference (CCI) and improves the system sum-rate (SR) performance. The proposed scheme compared with some traditional schemes invented from the duration of 2004–2010.

Wang (2012) presented a receiver combiner bank (RCB) for the MIMO system for MU–CCI. He also discussed the some receive combining strategies to increase the received SINR for MIMO–RCB. The author simulated the MIMO channel for two transmitters and two receivers and gives the higher average received SINR concerning conventional and previously invented combiners. The research duration of conventional and previously invented combiners from 1976–2010 is used by the author.

Wang (2013) also presented another RCB for MIMO systems. This MIMO receiver used to suppress the CCI and applied it to the cognitive radio networks. The author also proposed a new algorithm of variable SINR-based joint weight adjustment and power control for MIMO–CB.

Mendez-Rial et al. (2015) presented dictionary-free HPC for the mmWave MIMO systems. The mmWave MIMO systems have limitations of high-cost and power consumption of the radio-frequency (RF) chain and data converters. The authors proposed decoupled hybrid precoding and Greedy hybrid precoding to overcome the limitations of MIMO systems. They also proposed the Greedy hybrid precoding algorithm and simulated for the narrowband clustered channel model. The proposed algorithm gives the higher SE concerning the previously developed algorithms from the duration from 1999–2014. Also, the spectral efficiencies are closer to the unconstrained solution.

Chen (2015) explained the novel an iterative hybrid transceiver design algorithm for mmWave MIMO systems. The investigated algorithm updates the phases of phase shifters used in the RF combiners or precoders. The proposed algorithm also minimizes the weighted sum of squared residuals between the optimal full-based design and the hybrid design. The proposed algorithm is also simulated under the mmWave MIMO system model. The 64 transmitting antennas and 16 receiving antennas are used for the simulation model. The proposed algorithm gives the optimum result of the sum rate w.r.t. the SNR and average speed of previously developed algorithms from 1965–2014.

Son et al. (2015) investigated the maximum SINR based receive combiner for cognitive MU–MIMO systems. The researchers also proposed the optimal RCD with interference beam information. The performance of this model was evaluated by the four receive antenna combining techniques and a reference system in the form of SR. The SR of cognitive users is dependent on inter-primary base station interference (IPBSI), MUI, and effective desired channel gain (EDCG). After the comparison of simulation results and previously developed models from 1999–2013, the proposed model gives superiority results.

Lopez-Valcarce et al. (2016) proposed a new design/model of HPC for mmWave MIMO systems including the power constraints (Lopez-Valcarce et al. 2016) of per-antenna. The RF analog processing is also implemented phase shifters but previous hybrid transceiver designs consider the maximum of mutual information from 1962–2016. The previous works also present the decoupling of the designs of precoders and combiners with total power constraints. The proposed work also maximizes the SE by HPC designing under pre-antenna constraints.

Ahmed et al. (2017) explored a joint combiner for massive MIMO (Ahmed et al. 2018a) using a genetic algorithm (GA). The proposed joint combiner is based on the bit-allocation design for massive MIMO systems. The authors also explore the expression for the combiner of a MIMO receiver equipped with an MMSE estimator. The proposed channel model was simulated for the GA search and results were compared with some traditional and conventional algorithms. Traditional and conventional algorithms belong to the duration of 2005–2016. The simulation results are shown in the form of cost function and reduce until 17.3% when they had 8 RF paths for genetic algorithm. When the number of RF paths became 12 the cost function reduces by 1.5%. This concludes that the GA-based combiners reduced the CC.

Tian et al. (2017) presented HPC design in millimeter-wave MIMO systems for secure transmission. The proposed design is used to reduce the propagation loss of the channel using HPC transceiver architecture for MIMO systems. The authors determine the security rate of proposed precoders and combiners concerning SNR and also compared with the existing precoders and combiners invented from 2010–2017. The simulation results of the proposed algorithm demonstrated significant performance improvement as compared to other hybrid beam-forming algorithms.

Wang et al. (2017) investigated the novel iterative HPC design for mmWave MU–MIMO systems. The proposed algorithm enhances the performance at each iteration through the given combined design of the uplink and downlink precoders and combiners. The simulation results give the enhanced performance of the proposed design of precoders and combiners as compared with the existing precoders and combiners' designs. The existing precoders and combiners' designs investigated from 2014–2016.

Ni et al. (2017) invented the design of the HPC for multi-stream data transmission in point-to-point massive MIMO systems. The method involved to design the precoders and combiners is known as non-convex matrix decomposition. The proposed model is simulated and compared with some existing models of the precoders and combiners invented from 1996–2014 and the proposed model gives the higher SE using a matrix decomposition-based hybrid processing scheme.

Li et al. (2017) investigated the joint HPC design for multi-stream transmission in mmWave MIMO systems. The authors also analyze the complexity of the proposed joint HPC design. The proposed work also provides the comparative analysis of CC with other already investigated codebook-based schemes and these schemes are invented from the period 2011 to 2016. The proposed channel model was also simulated and analyzed for the SE and SR w.r.t. the SNR, number of transceiver antennas, and number of data streams in the fully connected structure. The simulation results give the optimum or higher SE and SR for the MIMO systems.

Ahmed et al. (2018b) presented the SVD method-based ADC bit-allocation and combiner design for the SU mmWave massive MIMO systems. This work ensures the optimal receiver performance in the form of mean standard error sense. The Camer–Rao lower-bound approaches used to evaluate the expression for the MSE. The proposed mmWave channel model simulated for the 64 QAM data symbols. The MSE analyzed the proposed model to optimize channel performance. This model gives the optimized MSE w.r.t. SNRs and also reduces the CC at a high level. The results were compared with the previously investigated models from the year 1993–2017. The number of complex multiplications reduces up to 0.05% and 0.0007% for the number of paths 8 and 12, respectively.

Wang et al. (2018) investigated the HPC design with low-resolution phase shifters in mmWave MIMO systems The proposed channel model-simulated and compared with the previously developed models from 2007–2017. It is a well-organized iterative algorithm that designs the low-resolution analog precoders and combiners for each data stream. Therefore, digital precoders and combiners were computed and enhance the SE based on the effective baseband channel.

Rodriguez-Fernandez et al. (2018) presented the frequency domain-based compressive channel estimation for frequency selective hybrid mmWave MIMO systems. It gives the optimized design of precoders and combiners under mutual information and SNR. Different types of algorithms are evaluated and computed the CC of the MIMO systems to enhance their performance. The MMSE, SE, and CC parameters of the proposed channel simulation model were compared with the traditional or conventional channel simulation model investigated from 1993–2016 and give the optimized result to enhance the performance of the MIMO system.

Li et al. (2019) investigated the novel iterative HPC design for mmWave MIMO–OFDM systems. The authors apply compressive sensing technology to estimate the efficient MIMO-OFDM system. The proposed channel simulation model maximizes the SE w.r.t. SNR as compared with the already investigated models from 2003–2017.

Zhang et al. (2019) give a new design of HPC for SU mm-Wave MIMO systems. The proposed design can be used in the wideband systems with OFDM modulation. The proposed HPC design also simulated with the proposed channel model. The simulation results and the mathematical

Table 1. Comparative data of combiners for the massive MIMO systems.

S.N.	Outcomes/Short Description	Simulation Analysis Parameters	Publication Year, Reference	Duration involved in their reference
1.	The packet error rate (PER) gives the optimum results for the proposed GD model and list sphere decoder (LSD) w.r.t. conventional models.	PER vs. SNR, LSD	2010 (Moon et al. 2010)	1982–2009
2.	The proposed model of this paper gives the higher system SR w.r.t. the traditional models.	System SR vs. number of users and SNR	2011 (Li et al. 2011a,b)	2004–2010
3.	The proposed combining method gives the higher SINR w.r.t. the previously developed methods.	Average SINR vs. the number of users	2012 (Wang 2012)	1976–2010
4.	The proposed RCB method of this paper gives the higher SINR w.r.t. the conventional methods.	Average SINR of secondary user vs. the number of users	2013 (Wang 2013)	1991–2011
5.	The proposed design of HPC gives the optimum result w.r.t. traditional designs.	SE vs. SNR	2015 (Mendez-Rial et al. 2015)	1999–2014
6.	The proposed iterative hybrid design gives a higher rate of w.r.t. conventional designs.	Achieved rate vs. SNR and angle spread	(Chen 2015)	1965–2014
7.	The proposed receiver combiner maximizes the SR w.r.t. previously developed combiners.	SR vs. the number of transmitting antennas and SNR	2015 (Son et al. 2015)	1999-2013
8.	The proposed HPC gives the optimized result w.r.t. some traditional designs.	SE vs. SNR	2016 (Lopez-Valcarce et al. 2016)	1962–2016
9.	The joint combiner gives the optimized value to the MSE using the genetic algorithm w.r.t. previously developed algorithms.	MSE vs. SNR	2017 (Ahmed et al. 2018a)	2005–2016
10.	The secrecy rate and SE both are optimized for the proposed HPC design w.r.t. conventional designs.	Secrecy rate vs. SNR, SE vs. MIMO system parameters	2017 (Tian et al. 2017)	2010–2017
11.	The proposed iterative HPC design gives the optimized values of the SR and BER w.r.t. traditional HPC designs.	SR vs. SNR and number of users, BER vs. SNR	2017 (Wang et al. 2017)	2014–2016
12.	The proposed hybrid RF and HPC model gives the higher SE based on the SVD w.r.t. traditions models.	SE vs. SNR	2017 (Ni et al. 2017)	1996–2014
13.	The SR and SE performance of the joint HPC design is optimized (maximize) w.r.t. some traditional designs.	SR vs. SNR and number of users, SE vs. SNR and number of users	2017 (Li et al. 2017)	2011–2016
14.	The SVD based combiner design minimizes the MSE of the proposed massive MIMO system.	MSE versus SNR	2018 (Ahmed et al. 2018b)	1993–2017
15.	The proposed HPC design gives the optimized values of the analysis parameters SE and SR w.r.t. many traditions previously developed designs.	SE vs. SNR and number of antennas, SR vs. SNR and number of users	2018 (Wang et al. 2018)	2007–2017

Table 1. Continued.

16.	The proposed hybrid MIMO system minimizes the normalized MSE and maximizes the SE.	Normalized MSE vs. SNR, SE vs. SNR	2018 (Rodriguez-Fernandez et al. 2018)	1993–2016
17.	The proposed iterative fully digital HPC design increases the SE w.r.t. previously developed designs.	SE vs. SNR	2018 (Li et al. 2019)	2003–2017
18.	The proposed HPC design gives the maximum value of the SE w.r.t. traditional HPC designs.	SE vs. SNR	2019 (Zhang et al. 2019)	2003–2018
19.	The precoder and combiner design give the optimized value of the SE based on CNN w.r.t. conventional precoder and combiner designs.	SE vs. SNR	2019 (Elbir 2019)	2000–2019

analysis of the proposed algorithm can achieve near to the optimal performance with low CC for mmWave MIMO systems w.r.t. the previously investigated algorithms from 2003–2018.

Elbir (2019) investigated the convolutional neural network (CNN) based on HPC design in mmWave MIMO systems. The proposed model was designed and simulated for the SU mmWave MIMO system and based on the CNN framework for HPC design. It composed the two CNNs with eight layers which have identical structures except for the last layer. The performance of the CNN framework based on hybrid beam-forming via deep learning evaluated and compared with the models investigated from 2000–2019. The proposed architecture provides better SE as compared to the optimized based and greedy based algorithm.

Table 1 presents the comparative study of the different types of massive MIMO combiners. Many analyses and simulation parameters are used by the researchers to improve the performance of the massive MIMO channel model.

4 RESEARCH ISSUES AND FUTURE SCOPE

As per the comparative study of different types of Massive MIMO combiners, it is found that, if massive MIMO systems have higher channel noise, it will have lower SINR and SNR after the signal passes through RCB. If we decrease the channel noise at a higher level to lower level, it will provide higher SINR and SNR for modified massive MIMO systems. In future research work, an updated massive MIMO system model will be presented to reduce the channel noise at the higher level w.r.t. the present level of combiners. Therefore, it will increase the SINR and SNR for updated massive MIMO systems.

5 CONCLUSION

MIMO technology utilized multiple transmitting antennas and multiple receiving antennas to attain higher SE but nowadays massive MIMO is a recent trend in the field of the wireless communication system of 5G. The capacity of wireless networks has increased data traffic, primarily due to improving SE. Massive MIMO also has several advantages like high SE, low BS noise interference, high SINR, but also has some major challenges like a large number of radio-frequency chains, high cost, high power consumption, apart from these challenges MIMO systems are most desirable of the next-generation wireless communication systems for high data rates.

The precoders and combiner are an important part of MIMO systems to generate the beamforming but the presently optimized result of HPC is one of the recent challenges in the field of MIMO communication systems. So, this review paper presents a comprehensive study of different types of combiners. This paper includes the present research in the field of combiners in the last 10 years by many researchers. Many study parameters are involved in this research but the maximum study parameters by the researchers were SE, SINR, and SS. This paper concludes that massive MIMO systems are most important as per the requirement of our present wireless communication system. The researchers are investigating the optimized channel model for the HPC day-by-day to enhance the performance of the massive MIMO wireless communication system.

REFERENCES

Abuhasel K. A. and M. A. Khan, (2020),"A Secure Industrial Internet of Things (IIoT) Framework for Resource Management in Smart Manufacturing," in IEEE Access, vol. 8, pp. 117354–117364, 2020, doi: 10.1109/ACCESS.2020.3004711.

Ahmed, I.Z., Sadjadpour, H., and Yousefi, S., (2018a). A joint combiner and bit allocation design for massive MIMO using genetic algorithm. *In*: *Conference Record of 51st Asilomar Conference on Signals, Systems and Computers, ACSSC 2017*. Institute of Electrical and Electronics Engineers Inc., 1045–1049.

Ahmed, I.Z., Sadjadpour, H., and Yousefi, S., (2018b). Single-user mmWave massive MIMO: SVD-based ADC bit allocation and combiner design. *In*: *SPCOM 2018 — 12th International Conference on Signal Processing and Communications*. Institute of Electrical and Electronics Engineers Inc., 357–361.

Ayach, O. El, Rajagopal, S., Abu-Surra, S., Pi, Z., and Heath, R.W., (2014). Spatially sparse precoding in millimeter wave MIMO systems. *IEEE Transactions on Wireless Communications*, 13 (3), 1499–1513.

Chen, C.E., (2015). An iterative hybrid transceiver design algorithm for millimeter wave MIMO systems. *IEEE Wireless Communications Letters*, 4 (3), 285–288.

Elbir, A.M., (2019). CNN-Based Precoder and Combiner Design in mmWave MIMO Systems. *IEEE Communications Letters*, 23 (7), 1240–1243.

Gao, X., Dai, L., Han, S., Chih-Lin, I., and Heath, R.W., (2016). Energy-Efficient Hybrid Analog and Digital Precoding for MmWave MIMO Systems with Large Antenna Arrays. *IEEE Journal on Selected Areas in Communications*, 34 (4), 998–1009.

Hassan, Y., Kuhn, M., and Wittneben, A., (2015). Group decoders for correlated massive MIMO systems: The use of random matrix theory. *In*: *IEEE Vehicular Technology Conference*. Institute of Electrical and Electronics Engineers Inc.

Kathuria J., Khan M.A., Abraham A., Darwish A. (2014) Low Power Techniques for Embedded FPGA Processors. In: Khan M., Saeed S., Darwish A., Abraham A. (eds) Embedded and Real Time System Development: A Software Engineering Perspective. Studies in Computational Intelligence, vol 520. Springer, Berlin, Heidelberg. https://doi.org/10.1007/978-3-642-40888-5_11

Khan M. A. (2020), An IoT Framework for Heart Disease Prediction Based on MDCNN Classifier, in IEEE Access, vol. 8, pp. 34717-34727, 2020. DOI: 10.1109/ACCESS.2020.2974687

Khan, MA, Abuhasel, KA. (2020).Advanced metameric dimension framework for heterogeneous industrial Internet of things. Computational Intelligence. 2020; 1– 21. https://doi.org/10.1111/coin.12378

Khan M.A, and Algarni F., (2020) "A Healthcare Monitoring System for the Diagnosis of Heart Disease in the IoMT Cloud Environment Using MSSO-ANFIS," in IEEE Access, vol. 8, pp. 122259-122269, 2020, doi: 10.1109/ACCESS.2020.3006424.

Khan, I. and Singh, D., (2018). Efficient compressive sensing based sparse channel estimation for 5G massive MIMO systems. *AEU — International Journal of Electronics and Communications*, 89, 181–190.

Khan, M. A., Quasim, M. T, et.al, (2020), A Secure Framework for Authentication and Encryption Using Improved ECC for IoT-Based Medical Sensor Data, in IEEE Access, vol. 8, pp. 52018-52027, 2020. DOI: 10.1109/ACCESS.2020.2980739

Khan M.A. et al., (2020), Decentralised IoT, Decenetralised IoT: A Blockchain perspective, Springer, Studies in BigData, 2020, DOI: https://doi.org/10.1007/978-3-030-38677-1

Larsson, E.G., Edfors, O., Tufvesson, F., and Marzetta, T.L., (2014). Massive MIMO for next generation wireless systems. *IEEE Communications Magazine*, 52 (2), 186–195.

Li, G., Zhang, X., and Yang, D., 2011b. Joint combiner and precoding in MU-MIMO downlink systems with limited feedback and user selection. *In*: *2011 IEEE GLOBECOM Workshops, GC Wkshps 2011*. 750–754.

Li, G., Zhang, X., Liu, X., and Yang, D., (2011a). Joint combiner and precoding in MU-MIMO downlink systems with limited feedback. *In*: *IEEE Vehicular Technology Conference.*

Li, M., Liu, W., Tian, X., Wang, Z., and Liu, Q., (2019). Iterative hybrid precoder and combiner design for mmWave MIMO-OFDM systems. *Wireless Networks*, 25 (8), 4829–4837.

Li, M., Wang, Z., Tian, X., and Liu, Q., (2017). Joint hybrid precoder and combiner design for multi-stream transmission in mmWave MIMO systems. *IET Communications*, 11 (17), 2596–2604.

Li, P., (2014). Data aided channel estimation in massive MIMO systems. *In*: *2014 International Workshop on High Mobility Wireless Communications.* 3.

Lopez-Valcarce, R., Gonzalez-Prelcic, N., Rusu, C., and Heath, R.W., (2016). Hybrid precoders and combiners for mmwave MIMO systems with per-antenna power constraints. *In*: *2016 IEEE Global Communications Conference, GLOBECOM 2016 - Proceedings.* Institute of Electrical and Electronics Engineers Inc.

Marzetta, T.L., (2015). Massive MIMO: An introduction. *Bell Labs Technical Journal.*

Masood, M., Afify, L.H., and Al-Naffouri, T.Y., 2015. Efficient collaborative sparse channel estimation in massive MIMO. *In*: *ICASSP, IEEE International Conference on Acoustics, Speech and Signal Processing - Proceedings.* Institute of Electrical and Electronics Engineers Inc., 2924–2928.

Maza, B.P., Dahman, G., Kaddoum, G., and Gagnon, F., (2020). Average Vector-Symbol Error Rate Closed-Form Expression for ML Group Detection Receivers in Large MU-MIMO Channels with Transmit Correlation. *IEEE Access*, 8, 45653–45663.

Mendez-Rial, R., Rusu, C., Gonzalez-Prelcic, N., and Heath, R.W., (2015). Dictionary-free hybrid precoders and combiners for mmWave MIMO systems. *In*: *IEEE Workshop on Signal Processing Advances in Wireless Communications, SPAWC.* Institute of Electrical and Electronics Engineers Inc., 151–155.

Moon, S.H., Jeong, J., Lee, H., and Lee, I., (2010). Enhanced group-wise detection with a new receive combiner for spatial multiplexing MIMO systems. *IEEE Transactions on Communications*, 58 (9), 2511–2515.

Ngo, H.Q. and Larsson, E.G., (2015). Blind estimation of effective downlink channel gains in massive MIMO. *In*: *ICASSP, IEEE International Conference on Acoustics, Speech and Signal Processing - Proceedings.* Institute of Electrical and Electronics Engineers Inc., 2919–2923.

Ni, W., Dong, X., and Lu, W.S., (2017). Near-Optimal Hybrid Processing for Massive MIMO Systems via Matrix Decomposition. *IEEE Transactions on Signal Processing*, 65 (15), 3922–3933.

Pappa, M., Ramesh, C., and Kumar, M.N., (2018). Performance comparison of massive MIMO and conventional MIMO using channel parameters. *In*: *Proceedings of the 2017 International Conference on Wireless Communications, Signal Processing and Networking, WiSPNET 2017.* Institute of Electrical and Electronics Engineers Inc., 1808–1812.

Quasim ,M. T.,Khan M. A, et.al, (2019), Internet of Things for Smart Healthcare: A Hardware Perspective, 2019 First International Conference of Intelligent Computing and Engineering (ICOICE), Hadhramout, Yemen, 2019, pp. 1-5. DOI: 10.1109/ICOICE48418.2019.9035175

Quasim, M.T., Khan M.A, Algarni F., Alharthy A., Alshmrani G.M.M, (2020) , Blockchain Frameworks. In: Khan M., Quasim M., Algarni F., Alharthi A. (eds) Decentralised Internet of Things. Studies in Big Data, vol 71. Springer, DOI: https://doi.org/10.1007/978-3-030-38677-1

Rodriguez-Fernandez, J., Gonzalez-Prelcic, N., Venugopal, K., and Heath, R.W., (2018). Frequency-Domain Compressive Channel Estimation for Frequency-Selective Hybrid Millimeter Wave MIMO Systems. *IEEE Transactions on Wireless Communications*, 17 (5), 2946–2960.

Santumon, S.D., and Sujatha, B.R., (2012). Space-time block coding (STBC) for wireless networks. *International Journal of Distributed and Parallel Systems*, 3 (4), 183.

Shariati, N., Björnson, E., Bengtsson, M., and Debbah, M., (2013). Low-complexity channel estimation in large-scale MIMO using polynomial expansion. *In*: *IEEE International Symposium on Personal, Indoor and Mobile Radio Communications, PIMRC.* 1157–1162.

Shariati, N., Bjornson, E., Bengtsson, M., and Debbah, M., (2014). Low-complexity polynomial channel estimation in large-scale MIMO with arbitrary statistics. *IEEE Journal on Selected Topics in Signal Processing*, 8 (5), 815–830.

Son, H., Kim, S., and Lee, S., (2015). Maximum SINR-Based Receive Combiner for Cognitive MU-MIMO Systems. *IEEE Transactions on Vehicular Technology*, 64 (9), 4344–4350.

Tian, X., Li, M., Wang, Z., and Liu, Q., (2017). Hybrid Precoder and Combiner Design for Secure Transmission in mmWave MIMO Systems. *In*: *2017 IEEE Global Communications Conference, GLOBECOM 2017 - Proceedings.* Institute of Electrical and Electronics Engineers Inc., 1–6.

Wang, J.T., (2012). Receive combiner bank for MIMO system under multi-user cochannel interference. *IEEE Communications Letters*, 16 (3), 328–330.

Wang, J.T., (2013). MIMO system with receive-combiner bank and power control for cognitive radio networks. *IEEE Transactions on Vehicular Technology*, 62 (8), 3767–3773.

817

Wang, Z., Li, M., Liu, Q., and Swindlehurst, A.L., (2018). Hybrid Precoder and Combiner Design with Low-Resolution Phase Shifters in mmWave MIMO Systems. *IEEE Journal on Selected Topics in Signal Processing*, 12 (2), 256–269.

Wang, Z., Li, M., Tian, X., and Liu, Q., (2017). Iterative Hybrid Precoder and Combiner Design for mmWave Multiuser MIMO Systems. *IEEE Communications Letters*, 21 (7), 1581–1584.

Xu, F., Xiao, Y., and Wang, D., (2014). Adaptive semi-blind channel estimation for massive MIMO systems. *In*: *International Conference on Signal Processing Proceedings, ICSP*. Institute of Electrical and Electronics Engineers Inc., 1698–1702.

Yokota, Y. and Ochi, H., (2015). An averaged-LLR Group Detection for higher-order MIMO MLD. *In*: *14th International Symposium on Communications and Information Technologies, ISCIT 2014*. Institute of Electrical and Electronics Engineers Inc., 21–25.

Zhang, R., Zou, W., Wang, Y., and Cui, M., (2019). Hybrid precoder and combiner design for single-user mmWave MIMO systems. *IEEE Access*, 7, 63818–63828.

Smart Computing – Khan et al (Eds)
© 2021 Taylor & Francis Group, London, ISBN 978-0-367-76552-1

Wideband antenna for medical implant in medical device radio communication service band

Pinku Ranjan
ABV-Indian Institute of Information Technology & Management, Gwalior, India

Sneha Chand
Department of Electrical Engineering, IIT Madras, Chennai, India

Abhay Krishna Yadav
Dept. of Vocational Education and Skill Development, U. P., India

Surjeet Singh Patel
G. B. Pant Institute of Engineering and Technology (GBPIET) Pauri Garhwal, Uttarakhand, India

ABSTRACT: This paper presents the design of a wideband medical-grade antenna that operates at 300–440 MHz. The proposed design has been successfully shown operating in the desired Medical Device Radio Communications Service band application. The design is unique in its style to accomplish antenna miniaturization. The antenna proposed has dimensions of 18 mm × 10 mm × 1.6 mm. The substrate has been used in Epoxy FR4 (Dielectric constant 4.4). It provides good bandwidth of 140 MHz, which can be good for medical applications. The proposed antenna provides sufficient bandwidth as well as radiation characteristics for desired medical applications.

1   INTRODUCTION

Millions around us today suffer from chronic diseases such as diabetes, Alzheimer's, cancer, and others with severe health issues like heart disorders, tumors, and critical injuries. Many health-care applications have been developed using Internet of Things (IoT) to make the system smarter (Abuhasel 2020; Khan 2020a–2020e; Quasim 2019, 2020). The most significant aspect is the early detection of these fatal diseases before it leads to many complications (Kim and Yahmat-Samii 2004; Kiourti et al. 2014). Implanted wireless devices such as drug pumps, cardiac defibrillators, neuro-stimulators, biventricular pacemakers, etc. are being used in the human body and found to be very useful in the detection of such situations. Therefore, several related antennas have been designed in the literature. Further antennas were designed with greater abilities like reconfigurable radiation pattern antennas to enhance the radiation efficiency in a particular direction due to application needs. A great range of antenna in telemetry and other areas can also be seen. Each design has its pros and cons, but high-frequency radio-frequency (RF) transmissions equip us with long-range and high data rates for in- and around-body wireless devices. The popular and similar antennas in this group are wire antennas, planar printed antennas, and conformal printed antennas.

The conventional inductive link for communication was falling out in this field, hence RF bands were established to overcome these limitations. The two major bands in this area are the Industrial, Scientific, and Medical band (ISM Band: 433 MHz, band for medical purposes) and Medical Device Radio-communications Service band (MedRadio band: 400–450 MHz).

These bands conduct well in humans providing a good data rate and a range up to 2 m for communication purposes. A medical implant communication system (MICS) network consists of two major devices: one the implant inside the patient and the otherm if present, outside the body

DOI 10.1201/9781003167488-101

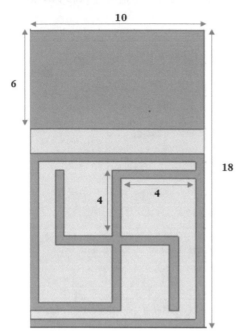

Figure 1.   Bottom view.

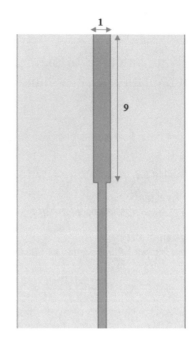

Figure 2.   Top view.

which can be a computer. The implant essentially acts as a sensor, sensing the data. The computer connected to the implant majorly collects data and if required sends a command. The computer is then connected to the Internet to avail of this data anytime and anywhere. The patient's family as well as health professionals can now monitor the patient.

Our designed antenna structure works well in the defined band of 300–440 MHz for the Medical Device Radio-communications Service band with bandwidth of 140 MHz. Its design and analysis have been discussed in two phases: pre-phase and post-phase. The rest of the paper is organized as follows. Section 2 addresses design elaboration and Section 3 presents the comparisons between different structures. Finally, Section 4 provides the conclusion.

2   ANTENNA DESIGN AND CONFIGURATION

The dimensions of the proposed antenna are seen in Figures 1 and 2 for the bottom view and top view, respectively. The radiating patch design and the ground plane have been depicted in the following figures. From Figures 1 and 2 it is clear that the antenna has a unique design with dimensions of the substrate as 18 mm × 10 mm × 1.6 mm. The antenna is fabricated on FR4 substrate of thickness 1.6 mm, and is of relative permittivity 4.4 F/m. Figure 2 gives the proper characteristics of the radiating patch with the microstrip feed line. The proposed design has two stages viz pre- and post-stages, respectively.

In pre-design, a monopole antenna is proposed where the behavior of a microstrip patch antenna is simulated for the monopole radiation pattern. This pattern can be depicted in the polar radiation graph shown in Section 3. In this design, the microstrip feed line is connected to the swastika design at the bottom through a cylindrical hole in the substrate to join both the layers. Several designs were optimized, mostly trying to fit the monopole antenna in a small area by spiraling it or giving it confined pattern, these traditional methods failed to achieve wideband radiation, and after several optimizations proposed design met the expectations.

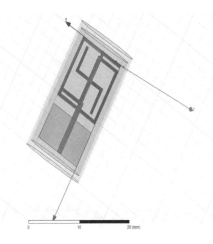

Figure 3.   Proposed antennas are encapsulated in a biocompatible material.

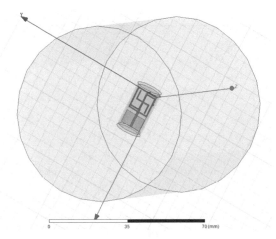

Figure 4.   The capsule placed inside a cylinder mimicking the human body as a phantom.

Finally, it has been seen that a feed line of width 1 mm squeezing to 0.5 mm halfway with a length of 18 mm, and the input impedance of 50Ω. The thickness of the substrate is 1.6 mm and that of the ground is 0.035 mm, over the rectangular patch having width 10 mm and a length of 18 mm. The swastika shape is designed with similar strips having a width of 0.5 mm and length 4 mm; all the symmetric hands are then joined to attain the swastika pattern. The widespread of each hand gives a better radiation pattern and minimizes conducting losses which help to maintain better gain. This overall design consideration is to enhance the radiation pattern. The performance of the proposed antenna is evaluated on the Ansoft HFSS simulation software.

The different stages of *Post-Design* are discussed below/

Stage 1: Here the antenna is encapsulated in a biocompatible material, as shown in Figure 3, which is Rogers RT/ droid 5870(tm), with a permeability = 1, permittivity = 2.33.

Stage 2: This capsule is further placed inside a cylinder, mimicking the human body, as shown in Figure 4, hence assigned material is called Phantom with Relative Permittivity = 46.7 and permeability = 1.

Stage 3: Lastly, the entire design is placed inside an air-box as shown in Figure 5.

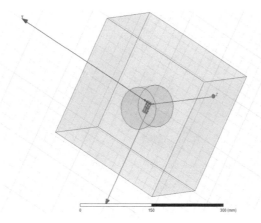

Figure 5.   The proposed antenna and a phantom kept inside an air-box.

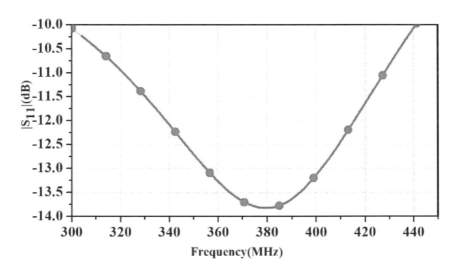

Figure 6.   S-parameters of the proposed antenna.

3   RESULTS AND DISCUSSION

The designed antenna has been analyzed for various parameters through a simulation-like input characteristics, far-field, gain, and current distribution. The proposed antenna provides a wide bandwidth of 300–440 MHz, which has wide applications in the biomedical area. From Figure 6 it can be observed that the antenna is resonating for a range of frequencies from 300–440 MHz. The graph depicts the return loss is less than 90% as the curve lies below −10 dB which is the basic definition of the S_{11} (return loss) plot. A bandwidth of 150 MHz is achieved by the proposed design and at resonant frequency 380 MHz. The antenna has an Omni-directional radiation pattern. From Figure 7, it is depicted that for H-plane; it has a monopoly-like radiation pattern and for E-plane dipole like pattern. Cross-polarization measure is quite low compared to the co-polarization measure. Three-dimensional radiation patterns have been also shown in Figure 8. The proposed antenna has a peak gain of 2.5 dB in the operating frequency band.

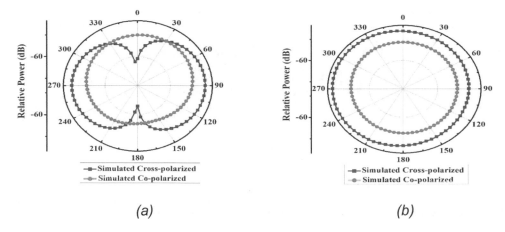

Figure 7.   The radiation pattern of the proposed antenna for (a) E-plane and (b) H-plane at resonant frequency 380 MHz.

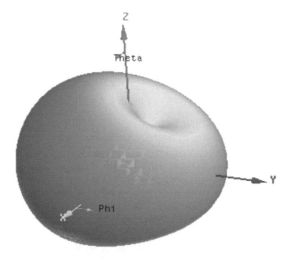

Figure 8.   3-dimensional radiation pattern of the proposed at resonant frequency 380 MHz.

4   CONCLUSION

There are two major bands are available for medical applications Industrial, Scientific, and Medical band (ISM Band: 433 MHz, band for medical purposes) and Medical Device Radio-communications Service band (MedRadio band: 400–450 MHz). The proposed antenna provides 300–440 MHz with 140 MHz wide bandwidth for the desired application.

REFERENCES

Abuhasel K. A. and M. A. Khan, (2020), "A Secure Industrial Internet of Things (IIoT) Framework for Resource Management in Smart Manufacturing," in IEEE Access, vol. 8, pp. 117354–117364, 2020, doi: 10.1109/ACCESS.2020.3004711.
Chow E. Y., Chlebowski A. L., Chakraborty S., Chappell W. J., and Irazoqui P. P. (2010). Fully wireless implantable cardiovascular pressure monitor integrated with a medical stent. IEEE Trans. Biomed. Eng., vol. 57, no. 6, pp. 1487–1496.

Chow E. Y., Morris M. M., and Irazoqui P. P. (2013). Implantable RF medical devices: The benefits of high-speed communication and much greater communication distances in biomedical applications. IEEE Microw. Mag., vol. 14, no. 4, pp. 64–73.

Duanand Z. and Xu L. (2017). Dual-band implantable antenna with circular polarization property for ingestible capsule application. Electron. Lett., vol. 53, no. 16, pp. 1090–1092.

Jung Y. H., Qiu Y., Lee S., Shih T.Y., Xu Y. 2016. A compact parylene-coated WLAN flexible antenna for implantable electronics IEEE Antenna Wireless Propag. Lett., vol. 15, pp. 1382–1385.

Karacolak T., Hood A. Z., and Topsakal E. (2008). Design of a dual-band implantable antenna and development of skin mimicking gels for continuous glucose monitoring. IEEE Trans.Microw. Theory Tech., vol. 56, no. 4, pp. 1001–1008.

Kathuria J., Khan M.A., Abraham A., Darwish A. (2014) Low Power Techniques for Embedded FPGA Processors. In: Khan M., Saeed S., Darwish A., Abraham A. (eds) Embedded and Real Time System Development: A Software Engineering Perspective. Studies in Computational Intelligence, vol 520. Springer, Berlin, Heidelberg. https://doi.org/10.1007/978-3-642-40888-5_11

Kim J. and Yahmat-Samii Y. (2004). Implanted antennas inside a human body: Simulations, designs, and characterizations. IEEE Trans. Microw.TheoryTech., vol. 52, no. 8, pp. 1934–1943.

Kiourti, K. Psathas, and Nikita K. S. (2014). Implantable and ingestible medical devices with wireless telemetry functionalities: A review of current status and challenges. Bioelectromagnetics, vol. 35, no. 1, pp. 1–15.

Khan M. A., (2020), An IoT Framework for Heart Disease Prediction Based on MDCNN Classifier, in IEEE Access, vol. 8, pp. 34717–34727, 2020. DOI: 10.1109/ACCESS.2020.2974687

Khan, MA, Abuhasel, KA. (2020).Advanced metameric dimension framework for heterogeneous industrial Internet of things. Computational Intelligence. 2020; 1–21. https://doi.org/10.1111/coin.12378

Khan M.A, and Algarni F., (2020) "A Healthcare Monitoring System for the Diagnosis of Heart Disease in the IoMT Cloud Environment Using MSSO-ANFIS," in IEEE Access, vol. 8, pp. 122259–122269, 2020, doi: 10.1109/ACCESS.2020.3006424.

Khan, M. A., Quasim, M. T, et al, (2020), A Secure Framework for Authentication and Encryption Using Improved ECC for IoT-Based Medical Sensor Data, in IEEE Access, vol. 8, pp. 52018–52027, 2020. DOI: 10.1109/ACCESS.2020.2980739

Khan M.A. et al., (2020), Decentralised IoT, Decenetralised IoT: A Blockchain perspective, Springer, Studies in BigData, 2020, DOI: https://doi.org/10.1007/978-3-030-38677-1

Liu Y., Chen Y., Lin H., and Juwono F. H. (2016). A novel differentially fed compact dual-band implantable antenna for biotelemetry applications. IEEE Antenna Wireless Propag. Lett., vol. 15, pp. 1791–1794.

Nguyen V. T. and Jung C. W. (2016). Radiation-pattern reconfigurable antenna for medical implants in MedRadioband. IEEE Antennas Wireless Propag. Lett., vol. 15, pp. 106–109.

Quasim, M. T., Khan M. A, et al, (2019), Internet of Things for Smart Healthcare: A Hardware Perspective, 2019 First International Conference of Intelligent Computing and Engineering (ICOICE), Hadhramout, Yemen, 2019, pp. 1–5. DOI: 10.1109/ICOICE48418.2019.9035175

Quasim, M.T., Khan M.A, Algarni F., Alharthy A., Alshmrani G.M.M, (2020), Blockchain Frameworks. In: Khan M., Quasim M., Algarni F., Alharthi A. (eds) Decentralised Internet of Things. Studies in Big Data, vol 71. Springer, DOI: https://doi.org/10.1007/978-3-030-38677-1

Shults M. C., Rhodes R. K., Updike S. J., Gilligan B. J., and Reining W. N., (1994). A telemetry-instrumentation system for monitoring multiple subcutaneously implanted glucose sensors. IEEE Trans. Biomed. Eng., vol. 41, no. 10, pp. 937–942.

Smart Computing – Khan et al (Eds)
© 2021 Taylor & Francis Group, London, ISBN 978-0-367-76552-1

Investigation of compact MIMO antenna for WLAN application

Pinku Ranjan, Vivek Kumar, Shubham Singh & Swati Khandare
ABV-Indian Institute of Information Technology & Management, Gwalior, India

Abhay Krishna Yadav
Department of Vocational Education and Skill Development, U.P., India

Surjeet Singh Patel
G.B. Pant Institute of Engineering and Technology (GBPIET), Pauri Garhwal, Uttarakhand, India

ABSTRACT: In this paper, a compact dual port Multiple-Input Multiple-Output (MIMO) antenna for WLAN application is designed. An antenna is etched on 15 mm × 30 mm × 1.6 mm FR4 substrate which is cheap and easily available. This paper focuses on a small antenna size offering mutual coupling < -10 dB between frequencies 4.82 GHz to 6 GHz with low return loss and good diversity performance. The simulation result shows the designed antenna is suitable for WLAN application in 5 GHz band (5.15–5.84 GHz). In MIMO antenna technology, diversity performance analysis based on envelope correlation coefficient (ECC), diversity gain, and total active reflection coefficient (TARC) is an important aspect which is also simulated and discussed in this paper.

1 INTRODUCTION

The Federal Communication Commission (FCC) has allowed 3.1–10.6 GHz unlicensed band for UWB communication, which is grouped based on application is mentioned in Table 1.

In a wireless communication system, a single antenna design faced disadvantages of low data rate, multipath fading, and interference which are finally countered by Multiple-Input Multiple-Output (MIMO) antenna technology. In Section 2, this paper explains a proposed antenna design which is basically 2 port MIMO antenna fabricated on FR4 substrate having dimension 15 mm × 30 mm × 1.6 mm which is compact and useful for WLAN application at low cost. The radiating element also occupies less space featuring low correlation coefficient and good diversity performance. The ground with curved edges along with rod like stub and rectangular slot is carved to get the desired WLAN frequency band and low mutual coupling between antenna elements. Section 3 discusses simulation results. S-parameters (S11/S12/S21/S22) briefs about the return loss and mutual coupling. There is an inverse relation between return loss and gain. Hence, the less the return loss the more the gain, which is the desired outcome. Currently, mutual coupling < -10 dB

Table 1. Application of frequency spectrum.

Application	Spectrum (GHz)
Bluetooth	2.40–2.484
WiMAX	3.40–3.69
WLAN	5.150–5.825
UWB	3.10–10.80

DOI 10.1201/9781003167488-102

Table 2. Electrical properties of the FR4.

sr	4.4
μr	1
$\tan \delta s$	0.02

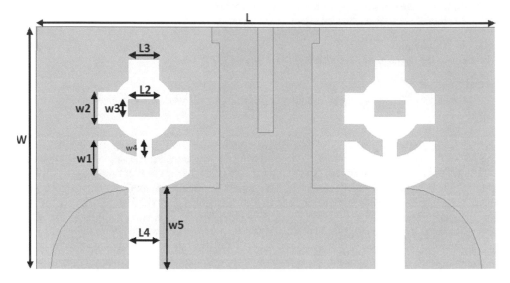

Figure 1. Top view of the proposed antenna.

is acceptable for MIMO antenna system working in sub-6 GHz. Several decoupling structures such as neutralization line, protruded ground plane, and etched slot are available are advantageous in providing isolation between the antenna elements; on the other hand, it increases the complexity. Hence, designing compact MIMO antenna with good isolation is the need of the hour. MIMO antenna performance could not be justified unless diversity parameters such as ECC, diversity gain, and TARC are not analyzed. This paper discusses on the important factors affecting antenna performance. Focusing mainly on 5 GHz band which is suitable for WLAN application, this paper discusses the respective antenna design. Finally, Section 4 provides a conclusion which compares the design with references.

2 ANTENNA DESIGN AND PARAMETERS

Designing a MIMO antenna with compact size, high gain, and high isolation is a challenging task for any portable application. This paper presents a dual-port MIMO antenna with substrate size [W × L × h] $mm3$. The top view of the proposed antenna fabricated on FR4 substrate is shown in Figure 1 and important electrical properties of the FR4 is mentioned in Table 2.

Figure 1 indicates the top view of the proposed antenna and the identical radiating patch distanced by D, embedded on the top of the substrate. The patch is fed with a 50-ohm rectangular strip of width w5 and length L1.

Figure 2 shows the bottom view of the proposed antenna design which consists of ground plane with length g1 with curved edges (modified by circular planes) at both the extreme ends on left and right. A narrow slot (s1 × s2) mm^2 carved on the ground plane provides suitable gain and isolation between the antenna elements [2]. Final optimized parameters of the proposed antenna design simulated in HFSS 13.0 are listed in the Table 3.

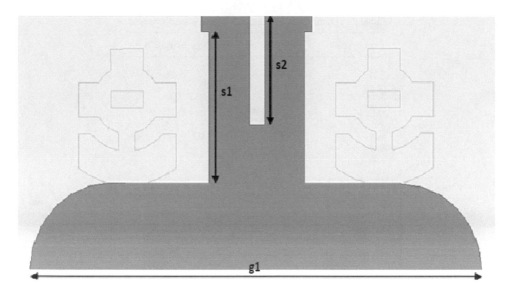

Figure 2. Bottom view of the proposed antenna.

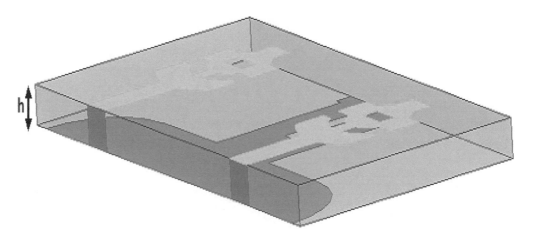

Figure 3. Side view of the proposed antenna.

3 SIMULATION RESULTS AND DISCUSSION

The discussed simulation in this paper result includes S-Parameters, Radiation Pattern, Gain, Current Distribution, and Diversity Performance (ECC and TARC). In Figure 4, S11/S12/S21/S22 plots have been shown. These parameters define the effectiveness of the designed antenna.

In terms of return loss and isolation between antenna elements, the designed antenna resonates at frequency 5.77 GHz giving very low return loss of approximately −37.9 dB. Bringing the focus toward WLAN application the suitable frequency band is 5.15–5.825 GHz and the objective of getting high gain is achieved in this frequency band with mutual coupling (S12,S21) ranging from ¡−10 dB at 4.81 GHz to approximately −14.3 at 6 GHz. Mutual coupling below −10 dB is considered suitable for MIMO antenna [4].

Figure 5 shows the four different phases involved in the design process of the proposed antenna. From S-parameters, impedance bandwidth can be observed to be ranging from 4.39–7.32 GHz and

Table 3. Optimized parameters of the proposed antenna.

Parameters	Dimensions (mm)
W	15
L	30
w1	2
w2	2
w3	1
w4	1.02
w5	5.1
L1	2
L2	2
L3	2
g1	28.1
g2	8.9
s1	1
s2	6.5
D	16

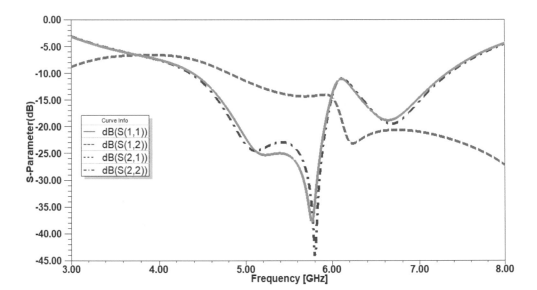

Figure 4. S-Parameters of the proposed antenna.

the frequency band of interest is 5.15–5.82 GHz for WLAN application. The Gain (total) achieved is between 3.48–3.87 dB as shown in Figure 6.

3.1 Diversity performance

Moving further on diversity performance of the proposed antenna ECC, TARC, and DG (Diversity Gain) have been analyzed. Theoretically, ECC in terms of isolation is given by Equation [6]:

$$ECC(abs) = |S_{11}^* S_{22} + S_{21}^* S_{22}|^2 / ((1 - |S_{11}|^2 - |S_{21}|^2)(1 - |S_{22}|^2 - |S_{12}|^2))$$

The lower the ECC the higher the directive gain will be [6]. The achieved ECC is less than 0.001 in the frequency range 5–6 GHz which is much lower than the limit 0.5, as shown in Figure 7.

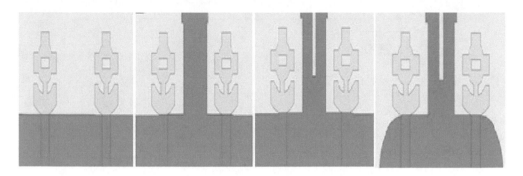

Figure 5.   Design phase of the proposed antenna 1, 2, 3, and 4, respectively.

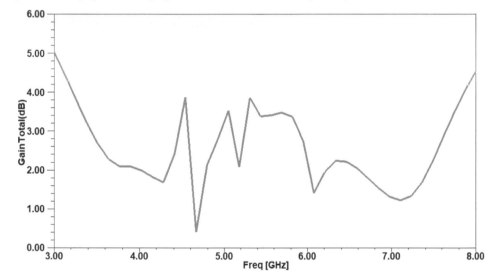

Figure 6.   Gain (dB) vs. frequency (GHz) curve of the proposed antenna.

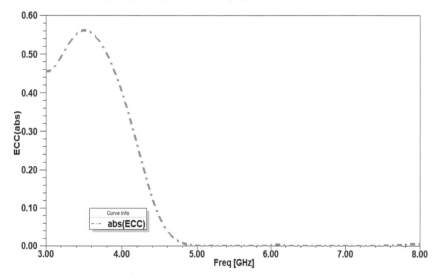

Figure 7. ρe vs. Freq. (GHz) curve of the proposed antenna.

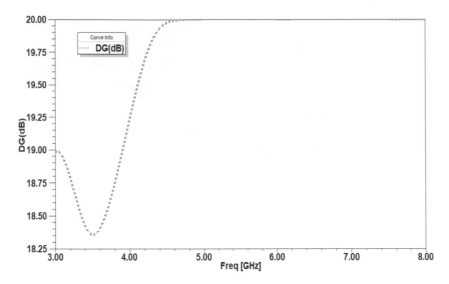

Figure 8. DG vs. frequ.ency (GHz) curve of the proposed antenna.

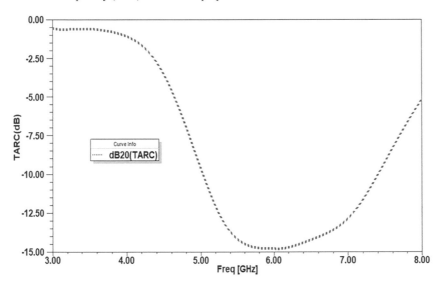

Figure 9. TARC (dB) vs. frequency (GHz) curve of the proposed antenna.

The second important parameter DG is calculated using the formula:

$$DG = 10\sqrt{(1 - ECC^2)}$$

The achieved DG is greater than 20 dB in the desired frequency band 5–6 Hz, as shown in Figure 8.

For a multiport antenna system, a new parameter TARC has been introduced to illustrate the apparent power loss of the overall MIMO system. TARC is given by the equation:

$$TARC = \sqrt{((S_{11} + S_{22})^2 + (S_{21} + S_{22})^2)/2}$$

From Figure 9, it can observe that the TARC obtained is <0 dB which is desirable for the MIMO system.

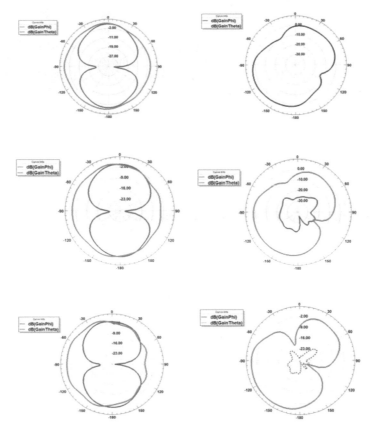

Figure 10. Radiation pattern for proposed antenna design for E-plane and H-plane at frequencies 5.15 GHz, 5.5 GHz, and 5.77 GHz, respectively.

Table 4. Comparison with other published work.

Comparison with previously published work

Paper	Year	Substrate	No.of Size (mm^3)	Ports	Return Loss (dB)	Mutual Coupling (dB)	ECC
Ameen et al.	2016	FR4	$70 \times 30 \times 3.2$	2	-25	<-20	0.05
Ding et al.	2018	FR4	$13.5 \times 32 \times 0.8$	2	-25	<-15	Not Given
Alex at el.	2018	FR4	$30 \times 40 \times 1$	2	<-15	<-15	<0.5
Kumar et al.	2020	FR4	$35 \times 35 \times 0.8$	2	<-21	<-19	<0.014
Proposed Work	2020	FR4	$15 \times 30 \times 1.6$	2	<-37	-14.3	<0.001

3.2 *Radiation pattern*

Figure 10 shows the different 2D radiation patterns for the proposed antenna for E-plane and H-plane at frequencies 5.15 GHz, 5.5 GHz, and 5.77 GHz covering the higher frequency band of WLAN spectrum. The radiation efficiency obtained with the proposed design is 98.02%.

4 CONCLUSION

There are numerous papers which have been published on compact MIMO antenna for WLAN application covering 5 GHz frequency band using FR4. Comparisons with few references have been summarized in Table 4. The comparison shows that the proposed design is better in terms of size, return loss, and diversity performance.

REFERENCES

Alex L. and Amma S. (2018). Compact Inverted U Shaped Slot Triple Band MIMO Antenna for WLAN and WiMAX Applications. *Second International Conference on Inventive Communication and Computational Technologies (ICICCT),* Coimbatore, pp. 1034–1036.

Ameen M. et al. (2015). A compact S-shaped 2 × 1 MIMO antenna for WLAN/WiMAX applications," *IEEE Applied Electromagnetics Confer- ence (AEMC),* Guwahati, pp. 1–2.

Biswas Arumita, Gupta Vibha Rani. (2019). Design and Development of Low Profile MIMO Antenna for 5G New Radio Smartphone Appli- cations. *Wireless Personal Communications, Springer,* 111, pp. 1695–1706.

Cui S., Jiang W. and Gong S. X. (2011). Compact dual-band monopole antennas with high port isolation *Electronics Lett.* vol. 47, No. 10, pp. 203–204.

Ding C. et al. (2018). A Compact Dual-Band MIMO Slot Antenna for WLAN Applications. *IEEE International Symposium on Antennas and Propagation USNC/URSI National Radio Science Meeting,* Boston, MA, pp. 461–462.

Federal Communications Commission, Washington, DC, USA. (2002). *Federal Communications Commission revision of Part 15 of the Commission's rules regarding ultra-wideband transmission system from 3.1 to 10.6 GHz,"* ET-Docket, pp. 98–153.

Kathuria J., Khan M.A., Abraham A., Darwish A. (2014) Low Power Techniques for Embedded FPGA Proces- sors. In: Khan M., Saeed S., Darwish A., Abraham A. (eds) Embedded and Real Time System Development: A Software Engineering Perspective. Studies in Computational Intelligence, vol 520. Springer, Berlin, Heidelberg. https://doi.org/10.1007/978-3-642-40888-5_11

Kumar A. Saurabh, Rathore P. Singh and Meshram M. Kumar. (2020). Compact wideband four-element MIMO antenna with high isolation. *Electronics Letters,* vol. 56, no. 3, pp. 117–119.

Ren J., Hu W., Yin Y. and Fan R. (2014). Compact Printed MIMO Antenna for UWB Applications," *IEEE Antennas and Wireless Propagation Letters,* vol. 13, pp. 1517–1520.

Chandel Richa, Gautam Anil Kumar and Rambabu Karumudi. (2018). Tapered Fed Compact UWB MIMO-Diversity Antenna with Dual Band-Notched Characteristics. *IEEE Transactions on Antennas and Propagation,* vol. 66, no. 4, 1677–1684.

Smart Computing – Khan et al (Eds)
© 2021 Taylor & Francis Group, London, ISBN 978-0-367-76552-1

Evaluating the effect of aliasing on the system throughput in a wideband cognitive radio networks

Sandeep Srivastava
Department of Master of Computer Application, G. L. Bajaj Institute of Technology and Management, Greater Noida, Affiliated to AKTU Lucknow, India

Pramod Kumar Srivastava
Department of Mathematics, Rajkiya Engineering College, Azamgarh, Affiliated to AKTU Lucknow, India

Deepak Gupta
Department of Master of Computer Application, G. L. Bajaj Institute of Technology and Management, Greater Noida, Affiliated to AKTU Lucknow, India

ABSTRACT: Cognitive Radio (CR) technology is one such technology which has gained popularity by increasing the opportunity of spectrum access for secondary users with wideband spectrum sensing. The communicative preference of the wideband spectrum for the frequency-domain sparsity, a wideband spectrum sensing- (WSS) compressed sensing blueprint make the spectrum energy efficient but involves the aliasing noise in the signal and also affect the throughput of the signal. In this paper, the problem is formulated in three section: (1) sense the spectrum in a multichannel communication environment using relatively low sampling rates; (2) show the effect of throughput on low sampling rate; and (2) is to set a threshold over which the spectrum is energy efficient as well as the aliasing effect being tolerable and probability of missed detection is minimum. Based on simulation and analysis, we identified a threshold point where the signal distortion and probability of missed detections are minimum and throughput decreases on increasing sensing time

Keywords: Cognitive radio network, Wideband spectrum sensing, Digital alias-free signal processing

1 INTRODUCTION

The need for higher data rates is increasing for the increased progress of voice-only communication to multimedia-type applications. Due to some constraint over the natural frequency spectrum, it is clear that the present static frequency allocation schemes cannot fulfill the needs of all the devices with increased maximum data rates. So new and inventive techniques are required so that it can exploit and reuse the free spectrum. Cognitive radio is one of those solution to solve spectrum limitation by introducing the new and practical management for present frequency bands that are not massively engaged by certified or primary users. Now our paper describes the explanation followed by Federal Communications Commission (FCC): "Cognitive Radio: A System that senses its functional electromagnetic environment and can dynamically and autonomously adjust its radio operating parameters to modify system operation, such as maximize throughput, mitigate interference, facilitate interoperability, access secondary markets. Subsequently, one important issue of cognitive radio is related to autonomously exploiting regionally unused spectrum to offer new paths to get entry of spectrum [1]. It is notable that there will be more opportunity for the secondary users (SUs) to access if the greater bandwidth of spectrum is detected. Therefore, the wideband spectrum sensing (WSS) scheme [2] is causing attention as a useful and effective approach for detecting multiple bands simultaneously.

DOI 10.1201/9781003167488-103

As we understand, WSS may be without problems completed in neighborhood sensing, which means it could be applied through any SU independently Hence, WSS is perfectly suitable with a large number of SUs on a large scale [3].

If evaluating the traditional WSS schemes with the compressed spectrum sensing scheme sampling rate is reduced on the sub-Nyquist rate and sensing the time period is shorter; both the schemes are favorable to energy saving. Although the compressed sensing has been cautioned to lessen the sampling rate in WSS, and increase the maximum energy performance as we increase the energy efficiency the aliasing effect will also increase and throughput will also be affected. This is the basic idea for this research paper to put a threshold so that the energy efficiency will increase and an aliasing effect will also be tolerable and the throughput could be maximum.

In this paper, we use a technique that is to sense the activity of the channels in multichannel communication environment based on the digital alias-free signal processing (DASP) approach. The spectrum detection approach that will be adopted and predicated on estimating the spectrum of the incoming sign and sensing its significance. The problem related to estimating the spectrum using non-uniformly sampled data has been already studied in a few publications [4]. We found except [5, 6] there is no paper taken into account with the presence of noise. So the results examined there should be taken with caution when applied to practical situations [7].

The major contributions and requirements of this paper can be summarized as follows.

(i) The wideband spectrum should be sparse in nature and the received SNR should be greater than the lower limit of SNR.
(ii) We introduce a digital alias-unfastened sign processing (DASP) technique for WSS in a CR network because the compressed sampling is followed in each sampling channel to wrap the sparse spectrum occupancy map and the consequences caused by compressed sampling are analyzed.
(iii) We endorse applying a distinct compressive rate in one-of-a-kind sampling channels (equivalently special CRs) for enhancing the spectrum-sensing performance and to research the impact of noise.
(iv) We examine the effect of throughput as we increase the sensing time.

2   WIDEBAND SPECTRUM SENSING SCHEME

2.1   Network Mode

In previous studies, researchers have followed this network mode. These are the basic condition for the spectrum to have and compressed sensing is applied on this network.

2.2   Throughput

The principle favorable position of WSS is its capacity to give better opportunistic throughput RO than meet grave Quality of Service (QoS) prerequisites for the network secondary users. The opportunistic spectrum gets to operation at a CR includes spectrum sensing taken after by transmitting over the distinguished empty subband(s).

Let $T_{total} = T_{st} + T_{ot}$ be the total access time comprising of the sensing functionality time slot T_{st} and the opportunistic transmission schedule time T_{ot}. It is noticed that the sensing time T_{st} is expected to join the associated processing time influenced by the detectors' complexity, computational cost, and the available processing resources at the SU:

$$T_{st} = \frac{T_{total} - T_{st}}{T_{total}} R_o \qquad (1)$$

2.3 Problem Formulation

Assume L to be the aggregate number of channels over which information is transmitted in a multichannel communication system. Each channel has a bandwidth of B_c, thus the total data transmission to be checked is $B = LB_c$. All channels' central frequencies are known. We expect that the most extreme channel occupancy is low. Our assignment is to deliver a calculation fit for examining the bandwidth B and distinguish which channel(s) are active. The algorithm will apply on sampling rates significantly less than 2B. Our aim is to use a sampling rate which is smaller than 2B but of course to above $2B_A$. Almost a similar task has been already solved in paper [8] by using universal sampling. So that, here in this paper, we have searched for algorithms that avoid huge computational costs solutions proposed in [8].

2.4 Spectrum Estimators

We are considering DASP techniques which are a combination of two steps: signal sampling (non-uniformly) and the second one is calculating its spectrum with the aid of unbiased estimators. The objective of such estimators is given by:

$$Xw(f) = \int_{t_o}^{t_o+T} x(t)w(t)e^{-j2\pi ft}\,\mathrm{d(t)} \tag{2}$$

Here, t_o be the initial time instant of the analyzed signal and T is its width. The windowing function w(t) is normally used to suppress the known Gibbs phenomenon.

In this section, we will review a set of available spectrum estimators and reject the ones that are less appropriate for our purpose. In previous papers, researcher have introduced estimators that are completely based on a total random sampling scheme in which sampling instants are identically distributed, independent random variables whose Probability Distribution Functions (PDFs) include the whole signal with observation window $[t_o, t_o + T]$. In [9], two estimators were proposed: Weighted Sampled (WS) and Weighted Probability (WP). At the end, the sampling instants PDFs depend on the used windowing function w(t).

Again, researchers have introduced estimators that use stratified and antithetical stratified sampling. The two methods present in these papers divides the signal analysis window into sub-intervals under which sample(s) with uniform PDFs are taken. We will refer to those two schemes by jitter sampling thereafter. Therefore, the remaining candidates are the WS and the two estimators that utilize jitter sampling (stratified-antithetical sampling with equal time partitions).

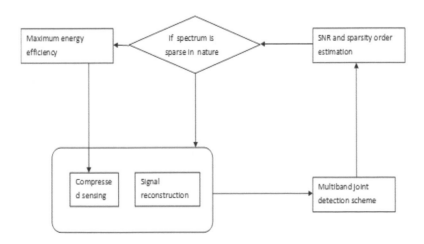

3 SPECTRUMESTIMATORS PERFORMANCE IN PRESENCE OF NOISE SPECTRUM SENSING

Spectrum estimators which we have studied in [7–13] those all were evaluated in noise-free environments. Although most of the data transmission systems are related to noise which affects and also limits the performance of the system? Noise is commonly known as zero mean Added White Gaussian Noise (AWGN). Therefore, the transmitted signal which is composed of data x(t) and noise n(t) is represented as $y(t) = x(t) + n(t)$. In this section, we will evaluate the effect of noise on the unbiased nature of the WS estimators and its accuracy also. The given results are related to the estimators that will use jitter (stratified-antithetical) sampling. The samplings used in WS approaches are do not depend on each other and they have identical PDFs which are represented as:

$$Pws(t) = \left\{ \begin{array}{ll} 1 \div T & t \in (t_o, t_o + T) \\ 0 & elsewhere \end{array} \right\} \tag{3}$$

WS estimator is defined by:

$$X_{ws}(f) = \frac{T}{N} \sum_{n=1}^{N} \left(y(t_n) \, w(t_n) e^{-j2\pi f t n} \right) \tag{4}$$

where N is the number of the taken samples.

3.1 Unbiased Spectrum Estimator

Here, in this following subsection, we will show that the WS estimator is still unbiased even in the presence of noise. The expected value of the estimators is calculated regards the sample points also the added noise. We noticed that every component of the summation in (3) do not depend on each other and ideally distributed random variables with identical PDFs, hence:

$$E[X_{ws}(f)] = TE[\{x(t) + n(t)\} w(t) e^{-j2\pi f t}] \tag{5}$$

Therefore, the estimator is unbiased.

According to Chebychev's inequality, the standard deviation is directly related to the accuracy which states that

$$\Pr\{|X - E[X]| \geq \varepsilon\} \leq \frac{\sigma^2}{\varepsilon^2} \tag{6}$$

Here, X is a random variable and $\varepsilon > 0$. In this subsection we will calculate the effect of the noise factor on the basis of standard deviations of the WS estimator. The variance is defined as:

$$\sigma^2(f) = E\left[|X_{ws}(f)|^2\right] - |X_w(f)|^2 \tag{7}$$

$$Now \; |X_{ws}(f)|^2 = \frac{T^2}{N^2} \sum_{n=1}^{N} \sum_{m=1}^{N} y(t_n) \, y(t_m) \, w(t_n) \, w(t_m) e^{-j2\pi f(t_n - t_m)}$$

The expected value of (7) informs the sampling instants and the added noise is evaluated in two stages: when indices are identical, i.e., n = m and when they are different, hence:

$$|X_{ws}(f)|^2 = \frac{T^2}{N^2} \sum_{n=1}^{N} \sum_{m=1}^{N} y(t_n) \, y(t_m) \, w(t_n) \, w(t_m) \, e^{-j2\pi f(t_n - t_m)} + \frac{T^2}{N^2} \sum_{n=1}^{N} y^2(t_n) \, w^2(t_n) \tag{8}$$

However, the sampling instants are non-identical and with identical distributions, we can combine (4) and (5) and use it. For n = m, expected value of (8) can be written as:

$$\frac{T^2}{N}\{E[x^2(t)w^2(t)] + E[n^2(t)w^2(t)]\} = \frac{T}{N}\{E_{ws} + \sigma^2 Ew\} \tag{9}$$

where E_{ws} and Ew represent the energy of the windowed signal and the area of the used window, respectively. They are defined by:

$$E[x^2(t)w^2(t)] = \frac{1}{N}\int_{t_o}^{t_o+T}[x(t)w(t)]^2 dt = \frac{Ews}{T} \tag{10}$$

$$E[n^2(t)w^2(t)] = \frac{\sigma^2}{N}\int_{t_o}^{t_o+T}w^2(t)dt = \frac{\sigma^2 Ew}{T} \tag{11}$$

When n $\neq$ m, the expected value of (8) yields: $\frac{(N-1)}{N}|Xw(f)|^2$. Then

$$E[|Xws(f)|^2] = \frac{T\{E_{ws} + \sigma^2 Ew\}}{N} + \frac{(N-1)}{N}|Xw(f)|^2 \tag{12}$$

By putting Equation (11) into (6) we obtain:

$$\sigma^2(f) = \frac{E_{ws} + \sigma^2 Ew}{\alpha} - \frac{|Xw(f)|^2}{N} \tag{13}$$

where $\alpha = N/T$ is the average sampling rate. Hence,

$$\sigma(f) = \sqrt{\frac{E_{ws} + \sigma^2 Ew}{\alpha} - \frac{|Xw(f)|^2}{N}} \tag{14}$$

$$\sigma_{ws,max} = (E_{ws} + \sigma_o^2 E_w)/\alpha \tag{15}$$

$\sigma_{ws,max}$ Could be describing as a white-noise like error that is inversely proportional to α. This error is representing the effect or consequences of noise and aliasing on the estimator's accuracy and its relation to the spectrum of the signal $X_w(f)$ is described by Chebychev's inequality [15–17].

4   OVERALL ANALSIS OF PERFORMANC AND SIMULATION

In this section, we are analyzing the spectrum that is under sampled and the effect of throughput with the low sampling rate and also sense the spectrum to analyze the effect of aliasing noise with three different conditions of compression rate. Our goal is to sense the spectrum of a multichannel communication system that consists of 10 channels (L = 10) that are 2 KHz each (Bc = 2 KHz). The monitored range of frequencies, i.e., system bandwidth stretches from f = [500, 1000, 2000] Hz.

In Figure 1, we consider the compression rate = 0.25, which shows the under sampled sinusoidal signal. In Figure 2, the compression rate $\delta = 0.5$, and in Figure 3 the compression rate $\delta = 1$. We can see as we are increasing the compression rate ($\delta \in 0, 1$) the sinusoidal signal gets more distorted because of aliasing effect. In Figure 4, on increasing the sensing time the throughput is fallen down. In Figure 5, there is combine effect of aliasing noise and AWGN with three different compression rates. The graph is between probability of false alarm and probability of detection which is showing that at minimum value of compression rate that is $\delta = 0.25$ the signal is less distorted and because of that the probability of missed detection is almost negligible. As increasing the value of compression rate the signal get more distorted and probability of missed detection is high but after reaching at

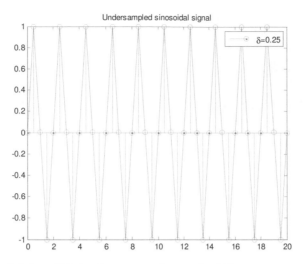

Figure 1.   Undersampled sinusoidal signal at compression rate $\delta = 0.25$.

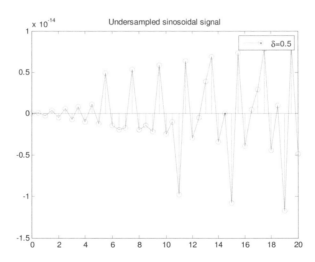

Figure 2.   Undersampled sinusoidal signal at compression rate $\delta = 0.5$.

threshold point, value of missed detection starts decreasing. And that is the basic idea behind this paper is to set a threshold value to avoid the missed detection and correctly sense the spectrum [17–20].

5   CONCLUSION

As mentioned earlier in this paper, the increment in compression rate will provide the energy-efficient network but also increase the aliasing effect and affect the throughput of the network. In Figures 1–3, we can clearly see the effect of compression rate (as increasing the value of δ signal get more distorted than the previous one).

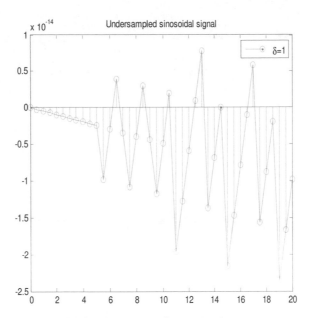

Figure 3.   Undersampled sinusoidal signal at compression rate $\delta = 1$.

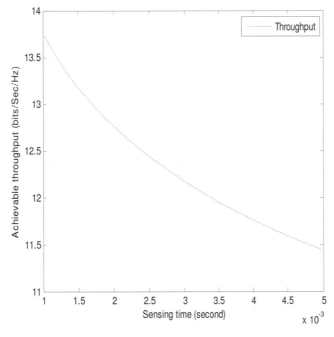

Figure 4.   Throughput vs. sensing time.

In Figure 4 is a graph that is between throughputs vs. sensing time. Increasing the sensing time decreases the value of throughput (sensing time will increase when we increase the compression rate means signals get more distorted because of noise). Finally, Figure 5 explains the effect of noise that is AWGN and aliasing noise which is showing a threshold point whose value is approximately 0.5 after which the probability of missed detection starts decreasing.

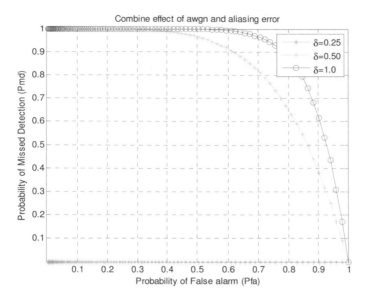

Figure 5.   Combine effect of noise with three different compression rate $\delta = 0.25, 0.5, 1$ showing a threshold point whose value is approximately 0.5 after which the probability of missed detection starts decreasing.

REFERENCES

[1] T. Yucek and H. Arslan, "A survey of spectrum sensing algorithms for cognitive radio applications," IEEE Communications Surveys & Tutorials, vol. 11, no. 1, pp. 116–130, 2009.

[2] J Meng, W Yin, HH Li, E Hossain, Z Han, Collaborative spectrum sensing from sparse observations in cognitive radio networks. IEEE J. Sel. AreasCommun. 29(2), 327–337 (2011)

[3] Sharma, Sandeep, Jitendra Singh, Rahul Kumar, and Abhilash Singh. "Throughput-save ratio optimization in wireless powered communication systems." In 2017 International Conference on Information, Communication, Instrumentation and Control (ICICIC), pp. 1–6. IEEE, 2017.

[4] Kumar, Rahul, and Abhilash Singh. "Throughput optimization for wireless information and power transfer in communication network." In 2018 Conference on Signal Processing And Communication Engineering Systems (SPACES), pp. 1–5. IEEE, 2018.

[5] Sandeep Srivastava, Rudra Pratap Ojha, Pramod Kumar Srivastava and Deepak Gupta Singh." Downlink Performance Improvement Using Base Station Cooperation for Multicell Cellular Networks.

[6] Singh, Abhilash, Sandeep Sharma, Jitendra Singh, and Rahul Kumar. "Mathematical modelling for reducing the sensing of redundant information in WSNs based on biologically inspired techniques." Journal of Intelligent & Fuzzy Systems Preprint (2019): 1–11.

[7] Zhao, Q., Wu, Z. & Li, X., "Energy efficiency of compressed spectrum sensing in wideband cognitive radio networks,"EURASIPJ Wireless Com Network (2016) 2016: 83. doi:10.1186/s13638-016-0581-9

[8] E. Masry, "Random Sampling Estimates of Fourier Transforms: Antithetical Stratified Monte Carlo," IEEETrans. Signal Process., vol. 57, pp.149–204, 2009.

[9] N. R. Lomb, "Least-squares frequency analysis of unequallyspaced data", Astroph. Space Sc., vol. 39, pp. 447–462, 1967.

[10] B.I.Ahmad; A.Tarczynski, "Spectrum sensing in multichannel communication systems using randomized sampling schemes," in the proc. of IEEE 17th European Signal Processing Conference Pages, pp. 1690–1694, 2009.

[11] P. Feng and Y. Bresler, "Spectrum-blind minimum-ratesampling and reconstruction of multiband signals", IEEE Int.Conf. Acoustics, Speech and Signal Processing, Atlanta, GA,May 1996, pp.1688–1691.

[12] Tarczynski and N. Allay, "Spectral Analysis of randomlysampled signals: suppression of aliasing and samplerjitter," IEEE Trans. Signal Process., vol. SP-52, pp. 3324–3334, Dec. 2004.

[13] Tarczynski and D. Qu, "Optimal random sampling forspectrum estimation in DASP applications," Int. J. Appl. Math. Comput. Sci, vol. 15, No. 4, pp. 463–469, 2005.

[14] E. Masry, "Random sampling of deterministic signals:statistical analysis of Fourier transforms estimates," IEEE Trans. Signal Process., vol. 54, pp.1750–1761, 2006.

[15] E. Masry, "Random Sampling Estimates of FourierTransforms: Antithetical Stratified Monte Carlo," IEEE Trans. Signal Process., vol. 57, pp.149–204, 2009.

[16] Patil, Vinayak, and Chetna Singhal. "Throughput Improvement in Hybrid MIMO Cognitive Radio Using Simultaneous Narrowband and Wideband System." In 2019 11th International Conference on Communication Systems & Networks (COMSNETS), pp. 285–290. IEEE, 2019.

[17] Kerdabadi, Mohammad Sadeghian, Reza Ghazizadeh, Hamid Farrokhi, and Maryam Najimi. "Energy consumption minimization and throughput improvement in cognitive radio networks by joint optimization of detection threshold, sensing time and user selection." Wireless Networks 25, no. 4 (2019): 2065–2079.

[18] Datta, Teethiya, Shohely Tasnim Anindo, and Sk Shariful Alam. "Detection Performance Analysis for Wideband Cognitive Radio Network: A Compressive Sensing Approach." In 2019 International Conference on Computer, Communication, Chemical, Materials and Electronic Engineering (IC4ME2), pp. 1–4. IEEE, 2019.

[19] Schaefer, Andrew F., and Mark Fowler. "Unique Compressive Sampling Techniques for Wideband Spectrum Sensing." In 2019 IEEE National Aerospace and Electronics Conference (NAECON), pp. 46–53. IEEE, 2019.

[20] Ahmad, Bashar I. "A Survey of Wideband Spectrum Sensing Algorithms for Cognitive Radio Networks and Sub-Nyquist Approaches." arXiv preprint arXiv:2001.02574 (2020).

[21] Kathuria J., Khan M.A., Abraham A., Darwish A. (2014) Low Power Techniques for Embedded FPGA Processors. In: Khan M., Saeed S., Darwish A., Abraham A. (eds) Embedded and Real Time System Development: A Software Engineering Perspective. Studies in Computational Intelligence, vol 520. Springer, Berlin, Heidelberg. https://doi.org/10.1007/978-3-642-40888-5_11

Smart Computing – Khan et al (Eds)
© *2021 Taylor & Francis Group, London, ISBN 978-0-367-76552-1*

Design and tuning of PID controller for an inherently unstable system

P. Swarnkar

Maulana Azad National Institute of Technology, Bhopal, Madhya Pradesh, India

H. Goud

IPS Academy, Institute of Engineering & Science, Indore, Madhya Pradesh, India

ABSTRACT: A desired performance of any process depends on the control action taken by the controller. Control system engineering is mainly concerned with understanding and controlling the process governed by any system to accomplish an objective and to provide useful economic products for society. Many practitioners and researchers in the field of control agree that controller design can be quite laborious in cases where the plant is unstable. The controller synthesis becomes a challenge for such systems because there are certain design and closed-loop performance limitations that narrow the range of feasible solutions. These constraints reflect in overshoots, peaks in sensitivity functions, and closed-loop band width. Choice of control structure and the design approach depend considerably on a priori knowledge of the process dynamics and system requirements. This paper mainly focuses on design and tuning of Proportional Integral Derivative (PID) controller for an unstable system. A comparative analysis of different conventional and real-time tuning methods is also presented based on detailed simulation studies. The study shows the effectiveness of suitable tuning method to control the unstable system for obtaining the desired performance out of it.

1 INTRODUCTION

As the complicacy of system is increasing day-by-day, design and tuning of controllers become a challenging task for the researchers. Human efforts and intervention are constantly replaced by actions of machines, i.e., automation. The automatic control, based on its control action, can be divided in two major categories:

- conventional control, with fixed parameters of the controller irrespective of the variations in the system.
- advanced control, with real time adjustment and tuning of the controller according to the variations in system or in environment.

Conventional controllers are mainly designed to control the linear time invariant (LTI) systems, where the parameters of the system are not the function of time (Goud & Swarnkar 2019a,2019b). As the complexity of the system is increased, the assumption of LTI nature for the system no longer holds. Tuning of the controller under such condition is also a complicated task using conventional tuning methods. Many adaptive control techniques, however, have been proposed in the last few decades to overcome this problem (Swarnkar et al. 2014; Goud & Swarnkar 2018; Swarnkar et al. 2010). Among several alternative design solutions of controllers obtained by different tuning methods, some control laws are superior to others so far as the performance specification are concerned. This leads to the problem of optimal control, where among all possible control algorithms, the algorithm that optimizes the performance specification should be chosen.

Getting the optimized controller becomes even more difficult under the situations where process parameters changes with time or environmental conditions, and with large variations in input or

DOI 10.1201/9781003167488-104

load. Many process industries also face the stability problem with the complicated process control systems. As an example, exothermic reactors, where heat produced by chemical reaction increases the temperature which, in turn, increases the rate of reaction, and hence the entire system becomes unstable (Albertos et al. 1997). Many industrial processes and highly nonlinear systems like robots require continuous monitoring and tuning of their controllers (Yufka & Yazici 2010; Babu & Warnalath 2017). In an electrical power system, such problems may encounter with the condition of subsynchronous resonance, ferro-resonance, or voltage collapse.

The controller for such systems should adapt changes in the process and transfer them in control algorithm such that the performance of control system is not degraded in spite of variations in the process. This gives rise to the problem of designing adaptive controller which tunes its parameter according to requirement of system (Goud & Swarnkar 2019a).

This paper deals with tuning and design of a Proportional Integral Derivative (PID) controller for an unstable system. Pure unstable modes usually occur in system a such as flight system, inverted pendulum system, etc. The aim of this study is to control the unstable system using a PID controller which is tuned by conventional and advance online tuning methods. The performance of system is then compared with both conventional fixed gain PID controller and advance online tuned controller.

2 CONVENTIONAL CONTROL ACTION

A PID controller is the most popularly used controller in all industrial and process control applications. Simple design, easy control algorithm, and convenient tuning methods are the main reasons for its popularity. PID controllers were first developed by Elmer Sperry in 1911 for automatic ship steering. The first published theoretical analysis of a PID controller was by Russian American engineer Nicolas Minorsky in 1922. The conventional control scheme may be closed-loop or open-loop. The automatic control systems are closed loop in nature. The general block diagram of a closed-loop control system is shown in Figure 1.

The control process involves the estimation of error signal between the reference input and actual output of the plant to be controlled. This error signal then becomes the input for the controller. Controller output is known as the actuating signal which in turn actuates the actuator so that it can generate a manipulated variable in to cause the possible changes in the plant. These changes drag the system towards its optimal performance. The performance of the system is evaluated in terms of time response specifications such as rise time, peak time, maximum overshoot, settling time, and steady state error. These performance indices become the basis for suitable controller design. There are three basic modes of control: proportional, integral, and derivative on which control action takes place. Table 1 discusses the properties of these three control actions in detail. Parameters (gain and time constant) of these controllers decide the amount of control action taken by the controller in order to improve the overall performance of the system. Selection of these parameters therefore

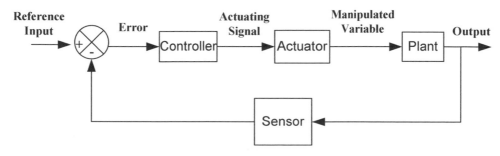

Figure 1.   Closed-loop control system.

is an important task for the controller. In conventional control once these parameters are decided they then remain fixed throughout the process irrespective of the variations in the system.

In PID controller, the control signal generated by the controller is defined as

$$u(t) = K_p e(t) + K_i \int e(t)dt + K_d \frac{de(t)}{dt} \tag{1}$$

The transfer function of PID controller is defined as

$$G_{PID}(s) = \frac{U(s)}{E(s)} = K_p + \frac{K_i}{s} + sK_d \tag{2}$$

K_p is the gain of proportional controller, K_i is the gain of Integral controller, and K_d is the gain of derivative controller. $e(t)$ is the error signal and $u(t)$ is the control signal. These gains fix the role of each individual controller in the process. Correct choice of these gains is actually the base for the perfect controlling (Goud & Swarnkar 2019a, Yufka & Yazici 2010).

Table 1. Control action and their properties.

	P Controller	PI Controller	PD Controller
Control Action	$u(t) = K_p e(t)$	$u(t) = K_p e(t) + K_i \int e(t)dt$	$u(t) = K_p e(t) + K_d \frac{de(t)}{dt}$
Transfer Function	$G_P(s) = \frac{U(s)}{E(s)} = K_p$	$G_{PI}(s) = \frac{U(s)}{E(s)} = K_p + \frac{K_i}{s}$	$G_{PD}(s) = \frac{U(s)}{E(s)} = K_p + sK_d$
Advantages	1. Improves the speed of sluggish response of the over damped system. 2. Reduces the steady state error. 3. Stable but does not necessarily ensure that the measured variable is always at the desired value.	1. Reduces the steady state error. 2. Increases the system accuracy 3. Eliminates the offset.	1. Reduces the overshoot. 2. Improves the transient response. 3. It has anticipatory nature to anticipate what the controlled condition is going to do. 4. It has a smaller recovery time. Control is stable.
Disadvantages	1. Causes offset. 2. Increases the maximum overshoot.	1. Less effective during a transient period. 2. Long recovery time 3. Response is slow for rapid changes. 4. Increment of gains beyond the limit may enhance the overshoot and may cause the poor stability.	1. Amplifies the noise signals. 2. May cause the saturation effect in magnetic circuits used in actuator. 3. It does not reduce the steady state error or even it is not effective after transient period. 4. It has some offset.
Application where	1. Load changes are small. 2. Offset can be tolerated. 3. Error signal is very small and there is need of amplification.	1. Offset must be eliminated 2. Integral saturation due to sustained deviation is not objectionable. 3. High degree of accuracy is required.	1. It is necessary to minimize the amount of deviation caused by plant load changes. 2. Maximum overshoot has to be reduced.

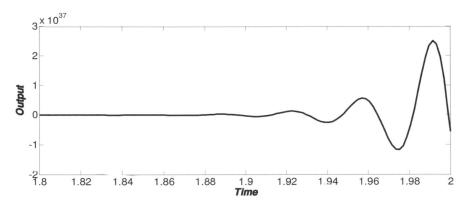

Figure 2. Time response characteristic of third-order unstable system.

3 UNSTABLE SYSTEM MODEL

Controller design of unstable systems could be attempted using many of the methods applicable to ordinary stable system, but the results may not be satisfactory. Controller design for a stable system is based on many linear assumptions when applied to unstable system practically may fail completely. This situation therefore demands careful and sensible design of a controller. The plant, which is now taken for the study of controllers, is the third-order unstable plant with feed forward transfer function

$$G(s) = \frac{1000}{(1 + 0.01s)(0.01s^2 + s)} \quad (3)$$

and feedback transfer function $H(s) = 1$.

The conventional and advanced control schemes are now applied to test their feasibility and applicability for such uncontrolled systems. The step response of the system without any controller is shown in Figure 2.

It can be observed that oscillations of system are increasing with time and making the system unstable. In unstable system the amount of overshoot is closely related to rise time. Surprisingly, the longer the rise times the higher the overshoots, which is contrary to the case of stable plants. A bode plot is shown for the loop transfer function in Figure 3. The gain crossover frequency (ω_g) is 200 rad/sec whereas the phase cross-over frequency (ω_p) is 100 rad/sec. The gain and phase margins obtained by the plot are -13.9 dB, $-37°$, respectively. Negative values of margins show the instability of the system.

To check the stability range with respect to feed-forward gain of the system, the root locus plot is also shown in Figure 4. This plot shows a very small stability range for the plant under consideration. System becomes marginally stable for feedforward gain of 0.2 only, beyond this system becomes unstable.

4 TUNING OF PID CONTROLLER BY ZIEGLER–NICHOLS'S SECOND METHOD

This section presents the use of Ziegler–Nichols (Z–N) method of PID controller tuning. Ziegler and Nichols described simple mathematical procedures, the first and second methods, respectively, for tuning PID controllers. These procedures are now accepted as standard in control systems practice. The first method is applied to plants which have the step responses of a typical first-order system with transportation delay. The second method is basically for oscillatory system, but in this study it is used to apply on the unstable system having oscillations of increasing magnitude. The second method of Ziegler–Nichols is therefore applied with following steps.

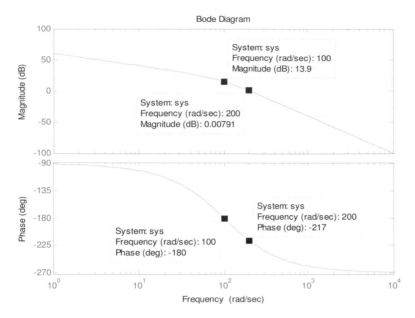

Figure 3. Bode plot for third-order unstable system.

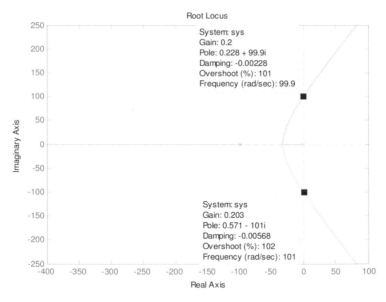

Figure 4. Root locus plot for third-order unstable system.

- First the gains of integral and derivative controller (K_i and K_d) are reduced to zero.
- Gain of proportional K_p controller is then increased gradually till the response will show the sustained oscillations.
- This critical value of K_p is either calculated by the time response characteristic or by Routh–Hurwitz criteria.
- The critical value K_p and the corresponding period of sustained oscillation T_c decides the value of three controller gains (Albertos et al. 1997; Babu & Warnalath 2017; Yufka & Yazici 2010).

Table 2. Calculation of controller gains.

	K_p	K_i'	K_d'
P	$0.5K_c = 1000000 = K_p \times 107$	0	0
	$K_p = 0.1$		
PI	$0.45K_c = 900000 = K_p \times 107$	$1.2/T_c = 19.0961$	0
	$K_p = 0.09$		
PID	$0.6K_c = 1200000 = K_p \times 107$	$2/T_c = 31.8268$	$0.125T_c = 7.855 \times 10 - 3$
	$K_p = 1.2$		

For the unstable system under consideration, the feedforward transfer function is defined by Equation (3), so the overall transfer function for unity feedback is given by

$$T(s) = \frac{G(s)}{1 + G(s)} = \frac{10^7}{(s^3 + 200s^2 + 10000s + 10^7)} \tag{4}$$

If the K′ is the unknown forward path gain, then the system can be defined as

$$T(s) = \frac{K}{(s^3 + 200s^2 + 10000s + K)} \tag{5}$$

where $K = K' \times 10^7$

The value of the forward path gain K is increased till the sustained oscillations appear. This critical value of K can also be found by applying the Routh–Hurwitz criteria. The Routh array for the critical value of K is given as follows:

s^3	1	10000
s^2	200	K
s^1	(2000000-K)/200	–
s^0	K	

Critical value of $K = K_c = 2000000 = K' \times 107$

$K' = 0.2$ (as shown in root locus), at this value of K', the system will show the sustained oscillations. The auxiliary equation is given by

$$A(s) = 200s^2 + K_c = 0 \tag{6}$$

which gives s $= 100j$, so the frequency of sustained oscillations, $\omega = 100$ rad/sec, Period of sustained oscillation, $T_c = 2\pi/\omega = 0.06284$ sec. Transfer function of controller is defined as

$$G_c(s) = K_p \left(1 + \frac{K_i'}{s} + K_d's\right) = K_p + \frac{K_i}{s} + K_d s \tag{7}$$

Table 2 shows the calculation of controller gains for P, PI, and PID controllers as per the Z–N second method of PID tuning. Final values of gains K_p, K_i, and K_d are given in Table 3.

Now the unstable system under study is controlled by using PI and PID controllers.

4.1 System response with PI controller

The PI controller designed by Z–N method is now applied to the third-order unstable system. The system becomes stable, but the value of maximum overshoot is beyond the limit (94%) and the settling time is also very high (1.25 sec). The time response characteristic of the system with PI controller is shown in Figure 5.

Table 3. Controller gains.

Controller	K_p	$K_i = K_i' \times K_p$	$K_d = K_d' \times K_p$
P	0.1	0	0
PI	0.09	1.7186	0
PID	1.2	38.1921	9.426×10^{-3}

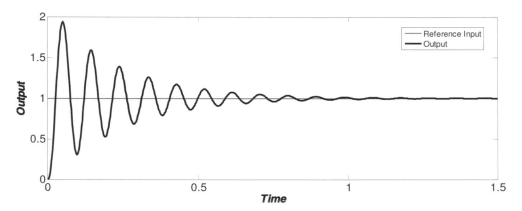

Figure 5. Time response characteristic with tuned PI controller for unstable system.

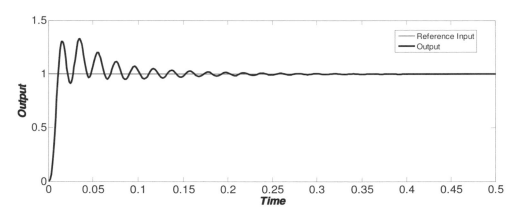

Figure 6. Time response characteristic with tuned PID controller for an unstable system.

4.2 *System response with PID controller*

To improve the transient response derivative term is included with the controller. The PID controller is now applied to the unstable system under observations. The time response characteristic of the system with PID controller is shown in Figure 6.

The clear improvement in system characteristic can be observed with the application of PID controller. Remarkable decrement in maximum overshoot and the settling time is achieved in this case. The overshoot is reduced to 33% and settling time to 0.35 sec. Still the response is not smooth, and oscillations are there in the characteristic.

Table 4. PID tuning rules.

Rule	Controller	k_C	τ_i	τ_d
Tyreus–Lyben	PI	$\dfrac{k_u}{3.2}$	$T_u \times 2.2$	–
	PID	$\dfrac{k_u}{3.2}$	$T_u \times 2.2$	$\dfrac{T_u}{6.3}$
Shinskey Method	P	$\dfrac{k_u}{2}$	–	–
	PI	$\dfrac{k_u}{2}$	$\dfrac{T_u}{2.2}$	
	PID	$\dfrac{k_u}{4}$	$\dfrac{T_u}{2}$	$\dfrac{T_u}{8.3}$
Damped Oscillation Method	P	$k_u \times 1.1$	–	–
	PI	$k_u \times 1.1$	$\dfrac{T_u}{2.6}$	–
	PID	$k_u \times 1.1$	$\dfrac{T_u}{3.6}$	$\dfrac{T_u}{9}$

5 TUNING OF PID CONTROLLER BY TYREUS–LUYBEN, SHINSKEY, AND DAMPED OSCILLATION METHODS

5.1 *Tyreus–Luyben method*

The process of Tyreus–Luyben and Z–N method is quite similar, but the final controller parameters settings are different. This method process has only PI and PID controller setting. It is also based on the ultimate period and gain which is shown in the Table 4. The property of this method is similar to Z–N method such as time-consuming and drives the system to margin if instability occurs. Tyreus–Luyben method is applied with following steps (Yufka & Yazici 2010).

- Assume $K_d = 0$ and $K_i = 0$, system is proportional.
- Take the characteristic equation and by using Routh criteria find the value of $K_p = K_u$
- Using characteristic equation and Routh criteria find the value of T_u.
- Find out the values of controller gains using Table 4.

5.2 *Shinskey method*

The Shinskey method is another PID controller parameter tuning method which provides relation in the aspect of performance between compensating noises as well as changes in the set point. It requires a lead-lag unit in the set point which is obtained by a graphical procedure. The values of $K_p, K_i,$ and K_d obtained by this method are given in Table 4 (Yufka & Yazici 2010).

5.3 *Damped oscillation method*

This tuning technique is basically used for solving the problems of marginal stability appear in the system. The frequency of oscillation (gain at damping ratio is 1/4) is received in this technique which is similar to the Z–N technique but the computational procedure for PID parameters is different as shown in Table 4. Tuning parameters of this method assume here are K_u is proportional gain and T_u is period of oscillation (Oladimeji et al. 2016).

5.4 *System response with PID controller*

The time response characteristic of the unstable system controlled with the above-mentioned methods are shown in Figure 7. A noticeable improvement in system characteristics can be seen with

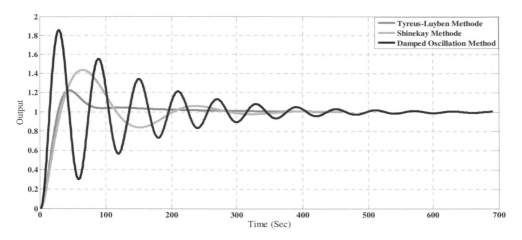

Figure 7.   Time response characteristic with different tuning techniques for an unstable system.

Table 5.   Controller gains.

Parameters	Tyreus–Lyben	Shinskey	Damped Oscillation
K_p	0.0909	0.0500	0.2200
K_i	0.6577	1.5915	12.6051
K_d	9×10^{-4}	6.9×10^{-4}	0.0015

the application of PID controller. The performance of the unstable system is analyzed in terms of rise time t_r, peak time t_p, settling time t_s, and overshoot. By using of the Tyreus–Lyben PID tuning method maximum overshoot is decreased to 22.3% and settling time to 0.203 sec which is comparatively better than other conventional methods. Table 5 shows the values of the PID controller parameters obtained by different conventional tuning methods. Table 4 shows that step response parameters like settling time, rise time, overshoot, and peak times are reduced due to the summation of the Tyreus–Lyben, Shinskey, and Damped Oscillation Conventional PID tuning methods.

5.5   Limitations of conventional controller

1. Tuning methods are dependent on the characteristic of the plant to be controlled, type of the controller, and practical experience of designer.
2. These methods are off-line methods. Once the controller parameters are set they cannot be changed during the process.
3. Conventional control system is not able to cope-up with the situation, like
   - Loads, inertias, and other forces acting on system change drastically.
   - Possibility of unpredictable and sudden faults.
   - Possibility of frequent or unanticipated disturbances

6   CONCLUSION

Performance improvement of stable system is convenient, but the controlling of uncontrolled system is a difficult task for controllers. If the gain and phase margins (of negative values) for unstable system have high magnitudes, then the performance improvement of such system is not easy for conventional fixed gain controllers. Tuning of the PID controller is a challenging task for such

Table 6. Comparative performance analysis with conventional tuning methods.

Tuning Method	Conventional Methods				
	Ziegler–Nichols		Tyreus–Lyben	Shinskey Method	Damped Oscillation
Specifications	PI	PID	PID	PID	PID
Rise Time (sec)	0.012	0.0125	0.0171	0.0225	0.929
Peak Time (sec)	0.05	0.02	0.0407	0.0663	0.028
Maximum overshoot	94%	33%	22.3%	43.6%	85.9%
Settling Time (sec)	1.25	0.35	0.203	0.348	0.51

unbounded systems. With detailed simulation studies this paper shows the design and implementation of conventional and advanced PID controller for controlling the highly unstable system. Unstable system is not only showing the bonded output but performance is also quite satisfactory with the adaptive schemes. The performance of the system based on time response specifications is summarized in Table 6 which shows the importance of suitable tuning of controller for obtaining the optimal performance of uncontrolled system. Performance of such conventional controllers can be used to understand complex behaviors of the system. ZN–PI response yields higher damping oscillations which can be slightly overcome by using ZN–PID. It is clearly shown that the Tyreus–Lyben PID controller provides robust dynamic controlled response of chosen unstable system compared to other conventional controllers. The overshoot (22.3%) and settling time (0.203 sec) are under prescribed limit with Tyreus–Lyben PID tuning method.

REFERENCES

Albertos, P. Strietzel, R. Mort, N. 1997. Control engineering solution-a practical approach, *The Institutions of Electrical Engineers.* London, United Kingdom.
Babu, R. & warnalath, R. 2017. Comparison of Different Tuning Methods for pH Neutralization in Textile Industry. *Journal of Applied Sciences*, 17(3):142–147.
Goud, H. & Swarnkar P. 2018. Signal Synthesis Model Reference Adaptive Controller with Artificial Intelligent Technique for a Control of Continuous Stirred Tank Reactor. *International Journal of Chemical Reactor Engineering.* 17(2):1–11.
Goud, H. & Swarnkar P.2019a. Investigations on Metaheuristic Algorithm for Designing Adaptive PID Controller for Continuous Stirred Tank Reactor. MAPAN-*Journal of Metrology Society of India,* Vol. 34(1): 113–119.
Goud, H. & Swarnkar, P., 2019b. Signal Synthesis Model Reference Adaptive Controller with Genetic Algorithm for a Control of Chemical Tank Reactor. International *Journal of Chemical Reactor Engineering,* 17(5):1–11.
Kathuria J., Khan M.A., Abraham A., Darwish A. (2014) Low Power Techniques for Embedded FPGA Processors. In: Khan M., Saeed S., Darwish A., Abraham A. (eds) Embedded and Real Time System Development: A Software Engineering Perspective. Studies in Computational Intelligence, vol 520. Springer, Berlin, Heidelberg. https://doi.org/10.1007/978-3-642-40888-5_11
Oladimeji, I. Yahaya, Z. & Saad, N. 2016. Comparative studies of PID controller tuning methods on a DC-DC boost converter. In *2016 6th International Conference on Intelligent and Advanced Systems (ICIAS)*: 1–5.
Swarnkar, P. Jain, S. & Nema, R. K. 2010. Effect of adaptation gain on system performance for model reference adaptive control scheme using MIT rule. *International journal of World Academy of Science, Engineering and Technology.* 4(10): 621–627.
Swarnkar, P. Jain, S. & Nema, R. K. 2014. Adaptive Control Schemes for Improving the Control System Dynamics: A Review. *IETE Technical Review (published by Taylor & Francis).* 31(1): No. 17–33.
Yufka, A. & Yazici, A. 2010. An Intelligent PID Tuning Method for an Autonomous Mobile Robot, *International workshop on Unmanned vehicles*, Turkey:130–133.

Smart Computing – Khan et al (Eds)
© 2021 Taylor & Francis Group, London, ISBN 978-0-367-76552-1

Power quality issues in grid-integrated renewable energy systems and their mitigation using UPQC

Yudhisthir Pandey & Aman Singh

Department of Electrical Engineering, Rajkiya Engineering College, Ambedkar Nagar, U.P, India

ABSTRACT: Increasing automation in the power sector, extending energy demand, increasing the number of electric vehicles, and the need for green energy sources have made it necessary for us to go with renewable energy sources for fulfilling our needs in an efficient and sustainable way. This all takes us to a distributed generation, i.e., generation of electric power in kW to MW size in the vicinity of load unlike the conventional way of centralized power generation of a size about 100's of MW. But integration of these renewable energy sources through distributed generation (DG) to a grid system involves several problems related to power quality because of the unpredictable, irregular, and discontinuous nature of renewable energy resources. Power quality now is an important factor for deciding the cost of electricity and it is needed to be up to a standard level to work efficiently sustain the equipment's lifespan. Thus, it required that generated power from renewable energy sources is well conditioned before it is fed to its users. This paper covers a literature review on emerging power quality (PQ) problems in the grid-integrated DG systems, parameters for good power quality, and a few mitigation techniques to improve power quality with a special focus on the unified power quality conditioner (UPQC) method.

1 INTRODUCTION

Conventional sources of power generation are now facing many problems which include the inadequacy of fossil fuels, high carbon emission by using conventional resources, harmful impacts on living beings, etc. Also, a huge power loss is associated with the transmission of electrical energy over long distances in the centralized power generation system (Naimul 2019). This has led the sector to look for distributed generation (DG) using renewable energy resources as an alternative to conventional resources (Sonali 2016). Wind turbines and solar PV systems comprise more than half of the total energy produced by all renewable energy sources. Renewable energy generation system differs from conventional power generation system therefore, it is very sophisticated to connect renewable energy power generation systems to the power grid (Xiaodong 2016). The power produced by renewable sources varies with varying environmental conditions (Chen 2001). Increasing renewable energy penetration to the grid has led to various power quality (PQ) problems. These PQ problems are mostly because of the use of power electronic devices having high switching frequency (Sonali 2016). A lot of research has been already done on power quality issues emerging upon the integration of renewable energy sources to the power grid and their best possible solutions. The main objective of this paper is, to sum up, all the important information about the PQ problems coming in the integration of any DG system to a grid and their existing technical solutions to support any future research in this direction. First, we have described the structure of the grid-connected Photovoltaic Solar Plant and Wind Energy Power Plant. Then we have mentioned the most important PQ issues that need to be kept under limits for the healthy operation of appliances at the user end and then in the next section we have covered few useful techniques of mitigation of these PQ issues with a special focus on the unified power quality conditioner (UPQC) method.

DOI 10.1201/9781003167488-105

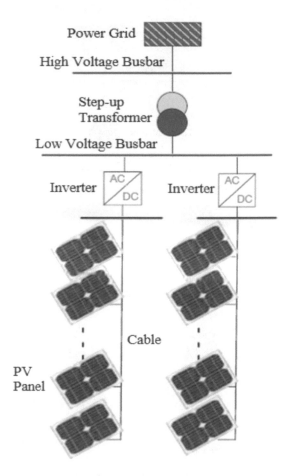

Figure 1.   Solar PV system connected to a grid.

2   STRUCTURE OF GRID-CONNECTED RENEWABLE ENERGY SOURCES (SOLAR AND WIND TURBINES)

In the system of DG shown, even operating it as proposed in can effectively condition the generated power such that PQ parameters could be maintained as per utility standards without adding any additional power conditioning equipment (Chen 2001).

2.1   *Solar PV system*

The outline of any Solar photovoltaic (PV) power plant connected to a grid is shown in Figure 1 (Madhu Mathi & Sasiraja 2017). Western Electric Coordinating Council (WECC) suggests to represent the equivalent of a solar PV plant by a single generator linked to the power transmission system Solar PV system integrated to a grid can be of two types, either it is residential or commercially laid system or Solar PV plant installed in a large area with capacity even more than 100 MW (International 2012).

2.2   *Wind energy system*

As the structure of solar PV power, a general configuration of wind power has been shown in Figure 2 (Madhu Mathi & Sasiraja 2017). Representation of Wind Power plant in any power system can

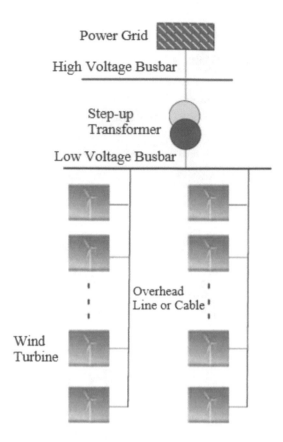

Figure 2.   Wind power system connected to a grid.

be done in 2 ways (WECC 2014), one is to represent the plant by only 1 wind turbine and the other option is to represent it by multiple wind turbines (Muljadi et al. 2006). According to WECC in general representation, we can use single turbine representation (Pooja 2018), but studies have shown that we need multiple turbine representation for modeling of large wind power plants. This is because multiple wind turbine gives us reliability to represent a few important characteristics of such a big power plant (Chen 2001).

3   POWER QUALITY PROBLEMS IN DISTRIBUTED GENERATION

Almost 2/3 of all problems related to PQ are because of faulty connections (WECC 2010). Voltage, power factor, flickers, and fluctuations, noise, and harmonics are few important parameters of the power quality of any power system (Sonali 2016). Variation in any of these parameters from the limits of their standard values as per PQ standards- IEEE Standard 519–2014 (IEEE 2014), IEEE Standard 929–2000 (IEEE 2000), and IEEE Standard 1453–2004 (IEEE 2004) is permissible otherwise it may harm load side equipment's very badly.

3.1   *Frequency deviation*

A very slight change in frequency from its ideal value is termed as frequency deviation. Although this deviation is very small in comparison to the actual value of frequency even that much deviation may have a very bad effect on our power system (WECC 2010).

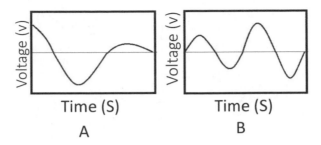

Figure 3. (A) Sag and (B) swell.

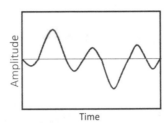

Figure 4. Harmonic distortion.

3.2 *Voltage dip & swell*

Voltage dip is also known as voltage sag; it is the sudden drop down of voltage to a level between 10–90%. Similarly, a sudden rise in voltage that makes it up to 10% above the normal value is known as voltage swell. This voltage sag and swell are alive for a very short period, i.e., about half of the cycle to 1 sec or tens of milliseconds to hundreds of milliseconds (Velayutham 2015). Examples of sag and swell have been shown in Figure 3 (Velayutham 2015).

3.3 *Harmonics*

Harmonics are said to be the most affecting one out of them all listed PQ problems. Its influences on PQ have been described in Almeida et al. (2013). Harmonics is the addition of several waves with different phases and magnitude values but with a frequency that would be multiple of fundamental frequency or say power frequency of the system (WECC 2010). The main reason behind the intro-duction of harmonics in the system is the use of power electronics devices for various applications in DG systems (Xiaodong 2016). A graph showing harmonics has been shown in Figure 4 (Almeida et al. 2013).

3.4 *Power system transients*

This includes voltage spike, notch, and impulse. These transients refer to a sudden increase of voltage which may be up to thousands of volts for a period of few microseconds to few milliseconds (Almeida et al. 2013).

3.5 *Poor power factor*

The power factor refers to the cosine of the phase angle difference between voltage and current at the load end. Current waves having harmonics in it would lead to poor power factor (WECC 2010).

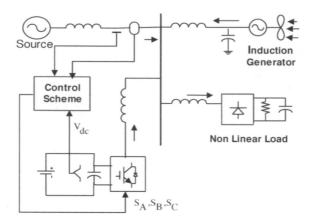

Figure 5.   Diagrammatic representation of STATCOM.

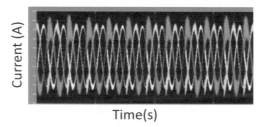

Figure 6.   Current at load side without compensation.

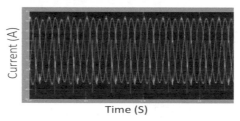

Figure 7.   Current at load side with compensation.

4   FEW TECHNIQUES OF POWER QUALITY IMPROVEMENT

4.1   *Static Compensator (STATCOM)*

STATCOM is a Shunt device, i.e., it is connected in Shunt with the line with current-controlled voltage source inverter STATCOM can be used to get rid of the harmonics present in source current. This inverter injects current in the system such that it will neutralize the harmonic as well as reactive part of nonlinear load and induction generator current. STATCOM system ensures good quality power at the point of common coupling (PCC). Figure 5 shows the diagrammatic representation of STATCOM & simulation results based on it has been shown in Figures 6 and 7 (Sheeraz 2017).

4.2   *Dynamic Voltage Restorer (DVR)*

Dynamic Voltage Restorer (DVR) injects the compensation voltage in the bus voltage through the transformer & improves the voltage profile so that the load voltage is balanced and does not contain any sag, swell, or harmonics. PQ problems like 30% sag depth or swell of 10% can be easily mitigated using DVR. Important parts of the DVR structure are transformer, harmonic filter,

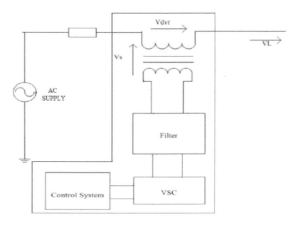

Figure 8. DVR series connected topology.

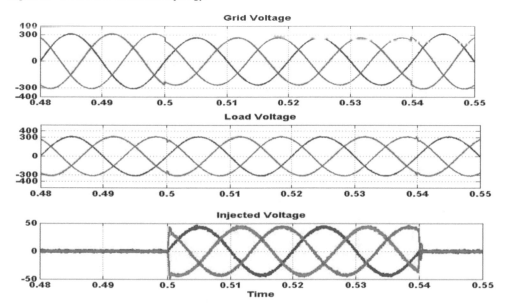

Figure 9. Voltage sag of 0.0398 sec was introduced (between 0.5 sec to 0.54 sec); (a) grid voltage; (b) load voltage before compensation; and (c) injected voltage; (d) balanced load voltage.

voltage source converter. Series connection topology of DVR has been shown in Figures 8 and simulation results related to it in Figure 9 (Rini 2016).

4.3 *Unified Power Quality Conditioner (UPQC)*

Unified Power Quality Conditioner (UPQC) is a hybrid of series active power filter (APF) and shunt APF. Shunt APF helps in mitigating the PQ problems introduced by the harmonics in load side current while series APF helps in solving the voltage related problem on the source side. Thus, UPQC aims at maintaining almost sinusoidal voltage and current at the site of its installation (Chen 2001). Thus, UPQC solves problems related to current as well as voltage also. The general configuration of the UPQC System has been shown in Figure 10 (Sushma 2012). Simulation result based upon this has been shown in Figures 11 and 12 (Sandhya 2013).

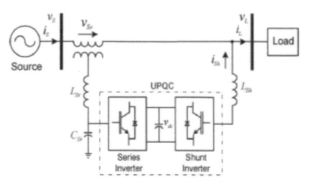

Figure 10. UPQC placement in a distribution system.

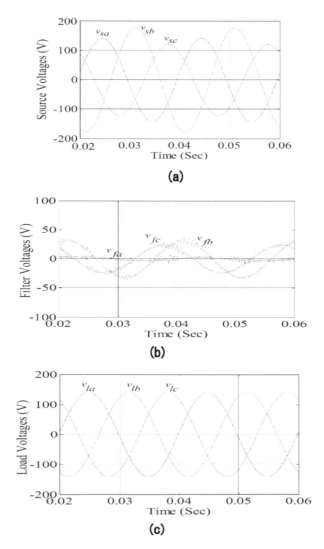

Figure 11. (a) Source voltage; (b) injected voltage (or say filter voltage); and (c) balanced load voltage.

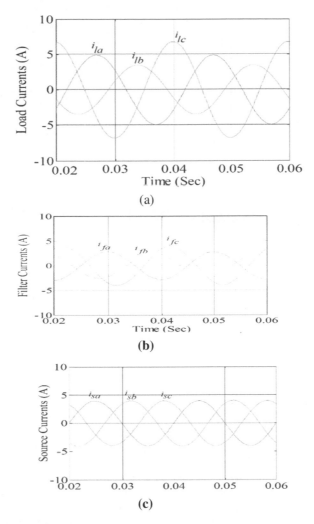

Figure 12. (a) source current; (b) injected current (or say filter current); and (c) balanced load current.

4.4 *Planning of farms*

Studies show that even the installation of renewable energy systems in a properly planned way may help to improve the PQ of generated power.

4.4.1 *Increasing the number of installations in farm*
Installing a collection of more no of the wind turbines results in a positive effect on PQ. This is because of the reduction in the impact of wind turbulence on the turbines as it does not hit all of them at the same instant of time. Figure 13 shows the comparison of the generated power curve under two different conditions. One of these curves represents the Total power generated curve when only 5 wind turbines were installed on the farm while the other one shows the total power generated curve for 10 wind turbines installed in the same plant (Prabha 1994).

4.4.2 *Spreading farm over wider area*
Spreading the installation area of power generating units of any DG system helps in the improvement of PQ as changing weather conditions do not have an impact on all the units. Thus, variation in

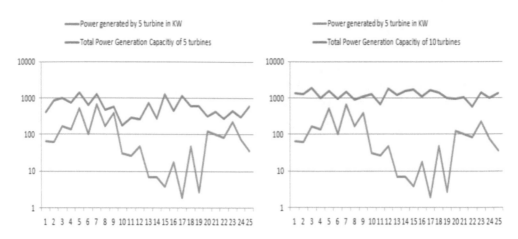

Figure 13. Comparison of power generated when ten turbines operated in aggregation to when only five operating in aggregation.

output power from the farm will have less variation in maximum and minimum values (Sonali 2016).

5 CONCLUSION

Electrical energy generation from renewable energy sources is increasing with a high rate but the important thing is to maintain the system's stability and reliability which is affected by the PQ problems arising upon the integration of renewable energy sources to the power grid. In this paper, we discussed a few important parameters of good PQ and the PQ issues arising in the system when the values of these parameters deviate from their ideal values. Further, we discussed the general structure of grid-connected renewable energy systems and a few methods to improve the PQ of the system to make the system more stable and reliable. Little information about STATCOM, DVR, and UPQC has also been covered in this paper. Even installing the plant in a planned way can help us to improve Power quality. As we have seen in the waveform results, that while STATCOM mitigates only current related PQ problems and DVR mitigates the only voltage-related PQ problems, on the other hand UPQC improves both current as well as voltage that reaches the user end. Thus, we find UPQC as a better mitigation device for the improvement of PQ. This literature review on PQ issues in grid-integrated renewable energy systems would surely support to go for any research or engineering efforts in this field.

REFERENCES

T. Ackermann. 2005, A book on Wind Power in Power Systems. Wiley Publication.
Almeida, L. Moreira, J. Delgado. 2013, Power Quality Problems and New Solutions, ISR Department of Electrical and Computer Engineering University of Coimbra, PloII, 3030–290 Coimbra (Portugal).
Z. Chen. 2001, Grid Power Quality with Variable Speed Wind Turbines. IEEE TRANSACTIONS ON ENERGY CONVERSION, VOL. 16, NO. 2.
K. Geetha, B. Sangeetha. 2013, Application of Artificial Intelligent Technique to Power quality issues in Renewable Energy. International Conference on Renewable Energy and Sustainable Energy.
Naimul Hasan, Ibraheem Nasiruddin, Yudhishthir Pandey. 2019, A Novel Technique for Transmission Loss Allocation in Restructured Power System. Journal of Electrical Engineering & Technology.
IEEE Recommended Practice and Requirements for Harmonic Control in Electric Power Systems, IEEE Std 519–2014.

IEEE Recommended Practice for Measurement and limits of voltage fluctuations and Associated Light Flicker on AC Power Systems, IEEE 1453–2004.

IEEE Recommended Practice for Utility Interface of Photovoltaic (PV) Systems, IEEE 929–2000.

Rini Ann Jerin. A Palanisamy. K, Umashankar. S, Thirumoorthy.A.D. 2016, Power Quality Improvement of Grid Connected Wind Farms through Voltage Restoration Using Dynamic Voltage Restorer. international journal of renewable energy research.

Sheeraz Kirmani, Brijesh Kumar. 2017, Power quality improvement by using STATCOM control scheme in wind energy generation interface to grid. International Conference on Power and Energy Engineering.

Sonali N. Kulkarni, Prashant Shingare. 2016, A review on power quality challenges in renewable energy grid integration. International Journal of Current Engineering and Technology.

Prabha Kundur. 1994, Power System Stability and Control. McGraw-Hill.

Xiaodong Liang. 2016, Emerging Power Quality Challenges Due to Integration of Renewable Energy Sources.

Madhu Mathi. M. A, Sasiraja. R. M. 2017, Improvement of Power Quality in the Distribution System by Placement of UPQC. International Journal of Engineering Science and Computing. International Electrotechnical Commission (IEC) White Paper. 2012, Grid Integration of Large-Capacity Renewable Energy Sources and Use of Large-Capacity Electrical Energy Storage. Geneva, Switzerland.

E. Muljadi, C.P. Butterfield, J. Chacon, and H. Romanowitz. 2006, Power Quality Aspects in a Wind Power Plant. IEEE Power Engineering Society General Meeting.

Sushma Parihar, Laith O. Maheemed, D.S. Bankar. 2012, The Unified Power Quality Conditioner Technique in Wind Energy Conversion System. International Journal of Advanced Engineering Technology.

Pooja Patel, Dr. Vijay Bhuria. 2018, Power Quality Issues in Grid Integrated Solar and Wind Hybrid System: A Review. IJEDR.

K. Sandhya, Dr.A. Jayalaxmi, Dr.M.P. Soni. 2013, Design of Unified Power Quality Conditioner (UPQC) for Power Quality Improvement in Distribution System. IOSR Journal of Electrical and Electronics Engineering (IOSR-JEEE).

C. Sankaran. 2002, Power Quality. CRC Press.

Velayutham. 2015, Expert talk on Power Quality (PQ) Issues in Smart Grid and Renewable Energy Sources, Ex-Member, MERC, at SGRES, CPRI, Bangalore. WECC Renewable Energy Modeling Task Force. 2010, WECC Wind Power Plant Dynamic Modeling Guide. Western Electricity Coordinating Council Modeling and Validation Work Group.

WECC Renewable Energy Modeling Task Force. 2014, WECC PV Power Plant Dynamic Modeling Guide. Western Electricity Coordinating Council Modeling and Validation Work Group.

Smart Computing – Khan et al (Eds)
© 2021 Taylor & Francis Group, London, ISBN 978-0-367-76552-1

Comparative performance analysis of different schemes in IEEE802.11n wireless LAN on MAC layer

Amiteshwar Bhalavi

Department of Electronics and Telecommunication, IET, DAVV, Indore, India
Department of Electronics and Communication, IPS Academy, IES, Indore, India

Sanjiv Tokekar & Ankit Saxena

Department of Electronics and Telecommunication, IET, DAVV, Indore, India

ABSTRACT: Wireless Local Area Network (WLAN) provides multiple and high throughput rate to the users. IEEE802.11 WLAN standards offer a high range of channel bandwidth for future media applications. The standard offered new capabilities to physical layer (PHY) and medium access control (MAC) layer that enhance throughput, i.e., the WLAN combines the MAC layer resources and allocates to a single user which directly improves the throughput performance. In this paper, we present the comparative throughput performance of the network under different configurations such as a network without MAC Packet Data Unit (MPDU) aggregation, a network with MAC Service Data Unit (MSDU), a network with MPDU and MSDU, and a network with MPDU aggregation. We use performance metrics to measure the performance are throughput and packet delay. In results we found that the aggregation of MPDU and MSDU improves the performance of the network.

1 INTRODUCTION

Wireless LANs (WLANs) based on the IEEE 802.11a (Telecommunications and Information Exchange between Systems Standard,) and 802.11g (Draft IEEE Standard) physical layer standards support multiple data rates. This enables the wireless access point to select the appropriate transmission rate depending on the required quality of service and the radio channel conditions as shown in Figure 1. For a high-speed network, maximize the throughput or minimize the transmission delay is always a prime concern. However, in a wireless network the distance between wireless stations is not fixed. It varies with user mobility that leads to an excessive number of re-transmissions. This may result degradation of WLAN performance.

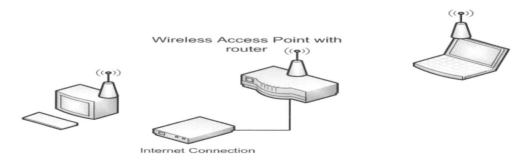

Figure 1. Network diagram.

DOI 10.1201/9781003167488-106

In order to maintain the Quality of Service (QoS) for trustworthy data communication over the channel with measuring bit error rate the IEEE 802.11 standards has been designed (IEEE 802). The MAC layer plays an important role for achieving high throughput. In order to get high throughput, the existing overheads at the MAC layer need to be reduced which is one of the bottlenecks for improving throughput. Distributed coordinate function (DCF) is the fundamental function to access the medium provided by MAC layer (Bianchi 2000) and it incorporates different schemes like Burst ACK, Block ACK, and Aggregation for reducing overheads.

Although improved performance of throughput is obtained using these schemes but it could not cope up with want of high-quality multimedia applications since in such applications involves MIMO which also accounts for high overhead thereby lower MAC efficiency and negatively affected the quality parameter of the multimedia service (Marroufi et al. 2007; Kljujic & Radivojevic 2009; Hoffmann & Kays 2010; Li et al. 2009). In order to overcome these limitations the two frame aggregation techniques: the A-MPDU (Aggregated MAC Protocol Data Unit) and the A-MSDU (Aggregated MAC Service data unit) has been included in 802.11n where for reducing the number of headers the \load" of a number of frames is combined into only one (IEEE std 802.11n-2009).

2 RELATED WORK

In Xiao (2004) the authors offered new mechanisms for better throughput performance of IEEE 802.11n at the MAC layer. In Vitsas et al. (2004), the authors confirmed that a complete solution for enhancing performance in QoS applications can be obtained by combining the packet bursting with priority mechanisms. In Liu et al. (2005), the authors investigated that the channel utilization improves considerably with bi-directional frame aggregation. In Abraham et al. (2005), the authors presented an overview of MAC and physical layer enhancements to improve channel utilization. In Kuppa & Dattatreya (2006) the authors illustrate the impact of aggregate size on channel utilization over a wide range of operating conditions and reported that there is no unique aggregate size that maximizes utilization under all scenarios. This motivates the need for a dynamic assignment of aggregate size. In Ginzburg et al. (2007), the authors investigated how the aggregation size, the packet error rate, and the PHY settings have an effect on the MAC throughput under TCP and UDP traffic. In Skordoulis et al. (2008), the authors explain how Aggregation is performed by using a single block of Acknowledgment (ACK) frame to exchange multiple MPDUs. In Sharon & Alpert (2017), the authors show how to aggregate the numbers of frames into a one frame. In Saldana et al. (2017), the authors studied the trade-off between the throughput improvement and the extra latency that come as a outcome of frame aggregation in 802.11 WLANs. Three solutions, based on prioritization, limiting the maximum A-MPDU size, and using central coordination of the aggregation have been studied and discussed. A trade-off appears: if the maximum delay of real-time services has to be reduced, a penalty in the throughput of TCP connections will appear. Ku et al. (2016) proposed an algorithm to improve throughput by selecting an optimal fragment length for the MPDU technique depending on various channel conditions. In order to recognnize optimal fragment length based on the time of the MSDU technique. The author in Ku et al. (2016) presented an algorithm. In Nomura et al. (2015), the author planned a hybrid aggregation algorithm that improves the throughput by providing the minimum frame error rate compared with MSDU aggregation. In Qian et al. (2017), the authors recommended a new aggregation method to improve the throughput by modifying both the upper and lower MAC sub-layers). In Anwar et al. (2013), the authors anticipated an MSDU aggregation scheme, namely ra-MSDU, which enables sub frame integrity check and re-transmission at the MSDU level by using implicit sub frame sequence control mechanism to manage the ordering of the frames at the receiver side without any additional sequence numbers. In Emmanuel et al. (2013), the authors accomplished that both A-MPDU and A-MSDU frame aggregation methods can support high-quality scalable video streaming, even when the system is heavily loaded. In Yuki et al. (2015), the authors proposed a new hybrid aggregation scheme by controlling the number of aggregate MSDUs for A-MSDU and also revealed that the proposed hybrid aggregation scheme can reduce the frame error probability and improve the throughput more efficiently than conventional aggregation scheme.

2.1 *Problem discussion*

The authors in Makhlouf et al. (2014) address the resource allocation problem for WLANs and offered a dispersed way out that can be used to find out the optimal scheduling in a practical system. For further improvement we focused on studying existing solutions and analyses the impact of aggregation with multiple data units.

2.2 *Major contribution of this work*

This work yields new conclusions on WLAN performance in practical systems providing:

1. A study of different configurations exists on the data layer.
2. We use packet delay and throughput performance metrics for analysis of four different configured WLAN's network with multiple distances between access point and station.

2.3 *Outline*

Section 3 describes the background of WLAN in terms of layered structure. Section 4 describes experimental setup and performance measurement. Sections 5 and 6 demonstrates the results and conclusion in the last section.

3 PRELIMINARIES

Figure 2 describes the structure of A-MSDU where MSDU consists of MSDU header with padding. MSDU formed by combining the Destination Address (DA), the Sender Address (SA), and the length of the MSDU. The MSDU arrives from Logical Link Control layer. The drawback associated with A-MSDU is error-prone channels which cannot be avoided. When MSDUs are combined with multiple MSDU in single Frame Check Sequence (FCS) the whole MSDUs need to be retransmitted if any of the frames got corrupt (Yazid, et al. 2016). In Aggregated MPDU, we combine multiple MPDU with single physical header. The basic structure is shown in Figure 3 (Yazid et al. 2016). Figure 4 shows the hybrid aggregation of A-MSDU and A-MPDU in limited capacity. This is special type of structure where both A-MSDU and A-MPDU units are combined at predefined frame length (Yazid et al. 2016).

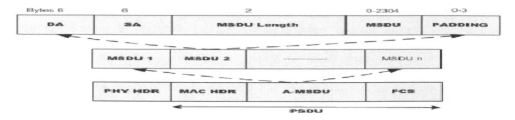

Figure 2. The layered format between MAC and PHY for Aggregate MSDU (Yazid et al. 2016).

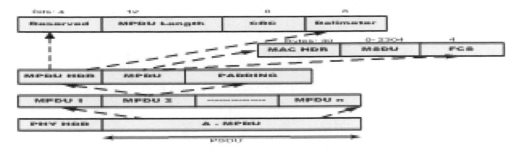

Figure 3. The frame structure for Aggregate MPDU (Yazid et al. 2016).

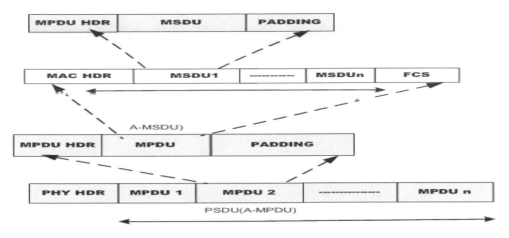

Figure 4. The frame structure for hybrid A-MSDU/A-MPDU aggregation (Yazid et al. 2016).

4 EXPERIMENTAL SETUP AND PERFORMANCE METRICS

4.1 *Network design*

Wireless network design is shown in Figure 5, that is conjured in four independent WLAN's configurations named as Aggregation Disabled (Aggregation (D)), only MSDU (MPDU (D) MSDU(E)), the two-level of Aggregations (MPDU (E), MSDU(E)), and only Aggregation MPDU (MPDU (E). We described the individual network con figuration in Figures 6, 7, 8, and 9, where Network A as \Aggregation MPDU (MPDU (E)), Network B as \Aggregation Disabled", Network C as \MPDU Disabled (D), MSDU Enabled (E)", and Network D as \MPDU (E), MSDU Enabled (E))". We configured network IP addresses for network A, as access point with IP (192.168.1.2) and User/Station of network A with (192.168.1.1), for network B, as access point with IP (192.168.2.2) and User/Station of network B with (192.168.2.1), for network C, as access point with IP (192.168.3.2) and User/Station of network C with (192.168.3.1), and for network D, as access point with IP (192.168.4.2) and User/Station of network D with (192.168.4.1).

To monitor the network performnce, we initiate traces for the flow monitor. Figure 6 shows the Wireless network as Aggregation (D) in which first block represents the SSID (service set identifier) of network B. The second block denotes that physical channel number is selected as 40. The third block represents that MPDU value is set to zero. The fourth block shows that station B is installed on network and station B id is 1. In the fifth block type of MAC layer has been set through beacon generation.

In the sixth block, device B is installed which is paired with channel one. Figure 7 shows the Wieless network as as only MSDU (MPDU (D) MSDU (E)), where the first block represents the

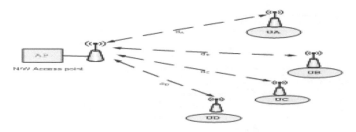

Figure 5.　Wireless LAN Network setup graph.
UA, UB, UC, UD: User in particular network
AP: Access Point connected with Internet

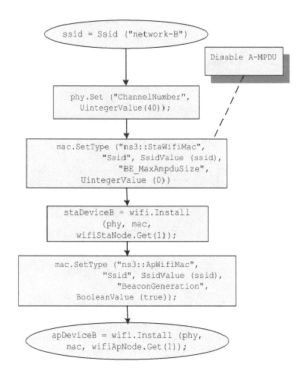

Figure 6.　Wireless LAN network configuration as aggregation (D).

SSID (service set identifier) of network C. The second block denotes that physical channel number is selected as 44. The third block represents that MPDU value is set to zero and MSDU value is set to 7395 bytes. The fourth block shows that station C is installed on the network and station C id is 2. In the fifth block type of MAC layer has been set through beacon generation. In the sixth block, device C is installed which is paired with channel two. Figure 8 shows the wieless network as two levels of Aggregations in which the first block represents the SSID of network D. The second block denotes that physical channel number is selected as 48. The third block represents that MPDU value is set to 32,768 bytes and MSDU value is set to 3,839 bytes.The fourth block shows that station D is installed on network and station D ID is 3. In the fifth block, type of MAC layer has been set through beacon generation. In the sixth block, device D is installed which is paired with channel three. Figure 9 shows the wireless network as Aggregation MPDU in which the first block represents the SSID of network A. The second block denotes that physical channel

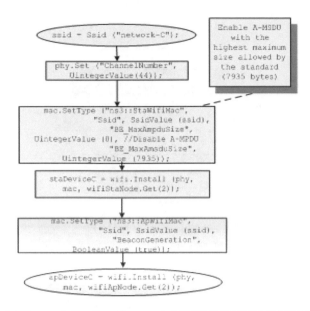

Figure 7. Wireless LAN network Configuration as only MSDU (MPDU (D) MSDU (E).

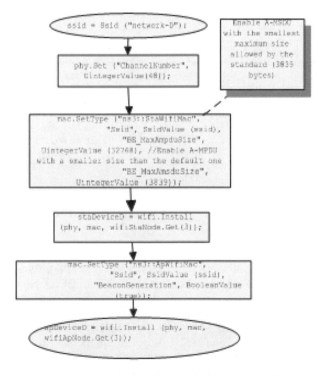

Figure 8. Wireless network configuration as two levels of Aggregation (MPDU (E), MSDU (E)).

number is selected as 36. The third block represents that Statin A SSID is mapped with MAC layer. The fourth block shows that station A is installed on network and station A ID is zero. In the fifth block, type of MAC layer has been set through beacon generation. In the sixth block, device A is installed which is paired with channel zero.

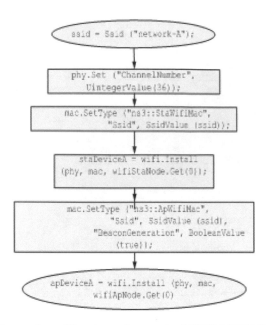

Figure 9.   Wireless LAN network configuration as Aggregation MPDU (MPDU (E).

Table 1.   Network parameter used in the experimental setup.

Parameter	Values
Carrier Frequency (Hz)	518 MHZ
RF Bandwidth (Hz)	2 MHZ
Payload Length	1472 bytes
WIFI PHY Standard	IEEE 80211n 5 GHZ
Mobility	Constant
Control/Data Mode	HtMcs0 "OFDM 6MBPS"
Distance Between Access Point and User	20 m

4.2   Implementation of WLANs

For implementation of WLANs we referred different simulations such as Network Simulator-2 (NS-2) (N.Simulator, NS2), NS-3(NSNAM, Network Simulator NS3), Omnettp (OMNET ++ Discrete Event Simulator), and MATLAB (MATLAB LTE TOOL BOX). However, we found that NS-3 is better for evaluation under the design. We described the individual network configurations with different IP addresses to measure in Figure 5, Network A as \MPDU Aggregation Enabled", Network B as \Aggregation Disabled", Network C as \MPDU Disabled and MSDU Enabled", and Netwok D as \MPDU Enaabled and MSDU Enabled". To monitor the network performance, we initiate traces for flow monitor. Table 1 describes the other network parameters used in the simulation. We used an identical parameter for multiple iterations and configurations of *network*.

4.3   Performance metrics

To identify the performance of individual network setup we have selected performance metrics as Throughput, Packet Delay, and Signal to Noise Ratio (SNR). Further described as below.

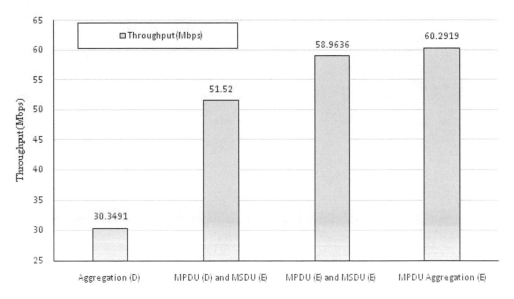

Figure 10. Comparison of throughput performance of four different network at a constant distance of 20 m apart from access point (AP) and user equipment (UE).

Throughput:
It is described as a number of bits transferred (in Mbps) from access point to user in the network.

$$\text{Throughput} = \frac{(\text{Total Packet} * \text{PayLoad Size})}{\text{Simulation Time}}$$

Packet Delay:
Packet delay is a transmission delay used to describe the amount of time required by packets to travel between source to destination, measured in millisecond (ms). In the paper, we used the mean packet delay.

Signal to Noise Ratio:
It is described as the ratio of signal power and noise power. In the network we measured both power at downlink, i.e., at user end. For mathematical calculation we measured SNR in dB.

$$\text{SNR} = \frac{\text{Signal Power}}{\text{Noise Power}}$$

5   RESULT ANALYSIS

We evaluate the performance of four independent WLANs under a common setup with different distances between access point and user/station. Figure 10 shows the throughput of individual network configurations. We found that the MPDU Aggregation enable network offered twice the throughput in comparison. And another configurations throughput lies in between them. Furthermore, two-level aggregation (MPDU (E) and MSDU (E)) also offers comparable throughput with MPDU Aggregation.

Figure 11 shows the packet delay of individual network configurations. We found that the MPDU Aggregation enable network offered nearly half the packet delay in comparison. And another

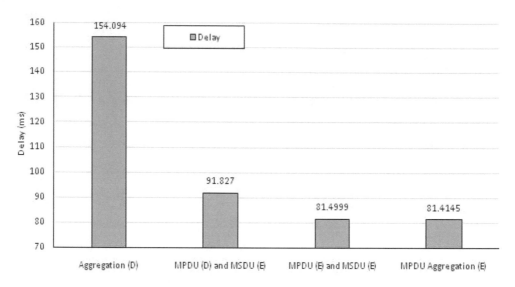

Figure 11. Comparison of mean packet delay performance of the four different networks at a constant distance of 20 m apart from Access Point (AP) and User Equipment (UE).

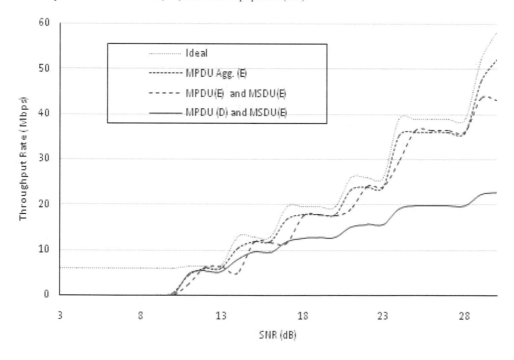

Figure 12. Performance comparison of data rate (Mbps) v/s SNR ratio (db) of the networks at constant distance of 20 m apart from access point (ap) and user equipment (ue) with respect to ideal networks as per IEEE 802.11n.

configurations packet delay lies in between them. Furthermore, two-level aggregation (MPDU (E) and MSDU (E)) also offers comparable packet delay with the MPDU Aggregation.

Figure 12 shows the throughput rate with respect to SNR of the individual network configurations. We found that the MPDU Aggregation enable network offered twice the throughput rate at a particular value of SNR, in the comparison. Another configuration throughput rate lies in between them. Furthermore, two-level aggregation (MPDU (E) and MSDU (E)) also offers comparable throughput with MPDU Aggregation.

6 CONCLUSION

In this paper, we conclude the comparatively performance of different WLAN networks configured at the MAC layer as aggregation disabled, MSDU enabled, MPDU and MSDU enabled, and MPDU aggregation enabled WLAN network. We found that the worst performance of aggregation disabled WLAN network. The MSDU enabled network shows improvement in throughput by 69%, MSDU and MPDU enabled network shows improvement in throughput by 94%, and MPDU aggregation WLAN network improved by 98% while comparing with aggregation disabled WLAN. For packet delay, MSDU enable network reduces packet delay by 41%, MSDU and MPDU enabled network reduces packet delay by 48%, and MPDU aggregation WLAN network reduces the delay by 49%. Similarly, we found that the network performance of MPDU aggregation and MPDU with MSDU network is better in terms of throughput rate and signal to noise ratio. We found that the MPDU aggregation perform better among others network in all aspects, as it overcomes the limitation of overhead between the MPDU and MSDU.

REFERENCES

Abraham, S., Meylan, A., Nanda, S. 2005. 802.11n MAC design and system performance.In Proceedings of International Conference on Communications, pp. 2957–2961.

Anwar Saifa, B., Mohamed, Othmana 2013. A Reliable A-MSDU Frame Aggregation Scheme in 802.11n Wireless Networks. The 4th International Conference on Emerging Ubiquitous Systems and Pervasive Networks (EUSPN-2013).

Bianchi, G. 2000. Performance analysis of the IEEE 802.11 distributed coordination function. IEEE J. Sel. Areas Commun. 18 (3), pp. 607–614.

Emmanuel Marcio, W., Jaime Guilherme, D. G., De Marca José Roberto, B. 2013.On The Use of IEEE 802.11n Frame Aggregation for Efficient Transport of Scalable Video Streaming. IEEE WCNC (2013) pp. 1079–1084.

Ginzburg, Boris, Kesselman, Alex. 2007. Performance analysis of A-MPDU and A-MSDU aggregation in IEEE 802.11n. IEEE Sarnoff Symposium 2007, pp. 1–5.

Hoffmann, O., Kays, R. 2010.Efficiency of frame aggregation in wireless multimedia networks based on IEEE 802.11n.IEEE 14th International Symposium on Consumer Electronics (ISCE), 2010, pp. 1–5.

IEEE802,[Online]. Available:http://www.ieee802.org/16/pubs/80216e.html. [Accessed 01 07 2017].

IEEE Std 802.11n-2009 (Amendment to IEEE Std 802.11-2007 as amended by IEEE Std 802.11k-2008, IEEE Std 802.11r-2008, IEEE Std 802.11y-2008, and IEEE Std 802.11w-2009) – IEEE Standard for Information technology–Telecommunications and information exchange between systems–Local and metropolitan area networks–Specific requirements Part 11: Wireless LAN Medium Access Control (MAC) and Physical Layer (PHY) Specifications Amendment 5: Enhancements for Higher Throughput.

Kljujic, J.S., Radivojevic, M. R. 2009.Testing of multimedia content transmission in wireless 802.11n network, Telecommunication in Modern Satellite, Cable, and Broadcasting Services. 9th International Conference on TELSIKS'09, pp. 552–555.

Ku, E., Chung, C., Kang, B., Kim, J. 2016.Optimal frame size analysis for fragmentation and aggregation algorithm. Proceedings of IEEE conference in Region 10 (TENCON), IEEE, pp. 3228–3231.

Ku, E., Chung, C., Kang, B., Kim, J. 2016.Throughput enhancement with optimal fragmented MSDU size for fragmentation and aggregation scheme in WLANs. Proceedings of IEEE conference in SoC Design Conference (ISOCC), pp. 287–288.

Kuppa, S., Dattatreya, G.R. 2006.Modeling and analysis of frame aggregation in unsaturated WLANs with Finite buffer stations.To appear in Proceedings of IEEE ICC'06, pp. 967–972.

Li, Tianji, Ni, Qiang, Malone, D., Leith, D., Xiao, Qiang, Turletti, T. 2009. Aggregation with Fragment Retransmission for Very High-Speed WLANs. Transactions on Networking, IEEE/ACM, 17(2), pp. 591–604.

Liu, Changwen, Stephens, Adrian P. 2005. An analytical model for infrastructure WLAN capacity with bidirectional frame aggregation.In Proceedings of Wireless Conference on Networking and Communications, pp. 113–119.

Makhlouf, A. B., Hamidi, M. 2014. Dynamic Multiuser Sub-Channels Allocation and Real-Time Aggregation Model for IEEE 802.11 WLANs.IEEE Transactions on Wireless Communications, 13(11), pp. 6015–6025.

Marroufi, S., Ajib, W., Elbiaze 2007. Performance evaluation of new MAC Mechanism for IEEE 802.11n.First international GIIS (Global information Infrastructure symposium), pp. 39–45.

MATLAB LTE TOOL BOX, [Online]. Available: https://www.mathworks.com/products/matlab.html. [Accessed 01 Jan 2017].

Nomura, Y., Mori, K., Kobayashi, H. 2015. Efficient Frame Aggregation with Frame Size Adaptation for Next Generation MU-MIMO WLANs. Proceedings of 9th International conference in Next Generation Mobile Applications, Services and Technologies, pp. 288–293.

N.Simulator, NS2, [Online]. Available: https://www.isi.edu/nsnam/ns/.

NSNAM, Network Simulator NS3 [Online]. Available: https://www.nsnam.org/docs/models/html/lte-design.html.[Accessed 01 June 2017].

OMNET ++ Discrete Event Simulator [Online]. Available: https://omnetpp.org/. [Accessed 01 July 2016].

Qian, X., Wu, B., Ye, T. 2017. Enhanced aggregation scheduler design in industrial 802.11 devices. Journal of Electronics Letters, 53(15), pp. 1073–1075.

Saldana, J., Ruiz-Mas, J., Almodóvar, J. 2017. Frame Aggregation in Central Controlled 802.11 WLANs: The Latency Versus Throughput Tradeoff. IEEE Communications Letters, 21(11), pp. 2500–2503.

Sharon, O., Alpert, Y. 2017. Single User MAC Level Throughput Comparison: IEEE 802.11 ax vs. IEEE802.11 ac. Journal of wireless sensor network, 9, pp. 166–177.

Skordoulis, D., Ni, Q., Chen, H. H., Stephens, A. P., Liu, C., Jamalipour, A. 2008.IEEE 802.11 n MAC frame aggregation mechanisms for next generation high-throughput WLANs. Journal of IEEE Wireless Communications, 15(1), pp. 40–47.

Standard, Draft IEEE Standard for Information Technology Telecommunications and Information Exchange between Systems Local and Metropolitan Area Networks Specific Requirements Part 11: Wireless Medium Access Control (MAC) and Physical Layer (PHY) Specifications:Am,[Online]. Available:http://ieeexplore.ieee.org/document/4040930/.[Accessed 01 June 2017].

Telecommunications and Information Exchange Between Systems – Local and Metropolitan Area Networks – Specific Requirements Part 11: Wireless LAN Medium Access Control (MAC) and Physical Layer (PHY) Specification,[Online]. Available:http://ieeexplore.ieee.org/document/4140843/. [Accessed 01 05 2017].

Vitsas, V., Chatzimisios, P., Boucouvalas, A. C., Raptis, P., Paparrizos, K., Kleftouris, D. 2004. Enhancing performance of the IEEE 802.11 Distributed Coordination Function via packet bursting.In Globecom Workshops, pp. 245–252.

Xiao, Yang 2004.Packing mechanisms for the IEEE 802.11n wireless LANs.In Proceedings of Globecom, pp. 3275–3279.

Yazid, M., Medjkoune-Bouallouche, L., Atssani, D. 2016.Performance Study of Frame Aggregation Mechanisms in the New Generation Wi-Fi. In 10th Workshop on Verification and Evaluation of Computer and Communication System, Tunis, Tunisia, 2016.

Yuki, Chosokabe, Tatsumi, Uwai, Yuhei, Leonardo Lanante, Jr. 2015. A Channel Adaptive Hybrid Aggregation Scheme for Next Generation Wireless LAN. IEEE WCNC (2015), pp. 153–158.

Smart Computing – Khan et al (Eds)
© *2021 Taylor & Francis Group, London, ISBN 978-0-367-76552-1*

Multi-hop zonal-based hybrid routing protocol for heterogeneous wireless sensor network using fuzzy technique

Kritika Mishra & A.K. Daniel
CSE, Madan Mohan Malviya University of Technology, Gorakhpur, India

ABSTRACT: The continuous development and progress of wireless networks' and sensor networks' innovation have gradually become an attractive technology to encourage individual's lives. Due to the extensive utilization of sensor lifetime on real time and effective data has become a basic concern. The lifetime of a network is limited to the energy of nodes as a key factor for designing a network's lifetime. Clustering is an effective method of topology control for reducing energy consumed by the sensor nodes to increase the network lifetime. This paper proposes multi-hop zonal-based hybrid routing protocol for heterogeneous nodes. The given area is divided into zones and randomly deploying two nodes, one as normal and the one as an advance node. The advance node send data through clustering and Normal nodes transfer information directly to base station. The cluster head elections are premise on residual energy and distance factor of cluster nodes using fuzzy logic concept. The proposed protocol is implemented and contrasted with SEP protocol. The simulation results show the that proposed work decreases consumption of energy. The proposed protocol prolongs network lifetime and stability of network.

Keywords: Zone, clustering, routing, fuzzy logic, Lifetime.

1   INTRODUCTION

A Wireless Sensor Network (WSN) generally collects a vast quantity of sensors that are randomly placed in the network. WSNs are used widely in the identification, situation control, and environmental monitoring. The main challenge of such networks is the limited energy of sensors. One of the most effective solutions is to use clustering techniques. In WSN, various protocol likes LEACH (Mahajan & Malhotra 2011), SEP (Smaragdakis et al. 2004), and TEEN (Manjeshwar & Agrawal 2001) are used to enhance the network lifetime. Hierarchical protocol is used as a cluster of the nodes and cluster head node (CH) that aggregate the information to save energy. In hierarchical routing protocol, clusters are formed and in each CH are allocated. CH collects the data from the network, aggregate the data, and transfer it to base station (BS) (Mahajan & Malhotra 2011; Heinzelman et al. 2000). Networks are categorized into two types: (a) homogeneous sensor network and (b) heterogeneous sensor network. Nodes in the organization having the same energy are homogeneous network and node having different energies from one another are a heterogeneous network. In the WSN cluster are two types: static and dynamic. This paper proposed a multi-hop zonal-based hybrid routing protocol to reduce energy utilization. The system is divided into multiple zone and different types of sensor nodes as advanced node and normal nodes, placed in a field. The network is divided into five zones (Zone1 to Zone5). Each nodes sense data from its surrounding and send to CH process it and transmit the information to BS using one-hop and/or multi-hop transmission (Chang & Tassiulas 2000; Michail & Ephremides 2000). The normal node transfer information directly to destination (BS) and advance node utilizes clustering technique to transfer information to BS using Multi-hop routing protocol (Torghabeh 2010; Chaturvedi et al. 2017; Narayan et al. 2020). Fuzzy logic technique used two parameters: distance to BS and residual energy of the nodes in zone/network to select the CH. This reduces the energy for the selection of CH (Latif et al. 2013; Sugihara & Gupta 2011). The hybrid routing approach enhance the network lifetime. Hence, the network life increased (Torghabeh 2010). This paper presents an extensive evaluation of the methodology used in cluster-based routing protocols along with evaluation of the clustering characteristics of these methods.

This paper also proposes a new viewpoint and classification to evaluate parameters and features of methods. The rest of the article is outlined as follows. In Section 2, we introduce the proposed work and algorithm to solve the issue is given in Section 3. The proposed model to solve the issue is given in Section 4, the link restoration technique is in Section 5, and the comparative results are discussed in Section 6. Finally, future work and conclusion are discussed in Sections 7 and 8, respectively.

2   RELATED WORK

WSN contains a huge number of sensors with the computational power to communicate with each other at radio frequencies. One of the most effective solutions is to use clustering techniques. Therefore, clustering and cluster-based routing protocols were analyzed in this paper. There are various routing protocols available that used to decrease energy consumption in an WSN.

LEACH protocol requires randomized rotation for local CH in the network. They are executed only in a homogenous surrounding. So, it does not work in a heterogeneous environment (Heinzelman et al. 2000).

In the SEP protocol having two sorts of sensor nodes, one is advance node and the another is normal node for data transmission. Election of CH is located on weighted probability. Super nodes consider high possibility to elect CH than normal nodes. The head node (CH) is elected premise on residual energy of node and SEP protocol doesn't guarantee deployment of nodes efficiently in network (Smaragdakis et al. 2004).

In cost arrangements of nodes for different transmission modes are minimized deployment in heterogeneous network. The amount of the initial battery energy is decided by cost of the CH device for rely upon member and transmission mode (Soro & Henizelman 2005).

In TEEN protocol is a reactive protocol for homogenous surrounding, where the node reacts immediately and appropriately for time basic application. Hard and soft thresholds are introduced in TEEN protocol which saves energy in network and minimize number of transmission (Manjeshwar & Agrawal 2001).

In E-SEP protocol is a three-level heterogeneities. E-SEP has intermediate nodes. The energy lying in the middle of normal nodes and advance nodes. The nodes do not hold any parameter for the CH election. The nodes are elected premise on criteria of remaining energy (Aderohunmu & Deng 2009).

In RBHR protocol having two nodes as Normal nodes and Advance nodes. Normal nodes transfer information directly to BS and are near to BS because they have less energy contrast to advance nodes. Advance node uses clustering technique for transferring information to BS. This approach uses efficient utilization of energy to improve network life time (Maurya et al. 2014).

3   PROPOSED MODEL

In this paper, the methods of clustering topology were reviewed. In clustering, every cluster consists of a group of sensor nodes. It consists of two sorts of nodes: member nodes and a cluster head. The node collects information from its surrounding and then transfer it to CH. Based on an information routing mechanism, the CH aggregates and transmits data to another.

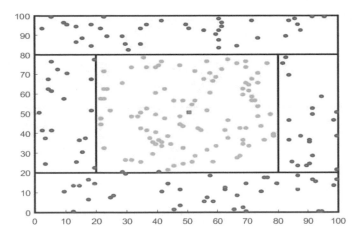

Figure 1. Network architecture.

3.1 *Proposed protocol for clustering*

The sensor network deployed in a square region of the dimensions $A * A$ is considered and the BS is supposed to be at the center. The network is divided into several zone consisting of two sorts of sensor nodes as normal and advance node, premise of energy parameter. Advance nodes consist λ $(\lambda > 1)$ times longer energy than normal nodes. The advance sensor nodes are deployed far from the BS and normal sensor nodes are deployed close to BS. The advance node zone is further divided into number of sub zone leveled into the cluster. The optimal CH are chosen on premise of distance parameters and residual energy. The experimental results display that proposed protocol minimizes the energy utilization, load through the selection of optimal cluster heads than existing approach.

3.1.1 *Deployment of zones*

The proposed protocol partition the target region into several zones as $Z = Z_1, \ldots Z_{s-1}$ to deploy the advance nodes and the zones Zs is used for the deployment of normal node. The advance nodes zone is partitioned into equal size levels shown in Figure 1 where $zone_1$ is closest to the BS.

3.1.2 *Multipath routing in advance node zones*

The advances nodes are placed far from the BS, so it uses multi-path routing mechanism for information transmission. The CH of each zone level (l_0) transfers the information to its above level l_{o-1} cluster head, and so on. The route discovery is done on premise of residual energy parameters and distance parameters i.e.s CH which is near, energy is higher, and distance is less is chosen as the next node for the information transmission.

3.1.3 *Clustering in advance node zones applying fuzzy technique*

The proposed routing protocol consists of following phases: formation of cluster, CH selection, aggregation, and data transmission. The first two phases constitute setup phase in which cluster head election is done among sensor nodes. The next phase is steady phase in which aggregation is performed on the sensed data and final phase is the data transmission. This approach uses fuzzy inference mechanism for CH election. Fuzzy logic controller compromises of fuzzifier, inference engine, fuzzy rule base, and defuzzifier (Maurya et al. 2014; Singh & Daniel 2015).

The network architecture shown in Figure 2 is represented by green dots for normal nodes in between $20 < x \leq 80$ and $20 < y \leq 80$ is Zone5, and blue dots are the super nodes in $0 < x \leq 100$

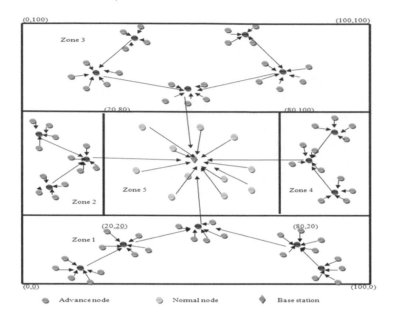

Figure 2. Scenario of wireless sensor network.

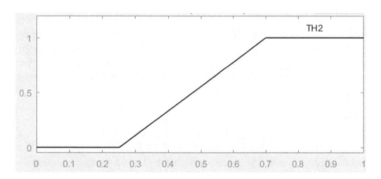

Figure 3. Graph with maximum and minimum threshold value of input variables.

and $0<y\leq20$ is Zone1, $20<x\leq20$ and $20<y\leq80$ is Zone2, $80<x\leq100$ and $80<y\leq100$ is Zone3, $80<x\leq100$ and $80<y\leq80$ is Zone4, and the red dot is the BS.

3.2 *Election of CH using fuzzy logic*

The proposed protocol used to upgrade balance the CH in the network. Fuzzy logic is required for the clustering technique. For the election of CH, two kinds of variables are used, Dis(D) and Res_Energy (RE) of the node used in fuzzy logic (Figure 3).

$$Dis = \{(d, \mu_{dis}(d))\}, d \in D$$

$$Res\_Energy = \{(e, \mu_{EN}(e))\}, e \in RE$$

Table 1.　Input variable.

Input	Membership		
Dis	close	Satisfactory	Far
Res_Energy	Less	Med	High

Table 2.　Output function.

Output	Membership
Cluster head formation probability	Highest, V-High, High, Med-High, Med, Med Less, Less, V-less, Lessen

Where, D indicates the universal discourse of Dis and RE indicates the universal disclosure of Res_Energy. The component of set D (Dis) is d & μ_{dis} (d) are the membership variable of the Dis and set RE (Res_Energy) is e and μ_{EN} (e) are membership function for the RE sets:

$$\mu(d) = \begin{cases} 1 & \text{if } D(d) \leq TH1 \\ D(d) - TH1/(TH2 - TH1) & \text{if } TH1 \leq D(d) \leq TH2 \\ 0 & \text{if } D(d) \geq TH2 \end{cases}$$

$$\mu(E) = \begin{cases} 1 & \text{if } RE(d) \leq TH1 \\ TH1 - RE(E)/(TH1 - TH2) & \text{if } TH1 \leq RE(E) \leq TH2 \\ 0 & \text{if } RE(E) \geq TH2 \end{cases}$$

where
TH1 = Threshold variable is min
TH2 = Threshold variable is max

3.2.1　*Rule classification for CH election*

In the proposed protocol, for election of CH in the advance nodes fuzzy logic technique is utilized. Here, two input parameter variable that is Distance and Residual energy (RE) of nodes. Table 1 used three membership functions which display degree of input function and Table 2 are the probable output functions.

The precedence functions of the input variable:

RE > Distance

The precedence order of the output member ship functions are:

Highest > VHigh > High > Med High > Med > Med Less > Less > Very Less > Lessen

The rule set is explained and aggregation of given fuzzy rules to achieve fuzzy output given in Table 3.

Rules has been explained:

Table 3.   Rule set.

Rule 1:
IF Dis is Close AND Res_energy is Less THEN membership is Less.
Rule 2:
IF Dis is Close AND Res_energy is Med THEN membership is Very High.
Rule 3:
IF Dis is Close AND Res_energy is High THEN membership is Highest.
Rule 4:
IF Dis is Satisfactory AND Res_energy is High THEN membership is Med.
Rule 5:
IF Dis is Satisfactory AND Res_energy is Low THEN membership is Med High.
Rule 6:
IF Dis is Satisfactory AND Res_energy is Med THEN membership is High.
Rule 7:
IF Dis is Far AND Res_energy is Less THEN membership is Lessen.
Rule8:
IF Dis is Far AND Res_energy is Med THEN membership is Very Less.
Rule 9:
IF Dis is Far AND Res_energy is High THEN membership is Med Less.

3.3   *Algorithm for proposed work for information transmission*

Table 4.   Transmission routing protocol.

CH = Cluster Head; CM = Cluster Member; BS = Base station
1.   Begin
a)   Network = A X A meter
b)   Number of nodes in the network = n
c)   m = Fraction of total number of nodes with α times
          more energy are super node.
d)   Super node = n * (1 − m)
e)   Sensor nodes set in different zones Z1, . . .Z4.
f)   Super nodes are placed in zones Z1, Z2, Z3, Z4
g)   Normal nodes are placed in zone Z5
2.   CH sense the data from every CH in the zone
3.   If(nodes = normal nodes) then
4.   Node sense data from environment
5.   Normal nodes transfer information directly to base station.
6.   Else(nodes = advance nodes)
7.   Cluster formation among super nodes.
8.   CH election using fuzzy logic technique.
9.   CH formation [$CM_1, CM_2, ... CM_n.$]
10.   CM sensed the data and data sends to CH
11.   If (CH distance < transmission range)
12.   Cluster Head sends data to BS
13.   Else
14.   if (CH distance > transmission range) then
15.   CH using multi hop communication through neighboring CH
16.   CH transmit data to BS
17.   End

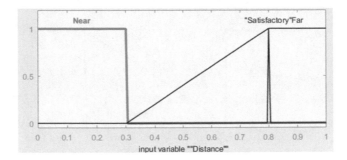

Figure 4.   Graph representing membership variables of input variable "Distance".

Table 5.   Degree of membership of distance.

Distance	Degree of Membership
20	1
35	1
45	0.25
55	0.75
80	0

4   SYSTEM ANALYSIS

We assume five advance nodes. Let us consider a set of advance node distance from BS are:

$$D = \{20, 35, 45, 60, 70\}$$

Now consider set of Res_Energy of node as:

$$RE = \{0.3, 0.4, 0.5, 0.8, 0.85\}$$

A membership function for node distance to BS (Figure 4)

$$\mu(d) = \begin{cases} 1 & \text{if } D(d) \leq 40 \\ D(d) - 40/(60 - 40) & \text{if } 40 \leq D(d) \leq 60 \\ 0 & \text{if } D(d) \geq 60 \end{cases}$$

A membership function of Res_Energy nodes (Figure 5):

$$\mu(E) = \begin{cases} 0 & \text{if } RE(E) \leq 0.3 \\ (RE(E) - 0.3/(0.8 - 0.3)) & \text{if } 0.3 \leq RE(E) \leq 0.8 \\ 1 & \text{if } RE(E) \geq 0.8 \end{cases}$$

Table 5. Distance {20, 35, 45, 55, 70} and degree of membership are {1, 1, 0.25, 0.75, 0} independently. As per the fuzzy member ship we can define as Distance (D) = {20|close, 35|close, 45|Satistactory, 55|Satisfactory, 70|Far}.

Table 6. Residual Energy {0.3, 0.4 0.5, 0.8, 0.9} and Degree of Membership {0, 0.2, 0.4, 1, 1} independently. As per the fuzzy membership, we can define Residual Energy (RE) = {0.3|Less, 0.4|Med, 0.5|Med, 0.8|High, 0.9|High}

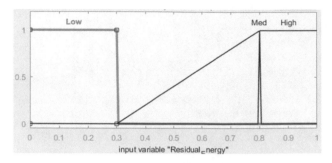

Figure 5.   Graph representing membership variable of input variable "Res_Energy".

Table 6.   Degree of membership of Res_energy.

Res_Energy	Degree of Membership
0.3	0
0.4	0.2
0.5	0.4
0.8	1
0.9	1

Table 7.   Max rule data.

D RE	20	35	45	55	80
0.3	0	0	0	0	0
0.4	0.2	0.2	0.2	0.2	0
0.5	0.4	0.4	0.25	0.4	0
0.8	1	1	0.25	0.5	0
0.9	1	1	0.25	0.5	0

Table 8.   Output table.

D RE	20	35
0.8	1	1
0.9	1	1

Applying MIN Rule on Tables 5 and 6, the output of the system is shown in Table 7
Applying MAX Rule on Table 7 we get the output in Table 8.

$Dis_1 = 20$ and $Res\_energy_1 = 0.8$ and
$Dis_2 = 35$ and $Res\_energy_2 = 0.8$
$Dis_1 = 20$ and $Res\_emergy_1 = 0.9$ and
$Dis_2 = 35$ and $Res\_energy_2 = 0.9$

The advance node elected for the CH can be any of the above rule.

Table 9. Result with AND fuzzy computation.

S. No	Distance	Membership Function	Res_ Energy	Membership Function
1	20	Close	0.8	High
2	35	Close	0.8	High
3	20	Close	0.9	High
4	35	Close	0.9	High

Table 10. Simulation variance.

Total number of Advance node	50
Total number of Normal node	50
Advance node in zone 1	15
Advance node in zone 2	15
Advance node in zone 3	10
Advance node in zone 4	10
Normal node in zone 5	50

Table 11. Energy level.

Variables	**Vales**
Initial energy E_0	0.5J
Initial energy of advance node	$E_0 (1+\alpha)$
Energy factor α	1
Transmitter/Receiver Electronics E_{elec}	50 nJ/bit
Transmit Amplifier at a short distance E_{fs}	10 pJ/bit/m^2
Transmit Amplifier at a longer distance E_{amp}	0.0013 pJ/bit/m^4
Data aggregation	
E_{DA}	5 nJ/bit/report

5   SIMULATION AND RESULT

On the basis of analytical work illustrate in a previous section, the simulations were performed in MATLAB. The simulation has been done in multi-path routing in load balancing zones based clustered for heterogeneous wireless sensor network using fuzzy technique, in the network whose area is 100×100 m2. Let us consider that the quantity of sensors nodes (n) are 100 and both nodes, normal and advance, are arbitrarily deployed in the network. To set normal nodes and advance nodes we assigned half of the total nodes to each of them. The simulation variance has been portrait in Table 10 and arrangements of nodes in various zones as per to their energy level described in Table 11. Proposed protocol is being compared with SEP in heterogeneous environment (Figures 6–10).

We thought about the normal aftereffect of SEP and MH-ZBHR that are described in Table 12. From Figures 4–7, we conclude the simulated result of network lifetime and normal nodes lifetime contrasted with SEP and MH-ZBHR is reached out by 93.61% and 29.40%.

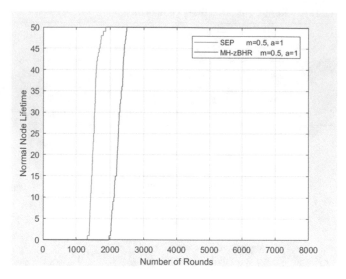

Figure 6. Normal node lifetime of SEP and MH-ZBHR.

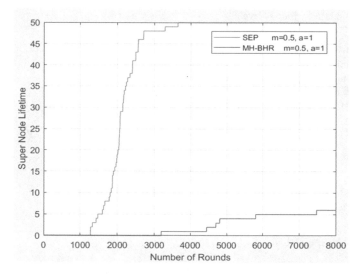

Figure 7. Super node lifetime of SEP and MH-ZBHR.

6 CONCLUSION

This paper proposed a multi-hop zonal-Based hybrid routing protocol for heterogeneous WSN using Fuzzy technique. When contrasted and the past SEP protocol, this method gives better result. Hence, in this protocol the stability period is improved, appeared in Table 12. It reduces energy used by the sensors and increase network lifetime.

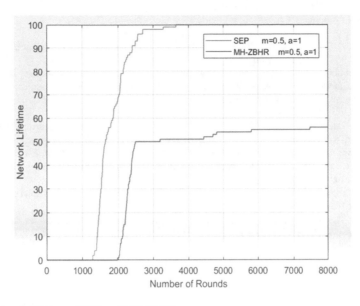

Figure 8.   Network lifetime of SEP and MH-ZBHR.

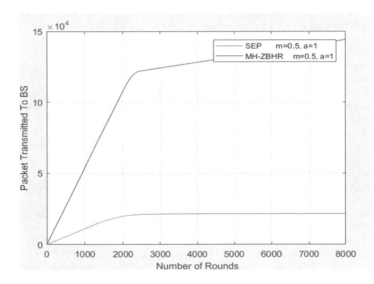

Figure 9.   Packet transmitted to BS of SEP and MH-ZBHR.

Table 12.   Performance comparision table.

Performance Metric	SEP	MH-ZBHR
Network lifetime (number of round after all node dead)	3698	7547
Advance node lifetime (number of round after all advance node dead)	3698	7547
Normal node lifetime (number of round after all normal node are dead)	1986	2570
Throughput (total number of packet transferred to BS)	21489	152134

REFERENCES

Aderohunmu F.A, & Deng J.D. 2009, An enhanced stable election protocol (SEP) for clustered heterogeneous WSN (No. 2009/07). *Discussion Paper Series.*

Chang J.H. & Tassiulas L. 2000, Energy conserving routing in wireless ad-hoc networks. *In: IEEE INFOCOM.*

Heinzelman W, Chandrakasan A & Balakrishnan H. 2000, Energy-efficient communication protocols for wireless microsensor networks. *In: Proceedings of the 33rd Hawaii International Conference on Systems Science. vol. 8, pp. 3005–3014.*

Singh Kalpana & Daniel A. K, 21-22 Feb 2015. Load Balancing in Region Based Clustering for Heterogeneous Environment in Wireless Sensor Networks using AI Techniques. *In IEEE. 5th International Conference on Advanced Computing & Communication Technologies ACCT, pp. (641–646), Rohtak, Haryana.*

Latif K, Ahmad A, Javaid N & Khan Z.A. Mar 2013, Divide and rule scheme for energy efficient routing in wireless sensor networks. *In: 4th International Conference on ANT.*

Mahajan S & Malhotra J. 2011, Energy efficient control strategies in heterogeneous wireless sensor networks: a survey, *Int. J. Comput. Appl. (0975–8887) 14(6).*

Manjeshwar A & Agrawal D. 2001, TEEN: a routing protocol for enhanced efficiency in wireless sensor networks. *In: Proceedings of 1st International Workshop on Parallel and Distributed Computing Issues in Wireless Networks and Mobile Computing, San Francisco.*

Michail A & Ephremides A. 2000, Energy efficient routing for connection-oriented traffic in ad-hoc wireless networks. *Technical Report, Department of Electrical and Computer Engineering and Institute for Systems Research, University of Maryland.*

Singh Ravendra, Gupta Itika & Daniel A.K, 2014. Position Based Energy- Efficient Clustering Protocol under Noisy Environment for Sensor Networks using Fuzzy Logic Techniques. *Science and Information Conference, London, UK.*

Smaragdakis G, Matta I & Bestavros A. 2004, SEP: a stable election protocol for clustered heterogeneous wireless sensor networks. *In: Proceedings of 2nd International Workshop on Sensor and Actor Network Protocols and Applications. (SANPA'2004).*

Maurya Sonam & Daniel A. K, 2014a. RBHR: Region-Based Hybrid Routing Protocol for Wireless Sensor Networks Using AI Technique. *In proceedings of AISC Series of SPRINGER, 4th International Conference on Soft Computing For Problem Solving. (SocProS-2014).*

Maurya Sonam & Daniel A.K, 2014b. Hybrid Routing Approach for Heterogeneous Wireless Sensor Networks Using Fuzzy Logic Technique. *Fourth International Conference on Advanced Computing & Communication Technologies ACCT, in 2014. pp. (202–208).*

Maurya Sonam & Daniel A.K. 2014c. RBHR: Region – Based Hybrid Routing Protocol for Wireless Sensor Networks Using AI Technique. *In 4th International conference on Soft Computing for Problem Solving. NIT Silchar, Assam.*

Soro S & Henizelman W.B. Apr 2005, Prolonging the lifetime of wireless sensor networks via unequal clustering. *In: Proceedings of 5th IEEE International Workshop on Algorithms for Wireless Mobile Ad Hoc and Sensor Networks, Denver, Colorado.*

Sugihara R, & Gupta R. 2011, Sensor localization with deterministic accuracy guarantee. *In: Proceedings of IEEE INFOCOM, pp. 1772–1780.*

Torghabeh N.A. 07 Aug 2010, Cluster head election using a two-level fuzzy logic in wireless sensor networks. *In: 2nd International Conference on Computer Engineering and Technology IEEE, vol. 2.*

Narayan Vipul & Daniel A.K. Feb 14-15,2020, Energy Efficient Two Tier Cluster Based Protocol For wireless Sensor Network. *International Confrence on Electrical and Electronics Engineering (ICE3-2020) IEEE.*

Author index